Essays on Music

Essays on Music

THEODOR W. ADORNO

Selected, with Introduction, Commentary, and Notes
BY RICHARD LEPPERT
New translations by Susan H. Gillespie

University of California Press
BERKELEY   LOS ANGELES   LONDON

University of California Press
Berkeley and Los Angeles, California

University of California Press, Ltd.
London, England

Library of Congress Cataloging-in-Publication Data

Adorno, Theodor W., 1903–1969.
  Essays on music / Theodor W. Adorno ; selected, with introduction,
commentary, and notes by Richard Leppert ; new translations by Susan
H. Gillespie.
     p.   cm.
  Includes bibliographical references and indexes.
  ISBN 0-520-22672-0 (alk. paper).—ISBN 0-520-23159-7 (pbk. : alk.
paper)
    1. Adorno, Theodor W., 1903–1969—Criticism and interpretation.
2. Music—Philosophy and aesthetics.   I. Leppert, Richard D. II. Gillespie, Susan H. trl III. Title.

ML423.A33 A63   2002
780—dc21   2001044601

Manufactured in the United States of America
10 09 08 07 06 05 04
10 9 8 7 6 5 4 3

The paper used in this publication is both acid-free and totally chlorine-
free (TCF). It meets the minimum requirements of ANSI/NISO Z39.48-
1992 (R 1997) *(Permanence of Paper).*♾

Contents

Preface and Acknowledgments   vii

Translator's Note   xiii

Abbreviations   xvii

Introduction (by Richard Leppert)   1

1. LOCATING MUSIC: SOCIETY, MODERNITY, AND THE NEW
   Commentary (by Richard Leppert)   85
   Music, Language, and Composition (1956)   113
   Why Is the New Art So Hard to Understand?* (1931)   127
   On the Contemporary Relationship of Philosophy and
   Music* (1953)   135
   On the Problem of Musical Analysis (1969)   162
   The Aging of the New Music (1955)   181
   The Dialectical Composer* (1934)   203

2. CULTURE, TECHNOLOGY, AND LISTENING
   Commentary (by Richard Leppert)   213
   The Radio Symphony (1941)   251
   The Curves of the Needle (1927/1965)   271

An asterisk (*) following a title indicates that the essay is here translated into
English for the first time.

The Form of the Phonograph Record (1934)   277

Opera and the Long-Playing Record (1969)   283

On the Fetish-Character in Music and the Regression of
Listening (1938)   288

Little Heresy* (1965)   318

3. MUSIC AND MASS CULTURE

Commentary (by Richard Leppert)   327

What National Socialism Has Done to the Arts (1945)   373

On the Social Situation of Music (1932)   391

On Popular Music [With the assistance of George Simpson]
(1941)   437

On Jazz (1936)   470

Farewell to Jazz* (1933)   496

Kitsch* (c. 1932)   501

Music in the Background* (c. 1934)   506

4. COMPOSITION, COMPOSERS, AND WORKS

Commentary (by Richard Leppert)   513

Late Style in Beethoven (1937)   564

Alienated Masterpiece: The *Missa Solemnis* (1959)   569

Wagner's Relevance for Today (1963)   584

Mahler Today* (1930)   603

Marginalia on Mahler* (1936)   612

The Opera *Wozzeck** (1929)   619

Toward an Understanding of Schoenberg* (1955/1967)   627

Difficulties* (1964, 1966)   644

Bibliography   681

Source and Copyright Acknowledgments   709

Index   713

Preface and Acknowledgments

In his text, the writer sets up house. Just as he trundles papers,
books, pencils, documents untidily from room to room, he creates
the same disorder in his thoughts. They become pieces of furniture
that he sinks into, content or irritable. He strokes them affectionately,
wears them out, mixes them up, re-arranges, ruins them.

Theodor Adorno, Minima Moralia

Theodor Wiesengrund Adorno (1903–1969) was one of the principal figures associated with the Frankfurt School and the founding of Critical
Theory; he wrote extensively on culture, society, the Enlightenment, modernity, aesthetics, literature, philosophy, and—more than any other
subject—music. Of all major twentieth-century social theorists none is
identified with music more than Adorno, and of all music analysts Adorno
is the most widely influential in other fields. To this day, he remains the
single most influential contributor to the development of qualitative musical sociology, just as he is by far the most important writer on musical
aesthetics—as well as aesthetics generally—in the past century. His nuanced and distinctly interdisciplinary and intertextual readings of musical
works, commonly provocative and often controversial, remain both fresh
and insightful, all of which gives Adorno broad claim to his increasing
force in music studies.

This volume makes available for the first time a general collection in
English of Adorno's essays on music that surveys the breadth of his work,
and at the same time provides detailed background commentary. The
twenty-seven Adorno essays included here—some short, others long—are
divided into four major sections, preceded by a general introduction.

The introduction provides a biographical sketch and background to the
intellectual tradition within which Adorno's thought developed. Critical
Theory and dialectics in particular are highlighted in an account of
Adorno's overriding concern with the social and cultural impact of late
modernity on the subject. Adorno's paradoxical position on political praxis
and the social role of the intellectual is considered, as well as his position—
closely related—on history and human suffering. The introduction incorporates consideration of Adorno's famously difficult writing.

I have provided commentaries to each of the book's four major divisions in an attempt to situate the music essays in relation to Adorno's other work, musical and otherwise, and with regard to the secondary literature that has emerged in response to Adorno.

Part 1, "Locating Music: Society, Modernity, and the New," constitutes an overview of Adorno's articulation of music in modernity, broadly conceived, focused on music's twin relation to history and the cultural production of its social-semiotic meaning. Included is an important essay wherein Adorno accounts for his claim that philosophy is fundamental to musical understanding. In particular, the essays in this section emphasize Adorno's lifelong and socially principled commitment to new music.

Part 2, "Culture, Technology, and Listening," marks Adorno's interest in and concern for the social and cultural consequences of modern mass media technology, in particular as regards what he considered the (mostly) regressive effects on subject formation brought about by the radio broadcast and phonographic reproduction of music, and the impact of both technologies on listening habits. Included as well are late essays in which Adorno moderates his position by articulating the potentially progressive import of these technologies.

Part 3, "Music and Mass Culture," includes Adorno's most important—and controversial—critiques of popular music, as well as what he took for jazz, in addition to musical kitsch of various sorts. Adorno's critique of mass culture is an engagement with a modernity that, whatever the music, is organized through what he regarded as production processes increasingly predetermined by centralization and profit—at the expense of truth, individuality, subjectivity, and emancipation.

Part 4, "Composition, Composers, and Works," includes essays on the six composers about whom Adorno wrote the most—invariably dialectically: Beethoven, Wagner, Mahler, Schoenberg, Berg, and Stravinsky. Adorno's musical interests were almost exclusively confined to the study of Western modernity, beginning with the rise of the bourgeoisie in the wake of the French Revolution and ending with the music of his own historical moment. Though his interest in twentieth-century music, at least in the classical sphere, was always "presentist"—in his last years, for example, he often wrote about composers such as Boulez, Cage, and Stockhausen—every generation of composers subsequent to Schoenberg was measured against the standard established by the Second Viennese School, Schoenberg especially, just as Schoenberg was measured against Beethoven, Wagner, and Mahler. Among these six composers Adorno admired four, Beethoven, Mahler, Schoenberg, and Berg, and aggressively critiqued two, Wagner and Stravinsky, while acknowledging their (deeply flawed) genius. The volume ends with a lengthy essay focused on the challenges faced alike by late-modern composers and listeners.

⟨⟩

"No one who has wrestled with the angel of Adorno's prose emerges without some part of him out of joint."[1] With this consequential observation very much in mind, I express my deepest gratitude to Susan H. Gillespie, at Bard College, who has translated fifteen of the twenty-seven Adorno essays collected in this volume. I can't imagine a more stimulating and genuinely pleasurable collaboration. Nothing involved in the labors of producing this volume has given me more pleasure than our many exchanges about the German language and Adorno's use of it; I greatly admire Susan's extraordinary sensitivity to—and insight into—both.

The other translators whose work is represented likewise deserve my thanks: Wes Blomster, Jamie Owen Daniel, Robert Hullot-Kentor, Thomas Y. Levin, Max Paddison, Duncan Smith, and Frederic Will.

My research assistant throughout the project, David Jenemann, deserves special praise and thanks for his tireless efforts to meet what must have seemed an endless string of requests for material. I deeply respect David's skill in the use of libraries and data bases, his endless patience in fact checking, and his perpetual good humor. Suffice to say that this volume would have been considerably delayed and diminished without David's participation.

In recent years I have taught five doctoral seminars on Adorno; the depth of understanding I gained from the sixty or so students who, with me, worked their way through great quantities of Adorno's work is difficult to measure but very considerable indeed. I'm certain that I would never have undertaken this volume without the intellectual stimulus and growth provided me by these young professionals and enthusiastic colleagues.

I owe a great deal to a number of musicologists who have variously assisted me. First, and foremost, is Rose Rosengard Subotnik. As is very well known, Rose's landmark studies on Adorno, beginning in the 1970s, literally brought Adorno to the attention of American musicology, and at a time when few were either aware of his work or all that much interested in finding out about it; indeed, she carried out her path-breaking efforts at considerable personal cost to her since-distinguished career. It is not

1. Harvey Gross, "Adorno in Los Angeles: The Intellectual in Emigration," *Humanities in Society* 2 no. 4 (Fall 1979), p. 350 n. 1.

going too far to say that without her, American musicology would have denied itself Adorno's musical writings for a decade or more, notably to the detriment of the discipline. Her brilliant readings of Adorno constitute the foundation for my own work. Rose, Lydia Goehr, and Susan McClary read my commentary and provided numerous suggestions; and each of them responded to strings of queries. I'm deeply grateful for their close and critical reading, and for the generosity with which they gave of their time.

Other colleagues have likewise offered valuable assistance, criticisms, and insights, for which I am immensely grateful. Larry Kramer, Rob Walser, and Otto Kolleritsch all provided helpful suggestions for tracking down details of some of the more thorny or obscure of Adorno's references. Jim Deaville, Jane Fulcher, Gary Tomlinson, and Nancy van Deusen provided a number of important suggestions for the basic organization and scope of the book. Finally, I'm grateful to the scholars, their names unknown to me, who provided consistently thoughtful reader-reports.

Several faculty colleagues at the University of Minnesota were particularly helpful: Jochen Schulte-Sasse and Gary Thomas engaged me in numerous, and often lengthy, conversations about Adorno's German and related translation issues; I am extremely indebted to both of them. Thomas Pepper provided valuable assistance on some literary references. Jack Zipes and Jochen Schulte-Sasse provided critical advice on licensing issues.

My department colleagues Kate Porter, David Meissner, and Anne Fredrickson provided staff assistance throughout the research and writing; I'm grateful to each of them for their tireless support.

I wish to express my thanks to the American Council of Learned Societies for the Fellowship awarded me for this project, which, together with sabbatical support from the University of Minnesota, provided a year's uninterrupted time to complete the volume. The Graduate School of the University of Minnesota generously assisted with a grant-in-aid-of-research.

My editors at the University of California Press, Mary Francis and Lynne Withey, have been everything an author could wish for: supportive, timely, forgiving, and an endless source of ideas, as well as invariably efficient in helping me with numerous details of publication. It's hard to give adequate account to the consummate professionalism of Lynne and Mary. I am likewise grateful to Steve Gilmartin for his attentive and sensitive text editing, and to Lawrence Fuchsberg for his editorial suggestions and careful indexing. Kate Warne saw through the book's final production with enormous skill. David Jenemann and Andrew Knighton, with endless good cheer and attentiveness, assisted with the proofreading.

I express my thanks to Dr. Rolf Tiedemann, Director of the Theodor W. Adorno Archiv, and to Suhrkamp Verlag, for their kind permission to publish Adorno's essays. Dr. Petra Christina Hardt, at Suhrkamp, was most helpful in arranging licensing. My thanks as well to the journals and other publishers who granted permission to reprint previously translated essays. I am grateful for the tireless assistance provided by the University of Minnesota Libraries, the Columbia University Rare Book and Manuscript Library, and the Columbia University Archives.

Ann: as always. Thus I reach the point where words fail.

Adorno often used foreign words, English especially. In the essays that follow, English words that appeared in the German text are italicized and followed by an asterisk (*).

The essays in this volume follow Adorno's original paragraph formatting. In certain essays Adorno inserted spaces between paragraphs, which seem to signal a more distinct break than paragraphs separated only by first-line indentations. Indeed, spatial breaks are typical to those essays which are essentially aphoristic in design.

In each of the four sectional commentaries, titles of Adorno essays included in this volume are given in small capitals, followed by the page numbers. Page numbers to quotations from essays included in this volume are given in parentheses in the text, rather than in the footnotes.

Richard Leppert, June 2001

Translator's Note

Hartmut Scheible's pithy and useful brief introduction to Adorno's life and work[1] opens with the observation that, biographically, Adorno's familiarity with and closeness to music were more deeply rooted and profound than his familiarity with and closeness to philosophy. The emblem of this closeness to music is a scene that Scheible cites from an essay Adorno wrote at the end of 1933 called "Four-Hands, Once Again" [GS, vol. 17, pp. 303–06; the following passage is my translation]. The child Adorno is playing piano four-hands with his mother:

> The music that we are accustomed to call classical, I learned as a child by playing piano four-hands. There was little, among the symphonic and chamber music repertoire, that wouldn't have been part of our domestic life thanks to the broad rectangular volumes, all bound in green by the bookseller. . . . Music for four hands—that was music with which one could get along, could live, before the musical compulsion itself imposed loneliness and secret handiwork. . . . He [the child Adorno] always truly had to work for the symphony in order to acquire it; he was not allowed, the way he was with his lyrical pieces by Grieg, to modify the tempo and dynamics at will, but had to orient himself to the score and markings of the work, if he didn't want to lose the connection with the partner.

The intimate scene comes to mind as a metaphor for the pleasure and challenge of translating Adorno—translation as performance, specifically musical performance.[2] In performance, as the above description reminds

1. Hartmut Scheible, *Theodor W. Adorno: Mit Selbstzeugnissen und Bilddokumenten* (Reinbeck bei Hamburg: Rowohlt, 1989). The following references are to pp. 8 (quote) and 17.
2. For a consideration of the role of musicality in Adorno's writing, see my

us, it is not only the so-called content of the text that matters, its semantic meaning in the narrow sense, or the melodies, harmonies, and divisions of the musical score, but also its rhetorical and gestural meanings, its performance indications and dynamics. Of course, the written text bears no explicit performance markers, so the translator must listen all the more carefully in order not to lose the connection with the imaginary Adorno, the elder "partner" who leads. In particular, she must be acutely aware of the gestural, rhetorical, and poetic uses of language that are the key to the author's intentions in the work, its performativity.

In translating the essays collected in this book, and elsewhere, I have tried to listen hard for the performative aspects of Adorno's texts, and to play them again in English. This has meant paying special attention to preserving, as much as possible, the ambiguities through which the text remains open to interpretation, while also, inevitably, interpreting it. It has meant acknowledging the text's rhythms and stresses, its oblique references to other texts and contexts, its use of rare or poetic words and frequent neologisms, and also certain more pervasive differences in mood, for example between the short, scherzo-like sketches and the longer, more symphonic essays. It has meant keeping a sharp eye out for such rhetorical moves as the frequent use—always with an ironic overtone—of terms in English and French; the often unusual sentence order, which lends striking emphasis to the language; and the careful, sometimes rather concealed but always provocative use of metaphor, for example in Adorno's borrowing of the technical term "point of interference" [*Indifferenzpunkt*], drawn from wave theory, to describe the interaction of the ideal and the profane in Mahler's music.[3]

Because of the prominence of aspects of performativity, Adorno's language does not lend itself well to abstraction, summary, or abridgement; this may well be one reason why he is considered "difficult." To this I would respond that Adorno's essays are difficult in precisely the ways that works of musical composition are difficult—they are uninterpretable without a full rendition of their complexity.

Of course, all this should be understood in light of the need to produce a translation that works both acoustically and semantically in English. The translator can go with Adorno to the threshold of incomprehensibility, but no further; and the language can accommodate only so much awkwardness

---

essay "Translating Adorno: Language, Music, and Performance," *Musical Quarterly* 79 no. 1 (Spring 1995), pp. 55–65.

3. "Mahler Today," p. 605.

without losing its charm. The most obvious practical consequence of this is that it is frequently necessary, and appropriate, to alter the word order or break up long sentences. To approach but respect the boundaries of English does not imply any general criterion of "readability" and does not have to lead to a normalization of the text.

I would like to thank Richard Leppert most warmly for his careful editing and expert attention to the many historical references that play such an important role in situating Adorno's comments; and Burt Brody, whose advice on physics has been invaluable on many occasions.

Susan H. Gillespie, December 2000

Abbreviations

The following abbreviations are used for major works by Adorno cited in notes and the bibliography. For full reference, see the bibliography (Adorno: Primary Sources Consulted).

AB	*Alban Berg: Master of the Smallest Link*
AT	*Aesthetic Theory*
B	*Beethoven: The Philosophy of Music*
CC	*The Complete Correspondence, 1928–1940* [Adorno and Benjamin]
CF	*Composing for the Films* [Adorno and Eisler]
CM	*Critical Models: Interventions and Catchwords*
DE	*Dialectic of Enlightenment* [Adorno and Horkheimer]
GS	*Gesammelte Schriften*
ISM	*Introduction to the Sociology of Music*
ISW	*In Search of Wagner*
M	*Mahler: A Musical Physiognomy*
MM	*Minima Moralia: Reflections from Damaged Life*
ND	*Negative Dialectics*
NL	*Notes to Literature*
PNM	*Philosophy of Modern* [i.e., New] *Music*
PR	*Prisms*
QF	*Quasi una fantasia: Essays on Modern Music*
SDE	*The Stars Down to Earth and Other Essays on the Irrational in Culture*
SF	*Sound Figures*

Introduction
Richard Leppert

LIFE AND WORKS

Adorno was a genius; I say that without reservation. . . . [He] had a presence of mind, a spontaneity of thought, a power of formulation that I never have seen before or since. One was unable to grasp the emerging process of Adorno's thoughts; they emerged, as it were, finished. That was his virtuosity. . . . When you were with Adorno you were in the movement of his thought. Adorno was not trivial; it was denied him, in a clearly painful way, ever to be trivial. But at the same time, he lacked the pretensions and the affectations of the stilted and "auratic" avant-garde that one saw in George's disciples. . . . By all notable standards, Adorno remained anti-elitist. Incidentally, he was a genius also in that he preserved certain child-like traits, both the character of a prodigy and the dependence of one "not-yet-grownup." He was characteristically helpless before institutions or legal procedures.

Jürgen Habermas, "A Generation Apart from Adorno"

Theodor Wiesengrund Adorno was born in Frankfurt am Main on 11 September 1903.[1] He died from a heart attack just short of his sixty-sixth birthday on 6 August 1969 while on vacation in Switzerland.

---

1. For additional information concerning Adorno's biography, see Martin Jay, *The Dialectical Imagination: A History of the Frankfurt School and the Institute of Social Research, 1923–1950* (Boston: Little, Brown, 1973); Martin Jay, *Adorno* (Cambridge: Harvard University Press, 1984); Gerhard Knapp, *Theodor W. Adorno* (Berlin: Colloquium, 1980); Hartmut Scheible, *Theodor W. Adorno: Mit Selbstzeugnissen und Bilddokumenten* (Reinbek bei Hamburg: Rowohlt, 1989); Rolf Wiggershaus, *The Frankfurt School: Its History, Theories, and Political Significance*, trans. Michael Robertson (Cambridge: MIT Press, 1995); and Rolf Wiggershaus, *Theodor W. Adorno* (Munich: C. H. Beck, 1987). This last study is princi-

Adorno's father, Oskar Wiesengrund (1870–1946), was a wine merchant and an assimilated Jew who converted to Protestantism at about the time of his son's birth. The family was well off. Adorno was an only child whose youth was as sheltered as it was happy. As Martin Jay put it, "His childhood provided him a model of happiness whose memory served as a standard against which he would measure all subsequent disappointments."[2] His mother, Maria Calvelli-Adorno della Piana (1864–1952), was Catholic, and it was her family name that Adorno exchanged for Wiesengrund (and Wiesengrund-Adorno, adopted in the mid 1920s) in 1938.[3] Also living in the household throughout Adorno's childhood was his mother's unmarried sister, Agathe Calvelli-Adorno (1868–1935). Adorno referred to both as Mother. Maria had been a very successful professional singer, her career ending with her marriage. Agathe had been a successful professional pianist; she had accompanied singer Adelina Patti in numerous recitals.

Adorno's intellectual training was rigorous and came early. By age fifteen, he began a long period of study—occupying Saturday afternoons—of Kant's *Critique of Pure Reason* mentored by family friend Siegfried Kracauer (1889–1966), who at the time was editor of the *Frankfurter Zeitung*. By Adorno's own account, the Kant study sessions went on "for years." By 1923 Kracauer and Adorno were studying Goethe's *Elective Affinities* and, thereafter, the first draft of Walter Benjamin's essay on this work.[4] Hauke Brunkhorst states the impact of the Kant studies as "the key

---

pally an introduction to Adorno's thought, though some biographical information is also provided. I have drawn, in part, on all of these texts for many of the biographical details reported in what follows.

2. Jay, *Adorno*, p. 25.

3. Concerning a degree of controversy about the name change, see Jay, *Adorno*, p. 34. Hannah Arendt judged the decision, in Jay's words, as "evidence of an almost collaborationist mentality." But Adorno's friend Friedrich Pollock "has claimed that it was on *his* initiative that the name change took place" (p. 34).

4. Leo Lowenthal, "Recollections of Theodor W. Adorno" (1983), trans. Sabine Wilke, in *An Unmastered Past: The Autobiographical Reflections of Leo Lowenthal*, ed. Martin Jay (Berkeley and Los Angeles: University of California Press, 1987), p. 205. Martin Jay, "Adorno and Kracauer: Notes on a Troubled Friendship," in *Permanent Exiles: Essays on the Intellectual Migration from Germany to America* (New York: Columbia University Press, 1985), p. 218, describes the early friendship as "rooted in a Platonically erotic attraction." The friendship was complicated by intellectual disagreements already by the 1930s. See also, in the same volume, Jay, "The Extraterritorial Life of Siegfried Kracauer," pp. 152–97. Though the two remained friends most of their lives (Kracauer died in 1966), during the last few years the very serious differences that emerged over each other's work in the end put a serious strain on the relationship, which Jay outlines in detail, principally based on extensive notes Kracauer wrote concerning his last two face-to-

work in Adorno's intellectual development. The idea of a negative dialectic, which is Adorno's most unique philosophical contribution, owes much to it."[5] Adorno himself acknowledged as much: "I am not exaggerating in the slightest when I say that I owe more to this reading [of Kant] than to my academic teachers."[6]

Leo Lowenthal (1900–1993), later the distinguished sociologist of literature, whom Adorno met in 1921, also studied with Kracauer. In a letter to Lowenthal of 4 December 1921, Kracauer mused about their mutual friend: "Something incomparable puts him in a position over both of us, an admirable material existence [referring to Adorno's family's wealth] and a wonderfully self-confident character. He truly is a beautiful specimen of a human being; even if I am not without some skepticism concerning his future, I am surely delighted by him in the present." Lowenthal, late in life, described Adorno at eighteen in more personal terms as "a delicate, slender young man. Indeed, he was the classical image of a poet, with a delicate way of moving and talking that one scarcely finds nowadays. We would meet either at a coffee house—mostly at the famous Café Westend at the opera, where intellectual *enfants terribles* met—or at one or the other of our parents' places. Naturally, I knew Adorno's parents well, also his aunt Agathe. It was an existence you just had to love—if you were not dying of jealousy of this protected beautiful life—and in it Adorno had gained the confidence that never left him his entire life."[7]

With Kracauer's guidance Adorno notes that he experienced Kant "from the beginning not as mere epistemology, not as an analysis of the conditions of scientifically valid judgments, but as a kind of coded text from which the historical situation of spirit could be read, with the vague expectation that in doing so one could acquire something of truth itself." No

---

face meetings with Adorno in 1960 and 1964, both of which ended badly. Further, Kracauer took offense at Adorno's somewhat backhanded seventy-fifth birthday tribute, first given as a radio lecture in 1964 and soon thereafter published: "The Curious Realist: On Siegfried Kracauer," NL, vol. 2, pp. 58–75. Jay reports, "Adorno and Kracauer," p. 235, that Kracauer attached the following note to his copy of the Adorno text: "this emotionally laden, slanderous article of TWA who does not shrink from telling falsehoods." Kracauer's reaction is overwrought, though he correctly recognized Adorno's between-the-lines critique of his one-time mentor.

5. Hauke Brunkhorst, "Theodor W. Adorno: Aesthetic Constructivism and a Negative Ethic of the Non-Forfeited Life," trans. James Swindal, in *The Handbook of Critical Theory*, ed. David M. Rasmussen (Oxford: Blackwell, 1996), pp. 307–08.

6. Adorno, "Curious Realist," p. 58.

7. Lowenthal, "Recollections of Theodor W. Adorno," p. 203.

less important, Adorno noted that "What pressed for philosophical expression in [Kracauer] was an almost boundless capacity for suffering: expression and suffering are intimately related. Kracauer's relationship to truth was that suffering entered into the idea—which usually dissipates it—in undistorted, unmitigated form; suffering could be rediscovered in ideas from the past as well."[8] The question of suffering, and the responsibility of both philosophy and art to address it, remained with Adorno his entire career.

In 1921, at age eighteen, Adorno entered Frankfurt's Johann Wolfgang Goethe University, where he studied philosophy, sociology, psychology, and music. He completed a doctorate in philosophy just three years later at age twenty-one. During these years he met and formed friendships with two men of particular importance to his later professional and intellectual life, respectively: in 1922 Max Horkheimer (1895–1973), eight years Adorno's senior; and in 1923 Walter Benjamin (1892–1940), eleven years older. By the late 1920s Adorno was also acquainted with a number of other heterodox Marxists, including Ernst Bloch, Bertolt Brecht, Herbert Marcuse, and Kurt Weill.

As an adolescent, Adorno's musical training included piano lessons from Bernhard Sekles, also the teacher of Hindemith. As a young man he seriously entertained the possibility of a career as a composer and concert pianist. He acted on this ambition in January 1925 with a move to Vienna, after having been deeply affected by excerpts from Berg's *Wozzeck*, prior to the opera's world premiere, played at a concert in Frankfurt, where he also met Berg. Berg accepted him as a composition student and gave him lessons twice weekly.[9] Adorno also took additional piano training from Eduard Steuermann, a champion of twentieth-century piano works, who like Berg was part of the Schoenberg circle.

Adorno did not find Vienna to his liking. Moreover, the Schoenberg "circle," which he hoped to join, turned out to be not much of one. Schoenberg himself was remote personally and inaccessible physically, having moved outside the city to Mödling following his second marriage; and in

8. Adorno, "Curious Realist," pp. 58–59.
9. For an amusing account of an early encounter between Berg and Adorno at the composer's home in Vienna in 1925—the young and awe-struck Adorno vastly overstaying his welcome, even to the point of following Berg and his wife to a concert and joining them, uninvited, in their box, all the while talking incessantly at the patient but exhausted Berg—see Christopher Hailey, "Defining Home: Berg's Life on the Periphery," in *The Cambridge Companion to Berg*, ed. Anthony Pople (Cambridge: Cambridge University Press, 1997), pp. 15–16.

1926 Schoenberg moved to Berlin. Not least, Schoenberg and Adorno did not hit it off, despite Adorno's admiration for the composer's music. Adorno returned to Frankfurt in the summer of 1925, though he traveled back to Vienna on and off until 1927, maintaining his contacts and publishing music criticism, notably in the music journals *Pult und Taktstock* and *Anbruch;* for the latter he acquired an editorial position with Berg's help in 1929 which he retained until 1932.[10] Both journals championed new music. Adorno's career in music journalism in fact predated his Vienna experience—and vastly exceeded his publication in philosophy, the first philosophical essay appearing only in 1933. Between 1921, while still a teenager, and 1931 he published dozens of opera and concert reviews, reviews of published new music, as well as essays on aesthetics, and heavily favoring new music.[11] Thus in 1922, at nineteen, he praised in print Schoenberg's *Pierrot lunaire* (1912) in the *Neue Blätter für Kunst und Literatur.* During the late 1920s and early 1930s he and Ernst Krenek carried on in-print debates about free tonality and serialism, and problems of musical form and genre; he also collaborated with violinist Rudolf Kolisch on developing a theory of musical performance.[12]

Returning to Frankfurt at twenty-four, Adorno began his association with the Institute of Social Research, founded in 1923, with which Horkheimer was already connected—only after the Second World War was the Institute's work referred to as the "Frankfurt School." Adorno's first publication for the Institute came in 1932, with the essay "On the Social Situation of Music," included in this volume; it appeared in the first issue of the Institute's journal, *Zeitschrift für Sozialforschung.* Adorno formally joined the Institute only in 1938, during its American exile.

The right to teach in German universities depends on the *Habilitationsschrift,* a kind of second dissertation. Adorno's first attempt ("The

10. For a list of the essays Adorno published in these journals during this period, see Max Paddison, *Adorno's Aesthetics of Music* (Cambridge: Cambridge University Press, 1993), pp. 333–36. Paddison points out (p. 23) that during this time Adorno was in direct contact with a number of composers besides Berg and Schoenberg, including Webern, Hindemith, Eisler, Weill, and Krenek. Concerning his important letter exchanges with Krenek, especially during the 1920s and 1930s, over twelve-tone music and the concept of musical material, see pp. 81–97; Adorno and Ernst Krenek, *Briefwechsel,* ed. Wolfgang Rogge (Frankfurt am Main: Suhrkamp, 1974); and Adorno and Ernst Krenek, "Arbeitsprobleme des Komponisten: Gespräch über Musik und soziale Situation" (1930), GS, vol. 19, pp. 433–39.

11. See GS, vol. 19.

12. Max Paddison, *Adorno, Modernism and Mass Culture: Essays on Critical Theory and Music* (London: Kahn and Averill, 1996), p. 3. For the *Pierrot lunaire* review, see GS, vol. 19, pp. 11–14.

Concept of the Unconscious in the Transcendental Theory of Mind") in 1927 was rejected by his advisor, philosopher Hans Cornelius. His second effort, successful, concerned Kierkegaard ("Kierkegaard: Construction of the Aesthetic") and constituted one of the early critiques of Existentialism. Paul Tillich, the theologian, was Adorno's official advisor on this project, since Cornelius had left the university, emigrating to Finland. Adorno's Kierkegaard study was published in 1933, on the very day that Hitler assumed office.

The Marxist orientation of the Institute of Social Research was well known and in no sense disguised; moreover, its members were almost exclusively Jewish. On 30 January 1933, the day of Hitler's ascendancy, the house shared by Horkheimer and Friedrich Pollock in a Frankfurt suburb was seized by Hitler's SS.[13] The Institute itself was searched and closed by the police on 13 March. In July the Gestapo office in Berlin sent notice of the confiscation of "Communist property," charging that the Institute "has encouraged activities hostile to the state."[14] Most of its sixty-thousand-volume library was confiscated. (The Institute's substantial private endowment had been transferred to Holland two years earlier and was later moved again to the United States, thereby protecting it from seizure.) In September, on his thirtieth birthday, Adorno's right to teach, the *venia legendi*, was revoked by the Nazi government, and he moved, briefly, to Berlin.[15] (To that point in his career Adorno had principally supported himself, however poorly, by journalistic music criticism, rather than teaching.)[16]

Horkheimer, who had assumed the directorship in 1931, and his colleagues initially moved the Institute to Geneva, where a branch office had been established the same year as Horkheimer became director—until the start of the war there were also branch offices in Paris and London. In May 1934 Horkheimer traveled to New York and secured an affiliation for the Institute with Columbia University. Soon thereafter, Horkheimer was joined by Leo Lowenthal, Herbert Marcuse, and Friedrich Pollock.

13. Richard Wolin, *The Terms of Cultural Criticism: The Frankfurt School, Existentialism, Poststructuralism* (New York: Columbia University Press, 1992), p. 47.

14. Cited in Wiggershaus, *Frankfurt School*, p. 128.

15. Gillian Rose, *The Melancholy Science: An Introduction to the Thought of Theodor W. Adorno* (New York: Columbia University Press, 1978), p. 9.

16. Evelyn Wilcock, "Adorno's Uncle: Dr. Bernard Wingfield and the English Exile of Theodor W. Adorno, 1934–38," *German Life and Letters* 49 no. 3 (July 1996), p. 327.

In 1934 Adorno left Germany for England, dividing his time between London and Oxford where he studied at Merton College. (His entry to Merton was supported by references from philosopher Ernst Cassirer and musicologist Edward Dent; Adorno had written to Alban Berg for the favor of intervening with Dent, whom Adorno had met through the International Society for New Music.)[17] Thereafter, Adorno made numerous trips back to Germany, some quite extended, in particular to see Gretel Karplus (1902–1993) in Berlin, whom he married in 1937. It was possible for Adorno to return to Germany more or less freely for two reasons. First, he was not politically active, nor was he a member of the Institute; second, he was, as Rolf Wiggershaus puts it, " 'only' a 'half-Jew' ";[18] the Nuremberg Laws of 1935 treated *Mischlinge* like Adorno more leniently than "full" Jews.[19] Leo Lowenthal accounts for Adorno's reluctance to leave Germany as typical of the assimilated German-Jewish middle class, the upper middle class especially. "Adorno had such an incredibly hard time finally leaving Germany (we had to drag him almost physically); he just couldn't believe that to him, son of Oskar Wiesengrund, nephew of aunt Agathe, and son of Maria, anything might ever happen [i.e., so secure and happy was his childhood], for it was absolutely clear that the bourgeoisie would soon become fed up with Hitler. This kind of naïve unfamiliarity with the real world—particularly that of Germany and the at-first complicated and then not-so-complicated relations of Christians and Jews—must be borne in mind if one is to fully understand Adorno's personal history."[20]

In June 1937 Adorno briefly visited the United States for the first time, at the urging of Horkheimer. Adorno and Gretel emigrated in February 1938, thanks to a part-time position established for him by Horkheimer in the music division of the Princeton University Radio Research Project.[21] Adorno remained in New York until November 1941, when he moved to

17. Ibid., pp. 330–31.
18. Wiggershaus, *Frankfurt School*, p. 128.
19. See further Wilcock, "Adorno's Uncle," p. 338; and Evelyn Wilcock, "Alban Berg's Appeal to Edward Dent on Behalf of Theodor Adorno, 18 November 1933," *German Life and Letters* 50 no. 3 (July 1997), pp. 365–68.
20. Lowenthal, "Recollections of Theodor W. Adorno," p. 204.
21. Adorno later succeeded in getting his parents out of Germany, but not before both had been arrested. His father's offices were destroyed and his property seized. See CC, p. 298, letter from Adorno to Benjamin, written from New York, 1 February 1939, describing his parents' incarceration and subsequent release. His parents emigrated to Cuba shortly thereafter, and to the United States early in 1940.

Los Angeles, following Horkheimer who had gone West for health and climate reasons several months earlier.[22] Adorno's nearly eight-year California exile was intellectually highly productive. Indeed, in a 1957 letter to Lowenthal he confided that "I believe 90 percent of all that I've published in Germany was written in America."[23]

Major works written during this period include *Dialectic of Enlightenment* (1944) written with Horkheimer at the beginning of his stay, and, at the end, *The Authoritarian Personality* (1950), a multi-person collaboration with Adorno the senior author.[24] *The Authoritarian Personality*, by far the largest monograph Adorno wrote in English, was part of a series of projects that fell under the heading *Studies in Prejudice*, sponsored by the American Jewish Committee, which had hired Horkheimer to direct its Department of Scientific Research. Between these two major collaborative projects came *Minima Moralia: Reflections from Damaged Life*, completed by 1946 but published only in 1951. Dedicated to Horkheimer, it is Adorno's most personal book, an often deeply moving analysis of late modernity viewed through the condition of exile. At about the same time, he collaborated with Hanns Eisler on *Composing for the Films* (1947), the first monograph on film music. *Philosophy of Modern Music* (Adorno's German title is more accurately rendered "New Music"), a highly influential—and controversial—account of music by Schoenberg and Stravin-

22. Adorno's distinctly modest house, which he rented, is at 316 S. Kentor Avenue, in Brentwood. Horkheimer lived nearby in a bungalow, no longer standing, at 13524 D'Este Drive. For a map to the homes of the émigrés, see the exhibition catalogue by Stephanie Barron, with Sabine Eckmann, *Exiles + Emigrés: The Flight of European Artists from Hitler*, Los Angeles County Museum of Art (New York: Harry N. Abrams, 1997), pp. 358–61. In the immediate area (Brentwood, Santa Monica, and Pacific Palisades) lived Hanns Eisler, Ernst Toch, and Thomas Mann, who resided in two different houses during his California years; Arnold Schoenberg, whose house is just down the block from the site where formerly stood the house belonging to O. J. Simpson; and Bertolt Brecht, who occupied two different houses about a block apart in Santa Monica. Stravinsky, in West Hollywood, was a bit farther away, and in any event not part of the German Jewish community. Rachmaninoff and Artur Rubinstein lived in Beverly Hills, as did Bruno Walter. For an account of Adorno's Southern California experience as read through MM, see Nico Israel, "Damage Control: Adorno, Los Angeles, and the Dislocation of Culture," *Yale Journal of Criticism* 10 no. 1 (Spring 1997), 85–113.

23. Quoted in Martin Jay, "The Frankfurt School in Exile," in *Permanent Exiles: Essays on the Intellectual Migration from Germany to America* (New York: Columbia University Press, 1985), p. 41.

24. For an overview of this project, see Wiggershaus, *Frankfurt School*, pp. 408–30. See also David Norman Smith, "The Beloved Dictator: Adorno, Horkheimer, and the Critique of Domination," *Current Perspectives in Social Theory* 12 (1992), pp. 195–230.

sky, appeared in 1949, though part of it was written several years earlier. *In Search of Wagner,* parts of which he had published in essay form in 1939, appeared in 1952.

During the war years, Adorno came into close contact with fellow émigré Thomas Mann, then writing his great novel *Doctor Faustus: The Life of the German Composer Adrian Leverkühn as Told by a Friend,* a sustained critique of Nazism using the fictional composer's biography and work as a metaphor for Germany's cultural decline. In 1943 Mann read both Adorno's Wagner manuscript, and the Schoenberg essay that constitutes the first part of *Philosophy of Modern Music.* Mann, much impressed, informally secured Adorno's services as de facto principal musical advisor to the novel, which among other things, involved Adorno's coaching Mann on Schoenberg's twelve-tone technique,[25] for which he received Mann's public expression of gratitude in his monograph account of the writing of the novel, *The Story of a Novel: The Genesis of Doctor Faustus.*[26] Mann's reaction to reading Adorno's Schoenberg essay: "Here indeed was something important. The manuscript dealt with modern music both on an artistic and on a sociological plane. The spirit of it was remarkably forward-looking, subtle and deep, and the whole thing had the strangest affinity to the idea of my book, to the 'composition' in which I lived and moved and had my being. The decision was made of itself: this was my man. . . . His knowledge of tradition, his mastery of the whole historical body of music, is enormous. An American singer who works with him said to me: 'It is incredible. [Adorno] knows every note in the world.' "[27]

25. Schoenberg—living in the same neighborhood—was not amused, taking particular umbrage at the lack of attribution of the compositional procedure to himself. This complaint was in turn responded to by Mann in the first American edition, *Doctor Faustus: The Life of the German Composer Adrian Leverkühn as Told by a Friend,* trans. H. T. Lowe-Porter (New York: Alfred A. Knopf, 1948), p. [512]. Following the novel's last page, Mann added the following text as an "Author's Note": "It does not seem supererogatory to inform the reader that the form of musical composition delineated in Chapter XXII [pp. 185–94], known as the twelve-tone or row system, is in truth the intellectual property of a contemporary composer and theoretician, Arnold Schönberg. I have transferred this technique in a certain ideational context to the fictitious figure of a musician, the tragic hero of my novel. In fact, the passages of this book that deal with musical theory are indebted in numerous details to Schönberg's *Harmonielehre.*"

26. Thomas Mann, *The Story of a Novel: The Genesis of Doctor Faustus,* trans. Richard Winston and Clara Winston (New York: Alfred A. Knopf, 1961). See especially the references to Adorno on pp. 40–48, 63, 94–95, 102–03, 150–56, 221–23.

27. Ibid., pp. 43, 45. Mann not only read Adorno's work on Wagner and Schoenberg but also from his Beethoven aphorisms, part of a book never completed

During the late 1940s Horkheimer, Pollock, and Adorno gradually reached a decision to return to Frankfurt and reestablish the Institute. Horkheimer made a brief exploratory visit in April 1948, and for a longer time during the spring and summer of 1949. In 1950 Horkheimer, together with Pollock, resettled there, though he made a number of return visits to the United States in subsequent years. The Institute's new home, located near the ruins of its prewar structure, officially reopened in 1951. Adorno's first return to Germany since his departure in 1938 came in November 1949; he was now forty-six. The Germany, and the university, to which Horkheimer, Pollock, and Adorno returned was profoundly different from what they had experienced before the war, as Wiggershaus summarizes:

> They saw themselves as Jews, as left-wing intellectuals and as critical sociologists in an environment which had been more or less completely purged of people like themselves, and in which all the signs had long since been pointing clearly to the restoration of the old order. The unique symbiosis represented by German-Jewish culture [whose liberal traditions had been a marked feature of Frankfurt University prior to Nazism] had been irreversibly destroyed. Apart from Horkheimer and Adorno, none of the distinguished lecturers or professors from the heyday of Frankfurt University—the last years of the Weimar Republic—returned. Horkheimer, Adorno and Pollock could count on being met with patience and good intentions precisely because they were, and remained, the exceptions.[28]

Indeed, there was resentment toward the returned Jewish émigrés. In 1953 Adorno was given a tenured faculty position, but as a special case—the precise title was "Extraordinary Chair of Philosophy and Sociology"—as a form of compensation and restitution. But Adorno's position, even in official university language, came to be called the "Compensation Chair," the very name of which in German *(Wiedergutmachungslehrstuhl)* is rendered absurd by the extraordinary length of the coinage.[29] In 1957, only

---

and published posthumously as a lengthy fragment. Mann acknowledges the incorporation of Adorno's Beethoven commentary (pp. 46–48). Adorno also played for Mann the entire Sonata op. 111 "in a highly instructive fashion," following which, over a period of three days, Mann revised his discussion of the sonata in the novel (chapter 8, pp. 49–69). "Into the poetic little illustrative phrases I wrote for the arietta theme I slipped Adorno's patronymic, *Wiesengrund (Meadowland),* by way of showing my gratitude" (p. 48).

28. Wiggershaus, *Frankfurt School*, p. 431.

29. Ibid., p. 466, Wiggershaus points out that "restitution and compensation to the victims of the Nazi regime had been forced on the Federal Republic by the Western Allies." Regarding anti-Semitic responses to returning Jews, see p. 467.

after forcing the issue (and despite his qualifications—or, for that matter, fame), he was finally granted a full professorship.[30]

Between October 1952 and August 1953, Adorno was (unhappily) back in Los Angeles—after which he never again returned to the United States, although at the time of his death he was preparing to deliver a series of lectures at Princeton. Horkheimer had signed a research contract with the Hacker Foundation, the brainchild of Friedrich Hacker, a Viennese-born psychiatrist who had opened a clinic in Beverly Hills. The matter was mutually beneficial. Hacker "hoped to gain an academic reputation and advertising for his clinic through collaboration with the leading members of the Institute of Social Research";[31] and the Institute's principal figures needed the funding that Hacker was able to provide. Adorno was sent to fulfill the contract; he also needed to return to the United States, else lose his American citizenship which was in fact subsequently surrendered. Under sponsorship from the Hacker Foundation, Adorno produced two studies on popular culture, "The Stars Down to Earth," a monograph-length essay on popular astrology, and the much shorter foray into television, "How to Look at Television."

In his essay "On the Question: 'What Is German?'" originally a radio lecture delivered in 1965, Adorno moved from a broad critique of national identity and its collectivizing tendencies to a much more personal account, in the second half, of his decision after the war to return to Germany. He acknowledges that "At no moment during my emigration did I relinquish the hope of coming back. . . . I simply wanted to go back to the place where I spent my childhood, where what is specifically mine was imparted to the very core. Perhaps I sensed that whatever one accomplishes in life is little other than the attempt to regain childhood."[32] But of course the reasons were more complicated. Adorno played up the ordinary European disdain

30. Ibid., p. 467: Adorno "had never had an offer of a chair from any other university, which would have strengthened his position at Frankfurt. Nor did he ever receive such an offer later on. Once again, Adorno suffered the old Jewish experience of being simultaneously privileged and nevertheless stigmatized and vulnerable."

31. Ibid., p. 456.

32. Adorno, "On the Question: 'What Is German?'" CM, pp. 209–10. Adorno is, of course, playing off the title of Wagner's essay "What Is German?" in *Richard Wagner's Prose Works*, trans. William Ashton Ellis (1895; reprint New York: Broude Brothers, 1966), vol. 4, pp. 149–69. See also Thomas Y. Levin, "Nationalities of Language: Adorno's *Fremdwörter*, An Introduction to 'On the Question: What Is German?'" *New German Critique* 36 (Fall 1985), pp. 111–19; and Russell A. Berman, *Modern Culture and Critical Theory: Art, Politics, and the Legacy of the Frankfurt School* (Madison: University of Wisconsin Press, 1989), p. 184.

for American commercialism "because it has produced nothing but refrigerators and automobiles while Germany produced the culture of the spirit." But this polemical remark was actually one he intended to undercut. The issue was not America or its commercialism. Indeed, in America, he pointed out, "there also flourishes sympathy, compassion, and commiseration with the lot of the weaker. The energetic will to establish a free society—rather than only apprehensively thinking of freedom and, even in thought, degrading it into voluntary submission [i.e., as he sees European experience]—does not forfeit its goodness because the societal system imposes limits to its realization. In Germany, arrogance toward America is inappropriate. By misusing a higher good, it serves only the mustiest of instincts."[33]

Adorno made abundantly clear that his American experience was fundamentally, if not surprisingly, shaped by his life before exile, just as his life's work after his return to Germany was reshaped by his years in America.[34] High among his reasons for returning to Germany was the desire to be immersed in his native language, not least due to frustrations with

33. Adorno, "On the Question: 'What Is German?'" p. 210.
34. Lydia Goehr, "Music and Musicians in Exile: The Romantic Legacy of a Double Life," in Reinhold Brinkmann and Christoph Wolff, eds., *Driven into Paradise: The Musical Migration from Nazi Germany to the United States* (Berkeley and Los Angeles: University of California Press, 1999), p. 70, notes what she terms the duality of home and estrangement, "less in mutually excluding than in doubling terms. Estrangement (linked to freedom, reflectiveness, and openness) and home (linked to understanding, identity, and involvement) capture in their mutual mediation a complex and constructive modernist attitude that persons may take in relation to the society in which they live." And she points to the duality as productive: "This dual perspective, in other terms, allows us to see past a polarization that forces us to conclude either that creativity demands estrangement or that it demands home, and allows us to conclude instead that, if it demands either, then it most likely demands both."

Martin Jay, "Adorno in America," *New German Critique* 31 (Winter 1984), pp. 157–82, provides an excellent overview of Adorno's alienation from American culture during his years in the United States, but also a clear indication of the powerful intellectual impact of this experience subsequent to his return to Germany, p. 165: "In summary, although it might be said that while in America, Adorno tended to interpret his new surroundings through the lens of his earlier experience, once back home, he saw Germany with the eyes of someone who had been deeply affected by his years in exile. Negatively, this meant an increased watchfulness for the signs of an American-style culture industry in Europe. Positively, it meant a wariness of elitist defenses of high culture for its own sake, a new respect for the value of democratic politics, a grudging recognition of the emancipatory potential in certain empirical techniques, and a keen appreciation of the need for a psychological dimension in pedagogy." Jay provides a useful history of Adorno's reception in the United States up to the early 1980s. See also Martin Jay, "The Permanent Exile of Theodor W. Adorno," *Midstream* 15 (December 1969), pp. 62–69, written

American academic publishing. He relates a particularly telling experience involving an American editor, "incidentally a European emigrant," who wanted to publish a portion of *Philosophy of Modern Music* in English translation, a draft of which Adorno prepared for him to consider. The result was rejection on grounds that it was "badly organized." And also he relates a tale about an essay, "Psychoanalysis Revised," that was virtually rewritten by copy editors of an American professional journal in an effort to achieve stylistic uniformity in the issue ("The entire text had been disfigured beyond recognition").[35]

From 1955 until his death in 1969, Adorno's publication proceeded at an astounding pace. Taken as a whole, the sheer quantity of his oeuvre is staggering. The German Collected Edition (twenty volumes, printed in twenty-three) comprises more than ten thousand pages, of which more than four thousand concern music; put differently, if pedantically, something over three million words in all, of which a million concern music. And much more remains to be published. The *Nachlass,* slowly appearing, is estimated to equal the length of the *Gesammelte Schriften* when complete.[36] Besides *In Search of Wagner* and *Philosophy of Modern Music,* which concerns Schoenberg and Stravinsky, Adorno wrote monographs on Berg (1956) and Mahler (1960). He left unfinished a virtually career-long

---

shortly after Adorno's death and serving as a kind of personal account of Jay's brief acquaintance with Adorno as well as introduction to his work for English readers at a time when none of the major monographs was available in English, apart from *The Authoritarian Personality* (1950), itself a collaborative project and distinctly atypical of Adorno's corpus taken as a whole. Harvey Gross, "Adorno in Los Angeles: The Intellectual in Emigration," *Humanities in Society* 2 no. 4 (Fall 1979), pp. 339–51, includes a memoir of a personal encounter with Adorno in 1948, and otherwise reads parts of MM against his life in exile.

35. Adorno, "On the Question: 'What Is German?'" pp. 210–11. The remainder of the essay discusses German as a philosophical language—not to promote it as such but, rather, to explain what German allows Adorno as a native speaker that he cannot gain access to via a foreign tongue. For other comments by Adorno on the exile experience, see Stephen Hinton, "Hindemith and Weill: Cases of 'Inner' and 'Other' Direction," in Reinhold Brinkmann and Christoph Wolff, eds., *Driven into Paradise: The Musical Migration from Nazi Germany to the United States* (Berkeley and Los Angeles: University of California Press, 1999), pp. 276–77 n. 56, summarizing a lecture Adorno read to the Jewish Club of Los Angeles on 27 May 1945 entitled "Fragen an die intellektuelle Emigration." In a letter to Benjamin, 13 March 1934, CC, p. 32, Adorno comments: "I am spending a great deal of time learning English. Learning a foreign language when you are an adult must count amongst the strangest of experiences"; see also p. 54, a letter to Benjamin, 6 November 1934, in which Adorno, proffering advice to his friend, stresses the importance of writing in one's native language.

36. For details, see "Editorisches Nachwort," GS, vol. 20.2, pp. 826–28.

project on Beethoven—first published more than twenty years after his death and only recently translated into English—*Beethoven: The Philosophy of Music*. He supervised publication of six essay collections devoted solely to music: *Dissonanzen* (1956), *Sound Figures* [1959, *Klangfiguren*], *Der getreue Korrepetitor* (1963), *Quasi una fantasia* (1963), *Moments musicaux* (1964), and *Impromptus* (1968) . The collection *Prisms* appeared in 1955, containing several important music essays in addition to others on a variety of subjects. He also published a loosely structured monograph on musical sociology, *Introduction to the Sociology of Music* (1962). The range of these collections is noteworthy: composers from Bach to Boulez, but focusing on the nineteenth century, Beethoven especially, and on the twentieth century up to the 1960s; specific musical works; the institution of early music (leading the way into the "authenticity debates" of the 1980s); compositional procedure; musical form; radio music; jazz; and kitsch; chamber music; opera; new music; popular and light music; conductors and conducting; musical nationalism; the role of the critic; recording technology; types of musical conduct; a theory of listening and listeners; and music pedagogy to touch on only some of the most important *topoi*.[37] Besides performance reviews and reviews of published music, he also published book reviews between 1930 and 1968.[38] Adorno also composed music much of his adult life, beginning before he went to Vienna in 1925 to study composition with Alban Berg and continuing through the 1930s and 1940s, during his exile in both England and the United States. In 1926 Berg confided to Schoenberg in a letter that he found "Wiesengrund's work *very good* and I believe it would also meet with your approval, should you ever hear it. In any event, in its seriousness, its brevity, and above all in the absolute purity of its entire style it is worthy of being grouped with the Schönberg school (and nowhere else!)."[39] Thomas Mann noted that Adorno was composing music during their association in Southern California during the 1940s.[40]

---

37. Adorno's concerns were almost exclusively Western European, and he rarely investigated music prior to Bach. His Eurocentrism has often been noted. See, for example, Edward W. Said, *Musical Elaborations* (New York: Columbia University Press, 1991), pp. xviii–ix, 54–55.

38. For a complete list of his opera and concert reviews, see GS, vol. 19, pp. 648–50; the book reviews, on pp. 341–430.

39. Berg was specifically discussing Adorno's First String Quartet. Alban Berg and Arnold Schoenberg, *The Berg-Schoenberg Correspondence: Selected Letters*, ed. Juliane Brand, Christopher Hailey, and Donald Harris, trans. Juliane Brand and Christopher Hailey (New York: Norton, 1987), p. 355.

40. Mann, *Story of a Novel*, p. 39. On Adorno, the composer, see René Lei-

Adorno's position as an advocate of avant-garde music was at once reflected and secured by his frequent participation, whether as a composition course director or discussant, in the Darmstadt International [Summer] Vacation Courses on New Music which he attended over nine summers between 1950 and 1966.[41] *Philosophy of Modern Music,* published in Germany in 1949, had a significant impact on the postwar generation of avant-garde composers active at Darmstadt—one reflection of which was that Adorno's own compositions were performed with some regularity during

---

bowitz, "Der Komponist Theodor W. Adorno," in *Zeugnisse: Theodor W. Adorno zum sechzigsten Geburtstag* (Frankfurt am Main: Europäische Verlagsanstalt, 1963), pp. 355–59; Sigfried Schibli, *Der Komponist Theodor W. Adorno* (Frankfurt am Main: Frankfurter Bund für Volksbildung, 1988); Dieter Schnebel, "Einführung in Adornos Musik," in *Adorno und die Musik,* ed. Otto Kolleritsch (Graz: Universal Edition, 1979), pp. 15–19; and, especially, Heinz-Klaus Metzger and Rainer Riehn, eds., *Theodor W. Adorno: Der Komponist,* Musik-Konzepte 63–64 (Munich: Edition Text + Kritik, 1989). This last volume comprises twelve essays concerning Adorno's compositions, including songs; pieces for female chorus; his *Kinderjahr,* an arrangement for small orchestra of six pieces from Schumann's *Album für die Jugend* op. 68, for solo piano (1848); *Zwei Stücke für Streichquartett;* and *Sechs kurze Orchesterstücke.* A complete catalogue of Adorno's compositions is provided (pp. 144–46), including unpublished work. The earliest dated composition is from 1918, when Adorno was only fifteen, and the latest from 1946. Most of his compositions date from the 1920s and 1930s.

Adorno left unfinished an opera based on *The Adventures of Tom Sawyer* called *Der Schatz des Indianer-Joe. Singspiel nach Mark Twain,* edited with an afterword by Rolf Tiedemann (Frankfurt am Main: Suhrkamp, 1979), a facsimile of the fragments, based on his own libretto written over a ten-month period beginning in November 1932. Adorno's only completed music for the piece was "Two Songs for Voice and Orchestra," published in the two-volume edition of Adorno's music (which contains twelve works in all, most of which are multi-part collections of short pieces—lieder, especially, but also choral works, pieces for string quartet, and a few pieces for orchestra, including arrangements): Adorno, *Kompositionen,* ed. Heinz-Klaus Metzger and Rainer Riehn (Munich: Edition Text + Kritik, 1980), vol. 2, pp. 63–72. Benjamin, notably critical of the libretto, exchanged several letters with Adorno on the matter. See CC, pp. 23–28; the letters date from late January to mid March 1934. In a letter to Benjamin, 13 March 1934, CC, p. 31, Adorno commented on his lack of success in getting his music published.

Adorno compositions employed both free tonality and serial techniques. Several compositions have recently been released on CD: (1) *Kompositionen,* Wergo WER 6173–2, currently out of print; (2) *Works for String Quartet,* DeutschlandRadio CPO 999 341–2, includes Six Studies for String Quartet (1920), the String Quartet (1921), and Two Pieces for String Quartet op. 2; and (3) *Schumann,* BIS-CD-1055, includes the *Kinderjahr* arrangement.

41. See Gianmario Borio, "Die Positionen Adornos zur musikalischen Avantgarde zwischen 1954 und 1966," in *Adorno in seinen musikalischen Schriften* (Rogensburg: G. Bosse, 1987), pp. 163–64, detailing Adorno's Darmstadt activities in 1950–51, 1954–57, 1961, 1965–66.

this period, though in fact most were written before 1945. And this despite the fact that Adorno was highly critical of the canonic status that serial compositional procedures attained in the aftermath of Schoenberg and Webern, a critique which was, in fact, explicitly voiced in *Philosophy of Modern Music* and later in "The Aging of the New Music," included in this volume. Indeed, Adorno welcomed aleatoric composition, exemplified in 1957 by Karlheinz Stockhausen *(Klavierstück XI)*[42] and Pierre Boulez (his lecture "Alea," that is, "Dice"), each breaking with his earlier serialist phase.[43]

Following Horkheimer's retirement in 1958, Adorno assumed director-

42. Though Stockhausen had been giving lectures at Darmstadt since 1953, it was only in 1957 that he was first invited to teach composition there. *Klavierstück XI* is organized so that the pianist determines its form each time it is performed.

43. See Pierre Boulez, "Alea," trans. David Noakes and Paul Jacobs, *Perspectives of New Music* 3 no. 1 (Fall/Winter 1964), pp. 42–53. Boulez speaks on behalf of a balance between composition and chance, p. 45: "Composition ought to reserve at every moment surprises and ways of its own regardless of all the rationality that must be imposed in other respects in order to attain an unquestionable solidity." He derides "pure" chance as much as he does integral serialist full-control efforts, regarding both as fetishistic. His critique of integral serialism parallels Adorno's, p. 43: "Schematization, quite simply, takes the place of invention. . . . [The result is] a fetishism of numbers, leading to pure and simple failure. We plunge into statistical lists that have no more value than other lists." Boulez taught annually at Darmstadt from 1955 to 1967. See his balanced and often appreciative commentary on Adorno, "L'informulé," *Revue d'esthétique* 8 (1985), pp. 25–29, which concludes: "Adorno, que l'on a souvent accusé d'être exagérément abscons, je le trouve, moi, un professeur de réalité, cette réalité qui annihile le dilettantisme, absolument"; and also his memorial verse following Adorno's death, "T. W. Adorno," in Pierre Boulez, *Orientations: Collected Writings by Pierre Boulez*, ed. Jean-Jacques Nattiez, trans. Martin Cooper (Cambridge: Harvard University Press, 1986), pp. 517–18.

Wiggershaus, *Frankfurt School*, pp. 512–17, provides a basic account of Adorno's Darmstadt involvement and related position on the musical avant-garde. See also two recent collections: (1) Heinz-Klaus Metzger and Rainer Riehn, eds., *Darmstadt-Dokumente I*, Musik-Konzepte Sonderband: Die Reihe über Komponisten (Munich: Edition Text + Kritik, 1999), which includes a long essay by Adorno not included in the GS, "Funktion der Farbe in der Musik," a 1966 Darmstadt lecture, and also the transcript of a 1966 planning session for a conference on the theme "Time in New Music." The participants were Adorno, György Ligeti, Rudolf Stephan, Herbert Brün, and Wol Rosenberg (pp. 313–29). Included are a number of photographs of Adorno at Darmstadt. (2) Markus Grassl and Reinhard Kapp, eds., *Darmstadt-Gespräche: Die Internationalen Fereinkurse für Neue Musik in Wien* (Vienna: Böhlau, 1996). Half of the text is devoted to eleven lengthy oral-history interviews of Darmstadt participants, and half to documents, including letters and postcards, newspaper articles, concert reviews, and new-music concert programs (1946–68); an extensive bibliography is provided. There are numerous references throughout the book to Adorno's involvement.

ship of the Institute for Social Research (he had been Horkheimer's co-director since 1955), a post he retained until his death. Between 1958 and 1965, Adorno produced four volumes of essays on a broad array of literary topics, *Notes to Literature I-IV*. His philosophical monographs from this period include *Against Epistemology: A Metacritique* (1956), a critique of Husserl and phenomenology; and *The Jargon of Authenticity* (1964), attacking Heidegger and other proponents of Existentialism. *Negative Dialectics*, a sustained critique of canonic Western philosophy and metaphysics from Kant and Hegel to Husserl, Heidegger, and Sartre, appeared in 1966. Not quite finished at the time of his death was *Aesthetic Theory*. And there is much more that I have not mentioned, including several other essay collections, and many single essays.

Often lost sight of in American consideration of Adorno, likely due to the difficulty of his major philosophical works, is that he was in every sense a public intellectual. Thus between 1950 and 1969 he was heard on more than 160 radio programs on highly varied subjects, including music. Other topics included matters of general political interest, such as the state of German public education and the question of historical memory in the light of National Socialism. He spoke about philosophy, his experiences as an émigré in America, and even free time (leisure and "hobbies," a word he spoke in English, and which he disparaged). Often Adorno revised the radio lectures for publication, principally in popular journals, and later collected them in paperback editions. As Henry W. Pickford notes, "His engagement in the mass media was a logical consequence of his eminently practical intentions to effect change."[44]

Adorno's regular lectures at his university were widely attended, some filling lecture halls seating one thousand. And of course he often lectured at other German academic institutions. In short, he was a major intellectual

44. Henry W. Pickford, "Preface," CM, p. ix. See further Gerd Kadelbach, "Persönliche Begegnungen mit Theodor W. Adorno im Frankfurter Funkhaus," in *Politische Pädagogik: Beiträge zur Humanisierung der Gesellschaft*, ed. Friedhelm Zubke (Weinheim: Deutscher Studien, 1990), pp. 49–56, a memoir of Adorno's editor at Hessischer Rundfunk in Frankfurt, regarding Adorno's attention to making his radio commentaries accessible to listeners. Some sense of this may be gleaned from the published transcript of a question and answer period following a public lecture, "The Meaning of Working through the Past," CM, pp. 295–306. Adorno's "public" writing appeared in the following notably diverse venues, among others: *Akzente, Darmstädter Echo, FAZ, Deutsche Post, Frankfurter Hefte, Frankfurter Neue Presse, Frankfurter Rundschau, Merkur, Der Monat, Neue Zürischer Zeitung, Neue Rundschau, Rundfunk und Fernsehen, Sender Freies Berlin, Der Spiegel, Volkshochschule im Westen,* and *Die Zeit.*

force in both academic and public spheres. In the words of his friend Leo Lowenthal—who chose to remain in the United States after the war and achieved a notably distinguished career at Berkeley—Adorno was "Germany's most prominent academic teacher and outstanding citizen of the Western-European avant-garde."[45]

The left student movement of the late 1960s produced a dramatic change in Adorno's fortunes among the very students much influenced by his philosophical and sociological writings. Adorno had refused to join the student protests in Frankfurt in 1969. Worse, on 31 January he had called in the police to end what he mistakenly thought was a student occupation of the Institute (in fact, the seventy-six students arrested had merely been looking for a place to meet). Matters came to a final head in April when three women activists of the SDS interrupted Adorno's philosophy lecture ("An Introduction to Dialectical Thinking") by surrounding him at the podium, bearing their breasts, simulating caresses, and "attacking" him with flowers. As Martin Jay described it, "Adorno, unnerved and humiliated, left the lecture hall with the students mockingly proclaiming that 'as an institution, Adorno is dead.'"[46] His physical death from a heart attack followed four months later.

CRITICAL THEORY

Whoever doesn't entertain any idle thoughts doesn't throw any wrenches into the machinery.

> Theodor Adorno, "The Meaning of Working
> through the Past"

Critical Theory—the designation comes from Adorno's friend and mentor Max Horkheimer in an essay published in 1937[47]—is constituted as a loose

45. Leo Lowenthal, "Theodor W. Adorno: An Intellectual Memoir," in *An Unmastered Past: The Autobiographical Reflections of Leo Lowenthal,* ed. Martin Jay (Berkeley and Los Angeles: University of California Press, 1987), pp. 189–90.

46. Jay, *Adorno,* p. 55. A highly detailed and consistently fascinating documentary account of this history is contained in a recent massive study, which includes numerous photographs: *Frankfurter Schule und Studentenbewegung: Von der Flaschenpost zum Molotowcocktail, 1946–1995,* ed. Wolfgang Kraushaar, 3 vols. (Hamburg: Rogner and Bernhard, 1998). Very heavy coverage is incorporated regarding the student protest movement from 1967 to 1969; Adorno's presence looms large. For briefer accounts see Wiggershaus, *Frankfurt School,* pp. 609–36; and Scheible, *Theodor W. Adorno,* pp. 141–46, which includes photographs of Adorno taken during this period.

47. Max Horkheimer, "Traditional and Critical Theory," trans. Matthew J.

amalgamation of philosophical principles rather than as either a neatly packaged system or a methodological recipe.[48] In what follows I lay out the defining issues and the social and cultural stakes to which these principles respond. To be sure, Frankfurt School Critical Theory evolved over time and was never regarded as a seamless entity. Nonetheless, some basic parameters are clear and well established.

Horkheimer's lengthy essay, "Traditional and Critical Theory" (1937), is a good place to start. He opens the text with a question: "What is 'theory'?" and immediately proceeds to provide the "traditional" answer, articulated as an outgrowth of scientific method employed in the natural sciences but also adopted by the social sciences—for which, as he will argue, traditional theory is sorely inadequate. "Theory for most researchers is the sum-total of propositions about a subject, the propositions being so linked with each other that a few are basic and the rest derive from these. The smaller the number of primary principles in comparison with the derivations, the more perfect the theory. The real validity of the theory depends on the derived propositions being consonant with the actual facts."[49] The inadequacy of traditional theory, Horkheimer argues, lies in its "assiduous collecting of facts"—not in the facts themselves but the invisibility and even irrelevance of the historicity of facts, and of the fact-perceiving human subject: "The facts which our senses present to us are socially preformed in two ways: through the historical character of the object perceived and through the historical character of the perceiving organ. Both are not simply natural; they are shaped by human activity, and yet the individual perceives himself as receptive and passive in the act of perception."[50]

Horkheimer's intention is not to attack scientific method but to delineate its inadequacy in theorizing the social, cultural, and political realms of human experience. Stated simply, traditional theory cannot address the

O'Connell, in *Critical Theory: Selected Essays* (New York: Continuum, 1986), pp. 188–243.

48. Susan Buck-Morss, *The Origin of Negative Dialectics: Theodor W. Adorno, Walter Benjamin, and the Frankfurt Institute* (New York: Free Press, 1977), p. 65: "Critical Theory was never a fully articulated philosophy which members of the Institute applied in an identical fashion. It was far more a set of assumptions which they shared, and which distinguished their approach from bourgeois, or 'traditional,' theory."

49. Horkheimer, "Traditional and Critical Theory," p. 188.

50. Ibid., pp. 190, 200.

fact and problem of the social totality precisely because the social totality develops less from the relation of fact to fact and more from the relation of fact to value. Further, fact and value are invariably history-laden, and the "facts" of history become facts not as the result of some natural order but because they are made so, indeed even willed so, by the social orders that prevail in a given time and place, which is to suggest that a social or cultural "fact" is not necessarily either permanently or universally so regarded. Moreover, the thinking subject—who will produce or define social "facts"—is never external to the processes for which explanation is sought. The scholar-subject is not autonomous; to assume autonomy is blindly to accept as "natural" fact the ideology of the Cartesian ego itself (the mind "is not cut loose from the life of society; it does not hang suspended over it").[51] In short, as Christoph Menke accounts for this issue, "The limits that Horkheimer sees imposed on traditional theory derive from the fact that it cannot grasp itself—its own functioning—as theory: it is not reflexive."[52]

Horkheimer provides an example in the modern intellectual division of labor: "In society as it is, the power of thought has never controlled itself but has always functioned as a nonindependent moment in the work process, and the latter has its own orientation and tendency."[53] Thought in modernity is fundamentally instrumental. And further, thought is marked by social privilege; it bears the mark of society's lack of equality. That some individuals are intellectuals occurs in relation to the denial of the intellectual practice to others, and this social fact affects thought itself. Expressed in more global language, the happiness of some comes about via the denial of happiness to others; it is this crucial mediation of happiness that is erased unless the "fact" of happiness is examined in relation to value and history.

The Marxian insight that drives Horkheimer's concern is the demand for equal justice. But unlike Marx he does not see a rising up of the proletariat (neither did Adorno). That the poor and oppressed deserve, or for that matter might even demand, justice does not constitute its guarantee.

51. Ibid., p. 223.
52. Christoph Menke, "Critical Theory and Tragic Knowledge," trans. James Swindal, in The Handbook of Critical Theory, ed. David M. Rasmussen (Oxford: Blackwell, 1996), p. 59. Frederic Jameson, "Introduction to T. W. Adorno," in The Legacy of the German Refugee Intellectuals, ed. Robert Boyers (New York: Schocken, 1972), p. 141, makes a similar point, noting that what Adorno regarded as dialectical thinking involved the "attempt to think self-consciously about our own thought while we are in the act of thinking about some object, to be both conscious and self-conscious at the same time."
53. Horkheimer, "Traditional and Critical Theory," p. 212.

Indeed, Horkheimer notes that the situation of social degradation and domination is "no guarantee of correct knowledge." Accordingly, he insists on the responsibility of the intellectual to "be a critical, promotive factor in the development of the masses."[54] The critical theoretician's role is to help change society by explaining it—but all the while remembering that his or her own position of relative intellectual privilege ironically exemplifies the very problem for which redress is sought.

Horkheimer acknowledges the utopian character of Critical Theory; its goal is not the perpetuation of present society but society's transformation.[55] Or, as he expressed it elsewhere, "The real social function of philosophy lies in its criticism of what is prevalent."[56] Nonetheless the extreme difficulty of effecting progressive change was recognized by Horkheimer, not least in light of Stalinism and National Socialism. Salvaging the possibility of thought itself appeared to be an enormous challenge: anti-reason seemed to drive modernity toward dystopian fulfillment. As he pointed out, "the first consequence of the theory which urges a transformation of society as a whole is only an intensification of the struggle with which the theory is connected."[57] Adorno, in *Negative Dialectics*, voiced what he saw as an increasing prohibition on thought itself: "When men are forbidden to think, their thinking sanctions what simply exists. The genuinely critical need of thought to awaken from the cultural phantasmagoria is trapped, channeled, steered into the wrong consciousness. The culture of its environment has broken thought of the habit to ask what all this may be, and to what end; it has enfeebled the question [of] what it all means—a question growing in urgency as fewer people find some such sense self-evident, as it yields more and more to cultural bustle."[58]

54. Ibid., pp. 213–14.
55. Ibid., p. 218. David M. Rasmussen, "Critical Theory and Philosophy," in *The Handbook of Critical Theory*, ed. David M. Rasmussen (Oxford: Blackwell, 1996), p. 12: "The ancient assumption that the purpose of reflection was for knowledge itself, allied with the further assumption that pure contemplation was the proper end of the human subject, was replaced by another end of reflection also to be derived from classical thought, but with its own peculiarly modern twist; theory when allied with praxis has a proper political end, namely, social transformation." Rasmussen's essay traces the history of Critical Theory from its origins in classic German philosophy through Jürgen Habermas.
56. Max Horkheimer, "The Social Function of Philosophy," in *Critical Theory: Selected Essays*, trans. Matthew J. O'Connell et al. (New York: Continuum, 1986), p. 264.
57. Horkheimer, "Traditional and Critical Theory," p. 219.
58. ND, pp. 85–86.

Critical Theory, responding to the specific historical circumstances of Western modernity, constitutes a Marxian-indebted critique of exchange economy and its impact on the subject and society—though Adorno's critical-theoretical practice, by contrast with most of his Frankfurt School compatriots, involved socio-cultural rather than socio-economic critique. Here is Horkheimer's summary statement: "The critical theory of society is, in its totality, the unfolding of a single existential judgment. To put it in broad terms, the theory says that the basic form of the historically given commodity economy on which modern history rests contains in itself the internal and external tensions of the modern era; it generates these tensions over and over again in an increasingly heightened form; and after a period of progress, development of human powers, and emancipation for the individual, after an enormous extension of human control over nature, it finally hinders further development and drives humanity into a new barbarism."[59] The "point" of Critical Theory develops from the presupposition of freedom, even to the extent that general freedom does not yet exist.[60] As Horkheimer states near the end of his essay, Critical Theory "has no specific influence on its side, except concern for the abolition of social injustice."[61]

Critical Theory stands in opposition to closed philosophical systems—Hegel's is a prime example—precisely because of the idealism that governs such systems' operation. That is, Critical Theory opposes philosophical systems designed to achieve a "logical" closure or absolute truth without necessary reference to the reality that stands outside thought itself. Thus the "totality" achieved in Hegel's dialectical overcoming of contradiction is at heart false to the extent that its philosophical logic fails to address actual social contradiction. Critical Theory by contrast draws attention to social contradiction—material existence—expressed as antagonism and suffering, not only by what it attends to and "says" but also by how it speaks: in fragments, aphorisms, short forms, in a word, anti-systematically, and by formulating a negative dialectics, in opposition to the (positive) dialectics of the Hegelian model, a topic I'll pursue later.

---

59. Horkheimer, "Traditional and Critical Theory," p. 227.
60. Cf. Adorno, "Why Still Philosophy," CM, p. 10: "If philosophy is still necessary, it is so only in the way it has been from time immemorial: as critique, as resistance to the expanding heteronomy, even if only as thought's powerless attempt to remain its own master and to convict of untruth, by their own criteria, both a fabricated mythology and a conniving, resigned acquiescence on the other of untruth. It is incumbent upon philosophy . . . to provide a refuge for freedom."
61. Horkheimer, "Traditional and Critical Theory," p. 242.

Critical Theory seeks to conjoin philosophy with social analysis, the practice governed by a materialist, as opposed to idealist, dialectics, the ultimate
concern being human happiness.[62]

Now to Adorno. The parameters that define his thought are several,
and their principal features have been mapped by Martin Jay:[63] Marxism
of a distinctly heterodox variety; aesthetic modernism; what Jay names
"mandarin cultural conservatism," in particular reference to Adorno's
writing on mass culture (Jay's position here is, in my judgment, too baldly
stated, as I shall discuss later); a "Jewish impulse," particularly notable
after the onset of the war and the horrors of the Holocaust—the first
sustained discussion by Adorno of anti-Semitism appears in *Dialectic of
Enlightenment;* and, finally, what Jay names "Deconstructionism," as
much as anything, I think, reflecting the moment Jay's Adorno monograph
was written.[64]

Finally, Adorno's thought reflects his reading of Freud,[65] and the place

62. See further Jay, *Dialectical Imagination,* pp. 41–85. For a good account of
Adorno's critique of philosophy, see Peter Uwe Hohendahl, *Prismatic Thought:
Theodor W. Adorno* (Lincoln: University of Nebraska Press, 1995), pp. 217–42.

63. Jay, *Adorno,* pp. 15–23.

64. Fredric Jameson, *Late Marxism: Adorno, or, the Persistence of the Dialectic*
(London: Verso, 1990), p. 247, argues against Adorno's reputed postmodernism
avant la lettre—while acknowledging that Adorno "included a place for the possible emergence of postmodernism." Jameson aptly, if bitterly, comments on
Adorno in light of the postmodern condition: "The question about poetry after
Auschwitz has been replaced with that of whether you could bear to read Adorno
and Horkheimer next to the pool" (p. 248). Tetsuo Kogawa, "Adorno's 'Strategy
of Hibernation,'" *Telos* 46 (Winter 1980–81), pp. 147–53, parses Adorno's restatement in ND of the Auschwitz comment, "All post-Auschwitz culture, including
its urgent critique, is garbage" (p. 367) as a "strategic critical gesture within the
context of the culture industry" (p. 151). See also on Adorno's supposed relation
to postmodernism Lambert Zuidervaart, *Adorno's Aesthetic Theory: The Redemption of Illusion* (Cambridge: MIT Press, 1991), pp. 248–74; Ben Agger, *A Critical
Theory of Public Life: Knowledge, Discourse and Politics in an Age of Decline*
(London: Falmer Press, 1991), pp. 19–42; Rainer Nägele, "The Scene of the Other:
Theodor W. Adorno's Negative Dialectic in the Context of Poststructuralism," in
Postmodernism and Politics, ed. Jonathan Arac (Minneapolis: University of Minnesota Press, 1986), pp. 91–111; Albrecht Wellmer, *The Persistence of Modernity:
Essays on Aesthetics, Ethics, and Postmodernism,* trans. David Midgley (Cambridge: MIT Press, 1991); Joel Whitebook, "From Schoenberg to Odysseus: Aesthetic, Psychic, and Social Synthesis in Adorno and Wellmer," *New German Critique* 58 (Winter 1993), pp. 45–64; and Christopher Rocco, "Between Modernity
and Postmodernity: Reading *Dialectic of Enlightenment* against the Grain," *Political Theory* 22 no. 1 (February 1994), pp. 71–97.

65. Critical Theory's linking of Marxian thought to Freudian psychoanalysis
was nothing short of intellectually audacious in the late 1920s and early 1930s,

he defined for psychology in his social theory, notably pertinent in light of what Jay has termed "the unexpected rise of an irrationalist mass politics in fascism, which was unforeseen by orthodox Marxists."[66] In point of fact, Adorno's principal interest in psychoanalysis was its de facto delineation of social trauma. To mark social trauma constituted a step toward the healing of the individual within society, to the extent that diagnosis precedes cure. But this is not to suggest that Adorno's interest was with psychoanalytic therapy, which addressed the individual psyche and whose healing remained distinct from the social whole. The diagnosis Adorno sought was social not individual, though the specific detail of individual psychosis could in turn inform social diagnostics. As he put it in the Dedication of *Minima Moralia*, "society is essentially the substance of the individual."[67] (Adorno's social psychology is in fact much governed by a study of the family, as a kind of middle ground between the individual and the larger society.)[68] More important for Adorno, Freudian psychoanalysis, ahistorical and based on a biological premise, nonetheless "expressed, at least metaphorically, one aspect of the nonidentity of man in an unreconciled totality."[69]

During the early 1940s, while living in Southern California, Adorno and Horkheimer jointly authored a text they first named *Philosophical Fragments* in a 1944 mimeographed edition, and later *Dialectic of Enlightenment* when the text was formally published in a revised version in Amsterdam in 1947; the book first appeared in English only in 1972.[70] Douglas

---

when, in Germany, Freud's work was anything but commonly accepted. See Joel Whitebook, "Fantasy and Critique: Some Thoughts on Freud and the Frankfurt School," in *The Handbook of Critical Theory*, ed. David M. Rasmussen (Oxford: Blackwell, 1996), pp. 287–88.

66. Jay, *Adorno*, p. 85.

67. MM, p. 17.

68. See Jay, *Dialectical Imagination*, pp. 76–112.

69. Jay, *Permanent Exiles*, p. 25.

70. On the specifics of the Horkheimer-Adorno collaboration, see James Schmidt, "Language, Mythology, and Enlightenment: Historical Notes on Horkheimer and Adorno's *Dialectic of Enlightenment*," *Social Research* 65 no. 4 (1998), pp. 807–38, including a comparison between the mimeographed first version and final published text, as well as background concerning a planned but never realized companion volume that would have served as a "positive theory of dialectics" explaining how, in Horkheimer's words, the "'rescue of the enlightenment' might be accomplished" (p. 811); and Robert Hullot-Kentor, "Back to Adorno," *Telos* 81 (Fall 1989), pp. 7–9; regarding the problematic nature of Cumming's translation, see pp. 27–29. Hullot-Kentor has retranslated the first excursus of DE, "Odysseus or Myth and Enlightenment," *New German Critique* 56 (Spring/Summer 1992), pp. 109–41.

Kellner comments that *Dialectic of Enlightenment* "provides the first critical questioning of modernity, Marxism and the Enlightenment from within the tradition of critical social theory," thereby anticipating by several decades postmodernism's critique of modernity.[71] The book is unconventionally structured and in a way that reflects the function of writing as Adorno understood it, though it might likewise be argued that the text is something of a hybrid, perhaps the result of an amalgamation of two quite different narrative styles: Horkheimer's distinctly the more conventional, organized in standard essay or chapter format; Adorno's the opposite, markedly more constellational, fragmented, and aphoristic. Elements of both are replete throughout the text.

The book opens conventionally, with an introduction, followed by a chapter on "The Concept of Enlightenment." Thereafter, chapter organization is interrupted by two paired sections called "Excursus," each of chapter length and on topics seemingly far removed from an investigation of (modern) enlightenment: *The Odyssey* and the Marquis de Sade. What follows next is still more jarring in light of the immediately preceding excursuses, namely, the much-cited chapter on "The Culture Industry: Enlightenment as Mass Deception," followed in turn by a chapter on anti-Semitism. At the end the text fragments radically in a lengthy section simply named "Notes and Drafts," organized as a series of twenty-four aphorisms, similar to those in *Minima Moralia*, which Adorno was beginning to write at the time. The book's organization, philosophically and socially grounded, is anti-philosophical to the extent it abandons any model of closed systematic investigation in its attempt to understand modernity. Nonetheless, it is fundamentally philosophical within the context of Critical Theory's critique of traditional philosophical practice. As regards both its narrative structure and its stance on history, the book is of singular importance for understanding Adorno.

The Marxian foundation of Critical Theory is shifted away from class conflict to what Adorno and Horkheimer regard as something more fundamental, namely, the subject's historical relation to nature as one of conflict which turns the subject against others and, ultimately, against the self. "What men want to learn from nature is how to use it in order wholly to dominate it and other men.[72] That is its only aim. Ruthlessly, in spite

71. Douglas Kellner, "Critical Theory Today: Revisiting the Classics," *Theory, Culture and Society* 10 no. 2 (May 1993), p. 50.
72. Adorno only occasionally wrote directly on gender issues, as in MM, pp. 90–96, 169–74, and in DE, pp. 110–12, 247–50. But critics have pointed out that

of itself, the Enlightenment has extinguished any trace of its own self-consciousness." And later: "Enlightenment is totalitarian."[73] This, in essence ultimate, conflict, in other words, long predates capitalism. As Adorno and Horkheimer (in)famously argue, the fundamental forms of domination that organize modernity have their roots in the primordial efforts of human beings to survive in a nature—primordial totality—of which they are at once a part yet deeply alienated from and fearful.

And yet human subjects lament the very separation from nature upon which their subjectivity is ultimately grounded. Thus by the principle Adorno and Horkheimer articulate, the designation of national parks which first occurred during the heyday of the Industrial Revolution—itself signaling a kind of final triumph over nature—directly responded to the fractured relation of the subject to nature; the setting aside of small and as yet "untamed" geographies signified less a nostalgic return to nature than a material acknowledgment of the permanence of the fracture, in the same way that salvage anthropology in essence picks among the graves and ruins to remember what "advanced man" has destroyed to become advanced. In this sense, of course, charity—compassionate conservatism—falls in line as a substitute for justice, not to alter the foundation of domination[74] but to make injustice more tolerable to some people's stomachs and other people's conscience.

The driving theme of *Dialectic of Enlightenment* is the ironic regression of enlightenment, reason's alleged goal, into myth, whose deadly consequences at the level of the subject and society were so dramatically enacted in the Aryan myths of the Third Reich. The book's "purpose" was to produce a critique that made visible enlightenment's internal contradictions, the recognition of which would necessarily constitute the first step in rescuing enlightenment from itself—from its unrecognized debased form. In this regard, for all its often cited pessimism, *Dialectic of Enlightenment* is at heart utopian.

---

his conception of subjectivity is resolutely a male bourgeois model. See Sabine Wilke and Heidi Schlipphacke, "Construction of a Gendered Subject: A Feminist Reading of Adorno's *Aesthetic Theory*," in *The Semblance of Subjectivity: Essays in Adorno's Aesthetic Theory*, ed. Tom Huhn and Lambert Zuidervaart (Cambridge: MIT Press, 1997), pp. 287–308. See also Maggie O'Neill, ed., *Adorno, Culture and Feminism* (London: Sage, 1999).

73. DE, pp. 4 [translation modified], 6.

74. Competition is domination's twin. The necessity of the struggle for survival, and for risk-taking in the name of personal advancement, become "the postulate of a moral excuse for profit" (DE, p. 62).

The fundamental rhetorical device of *Dialectic of Enlightenment* is ex-aggeration, embodied in the vast historical sweep from Homer to the mov-ies, in an implicitly unbroken historical thread, as exemplary of domina-tion to the point of self-domination—a gesture narratologically as effective as it was grist for subsequent criticism.[75] As Susan Buck-Morss points out: "The polemical, iconoclastic intent of the study is the reason why it focused on two sacred cows of bourgeois rational thought, the harmonious age of ancient Greece and the eighteenth-century Enlightenment. These mo-ments of an idealized past were juxtaposed to the most barbaric, most irrational phenomena of the present in order to demythologize the present and the past's hold over it."[76] Not the least of the book's intent is the effort to dismantle the self-satisfied ideology that structures the heart of histor-icism, the myth of history as progress, which itself underwrites the ideo-logical ground of modernity as the supposed realization of the Enlight-enment.

Though both Adorno and Horkheimer were modernists to the core, they attack the degree to which modern enlightenment is defined in terms of technological achievement. Neither was nostalgic for a supposed lost Golden Age, whether that of Homeric myth or the progressive moment of the bourgeois revolution in the early decades of the nineteenth century ("The task to be accomplished is not the conservation of the past, but the redemption of the hopes of the past").[77] Technological achievement as such

75. For a particularly well known example, see Jürgen Habermas, "The En-twinement of Myth and Enlightenment: Re-Reading *Dialectic of Enlightenment*," trans. Thomas Y. Levin, *New German Critique* 26 (Spring/Summer 1982), pp. 13–30. For a response, in turn, to Habermas, see Karin Bauer, *Adorno's Nietzschean Narratives: Critiques of Ideology, Readings of Wagner* (Albany: State University of New York Press, 1999), pp. 32–39. Critics of *Dialectic of Enlightenment*, Haber-mas notable among them, have not gone unanswered, however. See, for example, Peter Uwe Hohendahl, "*Dialectic of Enlightenment* Revisited: Habermas's Critique of the Frankfurt School," in *Reappraisals: Shifting Alignments in Postwar Critical Theory* (Ithaca: Cornell University Press, 1991), pp. 99–130; Hullot-Kentor, "Back to Adorno," pp. 5–29; and more general defenses by Jack Zipes, "Adorno May Still Be Right," *Telos* 101 (Fall 1994), pp. 157–67; and Kellner, "Critical Theory Today," pp. 43–60. For an overview of *Dialectic of Enlightenment*, see Simon Jarvis, *Adorno: A Critical Introduction* (New York: Routledge, 1998), pp. 20–43.

76. Buck-Morss, *Origin of Negative Dialectics*, p. 61. Cf. Robert Hullot-Kentor, "Notes on *Dialectic of Enlightenment*: Translating the Odysseus Essay," *New German Critique* 56 (Spring/Summer 1992), pp. 106–07, who suggests that the decision by Adorno and Horkheimer to employ the Odysseus story is rooted in the fact that since the eighteenth century, German intellectuals considered both themselves and Germany "as the bearer of the Hellenic torch."

77. DE, p. xv. See Michael Löwy and Eleni Varikas, "'The World Spirit on the

is a neutral element in their critique. Rather, it is the fetishization of technological achievement, and how technology comes to be made a fetish, that locates their concern. The real issue is instrumental reason and its function in domination: "Reason itself has become the mere instrument of the all-inclusive economic apparatus. It serves as a general tool, useful for the manufacture of all other tools, firmly directed towards its ends, as fateful as the precisely calculated movement of material production, whose result for mankind is beyond all calculation. At last its old ambition, to be a pure organ of ends, has been realized."[78] That is, reason instrumentalized is reason not concerned with social truth and its implications for social justice, but reason of the bottom line, whether in economics or cultural politics—reason degraded to wit, smarts, and especially cunning,[79] which functions as a tool on behalf of the self, not the other. Instrumental reason serves as agent in the subject's war on nature, broadly understood. Reason's "cunning *[List]* consists in turning men into animals with more and more far-reaching powers, and not in establishing the identity between subject and object."[80]

Adorno and Horkheimer argue that the dilemma of instrumental reason functions as a defining principle in Western history as far back as written records survive. Instrumental reason, the determinate agent in domination—so they scandalously argue—determines the primordial hero of Western history, Odysseus himself, in essence the First Modern Man, the hero as relentless Can-Do specialist of the ancient world. His cunning defeats Polyphemus, and by techniques of wanton cruelty;[81] his wit saves him from the Sirens, but only at the expense of his men whose ears he orders stopped up with wax to render them deaf to the Sirens' song, whose pleasure he denies them not for their own good, to avoid being drawn thereby to the rocks, but so that he can hear the song without risk to

---

Fins of a Rocket': Adorno's Critique of Progress," trans. Martin Ryle, *Radical Philosophy* 70 (March/April 1995), pp. 9–15.

78. DE, p. 30.

79. The first and last aphorisms in the "Notes and Drafts" section address cunning. The first, "Why It Is Better Not to Know All the Answers" ["Gegen Bescheidwissen"], pp. 209–211, concerning "cleverness" *[Gescheitsein]*; and "The Genesis of Stupidity" ["Zur Genese der Dummheit"], pp. 256–58 ("Stupidity is a scar" of a child's unanswered queries and unfulfilled needs). Cf. Adorno, "Notes on Philosophical Thinking," CM, p. 132: "Stupidity is nothing privative, not the simple absence of mental ability, but rather the scar of its mutilation."

80. DE, p. 223, from the aphorism "On the Critique of the Philosophy of History."

81. Ibid., pp. 64–69.

himself. Good planner, he buys himself some insurance by ordering his
men to tie him securely to the mast, a gesture that also "pays" for the
pleasure through a gesture of self-renunciation. Odysseus's ears are un-
stopped; he hears the song, but cannot act on the desires thereby lavishly
produced. Lashed to the mast, he is at once the simulacrum of phallic power
and self-rendered impotence.[82] Desire for desire is a recurring trope, as is
desire's defeat through seemingly perpetual deferral, the Weberian Prot-
estant work ethic *avant la lettre*. "The history of civilization is the history
of the introversion of sacrifice. In other words: the history of renunciation.
Everyone who practices renunciation gives away more of his life than is
given back to him: and more than the life that he vindicates."[83]

Fear, and fear's resentment, is the dominant trope of *Dialectic of Enlightenment*: Polyphemus is feared hence blinded; the self is feared and
disciplined; the Jew Other is feared and destroyed. Put differently, humankind's long "modernity" is constituted by a radical act of othering, in
which each instance of the other exists either to serve or be destroyed.[84]
Fear's causes are real. The human being in a primordial state confronts the
world at once as provider and threat. Language initiates the process of
ordering nature's apparent randomness and, worse, chaos. Myth narrates
an order, via an already advanced form of reason—but not advanced
enough. The language-act of myth is a device for coping with nature, not
controlling it. The subject (in actuality not yet a subject) functioning under
the order of myth only "imagines himself free from fear when there is no
longer anything unknown." Enlightenment supplants myth, itself a lesser
form of enlightenment but enlightenment nonetheless: "Enlightenment is
mythic fear turned radical." Enlightenment supersedes myth, by means of

82. Ibid., pp. 34, 59.
83. Ibid., p. 55. Cf. p. 57: "He just pulls through; struggle is his survival; and
all the fame that he and the others win in the process serves merely to confirm
that the title of hero is only gained at the price of the abasement and mortification
of the instinct for complete, universal, and undivided happiness."
84. Hullot-Kentor, "Notes on *Dialectic of Enlightenment*," p. 102. "What *Dialectic of Enlightenment* discerns as the reason for thought's capitulation deserves
blunt statement because even if it is a discovery that everyone has made at some
point it puts its finger on the origins of conformist thinking with rare candor:
thought conforms out of fear. And it is not just that thought balks at disturbing
insights but that thought itself develops as an organization of fear that progressively conforms to what it would master." Cf. DE, p. xiv: "The dutiful child of
modern civilization is possessed by a fear of departing from the facts which, in the
very act of perception, the dominant conventions of science, commerce, and politics—cliché-like—have already molded; his anxiety is none other than the fear of
social deviation."

which the subject controls nature absolutely. Enlightenment is determined by the need for nothing to escape its insight: "Nothing at all may remain outside, because the mere idea of outsideness is the very source of fear."[85] But to banish fear, through enlightenment, leads as well to the banishment of pity. Enlightenment is relentless, its demands total. The world must be rationalized, myth banned for its sin of fiction. The elimination of "outsideness" demands the identification of the Other, all others, and by whatever means necessary, the most efficient of which is reason instrumentalized, reason put to the task of naming, labeling: controlling. The modern forms of identification numbers—whether registered on magnetic disk or tattooed on one's arm—mark the outer limits of the territory. This is the form of rationality that conjoins Odysseus and Sade, whose accounts of the body involve systematically cataloguing its orifices and demonstrating their functionality for others' pleasure with imaginative—yet disciplined—concentration:[86] a modernity of sex in which the subject effectively others itself in the most fearsome manner that the human mind can envision—fully codified, a systematic law of outrage. Reason reverts, reasonably, under the circumstances, to its own other: Cartesian duality is enacted without mercy, the mind and body[87] in an embrace defined by hatred via the allegory of rape. The exchange principle is here worked out in an economy of hungry and degraded flesh, and the world is organized into binary principles: strong and weak, agents and their victims. "Enlightenment has relinquished its own realization."[88] And yet the antidote to instrumentalized reason is reason—the paradox and contradiction at the heart of the dialectic of enlightenment. As Adorno pointed out in *Negative Dialectics*, "Today as in Kant's time, philosophy demands a rational critique of reason, not its banishment or abolition."[89]

To summarize: enlightenment and domination are co-dependent. And in the end, the survival that accrues by othering nature produces at the same moment an othering of the self: "As soon as man discards his aware-

85. DE, p. 16.
86. Ibid., p. 88: "Sade realized [the affinity between knowledge and planning] empirically more than a century before sport was conceived. The teams of modern sport, whose interaction is so precisely regulated that no member has any doubt about his role, and which provide a reserve for every player, have their exact counterpart in the sexual teams of *Juliette*, which employ every moment usefully, neglect no human orifice, and carry out every function."
87. Regarding the love-hate relationship with the body, see the aphorism "The Importance of the Body," DE, pp. 231–36.
88. DE, p. 41.
89. ND, p. 85.

ness that he himself is nature, all the aims for which he keeps himself alive—social progress, the intensification of all his material and spiritual powers, even consciousness itself—are nullified, and the enthronement of the means as an end, which under late capitalism is tantamount to open insanity, is already perceptible in the prehistory of subjectivity. Man's domination over himself, which grounds his selfhood, is almost always the destruction of the subject in whose service it is undertaken."[90]

Adorno's position on natural beauty, which deeply informs both his social and aesthetic theory, is anchored in these concerns. "Nothing in the world is worthy of attention except that for which the autonomous subject has itself to thank."[91] In this regard, nature is lacking. Yet human subjects, by nature *of* nature, thereby are constituted by a lack of their own making. Adorno argues that authentic artworks silently hail natural beauty, which, like nature, is not directly available to us to the extent that "nature" is both pre-determined and pre-structured by history (just as language itself is historical). (Our longing for nature—for example, ecological regard, wilderness preservation, but also art, in Adorno's argument—is a projection of a lack that develops alongside our separation from and domination of nature.) Adorno suggests that the lack of interest in natural beauty in nineteenth-century aesthetics is part and parcel of the larger historical separation he critiques.[92] "The concept of natural beauty rubs on a wound."[93] Art is called upon to answer for natural beauty, in effect to substitute for it; art—wholly artifactual, that is, literally unnatural—by this means enacts or perpetuates the attack on nature. And yet art does more, for it acknowledges the natural beauty that the subject has otherwise degraded yet nonetheless desires in its nonexistent "perfect" state, and it reflects on this fact. Art, as Adorno put it, "want[s] to keep nature's promise. . . . What nature strives for in vain, artworks fulfill."[94] Natural

90. DE, p. 54.
91. AT, p. 62.
92. Adorno is thus bluntly positioning himself against Hegel, whose disregard for nature is well known. On this point, see AT, pp. 63, 75–77; and Richard Wolin, "Utopia, Mimesis, and Reconciliation: A Redemptive Critique of Adorno's *Aesthetic Theory*," *Representations* 32 (Fall 1990), p. 42.
93. AT, pp. 61–62. See also Heinz Paetzold, "Adorno's Notion of Natural Beauty: A Reconsideration," in *The Semblance of Subjectivity: Essays in Adorno's Aesthetic Theory*, ed. Tom Huhn and Lambert Zuidervaart (Cambridge: MIT Press, 1997), pp. 213–35.
94. AT, pp. 62, 65–66. "Under its optic, art is not the imitation of nature, but the imitation of natural beauty" (p. 71).

beauty, he insists, is "the trace of the nonidentical in things under the spell of universal identity."[95]

DIALECTICS

The true nihilists are the ones who oppose nihilism with their more and more faded positivities, the ones who are thus conspiring with all extant malice, and eventually with the destructive principle itself. Thought honors itself by defending what is damned as nihilism.

Adorno, *Negative Dialectics*

Adorno's critique of philosophy was isomorphic with his critique of society. The truth of modern society, for Adorno, was its falseness through and through. Modernity was structured around the commodity fetish and a commodified subjectivity which together functioned in a deadly, mutually self-sustaining embrace. Philosophy's role—in effect, philosophy's social and ethical responsibility—was to conceptualize this condition: "Conscience," Adorno wrote in *Negative Dialectics*, "is the mark of shame of an unfree society."[96] But philosophy's ability in so doing was doubly compromised; first, by its own history, which in the West was fundamentally idealist with its idealism in turn systematically totalizing and self-referential; second, philosophy, an act of language, failed to reveal the truth that it claimed, a principal cause of which was philosophy's conventionalized practice of treating language—hence thought itself—as a transparent mechanism, in essence autonomous from its own historical contingency. Under present conditions in particular, Adorno argued, thought—notably including his own—was deeply compromised by the forces driving modernity, as he acknowledged at the very beginning of *Negative Dialectics*, his greatest philosophical work: "No theory today escapes the marketplace. Each one is offered as a possibility among competing opinions; all are put up for choice; all are swallowed. There are no blinders for thought to don against this, and the self-righteous conviction that my own theory is spared that fate will surely deteriorate into self-advertising."[97] Today the awful phrase "marketplace of ideas" rarely provokes critique, so second-nature is the reduction of human activity to the metaphor of consumerism. The truth or falsity of ideas is collapsed under the myth that free subjects may simply pay their money and make a choice, pre-

95. Ibid., p. 73.
96. Ibid., p. 275.
97. Ibid., p. 4.

sumably because our self-engendered consumer-alert function will guide us to choose wisely. Adorno's point is that the social reality determining the marketplace metaphor, and myriad others like it, locates itself in the very soul of language, and by this means corrupts the ability to think beyond the parameters thereby established. In *Negative Dialectics* Adorno acknowledged the impact on thought of a society governed by the fetish of the bottom line: "We like to present alternatives to choose from, to be marked True or False. The decisions of a bureaucracy are frequently reduced to Yes or No answers to drafts submitted to it; the bureaucratic way of thinking has become the secret model for a thought allegedly still free. But the responsibility of philosophical thought in its essential situations is not to play this game."[98]

Truth is the result of an immense struggle against multiple levels of self-deceit: in particular, the self-defeating notion of a non-contradictory form of subjecthood, founded on the ideology of personal autonomy, together with the self-deceitful belief that one can unproblematically think outside the mediating impact of general falsehood, though the urgent social need to do so was philosophy's justification.[99] Indeed, for Adorno, the practice of philosophy represented an explicitly personal struggle against instrumental reason. Philosophy, in other words, was necessary to Adorno as a condition for his own subjecthood.

The challenge he set for himself was to write a philosophy that did not replicate that which the practice otherwise sought to confront: general and seemingly overwhelming falsehood. Borrowing from a distinction that had a lengthy history in German philosophy (Kant and Hegel, notably), Adorno distinguished between two forms of reason: *Verstand* and *Vernunft*. The former, essentially, refers at best to something like common sense, though in its darker forms it degenerates into cunning; it provides the foundation for instrumental reason—reason of the bottom line. *Vernunft*, the higher form, is coterminous with Adorno's sense of dialectical thought. Dialectics, for Adorno, was a language-act by means of which suppressed details were made visible, palimpsests read, and otherness articulated instead of subsumed. Dialectics retrieved leftovers—particulars— from the universalizing tendencies of concepts that conventionally determine philosophical practice. "The name of dialectics says no more, to begin with, than that objects do not go into their concepts without leaving a

98. Ibid., p. 32.
99. Ibid., p. 18: "The freedom of philosophy is nothing but the capacity to lend a voice to its unfreedom."

remainder, that they come to contradict the traditional norm of adequacy."[100] The goal of dialectics was utopian, reflecting the effort to preserve the *promesse de bonheur*, a phrase borrowed from Stendhal, through self-reflexive thought that confronted social contradiction. Dialectics attempted to preserve nonidentity in the face of a seemingly overwhelming identity—that is, to preserve difference in the face of its increasingly pervasive abolition.[101]

Dialectics' "agony is the world's agony raised to a concept. . . . Dialectics serves the end of reconcilement."[102] Adorno held that the domination of nature—nature broadly understood as that other which stands apart from the subject, and upon which the possibility of the subject ironically depends—is, in the end, destructive of both humankind and nature ("No universal history leads from savagery to humanitarianism, but there is one leading from the slingshot to the megaton bomb").[103] The rupture from nature that produced "Man" (in Foucault's sense: man as a cultural construct)[104] will in the end be man's undoing, unless a reconciliation can be staged. For this to occur two connected premises must guide thought: first, that the subject is also an object, that is, part of the very nature over which the subject claims dominion; second, that the object—nature, the object world external to the self—ultimately stands outside the totality of the subject's conceptual grasp, as it were, as a *remainder*. To recognize this ungraspable leftover, and indeed to think the self in the context of the object, marks the first step toward a possible reconciliation of subject and object, the subject and its other.[105] Adorno's concern was to retain in thought the object's fundamental particularity against its universal analogue captured in concepts.[106]

Hegel's pursuit of philosophical truth recognized contradiction as a component part of the whole. His dialectics articulates *thesis* as a category of preliminary affirmation and unification which recognizes apparent

100. Ibid., p. 5.
101. Ibid.: "Dialectics is the consistent sense of nonidentity."
102. Ibid., p. 6.
103. Ibid., p. 320.
104. Michel Foucault, *The Order of Things: An Archaeology of the Human Senses* (New York: Vintage, 1970).
105. ND, p. 183.
106. Buck-Morss, *Origin of Negative Dialectics*, p. 77: "Crucial to 'negative dialectics' was not only the object's nonidentity with itself, but its nonidentity with the knowing subject, the mind and its logical processes. . . . This level of [the object's] nonidentity found expression in [Adorno's] term 'unintentional truth.'"

unity. But every thesis contains its own *antithesis*—contradiction—defined by a negation of the affirmation, as well as differentiation. Whereas the first stage, thesis, is dogmatic (as it were received wisdom), antithesis is skeptical, and structured by "negative reason." In *Phenomenology of Spirit* (1807) Hegel speaks of negative dialectics' skepticism as

> a moment of self-consciousness, to which it does not *happen* that its truth and reality vanish without its knowing how, but which, in the certainty of its freedom, *makes* this "other" which claims to be real, vanish. What Skepticism causes to vanish is not only objective reality as such, but its own relationship to it, in which the "other" is held to be objective and is established as such, and hence, too, its *perceiving*, along with firmly securing what it is in danger of losing, viz. *sophistry*, and the truth it has itself determined and established. Through this self-conscious negation it procures for its own self the certainty of its freedom, generates the experience of that freedom, and thereby raises it to truth.[107]

Hegel advances a third stage, *synthesis*, wherein the dialectic turns positive once more, though reconfigured in light of the skeptical second stage. Ultimately, negation is philosophically overcome and a resolution achieved. It is at the level of this third stage where Adorno parts company with Hegel, precisely due to the fundamental idealism of the exercise, where a *philosophical* truth has no necessary connection to the truth of material reality. Accordingly, whereas Hegel could claim that "The True is the whole,"[108] Adorno countered in *Minima Moralia* that "The whole is the false."[109] That is, the truth about totality was its actual falseness, resolution to which could not be achieved in idealist pronouncement as an act of language, or, in Buck-Morss's words, "reason and reality did not coincide. . . . Because the contradictions of society could not be banished by means of thought, contradiction could not be banished within thought either."[110] Not coincidentally, in Adorno's aesthetic theory contradiction

107. G. W. F. Hegel, *Phenomenology of Spirit*, trans. A. V. Miller (Oxford: Oxford University Press, 1977), p. 124.

108. Ibid., p. 11.

109. MM, p. 50.

110. Buck-Morss, *Origin of Negative Dialectics*, p. 63; and p. 189: "The whole point of his relentless insistence on negativity was to resist repeating in thought the structures of domination and reification that existed in society, so that instead of reproducing reality, consciousness could be critical, so that reason would recognize its own nonidentity with social reality, on the one hand, and material nature's nonidentity with the categorizing consciousness that passed for rationality, on the other."

lies at the heart of any art which has any claim to truth. "A successful work," he pointed out, "is not one which resolves objective contradictions in a spurious harmony, but one which expresses the idea of harmony negatively by embodying the contradictions, pure and uncompromised, in its innermost structure."[111]

In 1960 Herbert Marcuse published "A Note on Dialectic" as a new preface to the second edition of *Reason and Revolution* (1941). He opens the text by expressing the hope that his book will contribute to the revival of a mental faculty "in danger of being obliterated: the power of negative thinking,"[112] almost certainly a wry reference to the then-popular Sunday affirmations of the radio preacher Reverend Dr. Norman Vincent Peale, whose signature phrase was "the power of positive thinking," a line about strictly personal do-it-yourself self-fulfillment.[113] The ethical claim of negative thought, by contrast, is determined by a fundamentally social purpose. "The negation which dialectic applies to ['facts'] is not only a critique of conformistic logic, which denies the reality of contradictions; it is also a critique of the given state of affairs on its own grounds—of the established system of life, which denies its own promises and potentialities."[114] Marcuse's concern, mirroring Adorno's, is to connect objective fact to social-subjective value, to insist on the defining impact of one on its other, and, not least, to foreground the historicity of the relationship. Dialectical thought begins with a social concern, namely, "the experience that the world is unfree; that is to say, man and nature exist in conditions of alienation, exist as 'other than as they are,' "—to which Marcuse appends a

111. Adorno, "Cultural Criticism and Society," PR, p. 32.
112. Herbert Marcuse, "A Note on Dialectic," in *The Essential Frankfurt School Reader*, ed. Andrew Arato and Eike Gebhardt (New York: Continuum, 1982), pp. 444–51.
113. Peale's tag line has more recently been adapted by television evangelist Reverend Robert H. Schuller as "possibility thinking." Both preachers connect affirmation to a popular form of religious existentialism, whose secular analogue Adorno critiqued in *The Jargon of Authenticity* as both supremely idealist, self-serving, and asocial. Adorno's argument hinged on the point that the authentic self was impossible in the face of general inauthenticity, which could not be escaped, as it were, by either thought or self-will, and which was structured on a degraded model of the bourgeois subject—a self-promoting individuality. As he put it in MM, p. 39, "Wrong life cannot be lived rightly."
114. Marcuse, "A Note on Dialectic," p. 445. Cf. ND, pp. 144–45: "To proceed dialectically means to think in contradictions, for the sake of the contradiction once experienced in the thing, and against that contradiction. A contradiction in reality, it is a contradiction against reality."

corollary: "Any mode of thought which excludes this contradiction from its logic is a faulty logic."[115]

Marcuse identifies a central component of negative dialectics, what Adorno called "immanent criticism": the critical power of negative dialectics was not the result of applying philosophical categories from the outside, so to speak, but the result of critiquing facts and concepts on the very basis of their own terminology and established processes. Further, as Adorno expressed the point in *Minima Moralia*, "the dialectic advances by way of extremes, driving thoughts with the utmost consequentiality to the point where they turn back on themselves, instead of qualifying them."[116]

The function of dialectical thought, Marcuse summarizes, "is to break down the self-assurance and self-contentment of common sense, to undermine the sinister confidence in the power and language of facts, to demonstrate that unfreedom is so much at the core of things that the development of their internal contradictions leads necessarily to qualitative change: the explosion and catastrophe of the established state of affairs."[117] He ends his remarks with an implicit homage to Adorno: "No method can claim a monopoly of cognition, but no method seems authentic which does not recognize that these two propositions are meaningful descriptions of our situation: 'The whole is the truth,' and the whole is false."[118]

If philosophy was at the heart of Adorno's effort to imagine a subject worthy of the name, his philosophical practice functioned against philosophical tradition—which tradition, he argued, ultimately promoted the untruth against which he struggled. The immanent difficulty of succeeding at this practice was not lost on him. The penultimate aphorism in *Minima Moralia*, in effect, looking back over the 151 preceding fragments, reviews the anti-philosophical philosophical practice the book engages and issues a *"Warning: not to be misused."* Dialectical thought has served historically as "a refuge for all the thoughts of the oppressed, even those unthought by them," he insists, but dialectical thought also has the capacity to poison itself. "As a means of proving oneself right [dialectical thought] was also from the first an instrument of domination, a formal technique of apologetics unconcerned with content, serviceable to those who could pay: the

---

115. Marcuse, "A Note on Dialectic," p. 446.
116. MM, p. 86. The next sentence reads: "The prudence that restrains us from venturing too far ahead in a sentence, is usually only an agent of social control, and so of stupefaction."
117. Marcuse, "A Note on Dialectic," p. 447.
118. Ibid., p. 451.

principle of constantly and successfully turning the tables. Its truth or untruth, therefore, is not inherent in the method itself, but in its intention in the historical process."[119]

Adorno is haunted by the potential for untruth in the pursuit of untruth's truth, tinged not least with the fact that thinking itself is always already in modernity marked by cultural and economic privilege. Earlier in *Minima Moralia*, in an aphorism titled "Bequest," he tempers his enthusiasm for dialectic's socially progressive potential: "Dialectical thought is an attempt to break through the coercion of logic by its own means. But since it must use these means, it is at every moment in danger of itself acquiring a coercive character: the ruse of reason would like to hold sway over the dialectic too."[120]

Adorno frequently voiced this concern in later years, whenever the project of philosophy came under his scrutiny. Thus in the essay "Why Still Philosophy," first given as a radio lecture, he expands the caveat:

> A philosophy that would still set itself up as total, as a system, would
> become a delusional system. Yet if philosophy renounces the claim
> to totality and no longer claims to develop out of itself the whole that
> should be the truth, then it comes into conflict with its entire tradition.
> This is the price it must pay for the fact that, once cured of its own
> delusional system, it denounces the delusional system of reality. . . .
> After everything, the only responsible philosophy is one that no
> longer imagines it had the Absolute at its command; indeed philosophy
> must forbid the thought of it in order not to betray that thought,
> and at the same time it must not bargain away anything of the emphatic
> concept of truth. This contradiction is philosophy's element. It
> defines philosophy as negative.[121]

---

119. MM, p. 244.
120. Ibid., p. 150.
121. Adorno, "Why Still Philosophy?" p. 7. In MM, pp. 26–28, on the related matter of the practicing philosopher, Adorno commented, "He who stands aloof runs the risk of believing himself better than others and misusing his critique of society as an ideology for his private interest. While he gropingly forms his own life in the frail image of a true existence, he should never forget its frailty, nor how little the image is a substitute for true life. . . . His own distance from business at large is a luxury which only that business confers. This is why the very movement of withdrawal bears the features of what it negates. . . . Private existence, in striving to resemble one worthy of man, betrays the latter, since any resemblance is withdrawn from general realization, which yet more than ever before has need of independent thought. There is no way out of entanglement. The only responsible course is to deny oneself the ideological misuse of one's own existence, and for the rest to conduct oneself in private as modestly, unobtrusively and unpre-

The last aphorism of *Minima Moralia*, no. 153, is named "Zum Ende."[122] I want to risk quoting the entire aphorism, since it decisively marks Adorno's commitment alike to negative dialectics and to the social stakes that determine the necessity of this philosophical choice. The aphorism aptly, and gracefully, demonstrates Adornian dialectics at work.[123] Movingly, the aphorism is saturated with Benjamin's utopian projection of social redemption, personally ironic to Adorno, without question, as regards his friend's then-still-recent politically motivated suicide. "Zum Ende" recapitulates the critical themes of *Minima Moralia:* the history of damaged life, but not a life relinquished; life clinging to hope in the face of catastrophe via the lifeline of critical thought: the insistence on thinking critically—negatively—to think something better. Adorno reiterates the image of enlightenment, and its corollary, philosophical intentionality. And in the process of defining one last time the necessity of negativity, he retains, at the end of "Zum Ende," negativity itself. There is, in the end, no ultimate escape in thought from the conditions that destroy thought. Such is the condition for thought's possibility.

> The only philosophy which can be responsibly practised in face of despair is the attempt to contemplate all things as they would present themselves from the standpoint of redemption. Knowledge has no light but that shed on the world by redemption: all else is reconstruction, mere technique. Perspectives must be fashioned that displace and estrange the world, reveal it to be, with its rifts and crevices, as indigent and distorted as it will appear one day in the messianic light. To gain such perspectives without velleity or violence, entirely from felt contact with its objects— this alone is the task of thought. It is the simplest of all things, because the situation calls imperatively for such knowledge, indeed because

---

tentiously as is required, no longer by good upbringing, but by the shame of still having air to breathe, in hell."

122. MM, p. 247. Edmund Jephcott has translated this as "Finale," which carries rather too much a valence of finality and neat conclusion, clearly not intended by Adorno. At the same time, however, Jephcott's choice of word appropriately acknowledges the notable importance of musical referents scattered throughout MM and, at least as important, the quasi-musical structure of many aphorisms, where narrative design recalls, variously, theme and variations and the kind of sonata structure found in Beethoven—even second developments.

123. Terry Eagleton, "Art After Auschwitz: Theodor Adorno," in *The Ideology of the Aesthetic* (Oxford: Basil Blackwell, 1990), p. 342: "All Marxist philosophers are supposed to be dialectical thinkers; but with Adorno one can feel the sweat and strain of this mode alive in every phrase, in a language rammed up against silence where the reader has no sooner registered the one-sidedness of some proposition than the opposite is immediately proposed."

consummate negativity, once squarely faced, delineates the mirror-image of its opposite. But it is also the utterly impossible thing, because it presupposes a standpoint removed, even though by a hair's breadth, from the scope of existence, whereas we well know that any possible knowledge must not only be first wrested from what is, if it shall hold good, but is also marked, for this very reason, by the same distortion and indigence which it seeks to escape. The more passionately thought denies its conditionality for the sake of the unconditional, the more unconsciously, and so calamitously, it is delivered up to the world. Even its own impossibility it must at last comprehend for the sake of the possible. But beside the demand thus placed on thought, the question of the reality or unreality of redemption itself hardly matters.

HISTORY: WALTER BENJAMIN

The need to lend a voice to suffering is a condition of all truth.

Adorno, *Negative Dialectics*

Corollary to Adorno's dialectics is his concern to connect philosophy to history—but history of a particular kind, one which chooses to remember what is conventionally forgotten: in essence, history's victims. Adorno's sense of the writing of history registers the influence of Walter Benjamin, whose views are encapsulated in his "Theses on the Philosophy of History," a series of eighteen aphorisms drafted shortly before his death in 1940.[124]

Benjamin attacks historicism, the doctrine of history as progress, which he regards at best as highly selective, socially regressive remembering. His concern is that history all too conventionally conforms to tradition, choosing to remember only that which responds to the requirements of the elite and powerful. The danger to the truth of history, he noted, is that history largely belongs to the victors, in whose interest the past is normalized and, in effect, made to affirm the here and now. "Only that historian will have the gift of fanning the spark of hope in the past who is firmly convinced that *even the dead* will not be safe from the enemy if he wins. And this enemy has not ceased to be victorious."[125] The task of the historian, Benjamin insists, is "to brush history against the grain."[126]

124. Walter Benjamin, "Theses on the Philosophy of History," in *Illuminations*, ed. Hannah Arendt, trans. Harry Zohn (New York: Schocken, 1969), pp. 253–64. The essay was first published in 1950. Benjamin gave the manuscript to Hannah Arendt shortly before his death.

125. Ibid., p. 255, original emphasis.

126. Ibid., p. 257. In a later section, p. 262, Benjamin provides a still more vivid

Benjamin, devoted to art, quickly turns his eye to culture to argue his point. Long enjoying a kind of ideological free ride as the ultimate mark of European bourgeois social distinction and achievement, as it were the sign of the mature subject, art—or to be more precise, what he polemically calls "the spoils"—is scrutinized for the immanent social inequality that stains its soul. "Cultural treasures," he suggests, are viewed by the historical materialist "with cautious detachment"; their origin cannot be contemplated "without horror. They owe their existence not only to the efforts of the great minds and talents who have created them, but also to the anonymous toil of their contemporaries. There is no document of civilization which is not at the same time a document of barbarism."[127]

Above all, "it is the sufferings of men that should be shared," Adorno wrote in *Minima Moralia*, a responsibility that constituted a principal function of art.[128] He later made this same point by way of a rhetorical query: "But then what would art be, as the writing of history, if it shook off the memory of accumulated suffering."[129] This is the ending of Adorno's last, and unfinished, major work, *Aesthetic Theory*. Reason can conceptualize suffering but, Adorno noted, it cannot express its experience.[130] That responsibility falls to art, which can "anticipate emancipation, but only on the basis of a solidarity with the current state of human

---

image: "The historical materialist leaves it to others to be drained by the whore called 'Once upon a time' in historicism's bordello. He remains in control of his powers, man enough to blast open the continuum of history." Cf. Adorno, "Why Still Philosophy," p. 17: "Whatever wants nothing to do with the trajectory of history belongs all the more truly to it. History promises no salvation and offers the possibility of hope only to the concept whose movement follows history's path to the very extreme." See also the excellent discussion of Benjamin's "Theses" by Rolf Tiedemann, "Historical Materialism or Political Messianism? An Interpretation of the Theses 'On the Concept of History,'" in *The Frankfurt School: Critical Assessments*, ed. Jay Bernstein (London and New York: Routledge, 1994), vol. 2, pp. 111–39.

127. Benjamin, "Theses on the Philosophy of History," p. 256. The impact of this passage on Adorno is striking, typical indications of which include the following: MM, p. 111: "Every work of art is an uncommitted crime"; AT, p. 187: "Greatness is the guilt that [art] works bear, but without this guilt they would remain insufficient"; and p. 234: "Artworks are, a priori, socially culpable, and each one that deserves its name seeks to expiate this guilt."

128. MM, p. 26.

129. AT, p. 261.

130. See further Rainer Forst, "Justice, Reason, and Critique: Basic Concepts of Critical Theory," in *Handbook of Critical Theory*, ed. David M. Rasmussen (Oxford: Blackwell, 1996), p. 151.

existence."[131] In the late essay "Why Still Philosophy" (1962), Adorno summarized the urgency that drove his practice: "Philosophy must come to know, without any mitigation, why the world—which could be paradise here and now—can become hell itself tomorrow. Such knowledge would indeed truly be philosophy."[132]

THE CULTURE INDUSTRY

Mass culture is a kind of training for life when things have gone wrong.

Adorno, "The Schema of Mass Culture"

Adorno distrusted any concept of culture that forgot its tainted origins in social inequality, and he further held that to celebrate culture only for its transcendence of, and autonomy from, material concerns undercut culture's critical and progressive potential. He insisted that Culture and culture alike bore the scars of modernity, though the social impact on subjects of "high" culture and "low" were often significantly different. He further argued that within the guise of modern technological society all culture, high and low, was profoundly marked by mass culture. These general concerns focused Adorno's attention throughout his career, but his first sustained discussion of the topic was the essay, included in this volume, "On the Social Situation of Music" (1932), followed later by the famous chapter from *Dialectic of Enlightenment*, "The Culture Industry: Enlightenment as Mass Deception,"[133] written with Max Horkheimer while living next to

131. Rasmussen, "Critical Theory and Philosophy," p. 30.

132. Adorno, "Why Still Philosophy," p. 14. Cf. the opening of ND, p. 3: "Philosophy, which once seemed obsolete, lives on because the moment to realize it was missed."

133. DE, pp. 120–67. See also an earlier essay by Max Horkheimer, "Art and Mass Culture," *Studies in Philosophy and Social Science* 9 (1941), pp. 290–304, published in English in the final issue of the Institute's journal following the move to New York. The bibliography on the Culture Industry essay is very large; among the most useful studies are David Held, *Introduction to Critical Theory: Horkheimer to Habermas* (Berkeley and Los Angeles: University of California Press, 1980), pp. 77–109; Jay, *Dialectical Imagination*, pp. 173–218; Jarvis, *Adorno*, pp. 72–89; and in particular the recent monograph by Deborah Cook, *The Culture Industry Revisited: Theodor W. Adorno on Mass Culture* (Lanham, MD: Rowman and Littlefield, 1996).

Adorno's work subsequent to the Culture Industry essay often repeats its principal arguments. A volume of Adorno essays, edited by J. M. Bernstein, *The Culture Industry: Selected Essays on Mass Culture* (London: Routledge, 1991), collects several of the most important: "The Schema of Mass Culture," "Culture Industry

Hollywood in the early 1940s, and reflecting their earlier experience in Weimar Germany as well as their current situation in California.[134]

The principles that organize the "Culture Industry" (CI) argument fundamentally shape virtually all of Adorno's subsequent thought, especially his later essays on mass and popular culture, although near the end of his life he modified his original position to some degree, as I will discuss later. Given the centrality of this essay to Adorno's lifelong study of culture generally, especially the tension between high culture and popular/mass culture, and the essay's centrality to popular culture studies to this day (whether praised or condemned, it is not ignored), I want to take some care in delineating the essay's most important claims.

First the name. Adorno and Horkheimer consciously substituted "culture industry" for mass (or popular) culture, terms already then current, on the grounds that "mass" and "popular" were strictly ideological (that is, false consciousness), that these terms disguised the true nature that lay behind them: a culture that was administered from above, rather than one emerging from below. Mass culture, as they saw it, was fundamentally imposed, not chosen ("Whoever speaks of culture speaks of administration as well").[135] Adorno and Horkheimer mince no words about their theory

---

Reconsidered," "Culture and Administration," "How to Look at Television" (a somewhat unusual essay to the extent that Adorno directly states a pedagogical intent for the medium's improvement; as he puts it at the start, "our approach is practical"), "Transparencies on Film," and "Free Time," besides several others. Other related essays include "Prologue to Television," and "Television as Ideology," both in CM; and "Theory of Pseudo-Culture," trans. Deborah Cook, *Telos* 95 (Spring 1993), pp. 15–38.

134. Martin Jay, "Mass Culture and Aesthetic Redemption: The Debate between Max Horkheimer and Siegfried Kracauer," in *On Max Horkheimer: New Perspectives*, ed. Seyla Benhabib, Wolfgang Bonss, and John McCole (Cambridge: MIT Press, 1993), pp. 365–66, points out that mass culture debates emerged in Germany immediately after World War I, if not before. See also on this point John Willett, *The New Sobriety, 1917–1933: Art and Politics in the Weimar Period* (London: Thames and Hudson, 1978). For an account of the historical, political, cultural, and intellectual situation in the U.S. at the time of Adorno's emigration, see Hohendahl, *Prismatic Thought*, pp. 21–44.

135. This is the opening line from Adorno's 1960 essay "Culture and Administration," p. 93. Adorno accounted for the decision to use the phrase "culture industry" in DE in the essay "Culture Industry Reconsidered," p. 85: "In our drafts we spoke of 'mass culture.' We replaced that expression with 'culture industry' in order to exclude from the outset the interpretation agreeable to its advocates: that it is a matter of something like a culture that arises spontaneously from the masses themselves, the contemporary form of popular art. From the latter the culture industry must be distinguished in the extreme."

of total administration; in the opening paragraph they refer to its possessing a steel-like rhythm *[stählernen Rhythmus]*, as though functioning
in stiff and perpetual motion. The essay itself, however, as Frederic
Jameson has pointed out, is "not a theory of culture but the theory of
an *industry*, of a branch of the interlocking monopolies of late capitalism
that makes money out of what used to be called culture. The topic here is
the commercialization of life,"[136] in effect the integration of the individual
into the exchange principle.[137]

The essay's lengthy opening paragraph, seldom remarked upon in any
critical literature, does not concern mass culture in the ways we have come
to expect. Instead, it's structured as a kind of urban allegory using architecture and urban development, housing especially, as the defining trope.
That is, whereas "culture" is conventionally understood at once as super-
structural and spiritual/immaterial to the extent that its appeal is to the
mind and spirit, Adorno and Horkheimer conversely—perversely—talk
about the mundane and notably material: where people live. They cite the
power of international capital to define cities and the people in them: monumental gleaming business towers juxtaposed to slums, and on the out-
skirts flimsily built bungalows (with which Adorno was personally familiar
in the new development where he lived in Brentwood), which they liken

136. Jameson, *Late Marxism*, p. 144, original emphasis. Adorno, "Culture Industry Reconsidered," pp. 87–88, commented that the phrase "culture industry"
should not be "taken too literally," that it referred to two interrelated factors, the
standardization of the CI products and the rationalization of the CI's distribution
techniques (advertising is the classic driving force) but not to the production process properly speaking, where, despite the obvious impact of industrialized production, the continued existence of individual forms of production remained evident.

137. In the 1970s, Senate Watergate Hearings chairman, North Carolina's Sen-
ator Sam Ervin, lionized by the media for his down-home, plainspoken fairness
and integrity, made fungible each of these assets. Not long after the conclusion of
the hearings, he was among the first, in what would become a long line of celebrities, to sell himself to the "Don't leave home without it" American Express Card
advertising campaign. Along similar lines, the Pope's January 1999 visit to Mexico
City, proclaimed as an opportunity to critique the widening gap between rich
nations and poor, was underwritten by Pepsi and two dozen other corporations—
with no apparent irony—whose logos were prominently displayed around Mexico
City and at the Pope's appearance sites. Potato-chip snack packs included ten different images of the Pope and the Virgin of Guadalupe printed on stamps that
could be put into an album, separately purchased. The story was very widely
reported. See, for example, Andrew Downie, "Papal Visit: Vatican's Endorsement
Deal Leaves Many Mexicans Uneasy," *The Houston Chronicle*, 22 January 1999,
p. 18; and Michael McCaughan, "Pope's Visit Gives Some a Chance for Financial
Gain," *The Irish Times*, 21 January 1999, p. 13.

to the stage-set buildings of world (trade) fairs functioning to praise technical progress, and thereafter to be discarded "like empty food cans." Not least, they cite planned housing projects, said to promote the ideal of the autonomous (private) individual, yet defined by mass-production monotony: cookie-cutter dwellings, with the strictest economy of permissible living space, and convenient to the centers of production (work) and consumption (leisure, pleasure), both determined by the labor of the projects' inhabitants. Macrocosm and microcosm mirror one another in a model of culture that advertises the subject (individuality), whose particular identity nonetheless is intended to merge perfectly with the general, thereby promoting identity solely as a mirage. These striking Marxian images emphasize a homology between the material and the cultural: "Under monopoly all mass culture is identical."[138]

The CI essay is organized around a central paradox: "To speak of culture was always contrary to culture."[139] In modernity, culture rendered self-reflexive is culture for sale; culture "spoken of" has regressed to its own advertising, functioning spatially as a terrain for maximizing economic development and the social structures to achieve it. Once named, in other words, culture is transformed from a process to a product. Culture becomes business,[140] and as such it requires administration at once to render it "safe" for consumption, and so that it will in fact be consumed.[141]

The account of the CI is principally a critique of mass entertainment—movies, music, radio, magazines, etc.—to whose impact, Adorno and Horkheimer argue, no one remains immune. Film more than any other form of mass entertainment constitutes the material for their ensuing critique. Adorno and Horkheimer dismiss the claim that the entertainment industries simply give people what they want, that they are (democratically) sensitive to general needs. They argue that the CI instead acts as a

138. DE, p. 121.
139. Ibid., p. 131.
140. Leo Lowenthal, "The Left in Germany Has Failed" [interview with Peter Glotz], trans. Benjamin Gregg, in *An Unmastered Past: The Autobiographical Reflections of Leo Lowenthal*, ed. Martin Jay (Berkeley and Los Angeles: University of California Press, 1987), p. 253: "What we've been calling mass culture, or as Adorno and Horkheimer more appropriately dubbed it, the culture industry, is a business. Whether the business is run by parties or warehouses or chemical concerns is irrelevant. It is not the advancement of new knowledge that counts, but the introduction of products into the market."
141. DE, p. 131: "Culture as a common denominator already contains in embryo that schematization and process of cataloging and classification which bring culture within the sphere of administration. And it is precisely the industrialized, the consequent, subsumption which entirely accords with this notion of culture."

"circle of manipulation and *retroactive* need."[142] In *Minima Moralia* Adorno reiterated the point: "The culture industry not so much adapts to the reactions of its customers as it counterfeits them. It drills them in their attitudes by behaving as if it were itself a customer."[143] The result, they argue, is the shaping of human identity by cultural "products" that are fully standardized, ever the same. Identity itself, formed in the image of the CI's products, tends toward the identical. The industry "robs the individual of his function. Its prime service to the customer is to do his schematizing for him."[144] The products of the CI, including by implication the human subjects shaped by the CI, lose all relation to spontaneity; as much as possible, even the reactions to mass art are as pre-planned, however imperfectly, as the cityscape described in the essay's opening paragraph. And planned first for profit: business (the word the industry uses to describe itself, just as it describes its production as product—to this day both films and recordings are thus conventionally referred to).

However, they did not mean to suggest that every "product" is literally the same. On the contrary, they argued that difference is structured into and explicitly manifested by the products but often only as a marketing technique endlessly promising claims for the new, commonly without providing it. Adorno and Horkheimer point to the CI's differential catering to the various social-class sectors—what they name "obedience to the social hierarchy."[145] Thus, in terms of our own time, a Chevy is not a Buick; a tabloid is not *Newsweek*. But nor are they as utterly different as their respective advertising claims might suggest. Given models of the Chevy and Buick share the same chassis; and the sensational celebrity features of *National Enquirer* are commonly matched, if slightly dressed up, in the "respectable" weekly news magazine's stories. None of this is this left to chance nor can it be, given the demands of the bottom line. Consumer "choice" and market research are conjoined in a perpetual embrace. "Consumers appear as statistics on research organization charts, and are divided by income groups; . . . the technique is that used for any type of propaganda."[146] (Marcuse once sarcastically noted that "choice" meant the free-

142. Ibid., p. 121, emphasis added.
143. MM, pp. 200–01, aphorism 129, "Service to the Customer" ["Dienst am Kunden"].
144. DE, p. 124. Cf. p. 127: "The might of industrial society is lodged in men's minds. . . . The culture industry as a whole has molded men as a type unfailingly reproduced in every product."
145. Ibid., p. 131.
146. Ibid., p. 123.

dom to choose between brands of toilet paper.)[147] The true "value" of the consumer is to consume what's offered. Adorno and Horkheimer attack the sameness and standardization in the products of the CI and the identification by subjects with what is offered, invariably in the name of free choice: the invitation to conceptualize one's subjecthood as the replication of the identical which, to be sure, claims to be different. The CI "consists of repetition."[148]

Critics of this position have conventionally argued on two complementary fronts: first, that the claim is inappropriately totalizing; second, in almost inevitable linkage, that Adorno (principally Adorno) directly or indirectly asserts an offensively elitist apologia for high culture—a charge often linked to his biography as an upper bourgeois German—a particularly reductive charge based on the accident of birth. Clearly, the limitations of Adorno and Horkheimer's sweeping critique of mass culture are real. But that reality is woefully inadequate as grounds for the dismissal of the critique's substantive principal claims. Too often ignored is the centrality of the mass-culture critique of high art itself mounted by Adorno throughout his career; as Fredric Jameson has pointed out: "The force of the Adorno-Horkheimer analysis of the culture industry . . . lies in its demonstration of the unexpected and imperceptible introduction of commodity structure into the very form and content of the work of art itself."[149] The distinction Adorno maintained between art and mass culture

147. Cook, *Culture Industry Revisited*, p. 123.

148. DE, p. 136. A year 2000 national print-media and television advertisement for Dodge cars and trucks is staged around a single word: "Different." Cf. Adorno, "Prologue to Television," p. 55: "The culture industry grins: become what you are, and its deceit consists precisely in confirming and consolidating by dint of repetition mere existence as such, what human beings have been made into by the way of the world. The culture industry can insist all the more convincingly that it is not the murderer but the victim who is guilty: that it simply helps bring to light what lies within human beings anyway."

149. Fredric Jameson, "Reification and Utopia in Mass Culture," *Social Text* 1 (1979), p. 132. Zipes, "Adorno May Still Be Right," p. 158, with reference to the charge that Adorno was an elitist because he somehow denounced not only mass culture but the masses as well, points out that Adorno in fact wrote on the masses' behalf, "for he wanted to make everyone aware of what the masses have become and to prompt his readers *not* to succumb to the culture industry. In short, Adorno spoke out in behalf of individuality, originality, uniqueness, and particularism. . . . As far as he was concerned, anyone could belong to the masses, and practically everyone did, while thinking they were actually distinct and original." This essay addresses the role played by the CI in the socialization of children for lives of consumption and cultural obeisance.

is that whereas artworks are *also* commodities, the products of the CI are commodities through and through.[150]

Much of the essay addresses pleasure as a component form of happiness. Its authors argue that the pleasure proffered by the CI is entertainment (not enlightenment), and specifically amusement, which under prevailing conditions in the industrialized world they regard as "the prolongation of work," that is, at once an escape device from the mechanized work process (the factory assembly line is their prevailing metaphor) and a momentary but administered means of getting oneself ready to go back for more. But worse, and this is their principal point, CI amusements replicate in over-determined fashion the semiotic codes upon which the work life itself depends, albeit in aestheticized form. "What happens at work, in the factory, or in the office can only be escaped from by approximation to it in one's leisure time."[151]

Pleasure, as they put it, "hardens into boredom because, if it is to remain pleasure, it must not demand any effort and therefore moves rigorously in the worn grooves of association. No independent thinking must be expected from the audience: the product prescribes every reaction: not by its natural structure (which collapses under reflection), but by signals. Any logical connection calling for mental effort is painstakingly avoided."[152] In the end, "The culture industry perpetually cheats its consumers of what it perpetually promises." The promise of pleasure remains just that, an illusory spectacle. "All it actually confirms is that the real point will never be reached, that the diner must be satisfied with the menu."[153]

Adorno remarked in *Minima Moralia* that "Every visit to the cinema leaves me, against all my vigilance, stupider and worse."[154] What does he intend by this notably provocative statement? The CI essay condemns the disconnect between the bought pleasure of the movie palace and the life led upon exit from the theater. "The unemployed in the great cities find coolness in summer and warmth in winter in these temperature-controlled locations." Good. But not enough. "Otherwise, despite its size, this bloated pleasure apparatus [i.e., the entertainment machine] adds no dignity to men's lives."[155] Adorno often commented that modernity possesses the technical means to reduce, if not eradicate, human suffering, yet modern-

150. Adorno, "Culture Industry Reconsidered," p. 86.
151. DE, p. 137.
152. Ibid.
153. Ibid., p. 139.
154. MM, p. 25.
155. DE, p. 139, translation modified.

ity's technological accomplishments were used more commonly to promote regressive ends, for profit above all else. His point is that the "pleasure" of the entertainment is coterminous with the physical comfort purchased by the price of the ticket. The physical benefit is temporary; the mental/spiritual benefit is nonexistent. The entertainment aesthetically replicates life, or as life would be if life's mysteries had deemed differently. (Adorno had of course watched the classic escapist Depression-era Hollywood movies, often comedies, that stylishly celebrated wealth in the midst of general misery.) With rare exceptions actual external social conditions are at best lamented through their film simulacra rather than critiqued. (Even in films like John Ford's social epic *The Grapes of Wrath* [1940], the blind force of weather is as much the culprit as the law enforcement acting on behalf of landowners and banks; indeed, economic forces, while directly referenced, are nonetheless strikingly mystified by explanations that suggest that reality is driven by blind fate, with no one to be blamed.)[156] In short, lament is passively internalized, as in the commonplace bumper sticker that reads "Shit Happens"—never to be found on new vehicles but on what are known to the trade as "transportation thrifties"—as opposed to the non-stoical and implicitly less preconditioned "Shit is Caused,"[157] which bumper sticker to my knowledge does not exist. The former mirrors perfectly the smiley face, the automatic-response and semiotically empty "Have a nice day," and the tuneful proclamation "Don't Worry, Be Happy"—what Adorno called the " 'keep smiling' attitude."[158] Or the ironic reverse, government sponsored, in the form of the advertising slogan for the State Lottery: "It could happen," a promise commonly bought

156. The film opens with the following text that frames the subsequent narrative: "In the central part of the United States of America lies a limited area called 'The Dust Bowl,' because of its lack of rain. Here drought and poverty combined to deprive many farmers of their land. This is the story of one farmer's family, driven from their fields by natural disasters and economic changes beyond their control [in reference to large-scale mechanized farming that supplants sharecropping] and their great journey in search of peace, security, and another home." Adorno and Horkheimer acknowledge that films conventionally, and very directly, treat the subject of human deprivation and the plight of the poor; they argue that this trope provides the opportunity to present society's alleged underlying "heart of gold." See DE, pp. 149–52.

157. Adorno, "Schema of Mass Culture," p. 83: "The neon signs which hang over our cities and outshine the natural light of the night with their own are comets presaging the natural disaster of society, its frozen death. Yet they do not come from the sky. They are controlled from earth. It depends upon human beings themselves whether they will extinguish these lights and awake from a nightmare which only threatens to become actual as long as men believe in it."

158. Ibid., p. 82.

with a substantial portion of their minimum-wage earnings by the desperate poor trying to improve the 85,000,000-to-1 odds of winning. "Pleasure promotes the resignation which it ought to help to forget."[159]

Adorno and Horkheimer, following Marx, argue that consumption is organized by exchange value (not use value), especially through advertising commodities that gain fetishistic hold over subject-consumers,[160] creating a psychological dependency on false needs, in regard to which Adorno and Horkheimer borrowed Leo Lowenthal's now-famous expression that the CI functioned as "psychoanalysis in reverse," that is (as Lowenthal put it), as a device "to keep people in permanent psychic bondage."[161] Advertising's surface-level semiotics are driven by the endless effort to promote individuality, promising the opportunity for the consumer to stand separate from everyone else, hence repeating in radical form the claims to individual uniqueness that define the idealized modern subject. Yet the uniqueness promised by advertising will ultimately succeed only if that individuality is acquired, via purchase, by masses of other "individuals"(if the product doesn't sell in sufficient numbers, it is withdrawn, hence cannot be acquired). Accordingly, the very notion of modern identity, structured by consumerism—identities bought—is built on a spurious foundation. The appeal, by definition necessarily renewed endlessly, is to what we are *not* but want with increasing desperation to be: truly individual. But if we consume in the manner intended we become less like what is promised—we tend toward those around us, whose very likeness we are attempting to be different from: the crowd (anti-subjects, as it were). Not surprisingly, the stakes perpetually get raised, evident, for example, in recent trends in body art, where multiple tattooing and multiple piercing, a process of radical addition, becomes the perfect premise of the ideology that itself drives the multiple economies of modernity: more. More of *this* will make me more of Me and less of Them. And so on.[162]

159. DE, p. 142.
160. Sut Jhally, "Advertising as Religion: The Dialectic of Technology and Magic," in *Cultural Politics in Contemporary America*, ed. Ian Angus and Sut Jhally (New York: Routledge, 1989), pp. 221–22: "The fetishism of commodities consists in the first place of emptying them of meaning, of hiding the real social relations objectified in them through human labor, to make it possible for the imaginary/symbolic social relations to be injected into the construction of meaning at a secondary level. Production empties. Advertising fills. The real is hidden by the imaginary. . . . The hollow husk of the commodity-form needs to be filled by some kind of meaning, however superficial. This is why advertising is so powerful."
161. Lowenthal, "Theodor W. Adorno," p. 186.
162. Culture itself is a commodity; fully subject to the law of exchange, it

Charlie Chaplin—whose work Adorno admired[163]—in *Modern Times* (1936) comically represented the mind-numbing repetition of modern life via the well-worn metaphor of the assembly line, where the Little Tramp in the climactic shop-floor scene pretty much literally is made a cog in industry's wheel. The work day extends limitlessly in the film. The lunch break constitutes an opportunity for an experiment with an automatic (worker) feeding machine, which of course goes completely haywire. Chaplin's character himself goes haywire late in a day entirely spent tightening large nuts with two huge wrenches that are virtually appendages of his own hands; even when he leaves the assembly line he continues attempting to tighten anything that looks remotely like a nut—as though he were an extension of a perpetual motion machine in spite of himself. Outside the factory, seeing a buxom woman coming toward him whose dress has strategically placed (bosom) buttons, he makes a move, as if unconscious, to tighten them, comically much to her horror.

Modern Times illustrates the functionality of twin concepts in Adorno's thinking about the relation between the commodity and the subject: productive forces and relations of production, both described in his essay "Is Marx Obsolete?" (c. 1968). He points out that modern (implicitly First World) societies' productive forces are industrial through and through, and

---

"amalgamates with advertising." And "advertising becomes art and nothing else" (DE, pp. 161, 163). In advance of the phenomenon, Adorno and Horkheimer accounted for the bizarre logic that stirs millions of television viewers to devote particular attention to the high-end ads produced annually for the Super Bowl—which not coincidentally are treated as national news stories. Indeed, the degree to which advertising has become naturalized in our consciousness as an homology to other forms of mass entertainment is evident in the Clio Award–winning ads shown in retrospectives by contemporary art museums.

Rose Rosengard Subotnik shared the following anecdote in a private communication: "I date a turning point in the culture back to the summer of 1965, when I was a counselor for prepubescent kids—say 10–12, at Camp Peter Pan, in Foxboro, Mass. Though I'd been at camps, first as a camper then as a counselor, all my life, it was in that setting that I saw kids, for the first time, act out commercials in games of Charades. In fact the change was very sudden: they didn't just include commercials as one of many mediums (such as book titles, movie titles, etc.)—commercials were the ONLY medium they used; it seemed suddenly to be the only medium they had in common. The ex. that sticks in my mind was some product that came hurtling through like a White Tornado—or conceivably like a White Knight, since the hero was supposed to be on horseback waving a sword. The kids laughed uproariously at that one; they loved it. I was baffled, as in those days—I was in graduate school—I didn't watch television."

163. See Adorno, "Chaplin Times Two," trans. John MacKay, *Yale Journal of Criticism* 9 no. 1 (Spring 1996), pp. 57–61.

tend "towards a totality" extending well beyond the realm of labor into "what is called culture." Comportment generally imitates an industrial model in its relations of production; mimetically, subjects are "appendages of machinery . . . compelled as they are to adjust themselves and their innermost feelings to the machinery of society, in which they must play their rôles and to which they must shape themselves with no reservation."[164]

Identification with the commodity form, fundamental to the theory driving the CI essay, manifests itself in our own rather more advanced state of technological postmodernity in the recent spate of game shows, whether on the major networks or cable. What passes for knowledge are facts and only facts—an obvious given—but what facts: mostly about the products of the CI itself. A perfect circle. Facts external to entertainment are introduced usually only at the higher levels, where some real cash might be given away. There is of course an alternate form, the higher-class variety such as "Jeopardy" or, still classier, the original, though rigged, "Twenty-One." But the only fundamental difference is the "higher-class" of facts themselves—questions about literature and the other arts, science, politics, etc. The point is that knowledge by default is defined as a storehouse of raw data, otherwise unrelated, and for the most part concerning mass entertainment. If this is what you know, it may well be worth something, worth calculated as cash-on-the-spot payments literally waved in front of contestants on shows like ABC's "Who Wants to Be a Millionaire" and Fox Television's "Greed." The issue in question is not whether high-class facts are better than their low-class cousins. Adorno and Horkheimer argue that both forms of culture so hailed are degraded in the process. Put differently, the fragmentation that has gained status as a defining characteristic of the postmodern condition is mirrored in the epistemology of the television quiz show: factual, fun, good for a laugh, and maybe riches. But the knowledge gained from the effort to reach quiz-show candidacy (to pass the considerable hurdle of the auditions) is useful for precisely and only that purpose, a knowledge that leads full circle but does not break out, the human mind as data bank for high-stakes Trivial Pursuit.[165] As

164. Adorno, "Is Marx Obsolete?" trans. Nicolas Slater, Diogenes 64 (Winter 1968), p. 7. See also the discussion in Rose, Melancholy Science, pp. 118–20; and Paddison, Adorno's Aesthetics of Music, pp. 124–28, 187–213.

165. In regard to which the high-culture data lists published in recent years by E. D. Hirsch, something of a small industry, bear no fundamental difference; see E. D. Hirsch, Jr., Cultural Literacy: What Every American Needs to Know (Bos-

Adorno elsewhere put it, "However useful it might be from a practical point of view to have as much information as possible at one's disposal, there still prevails the iron law that the information in question shall never touch the essential, shall never degenerate into thought."[166]

Adorno and Horkheimer conclude by noting that the triumph of advertising occurs despite the fact that consumers "see through" what's offered to them.[167] Thereby acknowledged is the potential agency that remains available to the consumer-subject: seeing through—often tinged with irony and cynicism—is not a trivial "remainder" but neither is it sufficient to sustain, let alone produce, subjecthood. The resistant consumer is still interpellated into the cultural framework defined by the CI.[168]

ton: Houghton Mifflin, 1987); and, with Joseph F. Kett and James Trefil, *The Dictionary of Cultural Literacy,* 2d ed. rev. (Boston: Houghton Mifflin, 1993).

Regarding Adorno's view of this phenomenon as a form of psychological re-infantalization, see his "Analytical Study of the NBC *Music Appreciation Hour,*" *Musical Quarterly* 78 no. 2 (Summer 1994), pp. 374–75 n. 18. See also Miriam Hansen, "Mass Culture as Hieroglyphic Writing: Adorno, Derrida, Kracauer," *New German Critique* 56 (Spring/Summer 1992), p. 51: "Horkheimer and Adorno ascribe the effectivity of mass-cultural scripts of identity not simply to the viewers' manipulation as passive consumers, but rather to their very solicitation as experts, as active readers. The identification *with* the stereotype is advanced by the appeal to a particular type of knowledge or skill predicated on repetition" (original emphasis).

166. Adorno, "Schema of Mass Culture," p. 73. Adorno continues, p. 74: "The curiosity which transforms the world into objects is not objective: it is not concerned with what is known but with the fact of knowing it, with having, with knowledge as a possession. . . . Wrenched from all context, [facts are] detached from thought, they are made instantly accessible to an infantile grasp." And as if in anticipation of later television quiz shows: "The more participation in mass culture exhausts itself in the informed access to cultural facts, the more the culture business comes to resemble contests, those aptitude tests which check suitability and performance, and finally sport."

167. DE, p. 167. See Cook, *Culture Industry Revisited,* pp. 51–53. In "Culture Industry Reconsidered," p. 89, Adorno expands on this phenomenon: "It may also be supposed that the consciousness of the consumers themselves is split between the prescribed fun which is supplied to them by the culture industry and a not particularly well-hidden doubt about its blessings."

168. Alan Tomlinson, "Introduction: Consumer Culture and the Aura of the Commodity," in *Consumption, Identity, and Style: Marketing, Meanings, and the Packaging of Pleasure,* ed. Alan Tomlinson (London: Routledge, 1990), p. 13: "If we think we are free when our choices have in fact been consciously constructed for us, then this is a dangerous illusion of freedom. . . . There is a double danger in this illusion of freedom. First, consumer choice is highly constructed. Second, millions unemployed by anyone and uninvited by Visa are, simply and brutally, excluded from the sphere of freedom. Freedom of goods for some goes hand-in-

To be sure, not all subjects are the same, nor are all products of the CI. Adorno and Horkheimer recognize this fact, despite the rhetorical polemic they self-reflexively engage for strategic reasons. But their principal point underlying the hyperbolic claim is not easily dismissed: namely, that modern society is characterized by a general if hardly universal stunting of critical interest and intelligent engagement on the part of the subject, on the one hand, and by the promulgation of social lies on the part of the CI, on the other. Popular-resistance theory that emerged from British Cultural Studies made a responsible and necessary contribution when it insisted on human agency in the face of its appropriation by mass culture.[169] But we

hand with subordination for others." Or in the parlance of a recent MasterCard advertising campaign, "There are some things in life that money can't buy; for everything else there's MasterCard." The stuff that can't be charged is precisely, and only, those "things" that are literally immaterial—nonetheless still referenced in the ads as commodities.

169. See, for example, Stuart Hall, and Tony Jefferson eds., *Resistance through Rituals: Youth Subcultures in Post-War Britain* (London: Hutchinson, 1976); Dick Hebdige, *Subculture: The Meaning of Style* (London: Methuen, 1979); and John Fiske, *Understanding Popular Culture* (Boston: Unwin Hyman, 1989); *Reading the Popular* (Boston: Unwin Hyman, 1989); and, with John Hartley, *Reading Television* (London: Methuen, 1978). For a critique of the critique, centered on Fiske, see Jim McGuigan, *Cultural Populism* (London: Routledge, 1992), pp. 70–75. For an example of a notably strident critique of the CI essay, see Jim Collins, *Uncommon Cultures: Popular Culture and Post-Modernism* (New York: Routledge, 1989), who misreads the CI chapter as a nostalgic apologia for a lost high-cultural "best that has been thought and said" (see pp. 141–42). For a rather more nuanced assessment, which incorporates a critique of Collins, see Hohendahl, *Prismatic Thought*, pp. 119–48. For recent examples of work closer in spirit to Adorno's mass-culture critique, see Neil Postman, *Amusing Ourselves to Death: Public Discourse in the Age of Show Business* (New York: Viking, 1985); Stuart Ewen, *All Consuming Images: The Politics of Style in Contemporary Culture* (New York: Basic Books, 1988); and Stuart Ewen and Elizabeth Ewen, *Channels of Desire: Mass Images and the Shaping of American Consciousness* (New York: McGraw-Hill, 1982).

Andreas Huyssen, "Adorno in Reverse: From Hollywood to Richard Wagner," *New German Critique* 29 (Spring/Summer 1983), pp. 8–38, provides a thoughtful discussion of shortcomings of the CI essay, arguing that the "black-hole theory of capitalist culture" Adorno and Horkheimer advance is "both too Marxist and not Marxist enough. It is too Marxist in that it rigorously applies a narrow reading of Marx's theory of commodity fetishism (the fetish as a mere phantasmagoria) to the products of culture. It is not Marxist enough in that it ignores praxis, bypassing the struggles for meaning, symbols, and images which constitute cultural and social life even when mass-media try to contain them" (p. 15).

Huyssen further suggests that Adorno's theory wipes out the specificity of cultural products just as it imagines the consumer in a state of passive regression. (On balance, Adorno and Horkheimer argue against the consumer's passivity.) He further notes that if cultural products were only commodities and nothing more,

sometimes lose track of the fact that such resistance is simultaneously severely compromised, not only by the socio-economic and political forces against which resistance acts, but also by the degree to which subjects who resist are nonetheless always already defined by that against which they struggle. Subjects defined by the principles of markets and consumption are not free agents. As Martin Jay aptly notes: "The culture industry may well not be as totalitarian as Horkheimer and Adorno assumed in their bleaker moments. But whether it allows more than pockets of what one commentator has called 'artificial negativity' remains very much to be seen."[170] Whatever autonomy subjects possess is markedly circumscribed

---

and if their sole value were exchange value, "they would no longer even be able to fulfill their function in the processes of ideological reproduction" (reminding of the happiness that we don't have; by the lie immanent to their very form, in other words, they reveal the truth that they function to keep us from knowing—as Adorno himself remarked from time to time). Huyssen argues that the CI does fulfill public functions: "it satisfies and legitimizes cultural needs which are not all *per se* false or only retroactive; it articulates social contradictions in order to ho-mogenize them. Precisely this process of articulation can become the field of con-testation and struggle" (p. 15). Huyssen readily acknowledges that Adorno and Horkheimer's critical analysis of mass culture as a means of social control "ripped to shreds that mystifying veil cast over the culture industry by those who sell it as 'mere entertainment,' or, even worse, a genuinely popular culture" (p. 17).

170. Jay, "Mass Culture and Aesthetic Redemption," pp. 380–81. The source for the phrase "artificial negativity" is Paul Piccone, "The Crisis of One-Dimensionality," *Telos* 35 (Spring 1978), p. 45. Cf. Ben Agger, "On Happiness and the Damaged Life," in *On Critical Theory*, ed. John O'Neill (New York: Seabury, 1976), p. 23: "One-dimensional society contains no sensible criterion of unfulfilled actuality because reality contains every illusion and promise made by the ideology of limitless liberation. Adorno's particular genius was to have recognized the phe-nomenology of one-dimensionality in its most insidious and abstracted socio-cultural forms." See also Mike Wayne, "Television, Audiences, Politics," in *Behind the Screens: The Structure of British Broadcasting in the 1990s*, ed. Stuart Hood (London: Lawrence and Wishart, 1994), pp. 43–64.

For more on Adorno's position as regards agency—its reality and its limita-tions—under sway of the CI, see Stephen Crook, "Introduction: Adorno and Au-thoritarian Irrationalism," SDE, pp. 24–25. Relative to his discussion of the *Los Angeles Times* astrology column, Adorno recognized that its readers would delin-eate a gap between their own lives and the smooth life promised and, further, that readers may not actually even believe in astrology. But as Crook puts it, p. 16: "The fact that people do not 'believe in' astrology no more prevents them from attending to [the astrology] column than the fact that they do not 'believe in' advertising prevents them from functioning as consumers." Crook further points out, p. 25, that "the 'sense' people make is rarely within their entirely conscious control: sense-making puts into play a complex of background assumptions and motivations. Adorno's case is that the messages of propaganda and commodified culture work by resonating with those background factors so that the 'sense' which is made will typically tend towards dependency and conformism. To put it another

in precisely the same way that Adorno understood aesthetic autonomy. Both bear the wound.

"All objectification is a forgetting" [Alle Verdinglichung ist ein Vergessen]; so they remarked in the aphorism *"Le prix du progrès"* in the "Notes and Drafts" section of *Dialectic of Enlightenment.*[171] Borrowing Lukács's notion of reification,[172] Adorno and Horkheimer acknowledge a double objectification in the CI exposé, one of history and the other of the subject in history. Both become thing-like: facts—valorized principally for their "universal informational character."[173] As a corollary, the masses themselves are treated as an "object of calculation; an appendage of the machinery"[174]—the social stakes of which Adorno drives home in the con-

---

way, for Adorno it would be a stupendous analytical naivety to take anyone's 'tastes and pleasures' at face value as a simple datum."

Finally, Schmidt, "Language, Mythology, and Enlightenment," pp. 814–17, describes a car trip taken by Horkheimer across the West in 1940 during which, while traveling between Kansas and Colorado, he heard a Hitler speech on his car radio. As Schmidt relates, the experience crystallized for Horkheimer the unique relationship between language and mass communications systems at the heart of fascism. "Radio had an inherent tendency to reduce its audience to a passive and anonymous mass" (p. 815). Radio made Hitler's voice into that of a god. The propositional elements of his speeches were irrelevant; what mattered was his speeches' ritual character.

171. DE, p. 230. Rose, *Melancholy Science,* p. 48: "To say that consciousness is 'completely reified' is to say that it is capable only of knowing the appearance of society, of describing institutions and behaviour as if their current mode of functioning were an inherent and invariant characteristic or property, as if they, as objects, 'fulfil their concepts.' Therefore, to say that consciousness of society is completely reified implies that no critical consciousness or theory is possible."

172. Georg Lukács, *History and Class Consciousness: Studies in Marxist Dialectics,* trans. Rodney Livingstone (Cambridge: MIT Press, 1971), pp. 83–110. See also Ferenc Feher, "Rationalized Music and Its Vicissitudes (Adorno's Philosophy of Music)," *Philosophy and Social Criticism* 9 no. 1 (Spring 1982), pp. 54–55. Lukácsian reification designated, among other things, the virtual spiritualization of objects through a process of commodity fetishism, as well as the disintegration of human relations in favor of what Jameson, *Late Marxism,* p. 180, calls "thing-like ones (money, the 'cash-nexus')." In AT Adorno, contrarily, promotes a positive form of reification. Speaking on behalf of the object-nature of artworks (as the specific results of human labor), which to be sure coincides with their actual involvement in the commodity form under prevailing social conditions, art's materiality must be used against the spiritualization, hence mystification, that lies at the heart of commodification. Jameson, pp. 180–81: "What results, therefore, is a restless series of transfers whereby reification—for Adorno absolutely essential to the work of art—changes its valences as it passes from the social to the aesthetic (and vice versa)."

173. Adorno, "Schema of Mass Culture," p. 70.

174. Adorno, "Culture Industry Reconsidered," p. 85.

clusion to his late essay "Culture Industry Reconsidered" (1963): "If the masses have been unjustly reviled from above as masses, the culture industry is not among the least responsible for making them into masses and then despising them, while obstructing the emancipation for which human beings are as ripe as the productive forces of the epoch permit."[175]

In his 1960 essay "Culture and Administration," first delivered as a radio lecture, Adorno returned to the question of human agency set against the forces of the CI. While insisting on the reified nature of culture, rendered thing-like, itself a commodity, and on the reification of the human subjects under the administration of mass culture, Adorno pointed out that culture and administration alike ultimately refer back to living subjects. He insisted on the objective fact that human consciousness was not wholly in the grip of administered culture. Consciousness retained a degree of spontaneity: "For the present, within liberal-democratic order, the individual still has sufficient freedom within the institution and with its help to make a modest contribution to its correction."[176] Adorno elsewhere suggested, along somewhat similar lines, that subjects constitute what he termed "the ultimate limit of reification," and that on that account mass culture could never afford to relax its grip. "The bad infinity involved in this hopeless effort of repetition is the only trace of hope that this repetition might be in vain, that men cannot wholly be grasped after all."[177]

Adorno's monograph-length analysis of the *Los Angeles Times* astrology column, "The Stars Down to Earth," one of the two studies he produced for the Hacker Foundation during his final visit to the United States in 1952–53, provides detailed access to his critique of the CI, characterizing what he regards as the CI's impact on subjectivity and the social stakes that accrue.[178] He based his analysis on a collection of roughly three

175. Ibid., p. 92.
176. Adorno, "Culture and Administration," p. 113.
177. Adorno, "Schema of Mass Culture," p. 80.
178. SDE, pp. 34–127; the second study is "Television as Ideology," in which Adorno has relatively little to say about the visual medium itself; the study is a script and plot analysis of thirty-four television shows which Adorno describes as "of various genres and quality" (p. 59). Though he does not explicitly name any of the programs, one is obvious, "Our Miss Brooks," concerning which see pp. 61–62. See also Adorno, "Scientific Experiences of a European Scholar in America," trans. Donald Fleming, in *The Intellectual Migration: Europe and America, 1930–1960*, ed. Donald Fleming and Bernard Bailyn (Cambridge: Belknap Press of Harvard University Press, 1969), pp. 365–66, Adorno's memoir of the writing of these essays.

months of the daily columns (November 1952–February 1953), written by Carroll Righter, "Astrological Forecasts."[179]

First the general theme. Adorno recapitulates an argument advanced in *Dialectic of Enlightenment*, likening astrology to myth as a not-entirely-irrational effort to put the chaos of reality into order. Adorno names astrology a "secondary superstition": people "know" better but consult it anyway. Astrology is "pseudo-rational," providing what he terms "calculative though spurious adaptation to realistic needs."[180] Adorno suggests that belief in the stars as determinants of human happiness posits life as inscrutable and beyond our control, except for the avenue of compliance to its dictates—which happen to replicate the way things are anyway. Adorno thereby signals an unexpected dialectical reversal: the astrology column (unwittingly) describes a truth about the prevailing irrationality of society and the concomitant de-rationalization of society's subjects. Astrology fictionalizes—or, let us say, aestheticizes—social relations, but its celestial narrative, a faceless cosmic ventriloquism, uncannily replicates what its receiver already knows and experiences as social reality. The aesthetics in other words are always already shabby. What astrology promises with one hand, it takes back with the other. Its truth is its lie, which its advice matches: " 'To be rational' means not questioning irrational conditions, but to make the best of them from the viewpoint of one's private interests."[181] All advice is proffered to an imagined solitary individual; it is never social. To the extent that social interaction is authorized, it occurs solely as an opportunity to advance oneself. "Friends" are reified as a

179. Crook, "Introduction," suggests that the "Stars" essay suffers from two methodological flaws: "the rhetorical materials are treated as windows on the psychology of their audience, and the psychology of the audience is 'read off' from rhetorical materials. In addition, there is little evidence of any systematic sampling technique: . . . extracts from the column have been selected to illustrate themes whose representative character is not established." Crook acknowledges that these flaws are not due to Adorno's naïveté but instead reflect his suspicion of American empirical audience-research methods. "He came to believe that such research isolated a single moment of subjective response from the objective totality while privileging the conscious over the unconscious reaction" (p. 19). However, Adorno himself points out that "our results must by necessity be regarded as tentative. They provide us with formulations, the validity of which can and should only be established by reader research. . . . We must therefore be cautious not to treat our material dogmatically as a mirrored reflection of the reader's mind" (p. 40), something well beyond the scope of the project as funded by the Hacker Foundation, whatever Adorno's position on American empirical research methods.

180. SDE, p. 37.

181. Ibid., p. 43; see also pp. 44, 97–98, 116–17.

means to achieve one's own ends. Sociability, in other words, is ʳᵉᵈᵘᶜᵉᵈ to instrumental and private practicality. Life is best led by cutting a deal with the stars; implicitly, life is getting ahead by using others for this purpose. All of which is ordained by the cosmos: the universe, as it were, decrees the logic of capitalism, the achievement of profit, the survival of the economic fittest.[182]

The column's presentation of objective difficulties lays their cause at the doorstep of the individual whose task it is to overcome that for which he himself bears responsibility.[183] The advice tendered, geared to the individual, "implies that all problems due to objective circumstances such as, above all, economic difficulties, can be solved in terms of private individual behavior or by psychological insight, particularly into oneself, but also into others."[184] The stars, put differently, have birthed Dale Carnegie: *How to Win Friends and Influence People*[185] had been a best-selling tract since its first publication in 1937 and, by the 1950s, was a major staple in self-marketing and getting ahead. The book treats intersubjective relationships as a means to an end and little more, an early example in the long history of such books, which continue to find their way onto best-seller lists.

Adorno repeatedly critiques the lack of human spontaneity presumed—and, indeed, prescribed—by astrology-column advice. He centers the discussion on the interface between private life and public, organized around the bi-phasically divided day: the day designated for work and the night for family and leisure, as determined by the stars. As Adorno wryly notes, the bi-phasic approach to life promotes the perfect circularity of the economic system: a man's life "falls into two sections, one where he functions

182. Ibid., pp. 49, 102–08.
183. Ibid., p. 58: "The constant appeal of the column to find fault with oneself rather than with given conditions . . . is only one aspect of the ideal of social *conformity*, promoted throughout the column and expressed by the implicit, but ubiquitous rule that one has to adjust oneself continuously to commands of the stars at a given time"; and pp. 59–60: "The adage 'be yourself' assumes an ironical meaning. The socially manipulated stimuli constantly aim at reproducing that frame of mind which is spontaneously engendered by the *status quo* itself" (original emphasis).
184. Ibid., p. 57.
185. Dale Carnegie, *How to Win Friends and Influence People* (New York: Simon and Schuster, 1937). The book remains in print and is also currently available on audiocassette and CD. Adorno clearly knew the book to which he makes passing, sarcastic reference in CF, p. 53: "It is as though the process of rationalization of art and the conscious command of its resources were diverted by social forces from the real purpose of art, and directed merely toward 'making friends and influencing people.'"

as a producer and one where he functions as a consumer."[186] And in the end, pleasure has no justification for its own sake; if properly had, it will lead to "practical advantages."

Accompanying this outline for future achievement is what Adorno names "the monotonously frequent advice to 'be happy.' "[187] Addressed to men (though, as Adorno presumed, more likely read by women), the column counsels on relationships, especially marriage, and is designed to keep happy the at-home wife, the better to further the husband's economic goals. Marriage is a calculation. Spousal closeness is transformed into an economic ritual, an interpersonal investment: Valentine's Day, Mother's Day, birthday. "Togetherness is rationalistically promoted just as a further means of smoothing out things and keeping the partners together while the actual basis for their common *joie de vivre* seems to have gone. . . . The idea that one has to send flowers to one's wife not because one feels an urge to do so, but because one is afraid of the scene she makes if one forgets the flowers is mirrored by the empty and meaningless nature of the family activities which the columnist sets in motion."[188]

The column's rhetorical address plays off the mythology of the subject, with subjecthood treated as spectacle: "Display that keen mind of yours"— in essence, by repeatedly making a gesture of assent: "Yes, I will." The appeal to anxiety—the column's first principle—is the social truth that things are not what they should be. Like advertising, astrology rejects the past, finds inadequacy in the present, and points to a future. As such, it references the utopian by taking advantage of utopia's own mythic value. Further, the dissatisfaction that astrology invokes is real. If one follows astrology's dictates, all futures—like all fortune cookies—promise benefits. Astrology immanently certifies that "Shit happens," and it ascribes a cause: the failure of the isolated self. Astrology cannot address the social, only the personal. And the charge to the person is: adapt yourself, manipulate others; be in tune; be cunning. And not least, submit to the stars— whose motions guarantee the prevailing terrestrial (social) order. Be dependable—by being dependent.[189]

186. SDE, p. 71.
187. Ibid., p. 75.
188. Ibid., pp. 60–61, 100–01. The quotation is from p. 101. Cf. DE, p. 155.
189. Pete Brush, "Telephone Psychics See Money in Their Futures," *Los Angeles Times*, 28 March 1997, p. D7. Described in 1997 as the "anchor of the 1–900 industry," telephone psychics at the time were estimated to be a $300-million-a-year business, helping to fill the coffers of long-distance carriers like AT&T and

In his late essay "Free Time" (1969), much of it addressing the issue of "hobbies," Adorno turns his gaze to the body, specifically the body on the beach, and the cultural politics of people preparing themselves to be looked at. He connects such bodies to the advertising for the cosmetics and leisure industries, and to the inculcation of a form of self-desire and drive. The example is tanning. "An exemplary instance is the behavior of those who let themselves roast brown in the sun merely for the sake of a tan, even though dozing in the blazing sun is by no means enjoyable, even possibly physically unpleasant, and certainly makes people intellectually inactive. With the brown hue of the skin, which of course in other respects can be quite pretty, the fetish character of commodities seizes people themselves; they become fetishes to themselves. . . . The state of dozing in the sun represents the culmination of a decisive element of free time under the present conditions: boredom."[190] Boredom, he clarifies, is a social phenomenon; it is "objective desperation"—an objective condition of Western subjectivity.[191]

WRITING

> For a man who no longer has a homeland, writing becomes a
> place to live.
>
> Adorno, *Minima Moralia*

Adorno was a supremely careful writer. Rolf Tiedemann, Adorno's assistant during the early 1960s, reported that Adorno invariably carried a small notebook in which he jotted down ideas, and which he later used as a source for dictation. The dictated pages were typed double-spaced and with wide margins. Sentences were often incomplete. "He then revised the typed pages, sometimes until none of the typed material was left and everything had been replaced with handwriting. This process was repeated sometimes up to four times."[192]

MCI, as well as the psychic networks proper. Founded in 1990 by Michael Lasky, "Psychic Friends" by 1997 was fielding between 7,500 and 10,000 calls per day, according to the *Times* report. Despite the hard-sell promise, replete with testimonials, of good things happening to those who call (invest) by spokeswoman Dionne Warwick, the late-night cable infomercials carried the expected legal disclaimer "for entertainment purposes only."

190. Adorno, "Free Time," CM, pp. 170–71.
191. Ibid., p. 171.
192. Wiggershaus, *Frankfurt School*, p. 598. Pickford, "Preface," pp. x, 315 n. 5, points out that most of the essays in Adorno's late collection *Critical Models:*

Though famously difficult, a great deal of Adorno's writing is in short form;[193] many examples, pointedly aphoristic, are not more than a few pages long. The 153 aphorisms constituting *Minima Moralia*, for example, vary in length from a single brief paragraph to as many as six pages (most are one or two pages); and much the same is true for the last section ("Notes and Drafts") of *Dialectic of Enlightenment*. Adorno's free-standing essays seldom exceed thirty pages and are often shorter. At the opposite end of the spectrum are the two late monographs, Adorno's longest, *Negative Dialectics* and *Aesthetic Theory*. The former is organized, conventionally, into three large parts, two of which are further subdivided into chapter-like sections. The nearly four hundred pages of *Aesthetic Theory*, more extreme, appear entirely without chapter division.[194]

Adorno's writing intentionally thwarts effortless reception by passive readers—which not coincidentally parallels his understanding of the resistant quality of socially "true" music.[195] In particular, it resists the "logic" of systematized argument, defined by the expectation that point A leads directly and inevitably to point B. In the words of Ben Agger: "Critique

---

Interventions and Catchwords (1963; 1969) exist in three to seven typescript versions, and notes that Adorno often reworked an essay as many as a dozen times.

193. Many of Adorno's radio lectures, revised for later publication, are notably "straightforward" and present few reading challenges. Adorno's name has been invoked in recent debates focused on academic writing, and by proponents on opposing sides; a defining issue centers on scholars' responsibilities to the larger public. The basic positions are well outlined by James Miller, "Is Bad Writing Necessary? George Orwell, Theodor Adorno, and the Politics of Language," *Lingua Franca* 9 no. 9 (December/January 2000), pp. 33–44.

194. Unfortunately, English translations of both monographs undercut Adorno's purpose by inserting headings, as readers' guides, throughout the texts. However, a recent second English translation of *Aesthetic Theory*, by Robert Hullot-Kentor, published in 1997, duly restores Adorno's original. Robert Hullot-Kentor, "Translator's Introduction," AT, p. xiv, comments on the 1984 translation of *Aesthetic Theory*: "Paragraph indentations were distributed arbitrarily throughout, completing the image of a monodirectional sequence of topic sentences that could be followed stepwise from chapter 1 through chapter 12. This subordinated the text's paratactical order to a semblance of progressive argumentation that offered to present the book's content conveniently. This device provided a steady external grip on the book's content while causing it to collapse internally." On the challenge of translating Adorno, see the aptly named introduction by Samuel Weber, "Translating the Untranslatable," PR, pp. 9–15.

195. Paddison, *Adorno's Aesthetics of Music*, p. 18, points out that Adorno's "tendency to proceed by means of tersely constructed, mutually contradictory assertions [is] designed in part to disrupt normal reading habits and to 'shock' the reader into an active relationship with the text."

must wrestle with the mystifications of ordinary and disciplinary language in order to wrest language from its straitjacket in the straightforward."[196] Nowhere is this more evident than in Adorno's use of paratactical devices as a principal means by which to organize argument at the level of paragraphs, some of which may consist of only a few sentences, though lengthy paragraphs, often several pages long, are more characteristic.[197] Of whatever length, both Adorno's individual sentences and paragraphs are commonly organized by parataxis, that is, an internal arrangement that avoids the use of either coordinating or subordinating elements. The result, as Susan H. Gillespie aptly explains, "is a grammatical trope that, like the 'broken-off parables' [in Kafka], creates a kind of disjunction and nonspecificity that undermine logical clarity and causality, leaving room for a certain vagueness, and for interpretation."[198]

The anti-systematic impulse evident in Adorno's use of parataxis reflects his critique of Western philosophical discursive traditions, to be sure, but at a more fundamental level it constitutes a reaction to the general instrumentalization of language in modernity. "Defiance of society," he once remarked, "includes defiance of its language."[199] Adorno employed two closely related organizational principles in his writing to accommodate this goal: force-field *(Kraftfeld)* and constellation. By the former he meant, in the words of Martin Jay, "a relational interplay of attractions and aversions that constituted the dynamic, transmutational structure of a complex phenomenon." By the latter, an astronomical term that he borrowed from Walter Benjamin, he meant "a juxtaposed rather than integrated cluster

196. Agger, *Critical Theory of Public Life*, p. 83.

197. Robert Hullot-Kentor, "The Philosophy of Dissonance: Adorno and Schoenberg," in *The Semblance of Subjectivity: Essays in Adorno's Aesthetic Theory*, ed. Tom Huhn and Lambert Zuidervaart (Cambridge: MIT Press, 1997), p. 312: "He spoke by starting at the top of a full inhalation, which he followed down to the last oxygen molecule left in his lungs, and his written style perfected dozen-page paragraphs hardened to a gapless and sometimes glassy density, as if the slightest hesitancy for an inhalation or any break for a new paragraph would have irretrievably relinquished the chance of completing the thought."

198. Susan H. Gillespie, "Translating Adorno: Language, Music, and Performance," *Musical Quarterly* 79 no. 1 (Spring 1995), p. 57. Gillespie further suggests that Adorno's writing is musical, though not in the acoustic sense, and she cites Adorno's lengthy essay on the late work of Friedrich Hölderlin, which Adorno greatly admired, describing the poet's "musiclike" use of parataxis. See Adorno, "Parataxis: On Hölderlin's Late Poetry," NL, vol. 2, pp. 109–49.

199. Adorno, "The George-Hofmannstahl Correspondence, 1891–1905," PR, p. 225.

of elements that resist reduction to a common denominator, essential core, or generative first principle."[200] The astronomical constellation posits a relation on the basis of observable proximity. But at the same time, the relation has a certain metonymic or even arbitrary quality (why link *these* stars and not those?). Nonetheless, once the relation is demonstrated something heretofore invisible becomes apparent, and an insight is produced.[201] (Terry Eagleton: "Every sentence of [Adorno's] texts is thus forced to work overtime; each phrase must become a little masterpiece or miracle of dialectics, fixing a thought in the second before it disappears into its own contradictions.")[202]

Exaggeration, central to Adorno's writing, brought dialectical tensions into bold relief as component parts of a force-field or constellation, rather than smoothing them over—the use of which harbors what Max Paddison describes as "a quite deliberate irritation value. [Adorno's] intention is not to restore an illusory equilibrium, wherein all tension . . . between the extremes is conveniently neutralized."[203] In one of the most trenchant sentences in *Minima Moralia*, Adorno remarked, "The splinter in your eye is the best magnifying-glass,"[204] an aphorism which itself constitutes a two-element constellation: eye, and magnifying glass used to improve seeing, but here a shattered lens whose shard is stuck in the eye. The result is a new form of "seeing." Whereas the conventional usage is instrumental, eye *and* magnifying glass combined as a tool, in Adorno's constellation this usage is provoked, contradicted, and rendered paradoxical. Seeing now is not a matter of optical mechanics but insight, the driving force behind

200. Jay, *Adorno*, pp. 14–15. Adorno's objection to philosophical idealism's notion of a "generative first principle" is its erasure of history. See further Zuidervaart, *Adorno's Aesthetic Theory*, pp. 46–48.

201. Zuidervaart, *Adorno's Aesthetic Theory*, p. 61, notes that "Constellations let concepts interrelate in such a way that both the sociohistorical essence of phenomena and their unique identities can emerge." Cf. Buck-Morss, *Origin of Negative Dialectics*, p. 96: Adorno's "central effort was to discover the truth of the social totality (which could never be experienced in itself) as it quite literally *appeared* within the object in a particular configuration" (original emphasis). For a detailed discussion of Adorno's constellational writing, see pp. 96–110; and Jarvis, *Adorno*, pp. 175–92.

202. Eagleton, "Art after Auschwitz," p. 342. For Adorno's own comments on the uses of exaggeration, see "Meaning of Working through the Past," p. 99; and "Opinion Delusion Society," p. 108: "All thinking is exaggeration, in so far as every thought that is one at all goes beyond its confirmation by the given facts."

203. Paddison, *Adorno, Modernism and Mass Culture*, p. 84.

204. MM, p. 50, aphorism 29, "Dwarf Fruit."

which in this instance is pain, made more urgent by the metaphor's strong affiliation with both somatic experience and, in essence, history.[205]

The essay form, Adorno's favorite, permits spontaneity and even (intellectual) play, that is, thought and writing that in their own form replicate both the spirit of emancipation and a constitutive part of the realized subject. Anti-dogmatic, the essay's "method" is to proceed "unmethodically."[206] As a structure for philosophical thought, the essay is not predetermined by a philosophical first principle; the thought it reflects arises more directly from the material it studies and less from the concepts that precede the material and which always threaten to overwhelm it. (The essay does not reject concepts; indeed, it cannot do without them. But concepts must be interwoven with experience "as in a carpet.")[207] The essay—in a sense *ideally* unsystematic, spontaneous, fragmented—formally constitutes itself less as a magnifying glass, more as a splinter in the eye. Its tendency is critical, its purpose "to move culture to become mindful of its own untruth."[208]

Adorno's writing is often peppered with foreign words, and their use was of sufficient significance that he produced two essays on the matter, both published in *Notes to Literature:* "On the Use of Foreign Words" and "Words from Abroad."[209] In the first of these essays Adorno outlines what he terms "a determined defense of the use of foreign words." What he

205. David Martin, "Dr. Adorno's Bag of Tricks," *Encounter* 47 no. 4 (October 1976), p. 70, points out that Adorno's work is neither philosophy nor sociology but belongs rather "to a class of philosophical reflection on society and on social fact rejecting both reflection and fact conceived in themselves. Merely to reflect on the given is simply to reflect the given; merely to reflect (i.e., mirror) the given is to leave everything as it is and claims to be. Philosophy conceived as pure reflection may achieve a systematic, rounded exposition, and science as the mirror of the given may also achieve systematisation. But the complicated reflexives of the critical dialectic have to work backwards, forwards, and across themselves, making every partial truth less partially true in light of its negation and in further light of a negation of that negation."
206. Adorno, "The Essay as Form," NL, vol. 1, p. 13. The essay is among Adorno's most important concerning writing. See further Shierry Weber Nicholsen, *Exact Imagination, Late Work: On Adorno's Aesthetics* (Cambridge: MIT Press, 1997), pp. 105–10; and Rose, *Melancholy Science,* pp. 14–15.
207. Adorno, "Essay as Form," p. 13.
208. Ibid., p. 20. Martin, "Dr. Adorno's Bag of Tricks," p. 70, refers to Adorno's writing as a process of unmasking, achieved in large part by his fragmentary form of writing. "Nothing is as it seems, and truth is paradoxically layered. You can only break through to truth by exposing the paradoxes and masquerades at each layer and setting them against other masquerades and paradoxes."
209. Adorno, "On the Use of Foreign Words," NL, vol. 2, pp. 286–91; and

seeks is "to release their explosive force: not to deny what is foreign in them but to use it."[210] Foreign words serve to explode the supposed transparency of language itself, to remind the reader of the history, contingency, and difference that language subsumes. Thus in *Minima Moralia* he comments that "German words of foreign derivation are the Jews of language,"[211] which is to suggest that language assimilates difference (the other) which it then uses for its own purpose. Adorno, by using unassimilated foreign words, seeks to promote the otherness of language, and to re-historicize its use rather than promote a supposedly natural transparency. Foreign words constitute for Adorno "the incursion of freedom" into writing; they have legitimacy "as an expression of alienation itself, and also as the transparent crystals that may at some future time explode human beings' dreary imprisonment in preconceived language."[212]

Adorno's enemy is the language of "communication," today perhaps best encapsulated in the common urge to "get to the point," or "indicate the bottom line"—writing in the service of instrumentality, of time-is-money "practicality." His position hinges on the insight that the extreme forms of "communication" ideology defining the goals of "plain" usage have been fully incorporated not only into the practice of writing but into language itself. Thought takes too long. Profit cannot wait on discourse—not the least explanation for the now ubiquitous phenomena of television sound bites, "factoids," and print-media sidebars: "information" at a glance.[213]

Adorno's attraction to foreign words develops from their promise of "escape from the sphere of what is always the same, the spell of what one is and knows anyway."[214] Adorno sees the foreign word as effecting a "beneficial interruption of the conformist moment of language,"[215] upon which claims of its "natural" character depend. The foreign word momentarily denaturalizes language. Adorno's writing explicitly, and carefully,

---

"Words from Abroad," NL, vol. 1, pp. 185–99. See also Nicholsen; *Exact Imagination*, pp. 84–89.

210. Adorno, "On the Use of Foreign Words," p. 286.
211. MM, p. 110.
212. Adorno, "On the Use of Foreign Words," p. 289.
213. Nicholsen, *Exact Imagination*, p. 67: "Communication serves as a form of social control in which human beings are treated as potential customers."
214. Adorno, "Words from Abroad," p. 187. He continues: "National groups who want one-dish meals even in language find this response hateful. It is from this stratum that the affective tension that gives foreign words their fecund and dangerous quality arises, the quality that their friends are seduced by and their enemies sense more readily than do people who are indifferent to them."
215. Ibid., p. 189.

attempts to makes us self-reflexive about what Nietzsche referred to as the prison-house of language[216]—the degree to which language, with its historical immanence, speaks us. The greater the self-reflexivity as to the fundamentally *interested* nature of language, the greater chance the subject has to use language against its naturalized perpetuation of falsehood and the promulgation of domination. That language is increasingly defined by the functions and purpose of the CI, as Adorno saw it, made his own radical usage more urgent.[217]

Herbert Marcuse once confessed in an interview that there were many things in Adorno's writing that he didn't understand. But in the same breath Marcuse defended his friend's writing: "Ordinary language, ordinary prose . . . expresses so much the control and manipulation of the individual by the power structure, that in order to counteract this process you have to indicate already in the language you use the necessary rupture with conformity. Hence [Adorno's] attempt to convey this rupture in the syntax, the grammar, the vocabulary, even the punctuation. Now whether this is acceptable or not I don't know. The only thing I would say is that there lies an equally great danger in any premature popularization of the terribly complex problems we face today."[218]

PRAXIS

The limitations of art proclaim the limits of politics.

Adorno, *Quasi una fantasia*

Georg Lukács: "A considerable part of the leading German intelligentsia, including Adorno, have taken up residence in the 'Grand Hotel Abyss,'

216. Friedrich Nietzsche, *Werke*, ed. Karl Schlechta (Munich: C. Hanser, 1954–65), vol. 3, p. 862, from the *Nachlass* of the 1880s. My thanks to Jochen Schulte-Sasse for locating this phrase for me. Adorno, "Words from Abroad," p. 189, paraphrasing Nietzsche, comments that the foreign word reminds us that language "imprisons those who speak it."

217. Adorno was sensitive to the potential for a kind of elitist one-upmanship incorporated into the use of foreign words. He made clear that foreign words are only justified when a native word cannot substitute. On both points, see "Words from Abroad," p. 192.

218. Herbert Marcuse, "Marcuse and the Frankfurt School: Dialogue with Herbert Marcuse" [interview with Bryan Magee], in *Men of Ideas* by Bryan Magee (New York: Viking Press, 1978), p. 73. Thanks to Christopher Swift for drawing my attention to this comment. Lowenthal, "Recollections of Theodor W. Adorno," pp. 206–07, with warm humor, repeats a story from Kracauer, who, during Adorno's youth, imagined that if Adorno ever declared his love to a young woman, she would have little chance of understanding him unless she had read all of Kierkegaard.

which I described in connection with my critique of Schopenhauer as 'a beautiful hotel, equipped with every comfort, on the edge of an abyss, of nothingness, of absurdity. And the daily contemplation of the abyss between excellent meals or artistic entertainments can only heighten the enjoyment of the subtle comforts offered.' "[219] Lukács's oft-quoted rejoinder agonistically echoes a chorus of similar critiques of Critical Theory on grounds of its purported absence of a social agenda. The Frankfurt intellectuals, so the story goes, recognized suffering, and Adorno, their most famous postwar "spokesman," responded with aesthetics. Lukács adds a nasty twist: Adorno and his crowd enjoyed the good life while philosophically savoring the pessimism triggered by the misery they recognized. Lukács in other words virtually makes the accusation of *Schadenfreude*.[220]

Critical Theory's lack of a social program for change was attacked from within as well, notably of course by Adorno's most famous student, Jürgen Habermas. And since Adorno's death this issue in particular has been endlessly invoked. Hans-Jürgen Krahl sums up the usual argument: "Adorno's

219. Georg Lukács, *Theory of the Novel: A Historico-Philosophical Essay on the Forms of Great Epic Literature*, trans. Anna Bostock (Cambridge: MIT Press, 1971), p. 22, from the preface (dated July 1962) to the reissue of the original 1920 German edition, published in 1968. For a concise account of the intellectual gulf separating Adorno from Lukács, especially as regards the relation of theory to praxis, see Irving Wohlfarth, "Hibernation: On the Tenth Anniversary of Adorno's Death," *Modern Language Notes* 94 no. 5 (December 1979), pp. 967–70. Adorno himself produced a lengthy critique of Lukács; see "Extorted Reconciliation: On Georg Lukács' *Realism in Our Time*," NL, vol. 1, pp. 216–40. Adorno admired much in Lukács's early work (*Soul and Form, The Theory of the Novel,* and *History and Class Consciousness*) and unrelentingly attacked the writings from the early 1920s and thereafter, "when Lukács' objectivism yielded . . . to official communist doctrine" (p. 216). Adorno's disdain centers on Lukács's attack on modernist art, and his stance toward socialist-realist art, which Adorno regarded as agitprop kitsch. See Eugene Lunn, *Marxism and Modernism: An Historical Study of Lukács, Brecht, Benjamin and Adorno* (Berkeley and Los Angeles: University of California Press, 1982), pp. 130–31 ("Lukács's position [on literature] came close to a dignified, sophisticated version of Soviet party doctrine," p. 131).

220. Hullot-Kentor, "Back to Adorno," p. 11, has responded: "The charge of pessimism is more pessimistic than any pessimism it claims to perceive. Even pessimism is dialectical, and especially in Adorno's case the relentlessness of his life's work can hardly be attributed to a lack of hope for change, but only to the most naïve optimism, which was continually transformed—by the refusal to compromise—into an instrument of cognition." He continues: "This dialectic of pessimism was opaque to a whole group of people who worked with Adorno at the Institute for Social Research, and who commented often on how strange it was that someone who wrote 'like that,' who worked with such intense seriousness, could at other times be so *albern* (silly, absurd)."

inability to confront the problem of organization points to an objective inadequacy in his theory, which nevertheless assumes social praxis as a central category in epistemology and social theory."[221]

Student movement protests, the dramatic social flash point as regards widespread public critique of Critical Theory and Adorno, began in Germany in 1966, focused on federal school and social reform, but reached crisis proportions in June 1967 when a student, Benno Ohnesorg, was killed by a plainclothes policeman during a protest in Berlin over a visit of the Shah of Iran. Shortly after Ohnesorg was shot, Adorno publicly demanded a thorough inquiry—as Rolf Wiggershaus describes it, "This was virtually the only 'intervention' of this sort that he engaged in during his whole career as a professor."[222] Adorno's refusal thereafter to become directly involved was seen by some as an ivory tower response, or worse, a betrayal of the ideals underlying Critical Theory, which had provided students with their intellectual training in social justice and cultural critique. Critical Theory seemed to fail in practice.[223]

The "problem" was not merely some sort of psychic incapacity or other personal failing on Adorno's part to "get involved"; his position mirrors the history, and historical moment, of Critical Theory generally. By the 1930s it was quite apparent to members of the Institute that progressive

---

221. Hans-Jürgen Krahl, "The Political Contradictions in Adorno's Critical Theory," *Telos* 21 (Fall 1974), p. 165. Russell A. Berman, "Adorno, Marxism and Art," *Telos* 34 (Winter 1977–78), p. 158: Adorno's "aesthetic theory must be understood as a camouflaged social theory in self-imposed exile." Berman's reading is highly critical: "The truth is not the whole, Adorno knew, yet for him the artwork's truth was wholly negative. Nothing could bind art more fundamentally to the forces of domination. . . . Huddled in its monadicity, Adorno's artwork becomes an embellishment of corporate liberalism because it refuses to risk contamination. Yet precisely that wager is the prerequisite of emancipation" (p. 166).

222. Wiggershaus, *Frankfurt School*, p. 620. For a detailed account of these events, see pp. 609–36.

223. The literature on the theory-praxis relation in regard to Critical Theory is substantial. For a summary of the various positions, see Zuidervaart, *Adorno's Aesthetic Theory*, pp. 20–22, 134–41, and 146–49. Michael Sullivan and John T. Lysaker, "Between Impotence and Illusion: Adorno's Art of Theory and Practice," *New German Critique* 57 (Fall 1992), pp. 87–122, provide a particularly effective defense of Adorno and his "turn" toward aesthetics, on the ground that his aesthetic theory defines how artworks preserve the tension between subject and object, and by that means challenge the dominating tendencies of the dialectic of enlightenment. Buck-Morss, *Origin of Negative Dialectics*, pp. 24–42, 82–85, provides a nuanced account of Adorno's position. See Agger, *Critical Theory of Public Life*, for an attempt to rethink the lessons of Critical Theory in light of the postmodern condition, especially as regards political and social praxis.

political change was out of the question. Europe was under the sway of two equally abhorrent models: one fascist, the other Stalinist, both murderous. In America, as they would soon discover, with the grips of the Depression still evident but loosening, liberal democracy marked by the impact of the CI hardly suggested to them a hopeful alternative. And they had long since given up on Marx's notion of a class-based proletarian revolution. In short, Critical Theory became an address to an uncertain future—what Adorno called *"Flaschenposten,"* or "messages in bottles," tossed out to sea in hopes of their later being found.[224] Critical Theory moved away from a critique of political economy in favor of a critique of instrumental reason, in an effort to protect at all costs the ideals—as opposed to the actuality—of the Enlightenment and so as to refuse the ultimate debasement of rationality, which guaranteed cataclysm.

As Irving Wohlfarth remarks, "The implacable logic of world-historical disaster is always counterpointed in Adorno's thinking by the conviction that it could be otherwise."[225] It was art that for Adorno posited an "otherwise" to the present. He expressed it, very much focused on the question at hand, in the essay "Commitment" (1962): "As pure artifacts, products, works of art . . . are instructions for the praxis they refrain from: the production of life lived as it ought to be."[226] A truly "committed" art is not, for Adorno, agitprop. Indeed, his own stance against political art is politically grounded, as Simon Jarvis has pointed out: "The danger for politically committed art is that it will end up as bad art without becoming good politics either."[227] Adorno insisted that art's function is practical only to

---

224. MM, p. 209. The source for the aphorism seems to be the following anecdote told by Hanns Eisler. At the beginning of the war some of the émigré Institute members were on the beach in Southern California when suddenly Adorno, overcome with melancholy, said: "We should throw out a message in a bottle." To which Eisler responded—with sardonic humor—that the message should read: "I feel so lousy." From Leo Lowenthal, "The Utopian Motif in Suspension: A Conversation with Leo Lowenthal," interview by W. Martin Lüdke, trans. Ted R. Weeks, in *An Unmastered Past: The Autobiographical Reflections of Leo Lowenthal*, ed. Martin Jay (Berkeley and Los Angeles: University of California Press, 1987), p. 237. Wolin, *Terms of Cultural Criticism*, p. 28: "The wager on Critical Theory's future as a potential revolutionary avant-garde seems both self-serving and grandiose. But it is this conception of Critical Theory as a refuge of truth in an era in which the objective social situation had repulsed the 'true' by failing to 'realize philosophy' that increasingly defined its self-understanding."

225. Wohlfarth, "Hibernation," p. 961.

226. Adorno, "Commitment," NL, vol. 2, p. 93.

227. Jarvis, *Adorno*, p. 121; see further pp. 188–92.

the extent that it constitutes a resistance indirectly through its aesthetic comportment;[228] in *Aesthetic Theory,* with Brecht clearly in mind, he suggested that artworks which strive to intervene politically have the effect of—as he put it in English—"preaching to the saved," then adding, "Artworks exercise a practical effect, if they do so at all, not by haranguing but by the scarcely apprehensible transformation of consciousness; in any case agitative effects dissipate rapidly."[229]

In 1979 Leo Lowenthal commented on Lukács's witty "Grand Hotel Abyss" jab at the comfortable existence of Adorno and company: "I have never heard that miserable living conditions and substandard nutrition are necessary prerequisites for innovative thought. If Marx and Nietzsche at times suffered insults of material deprivation, their theoretical creativity survived, not because of but despite such painful conditions. I might also add that Georg Lukács found his own ways of comfortable survival in a political environment where many other heretic Marxists, who were not privy to Lukács's strategy of adaptive behavior, had heir heads chopped off."[230] In this memoir Lowenthal staunchly defends Adorno's position, in the short run, in opposition to the demands that he join the student protest and, in the long run, as regards the function of Critical Theory. He sums up his position on both counts with a comment about Marx: "Imagine for a moment Marx dying on the barricades in 1849 or 1871: there would be no Marxism, no advanced psychological models, and certainly no Critical Theory. The call to arms the ultraradical disciples directed at their teachers—legitimate as their intentions may have been—has merely produced excesses, the consequences of which have become only too obvious in the troubled state the New Left finds itself in today."[231]

In *Negative Dialectics* Adorno several times addressed the theory-praxis relation, stressing the primacy of thought, and acknowledging the need for praxis, but refusing to link one to the other, especially in light of the commonplace demand that theory serve practice: "The call for unity of theory and practice has irresistibly degraded theory to a servant's role, removing the very traits it should have brought to that unity. The visa stamp of practice which we demand of all theory became a censor's placet. Yet whereas theory succumbed in the vaunted mixture, practice became

228. Adorno, "Commitment," pp. 79–80.
229. AT, pp. 242–43.
230. Lowenthal, "Theodor W. Adorno," p. 191.
231. Ibid., p. 193.

nonconceptual, a piece of politics it was supposed to lead out of; it became the prey of power. . . . The recovery of theory's independence lies in the interest of practice itself."[232]

In the face of the student attacks on what they regarded as his quietism, Adorno wrote a brief essay at the end of his life, "Resignation" (1969), in which he staked out one last time the argument for a position that he had in essence maintained his entire career. He summarized the charges against him: "One should join in. Whoever only thinks, removes himself, is considered weak, cowardly, virtually a traitor."[233] In the course of the essay he reiterates the arguments I have outlined above, drawing from earlier writings. He concludes with the following, returning to a concern that lies at the heart of Critical Theory, human happiness: "The happiness that dawns in the eye of the thinking person is the happiness of humanity. The universal tendency of oppression is opposed to thought as such. Thought is happiness, even where it defines unhappiness: by enunciating it. By this alone happiness reaches into the universal unhappiness. Whoever does not let it atrophy has not resigned."[234]

A social theory that so distinctly foregrounds and valorizes the aesthetic is hardly one bound to please subjects shaped by the thoroughly saturated *Realpolitik* of the Cold War and its aftermath and a century's worth of more or less global mass culture imperiously linked to the modes and values of advertising. Aesthetics, except for aestheticized politics in its

232. ND, p. 143; see also p. 408. As Rose Rosengard Subotnik has conveyed to me, "one could perhaps say that Adorno's praxis lay in the very disinterestedness that kept alive the notion, and thereby the possibility, of freedom in the aesthetic (as defined initially by Kant)" [private communication]. Cf. Adorno, "Why Still Philosophy," p. 14: "Praxis, whose purpose is to produce a rational and politically mature humanity, remains under the spell of disaster unless it has a theory that can think the totality of its untruth. It goes without saying that this theory should not be a warmed-over idealism but rather must incorporate societal and political reality and its dynamic." See similar remarks made during an interview in *Der Spiegel* following the student protests. The English translation of this interview was published as: "Of Barricades and Ivory Towers," *Encounter* 33 no. 3 (September 1969), pp. 63–69. Adorno, "Marginalia to Theory and Praxis," CM, pp. 277–78, noted that the wide circulation of his books such as *The Authoritarian Personality* and *Dialectic of Enlightenment* exerted "practical influence," despite their being written without practical intentions. In the same essay, p. 261, he comments, "Thinking is a doing, theory a form of praxis; already the ideology of the purity of thinking deceives about this. Thinking has a double character: it is immanently determined and rigorous, and yet an inalienably real mode of behavior in the midst of reality."

233. Adorno, "Resignation," CM, p. 290.

234. Ibid., p. 293.

myriad forms, is hardly regarded as a Midas horde by either the political right or left. The radical quality of Adorno's aesthetic theory is that it redefines the enterprise of aesthetics by insisting on its link not to beauty as such but to the "beauty" of human emancipation.[235]

TRADITION

Art today is scarcely conceivable except as a form of reaction that anticipates the apocalypse.

Adorno, *Aesthetic Theory*

What in the end has Adorno handed down? What is the "state" of his work today? There is no simple response to these questions. In the decade following his death in 1969 it's fair to say that Adorno's life's work in philosophy, sociology, music, and aesthetics was eclipsed in Germany in large part by the work of Jürgen Habermas, his former student, and also by historical realities in the Federal Republic. Whereas students in the late 1960s had attacked Adorno for what they perceived as his political quietism (from their point of view, in essence, his conservatism), within a very few years, posthumously, he was discredited by the political right as an intellectual father to the radical, and violent, left that emerged in Germany during the 1970s.[236] Adorno's "politics," by which his oeuvre as a whole was implicitly judged seemed either out of date or dangerous, or both.

Though a very major figure in new music circles extending out from the Darmstadt Summer Courses, Adorno's position in German musicology was something else again. In a discipline somewhat noted for aesthetic and epistemological conservatism, Adorno's sociology of music was distasteful

235. Richard Wolin, "Benjamin, Adorno, Surrealism," in *The Semblance of Subjectivity: Essays in Adorno's Aesthetic Theory*, ed. Tom Huhn and Lambert Zuidervaart (Cambridge: MIT Press, 1997), p. 94: Emancipation isn't simply a matter of changing the means of production but is instead one of the *"transformation of life in its totality*, that is, in its cultural, psychological, and everyday aspects, as well as its economic and political forms" (original emphasis). Wolin, "Utopia, Mimesis, and Reconciliation," p. 43, notes that "Art is the utopian reenchantment of radically disenchanted social totality. It serves as irrefutable proof of the fact that the existing universe of facts is not all there is." Recognizing the dangers of postmodernism, not least its anti-historicity and foundation in markets, advertising, and fashions of myriad sorts, Wolin nonetheless posits its potential in what he terms a "democratized" aesthetic sensibility to the extent that this sensibility, functioning at the level of everyday experience, has incorporated "an aesthetics of rupture, discontinuity, defamiliarization, and disenchantment—in sum, the 'ideology-critical' function Adorno attributes to authentic works of art" (p. 47).

236. See Hohendahl, *Reappraisals*, pp. 75–80.

to the degree that he cast his unrelenting critical gaze especially at the German musical canon—for which in other circles he has since been criticized for his seeming blindness to the non-German—and did so by means alien to the established traditions of German musicology. His work was anti-positivistic, dialectical, and relentlessly hermeneutical—in a word, philosophical; it was fundamentally qualitative, hence set against a resolutely established quantitative disciplinary practice.

Adorno's sociology worked from both the outside and the inside of musical works. "Outside" musical texts, he looked at social practices, but here he upset musicological convention by his relative lack of interest in empirical research, though Adorno knew well the "basic facts" of music history, to be sure. But he insisted on the inadequacy of musical facts as such to the understanding of music—precisely the argument in musicology that emerged in full-blown form only in the mid 1980s, but was nonetheless foreshadowed during the last decade of Adorno's life in his critique of positivism, especially as represented by British philosopher Karl Popper.[237] "Inside" the musical text, Adorno committed to what he named "immanent criticism," analyzing objective musical details in relation to one another, that is, to musically specific compositional procedures, and also interrogating them as objectively subjective engagements with the reality external to the musical text, a kind of musical hermeneutics that the discipline of musicology only slowly accepted as legitimate, and not without continuing controversy. Stated forthrightly, Adorno's work pursues music's meaning as produced through the complicated interplay of the work's own specificity—which develops in response to the demands of its musical material, the outgrowth of society and history—and meaning that results from the social-historical site the music occupies, both in the time of its making and in the ever-changing present.

Adorno refused the academic separation of history, sociology, philosophy, and aesthetics, though he obviously experienced their actual institutional disciplinary division. He was a member of a sociology department;

237. Agger, *Critical Theory of Public Life*, p. 24: Adorno regarded positivism as "a worldview of adjustment. Positivism suggests that one can perceive the world without making assumptions about the nature of the phenomena under investigation. Its notion that knowledge can simply reflect the world leads to the uncritical identification of reality and rationality. One experiences the world as rational and necessary, thus deflating attempts to change it. Instead, the critical theorists attempt to develop a mode of consciousness and cognition that breaks the identity of reality and rationality, viewing social facts not as inevitable constraints on human freedom. . . . but as pieces of history that can be changed." On the positivism dispute with Karl Popper, see Wiggershaus, *Frankfurt School*, pp. 566–82.

he didn't train musicologists. Within the academy of postwar Germany, aesthetics, an overriding concern to Adorno, was not precisely a hot topic, and from Adorno's point of view for very good reason, as he polemically wrote in the "Draft Introduction" to *Aesthetic Theory:* "Philosophical aesthetics found itself confronted with the fatal alternative between dumb and trivial universality on the one hand and, on the other, arbitrary judgments usually derived from conventional opinions. . . . The reason for the obsolescence of aesthetics is that it scarcely ever confronted itself with its object."[238] It was precisely the failures of philosophy and aesthetics that led Adorno in pursuit of both—and at the end of his life at a time when the academy was losing both faith and interest in these subjects.

On its appearance in 1970, a year after Adorno's death, *Aesthetic Theory* failed to attract the kind of attention that would likely have occurred had it appeared perhaps five years earlier. A clear sense of the decline in Adorno's intellectual stock is particularly notable by the mid-1970s, the flavor of which can be gleaned from a strident and dismissive review of the 1973 English translation of *Negative Dialectics* published in the British left-wing journal *New Society,* titled "Frankfurters."[239] "Is the Frankfurt school really in fashion?" D. G. MacRae, the author, rhetorically asks. The valence of "intellectual fashion" is forthright; MacRae dismisses the body of work as a whole as "too historically specific, too local, too incidental, to be accessible other than as an object of historical attention," to which he immediately adds that it wasn't even "intrinsically good enough for the effort [of studying it as a historical phenomenon] to be worthwhile." But then MacRae qualifies himself as he launches into the review proper. What he really means by "Frankfurters" is Adorno, whose book he characterizes as "preposterous." "To be a disciple of Frankfurt in 1974, in south London or Newcastle, is as silly as trying to be a Viking or an imperial Chinese bureaucrat." *Negative Dialectics* is directly assessed in two brief paragraphs. Especially notable is the reviewer's venom toward Adorno personally and his lack of hesitation to engage in an ad hominem appraisal in a book review. MacRae met Adorno once and found him "the most arrogant, self-indulgent (intellectually and culturally) man I had ever met. Some 20 years later, I can think of additional claimants for that position, but I doubt if they are serious rivals." In the end, MacRae grudgingly attributes to *Negative Dialectics* "some merits," but "mainly," he

238. AT, p. 333.
239. D. G. MacRae, "Frankfurters," *New Society* 27 no. 59 (28 March 1974), p. 786.

closes, "there is intellectual narcissism and self-indulgence, mitigated by a not unattractive statement of Adorno's own posture," presumably an acknowledgment of Adorno's self-reflexivity as a philosopher. Suggesting that *Aesthetic Theory* is "not worth the effort," he ends: "this book conveys a dreadful, negative truth about the vanities of the learned mind in our century." By MacRae's account, the small extent to which Adorno seemed interesting was solely as an historical figure whose time had passed.

Critical Theory—by the late 1960s coterminous with Adorno—seemed to have one foot firmly planted at the door of irrelevance and the other at the door of political regression by default. Adorno's comedown, which came about less by dealing with him than deciding, in the words of MacRae, that he just wasn't any longer "worth the effort," was exacerbated in the English-speaking world by few translations, poor translations, and, not least, Adorno's dependence on the German intellectual and philosophical tradition, which was little known and less appreciated in the UK and, especially, North America. At least as problematic was his dialectical, constellational, and intentionally hyperbolic writing, and, of course, his unremitting enmity (or so it appeared) toward popular culture, as that position began to be known via the first major work translated into English (1972), *Dialectic of Enlightenment*, and its since endlessly anthologized chapter on the Culture Industry. Adorno's CI critiques became widely available in English at precisely the moment that popular culture studies came into their own in the British and American academy. Adorno was greeted as the devil.

Adorno's vast corpus of musical writings hardly had an impact outside Germany, apart from the notable exception of his frequent appearances at Darmstadt, where his work on new music was widely received by an international body of composers. The nearly total absence of English translations of Adorno's work at the time of his death began to be rectified, slowly, in the course of the 1970s, principally in the journal *Telos*, and slightly later, in *New German Critique*; both journals included key music essays among those they published. The major philosophical works were translated first in a trickle, a bit faster in the 1980s, and quite dramatically in the 1990s—to the point where the earliest translations, often lamentably flawed, of major monographs are now being retranslated. The translation of Adorno's music writing has followed a similar trajectory, especially in the past decade. The demand for Adorno in English is clearly related to the qualitative (as opposed to the long-established quantitative) tendency in musicology that emerged in the 1980s, together with a new-found respect for music criticism (in regard to both, musicology followed the literary disciplines by nearly a generation; indeed, literary theory played a significant role in producing the changes that have occurred in musicology). Adorno's insistence on aesthetics generally, and music especially, as social discourses—as social agents—provided music scholars with a means to rethink the very purpose of their practice—a means by which to address a discipline that seemed increasingly to be of little interest to anyone besides themselves (for reasons, to be sure, by no means solely the fault of musicology's then-dominant intellectual paradigms, as would be clear from any reading of Adorno on the nature of modernity and the general dominance of the commodity form on all life, including the life of the mind). Simply stated, Adorno's musical thought constituted an engaged praxis that precisely attempted to understand how music itself functions as praxis. He defined his life's work, in other words, around pertinent questions about modern Western musical life, seemingly in perpetual crisis, the varying accounts of which are almost limitless: the death of classical music, the still-birth of new music, the colonization of all music by its commodification as "cultural product," the loss of audience, the decline of musical education in the schools, etc. Indeed, even Adorno's severe attacks on popular musics spurred important debate; he perceived earlier than virtually any other major scholar the social and cultural impact of popular art, and he developed a theoretical language for delineating the matter. Unlike musicology, in other words, Adorno did not ignore the popular but wrote extensively about it a full fifty years before popular music made its way into the academy as a legitimate object of study.

In music studies, Adorno's "star" has risen higher now than at any time during his life, his Darmstadt influence notwithstanding, in light of which I return to the first question I posed at the beginning of this section: What, in the end, has Adorno handed down? My response develops from a reading of Adorno's short essay, "On Tradition" (1966).[240] Adorno opens with etymology: *tradere*, to hand down, an implicit reference to generational continuity, physical proximity, and immediacy—virtually a familial relation. His purpose, as Eva Geulen notes, is to inquire into the tradition of tradition;[241] he immediately renders the term paradoxical: "Tradition is opposed to rationality, even though the one took shape in the other. Its

240. Adorno, "On Tradition," *Telos* 94 (Winter 1993–94), pp. 75–82.
241. Eva Geulen, "Theodor Adorno on Tradition," in *The Actuality of Adorno: Critical Essays on Adorno and the Postmodern,* ed. Max Pensky (Albany: State University of New York Press, 1997), p. 187.

medium is not consciousness but the pregiven, unreflected and binding existence of social forms—the actuality of the past; unintentionally this notion of binding existence was transmitted to the intellectual/spiritual sphere."[242]

In this sense, tradition has a kind of social-aesthetic dimension to the extent that it binds person to person; it acts as a force of reconciliation. But in modernity tradition is out of its element; it is "incompatible with bourgeois society," where the exchange principle has rendered tradition itself little more than an instrumentally rationalized advertising ploy. Adorno points to the loss of temporal continuity in common experience, wherein history is reduced to the Now of seasonal fashion. Tradition is invoked as a form of reassurance that nothing really has changed in the face of the myriad and fundamental social disruptions that define late modernity, or, conversely and perversely, tradition's loss is invoked but ironically blamed on social and political resistance to modernity's disruptive and regressive change—the Family Values slogans of the 1980s were a perfect manifestation. The very fact that tradition, in certain nostalgic and mythic forms, is the mantra of the political right marks the self-consciousness with which tradition must now be remembered, as opposed to being experienced or lived.[243] Under the social, cultural, and historical impact of the commodity form, tradition in its "classic" definition can only be advertised and, in a sense, literally purchased. Tradition's soul inhabits products: Brady-Bunch remakes, "That 70s Show"; retro designs for here and now, including model-year 2000 automobiles made to look like 1930s sedans (Chrysler's PT Cruiser), otherwise known only from old black-and-white movies; remakes of the '60s VW Beatle, with the genteel addition of a bud vase bracketed to the dashboard in homage to the Flower Power youth of its presumed, nostalgia-ridden middle-aged buyers. And so on.

And yet: "To complain [about the loss of tradition] and to recommend tradition as a cure is entirely useless. This contradicts the very essence of tradition. Utilitarian rationality—the consideration of how nice it would be to have a tradition in a world allegedly or actually lacking any coher-

242. Adorno, "On Tradition," p. 75.
243. Anthony Giddens, *The Nation-State and Violence*, vol. 2 of *A Contemporary Critique of Historical Materialism* (Berkeley and Los Angeles: University of California Press, 1985), p. 12, points out that in traditional societies, "especially in small oral cultures, 'tradition' is not known as such, because there is nothing that escapes its influence and, therefore, nothing with which to contrast it." Tradition in other words is a phenomenon of history and modernity.

ence—cannot prescribe what it invalidates."[244] Lost tradition cannot be reproduced aesthetically, though Adorno insists this is precisely what society attempts.

In its assigned task to assure us that we really are who we claim to be, tradition also engages difference: it works to extinguish otherness and is appealed to as a kind of universalized value. Thus, in extreme form, the otherness of the Jew is "overcome" by appeal to mythic Aryan "tradition": cultural solidarity, as national product, achieved by erasure. A society structured on a foundation of extreme inequality attempts to suture its gaps by the claim to oneness, by which means otherness is renamed. Accordingly, publicly to reference the increasingly obscene gap between the richest 5 percent of Americans and the rest of the population is anti-traditional: it flies in the face of the myth of the Melting Pot, the ultimate tradition that defined "us."[245] The temerity to mention radical inequality is to "engage in class warfare" and is hence un-American, anti-traditional.

And so with the aesthetic. "Society applies tradition systematically like an adhesive; in art, it is held out as a pacifier to soothe peoples' qualms about their atomization, including temporal atomization. . . . Manipulated and neutralized by the bourgeois principle, tradition eventually turns into a toxin. As soon as genuine traditional aspects of culture—significant art works of the past—are idolized as relics they degenerate into elements of an ideology which relishes the past so that the present will remain unaffected by it, at the cost of increasing narrowness and rigidity."[246] The appeal

244. Adorno, "On Tradition," p. 76.
245. In MM, pp. 102–03, Adorno comments: "Abstract utopia is all too compatible with the most insidious tendencies of society. That all men are alike is exactly what society would like to hear. It considers actual or imagined differences as stigmas indicating that not enough has yet been done; that something has still been left outside its machinery, not quite determined by its totality. . . . An emancipated society, on the other hand, would not be a unitary state, but the realization of universality in the reconciliation of differences." He ends this aphorism, "Mélange," with the following: "The melting-pot was introduced by unbridled industrial capitalism. The thought of being cast into it conjures up martyrdom, not democracy."
246. Adorno, "On Tradition," pp. 76–77. Cf. Herbert Marcuse, "Remarks on a Redefinition of Culture," in *Science and Culture: A Study of Cohesive and Disjunctive Forces*, ed. Gerald Holton (Boston: Houghton Mifflin, 1965), p. 225: "Culture is redefined by the existing state of affairs: the words, tones, colors, shapes of the perennial works remain the same, but that which they expressed is losing its truth, its validity; the works which previously stood shockingly apart from and against the established reality have been *neutralized as classics;* thus they no longer preserve their alienation from the alienated society" (emphasis added).

by artists to the past is fraught with danger precisely to the extent that modernity has rendered tradition a thing, ore to be mined for future product. "False tradition," Adorno warns, "wallows in false wealth,"[247] a principle that defines Adorno's sustained critique of musical neo-classicism which he derides as the fabrication of "arts and crafts," ready-made procedures, pre-molded. Adorno's larger point is that "tradition" rendered thing-like constitutes a self-conscious act of remembering in order to forget, in which the need to remember is trumped by the double appeal of nostalgia and nostalgia's commodity value. In aesthetics, the end result is not *l'art pour l'art* but something worse: art for sale and explicitly under false pretense, an art which fails to engage the present by pretending an idealized "past" (a never-never past) impotent to shape the future except to the extent that it authorizes the modernity (or postmodernity) against which it otherwise supposedly acts.

And yet: the market-driven appeal to tradition recognizes, and of course appeals to, an acute sense of loss that is real. The dominant here-and-now of a society increasingly divided economically and culturally is, after all, the constituent result of its own set of traditions: truly traditional to the extent that they are so deeply entrenched, naturalized, and non-reflexive. But they are not traditional insofar as the traditional ethical import of the word "tradition" conventionally presupposes; hence, the appeal to a false tradition rendered ideological through and through. "Thus tradition today poses an insoluble contradiction. There is no tradition today and none can be conjured, yet when every tradition has been extinguished the march toward barbarism will begin."[248] The dialectical paradox of tradition replicates the dialectics that organize modernity generally.

Adorno describes a condition of modern aporia that can neither be wished away nor passively accepted. Tradition must be confronted "with the most advanced stage of consciousness." He insists that there is no permanent canon *[keinen ewigen Vorrat]*: "But there is a relation to the past which, though not conservative, facilitates the survival of many works by refusing to compromise."[249] What does this mean?

Adorno remarks that what he called the "critical approach to tradition" does not turn its back on the past as no longer interesting, thereby reducing the past to the mere forebear of the here and now, the by-product of historicism, yesterday's news. What principally interests him about the

247. Adorno, "On Tradition," p. 77.
248. Ibid., p. 78.
249. Ibid., pp. 78–79.

past is that which has been "left along the way," that which has been forgotten or dismissed as outdated—what he elsewhere names as "scars."[250] New art does not ignore the past, as though "starting from scratch" but engages it via a "determinate negation" (which constitutes the basis of his position on Beethoven, Mahler, Schoenberg and Berg); thereby new art transforms tradition, working to collapse tradition's affirmative character, and remakes the meaning of past and present alike.[251] But the artist's relation to tradition necessarily remains fundamentally dialectical: "Tradition goes against the grain of every artist irritated by its ornamental character and its fabrication of meaning where there is none. Each remains true to this meaning by refusing to be deceived by it."[252] Adorno reiterates this theme in the essay's last sentence: "Only that which inexorably denies tradition may once again retrieve it."[253] In *Minima Moralia* he states the matter still more succinctly, and with specific regard for its implications for the human subject: "One must have tradition in oneself, to hate it properly."[254] Neil Lazarus comments that this aphorism's conceit "represents a uniquely illuminating and enabling rubric under which to think in a politically engaged fashion about intellectual and cultural practice today."[255] He continues, in what I take to be as sound an argument as I can imagine for the continued relevance, indeed urgency, of Adorno's work:

> The point for Adorno . . . is that while the tradition of European
> bourgeois humanism has always insisted upon its civility, has always
> gestured toward—even made a promise of—a universalistically

250. AT, p. 35: "The traces to be found in the material and the technical procedures, from which every qualitatively new work takes its lead, are scars: They are the loci at which the preceding works misfired. By laboring on them, the new work turns against those that left these traces behind." By this last remark Adorno means that the truth content of the artwork emerges from its dialectical relation to other artworks; as he puts it, "each artwork is the mortal enemy of the other."

251. Ibid., p. 22: "Aesthetic reflection, however, is not indifferent to the entwinement of the old and new. The old has refuge only at the vanguard of the new; in the gaps, not in continuity. Schoenberg's simple motto—If you do not seek, you will not find—is a watchword of the new."

252. Adorno, "On Tradition," p. 81.

253. Ibid., p. 82. Cf. AT, pp. 20–21: "The attitude of contemporary art toward tradition, usually reviled as a loss of tradition, is predicated on the inner transformation of the category of tradition itself." For the implications of this argument for philosophy, as Adorno understood it, see Jarvis, *Adorno*, pp. 150–53.

254. MM, p. 52.

255. Neil Lazarus, "Hating Tradition Properly," *New Formations* 38 (Summer 1999), p. 10.

conceived social freedom, it has never delivered on this promise, except, arguably, to the privileged few, and even then only on the basis of the domination of all the others. To hate tradition properly is in these terms very different from championing this exclusive (and excluding . . .) tradition; on the contrary, it is to keep faith with true universality, with the idea of a radically transformed social order, and to oppose oneself implacably to the false universality of modern (bourgeois) sociality. It is to use one's relative class privilege to combat all privilege, to shoulder the responsibility of intellectualism by "mak[ing] the moral and, as it were, representative effort to say what most of those for whom [one] say[s] it cannot see."[256]

256. Ibid., pp. 10–11. The internal quotation is from ND, p. 41. See also Seyla Benhabib, "Critical Theory and Postmodernism: On the Interplay of Ethics, Aesthetics, and Utopia in Critical Theory," in *The Handbook of Critical Theory,* ed. David M. Rasmussen (Oxford: Blackwell, 1996), pp. 327–31.

1

LOCATING MUSIC

Society, Modernity, and the New

Commentary

Richard Leppert

> As soon as one starts to discuss music, one enters the realm of thought, and no power on earth has the right to silence this.
>   Adorno, "Criteria of New Music"

As with a number of other philosopher-aestheticians, Adorno addressed questions about music's fundamental nature, which for him, as for others, invited consideration of musical meaning; the question of meaning in turn invited speculation about music's relation to language, the subject of the essay "MUSIC, LANGUAGE, AND COMPOSITION" (1956; this volume, pp. 113–26).[1] Adorno's overriding concern is modernity's social and cultural crisis, its impact on the human subject, and the role played by music. Music's role in modernity, for better or worse, appends to the import of its compositional "language." Adorno's argument will be that this language, both meaningful and immanently social, is itself in crisis as it variously responds to modernity in its present state.

The opening line, "Music is similar to language," drives the subsequent argument. Adorno is at pains to insist that music is socially meaningful, that it is more than merely a self-referential abstract acoustic phenomenon. Indeed, he assigns profound significance to musical sounds: "They say something, often something humane." Adorno insists, in a notably Benjaminian phrase, that music has a "theological aspect"; its meanings are "at once distinct and concealed." Music, in other words, is not the aesthetic transliteration of speech. It is something distinctly mystical; at the same time, it is a concrete, material practice. "It is demythologized prayer, freed from the magic of making anything happen, the human attempt, futile, as always, to name the name itself, not to communicate meanings" (p. 114). This is a crucial sentence marking Adorno's claim that music at heart is utopian: the expression of hope, which seeks to name the philosophical

---

1. Adorno also published the first half of this essay in QF, as "Music and Language: A Fragment," pp. 1–6.

(and spiritual) Absolute that nevertheless is unnamable (I will return to this later).[2] Music is the (concrete) voice of yearning for happiness, which cannot otherwise be directly annunciated, let alone realized.

Adorno stresses the similarities of music to language in order to outline how musical processes produce meaning—though he acknowledges that what music "says" cannot be abstracted from the music, as occurs with language, because music is not constituted by a sign system. Unlike language, music has no concepts, but like language it does possess a coherent and meaningful structure. As an "organized coherence of sounds," music is analogous to speech; it "has its sentence, phrase, period, and punctuation" (p. 113). Like language, music is "a temporal succession of articulated sounds." Its content is the "wealth of all those things underlying the musical grammar and syntax. Every musical phenomenon points beyond itself, on the strength of what it recalls, from what it distinguishes itself, by what means it awakens expectation" (p. 117). In this regard, Adorno suggests that music has something close to "primitive concepts," and cites as an example the "recurring symbols, insignia that bear the stamp of tonality" (p. 113)—in reference to the defining principles of harmony that have achieved the status of second nature in Western music during the period of common practice.

The sudden and somewhat jarring reference to tonality is rhetorically both striking and purposeful. Referencing tonality, a historically specific musical phenomenon, introduces history into the equation. And just as Adorno elsewhere argued the significance of the historicity of language, against the notion that language was simply a transparent medium of communication, he will argue here that musical language likewise sediments history—and also, in the case history of tonality, blinds us to that history in the glare of tonality's second-nature conventionality. He will later account for tonality's language-like functionality as a setup to argue its outmodedness, arguing that tonality in modernity fails to meet social need. As the established musical "language," tonality is reified, mechanical, and exhausted, like the language of instrumentalized communication. As such, tonality implicitly serves no other social function than to help anchor the status quo of an unjust society, by aestheticizing and naturalizing its fundamental ideological principles. By contrast, he regards socially

---

2. See Lambert Zuidervaart, *Adorno's Aesthetic Theory: The Redemption of Illusion* (Cambridge: MIT Press, 1991), pp. 125–28; and Shierry Weber Nicholsen, *Exact Imagination, Late Work: On Adorno's Aesthetics* (Cambridge: MIT Press, 1997), pp. 70–76.

progressive new music as directly engaging this issue—by denaturalizing tonality's second-nature status.[3]

Adorno points to the conventionality of chord function in tonal harmony in order to suggest that such "general symbols have the ability to merge with a particular context. They make room for musical specification" (p. 114). Within the specific context of a given use, harmonic function becomes less abstract, precisely what happens to concepts in language when set into particular contexts—though "the identity of these musical concepts lies in their own existence and not in something to which they refer." Despite its being "shot through with intentions," music is an "intentionless language." Yet, as regards meaning, had music none it would simply resemble an "acoustical kaleidoscope"; whereas, by contrast, if music were absolute signification it would cease to be music and "pass, falsely, into language" (all quotations, p. 114). In short, he argues, music signifies something definite, yet music's specific intentions remain veiled. Thus music lives—finds its life—in the gap between meaningfulness and meaninglessness.

Musical form is the result of a "gesture of judgment" (p. 115) which in turn gives the musical work its character of authenticity. But herein Adorno marks a warning. The more perfectly such judgments produce internal coherence—the more they seem to suggest that "this is the way it is"—the greater the music risks replicating the dominating logic it otherwise critiques. This then is the dialectic of musical enlightenment. To avoid this self-defeating trap, music must be realized against intentions: music's "similarity to language is fulfilled as it distances itself from language" (p. 117). Here is how Adorno puts the matter, in a paradoxical and complex formulation that attempts to preserve music's relative autonomy, the better to secure its position to engage, indirectly and by strictly musical means, socio-cultural critique: "The whole is realized against the intentions; it integrates them by means of the negation of each individual, indeterminate intention. Music as a whole rescues the intentions, not by diluting them into a more abstract, higher intention, but by readying itself, in the instant in which it crystallizes, to summon the intentionless. Thus, it is almost the antithesis of the kind of coherence that makes sense, even though it may appear as such in comparison to sensual immediacy" (p.

3. On Adorno's distinction between nature and second nature, both historically contingent, see Max Paddison, *Adorno's Aesthetics of Music* (Cambridge: Cambridge University Press, 1993), pp. 29–35, 53–54. His argument is influenced by the work of Lukács and Benjamin.

116). As Adorno argues later in the essay, music is riddle-like; it says something that the listener understands and yet doesn't. Like all art, music cannot be "pinned down as to what it says, and yet it speaks" (p. 122).

Max Paddison points out that Adorno uses the concept of form in two distinct ways: first, as normative (the conventional ways of doing things); second, as critical (the deviation from convention to create something new). Adorno thereby highlights the formal tension that results from sameness and difference, identity and nonidentity, within a structural whole by which means meaning results. Form constitutes a force-field of tensions. In Paddison's words, "It is the dynamic and oppositional relation to received formal norms within the structure of the musical work which enables the work to speak. At the same time, however, the received norms, as musical material, also carry with them the 'meanings' associated with their previous functionality." These meanings are recontextualized with the work, distancing the material from its previous functionality "without, however, being able to destroy its 'associative residues.' "[4]

Music's intentions, first and foremost, are musical; but because musical intentions themselves are always already at heart social, hence historical, this intentionless language engages intention. The truth content of its intentionless intentions is the expression of hope. Truth content [*Wahrheitsgehalt*], a critical concept for Adorno, is not what artworks mean "but rather what decides whether the work in itself is true or false,"[5] which is determined by the work's structural-procedural actuality. Truth content emerges from the technical manipulation of musical materials (in essence, their domination by the artist), which paradoxically gives to artworks something of the status of "natural" objects.[6] "Art is not nature, a belief that idealism hoped to inculcate, but art does want to keep nature's promise."[7] Autonomous artworks, in the apparent unity and totality of their

4. Max Paddison, "The Language-Character of Music: Some Motifs in Adorno," *Journal of the Royal Musical Association* 116 no. 2 (1991), pp. 275–78; quotation from p. 278. Cf. Adorno, "On Some Relationships between Music and Painting," trans. Susan H. Gillespie, *Musical Quarterly* 79 no. 1 (Spring 1995), p. 71: "Painting and music speak by virtue of the way they are constructed, not by the act of representing themselves; they speak all the more clearly, the more profoundly and thoroughly they are composed in themselves, and the figures of this essential form are their writing. . . . Écriture in music and painting cannot be direct writing, only encoded writing; otherwise it remains mere imitation."

5. AT, p. 130; see also p. 335.

6. Paddison, *Adorno's Aesthetics of Music*, p. 57: "The 'truth' of art appears to lie in this 'bringing to speech' of nature—a nature, however, which is itself the projection of that which has been repressed and rejected by society."

7. AT, p. 65.

formal structures, at least during the period of common practice, took on the illusion of both naturalness and spontaneity. The artwork's mimetic "naturalness," however, is artifactual, the result of labor, which in turn is informed by the social and historical.[8] Accordingly, Adorno rejects the notion that music is pure expression, insisting that it is also a form of cognition through which we can understand things about the world.

Mimesis—or mimetic expression—constitutes a central feature of Adorno's aesthetic theory. Though Adorno never directly explains his use of the term, his intent is clear enough. He considers mimesis "as an assimilation of the self to the other";[9] mimetic behavior, in other words, seeks to enact a reconciliation of subject to object. Mimetic activity occurs both in production (in music, both composing and performing) and in consumption (listening). The composer enacts mimesis through the rational manipulation of the musical materials, acknowledging what these materials demand in light of their own historicity. The composer's employment of the materials goes beyond convention specifically to engage convention, and thereby to restore the second nature of the conventional to the history that has shaped its conventionality. By this means the seemingly "natural" nature of the musical materials is also seen as immanently social. With the re-introduction of history and society, the composer's self-reflexive manipulation of the materials may posit the image (appearance or semblance) of a reconciliation of subject and object. By rendering second nature historically contingent and problematic, in other words, historical and social othering may be *aesthetically* transcended—though not transcended in actuality: the reconciliation is utopian.[10] "Wholly artifactual, the art-

---

8. Cf. Adorno, "To Describe, Understand and Explain" [1968 dialogue with Lucien Goldmann], in Lucien Goldmann, *Cultural Creation in Modern Society*, trans. Bart Grahl (St. Louis: Telos Press, 1976), pp. 135–36: "The work of art has a double character. It is simultaneously a 'social fact,' and also—and this is precisely what makes it a social fact—something else in relation to reality, something which is against it and somehow autonomous. This ambiguity of art, inasmuch as it belongs to society and inasmuch as it is different from it, leads to the fact that the highest level of art, its truth content and what finally gives it its quality as a work of art, cannot be a purely aesthetic matter. On the contrary, the truth content itself—and this is why I have said that basically only philosophy can grasp it—leads beyond the works precisely because it characterizes the moment of art in which art, in its truth, is more than art."

9. Nicholsen, *Exact Imagination*, p. 147; Nicholsen cites a number of passages in AT where the term is used in various contexts.

10. AT, p. 53: "In art the subject exposes itself, at various levels of autonomy, to its other, separated from it and yet not altogether separated. . . . That art, something mimetic, is possible in the midst of rationality, and that it employs its means,

work seems to be the opposite of what is not made, nature. As pure antithesis, however, each refers to the other: nature to the experience of a mediated and objectified world, the artwork to nature as the mediated plenipotentiary of immediacy. Therefore reflection on natural beauty is irrevocably requisite to the theory of art."[11]

In realizing music, the performer, through interpretation, likewise enacts the semblance of reconciliation, as does the (ideal) listener, to the extent that both understand the composition's mimetic comportment. This is to stress a critical feature of Adorno's aesthetic theory in a larger sense, namely, the centrality of thought at all stages. Philosophical reflection on the work is no less critical than the work itself if the work is to "speak"—if its own objecthood is to engage subjects. As Adorno stated, "The truth content of an artwork requires philosophy," but that truth emerges from the work, immanently; it is not "pumped into" the work. Or, as he put it, "Art awaits its own explanation.[12]

The enigmatic nature of the artwork is a direct outgrowth of its mimetic character, to the extent that artworks, while mimetic, are not conceptual. Artworks are produced by rationalized labor, but they act against instrumentalized reason, the ultimate tool of the domination of nature, of all that stands outside and against the subject. Reason constitutes the subject's sine qua non but also the subject's separation from nature, hence the schizoid separation from the self, since the subject is also at the same time a part of nature, as it were, in spite of its actions.[13] The artwork, rationalized, deflects the dominating impact of reason in order to posit an imagined kind of rational subjectivity that does not depend on maintaining a strict otherness to everything external to itself. Not the least means of imagining this reconciliation is through the artwork's expressiveness, which is at once

---

is a response to the faulty irrationality of the rational world as an overadministered world."

11. Ibid., p. 62.

12. Ibid., pp. 341, 353, respectively.

13. Martin Jay, "Mimesis and Mimetology: Adorno and Lacoue-Labarthe," in *The Semblance of Subjectivity: Essays in Adorno's Aesthetic Theory*, ed. Tom Huhn and Lambert Zuidervaart (Cambridge: MIT Press, 1997), p. 32: "Conceptual thought can be understood as an act of aggression perpetrated by a dominating subject on a world assumed to be external to it; it subsumes particulars under universals, violently reducing their uniqueness to typifications or exemplars of a general or essential principle. Mimesis, in contrast, involves a more sympathetic, compassionate, and noncoercive relationship of affinity between nonidentical particulars, which do not then become reified into two poles of a subject/object dualism."

artificial (expression is literally made, not "natural"), its apparent spontaneity being crucial to its being heard as expressive, though expressiveness results from the rational manipulation of musical materials. [14]

The second half of the essay more directly engages the relation of the musical work to history, focused on music of the twentieth century and what Adorno damningly terms this music's seeming "collective allergy to the primacy of similarity to language," notably, its common avoidance of the (productive) tension between music and language, in favor of a supposed "mere being-in-itself of its sound" (pp. 118, 117)—music, that is, shorn of the narcissistically expressive subjectivity often associated with late romanticism. Music true to the demands of its musical materials maintains the tension between itself and language (expression); indeed, the dialectical tension is itself crucial to musical truth. When new music, in rebelling against the nineteenth century, rebels against expression its gesture is self-defeating, a throwing of the baby out with the bathwater. In attempting to rid music of the excesses of solipsistic subjectivity by rigidly striving, by various means, for a supposed musical objectivism, new music represses or otherwise omits the past when what is called for, if musical truth is to emerge, is that the past be confronted so that it may be transcended.

Principally, what Adorno critiques are two moves in early-twentieth-century music, both exemplified by the work of Stravinsky, one toward primitivism (which erases history altogether in favor of mythic ritual), the other toward neo-classicism (which simply turns back the clock before the period of romantic hyper-expressiveness). Stravinsky's neo-primitivism supplants expression with ritual-like, obsessive rhythmic gesture; his later neo-classicism—what Adorno names a reversion to "sheer historicism"—references the musical materials of an earlier period, to Adorno's thinking, only as empty quotation (see part 4). By the half-century mark, new music had taken a further turn away from language via post-Webern radical serialism, which Adorno critiques as a music of "abstract negation . . . of mere omission. Through an ascetic taboo against everything that was linguistic in music, they hoped to be able to grasp pure musicality in itself . . . as the residue, as if whatever was left over was the truth" (p. 120).[15]

14. Zuidervaart, *Adorno's Aesthetic Theory*, pp. 111–12, citing AT: "Human expression is an objectified miming of pain and suffering and is permeated by moments of collectivity."

15. Adorno, "Berg's Discoveries in Compositional Technique," QF, p. 180, in reference to integral serialism, refers to "Webern transformed into a technological model." Regarding Adorno's admiration of Webern, see "Anton von Webern," SF,

Such music, organized by mathematical relationships, attempts to excise "subjectively mediated musical coherence" in the name of a pure objectivity—which for Adorno constitutes total reification: "the desire to be pure nature corresponds to the purely manufactured thing" (p. 121), the product of what he elsewhere wryly termed "tone-row engineers" *[Reihen-Ingenieure]*.[16] The point is that music "suffers" from its language-like nature, and this fact must be faced not escaped from, for the escape attempt ultimately abandons music to the machine of quasi-mechanized production, and promotes music's dehumanization.

Adorno offers a counterexample in Alban Berg, though he develops his argument by first citing Wagner. He credits Wagner with drawing vocal music closer to language. His assimilation of musical construction to the gestures of language helped advance the idea of great music "as a serious matter" and more than mere entertainment, and, not least, "created hitherto unimagined expressive values. . . . [Wagner] gave this music a dimension of bottomless depth."[17] Like Schoenberg, Berg emerges from Wagner's shadow; his operas are characterized by an expressiveness that confronts the expressive language-character that Wagner imposed on his vocal music. While paying strict attention to the demands of the vocal narrative, Berg realizes textual expressiveness by means of rigorously articulated musical forms adopted from instrumental music (in explicit tension with the Wagnerian compositional procedure). Berg thus engages tradition in order to transcend it; he does not pretend musically that tradition (history) doesn't exist.

Adorno, from his teens, was an outspoken advocate of aesthetic modernism, his early intellectual life having developed in the acoustical surroundings of the musical avant-garde—Schoenberg's Five Orchestral Pieces (1909), *Erwartung* (1909; premiered 1924), and *Pierrot lunaire* (1912); and Berg's *Wozzeck* (1925), among other works, were watershed compositions for his emerging aesthetic theory. During his adolescence and young adulthood he experienced first-hand new music's increasingly problematic relationship to its would-be audience, and he was keenly aware that the degree of audience estrangement from new music, and even hos-

---

pp. 91–105. "The whole of Webern's work revolves around the paradox of total construction as a means of achieving immediate utterance" (p. 94); "Webern's musical minimalism is founded on the expressive requirement that excludes any independent phenomenon that is not at the same time expressive. This economy comes to influence expression itself—to the point of silence" (p. 104).

16. Adorno, "The Aging of the New Music," this volume, p. 198.

17. Adorno, "Music, Language, and Composition," this volume, p. 123.

tility toward it, constituted an unparalleled situation by comparison with the reception of new European art music during much of the nineteenth century. His essay "WHY IS THE NEW ART SO HARD TO UNDERSTAND" (1931; pp. 127–34), written when he was twenty-eight, addresses the question sociologically.

Adorno's explanation, amplifying the line of argument outlined in the previous (though chronologically later) essay, is founded on the basic premise that the established conventions governing the production of older art are inappropriate for new art that attempts responsibly to confront its own historical moment. In short, although established conventions provide immediate access to the music, they obfuscate music's relation to society and history. "Art that lays claim to immediate general comprehensibility and social equivalency, on the basis of existing reality, necessarily possesses an ideological, concealing function" (p. 130). New music by contrast does not present the "immediacy of effect" (p. 128) that rendered earlier art so easily understandable—and palatable. This fact notwithstanding, despite real barriers to its understanding, new music has a good deal more to "say" to society, without regard to whether anyone cares to listen.

At the time Adorno wrote this essay, no issue loomed larger as definitive of the break between the musical past and present, and the estrangement of new music from its audience, than the supplanting of tonality by atonality and, later, serial technique, together with the corollary emancipation of dissonance. Adorno reiterates that tonality, which had defined the shape of music for two centuries, now principally served as affirmation of the aesthetic and social status quo, and for this reason did not meet the social-aesthetic demands of musical material.[18] Tonality has regressed to serve as a mechanism of affirmation for the here and now. Affirmative music, he later remarked, "takes the place of the Utopia it promises. By circling people, by enveloping them . . . and turning them as listeners into participants, it contributes ideologically to the integration which modern society never tires of achieving in reality. It leaves no room for conceptual reflection between itself and the subject, and so it creates an illusion of imme-

18. Adorno, "Music and New Music," QF, p. 257: "Bourgeois music was decorative, even in its greatest achievements. It made itself pleasant to people, not just directly to its listeners, but objectively, going far beyond them by virtue of its affirmation of the ideas of humanism. It was given notice to quit because it had degenerated into ideology, because its reflection of the world in a positive light, its call for a better world, became a lie which legitimated evil. The effect of canceling its contract reverberates in the most sensitive sublimations of musical form. Hence the right to speak of new music."

diacy in the totally mediated world, of proximity between strangers, of warmth for those who come to feel the chill of the unmitigated struggle of all against all."[19]

The production of art, he suggests, "behaves in a largely historical-dialectical fashion, to the extent that it expresses the tensions and contra-dictions of the existing relations . . . [and] calls for change." Accordingly, music today demands more than, say, tonality can offer. Atonal music, engaging both tonality and the immanent history it embeds, up-ends es-tablished convention, but at the cost of easy comprehensibility—which, ironically, is symptomatic of the very need the new music seeks to address, namely, that music with a claim to truth makes cognitive demands on listeners for which the prevailing social situation—mass consumer cul-ture—has not prepared them. Art consumption, Adorno points out, "largely lags behind [production] in unchanging existence"; its own pro-ductive force is minimal; it "only mirrors relations whose primary need is to maintain themselves" (p. 131). New music, radically denaturalized, stakes out a position counter to aesthetic and social norms alike. It demands attention; it isn't easily relegated to the background by audiences accus-tomed to a seamless homology between music and life, the one more or less unproblematically affirming the other. To be sure, affirmative music retains use value precisely to the extent that it affirms, but that use value is spurious in that it works against the ultimate, though unrecognized, interests of subjects whose subjecthood under prevailing circumstances re-mains largely unrealized. New music's use value is real to the extent that it expresses social truth; yet because this truth constitutes a critique of the here and now, its "practical" use value is commonly unrecognized—or is all too well recognized and on that account rejected as a threat to the second nature that underwrites modernity's present condition. To the extent that new music retains a "life" partly lived outside the bounds of mere con-sumerism, to the extent music still retains a breath of life as art, it presages an alternative to all-encompassing social instrumentality and the degra-dation of the subject that follows in tandem. As such art becomes an article of danger and resentment—as Adorno elsewhere remarked, "Music is re-alized in musical life, but that life conflicts with music."[20]

New art (by which Adorno means avant-garde art) insists on the reality, and centrality, of the gap between what art proffers—a glimpse of what is actually out of reach—and what audiences increasingly have come

19. ISM, p. 46.
20. Ibid., p. 119.

to expect from art, namely, the comfort that the gap can be closed by experiencing art. New art in other words refuses to deliver the package that art consumers believe they have bought. Or to construct the metaphor a bit differently, when the package is opened what's there is notably not what was ordered.

The modern habits of listening are at a standstill, Adorno claims, which is to say that listening has fallen increasingly behind the modern reality that new music confronts. The greater the distance between the two, the greater the rage against new art.[21] (I take up listening in greater detail in part 2.)

It is precisely *modernity's* incomprehensibility that art confronts, in one of two ways: either by attempting to stuff modernity back into the clothes of the pre-modern, pretending to a familiarity that is only ideological—in other words, denying reality—or by acknowledging modernity's radical strangeness (and estrangement) by direct confrontation via art techniques up to the task, thereby making critical sense of it. But to accomplish the latter, new art must make itself strange, because the techniques of old do not permit access to modernity, and this fact results in art's distance from an audience that social conditions regressively shape. In an art worthy of the name, production and consumption cannot be productively brought together, Adorno maintains, unless society itself changes. And he is clear that art itself is not going to change the world—its role is principally diagnostic.

Adorno closes with a comment about consumers, to the effect that their inability to comprehend new art results from social conditions defined by the coordination and complementarity of work and leisure, wherein leisure time is governed by the (as yet unnamed) Culture Industry: "The argument that the public wants kitsch is dishonest; the argument that it needs relaxation, at least incomplete." People's energies are diverted away from what might lead to a more humane subjecthood; that fact is the truth content of art, a truth so hard to understand.[22]

---

21. Cf. ibid., p. 120: "Even the purest and most consistent efforts, those of the musical avant-garde, run the risk of merely playing to themselves. They are exposed to that peril, which they can do nothing about, by their necessary renunciation of society. Neutralization and a loss of tension on the radical moderns' part are not due to their asociality but have been socially forced upon them: ears balk when they hear what would concern them."

22. Adorno, "New Music, Interpretation, Audience," SF, pp. 29–39, develops a series of concrete suggestions for the performance of new music intended to aid comprehension. For example, and following advice from Schoenberg and Berg on this score, he advocates playing unfamiliar works "rather slowly" so that audiences

"ON THE CONTEMPORARY RELATIONSHIP OF PHILOSOPHY AND MU-
SIC" (1953; pp. 135–61) is an important and detailed position paper in
which Adorno outlines the critical exchange between art and cognition, on
the one hand, and the relation of both to modern society and the subject,
on the other. The essay is bifurcated into two equal parts; the first is devoted to a general account of the philosophy-music relation; the second
principally concerns Schoenberg, whose music serves Adorno as a case
study of sorts for concretizing the more abstract discussion with which the
first part is principally occupied.

Published in the same year that Adorno reestablished himself permanently back in Germany after his long American exile, this article addresses the seemingly unending crisis of music in a modernity now shaped
by the Second World War and its recent aftermath; by the Cold War already unambiguously established as the "new world order"; by strident
anti-Communism (including McCarthyism directed against several of his
friends who had exiled themselves to the United States to escape Nazism);
and by the virtual globalization of mass culture and attendant consumerism. In short, the long history of both Western European and German
culture was at a watershed, pre-war Europe surviving as little more than
a memory. Though Adorno had neither interest in nor patience with attempts to revive a lost past, he did maintain a keen sense of the relation
of the past to an emerging future, which all too often seemed to preserve
and even promote the old injustices. New music confronted this history
but, as with all art worthy of the name, indirectly, and in light of the
postwar context, ever more problematically.

Struggling to maintain its autonomy, in an effort to retain its critical
non-affirmative stance in opposition to the here and now, music's relation
to society was fracturing. Its ability to communicate with immediacy was
lost, precisely because immediacy came at the price of co-option. Whether
music could still play any meaningfully progressive role in modernity's
future, whether it might bear any weight on behalf of humanity was an
urgent social and aesthetic question in equal measure. The right music

---

may more effectively absorb "the huge quantity of information that is conveyed
simultaneously and successively" (p. 32); he further suggests that attention to the
sensuous quality of the sound would serve to allay the listener's "stereotypical
belief that new music sounds awful and that's how it's supposed to be" (p. 33). His
larger point is the following: "Purists may talk of compromises with conformity
if they wish, and reject such concerns about performance as cowardly pandering
to audiences. Such purism is no more than a self-indulgent refusal to grapple with
a real problem" (p. 36).

could not create the right society, but the wrong music could indeed serve well the ends of further regression as a distraction from history's truth, as pleasant relaxation—a safety valve which cost the status quo nothing. The right kind of music, rightly understood, could serve progressive ends by expressing the truth behind "reality's" mask—a tall order, not least because composers and performers faced this challenge without benefit of the musical road map that had previously been at their disposal.[23] Indeed, the aporia of new music is realized "in the loss of a tradition that could be experienced even negatively," realized, in other words, in "technical, intellectual, and social disorientation" (p. 137). Adorno cites the silences that interrupt Webern's music as a sign of and response to the crisis, suggesting that Webern, rather than betraying music's essence by holding fast to existence, momentarily extinguishes it in order to remain true to its highest calling.

The crisis of new music pushes the demand for philosophically questioning what music is—and even fosters inquiry as to whether it has a right to exist. But the answer cannot be found in music itself as pure essence or first principle. What Adorno terms music's "dignity" is not revealed by the simple fact of its phenomenological reality, any more than its meaning can be directly or immediately accessed. Citing Schoenberg's remark that music says what only can be said through music, Adorno wryly emphasizes that music's character is at once enigmatical and "emphatically contingent. . . . Art as a whole is probably not amenable to this context of immanent explanations that asks everything that exists to show its passport" (p. 138). He later clarified this sentiment in *Aesthetic Theory:* "The enigmaticalness of artworks remains bound up with history. It was through history that they became an enigma; it is history that ever and again makes them such, and, conversely, it is history alone—which gave them their authority—that holds at a distance the embarrassing question of their raison d'être."[24]

---

23. Adorno's ideal musical philosopher is not, say, the academic musicologist or the "expert listener" but the performer, who realizes the music through a process of interpretation which itself is at once musical and philosophical. The challenge—and responsibility—of interpretation facing the performer must likewise be met by the listener. The challenge is both notable and unrelenting, for "Music gazes at its listener with empty eyes, and the more deeply one immerses oneself in it, the more incomprehensible its ultimate purpose becomes, until one learns that the answer, if such is possible, does not lie in contemplation, but in interpretation."

24. AT, p. 120. Richard Wolin, "Utopia, Mimesis, and Reconciliation: A Redemptive Critique of Adorno's *Aesthetic Theory,*" *Representations* 32 (Fall 1990),

Adorno argues that the enigmatical character of art is not its failure but an essential component of its being art in the first place. The residue of the uncertain is all the more critical under prevailing circumstance to the extent that it constitutes a resistance to music's instrumental utilization. The enigmatical is music's connection to the unattainable wherein lies utopia. During the long period of common practice, established convention made music's meaning appear self-evident; music's enigmatical character was more concealed. Today, when tradition no longer prescribes anything for music, music's enigmatic character reemerges, though it remains accessible only through attention to its historical characteristics and mediations. Music's relations to history, in other words, keeps music from being "utterly impoverished, abstract, and in the most real sense lacking in essence" (p. 141).

There is a distinctly pedagogical charge to Adorno's concern to define the music-philosophy relation, driven by his intention to undercut the charge that music is simply "a system of subjective projections and conventional notions" (p. 138). Modern music's loss of immediacy, critical to its truth content, can only be overcome by a process of interpretation rigorously attentive not only to musical processes as such, which could be revealed through formal analysis alone, but also to the history with which the processes are saturated. Music's processes, the result of human labor, are invariably always already socially anchored, and on that account they carry social meanings, though indirectly. Music's riddle, he suggests can only be solved by the person who plays the music "correctly, as something whole" (p. 139).

Adorno then turns to the language question, repeating but also further anchoring an argument advanced in "Music, Language, and Composition." "In music, what is at stake is not meaning, but gestures," which themselves are sedimented history. I take Adorno here to refer to the micro- and macrological ways in which music unfolds, established through a kind of grammar. The grammar itself reflects music's desire to "speak," yet it can only do so obliquely because it is not a language, only language-like. Like philosophy, music attempts to name, that is, strives for what Adorno calls "the absolute unity of object and sign," which in fact it cannot accomplish,

---

p. 39: "For unlike philosophy, the language of art is sensuous. Art's mode of articulation relies on images, sounds, and colors rather than the clarity of discursive argument. Consequently as vehicles of truth works of art are inherently 'enigmatic' *(rätselhaft)*. And it is precisely this enigmatic quality that beseeches, implores, and requires the *philosophical interpretation* of art. In other words, this dynamic alone mandates the necessity of *aesthetic theory*" (original emphasis).

since what results is only pure sound, though Adorno regards the effort itself as fundamentally utopian. "Music does not know the name—the absolute as sound—immediately, but, if one may express it this way, attempts its conjuring construction through a whole, a process" (p. 140). The process itself is rational, like language; music's unfolding bears a relation to philosophy.

Adorno connects music to history through a discussion of time in music, discursively constituted by the tension between music's own time and the historical time which it reflects back as appearance. In other words, musical time and empirical time exist in a dialectical relation in musical works. The stakes are high, and social: "Only history itself, real history with all its suffering and all its contradiction, constitutes the truth of music" (p. 147).

The implication is clear. Philosophical knowledge of music is not to be found in its supposed first-principle, ontological origin (the hopeless goal of idealist philosophy) but only from music's present, which of course contains a sedimented past. Thus Beethoven: Adorno argues that we can better understand his music if we begin with what confronts us in Beethoven today, than were we to limit our investigation to Beethoven's own milieu, because the current state of compositional processes "drastically extend the laws of construction that Beethoven's . . . work contained in encapsulated form during the nineteenth century. It is only from the vantage point of the most advanced production that light is shed on the entire species" (pp. 147–48).

In the second part of the essay, following his opening commentary on Schoenberg—principally a defense of the composer aimed squarely at young composers at mid-century for whom Schoenberg had taken on the role of graybeard ancestor—Adorno turns to the question of musical space, and to Schoenberg's work, both early and late. He suggests that spatiality is a prime component of tonal music (he cites Bruckner's symphonies), adhering alike to harmonic structure and instrumental sound, and delivering a kind of three-dimensional effect. As with modern painting, Schoenberg eclipses the third dimension in order to engage and critique the second nature of space. Space in other words is reformulated as a contested terrain precisely to the extent that it is rendered historical, hence contingent. Put differently, the would-be ontological naturalism of musical space is made strange: "Among the shocks that this music delivers, one of the ones that is surely of the essence is its denial, for the listener, of the feeling of inclusion, the spatial embrace. It sounds, to state it bluntly, like a beating" (p. 150). Adorno credits this intervention to Schoenberg, manifested in his atonal compositions that preceded his development of serial technique but which remain a characteristic dimension of his music thereafter, though by other means. For example, in the late work a new sense of space is achieved by the "disposition of color, the art of many-layered instrumentation intensified in the most extreme degree" (pp. 150–51; his example is drawn from *Moses und Aron*). The potential implication of Schoenberg's experiment is broad, namely, that instrumentation can stand in place for harmonic structures that had previously produced the effect of spatial depth.

Much of the essay confronts the crisis in new music around 1950 which, after all, has hardly abated even now, though the terms are somewhat if not wholly different. From Adorno's perspective, Schoenberg met history's challenge head on. He engaged the idiomatic conventional language of tonality by adopting atonality, and thereafter serialism, for the sake of rescuing expression from its late-romantic neutralization as an acoustic commodity. And now, after Schoenberg, with the integral serialism's domination of new music, expression itself is threatened in favor of music's "natural material," which emerges with "threatening purity" (p. 146)—music which seeks to erase subjectivity in favor of germ-free rationalization.[25] And yet, as Adorno carefully notes despite this critique, one cannot ultimately prejudge any technique, as it were, from above or beyond its use in a given work. The universal must take place within the particular, and it is the nature of the relation and tension between them that determines the legitimacy or illegitimacy of the endeavor. Thus with regard to serial and integral serialist composition, Adorno notes—via a corrective to his more rigid judgment in *Philosophy of Modern Music*—that new music's "organizational principles do not necessarily have to remain external to the musical events, so long as the latter create a compelling context purely from within themselves" (p. 152). Nonetheless, in the essay's final pages Adorno goes to some length to compare, unfavorably, the work of young composers around 1950, integral serialists, to Schoenberg's late works, where the *a priori* "demands" of serial technique are relaxed, giving greater sway to the musical material's expressive (subjective) demands. Adorno sees here the insistent reemergence of music's human, and hu-

25. Cf. Adorno, "Berg's Discoveries in Compositional Technique," p. 183. Adorno regards Berg's music as "the antipode to everything spick and span." He critiques the sometime tendency to associate Berg with "the cliché of the psychological late Romantic . . . [as] probably nothing but a defence against what might be termed the unhygienic aspect of his work: anything which is not clean as the bathroom must be sick."

mane, qualities, its ultimate raison d'être, and he quite obviously cautions members of the then-current (Darmstadt) avant-garde that they ignore this matter at enormous risk to their music's truth content (Boulez's work is named, presumably in reference to his integral serialist *Structure 1a* [1951]; Adorno's critique, directly or indirectly, got Boulez's attention, as his later compositions and statements confirm).[26]

Concluding the essay, Adorno refers to the "absurd, blindly violent element of the system," in light of which he insists on the need for a relentless self-reflexivity by composers—technical, intellectual and spiritual reflection (p. 158). Adorno amplifies this concern in *Introduction to the Sociology of Music*, by critiquing what he names this music's "unbridgeable distance from all empirical reality" and the corollary distancing from expression: "If something segregates itself to such an extent as if it no longer had any human content, if it thus indicts the inhuman condition, it is on the point of pitilessly forgetting that condition and becoming its own fetish. That is the ideological aspect of the radically technological, anti-ideological work of art."[27] Music's contemporary relation to philosophy, he concludes, is in essence "that of an independently unfolding truth"; but that truth can only be revealed by critique that occurs within the musical work itself, through the "law of form" (p. 158). (The critique of mid-century new music that Adorno engages here is taken up once again in his essay, "The Aging of the New Music," included in this volume).

"ON THE PROBLEM OF MUSICAL ANALYSIS" (1969; pp. 162–80) is transcribed from a taped talk that Adorno gave in Frankfurt at the Hochschule für Musik und Darstellende Kunst on 24 February 1969, about six months before his death. According to Max Paddison, who prepared the transcription and the English translation, Adorno likely delivered his remarks from minimal notes, his common practice. (Though strikingly literate, and

26. See Alastair Williams, *New Music and the Claims of Modernity* (Aldershot, UK: Ashgate, 1997), p. 50.

27. ISM, p. 187. See also related comments on the emergence of electronic music in Adorno, "Music and New Music," pp. 265–68. This essay, from 1960, concludes with a dialectical provisional assessment of early electronic experiments. Adorno singles out Stockhausen, and his *Gesang der Jünglinge* (1955–56), for particular praise. He sees in electronic music two contradictory tendencies: one toward extreme expressiveness, as in Stockhausen, the other toward the elimination of the composer's subjective intervention. See also Gianmario Borio, "New Technology, New Techniques: The Aesthetics of Electronic Music in the 1950s," *Interface: Journal of New Music Research* 22 no. 1 (1993), pp. 77–87, which includes a discussion of Adorno's writings on the subject.

the argument well articulated, the "essay" was not subjected to Adorno's characteristic practice of extensive revision.)[28] Its intent is explicitly pedagogical.

Addressing students, Adorno opens by reminding them of what they already know, that the word "analysis" when attached to music commonly signals the death of the music itself, wryly adding, "One can well say that the general underlying feeling toward musical analysis is not exactly friendly" (p. 162). His principal concern is the relation between analysis and interpretation in performance—an issue obviously relevant to his conservatory audience, though equally applicable to the act of listening, as he suggests at the essay's end. He cites the performer's needing to know the work "intimately" as a sine qua non for interpretation and suggests that such knowledge lies at the heart of analysis. This is a crucial move. Adorno's interest in analysis, directly linked to music's realization in performance, turns analysis into an active (and practical) exercise, itself a kind of musical "doing," an effort to bring music alive acoustically, cognitively, and subjectively. In other words, music's expressiveness is at once the result of subjectivity and rationalization (on the part of the composer, to be sure, but also the performer). Analysis becomes a critical component for bridging the subject-object gap that defines the challenge which must be faced for every performance-art form. "Analysis is itself a form in its own right, like translation, criticism and commentary, as one of those media through which the very work unfolds. Works need analysis for their truth content to be revealed" (p. 167).

The score represents the foundation for the process, obviously enough. But the score is the starting point and not the end. No score conveys full instructions for its realization; instead it provides *indications* to varying degrees, pertaining not to the notes but to the expressive character necessary for their appropriate realization—phrasing, dynamics, tempi, and the like. Citing Beethoven, and his relatively sparing, but precise, use of score markings, Adorno emphasizes the importance of knowing his music's processes in general in order to realize through performance the musical discourse of any particular work. Not least one needs a critical awareness of Beethoven's musical structure—not simply, say, that he used sonata form, but how his use of that formal schema functions in tension with its model.[29]

28. See Max Paddison's introductory comments in Adorno, "On the Problem of Musical Analysis," trans. Max Paddison, *Music Analysis* 1 no. 2 (July 1982), pp. 169–71.

29. Adorno, "Criteria of New Music," SF, p. 161, makes clear that no simple

Adorno emphasizes the importance of work-immanent analysis; as he put it in *Aesthetic Theory*, "Whoever refuses to reenact the work under the discipline it imposes falls under the empty gaze."[30] Of critical importance, analysis provides access, however limited, to the residue or surplus in art—that which in essence exceeds the quantifiable musical facts of the work—the precise "extra" that renders it art in the first place, and which constitutes the work's truth content. Aesthetic residue, as difficult to define as it is to locate precisely within works, defies analysis, yet demands analysis all the more; mediated by and manifested through the work's technical structure, it speaks to us "only musically."[31]

To clarify his argument, Adorno turns to a counter example of analysis common to certain popular forms of music appreciation that attempt to guide the listener effortlessly into (if not "through") the work, citing the well-known thematic guides by Hans von Wolzogen to Wagnerian operas and music dramas that catalogue and name leitmotifs.[32] Adorno's point is that such cataloguing serves less to promote access and understanding than to promote regression. Listeners are invited simply to identify the referent when it sounds in the orchestra (Ah! The Sword) rather than to follow anything of musical process beyond the level of its surface manifestation. Indeed, thematic recognition, in the absence of understanding thematic transformation, reduces the musical experience to something like an acoustical shopping spree, where the listener picks out the nicest version for gustatory delectation. By such means, an artwork's truth content is rendered invisible and, indeed, irrelevant.

homology exists between expression and meaning: "Meaningful music is not necessarily expressive. Expression, the mimetic element in music, the thing that . . . the music 'resembles,' is only one element of its meaning, and is to be held in tension with a further aspect, that of construction and logic. No doubt these opposed elements are dialectically interrelated."

30. AT, p. 120.

31. Ferenc Feher, "Negative Philosophy of Music—Positive Results," trans. Zoltan Feher, *New German Critique* 4 (Winter 1975), p. 104: *"The 'content' of the musical work is not something that exists outside of itself but is contained in its own organization,* an order embodied in this organization (or perhaps its disintegration in all its variations). However, the concept of every kind of order, every kind of structure, and every kind of totality is still 'external' to music, since it imposes itself upon the composer from the external world. Hence the work stands on its own as a window-less monad, a *being-for-itself,* yet at the same time it points beyond itself to the world where the idea of its organization originated—it is a *being-for-us"* (original emphasis).

32. For example, Hans von Wolzogen, *Guide to the Music of Richard Wagner's Tetralogy: The Ring of the Niebelung: A Thematic Key,* trans. Nathan Haskell Dole (New York: G. Schirmer, 1905). The guide was first published in German in 1876.

Adorno's principal point is to emphasize that music's truth is its "becoming." Art is processual, and without understanding the unfolding of each particular part of musical process, real understanding remains out of reach. In a temporal art this desideratum presents a notable challenge to analysis, to the extent that the work can only ultimately be understood after it is finished and silence ensues. That is, understanding comes from a looking backward at the music's forward movement. That we can only sort out the unfolding after it concludes is of course true for any temporal art form; but with music the challenge is greater to the extent that music is not, after all, a language of externally referring signs, but one whose referents are paradoxically at once wholly internal (immanently confined) yet invariably social. We don't have the "advantage" of words, as in a play, to guide us through the unfolding; we have only sounds, whose self-reflexive relations can only be understood in and of themselves and even then only after they have, so to speak, disappeared.

The ultimate point of analysis is to reveal a work's "problem," in essence its unique constellation of events or its force-field. (But there is a paradoxical cost that accompanies this exercise: analysis constitutes a reduction of the work, and to some extent the more "successful" the analysis, the greater the impact of the reduction.) The final goal, whatever the dangers of self-defeating reductiveness, is to recognize as precisely as possible how the music "realizes itself," which in turn demands a kind of analysis that is newly derived from each work—because the analysis follows the work, not the reverse. The goal of Adornian analysis is to come to the work in such a way that it reveals itself, rather than our revealing it, so to speak, by forcing it, reductively, into a mold (which principally drives Adorno's criticism of the Schenkerian "Fundamental Line" that occurs early on in the essay).

Max Paddison points to what he considers to be the limitations of Adorno's musical analyses. In particular, he critiques what he perceives as "the strange disparity between the sophistication and radicality of [Adorno's] aesthetics and sociology on the one hand, and on the other hand the lack of sophistication and the traditional character of his music-analytical method." Paddison suggests the cause for this disparity may lie in Adorno's "rather old-fashioned motivic-thematic formal analytical approach, with all its assumptions concerning the existence of separate categories like 'first subject,' 'transition section,' 'second subject,' etc., combined with a highly elaborated aesthetic theory which is founded on a notion of the dissolution and subversion of such apparently invariant formal categories." In the end, however, Paddison acknowledges that, despite the fragmentary nature and lack of precise technical detail in his musical analyses, Adorno "often succeed[ed] in spite of all in conveying a compelling sense of the music itself."[33] Leaving aside what I would argue is Paddison's somewhat essentialized articulation of how Adorno analyzes music, Paddison's final judgment compellingly makes the point about what really matters: the profound understanding of music and musical process that determines Adorno's writing. Adorno employed established analytical methods only to the extent that they served his larger purpose, beyond which he set off on his own—without regard to the established practices of musicological analysis, which he knew very well. (It's difficult to argue that Adorno's understanding of music would have been bettered by the systematic employment of any of the analytical means that enjoyed canonic status during his lifetime.) The result, far more often than not, was insight. Indeed, even when Adorno's analyses miss the mark, they cannot easily be dismissed but demand engagement.

That Adorno read scores, and in fact enjoyed the effort, is patently clear throughout his writing; his book on Mahler and the unfinished Beethoven project are notable in this respect. But what is clearer still is the fact that Adorno depended ultimately on his ears. He was an acute structural listener, and it is precisely the acoustical phenomenon of music that compelled him. Thus in the posthumous Beethoven book, I am repeatedly struck by his insight into tiny musical details—turns of musical phrase, a particular cadence, etc.—read against the whole, and displaying quite phenomenal sensitivity to how the music "works" internally in order to carry out what might be termed its musical-cultural work; in other words, his analysis is notably distinct from the established parameters set by analytical practice within the musical disciplines, if not now, certainly when Adorno was living.

In his Berg monograph Adorno speaks of the necessity to determine what he terms the objective properties of a composition's quality "by immersing oneself in the work as a whole and its microstructure."[34] What he means by this, in practice, is developing a general understanding of a work's formal apparatus, in relation to details. It's on the details that he concentrates. What he does not mean—ever—is a measure-by-measure

---

33. Paddison, *Adorno's Aesthetics of Music*, all quotations from pp. 169–70. See also the similar critiques by Diether de la Motte, "Adornos musikalische Analysen," in *Adorno und die Musik*, ed. Otto Kolleritsch (Graz: Universal Edition, 1979), pp. 52–63; and Harold Blumenfeld, "*Ad Vocem* Adorno," *Musical Quarterly* 70 no. 2 (Spring 1984), pp. 520–21.

34. AB, p. 35.

walk-through of the piece—the sort of thing I recall from graduate school days in the 1960s when a colleague of mine was required in a seminar devoted exclusively to the Bartók string quartets to label every single vertical structure with the supposedly appropriate chord designation, a grotesque and mind-numbing practice that virtually guaranteed his losing sight of the musical "forest" for the individual harmonic "trees"—to be sure, a fairly hyperbolic example of analytical pedantry. It is precisely this tradition against which Adorno's own analytical practice rebels, not because such data is *necessarily* meaningless but because it has under prevailing circumstances devolved into an exercise of trivial pursuit serving no higher purpose. Analysis for Adorno, as he himself states the matter, "focuses on those concrete moments that make up a piece of music. . . . It must be concerned with the flesh not the skeleton."[35] Picking up on the significance of the Berg monograph's subtitle, "Master of the Smallest Link," Adorno emphasizes Berg's compositional practice and the challenge of what he regards as responsible analysis: attention to the tiny particulars, always in a tense relation to the whole, by means of which the composition becomes, and ultimately reveals, itself. Simply stated, in his view, nailing down the technical details of a composition with a passionate intent to gather in succession every datum available to quantification will not on that account erase music's ultimate and immanent ambiguity, the enigmatical quality on the basis of which it gains status as art. It will instead obfuscate precisely this quality of the musical work. This is to suggest that quantification as such guarantees nothing in the way of understanding. Quantification does not constitute interpretation; it is instead the antecedent thereto. What Adorno critiques by contrast is the fetishization of data that results in technical analysis serving only its own end.[36]

One other matter. Adorno's analysis tends to cease at the point where

35. Ibid., p. 36.
36. See the excellent discussion by Rose Rosengard Subotnik, "Why Is Adorno's Music Criticism the Way It Is?: Some Reflections on Twentieth-Century Criticism of Nineteenth-Century Music," in *Developing Variations: Style and Ideology in Western Music* (Minneapolis: University of Minnesota Press, 1991), especially pp. 49–56: "Purely technical criticism seems even less capable than poetic criticism of capturing the essence of nineteenth-century music by becoming fully analogous with it, that is, analogous in the sense of evoking, even negatively through the character of its own incompleteness, some lost universe of interconnected mediums and events through which individual necessity might conceivably be guaranteed" (p. 51). See also Joseph Kerman's classic essay "How We Got into Analysis, and How to Get Out," in *Write All These Down: Essays on Music* (Berkeley and Los Angeles: University of California Press, 1994), pp. 12–32.

the musical-technical "event" or detail cannot be heard, where it would otherwise seem to exist only "on paper," or when to proceed with the analysis would produce no further insight into the work's immanence. This is not to suggest that Adorno's analyses invariably take the task to the appropriate point to elicit crucial meanings, nor that his readings are invariably correct.[37] If the ultimate purpose of analysis is to reveal a work's truth content, in essence the work's aesthetic comportment, the limitations of analysis are manifest to the extent that truth content does not lie waiting for its empirical demonstration. Despite the centrality of analysis to musical knowledge, what is most worth seeking through analysis will necessarily ultimately remain out of reach. Were that not the case, what was being analyzed would not be art.

"THE AGING OF THE NEW MUSIC" (1955; pp. 181–202), first presented as a lecture in 1954 at the Stuttgart Week of New Music, carries on much of the discussion I have outlined already but with a notable ferocity, attacking what Adorno saw as the elimination in then-new music of subjectivity and spontaneity in favor of an obsessive objectification that had regressed into its own fetish, though as Alastair Williams points out, Adorno's argument is weakened by a failure "to discuss in specific terms the repertoire to which he is referring."[38] The broad repertory of his concern, however, is not in doubt: post-Webern integral serialism but also what Adorno recognized as the general disintegration of twelve-tone technique into a system, in effect, a menu for what counted as new music. The cost was to music's critical edge, which disappears in a kind of blind affirmation of what is now only "officially" radical,[39] its "newness" commodified: "Twelve-tone technique has its justification only in the presentation of complex musical contents, which cannot otherwise be organized. Separated from this function, it degenerates into a deluded system" (pp. 184–85). Adorno argues that Schoenberg came to twelve-tone composition out

37. Numerous examples of Adorno's analyses of individual works are included in the GS, vol. 18.
38. Williams, *New Music and the Claims of Modernity*, p. 47. Heinz-Klaus Metzger, "Just Who Is Growing Old?" *Die Reihe 4: Young Composers* (Bryn Mawr, PA: Theodore Presser, 1960), pp. 63–80, critiques Adorno's essay on this point. Metzger likewise takes Adorno to task for giving comfort in this essay to reactionary critics of new music—unintentionally to be sure, though Metzger does not excuse Adorno on this account. Metzger's fundamental point is that the very music that Adorno himself championed is that which is growing old.
39. Elsewhere in the essay Adorno uses the phrase "radically empty" (p. 194); and in the same spirit remarks of "the arbitrariness of today's musical radicalism, the cheapness of being daring" (p. 190).

of a need, and even from desperation, at once personal and historical, to confront the aporia that led from tonality to atonality. "Trouble" started the moment twelve-tone technique was, in effect, summarily adopted as the road map for the future. The hegemony enjoyed by serialism in the academy generally, and at Darmstadt in particular, effectively gave the lie to the technique's truth. That is, once fully rationalized and actualized, twelve-tone composition became for Adorno an activity on autopilot. What for Schoenberg had been the musical engagement with the humane, was reduced to the same old (hence aging) affirmation of modern life as mathematical order, as dehumanized prefabrication. Indeed, Adorno argues that the new music of the previous half century retains a newness that much chronologically newer music inadvertently eschews. He suggests that the structural coherence of Schoenberg's compositions is compelled by the material itself, whereas with the avant-garde of the 1950s he hears "the arbitrariness of a radicalness for which nothing is any longer at stake," either emotionally or in actuality, "for almost no one gets excited anymore about that twelve-tone technique that is served up at all music festivals. It is tolerated as the private activity of specialists, a cultural necessity in some not quite clear fashion" (p. 185). New music reverts to privatization, though commonly under the protection of academic tenure.[40]

Music's truth content is realized in time and by means of its specific engagement with time. If modernity is organized by the bottom line, the metaphor for this principle is that "time is money." Since time is experienced as second nature, the more music de-naturalizes time, the more directly and meaningfully music engages modernity itself. Music, enacted through time and in tension with time's cultural given-ness, remakes our experience of time at once by "showing" time for what it has become, and, conversely, what it might otherwise be. Dystopia and utopia.

To elicit the historicity of time in music, for Adorno, requires music to refer to its own past, to evoke that past in order to transcend it. He hears this engagement in Schoenberg, Berg, and Webern, precisely to the extent that their compositions in one way or another function in direct tension with the musical system, tonality and its several teleological accouterments, that determines the aporia that new music must face. By contrast, in the new music of the 1950s' radical serialists Adorno "hears" history's absence, the past disappeared, and to this extent, this new music serves reification: forgetting. The nonidentical in Schoenberg becomes the new

40. See Susan McClary, "Terminal Prestige: The Case of Avant-Garde Music Composition," *Cultural Critique* 12 (Spring 1989), pp. 57–81.

identity; technique serves itself. Adorno hears in post-Webern serialism time stood still, as if it were locked in an eternal present, in effect a new myth. It is not going too far to suggest that he heard in this stasis the unwitting aesthetic analogue to the "promise" of the Thousand Year Reich: time halted in favor of the way things are, de facto "identification with the aggressor," or if one prefers a less horrific metaphor, art "set up as a nature reserve for the eternally human and of comfortable immediacy, isolated from the process of enlightenment" (p. 193).

The immanent dynamism of tonal music (for example, in sonata form the principle of thematic development) is coterminous with the social and cultural episteme that underwrites modernity even to the present, according to which space and time function in tandem as developmental parameters.[41] Tonal works engage time and space relations, whether affirmatively or critically. By contrast, the apparent stasis in integral serialist works, determined by what Adorno senses as developmental lack, might seem to critically engage the ideology underwriting development by simply refusing it. But Adorno argues against such a reading. New music that fails to develop fails on two *social* grounds. First, it refuses to acknowledge that time, as a social construct, does not stand still, and that to rigidify time merely serves to keep things in place. Secondly, it posits the human subject in precisely the same way, as a static being, cursed to be what now counts for Being. As a result, and ironically, musical stasis reinforces the status quo.

Reprising a theme Adorno often invoked, he suggests that expression has gained a bad reputation as the foundation of romanticism's lie, and that the new music confronts this misplaced blame by refusing expression altogether. Instead, what's called for is a confrontation with the *ideology* of expression, that is, with what underwrites expression's tendency toward affirmation. Adorno warns, in other words, not to throw the baby out with the bathwater. "What is needed is for expression to win back the density of experience," rescuing it from "ornament and empty gesture" (p. 191). So-called objectivism, "so vain about its lack of vanity" (p. 198), purges subjectivism in the purported name of progress; in effect it sees the subject as the enemy—a subject which under prevailing conditions hardly even exists—as though the subject prevents the musical material from realizing itself. The new objectivism responds to this misplaced assessment of blame with an overdetermined asceticism that, against its better judgment,

41. Donald M. Lowe, *The History of Bourgeois Perception* (Chicago: University of Chicago Press, 1982).

wounds an already wounded subjectivity that society generally finds intolerable. Asceticism protects the composer from getting his or her hands dirty; it inoculates the composer from the fearsome truth that art exists to reveal. Asceticism is the trail of crumbs left by someone desperate to find shelter as the consolation prize for refusing to pay heed to what might actually be sought. Music systematized is music practicing obedience, a music that measures itself against "an invisible canon of the permitted and the forbidden" (p. 196): in short, a music of fear. Fully rationalized, its resignation unwittingly expresses the dominant anti-rationality of a determined present. It "manages" the life it refuses to lead.

The subjectivity that Adorno seeks to rescue is realized through the subject's highly rationalized approach to music's formally organized materials. Musical structure reveals the human subject through the productive tension between the planned and the spontaneous; musical structure constitutes the semblance of a "realized" humanity, and reflects the will to freedom.[42] The subjective comes about, as Adorno puts it elsewhere, "as a consequence of ruthless reflection" of the objective subject matter on itself. That is, there must be a "technical reflection on technique," and not merely as the outgrowth of subjective intentions.[43]

The lengthy final essay in *Quasi una fantasia*, "Vers une musique informelle" (1961), takes up the fundamental problematic of new music in its confrontation with history one more time, beginning with a disclaimer—not precisely characteristic of Adorno—that his "membership [in] Schoenberg's Viennese school" doesn't confer "any particular authority on me or [permit me] to assert that as an initiate I had easy answers to these questions."[44] Adorno's purpose is to speak on behalf of an "a-serial" music, informal to the extent that it is not already fully systematized. Adorno confesses at the start that he will not be able to systematize

42. Cf. Adorno, "Music and Technique," SF, p. 198: "Inner experience and outer form are created by a reciprocal process of interaction." "The Aging of the New Music" is also discussed by Rolf Wiggershaus, *The Frankfurt School: Its History, Theories, and Political Significance*, trans. Michael Robertson (Cambridge: MIT Press, 1995), pp. 513–19; and by Robert Hullot-Kentor, "Popular Music and Adorno's 'The Aging of the New Music,'" *Telos* 77 (Fall 1988), pp. 86–94.

43. Adorno, "Music and Technique," p. 207.

44. Adorno, "Vers une musique informelle," QF, p. 270. Concerning the development of Adorno's late thought on new music after the Second World War, beginning with "The Aging of the New Music" and culminating with "Vers une musique informelle," given in Darmstadt in 1961, and "The Function of Color in Music," delivered in 1966, see Gianmario Borio, "Die Positionen Adornos zur musikalischen Avantgarde zwischen 1954 und 1966," in *Adorno in seinen musikalischen Schriften* (Rogensburg: G. Bosse, 1987), pp. 163–79.

his concept of the non-systematic; instead, he will "at least . . . attempt to stake out the parameters of the concept. What is meant is a type of music which has discarded all forms which are external or abstract or which confront it in an inflexible way. At the same time, although such music should be completely free of anything irreducibly alien to itself or super-imposed on it, it should nevertheless constitute itself in an objectively compelling way, in the musical substance itself, and not in terms of exter-nal laws."[45] Frustratingly abstract as this formulation may be, it contains nothing more—or less—than a fear of regression through adaptation to the formulaic—including formulaic adoption of, say, early-twentieth-century atonality in lieu of serialism. Indeed, as he later clarifies, his pur-pose is not achieved by restoration of an older tradition but by the devel-opment of equivalents suitable to the new material. In other words, music must move forward via self-reflexive engagement with the music materials of the here and now, which are always already rendered problematic by their historical locus.[46] The composer must exercise control over the ma-terial, in essence dominate it (rationally), paradoxically to rescue these materials from affirmative second-nature domination by instrumentalized reason and reification. "*Musique informelle*," Adorno suggests, "is not cultural neutralism, but a critique of the past" which by definition concerns the subject—what Adorno names as "the only component of art that is non-mechanical, truly alive."[47] He concludes, "the aim of every artistic utopia today is to make things in ignorance of what they are."[48] Art's truth content, that is, is constituted by the return to the repressed.

45. Adorno, "Vers une musique informelle," p. 272.

46. Cf. Rose Rosengard Subotnik, "The Challenge of Contemporary Music," in *Developing Variations: Style and Ideology in Western Music* (Minneapolis: University of Minnesota Press, 1991), p. 291: Composers "will have to recognize the ways in which all human statements actually operate within society, not as abstract structures with varying degrees of truth content but as elements in an ongoing discourse, inseparable from interpretation on all sides (the listener's and also the speaker's) in terms of numberless concrete values, associations, and needs."

47. Adorno, "Vers une musique informelle," pp. 305, 307.

48. Ibid., p. 322. See also Paddison, *Adorno's Aesthetics of Music*, p. 182. Adorno's "The Aging of the New Music" was not alone in provoking debate about the direction of avant-garde composition. Ian Pepper, "From the 'Aesthetics of Indifference' to 'Negative Aesthetics': John Cage and Germany, 1958–1972," *October* 82 (Fall 1997), pp. 31–47, provides a valuable glimpse into the discursive stew. The essay parses three primary documents from the period, also reprinted here, voicing reactions to Cage in Europe, written by men who had either studied with Adorno or were well acquainted with him: Heinz-Klaus Metzger, Konrad Boehmer, and Hans G. Helms. Their assessments of Cage, pro and con, notably reflect Adorno's then-recent writing about the state of new music—though not

In the short essay, "THE DIALECTICAL COMPOSER" (1934; pp. 203–9), Adorno posits Schoenberg's own career (up to 1934) as radically unsystematic, impossible to categorize as a whole: in short, as precisely engaged from one moment to the next with history as history itself unfolds. Further, each piece succeeds its predecessor by, in effect, challenging what came before. It is precisely the self-reflexive nature of Schoenberg's composition that Adorno most admires: Schoenberg's music does not critique the here and now as from a position on the outside; instead, his music critiques the here and now indirectly by confronting the musical past, including Schoenberg's own musical past. Schoenberg's every note, in other words, interrogates everything musical that preceded it, *particularly* Schoenberg's own composition. By this means, the composer directly acknowledges his own subject position, his own guilt in the perpetuation of the here and now, while at the same time struggling musically to reach beyond toward something better—and, precisely, by confronting the past. It is Schoenberg's unrelenting honesty that demands that he include himself, as it were, in his critique, even though the resulting "air of catastrophe" inspires fear of Schoenberg (p. 204). Adorno particularly valorizes how Schoenberg comports himself as a subject in relation to his musical material—in essence, his object; the two do not appear as wholly separate spheres; instead one engenders the other in a reciprocal—and always already historical—relation, and by that means they enact the semblance of reconciliation while at the same time blatantly confronting the history from which there is no escape.

----

invariably to adopt his position. Cage's own "Reflections of a Progressive Composer on a Damaged Society" is also reproduced.

Music, Language, and Composition

Music is similar to language. Expressions like musical idiom or musical accent are not metaphors. But music is not language. Its similarity to language points to its innermost nature, but also toward something vague. The person who takes music literally as language will be led astray by it.

Music is similar to language in that it is a temporal succession of articulated sounds that are more than just sound. They say something, often something humane. The higher the species of music, the more forcefully they say it. The succession of sounds is related to logic; there is a right and a wrong. But what is said cannot be abstracted from the music; it does not form a system of signs.

The similarity to language extends from the whole, the organized coherence of meaningful sounds, down to the single sound, the tone as the threshold of mere existence, the pure medium of expression. It is not only as an organized coherence of sounds that music is analogous to speech, similar to language, but also in the manner of its concrete structure. The traditional doctrine of musical forms has its sentence,[1] phrase, period, and punctuation. Questions, exclamations, subordinate clauses are everywhere, voices rise and fall, and, in all of this, the gesture of music is borrowed from the speaking voice. When Beethoven, referring to the performance of a bagatelle from op. 33, asks for "a certain speaking expression," he only emphasizes, in his reflection, an ever-present aspect of music.

The distinguishing element is commonly sought in the fact that music has no concepts. But quite a few things in music come rather close to the "primitive concepts" that are dealt with in epistemology. It makes use of recurring symbols, insignia that bear the stamp of tonality. If not concepts, tonality has, in any case, generated vocables: first the chords, which are always to be used in identical function, even worn-out combinations like the steps of a cadence, themselves often merely melodic phrases that re-formulate the harmony. Such general symbols have the ability to merge with a particular context. They make room for musical specification, as the concept does for individual things, and, like language, they are simulta-neously healed of their abstractness by the context. But the identity of these musical concepts lies in their own existence and not in something to which they refer.

Their invariance has become sedimented, a kind of second nature. This is what makes it so difficult for consciousness to separate itself from the tonality. But the new music rebels against the appearance that characterizes such second nature; it does away with the congealed formulae and their function, as mechanical, but not with the similarity to language itself—only its reified version, which misuses its individual elements as mere markers, disqualified signals of no less rigid subjective meanings. Musi-cally, too, subjectivism and reification correspond to each other, but their correlation does not describe conclusively the similarity of music to lan-guage in general. Today, the relationship of language and music has be-come critical.

In comparison to signifying language,[2] music is a language of a com-pletely different type. Therein lies music's theological aspect. What music says is a proposition at once distinct and concealed. Its idea is the form *[Gestalt]* of the name of God. It is demythologized prayer, freed from the magic of making anything happen, the human attempt, futile, as always, to name the name itself, not to communicate meanings.

Music aims at an intention-less language, but it does not separate itself once and for all from signifying language, as if there were different realms. A dialectic reigns here; everywhere music is shot through with inten-tions—not, to be sure, only since the *stile rappresentativo,* which used the rationalization of music as a means of coming to terms with its resem-blance to language. Music without any signification, the mere phenome-nological coherence of the tones, would resemble an acoustical kaleido-scope. As absolute signification, on the other hand, it would cease to be music and pass, falsely, into language. Intentions are essential to it, but they appear only intermittently. Music points to the true language as to a language in which the content itself is revealed, but for this it pays the price of unambiguousness, which has gone over to the signifying lan-guages. And as if to give it, the most eloquent of all languages, comfort for the curse of ambiguity—its mythical element—intentions stream into it. Time and again it points to the fact that it signifies something, some-thing definite. Only the intention is always veiled. Not for nothing did

Kafka, in several of his works, give to music a place that it had never before occupied in literature. He treated the meaningful contents of spoken, signifying language as if they were the meanings of music, broken-off parables—this in the most extreme contrast to the "musical" language of Swinburne or Rilke, which imitates musical effects and which is alien to the origins of music. To be musical means to innervate the intentions that flash forth, without losing oneself to them in the process, but taming them, instead. Thus, the musical continuum is constructed.

This brings us to interpretation. Both music and language require it in the same degree, and entirely differently. To interpret language means to understand language; to interpret music means to make music. Musical interpretation is the act of execution that holds fast to the similarity to language, as synthesis, while at the same time it erases every individual incidence of that similarity. Hence, the idea of interpretation belongs to music essentially and is not incidental to it. But to play music properly means, above all, to speak its language properly. This language demands that it be imitated, not decoded. It is only in mimetic practice—which may, of course, be sublimated into unspoken imagination in the manner of reading to oneself—that music discloses itself, never to a consideration that interprets it independent of the act of execution. If one wished to compare an act in the signifying languages with the musical act, it would more likely be the transcription of a text than its comprehension as signification.

In contrast to the cognitive nature of philosophy and the sciences, in art the elements that are brought together for the purpose of knowing are never combined into judgment. But is music in fact language without judgment? Among its intentions, one of the most urgent seems to be "That is the way it is"—the judicious, even judging, affirmation of something that is, however, not expressly stated. In the highest, as well as the most violent moments of great music, such as the beginning of the reprise of the first movement of the Ninth Symphony, this intention, through the sheer power of its coherence, becomes distinctly eloquent. It resonates in lower works as parody, for example in the C-sharp Minor Prelude by Rachmaninoff that keeps hammering "That is the way it is" from the first to the last measure, while lacking that element of becoming that could lead to the state of being whose existence it affirms, abstractly and to no avail.[3] Musical form, the totality in which a musical context takes on the character of authenticity, can hardly be separated from the attempt to create, for the nonjudging medium, the gesture of judgment. At times this succeeds so completely that the threshold of art is scarcely able to withstand the onslaught of logic's desire to dominate.

Thus, one is led to conclude that the differentiation of music and language will emerge not from their individual traits, but only from the entirety of their constitution. Or rather from their direction, their "tendency," the word used with the most extreme emphasis on the *telos*, with regard to music in general. Signifying language would say the absolute in a mediated way, yet the absolute escapes it in each of its intentions, which, in the end, are left behind, as finite. Music reaches the absolute immediately, but in the same instant it darkens, as when a strong light blinds the eye, which can no longer see things that are quite visible.

Music shows its similarity to language once more in that, like signifying language, it is sent, failing, on a wandering journey of endless mediation to bring home the impossible. Except that its mediation unfolds according to a different law from that of signifying language, not in meanings that refer to each other, but in their mortal absorption into a context that preserves meaning even as it moves beyond that meaning with every motion. Music refracts its scattered intentions away from their own power and brings them together into the configuration of the name.

To differentiate music from the mere succession of physical stimuli, we sometimes say that music has sense, or structure. To the extent that in music nothing is isolated, and everything only becomes what it is in its physical contact with what is closest and its spiritual contact with what is distant, in remembrance and expectation, that statement may be allowed to pass. But the sense of its coherence is not of the type that is made by signifying language. The whole is realized against the intentions; it integrates them by means of the negation of each individual, indeterminate intention. Music as a whole rescues the intentions, not by diluting them into a more abstract, higher intention, but by readying itself, in the instant in which it crystallizes, to summon the intentionless. Thus, it is almost the antithesis of the kind of coherence that makes sense, even though it may appear as such in comparison to sensual immediacy. This is the source of its temptation, in the fullness of its power, to pull back from all sense, to behave as if it were in fact the name immediately.

Schenker has cut the Gordian knot of the old controversy and declared himself against the aesthetics of expression as well as the aesthetics of form. Instead—like Schoenberg, whom he scandalously underrates—he has aimed at a concept of musical content. The aesthetics of expression mistakes the individual, ambiguously escaping intentions for the intentionless content of the whole; Wagner's theory falls short because it imagines the content of music as following from the expression of all musical moments infinitely extended; whereas to speak the whole is qualitatively different than to commit a single act of signification. The aesthetics of expression, where it is consistent, ends with the temptingly arbitrary act of substituting what has been understood ephemerally and by accident for the objectivity of the thing itself. The opposite thesis, however, that of the forms set in motion by sounding,[4] comes down to empty stimulus or the mere existence of something that reverberates, where this stimulus lacks the relationship of the aesthetic *Gestalt* to something that is not itself, through which it first constitutes itself as aesthetic *Gestalt*. Its simplistic and thus once again popular criticism of signifying language is paid for with the price of the artistic. Music does not exhaust itself in intentions; by the same token, however, no music exists without expressive elements: in music even expressionlessness becomes an expression. "Sounding" and "in motion" are almost the same thing in music, and the concept of "form" does not explain anything about what is concealed, but merely thrusts aside the question of what is represented in the sounding, moving context that is more than mere form. Form is only the form of something that has been formed. The specific necessity, the immanent logic of that act eludes the grasp: it becomes mere play, in which literally everything could be otherwise. But in truth, the musical content is the wealth of all those things underlying the musical grammar and syntax. Every musical phenomenon points beyond itself, on the strength of what it recalls, from what it distinguishes itself, by what means it awakens expectation. The essence of such transcendence of the individual musical event is the "content": what happens in music. If musical structure or form, then, are to be considered more than didactic schemata, they do not enclose the content in an external way, but are its very destiny, as that of something spiritual. Music may be said to make sense the more perfectly it determines its destiny in this way—not only when its individual elements express something symbolically. Its similarity to language is fulfilled as it distances itself from language.

Within music itself, music and language exist in a state of mutual tension. Music is reducible neither to the mere being-in-itself of its sound, nor to its mere being for the subject. Music is a means of cognition that is veiled both for itself and for the knowing subject. But it has this much, at least, in common with the discursive form of knowledge: it cannot be fully resolved in the direction of either the subject or the object, and each of them is mediated by the other. Just as those musics in which the existence of the whole most consistently absorbs and moves beyond its particular intentions seem to be the most eloquent, so music's objectivity, as the essence of its logic, is inseparable from the element within it that is similar to language, from which it derives everything of a logical nature. These categories are so thoroughly complementary that it is not, for instance, possible to maintain their balance by conceiving music as occupying a position equidistant between them. Rather, its success depends on the abandon with which it relinquishes itself to its extreme poles. This has been forcefully demonstrated in the history of the new music. Where it avoids the tension between music and language, it suffers the consequences.

The movement that is subsumed under the name of the new music could easily be represented from the perspective of its collective allergy to the primacy of similarity to language. At the same time, precisely its most radical formulations have tended more toward the extreme of similarity to language than toward the impulse that is hostile to it. With these formulations, the subject took aim against the burdensome, conventionalized weight of traditional material. But today it is evident that even those elements of the new music that, to a conventional way of thinking, are considered subjectivistic contain within them a second element that tends to work against the notion used in the nineteenth century to designate musical similarity to language—expression. The emancipation of dissonance is often identified with the untrammeled desire for expression, and the aptness of this equation is confirmed by the development from *Tristan* to *Elektra* to Schoenberg's *Erwartung*. But precisely in Schoenberg, the opposite also makes itself known early on. In one of his first works, the now much-beloved *Verklärte Nacht*, a chord occurs that sixty years ago was very shocking. According to the rules of harmony, it is not allowed: the ninth chord, in major, in an inversion that places the ninth in the bass, so that the resolution, the prime to that ninth, comes to lie above it; whereas the ninth, ostensibly, is meant to be heard as a mere suspension before the tonic. This chord, with its various possible resolutions, appears repeatedly in *Verklärte Nacht* at decisive turning points in the form in an intentionally nonorganic way. It creates caesuras in the idiom. In the First Chamber Symphony, Schoenberg proceeds in a similar way with the famous fourth chord, which is also not treated in traditional harmonic theory. It becomes the leading harmony and marks all the important divisions and articulations of the form. But it is precisely the expressive value of these chords that, in the context, is not essential. What is expressive and similar to language, rather, is that context itself. Eloquence of this nature tends to flow, so much so that it must have sounded to the composer's critical form-awareness like an unresistant merging. The musical material of the chromaticism does not contain the strong opposing forces of articulation required for plasticity of form and constructive "logic." In fact, the articulation of the chromatics in *Tristan* had remained problematic, and Wagner only did justice to it, in his later works, in a rather rough and restorative way by alternating diatonic and chromatic complexes. This results in discontinuities like the one between the wildness of most of Strauss's music in *Elektra* and its blissfully triadic conclusion. Schoenberg disdained any such option; hence, he had to find means of composition that would rise above the gliding of the chromatics without reverting back to a lack of differentiation. The solution lay precisely in those extraterritorial chords that had not yet been occupied by musical-linguistic intentions—a kind of musical new-fallen snow in which the subject had not yet left any tracks. The whole field of resolution made up entirely of fourth chords and their melodic transcription in the orchestral version of the First Chamber Symphony has been very aptly compared to a glacial landscape. In the last movement of the F-sharp Minor Quartet, the new chords have been inserted as literal allegories of "another planet."[5] It follows that the origin of the new harmony must be sought in the realm of the emphatically expressionless, as much as in the realm of expression, as much in hostility to language as in language—even though this hostile element, which is alien to the continuum of the idiom, repeatedly served to realize something that was linguistic in a higher degree, namely, the articulation of the whole. If the dissonant harmonics had not always also sought the expressionless, it would scarcely have been possible for it to be transformed into the twelve-tone technique, in which, after all, the linguistic values at first recede very strongly in favor of constructive ones. This is how profoundly the antithetical elements are intertwined with each other.

But this intertwining has not been realized in all new music. Much of the latter has absented itself, with modish phrases, from the dialectical effort and merely rebelled reactively against the linguistic element. It is not only to the ears of rancorous philistines that the music of the nineteenth and early twentieth century must have sounded as if it had forgotten what was best about itself, as if the progress of musical similarity to language had been paid for with the authenticity of music itself. The weakening of its constructive powers and of the consciousness of totality in favor of vivid details, in romanticism, was equated directly with the growth of expression and similarity to language. It was thought that simply by uprooting the latter it would be possible to regain what had been lost, without accepting the challenge of actually salvaging that best element

from the irrevocable state of both consciousness and material. Composers
fell into a state of what Hegel would have termed abstract negation, a
technique of consciously induced primitivism, of mere omission. Through
an ascetic taboo against everything that was linguistic in music, they hoped
to be able to grasp pure musicality in itself—a musical ontology, so to
speak—as the residue, as if whatever was left over was the truth. Or,
looked at in a different way, they repressed the nineteenth century instead
of transcending it in the manner in which Plato's Diotima describes dialectics: "the old worn-out mortality leaving another new and similar one
behind."⁶ If music's similarity to language really fulfills itself by distancing
itself from language, then this is attributable only to its immanent motion,
not to subtraction or the imitation of prelinguistic models that are always
revealed, in turn, as previous stages of the process between music and
language.

The attempt to do away with music's similarity to language was undertaken in two directions. One is the path taken by Stravinsky. By means
of an archaic reversion to musical models that seemed architectonic and
far removed from language, and a further process of alienation that eliminated from them everything that today sounds similar to language, pure
music, purified of all intentions, was supposed to result. But its intentionless character can only be maintained by doing violence to the origins that
are sought after in this way. Wherever the weight of the musical idiom is
apparent in the models, for example in the regular sequence of cadential
forms, the models are tweaked and twisted until they no longer disavow
the attempt. In this way, the pure essence of music is itself turned into a
subjective performance. The scars that result are accompanied by expression, ferments of an idiom made of convention that is by turns affirmed
and negated. The parodistic element—something eminently mimetic and
thoroughly similar to language—is inseparable from such musical hostility to language. It could not sustain itself at the apex of its own paradox-
icalness, where it had once executed the most astonishing balancing acts.
Becoming more moderate, it reverted to sheer historicism and sank, in its
reception by broader musical consciousness, to the depths of sanctimonious
pseudomorphosis, the unaffirmed gesture of affirmation. The substitution
of parodistic negation as absolute positivity, liberated from the superstructure of the subject, ends in mere ideology.

In its second, later form, the rebellion against musical similarity to
language desires nothing less than to catapult itself out of history altogether. It is difficult to exaggerate the rage against the musical element:
prisoners shaking the bars of their cells or people robbed of language driven

mad by the memory of speech. The indestructible traits of music that comprise its similarity to language are ostracized as the alien element in music, as mere distraction from its immanent logic, as if they, immediately and in themselves, were its perversion into a system of signs. In the heroic periods of the new music, the vehemence of the escape attempts—comparable to the tendency of early radical painting to absorb materials that mock all attempts at subjective inspiration, the fundamental phenomenon of montage—presents itself as an anarchic rebellion against the sense of musical coherence in general; the young [Ernst] Krenek's eruptions around the time of his Second Symphony are a case in point. Whereas this gesture, in Krenek, later manifests itself only in certain latent characteristics of composing against the grain, after the Second World War the same intention was revived and systematized by young composers whose starting point was their experience with the twelve-tone technique. In *Philosophy of New Music,* I had once observed that in Schoenberg the elements that are similar to language, to the extent that they form part of a musical coherence, remain essentially the same as in the tradition and thus contain a certain contradiction to the changes in the material.[7] From this same observation, the young composers jump to the conclusion of a tabula rasa. They want to liquidate the element of musical language in music, to end subjectively mediated musical coherence itself and create tonal relationships dominated by exclusively objective, that is, mathematical relationships. Consideration of any reproducible musical sense, indeed of the possibility of musical imagination itself, is irrelevant. The remainder is supposed to be the cosmically superhuman essence of music. Finally, the process of composition itself is rendered physical: diagrams replace the notes; formulae for the generation of electronic sound replace the act of composition which, itself, is ultimately seen as an arbitrarily subjective act.

But this objectivism in music turns into its opposite. The force that imagines it is overcoming the arbitrary rule of the subject, that obvious element of the possibility of doing everything differently—the very thing that had been striking fear into composers ever since its emergence during the romantic era, which, nevertheless, encouraged it—is identical with complete reification: the desire to be pure nature corresponds to the purely manufactured thing. The ontological region that lies beyond subjective accident is exposed as subjective mastery over nature that has been absolutized as a mere technique, in which the subject of absolute rule only divests itself of its own humanity and simultaneously fails to recognize itself. Nothing can sound more accidental than music that ostracizes the ultimate act of discrimination; the electronic production of sound, which thinks of itself as the voiceless voice of being itself, sometimes sounds like the droning of machinery. The utopia of a quasi supra-artistic art, which is to be had, it is true, only for the suspiciously low price of the substitution of alienated mechanical procedures for subjective effort, falls back into philistine tinkering of a sort not unlike the experiments with tone-color composition that were popular thirty years ago.[8] Aesthetic lawfulness, the essence of which consists precisely in its antithesis to causality, is confused with the latter; autonomy with heteronomy. The hope is that a natural law that is taken literally and, moreover, misunderstood will replace musical language's lost aesthetic authoritativeness. But with the proscription of everything that is even remotely similar to language, and thus of every musical sense, the absolutely objective product becomes truly senseless: objectively absolutely irrelevant. The dream of a wholly spiritualized music removed from the sullying influences of the animalistic nature of human beings awakens among rough, prehuman material and deadly monotony.

Music suffers from its similarity to language and cannot escape from it. Hence, it cannot stop with the abstract negation of its similarity to language. The fact that music, as language, imitates—that on the strength of its similarity to language it constantly poses a riddle, and yet, as non-signifying language, never answers it—must, nevertheless, not mislead us into erasing that element as a mere illusion. This quality of being a riddle, of saying something that the listener understands and yet does not understand, is something it shares with all art. No art can be pinned down as to what it says, and yet it speaks. Mere dissatisfaction with this fact will only undermine the principle of art without salvaging it as something else, for example discursive knowledge. While the idea of truth liberated from illusion remains essential to art, it is not within art's power to escape from appearance. Art comes closer to the idea of freedom from appearance by perfecting that appearance than it would by arbitrarily and impotently suspending it. Music distances itself from language by absorbing its peculiar strength.

The allergy to the linguistic element in music is inseparable, historically, from the turn away from Wagner. It refers, to use a metaphor from the Wagnerian world, to a wound that awakens the most violent emotions, at once unhealed and guilt-ridden. In fact, Wagner, with his radical demand for a declamation that would do justice to language, not only drew vocal music much closer to language than it had ever been before, and did so in a specifically mimetic way, but also assimilated musical construction itself to the gesture of language to the point of exaggerated clarity. What music lost in the way of autonomous development, and what surrogate qualities it assumed as a result of the unbroken repetition of gestures similar to language, I do not need to say. True, anti-Wagnerianism of the ordinary variety is less incensed about regressive, compositionally amorphous traits than about explosive characteristics and the unleashing of the language of music, its emancipation from innumerable conventional elements that no longer satisfied the critical ear; whereas, nowadays, the preference, in many cases, is for restoring that very convention by force, as it were, outwardly, to serve as a bond.

Following the irreparable collapse of the traditional formal cosmos, however, it was only the adaptation to language that salvaged for music something of the power it had possessed at the height of the Beethovenian attempt to reconcile the autonomous subject, from within that subject, with the traditional forms. Music's turn toward language in Wagner not only created hitherto unimagined expressive values, not only gave the musical material a wealth of the most highly differentiated qualities without which it can no longer survive, but also gave this music a dimension of bottomless depth. It may have been characterized by a boastful tragicality, something theatrical and self-dramatizing. It is easy to hold up the comparison of Bach, Beethoven, and Mozart as more metaphysically substantial, but all this does is to drown out, with difficulty, the truth of its own particular moment. The devalorization of metaphysical sense, which was reflected in Wagner's relationship to Schopenhauer, was appropriate to the state of social consciousness under developed capitalism; the thing that makes it inauthentic, the murky and despairing conflation of such negativity with the positivity of redemption, still did more honor to the determining historical experience than the fiction that humanity had been spared this experience. For Wagner, however, this experience was not some mere *Weltanschauung* lacking in compelling force; it left its stamp on the musical form *[Gestalt]* itself. The idea of great music, of music as a serious matter instead of ornament or private amusement, survived the nineteenth century solely as a result of the Wagnerian turn of music toward language. The most recent negation of the linguistic element in music reveals the need of weakness to abscond from that serious matter, as from an "unfolding of the truth." It was only thanks to the Wagnerian finds that the middle Strauss and then Schoenberg were able to plow over the field of the musical material in such a way that it finally became fertile again, of itself and not merely as decreed by an autonomous logic. Only music that has once been language transcends its similarity to language.

Let us recall the operas of Alban Berg. In them, autonomous musical logic reigns side by side with the element of Wagnerian musical language. But the two principles generate each other in alternation. The purely musical articulation, the dialectical, sonata-like form through which Berg retrieves those very elements—present in Viennese Classicism and sacrificed by Wagner—succeeds precisely on the strength of the ruthless immersion of music in language, both literally and figuratively. If, amidst all its constructive unity, Berg's music, as distinguished from the leveling tendencies that can be observed in the most diverse regions of the new music, insistently maintained the variety of individual musical contents that renders that unity a result, and substantial, then the sole reason is because his music obeys the text's intentions in every single one of its motions in order to tear the music loose from them once more through the organization of its coherence. In this way, it gains a kind of intervention, something like a process involving contending elements, and this is what constitutes its seriousness.

At any rate, the position of contemporary music toward the similarity of music to language can be indicated clearly enough to suggest the shape of what is needed. There is still a considerable divergence between the tonal material, which has been rationalized and disqualified in the name of the twelve-tone technique, and the musical-linguistic structures—from music's large forms down to its tiniest units, the typical motivic gestures—which those persevering and most advanced composers Schoenberg, Berg, and Webern have generated with this material and its qualities derived from tradition. But the problem—to employ this much-misused word, for once, in the strict sense—would be to resolve that divergence by advancing the compositional process.

This undertaking can begin at either pole. On the one hand, like the idea of form that fits the material, in architecture, or of functional form, the rationalized tonal material itself presses for principles of musical form, a musical language *sui generis*. This had only been neglected due to the preoccupation with preparing that material as an end in itself. The fact, for example, that development and developing variation became superfluous and were thrust back into the predisposition of the material bespeaks a compositional process that proceeds by segments and is articulated by "intonations," a stratification of the large forms according to their parts, each of which tends to be equidistant from the center. The result would be a music in which the immediacy of every moment outweighs the musical perspective and its form as mediated by expectation and memory. Before the discovery of the twelve-tone technique, Schoenberg had occasionally attempted something similar. Today, when one of the most gifted young composers, Pierre Boulez—who as one of the leading representatives of constructivism has always maintained a certain independence from its dogmas—takes his cue from Debussy as well as Webern, his instinct seems to lead him toward composition in segments. Such a reorganization of the musical structure according to the immanent laws of the material, as it unfolds, would also alter the entire language of music. Even the subtlest small articulations would be the result of tiny differentiations within the series, along with equally fine differentiations of the various forms of the series itself, and serial music would no longer have to speak as if its syntax were the one it inherited from tonality.

In the opposite case, the musical-linguistic forms can be similarly separated from the material and followed in their development, can be "constructed out," so to speak. This corresponds to Berg's practice and above all to that of the late Schoenberg, and also, oddly enough, to functional forms of music such as film scores. The task, in conscious mastery of the musical language, would be to crystallize out characters of a linguistic nature in themselves, Platonic ideas, as it were—of themes, transitions, questions and answers, contrasts, continuations abstracted from the musical material that was previously provided by tonality. Such a procedure is not without precedent; one could very easily find in Beethoven, whose compositional technique is much more rational than the irrationalism of our educational canon would have it, atomistic types of musical forms [*Gestalten*] that resemble a musical puzzle and are used over and over again and that are by no means conventional. They appear relatively independently of the flow of tonality, indeed of the progress of the individual compositions, and one of the elements of his art was to bring even these forms into harmony with the harmonic and formal progress of the whole.

But the attempts to wring its own separate language from the material, in the first case, and to treat language itself as material and make it self-reliant, in the second, converge in the free disposition over the means of composition. This is attained by the individual who abandons himself, in a kind of active receptivity, to that toward which the materials are striving on their own. This, however, would be nothing less than the mediation of subject and object. As one hears within the mere material the language that is enclosed within it, one becomes aware of the subject that lies concealed in that material; and as one breaks the linguistic elements, which without exception represent sedimented subjective feelings, out of their blind, quasi-primitive natural coherence and constructs them out oneself, purely, one does justice to the idea of objectivity that characterizes all language in the midst of its subjective signification. So, in the end, music and language, in their most extreme dissociation, may once more merge with one another.

(1956; GS, vol. 16, pp. 649–64)
Translated by Susan H. Gillespie

NOTES BY RICHARD LEPPERT

1. In German, the word for a musical movement, *Satz*, is the same as the word for sentence. [translator's note]

2. Throughout this essay, Adorno uses the phrase *meinende Sprache* to refer to ordinary spoken language. *Meinend*, in this usage, is quite idiosyncratic, which lends the phrase heightened importance. Semantically, it is related to *Meinung* (opinion); it should not be translated by its English cognate *meaning*, which is closer to the German *Bedeutung*. In the text, *meinende Sprache* has been rendered throughout as "signifying language." [translator's note]

3. Adorno discusses Rachmaninoff's C-sharp Minor Prelude with biting sarcasm in "Commodity Music Analysed," QF, pp. 38–40, describing it as infantile, a piece that cheaply strives for the easy effects of grandiosity ("the conjunction of heavy [musical] artillery and easy playability"), and best suited to children—and adults—suffering from the "Nero complex."

4. Adorno is referring to comments by Eduard Hanslick, in his treatise, *The Beautiful in Music* (1854), that "the essence of music is sound and motion," and that music's beauty "consists wholly of sounds artistically combined. The ingenious co-ordination of intrinsically pleasing sounds, their consonance and contrast, their flight and reapproach, their increasing and diminishing strength—this it is which, in free and unimpeded forms, presents itself to our mental vision." *The Beautiful in Music*, ed. Morris Weitz, trans. Gustav Cohen (Indianapolis: Bobbs-Merrill, 1957), pp. 46–47; based on the 7th German edition, this English translation first appeared in 1891. *The Beautiful in Music* is among the best known texts on music aesthetics produced during the nineteenth century. It reached ten editions (in German) by century's end, and was also translated into several other languages. Hanslick (1825–1904) was active as a music critic in Vienna throughout his adult life. He taught music appreciation at the University of Vienna for almost four decades. He was one of the most influential nineteenth-century anti-Wagnerians and a famous champion of Brahms.

5. The fourth movement of Schoenberg's String Quartet no. 2, op. 7, is based on a poem by Stefan George entitled "Entrückung" which contains the words "Ich fühle Luft von anderen Planeten" [I feel air from other planets].

6. From Plato's "Symposium," in *The Dialogues of Plato*, trans. B. Jowett (New York: Charles Scribner's Sons, 1905), vol. 1, p. 500. [translator's note]

7. See, for example, PNM, pp. 118–19.

8. See "The Aging of the New Music," p. 201 n. 12.

Why Is the New Art So Hard to Understand?[1]

Ladies and Gentlemen, I have posed the question why the new art is so hard to understand with a generality that immediately compels an explanation and a justification. You may object that neither is there a new art *per se*, in an intellectual context in which artistic efforts of every type overlap, nor can it be said of this new art, which does not exist as such, that it is hard to understand. I speak, therefore, only of that art which all of you experience as specifically modern in the sense that it is accompanied by the shock of its strangeness and enigmatic form, the shock that is actually the basis of all the talk about its being hard to understand. The catchwords expressionism, constructivism, futurism, cubism, atonality, surrealism—as empty, banal, and programmatic as they appear—may remind you of that shock as it was manifested at the time those artistic tendencies were emerging. Also—and this is precisely why I posed the question so vaguely and generally—I do not want to speak intrinsically about the conditions for the difficulty of understanding as we may encounter them in each of the various artistic tendencies individually. This would not only require a great wealth of detail, but would also, of necessity, lead deep into the discussion of professional problems that surely hold no interest for many of you—without even the possibility of coming up with a salient and uniform answer as a result. I pose the question from the outset, therefore, not for art itself and its concrete form, but for the public that finds itself confronted with it. I am asking sociologically, not aesthetically; I would almost like to direct the question to you yourselves, why you, as I may assume in your great majority, understand the new art with difficulty. Arguments like the cliché that the new art speaks to the understanding, while the old one also has to do with the emotions, to which it "gives" something, I take, in this context, as a symptom of the existing situation, by no means its explanation. For apart from the fact that the concepts "emotion" *[Gefühl]* and "understanding" *[Verstand]*, by-products of the great philosophy of an earlier era, should not be allowed to pass without having to show their visa, all they say here is that the older art possesses a certain immediacy of effect that makes it understand-able, while this immediacy is no longer present in the new art, and hence some kind of helping operations are required in order to penetrate into its center. The immediacy here is one of effect, not content—in other words understandability itself. The phrase about emotion and understanding is merely an unexamined and skewed reflection of the fundamental experi-ence of the difficulty of understanding new art, namely the experience that the production of art, its material, the demands and tasks that confront the artist when he works, have become divorced in principle from con-sumption, i.e., from the presumptions, claims, and possibilities of compre-hension that the reader, viewer, or listener brings to the works of art. When someone talks about the self-conscious specialization of modern artists, or when some Philistine rants against the ideal of *l'art pour l'art*—an ideal that supposedly always coincides with decadence and degeneration and other nefarious things—what he means is nothing but the alienation of production from consumption, the nowadays completely radical reification of all art, which removes it from immediate use and hence from immediate comprehensibility. The prevailing critique of this state of affairs usually presumes an isolated aberration—hence correctable by means of a so-called "recovery"—that is supposed to have something to do with some short-comings in the psychic makeup of modern artists, who are said to be root-less and alienated from nature. What is important, however, is, first, to acknowledge the necessary character of the situation itself, to grasp the fact that the roots nowhere reach deeper into the situation than in the case of so-called rootlessness. The reification of art is the result of a socio-economic development that transforms all goods into consumer goods, makes them abstractly exchangeable, and has therefore torn them asunder from the immediacy of use. The autonomy of art, its quality of being a law unto itself, the impossibility of arranging it at will according to the dictates of use, is, in contrast to the religious and ceremonial function of earlier artistic practice, the expression of that reification. It is a reification that we accept more or less lightheartedly where even consumer products retain something of their use value, but that is profoundly disturbing and denounces the entire situation as soon as the possibility of use vanishes entirely, and art, instead, wants to be seen merely as a mysterious sundial from whose face one imagines one can read the state of consciousness, without, oneself, any longer having power over it. To describe how this alienation came about would be nothing less than to sketch the history of our society. At a minimum, however, the enforced character of the situation can be seen in the fact that it scoffs at any correction coming from art—precisely because art is socially produced. The artistic products of a highly rationalized society can no more be made to revert to natural ones than the society itself can. The demand that art be designed to be generally understandable is, however, identical with the demand for this kind of reversion. That such reversion must remain dubious in its truth content, that the return to peasant and folk art in a country that is in the midst of the industrialization process leads to costumings and concealments of all kinds, but never to compelling production, is self-evident. It is all the more self-evident because in the face of liberated, emancipated consciousness bonds dissolve, are seen to be illusory, even where they are still present as such. They wither up even without being expressly attacked. If art is unable to recapture the lost character of immediacy, it is a result not of general cultural-philosophical awareness—which, ultimately, could always be contradicted by reality—but of the genesis of the production problems in art itself. For the process of differentiation, the progressive difficulty of artistic solutions, does not come from the private intellectual state of mind of the individual artists; nor does the social situation express itself mystically in the incomprehensibility of the works of art. Rather, technical differentiation, and with it the increase in difficulty, derives from the rationalization of the process of artistic production, namely from the fact that the artist, robbed of all prescribed norms, has to ask with every measure that he writes, every square centimeter of paint that he applies, whether it is right in just this way and just this spot. But the answer to this ceaseless questioning—in the material, and quite independent of the intellectual and emotional state of mind of the artist—is coterminous with differentiation and thus with increased difficulty. Perhaps I may elaborate with the help of the material to which I am closest, music. Attempts to simplify art music are not characterized as bad because they somehow fail to correspond to some general "situation," but rather because they are in contradiction to the material; because the chords, which are built in many layers and do not have a given function within a given key, cannot be repeated as arbitrarily as the old ones; or because rhythms that are constructed irregularly in themselves, as models, cannot be combined into regular, symmetrical forms. This differentiation does not exist in a vacuum, it is true; it is valid only relatively, as applied to the material. But the material itself is historically produced, and it is not possible to diverge at will from the material. Otherwise, those artists who want to escape from differentiation would be operating in an unbroken, immediate fashion using older material. But one can observe everywhere that this is not possible for them; that they hardly even try; that, where someone actually operates with older material, it is less the intention of the new simplification that is at work than an old and outmoded primitiveness. Thus the artists are forced to confront a difficulty, a differentiation, and hence at first an incomprehensibility from which they can escape only abstractly, namely programmatically and literarily.

Now, you may raise one weighty objection to this. If the reason for the difficulty of understanding the new art is located in the social conditions themselves, then—you will argue—it must transcend [aufheben] itself. For then the society that, through its own structure, makes the differentiation of artistic means necessary would, itself, have to be so differentiated that the understanding even of the most complicated art causes it no difficulty. The objection, plausible as it sounds, is conceived in a vacuum; above all, it is conceived undialectically—what I mean is that it is conceived without taking into account the real contradictions of the reality in which we live. The separation of production and consumption has precisely this consequence for art: that no equivalency such as is formulated by the objection can be present. Because art once burst the bonds of immediate use, [certain] developments impose themselves upon it, impose themselves socially as well, without these developments being connected, any longer, to the consciousness that actually prevails in the society. In a similar fashion, the development of mathematics may at one point have been produced socially by bourgeois autonomy, by the technical natural sciences, and yet, precisely within the logic of the principle of autonomy, have become ever more separate from society's understanding, become ever more "special." This dialectic is the real reason for the irreversibility of the artistic difficulties. Especially a view that interprets art radically in its social contingency must not believe that a phenomenon like reification and the difficulty of understanding art can be sublated [aufgehoben] in an isolated way; rather, such a view must know that serious change in this area can only emanate from the social conditions. But art that lays claim to immediate general comprehensibility and social equivalency, on the basis of existing reality, necessarily possesses an ideological, concealing function. The social situation can be formulated even more concretely. *Production* behaves in a largely historical-dialectical fashion, to the extent that it expresses the tensions and contradictions of the existing relations, suffers its own fate subject to their forces, and through its fate, which may not be concealed, calls for change. *Consumption*, however, largely lags behind in unchanging existence, because it is does not possess the force of production, which would point beyond what is unchanging; socially it is merely produced, without itself seriously helping to produce—at least in the aesthetic realm—and only mirrors relations whose primary need is to maintain themselves. The difficulty of understanding the new art has its specific basis in this necessity of consumer consciousness to refer back to an intellectual and social situation in which everything that goes beyond the given realities, every revelation of their contradictions, amounts to a threat. For this reason, the really useful art, which serves [the purpose of] distraction—entertainment reading and kitsch prints, sound film and hit dance tunes—is historically innocent and, despite all apparent timeliness of content, formally on a technical level that is long out of date. Here one might argue that the negative eternity of kitsch corresponds to a similar one of consumer consciousness; that it was always thus and not otherwise; that production always outstrips consumption. One can readily concede the tension between the two. Despite this, there is an unmistakable difference between the situation of contemporary art, for example, and the music of Wagner or the painting of impressionism at the time of its emergence. At that time, the lines connecting producers and consumers had not yet been cut, as it were, but merely wired in a more complicated way. But the image of material reality that impressionism ultimately brought forth was not different in principle from the one in which people existed on a daily basis, and in Wagner the preexisting schema of a harmony, which always grows out of tension and resolution, did not emerge from the work itself, but was still carried by social tradition. Hence the shock of incomprehensibility that went out twenty years ago from expressionism or cubism and especially from the futurist manifestoes was something qualitatively different from the agitation over Wagner's supposedly wrong notes, or the supposed daubings of the impressionists. The shock that accompanied the new artistic movements immediately before the war is the expression of the fact that the break between production and consumption became radical; that for this reason art no longer has the task of representing a reality that is preexisting for everyone in common, but rather of revealing, in its isolation, the very cracks that reality would like to cover over in order to exist in safety; and that, in so doing, it repels reality. Here the psychological question could be asked with some prospect of success. The lack of understanding toward the new art can probably be said—like every stupidity, perhaps—to be based essentially on a mechanism of repression. Historically, the new art goes beyond a reality that it does not, after all, have the power to change at will; while ideologically, reality itself must remain at a certain point in its own development, in order not to endanger itself. Its subconscious authorities, which perceive the threat in the new phenomena, secure themselves by proscribing understanding and calling a halt that is masked, after the fact, as resistance against intellectualization, abstraction, experiment, and whatever all the fine words may be.

From this dialectical situation, knowledge has conclusions to draw. Despite the insight into the compulsory character [of the process], it cannot be denied that the separation of art from reality endangers art itself. For even if art remains secluded, off by itself, it threatens to become ideological—to be self-satisfied in a muffled, petit bourgeois way, to forget its supportive human function, ultimately to become petrified into bad guildsmanship. But the danger cannot be overcome by arbitrary adaptation to the state of social consciousness, at the cost of aesthetic quality. Such adaptation, as has been suggested, is always tantamount, in a practical artistic sense, to a reversion to older, outlived and outdated ways of proceeding, and to take this path art would have to sacrifice the consciousness of itself—a sacrifice that cannot be expected of it. The economic production of the future can no more return to primitive, pre-division-of-labor forms of production, in order to avoid the alienation of human beings from consumer goods, than art can. This holds true no matter whether one is asking art to revert romantically to old forms of community, or, more logically, is denying art its right to exercise control over itself. For even the radicalism of such a procedure seems to have limits. The tension between guild-like, encapsulated art, on the one hand, and, on the other, the true *Gebrauchskunst*[2] that acquires its ease of understanding only by renouncing the rational through-construction of its production process—this tension cannot be resolved within art; it is established by the [social] relations within which we exist. But the problem does not, by any means, automatically disappear in other ways of life, either. In Russia, they thought at first that they could resolve it with the primitivism of peasant attitudes, and they rejected, as bourgeois, all art that was not immediately capable of being put to use. Today, they seem to have recognized that this was a case of leading production backward to an outdated standard of society, as was admittedly suggested by the preponderance of the agrarian population in Russia. They are beginning to cease their peasant-folkloristic efforts, and to demand work on contemporary material—contemporary, that is, in a rational, European sense. So far, the attempts to eliminate the difficulty of the new art have all made one mistake. Although they have occasionally acknowledged the dialectical character of production, its historical movement in contradictions, they always still think of consumption in its broad extent as static and unmoved. Although this static quality can certainly not be denied in the current situation, it may by no means be conceived of as an immutable law of nature. For example, if the disposition of work and leisure time were different than [it is] today; if people, independent of cultural privilege, could spend their leisure time occupied substantively and extensively with artistic matters; if a demonically precise mechanism of advertising and anesthetization did not, in every instant of their leisure, prevent them from occupying themselves with actual art—then in principle, the consciousness of consumers could be changed in such a way that they could understand new art without the new art having to be dumbed down on that account. The argument that the public wants kitsch is dishonest; the argument that it needs relaxation, at least incomplete. The need for the bad, illusory, deceptive things is generated by the all-powerful propaganda apparatus; but the need for relaxation, to the extent that it really—and today with justification—exists, is itself also a product of a circumstance that absorbs people's strength and time in such a fashion that they are no longer capable of other things. Let no one come back with a rejoinder about the slothful nature of human beings. For the suspicion is not so easily allayed that the consciousness of the person who responds in this way is more slothful than those on whose behalf he is responding.[3]

(1931; GS, vol. 18, pp. 824–31)
Translated by Susan H. Gillespie

NOTES BY RICHARD LEPPERT

1. Adorno adapted his title from the essay by Alban Berg, "Warum ist Schönbergs Musik so schwer verständlich?" first published in *Musikblätter des Anbruchs* in 1924, on the occasion of the composer's fiftieth birthday; reprinted in Willi Reich, *The Life and Work of Alban Berg*, trans. Cornelius Cardew (London: Thames and Hudson, 1965), pp. 189–204, given as "Why is Schönberg's Music So Difficult to Understand?" Berg's essay is built around the opening ten bars of Schoenberg's First String Quartet in D minor. Adorno had clearly digested this essay in detail; resonances between his essay and Berg's are obvious. That Berg's discusses Schoenberg's "difficulty" in terms of an early (1904–05) tonal work is, of course, intentional.

2. *Gebrauchskunst* has no exact English equivalent; "use art" or "functional art" is about as close as one can get. Adorno is playing off of the term *Gebrauchsmusik* coined in the early 1920s, and in widespread use immediately thereafter; the term referred to music that makes claims to having social utility, hence differ-

134 / Locating Music

entiates itself from *l'art pour l'art* aestheticism and the musical avant-garde. New music composed especially for musical amateurs, including for performance in the home, fell under the conventional meaning of the term; such music was often characterized by its relative simplicity and restrained expressiveness. Adorno tended to regard the results as more craft than art and as typical of a music that is ultimately concerned to keep faith with respectability and decorum. Adorno saw in the practices and function of *Gebrauchsmusik*, and what he here calls *Gebrauchskunst*, a link with what he would later name the Culture Industry (art in service of the broadcast and film industries, for example), on the one hand, and art as propaganda, on the other (what Adorno criticized in Brecht). Hindemith, as the most important composer of *Gebrauchsmusik*—despite his own eventual rejection of the term—was subject to a sustained critique in Adorno's writing on this account, but especially in his lengthy essay *"Ad vocem* Hindemith: Eine Dokumentation,"* GS, vol. 17, pp. 210–46, assembled from sections (most of which had previously been published) written in 1922, 1926, 1932, 1939, 1962, 1967, and 1968; and Adorno, "Gebrauchsmusik" (1924), GS, vol. 19, pp. 445–47.

3. Cf. Adorno's lecture-essay, "Difficulties," Part II (1966), this volume, pp. 644–79, much of which reconsiders the subject of this essay.

On the Contemporary Relationship of Philosophy and Music

The crisis of music, which needs no introduction, does not have to do merely with the difficulties of consistent and meaningful form-creation, not merely with the commercial hardening and leveling of musical life, not merely with the rupture between autonomous production and the public. Instead, all this has accumulated to the point where quantity is transformed into quality. The right of music—of all music—to exist at all is called into question. This is not to be understood as one of those all-too methodological forays into doubt whose "but nevertheless" one can already hear the moment they are uttered. Rather, it is confirmed by every experience that is not inclined to take the existence of the activity itself as its prior justification. You need only turn the knobs on the dial of a radio at random. If you are able to escape from the eternal sameness of the hit songs—whether trite or cynical—and find some so-called serious or, as it is known in the realm of informed barbarism, "classical" music, then the latter appears even in its difference, by virtue of the mere fact that it takes its place as one category among others, as an aspect of the monotony. At the first tone, you hear "serious music," the same way you receive the signal "religion" at the first tone from the organ. Through this classification, which is assigned to the phenomenon in advance, it already ceases to be what it claims to be—something in itself. It becomes a mere "for others," and well-meaning cultural rescue attempts do more to encourage the tendency than to weaken it. The *Third Program*[*1] only contributes still further to the neutralization of culture by making the existing intellectual division of labor also its own.

While the ever-present and inescapable music installs itself as a piece of concrete daily life, as one producer-standardized consumer good among others, and divests itself of everything that might go beyond service to and betrayal of the customer, it becomes comical. The pathos that clings to it even in its most extreme degradation, not to mention its autonomous phenomena, which unfold according to their own laws, the echo of the religious element even under conditions of the most extreme secularization, enters into contradiction with the detrition, the ubiquity, the character of a consumer good that it has universally assumed in society, and this contradiction evokes laughter. In one of the incomparable cinematic farces of the Marx Brothers, when thanks to some absurd complication an opera scene appears, in which one hears tragic arias illustrated by the clumsily grandiloquent, old-fashioned gestures of the singers, the effect is comparable to a demolition of the tragic stage, and the clowns immediately set to work and bring the scenery crashing down.[2] But that merely brings to mind harshly, through caricature, an aspect of music that, in truth, belongs to all its manifestations. It is just that belief in culture and the ideology of culture normally make us hesitant to express it; while at the same time the very humorlessness of the cultural scene, with all its affectations, its stubborn insistence on the dignity of music, unwittingly strains toward ridiculousness. The grotesque untruthfulness and inconsistency, as one can hear them, for example, in the diligent emotionality of the oratorio singer in his tuxedo, or in the well-attested positivity of the sound of the chorus, already begin to communicate themselves to the darkness of the basses, the outpouring of the violins, the veiled distance of the horn in great symphonic music, and only compositions that refuse ascetically to have anything to do with all that are still permitted a probationary period. Music that has merely to begin in order to define itself as an exception to normalized life, as a more elevated extreme, places itself, by dint of its always already potentially perceptible and nowadays complete integration into the average normalcy of a false life, in contradiction to the claim that its mere sounding inevitably makes.

Composers have the agonizing choice. They can play deaf and soldier on as if music were still music. Or they can pursue the leveling on their own account, turn music into a normal condition and in the process hold out for quality, when possible. Or they can ultimately oppose the tendency by a turn to the extreme, with the prospect of either being drawn in and leveled after all—as is already happening to Kafka nowadays—or becoming desiccated as a specialty. The extremely awkward situation of composing today derives from the decay of the raison d'être of music, the undermining of its possibility in general. This is communicated, then, in the decay of criteria; in the loss of a tradition that could be experienced even negatively; in technical, intellectual, and social disorientation. If contemporary music, in one of its most significant representatives (who is consequently unknown outside the most narrow circles), Anton von Webern, tenses for moments at a time and obeys a compulsion to be silent that is greater than even the composer's stubborn will to form, then music, in its interior structure, is reflecting its relationship to the conditions of its existence. Music that remains true to itself would rather not exist at all, would rather—in the most literal sense, as it so often appears in Webern's work—be extinguished, than betray its essence by holding fast to existence. The suspicion is justified that Eduard Steuermann[3] once expressed, namely that music, at least great music, whose concept extends from Bach via Beethoven to Schoenberg, is a transient category, bound up with the bourgeois era and fated to be forgotten. It is not unlike the way a jazz athlete, highly qualified in his particular specialty, who already finds it impossible to understand what was actually at stake, rejects serious music as *corny**, as an old-fashioned mixture of naïveté and affectation, and at the same time—having long since ceased to be content with pride at his own ignorance—goes so far as to declare himself an adherent of that music in the name of the *Weltgeist*.

If philosophy, now, attempts to get to the bottom of this state of affairs, it is almost inevitably forced to confront the question of what music, ultimately, is. All one has to do is to describe the characteristics of the crisis in one of the by now customary formulations, such as "radical endangerment," in order immediately to create a climate of self-satisfied unease. The response to radical endangerment is supposed to be concentration on the being of the thing that is being endangered, as such. One may wager that, in light of reflections like this, in the end it is music's own state of endangerment, simultaneously dark and consoling, that is unearthed as its essence. Previous to any critical epistemological reflection on the right and justification of such fundamental questions and questions of origin, there is the impossibility of identifying, in music, any singular category that would make possible an immediate determination of its meaning. In other words, it is impossible to determine in any comprehensive way the meaning of music, i.e., the thing by which it acquires its right to exist. Or we can express this slightly differently and say that there is something enigmatic that is apparent in all music. This is not fully explained by the psychological question why music has its stimulatingly strong effect. It has to do, rather, with the fact that there is absolutely no general moment to be found that would be capable of going beyond the description of music to indicate its meaning and justification. If, then, one gets close enough to music to make it seem alien; if, in other words, one does not conflate its existence as a phenomenon with its justification, then it becomes impossible to understand from what source it derives the dignity that has been accorded to it in our culture. For this reason, plenty of positivistically minded people—Nietzsche was not far from their point of view at times—have questioned whether music possesses any such dignity, at least in terms of music's being in itself, and have reduced music to a system of subjective projections and conventional notions.

The trivial, but not easily refutable distinction between the musical and the non-musical confirms music's specifically enigmatic character. That music does not speak at all to whole groups of aesthetically not insensitive people, that they have no idea what to do with it, while analogies in the realm of the visual arts or literature are rare, can certainly be explained to a considerable extent by the nature of these individuals, and by their childhood history, in particular. But at the same time it seems to indicate that the essence of music is not as clearly prescribed as that of other artistic media and that music, therefore, does not exercise the same compelling power over the receptive subject. If in fact music, in Schoenberg's remark, says something that can only be said through music,[4] then it assumes, as a result, a quality that is at once unfathomable and emphatically contingent. We will forebear to ask whether inquiring into the raison d'être of anything that is an image, and not reality, does not lead to the void; for art as a whole is probably not amenable to this context of immanent explanations that asks everything that exists to show its passport, none other than that very raison d'être. In the end, it is the raison d'être of every art to be unavailable to any raison d'être, i.e., to the justification of its own existence according to criteria of self-preservation, no matter how highly sublimated the latter may be. There is much to be said for the notion that every question of principle concerning the essence of an art is in vain or leads to a mere reiteration of the art's existence, once established. This is because the question itself is drawn from the very realm of self-justificatory, teleological rationality that art suspends. If philosophy were capable of determining the raison d'être of art, as it must admittedly always continue to attempt to do, and as it is asked to do by art itself, then art would in fact be completely absorbed into cognition [*Erkenntnis*] and would thus be outdated, in the strict sense.

It is, however, specific to music that its enigmatic character is emphasized by its distancing from the visually or conceptually determined world of objects; that this character is almost urged upon us by music itself. In language, as in the visual arts, this enigmatic character is hidden. In the case of linguistic forms, their participation in the medium that is simultaneously the medium of cognition *[Erkenntnis]* always lends them the appearance of something like "transparency" or comprehensibility. This is true no matter how much that which emerges as the meaning of a work of poetry or prose may differ from its "content"—that which, in Benjamin's words, has been *"gedichtet."*[5] In the visual arts, their constitution, in the external sense, which after all conveys the outer world of objects, diminishes their enigmatic character. The relationship to objects is merged with the content, even in the case of the associations of abstract painting. While such elements, in the non-musical arts, may ultimately reinforce irrationality by concealing it, in music this irrationality is located immediately within the phenomenon itself—something that, it is true, may perhaps also offer a point of departure for overcoming it. In any case, however, to recall the well-known alternative in musical aesthetics, the supposed happiness that is provoked by tonally moving forms[6] is much too thin and abstract a principle to serve as the foundation of a highly organized art form. If this were all there were to it, then there would be no difference between a kaleidoscope and a Beethoven quartet except the difference in material. On the other hand, the element of expression, in which people have perceived the corrective to Hanslick's above-cited principle, is too ambiguous, in every single isolated instance, and too vague to represent the content of music by itself. All music is characterized, first of all, by what happens to words, in language, only as a result of alienating concentration. Music gazes at its listener with empty eyes, and the more deeply one immerses oneself in it, the more incomprehensible its ultimate purpose becomes, until one learns that the answer, if such is possible, does not lie in contemplation, but in interpretation. In other words, the only person who can solve the riddle of music is the one who plays it correctly, as something whole. Its enigma apes the listener by seducing him into hypostasizing, as being, what is in itself an act, a becoming, and, as human becoming, a behavior.

In music, what is at stake is not meaning, but gestures. To the extent that music is language, it is, like notation in music history, a language sedimented from gestures. It is not possible to ask music what it conveys as its meaning; rather, music has as its theme the question, How can gestures be made eternal? In contrast, the search for the meaning of music itself, as something to be disclosed in the rational justification of its raison d'être, is revealed as a delusion, a pseudomorphosis into the realm of intentions, to which music, by virtue of its resemblance to language, misleads us. As language, music tends toward pure naming, the absolute unity of object and sign, which in its immediacy is lost to all human knowledge. In the utopian and at the same time hopeless attempts at naming is located music's relation to philosophy, to which, for this very reason, it is incomparably closer, in its idea, than any other art. But the name appears in music only as pure sound, divorced from its bearer, and hence the opposite of every act of meaning, every intention toward meaning. But music does not know the name—the absolute as sound—immediately, but, if one may express it this way, attempts its conjuring construction through a whole, a process. Therefore it is, at the same time, itself woven into the very process in which categories like rationality, sense, meaning, language have their validity. It is the paradox of all music that, as an effort toward that intentionless thing for which the inadequate word "name" was chosen, it unfolds precisely only by dint of its participation in rationality in the broadest sense. Sphinx-like, it fools the listener by constantly promising meanings, and even providing them intermittently—meanings that for music, however, are in the truest sense means to the death of meaning. Nor is music ever exhausted in these means. As long as music was played within a more or less closed context of tradition, such as that of the last 350 years, this irresolvable quality that it has, the fact that everything suggests meaning and nothing actually wants meaning, could be concealed. Within the tradition, the meaning of music was accepted, and it asserted itself, with the exception of the most manifest experiences of awe and astonishment, as self-evident. Today, however, when tradition no longer prescribes anything for music, its enigmatic character emerges, weak and needy, like a question mark—one that, admittedly, becomes blurred the moment anyone asks it to confess what it actually wants to communicate. For the name is no communication of an object.

This emergence of music's enigmatic character tempts one to pose the question of its being, while at the same time the process that brought it to this point forbids the question. Music, after all, does not possess its object, is not in command of the name; rather, it longs for it, and, in doing so, aims at its own demise. If music, for an instant, were to accomplish the thing around which the tones revolve, this would be its fulfillment and its end. Its relation to the thing that it cannot represent but would like to invoke is therefore endlessly mediated. The name itself is no more present for music than for human languages, and the theodicies that are so much in vogue just now and present music as a manifestation of the divine are blasphemies. They afford music the dignity of revelation, although music, as an art, is nothing but the secularly preserved form of prayer, which, in order to survive, forswears its object and surrenders it to thought. In such efforts to reach what is at once blocked and unattainable for it, music is, of necessity, endlessly mediated in itself. It has no being to which the person who is seduced by the enigma could refer. Rather, it draws the name closer, through the unfolded totality, the constellation of all its moments. Music's simple being, which would be accessible to a primal question if only it were to divest itself sufficiently of overlays and inessentials, is a *fata morgana*—no different from the Being from which philosophy, bored with its tedious investigations, hopes to suck gratification. The things that seem, to this type of inquiry, to be mere epiphenomena, camouflaging additions, incidentals from which the essence should be extracted, are precisely the unfolded life of music, in which it has its truth and in which its essence is, in fact, first determined. Only through its historical characteristics does music acquire its relation to the unattainable. Without historical mediations, understood as a mere principle or primal phenomenon, it would be utterly impoverished, abstract, and in the most real sense lacking in essence. Immediately before the conclusion of the first movement of Beethoven's sonata *Les Adieux*, when in a fleeting, vanishing association over the course of three measures the galloping of horses becomes audible as "meaning," this passage, which is more sublime than words can tell, says that this most transient of things, the ineffable sound of disappearance, holds more hope of return than could ever be disclosed to any reflection on the origin and essence of the form-seeking sound. Only a philosophy that would truly succeed, in the most intimate way, in securing such micrological figures from within the construction of the whole would come close to touching music's enigmatic character, without being able to flatter itself that it had resolved it. But if someone, instead, is of a mind to force music's secret directly and immediately, with the magic wand of primal words, he is left only with empty hands, tautologies, and sentences that, at best, provide formal constituents—if music even has something like a formal *a priori*. But the very essence of music will have vanished, usurped by the disposition of language and the concern about its supposed origins. For the relation of music to philosophy, what the Hegel of *Phenomenology of Spirit* described in his critique of the *prima philosophia*, of all absolute first principles, is eminently true.[7] [The fact] that what is first and original is not coterminous with the truth is something that can be said of no sphere of life with greater justification than of that art whose most sublime works virtually legitimate themselves by the fact that their truth does not emerge until the last measure—in Hegel's words, as a "result." For music, the nullity of the beginning becomes the motor of its own form.

There has been no lack of attempts at "inquiry" into the pure being of music, i.e., at the founding of a musical ontology. Given the paucity of statements that embrace all of music, to which such attempts must be restricted—however much they may protest against this and prize their abstractions as especially concrete—it is not difficult to come up with such a conception. Thus, for example, people have tried to spin out the essence of music from the observation that musical space and musical time constitute a separate continuum that is absolutely distinct from empirical space and empirical time. Similar, and very closely related to this, is the claim that music is a language *sui generis*. One feature that is peculiar to all such theses is that they remain in the most extreme and vague generality, and that despite their cautiousness when it comes to anything that might appear contingent and transitory they do not achieve the *a priori* truth to which they lay claim. That music is articulated separately is something it shares with art of every kind. The phenomenologist Donald Brinkmann went so far as to define the demarcation line between the aesthetic and the natural by referring to the aesthetic sphere as one that is free from the establishment of spatio-temporal facticity.[8] This definition is, itself, historical in essence, the secularized legacy of the magically separate, religious realm, a kind of disempowered magic-making, and hence interwoven with the overall dialectic of the Enlightenment. The separate aesthetic sphere, itself no *a priori*, is, then, by no means *a priori* capable of sustaining itself, and the historical movement of all art occurs, not least of all, by means of this susceptibility of the aesthetically pure. In the case of literature this is evident. But even in music, which after all has only driven separateness to an extreme, without monopolizing it, one can frequently find implied senses that themselves do not participate in the character of the aesthetic image—from the echo of march and martial music in great symphonic music, which contributes to its power in good and evil, down to the real, extra-aesthetic shocks and emotional sensations from whose protocols the new formal language of music crystallized. Despite all this, there is enough that remains specifically true about the reserve theory of music that what is "said" by music, if there is such a thing, evidently presents much greater obstacles to translation into other media than other art. Or, perhaps more accurately, to the extent that music provides the prototype of untranslatability, it is the first to make it evident in other artistic spheres, as well. A great musician who is shamefully misrepresented and ignored by the pre-classical, collectivist idiocy of today—Schumann—was the first to make the statement that the aesthetic of one art form is also that of the others. That romanticism proceeded precisely from music in setting out this program, which was then developed *ad absurdum* in the *Gesamtkunstwerk*, is no accident. Music put up the most stubborn resistance to the superficial unity of overall aesthetic development. With the growing integration of bourgeois culture in the nineteenth century, music had to perceive Schumann's claim as an urgent one, if it was not to fall victim to the verdict of a lack of cultivation, of craft-like, provincial narrowness. Nevertheless, the very historical extraterritoriality of music reminds us of an element in music that cannot be so easily integrated and that associates music with the dialectical ferment within the overall development. But this element, precisely as something that works antithetically within the process of the pan-European Enlightenment, may not be broken off from it, and above all may not be derived as an essential particularity from the constitution of the temporal art. Even if one were to remain on the basis of that most general characterization, the separate identity of musical space and musical time would have to be ascribed merely to the negation of the empirical, against which it establishes its boundaries; and it is precisely by virtue of such a polemic that empirical space and empirical time return within the internal composition of music as such. To accept this, one must take a look at the concrete complexion of music of various periods. Musical time is really musical—in other words not just the measurable time of the duration of a piece—only as time that is dependent on the musical content and in turn determines that content, the concrete means of transmission of the successive. But this musical time varies so completely from one type to the next that its over-arching idea would have to be limited to the most external aspect—the chronometric unit. That the temporal consciousness that is transmitted by the musical content of a vocal movement by Palestrina, a fugue from the *Well-Tempered Clavier*, the first movement of the [Beethoven] Seventh Symphony, a prelude by Debussy, or a quartet movement by Anton von Webern that has been reduced to twenty measures, is endlessly different, will be recognized even by the person who has remained completely aloof from superficial analogies like the expression "static music" propagated by neo-classicism. But this also already makes clear how little is grasped by a theory of musical invariance that thinks it can define the essential as that which remains. For the music of Webern and that of Bach, the experience of time that is specifically unique to it and that characterizes its structure may well be more essential than the fact that both unfold in time, or even that in both cases the musically established time does not coincide with that of its chronometric duration.

But just as the temporal form of every music, its inner historicity, varies historically, so this inner historicity also always reflects real, external time. After all, purely musical time, in its differentiation from the other one, always relates to the latter as the echo to the reflected sound. The actually dynamic developmental time of music, whose idea Viennese classicism crystallized—that time in which being itself is transformed into a process and, at the same time, its result—is not only genetically but substantively the very same time that constituted the rhythm of emancipated bourgeois society, which interpreted its own play of forces as stability. The relationship between Hegel's logic and Beethoven's method of composition, which can be demonstrated in detail, and which weighs all the more heavily because one must exclude any notion of influence, such as obtained, for example, between Schopenhauer and Wagner, is more than mere analogy. It is grounded in the historical constellations that form the organon of truth in both instances. And the position of philosophy vis-à-vis musical objectivity, i.e., the attempt to respond conceptually to the question of the enigmatic that music poses to its listeners, demands that these constellations be determined down to the most intimate details not only of the technical procedures but also of the musical characters themselves. Only by means of such mediations, and not in the immediacy of the question of pure being, can thought even begin to come close to what music is. Nor would it help very much to vary the attempt at a musical ontology in the direction of pulling oneself out of the supposed swamp of the ephemeral by one's own bootstraps, by declaring historicity itself to be the essence of music—something that the immanently process-oriented character of highly organized Western music tempts us to do. Rather, the time that is immanent in every music, its inner historicity, *is* real historical time, reflected as appearance. We may well suspect that music's attempt to possess the absolute consists in these very kinds of intellectual and spiritual sedimentations of real time. The attempt cannot even be imagined independently of this time. To develop this would be the task of a complete philosophy of music, which would find its model in the work of Beethoven, as it exists in light of the musically logical and real historical process that has since occurred with the work as it has with society.

The historical movement in which music, ostensibly the most irrational art, has its essence participates in the Enlightenment. Music is transformed from something merely existing into something intellectual and spiritual.

Only then does it find its truth with respect to existence—critical truth. However, this movement is coterminous with the progress of its reflection within itself, of its dominion over the merely natural—in short, with its increasing subjectivization and humanization. We merely give this situation a different twist when we identify the process as one of becoming language. Hence the ontological definition of music as a language *sui generis* is either so abstract that it says nothing more than that between the individual musical facts there exists an articulated context that is "logical" in its own way, as Harburger, for example, has attempted to demonstrate in his book on meta-logic.[9] Or the definition of music as language ends, once again, by branding an essentially historical, or in fact even *the* historical tendency of music as invariant. As previously stated, one of the favorite moves of present-day theories of being is to come to terms with historical dialectics, which in their authentic Hegelian formulation had just dissolved the concept of being, by absorbing history into being and, with a solemn gesture, celebrating transience as what is lasting. Now, the specifically linguistic character of music consists in the unity of its objectification, or, if you prefer, reification, with its subjectification; just as, everywhere, reification and subjectification are not mutually exclusive, but rather mutually determinant polar opposites. Since music, as Max Weber demonstrated in his posthumous sociology of music,[10] became integrated into the rationalization process of Western society, its linguistic character has become more pronounced. [This linguistic character] has a dual nature. On one hand, it involves the fact that music, by dint of its disposition over the natural material, is transformed into a more or less stable system, whose individual moments have a meaning that is at once independent of and open to the subject. All of music from the beginning of the age of figured bass until today forms a coherent "idiom" that is largely given by tonality, and that still exerts a persistent power even in the present-day negation of tonality. What is called "musical" in everyday parlance refers precisely to this idiomatic character, to a relationship to music in which the material, by virtue of its reification, has become second nature to the musical subject. On the other hand, however, the legacy of the pre-rational, magical, and mimetic also survives in the aspect of music that resembles language. In becoming linguistic, music has asserted itself as an organ of imitation, but now, in contrast to its early gestural and mimetic impulses of subjectively mediated and reflected imitation, [as] an imitation of the things that transpire inside human beings. The process of music's turn toward language *[Versprachlichung]* means its simultaneous transformation into convention and into expression. But insofar as the dialectic of the process of enlightenment consists essentially in the incommensurability of these two aspects, all Western music receives its contradiction from this dual character. The more music, as language, acquires power over and intensifies expression as the imitation of something gestural and pre-rational, the more, as its rational overcoming, it also works toward its dissolution. The contemporary crisis, the threat to music's right to exist, essentially results from the relation between these two moments. On the one hand, the objectivity of the signs has been dissolved; music ceases to be an idiom, to stand, in traditional forms, for something solidly traditional. But on the other, expression, whose intensification at first negated precisely the objectively traditional side of musical language, is also dissolved, becoming one with this objective element. Contemporary music is faced with an aporia. After breaking down the idiomatic element for the sake of pure, unreified, immediate expression, it is now no longer master of expression itself. In the end, the natural material emerges from the dialectic with threatening purity. The more music comes to resemble the structure of language, the more, at the same time, it ceases to be language, to say something, and its alienation becomes perfect at the instant when it becomes most human.

Among the motifs now perceptible in music of something that may come, its emancipation from language is not the last—the restoration, as it were, of its sounding, intentionless essence; the very thing that the concept of the name sought to describe, however inadequately. It is the overcoming of musical mastery over nature by way of its perfection. But in a situation in which the crisis of musical expression has become an excuse for apathy, and in which thinking that has dispensed with subjective reflection attempts to derive ontological advantage from this very thing, it is not superfluous to state that the emancipation of music from language cannot succeed by arbitrarily taking supposedly pre-linguistic structures as its models while abandoning music's own characters, which developed alongside language, or by imagining that Being would speak from within music if only the subject stops speaking and instead reverts to poorly quoted ornaments. The truth of music, in which it is able to go beyond language, is not the residue that remains behind after the credulously masochistic self-destruction of the subject; it could succeed only if the subject were also positively sublated [*aufgehoben*] in post-linguistic music. There is no lack of evidence for this possibility. But it can hardly be realized from the vantage point of music alone, but only in a changed relationship between it and society. Music cannot bring about such a relationship by itself, arbitrarily, for example by adapting itself to the consciousness of human beings. It would have to occur in society itself, and not for the sake of art. At the same time, however, we may well envisage the contemporary crisis of music as a crisis of its linguistic essence. Sometimes it almost seems as if, in comparison to music's latent, always still unrevealed, and yet ever-perceptible possibility, its approach to language, despite all its triumphs, were a kind of world-historical damage, as if the dignity of the greatest music, that of the late periods of Bach and Beethoven, derived from the fact that here music transcended its own character as language, in a manner comparable, say, to the way the poetry of the very late Hölderlin aims at a demolition of the sphere of linguistic meaning.[11] In this extreme, which is admittedly reached via technique, in particular by means of integral polyphony, in the abrupt moments in which the language of music, as such, becomes visible, shorn and defenseless, and in this very process ceases to be language, can be found the contemporaneity of the great late works for today's music. The only tradition in which it can place its trust is the fragmentary one of the works in which music breaks with all trust and all tradition.

II

Consideration of the contemporary relation of philosophy and music leads to the insight that the timeless essence of music must be viewed as a chimera. Only history itself, real history with all its suffering and all its contradiction, constitutes the truth of music. This, however, means nothing else than that one cannot acquire a philosophical knowledge of music by constructing its ontological origin, but only from the standpoint of the present. Only this makes possible the recognition of all those concrete and contradictory moments that were present only potentially in music's earlier phases. Since the truth of musical works themselves unfolds in time, it is no metaphorical exaggeration, nor is it the commonplace reference to the so-called living I-Thou relationship between subject and object, when one states that Beethoven, for example, is revealed much more readily when one starts from what confronts us today, as the construction of an antagonistic totality, and ultimately as its suspension, than if one were to confine oneself to the historical preconditions and immediate intentions from which this work once originated. But what today becomes visible in him, and similarly in Bach, is not the product of a more or less fluid intellectual history, but is determined right down to its details by the state that compositional processes have reached today—processes that drastically extend the laws of construction that Beethoven's or Bach's work contained in encapsulated form during the nineteenth century. It is only from the vantage point of the most advanced production that light is shed on the entire species.

Accordingly, an analysis of the current status of music itself should be as productive for philosophical insight, as, conversely, philosophical reflection is inseparable from the contemporary situation of music. The discussion of a few elements must suffice. Of necessity, one's thoughts are drawn to Arnold Schoenberg, the master of the new music, if indeed the title of "master," which derives from the realm of craft and has been shamefully abused by Wagnerian ideology, may still be employed today. One must speak of him not only in order to right at least a small part of the wrong that ignorance and conformism continued to do Schoenberg even in the very last moments of his life of integrity. However impotently, let us here affirm what even the general consciousness will one day be unable to deny, unless the notion of the morbidity of great music should come true with catastrophic speed. Schoenberg—and again the right words are lacking, because they have all been appropriated by the culture industry of celebrities and are worn out—was the true musical force of our era, and above everything else: a great composer. It is time to resist the phrases with which people demolish him. As a rule, what they come down to is simply that the critics project their own incapacity to understand Schoenberg's music, which is highly organized in a way that is without precedent and is at last emancipated from the element of musical stupidity, onto the music as an objection. In some cases, they even claim that on account of its advanced nature it lags behind the spirit of the times or its collective demands. They deal with Schoenberg's early works and all their wealth by classifying them, with the music-historical cliché, as late romantic post-Wagnerian. One might just as well dispose of Beethoven as a late-classicist post-Haydnerian. It is impossible to unravel in detail the nonsense of all these claims concocted from Philistinism, narrow-mindedness, incompetence, and spite. Anyone who has an ear for musical quality and whose trust in neo-classical ideology does not preclude the possibility of a spontaneous experience need only have a look at one of the works from the period of Schoenberg's breakthrough, such as the Second String Quartet or the relatively easy-to-perform Lieder op. 6, in order to cease being convinced by the verdicts of the teeming majority. But, at the same time, turning against this teeming majority also implies a self-correction. For *Philosophy of New Music*, whose dialectical method could not stop short of Schoenberg, has, for that very reason, been exploited on occasion by open or disguised musical reactionaries. This could only happen because the book did not follow its own principle as strictly as it would have been obliged to. Instead of always and everywhere relying unhesitatingly on the experience of the works, in certain sections it treated the material as such and its movement, above all the twelve-tone technique, in a quasi-abstract manner, independent of its crystallization in the works. In the process, aspects of the historical trend may have been revealed that could not have been so convincingly grasped in the individual work. But at the same time, inadvertently, it played into the hands of the prejudice that held Schoenberg for a mere reformer or forerunner, someone who provided a more polished and well-tuned *[stimmig]* set of tools, and whose own works one should treat as not very likeable school examples. The decisive thing, the interpretation of Schoenberg's compositions, still fell short. Thus the appearance was created that music should be completely and entirely dissolved into cognition *[Erkenntnis]*. But while the attempt at a penetrating knowledge *[Erkenntnis]* of music is absolutely required, the music itself, in its concreteness, sets the limits of the attempt, without which, to use Kafka's words, it degenerates into a facile, happy journey, the automated self-movement of the conceptual.[12] Schoenberg, who has been castigated for being an intellectual, but who, for all his rationalistic intellect, for good or evil, numbered among the naïve artists, himself often altered the general tendency of his style and technique through the individual work, in a way not commensurate with concepts of style. In his late works, in which he once again, perhaps for the last time, struggled for expression and inserted it into his constructions with allegorical harshness, one can enumerate the inevitable ruptures from the standpoint of the compositional process. But these ruptures, as in every significant late style, are themselves the organs of historical-philosophical truth. Schoenberg's endeavor continues to prove itself even in these shattering works of the final period, when the power of the once-fortunate hand seems to wane, and in which precisely this waning, leaving blank, enters into the service of expression; [it continues to prove itself] in the fact that, to borrow another expression from Hegel, at every new step of his work new immediacy emerged. No one who was present at the premiere of the dance around the golden calf from the opera *Moses und Aron*, the performance that only a few days before the master's death brought him, for the first time, full outward success with a twelve-tone work, could remain cold to [its] plasticity and drastic quality, one might almost say [its] simplicity of effect. The effect of the *Survivor from Warsaw* is no less powerful—a companion piece to Picasso's *Guernica*—in which Schoenberg made the impossible possible, standing up to the contemporary horror in its most extreme form, the murder of the Jews, in art. This alone would be enough to earn him every right to the thanks of a generation that scorns him, not least because in his music that inexpressible thing quivers that no one any longer wants to know about. If music is to escape from the nullity that threatens it, the very loss of the raison d'être I spoke about, then it can only hope to do so if it accomplishes what Schoenberg accomplished in the *Survivor from Warsaw*—if it confronts the utter negativity, the most extreme, by which the entire complexion of reality is made manifest.

Precisely in relation to the specific thing that the very late Schoenberg succeeded in accomplishing as a composer, there is something to be gained for philosophical knowledge *[Erkenntnis]*. Here we may refer back to the concept of musical space, as it has been developed, in particular, in the music psychology of Ernst Kurth.[13] This musical space is no more a fact of pure being than musical time. It springs from the collective implications of all music, the character of something that embraces groups of human beings, which gradually carried over to the sound as such. The phenomenon can only be described in analogies, but can be perceived very distinctly—unmistakable, for example, in Bruckner's symphonies. The spatial quality adheres to the harmonic structure and the instrumental sound; after all, these two musical dimensions always unfolded parallel to each other in the nineteenth century. Through the critique of tonal harmony, in which spatial consciousness had become sedimented, so to speak, so that certain chord combinations and above all modulatory relationships immediately seemed to constitute a musical space, this spatial consciousness had now been eliminated, in a way not so very dissimilar to the abolition of spatial perspective in modern painting. The musical space had shown itself to be an historical one, which could not outlive the necessary separation of music from all supporting collectivity. When an unprejudiced person listens to early works of free atonality, for example the especially aggressive third piano piece from Schoenberg's op. 11, he is assailed by the feeling, if it can be thus described, of spacelessness, of two-dimensionality. Among the shocks that this music delivers, one of the ones that is surely of the essence is its denial, for the listener, of the feeling of inclusion, the spatial embrace. It sounds, to state it bluntly, like a beating. This probably accounts for the often-remarked-upon gesture of rejection in the works from Schoenberg's expressionist phase. Now, in some of Schoenberg's late pieces, for example in the recent Dance around the Golden Calf, one becomes aware that, without borrowing anything from the traditional means of musical perspective, a new type of musical space is created solely through the disposition of color, the art of many-layered instrumentation intensified in the most extreme degree. The question may remain open whether [new] musical space is really opened up here, or whether it is merely the musical space of the past skillfully recreated. Nor [is it necessary to specify] how the collective pathos that announces itself in such a space might be legitimated. But the technical fact goes further than some statements in *Philosophy of New Music.* The section on twelve-tone music remained all-too beholden to its origins in the thesis that every musical dimension has its own essence, largely independent of the others. Accordingly, judgments are made about how the various dimensions fare in contemporary integral compositional technique. Instead, it seems as if nowadays, precisely because all the dimensions of composing have been reduced to the common denominator of internally coherent construction, one dimension could stand in for another. Forty years ago, it is well known that Schoenberg was already talking about *Klangfarbenmelodien*.[14] An analysis of the instrumentation of early lieder by Alban Berg discovered that the process of orchestration has a form-creating effect; that it either clarifies or actually creates the purely musical context, which to ordinary thinking appears to be something more or less linear [*zeichnerisch*]. This now applies much more broadly. If instrumentation in fact proves to be as constitutive of space as in Schoenberg's biblical opera fragment, then this means nothing less than that instrumentation can substitute for the harmonic structure that otherwise evoked the effect of depth. With this, the critique of the "chance nature" of twelve-tone harmony would be corrected to the extent that the functions that were performed in traditional music by its harmonic structure would be accomplished adequately by other means of composition, without necessarily falling into blindness and capriciousness.

But this change in the function of the individual material dimensions in their unification, as brought about by the twelve-tone technique, also affects the core of that technique, namely polyphony, from whose requirements, after all, the entire process is derived. In the history of more recent Western music, counterpoint and harmonic structure—this is worth repeating—are correlative concepts. It is customary to call counterpoint good when, along with complete independence of the simultaneous voices, their leading also makes harmonic sense. Now, the critique of twelve-tone music claims that the triumphal counterpoint of the late Schoenberg makes things too easy, so to speak, by dispensing with the corrective, its justification within the harmonic context. It is undeniable that this danger made itself very much felt in some of Schoenberg's pieces, above all from the early period of the twelve-tone technique, such as the wind quintet. But from this one should not impose a peremptory verdict. The philosophical interpretation of music, in particular, should be wary of performing what Schoenberg, in the title of a text, called the *"dance macabre* of principles."[15] There is a saying of his that is recounted to the effect that good counterpoint is only to be found where any thought of harmonic structure is completely forgotten. This formulation is as striking in its paradoxical simplicity as Schoenberg's pronouncements generally are, the moment they touch on anything really musical. He was the last to recommend some wild and uninhibited counterpointing at random, of the sort that young composers have sometimes pursued in the name of linear counterpoint. But the density of the relation among the several simultaneous voices, whether through similarity or contrast, but in any case through their enforced, thematically constructed, mutual relationship, may well reach such a high level of intensity that the question of harmonic progression becomes superfluous, as it was, by the way, in the greatest polyphonic instrumental works of Bach's late period, in which the power and unity of the voice leading do not eliminate the figured bass scheme of chord construction, in the manner of today, but rather make the listener forget it. Hence not only color, but to an even greater extent counterpoint, in other words the authentic medium of the new music, is capable of inheriting the mantle of harmonic structure and, by virtue of its own lawfulness, overcoming harmonic arbitrariness. In view of such accomplishments, which by no means derive from the rules and system of twelve-tone music, but rather arise out of the configuration of the works [themselves], technical works of art may not, after all, be as inevitably condemned to failure as *Philosophy of New Music* would have it. Their organizational principles do not necessarily have to remain external to the musical events, so long as the latter create a compelling context purely from within themselves. Referring back to the compositions themselves not only corrects some mistakes that creep in when one observes only the tendency of the material. It also makes clear that whatever the danger of violence and self-alienation in the most advanced music—the only music that is of serious account—the possibility of compelling works of art is greater than the false superiority of distance suspects. But this says something about genuinely philosophical inquiry into the raison d'être of music in the circumstances of today. Namely, there are a number of sound arguments that can be adduced for the claim that the self-dissolution of this raison d'être through the aesthetic rationalization process, the ever more drastic contradiction between the complete internal coherence of the work of art in itself and its equally complete incoherence in real social existence, does not have the last word. Already now, the most advanced musical works, as a consequence of that very rationalization, emit forces from within themselves that ultimately, perhaps, may heal the wounds that rationalization and perfection have inflicted on the work of art.

Such healing, admittedly, is reserved for the most advanced. Sedlmayr has cast doubt on the right "to identify Schoenberg as the only pure stage of music in our time, and to see everything that went beyond him—for example, the new works of a Hindemith and a Stravinsky—as already degenerate and reaction." He believes that in these works "a genuine need does make itself known, and that here, too, as in many other things, a so-called third way is being sought, even if these composers in fact have nothing convincing and similar to compare to Schoenberg's oeuvre, but only a bad compromise."[16] As little as, philosophically, one can defend strictly exclusionary thinking, and as thoroughly as one must contradict the totalitarian claims of aesthetic schools, with their constant tendency to lapse into violent sectarianism, Sedlmayr's pluralism remains equally dubious. The third way that he longs for represents nothing new in contemporary music, no addition of fresh musical characters. Rather, what is blooming along the third way demonstrates the very sterility of which the normative critics accuse progressive music, when they call it a dead end, making an all-too-hasty historical prognostication instead of first having a look at what is realized in it. The composers of the third way restrict their innovations, in each case, to just *one* dimension of the material, usually the so-called rhythm, or, to a lesser extent, the harmonic structure, so as to diverge only somewhat from the conventional, without, however, taking upon themselves the entire burden of following this through to its logical conclusion. But in everything else they allow themselves to be satisfied with the forcible, nowhere substantive repetition of something that is long since past, merely modified in the direction of the distinctive. Due to the specialistic narrowing of their techniques—the grotesque consequence of the modern division of labor—the products of these schools are befallen by a tedious similarity to each other and result in the kind of music-festival music that for almost thirty years has struck boredom into exhibitions of modern music. The possibilities that can be read in the very late Schoenberg, in other words the new liquification of composition due to the change in function of the previously stiffly separated musical dimensions, is denied to the more moderate schools. This is because they did not participate in the unification, but instead uncritically accepted the traditional separation of rhythm, melody, harmony, and counterpoint. As a result, with them one aspect cannot stand in truthfully for another.

They have, to put it in a vulgar way, not paid the price without which music—which has become problematic in its innermost existence—does not have even a chance of salvation. However it would be senseless to talk with such great pathos about the danger, on the one hand, and on the other to believe that it could be overcome by ignoring it, wriggling free of the burden, insisting self-righteously on one's own lack of concern and simplicity, and excusing oneself from the effort without which there is no way to face up to the pressure that weighs on music and that has assumed incalculable proportions. The point is not to linger over this because one school is supposed to be more correct than the other. But one must not become blind to the fact that Fascism has a lingering effect on the German intellectual climate by virtue of the widespread tendency to ward off reflections and tendencies—either as negativistic or as already belonging to the past—that seriously attack existing habits of thinking and feeling. Instead, people allow themselves to be satisfied with warmed-over cultural products or noncommittally unfathomable and, in their innermost content, profoundly restorationist efforts. The Communist stewards of culture, who are so committed to the people, are, for their part, only too content with this. It has to do with what psychoanalysis, which itself is repressed according to the same schema, has called defense mechanisms. We are not sufficiently certain of the positive nature of life as it continues after the end of the world, and probably also too much under the spell of unconscious feelings of guilt, for us to allow ourselves to be affected by anything that could make [our] precarious security falter. All the arguments that we find so near at hand when it is a matter of avoiding pain and negativity, from which no truth today can be separated, are nothing but so many acts of self-defense. It is because they only serve their purpose, instead of giving themselves over to something, that they are so powerless and thin. The reproach that is made against the new music in its advanced form, that it has no relationship to human beings and to reality, stands the facts on their head. Only in the memory of what one would rather not know about can one arrive at a relationship to the reality of this life, which is, so to speak, ours until it is revoked. But anything that plays along with reality and condescends to give the justification of a meaning to the way things are [*ihrer Sosein*] is after all only good for distracting us from it. It is no better than ideology in the strict sense, social illusion [*Schein*], false consciousness.

All this is not to preach some aesthetic optimism of a higher level or to pretend that music, or any art, could remedy that which is inflicted by the constitution of reality—and which the first task of art today is to recognize, unerringly and in its own way. To come back to the specifically musical, it is unclear whether one may, in fact, regard these extremely stimulating aspects of Schoenberg's late work and his technique as the first evidence of a higher immediacy that sublates *[aufhebt]* the pseudo-morphosis of music toward language. They may themselves be restorative in a sense that is, admittedly, sublimated in the extreme—attempts to hold fast to the musical-linguistic essence on the very threshold of the turn away from language by the material *[Entsprachlichung]*. That many people who heard the Dance around the Golden Calf were delighted by the strikingly operetta-like character of this ballet music makes the thought of such a restoration at any rate plausible. It cannot be taken lightly—the less so because the idea that music today could save itself with its own powers has something absurd about it, while at the same time it can scarcely be saved otherwise than with its own powers. If one speaks with younger physicists, one not infrequently encounters the statement that Einstein's relativity theory, in comparison to quantum mechanics, is actually classical physics. Schoenberg's achievement, which corresponds with Einstein's not only in the chronological sense, may one day similarly be considered classical music—taking the word not as it is used within the precincts of the culture industry, but in the sense of Schoenberg's subterranean but strict adherence to the Viennese School of work based on theme and variation. Probably the conventional separation of traditional and innovative moments is too mechanical altogether. Sustainable tradition is hardly ever a straight, unbroken, self-assured continuation or sequel. The only ones who would like to see it defined in this way are those traditionalists who invoke tradition because they have none. Tradition, rather, is always what Freud stated in a very profound passage of his late work on Moses and monotheism—a forgetting.[17] It asserts itself in the rejection of the very recent, not in the preservative adoption of achievements, the defense of property. It is only because Schoenberg cast out all the superficial elements of Viennese classicism, from the chord formulas and modulatory balance to the round, restrained sound and formal balance of the sonata form's recapitulations; only because at times he sacrificed even the principle of thematic work, which was so dear to him as a composer of quartets, that he asserted tradition in a substantive way, as opposed to wearing it down by mere imitation. Because he and his school destroyed the classical-romantic façade, he became capable of realizing the ideal of liberation, or, as he himself put it in his last book, of emancipating not only dissonance but the music that was exemplified in Beethoven and Brahms.[18] This emancipation made it possible, for the first time, to conceive the ideal of a pure through-construction of music in all of its aspects, toward which the most profound impulse of the tradition aims.

The principle, in Schoenberg, of the through-construction of the material, of the integral composition that his school strives for, collides with the linguistic character of music. The more purely its characters are justified only by their contexts, their mutual relations with each other, the less one can attribute to it the character of saying. That the very late Schoenberg, now, was not satisfied with liquidating the linguistic moments of music and replacing them with internal agreement *[Stimmigkeit]* in general, but instead wanted to make music once again ready as language, makes him susceptible to charges of restoration. In other words, his attempt at integration does not go far enough for some of the young composers. In fact, Schoenbergian rationalization leaves the rhythmic form free, for example, and to a great extent the melodic structure, as well. Hence there is room, as there is in traditional music, for so-called ideas or inspirations, for form-creation that is not bound by the material. For this reason, Schoenberg is systematically attacked as all too subjective—and not just by the neo-classicists. Precisely the aspect of his music that resembles human beings, the aspect through which he still communicates, in a refracted way, with tradition, is seen as a residue of arbitrariness by the zealots of objectivism who emerged out of his school. Thus, for example, the French composer Boulez, a student of Messiaen's, has worked out a system in which the rhythmic relationships are supposed to be strictly linked to the tonality of the construction. In the end, all the basic psychological facts of musical sound—its pitch, quality, intensity, duration, and color—are, as it were, inventoried and systematically combined in their contrasts and in continuous modification of all the possibilities that they allow. The end goal is for them to neutralize each other. In this way, not so very dissimilar to Stravinsky, a kind of static balance is intended to result. The resulting music, like some of the late works of Anton von Webern, sounds as if it were composed only of dissociated individual sounds. It leaves behind an impression of abstruseness; and according to the theory on which the music is based, the mood that was generated, at least for some people, was surely just misunderstanding. But one cannot entirely exclude the possibility that understanding came up against a limit. A person whose capacity to comprehend music has been formed in a profoundly musical-linguistic way may recognize the demise of the element of musical language, but he will be unable spontaneously to make the transition to music that has been cleansed of all language. Yet meanwhile the abstruseness of the subject seems more probable. One is reminded of a situation that must be described all the more candidly because it is not at all confined to music; rather, elements of it can be found in almost all contemporary intellectual movements—the element of the apocryphal, ridiculous, and foolishly far-fetched, of particular categories that have suddenly been blown up into totality. The problem of twelve-tone music may well require that we take account of this element, this murky sediment, which indeed, in the end, is the condition for the oddly broad impact that twelve-tone music has had in the very recent past. As much as one must see, in this impact, the result of an irresistible tendency of the thing itself, at the same time the rationalistic decree—Schoenberg emphasized that he did not find twelve-tone music, but rather invented it—has something infantile about it. The relation between progress and regression, which was developed in general in *Dialectic of Enlightenment*, does not flow first, musically, from the consequences of twelve-tone music. Rather, residues of craft, of the belief in the philosopher's stone, of roulette formulas are already present at its birth and follow its legitimation in the progress of the compositional process like a shadow. Anyone who, coming from free atonality, stumbled across Schoenberg's twelve-tone pieces well-nigh thirty years ago will also remember the impression of something crazily apocryphal that is so profoundly related to everything systematic. Later, this aspect was forgotten, and one day the second half of Schoenberg's entire oeuvre may very well be revealed as the effort to master this apocryphal element through musical self-consciousness. But today, when there is an entire twelve-tone school, it is breaking through again and fits very neatly into the general retrogression of consciousness. Kierkegaard's theologically oriented pronouncement from *Stages*[19] to the effect that where once the terrible abyss of the wolf's maw yawned there is now the arc of the railroad bridge, from which we cast a fleeting and comfortable glance into the depths, is a judgment against the twelve-tone composers who are popping up everywhere like mushrooms. The hope that the new musical means would escape from the absorption that perverts them was a vain one. The infectious readiness to surrender autonomy and take shelter under a roof, no matter how leaky, has given the twelve-tone procedure its enthusiastic followers. How cautiously Webern took up the new, multi-toned chords in his quartet pieces op. 5. He trembled so before their power that he did not for a moment make them into common coin. He held fast to every chord and, anxiously, let go of them only for the next sound, so to speak. This is the term of comparison by which one should measure the courage that again necessarily results from the progress of composition, and that has long since ceased to cost anything. The composers operate with the sounds as if these were the very same thirds that they were invented to oppose. The composers act like kings, but they have no blessings to give. The more unconcerned these attempts are, the more emphatically the accidental nature of their foundation emerges—the apocryphal character of the self-imposed rule. Usually what happens is that they adopt the row technique from Schoenberg, but not the infinitely rich, complex, and articulated structure of composition, whose realization provides the only measure of the row technique. Often, for example in the one-act opera of such an unquestionable talent as Luigi Dallapiccola, which was premiered in Frankfurt, twelve-tone technique recalls something that in mathematics is known as overdetermination.[20] Musical events of drastic simplicity, whose coherence is guaranteed by traditional means and which would not even require the twelve-tone technique, are also subjected to the row principle—from outside, as it were. The systematized avant-garde, organized into schools and heads of schools, is no less resigned than the conformists who write what people expect to hear. If the twelve-tone schools, in contrast, for example, to the neo-classicist tendencies, maintain a certain exclusivity and reject the understanding of the public, this is not ascribable to the radicalism that is precisely lacking in those who rely on the simplified and infallible system. Rather, it should be ascribed to the absurd, blindly violent element of the system, which is snatched from the vortex up to the surface. Relentless self-consciousness—technical and intellectual and spiritual reflection are all the same in this regard—is what the new music needs more than anything else, if, in its unsuspecting eagerness, it does not want to do its part, through what it takes for development, to destroy that raison d'être of all music for the sake of which it once suffered hatred and defamation. Something that was foreseeable in philosophy 150 years ago must now be criticized in art, especially music, whose essence, as that of an independently unfolding truth, proves to be so closely related to the essence of philosophy: only the critical path is now still open. But it does not consist in critique as it is exercised by consciousness vis-à-vis works that it encounters in an alien way. Rather, critique reveals itself as what it has always secretly been, the law of form of the works themselves.

(1953; GS, vol. 18, pp. 149–76)
Translated by Susan H. Gillespie

NOTES BY RICHARD LEPPERT

1. In state-supported European national radio, the Third Program, or network, is conventionally educational and is the usual locus for classical music broadcasting.

2. *A Night at the Opera* (1935), directed by Sam Wood; the Marx Brothers' first film for MGM. Written by George S. Kaufman and Morrie Ryskind. The demolished opera set is for *Il Trovatore*. See Lawrence Kramer, "Glottis Envy: The Marx Brothers' *A Night at the Opera*," in *Music and Meaning: Toward a Critical History* (Berkeley and Los Angeles: University of California Press, 2001), pp. 113–14.

3. Eduard Steuermann (1892–1964), pianist and composer, was Adorno's piano teacher in Vienna in 1925. Adorno wrote a tribute to him, "Nach Steuermanns Tod," GS, vol. 17, pp. 311–17. Steuermann was an active proponent of Schoenberg's music, which he often performed. He was a member of the ensemble formed by Schoenberg in Vienna in 1918, the Society for Private Musical Performances, dedicated to new music. He emigrated to the United States in 1938; he taught at Juilliard from 1952 until he died.

4. The idea that music says something that can only be said through music permeates Schoenberg's writings—and parallels Eduard Hanslick's famous dictum: "To the question: What is to be expressed with all this [musical] material? the answer will be: Musical ideas." From *The Beautiful in Music,* trans. Gustav Cohen, ed. Morris Weitz (Indianapolis: Bobbs-Merrill, 1957), p. 48. A sense of Schoenberg's position can be had in essays such as "Connection of Musical Ideas" (c. 1948) and "Brahms the Progressive" (1947), in *Style and Idea: Selected Writings of Arnold Schoenberg,* ed. Leonard Stein, trans. by Leo Black (New York: St. Martin's, 1975), pp. 287–88, and 398–441, respectively.

5. German "concentrated," or written as poetry. [translator's note]

6. Adorno is referencing Hanslick, *The Beautiful in Music,* p. 47: Music's "*nature is specifically musical.* By this we mean that the beautiful is not contingent upon nor in need of any subject introduced from without, but that it consists wholly of sounds artistically combined" (original emphasis).

7. G. W. F. Hegel, *Phenomenology of Spirit,* trans. A. V. Miller (Oxford: Oxford University Press, 1977), pp. 13–14. See further on this point, Adorno, *Hegel: Three Studies,* trans. Shierry Weber Nicholsen (Cambridge: MIT Press, 1994), pp. 10–13.

8. Donald Brinkmann, *Natur und Kunst: Zur Phänomenologie des ästhetischen Gegenstandes* (Leipzig: Rascher, 1938).

9. Walter Harburger, *Die Metalogik: Logik des überbegreiflichen Denkens, Begründung einer exakten Phänomenologie* (Munich: Musarion, 1919).

10. Max Weber, *The Rational and Social Foundations of Music,* ed. and trans. Don Martindale, Johannes Riedel, and Gertrude Neuwirth (Carbondale: Southern Illinois University Press, 1958).

11. See Adorno, "Parataxis: On Hölderin's Late Poetry," NL, vol. 2, pp. 109–49.

12. Franz Kafka, "Aphorismen-Zettelkonvolut" (1918–1920), in *Nachgelassene Schriften und Fragmente,* ed. Jost Schillemeit (Frankfurt am Main: S. Fischer, 1992), vol. 2, p. 123, aphorism 45: "Je mehr Pferde du anspannst, desto rascher gehts—nämlich nicht das Ausreissen des Blocks aus dem Fundament, was unmöglich ist, aber das Zerreissen der Riemen und damit die leere fröliche Fahrt" [The more horses you harness up, the faster it goes—not however the pulling of the stone from the foundation, which is impossible, but the tearing of the reins and with that emptiness (i.e., the freedom from constraints of the harness) the

happy journey]. In other words, one harnesses more horses in order to get the difficult job of moving a heavy stone done faster, but what really happens is that the harness breaks, the job doesn't get done, and the horses run merrily away.

13. Ernst Kurth (1886–1946), Austrian-born Swiss musicologist and theorist. Adorno refers to Kurth's *Musikpsychologie* (Berlin: Max Hesse, 1931), which links psychology and acoustics, and his monumental (1,300 pages) *Bruckner*, 2 vols., (Berlin: Max Hesse, 1925). See Lee A. Rothfarb, *Ernst Kurth as Theorist and Analyst* (Philadelphia: University of Pennsylvania Press, 1988), which, however, focuses principally on Kurth's work prior to these two later studies, namely, the *Grundlagen des linearen Kontrapunkts* (1917) and *Romantische Harmonik und ihre Krise in Wagners Tristan* (1920). Adorno published a short review of the *Musikpsychologie* in 1931, and a lengthy, and favorable, review in 1933; reprinted in GS, vol. 19, pp. 349, 350–58, respectively.

14. The term is Schoenberg's, from the *Harmonielehre* (1911), and involves timbre. Schoenberg's concern was to treat successive tone colors analogously to successive pitches; that is, he envisioned successive timbres as relational, hence a structural element in a composition much like melody, harmony, or rhythm. As is well known, in the Five Orchestral Pieces op. 16 (1909, rev. 1949), notably the third piece, originally titled "Farben," Schoenberg employed timbre in this manner. Webern made wider use of the idea, as in the first of the Five Pieces for Orchestra op. 10 (1913), and in his transcription of the ricercar from Bach's *Musikalisches Opfer*. Structural use of timbre is commonplace in integral serialist and electronic compositions by other composers. On the "invention" of *Klangfarbenmelodie*, see Schoenberg's 1951 short essay, "Anton Webern: *Klangfarbenmelodie*," in *Style and Idea*, pp. 484–85.

15. Arnold Schoenberg, "Totentanz der Prinzipien," written in 1915 and included in Schoenberg's *Texte* (Vienna: Universal-Edition, 1926), pp. 23–28.

16. Hans Sedlmayr (1896–1984), Austrian art historian who wrote about architecture, in particular, as well as painting. His books that concern modern art and which likewise contain some discussion of music are *Die Revolution der modernen Kunst* (Hamburg: Rowohlt, 1955), and *Art in Crisis* [*Verlust der Mitte* (1948)], trans. Brian Battershaw (London: Hollis and Carter, 1957). The passage Adorno cites does not appear in any of Sedlmayr's books, hence is presumably taken from a journal essay which I've not been able to locate.

17. Sigmund Freud, *Moses and Monotheism*, trans. Katherine Jones (New York: Vintage, 1939), p. 120: "In what sense, therefore, can there be any question of a tradition? In what form could it have existed? . . . I hold that the concordance between the individual and the mass is in this point almost complete. The masses, too, retain an impression of the past in unconscious memory traces. The case of the individual seems to be clear enough. The memory trace of early events he has retained, but he has retained it in a special psychological condition. One may say that the individual always knew of them, in the sense that we know repressed material. We have formed certain conceptions . . . of how something gets forgotten and how after a time it can come to light again. The forgotten material is not extinguished, only 'repressed.'" See also Adorno, "On Tradition," *Telos* 94 (Winter 1993–94), pp. 75–82.

18. Arnold Schoenberg, "Composition with Twelve Tones," in *Style and Idea: Selected Writings of Arnold Schoenberg*, ed. Leonard Stein, trans. Leo Black (New York: St. Martin's, 1975), pp. 216–17, 246.

19. Søren Kierkegaard, *Stages on Life's Way: Studies by Various Persons*, ed. and trans. Howard V. Hong and Edna H. Hong (Princeton: Princeton University Press, 1988). I have not located the passage to which Adorno refers, nor does the

Kierkegaard concordance locate such a passage: Alastair McKinnon, *Index Verborum til Kierkegaards Samlede Værker*, vol. 3 of *The Kierkegaard Indices* (Leiden: E. J. Brill, 1973).

20. Luigi Dallapiccola (1904–1975) wrote two one-act operas, *Volo di notte* (1940) and *Il Prigioniero* (1944–1948), both of which were given their stage premieres in Florence. The German premiere of *Il Prigioniero* occurred in Essen in 1954, shortly after this essay was first published.

On the Problem
of Musical Analysis

The word "analysis" easily associates itself in music with the idea of all that is dead, sterile and farthest removed from the living work of art. One can well say that the general underlying feeling toward musical analysis is not exactly friendly. The musician's traditional antagonism toward all so-called "dead knowledge" is something that has been handed down of old, and continues to have its effect accordingly. One will encounter this antipathy again and again, above all in the rationalization represented by that absurd though utterly inextinguishable question: "Yes, everything you say is all very well and good, but did *the composer himself* know all this—was the composer *conscious* of all these things?"

I should like to say straight away that this question is completely irrelevant: it is very often precisely the deepest interrelationships that analyses are able to uncover within the compositional process which have been unconsciously produced; and one has to differentiate here—differentiate strictly—between the object itself (that is, between what is actually going on within the object itself) and the way in which it may have arisen in the consciousness or unconsciousness of the artist. Otherwise one ends up arguing on the level of the retired operetta director in Hamburg who once, in the course of an analytical talk I was giving, came up with the question as to "whether Mozart had been conscious of all these things." This concern with the unconscious seems to go only too naturally with the profession of operetta director or operetta composer.

The invalidity of this grudge against analysis is obvious, I think, to the musical experience of each person who attempts to come to terms with his or her experience. I'll begin with the experience of the performer, or interpreter. If he does not get to know the work intimately, the interpreter— and I think every practicing musician would agree with me here—will not

be able to interpret the work properly. "To get to know something intimately"—if I may express it so vaguely—means in reality "to analyze":
that is, to investigate the inner relationships of the work and to investigate
what is essentially contained within the composition. One could well say
that, in this sense, analysis may be regarded as the home ground of tradition. If, with an eye for these things, one examines Brahms, then one
finds (and I regret that I have to refrain from showing this in detail here)
just how much his compositions (especially the later works, which I consider to be extraordinarily important and significant) are actually the product of the analysis of works of the past—especially those of Beethoven.
One sees how this music in itself would be unthinkable without the analytical process which preceded it. Thus the infinite motivic economy which
characterizes the technique of the later Brahms (whereby practically no
note occurs which is not in fact thematic) is really quite inconceivable
without the dissolving process of analysis—a process which is, at first
sight, apparently irreconcilable with such economy.[1]

I should like to bring your attention to a further basic requirement of
analysis here: that is, the reading of music. As everybody knows, this is a
matter which is much more complicated than simply knowing the five lines
and four spaces, the accidentals and the note-values—the whole system of
signs, everything, that is to say, which is represented graphically to be read
as the score (I won't go into more recent developments, where in many
cases notation is more precise, although in other cases is also more vague
in this respect). The signs and the music which they signify are never
directly one and the same thing. And in order to read notation at all, so
that music results from it, an interpretive act is always necessary—that is
to say, an analytical act, which asks what it is that the notation really
signifies. Already in such elementary processes as these, analysis is always
essentially present. The façade—i.e., the score as "picture" [das Noten-
bild]—has to be unraveled, dissolved [aufgelöst] (and this as reliably as
possible) in order to arrive at that which is indicated by the score. And
once such an analytical process has been set in motion (as is the case, for
example, with even the most elementary reading of notation), then such
an analytical process may not be stopped at will, as the result of some
resolve or other which insists that, whatever happens, one is not allowed,
for Heaven's sake!, to touch the unconscious. That correct reading of the
score is the prerequisite for correct interpretation is obvious, but is by no
means as self-evident as one might think. In the first place it is a feature
of earlier musical practice that decisive musical elements like tempo and
dynamics, and very often also phrasing, are not to be gathered from the

score at all, and have to be extrapolated. They are to be discovered from that which is *not* written—that is to say, from an analytical act. But such an analytical process is still needed even in the case of composers where the score is already highly formulated. In this connection I'm thinking particularly of Beethoven—and perhaps it is a good idea to consider this for a moment, as there are questions here which, in my opinion, are far too seldom reflected upon.

Beethoven is relatively sparing in his use of markings in his scores. Apart from the bare musical text itself there is not much in the way of markings; what there is, however, is extraordinarily precise and carefully thought out, and to some extent one needs to be familiar with certain Beethovenian *Spielregeln* [performance rules] in order to understand just how painstaking and precise the markings are. One needs to know, for example, that the marking *fp* within an overall *forte* field indicates that, after an accent, the *piano* dynamic should then continue to be played, whereas something like *sf* within such a context indicates that the overall dynamic *(f)* should continue. There is, moreover, the whole question of the interpretation of dynamic markings in general: whether they are absolute—e.g., whether *crescendi* always lead up to *forte*—or whether they are only relative within particular dynamically defined fields. This in itself is already an extraordinarily difficult problem in innumerable cases in traditional music, and can only be resolved—can only be answered—with recourse to the structure of the music. That is to say, therefore, that this is also an essentially analytical problem. Furthermore, the most important "rule" for the—if I may so term it—"elementary analytical reading" of Beethoven is that, in his case, each marking is basically valid up to the next marking, and that only when a new marking is quite clearly indicated may the performer depart from the dynamic previously indicated. But even such a rule as this—which, I would suggest, may in general be applied to Beethoven—needs constant re-examination against the structure of individual works.

Analysis is thus concerned with structure, with structural problems, and finally, with structural listening. By structure I do not mean here the mere grouping of musical parts according to traditional formal schemata, however; I understand it rather as having to do with what is going on, musically, *underneath* these formal schemata. But this is also something that one dare not oversimplify, and it is already possible to see here how big the problems of musical analysis are. For, contrary to widespread belief, even that which is going on underneath is not simply a second and quite different thing, but is in fact mediated by the formal schemata, and is partly, at any given moment, *postulated* by the formal schemata, while on the other hand it consists of deviations which in their turn can only be at all understood through their relationship to the schemata. Naturally enough, this refers most directly to that traditional music in which such all-encompassing general schematic relationships exist at all. The task we have before us, therefore, is the realization of this already complex relationship of *deviation* to *schema*, rather than just the one or the other alone; and as a first step in this direction it can well be said that what we understand as analysis is the essence of the investigation of this relationship.

Although forgotten today, partly due to certain follies of which he was guilty and partly due to his vulgar nationalism, Heinrich Schenker must surely, in spite of all, be given the greatest credit for having been the first to demonstrate that analysis is the prerequisite for adequate performance.[2] And within the Schoenberg circle, ever since the period of the *Verein für musikalische Privataufführungen*, this had already been placed quite consciously at the very center of performance practice. This was probably first realized most fully by the Kolisch Quartet,[3] the reason for whose famous practice and technique of playing from memory in some respects stems from the simple fact that, if one has really studied works thoroughly and taken the trouble to analyze them, then one can play them from memory as a matter of course. That is to say, if each performer in a quartet plays according to the score as a whole and does not merely follow his own part, then this, in effect, already implies such an intimate understanding of the work's structure that playing from memory is essentially the natural outcome. Schenkerian analysis, distinguished as it often is by its extraordinary precision, subtlety and insistence, really amounts to an attempt to bring music down to certain fundamental structures of the most basic kind, among which the central position is occupied by what he called the Fundamental Line *[Urlinie]*—a difficult concept which oscillates remarkably between step-progression *[Stufenfolge]* and basic thematic material. In relation to this Fundamental Line all else appears to Schenker as being, so to speak, quite simply fortuitous—a kind of additive *[Zusatz]*, as it were— and it is this, I think, that already marks out the limitations of the Schenkerian form of analysis. For, in reducing music to its most generalized structures, what seems to him and to this theory to be merely casual and fortuitous is, in a certain sense, precisely that which is really the essence, the being *[das Wesen]* of the music. If, to take a rather unsubtle example, you examine the difference between the styles of Mozart and of Haydn, then you will not expect to discover this difference in general stylistic models and characteristics of the formal layout (although very significant differ-

ences do exist between the Haydnesque and the Mozartian sonata form).
You will have to resort instead to examining small but decisive features—
little physiognomic characteristics—in the way the themes themselves are
constructed, features which, for Schenker, are of mere secondary importance but which make all the difference and constitute, in fact, the difference between Haydn and Mozart. Now what this means, therefore, is that
what constitutes the essence, or "Being," of the composition is for
Schenker more or less its very abstractness, in fact, and the individual
moments[4] through which the composition materializes and becomes concrete are reduced by him to the merely accidental and non-essential. Thus
such a concept of analysis intrinsically misses the mark, for if it is really
to reveal the specific structure of the work, as I have maintained, it has to
come to terms with precisely those individual moments which, in terms
of Schenker's reductive process, merely supervene and which for him,
therefore, are only of peripheral interest. He himself tried to defend himself against this criticism (of which he was naturally aware) and he particularly tried to justify the general nature of the Fundamental Line—or the
identity of Fundamental Lines—by reference to certain basic relationships
[*Urverhältnisse*] in the music—a point of view which disregards the thoroughly historical structure of all musical categories. But it also cannot be
denied that, as far as Beethoven is concerned, Schenker's methods hit upon
a valid moment; as Rudolf Stephan has remarked, the Schenkerian method
is actually only really fruitful in connection with Beethoven. The inadequacy of Schenker's approach can be seen very clearly in his attitude to
Debussy. As a Francophobe, Schenker repeatedly attacked Debussy in a
very shabby manner, and accused him (and others, including Richard
Strauss) of the destruction of the Fundamental Line, without being able
to see that, in Debussy's case, there are criteria for inner consistency and
musical cohesion which are entirely different from the requirements of
what he called the Fundamental Line, essentially derived as it is from the
harmonized chorale. But it is possible to learn something from all this
which I consider to be central to the whole idea of musical analysis: namely
that analysis must be immanent—that, in the first instance, the form has
to be followed a *priori*, so that a composition unfolds itself in its own terms.
Or, to put it another way, one has to allow the composition something in
advance: that is, one must let it assert itself, in order to be able to enter
into its structure analytically. It never seems to have occurred to Schenker
that his accusing Debussy of the destruction of the Fundamental Line could
in any way have been connected with the crisis in motivic-thematic composition (which Schenker had made total and absolute).

Now, to get back to Beethoven, for whom, as I said, the Schenkerian approach is, in a certain sense, legitimate. One can perhaps account for this to a certain extent as follows: due to its artistically planned indifference toward each of the individual aspects of the materials it uses, Beethoven's music amounts to something like a kind of "justification" *[Rechtfertigung]*[5] of tonality itself and of the forms associated with tonality. Beethoven, as it were, tried to reconstruct tonality through his autonomous and individualized music. In a manner not unlike Kant—where, if you will allow me a philosophical digression, the objectively given world of experience is thrown into question and has then to be recreated once more by the Subject and its forms—in Beethoven the forms (particularly the large, dynamic forms like the sonata) could be said to re-emerge from out of the specific process of the composition. It is actually tonality itself which, in Beethoven's case, is both theme as well as outcome, and in this sense the Schenkerian concept of the Fundamental Line to some extent correctly applies here. However, Beethoven's genius consists precisely in the fact that this process does not remain on a general level, but, on the contrary— and in a manner which corresponds exactly to the great tradition of German philosophy (the philosophy of Hegel above all)—it plunges itself from the most generalized and unspecific into the most extreme concretion in order thus to lead back to the binding forces of the Universal once more. The decisive factor in Beethoven's compositions is just this "way to concretion," and it is precisely here, because of this peculiar change of emphasis, that Schenker has not gone the whole way. But it is exactly in this direction that the way—the idea of analysis—really does lie: that is to say, composition understood as a "coherence," as a dynamic set of interrelationships. And it is within this set of interrelationships—if anywhere at all—that the meaning of the composition resides.

I should now like to draw a few conclusions from all this. Firstly, although analysis is certainly of decisive help in questions of performance and interpretation, it is not actually from interpretation that it is derived, but from the work itself. You could put it this way: analysis is itself a form in its own right, like translation, criticism and commentary, as one of those media through which the very work unfolds. Works need analysis for their truth content *[Wahrheitsgehalt]*[6] to be revealed. To return to Beethoven again: initially he achieved his effect through what I think has been called "titanism," or through his expressivity; and only by means of intensive structural analysis did it then later become clear why his music can, with good reason, be called beautiful and true, and also eventually where its limits were to be sought.

Aesthetic theories on music and, above all, aesthetic *programs* (that is to say, claims made for and judgments pronounced on music) are quite inconceivable without analysis. Analysis is to be understood as an organ not only of the historical momentum of the works in themselves, but also of the momentum which pushes beyond the individual work. That is to say, all criticism which is of any value is founded in analysis; to the extent that this is not the case, criticism remains stuck with disconnected impressions, and thus, if for no other reason than this, deserves to be regarded with the utmost suspicion.

If one takes Wagner's claim regarding music's "coming of age" seriously—that is, the inescapable relation of music to *reflection*—then with this the significance of analysis as something immanent to the works themselves must also increase correspondingly, and has indeed done so. Given the presence of living experience, music unfolds itself through analysis; it becomes fuller for this experience, richer rather than poorer. Any interpreter who has initially made music only from what, precritically [*vorkritisch*], is called "musicality," and who has then subsequently performed from an all-encompassing analytical consciousness, will, I think, have no difficulty in acknowledging here what an enrichment is to be discovered in the realization of hidden relationships which, so long as the work is not analyzed, cannot come to the fore.

An art aware of itself is an *analyzed* art. There is a kind of convergence between the analytical process and the compositional process—I have tried to show this in my book on Berg,[7] using him as a model whereby the music, in a certain sense, can be looked upon as being its own analysis. So, the less it is that works operate within a pre-existing medium and with pre-existing forms—and this is certainly the overall tendency in the development of modern music, particularly since *Tristan*—the more it is that, for the sake of their own "livingness" [*um ihres eigenen Lebens willen*], they are in need of specifically tailored analysis. A piece by Handel—broadly speaking—may to some extent be grasped without analysis; Beethoven's *Diabelli* Variations, on the other hand, are already much less likely to be understood without it, whereas the Bagatelles of Webern cannot be grasped at all in this way. If Webern's Bagatelles are performed unanalyzed, though with faithful attention to all markings in the score but without uncovering the subcutaneous relationships—a merely respectable rendering of the score as it stands, that is—then the result, as is not difficult to imagine, is utter nonsense [*ein vollkommener Galimathias*]. On the other hand, the moment these pieces are analyzed, and performed after having been analyzed, they make sense and the light dawns.[8] . . . If, without analysis, such music cannot be presented in even the simplest sense as being meaningful, then this is as much as to say that analysis is no mere stopgap, but is an essential element of art itself. As such it will only begin to be able to correspond to the status of art when it takes the demands of its own autonomy upon itself. Otherwise, in the words of Heinz-Klaus Metzger, it remains "mere tautology"—that is to say, a simple translation into words of that which everyone can hear in the music anyway. Analysis has to do with the remainder *[das Mehr]* in art; it is concerned with that abundance which unfolds itself only by means of analysis. It aims at that which—as has been said of poetry (if I may be permitted a poetic analogy)—is the truly poetic in poetry, and the truly poetic in poetry is that which defies translation. Now, it is precisely this moment which analysis must grasp if it is not to remain subordinate. Analysis is more than merely the facts, but is so only and solely by virtue of *going beyond* the simple facts by absorbing itself into them. Every analysis that is of any value, therefore—and anyone who analyzes seriously will soon realize this for himself—is a squaring of the circle. It is the achievement of imagination through faith; and Walter Benjamin's definition of imagination as "the capacity for interpolation into the smallest details" applies here.[9]

Now, the ultimate "remainder" over and beyond the factual level is the *truth content*, and naturally it is only critique that can discover the truth content. No analysis is of any value if it does not terminate in the truth content of the work, and this, for its part, is mediated through the work's technical structure. If analysis hits up against technical inconsistency, then such inconsistency is an index of the work's untruth—I have attempted elsewhere to demonstrate this in concrete terms in certain specific aspects of the music of Wagner[10] and of Richard Strauss.[11] At the moment, I wish only to put forward these thoughts in their theoretical generality, however—although with the immediate further qualification that the work of art insists that one put this question of truth or untruth *immanently* and not arbitrarily bring some yardstick or other of the cultural-philosophical or cultural-critical varieties to the work from outside.

I now want to come to the point I have really been leading up to so far: analysis, as the unfolding of the work, exists in relationship to the work itself and to its genre or "compositional archetype" *[Typus]*. This is perhaps most clearly to be seen in the first of the more primitive forms of analysis to have become generally effective—the so-called "guide literature" *[Leitfadenliteratur]* to the music of Wagner and the New German School, as associated with the name of Hans von Wolzogen.[12] Here the intention was simply to ease orientation in the kind of music which avoids traditional forms but which is held together by the drastic means of leitmotifs which, though admittedly varied, are always essentially recognizable. This aim is achieved by the simple procedure of picking out the leitmotifs, labeling them and identifying them in their different forms. (It may be noted in passing that this kind of analysis contradicts its own aim, and serves, in fact, to further that external, superficial type of listening which so characterizes the old-style Wagner listener, proud if he is able to recognize the "Curse Motif" in the *Ring* every time somebody gets murdered, given the necessary references—if he doesn't recognize it on the darkened stage anyway—while in doing so he misses what is really happening in the music.) This reified form of analysis, as represented by the "guide" to themes and motifs, serves a reified and false consciousness of the object. Because of its inadequacy, however, it has at least served to promote another, and much more justifiable, type of analysis—in particular that associated above all with the Viennese classics and for which Riemann could be said to have supplied the best-known examples. I am going to label this type "elemental analysis."[13] With progressive energy it turns to the smallest single elements from which a piece is built up—roughly in the same way in which knowledge, according to Descartes, has continually to divide up its object into the smallest possible elements. Now, just as the principle of *economy* can be said to dominate in the music of Viennese Classicism (that is, the Viennese tradition since Haydn, but particularly Beethoven and Brahms, and in a particular sense also Schoenberg and his school)—that is to say, that a maximum of different appearances has to be derived from a minimum of basic shapes *[Grundgestalten]*—so can the elemental type of analysis be seen, in fact, to have its support in that kind of music which can be categorized under the concept "motific-thematic" composition. Implied here there is also, of course, a hidden criticism of this type of composition, obligatory as it was for more than 150 years.

Elemental analysis confirms a suspicion which irritates everyone who persists in occupying himself with [motific-thematic] music: namely—and I'm going to say something blasphemous here—its similarity to the jigsaw puzzle, constructed as it is out of elements over against which dynamic development (which on the face of it predominates to such an extent in this music) reveals itself in many ways to be merely a contrived appearance. It could be said that the character of this aesthetic appearance (which even applies, in spite of all, to an art as far removed from illusion as music, and through which music has integrated itself into the development of European culture as a whole) has occurred as the consequence of an unceasing Becoming—or development—from out of itself *[aus sich Heraus-werdendes]*. In reality, however, such music could more accurately be said to have been "put together" in the quite literal sense of having been "composed," contrary to the impression more usually associated with it. And incidentally, this may also be said to a certain extent to apply to Bach, producing at times in his case—due to the absence of the aspect of Becoming—that impression of mechanicalness which can be dispelled only by an ideological effort [of interpretation] which actually glorifies the apparent mechanicalness as a special kind of logicality. Indeed, all Becoming in music is in fact illusory, insofar as the music, as *text*, is really fixed and thus is not actually becoming anything as it is already all there. Nevertheless, music is actually only a coherence when regarded as a Becoming, and in this there lies a paradox for musical analysis: analysis is, on the one hand, limited by what is actually fixed and available to it; but, on the other hand, it has to translate this back again into that movement as coagulated in the musical text. But the elemental type of analysis is also inadequate as far as Viennese Classicism is concerned. Schoenberg's sentence "music is the history of its themes" serves to remind us of this. May "Becoming" continue always to have its problematic existence!

All this applies particularly to Beethoven. In his case the germinal cells *[die Keime]* are very often—as initially stated—ingeniously indifferent, in order that they may smoothly *[bruchlos]* and seamlessly lead up to the whole; in fact, they simply represent the fundamental relationships of tonality itself. And it is particularly the case with Beethoven that, just for this very reason, it is much more important what the themes *become*— what happens to them and *how* they develop—than what the basic elements themselves actually are. The real weakness of analysis up to now lies in the fact that it neglects this moment of Becoming for the reduction [of music] to its elements. In this connection I would like to refer once more to what I said earlier about analysis being an essential prerequisite of criticism. I have just spoken of the indifference of the material in Beethoven. With Wagner, the basic motifs *[Urmotive]* which are supposed to represent the primeval world of Wotan and the Valhalla domain in the *Ring* are kept within a certain—how shall I put it?—undifferentiated, or unspecific Universality. But in Wagner's case they are not, by a long way, as legitimate as they are with Beethoven, because Wagner's individual motifs have the significance and weight of symbols and contain basically the whole idea of the germinal cell of the romantic lied. For this reason they have pretensions to a Beingness *[Sein]* in and for themselves much more than is ever the case with Beethoven. And this weakness, inherent in the themes and contradicting their own claim to just being there *[da zu sein]*, points, moreover, to their real weakness as regards substance, in view of what happens to them and what they become—something that one would not think of in connection with Beethoven, because with him the priority of *Becoming* over that which simply *is* is already established right from the start. Yes, a really true and adequate analysis would have to point out such differences, and it is possible to see from this how an analysis of this type merges into criticism, into critique.

Any adequate analysis of Beethoven has to grasp the music as an *event*, as "a something which is happening" *[als ein Geschehendes]*, and not only as the elements flanked by this event. In the recapitulation of the first movement of the Ninth Symphony, for example, it is not the return of the theme and the components, the basic constitutive elements *[Urbestandteile]* of which it is formed that matters; what is important is that this recapitulation appears as the result of the foregoing development. It is a similar situation in the *Appassionata* concerning the overwhelming effect of the recapitulation over the dominant pedal point in the first movement. Analysis would have to show why these kinds of effects are achieved, and not simply that here, at this point, this or that theme recurs. To demonstrate this is in reality extraordinarily difficult; but by the very posing of this question you may already be able to recognize that the tedium and aridity of analysis in general is a consequence of the fact that analysis has not yet really begun to grapple with its own problems—something, in fact, which should be its proper concern.

Now, from all that I've been saying so far it may have become plain to you just how much any particular kind of analysis and its legitimacy are actually themselves dependent upon the particular music which is being analyzed. It goes without saying that radical serial and aleatory music cannot be grasped by traditional analytical approaches, and particularly not by means of the elemental type of analysis, because concepts like dynamic coherence *[dynamische Sinnzusammenhang]*, or context of meaning, and so on are far removed from its basic assumptions. It is precisely here, when faced with aleatory and serial music, that analysis is frequently confused with the mere recording of facts. This then results in the kind of absurdity once reserved for me at Darmstadt, where a composer (who, to his credit, has since given up the vocation) showed me a composition which seemed to me to be the purest nonsense. When I asked him what this or that meant, what meaning, what kind of musical sense this or that particular phrase or development had, he simply referred me to correspondences between dynamic markings and pitches and so on—things which have nothing whatever to do with the musical phenomenon as such. This kind of description of the compositional process, of what the composer has done in the composition, is totally unproductive, just as are all those kinds of aesthetic examination which are unable to extract from a work any more than what has been put into it, so to speak—what it says in the Baedeker guide. All such approaches are doomed from the outset as worthless and irrelevant.

With so-called "athematic," free atonality the relationships are quite different, and I mention this precisely because I feel myself to be on much firmer ground here, analytically speaking, than when faced with serial and post-serial music. Here—and I'm thinking especially of Webern in this connection—one encounters once more particular transformations of the categories of traditional thematic-motific compositional methods. I have elsewhere attempted to develop this in some of the most daring of Webern's works, like the Bagatelles and the violin pieces.[14] Here the transmutation of the traditional (i.e., thematic-motivic) categories of musical coherence into something quite opposed to them can be traced and demonstrated. The thematic technique of developing variation—a technique which necessitates the unceasing derivation of the "new," indeed the radically new, from the "old"—is radicalized to become the negation of that which used to be called the thematic development or working-out. And it is this coherence—this transmutation—that analysis has to meet in such music. Its task, therefore, is not to describe the work—and with this I have really arrived at the central issue concerning analysis generally—its task, essentially, is to reveal as clearly as possible the problem of each particular work. "To analyze" means much the same as to become aware of a work as a force-field organized around a problem. Having said this, however, we must now be quite clear about one thing: whether we like it or not analysis is inevitably to some extent, of its very nature, the reduction of the unknown, the new—with which we are confronted within the composition and which we want to grasp—to the already known, inasmuch as it is the old. However, in that every modern composition contains an essential, inbuilt moment that combats this mechanism of the familiar and the known, insofar can it be said that the analysis of modern works is also always a betrayal of the work—although at the same time it is also actually demanded by the work itself. From this there also arises the question as to how analysis puts right this wrong it inflicts on the work; and the way to an answer lies, I believe, precisely in the fact that analysis serves to pinpoint that which I call the "problem" of a particular composition—the paradox, so to speak, or the "impossible" that every piece of music wants to make possible. (Rather as in Schoenberg's Phantasy for violin and piano, op. 47: how in the end the radically dynamic process of composition itself results in a composition in coordinated fields, and how the categories of the composition transform themselves into the balance, the equilibrium of those fields, and then finally, through this equilibrium, an effect is brought about which fulfills the dynamic.)[15] Once the problem—I was almost going to say the "blind spot"—of the work has been recognized, then the individual moments will thereby be clarified in a quite different manner than by the so-called reductive methods of traditional practice.

Now all this has to be differentiated, of course—and I must emphasize this—from the so-called holistic method of examination [*ganzheitliche Betrachtung*][16] so popular with the pedagogues. With musical compositions it is obviously the whole that matters; but the whole is not something which simply reduces the individual single moments to insignificance. The whole—if I may be permitted to express it in Hegelian terms—is itself the relation between the whole and its individual moments, within which these latter obtain throughout their independent value. Analysis exists only as the uncovering of the relationship between these moments, and not merely by virtue of the obtuse and aconceptual priority of the whole over its parts. It is particularly in new music, moreover, that analysis is concerned just as much with dissociated moments [*Dissoziationsmomente*], with the works' death-wish [*Todestrieb*]—that is to say, with the fact that there are works which contain within themselves the tendency to strive from unity back into their constituent elements—as it is concerned with the opposite process; and these are questions which have been totally neglected in the name of the so-called holistic method, within which there are usually disturbingly positivist implications. Just as analysis should no longer dare be of the elemental type, it is also equally wrong that it should disregard the individual moments and reduce them all to the same level of indifference by taking a rigid and overriding concept of the totality as its point of departure. If one really takes the whole as one's point of departure then also simultaneously implied here is the obligation to grasp the logic of the individual moments—that is, the concretion of the isolated musical instants. And correspondingly, if one takes the constituent elements as the point of departure one's task is to understand how these elements in themselves, and frequently in contradiction to each other, and then through this contradiction, also simultaneously generate the whole.

In this sense—that is, relative to whole and to part—analysis is always a double process. Erwin Ratz—to whom we are indebted for some excellent analyses of certain very complex movements by Mahler (the finale of the

Sixth Symphony and the first movement of the Ninth, for example)[17]—once formulated this very nicely in one of his analyses as follows: there are really two analyses always necessary; that which advances from the part to the whole—i.e., just like the way in which the innocent listener has no choice but to listen in the first instance, willy-nilly; and then that which, from the already-won awareness of the whole, determines the individual moments. And this is not merely a genetic difference, determined by the time-factor; the difference is also determined by the object—the compositional structure itself—in which these antithetical moments necessarily intermesh.

Moreover—and this is of further importance in distinguishing it from any totality cult *[Ganzheitskultus]*—the relationship of whole to part is *never* to be understood as the relationship of an all-embracing *[Umfassenden]* to an all-embraced *[Umfassten]*, but is, instead, dynamic, which is to say a process. This means to say; on the one hand, that—in music, as an art which unfolds through time—all moments have, generally speaking, something evolving about them, something becoming, and thus reach out beyond themselves. The sense and aim of an analysis which takes the individual moment as its point of departure is not only—as tends mostly to be the case—the indication and fixing of the individual moments (or more extreme, their mere recognition); it is also the indication of that within them which propels them onward. Take, for example, the well-known counter-subject to the first theme of Mahler's Fourth Symphony:[18]

Already, right from the very beginning, one has to listen to this in terms of the direction it wants to go in and for which it yearns, in terms of the fact that it is striving ultimately beyond itself toward the high B,[19] in order to fulfill itself; and if one doesn't hear this in its individual elements, if one doesn't hear the theme's own directional tendency within each single element, then the description of the individual moments can already, for this very reason, be said to have missed the point.

If one analyzes the main theme of the first movement of the *Eroica*, for example, then one sees that the point which occurs almost immediately and leaves the music hanging suspended on the C#—that damming-up of forces which invests the initial *Grundgestalt* with tension after its first few bars—is decisive and of much more importance than the indifferent broken major triad with its closing minor seconds, the so-called material of this theme (and of most of the themes of the so-called Viennese Classics).

On the other hand, attention has also to be paid to the way in which the individual motifs are pre-formed by the whole, as is mostly the case with Beethoven. Beethoven's music is not in fact formed, or built up, out of themes and motifs at all, as the elemental type of analysis would lead us to believe; it is rather that these themes and motifs are instead already— I almost said prepared, anachronistically, as one talks of prepared piano: they adapt themselves to become part of the pervading idea of the whole. Beethoven's work was, in fact—as may be easily recognized from the sketchbooks—essentially to tinker with the themes and motifs until they finally became capable of meeting their function within the whole. In reality this function always has priority in Beethoven, although it seems as though everything develops out of the motive-power *[Triebkraft]* of the individual elements. And in this his music is no mere analogy for, but is in fact directly identical to, the structure of Hegelian logic. While one should not overvalue the genesis of music [i.e., the way in which it comes into being] and should not, above all, confuse it with the inner dynamics of the composition, with Beethoven, at least, this genesis nevertheless suffices to demonstrate just how much the conception of a whole dynamically conceived in itself defines its elements, and how, through this, the task facing analysis right from the start will naturally be totally different from that which the elemental type of analysis makes it out to be.

All in all, therefore—if you will allow me a very rough generalization— two types of music can be distinguished: 1) the kind which goes, in principle, from above to below, from totality to detail; and 2) the kind which is organized from below to above. Thus, according to which of these dominates the structure of the music, the same will correspondingly direct the analysis itself. If I may speak from my own experience for a second: I hit upon the necessity for extensive modifications to the concept of analysis through the study of the music of my teacher, Alban Berg. The Berg analyses which I wrote some thirty years ago, directly after his death, were traditional analyses of the kind which brings the "whole" down to the smallest possible number of what one calls germinal cells and then shows how the music develops out of them.[20] And there is no question but that Berg himself, from his own understanding [of the term], would also still have approved of this traditional kind of analysis. However, as I came to revise and prepare the book last year [1968], and so to occupy myself with Berg's music with renewed intensity, I saw something that I had, of course, dimly sensed for a long time: namely, that Berg's music is not at all a Something *[ein Etwas]* which forms itself, so to speak, out of a Nothingness *[ein Nichts]* of the smallest possible, undifferentiated component elements. It only seems like this at first glance. In reality it accomplishes within itself a process of permanent dissolution[21] rather than achieving a "synthesis"—a term which any self-respecting person should hardly be able to get past his lips these days. So then, not only does Berg's music start out from the smallest component elements and then immediately further subject these to a kind of splitting of the atom, but the whole character of his music is that of permanent re-absorption back into itself. Its Becoming, if I may term it thus—at all events, where it crystallizes-out its idea in its purest form—is its own negation. This means that such a structuring of the inner fiber of a music also calls for an analytical practice completely different from the long-established motivic-thematic approach—and I should like expressly to say that it was in the Berg book that I became particularly aware of this necessity. However, I don't in the slightest flatter myself as in any way having succeeded in fulfilling this demand, and what I say here as criticism of analysis in general also applies without reservation as a criticism of all the countless analyses that I myself have ever produced.

Analysis, therefore, means much the same as the recognition of the way in which the specific, sustaining structural idea of a piece of music realizes itself; and such a concept of analysis would need essentially to be derived from each work anew. Nevertheless, I have no wish to stop short here with this demand for the absolute singularity or absolute individuation of analysis. There also lies in analysis a moment of the universal, the general *[des Allgemeinen]*—and this goes with the fact that music is certainly also, in essence, a language—and it is, furthermore, precisely in the most specific works that this moment of universality is to be sought. I might attempt to summarize or codify this universality in terms of what I once defined as the "material theory of form in music" *[materiale Formenlehre der Musik]*: that is, the concrete definition of categories like statement *[Setzung]*, continuation *[Fortsetzung]*, contrast *[Kontrast]*, dissolution *[Auflösung]*, succession *[Reihung]*, development *[Entwicklung]*, recurrence *[Wiederkehr]*, modified recurrence *[modifizierter Wiederkehr]*, and however such categories may otherwise be labeled. And so far not even the beginnings of an approach have been made regarding such a "material theory of form" (as opposed to the architectonic-schematic type of theory). These [i.e., dialectical] categories are more important than knowledge of the traditional forms as such, even though they have naturally developed out of the traditional forms and can always be found in them. Were this conception of analysis such as I have in mind, and which is in accordance with structural listening—were this conception to be consistently realized, then something else, a further level, something like such a "material theory of musical form," would necessarily emerge out of it. It would not, to be sure, be fixed and invariable—it would not be a theory of form for once and always, but would define itself within itself historically, according to the state of the compositional material, and equally according to the state of the compositional forces of production.

The crisis in composition today—and with this I should like to close—is also a crisis in analysis. I have attempted to make you aware of why this is the case. It would perhaps not be too much of an exaggeration to say that all contemporary musical analyses—be they of traditional or of the most recent music—have remained behind the level of contemporary musical consciousness in composition. If analysis can be raised to this level without thereby lapsing into a vacuous obsession with musical fact-collecting, then it will, in its turn, very probably be capable of reacting back on to, and critically affecting, composition itself.

(1969)

Translated by Max Paddison

NOTES BY MAX PADDISON

This text is a revised version by Max Paddison of the original translation he made from his own transcription from a tape recording of a lecture, "Zum Probleme der musikalischen Analyse," delivered by Adorno on 24 February 1969 at the Hochschule für Musik und Darstellende Kunst, Frankfurt am Main, a few months before his death. The original translation was published, with an introduction by Max Paddison, in *Music Analysis* 1 no. 2 (July 1982), pp. 169–87. The German text of the translation was published for the first time in the journal of the Adorno-Archiv, *Frankfurter Adorno Blätter* 7 (2001), pp. 73–89.

1. It may seem that Adorno is contradicting himself here. What he means is that, although the motific economy of the later Brahms is dependent upon the analysis which preceded it, there does at first sight appear to be something irreconcilable about these two processes. That is to say, on the one hand, there is the process of composition and integration which attempts to conceal the technical steps which went into its own construction, while, on the other hand, there is the step-by-step process of analysis which, through dissection, dissolution, and "disintegration," attempts to reveal and lay bare the technical structure of the integrated work once more.

2. It has to be remembered that Adorno is speaking in 1969, but Schenker still remains relatively neglected in Germany.

3. The Society for Private Musical Performances, founded by Schoenberg, and dedicated to the performance of modern works, functioned in Vienna from 1918 to 1921, during which time 117 concerts were given. The Kolisch Quartet, founded

by Rudolf Kolisch in 1922, premiered chamber music by Schoenberg, Berg, Webern, and Bartók. The Society's prospectus, drafted by Berg, is reprinted in Willi Reich, *The Life and Work of Alban Berg*, trans. Cornelius Cardew (1965; reprint, New York: Da Capo, 1982), pp. 46–49.

4. "Moment" in this sense refers to the German *das Moment*, defined in Martin Jay, *The Dialectical Imagination: A History of the Frankfurt School and the Institute of Social Research, 1923–1950* (Boston: Little, Brown, 1973), p. 54, as "a phase or aspect of a cumulative dialectical process. It should not be confused with *der Moment*, which means a moment in time in the English sense."

5. Although "justification" is perhaps an unexpected word in this context, it is nevertheless the correct translation of *Rechtfertigung* here. It seems clear enough what Adorno means.

6. "Truth content" *[Wahrheitsgehalt]* is a difficult concept as Adorno uses it. The following two quotations from Adorno's AT may help to provide a few clues: "The truth content of artworks is the objective solution of the enigma posed by each and every one. . . . It can only be achieved by philosophical reflection. This alone is the justification of aesthetics [and, by implication, analysis; pp. 127–28]. Art is directed toward truth, it is not itself immediate truth; to this extent truth is its content. By its relation to truth, art is knowledge; art itself knows truth in that truth emerges through it" [p. 282]. The notion of "truth content" ties up with the conception of the artwork as being primarily a form of *cognition*, of knowledge (albeit, in the case of music, in purely musical-structural terms). This particularly Hegelian position of Adorno's calls to mind Schoenberg, in chapter 6 of *Fundamentals of Musical Composition* (cf. Alexander Goehr, "Schoenberg's *Gedanke* Manuscript," *Journal of the Arnold Schoenberg Institute* 2 no. 1 [October 1977], p. 16): "The real purpose of musical construction is not beauty, but intelligibility." It is tempting also to connect the "truth content" of the work with the "problem" around which the work, as "force-field," forms itself (see p. 173 of the present translation).

7. AB. Parts of this book originally appeared as contributions to Willi Reich's *Alban Berg: mit Bergs eigenen Schriften und Beiträgen von Theodor Wiesengrund-Adorno und Ernst Krenek* (Vienna: Herbert Reichner, 1937).

8. In an aside (which I have omitted in the text) Adorno suggests we follow up the points he is making here by referring to the chapter on Webern's Bagatelles for String Quartet, op. 9, in *Der getreue Korrepetitor*, GS, vol. 15, pp. 277–301.

9. See Susan Buck-Morss, *The Origin of Negative Dialectics: Theodor W. Adorno, Walter Benjamin, and the Frankfurt Institute* (New York: Free Press, 1977), pp. 91–93, 106–07. In an aside Adorno mentions at this point that Walter Benjamin's son is present in the audience.

10. ISW. See also "Zum 'Versuch über Wagner,'" GS, vol. 13, pp. 497–508; "Wagner's Relevance for Today," this volume, pp. 584–602; and "Nachschrift zu einer Wagner-Diskussion," GS, vol. 16, pp. 665–70.

11. Adorno, "Richard Strauss: Born June 11, 1864," trans. Samuel Weber and Shierry Weber, *Perspectives of New Music* 3 (Fall/Winter 1965), pp. 14–32 and 4 (Spring/Summer 1966), 113–29.

12. See p. 103 n. 32.

13. There are problems in finding an adequate translation for Adorno's term *Elementaranalyse*. "Formal-motivic analysis" perhaps comes as close as anything. However, I have opted for "elemental analysis" in the text, unsatisfactory as it is, as I felt it necessary to retain the notion of "element," "elementary," and "elemental," in the sense of "reduction to constituent elements."

14. See n. 8.

15. Adorno is probably referring to the fact that Schoenberg composed the violin part of op. 47 before the piano part.

16. Adorno is certainly referring to *Gestalt* psychology here—but in particular, it would seem, to that school of *Gestalt* known as *"Ganzheitspsychologie"* (i.e., the Second Leipzig School of *Gestalt* Psychology associated with Felix Krueger). This was a diluted form of *Gestalt* which deified the whole over its parts.

17. Erwin Ratz, "Zum Formproblem bei Gustav Mahler: eine Analyse des ersten Satzes der IX. Symphonie," *Musikforschung* 8 (1955), pp. 169–71; and "Zum Formproblem bei Gustav Mahler: eine Analyse des Finales der VI. Symphonie," *Musikforschung* 9 (1956), pp. 156–71.

18. Adorno simply sings his example at this point. It is the five-note motif, which appears in the clarinets and bassoons at bar 20 of the first movement of Mahler's Fourth Symphony.

19. The "high B" referred to by Adorno is most certainly that in the cellos in bar 94, the high point of this "counter-subject" (i.e., the five-note motif referred to in note 18 above) as it is ultimately extended in the cellos in bars 90–101. Adorno seems to have expected a lot from his audience, that they should be able to make this connection on the spot, from the rather sparse indications he gives.

20. See n. 7.

21. It is not easy to find a satisfactory translation for *Auflösung*, as it can mean, among other things, disintegration, solution, and also liquidation. I have decided on *dissolution* as this is the term used by Alexander Goehr, "Schoenberg's *Gedanke* Manuscript," pp. 4–25. It is illuminating to consider Schoenberg's use of the term *Auflösung* (as well as of the term *liquidieren*) in the following extract from the *Gedanke* manuscript (p. 24): "Dissolution *[Auflösung]* is the exact counterpart of establishment *[Aufstellung]*, firm formation, shaping. If in these the main objective is, through variation of the basic shapes *[Gestalten]*, to bring out their characteristics as sharply as possible, to interconnect the single *Gestalten* as closely as possible, to keep the tension among the tones high, the most important thing in dissolution is to drop all characteristics as fast as possible, to let the tensions run off and to liquidate *[liquidieren]* the obligations of the former *Gestalten* in such a way that there will be, so to speak, a 'clean slate,' so that the possibility for the appearance of other materials is given."

The Aging of the New Music

To speak of the aging of the New Music seems paradoxical.[1] Yet music that has its essence in the refusal to go along with things as they are, and has its justification in giving shape to what the conventional superficies of daily life hide and what is otherwise condemned to silence by the culture in-dustry—which threatens to acquire New Music as a wholly owned sub-sidiary—precisely this music has begun to show symptoms of false sat-isfaction. The malicious objection of reactionaries that scholasticism has crept into modernism and is spreading can only be met by the critical reflection sedimented in the works themselves. The concept of New Music is incompatible with an affirmative sound, the confirmation of what is, even if this were beloved "Being" itself. When music for the first time came to completely doubt all that, it became New Music. The shock it dealt to its audience in its heroic period—at the time of the first performance of the *Altenberg* Songs of Alban Berg or the first performance of the *Sacre du printemps* of Stravinsky in Paris[2]—cannot simply be attributed to un-familiarity and strangeness, as the good-natured apology would have it; rather, it is the result of something actually distressing and confused. Who-ever denies this and claims that the new art is as beautiful as the traditional one does it a real disservice; he praises in it what this music rejects so long as it unflinchingly follows its own impulse.

The aging of the New Music means nothing else than that this critical impulse is ebbing away. It is falling into contradiction with its own idea, the price of which is its own aesthetic substance and coherence. The "sta-bilization of music," the danger of the dangerless noticeable as early as 1927,[3] became even stronger after the world catastrophe. Indeed, on no account, as another cliché would have it, has the fermenting must clarified into ripe, sweet wine. No valid accomplishment, no rounded masterpiece, took the place of the excesses of certain devotees of *Sturm und Drang.* The striving for masterpieces is part of that conformism renounced by New Music. While the aficionados of modernism, whom one meets on every side nowadays, forget what the whole really should be, the quality and binding force of musical works evaporate; the waning of inner tension and the waning of formative power are interrelated, and have the same root. One could hardly claim that the creations of the mid-twentieth century are superior to *Pierrot lunaire, Erwartung, Wozzeck,* the lyrics of Webern or the early outbursts of Stravinsky and Bartók. Even if in the meantime the raw material of composition was purified of slag and unhomogeneous vestiges of the past, and if somehow the possibility developed of a rigorous new musical phrase, it is still questionable whether such a purification of all disturbing intrusions would be of service to the cause of music, and not simply to a technocratic attitude, in whose eager concern for consistency something entirely too binding, violent, and unartistic announces itself. In any case, advances in the material have hardly benefitted the quality of the works that use them. A blind belief in progress is required not to notice how little progress has been made since the early twenties, how much has been lost, how tame and in many respects how impoverished most music has become. This must be pointed out without hesitation by whoever keeps faith with the New Music and hopes to help it better than by accommodation to the *Zeitgeist,* to the servile acknowledgment of the status quo.

Neither was radical music replaced by a less embattled music, as those theories that appeal to the wisdom of the course of the generations would like to convince their contemporaries; music did not find its way comfortably back to the tradition that had been demolished by the atonal revolt. To argue this position theoretically would be as senseless as the praxis of that moribund music that copies the music of the ages and polishes it up with a scattering of false notes. It is already questionable whether the forgetting of Bach and the victory of the "gallant style" two hundred years ago were such a healthy reaction and positive force as music history so frequently declares them to have been. Whoever reflects on the course of musical history should also consider this: that although the development of eighteenth-century homophony was fundamental for the work of Haydn and Mozart, still the loss of a living Bach tradition created great difficulties for the Vienna composers, difficulties resulting in true defects of composition that are only now becoming recognizable.[4] It is perfectly certain, however, that the music that currently makes up the greater part of what is composed, and which might be called Music Festival music, did not give expression to a freshly burgeoning primary experience, as was the case in spite of everything after Bach's death. On the contrary, this Music Festival music feeds essentially off of the discoveries of the New Music, while at the same time treating it arbitrarily, indifferently, thinning it out, bending it out of shape. Perhaps a drastic analogy from literature may be permitted here. It is drawn from a work whose spiritual origins are allied with those of the New Music: *The Last Days of Mankind* by Karl Kraus.[5] He was close to Strindberg, who often referred to Kraus gratefully as a spiritual ally. The first edition of Kraus's drama contained a title-page picture of the execution of the deputy Battisti, accused by the Austrians of spying: in the center was a ghoulish photograph of a merrily laughing hangman. That picture—along with another that was, if possible, even more shocking—was left out of the new edition published after the Second World War. As a result of this seemingly superficial change something decisive was transformed in the work. A similar transformation, a little less crass, occurred in New Music. The sounds remain the same. But the anxiety that gave shape to its great founding works has been repressed. Perhaps that anxiety has become so overwhelming in reality that its undisguised image would scarcely be bearable: to recognize the aging of the New Music does not mean to misjudge this aging as something accidental. But art that unconsciously obeys such repression and makes itself a game, because it has become too weak for seriousness, renounces its claim to truth, which is its only raison d'être. When this art asserts the superiority of its exalted spirit over the confusions of mere existence it achieves nothing more than an alibi for its own bad conscience. More than a hundred years ago Kierkegaard, speaking as a theologian, said that where once a dreadful abyss yawned a railroad bridge now stretches, from which the passengers can look comfortably down into the depths. The situation of music is no different. Even if the historical force behind this development were so overpowering that it made all resistance vain, it would at the very least be worth destroying the illusion that such art is still what it claims to be, or is held to be, in a trade whose standard is conformity.

Included here are not only camp followers and epigones, of whom there have always been plenty. The symptoms have worked their way into the compositions of the most gifted and, according to their own principles, most uncompromising composers. Cases like those of Stravinsky and Hindemith, who more or less explicitly abjured what filled their youth, what in them was once so fascinating, are not at issue here. Their restorative efforts, just like those of certain converted surrealist painters, are in any case, from a cultural-philosophical standpoint, a renunciation of the concept of New Music. They stick to the deceptive image of a *musica perennis*.

But even Béla Bartók, from whom such inclinations were very distant, began at a certain point to separate himself from his own past. In a speech given in New York, he explained that a composer like he, whose roots were in folk music, could ultimately not do without tonality—an astounding statement for the Bartók who unhesitatingly resisted all populist temptations and chose exile and poverty when the shadow of Fascism passed over Europe. In fact his later works, like the [Second] Violin Concerto, actually count as traditional music, though indeed they are not cramped and narrow resurrections of a distant past, but almost unabashed continuations of Brahms: they are late, posthumous masterpieces, certainly, but domesticated, no longer heralds of the threateningly eruptive, the ungrasped. The development of his work has a peculiar retrospective effect. In its light many of his most radical compositions, like the First Violin Sonata, appear much more harmless than their sound and harmonies. What once seemed like a prairie fire ultimately reveals itself as a Czardas, so that even the rather obvious piano composition *Im Freien* sounds today like dried-out Debussy, a sort of corroded mood music: Bartók's guardian angel is Liszt's *Mazeppa*.[6] Even among those who were once leaders of New Music, more than one lagged behind his avant-garde claims, more than one lived to some degree beyond his spiritual-cultural means. The naïveté of the musical specialist, who attends to his metier without actually participating in objective spirit, is partially responsible for this. The rift between society and the New Music runs through modern musicians themselves in more ways than one. While they embrace New Music as if it were an unavoidable task, their own inculcated taste balks against it; their musical experience is not free from the element of the non-contemporaneous. As soon as they were struck by the failures of the music of the past, those especially capitulated who had unhesitatingly taken up the New because they knew too little about the Old.

Thus the aging of the New Music is to be taken much more seriously than as a simple revolt or as the appeasement after which the classical ideal yearns. There is no sense in pointing, today, to the feebleness of neoclassicism; in the face of the pallor and monotony of the recent works of this school, the more talented young composers are obviously repelled. All the more urgent therefore to understand the present situation of what now attracts the disgruntled and rebellious: twelve-tone technique. Schoenberg's own misgivings are enlightening for anyone who is no more pleased by the popularity of twelve-tone technique—as historically necessary as ever—than, say, by the popularity of Kafka. Twelve-tone technique has its justification only in the presentation of complex musical contents, which

cannot otherwise be organized. Separated from this function, it degenerates into a deluded system. While New Music, and particularly Schoenberg's achievement, is stamped as twelve-tone composition, and thus hand-
ily pigeonholed, the fact that a very large and perhaps, qualitatively, the
decisive part of this production was composed prior to the invention of
this technique or independently of it, should give reason to pause. Schoenberg himself consistently refused to teach what the music marketplace had
falsified into a system. One may think, for instance, of Anton von Webern's Five Movements for String Quartet, op. 5, which today sounds as
contemporary as on its first day,⁷ and technically has not been surpassed.
These movements, whose composition now lies forty-five years in the past,
had already broken with tonality; they know, as one says, only dissonances;
they are not dodecaphonic. A shudder surrounds each of these dissonances.
They are felt as something uncanny, and are introduced by their author
with fear and trembling. Right into the treatment of the sounds it is possible to follow how carefully Webern lay hold of them. Only with hesitancy does he separate himself from each and every sound; each one he
holds fast until its expressive values are exhausted. He shrinks away from
ruling sovereignly over them while at the same time he respects his own
discoveries. This is not the least source of the undiminished power of
Webern's tenderness. Now, to be sure, the quality of occurring "for the
first time" cannot be preserved. One must renounce it, go beyond it, as
soon as those fresh effects have become sedimented and rigidified. But
everything depends on whether such chords can free themselves from the
spell of their isolation—can shoot together as large totalities in which they
assert themselves—or if they simply renounce their individual character,
if they are manipulated as though they were without significance. In the
leveling and neutralization of its material, the aging of the New Music
becomes tangible: it is the arbitrariness of a radicalness for which nothing
is any longer at stake. Without stakes in a double sense: neither emotionally, because through the inhibition vis-à-vis such chords and the happiness in them their substance, their power of expression, their relation to
the subject has been lost; nor in actuality, for almost no one gets excited
anymore about that twelve-tone technique that is served up at all music
festivals. It is tolerated as the private activity of specialists, a cultural necessity in some not quite clear fashion, entrusted wholly to the experts;
no one is actually challenged, no one recognizes himself in it, or senses in
it any binding claim to truth. Twelve-tone technique cannot be conceived
without its antithesis, the explosive power of the musically individual,
which even today still lives in Webern's early works. Twelve-tone tech-

nique is the inexorable clamp that holds together what no less powerfully strives to break apart. If it is employed without being tested against such contrary forces, if it is employed where there is nothing counteracting it to be organized, then it is simply a waste of energy. Judgment is passed over innumerable contemporary twelve-tone compositions by the fact that in them relatively simple musical occurrences stand in a relatively simple musical interrelation, the establishment of which by no means demanded serial technique in the first place. Such technique becomes what in mathematics is called the convergence of an equation, a simple error.

Yet among the intransigent, who would as far as possible like to pursue consequentiality beyond Schoenberg, one meets a remarkable mixture of sectarianism and academicism. Among the major exponents of the New Music, including Schoenberg himself, it is not difficult to uncover traditional elements, particularly in its musical language, that is, in its expressive character and the inner construction of the music, in contrast to the entirely transformed musical material itself. This is crudely evident in Schoenberg's opera fragment *Moses und Aron,* which had its first concert performance a few years ago in Hamburg.[8] In matters of staging, text, expression, its broad gestures, it remains true to the traditional style of musical drama in spite of all its purely musical innovations. The same could be demonstrated with the greatest detail in Schoenberg's compositional techniques: thematic construction, exposition, transitions, continuation, fields of tension and release, etc., are all scarcely distinguishable from traditional, especially Brahmsian, techniques, even in his most daring works. It is hardly possible to conceive of composition of a high order other than as the most detailed meaningful articulation of the appropriate musical material. But the available materials, right up to the present, have all grown out of the soil of tonality. When they are transferred to nontonal material, certain inconsistencies result, a kind of break between musical subject-matter and the forming of the music. Schoenberg's musical sovereignty enabled him to master this break. But the antagonisms with which he saw himself confronted are not to be silenced. For all of those features to which he held fast with sublime naïveté—such as certain figures of the early tonal First Chamber Symphony that were maintained in the later twelve-tone Fourth Quartet[9]—cannot, with regard to their function, simply be transposed out of their original soil. The very concept of a transition, for example, presupposes various harmonic levels of modulation; stripped of its harmonic task it withers up all too easily into a formal reminiscence. Even the central category—the theme—is difficult to maintain when, as in twelve-tone technique, every tone is equally determined, equally thematic; in twelve-tone compositions themes persist largely as rudiments of an older period. On the other hand, it is only by means of these and related traditional categories that the coherence of the music, its sense, the authentic composition, in so far as it is more than mere arrangement, has been preserved in the midst of twelve-tone technique. Schoenberg's conservatism in this respect is not attributable to a lack of consistency, but to his fear that composition would otherwise be sacrificed to the prefabrication of the material. His most recent followers blithely short-circuit the antinomy that he rightly tried to deal with. They are intentionally indifferent to whether the music makes sense and is articulated—a consideration that caused Schoenberg's hesitations—and believe that the preparation of tones is already composition as soon as one has dismissed from composition everything by which it actually becomes a composition. They never get farther than abstract negation, and take off on an empty, high-spirited trip, through thinkably complex scores, in which nothing actually occurs; this seems to authorize them to write one score after another, without any constraints at all.

This development already set in with Schoenberg's pupil, Anton von Webern. His later works, which precisely in their skeletal simplicity are extremely difficult, attempt to overcome the contradiction by fusing the fugue and the sonata. These last works attempt to organize the musical-linguistic means so entirely in accordance with the new subject-matter, the twelve-tone rows, that he occasionally comes very close to renouncing the musical material altogether and reducing music to naked processes in the material, to the fate of the rows as such, though admittedly without ever completely sacrificing musical meaning entirely. Recently a group of composers have pursued this direction farther. At their head stands Pierre Boulez, student of Messiaen and Leibowitz, a highly cultured and exceptionally gifted musician, with the highest sense of form and with a power that is communicated even where he disavows subjectivity altogether.[10] He and his disciples aspire to dispose of every "compositional freedom" as pure caprice, along with every vestige of traditional musical idiom: in fact, every subjective impulse is in music at the same time an impulse of musical language. These composers have above all attempted to bring rhythm under the strict domination of twelve-tone procedure, and ultimately to replace composition altogether with an objective-calculatory ordering of intervals, pitches, long and short durations, degrees of loudness; an integral rationalization such as has never before been envisaged in music. The capriciousness of this legalism, however, the mere semblance of objectivity in a system that has simply been decreed, becomes apparent in the inap-

188 / Locating Music

propriateness of its rules to the structural interrelations of the music as it
develops, relations that rules cannot do away with. The merely thought
up is always also too little thought out. The basis of this serialism is a
static idea of music: the precise correspondences and equivalences that total
rationalization requires are founded on the presupposition that the identical element that recurs in music is indeed actually equivalent, as it would
be in a schematic spatial representation. The static pattern of notes is confused with the event that the notes signify. But as long as music takes place
entirely in time, it is dynamic in such a way that in the course of the music
the identical becomes non-identical just as the non-identical can become
the identical as, e.g., in an abbreviated reprise. What is referred to as the
architecture of great traditional music rests precisely on these effects, not
on musical relations defined by geometrical symmetry. The most powerful
effects of Beethoven's form depend on the recurrence of something, which
was once present simply as a theme, that reveals itself as a result and thus
acquires a completely transformed sense. Often the meaning of the preceding passage is only fully established by this later recurrence. The onset
of a reprise can engender a feeling of something extraordinary having
occurred earlier, even if the perceived event cannot in the slightest be
located at that specific point. The pointillist constructivists not only rob
themselves of these possibilities of authentic form, they fail to see that
against their own will temporal interrelations are established and give a
completely transformed local value to what on paper seems to be an identical repetition. The secure balance, which these composers have calculated
on the page, has not actually been achieved. Their overblown concern for
security destroys their security: because the balance of the musical elements works together only too well, from a static point of view, it is over-
turned by the immanent dynamics of the music. The balance gets lost in
the actual course of the music, the one thing of aesthetic importance here.

The loss of tension is not merely a symptom of aging, but can be traced
all the way back to the origins of New Music: what has today become
evident casts its shadow back over the heroic period. The expressionist
Schoenberg was allied with *Der Blaue Reiter;* songs by him, Webern, and
Berg were published there, and Kandinsky's manifesto, "On the Spiritual
in Art," also includes the impulse of atonality.[11] Music wanted finally to
do justice to the Kantian precept that nothing sensuous is sublime, and
the more the market debased music into a childish game, the more emphatically true music pressed toward maturity through spiritualization.
Music had to pay a price for this, which Valéry suspected was the case
with all new art. In New Music this price is its senescence. The emanci-

pation from pre-established forms and structures of musical material was predicated on a presupposition, common to expressionist painting insofar as the latter based the spiritualization of its technique on the idea that all colors as such, that the material elements of painting in themselves, have meaning. The totally new, many-layered sounds of the New Music were conceived of as bearers of expression. And this they were, but in a mediated way, not immediately. Their individual values depended partly on their relation to traditional sounds that they negated and through this negation preserved in memory, and partly on the position of the sounds in the structure of the compositions as a whole, which they at the same time contributed to changing. On account of their newness, however, the expressive qualities were at first attributed to isolated phenomena of the sounds themselves. This was the origin of a superstitious belief in intrinsically meaningful primitive elements, which in truth owe their existence to history, and whose meaning is itself historical. Even radically minded artists barely withstood such superstition, and easily slipped over into what was most antipathetic to them, namely arts and crafts: cold-blue sounds, an evil red, are not at all so different from the noble materials of batik veils carried in rhythmical gymnastics. Thoroughly arts and crafts concerns like those involving *Tonfarbenmusik*,[12] which became popular some thirty years ago, early on emphasized that side of expressionism: the modernistic side, as opposed to that of modernity. In fact, what is produced today under the headings of pointillistic music and integrally rationalized music is only too closely related to *Tonfarbenmusik* and the like: infatuation with the material along with blindness toward what is made out of it resulting from the fiction that the material speaks for itself, from an effectively primitive symbolism. To be sure, the material does speak but only in those constellations in which the artwork positions it; it was this capacity to organize the material and not the mere discovery of individual sounds that from the very start constituted Schoenberg's greatness. The inflated idea of the material, however, which clings tenaciously to life, misleads a composer into sacrificing the ability, insofar as he has it, to form constellations and encourages him to believe that the preparation of primitive musical materials is equivalent to music itself. Something purely irrational is hidden in the midst of rationalization, a confidence in the meaningfulness of abstract material, in which the subject fails to recognize that it, itself, releases the meaning from the material. The subject is blinded by the hope that those materials might lead it out of the exile of its own subjectivity. As long as New Music was alive, it mastered this illusion through the power of form; today it is losing that power, and it explains away its formal powerlessness as a triumph of cosmic substantiality. The situation, like that of restorative literature, borders closer on *art nouveau* than has been imagined.

At the same time, of course, the expansion of musical material has gone ahead limitlessly. The trust in the eloquence of the subject matter *[Stoff]* was always allied with a second form of trust: the trust that the discovery of intentionless layers, like new snow still unmarked by the imprint of the subject and the objectivation of the subject's traces in the form of conventionalizations of expression, would make pure immediacy possible. But if one leaves out of consideration the bichromatic subdivisions of the tonal system—which were never accurately absorbed by the hearing of even the most refined composers, subdivisions that sound like chromatics that have been further divided up and thus run counter to the effort of New Music to establish independent secondary degrees of the scale—then the possibilities of new sounds within the sphere of the twelve equally tempered halftones are virtually exhausted. It is not that all the sound combinations have already been used: ever since the emancipation from the system of triads their mathematical possibilities have been virtually unlimited. The issue here, however, is that of quality, not quantity. What is actually composed, and what is not composed, out of these combinations is already a matter of accident; the important fact is that the space has been staked out, and no additional sound would actually alter the musical landscape. Perhaps such alteration was only possible vis-à-vis still valid restrictions. When the mature Wagner added the minor fourth to the diminished-seventh chord,[13] and when Schoenberg in his *Verklärte Nacht* used the forbidden last inversion of the ninth chord, the potential of such chords unfolded into what Webern called a sea of never-heard sounds, a sea onto which *Erwartung* ventured. No sound today could so easily announce the claim of never before having been heard. If an insatiable composer were to go hunting for such a sound, he would fall victim to that powerlessness that always sets in as soon as musical material is no longer broadened by an inner compulsion but is instead ransacked in the interest of turning up new sensory stimulation. The arbitrariness of today's musical radicalism, the cheapness of being daring, is the direct result of the fact that the absolute boundary of the historical tone-space of Western music has evidently been reached; every conceivable particular tonal event is strikingly predictable and prefabricated while at the same time no strong impulse stirs to break out of the boundaries of this tone-space, nor is there any evidence of people having the ability spontaneously to hear outside of that tone-space. The efforts to achieve the total rationalization of music, however, are themselves dependent upon this boundary of listening—which is the boundary of the rationalization of music—in so far as these efforts continue to measure themselves by the idea of a space that is open and infinite and to be tamed, even though there is no longer any musical frontier. Thus the effort to rationalize music completely has something useless and frantic about it; it applies to a chaos that is no longer chaotic. It is time for a concentration of compositional energy in another direction; not toward the mere organization of material, but toward the composition of truly coherent music out of a material however shorn of every quality.

Something in the total rationalization of music seems to appeal strongly to young people. They find their own reflection in the new widespread allergy toward every kind of expression, an allergy that the iconoclastic exponents of "pointillist" music share with their conservative opponents, as with the historicist interpreters of Bach or the collectivist camp followers of the youth movement. Yet the implicit equation of expression with romanticism, or with *art nouveau,* is false, and the rejection of expression simply sounds avant-garde. It is not expression as such that must be exorcised from music, like an evil demon—otherwise nothing would be left except the designs of resounding forms in motion—rather the element of transfiguration, the ideological element of expression, has grown threadbare. This ideological element is to be recognized in what fails to become substantial in the musical form, what remains ornament and empty gesture. What is needed is for expression to win back the density of experience, as was already tried during the expressionist period, though without being satisfied with parading the cult of inhumanity under the guise of the cult of humanity. This touches on one of the decisive anthropological grounds for the aging of New Music: young people no longer trust in their youth. Anxiety and pain have grown to an extreme degree, and can no longer be controlled by the individual psyche. Repression becomes a necessity, and this repression, not the positiveness of some higher state of modesty and self-discipline, stands behind the idiosyncratic rejection of expression, which is itself one with suffering. Every impulse not already comprehended under collective schemata necessarily brings to mind what cannot be admitted to consciousness, and is therefore itself forbidden. Aesthetic objectivity, which flourishes on such unsteady ground, is the most extreme antagonist of the bindingness that aesthetic objectivity usurps. All the same, in the form of those works under discussion here, too much of the present state of consciousness and unconsciousness has been sedimented for these art works to be dismissed as irrelevant. But precisely the substance [*Gehalt*] of this consciousness is untruth. Many compositions of this kind give a suggestion of expression, as does any consistent work, no matter how absurd it may be. And absurdity is the direction of things. These compositions are musically meaningless in the rigorous sense of the word: their logic, construction, and inner nexus refuse any living, hearing actualization, the standard of every measure of music including that of Schoenberg. If the traditional concept of musical meaning was based on the resemblance of music to speech, and if in its explosions the revolutionary works of the New Music rebelled against meaning in order to shake off any resemblance to speech, and to actualize the usually slackly employed concept of absolute music, still the very explosions of New Music remain elements of a nexus of meaning. Even meaninglessness can become meaningful, as a contrast to and negation of meaning, just as in music the expressionless is a form of expression. But the newest musical efforts have nothing to do with this. In them meaninglessness becomes the program, though sometimes dressed up with Existentialism: in place of subjective intention, Being itself is supposed to be heard. But as a result of the abstract compositional procedures in which it originates, this music is anything but that of primal sources; it is subjectively and historically mediated to the extreme. But if this music is not the pure voice of Being, what then is the raison d'être of this purified music? Its schematic organization takes the place of the raison d'être, and the organization of material becomes a substitute for the renounced goal. As a result of the atomistic disposition of musical elements, the concept of musical coherence [*Zusammenhang*] is liquidated, a concept without which nothing like music really exists. The cult of rigid consistency terminates in idolatry; the material is no longer worked through and articulated in order to be amenable to artistic intention; instead the arrangement of the material becomes the sole artistic intention, the palette becomes the painting. Thus, in an ominously symbolic way, the rationalization of art tips over into chaos.

The belief that through the rationalization of its materials music enters a new scientific stage is naïve; it is one of those hypotheses by which artists undertake to justify, in an amateurishly intellectual way, what they have already begun to do. In the history of spirit [*Geist*], the relation between art and science is never slack, as if with progressive rationalization art would change into science and take part in its triumph. Art, and above all music, is the effort to preserve in memory and cultivate those split-off elements of truth that reality has handed over to the growing domination of nature, to scientific and technological standards that permit no exceptions. Art's effort has no place for any exalted terrain of the unconscious, no cozy little corners in the bright electrified world. Even as determinate negation, what art says is itself part of the world and subordinate to the law of enlightenment. The barbaric middle-class separation of feeling from understanding is only externalized when art is set up as a nature reserve for the eternally human and of comfortable immediacy, isolated from the process of enlightenment. The authentic artists of this age, Valéry above all, have not only obeyed the technologization of the artwork, but accelerated it; the whole development of modern music, since Richard Wagner, would be unthinkable without the determined absorption of technique in the broadest sense. But the result of this, as well as of the seemingly scientific methods such as impressionism and pointillism imported into painting, is not that art has been transformed into science or technology. The aim of the introduction of these technical elements is not the real domination of nature but the integral and transparent production of a nexus of meaning [Sinnzusammenhang]. When such transparency lets nothing glimmer through, when it is not a medium of artistic content [Gehalt] but an end in itself, it loses its raison d'être. Valéry himself forcefully emphasized this. The aesthetic rationality of the materials neither reaches their mathematical ideal nor dominates reality: it remains the mimesis of scientific procedures, a kind of reflex to the supremacy of science, one that casts into an even sharper light the difference of art from science the more that art shows itself to be powerless vis-à-vis the rational order of reality. Scientific art, art that would be nothing more than scientific, would be an arts and crafts analogue, no matter how rigorously it were organized. The necessity, indeed the justification, of musical construction is bound to what is to be constructed, to the composition, not to the mere fulfillment of self-posited mathematical norms, whose arbitrariness is only too easy to prove. The meaning of "technology" outside of the boundaries of the aesthetic sphere, of the sphere of play and semblance, is that of the performance of a real function: the reduction of labor. Since today as always the artwork lays claim to a sphere separate from that of practical cause-and-effect relationships, it can have nothing to do with technology in this sense, but must fulfill its own immanent order even where it participates in technique. If art forgets this, it becomes a poor third, aesthetically empty and objectively powerless, deluded hobby work. The vain hope of art, that in the disenchanted world it might save itself through pseudomorphosis into science, becomes art's nemesis. Its gesture corresponds to what is psychologically termed identification with the aggressor. The mannerisms of a machine shorn of any utility only accentuate its uselessness in the midst of universal utility, a uselessness from which art's bad conscience derives, as well as much that art credits to itself as a triumph over romanticism. The work of Edgard Varèse bears witness to the possibility of musically mastering the experience of a technologized world without resort to arts and crafts or to a blind faith in the scientization of art. Varèse, an engineer who in fact really knows something about technology, has imported technological elements into his compositions, not in order to make them some kind of childish science, but to make room for the expression of just those kinds of tension that the aged New Music forfeits. He uses technology for effects of panic that go far beyond run-of-the-mill musical resources.

Vain is the hope that through mathematical manipulations some pure musical thing-in-itself might come into being. One thinks that one is following the laws of nature, whereas the organizations of the material, however cosmically they gesture, are themselves already the product of human arrangements as are tempered tuning and the equality of the octave. Deluded, man sets up something artifactual as a primal phenomenon, and prays to it; an authentic instance of fetishism. This mentality has something infantile about it, for all its purity of intention. It is the passion of the empty, perhaps the gravest symptom of aging. Alienated and pre-established rules are blindly followed—as a good schoolboy might follow them—excluding any tension with subjectivity, without which there is as little art as truth. As certain as it is that New Music must bring the language of music and the material of music into full congruence, this congruence is not to be achieved by simply abrogating the language of music and abandoning the remains—shorn of every qualitative distinction—to their own devices, nor by simply spinning a web of schemata around this remainder instead of penetrating it. One is reminded of that popular etymology that translates "radical" as "radically empty." Artistic consistency, the fulfillment of the work's own obligation—without which aesthetic seriousness is inconceivable—is not there for its own sake, but in order to present what was once called the artistic idea, and what in music might be better called the composed. In music, however, that is all construction, nothing at all is composed any more. Music regresses to the pre-musical, the pre-artistic tone. Many of its adepts logically pursue *musique concrète*[14] or the electronic production of tones. But to date, electronic music has failed to fulfill its own idea; even though it theoretically disposes over the continuum of all imaginable sound colors, in actual practice—similar to the musical tin-can taste familiar from the radio, only much more extreme than that—these newly won sound colors resemble one another monotonously, whether because of their virtually chemical purity, or because every tone is stamped by the interposition of the equipment.

It sounds as though Webern were being played on a Wurlitzer organ. The compulsion toward leveling and quantification seems in electronic music to be stronger than the goal of qualitative freedom and release. Of course it is quite possible that the narrowness and limitation of technological development in contemporary society bears more responsibility than does technology itself for the present state of affairs.

There is no need to fear the objection that this criticism of the situation of music is a throwback to Schoenberg, and is unable to get beyond him, Berg, and Webern, and that it will ultimately serve reactionary forces. Even within the sphere of New Music the articulation of critical thought is often sabotaged by the remark that such ideas might benefit the opposition. This argument secretly resembles the thought control exercised in totalitarian states. The real danger is not insights that opponents can make use of, but rather mindless apologetics that strengthen the dubious and thereby actually admit that the opposition is right. The formulaic reproach of a desired return to the twenties, after the inconvenient interruption of the Third Reich, is unquestionably grotesque. Besides one could only speak of a return if in the meantime there had been some progress. This going forward, however, was itself essentially a going backward, and musically Schoenberg's generation bequeathed innumerable tasks that remain unfulfilled. On the other hand the geological shifts that have taken place since then are such that nobody could step outside of them, no matter how earnestly he wanted to devote himself to a time that already appeared riddled with crises and yet was a paradise compared to what was to come. The reproach that the critics have not understood the most recent compositions of unchecked rationalization can hardly be maintained because such musical reasoning wants only to be demonstrated mathematically, not understood. If one asks after the function of some phenomenon within a work's total context of meaning [Sinnzusammenhang], the answer is a further exposition of the system. It would indeed be small comfort to imagine that, as happened in the seventeenth century, meaning might someday be imposed by future composers on new musical means, waiting to be conquered. It will hardly make sense today, the fusion of material and work having already been achieved, that artistic means could first be mechanically invented then later find their proper employment, anymore than this possibility could be ruled out a priori. Such an idea would eternalize the separation of musical language from musical materials, if not indeed from the musical subject-matter and the aesthetic aim toward which the rectification of New Music labored so hard. Musical material never comes to life independently of the substance [Gehalt] of the art work:

except barbarically. In music, the concepts of progress and reaction should no longer be applied automatically solely to the material, which has obviously long enough been the bearer of the progress of musical meaning itself. The concept of progress loses its justification when composition turns into a mere hobby: when the subject, whose freedom is the precondition of all advanced art, is driven out; when a violent and external totality, hardly different from political totalitarianism, acquires the reins of power. The combination of technical-specialist stubbornness, which outlaws the need for expression, with a state of mind that in fact no longer even knows this need mirrors, at best passively, the fatality of the age, which this music wants to resist. It does not call this age by its name. The best this music is capable of are pieces that spring from a sometimes highly developed knowledge of what today constitutes technical necessity. In these works every measure bears witness to the concern of how music must appear if it is to be invulnerable to all imaginable objections. These are school pieces, paradigms. They measure themselves against an invisible canon of the permitted and the forbidden, and that alert control, which this canon certainly demands, is all that remains of composition. This music sounds as though its only origin were the fear of composing a wrong note that a schoolmate might stumble on and criticize. Musical logic becomes a caricature of logic, one that is certainly implicit in it from the start, in the rigid interdiction of anything that the system finds foreign, the latter being left to atrophy. Already in the first measure the listener senses with resignation that he has been turned over to an infernal machine, which will run its course mercilessly, until fate has completed its cycle and he can breathe again.

To be sure most of the younger twelve-tone composers are less demanding. Unfamiliar with the real accomplishments of the Schoenberg School and in possession only of the rules of twelve-tone composition, which have become apocryphal through separation from its accomplishments, these young people amuse themselves with the juggling of tone rows as a substitute for tonality, without really composing at all. This touches on a genuinely paradoxical situation: the disappearance of tradition within New Music itself. The innovators, Schoenberg, Bartók, Stravinsky, Webern, Berg, even Hindemith, were all raised on traditional music. Their idiom, their critical stance, their resistance, all crystallized around that tradition. This tradition is no longer a living part of their successors. In its place they turn what is in itself a critical musical ideal into an artificially positive one, without summoning up the spontaneity and effort that it requires. This failing can hardly be cast as a reproach. The training of

composers, especially in conservatories and advanced schools of music, has
remained frozen at the level of traditional tonality, and scarcely offers the
student any serious technical standards by which to judge New Music.
Therefore, in their search for authority, students rely on favorite and impressive models of the New Music, without being able to judge, in their
own works whether they are doing justice to the inner demands of those
models or whether they are simply imitating them externally and depending on means that once proved effective and that for this very reason
are no longer effective. While many so-called professional musicians have
not kept up, and cannot pass on what has remained foreign to them, the
older tradition, tonal music, is so ragged that it only inadequately reaches
today's young musicians. There is reason to suspect that those who have
not mastered the new material are also unable to control the older, that
they cannot compose an irreproachable, four-voice Palestrina setting, and
in many cases can hardly harmonize out a chorale. The pedagogical virtues
of the academy have been lost without the realm of freedom having been
entered.

Even music criticism hardly helps. Critics and composers only rarely
meet on the same level. Most critics are even less able than the averagely
educated musician to judge a demanding new score according to its inner
coherence, its level of form, its individual power. Instead they fulfill their
service with substitutes such as reports about their chance pleasure or
displeasure in the music, or provide journalistic information. The critic
more or less routinely brings forth everything possible about the impression a work makes, its history, style, and author without carrying out what
the name of his profession demands: critique, making a judgment, debatable though that judgment might be. Many derive their criteria from the
limits of their own understanding and denounce everything opaque to
them as intellectual and abstract, music for the drawing board, not for the
ear. Others, whose education is more historical than practical, draw their
standards from this history and content themselves with reminiscences,
or with clichés drawn from folk or youth movements, embracing the norm
of community for community's sake in spite of the fact that contemporary
society militates against collectively confirmed music. Recently, many critics have overcompensated for their lack of musical comprehension: in order
not to miss the birth of a new genius, they indiscriminately praise everything that could perhaps be important. This only contributes to the general
disorientation and helps produce a culture of musical mish-mash. The de-
testable ideal of a moderate modernism gains currency, fostering on both
sides problematic compromise-solutions between tradition and the new.

The new musical material, emptied of its sense, is transformed into deadening stimuli by its endless repetition. Scarcely felt is the obligation of achieving that uniqueness of the work, that unrepeatableness enjoined on musical composition by the emancipation of music from all pre-established form. Most composers, who do not swear by exactitude, are content to produce further examples of various types of compositions established by composers such as Bartók, Stravinsky, and Hindemith, without recognizing that these types do not define a space inside of which one can move with pre-established assurance, and that what matters is exclusively the production of new types, or rather new characters. On the other hand this disorganization of the new musical means has disorganized the traditional ones. A virtue has been made out of this disorganization in the form of a sort of all-purpose musical language, in which quasi-literary effects, in particular a thoroughly baseless and cheap irony, claim first place. Pseudo-intellectuality and cultural-political knowledgeability replace genuine artistic realization. Music that strikes up the pose of a tradition that is no longer substantive, and even technically no longer present, has no advantage over the techniques of the tone-row engineers. Such music is simply making things a little more comfortable for itself and its followers.

All of these inner aesthetic tendencies accord precisely with those of society as a whole, although the mediation between the two realms is not at every point transparent. Society not only influences artists externally, not only supervises them—although there is enough of that—it also brings forth the individuals and forms of objective spirit [Geist] that are the artist's own essence.[15] As if objectivity were the result of a kind of subtraction, the exclusion of an ornament, and were nothing other than a residue, it is supposed that through an absence of subjectivity one would be empowered with an objectively binding force, the destruction of which is blamed on the preponderance of a subjectiveness that in fact no longer exists. Yet all aesthetic objectivity is mediated by the power of the subject, which brings an object [Sache] entirely to itself. Objectivism, which is so vain about its lack of vanity, and so facilely considers itself morally superior, self-righteously puts a premium on the deficiencies of its exponents. It thrives on the tempting ideology that one need only capitulate to the overpowering, senseless force of existence, in order to share in an authenticated cosmos. But the overcoming of a non-existent self is an all too comfortable course, as is evident in what today's alleged asceticism is bringing to maturity. The symptoms of the aging of the New Music are in social terms those of the contraction of freedom, the collapse of individuality that helpless and disintegrated individuals confirm, approve, and do once again to themselves. In this there is a fatal resemblance between the radicals—who turn themselves over to what they mistakenly consider the inner law of the material, and who enthusiastically subtract themselves from the picture—and those who have crawled away into the ruins of a bygone tradition, or who trump up a supra-individually sanctioned aesthetic realm that in fact merely corresponds to the ideal of weakened and anxious individuals. Nobody really takes a chance any more; all are looking for shelter. The brutal measures taken by the totalitarian states, measures that over-control music and attack all deviation as decadent and subversive, give tangible evidence of what happens less visibly in non-totalitarian countries, of what transpires, indeed, in the interior of art as well as within most human beings. In the face of such profound damage, nothing would be more foolish than to moralize. The primitive fact of the matter cannot be kept silent, that today the alienation between music and the public has so rebounded against music that the material existence of serious musicians is seriously threatened. They are compelled to produce compromised compositions that, given the inescapable necessity of the very same alienation, must themselves turn out powerless and false. The daily existence of Webern and Berg was precarious even in their own time. They only got by thanks to the economic backwardness of their homeland, which in many ways was still pre-capitalist and offered loopholes for activities that had no exchange-value. Berg passed the last years of his life in material need, after the possibility of performances in Germany had been cut off. Anyone unwilling to volatilize comfortably the aging of the New Music as a chapter in cultural history must think it together with the real suffering of men, not the least of whose terror—as Theodor Haecker[16] put it—is that they are no longer even permitted to articulate their condition. Today, artists like Berg or Webern would hardly be able to make it through the winter. If there were such artists, they would either have to play along and in some way or other learn to toe the line, or at least become the leader of a deluded group of disciples and thus in protest against collectivization become the hostages to a second and scarcely less dubious collectivization.

The current paralysis of musical forces represents the paralysis of all free initiative in this over-managed world, which will not tolerate anything that would remain outside of it or at least not be integrated as an element of opposition. All this must be brought unsparingly to consciousness, for the sake of the possibility of something better. Whether it will do any good is highly questionable; for the foundation of music, as of every art, the very possibility of taking the aesthetic seriously has been deeply shaken. Since the European catastrophe, culture hangs on like houses in the cities accidentally spared by bombs or indifferently patched together. Nobody really believes in "culture" any more, the backbone of spirit *[Geist]* has been broken, and anyone who pays no attention to this and acts as though nothing had happened, must crawl like an insect, not walk upright. The only authentic artworks produced today are those that in their inner organization measure themselves by the fullest experience of horror, and there is scarcely anyone, except Schoenberg or Picasso, who can depend on himself to have the power to do this. Even so, the earnestness that would rather renounce art than put it in the service of a debased contemporary reality may itself be only a disguised form of adaptation to an already universal attitude of a praxis: submission to a praxis that aspires to the given without in any way going beyond it. Though today all art has and must have a bad conscience to the extent that it does not make itself stupid, nevertheless its abolishment would be false in a world in which what dominates needs art as its corrective: the contradiction between what is and the true, between the management of life and humanity. The possibility of winning back the power of artistic resistance depends on not shrinking from the fact that what is objectively, socially required is now preserved exclusively in hopeless isolation. Only one who was prepared to work in isolation, to support himself by no delusive laws and necessities, would perhaps be granted something more than mirroring the helplessly solitary.

(1955; GS, vol. 14, pp. 143–67)

Translated by Robert Hullot-Kentor and Frederic Will

NOTES BY ROBERT HULLOT-KENTOR AND FREDERIC WILL; ADDITIONAL NOTES BY RICHARD LEPPERT [RL]

1. A peculiar, abbreviated and completely confabulated paraphrase of Adorno's essay, translated from the French, was published in *The Score* in December 1956. An essay by Heinz-Klaus Metzger, "Just Who Is Gowing Old?" *Die Reihe 4: Young Composers* (Bryn Mawr, PA: Theodore Presser, 1960), pp. 63–80, incorporated several newly translated passages of Adorno's essay. This latter translation has been usefully consulted on several occasions.

2. In 1912 and 1913, respectively.

3. Adorno is apparently referring to an essay "Die stabilisierte Musik," which he wrote in 1927. In this essay, a review of a Frankfurt music festival of that year, he writes that "Music has come into harmony with the world *[stabilisert sich mit der Welt]*; should anyone be surprised that the music has gotten worse?" GS, vol. 19, p. 101. What is strange about this reference is that this essay was only published posthumously. Adorno, however, wrote a great number of articles in these early years and did not always keep clearly in mind what of his work had been published and what had not. Many essays were only published posthumously.

4. Adorno is referring to difficulties in the relation of counterpoint and harmony. See his "Die Funktion der Kontrapunkt in der neuen Musik," GS, vol. 16, pp. 155–62, for a discussion of the relation of Schoenberg and Bach.

5. Karl Kraus wrote his sprawling satiric tragedy on World War I, *The Last Days of Mankind*, during the war, completing the text in 1922. The play consists of a prologue and five acts, with approximately 500 characters both fictional and real—among the latter are two Austrian emperors, the last German kaiser, and Hindenburg. The play, nearly 800 pages long, takes place across Europe, in cities (Vienna, Berlin), on a mountain top, and even underwater on a U-boat. Cesare Battisti (1875–1916) was an Austrian journalist; he founded the journal *Il Popolo* in which he attacked the Austrian dictatorship. He joined anti-Austrian forces during the war and was wounded, captured, and hanged as a traitor by the Austrians. [rl]

6. Mazeppa, the Ukrainian cossack, whose insurrection and death is the material of Liszt's symphonic poem (1854) of the same name.

7. It was composed in 1909; in 1930 it was transcribed for string orchestra.

8. Only the first two of the three acts of this opera are complete (1930–32), and they were first presented in 1954.

9. In 1906 and 1937, respectively.

10. René Leibowitz (1913–1972) studied with Schoenberg, Webern, and Ravel in the early 1930s. He conducted new works by members of the Second Viennese School. Boulez studied with him immediately after the Second World War. [rl]

11. The friendship between Schoenberg and Kandinsky is well documented, in particular by their exchange of letters written between 1911 and 1914 during a critical time in the development of both men's work. See *Arnold Schoenberg, Wassily Kandinsky: Letters, Pictures and Documents*, ed. Jelena Hahl-Koch, trans. John C. Crawford (London: Faber and Faber, 1984); the letters in this volume were written between 1911 and 1936. Kandinsky's *Über das Geistige in der Kunst*, a pamphlet-manifesto theory of art, and Schoenberg's *Harmonielehre* are contemporanous (1911–12). Paintings by Schoenberg were included in the first group exhibition of *Der Blaue Reiter* organized by Kandinsky and Franz Marc in Munich, 1911–12. Kandinsky's tract is available in English as *Concerning the Spiritual in Art* (New York: George Wittenborn, 1947), a re-translation by Francis Golffing of the 1914 translation by Michael Sadleir authorized by Kandinsky. Kandinsky references music—Wagner, Debussy, Mussorgsky, Scriabin, and, in particular, Schoenberg (citing the *Harmonielehre*): "Schönberg is endeavoring to make complete use of his freedom and has already discovered mines of new beauty in his search for spiritual structure. His music leads us to where musical experience is a matter not of the ear, but of the soul—and from this point begins the music of the future" (p. 36). [rl]

12. "*Tonfarbenmusik*" [tone-color music] develops correspondances between sounds and colors, which was an important movement in the first part of the twentieth century. Schoenberg's *Die glückliche Hand* (1910–1913), for example, prescribes colors to be projected onto a screen onstage during a performance. See also p. 122.

13. The *Tristan* chord.

14. This is Pierre Schaeffer's term for the music he created in his famous laboratory, beginning in 1948. "*Musique concrète*," in opposition to "abstract music," music represented on paper, was constructed from recorded sounds (for example, train and sea noises).

15. "*Wesen oder Unwesen.*" This phrase cannot be properly translated, though "order or disorder" does catch one corner of the thought within the bounds of its rhetoric.

16. Theodor Haecker (1879–1945) was a philosopher, journalist, and translator, and a Catholic convert. He was forbidden to speak publicly by the Nazis in 1935 and also forbidden to publish. For an account of his life and work, see the [unattributed] introduction to Haecker's book of 717 aphorisms written between 1939 and 1945, *Journal in the Night*, trans. Alexander Dru (London: Harvill, 1950), pp. xi–xlvi. *Journal in the Night* makes repeated reference to Christian ethics, often in the context of a critique of Nazism and its self-presentation to the German people through mass-media propaganda efforts. [rl]

The Dialectical Composer

The resistance to Schoenberg has its most evident reason in the fact that every work from his hand, and certainly every phase in the history of his music, confronted us with new enigmas that could not be mastered with knowledge of what went before, or even of his own most recent production. Here, it was the overwhelming nature of the apparatus that was shocking; there, its minimal quality that gave cause for alarm. Here, it was the wealth of harmonic relations, apparently impossible for the ear to follow; there, the unbridgeable gulf between self-empowered, baldly signifying sounds. Here, the bottomless riches of the counterpoint caused confusion; there, a threatening simplicity demolished the decorative harmonic polyphony of late romanticism. Here, it was the explosive character of the expression, which in the visions of fear, in *Erwartung* and *Die glückliche Hand*, broke through all beautiful appearance with immediate truth; there, the metallic remoteness of the twelve-tone pieces, which largely resisted human expression and thus frightened off all merely human empathy. That what was playing between the extremes in this way remained difficult was not a consequence of the technical innovations. Before long, these were picked up by others, imitated, and cleverly made over into harmless counterfeits, so that even in their original, alienating form they might ultimately be revealed as meaningful. What is difficult, rather, is the movement between the extremes itself. For just as it fails to provide a safe center for enjoyment, it also radically refuses to submit to the categories with which intellectual history, no matter how progressive it would like to seem, inevitably and in a banal way seeks to create unity in the variety of an artist's work—the categories of development and the organic. Although each work by Schoenberg follows the previous one in a compulsory way, they by no means grow out of each other. They emerge from each other not in small-

est intervals, but in reversal—it is no accident that he titled a truly prototypical orchestral piece "Peripetie."[1] Never, in Schoenberg, does a bud
unfold into a blossom. Models—often vocal compositions—are constructed, and then, following them, the great instrumental pieces are completed. But the questions that their material leaves behind, as it emerges
from composition, are hardly ever answered in calm progression, but instead with catastrophes. The answer destroys the question and the material
from which it emerged; it sets truly new music. Not the unaccustomed
sounds, no, it is the rhythm of the extremes, the air of catastrophe that
has inspired the fear of Schoenberg. This rhythm does not merely dominate the history of Schoenberg's oeuvre in the abstract. It inhabits almost
every one of his pieces, down to the most hidden compositional cells. The
Lieder op. 6 already do not spin out a motif, Wolfishly,[2] developing sequences and mediating. They are constructed, down to their smallest details, out of contrasts, which only become an integrated form by virtue of
the force of the extreme—at which point, admittedly (and this is Schoenberg's secret), they prove to be profoundly identical. The couple of introductory bars for piano of "Lockung" could be considered, today, in light
of Schoenberg's entire oeuvre, as a monad that abruptly, somewhere between an outbreak and a rigid halt, presents the whole—Schoenberg's
style, and also the movement that he makes in it from one work to the
next.

The determined enemies who understood this sooner and better than
those friends who hastened to give him a place in the history of musical
development, in the process made the astonishing discovery of the relationship of the early works to Wagner, and later hoped to jettison him as
an outmoded way station in a historical process whose world spirit is embodied in [Fritz] Jöde.[3] With this, it is true, they lost sight of Schoenberg's
specific essence, on the field they surveyed so commandingly. Along with
Schoenberg's specific character, they also relinquished the historical element that broke through with him. Old Riemann, with his hate-filled
formula about the "addiction to achieving the unheard-of," actually came
closer there.[4] His hatred at least reflects something of the thoroughgoing
change in musical consciousness which Schoenberg brought about and
which the others, in their version of music history, deny in order to escape
it. If Riemann actually meant to explain away his shock, psychologically,
with the "addiction to achieving the unheard-of," he precisely failed to hit
the mark with Schoenberg. In Schoenberg we are not dealing with arbitrary behavior or the preferences of a subjective, unfettered artist, the way

people once tried to label him as an "Expressionist," for example; nor, equally, are we dealing with the work of a blind craftsman who follows after his material with a calculator, no longer intervening in it spontaneously. Instead, what truly characterizes Schoenberg, and what must be seen as the source of his stylistic history and his techniques, as well as of all potentially serious insight, is a very exemplary change, both in principle and historically, in the way the composer behaves toward his material. He no longer acts like its creator, nor does he obey its ready-made rules. "The greatest strictness is also the greatest freedom"—this saying by [Stefan] George, the poet, who was touched to the quick by Schoenberg's music, in the most creative contradiction, serves as the motto of his works and took on a meaning that places George far away from the Classicist aesthetic from which he may have emerged.[5] It becomes the program of this new type of behavior by the composer, which today has already changed music, and tomorrow may bring about a change in its relation to society.

This meaning, however, may be called dialectical. In Schoenberg, the contradiction between strictness and freedom is no longer transcended in the miracle of form. It becomes a force of production; the work does not turn the contradiction toward harmony, but conjures up its image, again and again, looking for duration in its cruelly ravaged traits. "Patchwork, like everything else," the Master wrote in a dedication copy of his choral works. For it is—to use another of his formulations—no contradiction in "mentality," in mere subjectivity that vacillated there between form and expression, until, through its subjective mediation, it would bring them to reconciliation. It is a contradiction for cognition [*Erkenntnis*], the cognition that he, wiser than any composer before him, set down as a corrective to mentality; a contradiction not inside the artist, but between the power in him and what he found before him; or, if I may express it in philosophical terms, a contradiction between subject and object. Subject and object— compositional intention and compositional material—do not, in this case, indicate two rigidly separate modes of being, between which there is something that must be resolved. Rather, they engender each other reciprocally, the same way they themselves were engendered—historically. The author approaches the work the way Oedipus approached the Sphinx, as a person who must solve riddles. Where is this harmony heading, he asks, and feels his way into the "emotional life of sound." What is decoration, and what is in the nature of the thing itself? He removes ornaments and symmetries that, for this harmony and this counterpoint, were becoming separated from the thing itself. How is it possible to do away with the rupture between exposition and variational development, which has become senseless following the disintegration of the sonata's tonal unity? How, in the harmonic-melodic structure, can one do away with the greater stress on one tone than another, which since emancipation has become false? How can one do away with the divergence of the horizontal and vertical elements?— And he develops, as a brief, precise answer, the twelve-tone technique. Indeed, it might often seem as if the old "creativity" of the artist has become entirely concentrated in those answers, in tiny strokes that are inserted to fulfill the immanent demands of the material. But the productive power of these answers is revealed in the fact that in their light the question itself disintegrates and disappears. The de-riddled Sphinx falls into the abyss of the has-been. The Chamber Symphony—in contrast to Reger,[6] for example—had constructed out tonality with the greatest firmness, instead of softening it up. But the means with which this occurred, adjacent tonalities, fourths, and whole-tone rows that hold the final E major together like brackets, have such power that they do not remain collected, as a result, but become free; hence, following this E major, there is no more chromaticism and dominance-tonality,[7] but the tonality-free harmonic world. In the works for the stage, expression sweeps the last external symmetry away; but the untrammeled sound that it unleashes offers itself up for construction, already in *Pierrot*. And retrospectively, then, again and again, the analytical eye can locate the answer that has been won, in the form of the question itself.

Conversely, the "material" that he casts off, by obeying it, is no static and unvarying natural material. Already before the war, in his harmonic theory, Schoenberg responded with unerring sureness to Debussy's "back to nature," which believed in the primacy of simple overtone relations, with the formula "forward to nature"—a nature that is essentially historical, whose archaic "In-itself" is distorted and unable to assert its right other than in the claims it makes on the composer as compositional material, but hence precisely as historical. The questions and anomalies against which he has to measure himself are, in their totality, nothing but the marks of that very historical process, as whose executor he encounters it. If, in relation to compositional subjectivity, they are thought to possess any objective character at all, this is because, unconsciously and often secretly enough, they bear within themselves the social authority that the composer must engage as his inescapable task, precisely in those realms of strictness and freedom where a superficial gaze least suspects it. One day, it will be one of the most important tasks of a conscientious interpretation of Schoenberg to point out—against all the ridiculous phrases about the lonely *artiste*, constructor, and intellectual—the real social significance that every compositional mark by his hand imposes more truly than the sociological musics that, in order to serve contemporary society, call up the ghosts of predecessors and thereby forget the future reality.

One could object that the dialectical relationship between artist and material has been in force, in truth, ever since the material of art achieved thing-like autonomy in relation to human beings. That remains undisputed. But what is entirely new is that in Schoenberg this dialectic has achieved its Hegelian "self-consciousness," or, better, its measurable and exact showplace: musical technology. In the light of the knowledge that his music brings about, it is possible to make judgments of right and wrong about the reciprocal production of subject and object. No impulse of the imagination, no claim of the given that does not have its decidable technical correlate. But as subject and object confront each other within the sphere of technical consistency *[Stimmigkeit]*, and are subjected to control precisely in their mutual dependence, their dialectic, as it were, has freed itself from its blind state of nature and become practicable—the greatest strictness, namely the unbroken one of technique, ultimately really does stand revealed as the greatest freedom, namely that of the human being over his music, which once began mythically, softened into reconciliation, confronted him as form, and finally belongs to him by virtue of a behavior that takes possession of it by wholly belonging to it. After Schoenberg, the history of music will no longer be fate, but will be subject to human consciousness. Not to a mathematical, extrinsic play of numbers, as those people claim who would like to backdate the twelve-tone technique to that of the Pythagorean era, without hearing that each of the computational rules of the former owes its existence solely to the technological requirements of a wakeful ear and an exact imagination, but rather to a consciousness that changes itself along with reality, on which it knows itself to be dependent, and in which it still intervenes. This consciousness struggled free of the abyss of the subconscious, of dream and desire, fed itself on its material like a flame, until the light of a true day transformed all the contours of music. This is its greatest success between the extremes, no longer play, but truth itself. This success places the name of Schoenberg, the greatest living musician, in the landscape of the one who first found the conscious sound for the dream of freedom: Beethoven.

(1934; GS, vol. 17, pp. 198–203)
Translated by Susan H. Gillespie

NOTES BY RICHARD LEPPERT

1. *The American Heritage Dictionary of the English Language*, s.v. "Peripe-
teia": "an abrupt or unexpected change in the course of events or situation, especially in a literary work." Adorno's reference is to the fourth piece of Five Orchestral Pieces op. 16 (1909). In a diary entry from 27 January 1912, Schoenberg comments that Peters, his publisher, wants titles for each of the pieces "for publisher's reasons." He is reluctant to provide them since he "said" what he
wanted with the music itself: "If words were necessary they would be there in
the first place. But art says more than words." So he provides words to satisfy
the publisher but chooses ones that "give nothing away." After listing "Peripetie
[sic]" he adds in parentheses, "general enough, I think." Quoted from John Ru-
fer, *The Works of Arnold Schoenberg: A Catalogue of His Compositions, Writings and Paintings*, trans. Dika Newlin (New York: Free Press of Glencoe, 1963),
p. 34.

2. That is, as does the late-romantic Austrian lieder composer Hugo Wolf
(1860–1903).

3. Fritz Jöde (1887–1970), influential German music educator and avid pro-
moter of folk music and folk dance. He published books on music education and
collections of German folk songs.

4. Hugo Riemann (1849–1919), German musicologist. In his famous *Musik-
Lexikon*, ed. Alfred Einstein, 10th ed. (Berlin: Max Hesse, 1922), p. 1157, Riemann
praises the composer's early works—specifically, the *Gurrelieder* and the First
String Quartet—for what he calls their expressive power in the *Tristan* tradition;
the First Chamber Symphony is likewise lauded. But thereafter Riemann somewhat cautiously suggests that Schoenberg has gone overboard as the moderns'
modern—pushing expression further and further, in essence to the point of its
being unchecked *[Unkontrollierbarkeit]*, while nonetheless acknowledging the
composer's integrity. The 8th edition (1916) includes Schoenberg's biography for
the first time; here Riemann openly criticizes the *Harmonielehre*—music theory
was, of course, an arena where Riemann had built much of his substantial career.
Schoenberg, no surprise, later returned the criticism in kind; see William Thomson,
Schoenberg's Error (Philadelphia: University of Pennsylvania Press, 1991), p. 52
n. 1.

5. Adorno greatly admired the German poet Stefan George (1868–1933) while
recognizing regressive elements in both his work and its reception. (See Adorno,
"Stefan George," NL, pp. 178–92.) Though George wrote almost exclusively lyrical
poetry, his work is distinguished by its structural discipline, which Adorno recognized as well in Schoenberg. Adorno saw in both artists' work an intense expressiveness, coupled with a high degree of structural integrity. In 1908–09,
Schoenberg set to music (op. 15) fifteen of the thirty-one poems in George's 1895
collection *Buch der Hängenden Gärten*. Schoenberg also used George texts for the
third and fourth (vocal) movements of his String Quartet op. 10 (1907–08). The
passage, which Adorno slightly misquotes, apparently writing from memory, appears in Stefan George *Tage und Taten: Aufzeichnungen und Skizzen*, in *Sämtliche
Werke* (Stuttgart: Klett-Cotta, 1982–98), vol. 17, p. 69, the seventh of ten aphorisms, titled "Über Dichtung": "Strengstes maass ist zugleich höchste freiheit,"
which Adorno gives as: "Höchste Strenge ist zugleich höchste Freiheit" (GS, vol.
17, p. 200).

6. See p. 323 n. 4.

7. Adorno's invention of the term *Dominanz-Tonalität* neatly sums up his critique of the domination of compositional practice by traditional key structures, and the principal feature of those key structures, namely, their reliance on the chords known "tellingly" as tonic and dominant. [translator's note]

2

CULTURE, TECHNOLOGY,

AND LISTENING

Commentary
Richard Leppert

The bourgeois want art voluptuous and life ascetic; the reverse
would be better.

Adorno, Aesthetic Theory

Adorno arrived in New York in February 1938, having accepted a half-
time appointment, arranged by his friend Max Horkheimer, to work on
the Princeton (University) Radio Research Project, funded by the Rockefeller Foundation. Paul Lazarsfeld,[1] head of research, employed Adorno.
(Actual work took place at Lazarsfeld's own small research institute in
Newark, New Jersey, located in a former brewery building.) Adorno
headed the radio music programming division (the other divisions focused
on book reading, news, and politics); music received particular attention

---

1. Although the Project was originally awarded to Princeton University in
1937, it was transferred to Columbia University in 1939. Concerning Lazarsfeld
and his career in communications research, see Anthony Heilbut, *Exiled in Paradise: German Refugee Artists and Intellectuals in America from the 1930s to the
Present* (Berkeley and Los Angeles: University of California Press, 1983, and with
a new postscript, 1997), pp. 95–100. See also Lazarsfeld's own account of his Princeton Radio Project work: Paul F. Lazarsfeld, "An Episode in the History of Social
Research: A Memoir," in *The Intellectual Migration: Europe and America, 1930–
1960,* ed. Donald Fleming and Bernard Bailyn (Cambridge: Belknap Press of Harvard University Press, 1969), esp. pp. 304–34; concerning Adorno, see pp. 322–25.
David E. Morrison, "Kultur and Culture: The Case of Theodor W. Adorno and
Paul F. Lazarsfeld," *Social Research* 45 no. 2 (Summer 1978), pp. 331–55, provides
a detailed account of the Radio Project and the Lazarsfeld-Adorno collaboration,
principally based on information found in Lazarsfeld's personal papers archived at
Columbia University and personal interviews with Lazarsfeld and others involved
in the Project (Adorno had died by the time the study was researched). See also
by David E. Morrison, "The Beginning of Modern Mass Communication Research," *Archives Européennes de Sociologie* 19 no. 2 (1978), pp. 347–59, an
account of Lazarsfeld's early work in America, with passing reference to
Adorno. Rolf Wiggershaus, *The Frankfurt School: Its History, Theories, and
Political Significance,* trans. Michael Robertson (Cambridge: MIT Press, 1995),
pp. 236–46, provides a good account of the working relationship between Adorno
and Lazarsfeld.

during the Project's early phase. Adorno's involvement in the Project lasted until late 1939 or 1940,[2] when funding was cut off for the music research, in no small part because of dissatisfaction with Adorno's unremitting critique of the Project's empirical methods. As the result of his involvement in the Radio Project, Adorno produced four essays, only one of which, "The Radio Symphony," was published as part of the Project's official proceedings, in a volume called *Radio Research 1941* (1941), co-edited by Lazarsfeld and Frank N. Stanton.[3]

Adorno arrived in the United States already keenly sensitive to the social and cultural power of modern communications media, radio especially, having witnessed close at hand the uses to which they were put in Germany.[4] In America, radio, though still relatively new, was already well established and of considerable concern as a shaping influence on national consciousness. U.S. commercial broadcasting had begun in 1920, and by

2. Lazarsfeld, "Episode in the History of Social Research," p. 324, indicates that "the renewal of the Rockefeller grant in the fall of 1939 provided no budget for continuation of the music project." Adorno, "Scientific Experiences of a European Scholar in America," trans. Donald Fleming, in *The Intellectual Migration: Europe and America, 1930–1960*, ed. Donald Fleming and Bernard Bailyn (Cambridge: Belknap Press of Harvard University Press, 1969), states the dates in two different ways: on p. 351, he indicates that his involvement lasted from 1938 to 1940; on p. 355 he remarks: "In 1941 my work at the Princeton Radio Project . . . came to an end." On 29 February, 1940, Adorno wrote to Benjamin that he was "finally free" of the Radio Project (CC, p. 322). Finally, Morrison, "Kultur and Culture," p. 351, quotes from letters written by Lazarsfeld in June 1941 indicating his final unsuccessful attempts to convince the Rockefeller Foundation to continue funding for Adorno and the music part of the Radio Project.

3. The other essays written by Adorno during his involvement in the Princeton Radio Project are: "On Popular Music," which first appeared in *Studies in Philosophy and Social Science* 9 (1941), pp. 17–48, the final issue, in English, of the Institute's journal following its move to Columbia; the essay is included in part 3 of this volume, pp. 437–69; "A Social Critique of Radio Music," *Kenyon Review* 7 no. 2 (Spring 1945), pp. 208–17, first delivered as a lecture to the Radio Project staff in 1939; it outlines the rudiments of Adorno's theoretical position; the fourth and largest piece, which was only recently published: "Analytical Study of the NBC *Music Appreciation Hour*," *Musical Quarterly* 78 no. 2 (Summer 1994), pp. 325–77, is based on Adorno's original unedited transcript found among Lazarsfeld's papers in the archives at Columbia University.

Adorno planned but never completed a volume on radio theory. Two volumes of related projects form part of the *Nachlass*: (1) *Zu einer Theorie der musikalischen Reproduktion: Aufzeichnungen, ein Entwurf und zwei Schemata*, ed. Henri Lonitz (Frankfurt am Main: Suhrkamp, 2001); (2) *Current of Music: Elements of a Radio Theory*, ed. Robert Hullot-Kentor, forthcoming.

4. See Horst J. P. Bergmeier and Rainer E. Lotz, *Hitler's Airwaves: The Inside Story of Nazi Radio Broadcasting and Propaganda Swing* (New Haven: Yale University Press, 1997).

1922 commercially sponsored programming was initiated, with sponsored national network programming following in 1928.[5] By 1939, while Adorno was working on the Radio Project, 774 stations were broadcasting in the United States, forty of them at 50,000 watts.[6]

Paul Lazarsfeld (1901–1976) arrived in America from his native Austria in 1933. His sociological research involved the study of markets and was specifically geared for use by business. For example, in 1937, prior to the start of the Radio Project, Lazarsfeld, by his own account, helped organize studies on "How Pittsburgh Women Decide Where to Buy Their Dresses" and "How Pittsburgh Drivers Choose Their Gasoline." ("The first study once made me a house guest of a local Pittsburgh tycoon, Edgar Kaufmann, and the second brought me into repeated contact with Paul Mellon.")[7] In a co-authored paper published in 1935, he succinctly described the practical application of his work as providing the *"knowledge by means of which to forecast and control consumer behavior."*[8] As Anthony Heilbut points out, Lazarsfeld, from his position at Columbia University whose faculty he joined in 1939, "turned his methods to marketable use by surveying listening habits for advertising agencies and sponsors."[9] Adorno, simply put, regarded such activity as the promotion of mass manipulation.

Near the end of his life Adorno drafted a memoir of his American experience. Writing about the Radio Project, he noted that he regarded his own endeavor to be at once philosophical and sociological, a reflection of the fact that throughout his career he "never rigorously separated the two disciplines"; he further indicated that "I considered it to be my fitting and objectively proffered assignment to *interpret* phenomena—not to ascertain, sift, and classify facts and make them available as information."[10] He

5. Henry L. Ewbank and Sherman P. Lawton, *Broadcasting: Radio and Television* (New York: Harper and Brothers, 1952), p. 48.

6. Edgar A. Grunwald, ed., *Variety Radio Directory 1939–1940* (New York: Variety, 1939), p. 569.

7. Lazarsfeld, "Episode in the History of Social Research," p. 298.

8. Arthur W. Kornhauser and Paul F. Lazarsfeld, "The Techniques of Market Research from the Standpoint of a Psychologist," Institute of Management Series, no. 16 (New York: American Management Association, 1935), p. 4, original emphasis; and p. 15: "Buying behavior is largely a reflection of people's attitudes—attitudes toward the product itself, attitudes toward the selling and advertising methods, attitudes toward all sorts of life situations into which the product enters."

9. Heilbut, *Exiled in Paradise*, pp. 94–97; quotation from p. 97.

10. Adorno, "Scientific Experiences of a European Scholar in America," p. 339, original emphasis. Morrison, "Kultur and Culture," pp. 341–42, argues that Adorno's critique is unfounded, but the counter-argument he provides strikes me an inadequate. Essentially, Morrison points out that the Project as a whole sought

quickly recognized the gulf separating his concerns from those of the Radio Project: "This much I did understand: that it was concerned with the collection of data, which were supposed to benefit the planning departments in the field of the mass media, whether in industry itself or in cultural advisory boards and similar bodies. For the first time, I saw 'administrative research' before me." Adorno noted that the Project's charter, which stipulated that research be framed by the commercial radio system, implied that "the system itself, its cultural and sociological consequences and its social and economic presuppositions were not to be analyzed." To which Adorno wryly understates, "I cannot say that I strictly obeyed the charter."[11]

Adorno's critique of American sociology's empirical bent was straightforward: he recognized it less as empirical (objective) than as fundamentally ideological.[12] The Radio Project as a whole was based on listener response surveys, about which Adorno lodged several complaints. He argued that to proceed from listener reactions as though they were the ultimate source of sociological knowledge was fundamentally misguided; the results obtained were bound to be superficial. The surveys failed to investigate the actual degree of spontaneity and directness of the subjective reactions of the survey's subjects; further, there was no attention paid to the impact of the survey's design itself in eliciting particular responses; nor was there any concern with what Adorno termed "the objective implications of the material with which listeners were confronted." Finally, the surveys left undetermined "how far comprehensive social structures, and even society as a whole, came into play."[13]

Adorno criticized sociological research that de-historicized human subjects and their opinions; he separated himself from research he regarded as interested only in symptoms but not causes. If the Radio Project's prin-

to study the relation between radio and the social system. But this, after all, was not Adorno's point. The issue was how the social connection was to be accurately established when the techniques for doing so were, from his perspective, fundamentally flawed.

11. Adorno, "Scientific Experiences of a European Scholar in America," pp. 342–43.

12. See Adorno, "Sociology and Empirical Research," in Critical Sociology: Selected Readings, trans. Graham Bartram, ed. Paul Connerton (Harmondsworth, UK: Penguin Books, 1976), pp. 256–57. This essay, first published in 1957, lays out Adorno's critique of quantitative sociology in detail.

13. Adorno, "Scientific Experiences of a European Scholar in America," pp. 343–44.

cipal concern was to determine what listeners thought about radio programming, Adorno's interest lay in determining the process by which their
opinions were formed in the first place, including the impact on listeners
of radio itself. At a more basic level, he pointed to what he regarded as
elementary methodological flaws in the way that empirical data was produced: "If a questionnaire asking members of the public about their musical tastes gives them the choice of the categories 'classical' and 'popular,'
it is with the justifiable certainty that the people concerned listen according
to these categories. . . . As long as the social determinants of this sort of
reaction are omitted from the survey, the conclusions it comes to, though
correct, are at the same time misleading; they suggest that the division of
musical experience into 'classical' and 'popular' is a final one, somehow
part of the natural order of things."[14] Lazarsfeld, despite his openness about
directly serving industry, more or less posited his work as apolitical objective data gathering; Adorno, having none of this, had the temerity to draw
attention to the social forces underwriting the subjects studied and the
ideological foundation immanent to the research itself, notably embedded
in its purportedly objective methodology. Adorno's memoir tells of the
(now common) use of a machine that allowed a listener to indicate likes
and dislikes during a musical performance by pushing a button, and asks
how such data so gathered can be responsive to the complexity of the
problem the technique purports to measure. He argues that the supposedly
spontaneous reactions to music were not natural but were culturally produced, hence historical.[15] Therein lay the real story, of little apparent interest to anyone but himself: Adorno sensed that his colleague's concern
with music was defined by its role as "a mere stimulus"[16] for the supposedly spontaneous reactions the Project hoped to measure. By contrast,
Adorno's concern was to take from the given of subjective reactions the
opportunity to discover objective determinants—yet not for the purpose
of market manipulation that underwrote the Radio Project, but for his
prevailing concern with human liberation: "The unfreedom of the methods
serves the cause of freedom by bearing silent witness to the unfreedom
that prevails in reality."[17]

14. Adorno, "Sociology and Empirical Research," pp. 244.
15. Adorno, "Scientific Experiences of a European Scholar in America," p. 344.
16. Ibid., p. 349.
17. Adorno, "Sociology and Empirical Research," p. 243. Cf. MM, p. 44: "Since
Utopia was set aside and the unity of theory and practice demanded, we have
become all too practical. Fear of the impotence of theory supplies a pretext for

Adorno's research focused on a problem not readily responsive to Lazarfeld's *modus operandi* of subject interviews and questionnaires: "something specifically musical impeded my progress from theoretical considerations to empiricism—namely the difficulty of verbalizing what music subjectively arouses in the listener, the utter obscurity of what we call 'musical experience'."[18] The result was his essay "THE RADIO SYMPHONY" (1941; pp. 251–70), subtitled "An Experiment in Theory"—largely concerning Beethoven—addressing the question "what radio transmission does musically to a musical structure or to different kinds of music" (p. 251). Adorno's fundamental insight is that radio (meaning AM-band broadcast) is not a neutral or transparent technology for sound transmission. He gets at the issue in two complementary ways as regards music, in essence considering sound production as well as its consumption by listeners. Regarding the former Adorno points to radio's ever-present background noise, what he named radio's "hear-stripe," as a factor of technological interference between the broadcast live performance and the radio listeners' ears.[19] In the as yet unpublished "Memorandum: Music in Radio" from 1938, a 161-page mimeograph produced for Lazarsfeld, Adorno discusses the "hear-stripe" in detail. He likens radio background noise to what's heard on a 78-rpm recording at the start, before the music begins,

---

bowing to the almighty production process, and so fully admitting the impotence of theory." It is not the case, however, as has often been ascribed, that Adorno maintained a total disregard for empirical research. See his comments, including self-criticism, in "Scientific Experiences of a European Scholar in America," pp. 352–53, which includes the following: "I may sum up by saying that empirical investigations are not only legitimate but essential, even in the realm of cultural phenomena. But one must not confer autonomy upon them or regard them as a universal key. Above all, they must themselves terminate in theoretical knowledge. Theory is no mere vehicle that becomes superfluous as soon as the data are in hand." See further on this point, Martin Jay, *The Dialectical Imagination: A History of the Frankfurt School and the Institute of Social Research, 1923–1950* (Boston: Little, Brown, 1973), pp. 221–23, 250–51.

18. Adorno, "Scientific Experiences of a European Scholar in America," p. 344.

19. Adorno later acknowledged that high fidelity and stereophonic technologies met this concern. See Adorno, "Scientific Experiences of a European Scholar in America," p. 352. Thomas Y. Levin, "The Acoustic Dimension: Notes on Cinema Sound," *Screen* 25 no. 3 (May/June 1984), pp. 66–68, suggests that the proper term would be "hear-strip" (not stripe); he maintains that Adorno's phrase indicates an analogy between background broadcast noise and the noise produced on the optical track (dust, scratches) in film "creating a constant very low level but audible 'current' of noise" (p. 66). In CF, pp. 86–87, Adorno and Eisler refer to a "running thread" [*Streifenhaftes*] and also the more conventional "sound track" [*Klangstreifen*]. They also repeat the matter of background noise on p. 110.

groove noise, which then recedes—but does not disappear—once the music starts. "This slight, continuous and constant noise is like a sort of acoustic stripe," which Adorno then likens to film noise. (A more recent technological analogue is tape hiss.) His interest in the "hear-stripe" involves more than any overt listener distraction it might produce. He posits that the "hear-stripe" likely changes the listener's relation to the music to the extent that the music "appears to be projected upon the stripe and is only, so to speak, like a picture upon that stripe." In other words, music, though performed live over radio, is compromised by a second-order presence, a technological filter whose effects, Adorno believes, may function only at the level of the unconscious.[20]

Writing in the "Memorandum," Adorno bluntly amplifies his concern about the interface between music and broadcast technology, and at the same time shifts his gaze toward ideological factors shaping music reception: "Music in [sic] radio always sounds a bit like 'news.' It sounds like something which is told to you by an unseen informer rather than sounding like an objectivated work of art with which you are presented. The listener has the feeling, not that he is being confronted with the music itself, but that he is being told something about the music, or being introduced to music by radio. It does not sound like Beethoven's music itself, but like 'now you will hear something about Beethoven'; a tendency which, by the way, is emphasized not only by the way music is announced over the radio, but especially in the case of serious music by the ever-reappearing tendency to regard it as an 'educational feature' of radio."[21]

Reacting specifically against the commonsensical and well-advertised claims for radio as a technological means by which to help realize democratic ideals—by making available to the masses, and without cost, the great musical treasures heretofore conventionally associated with economic privilege—Adorno pursued a line of argument advanced in his just-published "Fetish-Character" essay (discussed below), suggesting that the radio symphony did nothing to help liberate the masses but instead con-

---

20. Adorno, "Memorandum: Music in Radio" (unpublished; Paul F. Lazarsfeld papers, Columbia University, dated June 1938), pp. 30–31; see also pp. 23–24. Cf. Virgil Thomson, *The Musical Scene* (New York: Alfred A Knopf, 1945), p. 259, in a review (24 May 1943) of a New York Philharmonic all-Beethoven program conducted by Bruno Walter, broadcast from Carnegie Hall; listening from home—in what he wryly named "a pleasantly domestic ceremony"—Thomson noted that the music was "accompanied by those intermittent frying noises that my instrument likes to add to everything."

21. Adorno, "Memorandum: Music in Radio," p. 37.

tributed to their further regression as subjects of domination by market manipulation. The "freedom" dealt out in the name of "Culture" was administered; the cultural negativity of artworks—that which ran counter to culture's (marketed) claims—was transformed into wholly affirmative cultural product. In short, he argued that the radio symphony promoted the fetishizing of culture itself.[22]

Adorno's essay sets its sights on a single example, Beethoven, and one work, the Fifth Symphony, for several reasons. First, as Adorno seeks to demonstrate, the Fifth is an artwork of notable distinction. In developing an argument about the shortcomings of radio music, the stakes, in effect, are greater, the greater the artwork being broadcast. Second, he wryly acknowledges that Beethoven himself is "the standard classic of cultural sales talk in music" (p. 253). He will demonstrate that radio helps reduce the Fifth Symphony to precisely that. Third, his critique of radio music is tied intimately to what happens within the music itself, what Adorno refers to as "the problem of the fate of the 'integral form'" (p. 253) when broadcast on (AM) radio.

Beethoven on radio, he asserts, is Beethoven reduced to mere entertainment. Characterizing the work itself as possessing "a particular intensity and concentration" (p. 254)—a formal process containing nothing extraneous, everything integral—Adorno argues that Beethoven's music demands something from listeners: "Structurally, one hears the first bar of a Beethoven symphonic movement only at the very moment when one hears the last bar" (p. 255). One might reasonably take Adorno's position on structural listening as both unreasonable (who but trained musicians can hear Beethoven in the manner he prescribes?) and/or elitist (what is implied as regards the socio-economic status required to gain such knowl-

---

22. Thomson, *Musical Scene*, p. 251, echoed Adorno, and expanded on his argument, pointing to music's inescapability: "It is harder today in the United states to avoid music than to hear it" (and this in 1943): we are "bathed" in music all day long. "Never before has civilized humanity lived in an auditory décor, surrounded from morn till night, from cradle to coffin, by planned sound." He agrees that as a "cultural opportunity for all, this is a fine thing." But there is a dark side: "As forced consumption of everything by everybody, it is a horrid thing. One used to have to work hard to keep in touch with the cultural tradition. Today educated people are obliged to immure themselves in order to avoid suffocation from constant contact with it." Put in Adornian terms, the utopian element of cultural tradition, something to which the individual had to aspire, is today served up, freely as it were, as Cultural Goods, with all the spirituality of Muzak, and the unavoidability of death and taxes. The same topic, but concerning the current situation, is addressed by J. Bottum, "The Soundtracking of America," *Atlantic Monthly* (March 2000), pp. 56–70.

edge?).[23] But the matter is not so simple. Adorno was keenly sensitive to the history of privilege and elitism that accrued to the history of art, but that fact by itself could not for Adorno stand as good reason to disparage art—and art's truth content. Put differently, if art's own (internal) resistance to the regressive nature of its origins was to be realized in the act of reception, the act of reception must meet the artwork's immanent demands for this to occur.

Adorno argued that there were pedagogical means by which to accomplish this goal that could be made available through radio. This matter, in essence, is the principal subject of his lengthy essay, "Analytical Study of the NBC *Music Appreciation Hour.*" The "Music Appreciation Hour," hosted by Walter Damrosch, was broadcast weekly from 1928 to 1942; it was addressed to children. Adorno's position is blatantly stated in the opening sentence: "The purpose of the present study is to point out that radio, at its 'benevolent' best, in a nation-wide, sustaining program of purely educational character, fails to achieve its aim—namely, to bring people into an actual life relation with music."[24] Adorno's data was not the kids who

23. Two essays are critical to any discussion (and critique) of structural listening: the now-classic by Rose Rosengard Subotnik, "Toward a Deconstruction of Structural Listening: A Critique of Schoenberg, Adorno, and Stravinsky," in *Deconstructive Variations: Music and Reason in Western Society* (Minneapolis: University of Minnesota Press, 1996), pp. 148–76, 245–52; and a more recent essay by Olle Edström, "Fr-a-g-me-n-ts: A Discussion on the Position of Critical Ethnomusicology in Contemporary Musicology," *Svenskt Tidskrift för Musikforskning* 79 (1997), no. 1, pp. 9–68. Both Subotnik and Edström point out that little music can actually lay claim to the autonomy principle, critical to the demand for structural listening; it cannot be applied to Western musical structures prior to the nineteenth century, to say nothing of the music produced elsewhere in the world. Further, structural listening is fundamentally applicable to instrumental music and not vocal. Both Schoenberg and Adorno stress the point that structural listening is directed toward the discernment of development in musical structures, notwithstanding the fact that development is a foundation principle of "very little music" (Subotnik, p. 159). Subotnik argues that structural listening "depreciates the value of sound with unusual explicitness" (p. 161)—though in fact Adorno did not invariably ignore what Subotnik terms music's "sensuous actuality" (p. 163), as is evident, for example, in his various commentaries on Alban Berg, on orchestral color in Wagner, and in his essays on new music, "Vers une musique informelle," QF, pp. 269–322; and "New Music, Interpretation, Audience," SF, pp. 29–39. Concerning the retrospective quality of structural listening, Max Paddison, *Adorno's Aesthetics of Music* (Cambridge: Cambridge University Press, 1993), p. 195, points out that Adorno "maintains that it is only in light of later musical production that the constructive unity of such earlier works [i.e., an early Beethoven piano sonata] has become clearly recognizable."

24. Adorno, "Analytical Study of the NBC *Music Appreciation Hour,*" p. 326 (see n. 4, above).

listened but, principally, the pedagogical print materials NBC released in 1939–40, a *Teacher's Guide*[25] and four sets of *Student's Worksheets*, published by Columbia University Press. He argued that the program and its supplementary pedagogical material shortchanged young listeners by shortchanging music; the result was the creation of "a fictitious musical world" based on ready-made labels, pre-digested values, stereotyped attitudes, the whole reduced to the inculcation of star performers and star composers—musical personalities, musical Hollywood. The end result, summarized in a phrase on the report's second page, is "the promotion of musical Babbittry."[26] This was hardly an assessment to be regarded as music to the ears of the broadcast industry. Small wonder the study remained in manuscript form.

Adorno sees the problem in systemic terms, the result of a medium organized "as an economic enterprise in an ownership culture." Commercial radio's function is to produce profit; public good, such as may result, is ancillary, even accidental to the profit motive. His own concern is driven by what he repeatedly terms an "actual life relation with music," tacitly acknowledging his concern for music's significance in the formation of humane subjects. For this to occur, as he argues at length, the student must get from the outside of music to its inside; in short, music must be understood on music's terms.[27] He insists that if, for pedagogical reasons, the entire truth cannot be told, at least nothing false should be substituted, precisely what he believes is conventional practice. He cites as an example a lesson plan for *Tristan und Isolde* whose plot is distorted so as to avoid mentioning the lovers' illicit sexual relationship:

25. Ibid., p. 373 n. 1: "The *Teacher's Guide* is meant to be used by classroom teachers in schools where the Music Appreciation Hour is a lesson on Friday afternoons."

26. Ibid., pp. 326–27. "Good musical education postulates respect for the work. . . . It is not loaded with inculcating maudlin respect for the composer" (p. 358); "The authoritarian structure of this type of musical education promotes a cult of persons instead of an understanding of facts" (p. 353); "The Music Appreciation Hour strives to cast a spell around the conductor" (p. 361). See also his remarks on Toscanini on radio in DE, pp. 159–61, and ISM, pp. 104–17, essentially a social-psychoanalytic reading of the relation of the conductor to his orchestra, read as dominator to dominated.

27. Adorno, "Analytical Study of the NBC *Music Appreciation Hour*," p. 326. Cf. Adorno, "Some Ideas on the Sociology of Music," SF, p. 2: "A sociology of music has a dual relationship to its object: an internal and an external dimension. Any social meaning inherent in music is not identical with that music's place and function in society."

The Music Appreciation Hour voices the idea that [the lovers] simply suffer, because for reasons of conventional morality they cannot get together. As a matter of fact, they do get together, and adultery is the presupposition of the whole "Tristan" plot. If one is afraid to speak about adultery, one should not speak about "Tristan." One had better not even play it. The assumption, however, that an adolescent would not suspect the true story when faced with the plot . . . is absurd. But talking about "Tristan" in a coy, old-maidish manner necessarily creates an atmosphere of giggling and dark stair-cases. The idea that young people would be "corrupted" by "Tristan," when they can get *Film Fun* at any newsstand, is preposterous as well as hypocritical. But this is only one consequence of the gerontocratic attitude which does not recognize children and adolescents as people.[28]

Elsewhere, Adorno critiques musical explanations that he regards as "absolutely incomprehensible" to children. He takes on the lessons' historicist approach to music history, including a marked tendency to organize chronology against a musical telos of simple (early music) to complex (post-Bach). And so on. In each instance Adorno articulates the consequences that accrue to the pedagogy he laments, and also offers counter-strategies for more responsible musical education. His own program is proto-Freirean[29] *avant la lettre:* "It is far more fruitful to start from what is known to be the actual standard of musical consciousness within the pupil—from what he, himself, considers as his 'normal' musical language"; instead, what Adorno recognizes is a lot of "erudite babbling" which the student is encouraged to emulate.[30]

---

28. Adorno, "Analytical Study of the NBC *Music Appreciation Hour,*" p. 345; the comments concerning truthful pedagogy appear on p. 329. "Children are particularly sensitive when they feel betrayed by adults, and the child who waits for the instrumental personality which then does not appear [Adorno is critiquing Damrosch's technique of teaching individual instruments as "personalities"] must necessarily feel that adults talk nonsense to him and betray him" (p. 330).

29. Paulo Freire, *Pedagogy of the Oppressed* (1970), trans. Myra Bergman (New York: Seabury, 1972).

30. Adorno, "Analytical Study of the NBC *Music Appreciation Hour,*" pp. 338, 344, respectively. See further concerning Adorno's interest in education, "Philosophy and Teachers," CM, pp. 19–35; and in the same volume, "Education after Auschwitz," pp. 191–204, and "Taboos on the Teaching Vocation," pp. 177–90, which examines the cultural history of aversion to the teaching vocation and its impact on German public (pre-university) education; Adorno ends by stating that schools must promote what he terms the "debarbarization of humanity." "Education after Auschwitz," first given as a 1966 radio lecture, opens as follows: "The premier demand upon all education is that Auschwitz not happen again. . . .

Adorno was sensitive to the intersubjectivity immanent to the symphonic (live) performance space, specifically, the concert hall, and public listening. The snobbism common to the concert audience was not lost on him, but neither was the concert's utopian potential as a site where could be realized artworks that offered something besides the iteration of the privilege upon which they necessarily depend. The radio performance, by contrast, "democratically" available to anyone with a radio set, is resolutely nonetheless privatized; the radio listener's intersubjective relation to others is lost, beyond those gathered in front of the console, and even this limited form of intersubjectivity is further constrained by the myriad distractions of the domestic interior. Virgil Thomson makes a similar argument, writing in 1943: "And though many concerts are broadcast from places where there are a live audience as well as live performers, the private listener is no part of that audience. For him it is just another element in a far-away show. He cannot applaud with it and whistle with it and talk back to it and ask for an encore. He can only listen to the whole thing or else turn it off, take it or leave it as he would a book."[31]

For Adorno, writing in "The Radio Symphony," the "experience of symphonic space" (p. 257) is a categorical necessity, because without it the merging with or absorption by the symphony cannot occur. The small sound of the 1930s radio, its lack of ability to "enclose" the listener, con-

---

Every debate about the ideals of education is trivial and inconsequential compared to this single ideal: never again Auschwitz. It was the barbarism all education strives against." Adorno's concern is early childhood education as well as what he calls a "general enlightenment" that provides "an intellectual, cultural, and social climate in which a recurrence would no longer be possible, a climate, therefore, in which the motives that led to the horror would become relatively conscious" (p. 194).

Leo Lowenthal, "The Left in Germany Has Failed" [interview by Peter Glotz], trans. Benjamin Gregg, in *An Unmastered Past: The Autobiographical Reflections of Leo Lowenthal*, ed. Martin Jay (Berkeley and Los Angeles: University of California Press, 1987), defends Adorno's position on musical pedagogy in two related comments: "If Mozart and Beethoven are played over and over again for a listener who isn't able to appreciate the music, or if they're played as background music in cafés, department stores, restaurants, at the hairdresser's or dentist's, then I fail to see anything particularly valuable in it. That's really nothing but the desire to be part of the action" (p. 254); "I only know that if you don't want to teach a person how to experience aesthetic products, then all this information—mere popularization—backfires and only strengthens the tendency toward cheap, passively enjoyable amusement. Hence, without genuine—if you'll excuse the word—*education* of people to aesthetic experience, then a kind of popularization that would be at all meaningful is impossible" (p. 256, original emphasis).

31. Thomson, *Musical Scene*, p. 251.

) stituted a fatal technical flaw. Thus Adorno critiques radio's inability to preserve the crucial role played by structural dynamics in Beethoven's music. Indeed, much of his argument against radio is the loss of dynamic and timbral nuance crucial to Beethoven's compositional process. Gradation is lost; extremes prevail. "While exaggerating conspicuous contrasts, radio's neutralization of sound colors practically blots out precisely those minute differences upon which the classical orchestra is built" (p. 260). What Adorno is getting at, in terms of 1930s broadcasts, is somewhat akin to today's listening experience in automobiles, with the background noise of the heating or air conditioning, the motor and the road. Soft passages are clear only if played at very high volumes, leading to ear-shattering dynamic levels in loud passages. Fundamental distortion. Virgil Thomson makes a complementary observation regarding Beethoven on radio. He suggests that if the listener were without memories of what Beethoven sounded like in the concert hall, "one would have strange ideas indeed about them" based on what emerges from the speaker: "Beethoven, heard over the radio, sounds disjointed and picayune." His review, "Beethoven in the Home," continues:

> The limited dynamic range that a microphone will carry has something to do with this distortion; and so, I imagine, has the placing of the microphones. Yesterday, for instance, the fortes all lacked background, as if the violins were too close; and so the essential majesty of Beethoven, which comes from his constant contrasts of loud and soft, was reduced both by the radio's inability, at best, to transmit a really loud ensemble of musical sounds and by the fact that the bottom was out of these, even in their toned-down state. There was continuity in the rhythmic layout but no real strength in the dynamic pattern or any massiveness in individual chords. The lyrical passages came off prettily, as they always do in broadcast music; but the dynamic eloquence that constitutes such a large part of Beethoven's thought sounded puny.[32]

32. Ibid., pp. 259–60. Arnold Schoenberg makes a similar point; see "Modern Music on the Radio," an essay from 1933, in *Style and Idea: Selected Writings of Arnold Schoenberg*, ed. Leonard Stein, trans. Leo Black (New York: St. Martin's Press, 1975), pp. 151–52. Commenting that radio's acoustic limitations favor music's high register, he likens the sound to that of "a lady sawn in half." Schoenberg suggests that radio technology should favor new music to the extent that so much of it is "thinly scored," and transmits with less loss of aural quality than is the case with thickly scored music. He agrees with Adorno's position that further advances in radio technology will not be driven by radio's serving art but only the market ("something which can be mass-produced and thrown cheaply onto the market, and which can be brought out at least once a year in a new fashionable

What results in reception, Adorno claims, is "atomized listening," otherwise known as listening for the good parts, about which more later. The artwork is pulled apart, made episodic, a collection of brief quotations: "What is heard is not Beethoven's Fifth but merely musical information from and about Beethoven's Fifth" (p. 262), what elsewhere Adorno referred to as music's "gustatory qualities," in essence cultural advertising, "the ideal of Aunt Jemima's ready-mix for pancakes extended to the field of music."[33] An experience of musical process is lost to musical product, taking the form of remembered thematic snippets. The theme itself, not what happens to it in the artwork, is privileged; listeners taught to claim the theme as cultural property promote "a fetishism of ownership."[34] Essentially, Adorno is suggesting, as he suggested in *Dialectic of Enlightenment*, that we're denied the food while being handed the menu. And the menu becomes a souvenir possessing cultural cachet, treasured in lieu of the actual nourishment—and pleasure—that it otherwise promises to deliver. The very listeners for whom this purported democracy of culture is promulgated are cheated of the very thing to which they may now lay claim—as Cultured Consumers. "Who are the 'we'?" Adorno asks at one juncture,[35] declaiming radio's immanent "social authoritarianism" (p. 264).

---

version that makes the earlier ones valueless, until the whole world loses interest. This is a sad and hope-destroying phenomenon").

33. Adorno, "Social Critique of Radio Music," p. 211. See also Adorno, "Über die musikalische Verwendung des Radios," GS, vol. 15, pp. 369–401, which recuperates material developed for the Princeton Radio Project; an extract from this essay on Beethoven is translated and reprinted in B, pp. 118–22.

34. Adorno, "Analytical Study of the NBC *Music Appreciation Hour*," p. 352. Cf. pp. 358–59: "A theme isolated solely for the purposes of recognition and identification, is no longer part of the living musical process, but is a thing owned. . . . The pleasure involved consists of a fetishistic hoarding of information about music, which one enjoys as a miser enjoys the gold he has accumulated. . . . Music, instead of being 'lived' by the listener, is actually transformed into property." See also p. 375 n. 27, for Adorno's scathing critique of the then-famous book by Sigmund Spaeth, prominent guru of music appreciation, *Great Symphonies: How to Recognize and Remember Them* (Garden City, NY: Garden City Publishing, 1936). Spaeth attaches text to prominent symphonic themes as a mnemonic device; thirty-six works from the standard repertory are thus parsed; for example, p. 91, "I am your fate! Come, let me in!" for the opening of Beethoven's Fifth Symphony. The book remains in print, a 1972 edition by Greenwood Publishing. Adorno commented on this book in the 1959 essay "Theory of Pseudo-Culture," trans. Deborah Cook, *Telos* 95 (Spring 1993), pp. 31–32: "The idiotic words [added by Spaeth to the musical themes] sung have nothing to do with the content but attach themselves like leeches to the effect of symphonic works, testifying conclusively to the fetishism of pseudo-culture in relation to its objects."

35. Adorno, "Analytical Study of the NBC *Musical Appreciation Hour*," p. 355.

Fundamentally, Adorno's critique drives toward the following conclusion: "Music under present radio auspices serves to keep listeners from criticizing social realities; in short, it has a soporific effect upon social consciousness." And in a bitter reference to the gap between radio-administered Cultural Goods and ordinary lives, he has the temerity to point out:

> The illusion is furthered that the best is just good enough for the man in the street. The ruined farmer is consoled by the radio-instilled belief that Toscanini is playing for him and for him alone, and that an order of things that allows him to hear Toscanini compensates for low market prices for farm products; even though he is ploughing cotton under, radio is giving him culture. Radio is calling back to its broad bosom all the prodigal sons and daughters whom the harsh father has expelled from the door. In this respect radio music offers a new function not inherent in music as an art—the function of creating smugness and self-satisfaction.[36]

All this notwithstanding, Adorno notably moderated his position on radio music years later back in Germany—just how much is perhaps best exemplified by a radio broadcast in 1965 called "Beautiful Passages" *(Schöne Stellen)*, a nearly two-hour program replete with fifty-two recorded musical examples interspersed with Adorno's commentary, literally favorite musical bits, in which atomization of musical works, though not atomistic listening, defines the program's format.[37] Adorno's point, how-

36. Adorno, "A Social Critique of Radio Music," pp. 212–13. The allusion to the ruined farmer is a direct reference to another Radio Project report, published in the same volume as Adorno's "The Radio Symphony," by William S. Robinson: "Radio Comes to the Farmer," in *Radio Research 1941*, ed. Paul F. Lazarsfeld and Frank N. Stanton (New York: Duell, Sloan and Pearce, 1941), pp. 224–94, by far the longest in the volume. It accounts for the listening habits of farmers in one county in each of two Midwestern states, Illinois and Nebraska. Music is not referenced, but there is a section on "Radio as a Medium for Cultural Education," pp. 245–51.

The volume includes two other essays on music by other project participants, of whom Adorno spoke favorably (see "Scientific Experiences of a European Scholar in America," pp. 353–55): Duncan MacDougald, Jr., "The Popular Music Industry," pp. 65–109; and Edward A. Suchman, "Invitation to Music: A Study of the Creation of New Music Listeners by the Radio," pp. 140–88. The other reports concerned "Foreign Language Broadcasts over Local Radio Stations" and "Radio and the Press among Young People." Adorno's essay, no surprise, is the shortest of all of them.

37. Adorno, "Schöne Stellen," GS, vol. 18, pp. 695–718. The lecture is discussed by Thomas Y. Levin, "For the Record: Adorno on Music in the Age of Its Technological Reproducibility," *October* 55 (Winter 1990), p. 45; Shierry Weber

ever, is not to sell to listeners fifty-two lovely musical snippets but to discuss musical meaning and expression by means of the significance of musical particulars. Loveliness, in other words, is not necessarily self-evident, and it is contextual, as well as discursive. Still, Adorno's focus on detail under these circumstances leads him to explain, and valorize, music on terms other than those required by structural listening, which by def-inition is fundamentally different from listening to musical details in iso-lation from their larger whole as would necessarily ensue in such a radio broadcast.[38]

The opening chapter to *Introduction to the Sociology of Music* (1962), "Types of Musical Conduct,"[39] outlines a typology of listeners, rooted in the principle of structural listening, that is, by listening that concentrates on musical content via music's structural unfolding in time. Adorno names eight types, beginning with the expert and ending with what he names the "entertainment listener."[40] Each is rife with shortcomings; all forms of

---

Nicholsen, *Exact Imagination, Late Work: On Adorno's Aesthetics* (Cambridge: MIT Press, 1997), pp. 19–20; and Helmut Haack, "Adornos Sprechen über Musik," in *Adorno und die Musik*, ed. Otto Kolleritsch (Graz: Universal Edition, 1979), pp. 37–51.

38. Nonetheless, in AT, pp. 187–88, Adorno commented that "whoever lacks an appreciation for beautiful passages . . . is as alien to the artwork as one who is incapable of experiencing its unity. All the same, such details gain their luminosity only by virtue of the whole." Adorno, "Memorandum: Music in Radio," pp. 142–43, strongly advocates the broadcast of orchestral rehearsals of classical music, designed to convey "an idea not only of the manner in which a performance is constructed but also to show how the composition itself is constructed"—a goal strikingly similar to Leonard Bernstein's 1950s televised young persons' concerts.

39. ISM, pp. 1–20.

40. The full typology is: (1) the expert listener; (2) the good listener; (3) the culture consumer; (4) the emotional listener; (5) the resentment listener; (6) the jazz expert and jazz fan (in fact, similar to type five); (7) the entertainment listener; and (8) the indifferent, the unmusical or the anti-musical. Among the Lazarsfeld papers at Columbia University is a seventeen-page typescript by Adorno titled "A Typology of Music Listening," dating from the Princeton Radio Research period (the later book chapter reprises much of what is contained in this manuscript), listing eleven listener types; it also contains suggestions for empirically determin-ing the type to which a given listener belongs. The types are: (1) the fully conscious or musical expert; (2) the "good musical listener" (the quotation marks here and hereinafter are Adorno's); (3) the "erudite" or "informed"; (4) the "emotional"; (5) the "sensuous"; (6) the type for whom every music is "entertainment"; (7) the time-killer; (8) the jitter-bug; (9) the musical sportsman or the man with a knack; (10) the musically indifferent; and (11) the anti-musical.

See further Paddison, *Adorno's Aesthetics of Music*, pp. 207–13. The essay by Suchman, "Invitation to Music" repeatedly cites Adorno's Project work. Such-

listening bear, differentially, the mark of an antagonistic social totality—aspects of the social wrongs that determine modernity. The "expert listener" is the ideal type to the extent that he or she is fully conscious, misses nothing, and "at each moment, accounts to himself for what he has heard." Quantitatively such listeners are "probably scarcely worth noting."[41] The "upper ranks" of the typology typically gain expertise from social privilege. For example, Adorno associates type three, the "culture consumer," with the "upper and uplifted" bourgeois symphony and opera crowd whose social prestige is in part both reflected in and perpetuated by showing up—people who "posture as elitists hostile to the mass," and who are highly antagonistic to new music as well, a group which "to a great extent determines the official life of music."[42] "My point," Adorno comments, "is neither to disparage representatives of the described listening types negatively nor to distort the picture of reality by deriving judgments on the world situation from the present dubious state of listening to music. To posture mentally as if mankind existed for the sake of good listening would be a grotesque echo of estheticism, just as the converse thesis, that music exists for mankind, merely puts a humane face on the furtherance of thought in exchange categories—a way of thinking to which everything that exists is only a means for something else, a way that degrades the truth of the matter and thus strikes the very men it attempts to please."[43]

---

man's debt to Adorno is obvious from his own abbreviated typology of listening, and from his conclusions about listening. Suchman's study, unlike Adorno's, is empirical; it is based on data gathered from subscribers to *Masterwork Bulletin*, published bimonthly for classical-music listeners by WNYC, a noncommercial station operated by the City of New York, fundamentally a play list for the station's "Masterwork Hour" program.

Suchman points out in his opening, pp. 140–41, that broadcasters have impressive statistics as to the amount of radio time given to serious music, and that educators see in these figures the near fulfillment of a dream of mass education for millions. He then cites "one voice of dissent" which can be "faintly heard. This comes from the musical expert,"—he means Adorno—and suggests that "familiarity does not mean understanding—in fact, familiarity without knowledge may be an enemy of true appreciation. The happy accord between the broadcaster and the educator has been challenged" (p. 141). In the end he arrives at a conclusion identical to Adorno's.

41. ISM, pp. 4–5.
42. Ibid., pp. 6–7.
43. Ibid., p. 18. For an attempt to relate a portion of Adorno's typology to actual listeners, see Fred B. Lindstrom and Naomi Lindstrom, "Adorno Encounters Cu-Bop: Experimental Music as a Task for Critics and Their Audiences," *Sociological Perspectives* 29 no. 2 (April 1986), pp. 284–304.

Adorno's radio research essay met with little approval, and less notice,[44] though one well-established writer, B. H. Haggin, music critic for *The Nation*, reacted heatedly, his invective tinged with anti-German wartime fervor: "I find it difficult to write temperately about the motivation, the method, the results of the Adorno performance—of the aggressive ostentation and triumphant assurance in the display of his powers that leap out at one from his use of one of the methods of the German system-grinders and concept-spinners to produce the conclusions that [Virgil] Thomson welcomes 'with cries of joy.'" Complaining that Adorno takes facts and translates them into statements "with new meanings which become increasingly remote from fact," he ends by damning what he regards as Adorno's producing "a climax of triumphant ferocity in musico-socio-psychological concept and jargon."[45] Not content to leave the matter there, Haggin returned to Adorno a few months later in a lengthy review of a book by Herbert Graf, *The Opera and Its Future in America*. Complaining that Graf's "performance is typical of German writing," he both amplified the point and found an opportunity to cite Adorno: "The striking thing about German writing is the combination of its pedantic fact-grubbing with a concept-spinning so freed from connection with fact, sometimes, as to become utterly fantastic, and indeed often manipulating facts, and misrepresenting them, for its purposes. An extreme example of this writing was Adorno's discussion of the effect of radio on the symphony."[46]

Adorno was a critical modernist who understood modernity in specific

44. Among the five reviews of *Radio Research 1941* I've located only one, by B. H. Haggin (see the next footnote), that addresses Adorno's contribution. The other reviews appear in *The Booklist* (15 February 1942), p. 205; *Saturday Review* (7 March 1942), p. 14; *Sociology and Social Research* (July/August 1942), pp. 563–64; and *Yale Review* 31 no. 3 (March 1942), pp. 643–44.

45. B. H. Haggin, *Music in the Nation* (New York: William Sloan Associates, 1949), p. 93. The review first appeared in *The Nation* on 30 May 1942. Haggin continues later in the essay: "It isn't only [Virgil] Thomson who utters cries of welcome; Adorno's tripe is the sort of thing that social science research institutes, foundations, and journals go for" (p. 94). On this point, to say the least, Haggin was precisely wrong. (I have not been successful in locating Thomson's review of Adorno's essay to which Haggin alludes.) See also Michael Wood, "Adorno's Ascetic Formula," *Kenyon Review* 18 nos. 3–4 (Summer/Fall 1996), pp. 223–26, which provides a summary of Adorno's main points as well as a brief critique of the essay's limitations: chiefly that "Adorno seems to think the medium must be static, technically and sociologically fixed in its properties" (p. 225).

46. Haggin, *Music in the Nation*, p. 107, from a review originally published in two parts, 25 July and 10 October 1942.

relation to its prehistory, especially the Western European nineteenth century, which was marked by astounding technological change that transformed society, culture, and the human subject: internationally linked railroad systems; instantaneous communication via telegraph and later telephone; photography and later motion picture photography; mass-market daily newspapers and popular mass-circulation magazines; sound recording, and the like. Global time standardization helped regularize experience; particularly dramatic in this regard was the precise delineation of the work day and the discipline thereby imposed on the body.

The full impact of technology on modernity and modern consciousness was foremost realized via its demonstrated capacities in war, which for many erased forever any remnants of the myth of a technological Golden Age, and for others was openly celebrated. The Futurist fascist poet F. T. Marinetti was among the latter. Thus he confides to his friend and fellow Futurist Luigi Russolo, in an orgasmic ecstasy of words piled atop one another, taking pleasure in the sonorities of the battle at Adrianapolis, Turkey, in October 1912, which he witnessed: "What a joy to hear to smell completely *taratatata* of the machine guns screaming a breathlessness under the stings slaps *traak-traak* whips *pic-pac-pum-tumb* weirdness leaps 200 meters range Far far in back of the orchestra pools muddying hyffing goaded oxen wagons"—eliciting the following promotion from Russolo, "We want to give pitches to these diverse noises, regulating them harmonically and rhythmically."[47] Adorno shared very little with Marinetti and Russolo, but like them he insisted that modern music must face, in essence, the consequences of noise. Whereas Marinetti in particular celebrated noise as an allegorical apotheosis of domination and cruelty, Adorno engaged it as an expressive source for articulating a dual critique of domination and bourgeois historicism, the latter an explanatory paradigm serving, ideologically, to define and defend the former. Put differently,

47. Luigi Russolo, *The Art of Noises*, Monographs in Musicology, no. 6, trans. Barclay Brown (New York: Pendragon Press, 1986), pp. 26–27, quoting Marinetti. Marinetti published his poetic account of the experience in *Zang Tumb Tumb* (1914), employing onomatopoeias and a variety of different typefaces, from small to very large, in an effort to represent as graphically as possible the sounds of war. The letter-passage quoted reflects his so-named "words-in-freedom" style. He celebrated the outbreak of the First World War; and in 1915 he produced a volume of poems called *Guerra sola igiene del mundo* [War the Only Hygiene of the World]. Later, Marinetti was an active supporter of Mussolini. See further Cinzia Sartini Blum, *The Other Modernism: F. T. Marinetti's Futurist Fiction of Power* (Berkeley and Los Angeles: University of California Press, 1996).

Adorno's approach to noise, so far as compositional practices and semiotics are concerned, was dialectical; Marinetti's was at once affirmative and fascistic.

Technology was a principal determinant in music's consumption, just as the impact of technology on consumption in turn affected musical production. With the advent of sound recording and, later, radio broadcasting, music's potential as a consumer product was realized—but not in fact for the first time. Indeed, and as Adorno understood, music underwrote the principle of consumerism during the early heyday of the Industrial Revolution that anchored commonplace understandings of the very nature of modernity. For example, the history of piano design, manufacture, and distribution in the course of the nineteenth century appropriately serves not only as a perfect metaphor of capitalist economic principles in operation but also as an agent of capitalism's political, economic, and ideological success.[48] Manufactured on a massive scale for a seemingly insatiable audience of consumers, the domestic piano bespoke a principal contradiction of nineteenth-century bourgeois society. High-caste pianos with elaborately decorated cases virtually fetishized conspicuous materialism; at the same time the music to be played on the instrument was valorized precisely because of its immateriality, to the nineteenth century the sine qua non of music's supposedly socially transcendent autonomy. Whatever its aesthetic correlatives, the piano was a consumer product whose presence helped to define familial prestige akin to that of today's family-room "entertainment centers," not for nothing so-named, in advertising lingo that teaches us to focus our eyes on the screen and ears on the speakers to learn what's for sale, in exchange for the shows and music that come along as loss leaders.

However, the technology that particularly interested Adorno did not involve changes in the design and manufacture of musical instruments.

48. Cyril Ehrlich, *Social Emulation and Industrial Progress—The Victorian Piano*, New Lecture Series, no. 82 (Belfast: Queen's University, 1975), notes that "by 1910 there were some two to four million pianos in Britain—say one instrument for every ten to 20 people. Since few households contained more than one piano, even the lowest estimates imply that ownership was not confined to the middle classes" (p. 7). On the merchandising of pianos in the United States, see Craig H. Roell, *The Piano in America, 1890–1940* (Chapel Hill: University of North Carolina Press, 1989), pp. 139–82; and Christine Merrick Ayars, *Contributions to the Art of Music in America by the Music Industries of Boston, 1640 to 1936* (New York: H. W. Wilson, 1937), pp. 99–101. David Wainwright, *Broadwood, by Appointment: A History* (London: Quiller Press, 1982) contains valuable information about that firm's sales history, prices, and merchandising techniques.

Instead, it was the impact of technologies of sound transmission and recording that drew his attention. Three remarkable essays, all brief, address the impact of sound recording on listening: "The Curves of the Needle" (1927; revised 1965), "The Form of the Phonograph Record" (1934), and "Opera and the Long-Playing Record" (1969).[49]

"THE CURVES OF THE NEEDLE" (1927/1965; pp. 271–76), written when Adorno was twenty-four, is distinctly strange, and strange for Adorno. The essay is difficult to grasp except in broad—albeit uncertain—terms. What's clear is that the young writer is at once fascinated and troubled by the phonograph, his concern seemingly centered on the machine's intervention between a work's performance and the listener—as well as serving as a substitute for (amateur) self-performance on the part of bourgeois consumers who, in effect, "own" musical sound but do not themselves make it. ("The gramophone belongs to the pregnant stillness of individuals," p. 272; and "With its movable horn and its solid spring housing, the gramophone's social position is that of a border marker between two periods of musical practice," p. 273.) Much of the essay is imagistic and vague, at times almost free-associational, reflecting, I suspect, a kind of theoretical uncertainty as to the cultural import of the apparatus (Adorno's later revision—the version included in this volume—does not excise this quality). By 1927, when Adorno wrote this essay, commercial recordings had been available for thirty years, and the impact on listening habits and musical consumption was apparent but nonetheless not well researched.[50]

49. These essays are the subject of an important, detailed discussion by their English-language translator, Levin, "For the Record," pp. 23–47 (see n. 37, above). In what follows, for the most part, I stress somewhat different features of these essays than Levin. See Georgina Born, "Against Negation, for a Politics of Cultural Production: Adorno, Aesthetics, the Social," *Screen* 34 no. 3 (Fall 1993), pp. 226–31, for a critique of Levin's essay.

50. When Adorno joined the editorial board of the Viennese journal *Anbruch* in 1929, he proposed a new regular feature to be called "*Mechanische Musik*" devoted to discussions of music and machines, and addressed to consumers, as an initial effort to meet this need. See Levin, "For the Record," pp. 26–30. See also Thomas Y. Levin, with Michael von der Linn, "Elements of a Radio Theory: Adorno and the Princeton Radio Research Project," *Musical Quarterly* 78 no. 2 (Summer 1994), pp. 318–19. Barbara Engh, "After 'His Master's Voice,'" *New Formations* 38 (Summer 1999), p. 54, borrowing from Roland Barthes' comments on the impact of photography, suggests that the phonograph "represents an anthropological revolution in human history—not just another in a series of technological innovations, but one which profoundly interrupts and problematises what it means to be human. The phonograph dissociated the voice and embodied consciousness, which formerly had been thought to be so coterminous as to virtually define each other."

He expresses concern with the phonograph's effect of further privatizing life (he refers to it as "a utensil of the private life," p. 272)—in essence, the Sony Walkman/Discman paradox, wherein the aesthetic labor of others is privately heard rather than experienced intersubjectively and socially as may occur in musical ritual, whether ecclesiastical or secular.

Acknowledging the earliest arguments, and advertising, for the phonograph, namely, its function as a sound archive, Adorno wryly notes his uncertainty as to the worth of bothering. That is, why construct an archive if no one seeks to enter the museum, this with presumed reference to the gap between the vast amount of music then available on disk—from Caruso to pop acts (he names high-profile examples)—and the implied absence of recorded serious new music, that music which, from his perspective, immanently engages technological culture, as opposed to a common circumstance whereby the technological apparatus itself may attract more attention than the music played on it—much in the spirit of audiophile fetishism of our own time. Thus Adorno describes the class-prestige attached to fancifully decorated horns typical to machines purchased by "better social circles," and describes them as "shrouds of the emptiness that people usually prefer to enshroud within themselves" (pp. 272–73). And later he says essentially the same thing about records, likening them to "virtual photographs of their owners, flattering photographs—ideologies" (p. 274), in other words, possessions by means of which identity itself is colonized.[51]

"THE FORM OF THE PHONOGRAPH RECORD" (1934; pp. 277–82), as the title suggests, considers the disk rather than the machine. Adorno here quite radically detours from the path taken in the previous essay, particularly regarding the question of the phonograph record as archive. The essay begins almost poetically with a physical description of the disk itself, building toward a particular image: "covered with curves, a delicately scribbled, utterly illegible writing" (p. 277). Allusion to writing provides him with the opportunity to liken the disk to a plate, or tablet, and this leads to the metaphor of archaic knowledge preserved for a later time, in this instance, a future beyond modernity. Adorno's image is distinctly spatial. The disk's flatness he equates with a two-dimensionality that references the third dimension, that is, the musical actuality—the performance, in

---

51. Rather the same point is articulated by Jacques Attali, *Noise: The Political Economy of Music*, trans. Brian Massumi (Minneapolis: University of Minnesota Press, 1985), pp. 87–132, concerning modern habits of the mass-collecting of recordings, what Attali terms stockpiling.

real and specific time captured on disk. "The phonograph record is not good for much more than reproducing and storing a music deprived of its best dimension, a music, namely, that was already in existence before the phonograph record and is not significantly altered by it" (p. 278). He points to the medium's technological liabilities, noting the constant breaks in the performance of a symphony (he uses the *Eroica* as his example) caused by having to change disks.[52] But he is really after something more important than technological limitations of this sort. His issue is storing—preservation—which he understands both literally and as an allegory.

He describes the phonograph record as presenting riddles—not in terms of the sound waves imprinted on the shellac but what he names the very "thingness" of the disk itself. Precisely because it is a thing, it can be possessed, but he reverses the terms of his critique of musical possession noted earlier in favor of preservation and, indeed, access, which he regards dialectically. He likens the phonograph record to the nineteenth-century photo and postage-stamp album, small things that gain our attention only if we wish to notice them, objects "ready to conjure up every recollection that would otherwise be mercilessly shredded between the haste and humdrum of private life." In particular, the recording captures the experiential parameter through which music is activated but which cannot be held onto: time itself "as evanescence, enduring in mute music" (p. 279). "There is no doubt that, as music is removed by the phonograph record from the realm of live production and from the imperative of artistic activity and becomes petrified, it absorbs into itself, in this process of petrification, the

---

52. Thomson, *Musical Scene*, pp. 249–50, in a short essay from 1943 called "Processed Music," in spite of nearly a decade of technological improvement beyond what Adorno knew in 1934, echoes his concern regarding the degree to which recordings alter musical sound—a foretaste of the debates occurring over the change from analogue to digital recordings, as well the change from the long-playing record to the compact disc. Emerging from the speaker, "this music is never wholly realistic. The electro-mechanical devices by which music is preserved or transmitted all give it a slight flavor as of canned food. The preserved stuff, however, is nourishing and incredibly abundant; and one could neither wish nor imagine its abolishment. . . . This does not mean that processed music is completely interchangeable with fresh. It will sustain life, of course, at least for brief periods; and some of it has a special charm of its own, like canned peaches, boxed sardines, and filets of anchovy." Thomson then catalogues what broadcast music lacks, using Beethoven as his example; he lists dynamic diminution especially, along with what he terms the "deformation of instrumental timbres." Obliquely, he cites Adorno: "These matters and their implications for culture are discussed in the published reports of Columbia University's Institute for Social Research."

very life that would otherwise vanish. The dead art rescues the ephemeral and perishing art as the only one alive. Therein may lie the phonograph record's most profound justification, which cannot be impugned by an aesthetic objection to its reification" [i.e., in this instance, commodification] (p. 279). The recording in other words functions as a kind of trace in hibernation, or what he would later call "messages in bottles" tossed into the sea of future history.

Thus Adorno's conclusion suggests that music which was *conveyed* by writing (notation) suddenly in the record *becomes* writing. By this means it loses its "immediacy" but gains something in exchange, "the hope that, once fixed in this way, it will some day become readable as the 'last remaining universal language since the construction of the tower [of Babel]'" (p. 279). The image of universality encapsulates his utopian concern for reconciliation of the subject with nature, described in the introduction, here mixed with a Benjaminian allegory of musical time in its problematic relation to empirical time—that is, history: "Ultimately the phonograph records are not artworks but the black seals on the missives that are rushing towards us from all sides in the traffic with technology; missives whose formulations capture the sounds of creation, the first and the last sounds, judgment upon life and message about that which may come thereafter" (p. 280). In this instance the same technology that serves to make possible the end of history might also provide the means for helping to rescue what technological modernity has either tossed aside or smothered.

"OPERA AND THE LONG-PLAYING RECORD" (1969; pp. 283–87), which appeared first in *Der Spiegel*, still further modifies earlier positions on the technologies associated with the mass communication of music. Geared for a large-market weekly news magazine, the essay is not much more than an aphorism. Its points are few but nonetheless significant, not least for the clarity with which Adorno re-imagines the progressive potential of what was, after all, an established commodity form. Adorno regards opera as a fading anachronism, kept on life support in opera houses catering to a culture-vulture bourgeoisie by one of two means, both calling forth opera's visual appeal and both perfect for the televisual age, though he doesn't explicitly make the connection: period-piece confections (his example is *Figaro* in a rococo staging), pretty and pretty tired, or updates, which upgrade operas into the present-future, with characters—as he puts it—"dressed in sweat suits" [*Turnanzügen*] (p. 284), the updating-as-shock further begging the questions "What's the

point? Why even bother doing it on stage?" Adorno valorizes music,
opera's "true object."[53] Opera on long-playing record excises the visual

53. For a detailed account of Adorno's critique of opera, see ISM, pp. 71–84,
where he assesses it "obsolete": "The dawning insight [that opera was already
passé by the 1930s] . . . was that in style, in substance, and in attitude the opera
had nothing to do any more with the people it had to appeal to if its outwardly
pretentious form was to justify the prodigal expense required." He suggests that
opera has been done-in by the movies' overdetermined naturalism, making "the
improbabilities served up in each opera, even if the hero was a machinist," appear
absurd (pp. 71–72). Adorno's nearly visceral reaction to opera in this chapter—
a music genre he knew very well—is linked to what he sees as its regressive
social role in modernity. Apart from Alban Berg, he is notably unimpressed by
the dominant opera composers of the first two-thirds of the century (Strauss, in
particular).

Adorno's distaste for the opera audience is striking and stems not least from its
common and extreme musical conservatism: "Hatred of things modern—much
more virulent in the opera audience than in that of the drama—combines with
obstinacy in praising the good old days. The opera is one of the stopgaps in the
world of resurrected culture, a filler of holes blasted by the mind. That operatic
activities rattle on unchanged even though literally nothing in them fits any more,
this fact is drastic testimony to the noncommittal, somehow accidental character
assumed by the cultural superstructure. The official life of opera can teach us more
about society than about a species of art that is outliving itself and will hardly
survive the next blow" (p. 83). In 1955, several years before Adorno drafted this
chapter, he published an essay called "Bourgeois Opera," later included in his essay
collection SF, pp. 15–28. This essay is the more thoughtful and less polemical of
the two, though similar arguments appear in both (for example, he wryly refers
to opera as "a bourgeois vacation spot," p. 23). In "Bourgeois Opera" Adorno
alludes to what he understands to be the progressive elements formerly ascribable
to the genre, namely, opera's appeal to myth and magic—a kind of remembrance
of things past, and a protest against the instrumentalization of reason typical of
modernity: "It would be appropriate to think of opera as the specifically bourgeois
genre that, in the midst of, and with the methods appropriate to, a world bereft of
magic, paradoxically endeavors to preserve the magical element of art" (p. 18). The
examples he considers include *Die Zauberflöte, Fidelio,* and *Der Freischütz.*

Adorno links the chasm separating opera audiences today from old operas to
the difference between the modern subject and the subject represented on stage.
Gary Tomlinson, *Metaphysical Song: An Essay on Opera* (Princeton: Princeton
University Press, 1999), p. 129, points out the limitations of this rather undialectical formula: "it appears to rely on an almost pop-psychological notion of identification as a straightforward, empathic bond entered into by an integral subject on
the basis of perceived affinities with some object." On the other hand, to give
Adorno his due, he's also getting at something larger, in two parts: first, he regards
the opera house as a museum that long ago ceased acquiring new works and which
increasingly fetishizes the old by, as it were, re-dressing the corpse and rearranging
the display rooms; second, his position is consistent with his larger argument,
discussed in "The Aging of the New Music" in part 1, concerning the aging of all
artworks. That is, a great deal of history has occurred since Violetta took up house-

distraction that lavishly celebrates operatic obsolescence, in favor of what he names the text, which by means of recording the auditor may listen to/read.

The long-playing recording permits experiencing an opera's temporal dimension without distraction (including those caused by record-change breaks of the 78-rpm era); alternately, it permits re-audition of parts in order for the listener to focus on musical details. Adorno does not critique the private listening experience in this instance, principally I suspect because he finds the "ritual of performance" (p. 285) within the opera house still more regressive. He does acknowledge the fetishization of possession that accrues to record collecting, but essentially writes it off as a fact of modern life: "But there remains hardly any means other than possession, other than reification, through which one can get at anything unmediated in this world—and in art as well" (p. 285).[54] While he seems to re-imagine the private listener in essentially positive terms, he nonetheless laments the condition of (pervasive) loneliness. That is, whether privatization is the result of turning away or of being turned away, it prevails. Adorno's listener in this instance is alone and lonely, but his solitude has been turned

---

keeping with young Germont, and Manon Lescaut with de Grieux. However nineteenth-century audiences may have envisioned the bourgeois social mores underwriting these texts, today they seem little more than historical conceits necessary to activate the plots.

54. Tomlinson, *Metaphysical Song*, p. 144, echoing Attali, *Noise*, re-articulates Adorno's more typical argument as to the opera recording as commodity which, to be sure, Adorno acknowledges in this late essay while uncharacteristically underplaying its significance. Tomlinson: "The psychological investment of the opera fan is now shunted away from a public relation with the performers and other audience members and instead directed toward a private interaction with material things: the CDs, the gratifyingly hefty libretto booklet, the audio equipment, the videotape, the TV screen. These grant access to the distant, resonating bodies they represent in an estranged form, equivalent to the film viewer's relation to movie stars. So it is no surprise that cults of voice of a qualitatively new sort have taken root alongside the supremacy of recordings."

More in line with Adorno's argument, Lydia Goehr, *The Quest for Voice: On Music, Politics, and the Limits of Philosophy* (Berkeley and Los Angeles: University of California Press, 1998), pp. 165–67, points to Glenn Gould's abandonment of the stage for the recording studio on the grounds, he thought, that recording would make possible a degree of fidelity to the work unrealizable in live performance. As Goehr makes clear, Gould was in part conscious of "the critical distance granted to listeners who, in the privacy of home, could listen to recordings in their own time and as individuals without their judgment or experience of the works being influenced by the authoritatively dressed performer or by 'the herd' judgment of status-conscious audiences" (pp. 165–66).

against loneliness through the trace of intersubjectivity inscribed on the record's grooves. In the instance at hand, technology provides an opportunity for its force to act against the interests which it characteristically serves.[55]

Similarly, in an essay first written in 1957 and later included in *Sound Figures*, "New Music, Interpretation, Audience," Adorno addresses the gap between new music and audiences and considers how to narrow it. At the end he turns his attention to radio and offers a view of its possibilities notably revised from what he had expressed while involved with the Princeton Radio Project. Speaking of the split between art and society, he suggests that new music should, in effect, use market forces against the market: "Snobbishness towards the mass media is idiotic. Only by changing the function of the mass media can the intellectual monopoly of the Culture Industry be broken; it cannot be accomplished by retreating into social impotence. Today the radio alone can provide a shelter for new music, separate as it is from the market, and can take up its cause, which is that

55. Late in life Adorno moderated his hostility to mass culture, evident for example in his essay "Transparencies on Film" (1966), trans. David J. Levin, in *The Culture Industry: Selected Essays on Mass Culture*, ed. J. M. Bernstein (London: Routledge, 1991), pp. 154–61. Adorno's modified position on (some) film was in response to the new independent cinema of the 1960s, and especially the work of Alexander Kluge, as traced by Miriam Hansen, "Introduction to Adorno, 'Transparencies on Film' (1966)," *New German Critique* 24–25 (Fall/Winter 1981–82), pp. 186–98: "Kluge refers to Adorno's fundamental mistrust of the visual immediacy of film which he and Horkheimer had diagnosed as one of the culture industry's most effective ideological mechanisms." What Adorno valorizes in the new cinema are the practices that rupture the seamlessness of representation, especially the radical use of montage, thereby breaking down what Hansen names "the obtrusive referentiality of the image flow" (p. 194). This notwithstanding, Adorno foresaw that montage was not a magic elixir for producing rupture, or shock; that radical montage has degenerated into a postmodern cliché of hip advertising, and a clichéd staple of music videos, certifies his misgivings. "Transparencies on Film" identifies film as a form of writing, hence similar to his comments about the phonograph record. The montage-writing that he sought to advance was, in effect, constellational. See Stuart Liebman, "On New German Cinema, Art, Enlightenment, and the Public Sphere: An Interview with Alexander Kluge," *October* 46 (Fall 1988), pp. 36–38, Kluge's personal memoir of Adorno.

In ISM, pp. 134–35, Adorno also writes about the phonograph record, echoing points about the advantages of repetitive listening, and emphasizing the possibility of making music very widely available, thereby allowing for the "potential abolition of educational privilege." Nonetheless, he acknowledges the hoarding aspect of classical music recording aficionados and the tendency of recording companies to focus their catalogues on war-horse classics and star performers, hence reproducing the fundamentals of base consumerism.

of human beings, in its battle against human beings. In the same way, radio can guarantee performances in which the music is truly realized."[56]

"ON THE FETISH-CHARACTER IN MUSIC AND THE REGRESSION OF LISTENING" (1938; pp. 288–317) is an extraordinary and wide-ranging essay less about listening, and more about the social conditions affecting listening and the impact of these "listening conditions" on music's relation to subjects. The essay is the result of a critical exchange of ideas between Adorno and Walter Benjamin in the form of several lengthy letters sent by Benjamin from his exile in Paris, and by Adorno from his exile first in London and Oxford and later New York. The so-named "Adorno-Benjamin Debate," whose story, long and complicated, constitutes one of the most important discussions of aesthetics produced in the twentieth century.[57] I want to trace the essentials of just one part of it, namely, the exchanges triggered by Benjamin's essay "The Work of Art in the Age of Mechanical Reproduction,"[58] which first appeared in print in the Institute of Social Research's journal, in French translation, in 1936. First reference to this essay occurs in the Adorno-Benjamin correspondence in a passing reference by Benjamin in January 1936, by which time the essay was already fully drafted, though Adorno hadn't yet seen it. On 27 February 1936, Benjamin sent Adorno a copy in German, together with an accompanying letter. Three weeks later, on 18 March, Adorno responded with a detailed and lengthy critique,[59] which would culminate two years later with

56. Adorno, "New Music, Interpretation, Audience," pp. 37–38. To be sure, Adorno does not address the question of whether anyone listens to what is transmitted. See also ISM, pp. 133–34, on potential progressive pedagogical contributions of the mass media relative to new music.

57. For thorough accounts of the dispute, see Susan Buck-Morss, *The Origin of Negative Dialectics: Theodor W. Adorno, Walter Benjamin, and the Frankfurt Institute* (New York: Free Press, 1977), pp. 136–84; Eugene Lunn, *Marxism and Modernism: An Historical Study of Lukács, Brecht, Benjamin, and Adorno* (Berkeley and Los Angeles: University of California Press, 1982), pp. 151–70; and Richard Wolin, *Walter Benjamin: An Aesthetic of Redemption* (New York: Columbia University Press, 1982), pp. 163–212. For brief summaries, see Wiggershaus, *Frankfurt School*, pp. 210–18; Lambert Zuidervaart, *Adorno's Aesthetic Theory: The Redemption of Illusion* (Cambridge: MIT Press, 1991), pp. 29–32; and Andrew Arato and Eike Gebhardt, "Esthetic Theory and Cultural Criticism," in *The Essential Frankfurt School Reader*, ed. Andrew Arato and Eike Gebhardt (New York: Continuum, 1982), pp. 215–19.

58. Walter Benjamin, "The Work of Art in the Age of Mechanical Reproduction," in *Illuminations*, ed. Hannah Arendt, trans. Harry Zohn (New York: Schocken Books, 1969), pp. 217–51, representing a revised second German version produced shortly after the one in French.

59. CC, pp. 127–33.

the publication of the "Fetish-Character" essay, written in New York—references to which thereafter continue to appear in the correspondence as late as the penultimate letter to Adorno by Benjamin, written a few months before his suicide in September 1940.

Benjamin's concern, stated in his essay's preface, is a theory of mass art "useless for the purposes of Fascism," and useful by contrast "for the formulation of revolutionary demands in the politics of art."[60] His argument hinges on the claim that modern reproductive technology, in the realm of mass entertainment/art, film especially, fundamentally alters the cultural landscape in socially progressive ways less by making mass art more or less democratically available (and inexpensive), more by the changed conditions of viewing engendered by the medium. Benjamin's point of departure is a comparison of two ways of viewing two different types of art: relatively private viewing of unique (original) artworks—paintings—on the one hand, and, on the other, communal or mass viewing of mass art—that is, film, of which there are any number of reproduced prints but in essence no original. Whereas paintings demand contemplation under ritualized viewing conditions, film by contrast invites distraction.[61] Films tend toward a high degree of referentiality—plot, narrative, settings, and bodies in gestural relationships, not to downplay the indexical photographic image as such. Movies in short were sufficiently "like life" that their reception no longer required rapt contemplation. They could be received by viewers as already familiar—rather like acetate acquaintances. And the settings in which they were watched, communally, and cheaply, did not inspire awe or, for that matter, ritual silence (audience interaction of the "Rocky Horror" type was not wholly an invention of the 1970s). An original artwork was available only under the special circumstances permitted by the established protocols, and at a single viewing site, and these conditions of viewing gave the work "cult value" and the quality of "unapproachability"; "True to its nature, it remains 'distant, however close it may be' ").[62] The film, lacking an original, rendered moot the protocol of reverential respect for all intents and purposes. Reproducibility, in Benjamin's words, replaced authenticity. What "withered" with the film, was

60. Benjamin, "Work of Art in the Age of Mechanical Reproduction," p. 218.
61. Ibid., p. 238: "Let us compare the screen on which a film unfolds with the canvas of a painting. The painting invites the spectator to contemplation; before it the spectator can abandon himself to his associations. Before the movie frame he cannot do so. No sooner has his eye grasped a scene than it is already changed. It cannot be arrested."
62. Ibid., p. 243 n. 5.

the artwork's "aura" (a word Benjamin places in scare quotes at its first appearance).[63]

Film advances "the liquidation of the traditional value of the cultural heritage," which Benjamin reads as a politically progressive diminution of privilege and intellectual domination. The spatial element resurfaces here; Benjamin speaks of the masses' desire to bring things " 'closer' spatially and humanely," in essence to have what has been denied them.[64] Freeing itself from ritual, the mechanically reproduced artwork "begins to be based on another practice—politics. . . . Mechanical reproduction of art changes the reaction of the masses toward art. The reactionary attitude toward a Picasso painting changes into the progressive reaction toward a Chaplin movie. The progressive reaction is characterized by the direct, intimate fusion of visual and emotional enjoyment with the orientation of the expert. Such fusion is of great social significance."[65]

As Richard Wolin put it, art's status as "an object of aesthetic enjoyment or satisfaction assumes a role subordinate to its function as an instrument of communication."[66] Distraction and contemplation are constituted by Benjamin as polar opposites as regards their political implications under the prevailing conditions of modernity. The man who stands in contemplation before an artwork, as Benjamin sees it, is passively "absorbed by it." Contemplative viewing, that is, is not envisioned as an active process, presumably because the artwork colonizes the viewer, though less by what it is, more because of what it has become (a cult object). The "distracted mass" by contrast "absorbs the work of art."[67]

Benjamin is especially attracted to montage and to the shock effects that can result from the technique, which he judges anti-auratic and functioning against both contemplation (one doesn't contemplate when shocked) and passivity (shock cannot be ignored). Put differently, so as to square the circle: shock is distracting. And here Benjamin learns from his friend Brecht: shock alienates, estranges. Accordingly, the viewer must actively attempt to make sense of what's happening. The viewer becomes a critic instead of a worshipper or believer.[68] Benjamin employs distraction as a mark of expertise among the masses; it signals the habitual. That is, dis-

63. Ibid., p. 221.
64. Ibid., pp. 221, 223.
65. Ibid., pp. 224, 234.
66. Wolin, *Walter Benjamin*, p. 189.
67. Benjamin, "Work of Art in the Age of Mechanical Reproduction," p. 239.
68. Wolin, *Walter Benjamin*, p. 190.

traction implies a level of expertise to which the mechanically reproduced artwork can appeal yet without colonizing the viewer. In other words, the viewer's interpretative agency is implicitly valorized by film and also, as it were, protected (through the replacement of aura by distraction). By honoring this agency film honors the masses as subjects and at the same time contributes to their subjecthood. The public is placed in the position of the critic—but "this position requires no attention. The public is an examiner, but an absent-minded one."[69]

In response, and referring to the study as "extraordinary," Adorno tells Benjamin that "there is not a single sentence here that I would not want to discuss with you in detail," were they in a position to meet face to face. Barring that possibility, Adorno identifies one "fundamental theme," his "passionate interest and total approval" of Benjamin's intention to de-mythify art, adding that his own work emphatically endorses "the primacy of [modern] technology, especially in music."[70] He then begins to elucidate his objections, which may be summarized as follows. First, Benjamin correctly recognizes a kind of Brechtian assignment of "magical aura" to high art (what he names in scare quotes the "autonomous work of art") and the implicit designation of such art, pro forma, as counter-revolutionary: simply, wholly, on the wrong side, so to speak. Adorno agrees with Benjamin (and Brecht) that a magical aura persists in the bourgeois artwork, pointing out that he has long criticized this very feature. But here he separates himself from Benjamin by insisting that the artwork is not *only* magically auratic but rather is inherently dialectical, that is, it "compounds within itself the magical element with the sign of freedom."[71] In a later letter to Benjamin (10 November 1938, from New York), likewise connected to their running dispute but this time concerning Benjamin's manuscript, "The Paris of the Second Empire in Baudelaire," part of the never-completed *Arcades* project, Adorno put the matter succinctly: "Unless I

69. Benjamin, "Work of Art in the Age of Mechanical Reproduction," pp. 240–41. Benjamin ends his essay with an epilogue addressing fascism and its aestheticization of politics. Not coincidentally he quotes one of Marinetti's celebrations of war ("War is beautiful because it initiates the dreamt-of metalization of the human body. War is beautiful because it enriches a flowering meadow with the fiery orchids of machine guns").

70. CC, pp. 127–28. Adorno here plays off the fact that in German the word *Technik* means both technology and technique. Adorno's interest in new techniques associated with new music is for him homologous to Benjamin's promotion of the socially progressive promise of film technology.

71. Ibid., p. 128.

244 / Culture, Technology, and Listening

am very much mistaken, your dialectic is lacking in one thing: media-tion."[72] Thus, with regard to autonomous artworks, Adorno reminds Ben-jamin of his own "emphatic endorsement of the primacy of technology, especially in music," as a means to transform this art as well, by de-fetishizing it. He suggests that the "pursuit of the technical laws of au-tonomous art"—the rigorous application of the compositional processes of new music, such as twelve-tone technique—are the means to this end. Adorno rejects the absolute nature of Benjamin's position: "The reification of a great work of art is not simply a matter of loss, any more than the reification of the cinema is all loss." In other words, dialectic critique must be applied to the low as well as to the high. Thus Adorno insists that cinema itself possesses aura "to an extreme and highly suspect degree"—the cult of stars, the site (not the neighborhood theater but the movie palace), and advertising hype (movie magazines, trailers).[73]

Adorno acknowledges the damage to artworks in commodity culture, just as he insists on the commodification of mass art. Both high and low "bear the stigmata of capitalism, both contain elements of change (but never, of course, simply as a middle term between Schoenberg and the American film). Both are torn halves of an integral freedom, to which, however, they do not add up."[74] Adorno accuses Benjamin of romanticiz-ing, placing what he names "blind trust in the spontaneous powers of the proletariat . . . which is itself [lamentably] a product of bourgeois society." That is, Adorno wonders aloud about the nature of the magic that will suddenly allow the downtrodden to become enlightened in the manner prescribed by Benjamin, through watching movies. Nazi cinema, sharp in his mind (cinema which Benjamin knew as well), suggests that Benjamin's enthusiasm is not warranted. Adorno then speaks of audience laughter which he, like Benjamin, has heard in the cinema. He finds it "anything but salutary and revolutionary," naming what he hears "bourgeois sa-dism" (not fundamentally different, say, from Jerry Springer audiences taking exquisite pleasure in the misery and self-shaming behavior of oth-ers). But with respect to the Little Tramp: "The idea that a reactionary individual can be transformed into a member of the avant-garde through an intimate acquaintance with the films of Chaplin, strikes me as simple

72. Ibid., p. 282.
73. Ibid., all quotations from pp. 128–30.
74. Ibid., p. 130. Adorno repeated this thought in the "Fetish-Character" essay, p. 293, and in "On the Social Situation of Music," p. 395.

romanticization. . . . You need only have heard the laughter of the audience at the screening of this film to realize what is going on."[75]

Benjamin's artwork essay addresses photography and film. Adorno via the "Fetish-Character" essay, and responding to Benjamin, addresses music. Whereas Benjamin's political theory of mass art argues for its liberating tendencies, Adorno's essay opens with a statement about mass consciousness and obedience. Both writers' essays speak to issues of production and consumption, but their emphasis is different. Arguably, Benjamin's is more concerned with the question of audience consumption, whereas Adorno is more directly focused on production. Benjamin speaks in detail about *how* audiences receive mass art, Adorno speaks in detail about *what* they are given to consume—and his examples come from both the classical and popular repertories, both commodified and by various means standardized, as he will argue—his point being to suggest that Benjamin's utopian conclusion is unwarranted and dangerously myopic as regards the very politics he espouses.

Adorno's overriding critique is based on what he regards as the standardized nature of what he names "musical goods," art reduced to product. He suggests that people listen to music as (before the fact) so much Muzak, which is to say that they barely listen at all, and precisely because they don't need to. They already know what they will hear even before they hear it. (And he ironically adds: "Schoenberg's music resembles popular songs in refusing to be enjoyed," p. 292.) Adorno is building toward an argument for contemplative listening—which he does not perceive as a passive exercise—focused on musical structure, such as I have discussed earlier with regard to "The Radio Symphony." Standardization, he argues, is driven by imitation which, by repeating, in essence musically speaks against the foundation of originality upon which individuality depends: "The liquidation of the individual is the real signature of the new musical situation" (p. 293), rather than the individual liberated per Benjamin. Adorno's larger claim is that all contemporary musical life is commodity dependent. There is no fundamental difference between the marketing of The Three Tenors and the Backstreet Boys, nor the music each group performs; indeed, not even their performance venues are markedly different. "The consumer is really worshipping the money that he himself has

75. Ibid., p. 130. See further on sadistic laughter, Miriam Hansen, "Of Mice and Ducks: Benjamin and Adorno on Disney," *South Atlantic Quarterly* 92 no. 1 (Winter 1993), pp. 32, 34–35, 52–54.

paid for the ticket to the Toscanini concert" (p. 296).[76] That is, the more that society is governed by the exchange principle, the more that exchange-value presents itself as the object of enjoyment. Conversely, Adorno commented that "every pleasure which emancipates itself from exchange-value takes on subversive features" (p. 297). Using Toscanini as his example, whose cultic star status regenerates him as a fetish, Adorno critiques what he terms the "barbarism of perfection," a form of fetishistic technocratic discipline and musical purity under the reign of a conductor's steely control. The result, he insists, is the loss of spontaneity to the degree that live performance already sounds recorded, in essence objectified, and standardized: "The new fetish is the flawlessly functioning, metallically brilliant apparatus as such, in which all the cogwheels mesh so perfectly that not the slightest hole remains open for the meaning of the whole. . . . The performance sounds like its own phonograph record" (p. 301).[77]

The first half of the "Fetish-Character" essay addresses Adorno's reading of music's fetishization, a critique principally centered on classical music. The last half is devoted to the regression of listening produced by music's fetishization. Adorno acknowledges that with mass communications technology, millions more people have access to music; his concern, however, is that their listening is "arrested at the infantile stage" (p. 303), a polemical comment charged against what he regarded as Benjamin's suggestion that filmgoers became both experts and critics. Adorno in effect wonders how this happens, particularly when what is consumed would from his perspective seem to dull nascent critical responses. Taking music,

76. Cf. Jean Baudrillard, "The Art Auction: Sign Exchange and Sumptuary Value," in *For a Critique of the Political Economy of the Sign*, trans. Charles Levin (St. Louis: Telos Press, 1981), pp. 112–22.

77. Regarding Toscanini, see also Adorno, "The Mastery of the Maestro," SF, pp. 40–53; he argues that the conductor's perfectionism favors craft over expression—what Adorno terms Toscanini's "technocratic hostility to the spirit" (p. 53); and "Analytical Study of the NBC *Music Appreciation Hour*," p. 376 n. 31. See also Joseph Horowitz, *Understanding Toscanini: How He Became an American Culture-God and Created a New Audience for Old Music* (New York: Alfred A. Knopf, 1987). Edward W. Said, *Musical Elaborations* (New York: Columbia University Press, 1991), pp. 18–21, while agreeing with the critical accounts of Toscanini by both Adorno and Horowitz, points to a significant "remainder"—and by means of a narrative that is notably Adornian: "There is something I think centrally missing in both their accounts of the Toscanini phenomenon. What stamps the still available 1938 performance by Toscanini of the *Eroica* is the absolute rigor of the logic that he lets unfold in Beethoven's music, and in so doing discloses a process, almost a narrative, that is irreducibly unique, eccentric, contrary to everyday life. So highly wrought is this that it feels like a clear aesthetic alternative to the travails of ordinary human experience" (p. 19).

like film a time-bound art form, Adorno turns Benjamin's notion of dis-tracted consumption on its head, in essence to ask: if one doesn't pay at-tention (whether because there is not much to pay heed to, as per musical standardization, or because the commodified nature of music is such that the music is less important than, say, the star conductor), one doesn't hear the music, or, as he puts it, one listens only atomistically. "Deconcentrated listening makes the perception of a whole impossible. All that is realized is what the spotlight falls on—striking melodic intervals, unsettling mod-ulations, intentional or unintentional mistakes, or whatever condenses it-self into a formula by an especially intimate merging of melody and text" (p. 305). What he's after is the musical analogue to TV channel surfing, in which quick surface impressions are created but no thorough sense of any one narrative whole is developed, an analogue—one could add—in which the differences among the multiple "channels" often extend little further than the musical parameters that distinguish Top 40 radio from, say, PBS's *Great Performances*. I've chosen my examples precisely for the same hyperbolic purpose that Adorno intended by his. That is, there are differences among the examples cited, and these are sometimes greater than the chosen examples otherwise serve to imply. But from Adorno's point of view, the prevailing trend is evident enough, and the best way to shake the reader's own assumed proclivities toward the trend is rhetorical exaggeration—precisely responding to the strategic exaggeration he rec-ognizes in Benjamin's counter-argument.

Adorno outlines two broad categories of music, classical or serious, and what he terms "light" music. When speaking of structural listening, his concern is music whose processural complexity defines the musical work's essence. Adorno recognizes a functional differentiation between classical music (ideally experienced by means of contemplative listening) and light music (for example, its "use" for dancing). But here he takes a different tack in his critique. The classical musics he alludes to are old works, pre-cisely because new music has gained no place in mass consciousness and made no inroads in mass distribution. Old music is in essence fixed in time but not fixed in reception, which has changed, or to be more precise, re-verted to a mode of attending appropriate to the low common denominator of background sounds. Light music by contrast is new but fully standard-ized, locked in the narrow perimeter of self-imitation, in which instance there remains nothing to listen for, because the listener has already heard it before its first audition. Adorno recognizes the potential for a progressive social function for both types of music, just as he insists that this function is not met by either. His argument is not about one music being inherently good and the other not, nor that listeners are inherently stupid. His claim is that listeners are made not born, that listening is a cultural practice, and that modernity has served the practice poorly, by turning music—all music, to every degree possible—into a thing, a market object. Listeners— and he means all listeners, whatever their social class or educational background—are in his words "betrayed," and the betrayal's cost is charged against their own subjectivity and identity: "Regressive listeners behave like children. Again and again and with stubborn malice, they demand the one dish they have once been served. A sort of musical children's language is prepared for them" (p. 307). It seems to me that what Adorno is getting at in this obviously inflammatory rhetoric is evident from the media-reception extremes of my own generation. On American Bandstand three or so long decades ago on-camera teenagers were daily asked to rate songs. The usual answers—whose very repetition on the air taught an entire generation how (little) to talk about the music—were, for a high rating: "It has a good beat." At least, in this instance, the kids were addressing the music itself; and since they were dancing, the beat was a good place to start. The fact that that's nearly the only thing ever said about the music strikes me as the mutual reinforcement of limitations then imposed alike on music and talk about music. A long generation later, on MTV's TRL (Total Request Live), like American Bandstand broadcast during the after-school time slot, teenage and young adult listeners gathered on the side-walk in Times Square, in front of the second-level picture-windowed MTV studios, are also interviewed. Day after day what's emphasized in their assessments of particular hits is not the music but the sexiness of the musicians in the video image. Of course, such commentary does not indicate that no one is listening; but it does make clear that musical discourse as such hardly exists as a valorized practice. Discourse has been transferred instead onto musicians' bodies, or body parts—ritualistically described as "hot"—in lieu of a discursive language with which to discuss the music itself. Adorno's point here is to undercut Benjamin's claim as to the de-mystifying effect of mass art. Adorno insists that no such disenchantment occurs, that "nothing survives in it more steadfastly than the illusion, nothing is more illusory than its reality" (p. 312).[78]

78. Adorno wrote to Benjamin from New York on 10 November 1938 that he had finished the "Fetish-Character" essay and that it had already gone to press. He added, "The work certainly bears the marks of haste in composition; but perhaps that is not entirely a bad thing" (CC, p. 286). The white-heat of his polemic— perhaps what he regarded as "not entirely a bad thing"—is particularly evident in the essay's last pages where he articulates a fairly stilted, ill-considered, and no-

In the end, two extremes are established: Benjamin's argument for the emancipatory force of mass art, and Adorno's fundamental denial of its actuality. Adorno maintained faith in rigorously avant-garde art, but this was art that in essence had very little audience; its impact was negligible, as well he knew. On the other hand, Adorno confronted (as Benjamin did not) the paradox of a potentially progressive political mass art: its tendency, which he saw in Brecht, of regressing to propaganda, with the result being little better than the forms of mass art which it opposed.[79] Both Adorno's and Benjamin's essays were written in the shadow of fascism, from positions of personal exile. Both men saw fascism as the symptom of a prevailing condition rather than as a political aberration. Miriam Hansen, writing recently—and brilliantly—on the Disney references in both essays (pithy exchanges concerning Mickey Mouse and Donald Duck), closes with the following: "Half a century later, in an age of cyborgs, global integration, and more sophisticated technological warfare, the questions posed by Benjamin and Adorno's debate on Disney are still with us, suggesting a line of inquiry that can help us defamiliarize the all-too-familiar opposition of high-modernist critique and postmodernist affirmation."[80]

-----

tably undialectical assessment of the ham radio operator, for whom he says any sound is as good as another, and of jitterbug dancing, which he likens to the reflex motions of "mutilated animals" (p. 309) in order to assert, rather heavy-handedly, an argument about dehumanization. The essay loses steam at the end through Adorno's overplaying of his generally impressive hand.

Benjamin provided Adorno with a reaction to the "Fetish-Character" essay in a very long letter from 9 December 1938 that for the most part responds to Adorno's earlier negative assessment of Benjamin's Baudelaire essay. Benjamin aptly recognized that in the "Art-Work" essay he had attempted to articulate the positive moments whereas [Adorno in his "Fetish-Character" essay] articulated the negative ones (CC, p. 295). On 1 February 1939, Adorno responded to Benjamin's letter in turn, notably remarking the essay's limitations: "I am all too aware of the weakness of the work. And this consists, to put it crudely, in the tendency to engage in Jeremiads and polemics." He then poses a question that remains to be addressed: "What will becomes of human beings and their capacity for aesthetic perception when they are fully exposed to the conditions of monopoly capitalism? But when I composed the essay, I was not yet psychologically capable of posing the question in such diabolical and behaviouristic terms. The piece must be seen essentially as an expression of my experiences here in America [then about one year's duration], which may well inspire me one day to grapple with something that we have both rightly felt was previously missing in our writings on mass art and monopoly capitalism" (CC, p. 305). That effort would be realized in California a few years later with the drafting of the Culture Industry chapter in DE. See further Adorno's self-critique of the essay, CC, p. 320.

79. See further Wolin, *Walter Benjamin*, pp. 207–12.
80. Hansen, "Of Mice and Ducks," p. 54.

In "LITTLE HERESY" (1965; pp. 318–24), Adorno returns to structural listening to offer a caveat to his own earlier arguments as regards the centrality of the artwork's aesthetic wholeness. Specifically, he insists on the importance of preserving the musical detail against the tendency of the whole to overwhelm it. He associates the detail in the artwork with the individual in society: just as the social collective is realized in and by individuals, so too is the work realized by the details of which it is composed. Adorno promotes preservation of a reciprocal relation between the two elements, part and whole, by means of which each is the more fully realized. Heard atomistically, the detail is rendered meaningless in its isolation. Conversely, heard solely as a building block of something larger, the detail surrenders any sense of its own spontaneity—which ultimately must be preserved if the whole is to express anything more than its own immanent structure.

In musical details Adorno hears the subject speaking, willingly bending toward the musical object (the whole) in order to make possible the work. Musical details, bending and blending their expressive character toward the whole while retaining their own specific character, permit the reenactment of reconciliation between subject and object, for Adorno the artwork's highest goal. In late modernity, when objective character as such is valorized over and above any form of subjectivity worthy of the name, his "little heresy" brushes against the grain: "The attention [now] paid to the whole has become one-sided and threatens to make the individual aspects, without which, after all, no musical whole has vitality, atrophy" (p. 320). The only responsible listening, he suggests, is one that recognizes and seeks to sustain the actual dialectical relation between the particular and the universal. It is by this means that the non-identical in the musical work—that particularity which marks resistance to standardization and desultory repetition—can survive. In short, Adorno's promotion of the detail betrays his fear of the force of modern totality replicated alike in artworks and in rigidly objectified forms of structural listening, whose responsible social purpose should, contrarily, be to refuse.

The Radio Symphony

An Experiment in Theory[A]

THE PROBLEM

To make a study of what radio transmission does musically to a musical structure or to different kinds of music would be a vast undertaking. It involves problems of a great many types and levels, concerning the material and the technicalities of transmission,[B] which can be solved only by the close collaboration of analytically minded musicians, social scientists, and experts on radio engineering. Here would appear the problem of the role played in traditional serious music by the "original"—that is, the live performance one actually experiences, as compared with mass reproduction on the radio. Or one would have to investigate to what extent the technical conditions of jazz in themselves establish a configuration of quasi-

A. The author wishes to express his indebtedness for editorial assistance to Josef Maier and George Simpson.

B. Of the related problems, which may very well basically affect the structure and the meaning of broadcast music, we refer only to one: the problem of the hear-stripe. Even if the set functions properly, the "current," namely, the thermal noises, can be heard. These continuous noises constitute a hear-stripe. The hear-stripe, which of course varies with the quality of the set, tends to disappear from the musical surface as soon as the performance takes shape. But it still can be heard underneath the music. It may not attract any attention and it may not even enter the listener's consciousness; but as an objective characteristic of the phenomenon it plays a part in the apperception of the whole.

One might venture to suggest that the psychological effect of the hear-stripe is somewhat similar to the awareness of the screen in the movies: music appearing upon such a hear-stripe may bear a certain image-like character of its own. Since at the present stage in technical development—particularly by means of FM—this undercurrent of noise is supposed to be abolished, the present study does not take into broader consideration this particular aspect of the field.

mechanized technique with quasi-subjective expression weirdly analogous to that of the actual mechanization of radio transmission with the quasi-expressive ballads with which our radio programs are jammed. Attention must be accorded to chamber music, which structurally is best suited to radio transmission but which, for socio-psychological reasons, is very rarely heard over the air.[c]

It is not our intention to do more than suggest the significance of such problems here. Instead of elaborating them systematically to their fullest extent, we restrict ourselves to one example analyzed in detail, in order to demonstrate concretely the implications as well as the complexity of the field. We are primarily concerned with pointing out the fact that serious music as communicated over the ether may indeed offer optimum conditions for retrogressive tendencies in listening, for the avalanche of fetishism which is overtaking music and burying it under the moraine of entertainment. The statement of the problem and the model analysis which we offer here are in the nature of a challenge to musical and social research. We are undertaking an experiment in theory.

The subject matter of this experiment in theory is the fate of the symphony and, more specifically, of the Beethoven symphony, when it is transmitted by radio. The reasons for this approach are sociological and musical. A typical statement exhibiting official optimism presents claims that today "the farmers' wives in the prairie states listen to great music performed by great artists as they go about their morning housework."[D] The Beethoven symphony is popularly identified with such great music. The truth or falsity of such complacent statements concerning the spreading of great music, however, can be gleaned only by an investigation into their presuppositions, namely, the naïve identification of a broadcast with the presentation of a live symphony.

The musical reasons for the choice of the symphony as instance become

---

C. The fact that a majority of listeners prefer "symphonic" music to chamber music can be accounted for as follows: (a) the factor of primitive and spectacular strength of sound, its "publicity character"; (b) a multicolored structure is more attractive to the untrained ear than a unicolored one; (c) the specific symphonic intensity and emphasis, a feature, in which chamber music is more or less lacking; (d) the structure of symphonic music of the "classical" period is often simpler than that of chamber music of the same period. This holds good particularly for the question of polyphony. The texture of classical chamber music is generally more polyphonous than that of symphonies. Polyphony, however, to most listeners is the main obstacle to understanding.

D. Dixon Skinner, "Music Goes into Mass Production," *Harper's Magazine*, April 1939, p. 487.

clear in the course of the analysis. Beethoven is selected not only because he is the standard classic of cultural sales talk in music, but also because his music exhibits most clearly some of the features we regard as particularly affected by radio transmission. Earlier symphonic music is less exposed to changes by radio because the problem of sound volume and the issue of dynamic development play a lesser role than in Beethoven; the later romantic symphony is less characteristic because it does not offer the central problem of the radio symphony: the problem of the fate of the "integral form."

CHARACTERISTICS OF THE SYMPHONY

Even those who optimistically assume that radio brings great symphonic music to people who never heard it before concede that symphonies brought to the overburdened hypothetical farmer in the Middle West are somewhat affected and deteriorated by radio transmission. But in principle, they maintain that these differences matter only to the musical snobs[E] who know so much about music in general and about symphonic music in particular. The finer shades and differences—so they say—are of no importance to the layman who must first become acquainted with the material. Better a symphony that is not quite as good as it is supposed to be in Carnegie Hall, than no symphony at all. Whoever dares to oppose such a view is likely to be regarded as an esthete who has no true sympathy for the needs and desires of the people. Yet the social analyst must risk being castigated as a misanthrope if he is to pursue social essence, as distinct from the façade.

Analysis of a radio symphony must rid itself of the commonsense view that the alterations brought about by radio have no significant bearing on

E. Cf. Robert West, *S-o-o-o-o You're Going on the Air!* (New York: Rodin, 1934), p. 56. [The passage Adorno has in mind is the following, pp. 56–57: "A certain class of listeners are loud in protest that the stations and the sponsors stoop to conquer. They demand that every one of the thousands of musical programs shall be exactly suited to their personal taste. They seek perfection in everything as they themselves define perfection. . . . Cynics need not fear that good music will be hacked to pieces and rendered futile over the air in the approaching years. Were Beethoven to live today to see his exalted vogue, he would no doubt gush with happiness. The Ninth Symphony can be repeated safely without becoming stale. With improvements in sound effects electrically, the audience will receive more than the usual fraction of melodic harmony communicated through the present-day receiver. He will be lifted literally to the skies by orchestral, choral and operatic works, where he today is but stirred to elementary emotion with limited delivery." (rl)]

the symphonic purpose. To begin with, it must cast off the conventional definition of symphony which asserts that it is merely a sonata for orchestra.[F] For insight into the changes a Beethoven symphony suffers in radio transmission depends upon the specific understanding of symphonic form as it crystallized and maintained itself in the comparatively short period of Haydn, Mozart, and Beethoven. This specific understanding is not furthered by analyzing the symphony in stereotyped terms such as exposition, development, repetition, or even more subtle ones such as the antagonism of the two main subjects of the exposition,[G] their "bridge," their conclusion, the way they develop and undergo their modified recurrence. However easy it may be to identify all those typical constituents of form in every Beethoven symphony, they are essential not abstractly, but only within the interplay of the inexchangeable content of each work. Such schematic identification actually is *too* easy: any approach starting from the mere recognition of those invariants, tends to deliver listening up to a mechanical process in which any symphony can be replaced by any other which has the same framework.

If reference to those terms does not add much in the actual following of a specific work, it is even less helpful in achieving an understanding of the meaning and function of symphonic form *per se*.

What characterizes a symphony when experienced in immediate listening, as distinct not only from chamber music, but also from orchestral forms such as the suite or the "tone poem," is a particular intensity and concentration. This intensity rests musically upon the incomparably

F. Cf. Paul Bekker, *The Symphony from Beethoven to Mahler* (Berlin: Schuster and Loeffler, 1918). Paper read before the Frankfurt Main Association for Modern Art, 1918, p. 8. [Adorno gives the title of this sixty-one-page monograph in English; it was in fact only available in German: *Die Sinfonie von Beethoven bis Mahler.* (rl)]

G. The "dualism" of themes, which is, by most commentators, urged as the main characteristic of the sonata form in general and the symphonic form in particular, actually plays only a minor role in Beethoven. Generally the "second" theme is by no means in marked contrast to the first theme (as it is, for instance, in the first movement of romantic symphonies even as early as Schubert's C Major and B Minor) but is carefully "mediated" with the first theme to avoid any sharp contrast which might endanger the unity of the whole movement. Further, in Beethoven the so-called second theme is very seldom "one" theme but, in most cases, a unity of manifold thematic ingredients so that it is often difficult to identify one particular thematic *Gestalt* as "the" second theme. This is especially apparent in one of Beethoven's most famous symphonic pieces, the first movement of the Ninth Symphony. The replacement of the actual Beethoven symphony by patterns of late romanticism is reflected even in the way in which musical commentators talk about it: they mistake it for Tchaikovsky.

greater density and concision of thematic relationships of the symphonic as against other forms. This density and concision are strictly technical and not merely a by-product of expression. They imply first a complete economy of craft; that is to say, a truly symphonic movement contains nothing fortuitous, every bit is ultimately traceable to very small basic elements, and is deduced from them and not introduced, as it were, from outside, as in romantic music.[H]

Secondly, this economy itself does not reside in a static identity, as in pre-classical music. It is not content with mere repetition, but is intrinsically bound up with variation. If everything in a Beethoven symphony is identical in its ultimate motifical content, nothing is literally identical in the sense of plain repetition, but everything is "different" according to the function it exercises within the development of the whole. A Beethoven symphonic movement is essentially the unity of a manifold as well as the manifoldness of a unity, namely, of the identical thematic material. This interrelationship of perpetual variation is unfolded as a process—never through mere "statement" of detail. It is the most completely organized piece of music that can be achieved. Every detail, however spontaneous in emphasis, is absorbed in the whole by its very spontaneity and gets its true weight only by its relation to the whole, as revealed finally by the symphonic process. Structurally, one hears the first bar of a Beethoven symphonic movement only at the very moment when one hears the last bar. Romanticism failed to produce symphonic works of this exacting character because the increase in importance of the expressive detail as against the whole, rendered impossible the determination of every moment by the totality. While listening to a typical romantic symphony one remains fully conscious, sometimes all too conscious,[I] of the time it consumes, despite

H. Extreme examples of this characteristic are evident in some few works of Beethoven in which the first and second themes are actually identical and only presented in a different mode, as in the first movement of the *Appassionata*. Such cases are exceptions, but only in the sense that they bring to the fore a tendency which operates to one degree or another latently throughout Beethoven's mature works. The identity of the basic motifical [sic] content of apparently widely divergent themes of a Beethoven movement can be demonstrated in a less obvious yet striking example—the *Waldstein* Sonata. Here the character of the second theme, in E major—its "cantability"—is actually very different from the character of the first theme in C major—its quick pulsation. Yet the second theme is based upon an "inversion" of the intervals of the first theme, within the space of a fifth. One may characterize this technique in Beethoven as that of universal variation. In later composers this technique has been employed only by Brahms and by the Schoenberg School to any large extent.

I. The famous slogan about Schubert's "heavenly lengths" applies to this fact.

the immensely progressive novelty of the details. With Beethoven it is different. The density of thematic interwovenness, of "antiphonic" work, tends to produce what one might call a suspension of time consciousness.

When a movement like the first of Beethoven's Fifth or Seventh Symphonies, or even a very long one such as the first of the *Eroica* is performed adequately, one has the feeling that the movement does not take seven or fifteen minutes or more, but virtually one moment. It is this very power of symphonic contraction of time which annihilates, for the duration of the adequate performance, the contingencies of the listener's private existence—thus constituting the actual basis of those experiences which, in commentator phraseology, are called the elatedness of an audience as a result of the sublimity of the symphony.

THE ROLE OF SOUND INTENSITY

To what extent are the inherent constituents of the Beethoven symphonic form realized by radio?

To start from the most primitive fact about symphonic music: it may be stated in terms of "absolute dynamics," the meaning of which is well known from the visual sphere, particularly from architecture. A cathedral acquires an essential condition of its actual function, as well as its aesthetic meaning, only in proportion to the human body. A model of a cathedral in table size is something totally different from the actual cathedral, not only quantitatively but also qualitatively. On the Campo Santo in Genoa, there is a tomb in the form of a diminutive imitation of the Milan dome. The building itself, which is of highly questionable architectural value, becomes plainly ridiculous in miniature: the impression one has is much like the one received upon seeing the sugar-coated architecture of wedding cakes. The question of absolute dimensions in architecture has its counterpart in music in the question of absolute dynamics.

The power of a symphony to "absorb" its parts into the organized whole depends, in part, upon the sound volume. Only if the sound is "larger," as it were, than the individual so as to enable him to "enter" the door of the sound as he would enter through the door of a cathedral, may he really become aware of the possibility of merging with the totality which structurally does not leave any loophole. The element of being larger may be construed comparatively in terms of the intensity range; that is to say, the intensity range of symphonic sound must be larger, because of the exigencies of symphonic form, than any musical range the individual listener can conceive of producing himself either by singing or playing.[J] Absolute symphonic dimensions, furthermore, carry with them the existence of an experience which it is difficult to render even in rough terms, but which is, nonetheless, fundamental in the apperception of [the] symphony and is the true musical objective of technical discussion of auditory perspective: the experience of symphonic space. To "enter" a symphony means to listen to it not only as to something before one, but as something around one as well, as a medium in which one "lives." It is this surrounding quality that comes closest to the idea of symphonic absorption.

All these qualities are radically affected by radio. The sound is no longer "larger" than the individual. In the private room, that magnitude of sound causes disproportions which the listener mutes down. The "surrounding" function of music also disappears, partly because of the diminutions of absolute dimensions, partly because of the monaural conditions of radio broadcasting. What is left of the symphony even in the ideal case of an adequate reproduction of sound colors, is a mere chamber symphony.[K] If the symphony today reaches masses who have never before been in touch with it, it does so in a way in which their collective aspect and what might be called the collective aspect of the symphony itself, are practically eliminated from the musical pattern—which becomes, as it were, a piece of furniture of the private room.

One must be careful not to derive therefrom a premature judgment on radio, or try to "save" music from it. The abolition of the "surrounding" quality of music on the radio, has its progressive aspects. This "surrounding" quality of music is certainly part of music's function as a drug, the

J. This largeness of sound has nothing to do with noisiness, but simply with the necessity for enclosing the listener. It is not a matter of loudness but of a wide range between minimum and maximum sound.

K. Here, as in innumerable other cases, radio is an executor of musical and social tendencies which have developed extraneous to it. In musical production itself, independent of radio, the form of chamber symphony and other hybrids between orchestra and chamber music, have gained an ever-increasing importance since Schoenberg's *Kammersymphonie* (1906). Whatever the merits of this development for composition itself, the transformation of a Beethoven symphony into a *Kammersymphonie* by radio certainly undermines what is conventionally regarded as a main asset of radio transmission, namely, its seemingly collective message. It is hard to reconcile the experience of collectivity with that of "chamber." The German musicologist, Paul Bekker, went so far as to define symphony by its collective message, by its community-building power.* Obviously, this theory loses its point when the situation of symphony listeners becomes one of complete atomization, such as symbolized by millions of individuals scattered among their various "chambers," at the same time as the symphony [that] they get is a chamber symphony. [* This discussion appears in Bekker, *Die Sinfonie von Beethoven bis Mahler*; with regard to Beethoven, see especially pp. 22–28, 31–32. (rl)]

criticism of which, inaugurated by Nietzsche and revived by such contemporary writers as Jean Cocteau, is justified and has been considerably furthered by radio.[1] The drug tendency is very clear in Wagner where the mere magnitude of the sound, into whose waves the listener can dive, is one of the means of catching the listeners, quite apart from any specific musical content. In Beethoven, where the musical content is highly articulate, the largeness of the sound does not have this irrational function, but is the more intrinsically connected with the structural devices of the work, and is therefore also the more deeply affected by broadcasting. Paradoxical as it may appear, a Beethoven symphony becomes more problematical as a broadcast than the music of a Wagner opera.

THREAT TO THE STRUCTURE

This may be made clear by such a well-known piece of music as the first movement of the Fifth Symphony. It is characterized by its simplicity. A very short and precise motif, the one with which it opens, is conveyed by an unabating intensity of presentation. Throughout the movement it remains clearly recognizable as the same motif: its rhythm is vigorously maintained. Yet there is no mere repetition, but development: the melodic content of the basic rhythm, that is to say, the intervals which constitute it, change perpetually; it gains structural perspective by wandering from one instrument or instrumental group to another and appearing sometimes in the foreground as a main event, at other times as a mere background and accompaniment. Above all, it is presented in gradations, dynamic developments, the continuity of which is achieved through the identity of the basic material. At the same time, this identity is modified by the different dynamic grades in which the basic motif occurs. Thus the simplicity of the movement is inextricably bound up with an elaborate richness of texture: the richness prevents the simple from becoming primitive, while simplicity prevents richness from dissipation into mere details. It is this unity within the manifold as well as this manifoldness within that unity which constitute the antiphonic work finally terminating in the suspension of time-consciousness. This interrelationship of unity and manifoldness, and not only the loudness of the sound, is itself affected by the dynamic reductions of radio.

First of all, the whole building up of the movement upon the one simple motif—the creation *ex nihilo*, as it were, which is so highly significant in Beethoven—can be made understandable only if the motif, which is actually nothing in itself, is presented in such a way that from the very beginning it is underscored as the substance of everything that is to come. The first bars of the Fifth Symphony, if rightly performed, must possess the characteristic of a "statement," of a "positing." This positing characteristic, however, can be achieved only by the utmost dynamic intensity. Hence, the question of loudness ceases to be a purely external one and affects the very structure of [the] symphony. Presented without the dynamic emphasis which makes out of the Nothing of the first bars virtually the Everything of the total movement, the idea of the work is missed before it has been actually started. The suspension of time-consciousness is endangered from the very beginning: the simple, no longer emphasized in its paradoxical nature as Nothing and Everything, threatens to degenerate into the trite if the "nothingness" of the beginning fails to be absorbed into the whole by the impetus of the statement. The tension is broken and the whole movement is on the verge of relapsing into time.

It is threatened, even more, by the compression of the dynamic range. Only if the motif can develop from the restrained pianissimo to the striking yet affirming fortissimo, is it actually revealed as the "cell" which represents the whole even when exposed as a mere monad. Only within the tension of such a gradation does its repetition become more than repetition. The more the gradation is compressed—which is necessarily the case in radio—the less this tension is felt. Dynamic repetition is replaced by a mere ornamental, tectonic one. The movement loses its character of process and the static repetition becomes purposeless: the material repeated is so simple that it requires no repetition to be understood. Though something of the tension is still preserved by radio, it does not suffice. The Beethoven tension obtains its true significance in the range from Nothing to All. As soon as it is reduced to the medium range between piano and forte, the Beethoven symphony is deprived of the secret of origin as well as the might of unveiling.

It could be argued that all these changes by radio turn the symphony into a work of chamber music which, although different from symphony, has merits of its own. A symphony, conceived in symphonic terms, however, would necessarily become a bad work of chamber music. Its symphonic simplicity would make itself felt as poverty in chamber music texture, as lack of polyphonous interwovenness of parts as well as want of extensive melodic lines developed simultaneously. Simplicity would cease to function in the symphonic way. Clearly, a Beethoven symphony played on the piano by four hands, although it is only a one-color reproduction, is to be preferred to a chamber music arrangement, because it still preserves something of the specifically symphonic attack by fingers striking the keys, whereas that value is destroyed by the softened chamber music arrangement, which, by virtue of its mere arrangedness, easily approaches the sound of the so-called salon orchestra. Radio symphony bears a stronger resemblance to the chamber music transcription than to the simple yet faithful translation into the mere piano sound. Its colorfulness is as questionable as it would be in a salon arrangement. For the sound colors, too, are affected on the air, and it is through their deterioration that the work becomes bad chamber music. Symphonic richness is distorted no less than symphonic simplicity. While trying to keep the symphonic texture as plain and transparent as possible, Beethoven articulates it by attaching the smallest units of motifical construction to as many different instruments and instrumental groups as possible. These smallest units together form the surface of an outspoken melody, while their coloristic differentiation realizes at the same time the construction and all its interrelationships underneath the surface. The finer the shades of motifical interrelationships within the construction, the finer necessarily the shades of changing sound colors. These essential subtleties more than anything else tend to be effaced by radio. While exaggerating conspicuous contrasts, radio's neutralization of sound colors practically blots out precisely those minute differences upon which the classical orchestra is built as against the Wagnerian, which has much larger coloristic means at its disposal.

Richard Strauss, in his edition of Berlioz' *Treatise on Instrumentation*, observes that the second violins—never quite so brilliant and intense as the first violins—are different instruments, so to speak, from the first.[L] Such differences play a decisive part in the Beethoven articulation of symphonic texture: a single melody, subdivided between first violins, second violins and violas, becomes plastic according to the instrumental disposition—that is to say, the elements of the melody which are meant to be decisive are played by the first violins while those intended rather as incidental are played by the second violins or violas. At the same time, their unity is maintained by the fact that they are all strings playing in the same tonal region. Radio achieves only unity, whereas differences such as those between first and second violins are automatically eliminated. Moreover, certain sound colors, like that of the oboe, are changed to such an extent that the instrumental equilibrium is thrown out of joint. All these colors are more than mere means of instrumental make-up, that is, are integral

---

L. Hector Berlioz, *Instrumentationslehre*, ed. Richard Strauss, 2 vols. (Leipzig: C. F. Peters, 1905), vol. I, p. 64.

parts of the composition which they as well as the dynamics articulate; their alteration consummates the damage wreaked by radio upon symphonic structure. The less articulate symphony becomes, the more does it lose its character of unity and deteriorate into a conventional and simultaneously slack sequence, consisting of the recurrence of neat tunes whose interrelation is of no import whatever. Thus it becomes ever more apparent why it is Beethoven who falls victim to radio rather than Wagner and late romanticism. For it is in Beethoven that the idea of articulate unity constitutes the essence of the symphonic scheme. That unity is achieved by a severe economy of means forbidding their reduction, which is inevitable by radio.

TRIVIALIZATION

In the light of the preceding analysis, the hackneyed argument that radio, by bringing symphony to those formerly unfamiliar with it, compensates for its slight alterations, tilts over into its opposite: the less the listeners know the works in their original form, the more is their total impression necessarily erroneously based on the specific radio phenomena delivered to them. And these phenomena are, in addition, far from being structurally consistent. One is tempted to call them contradictory in themselves. A process of polarization sets in through radio transmission of the symphony: it becomes trivialized and romanticized at the same time.

The trivialization of symphony, first of all, is bound up with its relapse into time. The compression of symphonic time is relaxed because the technical prerequisites have been made blunt. The time the radio symphony consumes is the empirical time. It is in ironic keeping with the technical limitations imposed by radio on the live symphony that they are accompanied by the listener's capacity to turn off the music whenever he pleases. He can arbitrarily supersede it—in contrast to the concert hall performance where he is forced, as it were, to obey its laws. It may be questioned whether symphonic elation is really possible or desirable. At any rate, radio expedites its liquidation. Its very sound tends to undermine the idea of spell, of uniqueness and of "great music," which are ballyhooed by radio sales talk.

But not only the spell and the high-flown notion of symphonic totality fall victim to mechanization. The decline of the unity, which is the essence of symphony, is concomitant with a decay of the manifold comprehended by it. The symphonic particulars become atoms. The tendency toward atomistic listening obtains its exact and objective technical foundation through radio transmission.[M] The meaning of the music automatically shifts from the totality to the individual moments because their interrelation and articulation by dynamics and colors is no longer fully affected. These moments become semi-independent episodes, organized mainly by their chronological succession.

The symphony has often been compared with the drama. Though this comparison tends to overemphasize the dualistic character, the dialogue aspect of symphony, it must still be admitted that it is justified in so far as symphony aims at an "intensive" totality, an instantaneous focusing of an "idea" rather than an extensive totality of "life" unfolding itself within empirical time.[N] It is in this sense that radio symphony ceases to be a drama and becomes an epical form, or, to make the comparison in less archaic terms, a narrative. And narrative it becomes in an even more literal sense, too. The particular, when chipped off from the unity of symphony, still retains a trace of the unity in which it functioned. A genuine symphonic theme, even if it takes the whole musical stage and seems to be temporarily hypostatized and to desert the rest of the music, is nonetheless of such a kind as to impress upon one that it is actually nothing in itself but basically something "out of" something else. Even in its isolation it bears the mark of the whole. As this whole, however, is not adequately realized in the phenomenon that appears over the air, the theme, or an individual symphonic moment, is presented like something from a context itself blurred or even absent. In other words, through radio, the individual elements of symphony acquire the character of quotation. Radio symphony appears as a medley or potpourri in so far as the musical atoms it offers up acquire the touch of having been picked up somewhere else and put together in a kind of montage. What is heard is not Beethoven's Fifth but merely musical information from and about Beethoven's Fifth. The commentator, in expropriating the listener's own spontaneity of judgment by prating about the marvels of the world's immortal music, is merely the

M. This tendency is perhaps the most universal of present-day listening on the sheerly musical level. It is furthered by features as divergent as musical recognition contests that put chief emphasis on the isolated detail, the "theme," just as books that tell the reader how to memorize the main tunes of famous symphonies by subjecting them to certain words, and the standardization of popular music where the whole is so stereotyped that only the detail fetches the listener's attention.

N. Cf. Georg Lukács, *The Theory of the Novel* (Berlin: Paul Cassirer, 1920), p. 31. [Adorno gives the title in English; the edition cited was in fact published in German: *Die Theorie des Romans: Eine geschichtsphilosophischer Versuch über die Formen der grossen Epik.*(rl)]

human executor of the trend inherent in music on the air, which, by reassembling fragments from a context not itself in evidence, seems to be continually offering the reassurance: "This is Beethoven's Fifth Symphony." The image character of radio cannot be altogether explained by abstract reference to physical conditions alone, but these conditions must be shown at work on the symphonic structure, wreaking havoc on musical sense.

QUOTATION LISTENING

The issue of "quotation" is inseparably bound up with the structure and significance of symphonic themes themselves. Sententious precision which summarizes the meaning of preceding dramatic development or situation, is an age-old ingredient of dramatic structure. The sententious passages, by reflecting upon the action, detach themselves from the immediacy of the action itself. Through this detachment they become reified, emphasized, and facilely quotable. The abstract generality of maxims for practical life into which they translate the concrete idea of the drama brings them close to the banal. At times the sententious moments supersede concrete dramatic sense altogether. There is the revealing joke about elderly ladies who express delight in *Hamlet* with the single reservation that it consists of quotations. In the realm of music radio has realized a similar tendency and has transformed Beethoven's Fifth Symphony into a set of quotations from theme songs.

The symphonic theme of the Beethoven period may structurally very well be compared with the sententious element of the drama. It consists in most cases of the triad. It is based on the triad harmonically and it circumscribes the triad melodically. As the triad is the general principle of major-minor tonality, the triadic theme has a touch of "generality" itself; it is, to a great extent, interchangeable with other triadic themes. The striking similarity between the material of movements as totally different as the finale of Mozart's G Minor Symphony from the scherzo of Beethoven's Fifth, bears witness to this generality. This generality of symphonic theme is balanced by its precision, which is in the main achieved by one short and distinct rhythmical formula apt to be remembered as well as to be repeated. Musical commentators have often compared symphonic themes with mottoes in literature, and German musicology frequently alludes to "head motifs" *(Kopfmotive)* as opening a symphonic movement.

All this points up the sententious character of the symphonic theme. It is this character that offers the theme up to the process of trivialization by radio. The triviality characteristic of live symphonic themes serves a double purpose: that of "generality" transcending the specific case in which they appear, and their existence as a mere material for self-development. Radio interferes with both these purposes. Being atomized, the symphonic theme fails to show its "generality." It calls for significance just as it is. From the viewpoint of consistent symphonic construction it would be possible to imagine a substitute for the famous second theme of the first movement of Schubert's B Minor Symphony—the so-called "Unfinished." The radio listener who does not care much for the movement and waits for the theme would get the shock of his life if it were replaced by another. Moreover, the theme that sticks out because it has lost its dynamic function, can no longer fulfill its truly musical role—which is to serve as a mere material of what follows—as soon as everything that follows is visualized only from the viewpoint of the undeveloped material of the theme. Hence, in the isolation of the symphonic theme, only the trivial remains. And in turn it is the triviality of the symphonic detail which makes it so easy to remember and own it as a commodity under the more general trademark of "culture."

For by sounding like a quotation—the quintessence of the whole—the trivialized theme assumes a peculiar air of authority, which gives it cultural tone. Only what is established and accepted as a standard social value is quoted, and the anxiety of the listeners to recognize the so-called Great Symphonies by their quotable themes is mainly due to their desire to identify themselves with the standards of the accepted and to prove themselves to be small cultural owners within big ownership culture. This tendency again springs from the "electrocution" of symphony by radio, without taking into account radio's social authoritarianism. It has already been mentioned that radio tends to present symphony as a series of results rather than a process. The more a particular result is set off against the process in which it gains creation, the more it ceases to be "the problem" of its own treatment. Within the symphonic process the theme has its fate. It is "disputed"; by radio the theme becomes definite. In the process of symphonic development it is not conceived as something rigid but fluent, even in its seemingly dogmatic first presentation. By radio even its musically remote transformations sound like themes of their own. If one could say, exaggeratedly, that in symphonic music nothing is theme and everything is development—which holds good literally for some modern symphonic music, particularly for Mahler—one could say as well that by radio everything becomes "theme." The emphasis which every symphonic moment acquires through the radio voice is unlike the emphasis which the symphonic theme possesses in its live "positing." As positing, it owes its emphasis to the potentiality for process which it contains within itself. By radio it becomes emphasized because that process has been broken through and the theme absolutizes itself in its mere present subsistence, in its being as it is. It is this literal-minded and pharisaical self-righteousness of the theme which transforms it into quotation.

It must be emphasized that the substitution of quotation for reproduction does not mean a greater faithfulness to the original but just the opposite. Quotation is reproduction in its decline. While genuine reproduction would stand in a tension-like relation to its object and realize it by again "producing" it, quotation-reproduction sheds all spontaneity, dissolves all tension toward the object and seizes upon all particulars of the object as fixed and reified items. It is essential to the object, that is, the symphonic original, that it be reproduced in the sense of being produced again rather than of being photographed in degenerated colors and modified proportions. A Beethoven symphony is essentially a process; if that process is replaced by a presentation of frozen items, the performance is faithless even if executed under the battle cry of the utmost fidelity to the letter.

ROMANTICIZATION

Radio symphony promotes the romanticization of music no less than its trivialization. The authoritarian theme, the "result" replacing the process and thus destroying symphonic spell, acquires a spell of its own. History of symphonic musical production after Beethoven itself reveals a shift from the totality aspect to the detail, which bears a strong resemblance to the shift which the Beethoven symphony suffers through radio. The shift after Beethoven took place in the name of subjective expression. Lyrical expression tends to emphasize the atom and separate it from any comprehensive "objective" order. Radio disintegrates classical music in much the same way as romanticism reacted to it. If radio atomizes and trivializes Beethoven, it simultaneously renders the atoms more "expressive," as it were, than they had been before. The weight which falls upon the isolated detail conveys to it an importance that it never has in its context. And it is this air of importance that makes it seem to "signify" or express something all the time, whereas in the original the expression is mediated by the whole. Consonantly, radio publicity proclaims the "inspiration" of symphonic themes, although precisely in Beethoven the movement, if anything, is inspired and not the theme. It is the romantic notion of melodic inventiveness which radio projects upon classical music strictly so-called. Details are deified as well as reified.

This has paradoxical consequences. One might expect that radio, since it affects the freshness of sound colors, makes them less conspicuous than in live music. Precisely the opposite is true. Together with the structural totality there vanishes in radio the process of musical spontaneity, of musical "thinking" of the whole by the listener. (The notion of musical thinking refers to everything in musical apperception that goes beyond the mere presence of the sensual stimulus.) The less the radio phenomenon evokes such thinking, the greater is the emphasis on the sensual side as compared with live music, where the sensual qualities are in themselves "better." The structural element of music—the element that is defamed by many listeners as "intellectual" though it constitutes the concreteness of the musical phenomenon even more than the sound—is skipped over, and they content themselves with the stimuli remaining, however shopworn these stimuli may be. In romantic music and even in romantic interpretation of Beethoven, those stimuli actually were the bearers of musical "expression." Deteriorated as they are now, they still maintain something of their romantic glamour. Certain of them today, through the radio, assume such a glamour even though they never had it before, because their institutionalization casts about them a social validity which listeners credit to the music. That is why the atoms, sentimentalized by radio through the combination of triviality and expressiveness, reflect something of the spell which the totality has lost. To be sure, it is not the same spell. It is rather the spell of the commodity whose value is adored by its customers.

In the symphonic field those works surrender themselves to radio most readily which are conglomerates of tunes of both sensual richness and structural poverty—tunes making unnecessary the process of thinking which is anyhow restrained by the way the phenomenon comes out of the radio set. The preference for Tchaikovsky among radio listeners is as significant a commentary on the inherent nature of the radio voice as on the broader social issues of contemporary listening habits. Moreover, it is very likely that Beethoven is listened to in terms of Tchaikovsky. The thesis that music by radio is no longer quite "serious" implies that radio music already prejudices the capacity to listen in a spontaneous and conscious way. The radio voice does not present the listeners with material adequate to such desiderates. They are forced to passive sensual and emotional acceptance of predigested yet disconnected qualities, whereas those qualities at the same time become mummified and magicized.

IS SYMPHONIC MUSIC "SPREAD"?

This shows the necessity for starting from the sphere of reproduction of musical works by radio instead of from an analysis of listeners' reactions. The latter presupposes a kind of naïve realism with respect to such notions as symphony or "great music" on the air. If that music is fundamentally different from what it is supposed to be, listeners' statements about their reactions to it must be evaluated accordingly. There is no justification for unqualifiedly accepting the listener's word about his sudden delight in a Beethoven symphony, if that symphony is changed the very moment it is broadcast into something closely akin to entertainment. Further, the analysis invalidates the optimistic idea that the knowledge of the deteriorated or even "dissolved" radio symphony may be a first step toward a true, conscious and adequate musical experience. For the way a symphony appears by radio is not "neutral" with regard to the original. It does not convey a hollow one-colored effigy which can be "filled" and made more concrete by later live listening. The radio symphony's relation to the live symphony is not that of the shadow to the robust. Even if it were, the shadow cannot be given flesh by the transfusion of red blood corpuscles. The changes brought about by radio are more than coloristic; that they are changes of the symphony's own essential structure means not only that this structure is not adequately conveyed but that what does come out opposes that structure and constitutes a serious obstacle against its realization. Beethoven's musical sense does not match with the postulates it evokes itself when transmitted on the air. Reference may again be made to the coloristic element. The radio phenomenon produces an attitude in the listener which leads him to seek color and stimulating sounds. Music, however, composed in structural rather than coloristic terms does not satisfy these mechanized claims. The color of a Beethoven symphony in live performance as well as by radio is incomparably less radiant, more subdued not only than those of Wagner, Richard Strauss, or Debussy, but poorer even than the supply of current entertainment. Moreover, the coloristic effects which Beethoven achieves are valid only against the ascetic background of the whole. The cadenza of the oboe in the beginning of the repetition of the first movement of the Fifth Symphony is striking only as a contrast to the bulk of the strings: as a coloristic effect in itself it would be "poor," and it is the misinterpretation of such relations which leads some of today's happy-go-lucky routine musicians, who are nothing but competent, to such ingenuous statements as that Beethoven was not able to score well. If radio, however, brings into the limelight just such particles as the oboe cadenza, may it not actually provoke those opinion statements and even a resistance within the listeners—a resistance which is only superficially compensated by the official respect for established values—because the symphony fails to satisfy the very same demands which it seems to raise? But the resistance goes beyond unfavorable comparisons between the full seven-course dinner in color of [Paul] Whiteman's rendition of the *Rhapsody in Blue* and the frugal meal of the symphony in black and white consumed, as it were, as a meal merely. The transformation of the symphonic process into a series of results means that the listeners receive the symphony as a ready-made piecemeal product which can be enjoyed with a minimum of effort on his part. Like other ready-made articles, radio symphony tends to make him passive: he wants to get something out of it, perhaps to give himself up to it, but, if possible, to have nothing to do with it, and least of all to "think" it. If it is true that the experience of the actual meaning of symphonic structure implies something like an activity of concrete musical thinking, this thinking is antagonized by radio presentation. It is significant that the same listeners who are allegedly overwhelmed by symphonic music are also ever ready to dwell upon what they call their emotions as against what they call "intellectual" in music. For it is as certain that actual musical understanding, by transcending the isolated, sensual moments of music and categorizing them by the interconnection of the past and the coming within the work, is bound to definite intellectual functions, as it is certain that the stubborn and spiteful adherence to one's private emotional sphere tends to build a wall against these experiences—the very experiences by which alone a Beethoven symphony can be properly understood. Great music is not music that sounds the best, and the belief in that sound is apt to tilt over into frank hostility against what, though mediated by the sound, is more than sound. It is highly doubtful if the boy in the subway whistling the main theme of the finale of Brahms's First Symphony actually has been gripped by that music. By the way he picks out that tune he translates it into the language of only a few. It may well be that this translation falls into an historical process, the perspectives of which go far beyond the limits of traditional aesthetics.

If this be true, one should not speak about spreading music while that spreading implies the abnegation of the same concepts of musical classicism, in the name of which serious music is handled by radio. At least no responsible educational attempt can be built directly upon radio symphony without taking into consideration that the radio symphony is not the live symphony and cannot therefore have the same cultural effect as the live symphony. No such educational attempt is worth undertaking that does not give the fullest account of the antagonistic tendencies promulgated by serious music in radio.

(1941)

NOTE BY RICHARD LEPPERT

Adorno wrote this essay in English. Occasionally, he failed to catch typos (such as "life" for "live" in reference to musical performances, in the first and third paragraphs; and "form" when he intended "from"). In a few instances he simply misspelled words. I have corrected these errors and also have changed his occasional use of British orthography to American.

Adorno's punctuation is sometimes incorrect, in particular as regards misplaced commas that confuse the reader or distort meaning; I have corrected these mistakes. Finally, Adorno liked to employ a comma and dash together (a practice common to his written German, even in instances where conventional practice—which differs in this regard from English—would not require it). I have retained whichever one of the two marks that seemed best to fit the context.

1. Friedrich Nietzsche, *The Birth of Tragedy,* in *The Birth of Tragedy and the Case of Wagner,* trans. Walter Kaufmann (New York: Vintage, 1967), p. 25: "Contemporary *German music,* which is romanticism through and through and most un-Greek of all possible art forms—moreover, a first-rate poison for the nerves, [is] doubly dangerous among a people who love drink and who honor lack of clarity as a virtue, for it has the double quality of a narcotic that both intoxicates and spreads a *fog.*" The passage is from section 6 of the "Attempt at Self-Criticism," added to the text in 1886, hence following his break with Wagner as the text bitingly reflects. *The Birth of Tragedy* (1872) was Nietzsche's first book. Jean Cocteau's (1889–1963) opium addiction is detailed in his *Opium: The Diary of a Cure,* trans. Margaret Crosland and Sinclair Road (London: Peter Owen, 1957); the text is a set of notes written in 1929 with additions made the following year when the book was at proof stage. It includes a variety of references to modern music. Cocteau's *A Call to Order,* trans. Rollo H. Myers (London: Faber and Gwyer, 1926), based on texts written between 1918 and 1926, includes the brief *Cock and Harlequin,* first published separately in 1918, consisting of aphorisms on art in general and music in particular, by Bach, Beethoven, Wagner, Bizet, Saint-Saëns, Musorgsky, Puccini, Debussy, Satie, Strauss, Stravinsky, and Schoenberg, among others. Cocteau's allusion to music as a drug comes in a short section concerning Nietzsche and Wagner and, obviously, replicates Nietzsche's position: "There are certain long works which are short. Wagner's works are long works which are long, and *long-drawn-out,* because this old sorcerer looked upon boredom as a useful drug for the stupefaction of the faithful" (p. 14). The *Cock and Harlequin* was something of an aesthetic manifesto for modern French music, and notably for Les Six (Auric, Durey, Honegger, Milhaud, Poulenc, and Tailleferre). Cocteau wrote in specific

opposition to German music, as evident, for example, in his comment on Schoenberg: "Schoenberg is a master; all our musicians, as well as Stravinsky, owe something to him, but Schoenberg is essentially a blackboard musician" (p. 15). In particular, Cocteau writes at length about, and with great admiration of, Satie, whose early career he actively and successfully promoted. The text also includes laudatory comments about music by various of Les Six composers as well as Stravinsky.

The Curves of the Needle

Talking machines and phonograph records seem to have suffered the same historical fate as that which once befell photographs: the transition from artisanal to industrial production transforms not only the technology of distribution but also that which is distributed. As the recordings become more perfect in terms of plasticity and volume, the subtlety of color and the authenticity of vocal sound decline as if the singer were being distanced more and more from the apparatus. The records, now fabricated out of a different mixture of materials, wear out faster than the old ones. The incidental noises, which have disappeared, nevertheless survive in the more shrill tone of the instruments and the singing. In a similar fashion, history drove out of photographs the shy relation to the speechless object that still reigned in daguerreotypes, replacing it with a photographic sovereignty borrowed from lifeless psychological painting to which, furthermore, it remains inferior. Artisanal compensations for the substantive loss of quality are at odds with the real economic situation. In their early phases, these technologies had the power to penetrate rationally the reigning artistic practice. The moment one attempts to improve these early technologies through an emphasis on concrete fidelity, the exactness one has ascribed to them is exposed as an illusion by the very technology itself. The positive tendency of consolidated technology to present objects themselves in as unadorned a fashion as possible is, however, traversed by the ideological need of the ruling society, which demands subjective reconciliation with these objects—with the reproduced voice as such, for example. In the aesthetic form of technological reproduction, these objects no longer possess their traditional reality. The ambiguity [Zweideutigkeit] of the results of forward-moving technology—which does not tolerate any constraint—

271

confirms the ambiguity of the process of forward-moving rationality as such.

The relevance of the talking machines is debatable. The spatially limited effect of every such apparatus makes it into a utensil of the private life that regulates the consumption of art in the nineteenth century. It is the bourgeois family that gathers around the gramophone in order to enjoy the music that it itself—as was already the case in the feudal house-hold—is unable to perform. The fact that the public music of that time—or at least the arioso works of the first half of the nineteenth century—was absorbed into the record repertoire testifies to its private character, which had been masked by its social presentation. For the time being, Beethoven defies the gramophone. The diffuse and atmospheric com-fort of the small but bright gramophone sound corresponds to the hum-ming gaslight and is not entirely foreign to the whistling teakettle of bygone literature. The gramophone belongs to the pregnant stillness of individuals.

If one were to be thoroughly rigorous, the expression "mechanical music" is hardly appropriate to talking machines.[1] The mechanism of the gramo-phone affects only the reduced transmission, adapted to domestic needs, of preexisting works. The work and its interpretation are accommodated but not disturbed or merged into each other: in its relative dimensions the work is retained and the obedient machine—which in no way dictates any formal principles of its own—follows the interpreter in patient imitation of every nuance. This sort of practice simply assumes the unproblematic existence of the works themselves as well as the interpreter's right to that freedom, which the machine accompanies with devout whirring. Yet both of these are in decline. Neither the works (which are dying out) nor the interpreters (who are growing silent) obey the private apparatus any more. Interpretations whose subjective aspect had been eliminated—as is virtu-ally the case in works by Stravinsky[2]—do not require any further repro-duction; the works that in themselves are in need of free interpretation begin to become unreproducible. The archival character of records is read-ily apparent: just in time, the shrinking sounds are provided with herbaria that endure for ends that are admittedly unknown. The relevance of the talking machines is debatable.

The transformation of the piano from a musical instrument into a piece of bourgeois furniture—which Max Weber accurately perceived—is recurring in the case of the gramophone but in an extraordinarily more rapid fashion.[3] The fate of the gramophone horns marks this development in a striking manner. In their brassness, they initially projected the mechanical being of the machines onto the surface. In better social circles, however, they were quickly muffled into colored masses or wood chalices. But they proceeded to make their way into private apartments, these fanfares of the street, loudspeakers and shrouds of the emptiness that people usually prefer to enshroud within themselves. In Max Beckmann's postwar paintings, these drastic symbols are still recorded.[4] The stabilization subsequently excises these disturbers of the peace with a gentle hand; the last ones still drone out of bordello bars. In the functional salon, the gramophone stands innocuously as a little mahogany cabinet on little rococo legs. Its cover provides a space for the artistic photograph of the divorced wife with the baby. Through discrete cracks comes the singing of the Revelers,[5] all of whom have a soul; baby remains quiet. Meanwhile, the downtrodden gramophone horns reassert themselves as proletarian loudspeakers.

With its movable horn and its solid spring housing, the gramophone's social position is that of a border marker between two periods of musical practice. It is in front of the gramophone that both types of bourgeois music lovers encounter each other. While the expert examines all the needles and chooses the best one, the consumer just drops in his dime—and the sound that responds to both may well be the same.

In Nice, on the other side far away from the big hotels, there is a locale where, with considerable effort, one extracts some publicity from the gramophone whose private character is conserved in French fashion. There, along the walls in sealed glass cases, one finds twenty gramophones lined up one next to another, each of which doggedly services one record. The gramophones are operated automatically by inserting a token. In order to hear something, one has to put on a pair of headphones: those who don't pay hear nothing. And yet, one after another, everyone hears. In this manner the use of radio technology penetrates the tenaciously preserved sphere of the gramophone and explodes it from within. Audience and object alike are petit bourgeois girls, most of them underage. The big attractions are a screeching record by Mistinguett[6] and the lewd *chansons* of a baritone who rhymes the impotent Siméon with his large pantalons. Both text and music hang on the wall above. The girls wait for someone to approach them.

The dog on records listening to *his master's voice*[*7] off of records through the gramophone horn is the right emblem for the primordial affect which the gramophone stimulated and which perhaps even gave rise to the gramophone in the first place. What the gramophone listener actually wants to hear is himself, and the artist merely offers him a substitute for the sounding image of his own person, which he would like to safeguard as a possession. The only reason that he accords the record such value is because he himself could also be just as well preserved. Most of the time records are virtual photographs of their owners, flattering photographs—ideologies.

The mirror function of the gramophone arises out of its technology. What is best reproduced gramophonically is the singing voice. Here, "best" means most faithful to the natural ur-image and not at all most appropriate to the mechanical from the outset. But good records want, above all, to be similar.

Male voices can be reproduced better than female voices. The female voice easily sounds shrill—but not because the gramophone is incapable of conveying high tones, as is demonstrated by its adequate reproduction of the flute. Rather, in order to become unfettered, the female voice requires the physical appearance of the body that carries it. But it is just this body that the gramophone eliminates, thereby giving every female voice a sound that is needy and incomplete. Only there where the body itself resonates, where the self to which the gramophone refers is identical with its sound, only there does the gramophone have its legitimate realm of validity: thus Caruso's uncontested dominance. Wherever sound is separated from the body—as with instruments—or wherever it requires the body as a complement—as is the case with the female voice—gramophonic reproduction becomes problematic.

With the advent of the gramophone, absolute pitch runs into difficulties. It is almost impossible to guess the actual pitch if it deviates from the original one. In that case, the original pitch becomes confused with that of the phonographic reproduction. For as a whole, the sound of the gramophone has become so much more abstract than the original sound that again and again it needs to be complemented by specific sensory qualities of the object it is reproducing and on which it depends in order to remain at all related to that object. Its abstraction presupposes the full concreteness of its object, if it is to become in any way graspable, thereby circumscribing the domain of what can be reproduced. Phonographic technology calls for a natural object. If the natural substance of the object is itself already permeated by intentionality or mechanically fractured, then the record is no longer capable of grasping it. Once again the historical limits of the talking machines are inscribed upon them.

The turntable of the talking machines is comparable to the potter's wheel: a tone-mass *[Ton-Masse]*[8] is formed upon them both, and for each the material is preexisting. But the finished tone/clay container that is produced in this manner remains empty. It is only filled by the hearer.

There is only one point at which the gramophone interferes with both the work and the interpretation. This occurs when the mechanical spring wears out. At this point the sound droops in chromatic weakness and the music bleakly plays itself out. Only when gramophonic reproduction breaks down are its objects transformed. Or else one removes the records and lets the spring run out in the dark.

(1927/1965; GS, vol. 19, pp. 525–29)
Translated by Thomas Y. Levin

NOTES BY THOMAS Y. LEVIN

This essay, written in 1927 and published in 1928, was reprinted in 1965 with the following note by Adorno: "It goes without saying that over the course of forty years, insights into a technological medium become outdated. On the other hand, even at that time there was already a recognition of aspects of the transformed character of experience which, even as it was caused by technology, also had an effect on that very same technology. The motifs have been retained unchanged and with no attempt to cover up the temporal distance; the author made changes in the language to the extent that he deemed it necessary."

1. Adorno is referring here to the use of the term in such vanguard musico-logical debates of the time as H. H. Stuckenschmidt's 1926 article on "Mechanische Musik" in a special issue of the Prague music journal *Der Auftakt: Musikblätter für die Tschechoslowakische Republik* on "Music and Machine," vol. 6 no. 8 (1926), pp. 170–73. The tenacity of this designation, Adorno's objections notwithstanding, is indicated by its employment as late as 1930 in the title of a special issue of *Der Auftakt* (vol. 10 no. 11) devoted to "Mechanical Music."

2. For a discussion of what Adorno described as Stravinsky's "hysterically ex-aggerated suspicion of the subject" and the consequent attempt on the part of the composer to excise all traces of subjectivity in his works, see Adorno's 1962 essay "Stravinsky: A Dialectical Portrait," QF, pp. 145–75, and especially pp. 162–63.

3. For an illustrated discussion of this development, see Graham Melville-Mason, "The Gramophone as Furniture," in *Phonographs and Gramophones: The Edison Phonograph Centenary Symposium* (Edinburgh: The Royal Scottish Museum, 1977), pp. 117–38.

For Weber's remarks on the piano, see Max Weber, *Die rationalen und sozio-logischen Grundlagen der Musik* (1921), which is included as an appendix in Max Weber, *Wirtschaft und Gesellschaft*, ed. Johannes Winckelmann, 4th ed. (Tübingen: J. C. B. Mohr, 1956), vol. 2, pp. 925–28, and which has been reprinted as a separate volume (Tübingen: J. C. B. Mohr / Paul Siebeck, 1972), pp. 73–77. An English translation by Don Martindale, Johannes Riedel, and Gertrude Neuwirth was published under the title *The Rational and Social Foundations of Music* (Carbondale: Southern Illinois University Press, 1958). The section relevant to the current context is also available in a translation by Eric Matthews entitled "The History of the Piano," in *Max Weber: Selections in Translation*, ed. W. G. Runciman (Cambridge: Cambridge University Press, 1978), pp. 378–82.

4. See, for example, the 1920 lithograph *Möbliert* from the *Stadtnacht* series, as well as the 1924 painting *Stilleben mit Grammophon und Schwertlilien*, in Max Beckmann, *Frankfurt 1915–1933*, ed. Klaus Gallwitz (Frankfurt am Main: Städtische Galerie, 1983).

5. The Revelers were the most popular singing act of the latter half of the 1920s in vaudeville and cabaret, on the air, and on records. Originally known as the Shannon Quartet, the group consisted of Lewis James and Franklyn Baur (tenors), Elliot Shaw (baritone), and Wilfred Glenn (bass); in 1924 they were joined by the baritone, piano accompanist, and arranger Ed Smalle. Best known as The Revelers, the name under which they recorded for Victor (HMV) Records, the quintet also made records as The Merrymakers (on the Brunswick label) and as The Singing Sophomores (on Columbia Records). Members of the group also sang—often anonymously—as duos, trios, and quartets on hundreds of cuts by dance bands of all sorts from the mid-1920s to the mid-1930s.

6. Mistinguett (1875–1956) was the stage name of Jeanne Florentine Bourgeois, a French chanson singer and actress who performed early in her career at the Folies-Bergères together with Maurice Chevalier and quickly became the leading lady of the Paris revue-theaters in the 1920s. Her autobiography is available in a translation by Lucienne Hill as *Mistinguett, Queen of the Paris Night* (London: Elek Books, 1954).

7. For a richly illustrated account of the HMV logo, see Leonard Petts, *The Story of "Nipper" and the "His Master's Voice" Picture Painted by Francis Barraud* (Bournemouth, UK: The Talking Machine Review International, 1973/1983).

8. Adorno here plays upon the untranslatable polyvalence of *Ton*, which in German means both "sound" or "tone" and also "clay." A *Ton-Masse* is thus a quantity or mass both of acoustic and of argillaceous material.

The Form of the Phonograph Record

One does not want to accord it any form other than the one it itself exhibits: a black pane made of a composite mass which these days no longer has its honest name any more than automobile fuel is called benzine; fragile like tablets, with a circular label in the middle that still looks most authentic when adorned with the prewar terrier hearkening to his master's voice; at the very center, a little hole that is at times so narrow that one has to redrill it wider so that the record can be laid upon the platter. It is covered with curves, a delicately scribbled, utterly illegible writing, which here and there forms more plastic figures for reasons that remain obscure to the layman upon listening; structured like a spiral, it ends somewhere in the vicinity of the title label, to which it is sometimes connected by a lead-out groove so that the needle can comfortably finish its trajectory. In terms of its "form," this is all that it will reveal. As perhaps the first of the technological artistic inventions, it already stems from an era that cynically acknowledges the dominance of things over people through the emancipation of technology from human requirements and human needs and through the presentation of achievements whose significance is not primarily humane; instead, the need is initially produced by advertisement, once the thing already exists and is spinning in its own orbit. Nowhere does there arise anything that resembles a form specific to the phonograph record—in the way that one was generated by photography in its early days. Just as the call for "radio-specific" music remained necessarily empty and unfulfilled and gave rise to nothing better than some directions for instrumentation that turned out to be impracticable, so too there has never been any gramophone-specific music.[1] Indeed, one ought to credit the phonograph record with the advantage of having been spared the artisanal transfiguration of artistic specificity in the arty private home.

Furthermore, from their phonographic origins up through the electrical process (which, for better and for worse, may well be closely related to the photographic process of enlargement), the phonograph records were nothing more than the acoustic photographs that the dog so happily recognizes. It is no coincidence that [in German] the term "plate" is used without any modification and with the same meaning in both photography and phonography.[2] It designates the two-dimensional model of a reality that can be multiplied without limit, displaced both spatially and temporally, and traded on the open market. This, at the price of sacrificing its third dimension: its height and its abyss.

According to every standard of artistic self-esteem, this would imply that the form of the phonograph record was virtually its nonform. The phonograph record is not good for much more than reproducing and storing a music deprived of its best dimension, a music, namely, that was already in existence before the phonograph record and is not significantly altered by it. There has been no development of phonographic composers; even Stravinsky, despite all his good will towards the electric piano, has not made any effort in this direction.[3] The only thing that can characterize gramophone music is the inevitable brevity dictated by the size of the shellac plate. Here too a pure identity reigns between the form of the record disc and that of the world in which it plays: the hours of domestic existence that while themselves away along with the record are too sparse for the first movement of the *Eroica* to be allowed to unfold without interruption. Dances composed of dull repetitions are more congenial to these hours. One can turn them off at any point. The phonograph record is an object of that "daily need" which is the very antithesis of the humane and the artistic, since the latter cannot be repeated and turned on at will but remain tied to their place and time.

Nevertheless, as an article, the record is already too old not to present us with its riddles, once one forgoes considering it as an art object and explores instead the contours of its thingness. For it is not in the play of the gramophone as a surrogate for music but rather in the phonograph record as a thing that its potential significance—and also its aesthetic significance—resides. As an artistic product of decline, it is the first means of musical presentation that can be possessed as a thing. Not like oil paintings, which look down from the walls upon the living. Just as these can hardly fit any more in an apartment, there are no truly large-format phonograph records. Instead, records are possessed like photographs: the nineteenth century had good reasons for coming up with phonograph record albums alongside photographic and postage-stamp albums, all of them herbaria of artificial life that are present in the smallest space and ready to conjure up every recollection that would otherwise be mercilessly shredded between the haste and hum-drum of private life. Through the phonograph record, *time* gains a new approach to music. It is not the time in which music happens, nor is it the time which music monumentalizes by means of its "style." It is time as evanescence, enduring in mute music. If the "modernity" of all mechanical instruments gives music an age-old appearance—as if, in the rigidity of its repetitions, it had existed forever, having been submitted to the pitiless eternity of the clockwork—then the evanescence and recollection that is associated with the barrel organ as a mere sound in a compelling yet indeterminate way has become tangible and manifest through the gramophone records.

The key to the proper understanding of the phonograph records ought to be provided by the comprehension of those technological developments that at one point transformed the drums of the mechanical music boxes and organs into the mechanism of the phonograph. If at some later point, instead of doing "history of ideas" *[Geistesgeschichte]*, one were to read the state of the cultural spirit *[Geist]* off of the sundial of human technology, then the prehistory of the gramophone could take on an importance that might eclipse that of many a famous composer.[4] There is no doubt that, as music is removed by the phonograph record from the realm of live production and from the imperative of artistic activity and becomes petrified, it absorbs into itself, in this process of petrification, the very life that would otherwise vanish. The dead art rescues the ephemeral and perishing art as the only one alive. Therein may lie the phonograph record's most profound justification, which cannot be impugned by an aesthetic objection to its reification. For this justification reestablishes by the very means of reification an age-old, submerged and yet warranted relationship: that between music and *writing*.

Anyone who has ever recognized the steadily growing compulsion that, at least during the last fifty years, both musical notation and the configuration of the musical score have imposed on compositions (the pejorative expression "paper music" betrays this drastically) will not be surprised if one day a reversal of the following sort occurs: music, previously conveyed by writing, suddenly itself turns into writing. This occurs at the price of its immediacy, yet with the hope that, once fixed in this way, it will some day become readable as the "last remaining universal language since the construction of the tower,"[5] a language whose determined yet encrypted expressions are contained in each of its "phrases."[6] If, however, notes were still the mere signs for music, then, through the curves of the needle on the phonograph record, music approaches decisively its true character as writing. Decisively, because this writing can be recognized as true language to the extent that it relinquishes its being as mere signs: inseparably committed to the sound that inhabits this and no other acoustic groove. If the productive force of music has expired in the phonograph records, if the latter have not produced a form through their technology, they instead transform the most recent sound of old feelings into an archaic text of knowledge to come. Yet though the theologian may feel constrained to come to the conclusion that "life" in the strictest sense—the birth and death of creatures—cannot be ascribed to any art, he may also tend to hold that the truth-content of art only arises to the extent that the appearance of liveliness has abandoned it; that artworks only become "true," fragments of the true language, once life has left them; perhaps even only through their decline and that of art itself. It would be then that, in a seriousness hard to measure, the form of the phonograph record could find its true meaning: the scriptal spiral that disappears in the center, in the opening of the middle, but in return survives in time.

A good part of this is due to physics, at least to Chladni's sound figures,[7] to which—according to the discovery of one of the most important contemporary aesthetic theorists—Johann Wilhelm Ritter referred as the script-like Ur-images of sound.[8] The most recent technological development has, in any case, continued what was begun there: the possibility of inscribing music without it ever having sounded has simultaneously reified it in an even more inhuman manner and also brought it mysteriously closer to the character of writing and language.[9] The panicked fear that certain composers express regarding this invention captures precisely the extraordinary threat to the life of artworks that emanates from it just as it already did from the gentler barbarism of the phonograph record albums. What may be announcing itself here, however, is the shock at that transfiguration of all truth of artworks that iridescently discloses itself in the catastrophic technological progress. Ultimately the phonograph records are not artworks but the black seals on the missives that are rushing towards us from all sides in the traffic with technology; missives whose formulations capture the sounds of creation, the first and the last sounds, judgment upon life and message about that which may come thereafter.

(1934; GS, vol. 19, pp. 530–34)
Translated by Thomas Y. Levin

NOTES BY THOMAS Y. LEVIN

1. The stakes involved in Adorno's resistance to the possibility of composition specific to what he himself called "the most important of all the musical mass media" are articulated in the opening lines of his essay "On the Musical Employment of Radio": "In the early 1920s, when radio was becoming generally established, there was much talk of radio-specific music. Such compositions had to be particularly light and transparent since it was held that not only anything massive but also everything complex could only be transmitted badly. Individual acoustic timbres such as the flute would stick out so badly that one would do well to avoid them. On the surface, such rules recalled those contemporary imperatives for both construction and functional forms that did justice to their materials. In truth, however, they ran parallel with the enthusiastic community-oriented slogans calling for simplification that had been launched around the same time in reaction to the alienating aspects of new music" ("Über die musikalische Verwendung des Radios," GS, vol. 15, p. 369).

2. In German this linguistic coincidence still resonates clearly since, analogous to the photographic plate, the word for the phonograph record is *Schallplatte* (literally "sound-plate").

3. Stravinsky, whose interest in mechanical instruments of all sorts dated back to his childhood, composed a study for pianola in 1917 for the Aeolian Company, London, whose exhibition of pianolas he had seen a few years earlier. This short, barely two-minute-long piece (which the composer orchestrated in 1928 under the title "Madrid" as the last section of his "Quatre Etudes pour Orchestre") was performed on 13 October 1921, in the Aeolian Hall in London and was subsequently published as roll #T-967B. In 1923, the year he signed a six-year contract with Pleyel in Paris to record his entire corpus on pianola rolls, Stravinsky also wrote an early instrumentation of *Les noces* for two cymbalons, harmonium, pianola, and drums. In a statement entitled "My Position on the Phonograph Record," published in 1930, Stravinsky calls not only for recording practices that take advantage of the plastic capabilities of phonographic reproduction, as the composer claims to have done in his records for the Columbia label; he also insists that "it would be of the greatest interest to produce music specifically for phonographic reproduction, a music which would only attain its true image—its original sound—through the mechanical reproduction. This is probably the ultimate goal for the gramophonic composer of the future" (Igor Stravinsky, "Meine Stellung zur Schallplatte," *Kultur und Schallplatte* 9 [1930], cited in *Musik und Gesellschaft* 1 no. 8 [1931], p. 32).

4. As early as the mid-1920s, articles discussing the prehistory of the gramophone were in fact being published in increasing number in the more progressive music journals of the time; see, for example, H. H. Stuckenschmidt, "Maschinenmusik," *Der Auftakt* 7 nos. 7/8 (1927), pp. 152–56; K. Marx, "Schallplatten-Geschichte," *Der Auftakt* 10 no. 11 (1930), pp. 241–43; and Günther Ziegler, "Musikautomaten," *Der Auftakt* 13 nos. 9/10 (1933), pp. 131–33.

5. See Walter Benjamin, *Ursprung des deutschen Trauerspiels*, in GS, vol. 1 (Frankfurt am Main: Suhrkamp, 1974), p. 387; translated by John Osborne as *The Origin of German Tragic Drama* (London: New Left Books, 1977), p. 214; translation slightly modified.

6. A play on the German word *Satz*, which means "phrase" and—in a musical context—the "movement" of a composition.

7. Ernst Florens Friedrich Chladni (1756–1827), a German physicist often called

the "father of acoustics" for his pioneering studies of the transmission of sound. The first to examine sound waves mathematically—as in his 1802 study entitled *Die Akustik,* published in Leipzig by Breitkopf und Härtel—Chladni experimented with vibrating plates of thin glass and metal covered with sand, noting that the sand remained in curved lines at the points where the plates did not quiver. These symmetrical patterns, the so-called Chladni figures, attracted popular attention, and in 1809 a demonstration was staged for Napoleon. In 1790 Chladni invented a musical instrument called the "euphonium," which was composed of glass rods and steel bars made to sound through rubbing with moistened fingers. Along with its contemporary, the "aiuton," invented by Charles Clagget, the euphonium was the first of numerous friction bar instruments, some with piano keyboards and horizontal friction cylinders or cones that acted on vertical bars, and others with bars stroked by the player's fingers or with a bow. For more on Chladni, see Mary Desiree Waller, *Chladni Figures: A Study in Symmetry* (London: G. Bell, 1961).

8. The German physicist Johann Wilhelm Ritter (1776–1810), often called the "father of electrochemistry," is credited with the discovery in 1801 of the ultraviolet region of the spectrum and in 1803 of the polarization of electrodes in batteries. Adorno here extends a concealed compliment to Walter Benjamin, who reviewed Ritter's treatment of Chladni in *The Origin of German Tragic Drama.* For further remarks on Ritter by Benjamin, see the introductory note to Ritter's letter to Franz von Baader included in Benjamin's epistolary compilation *Deutsche Menschen* (1936), in Benjamin, GS, vol. 4, pp. 176–77. For Ritter's discussion of Chladni, see Johann Wilhelm Ritter, *Fragmente aus dem Nachlasse eines jungen Physikers: Ein Taschenbuch für Freunde der Natur,* ed. J. W. Ritter [editorship fictitious], vol. 2 (Heidelberg: Mohr und Zimmer, 1810), pp. 227 ff. For a detailed study of Ritter, see Walter D. Wetzels, *Johann Wilhelm Ritter: Physik im Wirkungsfeld der deutschen Romantik* (Berlin and New York: Walter de Gruyter, 1973).

9. Adorno here is most likely referring to the more recent variations on the possibility of composing for mechanical pianos by inscribing directly upon the scrolls. This had been demonstrated as early as 1926 at a "Festival of Mechanical Music" in Donaueschingen where Ernst Toch and Gerhard Münch had composed pieces in this manner for a Welte-Mignon pianola. These works were "performed" by Paul Hindemith (who serviced the machine) together with a similarly generated work by Hindemith that served as an accompaniment to Oskar Schlemmer's "Triadic Ballet." See Dr. Erich Steinhard, "Donaueschingen: Mechanisches Musikfest," *Der Auftakt* 6 no. 8 (1926), pp. 183–86; on the history of the pianola, see Peter Hagmann, *Das Welte-Mignon-Klavier, die Welte-Philharmonie-Orgel und die Anfänge der Reproduktion von Musik* (New York: Peter Lang, 1984). In the late 1920s and early 1930s, the music journals were regularly reporting on a host of newly "invented," largely electric instruments such as Theremin's "Ätherwellenapparat," Dr. Friedrich Trautwein's "Trautonium," Helberger's "Hellerton," and Jörg Mager's "Sphärophon"; see, for example, Herbert Weisskopf, "Sphärophon: Das Instrument der Zukunft," *Der Auftakt* 6 no. 8 (1926), pp. 177–78; Hans Kuznitzky, "Neue Elemente der Musikerzeugung," *Melos* 6 (April 1927), pp. 156–60; Frank Warschauer, "Neue Möglichkeiten elektrischer Klangerzeugung," *Der Auftakt* 10 no. 11 (1930), pp. 233–35; and Edwin Geist, "Bedeutung und Aufgabe der elektrischen Musikinstrumente," *Melos* 12 (February 1933), pp. 49–52.

Opera and the Long-Playing Record

In the history of music it is not all that rare for technological inventions to gain significance only long after their inception. This was the fate of the valve horn with the chromatic scale, which did not become fully utilized until Wagner. The saxophone, a connecting link between woodwind and brass instruments, was already hesitantly used by Bizet,[1] but only entered the domain of serious music by means of a detour through jazz. A similar development now seems to be taking place with the phonograph record.

In music, *Technik* has a double meaning.[2] On the one hand, there are the actual compositional techniques and, on the other, there are the industrial processes that are applied to music for the purpose of its mass dissemination. The latter do not, however, remain completely external to the music. Behind both the technologico-industrial and the artistic discoveries there is the same historical process at work, the same human force of production. That is why they both converge.

As late as 1934 it still had to be claimed that, as a form, the phonograph record had not given rise to anything unique to it.[3] This may well have changed since the introduction of long-playing recordings, irrespective of whether, on the one hand, LPs might have been technologically possible from the very start and were only held back by commercial calculations or due to lack of consumer interest, or, on the other, one really only learned so late how to capture extended musical durations without interrupting them and thereby threatening the coherence of their meaning. In any case, the term "revolution" is hardly an exaggeration with regard to the long-playing record. The entire musical literature could now become available in quite-authentic form to listeners desirous of auditioning and studying such works at a time convenient to them.

The gramophone record comes into its own, however, by virtue of the fate of a major musical genre: the opera. It has been more than thirty years since any operas have been written for opera houses that—if one is allowed to insist on such high standards—manifested something of world spirit *[Weltgeist]*. The supply of traditional operas on the stages reserved for them has, however, become folderol for *opera fans**[*4] or cult objects for culture worshippers. Thus the tireless efforts to modernize operas in opera houses with new sets and new stagings—at the expense of their substance. This confrontation as surrealist tease has itself already become institutionalized, and rapidly loses its effect. In its heroic periods, modern music distanced itself from the production of opera for opera houses and groped toward a theater qualitatively different from the high bourgeois representation of the nineteenth century.[5] The current avant-garde has taken this up once again—probably most radically and convincingly by Kagel.[6]

When, almost forty years ago, audiences began to chuckle about Lohengrin's swan and the Germanic beards in the *Ring,* this was not due only to the inability of an already then sobered generation to experience art according to its stylistic principles, that is, in terms of its distance from the everyday. One sensed that, artistically, things just could not go on like this, that this very stylization was making opera into a marketable specialty item. The music of *Figaro* is of truly incomparable quality, but every staging of *Figaro* with powdered ladies and gentlemen, with the page and the white rococo salon, resembles the praline box,[7] not to mention the *Rosenkavalier* and the silver rose. If instead one sweeps away all the costuming and has the participants, copying the practices of contemporary dance, dressed in sweat suits or even timeless outfits, one cannot avoid asking, What's the point? Why even bother doing it on stage? One wants to spare Mozart from this.

It is obvious that Mozart's operas cannot be performed in oratorio fashion without an unintentionally comic effect. Television broadcasts of gala opera evenings do not make things any better. A million praline boxes are actually worse than one single one that still retains something of the childlike joy of blissful moments.[8] Radio operas merely produce the effect of a pale replica of the live performance, yet without relinquishing the claim to singularity that has become fatal. It is here that the LP makes its entrance as deus ex machina.

Shorn of phony hoopla, the LP simultaneously frees itself from the capriciousness of fake opera festivals. It allows for the optimal presentation of music, enabling it to recapture some of the force and intensity that had been worn threadbare in the opera houses. Objectification, that is, a con-

centration on music as the true object of opera, may be linked to a perception that is comparable to reading, to the immersion in a text. This
offers an alternative to that which opera does in the best case—and which
is just what an artwork ought not do—that is: cajole the listener. The form
of the gramophone record comes into its own as a form of sound figures.
The ability to repeat long-playing records, as well as parts of them, fosters
a familiarity which is hardly afforded by the ritual of performance. Such
records allow themselves to be possessed just as previously one possessed
art-prints. But there remains hardly any means other than possession,
other than reification, through which one can get at anything unmediated
in this world—and in art as well. One of the essential properties of operas,
particularly such as those from the later period by Wagner and Strauss, is
long temporal duration: they are sea voyages. LPs provide the opportunity—more perfectly than the supposedly live performance—to recreate
without disturbance the temporal dimension essential to operas.

The gramophone record becomes a form the moment it unintentionally
approaches the requisite state of a compositional form. Looking back, it
now seems as if the short-playing records of yesteryear—acoustic daguerreotypes that are already now hard to play in a way that produces a
satisfying sound due to the lack of proper apparatuses—unconsciously also
corresponded to their epoch: the desire for highbrow diversion, the salon
pieces, favorite arias, and the Neapolitan semihits whose image Proust
attached in an unforgettable manner to "O sole mio."[9] This sphere of music
is finished: there is now only music of the highest standards and obvious
kitsch, with nothing in between. The LP expresses this historical change
rather precisely.

At the time when music critic Paul Bekker was trying his hand as opera
house director, he may have been the first to have spoken of opera as a
museum.[10] Despite the fact that when Richard Strauss subsequently took
this up the result was reactionary, there is still something to it.[11] The form
of the LP makes it possible for more than a few musically engaged people
to build up such a museum for themselves. Nor need they fear that the
recorded works will be neutralized in the process, as they are in opera
houses. Similar to the fate that Proust ascribed to paintings in museums,[12]
these recordings awaken to a second life in the wondrous dialogue with
the lonely and perceptive listeners, hibernating for purposes unknown.

Of course, the LPs do bear the marks of the system within which they
are produced. This is true, first of all, of their rather steep prices, the
necessity of which—at least in Western countries—is doubtful. One notices many inadequacies in the LP that are probably the product of the

longstanding unequal relationship between the extramusical technology and music in itself. The most dubious of these shortcomings, all assurances to the contrary notwithstanding, still remains the manipulation of the sound. Another sensitive point is the practice of making cuts within an act, the unity of which ought to be respected at all costs. Plausible explanations will inevitably be proffered for all of these, as one can always comfortably argue against the ends from the standpoint of the means. Once the industry becomes fully aware of the ramifications of this invention, then mechanical reproduction might well be able to help resurrect opera in a decisive way at a time when it has become anachronistic in its own loci.

(1969; GS, vol. 19, pp. 555–58)
Translated by Thomas Y. Levin

NOTES BY THOMAS Y. LEVIN

1. Adorno is referring to Georges Bizet's employment of the saxophone in the two orchestral suites for *L'Arlésienne,* incidental music written in 1872 for a drama by Alphonse Daudet. The composer's hesitation regarding the new instrument is expressed in a prefatory note to the original edition where he explains that one can leave out the saxophone if one likes and have its part played instead by various other wind instruments.

2. In German, *Technik* refers both to artistic technique (in the sense of compositional style) and to technology. In his study of film music co-authored with Hanns Eisler, CF, Adorno articulates this distinction with regard to cinema as follows: "In the realm of motion pictures the term 'technique' has a double meaning that can easily lead to confusion. On the one hand, technique is the equivalent of an industrial process for producing goods: e.g., the discovery that picture and sound can be recorded on the same strip is comparable to the invention of the air brake. The other meaning of 'technique' is aesthetic. It designates the methods by which an artistic intention can be adequately realized" (p. 9 n. 3; compare also GS, vol. 15, p. 19 n. 2). For more on the question of musical technique, see Adorno's remarks in his 1958 essay "Musik und Technik," GS, vol. 16, pp. 229–48, translated by Wes Blomster as "Music and Technique," *Telos* 32 (Summer 1977), pp. 79–94.

3. Adorno is here referring to his own remarks made decades earlier in "The Form of the Phonograph Record." See pp. 277–82.

4. On Adorno's use of foreign words, see Thomas Y. Levin, "Nationalities of Language: Adorno's *Fremdwörter,*" *New German Critique* 36 (Fall 1985), pp. 111–19, my introduction to Adorno's essay "On the Question: 'What Is German?'"

5. Adorno is referring to works such as Berg's *Lulu* and Schoenberg's *Moses und Aron,* about which he notes elsewhere: "It is hardly a coincidence that since *Lulu* and *Moses und Aron* no operas have been written that were truly modern and simultaneously authentic ("Zu einer Umfrage: Neue Oper und Publikum," GS, vol. 19, p. 494). For more on Adorno's position on opera, see his 1955 essay "Bürgerliche Oper," GS, vol. 16, pp. 24–39, translated as "Bourgeois Opera," SF, pp. 15–28.

6. Following initial experiments in the 1950s with *musique concrète,* composer

Mauricio Kagel (born in Argentina in 1931) began experimenting with different electro-acoustic and audio-visual media, which he subsequently translated into various sorts of theatrical and multi-media performance pieces. Kagel also incorporated the theatrical aspect of performance itself as a new compositional parameter in traditionally nontheatrical genres such as the string quartet. One can find observations by the composer on his conception of opera in his introductory comments to the 1964 piece "Match für drei Spieler" entitled "Kaum eines Musikstückes" in Leo Karl Gerhartz, *Oper: Aspekte der Gattung* (Laaber: Laaber Verlag, 1983), pp. 188–95. See also Dieter Schnebel, *Mauricio Kagel: Musik, Theater, Film* (Cologne: Dumont Schauberg, 1970).

7. Probably a reference to the commercial exploitation of the iconography of classical stagings of Mozart operas on the boxes of "Mozartkugel" (Mozart Ball) chocolates.

8. For more extensive observations on the aesthetics and politics of music broadcasts on television, see Adorno's 1968 discussion with the editors of *Der Spiegel*, "Musik im Fernsehen ist Brimborium," and the subsequent polemical response to readers' letters, "Antwort des Fachidioten," GS, vol. 19, pp. 559–69 and 570–72.

9. See Marcel Proust, *The Fugitive*, in *Remembrance of Things Past*, vol. 3, trans. C. K. Scott Moncrieff, Terence Kilmartin, and Andreas Mayor (New York: Random House, 1981), pp. 677 ff.

10. Paul Bekker (1882–1937), turn-of-the-century German music critic at the *Berliner neueste Nachrichten, Berliner allgemeine Zeitung,* and the *Frankfurter Zeitung,* was an enthusiastic advocate of the music of Mahler, Schoenberg, Hindemith, Krenek, and Schreker. In 1925 he became director of the theater in Kassel and, after holding the same position at the Wiesbaden theater from 1927–1933, emigrated to New York to escape the Nazis in 1934 and died soon thereafter. An English version of his study, *The Story of Music,* translated by M. D. Herter Norton and Alice Kortschak, was published as early as 1927 (New York: Norton), followed by his *The Changing Opera,* translated by Arthur Mendel (New York: Norton), in 1935.

11. Adorno is referring to the anachronistic eighteenth-century period settings of Richard Strauss's opera *Der Rosenkavalier* (1909–1910). For further remarks by Adorno on Strauss, see "Richard Strauss: Born June 11, 1864," trans. Samuel Weber and Shierry Weber, *Perspectives of New Music* 3 (Fall/Winter 1965), pp. 14–32, and 4 (Spring/Summer 1966), pp. 113–29.

12. Adorno discusses Proust's position on the museum at some length in his 1953 essay "Valéry Proust Museum," republished in PR, pp. 173–85.

On the Fetish-Character in Music and the Regression of Listening

Complaints about the decline of musical taste begin only a little later than mankind's twofold discovery, on the threshold of historical time, that music represents at once the immediate manifestation of impulse and the locus of its taming. It stirs up the dance of the Maenads and sounds from Pan's bewitching flute, but it also rings out from the Orphic lyre, around which the visions of violence range themselves, pacified. Whenever their peace seems to be disturbed by bacchantic agitation, there is talk of the decline of taste. But if the disciplining function of music has been handed down since Greek philosophy as a major good, then certainly the pressure to be permitted to obey musically, as elsewhere, is today more general than ever. Just as the current musical consciousness of the masses can scarcely be called Dionysian, so its latest changes have nothing to do with taste. The concept of taste is itself outmoded. Responsible art adjusts itself to criteria which approximate judgments: the harmonious and the inharmonious, the correct and the incorrect. But otherwise, no more choices are made; the question is no longer put, and no one demands the subjective justification of the conventions. The very existence of the subject who could verify such taste has become as questionable as has, at the opposite pole, the right to a freedom of choice which empirically, in any case, no one any longer exercises. If one seeks to find out who "likes" a commercial piece [markt-gängiger Schlager], one cannot avoid the suspicion that liking and disliking are inappropriate to the situation, even if the person questioned clothes his reactions in those words. The familiarity of the piece is a surrogate for the quality ascribed to it. To like it is almost the same thing as to recognize it. An approach in terms of value judgments has become a fiction for the person who finds himself hemmed in by standardized musical goods. He can neither escape impotence nor decide between the offerings where everything is so completely identical that preference in fact depends merely on biographical details or on the situation in which things are heard. The categories of autonomously oriented art have no applicability to the contemporary reception of music; not even for that of serious music, domesticated under the barbarous name of classical so as to enable one to turn away from it again in comfort. If it is objected that specifically light music and everything intended for consumption have in any case never been experienced in terms of those categories, that must certainly be conceded. Nevertheless, such music is also affected by the change in that the entertainment, the pleasure, the enjoyment it promises, is given only to be simultaneously denied. In one of his essays, Aldous Huxley has raised the question of who, in a place of amusement, is really being amused.[1] With the same justice, it can be asked whom music for entertainment still entertains. Rather, it seems to complement the reduction of people to silence, the dying out of speech as expression, the inability to communicate at all. It inhabits the pockets of silence that develop between people molded by anxiety, work and undemanding docility. Everywhere it takes over, unnoticed, the deadly sad role that fell to it in the time and the specific situation of the silent films. It is perceived purely as background. If nobody can any longer speak, then certainly nobody can any longer listen. An American specialist in radio advertising, who indeed prefers to make use of the musical medium, has expressed skepticism as to the value of this advertising, because people have learned to deny their attention to what they are hearing even while listening to it. His observation is questionable with respect to the advertising value of music. But it tends to be right in terms of the reception of the music itself.

In the conventional complaints about declining taste, certain motifs constantly recur. There is no lack of pouting and sentimental comments assessing the current musical condition of the masses as one of "degeneration." The most tenacious of these motifs is that of sensuality, which allegedly enfeebles and incapacitates heroic behavior. This complaint can already be found in Book III of Plato's *Republic* in which he bans "the harmonies expressive of sorrow" as well as the "soft" harmonies "suitable for drinking," without its being clear to this day why the philosopher ascribes these characteristics to the mixolydian, Lydian, hypolydian and Ionian modes. In the Platonic state, the major of later Western music, which corresponds to the Ionian, would have been tabooed. The flute and the "panharmonic" stringed instruments also fall under the ban. The only modes to be left are "warlike, to sound the note or accent which a brave man utters in the hour of danger and stern resolve, or when he faces injury, defeat or death, or any other misfortune, with the same steadfast endurance." Plato's *Republic* is not the utopia it is called by the official history of philosophy. It disciplines its citizens in terms of its existence and will to exist even in music, where the distinction made between soft and strong modes was by Plato's time already little more than a residue of the mustiest superstition.[2] The Platonic irony reveals itself mischievously in jeering at the flute-player Marsyas, flayed by the sober-sided Apollo.[3] Plato's ethical-musical program bears the character of an Attic purge in Spartan style. Other perennial themes of musical sermonizing are on the same level. Among the most prominent of these are the charge of superficiality and that of a "cult of personality." What is attacked is chiefly progress: social, essentially the specifically aesthetic. Intertwined with the forbidden allurements are sensual gaiety and differentiating consciousness. The predominance of the person over collective compulsion in music marks the moment of subjective freedom which breaks through in later phases, while the profanation which frees it from its magic circle appears as superficiality. Thus, the lamented moments have entered into the great music of the West: sensory stimulation as the gate of entry into the harmonic and eventually the coloristic dimensions; the unbridled person as the bearer of expression and of the humanization of music itself; "superficiality" as a critique of the mute objectivity of forms, in the sense of Haydn's choice of the "gallant" in preference to the learned. Haydn's choice indeed, and not the recklessness of a singer with a golden throat or an instrumentalist of lip-smacking euphony *[geschlekten Wohllauts]*. For those moments entered into great music and were transformed in it; but great music did not dissolve into them. In the multiplicity of stimulus and expression, its greatness is shown as a force for synthesis. Not only does the musical synthesis preserve the unity of appearance and protect it from falling apart into diffuse culinary moments, but in such unity, in the relation of particular moments to an evolving whole, there is also preserved the image of a social condition in which above those particular moments of happiness would be more than mere appearance. Until the end of prehistory, the musical balance between partial stimulus and totality, between expression and synthesis, between the surface and the underlying, remains as unstable as the moments of balance between supply and demand in the capitalist economy. *The Magic Flute*, in which the utopia of the Enlightenment and the pleasure of a light opera comic song precisely coincide, is a moment by itself. After *The Magic Flute* it was never again possible to force serious and light music together.

But what are emancipated from formal law are no longer the productive impulses which rebelled against conventions. Impulse, subjectivity and profanation, the old adversaries of materialistic alienation, now succumb to it. In capitalist times, the traditional anti-mythological ferments of music conspire against freedom, as whose allies they were once proscribed. The representatives of the opposition to the authoritarian schema become witnesses to the authority of commercial success. The delight in the moment and the gay façade becomes an excuse for absolving the listener from the thought of the whole, whose claim is comprised in proper listening. The listener is converted, along his line of least resistance, into the acquiescent purchaser. No longer do the partial moments serve as a critique of that whole; instead, they suspend the critique which the successful aesthetic totality exerts against the flawed one of society. The unitary synthesis is sacrificed to them; they no longer produce their own in place of the reified one, but show themselves complaisant to it. The isolated moments of enjoyment prove incompatible with the immanent constitution of the work of art, and whatever in the work goes beyond them to an essential perception is sacrificed to them. They are not bad in themselves but in their diversionary function. In the service of success they renounce that insubordinate character which was theirs. They conspire to come to terms with everything which the isolated moment can offer to an isolated individual who long ago ceased to be one. In isolation, the charms become dulled and furnish models of the familiar. Whoever devotes himself to them is as malicious as the Greek thinkers once were toward oriental sensuality. The seductive power of the charm survives only where the forces of denial are strongest: in the dissonance which rejects belief in the illusion of the existing harmony. The concept of the ascetic is itself dialectical in music. If asceticism once struck down the claims of the aesthetic in a reactionary way, it has today become the sign of advanced art: not, to be sure, by an archaicizing parsimony of means in which deficiency and poverty are manifested, but by the strict exclusion of all culinary delights which seek to be consumed immediately for their own sake, as if in art the sensory were not the bearer of something intellectual which only shows itself in the whole rather than in isolated topical moments. Art records negatively just that possibility of happiness which the only partially positive anticipation of happiness ruinously confronts today. All "light" and pleasant art has become illusory and mendacious. What makes its appearance aesthetically in the pleasure categories can no longer give pleasure, and the *promesse du bonheur*, once the definition of art, can no longer be found except where the mask has been torn from the countenance of false happiness. Enjoyment still retains a place only in the immediate bodily presence. Where it requires an aesthetic appearance, it is illusory by aesthetic standards and likewise cheats the pleasure-seeker out of itself. Only where its appearance is lacking is the faith in its possibility maintained.

The new phase of the musical consciousness of the masses is defined by displeasure in pleasure. It resembles the reaction to sport or advertising. The words "enjoyment of art" sound funny. If in nothing else, Schoenberg's music resembles popular songs in refusing to be enjoyed. Whoever still delights in the beautiful passages of a Schubert quartet or even in the provocatively healthy fare of a Handel concerto grosso, ranks as a would-be guardian of culture among the butterfly collectors. What condemns him as an epicure is not perhaps "new." The power of the street ballad, the catchy tune and all the swarming forms of the banal has made itself felt since the beginning of the bourgeois era. Formerly, it attacked the cultural privilege of the ruling class. But today, when that power of the banal extends over the entire society, its function has changed. This change of function affects all music, not only light music, in whose realm it could comfortably enough be made light of as simply "gradual," as the result of the mechanical means of dissemination. The diverse spheres of music must be thought of together. Their static separation, which certain caretakers of culture have ardently sought—the totalitarian radio was assigned to the task, on the one hand, of providing good entertainment and diversion, and on the other, of fostering the so-called cultural goods, as if there could still be good entertainment and as if the cultural goods were not, by their administration, transformed into evils—the neat parcelling out of music's social field of force is illusionary. Just as the history of serious music since Mozart as a flight from the banal reflects in reverse the outlines of light music, so today, in its key representatives, it gives an account of the ominous experiences which appear even in the unsuspecting innocence of light music. It would be just as easy to go in the other direction and conceal the break between the two spheres, assuming a continuum which permits a progressive education leading safely from commercial jazz and hit songs to cultural commodities. Cynical barbarism is no better than cultural dishonesty. What it accomplishes by disillusion on the higher level, it balances by the ideologies of primitivism and return to nature, with which it glorifies the musical underworld: an underworld which has long since ceased to assist the opposition of those excluded from culture to find expression, and now only lives on what is handed down to it from above. The illusion of a social preference for light music as against serious is based on that passivity of the masses which makes the consumption of light music contradict the objective interest of those who consume it. It is claimed that they actually like light music and listen to the higher type only for reasons of social prestige, when acquaintance with the text of a single hit song suffices to reveal the sole function this object of honest approbation can perform. The unity of the two spheres of music is thus that of an unresolved contradiction. They do not hang together in such a way that the lower could serve as a sort of popular introduction to the higher, or that the higher could renew its lost collective strength by borrowing from the lower. The whole cannot be put together by adding the separated halves, but in both there appear, however distantly, the changes of the whole, which only moves in contradiction. If the flight from the banal becomes definitive, if the marketability of the serious product shrinks to nothing, in consequence of its objective demands, then on the lower level the effect of the standardization of successes means it is no longer possible to succeed in an old style, but only in imitation as such. Between incomprehensibility and inescapability, there is no third way; the situation has polarized itself into extremes which actually meet. There is no room between them for the "individual." The latter's claims, wherever they still occur, are illusory, being copied from the standards. The liquidation of the individual is the real signature of the new musical situation.

If the two spheres of music are stirred up in the unity of their contradiction, the demarcation line between them varies. The advanced product has renounced consumption. The rest of serious music is delivered over to consumption for the price of its wages. It succumbs to commodity listening. The differences in the reception of official "classical" music and light music no longer have any real significance. They are only still manipulated for reasons of marketability. The hit song enthusiast must be reassured that his idols are not too elevated for him, just as the visitor to philharmonic concerts is confirmed in his status. The more industriously the trade erects wire fences between the musical provinces, the greater the suspicion that without these, the inhabitants could all too easily come to an understanding. Toscanini, like a second-rate orchestra leader, is called Maestro, if half ironically, and a hit song, "Music, Maestro, Please*,"[4] had its success immediately after Toscanini was promoted to Marshal of the Air with the aid of the radio.

The world of that musical life, the composition business which extends peacefully from Irving Berlin and Walter Donaldson[5]—"*the world's best composer*"—by way of Gershwin, Sibelius and Tchaikovsky to Schubert's B Minor Symphony, labeled *The Unfinished**, is one of fetishes. The star principle has become totalitarian. The reactions of the listeners appear to have no relation to the playing of the music. They have reference, rather, to the cumulative success which, for its part, cannot be thought of unalienated by the past spontaneities of listeners, but instead dates back to the command of publishers, sound film magnates and rulers of radio. Famous people are not the only stars. Works begin to take on the same role. A pantheon of *best-sellers** builds up. The programs shrink, and the shrinking process not only removes the moderately good, but the accepted classics themselves undergo a selection that has nothing to do with quality. In America, Beethoven's Fourth Symphony is among the rarities. This selection reproduces itself in a fatal circle: the most familiar is the most successful and is therefore played again and again and made still more familiar. The choice of the standard works is itself in terms of their "effectiveness" for programmatic fascination, in terms of the categories of success as determined by light music or permitted by the star conductors. The climaxes of Beethoven's Seventh Symphony are placed on the same level as the unspeakable horn melody from the slow movement of Tchaikovsky's Fifth. Melody comes to mean eight-bar symmetrical treble melody. This is catalogued as the composer's "inspiration" which one thinks he can put in his pocket and take home, just as it is ascribed to the composer as his basic property. The concept of inspiration is far from appropriate to established classical music. Its thematic material, mostly segmented triads, does not at all belong to the author in the same specific sense as in a romantic song. Beethoven's greatness shows itself in the complete subordination of the accidentally private melodic elements to the form as a whole. This does not prevent all music, even Bach, who borrowed one of the most important themes of *The Well-Tempered Clavier*, from being examined in terms of the category of ideas, with musical larceny being hunted down with all the zeal of the belief in property, so that finally one music commentator could pin his success to the title of tune detective. At its most passionate, musical fetishism takes possession of the public valuation of singing voices. Their sensuous magic is traditional as is the close relation between success and the person endowed with "material." But today it is forgotten that it is material. For musical vulgar materialists, it is synonymous to have a voice and to be a singer. In earlier epochs, technical virtuosity, at least, was demanded of singing stars, the castrati and prima donnas. Today, the material as such, destitute of any function, is celebrated. One need not even ask about capacity for musical performance. Even mechanical control of the instrument is no longer really expected. To legitimate the fame of its owner, a voice need only be especially voluminous or especially high. If one dares even in conversation to question the decisive importance of the voice and to assert that it is just as possible to make beautiful music with a moderately good voice as it is on a moderately good piano, one will immediately find oneself faced with a situation of hostility and aversion whose emotional roots go far deeper than the occasion. Voices are holy properties like a national trademark. As if the voices wanted to revenge themselves for this, they begin to lose the sensuous magic in whose name they are merchandised. Most of them sound like imitations of those who have made it, even when they themselves have made it. All this reaches a climax of absurdity in the cult of the master violins. One promptly goes into raptures at the well-announced sound of a Stradivarius or Amati, which only the ear of a specialist can tell from that of a good modern violin, forgetting in the process to listen to the composition and the execution, from which there is still something to be had. The more the modern technique of the violin bow progresses, the more it seems that the old instruments are treasured. If the moments of sensual pleasure in the idea, the voice, the instrument are made into fetishes and torn away from any functions which could give them meaning, they meet a response equally isolated, equally far from the meaning of the whole, and equally determined by success in the blind and irrational emotions which form the relationship to music into which those with no relationship enter. But these are the same relations as exist between the consumers of hit songs and the hit songs. Their only relation is to the completely alien, and the alien, as if cut off from the consciousness of the masses by a dense screen, is what seeks to speak for the silent. Where they react at all, it no longer makes any difference whether it is to Beethoven's Seventh Symphony or to a bikini.

The concept of musical fetishism cannot be psychologically derived. That "values" are consumed and draw feelings to themselves, without their specific qualities being reached by the consciousness of the consumer, is a later expression of their commodity character. For all contemporary musical life is dominated by the commodity form: the last pre-capitalist residues have been eliminated. Music, with all the attributes of the ethereal and sublime which are generously accorded it, serves in America today as an advertisement for commodities which one must acquire in order to be able to hear music. If the advertising function is carefully dimmed in the case of serious music, it always breaks through in the case of light music. The whole jazz business, with its free distribution of scores to bands, has abandoned the idea that actual performance promotes the sale of piano scores and phonograph records. Countless hit song texts praise the hit songs themselves, repeating their titles in capital letters. What makes its appearance, like an idol, out of such masses of type is the exchange-value in which the quantum of possible enjoyment has disappeared. Marx defines the fetish-character of the commodity as the veneration of the thing made by oneself which, as exchange-value, simultaneously alienates itself from producer to consumer—"human beings." "A commodity is therefore a mysterious thing, simply because in it the social character of men's labor appears to them as an objective character stamped upon the product of that labor; because the relation of the producers to the sum total of their own labor is presented to them as a social relation, existing not between themselves, but between the products of their labor."[6] This is the real secret of success. It is the mere reflection of what one pays in the market for the product. The consumer is really worshipping the money that he himself has paid for the ticket to the Toscanini concert. He has literally "made" the success which he reifies and accepts as an objective criterion, without recognizing himself in it. But he has not "made" it by liking the concert, but rather by buying the ticket. To be sure, exchange-value exerts its power in a special way in the realm of cultural goods. For in the world of commodities this realm appears to be exempted from the power of exchange, to be in an immediate relationship with the goods, and it is this appearance in turn which alone gives cultural goods their exchange-value. But they nevertheless simultaneously fall completely into the world of commodities, are produced for the market, and are aimed at the market. The appearance of immediacy is as strong as the compulsion of exchange-value is inexorable. The social compact harmonizes the contradiction. The appearance of immediacy takes possession of the mediated, exchange-value itself. If the commodity in general combines exchange-value and use-value, then the pure use-value, whose illusion the cultural goods must preserve in completely capitalist society, must be replaced by pure exchange-value, which precisely in its capacity as exchange-value deceptively takes over the function of use-value. The specific fetish character of music lies in this quid pro quo. The feelings which go to the exchange-value create the appearance of immediacy at the same time as the absence of a relation to the object belies it. It has its basis in the abstract character of exchange-value. Every "psychological" aspect, every ersatz satisfaction, depends on such social substitution.

The change in the function of music involves the basic conditions of the relation between art and society. The more inexorably the principle of exchange-value destroys use-values for human beings, the more deeply does exchange-value disguise itself as the object of enjoyment. It has been asked what the cement is which still holds the world of commodities together. The answer is that this transfer of the use-value of consumption goods to their exchange-value contributes to a general order in which eventually every pleasure which emancipates itself from exchange-value takes on subversive features. The appearance of exchange-value in commodities has taken on a specific cohesive function. The woman who has money with which to buy is intoxicated by the act of buying. In American conventional speech, *having a good time** means being present at the enjoyment of others, which in its turn has as its only content being present. The auto religion makes all men brothers in the sacramental moment with the words: "That is a Rolls Royce," and in moments of intimacy, women attach greater importance to the hairdressers and cosmeticians than to the situation for the sake of which the hairdressers and cosmeticians are employed. The relation to the irrelevant dutifully manifests its social essence. The couple out driving who spend their time identifying every passing car and being happy if they recognize the trademarks speeding by, the girl whose satisfaction consists solely in the fact that she and her boyfriend "look good," the expertise of the jazz enthusiast who legitimizes himself by having knowledge about what is in any case inescapable: all this operates according to the same command. Before the theological caprices of commodities, the consumers become temple slaves. Those who sacrifice themselves nowhere else can do so here, and here they are fully betrayed.

In the commodity fetishists of the new model, in the "sado-masochistic character," in those receptive to today's mass art, the same thing shows itself in many ways. The masochistic mass culture is the necessary manifestation of almighty production itself. When the feelings seize on exchange-value it is no mystical transubstantiation. It corresponds to the behavior of the prisoner who loves his cell because he has been left nothing else to love. The sacrifice of individuality, which accommodates itself to the regularity of the successful, the doing of what everybody does, follows from the basic fact that in broad areas the same thing is offered to everybody by the standardized production of consumption goods. But the commercial necessity of concealing this identity leads to the manipulation of taste and the official culture's pretense of individualism, which necessarily increases in proportion to the liquidation of the individual. Even in the realm of the superstructure, the appearance is not merely the concealment of the essence, but proceeds of necessity from the essence itself. The identical character of the goods which everyone must buy hides itself behind the rigor of the universally compulsory style. The fiction of the relation between supply and demand survives in the fictitiously individual nuances. If the value of taste in the present situation is questioned, it is necessary to understand what taste is composed of in this situation. Acquiescence is rationalized as modesty, opposition to caprice and anarchy; musical analysis has today decayed as fundamentally as musical charm, and has its parody in the stubborn counting of beats. The picture is completed by accidental differentiation within the strict confines of the prescribed. But if the liquidated individual really makes the complete superficiality of the conventions passionately his own, then the golden age of taste has dawned at the very moment in which taste no longer exists.

The works which are the basis of the fetishization and become cultural goods experience constitutional changes as a result. They become vulgarized. Irrelevant consumption destroys them. Not merely do the few things played again and again wear out, like the Sistine Madonna in the bedroom, but reification affects their internal structure. They are transformed into a conglomeration of irruptions which are impressed on the listeners by climax and repetition, while the organization of the whole makes no impression whatsoever. The memorability of disconnected parts, thanks to climaxes and repetitions, has a precursor in great music itself, in the technique of late romantic compositions, especially those of Wagner. The more reified the music, the more romantic it sounds to alienated ears. Just in this way it becomes "property." A Beethoven symphony as a whole, spontaneously experienced, can never be appropriated. The man who in the subway triumphantly whistles loudly the theme of the finale of Brahms's First is already primarily involved with its debris. But since the disintegration of the fetishes puts these themselves in danger and virtually assimilates them to hit songs, it produces a counter tendency in order to preserve their fetish character. If the romanticizing of particulars eats away the body of the whole, the endangered substance is galvanically copperplated. The climax which emphasizes the reified parts takes on the character of a magical ritual, in which all the mysteries of personality, inwardness, inspiration and spontaneity of reproduction, which have been eliminated from the work itself, are conjured up. Just because the disintegrating work renounces the moment of its spontaneity, this, just as stereotyped as the bits and pieces, is injected into it from the outside. In spite of all talk of new objectivity, the essential function of conformist performances is no longer the performance of the "pure" work but the presentation of the vulgarized one with a gesture which emphatically but impotently tries to hold the vulgarization at a distance.

Vulgarization and enchantment, hostile sisters, dwell together in the arrangements which have colonized large areas of music. The practice of arrangement extends to the most diverse dimensions. Sometimes it seizes on the time. It blatantly snatches the reified bits and pieces out of their context and sets them up as a potpourri. It destroys the multilevel unity of the whole work and brings forward only isolated popular passages. The minuet from Mozart's E-flat Major Symphony, played without the other movements, loses its symphonic cohesion and is turned by the performance into an artisan-type genre piece that has more to do with the "Stephanie Gavotte"[7] than with the sort of classicism it is supposed to advertise. Then there is the arrangement in coloristic terms. They arrange whatever they can get hold of, as long as the decree of a famous interpreter does not forbid it. If in the field of light music the arrangers are the only trained musicians, they feel called on to jump around all the more unrestrainedly with cultural goods. All sorts of reasons are offered by them for instrumental arrangements. In the case of great orchestral works, it will reduce the cost, or the composers are accused of lacking technique in instrumentation. These reasons are lamentable pretexts. The argument of cheapness, which aesthetically condemns itself, is disposed of by reference to the superfluity of orchestral means at the disposal of precisely those who most eagerly carry on the practice of arrangement, and by the fact that very often, as in instrumental arrangements of piano pieces, the arrangements turn out substantially dearer than performance in the original form. And finally, the belief that older music needs a coloristic freshening up presupposes an accidental character in the relation between color and line, such as could be assumed only as a result of the crudest ignorance of Viennese classicism and the so-eagerly arranged Schubert. Even if the real discovery of the coloristic dimension first took place in the era of Berlioz and Wagner, the coloristic parsimony of Haydn or Beethoven is of a piece with the predominance of the principle of construction over the melodic particular springing in brilliant colors out of the dynamic unity. Precisely in the context of such parsimony do the bassoon thirds at the beginning of the third *Leonore* overture or the oboe cadenza in the recapitulation of the first movement of the Fifth achieve a power which would be irretrievably lost in a multicolored sonority. One must therefore assume that the motives for the practice of arranging are *sui generis*. Above all, arranging seeks to make the great distant sound, which always has aspects of the public and unprivate, assimilable. The tired businessman can clap arranged classics on the shoulder and fondle the progeny of their muse. It is a compulsion similar to that which requires radio favorites to insinuate themselves into the families of their listeners as uncles and aunts and pretend to a human proximity. Radical reification produces its own pretense of immediacy and intimacy. Contrarywise, the intimate is inflated and colored by arrangements precisely for being too spare. Because they were originally defined only as moments of the whole, the instants of sensory pleasure which emerge out of the decomposing unities are too weak even to produce the sensory stimulus demanded of them in fulfill-ment of their advertised role. The dressing up and puffing up of the in-dividual erases the lineaments of protest, sketched out in the limitation of the individual to himself over and against the institution, just as in the reduction of the large-scale to the intimate, sight is lost of the totality in which bad individual immediacy was kept within bounds in great music. Instead of this, there develops a spurious balance which at every step be-trays its falsity by its contradiction of the material. Schubert's "Serenade,"[8] in the puffed-up sound of the combination of strings and piano, with the silly excessive clarity of the imitative intermediate measures, is as non-sensical as if it had originated in a girls' school. But neither does the Prize Song from *Meistersinger* sound any more serious when played by a string orchestra alone. In monochrome, it objectively loses the articulation which makes it viable in Wagner's score. But at the same time, it becomes quite viable for the listener, who no longer has to put the body of the song together from different colors, but can confidently give himself over to the single and uninterrupted treble melody. Here one can put one's hands on the antagonism to the audience into which works regarded as classic fall today. But one may suspect that the darkest secret of arrangement is the compulsion not to leave anything as it is, but to lay hands on anything that crosses one's path, a compulsion that grows greater the less the fun-damental characteristics of what exists lend themselves to being meddled with. The total social grasp confirms its power and mastery by the stamp which is impressed on anything that falls into its machinery. But this affirmation is likewise destructive. Contemporary listeners would always prefer to destroy what they hold in blind respect, and their pseudoactivity is already prepared and prescribed by the production.

The practice of arrangement comes from salon music. It is the practice of refined entertainment which borrows its pretensions from the *niveau* of cultural goods, but transforms these into entertainment material of the type of hit songs. Such entertainment, formerly reserved as an accompa-niment to people's humming, today spreads over the whole of musical life, which is basically not taken seriously by anyone anymore and in all dis-cussion of culture retreats further and further into the background. One has the choice of either dutifully going along with the business, if only furtively in front of the loudspeaker on Saturday afternoon, or at once stubbornly and impenitently acknowledging the trash served up for the ostensible or real needs of the masses. The uncompelling and superficial nature of the objects of refined entertainment inevitably leads to the in-attentiveness of the listeners. One preserves a good conscience in the matter since one is offering the listeners first-class goods. To the objection that these are already a drug on the market, one is ready with the reply that this is what they wanted, an argument which can be finally invalidated by a diagnosis of the situation of the listeners, but only through insight into the whole process which unites producers and consumers in a diabolical harmony. But fetishism takes hold of even the ostensibly serious practice of music, which mobilizes the pathos of distance against refined entertainment. The purity of service to the cause, with which it presents the works, often turns out to be as inimical to them as vulgarization and arrangement. The official ideal of performance, which covers the earth as a result of Toscanini's extraordinary achievement, helps to sanction a condition which, in a phrase of Eduard Steuermann,[9] may be called the barbarism of perfection. To be sure, the names of famous works are no longer made fetishes, although the lesser ones that break into the programs almost make the limitation to the smaller repertoire seem desirable. To be sure, passages are not here inflated or climaxes overstressed for the sake of fascination. There is iron discipline. But precisely iron. The new fetish is the flawlessly functioning, metallically brilliant apparatus as such, in which all the cogwheels mesh so perfectly that not the slightest hole remains open for the meaning of the whole. Perfect, immaculate performance in the latest style preserves the work at the price of its definitive reification. It presents it as already complete from the very first note. The performance sounds like its own phonograph record. The dynamic is so predetermined that there are no longer any tensions at all. The contradictions of the musical material are so inexorably resolved in the moment of sound that it never arrives at the synthesis, the self-production of the work, which reveals the meaning of every Beethoven symphony. What is the point of the symphonic effort when the material on which that effort was to be tested has already been ground up? The protective fixation of the work leads to its destruction, for its unity is realized in precisely that spontaneity which is sacrificed to the fixation. This last fetishism, which seizes on the substance itself, smothers it; the absolute adjustment of the appearance to the work denies the latter and makes it disappear unnoticed behind the apparatus, just as certain swamp-drainings by labor detachments take place not for their own sake but for that of the work. Not for nothing does the rule of the established conductor remind one of that of the totalitarian Führer. Like the latter, he reduces aura and organization to a common denominator. He is the real modern type of the virtuoso, as *band leader** as well as in the Philharmonic. He has got to the point where he no longer has to do anything himself; he is even sometimes relieved of reading the score by the staff musical advisors. At one stroke he provides norm and individualization: the norm is identified with his person, and the individual tricks which he perpetrates furnish general rules. The fetish character of the conductor is the most obvious and the most hidden. The standard works could probably be performed by the virtuosi of contemporary orchestras just as well without the conductor, and the public which cheers the conductor would be unable to tell that, in the concealment of the orchestra, the musical advisor was taking the place of the hero laid low by a cold.

The consciousness of the mass of listeners is adequate to fetishized music. It listens according to formula, and indeed debasement itself would not be possible if resistance ensued, if the listeners still had the capacity to make demands beyond the limits of what was supplied. But if someone tried to "verify" the fetish character of music by investigating the reactions of listeners with interviews and questionnaires, he might meet with unexpected puzzles. In music as elsewhere, the discrepancy between essence and appearance has grown to a point where no appearance is any longer valid, without mediation, as verification of the essence.[A] The unconscious reactions of the listeners are so heavily veiled and their conscious assessment is so exclusively oriented to the dominant fetish categories that every answer one receives conforms in advance to the surface of that music business which is attacked by the theory being "verified." As soon as one presents the listener with the primitive question about liking or disliking, there comes into play the whole machinery which one had thought could be made transparent and eliminated by the reduction to this question. But if one tries to replace the most elementary investigative procedures with others which take account of the real dependence of the listener on the mechanism, this complication of the investigative procedure not merely makes the interpretation of the result more difficult, but it touches off the resistance of the respondents and drives them all the deeper into the conformist behavior in which they think they can remain concealed from the danger of exposure. No causal nexus at all can properly be worked out between isolated "impressions" of the hit song and its psychological effects on the listener. If indeed individuals today no longer belong to themselves, then that also means that they can no longer be "influenced." The opposing

A. Cf. Max Horkheimer, "Der neueste Angriff auf die Metaphysik," *Zeitschrift für Sozialforschung* 6 (1937), pp. 28 ff.

points of production and consumption are at any given time closely co-ordinated, but not dependent on each other in isolation. Their mediation itself does not in any case escape theoretical conjecture. It suffices to remember how many sorrows he is spared who no longer thinks too many thoughts, how much more "in accordance with reality" a person behaves when he affirms that the real is right, how much more capacity to use the machinery falls to the person who integrates himself with it uncomplainingly, so that the correspondence between the listener's consciousness and the fetishized music would still remain comprehensible even if the former did not unequivocally reduce itself to the latter.

The counterpart to the fetishism of music is a regression of listening. This does not mean a relapse of the individual listener into an earlier phase of his own development, nor a decline in the collective general level, since the millions who are reached musically for the first time by today's mass communications cannot be compared with the audience of the past. Rather, it is contemporary listening which has regressed, arrested at the infantile stage. Not only do the listening subjects lose, along with freedom of choice and responsibility, the capacity for conscious perception of music, which was from time immemorial confined to a narrow group, but they stubbornly reject the possibility of such perception. They fluctuate between comprehensive forgetting and sudden dives into recognition. They listen atomistically and dissociate what they hear, but precisely in this dissociation they develop certain capacities which accord less with the concepts of traditional aesthetics than with those of football and motoring. They are not childlike, as might be expected on the basis of an interpretation of the new type of listener in terms of the introduction to musical life of groups previously unacquainted with music. But they are childish; their primitivism is not that of the undeveloped, but that of the forcibly retarded. Whenever they have a chance, they display the pinched hatred of those who really sense the other but exclude it in order to live in peace, and who therefore would like best to root out the nagging possibility. The regression is really from this existent possibility, or more concretely, from the possibility of a different and oppositional music. Regressive, too, is the role which contemporary mass music plays in the psychological household of its victims. They are not merely turned away from more important music, but they are confirmed in their neurotic stupidity, quite irrespective of how their musical capacities are related to the specific musical culture of earlier social phases. The assent to hit songs and debased cultural goods belongs to the same complex of symptoms as do those faces of which one no longer knows whether the film has alienated them from reality or re-

ality has alienated them from the film, as they wrench open a great formless mouth with shining teeth in a voracious smile, while the tired eyes
are wretched and lost above. Together with sport and film, mass music and
the new listening help to make escape from the whole infantile milieu
impossible. The sickness has a preservative function. Even the listening
habits of the contemporary masses are certainly in no way new, and one
may readily concede that the reception of the prewar hit song
"Püppchen"[10] was not so very different from that of a synthetic jazz children's song. But the context in which such a children's song appears, the
masochistic mocking of one's own wish for lost happiness, or the compromising of the desire for happiness itself by the reversion to a childhood
whose unattainability bears witness to the unattainability of joy—this is
the specific product of the new listening, and nothing which strikes the ear
remains exempt from this system of assimilation. There are indeed social
differences, but the new listening extends so far that the stultification of
the oppressed affects the oppressors themselves, and they become victims
of the superior power of self-propelled wheels who think they are determining their direction.

Regressive listening is tied to production by the machinery of distribution, and particularly by advertising. Regressive listening appears as
soon as advertising turns into terror, as soon as nothing is left for the
consciousness but to capitulate before the superior power of the advertised
stuff and purchase spiritual peace by making the imposed goods literally
its own thing. In regressive listening, advertising takes on a compulsory
character. For a while, an English brewery used for propaganda purposes
a billboard that bore a deceptive likeness to one of those whitewashed brick
walls which are so numerous in the slums of London and the industrial
cities of the North. Properly placed, the billboard was barely distinguishable from a real wall. On it, chalk-white, was a careful imitation of awkward writing. The words said: "*What we want is Watney's*.*" The brand
of the beer was presented like a political slogan. Not only does this billboard give an insight into the nature of up-to-date propaganda, which sells
its slogans as well as its wares, just as here the wares masquerade as a
slogan; the type of relationship suggested by the billboard, in which masses
make a commodity recommended to them the object of their own action,
is in fact found again as the pattern for the reception of light music. They
need and demand what has been palmed off on them. They overcome the
feeling of impotence that creeps over them in the face of monopolistic
production by identifying themselves with the inescapable product. They
thereby put an end to the strangeness of the musical brands which are at

once distant from them and threateningly near, and in addition, achieve the satisfaction of feeling themselves involved in Mr. Know-Nothing's enterprises, which confront them at every turn. This explains why individual expressions of preference—or, of course, dislike—converge in an area where object and subject alike make such reactions questionable. The fetish character of music produces its own camouflage through the identification of the listener with the fetish. This identification initially gives the hit songs power over their victims. It fulfills itself in the subsequent forgetting and remembering. Just as every advertisement is composed of the inconspicuous familiar and the unfamiliar conspicuous, so the hit song remains salutarily forgotten in the half-dusk of its familiarity, suddenly to become painfully over-clear through recollection, as if in the beam of a spotlight. One can almost equate the moment of this recollection with that in which the title or the words of the initial verse of his hit song confront the victim. Perhaps he identifies himself with this because he identifies it and thereby merges with his possession. This compulsion may well drive him to recall the title of the hit song at times. But the writing under the note, which makes the identification possible, is nothing else but the trademark of the hit song.

Deconcentration is the perceptual activity which prepares the way for the forgetting and sudden recognition of mass music. If the standardized products, hopelessly like one another except for conspicuous bits such as hit lines, do not permit concentrated listening without becoming unbearable to the listeners, the latter are in any case no longer capable of concentrated listening. They cannot stand the strain of concentrated listening and surrender themselves resignedly to what befalls them, with which they can come to terms only if they do not listen to it too closely. Benjamin's reference to the apperception of the cinema in a condition of distraction is just as valid for light music.[11] The usual commercial jazz can only carry out its function because it is not attended to except during conversation and, above all, as an accompaniment to dancing. Again and again one encounters the judgment that it is fine for dancing but dreadful for listening. But if the film as a whole seems to be apprehended in a distracted manner, deconcentrated listening makes the perception of a whole impossible. All that is realized is what the spotlight falls on—striking melodic intervals, unsettling modulations, intentional or unintentional mistakes, or whatever condenses itself into a formula by an especially intimate merging of melody and text. Here, too, listeners and products fit together; they are not even offered the structure which they cannot follow. If atomized listening means progressive decomposition for the higher music, there is nothing more to decompose in the lower music. The forms of hit songs are so strictly standardized, down to the number of measures and the exact duration, that no specific form appears in any particular piece. The emancipation of the parts from their cohesion, and from all moments which extend beyond their immediate present, introduces the diversion of musical interest to the particular sensory pleasure. Typically, the listeners show a preference not merely for particular showpieces for instrumental acrobatics, but for the individual instrumental colors as such. This preference is promoted by the practice of American popular music whereby each variation, or "*chorus**," is played with emphasis on a special instrumental color, with the clarinet, the piano, or the trombone as quasi-soloist. This often goes so far that the listener seems to care more about treatment and "style" than about the otherwise indifferent material, but with the treatment validating itself only in particular enticing effects. Along with the attraction to color as such, there is of course the veneration for the instrument and the drive to imitate and join in the game; possibly also something of the great delight of children in bright colors, which returns under the pressure of contemporary musical experience.

The diversion of interest from the whole, perhaps indeed from the "melody," to the charm of color and to the individual trick, could be optimistically interpreted as a new rupture of the disciplining function. But this interpretation would be erroneous. Once the perceived charms remain unopposed in a rigid format, whoever yields to them will eventually rebel against it. But then they are themselves of the most limited kind. They all center on an impressionistically softened tonality. It cannot be said that interest in the isolated color or the isolated sonority awakens a taste for new colors and new sonorities. Rather, the atomistic listeners are the first to denounce such sonorities as "intellectual" or absolutely dissonant. The charms which they enjoy must be of an approved type. To be sure, dissonances occur in jazz practice, and even techniques of intentional "misplaying" [Falschspielens] have developed. But an appearance of harmlessness accompanies all these customs; every extravagant sonority must be so produced that the listener can recognize it as a substitute for a "normal" one. While he rejoices in the mistreatment the dissonance gives to the consonance whose place it takes, the virtual consonance simultaneously guarantees that one remains within the circle. In tests on the reception of hit songs, people have been found who ask how they should act if a passage simultaneously pleases and displeases them. One may well suspect that they report an experience which also occurs to those who give no account of it. The reactions to isolated charms are ambivalent. A sensory pleasure turns into disgust as soon as it is seen how it only still serves to betray the consumer. The betrayal here consists in always offering the same thing. Even the most insensitive hit song enthusiast cannot always escape the feeling that the child with a sweet tooth comes to know in the candy store. If the charms wear off and turn into their opposite—the short life of most hit songs belongs in the same range of experience—then the cultural ideology which clothes the upper-level musical business finishes things off by causing the lower to be heard with a bad conscience. Nobody believes so completely in prescribed pleasure. But the listening nevertheless remains regressive in assenting to this situation despite all distrust and all ambivalence. As a result of the displacement of feelings into exchange-value, no demands are really advanced in music anymore. Substitutes satisfy their purpose as well, because the demand to which they adjust themselves has itself already been substituted. But ears which are still only able to hear what one demands of them in what is offered, and which register the abstract charm instead of synthesizing the moments of charm, are bad ears. Even in the "isolated" phenomenon, key aspects will escape them; that is, those which transcend its own isolation. There is actually a neurotic mechanism of stupidity in listening, too; the arrogantly ignorant rejection of everything unfamiliar is its sure sign. Regressive listeners behave like children. Again and again and with stubborn malice, they demand the one dish they have once been served.

A sort of musical children's language is prepared for them; it differs from the real thing in that its vocabulary consists exclusively of fragments and distortions of the artistic language of music. In the piano scores of hit songs, there are strange diagrams. They relate to guitar, ukulele and banjo, as well as the accordion—infantile instruments in comparison with the piano—and are intended for players who cannot read the notes. They depict graphically the fingering for the chords of the plucking instruments. The rationally comprehensible notes are replaced by visual directives, to some extent by musical traffic signals. These signs, of course, confine themselves to the three tonic major chords and exclude any meaningful harmonic progression. The regulated musical traffic is worthy of them. It cannot be compared with that in the streets. It swarms with mistakes in phrasing and harmony. There are wrong pitches, incorrect doublings of thirds, fifth and octave progressions, and all sorts of illogical treatments of voices, sometimes in the bass. One would like to blame them on the amateurs with whom most of the hit songs originate, while the real musical work is first done by the arrangers. But just as a publisher does not let a misspelled word go out into the world, so it is inconceivable that, well-advised by their experts, they publish amateur versions without checking them. The mistakes are either consciously produced by the experts or intentionally permitted to stand—for the sake of the listeners. One could attribute to the publishers and experts the wish to ingratiate themselves with the listeners, composing as nonchalantly and informally as a dilettante drums out a hit song after hearing it. Such intrigues would be of the same stripe, even if considered psychologically different, as the incorrect spelling in many advertising slogans. But even if one wanted to exclude their acceptance as too farfetched, the typographical errors could be understood. On the one hand, the infantile hearing demands sensually rich and full sonority, sometimes represented by the abundant thirds, and it is precisely this demand in which the infantile musical language is in most brutal contradiction with the children's song. On the other hand, the infantile hearing always demands the most comfortable and fluent resolutions. The consequences of the "rich" sonority, with correct treatment of voices, would be so far from the standardized harmonic relations that the listener would have to reject them as "unnatural." The mistakes would then be the bold strokes which reconcile the antagonisms of the infantile listener's consciousness. No less characteristic of the regressive musical language is the quotation. Its use ranges from the conscious quotation of folk and children's songs, by way of ambiguous and half accidental allusions, to completely latent similarities and associations. The tendency triumphs in the adaptation of whole pieces from the classical stock or the operatic repertoire. The practice of quotation mirrors the ambivalence of the infantile listener's consciousness. The quotations are at once authoritarian and a parody. It is thus that a child imitates the teacher.

The ambivalence of the retarded listeners has its most extreme expression in the fact that individuals, not yet fully reified, want to extricate themselves from the mechanism of musical reification to which they have been handed over, but that their revolts against fetishism only entangle them more deeply in it. Whenever they attempt to break away from the passive status of compulsory consumers and "activate" themselves, they succumb to pseudoactivity. Types rise up from the mass of the impaired who differentiate themselves by pseudoactivity and nevertheless make the regression more strikingly visible. There are, first, the enthusiasts who write fan letters to radio stations and orchestras and, at well-managed jazz festivals, produce their own enthusiasm as an advertisement for the wares they consume. They call themselves *jitterbugs**, as if they simultaneously wanted to affirm and mock their loss of individuality, their transformation into beetles whirring around in fascination. Their only excuse is that the term *jitterbugs**, like all those in the unreal edifice of films and jazz, is hammered into them by the entrepreneurs to make them think that they are on the inside. Their ecstasy is without content. That it happens, that the music is listened to, this replaces the content itself. The ecstasy takes possession of its object by its own compulsive character. It is stylized like the ecstasies savages go into in beating the war drums. It has convulsive aspects reminiscent of St. Vitus' dance or the reflexes of mutilated animals. Passion itself seems to be produced by defects. But the ecstatic ritual betrays itself as pseudoactivity by the moment of mimicry. People do not dance or listen "from sensuality" and sensuality is certainly not satisfied by listening, but the gestures of the sensual are imitated. An analogue is the representation of particular emotions in the film, where there are physiognomic patterns for anxiety, longing, the erotic look; along with *keep smiling**; for the atomistic expressivo of debased music. The imitative assimilation to commodity models is intertwined with folkloristic customs of imitation. In jazz, the relation of such mimicry to the imitating individual himself is quite loose. Its medium is caricature. Dance and music copy stages of sexual excitement only to make fun of them. It is as if desire's surrogate itself simultaneously turned against it; the "realistic" behavior of the oppressed triumphs over his dream of happiness while being itself incorporated into the latter. And as if to confirm the superficiality and treachery of every form of ecstasy, the feet are unable to fulfill what the ear pretends. The same *jitterbugs** who behave as if they were electrified by syncopation dance almost exclusively [to] the good rhythmic parts. The weak flesh punishes the lies of the willing spirit; the gestural ecstasy of the infantile listener misfires in the face of the ecstatic gesture. The opposite type appears to be the eager person who leaves the factory and "occupies" himself with music in the quiet of his bedroom. He is shy and inhibited, perhaps has no luck with girls, and wants in any case to preserve his own special sphere. He seeks this as a radio ham *[Bastler]*. At twenty, he is still at the stage of a boy scout working on complicated knots just to please his parents. This type is held in high esteem in radio matters. He patiently builds sets whose most important parts he must buy readymade, and scans the air for shortwave secrets, though there are none. As a reader of Indian stories and travel books, he once discovered unknown lands and cleared his path through the forest primeval. As radio ham he becomes the discoverer of just those industrial products which are interested in being discovered by him. He brings nothing home which would not be delivered to his house. The adventurers of pseudoactivity have already organized themselves on a large scale; the radio amateurs have printed verification cards sent them by the shortwave stations they have discovered, and hold contests in which the winner is the one who can produce the most such cards. All this is carefully fostered from above. Of all fetishistic listeners, the radio ham is perhaps the most complete. It is irrelevant to him what he hears or even how he hears; he is only interested in the fact that he hears and succeeds in inserting himself, with his private equipment, into the public mechanism, without exerting even the slightest influence on it. With the same attitude, countless radio listeners play with the feedback or the sound dial without themselves becoming hams. Others are more expert, or at least more aggressive. These smart chaps can be found everywhere and are able to do everything themselves: the advanced student who in every gathering is ready to play jazz with machinelike precision for dancing and entertainment; the gas station attendant who hums his syncopation ingenuously while filling up the tank; the listening expert who can identify every band and immerses himself in the history of jazz as if it were Holy Writ. He is nearest to the sportsman: if not to the football player himself, then to the swaggering fellow who dominates the stands. He shines by a capacity for rough improvisations, even if he must practice the piano for hours in secret in order to bring the refractory rhythms together. He pictures himself as the individualist who whistles at the world. But what he whistles is its melody, and his tricks are less inventions of the moment than stored-up experiences from acquaintance with sought-after technical things. His improvisations are always gestures of nimble subordination to what the instrument demands of him. The chauffeur is the model for the listening type of the clever fellow. His agreement with everything dominant goes so far that he no longer produces any resistance, but of his own accord always does what is asked of him for the sake of the responsible functionary. He lies to himself about the completeness of his subordination to the rule of the reified mechanism. Thus, the sovereign routine of the jazz amateur is nothing but the passive capacity for adaptation to models from which to avoid straying. He is the real jazz subject: his improvisations come from the pattern, and he navigates the pattern, cigarette in mouth, as nonchalantly as if he had invented it himself.

Regressive listeners have key points in common with the man who must kill time because he has nothing else on which to vent his aggression, and with the casual laborer. To make oneself a jazz expert or hang over the radio all day, one must have much free time and little freedom. The dexterity which comes to terms with the syncopation as well as with the basic rhythm is that of the auto mechanic who can also repair the loudspeaker and the electric light. The new listeners resemble the mechanics who are simultaneously specialized and capable of applying their special skills to unexpected places outside their skilled trades. But this despecialization only seems to help them out of the system. The more easily they meet the demands of the day, the more rigidly they are subordinated to that system. The research finding that among radio listeners the friends of light music reveal themselves to be depoliticized is not accidental. The possibility of individual shelter and of a security which is, as always, questionable, obstructs the view of a change in the situation in which one seeks shelter. Superficial experience contradicts this. The "younger generation"—the concept itself is merely an ideological catch-all—seems to be in conflict with its elders and their plush culture precisely through the new way of listening. In America, it is just the so-called liberals and progressives whom one finds among the advocates of light popular music, most of whom want to classify their activity as democratic. But if regressive hearing is progressive as opposed to the "individualistic" sort, it is only in the dialectical sense that it is better fitted to the advancing brutality than the latter. All possible mold has been rubbed off the baseness, and it is legitimate to criticize the aesthetic residue of an individuality that was long since wrested from individuals. But this criticism comes with little force from the sphere of popular music, since it is just this sphere that mummifies the vulgarized and decaying remnants of romantic individualism. Its innovations are inseparably coupled with these remnants.

Masochism in hearing is not only defined by self-surrender and pseudo-pleasure through identification with power. Underlying it is the knowledge that the security of shelter under the ruling conditions is a provisional one, that it is only a respite, and that eventually everything must collapse. Even in self-surrender one is not good in his own eyes; in his enjoyment one feels that he is simultaneously betraying the possible and being betrayed by the existent. Regressive listening is always ready to degenerate into rage. If one knows that he is basically marking time, the rage is directed primarily against everything which could disavow the modernity of being with-it and *up-to-date** and reveal how little has in fact changed. From photographs and movies, one knows the effect produced by the modern grown old, an effect originally used by the surrealists to shock and subsequently degraded to the cheap amusement of those whose fetishism fastens on the abstract present. For the regressive listener, this effect is fantastically foreshortened. They would like to ridicule and destroy what yesterday they were intoxicated with, as if in retrospect to revenge themselves for the fact that the ecstasy was not actually such. This effect has been given a name of its own and repeatedly been propagated in press and radio. But we should not think of the rhythmically simpler, light music of the pre-jazz era and its relics as *corny**; rather, the term applies to all those syncopated pieces which do not conform to the approved rhythmic formula of the present moment. A jazz expert can shake with laughter when he hears a piece which in good rhythm follows a sixteenth note with a dotted eighth, although this rhythm is more aggressive and in no way more provincial in character than the syncopated connection and renunciation of all counter-stress practiced later. The regressive listeners are in fact destructive. The old-timer's insult has its ironic justification; ironic, because the destructive tendencies of the regressive listeners are in truth directed against the same thing that the old-fashioned hate, against disobedience as such, unless it comes under the tolerated spontaneity of collective excesses. The seeming opposition of the generations is nowhere more transparent than in rage. The bigots who complain to the radio stations in pathetic-sadistic letters of the jazzing up of holy things and the youth who delight in such exhibitions are of one mind. It requires only the proper situation to bring them together in a united front.

This furnishes a criticism of the "new possibilities" in regressive listening. One might be tempted to rescue it if it were something in which the "auratic" characteristics of the work of art, its illusory elements, gave way to the playful ones. However it may be with films, today's mass music shows little of such progress in disenchantment. Nothing survives in it more steadfastly than the illusion, nothing is more illusory than its reality. The infantile play has scarcely more than the name in common with the productivity of children. Otherwise, bourgeois sport would not want to differentiate itself so strictly from play. Its bestial seriousness consists in the fact that instead of remaining faithful to the dream of freedom by getting away from purposiveness, the treatment of play as a duty puts it among useful purposes and thereby wipes out the trace of freedom in it. This is particularly valid for contemporary mass music. It is only play as a repetition of prescribed models, and the playful release from responsibility which is thereby achieved does not reduce at all the time devoted to duty except by transferring the responsibility to the models, the following of which one makes into a duty for himself. In this lies the inherent pretense of the dominant music sport. It is illusory to promote the technical-rational moments of contemporary mass music—or the special capacities of the regressive listeners which may correspond to these moments—at the expense of a decayed magic, which nevertheless prescribes the rules for the bare functioning itself. It would also be illusory because the technical innovations of mass music really don't exist. This goes without saying for harmonic and melodic construction. The real coloristic accomplishment of modern dance music, the approach of the different colors to one another to the extent that one instrument replaces another without a break or one instrument can disguise itself as another, is as familiar to Wagnerian and post-Wagnerian orchestral technique as the mute effects of the brasses. Even in the techniques of syncopation, there is nothing that was not present in rudimentary form in Brahms and outdone by Schoenberg and Stravinsky. The practice of contemporary popular music has not so much developed these techniques as conformistically dulled them. The listeners who expertly view these techniques with astonishment are in no way technically educated thereby, but react with resistance and rejection as soon as the techniques are introduced to them in those contexts in which they have their meaning. Whether a technique can be considered progressive and *"rational*"* depends on this meaning and on its place in the whole of society as well as in the organization of the particular work. Technical development as such can serve crude reaction as soon as it has established itself as a fetish and by its perfection represents the neglected social tasks as already accomplished. This is why all attempts to reform mass music and regressive listening on the basis of what exists are frustrated. Consumable art music must pay by the sacrifice of its consistency. Its faults are not "artistic"; every incorrectly composed or outmoded chord bespeaks the backwardness of those to whose demand accommodation is made. But technically consistent, harmonious mass music purified of all the elements of bad pretense would turn into art music and at once lose its mass basis. All attempts at reconciliation, whether by market-oriented artists or collectively oriented art educators, are fruitless. They have accomplished nothing more than handicrafts or the sort of products with which directions for use or a social text must be given, so that one may be properly informed about their deeper background.

The positive aspect for which the new mass music and regressive listening are praised—vitality and technical progress, collective breadth and relation to an undefined practice, into whose concepts there has entered the supplicant self-denunciation of the intellectuals, who can thereby finally end their social alienation from the masses in order to coordinate themselves politically with contemporary mass consciousness—this positive is negative, the irruption into music of a catastrophic phase of society. The positive lies locked up solely in its negativity. Fetishized mass music threatens the fetishized cultural goods. The tension between the two spheres of music has so grown that it becomes difficult for the official sphere to hold its ground. However little it has to do with the technical *standards** of mass music, if one compares the special knowledge of a jazz expert with that of a Toscanini worshipper the former is far ahead of the latter. But regressive listening represents a growing and merciless enemy not only to museum cultural goods but to the age-old sacral function of music as the locus for the taming of impulses. Not without penalty, and therefore not without restraint, are the debased products of musical culture surrendered to disrespectful play and sadistic humor.

In the face of regressive listening, music as a whole begins to take on a comic aspect. One need only listen to the uninhibited sonority of a choral rehearsal from outside. This experience was caught with great force in a film by the Marx Brothers, who demolish an opera set as if to clothe in allegory the insight of the philosophy of history on the decay of the operatic form, or in a most estimable piece of refined entertainment, break up a grand piano in order to take possession of its strings in their frame as the true harp of the future, on which to play a prelude.[12] Music has become comic in the present phase primarily because something so completely useless is carried on with all the visible signs of the strain of serious work. By being alien to solid people, music reveals their alienation from one another, and the consciousness of alienation vents itself in laughter. In music—or similarly in lyric poetry—the society which judged them comic becomes comic. But involved in this laughter is the decay of the sacral spirit of reconciliation. All music today can very easily sound as *Parsifal* did to Nietzsche's ear. It recalls incomprehensible rites and surviving masks from an earlier time, and is provocative nonsense.[13] The radio, which both wears out music and overexposes it, makes a major contribution to this. Perhaps a better hour may at some time strike even for the clever fellows: one in which they may demand, instead of prepared material ready to be switched on, the improvisatory displacement of things, as the sort of radical beginning that can only thrive under the protection of the unshaken real world. Even discipline can take over the expression of free solidarity if freedom becomes its content. As little as regressive listening is a symptom of progress in consciousness of freedom, it could suddenly turn around if art, in unity with the society, should ever leave the road of the always-identical.

Not popular music but artistic music has furnished a model for this possibility. It is not for nothing that Mahler is the scandal of all bourgeois musical aesthetics. They call him uncreative because he suspends their concept of creation itself. Everything with which he occupies himself is already there. He accepts it in its state of *deprivation**; his themes are expropriated ones. Nevertheless, nothing sounds as it was wont to; all things are diverted as if by a magnet. What is worn out yields pliantly to the improvising hand; the used parts win a second life as variants. Just as the chauffeur's knowledge of his old secondhand car can enable him to drive it punctually and unrecognized to its intended destination, so can the expression of an exhausted melody, straining under the pressure of E-flat clarinets[14] and oboes in the upper register, arrive at places which the approved musical language could never safely reach. Such music really crystallizes the whole, into which it has incorporated the vulgarized fragments, into something new, yet it takes its material from regressive listening. Indeed, one can almost think that in Mahler's music this experience was seismographically recorded forty years before it permeated society. But if Mahler stood athwart the concept of musical progress, neither can the new and radical music whose most advanced practitioners give allegiance to him in a seemingly paradoxical way any longer be subsumed exclusively under the concept of progress. It proposes to consciously resist the phenomenon of regressive listening. The terror which Schoenberg and Webern spread, today as in the past, comes not from their incomprehensibility but from the fact that they are all too correctly understood. Their music gives form to that anxiety, that terror, that insight into the catastrophic situation which others merely evade by regressing. They are called individualists, and yet their work is nothing but a single dialogue with the powers which destroy individuality—powers whose "formless shadows" fall colossally on their music. In music, too, collective powers are liquidating an individuality past saving, but against them only individuals are capable of consciously representing the aims of collectivity.

(1938; GS, vol. 14, pp. 14–50)
Translation modified by Richard Leppert

NOTES BY RICHARD LEPPERT

1. Aldous Huxley (1894–1963) often commented on modern amusements along these lines. Thus in his essay "Work and Leisure," in *Along the Road: Notes and Essays of a Tourist* (New York: George H. Doran, 1925), p. 246: "The fact is that, brought up as they are at present, the majority of human beings can hardly fail to devote their leisure to occupations which, if not positively vicious, are at least stupid, futile and, what is worse, secretly realized to be futile"; and "The Problem of Leisure," in *Aldous Huxley's Hearst Essays*, ed. James Sexton (New York: Garland, 1994), pp. 101–02, first published in August 1932: "People who are constantly 'doing things' are constantly buying material objects, transportation and admissions to places of 'amusement.' . . . Taken out of the hands of private profit makers and run on scientific lines, the amusement industry could probably

be made to yield considerably higher returns in pleasure and distraction than it does today. . . . The trouble with the present system is that it treats man as though he were made for economics" (p. 102).

2. See Plato, *The Republic of Plato*, trans. A. D. Lindsay (New York: E. P. Dutton, 1957), Book III, pp. 99–102 (st. 398–99) for the full discussion of the Greek modes and their affects, from which Adorno draws.

3. The musical contest between Apollo and Marsyas pits a stringed instrument against a wind. The story allegorically associates Apollo's lyre with civilization: measured, rationalized, etc., and Marsyas's panpipes as its uninhibited Dionysian opposite—taken together, the sonoric enactment of the division of mind and body. Apollo wins by resorting to tricks and, finally, by lavishing flattery on the Muses who judge the contest; Apollo thereafter ties Marsyas to a pine tree and flays him alive.

4. "Music, Maestro, Please!" (1938), music by Allie Wrubel, text by Herb Magidson.

5. Walter Donaldson (1893–1947), popular-song composer, arranger, and lyricist; his songs include "My Mammy," "My Buddy," "Carolina in the Morning," "My Blue Heaven," and "Yes, Sir, That's My Baby."

6. Adorno's citation is from Karl Marx, *Das Kapital. Kritik der politischen Ökonomie*, 2nd ed. (Berlin, 1932), vol. 1, p. 77, from the famous opening chapter, "The Commodity." Cf. the slightly different translation of this passage in Karl Marx, *Capital: A Critique of Political Economy*, trans. Ben Fowkes (London: Penguin, 1976), vol. 1, pp. 164–65.

7. The *Stephanie Gavotte*, popular into the early twentieth century, was written by Alphons Czibulka (1842–1894), a Hungarian bandmaster and composer. The *Catalogue of Printed Music in the British Library to 1980* (London: K. G. Saur, 1983), vol. 15, pp. 91–92, lists numerous different arrangements of the piece, including for band, orchestra, two- and four-hand piano, and vocal versions with words added. The earliest version in the BL catalogue dates from 1876; most appeared in the 1880s; the latest is from 1934. I'm grateful to Otto Kolleritsch for identifying this (obscure-for-Americans) piece for me.

8. Schubert's several vocal serenades have been subjected to a great variety of instrumental arrangement, including harp, mandolin, Hawaiian guitar, and cornet. Given Adorno's reference to a girls' school, the saccharine arrangement of *Ständchen* he may have had in mind could be of D. 920 (1827) for contralto solo, female chorus, and piano on a text by Franz Grillparzer. (There is also a version for male voices.) Adorno's reference to its "aufgeplusterten Klang" would in that case refer to an arrangement that augments the composition with strings, or, more likely, replaces the vocal parts with a string orchestra—*Lieder ohne Worte*, so to speak. Larry Kramer suggested to me that another likely candidate is the once all-too-popular *Ständchen* setting in the *Schwanengesang* cycle, D. 957 (1828), which, as he aptly put it, "if arranged for strings and piano, would surely be enough to set Adorno's teeth on edge" (private communication).

9. Concerning Steuermann, see p. 159 n. 3.

10. The only reference I've located to a children's song titled "Püppchen" dates from 1929, text by Alfred Schönfeld, music by Jean Gilbert. Adorno, writing just prior to the start of World War II, refers to the tune as prewar, thus indicating a date prior to 1914.

11. Walter Benjamin, "The Work of Art in the Age of Mechanical Reproduction," in *Illuminations*, ed. Hannah Arendt, trans. Harry Zohn (New York: Schocken, 1969), especially pp. 222–23, 234–41. See also my commentary, pp. 240–50, above.

12. *A Night at the Opera* (1935); see p. 159 n. 2.

13. Nietzsche's reaction to *Parsifal* permeates *The Case of Wagner* (1888). The following are typical of Nietzsche's acerbic wit directed at the work of his one-time friend: (1) he refers to the character Parsifal "as a candidate for a theological degree, with secondary school education (the latter being indispensable for *pure foolishness*)" (section 9, p. 176); and (2) "Open your ears: everything that ever grew on the soil of *impoverished* life, all of the counterfeiting of transcendence and beyond, has found its most sublime advocate in Wagner's art . . . by means of a persuasion of sensuousness which in turn makes the spirit weary and worn-out. Music as Circe. His last work is in this respect his greatest masterpiece. In the art of seduction, *Parsifal* will always retain its rank—as *the stroke of genius* in seduction. . . . Never was there a greater master in dim, hieratic aromas" (first postscript, pp. 183–84). All citations are from Friedrich Nietzsche, *The Case of Wagner*, in *The Birth of Tragedy and The Case of Wagner*, trans. Walter Kaufmann (New York: Vintage, 1967).

14. Seven of Mahler's symphonies are scored to include the E-flat clarinet, nos. 1–3, 6–9, but Adorno seems likely to have had in mind the last movement of the Seventh Symphony (rev. ed.), at mm. 476 ff.

Little Heresy

Musical understanding, musical cultivation with a human dignity that means more than mere information content, is tantamount to the ability to perceive musical contexts, ideally developed and articulated music, as a meaningful whole. This is what is meant by the concept of structural listening, whose demands, critical of everything that is mired in the momentary, of bad naïveté, are emphatically and acutely with us nowadays. Atomistic listening, which loses itself weakly, passively, in the charm of the moment, the pleasant single sound, the easily graspable and recollectable memory, is pre-artistic. Because such listening lacks the subjective capacity for synthesis, it also fails in the encounter with the objective synthesis that every more highly organized music carries out. Atomistic behavior, which is still always the most widespread, and certainly the one on which so-called light music speculates and which it cultivates, merges with the naturalistic pleasures of the sense of taste, the de-artification[1] of art from which the latter, over the course of centuries, struggled free with considerable effort and always pending reversal. Since music, after all, lacks concepts, the person who listens atomistically is not capable of perceiving it sensually as something intellectual and spiritual [Geistiges]. This is how dilettantes behave, when, amid great movements of complex architecture, they pick out melodies that they think are beautiful, or that really are beautiful, for example secondary themes in Schubert, and, instead of following and further developing them, call, in an infantile manner, for their stultifying repetition. In this they are like the Austrian aesthetic philosopher who confessed that he had the "March of the Toreadors" from *Carmen* played for him all evening, over and over, without ever hearing enough of it. This is already the form of response appropriate for hit songs, regardless of whether the people who enjoy this genre and seek out the pearls that they think suit them may, in their own eyes, appear especially musical for this reason. The history of the music of the nineteenth century did them a favor in this regard. In late romanticism and the folkloristic schools, attention was increasingly focused on the solo melody *[Einzel-melodie]*, which, originally, and even as late as Schubert, had been subjectively lyrical. This melody made itself independent, as a brand name, to the detriment of the objective, constructive context of the musical whole. A music history that would not be satisfied with distinguishing between high and low music, but would see through the low as a function of the high, would have to trace the path that leads from the most drastic formulations of Tchaikovsky, such as the secondary theme of *Romeo and Juliet*, to the harmonically spiced favorite melodies from Rachmaninoff's piano concertos, to Gershwin, and from there on down into the bad infinity of entertainment. Musical cultivation must work against all this, in view of its overwhelming quantitative weight. I myself have been attempting to do so long enough, and probably even coined the concept of atomistic listening.

But musical insight, and experience, if it doesn't want to become idiotic out of conceit at its own level, must not stop at this. For in highly organized music, to which this kind of insight applies—and indeed applies all the more, the more highly organized the music is—the whole is in the process of becoming, not abstractly preconceived, not a pattern into which the parts merely need to be inserted. On the contrary, the musical whole is essentially a whole composed of parts that follow each other for a reason, and only to this extent is it a whole. This necessity is imposed by the limits of the possible in music comprehension, which does not become conscious of the whole, as something that extends in time, other than in its successive parts. The whole is articulated by relations that extend forward and backward, by anticipation and recollection, contrast and proximity. Unarticulated, not divided into parts, it would dissolve into mere identity with itself. To comprehend music adequately, it is necessary to hear the phenomena that appear here and now in relation to what has gone before and, in anticipation, to what will come after. In the process, the moment of pure present time, the here and now, always retains a certain immediacy, without which the relation to the whole, to that which is mediated, would no more be produced than vice versa.

Music education, in order to be able to withstand the entertainment music that is hammered into people by the culture industry and loudly acclaimed by docile *teenagers**, has been forced to place a one-sided emphasis on the hearing of the whole, at the cost of its articulation in details.

The anti-romantic tendencies in the development of serious music tended in the same direction. In the meantime, however, the situation has shifted, under pressure from the neo-classical and historicist ideal of sewing-machine objectivity. The attention paid to the whole has become one-sided and threatens to make the individual aspects, without which, after all, no musical whole has vitality, atrophy. The interpretations of the so-called youth music movement could be considered, from this perspective, as repressive measures in the service of the whole and in opposition to the details. They regard the latter, not entirely wrongly, as equivalent to the subject's interest in music, and fail to recognize that no musical objectivity at all can be established without passing through the subject. The whole, seen without reference to partial aspects and articulated relations, is not a whole; is abstract, schematic, and static. This kind of reactive perception, which is not receptive to spontaneous musical impulses, but instead immediately disciplines them, corresponds to a supply of undifferentiated, schematic music from the seventeenth and eighteenth centuries, which is not improved by the declaration, made with historically informed mien, that the category of individual style is not appropriate to it. For many years, the reactionary culture ideology of the youth movement has taken traits like this as its point of departure. Today, when this ideology has become transparent and is decaying, a steady eye for the musical particular, as a complement to structural listening and as its concretion, seems urgently *à propos*.

This turn is demanded by the truth content of the historical movement that music has experienced since the era of figured bass. It can be seen, in inevitably rough terms, as the dialectic between the musically universal and the musically particular; as the by no means conscious effort of the objective spirit to master the divergence between form and specific musical content, as this divergence largely coincides with that between society and the individual; to reconcile them. Without forcing the interpretation too far, the detail can be understood as the representative of the individual, and the whole as that of the universal, namely that which has received social approbation—no matter how much, at the height of Viennese classicism, and before that in Bach, the forms themselves might have seemed to be brought forth from within the free subject. It took a very long time until the subject reached the point where it was also present at the constitution and construction of the whole, in the Hegelian sense.[2] Not until the modern era did the ideal of a music begin to emerge in which the two extremes would be fused together. It is, meanwhile, questionable whether this ideal really is one; whether, in complete integration, both elements would not be destroyed without, as people think, being sublated *(aufge-hoben)* at a higher level. In contemporary music there is no lack of forms, or programs—and in many instances the forms have become their own program—in which the individual impulse no longer has a place in the dictatorially imposed structure, while the latter is merely something that has been set, and that lacks any objectivity of musical language that would extend beyond the individual work, as the language of tonal forms once did. Probably, integration, the longed-for reconciliation of the universal and the particular in aesthetic form, is impossible as long as the reality outside art remains unreconciled. Works of art, to the extent that they rise above society, are immediately overtaken by reality's urgent need. As long as reconciliation is only reconciliation in the image, it continues to have something feeble and beside-the-point about it. Accordingly, in great works of art, the tension would not only have to be resolved [ausgleichen] in the works themselves, as even Schoenberg thought, but would also have to be sustained throughout their course. This, however, says no less than that, precisely in the legitimate forms, the whole and the parts cannot be so fully merged into each other as an aesthetic ideal that is by no means limited to classicism demands. The right way to hear music includes a spontaneous awareness of the non-identity of the whole and the parts as well as of the synthesis that unites the two. Even in Beethoven, the resolution [Ausgleich] of this tension, which no one succeeded in achieving as well as he, because no one created a more powerful tension, took some doing. Only because in his work the parts are already patterned after the whole, are pre-formed by it, does identity, resolution, occur. The price for this is paid, on the one hand, by the decorative pathos with which the identity fortifies itself, and, on the other hand, by the carefully thought-out insubstantiality of the individual musical inventions, which drives the individual detail, from its inception, to outstrip itself, so that it can be transformed into something, and anticipates the whole into which the individual part is transformed and by which it is destroyed. The medium that made this undertaking possible was tonality, the universality whose typically intended ends, in Beethoven, are already the equivalent of the particular, the themes. With the irreversible downfall of tonality, this possibility is a thing of the past; it is also, since its principle has become transparent, no longer to be desired.

If the true musical whole does not impose a blind dominance of so-called form, but is rather result and process in one—very closely related, by the way, to the metaphysical conceptions of great philosophy—then it makes sense that the way to understand the whole would have to lead up from the individual part, as well as down from the whole. Musical experience is all the more impelled to take this route since there are no longer any overarching forms to which the ear could entrust itself blindly. The means to such experience is exact imagination *(exakte Phantasie)*. It opens up the richness of the individual detail, over which it lingers, instead of hastening past it to the whole, with the anxious impatience that is drummed into good musicians and that sours so much interpretation nowadays. But because the two do not merge fully into each other, the individual detail also acquires its own rights, which go beyond the whole. It acquires inner substance to the extent that music itself, in its idea, is more than culture, order, [or] synthesis. Much musical detail—and by no means, as historicism would have it, only since romanticism—retains a color that does not disappear into the whole. Sometimes one is inclined to look for the best things there. Details with this kind of dignity are like seals that attest to the authenticity of a text; one could compare them to names.[3] How greatly music is indebted to them can be seen where they are lacking, for example in the stream of music emanating from Max Reger, a kind of genius who, gliding along in unending chromaticism, virtually has no patience for details and who, with them, loses what is indelible, unrepeatable.[4]

Walter Benjamin's *One-Way Street* contains the following aphorism: "Citations in my work are like highwaymen along the road, who jump out, armed, and divest the loiterer of his conviction."[5] Musical quotations also possess something of this polemical force; which may be why Alban Berg once conceived a music journal that would have quoted parts of musical compositions the way Karl Kraus, punishingly, treated the press in the *Fackel*.[6] But the equivalent of the punishing power of quoted musical stupidity is the shining power of the quoted musical name.[7] The light of the beauty of the details, once perceived, destroys the appearance in which cultivation drapes music, and which is only too much at home with music's dubious aspect—as if it were already the joyful whole that humanity, up to now, denies itself. The image of the latter is more readily captured by the single, scattered measure than by the triumphal whole.[8]

(1965; GS, vol. 17, pp. 297–302)
Translated by Susan H. Gillespie

NOTES BY RICHARD LEPPERT

1. *Entkunstung*, a neologism. Adorno clearly intended the word to stand out in its oddity and artificiality. [translator's note]

2. Hegel maintained that neither the whole nor the universal were theologically or ontologically pre-given. Rather, he argued that the whole is the end result of the cultural activities of both individuals and a collective.

3. That is, the names of the text, or even names in general. Details are defining moments in a work; they have a life of their own as particulars; at the same time they constitute a central component of the larger whole, but into which they do not simply disappear. Adorno addressed musical details in his essay "Schöne Stellen" [Beautiful Passages].

4. The German composer Max Reger (1873–1916), whose brief career lasted only a quarter-century, produced a very large number of works for a contemporary composer—there are 147 opus numbers—hence Adorno's reference to the "stream of music emanating" from him. There are ample traces in Reger's music of the German-Austrian canon from Beethoven to Brahms and Wagner, with a sense of counterpoint that marks his admiration for Bach. Wagnerian chromaticism had a notable impact on Reger, to which Adorno obliquely alludes—it is chromaticism which stands out in Reger above all else, as it were, a single "detail" that encompasses entire compositions.

5. Walter Benjamin, *One-Way Street and Other Writings*, trans. Edmund Jepthcott and Kingsley Shorter (London: NLB, 1979), p. 95, translated as, "Quotations in my work are like wayside robbers who leap out armed and relieve the stroller of his conviction."

6. *Die Fackel* [The Torch] was a satirical journal founded by Kraus in 1899; from 1911 until his death in 1936, Kraus single-handedly edited and authored the journal—933 numbered issues in all. His unremitting and often scathing critique was directed squarely at Austrian society and its institutions, notably the popular press. Thus: "Why didn't Eternity have this deformed age aborted? Its birthmark is the stamp of a newspaper, its meconium is printer's ink, and in its veins flow ink"; "Newspapers have roughly the same relationship to life as fortune tellers to metaphysics"; and "The making of a journalist: no ideas and the ability to express them." Kraus's motto was "Was wir umbringen" [What we shall do in]. These and many other aphorisms appear in the collection *Half-Truths and One-and-a-Half Truths: Karl Kraus, Selected Aphorisms*, ed. and trans. Harry Zohn (New York: Carcanet, 1986), pp. 71–73. Concerning Kraus, see also p. 494 n. 12.

As Adorno relates in his "Reminiscence" of the composer, AB, p. 27, Berg "liked to send Kraus splendid atrocities, occasionally 'expanded and elaborated,' from music journalism; no doubt more than one such quotation found its way into the *Fackel*." Something of the sort of journal that Berg had in mind came to be in *23: Eine Wiener Musikzeitschrift*, edited by Berg's student Willi Reich from 1932 to 1937, who later produced critical biographies of both Berg and Schoenberg. *23*, which Adorno suggests was "probably Berg's idea" (p. 28), was published in Vienna; it championed new music, just as it relentlessly critiqued the musical old guard—and National Socialism—more or less in the same spirit as *Die Fackel*. (No surprise, the journal was banned following the Anschluss.) Adorno himself published a few essays in *23*, including "The Form of the Phonograph Record," included in this volume.

On Berg's friendship with Kraus, whom he held in considerable awe, see Andrew Barker, "Battles of the Mind: Berg and the Cultural Politics of 'Vienna 1900,'" in *The Cambridge Companion to Berg*, ed. Anthony Pople (Cambridge: Cambridge University Press, 1997), pp. 24–37; and Susanne Rode, *Alban Berg und Karl Kraus: Zur geistigen Biographie des Komponisten der "Lulu"* (Frankfurt am Main: Peter Lang, 1988). Rode, pp. 182–83, provides additional information about Berg's role in the formation of *23*. (Officially, the journal's name was derived from a section in the Austrian press law that authorizes the demand for the correction of erroneous statements that appear in print; but secretly, according to Willi Reich, the name "originated from Berg's 'fateful number' 23." See Willi Reich, *The Life and Work of Alban Berg*, trans. Cornelius Cardew (New York: Da Capo, 1982), pp. 81–82.

7. Adorno is borrowing from the essay by Walter Benjamin, "Karl Kraus," in *Reflections: Essays, Aphorisms, Autobiographical Writings*, ed. Peter Demetz, trans. Edmund Jepthcott (New York: Schocken, 1978), p. 268: "To quote a word is to call it by its name," regarding which see the following note.

8. Adorno dialectically returns to the question of the name as a kind of cultural capital attached both to a composer ("Beethoven," say) or a particular composition (Fifth Symphony); his concern is that when the work is obscured behind its name, we no longer hear the music except as an experience of its fame. Details can work to undercut this phenomenon, cause us to listen anew, as it were—even though details, separated from the whole, obviously run the risk of preserving the particular at the expense of the unified whole—thus the discussion of atomistic listening with which the essay opens. The ultimate point is, of course, that structural listening (the whole) and attention to the musical detail (the part as part of the whole) complement genuine musical understanding. Adorno borrows an insight from Benjamin's essay on Kraus, p. 269 (see previous note), regarding the power of the quotation (for Adorno, the musical detail): "In the quotation that both saves and chastises, language proves the matrix of justice. It summons the word by its name, wrenches it destructively from its context, but precisely thereby calls it back to its origin. It appears, now with rhyme and reason, sonorously, congruously in the structure of a new text."

Adorno's use of the terms *name* and *naming* has varying levels of complexity. Thus in the instance of a proper name, as a special linguistic category, object and word are quasi-identical. (A thing or a person can have only one proper name, which refers uniquely to that thing or person.) In this sense, names have a unique ontological status. Compare p. 114, above: "[Music's] idea is the form of the name of God"; p. 116: "Music refracts its scattered intentions away from their own power and brings them together into the configuration of the name"; and p. 140: "Music tends toward pure naming, the absolute unity of object and sign"; and "But the name appears in music only as pure sound, divorced from its bearer, and hence the opposite of every act of meaning, every intention toward meaning. But music does not know the name—the absolute as sound—immediately, but, if one may express it this way, attempts its conjuring construction through a whole, a process." Accordingly, when names, or details, or phrases are *quoted* (and perhaps when details are simply patched together or cranked out thoughtlessly) they are robbed of this particular kind of identity with the object, of this special status or transparency. They become ironic and, as in the Benjamin quotation, incapable of convincing.

Adorno may be saying that *some* (but not all) musical details have the status of names in an elevated sense. Thus, in the final sentences of this essay, the "shining power of the quoted musical name," likely corresponds to the "light of the beauty of the details." This suggests that compelling musical details—those with the kind of dignity referred to above—don't lose their special status, but resist being drawn into "the appearance in which cultivation drapes music." Hence they do more to salvage the truth-character of music than whole pieces that have been ingested by the Culture Industry, "triumphal wholes." My thanks to Susan H. Gillespie for her assistance with this issue.

3

MUSIC AND MASS CULTURE

Commentary

Richard Leppert

Art is the semblance of what is beyond death's reach.

Adorno, *Aesthetic Theory*

In March 1945 Adorno delivered a paper at a lecture series organized at Columbia University by the Sociology Department on the topic "The Aftermath of National Socialism: Cultural Aspects of the Collapse of National Socialism." The paper's title was "WHAT NATIONAL SOCIALISM HAS DONE TO THE ARTS" (pp. 373–90).[1] The tone is polemical, and the substance was not likely expected. On the eve of Allied victory in Europe Adorno is not celebrating before his American audience; he is warning. Adorno's fear is fascism's survival, music serving as his point of analysis. Dwelling neither on the ruins of Europe following Total War, nor on its uncountable victims, though acknowledging both, he addresses a future built on an implicitly American model of what he regards as manipulative consumerism, of domination by other means. His stated theme is the implications for America caused by what he names "the spirit of Fascism," which—as in *Dialectic of Enlightenment*—he locates in a history preceding the Third Reich, arching back to the nineteenth century and Richard Wagner and his later reception by the Nazi hierarchy, reprising themes from *In Search of Wagner*, parts of which by then were in print. Adorno is direct: Wagner's "music itself speaks the language of Fascism, quite apart from plots and bombastic words" (p. 375). But no sooner does he sum-

---

1. In this same series, papers were also delivered by Horkheimer, Pollock, and Lowenthal. See Rolf Wiggershaus, *The Frankfurt School: Its History, Theories, and Political Significance*, trans. Michael Robertson (Cambridge: MIT Press, 1995), pp. 384–85. Adorno's paper exists in two versions. The longer of the two is reprinted here. The second version, "The Musical Climate for Fascism in Germany," roughly two-thirds the length of the first, is reprinted in the GS, vol. 20.2, pp. 430–40. Much of the second version is identical to the first, but material is sometimes substantially rearranged, and new material is also incorporated.

marize his position on Wagner than he backs off from it, acknowledging that Wagner, long before Hitler, had ceased to be a significant force in German culture; he points to his own students in Frankfurt—mostly musicologists—who in 1932–33 were incapable of replicating the Siegfried motif ("the most famous of all Wagnerian *leitmotifs*"). The real point is to decry the gradual dumbing down of culture in modernity even among groups of the social elite. It's the symptom that concerns him, "the neutralization of culture in general and of the arts in particular" (p. 377), by their transformation into consumer goods.[2] He indicts the reduction of art to entertainment and amusement as a dehumanization of the subject, in betrayal of the Enlightenment ideals that determine so much of his thought. As in his radio essays, he turns to the impact of this process on children, who provide a powerful rhetorical example of innocence betrayed, and the commonplace symbol of the future on whose ultimate behalf the war was being fought. Adorno elicits the image of a domestic interior and a boy at bedtime hearing music on the sly: "The German boy of our age who has no longer heard, as his father might have, the *Kreutzer* Sonata played by friends of his parents, and who never listened passionately and surreptitiously when he was supposed to go to bed, does not merely miss a piece of information or something which might be recognized as being educational. The fact that he has never been swept away emotionally by the tragic forces of this music bereaves him somehow of the very life phenomenon of the humane" (p. 378).

We would miss the point to disregard this remark on account of the bourgeois privilege upon which the allegory depends—which Adorno often acknowledged. What Adorno valorizes in this tale is not privilege but a sociability and intersubjectivity constructed through musical performance: art as a source not for reconciliation but for reconciliation's promise, and at the same time the solicitation of the young into that realm of hope realized through what Adorno took to be art's truth content. What he imagines is the boy's recognition of a *promesse de bonheur*,[3] by means of the highest form of musical experience: its realization in performance.

2. Robert Hullot-Kentor, "The Impossibility of Music: Adorno, Popular and Other Music," *Telos* 87 (Spring 1991), p. 98: "The trade-mark of EMI, one of the several international corporations that bathes the globe in music, is: 'Music that means business.'"

3. Adorno, "Musical Climate for Fascism in Germany," p. 434; to make this point clearer, Adorno revised the statement quoted above in the text's second draft, as follows: "The fact that he has never been swept away emotionally by the tragic forces of this music bereaves him somehow of one of the strongest experiences of the *humane*" (original emphasis).

Later in the essay, Adorno shifts discussion from Wagner to Richard Strauss, who, he suggests, writes music "to be enjoyed as a stimulus for the nerves of the big but tired businessman," music like the rococo confection of *Der Rosenkavalier* "which proved to be so convenient for the taste of the German industrial upper class who got out of this work a mirrored reflection which made them look as if they were a legitimate aristocracy"[4] (p. 379). Thereafter Adorno turns to the counter examples of Schoenberg, Berg, and Webern, unlike Strauss without much audience, but keeping faith with the humanism Adorno heard in Beethoven, articulating not bourgeois comfort but fear, anguish, and suffering, and thereby maintaining "the link between music and philosophical truth" (p. 380).

Adorno readily acknowledges here and elsewhere the ugliness[5]—by conventional standards—of musical modernism, and the demand that, since the world (in 1945) is so ugly and terrifying, music should be beautiful. He sees this demand as congruent with fascist ideology (though hardly fascism itself), namely, a reversion, a turning one's back to reality. "The infantile twist is the forthright identification of ugly and beautiful in art with ugly and beautiful in reality," and, he continues, "it is just this taboo of expressing the essence, the depth of things, this compulsion of keeping to the visible, the fact, the datum and accepting it unquestioningly which has survived as one of the most sinister cultural heritages of the Fascist era" (p. 381).[6] The concerns expressed in this paper encapsulate themes organizing all of Adorno's work on musical mass culture.

4. Ibid., pp. 434–35. Adorno amplifies this remark; referring first to Strauss's translation of Nietzsche's philosophy into program music *(Also Sprach Zarathustra)*, he notes that: "One rather may say that this philosophy, as well as the estheticism of Oscar Wilde *[Salome]* or the religious symbolism of the *Frau ohne Schatten*, the Rococo of the *Rosenkavalier*, or the intimacy of the private life of the modern upper middle class, have been put on exhibition by Strauss in a gigantic sale of all cultural goods. They first have become neutralized . . . and are then transformed into consumer goods which are enjoyed as stimuli without being related to any ideas transcending the comfort offered by the world as it is."

5. See AT, pp. 45–53. This from p. 49: "The aesthetic condemnation of the ugly is dependent on the inclination, verified by social psychology, to equate, justly, the ugly with the expression of suffering and, by projecting it, to despise it. Hitler's empire put this theorem to the test, as it put the whole of bourgeois ideology to the test: The more torture went on in the basement, the more insistently they made sure that the roof rested on columns."

6. On the general topic of this essay, see also MM, pp. 106–08, aphorism 70, "Uninformed Opinion." Adorno several times returned to the image of infantilization, usually in conjunction with what he perceived as the regressive psychological effects of standardization and repetition in popular music, as in "The Schema of Mass Culture," in *The Culture Industry: Selected Essays on Mass Cul-*

Between 1932 and 1941, Adorno published most of his sustained essays on musical mass culture (all of the lengthy texts were published in the Institute's journal), though a few short pieces appeared during the 1920s, and a few lengthy essays much later, especially "Perennial Fashion—Jazz" (1953).[7] These include three short, aphoristic texts: "Farewell to Jazz" (1933), "Music in the Background," and "The Form of the Phonograph Record" (both 1934); and the major essays "On the Social Situation of Music" (1932), "On Jazz" (1936, using the pseudonym Hektor Rottweiler, the name in perfect homology with the tone of his critique, as well as a mode of self-protection in light of his periodic return trips to Germany),[8]

---

ture, ed. J. M. Bernstein (London: Routledge, 1991), p. 58: "The pre-digested quality of the product prevails, justifies itself and establishes itself all the more firmly in so far as it constantly refers to those who cannot digest anything not already pre-digested. It is baby-food: permanent self-reflection based upon the infantile compulsion towards the repetition of needs which it creates in the first place." The quasi-ritualized, entirely formulaic nature of monster-truck events and professional wrestling, where "real life" tends increasingly to imitate video games likely meets the criteria that define Adorno's point.

Rose Rosengard Subotnik, "Toward a Deconstruction of Structural Listening: A Critique of Schoenberg, Adorno, and Stravinsky," in *Deconstructive Variations: Music and Reason in Western Society* (Minneapolis: University of Minnesota Press, 1996), p. 167: "What drew Adorno to Schoenberg's music was not just its structural idealism but also the ugliness, by conventional standards, of its sound. . . . Adorno was sympathetic to Schoenberg's ugliness because he understood its cultural significance. And he understood this significance because he operated within the same set of concrete cultural assumptions, expectations, conventions, and values that Schoenberg did. He could listen to Schoenberg's music with the advantage of an insider's knowledge, not of a universal structure, but of a particular style." Subotnik points out that Adorno valorized Schoenberg's "ugliness" for its negative import, weighed against affirmative culture. But she wonders whether Adorno would have been likewise drawn to "the jagged qualities of grunge or punk rock or Laurie Anderson's music, while doubting that anything could have convinced him to view Leonard Bernstein's choice of the popular route as socially responsible." Richard Wolin, "The De-Aestheticization of Art: On Adorno's *Aesthetische Theorie*," *Telos* 41 (Fall 1979), p. 111, argues that Benjamin's notion of the de-auraticization of art becomes the concept of art's de-aestheticization in Adorno's AT: "Through the process of de-aestheticization, avant-garde art contests the counterfeit aura of reconciliation projected by affirmative art, that is, the conciliatory notion that culture should serve as the *ersatz* domain where the ideals that are denied by reified society can be realized." Wolin's article provides an excellent general reading of AT, especially as regards Adorno's engagement with traditional aesthetics.

7. Adorno, "Perennial Fashion—Jazz," PR, trans. Samuel Weber and Shierry Weber (Cambridge: MIT Press, 1981), pp. 119–32.

8. Martin Jay, *The Dialectical Imagination: A History of the Frankfurt School and the Institute of Social Research, 1923–1950* (Boston: Little, Brown, 1973), p. 185. Regarding "Rottweiler," see also n. 51, below.

and "On the Fetish-Character in Music and the Regression of Listening" (1938). As part of his Radio Project research, and with the help of his Radio Project assistant George Simpson,[9] he wrote (in English) "On Popular Music" (1941), which appeared in the last issue of the Institute's journal, published from New York, the only volume whose title and contents were in English *(Studies in Philosophy and Social Sciences)*. In this same issue he published a lengthy review essay of two recently published jazz monographs.[10] *Composing for the Films* was published in 1947, about which more later.

Adorno's essays on popular music and jazz constitute a notably small portion of his writings devoted to music, but they have generated passionate, often heated, response virtually from the moment they began to appear, and continuing to this day. Under the general rubric of mass culture, Adorno produced texts addressing "light music," essentially light classics (from nineteenth-century salon music to the fare of symphony orchestra pops concerts), popular music (essentially hit songs available on radio and disk, from standard-fare love songs to novelty numbers), jazz (essentially big-band dance music of the 30s and 40s, all the rage in Europe as well as America), and what he termed kitsch (not a separate genre, but a particular manifestation of the aforementioned types). Finally, he wrote on film music. In what follows, I want to suggest the outlines of his position in general and also in particular as regards these types of musical mass culture; in the course of the discussion I'll outline assessments (often negative) of Adorno's position, as well as suggest counter-arguments. Not the least difficulty with Adorno's approach to the music of mass culture is that his critique is less dialectical than is the case when he addresses art

9. Adorno, "Scientific Experiences of a European Scholar in America" trans. Donald Fleming, in *The Intellectual Migration: Europe and America, 1930–1960,* ed. Donald Fleming and Bernard Bailyn (Cambridge: Belknap Press of Harvard University Press, 1969), p. 351: "Officially, Simpson functioned as an 'editorial assistant.' In fact, he did a great deal more by making the first attempts to transform my distinctive efforts into American sociological language. . . . Simpson not only encouraged me to write as radically and uncompromisingly as possible, he also gave his all to make it succeed."

10. Theodor W. Adorno, with the assistance of Eunice Cooper, review of *American Jazz Music,* by Wilder Hobson, and *Jazz Hot and Hybrid,* by Winthrop Sargeant, *Studies in Philosophy and Social Science* 9 (1941), pp. 167–78. What Adorno finds in these monographs, especially Sargeant's, reinforces his own earlier assessments of the genre in "On Jazz." On Adorno's reading of these texts, and his dependence on them thereafter, see James Martin Harding, *Adorno and "A Writing of the Ruins": Essays on Modern Aesthetics and Anglo-American Literature and Culture* (Albany: State University of New York Press, 1997), pp. 98–100.

music—whatever his ultimate position on classical music, some of which he critiques severely.

"ON THE SOCIAL SITUATION OF MUSIC" (1932; pp. 391–436), published in the first issue of the Institute's journal, addresses modern music generally, classical and popular alike. The essay is organized by two tropes identified in the opening: all music today clearly sketches society's contradictions and flaws; and, the paradoxical corollary, all music today is separated from society by society's flaws. Music's inner life is dead to society which absorbs only its "ruins and external remains," in reference to music's devolution to commodity, its value determined by the market. Music is commodified, and as such its alienation from the subject is now complete. As the essay progresses, Adorno modifies the situation he describes in his opening, only to account for the same thing by other means: Some music escapes complete commodification, but only to be exiled from a society that has no use for it.

Music itself cannot correct what society has caused or become. Whether music can contribute to progressive social change remains an open question. But any music worthy of the name will attempt to do so "through the coded language of suffering" (p. 393), that is, by expressing social critique musically, through the realization of its own acoustic processes and potential: indirectly, as it were, and not as propaganda, which perforce by definition merely reenacts the domination which art's truth content demands be exposed for critique rather than disguised via aestheticization.[11] In what follows, Adorno articulates his position on the century's major European composers, centering the discussion first on the distinctions he will later trace in greater detail as regards Schoenberg and Stravinsky, but including as well précis accounts of Berg, Webern, Bartók, Kodály, Hindemith, Eisler, and, finally, Kurt Weill, who receives here a

11. Hullot-Kentor, "Impossibility of Music," p. 109: "The point of all his writings on art, in fact, is that aesthetic importance is defined by the intensity of its social content." Max Paddison, *Adorno's Aesthetics of Music* (Cambridge: Cambridge University Press, 1993), pp. 97–107, provides a detailed and well-nuanced reading of the major themes, critical to Adorno's later work, articulated in this essay. I have not attempted to replicate Paddison's fine analysis, though the tropes he discusses appear elsewhere in my commentary, but based on other of Adorno's writings. On Adorno's sociology of music more generally, see Wes Blomster, "Sociology of Music: Adorno and Beyond," *Telos* 28 (Summer 1976), pp. 81–112; and Edward Lippman, *A History of Western Musical Aesthetics* (Lincoln: University of Nebraska Press, 1992), pp. 472–88, principally a summary of PNM and ISM. For a brief summary of the history of musical sociology, see K. Peter Etzkorn "Sociologists and Music," in *Music and Society: The Later Writings of Paul Honigsheim*, ed. K. Peter Etzkorn (New York: John Wiley and Sons, 1973), pp. 3–40.

notably more sympathetic treatment than will be the case later, not least because in this early essay Adorno is considerably more in tune with a less mediated Marxist cultural critique than will soon and ever thereafter be the case.[12]

Whereas the essay's first half concerns musical production, that is, composition, the second half of the essay addresses music's reproduction and consumption. By reproduction, in this instance, Adorno means music's realization in performance. He outlines a sociology of the conditions for music, tropes explored at greater length thirty years later in *Introduction to the Sociology of Music*: the role of the conductor, the opera audience, and the ideology of musical consumption, and one composer, Richard Strauss, for whose music he reserved particular antipathy.

Paul Lazarsfeld was drawn to Adorno, on the basis of "On the Social Situation of Music,"[13] though he may have known the "Fetish-Character" essay as well. The last few pages of the "Social Situation" essay address musical mass culture, hence provide access to some of Adorno's earliest thinking on the matter, which he will amplify in later writings but not fundamentally change. He begins with "light music," to which he assigns a progressive social function, namely, satisfying "immediate needs . . . of all of society" (p. 425). That is, Adorno explicitly recognizes the potential for two kinds of socially responsible music: an art music that looks toward a future social reconciliation, and one which responds to the here and now, music that in essence "gives something" to listeners in the form of entertainment.[14] However, since this same light music is now as well "pure

12. Adorno, "On the Social Situation of Music," p. 409, the summary comment regarding Weill: "It is beyond question that Weill's music is today the only music of genuine social-polemic impact, which it will remain as long as it resides at the height of its negativity; furthermore, this music has recognized itself as such and has taken its position accordingly." But in a foretaste of what will be Adorno's later view, he adds in the next sentence, "Its problem is the impossibility of remaining at this height." In ISM, p. 233 n. 1, Adorno criticized "On the Social Situation of Music" for its "flat identification of the concept of musical production with the precedence of the economic sphere of production, without considering how far that which we call production already presupposes social production and depends on it as much as it is sundered from it."

13. Paul F. Lazarsfeld, "An Episode in the History of Social Research: A Memoir," in *The Intellectual Migration: Europe and America, 1930–1960*, ed. Donald Fleming and Bernard Bailyn (Cambridge: Belknap Press of Harvard University Press, 1969), p. 322.

14. In DE, p. 135, Adorno amplifies this position: "'Light' art as such, distraction, is not a decadent form. Anyone who complains that it is a betrayal of the ideal of pure expression is under an illusion about society. . . . Light art has been the shadow of autonomous art. It is the social bad conscience of serious art."

commodity," it is "the most alien of all music to society." That is, its sociability, so to speak, is a sham, a form of advertising. "It no longer expresses anything of social misery and contradiction, but forms rather in itself one single contradiction to this society . . . by falsifying the cognition of reality" (p. 425).

Adorno defines a crucial paradox of light music under mass cultural commodification. It is the music "at one and the same time . . . the closest to and the most distant from man." He compares such music to the day-dream, wherein people imagine something better. Light music, fully commodified, is daydream qua product, as it were, administered. It does not arise from the people themselves, but is brought to them by an industry. Turning to a novelty hit, "Who Rolled the Cheese to the Depot" ["Wer hat denn den Käse zum Bahnhof gerollt"], he posits the necessity for "highly exact interpretation," pointing to the inadequacy of established critical means developed for autonomous (i.e., art) music. That is, popular music cannot be studied as though it were art music that didn't make the grade. Instead, he argues, light music should be studied with respect to what he calls "an indication of the few, regressively preserved and obvi-ously archaic-symbolic *types* and figures with which vulgar music oper-ates" [*Vulgärmusik*, as in "common," though the more provocative "coarse" is likewise reasonable, given the general and intentional polemical tone of the essay] (p. 426). He describes basic musical tendencies deeply embedded and recurring in popular music.

The difficulty with this formulation is less its vagueness, and more its virtually structuralist-universalist tendency, which he "corrects" in part by what follows. Adorno calls for the investigation of recurring types of light music, and an account of changes occurring as the result of the his-torical circumstances of modernity. In other words, the ahistoricism of popular musical types (here tinged with a certain folk-like timelessness) must be historicized in terms of the present. Adorno is especially interested in the question of the social function of popular musics—which contrasts fundamentally with the functionlessness of avant-garde modern music as the result of the latter's autonomy from commercialized life, on the pos-itive side, and of its deeply conflicted relation to society which doesn't want it, on the negative. With popular forms, social function is dominant: as a commodity form and as something that people desire, if for the "wrong" reasons. Adorno insists that without a careful examination of social func-tion, light music cannot be known. In essence, he is calling for a new music sociology.

Here Adorno turns to what he terms the "radical tension" between art music and popular music that emerged with high capitalism (p. 427). He points to earlier times, when art music renewed itself by borrowings from below, as in *The Magic Flute*, where two distinctly different musical types exist in productive tension. He seems to see in such borrowings a kind of high-low, elite-folk exchange, a relation now shattered by the degree to which popular music is defined by commodity form, and art music by its extreme antipathy to society as it is.

Adorno argues that commodity music rigidly maintains its connection to art music, but to art music's older, outmoded, outdated, neutralized self (p. 428), and results from the process of industrialized production, together with the incessant demands of the market and intense competition—his example is not Tin Pan Alley but Austrian operetta and, later, film music. In short, it is the mechanization of the composition process itself that Adorno regards as definitive for the commodification of popular musics.

He closes the essay by turning briefly to jazz (here, dance music). His concern is to argue against the market, which presents this music as "new," by insisting that its musical techniques, principally borrowed from classical music of the nineteenth century, are in fact exhausted. (I'll comment on this later in regard to "On Jazz.") Adorno's greater interest is the impact of such music on listeners. He argues, at the level of social psychology, that popular music by nature of its musical-structural procedures, effects on the listener a sense of a false collectivity conducive to narcissism. Essentially, what he's getting at is the degree to which a popular piece, produced and marketed as a commodity, urges the listener into a false relation with the song and, via the song, with the market itself.[15] In other words, as with art music, Adorno insists on the social power of popular music, while arguing that this power acts regressively. Commodified music works to define subjects in the image of the commodity form, as products of

15. Florindo Volpacchio and Frank Zappa, "The Mother of All Interviews: Zappa on Music and Society," *Telos* 87 (Spring 1991), p. 129. Zappa dismisses the Sex Pistols in one word: "manufactured," to which Volpacchio protests that, though true, they were nonetheless "a serious inspiration for a new generation of rock musicians and audiences who saw in them precisely the potential of rock to challenge the corporate culture that had absolutely appropriated rock by the mid-1970s." Zappa's wry response: "Great, hum me one of their songs. Are we talking about music or are we talking about sociology? Basically, what you are describing to me is a commercial game which has been played. As far as I am concerned, this has nothing to do with music."

acoustical advertising. Adorno here errs to the extent that he universal-
izes light musics (all of a sort), and also insofar as he ascribes to popular-
music consumers habits of listening that are not necessarily warranted.
That is, he implicitly posits popular-music listeners as attentively focused on the musical material (as opposed to, say, less attentive background listening), since the degree of psychological dependency he describes would seem to require a type of listening more attentive than
mere osmotic absorption. Or, to put the matter somewhat differently,
the impact of popular musics, predominantly socially negative as he sees
it, seems to come about—paradoxically—without regard to how it's
heard: whether by careful listening or as so much background Muzak, or
as something of both. (Whereas Adorno insists that the impact of socially progressive art music can only be realized through structural listening—in essence through rapt concentration of the unfolding of a
work—structural listening isn't crucial for popular music because the
structures and procedures do not in fact require it.) He leaves unexplai-
ned precisely what kind of listening to popular music does occur in order
to produce the desultory effects he describes. Finally, Adorno's argument
is further compromised by the implication that mass-audience listeners
are always and everywhere the same.

The considerable strengths and weaknesses of this essay are palpable,
and both qualities emerge in greater detail in the major essays on popular
music and jazz that appear later, including "ON POPULAR MUSIC" (1941;
pp. 437–69). This essay is divided into three sections of unequal length.[16]
In the first, "The Musical Material," Adorno argues that popular music is
highly standardized, in essence cliché ridden. In the second, "Presentation
of the Material," he principally considers "plugging," that is, the marketing of music as a consumer product. In the third, and by far the longest
section, "Theory about the Listener," Adorno focuses on the impact of
popular music at the level of subject formation, maintaining that popular
music degrades the subject's individuality in favor of identity with a (false)
collective.

Adorno's critique of standardization, in the opening section of this essay, identifies numerous hit tunes as examples but without ever considering any one of them in detail. The reason for the lack of analysis rests

16. All of the principal arguments advanced in this essay reappear, with little
modification, and sometimes word for word in ISM (1962), the chapter "Leichte
Musik," given in the English translation as "Popular Music," pp. 21–38.

with Adorno's claim of ever-sameness, including a rigid structure (thirty-bar chorus, with the vocal range of a ninth) applied to songs of widely divergent types.[17] Adorno points to a book by Abner Silver and Robert Bruce, *How to Write and Sell a Song Hit* (1939), a kind of basic instruction manual for would-be amateurs aspiring to Tin Pan Alley (the book is cited in the first footnote of Adorno's essay). A few years later Robert Bruce published a still-more-telling variant, *How to Write a Hit Song and Sell It*, in which he comments: "It is sometimes difficult to realize that music, despite its nebulous distinction as 'one of the arts' is actually regarded as a commodity and is bought, exploited, distributed and sold in much the same way as other commodities including soap, food, cosmetics, cigarettes and automobiles."[18] Herein lies the overriding basis for Adorno's critique: songs for the masses are, first and foremost, goods for sale, and produced according to a quasi-industrial formula, though Adorno carefully notes that popular music does not actually employ industrial-production standards except in the distribution phases. The industrial terminology functions as an organizing metaphor for what he regards as the mold-like, formulaic functionality of standardization. In a later study Adorno commented that popular music "uses the types as empty cans into which the material is pressed without interacting with the forms. Unrelated to the forms, the substance withers and at the same time belies the forms, which no longer serve for compositional organization."[19] The metaphor of the mold resonates with Bruce's manual on writing a song hit. Here is the book's opening: "Writing a song is, in many ways, like baking a cake. Almost anyone can do it. On the surface it appears to be merely a matter of selecting the proper ingredients and putting them together according to some prescribed recipe" (to which he adds that it's actually not quite so simple).[20]

17. Adorno, "The Schema of Mass Culture," p. 62, distinguishes the standardization he critiques in popular music from his sense of genre-structures in serious music (e.g., sonata form): "Certainly every finished work of art is already predetermined in some way but art strives to overcome its own oppressive weight as an artifact through the force of its very construction. Mass culture on the other hand simply identities with the curse of predetermination and joyfully fulfills it."

18. Robert Bruce, *How to Write a Hit Song and Sell It* (New York: Lexington Press, 1945), p. 110.

19. ISM, p. 26. The insight is, of course, undercut to the degree that popular musics precisely transcend—if not outright ignore—this formal-procedural straitjacket, whether in Adorno's time, or our own.

20. Bruce, *How to Write a Hit Song and Sell It*, p. 3.

Bruce lays out "ten cardinal rules," each later explained in some detail, "the formula for a successful song," around 1945. They are:

1. The song must be in dance tempo.
2. The melody must be based on a short theme.
3. The melodic theme must conform to one of several patterns.
4. The melody should be simple enough to be sung, played and remembered by the average person.
5. The lyric idea should appeal to the majority of people.
6. The title should be short, catchy and up-to-date.
7. The lyric pattern should follow the melodic pattern.
8. The lyric "story" should build up the title.
9. The lyric and melody should be in the [s]ame mood.
10. Treatment of both lyric and melody should be original and novel.[21]

Adorno's music aesthetics acknowledges the power of song to express the subject, in essence to give voice to human yearning, desire, and sub-jecthood, and by a means (solo singing) that speaks directly through a singular subject. But in the instance of the mass-marketed pop hit, Adorno sees a utopian opportunity missed. Implicitly arguing against Benjamin's position articulated in his "Art-Work" essay, he suggests that the stan-dardization constraining the hit song dishonors music and the subject si-multaneously, by working, for example, against the commonly stated goals of song lyrics which, after all, so frequently evince human desire. Desire, at once personal and social, is thereby transformed into an advertising slogan by ever-same music that repeats endlessly, music which does not enlighten but anesthetizes.

Adorno regards song hits as entirely predictable except for small details, in essence the hook, on which hangs the greatest opportunity for market-ing success—a turn of phrase, a particular riff, a specific chord change, etc., which individualizes the piece, advertises its "uniqueness." Again, Robert Bruce: "There must be something about the song that provides an element of surprise and appeal and that distinguishes it from all other songs. This factor of novelty is gained, largely, by a new approach to a basically familiar idea. In other words, the successful songwriter uses the familiar and basic formulas but dresses them up with a new sauce and flavoring. The same framework may be used, time and again, providing the songwriter has

21. Ibid., pp. 8–9. Cf. the similar but not identical ten "Points for the Melody Writer," in Abner Silver, and Robert Bruce, *How to Write and Sell a Song Hit* (New York: Prentice Hall, 1939), pp. 69–70.

sufficient individuality in his approach and treatment."[22] Adorno regarded the function of the hook as pseudo-individualization. Whatever the detail, it never threatens the iron-clad model on which it's based. Further, the detail stands apart from the whole to the extent that it functions as a kind of advertisement for the lack of originality that otherwise characterizes the song. The whole, as it were, depends on the detail not as an aesthetic correlative but as a marketing ploy. Accordingly, as he wrote in "On Popular Music," "every detail is substitutable" (p. 440).

Standardization is not the product of pop simplicity (as opposed to, say, classical complexity). Indeed, Adorno suggests that the harmonic vocabulary of the common song hit is more varied than what occurs in much of the standard classical repertory (p. 442). And he argues similarly as regards other musical parameters. Instead, the issue is determined by the effects striven for, namely, "response-mechanisms wholly antagonistic to the ideal of individuality in a free, liberal society" (p. 442); that is, the issue is not the musical vocabulary but how it's used: repeatedly within well-established and expressively confined parameters. Further, he suggests, the structure and musical processes of the hit song function abstractly, without regard to the expressive demands of the text.

Bruce's advice to the would-be tunesmith: "The composer's task is to create an original melody that can be fully expressed within eight measures, that is so novel that it will not be regarded as hackneyed or imitative of other compositions and yet is sufficiently familiar to be pleasing to the ear."[23] The effect on the listener is a diminution of his or her own spontaneity (i.e., freedom, agency) by means of conditioned reflex. Indeed, the listener quickly becomes expert at the level of listening required to digest the pre-digested. Market success breeds market imitation, rather in homology with TV sitcom spin-offs. If one musical detail works, it will be picked up, repackaged, and sent out again over the radio and to the record shop. In the end, the musical conventions of the pop hit require so little of the listener that, as Adorno famously put it, "The composition hears for the listener" (p. 442).

The subject of the essay's second section, "Presentation of the Musical Material," is marketing, whose principal technique was called "plugging." Bruce's 1945 how-to book explains: "The song-plugger serves an important function in any publishing house. He acts in the same capacity as a salesman except that in his case the product is music, and his customers

22. Bruce, *How to Write a Song Hit and Sell It*, p. 66.
23. Ibid., p. 37.

are bandleaders, radio stars and other public performers. . . . To accomplish [his goals], the song-plugger must use all the devices of the super-salesman."[24] But this typical definition of "plugging" is insufficient for Adorno's purposes. Adorno is at least as interested in the ways that pop songs, in effect, plug themselves. In other words, plugging is homologous to standardization. "Plugging aims to break down the [listeners'] resistance to the musically ever-equal or identical" (p. 447), whether by means internal to the music (the hook is the defining feature though Adorno does not use the term) or external in the form of marketing. Part of plugging involves the assignment of star quality to performers. Adorno's examples are big-band leaders of the time; better examples today are the personality promotions for virtually all forms of popular musics that appear in magazines like *Teen People*, on one end of the spectrum, or, say, *Rolling Stone* or *Spin*, on the other, which market themselves as less adulatory and more critical but which depend on precisely the same techniques of star worship as do their less prestigious teen-mags. This is to say that the cult of personality is alive and well and of far greater social import in popular music than it is in the classical world, whose "real stars" are comparatively few and whose fans are negligible by comparison with the pop world. (To be sure, the repetitiveness of star-quality attributes in the marketing of celebrities unwittingly makes shabby the stars thereby created; all that changes are the faces, and the shrillness of the hype promoting them.)

In the essay "The Schema of Mass Culture" (1942), originally intended as part of *Dialectic of Enlightenment*, Adorno finds an architectural metaphor for his complaint about the repetitiveness of Tin Pan Alley songs. He compares them to mass-produced up-scale housing "which even standardize the claim of each one to be irreplaceably unique, to be a villa of its own. It is not the standardization as such which makes these houses from the nineteenth century look so uncanny today as much as the relentless repetition of the unrepeatable, all those pillars and bay windows, little stairs and turrets."[25]

In the volume *Radio Research 1941*, Adorno's essay "The Radio Symphony" is sandwiched between two other essays also addressing music, the first of which by Duncan MacDougald, Jr., "The Popular Music Industry," discusses plugging in detail, based on a substantial amount of

24. Ibid., pp. 118–19. See also Adorno, "A Social Critique of Radio Music," *Kenyon Review* 7 no. 2 (Spring 1945), pp. 215–16.
25. Adorno, "Schema of Mass Culture," p. 68.

empirical data, some of which is important to understand relative to Adorno's position on mass culture, capital concentration, and the social effects of both.[26] The essay's author directly credits Adorno's assistance, and examples and even phrasing found in "On Popular Music" appear throughout the text. What's fundamentally different is that Adorno's essay is the more abstractly theoretical, and MacDougald's the more empirical. Taken together, they reach identical conclusions. The essay's opening: "The object of this study is to contribute coherent and specific information about the way in which the popularity of hit songs is determined by the agencies controlling the popular music business."[27] The study's principal focus is on major publishers of sheet music, though the record industry is cited as well (at the time an average hit sold 250,000 records and 50,000 sheet music copies; "major hits" sold as many as 300,000 of sheet music and a half-million recordings).[28] The essay provides extensive detail about plugging practices in a variety of manifestations, from concerted efforts to get performers to play the songs to pushing new recordings onto radio playlists. It also cites data on industry concentration: among sixty popular music publishers, fifteen account for 90 percent of the hit market; and eight of the biggest publishers were either owned outright or directly controlled by major Hollywood film companies.[29] MacDougald also traces how a Tin Pan Alley song is made, which, as he puts it, "must not be viewed in terms of a spontaneous creation, but rather as a very practical, almost cold-blooded process carried out according to a standardized pattern based upon past success. Popular songs nowadays are more or less 'hacked-out,' a procedure which in a sense is similar to the working of jigsaw puzzles."[30]

26. Duncan MacDougald, Jr., "The Popular Music Industry," in *Radio Research 1941*, ed. Paul F. Lazarsfeld and Frank N. Stanton (New York: Duell, Sloan and Pearce, 1941), pp. 65–109. The other essay is by Edward A. Suchman, "Invitation to Music: A Study of the Creation of New Music Listeners by the Radio," pp. 140–88, discussed in part 2.

27. MacDougald, "The Popular Music Industry," p. 65.

28. Ibid., p. 71.

29. Ibid., pp. 73–76.

30. Ibid., p. 78. Paul Whiteman and Mary Margaret McBride, *Jazz* (New York: J. H. Sears, 1926), pp. 163–64: "But never let anybody tell you that the Alley is not business-like. There are as many yards of red tape wound about the 'Mammy' song that finally reaches you as there are about the automobile produced in any up-to-date factory. Tin Pan Alley is divided into departments with heads, super and under, clerks, secretaries, telephone operators and authors. It takes as many long-drawn-out conferences, house messages on blue, yellow, pink and green sheets of paper to run a song factory as it does to build a skyscraper. For the Tin

The final section of "On Popular Music," "Theory about the Listener," essentially traces what Adorno sees as a socially debasing form of mass psychology developing from mass listening. To the modern reader his account almost necessarily reads as overblown, however convincing in specific details, and the mass social psychology underlying the argument as too essentialist by half. Some background is necessary. Adorno wrote this essay in light of the impact of fascism and fascism's dependence on mass media for advancing its message. Once in America, Adorno quickly recognized the emergence of a still-later phase of mass communication's power, not so much directly at the level of politics as at the level of culture. He had witnessed what he regarded as mass psychosis at work in Germany; he feared its broader impact outside the state apparatus proper, driven by the overriding pursuit of profit. For Adorno, the subject's domination by the state through raw physical coercion and the subject's domination by cultural mechanisms—mass culture—were both socially destructive. Adorno correctly understood the power of mass media to shape taste, and he wasted no time insisting that the issue was not taste as such which, after all, only trivialized the issue, but mass culture's power to degrade the individual, hence again arguing specifically against Benjamin's position.[31] In other words, Adorno's concern with the psychological impact of culture on the masses was, precisely, making them mass—as it were, undifferentiated.

The impact of mass music on the listener, so Adorno argues, is to render recognition as the end instead of the means of listening. He posits that we make sense of a musical work by developing an understanding of what cannot be grasped by recognition alone; this is the "new" in music. Within a work, the recognized and the new function in a state of productive tension, each informing the other, the result of which is expression, which serves as the intersubjective link between composer, performer, and listener. The new constitutes difference and spontaneity, in essence: agency. But the new ultimately both means and matters only in relation to the old. It builds from what is already known and by that means transforms the old, thereby providing the subject with an insight at once personal, historical, historically critical, and of the present: an engagement with the

---

Pan Alley factory generally takes its product straight through from the first step to the last."

31. See Adorno's monograph-length essay "The Psychological Technique of Martin Luther Thomas' Radio Address," GS, vol. 9.1, pp. 7–141, written in English, concerning the then-prominent American anti-Semitic agitator and radio personality.

here and now. Adorno's critique of the hit song builds from an understanding that there is no "new"; the detail or hook that promulgates itself as such is nothing more than a variation of a cliché. Its "newness" fits altogether too well with what in the song is already recognized. Nothing is transformed; some already all too familiar spice is added to the same old dish.

There is a saving grace to Adorno's somewhat essentialized account of the workings of mass psychology. Repeatedly, he insists on a degree of agency retained by listeners under assault. Thus, in a section on distraction clearly aimed at Benjamin's promotion of distraction as a democratic phenomenon, he points to a problem facing mass marketers. If listeners don't pay any attention to the radio (would-be) hit, the song won't sell; but if attention is paid to it, "there is always the possibility that people will no longer accept it, because they [already] know it too well" (p. 459). Later, in a discussion of what he terms "emotional" listeners, he considers the Hollywood and Tin Pan Alley "dream factories," pointing to what can be gained from sentimental music, as it were, in spite of itself: listeners becoming "aware of the overwhelming possibility of happiness" and as a result daring "to confess to themselves what the whole order of contemporary life ordinarily forbids them to admit, namely, that they actually have no part in happiness" (p. 462).[32] (The social impact of this realization—a momentary insight—on the other hand, strikes Adorno as typically minimal.) Endless repetition naturalizes the state of popular music; even so Adorno posits resistance, however circumscribed: "This [situation] of course does not imply absolute elimination of resistance. But it is driven into deeper and deeper strata of the psychological structure. Psychological energy must be directly invested in order to overcome resistance. For this resistance does not wholly disappear in yielding to external forces, but remains alive within the individual and still survives even at the very moment of acceptance" (p. 464). Adorno's point here, however, is not to promote the resistance he acknowledges but, instead, to argue that the listener's very awareness of the dissatisfaction that in turn provokes resistance is suppressed by a spite that is directed inward: "The shame aroused by adjustment to injustice forbids confessions by the ashamed.

32. Cf. Adorno's comment in ISM, the chapter "Function," pp. 39–54, where the argument advanced is the following, p. 45: "Music as a social function is akin to the 'rip off' [Nepp], a fraudulent promise of happiness which, instead of happiness, installs itself. Even in regressing to the unconscious, functional [as opposed to autonomous] music grants a mere ersatz satisfaction to the target of its appeal."

Hence, they turn their hatred rather on those who point to their dependence than on those who tie their bonds" (pp. 464–65).

The last pages engage the jitterbug sensation which Adorno anthropomorphizes into jitterbugs: people transforming themselves into insects, whose frenetic behavior, in dance (to the music of Artie Shaw and Benny Goodman), he allegorizes as fury. He sees in "jitterbugs" the psychological internalization of an external order, the "endowment of musical commodities with libido energy" (p. 466). Adorno conflates a mass dance craze with collective conformity, and he reads it through the darkest possible lens. In essence, he conflates jitterbugs as culturally homologous with the mass rally and military parades in Germany—he cites, in a footnote, an invocation on a piece of sheet music to "Follow Your Leader, Artie Shaw" (p. 466 n. K).[33] Yet this notoriously overwrought comparison is too much even for Adorno, who ends his essay by suggesting that the process of internalization is not easy, that it requires tremendous effort by each individual to enact on oneself, against one's own ultimate interest. Subjects see through the lie, he suggests, but nonetheless reenact it as though it were the truth. He ends with a line that suggests an alternative use for the energy thus consumed: "To become transformed into an insect, man needs that energy which might possibly achieve his transformation into a man" (p. 468).

In the end, Adorno's crediting of the Culture Industry with take-no-prisoners power as regards the degradation of both musical taste and human subjectivity can be neither wholly subscribed to nor outright dismissed. When Adorno returned to popular music in his *Introduction to the Sociology of Music* he grudgingly admitted to the existence of a "few really good song hits"—registering them as "an indictment of what artistic music forfeited by making itself its own measure, without being able to make up the loss at will."[34] That is, the (for him rare) decent piece of pop music, by reason of being both good and popular, marks a link between

33. Adorno was not alone in producing the analogy. See J. Frederick MacDonald, "'Hot Jazz,' the Jitterbug, and Misunderstanding: The Generation Gap in Swing 1935–1945," in *American Popular Music: Readings from the Popular Press,* Vol. 1: *The Nineteenth Century and Tin Pan Alley,* ed. Timothy E. Scheurer (Bowling Green, OH: Bowling Green State University Popular Press, 1989), pp. 151–60. Among the examples MacDonald, p. 152, cites is that of a Barnard College economics professor who in 1938 suggested that the swing music dance craze could lead its adherents (the "jitterbugs") to "musical Hitlerism."

34. ISM, p. 36.

music and society that avant-garde music cannot claim except in the negative: social (true to what the social should mean but doesn't) but refusing society as it is. Elsewhere in the same essay he wryly commented that "there is still some good bad music left today, along with all the bad good music."[35] Wading through the apparent sarcasm, we can take his point that the "badness" common to popular music as a whole is not excused by the small amount of it that is notably good, in the same way that the aesthetic "goodness" pro forma ascribed to classical music masks the fact that enormous amounts of it are what he regarded as little more than trash.

Clearly, in the 1930s, as is the case today, popular music was produced outside the formulaic constraints Adorno described. Indeed, recent scholarship insists on a broad-based understanding of popular musicians as self-reflexive composers whose work not coincidentally often directly engages critique of mass culture.[36] In the end, it is the formulaic aspect of Adorno's own critique that distracts from the notable insights his work provides. An enormous quantity of popular musics is precisely what Adorno claimed—academic scholars are less wont to "defend" typical Top 40 hits than, say, Brian Eno, Peter Gabriel, or Laurie Anderson. That is, the popular musics typically celebrated by scholars represent something of a mass-culture avant-garde.[37] Few scholars (or fans, for that matter) are content to make sweeping claims for the alleged truth content of popular music in general. What tends to be valorized are specific instances, which quite commonly are exceptional.[38]

And yet, in the words of Robert Hullot-Kentor, "The instant popular

35. Ibid., p. 32.

36. Thus, to follow this line of argument, teenage musicians in garage bands need not seek to achieve economic penury for their labors in order to validate the authenticity of their social critique, any more than monetary gain guarantees expressive failure. See Jacques Attali, *Noise: The Political Economy of Music,* trans. Brian Massumi (Minneapolis: University of Minnesota Press, 1985), the chapter "Composing," pp. 133–48; and Florindo Volpacchio, "The Unhappy Marriage of Music and Emancipation: Reply to Kentor," *Telos* 87 (Spring 1991), pp. 118–23.

37. Richard Middleton, *Studying Popular Music* (Milton Keynes, UK: Open University Press, 1990), p. 37: As late as the early 1960s Carole King described New York City's song-factories in words not fundamentally different from the accounts that spurred Adorno's critique in the 1930s.

38. A few studies also engage the interface between music criticism and the academy, using the classical-popular divide as an opportunity to rethink the equation in terms of its implication for research and teaching, among the best of which is by Robert Fink, "Elvis Everywhere: Musicology and Popular Music Studies at the Twilight of the Canon," *American Music* 16 no. 2 (Summer 1998), pp. 135–79.

music is critically broached, eyes square off warily, waiting for the wrong line to be crossed, as if, in fact, the wrong line had already been crossed."[39] No one apparently crossed the line more than Adorno, and yet the terms of his critique of musical mass culture (indeed, of all the music he wrote about) have largely remained current even among those who most stridently oppose him. That is, music criticism has retained the aesthetic query that lies at the heart of Adorno's concern: is the music "authentic"?[40] The

39. Hullot-Kentor, "Impossibility of Music," p. 99. At the same time, the suspicion of popular music scholars can hardly be blamed in light of intellectually crude dismissals of popular music of the sort penned by Allan Bloom, *The Closing of the American Mind: How Higher Education Has Failed Democracy and Impoverished the Souls of Today's Students* (New York: Simon and Schuster, 1987); and Robert Pattison, *The Triumph of Vulgarity: Rock Music in the Mirror of Romanticism* (Oxford: Oxford University Press, 1987); Pattison's book is about lyrics and says little about music. Two recent studies of popular-music aesthetics should be noted: Simon Frith, *Performing Rites: On the Value of Popular Music* (Cambridge: Harvard University Press, 1996); and Theodore A. Gracyk, *Rhythm and Noise: An Aesthetics of Rock* (Durham, NC: Duke University Press, 1996), which includes a solidly argued chapter on Adorno.

40. Critiques of Adorno's popular music essays are pretty much legion, though, to be sure, his work likewise has its defenders. Among the more nuanced and balanced critiques are the following: Middleton, *Studying Popular Music*, pp. 34–63, notably thoughtful; Bruce Baugh, "Left-Wing Elitism: Adorno on Popular Culture," *Philosophy and Literature* 14 no. 1 (April 1990), pp. 65–78; Bernard Gendron, "Theodor Adorno Meets the Cadillacs," in *Studies in Entertainment: Critical Approaches to Mass Culture*, ed. Tania Modleski (Bloomington: Indiana University Press, 1986), pp. 18–36; Max Paddison, "The Critique Criticized: Adorno and Popular Music," in *Popular Music 2: Theory and Method*, ed. Richard Middleton and David Horn (Cambridge: Cambridge University Press, 1982), pp. 201–18; Richard Shusterman, "Form and Funk: The Aesthetic Challenge of Popular Culture," *British Journal of Aesthetics* 31 no. 3 (July 1991), pp. 203–13 (though rather more a critique of Pierre Bourdieu than Adorno); Deborah Cook, *The Culture Industry Revisited: Theodor W. Adorno on Mass Culture* (Lanham, MD: Rowman and Littlefield, 1996), pp. 39–44; Brian Longhurst, *Popular Music and Society* (Cambridge: Polity Press, 1995), pp. 3–14; Peter J. Martin, *Sounds and Society: Themes in the Sociology of Music* (Manchester: Manchester University Press, 1995), *passim*; and Keith Negus, *Popular Music in Theory: An Introduction* (Hanover, NH: Wesleyan University Press, 1997), pp. 36–65; this from p. 36: "The industry needs to be understood as both a commercial business driven by the pursuit of profit and a site of creative human activity from which some very great popular music has come and continues to emerge. The problem is trying to bring the two together: most theorists have tended to come down on the side of the corporate machine or the human beings." Among studies meeting the criteria advanced by Negus are Robert Walser, *Running with the Devil: Power, Gender, and Madness in Heavy Metal Music* (Hanover, NH: Wesleyan University Press, 1993); and Christopher Small, *Musicking: The Meanings of Performing and Listening* (Hanover, NH: Wesleyan University Press, 1998).

very same German idealism that serves as the basis for Adorno's concept of truth content continues to inform discussions of virtually all forms of Western music, popular-music research prominently included. The concept of "authenticity," long promoted in popular music studies, is after all a direct outgrowth of the idea of aesthetic autonomy defined by Adorno, via his notable mediation of Kant and Hegel as read through Marx and Freud. (Few popular-music genres have emerged without claiming an authenticity judged to be lacking in the music against which the new competes for status and attention. Hit status—actual mass popularity—is commonly perceived as deeply problematic, a clichéd sign of having sold out—ironically, to the same market upon which all popular culture, including new forms, depends for its popularity.)[41] In short, Adorno's contribution to popular music research is unimpeachable, despite the fact that he was no "fan" of popular music, held strong prejudices, didn't know a fraction of a repertory he attacked, and didn't change his mind (very much or often) on the topic— and has been dead a long while, "missing" (and earlier largely ignoring) the popular music of the last half century. The small obsession with Adorno on the part of popular-culture scholars is a tacit, if sometimes inadvertent, acknowledgment not only of the vitality of his ideas but also of the pervasiveness of the social and cultural conditions that produced his account in the first place.[42]

Adorno's pessimism about the future of the subject in the face of mass culture has inspired a great deal of critique, and some outright dismissal. But a counterclaim may also be responsibly voiced, in particular regarding the too easy and virtually automatic assignment of "resistance" to the regressive ideological tendencies of mass cultural products and also to the "resistant" uses that subjects make of them. In the words of Calvin Thomas:

> Those who rail against Adorno's critique of the culture industry would
> perhaps better serve the cause of human liberation . . . by focusing
> less on the vague possibilities of struggle supposedly provided by the

41. Gracyk, *Rhythm and Noise*, pp. 161–62, points to rock song lyrics which directly critique the notion of selling out, including (among a list of six examples), the Byrds' "So You Want to Be a Rock 'n' Roll Star" (1967), and Public Enemy's "Don't Believe the Hype" (1990).

42. Thus Middleton, *Studying Popular Music*, pp. 35, 57: "Anyone wanting to argue the importance of studying popular music has to absorb Adorno in order to go beyond him"; and "The *force* of Adorno's argument has to be admitted. . . . But, again, the argument is taken too far" (original emphasis).

"discontinuities" and "ruptures" of mass culture, and more on mass culture's predominant ideological functions: what it actually does, what type of world it continues to legitimate. Is it utopian—and hence fetishtically nostalgic—to imagine a world in which real atrocities and special effects, mass extermination and mass entertainment, are not indistinguishable and interchangeable details, mere simulacra? A world in which real human suffering and the body's pain are not offered up as high-camp moments of cheap entertainment and derisive contempt?[43]

Simply stated, in the end, Adorno heard right. And he heard wrong. Essentially what he missed, and not least because after the early 1940s he took little notice of popular music, is its hybrid nature, and certainly, in terms of the last forty years, he did not foresee its enormous variety and notable musical experimentation, self-reflexively acting against the tendency toward sameness structured into cultural practices generally.[44] Yet despite this considerable shortcoming in Adorno, few scholars have contributed as much to the advancement of critical studies of music and mass culture. Thus Bernard Gendron, who otherwise seriously engages what he regards as the deficiencies of Adorno's popular music research, duly gives Adorno his due: "Despite its failures and excesses, Adorno's 1941 essay 'On Popular Music' remains in my opinion one of the two or three most penetrating pieces on the subject; it addresses many important questions which are often neglected by those who tend to dismiss Adorno's work."[45]

Adorno's lengthy letter of 18 March 1936 to Benjamin, principally con-

43. Calvin Thomas, "A Knowledge That Would Not Be Power: Adorno, Nostalgia, and the Historicity of the Musical Subject," *New German Critique* 48 (Fall 1989), p. 174. Thomas Adam Pepper, *Singularities: Extremes of Theory in the Twentieth Century* (Cambridge: Cambridge University Press, 1997), p. 23, comments about the tendency to dismiss Adorno more generally because of his critique of popular culture. "Identification as a readerly strategy belongs to the New Old Right, which is why we don't have to throw out Adorno because he rejects, for example, Jazz: it is only the uncritical desire to seek a Master, thus to be a Slave, that would demand of a great thinker that his taste always be correct. It is silly enough, but the mistake is so often made that an error of such serious proportions could force an absolute reader-text estrangement or divorce. This is to miss the point of the notion of a—or of the—critical reader which Adorno promulgates, a notion which refuses to allow the reader off the hook. It also refuses to allow the reader simply to indulge in the (naïvely construed) aesthetic pleasure of turning our author into just another example of an irate parent on the other side of the generation gap."
44. See Terry Bloomfield, "Resisting Songs: Negative Dialectics in Pop," *Popular Music* 12 no. 1 (January 1993), pp. 13–31.
45. Gendron, "Theodor Adorno Meets the Cadillacs," p. 19.

taining his critique of the "Art-Work" essay, ends with a paragraph about his nearly finished "ON JAZZ" (1936; pp. 470–95), drafted during his English exile. Adorno tells Benjamin that he's making a return trip to Germany, where he hopes to finish it: "All of this is still uncertain, however, since I do not yet know whether I shall find the time or, more particularly, whether the nature of the study itself would allow me to dispatch it from Germany without risking considerable danger." Adorno writes that the essay, whose subject "is a very modest one, . . . offers a complete verdict on jazz, in particular by exposing the 'progressive' elements of the latter [i.e., with reference to Benjamin's position on film] (the appearance of montage, collective participation, the primacy of reproduction over production) as façades of something that is in truth utterly reactionary. I believe that I have succeeded in effectively decoding jazz and defining its social function. Max [Horkheimer] was very taken with the piece, and I can well imagine that you will be too."[46]

Adorno begins the essay by defining what he means by jazz, providing what he names "a crude orientation" to the subject: a type of dance music extant since World War I (the first jazz recording was released in 1917) and marked by "its decidedly modern character"—a quality much needing analysis, he adds. Adorno used "jazz" to refer in particular to big-band/orchestra dance music, then a veritable craze in Europe as well as America, by the likes of Guy Lombardo and Paul Whiteman (variously known as "King of Syncopation," "King of Jazz Rhythm," but especially as the self-proclaimed "King of Jazz")—in other words, hardly what today would characteristically be incorporated under the label.[47] The music was highly

46. CC, p. 132. See also Adorno's letter of 28 May 1936, p. 135. In the preface to his essay collection *Moments musicaux* (1964), GS, vol. 17, p. 11, Adorno comments that he gained detailed information concerning jazz from conversations with composer Mátyás Seiber who had taught a class on jazz at the Frankfurt Conservatory before 1933—that is, before the ascension to power of Hitler, after which such a class would not have been possible. Seiber emigrated to England where he and Adorno interacted during the period of Adorno's writing of the jazz essay. He died in 1960. See Nick Chadwick, "Mátyás Seiber's Collaboration in Adorno's Jazz Project, 1936," *British Library Journal* 21 no. 2 (Fall 1995), pp. 259–88. Chadwick accounts for Adorno's work on what he termed a jazz "exposé," which remains unpublished, for which Seiber provided some assistance and also offered a quite extensive critique which Chadwick fully quotes. Adorno's plan included provision, never carried out, for empirical research. The scope of the work was scaled back, following indication from Horkheimer that the Institute's energies had to be put elsewhere. The end result, of course, was a somewhat different essay: "On Jazz."

47. Thomas A. DeLong, *Pops: Paul Whiteman, King of Jazz* (Piscataway, NJ: New Century, 1983), p. ix: "Certainly by 1924 Whiteman's group was listened to

commercialized and enjoyed a mass market; in Max Paddison's apt phrase, it was epitomized by "slick arrangements."[48]

Adorno suggests that jazz music's newness is confined to the arena of sound and rhythm *(Klang und Rhythmus)*. He argues that jazz is an old costume with shiny new buttons. The new buttons coincide in particular with rhythmic syncopation, by which he means any form of beat displacement, and which in occasional virtuoso pieces "yield[s] an extraordinary complexity." By new sound Adorno refers to the extension of conventional performance techniques established by (classical) orchestral instruments, two in particular: the saxophone and trumpet. Performers play these "melody" instruments over a continuo-like ground, and in effect dirty the sound through the use of vibrato and other (unnamed) techniques of producing acoustical "interferences."[49] The fundamental point he strives to establish is that the modernity of jazz dance music is a surface manifestation that never exceeds the traditional (by which he means outmoded) salon and dance music of the previous century, as well as march music.[50]

---

and sought after more than any other musical organization in the United States." Whiteman's first recording was released in December 1920. By 1922 individual records were selling well over a million copies (p. 59). DeLong, p. 46, notes that Whiteman's popularity was so great for a time in the 1920s that he organized satellite bands under his name, maxing out at no fewer than nineteen (all of them dispersed by the decade's end). During 1923 the Whiteman orchestra played very successfully for five months in London. Whiteman's long history of radio broadcasts was inaugurated in 1929. In 1930, Universal Pictures filmed the Whiteman orchestra in the musical revue, *The King of Jazz*—the second "all-talking, all-color picture to emerge from Hollywood," at a record cost of nearly $2 million, though the film was a box-office failure (pp. 142–51). Regarding the impact of the big bands like Whiteman's on Adorno's understanding of what constituted jazz, see Wolfgang Sandner, "Popularmusik als somatisches Stimulans: Adornos Kritik der 'leichten Musik,'" in *Adorno und die Musik*, ed. Otto Kolleritsch (Graz: Universal Edition, 1979), pp. 126–27. It was, of course, Whiteman who commissioned and premiered George Gershwin's *Rhapsody in Blue*, orchestrated by Whiteman's arranger, Ferde Grofé, with Gershwin at the piano, at the famous Aeolian Hall concert in New York in 1924. (I will return to the question of just what music Adorno considered jazz.)

48. Max Paddison, *Adorno, Modernism and Mass Culture: Essays on Critical Theory and Music* (London: Kahn and Averill, 1996), p. 93.

49. Adorno, "On Jazz," p. 491, at the end of the essay returns to vibrato as produced by "the unbearable Wurlitzer organ" *[die unerträgliche Wurlitzer-Orgel]*, an expressive technique reduced to the mechanics of electronics: utterly mechanical, automated expression, as it were.

50. Cf. Adorno, "Perennial Fashion—Jazz," p. 127: "Anyone who mistakes a triad studded with 'dirty notes' for atonality, has already capitulated to barbarism." This essay, from 1953, in essence capping off his years in America, reprises all the

In other words, jazz does not break free from the history that enchains it musically, and it fails to do so precisely because it is in complicit historical relationship with commodity culture. Simply stated, he regards jazz as ideological through and through.

Adorno's concern with history informs the foundation of the essay. For example, he is notably conscious of the then-common arguments that jazz constituted a kind of musical renewal of exhausted Western musical traditions by an infusion of the prehistorical courtesy of Africa—thus the saxophone, to whose sound (as he correctly notes) was then widely ascribed, as it still is, a high degree of libidinal expressivity, giving acoustical shape to an imagined primitive subjectivity, thereby subjecting "the over-stimulated Western nerves to the vitality of blacks" (p. 471). He will have none of this. Adorno invokes race (and racism)[51] in order to critique the mythologization of time and space embedded in the otherness attributed to jazz. The saxophone, by the 1930s enjoying status as the instrument marking the newness (and exoticism) of jazz, was neither new nor exotic.

---

major points developed in "On Jazz." There is a small amount of "updating" of the musical examples; ideas advanced in the chapter on the Culture Industry from DE are evident, along with the social psychology research from *The Authoritarian Personality*.

51. Some scholars have read Adorno's comments on blacks and jazz as racist, a charge that is, frankly, absurd, and not least the result of careless reading. Thus William P. Nye, "Theodor Adorno on Jazz: A Critique of Critical Theory," *Popular Music and Society* 12 no. 4 (Winter 1988), p. 72: "Adorno's critical depreciation of this aspect of popular music [i.e., timbral improvisation and the uniqueness of sound achieved by virtuoso jazz musicians] reflects a myopic ethnocentrism toward non-European music in general, and perhaps a disguised racism when applied to jazz." On this and other occasional, and notably careless, outright or veiled charges of racism as regards Adorno's reading of jazz, see Harding, *Adorno and "A Writing of the Ruins,"* pp. 102–03, 110–11, which provides information on the charge as well as an apt refutation, including the point that Adorno's comments echo those of Ralph Ellison; see Evelyn Wilcock, "Adorno, Jazz and Racism: 'Über Jazz' and the 1934–7 British Jazz Debate," *Telos* 107 (Spring 1996), especially pp. 69–80, who makes abundantly clear that Adorno's position is explicitly anti-racist. She describes English racist attitudes, sometimes quite rabid, toward black music and musicians, and ironically often coterminous with anti-Semitism; she indicates that Adorno's views on the subject were likely shaped by discourse readily available in U.K. music magazines. Thus *Rhythm* (May 1935), pp. 17–18, published a xeno-phobic essay by Bruce Sievier against foreign composers: "Let us connect with the Empire, this Motherland—this England; and remember foreigners did not put us where we are. It was *pride of race* that won us our unusual position in the world. It was the dogged determination that we call the Bulldog breed" (original emphasis). Wilcock points to this text in relation to Adorno's decision to use the ironic pseudonym "Rottweiler" for his own jazz essay (see p. 71).

Invented around 1840 by the Belgian Adolphe Sax, it was occasionally used in nineteenth-century classical music and had long been a staple in military bands (albeit in France, Belgium, and especially England, but not in Germany; though Adorno doesn't mention it, John Philip Sousa helped establish the instrument's popularity in America during the last decade of the nineteenth century).[52] The saxophone is European through and through; the transposition onto its sound of racial otherness, at once denounced and desired for the supposed sexual prowess its sound conjures, Adorno implicitly regards as a racist reading of blacks as primitives, primitive on account of a purported sexual animality, an historical survival of nineteenth-century racist physiognomy. Adorno's pointing to the saxophone's use in European military music directly confronts this stereotype; he suggests that the saxophone equates with the disciplinary regimes of bourgeois modernity (the military machines that worked to guarantee the national identities and economic boundaries of capitalism) and not the sexual freedom imputed to people of color. (Near the essay's end Adorno returns to sexuality, playing off this earlier trope, but now with reference to "hot" jazz rhythms, which he describes—provocatively, hyperbolically, and variously—as masturbatory, prematurely ejaculatory, and impotent [p. 490],[53] in other words, a strategic rhetorical gesture at reconfiguring clichéd conflations of jazz dance music and sexual prowess.)

52. Philip Bate, "Saxophone," *The New Grove Dictionary of Music and Musicians,* ed. Stanley Sadie (London: Macmillan, 1980), vol. 16, pp. 534, 538–39. Adorno, "On Jazz," p. 485, associates march rhythms with the sounds of fascist military displays. In "Perennial Fashion—Jazz," p. 129, he is very direct on this matter: "While the leaders in the European dictatorships of both shades raged against the decadence of jazz, the youth of the other countries has long since allowed itself to be electrified, as with marches, by the syncopated dance-steps, with bands which do not by accident stem from military music. The division into shocktroops and inarticulate following has something of the distinction between party élite and the rest of the 'people.'"

53. Adorno is extremely provocative on this matter in the later essay, "Perennial Fashion—Jazz," p. 129. Arguing that the music produces ego weakness, he proclaims: "The aim of jazz is the mechanical reproduction of a regressive moment, a castration symbolism. 'Give up your masculinity, let yourself be castrated,' the eunuchlike sound of the jazz band both mocks and proclaims, 'and you will be rewarded, accepted into a fraternity which shares the mystery of impotence with you, a mystery revealed at the moment of the initiation rite.'" Clearly sensing in this remark less its provocative nature and more its surface absurdity, Adorno devotes most of a page to defending the claim, citing Freudian-slip-like high jinks of jazz musicians playing (in the sexual sense) with their instruments, and a reading of the biblical Samson and Delilah sexual narrative embedded into the stereotyped phrases "long hair" and "short hair" in reference to jazz musicians. In other words, Adorno hangs a great deal of psychoanalysis on not terribly much.

Adorno comments that the "extent to which jazz has anything at all to do with genuine black music is highly questionable; the fact that it is frequently performed by blacks and that the public clamors for 'black jazz' as a sort of brand-name doesn't say much about it, even if folkloric research should confirm the African origin of many of its practices" (p. 477). Acknowledging the possibility of African borrowings, Adorno in effect argues against any trace of social significance to the extent that the music is, in effect, profoundly "whitened." To the extent that Adorno knew big band music of the Paul Whiteman variety he has a legitimate point. (He also knew something of Duke Ellington; what he principally recognized was Ellington's debt to European impressionist composers, Debussy and Delius especially.)[54] Paul Whiteman's own account of how to put together a top-notch jazz orchestra is metaphoric. "Perhaps the most important item in the jazz equipment is that each player shall be American. It is better to be a native-born American and better still, if one's parents were born here, for then one has had the American environment for two generations and that helps a great deal in playing jazz. At least, the musician must be a naturalized citizen, which means a considerable residence and a knowledge of language and customs." Whiteman then catalogues the national origins of his own musicians. They are, he says, "of every kind of ancestry— Italian, German, French, English, Scandinavian. . . . What does matter is that they are all American citizens and nearly all native-born."[55] What they were not, of course, is African-American: not one.[56] Many of his players, much to Whiteman's delight, were "symphony men." In White-

---

For a scathing assessment of this matter, see Peter Townsend, "Adorno on Jazz: Vienna Versus the Vernacular," *Prose Studies* 11 no. 1 (May 1988), pp. 71–72. Nevertheless, there is an apt historical parallel, in nineteenth-century blackface minstrelsy, to the Freudian hermeneutic that Adorno applies to Whiteman-esque dance-band jazz. Arguably, both re-enact black cultural practice in a kind of white parody mixed with sexual panic. Eric Lott, "Love and Theft: The Racial Unconscious of Blackface Minstrelsy," *Representations* 39 (Summer 1992), pp. 33–37, discusses blackface minstrelsy as a form of symbolic castration of African-American men. On the importance of blackface minstrelsy to the history of jazz in relation to Adorno's critique, see Harding, *Adorno and "A Writing of the Ruins,"* pp. 115–16.

54. Adorno was not alone in his perspective. Discussing the fox-trot, Virgil Thomson, "Jazz," *American Mercury* 2 no. 8 (August 1924), pp. 465–67, argues along virtually identical lines to Adorno as to the homology of European classical musics and dance-band jazz; he notes African-American influence only in passing.

55. Whiteman and McBride, *Jazz*, pp. 237–38.

56. Whiteman did hire African-American musicians as composers and arrangers, concerning which, as well as the general issue of integration, see DeLong, *Pops*, pp. 102–03.

man's expensive and over-produced (and fairly dreadful) film of 1930, *The King of Jazz*, the final scene, a massive production number, visually traces the purported musical melting pot that is jazz—the opening and closing of which has Whiteman staring into the somewhat ominously whirling vortex in a global stew-pot—from which emerge appropriately costumed dancers executing Scottish reels, gypsy music, European salon music, and the like, in a lengthy multi-part romp around the musical globe but entirely excluding any hint of African or African-American culture. Whiteman's world is white and (ultimately) European. *Tout court.*[57]

In the end, Adorno argues that "Jazz is not what it 'is': its aesthetic articulation is sparing and can be understood at a glance. Rather, it is what it is used for, and this fact clearly brings up questions whose answers will require in-depth examination" (p. 472). Jazz promises a newness valorizing individuality and liberation (the image here depends on dance-band improvisatory solos structured into individual pieces). It doesn't deliver. Improvisatory moments are pre-planned to fit comfortably into the composition's preestablished character. Paul Whiteman: "As I have tried to indicate, the modern jazz orchestra is an efficient arrangement. Every member knows exactly what he is to play every minute of the time. Even the smears are indicated in the music."[58] The free moment of improvisation, which may momentarily create the desired effect of breaking free from the standardized event, in the end—rather like Bakhtin's notion of carnival—only certifies the grip of both the commodity form and the social formation upon which the commodity form ultimately depends.[59]

Adorno sees jazz functioning as a certification of the European bourgeoisie. It's played in the chic clubs, and danced to by people who have time to learn the steps, and for whom "jazz represents, somewhat like the evening clothes of the gentlemen, the inexorability of the social authority which it itself is, but which is transfigured in jazz into something original and primitive, into 'nature' " (p. 474). (Here he exhibits a degree of Marx-

57. There is, however, a distinct danger of invoking a reverse form of racial purity: good jazz = black jazz. The real point, of course, is that jazz is a hybrid, the result of a collision of cultures, races, classes, and genders. As Lee B. Brown, "Adorno's Critique of Popular Culture: The Case of Jazz Music," *Journal of Aesthetic Education* 26 no. 1 (Spring 1992), p. 27, aptly puts it: "When the purist is finally driven back to African music, he will find his prize [jazz] disappearing like smoke."

58. Whiteman and McBride, *Jazz*, p. 211.

59. Mikhail Bakhtin, *Rabelais and His World*, trans. Hélène Iswolsky (Bloomington: Indiana University Press, 1984).

ian bitterness rather more characteristic of Brecht.) The social function of jazz dance music for Adorno is the aestheticization of privilege by means of colonizing otherness and making it one's own. This is the point of Adorno's remark that dance band jazz is a Western urban "manufacture," wherein "the skin of the black man functions as much as a coloristic effect as does the silver of the saxophone," which he explicitly names "a confusing parody of colonial imperialism" [die verwirrende Parodie aus dem kolonialen Imperialismus] (pp. 477–78).[60] For Adorno, the fact that European jazz eventually became all the rage across the social spectrum marks a more general mass identification with the aggressor.

At various points throughout the essay Adorno hints at ways jazz musicians push against constraints. He readily acknowledges musicians' virtuosity in improvising, and he names "hot" jazz as "relatively progressive" (p. 475). Further, he points out that jazz contains an element of the progressive specifically denied art music; it "reintroduces" into the composition those who are "reproducing" (i.e., performing) it. In jazz "the reproducer has reclaimed his rights vis-à-vis the work of art—man has reclaimed his rights over the object" (p. 480).[61] Except that it isn't so. The constraints of function circumscribe full realization of the possibility. "Subjective proclamation" is controlled. The performer is "permitted to tug at the chains of his boredom, and even to clatter them, but he cannot break them" (p. 480); the music is always already "stabilized" by the Grand Tradition.[62]

60. Wilcock, "Adorno, Jazz and Racism," p. 73 n. 53, cites the libretto for Adorno's unfinished Mark Twain adaptation, *Der Schatz der Indianer Joe*, which contains a bitterly ironic exchange between Tom Sawyer and Huck Finn about the inevitably of the lynching of a black man since someone has to be punished "if the [white] doctor dies."

61. Miriam Hansen, "Of Mice and Ducks: Benjamin and Adorno on Disney," *South Atlantic Quarterly* 92 no. 1 (Winter 1993), p. 49, "Adorno discerns in jazz's momentary rebellion 'against patriarchal genitality' an affinity with the most advanced esoteric music (Berg, Schönberg) in which 'the partial drives are called up one by one.'"

62. In 1937 Adorno returned to this essay, while still in England, adding a few pages, the so-named "Oxford Additions," GS, vol. 17, pp. 100–08, a series of ten aphoristic free-standing paragraphs. It is the third of these statements, p. 101, that opens with the (in)famous line: "Jazz und Pogrom gehören zusammen." Harry Cooper, "On *Über Jazz:* Replaying Adorno with the Grain," *October* 75 (Winter 1996), p. 108, refers to the comment as "This adman's shock tactic is Nietzschean." But in fact Adorno's line is not gratuitous. In Germany, and in England, a common thread was established between jazz and both blacks and Jews. Thus Wilcock, "Adorno, Jazz and Racism," p. 79: "Anti-Semites seemed uncertain whether jazz

In the chapter on popular music in *Introduction to the Sociology of Music* (1962), Adorno is slightly more giving: "Within pop music jazz has its unquestioned merits. Against the idiotic derivatives from the Johann Strauss–type operetta it taught technique, presence of mind, and the concentration which pop music had discarded, and it developed the faculties of tonal and rhythmical differentiation. The climate of jazz freed teenagers from the stuffily sentimental utility music of their parents." Shortly thereafter he added, "Certainly, jazz has the potential of a musical breakout from this culture on the part of those who were either refused admittance to it or annoyed by its mendacity"—an opportunity mostly missed, he suggests. "Time and again, however, jazz became a captive of the culture industry and thus of musical and social conformism."[63]

Adorno's position, in effect that little of jazz escaped the Culture Industry, is indefensible, as has often been pointed out. Leaving alone the issue of jazz musicians at work before and during the big band era, such as Louis Armstrong, Adorno seems to have missed the fact that a great deal of jazz was not mass marketed; indeed, its lack of marketability was analogous to that of the musical avant-garde.[64]

---

was a Jewish invention with which Jews were poisoning the world or whether it was something they had stolen from blacks"—and Wilcock is speaking here not of German Nazis but of English music commentators.

For a short version of the main arguments advanced on "On Jazz," toned down by Adorno for inclusion in a one-volume encyclopedia, see "Jazz," in *Encyclopedia of the Arts*, ed. Dagobert R. Runes and Harry G. Schrickel (New York: Philosophical Library, 1946), pp. 511–13. In this essay Adorno directly acknowledges the impact on jazz of African-American music, spirituals, and blues.

63. ISM, pp. 33–34. For Adorno's own assessment of "On Jazz," written at the end of his life, see Adorno, "Scientific Experiences of a European Scholar in America," pp. 340–41.

64. See on this point, Theodore A. Gracyk, "Adorno, Jazz, and the Aesthetics of Popular Music," *Musical Quarterly* 76 no. 4 (Winter 1992), pp. 532–33, regarding a discussion of an early recording by Armstrong, as well as the work of jazz artists working in the '50s and '60s. Gracyk, p. 537, makes the point that Adorno's critique of jazz depends ultimately on a conception of the musical works derived from the classical music tradition, whereas "jazz is a *performer's* art. . . . [It] challenges the division between the musical work and its performance" (original emphasis). In fact, Adorno would agree, as is clear from numerous comments scattered through AT as regards music's realization in performance. Adorno's point about 1930s swing is that the music is more or less pre-interpreted in the sense that "improvisations" are at once pre-scripted and clichéd. For a critique of Adorno on the question of jazz improvisation, arguing that what counts in this regard is not what Adorno experienced in listening to Paul Whiteman, see Richard Quinn, "Playing with Adorno: Improvisation and the Jazz Ensemble," *Yearbook of Comparative and General Literature* 44 (1996), pp. 57–67. Quinn suggests that small-

It is appropriate at this juncture to return, briefly, to the question of what music Adorno knew as jazz at the time he produced his principal work on the subject. New research has helped to illuminate this issue and makes clear that Adorno knew quite precisely what he was talking about. The "jazz" in question was the popular dance music produced in the waning years of the Weimar Republic and also in England during Adorno's exile years there. And as J. Bradford Robinson has convincingly shown, it had everything to do with salon music and the military march, just as Adorno reported, and very little to do with non-swing American jazz and even less with African-American musics.[65] Robinson points out that, be-

---

ensemble jazz, in which improvisation and give-and-take exchange plays the central role, realizes Adorno's aesthetic arguments for music's responsibility to express a utopian sociality. In this instance, in other words, the relation of part to whole remains in productive tension both musically and in terms of the performance situation itself: the individual performer is part of a community of mutual respect and interdependence, where individuality itself is realized in association with and relation to one's others. See also Paul F. Berliner, *Thinking in Jazz: The Infinite Art of Improvisation* (Chicago: University of Chicago Press, 1994).

Regarding its popularity, Ulrich Schönherr, "Adorno and Jazz: Reflections on a Failed Encounter," *Telos* 87 (Spring 1991), p. 89, points out that "in fact jazz never had—perhaps with the exception of the swing era to which Adorno primarily refers—a social 'mass basis.'" He suggests that the work of musicians like Ornette Coleman, John Coltrane, Charles Mingus, and Anthony Braxton in the 1960s (while Adorno was still alive) met the criteria Adorno established for progressive music (p. 93). Schönherr favorably compares Coltrane's stunning version of the *Sound of Music* tune "My Favorite Things" to Adorno's take on Mahler's progressive use and transformation of kitsch; see pp. 94–96. In a similar vein, see Nick Nesbitt, "Sounding Autonomy: Adorno, Coltrane and Jazz," *Telos* 116 (Summer 1999), pp. 81–98, who suggests, p. 83, that Adorno's non-jazz musical aesthetics, especially regarding the avant-garde, offer "a wealth of insights into artistic and specifically musical processes capable of redirection to other musical objects," such as jazz. For an excellent account of bebop, see Scott DeVeaux, *The Birth of Bebop: A Social and Musical History* (Berkeley and Los Angeles: University of California Press, 1997).

65. J. Bradford Robinson, "The Jazz Essays of Theodor Adorno: Some Thoughts on Jazz Reception in Weimar Germany," *Popular Music* 13 no. 1 (January 1994), pp. 1–25. See also by the same author "Jazz Reception in Weimar Germany: In Search of a Shimmy Figure," in *Music and Performance during the Weimar Republic*, ed. Bryan Gilliam (Cambridge: Cambridge University Press, 1994), pp. 107–34. Wilcock, "Adorno, Jazz and Racism," expands on Robinson in a variety of helpful ways, characterizing the significant degree to which Adorno's jazz views were formed by experiences in both Germany and England during this period. Two other recent essays addressing Adorno's work on jazz, but not otherwise cited here, deserve mention: see Carol V. Hamilton, "All That Jazz Again: Adorno's Sociology of Music," *Popular Music and Society* 15 no. 3 (Fall 1991), pp. 31–40; and Adrian Rifkin, "Down on the Upbeat: Adorno, Benjamin and the Jazz Question," *Block* 15 (1989), pp. 43–47, both balanced accounts duly noting

cause of Allied trade restrictions imposed on Germany after World War I, American jazz recordings were not available before about 1926, and the same more or less held for sheet music. German jazz, as a result, was homegrown—and distinctly European. All its sub-genres were in place by the time of the first American jazz band's visit to Germany in 1924. Once available, it was white American jazz band music that became extremely popular, Paul Whiteman in particular, who left "an indelible mark on Weimar Germany's image of jazz. . . . Black American jazz, however, was still virtually uncharted territory."[66] As regards "improvisation," German musicians generally learned by rote from various "break manuals" (one of which was written by Mátyás Seiber, Adorno's jazz advisor). These same manuals—Seiber's included—also offered instruction on formulaic and simple syncopation of existing tunes.[67] The rebelliousness claimed for jazz in Germany was anything but, and Adorno was prescient to so insist. In Robinson's words, "Adorno recognized that the pompously inflated music of Whiteman's 'jazz symphony orchestra' was merely an attempt to reach out to a new circle of potential buyers who were willing to accept 'consumption as artistic enjoyment.' "[68] On the jazz dance craze and the issue of social class, Adorno also hit the mark; in Germany this was not music of or for the many but for the few. Requiring both training and leisure time, its reception began at the social apex, with the smart set, and worked its way gradually downward. In other words, by comparison with the rise of jazz in America, the class origins were reversed.[69]

---

both shortcomings and insights. Among the most sustained negatively critical assessments is Townsend, "Adorno on Jazz," which incorporates a detailed analysis of Adorno's use of polemical rhetorical devices, a use that Townsend, p. 70, characterizes as a form of argument that "is a spasmodic and uncomfortable mixture of the journalistically vague and the irrelevantly precise"; he suggests, p. 80, that Adorno's presentation "must be regarded as special pleading, primarily on behalf of his own exemption from the responsibilities of exposition and evidence, his own privileged access to psychological secrets."

66. Robinson, "Jazz Essays of Theodor Adorno," p. 6.

67. Ibid., p. 10. Wilcock, "Adorno, Jazz and Racism," p. 69, however, makes clear that while in England, during the time the jazz essay was drafted, Adorno experienced black jazz. Among other evidence, she cites a 1937 letter from Adorno to Horkheimer where he mentions going to a black night club in Soho; Wilcock suggests several possible establishments, where in each instance prominent African-American jazz musicians performed, including Coleman Hawkins, Fats Waller, Benny Carter and Dizzy Gillespie. She does not address implications that might arise as regards Adorno's general views on jazz from hearing such musicians perform.

68. Robinson, "Jazz Essays of Theodor Adorno," p. 16.

69. Ibid., pp. 18–19. Robinson concludes (p. 22): "What is left is a series of

In October 1933 the Nazis banned radio broadcasts of "Negerjazz." The same year Adorno wrote his first jazz "essay"—in fact, not much more than a lengthy aphorism, "FAREWELL TO JAZZ" (pp. 496–500), which opens with a reference to this "drastic verdict." Michael H. Kater, misreading the essay's import, comments: "Having hated jazz with a passion even at the end of the republic, early in the regime [Adorno] was enthused over the prospect of the Nazi authorities forbidding the music altogether—a strange position for a Jew."[70] What Kater fails to recognize is that Adorno clearly understood the "dance-band commercial jazz" widely available in Weimar Germany to have little to do with African or African-American culture,[71] as Adorno states in his first sentences: "For no matter what one wishes to understand by white or by Negro jazz, here there is nothing to salvage. Jazz itself has long been in the process of dissolution, in retreat into military marches and all sorts of folklore"—what he calls, later in the essay, "patriotic kitsch," and clearly associates with fascism.[72] His point is

brilliant sociological and aesthetic analyses of Weimar's popular music culture by a committed contemporary observer who understood, more than anyone else at the time, the peculiar origins, musical fabric, institutional prerequisites and foreordained demise of this uniquely German music." Cooper, "On *Über Jazz*," provides an often insightful critique of Adorno's essay, though he acknowledges, p. 128, that Adorno's analysis of Whiteman "is incisive indeed." Cooper's principal argument hinges on the difference between swing and hot jazz, and the fact that Adorno admitted no real distinction. However, it is clear that Cooper did not factor the research of Robinson or Wilcock into his analysis, which would have required him to moderate the unambiguous position he takes on Adorno, e.g., p. 108: "Adorno could not stop writing about jazz but could never focus on it either. . . . His furtive, repeated *glances* are the bad faith of the high-cultural fetishist. Why pretend otherwise?" (original emphasis). The principal counter-example to Whiteman that Cooper offers is Louis Armstrong, whom Adorno had heard—precisely how much is unknown, though not likely very much.

70. Michael H. Kater, *Different Drummers: Jazz in the Culture of Nazi Germany* (New York: Oxford University Press, 1992), p. 33.

71. Paddison, *Adorno, Modernism and Mass Culture*, p. 113: "Beneath its veneer, [this music] has a rhythmic scheme uncomfortably close to that of the military march (an ironic and thinly disguised reference to the Nazis' own love of martial music); and that jazz in this sense has little to do with black music, being rather at most a commercial exploitation of 'negro music' by whites." James Harding, *Adorno and "A Writing of the Ruins*," p. 103, argues directly counter to Kater, and from a firmer grounding both in Adorno's text and in the historical situation he confronted: "When one places Adorno's claims that jazz is 'not Black, not powerful, not dangerous . . . [nor] emancipatory' in the context of fascist Germany, Adorno's arguments refute point by point the hysteria to which the Nazis appealed when they banned jazz music."

72. Robinson, "Jazz Essays of Theodor Adorno," p. 20: "By 1933, then, the year in which Adorno published his first jazz essay, the regression of German dance

explicit: German jazz is about Germany, and nothing more—he calls it "bad arts and crafts" (p. 497). "Jazz no more has anything to do with authentic Negro music, which has long since been falsified and industrially smoothed out here, than it is possessed of any destructive or threatening qualities" (p. 496). Adorno regards this music as the product of music industrialization, utterly bereft of spontaneity, newness (which it nonetheless claims), and freedom of expression. He regards it, instead, as the shabby results of now-stereotyped formulae, better and fresher examples of which date from the nineteenth century in music by Brahms and Johann Strauss.

The essay's ending alludes to what jazz might have achieved but did not, namely, "the emancipation of the rhythmic emphasis from metrical time," what Adorno regarded as jazz's most significant, but failed, promise. Now, and in light of the radio ban, he suggests, there is nothing except the silence[73] of a vacuum, which might, however, prove instructive: "In it is expressed, wordlessly, like the alienation of art and society, a kind of overall state of reality that words are lacking to express. This vacuum may be wordless, but it is no false consciousness. Perhaps in the silence it will grow loud" (p. 499).

Between 1934 and 1940 Adorno wrote a series of musical aphorisms, first published in 1955, titled "Commodity Music Analysed" ["Musikalische Warenanalysen"]. The subject uniting them is kitsch. Here is the text's opening, an Adornian rhetorical tour de force, as notable for its concentrated expressive aptness as for its hilarity: "Gounod's *Ave Maria*: an Englishman has proposed this formula for music hall: *Put three half-naked girls on a revolving stage. Then play the organ**. This recipe is foreshadowed in the *Méditation*."[74] The aphorism's bitter humor is orga-

---

| music to the military march was complete. Adorno's commentary on this development betrays all the bitterness of one who suffered the full brunt of its consequences, and yet could claim that he had predicted it from the very start."

73. In "On Jazz," p. 485, Adorno indicates that the ban did not hold against march-like jazz which, to be sure, he does not find surprising, to the extent that it equates with fascist militarism, as he implies later in the essay, p. 491. He hears, in the momentary eccentricities of "hot" sections of jazz tunes, the faint echo of a persevering individuality—what he calls "the playful superiority of the individual over society." This individuality he regards as the rub, so far as the ban is concerned: "Only this ironic excess is suspect in jazz, and this is indicated by its hatred for squeaks and dissonance—but not the adaptation of syncopation; only it is eliminated within fascism, but not the model of its rhythmic development."

74. Adorno, "Commodity Music Analysed," QF, p. 37. The other aphorisms focus on Rachmaninoff's Prelude in C-sharp Minor, which Adorno describes as nothing more than "one long final cadence"; Dvořák's *Humoresque;* the slow

nized by Adorno's awareness of the relation of kitsch to the Culture Industry, and the CI's relation to history. Kitsch invokes a past that is nos-
talgically misremembered; as such kitsch is a means by which to forget—
but less to forget the past than the present. Kitsch offers consolation, not
so as to change anything but to make the anything of the here and now
slightly more tolerable. The past is "better," and analogous to children's
liquid aspirin, a sweet, syrupy inoculation against (perpetual) headache.
Adorno traces the reversals exercised by kitsch, necessary to produce forgetting as sweet remembrance.[75] Thus the Gounod, which he defines as "a
piece of sacred pop music featuring one of those Magdalenes notable
equally for their penitence and their seductiveness" (in reference to a long-
lived trope in European religious painting). "Overcome with remorse, they
reveal all." The Magdalene repents, so to speak, and displays herself for
our viewing pleasure, or, as Adorno puts it: "The soul delivers itself into
the hands of the Almighty with uplifted skirt"; "Saccharined religion becomes the bourgeois cloak for a tolerated pornography."[76]

Adorno views musical kitsch as both bad faith and bad conscience—
which he takes very seriously.[77] You want the shamelessly pious display

---

movement of the Tchaikovsky Symphony in E Minor, which Adorno regards as
cinema music before its time; and a piece of popular sheet music, "Penny Serenade"—he discusses the title-page image in commercial art moderne style ("adman's Cubism"), a southern street at night with a singer in the foreground wearing
a cowboy outfit and sombrero and holding a guitar, and placed so deep in shadow
that "it is uncertain whether he is a troubadour or the Lone Ranger"; standing at
the right and looking in at the scene is the man who popularized the tune, Guy
Lombardo, "looking like King Kong in a dinner-jacket." Adorno also discusses the
tune.

75. Adorno concludes the essay "Classicism, Romanticism, New Music," SF,
p. 122, with this passing critical allusion to kitsch: "What is wanted is not a peacefulness above all conflicts [typical to kitsch], but the pure, uncompromising representation of absolute conflict." In the essay "Criteria of New Music," SF, p. 194,
he amplifies his point: "The furious listener who wrote to his radio station after
hearing a performance of Stockhausen's *Gesang der Jünglinge* saying that the piece
had reminded him of atom bombs, whereas what he wanted from art was relaxation, exaltation, and edification, understood more in his subaltern repressiveness
than the sophisticated connoisseur who simply takes note of such music and weighs
up its merits in comparison to those of other products. In general, there is more
to be learned from sullen reactionaries than from moderate progressives who do
not allow anything that is not moderate to get anywhere near them."

76. Adorno, "Commodity Music Analysed," p. 37.

77. See Thomas Y. Levin, "For the Record: Adorno on Music in the Age of Its
Technological Reproducibility," *October* 55 (Winter 1990), pp. 27–28. Levin points
to Adorno's interest in pursuing the topic on a recurring basis in the Viennese

of Gounod, but Bach provides a foundation of precise disciplined musical rigor—as it were, body and soul reconciled forcibly. Bach provides the guarantee of aesthetic solidarity; Gounod provides, via text, tune, and violin obbligato, the feel good. The marriage is forced, which Adorno demonstrates by the ill fit between the Bach prelude and the words (e.g., "The climax comes, God alone knows why, with the [word] 'hora' ").[78]

In a longer series of aphorisms, part of the same volume, collected under the name "Motifs" (1927–37, 1951), Adorno suggests that "every great, authentic piece of musical kitsch . . . is capable of acting as the accompaniment to imaginary catastrophes."[79] (Whether explicitly drawn from the cinema or simply imagined, the examples he provides are notably cinematic, and include one of the Titanic sinking that uncannily recalls any number of scenes from the major movies on the subject from the 1950s to James Cameron's recent, particularly resplendent example of cinematic—and musical—kitsch. The aphorism in question was written in 1928.) Adorno's phrase expresses the seriousness which he accords the genre: kitsch comes in varieties of greater and lesser, authentic and inauthentic, and it semiotically underscores danger. His telescoped sentence is semantically slippery. Authentic kitsch: a phrase reminiscent of an advertising campaign in the 1980s for shopping-mall art emporia selling expensive "authorized Authentic Reproductions," duly copyrighted, of masterwork paintings from "The Nelson Rockefeller Collection." Selling, in other words, Real Fakes. Adorno is eliciting the reality of the truth in the lie, that is, that the truth of kitsch is its falseness, which every "authentic" example thereof represents before all else. The precise truth of the lie is the catastrophe which the kitsch-work accompanies, rather like the blindfold offered the man about to be shot.

In his aphoristic essay "KITSCH" (c. 1932; pp. 501–05), Adorno suggests that kitsch has the "quality of being unrealized, merely hinted at." In music it has the "character of a *model*," that is, the "outline and draft of objectively compelling, pre-established forms that have lost their content

---

journal *Anbruch*, following his appointment to the editorial board in 1929. Levin quotes Adorno on the importance of a dialectical approach to the topic (e.g., p. 28: "Kitsch must be played out and defended against everything that is merely elevated mediocre art, against the now rotten ideals of personality, culture, etc. On the other hand, however, one must not fall prey to the tendency . . . to simply glorify kitsch and consider it the true art of the epoch merely because of its popularity"). On this last remark see also MM, p. 147, aphorism 96, "Palace of Janus."

78. Adorno, "Commodity Music Analysed," pp. 37–38.
79. Adorno, "Motifs," QF, p. 16.

in history." And yet kitsch is also a form of remembering, however distorted and illusory, of what Adorno terms "a formal objectivity that has passed away" (p. 501). It is the moment of objectivity of kitsch that constitutes its justification. In "Commodity Music Analysed," Adorno commented that "kitsch contains as much hope as is able to turn the clock back. It is the depraved reflection of that epiphany which is vouchsafed only to the greatest works of art. Kitsch only forfeits its right to exist when it enters into a parasitical relationship to history, mimics its verdicts and finds itself forbidden to reverse them."[80] Kitsch, as stated earlier, evokes a future utopia but only by looking back at a past that is selectively (mis)remembered, thereby helping to stabilize the present toward which kitsch is otherwise deeply antagonistic. Great art, by contrast, Adorno suggests, stares history directly in the face and speaks the unspeakable—and sometimes the unbearable. By contrast, "the positive element of kitsch lies in the fact that it sets free for a moment the glimmering realization that you have wasted your life." In "Kitsch" he comments that kitsch has the social function of deceiving people about their own situation and that as such it is "essentially ideology" (p. 502). Kitsch offers life a "fairy-tale glow"; in musical terms, kitsch is encapsulated by hyper-romanticism (historically, the style of choice for cinema music), music which Adorno notes "only enables . . . a good cry."[81] The reasons to cry are real; crying itself will not address the problem.

Clement Greenberg, in his famous essay "Avant-Garde and Kitsch," first published in 1939, provided the classic account of the relationship between the terms invoked in his title, much of which resonates with Adorno's own position. Both understood kitsch as commercial, mass-produced, formulaic, standardized, and aesthetically and politically rearguard ersatz culture, which feeds off genuine culture but only for the purpose of enjoying the profits that might accrue from the recognition and/or patina of prestige and comfort that such culture might provide—of enjoying what Greenberg calls "vicarious experience and faked sensations." Kitsch, as he puts it, "pretends to demand nothing of its customers except their money—not even their time."[82]

---

80. Adorno, "Commodity Music Analysed," p. 43.

81. Ibid., p. 50.

82. Clement Greenberg, "Avant-Garde and Kitsch," in *Mass Culture: The Popular Arts in America*, ed. Bernard Rosenberg and David Manning White (Glencoe, IL: Free Press, 1957), p. 102. See Nancy Jachec, "Adorno, Greenberg and Modernist Politics," *Telos* 110 (Winter 1998), pp. 105–18, which considers each man's aesthetic theory in relation to political liberalism. See also Andreas Huyssen, *After*

Kitsch and art share common ground—too much for comfort. Both "escape" reality, art through its autonomy, kitsch through the reification that attends commodity fetishization. Both are permeated with history, but whereas art seeks to invoke history, and indeed to "brush it against the grain," the history to which kitsch responds is one that kitsch either erases or, more likely, seeks to make palatable. Further, as Adorno suggests in the aphorism "Art-object" in *Minima Moralia*, both kitsch and the artwork celebrate "freedom from nature." That is, representation is an effort to imitate and, by imitating, to overcome what is feared; representation permits us to overcome that which "imprisons [us] in toil." Art and kitsch alike, in other words, are the result of effort to dominate that which dominates us; by re-creating what we fear we symbolically break the compulsion to adapt. In both art and kitsch "freedom from nature is celebrated, yet remains mythically entrapped"—not overcome but seemingly so.[83] Kitsch lavishly relishes imitation; art hides the fact but utterly depends on it. Art separates itself from nature as absolutely as possible, though without succeeding: its proclaimed made-ness defines the very nature of the dominant subject who, by making, overcomes nature. Kitsch, art's bad conscience over the gap between the two, reminds art of the imitation that underlies art's every effort, and also art's privilege—class privilege notably.[84] "In the end indignation over kitsch is anger at its shameless revelling in the joy of imitation, now placed under taboo, while the power of works of art still continues to be secretly nourished by imitation. . . . [Kitsch] incurs hostility because it blurts out the secret of art and the affinity of culture to savagery."[85]

---

the Great Divide: Modernism, Mass Culture, Postmodernism (Bloomington: Indiana University Press, 1986), pp. 55–58, for a discussion and comparison of Adorno and Greenberg on mass culture. Adorno himself refers to Greenberg's essay in PNM, p. 10.

In another aphoristic essay, "Is Art Lighthearted?" (1967), NL, vol. 2, p. 249, Adorno attempted to define kitsch, again by comparing it to what he regarded as the authentic artwork: "Though attempts to define kitsch usually fail, still not the worst definition would be one that made the criterion of kitsch whether an art product gives form to consciousness of contradiction—even if it does so by stressing its opposition to reality—or dissembles it. In this respect seriousness should be demanded of any work of art. As something that has escaped from reality and is nevertheless permeated with it, art vibrates between this seriousness and lightheartedness. It is this tension that constitutes art."

83. MM, p. 225.

84. AT, p. 240: "Fidelity to the noble in art should be maintained, just as the noble should reflect its own culpability, its complicity with privilege."

85. MM, pp. 225–26. Cf. AT, p. 239: "Kitsch is not, as those believers in erudite

Composing for the Films, co-authored with composer Hanns Eisler, was published in 1947, though without Adorno's name.[86] Reading this book is somewhat frustrating when compared to Adorno's other work on music. Though his presence is evident throughout most of the book, and hence nearly all the basic ideas are familiar, it is unlike anything else he ever wrote. On the one hand, too much of the text reads too familiarly, repeating arguments about the Culture Industry and twentieth-century music worked out elsewhere and with greater nuance. On the other hand, *Composing for the Films* engages the social regression of the Culture Industry by means of a fairly explicit design for a progressive musical praxis

culture would like to imagine, the mere refuse of art, originating in disloyal accommodation to the enemy; rather, it lurks in art, awaiting ever recurring opportunities to spring forth."

86. CF. The book was originally written in German. Though the preface is dated 1944, the book actually appeared only three years later, in English. Eisler republished it in German and with changes in 1949 under his name alone. Adorno withdrew his name from the original edition in order to avoid involvement in Eisler's political troubles with the House Un-American Activities Committee (HUAC)—Eisler was ordered to testify on account of his brother, Gerhard, a Communist, who had been arrested for spying. Eisler for all intents and purposes was hounded from the U.S. and spent most of his remaining life in East Germany. Adorno published a second German version in 1969, based on the original manuscript, and using both his name and Eisler's. (The first English edition contains changes from the original German. The 1994 reprint is this version, hence the original German text from 1944 has yet to appear in English.) In the afterword to this edition, GS, vol. 15, pp. 144–46, Adorno suggests that Eisler's numerous changes effect an anti-American tone and serve to satisfy the Communist regime under which he was by then living. Adorno comments that without these changes it would have been very difficult for Eisler to have published the book in East Germany.

The details of co-authorship have never been fully sorted out. Without question, however, Adorno wrote a great deal of it; in private correspondence he claimed to have written nine-tenths of it. Not only is the book fully reflective of his ideas on music, music sociology, and the Culture Industry, but the style of the writing in much of the text is close to his as well. Concerning authorship, see Eberhardt Klemm, "Zur vorliegenden Ausgabe," in Theodor W. Adorno and Hanns Eisler, *Komposition für den Film*. Vol. 4 of Hanns Eisler, *Gesammelte Werke* (Leipzig: VEB Deutscher Verlag für Musik, 1977), pp. 5–24; Miriam Hansen, "Introduction to Adorno, 'Transparencies on Film' (1966)," *New German Critique* 24–25 (Fall-Winter 1981–82), p. 198 n. 34; Günter Mayer, "Adorno und Eisler," in *Adorno und die Musik*, ed. Otto Kolleritsch (Graz: Universal Edition, 1979), pp. 139–40; and Claudia Gorbman, "Hanns Eisler in Hollywood," *Screen* 32 no. 3 (Fall 1991), p. 274 n. 6; authorship of CF is also discussed in the book review by James Buhler and David Neumeyer of *Strains of Utopia* by Caryl Flinn and *Settling the Score* by Kathryn Kalinak, in *Journal of the American Musicological Society* 47 no. 2 (Summer 1994), pp. 369–70 n. 27.

within mass culture, something Adorno did not otherwise propose until very near the end of his life. (Eisler's own commitment to music's critical engagement with society at the level of the masses is well known. His association with and admiration of Brecht is evident in the book, and indeed he acknowledges Brecht in the preface.) But herein lies a problem. The very specificity with which Adorno and Eisler make practical recommendations to prospective film composers gives the text at times the oddly formulaic character of a how-to book, and this despite the authors' insistence that all musical decisions must ultimately be decided by careful attention to each individual film. As has often been noted, Adorno's own limited knowledge of film production processes limits the applicability of the insights offered[87]—though Eisler knew the process well and from the inside, having scored a number of films in prewar Europe and later in America (his experience in the Hollywood studio system assembly line was not a happy one).[88] The numerous practical recommendations for producing a socially responsible film score of the sort envisioned by Adorno and Eisler would have run headlong into the studios' well-established protocols as well as collided with standard film fare. As they pointed out, "Fundamentally, no motion-picture music can be better than what it ac-

87. See CC, p. 131, Adorno's letter to Benjamin on 18 March 1936, concerning the "Art-Work" essay. Adorno describes his impressions from a one-day visit around 1934 to a German film studio.

88. See CF, Graham McCann's comments, pp. xviii–xix. On the studio system and film music composing, see pp. xxiv–xxv. Concerning Eisler with regard to this text, and his experiences in the film industry, see Albrecht Betz, *Hanns Eisler Political Musician*, trans. Bill Hopkins (Cambridge: Cambridge University Press, 1982), pp. 176–83; and Hanns Eisler, *Hanns Eisler: A Rebel in Music, Selected Writings*, ed. Manfred Grabs (New York: International Publishers, 1978), pp. 90–92, from a lengthy radio talk titled "A Musical Journey through America" (1935), which Eisler read for a Strasbourg radio station during the First International Workers' Music Olympiad, describing his cross-country tour to major American cities. The broadcast was broken off, very near the end, when Eisler described the working conditions in Detroit at the Ford Motor Company's assembly plant, p. 92: "The working methods at Ford's are inhuman. Our writers and composers should be sent there to see this hell and tell the world what our times mean for some people in degradation, hopelessness and brutality." Also on Hollywood, see, in the same collection, "Hollywood Seen from the Left," also from 1935, pp. 101–05. Finally, see Eisler's short essay "From My Practical Work: On the Uses of Music in Sound Film" (1936), pp. 121–25, which certifies his early interest in developing a theory of film music—ideas repeated in CF. Finally, for an overview of Eisler's American émigré experiences, see Anthony Heilbut, *Exiled in Paradise: German Refugee Artists and Intellectuals in America from the 1930s to the Present* (Berkeley and Los Angeles: University of California Press, 1983, and with a new postscript, 1997), pp. 153–59.

companies. Music for a trashy picture is to some extent trashy, no matter how elegantly or skilfully [sic] it has solved its problems."[89] Essentially they propose film music that works against the film, a score that contradicts the affirmative character of the image and narrative, a music that more or less bites the hand feeding it. Eisler's own frustrations as a Hollywood film composer—despite his winning an Oscar for the score of *Hangmen Also Die* (1943)—could not have rendered him insensitive to the decided impracticality of his and Adorno's practical advice. (And this says nothing as to the problematics of consumer reception of such a score.)

Nonetheless, in a very real sense the book's weakness is its strength, to the extent that it represents a considered and original attempt to define a new aesthetic for film music, and not simply to argue for an autonomous musical practice, as it were, spliced onto a (commodified) film text. The authors attempted to square a circle, arguing for a film music well within the avant-garde traditions of new music. They define a non-autonomous musical practice that attempts somehow to retain the critical edge otherwise dependent on the musical autonomy they surrender.

The authors' critique of the film industry, within the general parameters of the CI, is acute and well taken. Both are keenly aware of the clichéd nature of classical film music of '30s and '40s Hollywood, and the causal factors leading to this condition. Film music is the result of a dual adaptation to the industry and convention. The music itself and the conditions under which it is produced are fully standardized—Tin Pan Alley with images. In the opening chapter—titled "Prejudices and Bad Habits"—Adorno and Eisler catalogue nine characteristic movie-music clichés, beginning with the leitmotif with which film music "is still patched together." (By way of more recent example, they have in mind the likes of John Williams's score for *Star Wars*, and the ubiquitous motif for Darth Vader.) Such themes "were drummed into the listener's ear by persistent repetition, often with scarcely any variation, very much as a new song is plugged or as a motion-picture actress is popularized by her hair-do." Since the leitmotif cannot be developed to its full musical significance, given the constraints of film narrative (short scenes, especially), it remains the same, without development, and leads to "extreme poverty of composition" at the same time that it numbs the listener.[90] The authors critique "melody and euphony" as a dominating and crude tunefulness, minimally expressive, notable solely for its easy intelligibility and as a "sign of utility"

89. CF, pp. 116–17.
90. Ibid., pp. 4, 6.

under the conditions of an industrial process. They see "the demand for melody at any cost and on every occasion" as that which, more than any-thing else, has "throttled the development of motion-picture music."[91] They critique the widespread industry prejudice that film music must be unobtrusive, playing a role subordinate to the screen image. By this con-vention, music's presence is often narratively determined as a kind of plot accessory—the hero, while waiting for his lover, turns on the radio. In addition to music's use as a plot accessory, it is also employed as an acoustic confirmation of a setting, often by means of stock effects: "Mountain peaks invariably invoke string tremolos punctuated by a signal-horn motif." Moonlight scene = *Moonlight* Sonata. And so on.[92]

Among the most interesting comments is their suggestion that, in an age dominated by the sense of sight as the principal path to knowing, hearing has lagged behind. They regard the ear as a passive organ when contrasted to the "swift, actively selective eye."[93] Pointing to the com-monplace that vision is distancing, and hearing both enveloping and com-munal, they suggest that this sensory gap may be exploited for progressive musical and social purposes. Since acoustical perception preserves to a greater degree the collective impact of orality, this suggests that film music could be put in service to undercut the false collectivity of mass culture itself, but only by means of a music that works against the grain. Con-ventional film music's standardization and conventionality reinforces the notion that a collective is always already in place. Such music's tendencies thus work against progressive interests. The resources of new music may be brought to bear against these tendencies—and here Adorno and Eisler mention as examples the music of Schoenberg, Bartók, and even Stravin-sky.[94] They later argue that music was introduced to films, in the era of silent pictures, as a specific antidote "against the picture."[95] In essence they

91. Ibid., pp. 7–9.
92. Ibid., pp. 13, 15. For a summary of their critique of standard film music, see Claudia Gorbman, *Unheard Melodies: Narrative Film Music* (Bloomington: Indiana University Press, 1987), pp. 106–08. Two excellent critical summaries of CF, incorporating assessments of the book's contributions to a theory of film music should be noted: Philip Rosen, "Adorno and Film Music: Theoretical Notes on *Composing for the Films*," *Yale French Studies* 60 (1980), pp. 157–82; and Thomas Y. Levin, "The Acoustic Dimension: Notes on Cinema Sound," *Screen* 25 no. 3 (May/June 1984), pp. 55–68.
93. CF, p. 20.
94. Ibid., p. 32.
95. Levin, "Acoustic Dimension," p. 60, points out that this argument flies in the face of conventional claims that music was introduced into silent films simply to drown out the noise of the projector.

allude to the uncanny nature of the simultaneously "living and nonliving" silent figures flickering on the screen, which possesses a "ghostly effect." Music, they suggest, gives life back to such figures, and helps the spectator to "absorb the shock."[96] In the silent era, muteness functions as a threat, an emptiness, a frustration exhibited directly on the screen by exaggerated gestures—pantomime—the impact of which is decidedly not cancelled by the captions that interrupt the action and that invariably and vastly condense intersubjective verbalization.

Adorno and Eisler point to the B-pictures' common sensationalism and dominant low-brow character as potentially progressive to the extent that such "cinematic trash" lays bare "the barbaric foundation of civilization"— presumably rather in the way highly sensationalized crime-and-detective magazines of the 1940s, lavishing both photographic and textual attention on grisly crimes, likewise exposed the underside of the American Dream. The popular sensationalism may "gain access to collective energies that are inaccessible to sophisticated literature and painting."[97] In this regard, later in the text, they explicitly acknowledge audience agency: "Even under the regime of the industry, the public has not become a mere machine recording facts and figures; behind the shell of conventionalized behavior patterns, resistance and spontaneity still survive."[98] Audience energy can be further harnessed in part with a musical score worthy of the visual scene: the narrative and visual shock may be critically reinforced acoustically, rather than smoothed over or made predictable, by musical cliché made affirmative.[99]

They equate the secret of all then-current film music with "the roar of MGM's lion": the music serves the function of the fanfare and sets the

96. CF, p. 75. See also Gorbman, *Unheard Melodies*, pp. 39–40; Rosen, "Adorno and Film Music," pp. 169–70; and Levin, "Acoustic Dimension," pp. 60–64. Levin points to the spatiality of musical sound, arguing that it provides a corporeality—even when recorded, as opposed to live performance—that cannot be achieved in the two dimensions of the screen image. Adorno and Eisler, CF, p. 75, insist that the advent of talkies did not erase this situation: the characters, now voiced, remain two-dimensional effigies, still lacking the depth that the spatially powerful acoustics of music can provide.

97. CF, p. 36.

98. CF, pp. 120–21.

99. Ibid., p. 43, Adorno and Eisler insist, however, that the techniques of new music cannot automatically be applied to produce this result: "For instance, certain novices might be ready to exhaust the listener with completely absurd twelve-tone compositions which seem advanced, whereas their sham radicalism would only weaken the effect of the motion picture." See also Rosen, "Adorno and Film Music," pp. 165–67.

tone of enthusiasm solicited from the audience. "Its action is advertising, and nothing else. It points with unswerving agreement to everything that happens on the screen, and creates the illusion that the effect that is to be achieved by the whole picture has already been achieved."[100] Among the techniques conventionally employed to this end is that of synchronizing image, narrative, and action to the score—Adorno and Eisler notably critique Sergei Eisenstein on this point.[101] They do not, conversely, advocate a lack of relation between the two. Instead they critique the underlying attitude that music serve as handmaiden to the affirmative indexicality of the screen image. Thus the image-score relation needs to act in a unified accord to critique the socio-cultural here and now, and against the "natural" tendencies of the visual medium itself. The technique they advocate, simply put, is montage—between image and score. Adorno and Eisler recommend exploiting the gap between the two, a kind of visual-acoustical back-and-forth that acknowledges, rather than attempts to cover up, the difference. What they seek to accomplish is a denaturalizing of the experience of viewership. Instead of music's serving as an over-determinate to the suturing proclivities of film in relation to the viewer, it should draw attention to the reality gap itself. The music, in other words, ought to defamiliarize, distance, or estrange the viewer—a bit of the Russian formalist Shklovsky and a bit of Brecht, as it were.[102] Here is how they put it: "Roughly speaking, all music, including the most 'objective' and nonexpressive, belongs primarily to the sphere of subjective inwardness, whereas even the most spiritualized painting is heavily burdened with unresolved objectivity. Motion-picture music, being at the mercy of this relationship, should attempt to make it productive, rather than to negate it in confused identifications."[103]

Good film music, they suggest, is marked by sensuousness, as opposed to transcendence and inwardness. Technically, film music should favor movement and color over formal development, which is inappropriate to film. Film music should sparkle and glisten [*sollte aufblitzen und funkeln*], since "sparkling variation and coloristic richness are also most readily compatible with technification."[104] They recommend a detailed planning of the

100. Ibid., p. 60.

101. Ibid., pp. 65–68.

102. See Gorbman, "Hanns Eisler in Hollywood," p. 276; Ben Brewster, "From Shklovsky to Brecht: A Reply," *Screen* 15 no. 2 (Summer 1974), 82–102; and Rosen, "Adorno and Film Music," pp. 171–74.

103. CF, p. 71.

104. Ibid., p. 133.

score in relation to the film, no surprise; what is surrendered for the sake of planning is, as Philip Rosen notes, style as such—but not spontaneity.[105] These effects are specifically geared toward the common brevity of any given scene, and hence the necessity for immediate effect as opposed to a slow unfolding, which is not possible (hence, the fundamental inappropriateness of such film music that repeats compositional principles and procedures from autonomous instrumental music). They conclude with the insight that defines the book's thesis: "By displaying a tendency to vanish as soon as it appears, motion-picture music renounces its claim that it is *there*, which is today its cardinal sin."[106]

The subject of "MUSIC IN THE BACKGROUND" (1934; pp. 506–10), a brief and extraordinary essay, is the everyday, utterly ordinary—and clichéd—live entertainment music of '30s cafés and pubs.[107] The aphoristic text provides an apt conclusion to Adorno's take on musical life under the pervasive conditions of mass culture. His concern, in essence, is musical ruins, whose sounds he pursues with both determination and sadness.

He opens the essay with a series of images of music now silenced in the administration and bustle of modern life. If one sings aloud on the street there's the risk of being arrested as a disturber of the peace; if one hums while in the car, the very lack of attention to the task of (hectic) driving may produce an accident. In short: "If you are looking for music, you have to step outside the space of immediate life, because it no longer is one, and find the lost immediacy where it costs the price of admission, at the opera, at a concert" (p. 506). Modern life, that is, is unmusical, and the only way

105. Ibid., pp. 79–83. Rosen, "Adorno and Film Music," p. 180, herein the utopian moment: "The musical expression of . . . [an aesthetic subject] would in fact be the achievement of a reconciliation of freedom and necessity, of subject and object, which Adorno had previously found accomplished only temporarily by Beethoven."

106. CF, p. 133, original emphasis. See also pp. 122–23, for an expanded restatement of this thesis. Gorbman, *Unheard Melodies*, p. 109, points out that the practical compositional advice offered by Adorno and Eisler is "precisely what Hollywood composers suggest: compose in short and flexible phrases to accommodate to the images, and so forth." Her ultimate assessment of the book is noteworthy, p. 108: "*Composing for the Films* is a remarkable work on the ideological situation of standard film music, written a quarter century in advance of mainstream film theory's parallel concerns with the cinematic apparatus."

107. See, on this general subject, Olle Edström, "'Vi skall gå på restaurang och höra musik': Om reception av restaurangmusik och annan 'mellanmusik'" ["'We Shall Go to a Restaurant and Listen to Musik': About Reception of Music Played in Restaurants and Other 'Middle Music'"], *Svensk Tidskrift för Musikforskning* (1989), pp. 77–112.

to recoup the loss is to see that life re-staged, on historical display, and in the elevated fashion of high art. The exceptions only serve to prove the rule.[108] Here Adorno takes an unexpected turn to the extent that he identifies places where ordinary musical life holds on and which he clearly valorizes: the restaurant and the bar. Here music still "belongs; it may have been shooed off the street, but not to the distant reaches of formalized art" (p. 507). It lives in the background—you don't have to bother listening—but it maintains a presence nonetheless as accompaniment to conversation. The crowd does not constitute an audience; it treats the music simply as "an objective event." And yet the music does something; music and people are "caught up and bound together" (p. 507).

Adorno hears in live-performance café music the remnant of a musical life, without the self-consciousness of formal art or, for that matter, the administered goods variously distributed through the reach of the Culture Industry. Well, not quite. Musically, there's nothing original, just pared down arrangements of stuff likely first intended for an orchestra. As he explains, it's not much, but it's something. "The café arranges bouquets of dead flowers." What we will hear, should we choose to listen to the background, are acoustic ruins, yet ruins awakened to "new, ghostly life" (pp. 508–09). The music-in-ruins "lights up" those who hear it, even though its glow is "netherworldly." When café music falls silent, its loss is instantly apparent: "it sounds as if a miserly waiter is turning off a couple of electric bulbs." The sad state of the late-modern transformation of Enlightenment ideals is allegorized as paltry electric illumination: "Background music is an acoustic light source" (p. 508). It shines, however dimly, on what might have been.

108. In ISM, p. 129, written nearly three decades after this essay, Adorno pointed out that nowadays music is no longer exceptional but instead is ubiquitous and a "part of everyday life," principally the result of mass cultural production. Nonetheless, he posits that music of substance retains its exceptional character.

What National Socialism
Has Done to the Arts

By talking about the legacy of National Socialism within the artistic life of Europe I do not intend to dwell on Nazi terror, or the annihilation of many artists and intellectuals in the conquered countries, nor on the administrative measures by which the Nazi regime has put every cultural activity into the service of the totalitarian setup. What we are concerned with is the after-effect of the Fascist era and its significance for America rather than the actions and crimes of the regime itself. Our attention is focused on those traces of the Nazi spirit which threaten to survive or to resurrect at a given opportunity. In order to understand these traces we have to cope with what might be called the spirit of Fascism, the structural changes which it has brought about throughout European society rather than with administrative measures which may be remedied. It should be said, however, that there is one aspect in crude reality which is beyond repair, namely the mass murder of intellectuals perpetrated by the Nazis, particularly in such countries as Poland. We do not yet know the extent to which intellectual and artistic groups in great parts of Europe have been liquidated. We do know, however, that the systematic drive carried out by the regime against all potential centers of intellectual resistance will leave its imprint upon the future. It is likely to result in a vacuum the impact of which on the whole cultural life cannot be foreseen. Though I am fully conscious, however, that, what National Socialism has done to art, is above all murder, I shall discuss today some less obvious aspects of the situation which seem to me of particular relevance, since they did not result from arbitrary actions of political gangsters but rather from developmental tendencies which are so deep-lying, that we may say that they have not only been brought about by National Socialism but are among its causes as well. In order not to lose ourselves in too vast a field I shall concentrate

373

on the fate of *music* which I had an opportunity to study most closely. I wish to emphasize, however, that music serves here merely as an example for much broader sociological aspects, not as an end in itself.

The idea that there are certain cultural trends which both belong to the presuppositions and to the effects of Fascism dictates the topics with which I have to deal. I shall first say something about the climate for Fascism in Germany as it showed itself throughout musical life in pre-Hitler days and I then shall point to some of the more obstinate effects of Hitlerism throughout the musical sphere. I am under the impression that we shall be able to understand the structural relationship between Fascism and culture the better the more deeply we are aware of the cultural roots of some of the most terrifying anti-cultural phenomena of our time. It would be naïve to assume that the indisputable destruction of German musical culture has been brought about solely by a kind of political invasion from the outside, by mere force and violence. A severe crisis, economic no less than spiritual, prevailed before Hitler seized power. Hitler was, in music as well as in innumerable other aspects, merely the final executor of tendencies that had developed within the womb of German society.

However, one can very well differentiate between artistic and philosophical phenomena which tend toward Fascism by themselves, and others which were claimed by the Nazis more or less arbitrarily, mainly on account of their prestige value. Moreover, one can clearly distinguish between names to which the Nazis paid only lip service, such as Goethe and Beethoven, and others who represent ideas which are the lifeblood of the Fascist movement, mostly comparatively obscure figures such as Ernst Moritz Arndt or Paul de la Garde.[1]

Nobody can escape the awareness of the deep interconnection between Richard Wagner and German supra-nationalism in its most destructive form. It may be good to recollect that there is an immediate link between him and official Nazi ideology. Wagner's standard-bearer and son-in-law, the Germanized Englishman Houston Stewart Chamberlain, was one of the first writers who combined aggressive pan-Germanism, racism, the belief in the absolute superiority of German culture—or you may rather say of German Kultur—and militant anti-Semitism. The Nazi bogus philosopher Alfred Rosenberg has confessedly borrowed most of his theses from Chamberlain's *Grundlagen des 19. Jahrhunderts*. The book had the blessing of the Bayreuth circle, and Chamberlain, as an old man, welcomed enthusiastically the National Socialist movement.[2]

The pedigree Wagner-Chamberlain-Rosenberg is more than just historical accident. Not only can we discover many elements of rubber-stamped Nazi doctrine in Wagner's theoretical writings, but we can also spot them, which is more important, throughout Wagner's works in more or less flimsy allegorical disguise. The whole plot of Wagner's *Ring* suggests some kind of a gigantic Nazi frame-up, with Siegfried as an innocent, lovable Teutonic hero who, just by chance, conquers the world and ultimately falls victim to the Jewish conspiracy of the dark dwarfs and those who trust their counsel.

Incidentally, it is ironical enough and not without deeper significance that even the downfall of Hitler is presaged in this metaphysical master plan. We may well say that the whole pan-German movement, consummated by Nazis, bore within itself an inkling of the doom it spelled, not only upon its foes but also upon itself. This inkling is not of an entirely irrational nature, but is tinged with an insight, however inarticulate it may have been, into the ultimate hopelessness of German imperialism within the given constellations of world power politics. No clear-sighted observer of the early days of Nazism in Germany can have failed to notice an element of uncertainty and even despair underneath the drunkenness of victories celebrated before they were won. It is quite possible that the ruthlessness and cruelty of the Nazi regime, so utterly ununderstandable to other nations is partly determined by this deep sense of futility of the whole adventure. The Hitlerian statement that if his regime should ever collapse he would slam the door so that the whole world could hear it, is indicative of something much farther reaching than it seems to express. When we speak of the destructiveness of the German mind we have to understand this not merely psychologically but also politically, in terms of the desperate character of the whole gamble. The Germans permanently anticipated, as it were, the revenge for their own downfall. This may suffice as an example for speculations on the innermost secrets of Nazi mentality and Nazi reality as suggested by the Wagnerian work.

A minute musical analysis of Wagner's works yields insight into the repressive, compulsory, blind and ultimately anti-individual way of his composing in a very concrete and tangible sense. His music itself speaks the language of Fascism, quite apart from plots and bombastic words.

Yet, we should not overrate the importance of Wagner as a formative element of Fascism. Apart from the fact that his work contains forces entirely antagonistic to those which I mentioned, his actual influence in Germany was definitely on the decline. True, he helped to prepare the climate for Fascism with the generation of our parents. The imagery of his works doubtlessly soaked through innumerable channels into the unconscious of most Germans. However, his work itself had largely ceased to be a living force. This holds for the artists as well as for the public. Since about 1910, at the latest, there started a revolt of all composers of any independence and talent against Wagnerism and all it entailed. One may easily regard anti-Wagnerism as the common denominator of all the different schools that have sprung into existence since the beginning of this century. Concomitantly, Wagnerian philosophy lost its hold on the intellectuals. But what happened with the audience at large is perhaps even more significant. The lack of knowledge of the Wagnerian work among the younger generation in Germany was simply astonishing. The spiritual demands of the *Weltanschauungsmusik,* the exacting length of the *Musikdrama,* the spirit of highfalutin' symbolism so incompatible with the positivist matter-of-factness spreading over the youth of the whole world—all this helped to bring Wagner into almost complete oblivion. His old Germans became associated with the idea of the "beaver" game. I can give you an example.

In the winter term of 1932–33, immediately before Hitler took over, I had to conduct at Frankfurt University a seminar on Hanslick's treatise *On the Musically Beautiful*[3]—which is essentially a defense of musical formalism against the doctrine of Wagner and the programmatic school. Although the seminar was focused on philosophical issues, the participants, about thirty, were mostly musicologists. In the first meeting I asked who was capable of writing the Siegfried motif, the most famous of all Wagnerian *leitmotifs,* on the blackboard. Nobody was.

This little event is symptomatic not only of the oblivion into which Wagner had fallen but of a much broader issue, which has something to do with the rise of Hitlerism and will by no means have been settled by his defeat. You may call it the decultivation of the German middle classes, demonstrated in the field of music but noticeable in every aspect of German life.

During the nineteenth century there existed certain groups which, without being professional musicians or artists, were in real contact with music and the arts, were moved by the ideas expressed by music, and were capable of a subtle and discriminating understanding. The attitude of writers such as Schopenhauer, Kierkegaard or Nietzsche toward music was not understandable without the existence of such a nucleus of musically truly cultured non-musicians. This nucleus has disappeared. Musical knowledge and understanding has become the privilege of experts and professionals.

I cannot go into the reasons for this process which is deeply connected with certain changes undergone by the whole German middle class. On the basis of their own material interests, they became more and more alienated from the same culture which their fathers and grandfathers had brought about. It is this decultivation, this loss of any life relationship with what is supposed to be the tradition of great German culture, upheld merely as an empty claim that has contributed more to the Fascist climate than the allegiance to even so nationalistic and chauvinistic an author as Richard Wagner.

We should be quite clear with regard to what we mean by this process of decultivation. It is not simply lack of knowledge or erudition, although the processes in question tend also to lower all acquaintance with the manifestations of culture in a most elementary sense. Nor is it the ever-increasing aloofness of artistic products from the empirical life of society, a process that can be dated back to the time when art lost its locus within the order of the all-embracing Catholic Church. I refer to something much more specific. It may be called the neutralization of culture in general and of the arts in particular.

Since philosophy in the broadest sense, the general consciousness of the people, has been brought more and more under the sway of science and technical civilization, the relationship between art and truth has been profoundly affected. There is no longer any unifying common focus between knowledge or science on the one hand and art on the other, as there is no common focus between science and philosophy or religion. Dr. Horkheimer has pointed this out in his lecture.[4] What has been called the "idea" of arts during the age of great speculative philosophy has come to be regarded as an obsolescent metaphysical prejudice. Instead of being a decisive means to express fundamentals about human existence and human society, art has assumed the function of a realm of consumer goods among others, measured only according to what people "can get out of it," the amount of gratification or pleasure it provides them with or, to a certain extent, its historical or educational value. This does not merely pertain to the products of today's cultural industry which are conceived and produced in terms of consumer goods anyway, but this generally also affects the present attitude toward traditional works. They are, and were long before the rise of Fascism, in a certain way "on exhibition," things to look at, maybe to admire, maybe to enjoy, perhaps even emotional stimuli, but they became within the general consciousness of the consuming audiences, more or less deprived of any intrinsic and compelling meaning of their own.

This has sucked their life blood away even if their façade was still intact in German opera houses, concert halls and art galleries. Their own essence was gradually lost, and they were experienced in terms of the want of entertainment which they had satisfied only incidentally. While the public apparently became their master who has the choice among the infinite variety of cultural goods, the public actually was the victim of this whole process since the works became mute to the listener and lost any deeper hold on his experience, his development and his philosophy. Ultimately consumption of the art became a mere appendage to the business interests of those who were in command of the market.

We can, therefore, not blame the masses for the process of decultivation, the broadest pattern of which I have tried to indicate. The loss of knowledge and interest in the products of art which may ultimately lead to a completely barbarian severance between serious artistic production and universal tastes is not a matter of degeneration or bad will but is the almost unavoidable consequence of the relegation of art into the realm of pure embellishment brought about by the technological development itself.

This process, however, does not only imply a crisis of the general relationship between arts and audience and concomitantly of art itself, which is condemned to an ever more threatening isolation, but it also has much more immediate social consequences. For the idea of compelling and objective truth, however differentiated its artistic and philosophical expression might have been, is inseparably bound up with the idea of humanism. German humanism was the most substantial counter-tendency against violent nationalism. This holds good for music above all. One may say that the cultural impact of music in Germany was the equivalent of the humanistic tradition in great French literature.

Humanistic philosophy permeates Beethoven's whole work and determines even the most subtle details of his musicianship. The lack of experience of this humanistic spirit—and here I mean experience in a deeper sense than the listening over the air to some standard performance of a standard work—reflects, viewed in broad social terms, a vacuum ready to absorb the arbitrarily superimposed doctrines of totalitarianism. The German boy of our age who has no longer heard, as his father might have, the *Kreutzer* Sonata played by friends of his parents, and who never listened passionately and surreptitiously when he was supposed to go to bed, does not merely miss a piece of information or something which might be recognized as being educational. The fact that he has never been swept away emotionally by the tragic forces of this music bereaves him somehow of the very life phenomenon of the humane. It is this lack of experience of the imagery of real art, partly substituted and parodied by the ready-made stereotypes of the amusement industry, which is at least one of the formative elements of that cynicism that has finally transformed the Germans, Beethoven's own people, into Hitler's own people.

This is not to say that musical culture in Germany simply died away.

It survived within some artists, and even during the first years of Hitlerism the average level of performance was often astonishingly high. But musical culture became under Hitler what it had started to become long before, a museum piece of an export article, somewhat reminiscent of the cultural function of the renaissance architecture in today's Italy. The tie between the idea of humanism, of music as an art, and the actual outward and inward life of the people, was definitely broken.

This is the most essential characteristic of the musical climate for Fascism in pre-Hitler Germany. It is certain to increase, not only in Germany, dangerously with the impoverishment of the European continent after the present war.

I wish to emphasize that the process in question does not merely engulf the attitude of the masses toward art, but artistic production per se and its inherent values. If we take a quick glance at the most successful German post-Wagnerian composer—as a matter of fact the only one whose fame is internationally established—Richard Strauss, there is clear evidence that the link with German humanism, in the sense I have discussed it right now, has ceased to exist. The fact that Richard Strauss at one time attempted to translate a philosophical work, Nietzsche's *Zarathustra*, into program music, is no proof to the contrary. One may rather say that philosophy, as well as religion or as the *l'art pour l'art* doctrine of symbolism, is for sale in Strauss's music, and that the very way it is treated as a subject matter destroys it as the true life basis of the works which so glibly deal with all kinds of philosophical ideals and values. Everything becomes a cultural good to be looked at, to be bought, to be enjoyed as a stimulus for the nerves of the big but tired businessman. This holds for the whole range of Strauss's *œuvre:* the Archaic Greece of *Elektra* and the smart pervertedness of *Salome,* the second-hand Goethe edition of the *Frau ohne Schatten,* and the rococo of the *Rosenkavalier* which proved to be so convenient for the taste of the German industrial upper class who got out of this work a mirrored reflection which made them look as if they were a legitimate aristocracy.

What remains, apart from such stimuli made to order of the quickly changing tastes of those German layers with whom Strauss identified himself, is a kind of cult of the *élan vital,* which has become, in the *Schwung* [swing, energy] of this music, almost synonymous with the spirit of success, recklessness and expansionism fitting only too well with imperialist Germany from Emperor Wilhelm to Hitler. If complete cynicism and relativism are among the foremost characteristics of Fascism, these characteristics come clearly to the fore in an author who is apparently so faithful a child of the liberal era as Richard Strauss. To be sure, his managerial broad-mindedness is quite irreconcilable with the narrow and petty bourgeois fanaticism of the Nazi movement. Yet he only put the seal under the secret text of his life-work when he grudgingly compromised with the Nazi government.

It is this spirit of pseudo-hedonistic complacency and shallow showmanship—in spite of all the virtuosity of the composer—against which everything rebelled that was productive and responsible in German musicianship. But it is also this very rebellion by which the great music which Germany has produced during this century, and of which the life-work of Arnold Schoenberg is representative, became definitely and radically antagonistic to the audience and to the whole sphere of commercialized musical life, of the official German *Musikleben.* It has often been alleged, and also repeated in this country, that it was a kind of guilt or an expression of snobbishness, of the ivory tower idea, that the real musical *avantgarde* in Germany lost more and more its touch with the audience. The work of Schoenberg, Berg, and Webern never became familiar to the non-musicians to any extent comparable with Wagner or even Strauss.

In a deeper sense, however, the *avantgarde* represented the true societal interests against blindness, spite and conventionalism of the actual audience. The musical discord, which became the symbol of so-called *Kulturbolschewismus,* and which is the conspicuous identification mark of the musical *avantgarde,* the supposed spirit of negativism and destruction, kept faith to [sic] Beethoven's humanism by expressing in an undiluted way the sufferings, the anguish, the fear, under which we live today long before the political crisis arose, instead of covering it up by idle comfort. It thus has maintained the link between music and philosophical truth. This does not only refer to the expressive sincerity of artists such as Schoenberg, but also to their purely musical qualities, their severe and undisguised construction shunning all ornamentation, embellishment, everything which is not strictly necessary. We know today how deeply the often denounced subjectivism of the so-called atonal *avantgarde* was bound up from the beginning with functionalism, with those tendencies within art which try to regain its real dignity by purifying it from all the remnants of romanticism which today are nothing but empty pretenses.

This is perhaps the appropriate moment to illustrate by a very specific example the danger of a survival of the Nazi spirit after its defeat. I mentioned before the idea of *Kulturbolschewismus* which served as a means to denounce every artistic impulse which threatened to shatter the conventional belief in the good and natural order of things. Today we find the heritage of this denunciatory notion among some of the sincerest foes of the Hitlerian system. The world has become so ugly and terrifying, so runs the argument, that art should no longer dwell upon distorted forms, discords and everything branded as being destructive, but should return to the realm of beauty and harmony. The world of destruction, terror and sadism is the world of Hitler. And art should show its opposition to it by going back to its traditional ideals.

The amazing similarity of such enunciations with those of the jailers would not be a counter-argument in itself, but it is highly indicative of the perseverance of the Nazi frame of mind, a perseverance which is not merely due to the minds of the intellectuals but to the situation as such. What is wrong about the argument is not that it sounds Hitlerian, but that it is infantile and expresses a general reversion of thinking which goes infinitely beyond the sphere of the arts—and hatred of thinking, hostility against the development of independent thought is what makes for Fascism.

The infantile twist is the forthright identification of ugly and beautiful in art with ugly and beautiful in reality, an identification in the style of the Hays Office which regards every unpolished villain on the screen as an encouragement of robbery on the street.[5] Thinking is endangered of losing the power of discriminating between imagery and reality. Goethe, who is supposed to have been a classicist, as well as Hegel, the conservative, knew that speaking out the negative, facing catastrophe and calling it by its name, has something wholesome and helpful in itself which could never be achieved by the pretense of a harmony borrowed from the surface phenomena and leaving the essence untouched.

It is just this taboo of expressing the essence, the depth of things, this compulsion of keeping to the visible, the fact, the datum and accepting it unquestioningly which has survived as one of the most sinister cultural heritages of the Fascist era, and there is real danger of a kind of pink pseudo-realism sweeping the world after this war, which may be more efficient but which is certainly not fundamentally superior to the art exhibitions commandeered by the Nazis.

Art should put against those restorative tendencies, even if they are clothed in terms of Parisian neo-classicism, the word of an Anglo-Saxon philosopher who certainly cannot be blamed for *Kulturbolschewismus*, namely Francis Bradley: "If everything is bad, it may be good to know the worst."[6]

Simultaneously however, we should not underrate the issue of aloofness and non-conformity of music, and of arts in general, with regard to its political importance. For this aloofness did not only keep it away from the market but also created a kind of resentment which belongs to the most significant phenomena of the German pre-Fascist cultural climate and which has its strong counterpart in anti-intellectualism and anti-highbrowism all over the world.

This resentment as well as the musical decultivation of the German middle classes resulted in certain ill-defined collectivistic tendencies of the pre-Fascist era. They found their quasi-positive expression in the so-called musical folk and youth movement. During the Third Reich, this movement came into a certain antagonism with the Party and seems to have been abolished or absorbed by the Hitler Youth. Nevertheless, there is no doubt that this movement had a strong affinity to the spirit of Nazism. No need to stress such obvious aspects as the connection between this musical collectivism and the Nazi folk ideology. But there are less obvious features to which I should like to draw your attention.

There is a strong repressive trend throughout this musical collectivism, a hatred against the individual, the supposedly refined and sophisticated. This hatred is an expression of envy of those whose individuality could not truly develop, rather than a desire for a true solidarity of men which would pre-suppose those very individual qualities which are taboo to the agitators of musical collectivism. There is, moreover, the wish for simplicity at any price, the contempt of the métier, the unwillingness to learn anything that requires persistent intellectual efforts—a kind of glorification of the supposedly plain, average man which may be transformed into a weapon against anyone and anything that does not conform to his standards.

There is, above all, the display of an aggressive spirit of community as an end in itself, played up artificially so as not to allow any questioning of its real meaning. The idea of collectivity is made a fetish, glorified as such, and only loosely connected with concrete social contents which may easily be changed with every turn of *Realpolitik.* This last element is perhaps the most important one. It bears witness to the calculated, synthetic nature of this supposed folk music. The more it pretends to be the expression of "we the people," the more certain we may be that it is actually dictated by very particularistic clique interests, intolerant, aggressive and greedy for power.

I have so far discussed underlying tendencies of German culture as manifested in the field of music which prepared the climate for Fascism or rather were indicative of the same social forces which ultimately made for political Fascism too. I dwelt on these aspects because we have reason to believe that it is they which are likely to persist, though in many ways modified, after Hitler's defeat. As far as the actual musical situation under Hitler is concerned, I confine myself to some brief remarks.

It would be erroneous to assume that there ever sprung into life a specific musical Nazi culture. What was profoundly changed by the system was the function of music which now openly became a means to an end, a propagandistic device or an ideological export article among many others. However, any attempts to create a music, intrinsically National Socialist by order, were limited to the most fanatic groups of the Nazi movement and never got hold of any responsible artist, nor of the bulk of the population, just as official Nazi poetry never became really popular.

As to the production of the younger generation of more or less fervent believers in the Nazi ideology a number of new names appeared, but what they actually achieved largely amounted to a feeble and diluted imitation of some of the better known composers of the Weimar era, particularly of those collectivist composers who had exercised a certain appeal to larger audiences, such as Hindemith or Kurt Weill. The latter's Jewish descent was no obstacle to one of the more successful Nazi opera composers, Mr. Wagner-Régeny, who copied Weill's style with all its mannerisms almost entirely.[7]

The most important characteristic of musical life under Hitler seems to me a complete stagnation, a "freezing" of all musical styles of composing and performing and of all standards of criticism, comparable to the freezing of wages under Hitler. Throughout cultural life the Nazis developed a kind of double-edged policy. On the one hand they raged against modernism and *Kulturbolschewismus;* on the other hand they disavowed what they themselves called fellow travellers, *Mitläufer,* that is to say those artists who tried to coordinate themselves quickly to the catchwords of the Nazi ideology without enjoying the privilege of being Party old-timers. Thus the compliant musicians and, above all, the composers, were left somewhat confused. Musical stagnation as well as that of art as a whole did not remain unnoticed by the more intelligent Nazis, and even Herr Rosenberg, who generally had to take an attitude of official optimism, once suggested the idea that there was no time for great artistic production today and that the energies formerly invested in the arts were now properly absorbed by technical and military ventures. This amounts to a forthright admission of artistic bankruptcy. Subsequently, the restrictions put upon composing were somewhat lifted in order to raise the artistic standards. As soon, however, as the Party allowed any bolder work to make its public appearance, the official Nazi critics spoke threateningly of *Kulturbolschewismus.*

Thus an atmosphere of total insecurity was brought about, comparable to the strange amalgamation of strictly enforced laws and arbitrary illegality so characteristic of the Third Reich. It exercized a paralyzing effect. The best a German artist could hope for was escape into what has been properly called *innere Emigration*, internal emigration. Whereas German artistic tradition had evaporated and artistic pioneering had been eliminated at the surface, the Nazis failed completely in building up even a façade of a musical culture of their own. The same people who always had blamed intellectual cliques for modernism in the arts, remained themselves a clique whose folk ideas proved to be even more distant from the life of the people than the most esoteric products of expressionism and surrealism. Paradoxical as it sounds, the Germans were more willing to fight Hitler's battles than to listen to the plays and operas of his lackeys. When the war catastrophe put an end to the remnants of public German musical life, it merely executed a judgment that was silently spoken since the Hitler gang had established its dictatorship over culture.

What then are we going to expect as an aftermath of the trends which I tried to point out to you? I do not intend to dwell on the question whether economic conditions in Europe as a whole and particularly in Central Europe will allow any artistic culture or whether the apathy of the population after the war will result in their becoming entirely disinterested [sic] in the arts. I do not think that the greatest danger lies here. There is no direct correlation between material wealth and artistic production, and one might easily imagine situations where material wealth and the tremendous machinery of cultural industry may be a threat to artistic spontaneity rather than an enhancement of it. The present stage of technical civilization may call for a very ascetic art developed in the loopholes of poverty and isolation, as counter-balance against the business culture which tends to cover the whole world. Instead of dwelling on the crude economic issues, I want to finish this lecture with an attempt to briefly formulate four of the deeper-going tendencies toward a survival of the Fascist spirit in the arts.

1.   The propagandistic aspect of all the arts which has been emphasized by the Nazis and which has destroyed almost completely artistic autonomy is not likely to disappear automatically. To be sure, European art after this war will not be allowed to serve the purpose of Fascist propaganda and the freedom of artistic creation will be restored at least formally. What is likely to remain, however, is the prevailing idea that art is essentially a force of manipulation, something that is to be directed this or the other way, that has to follow a set ideological pattern. The very fact that everything that

carries with itself associations of Fascism, however faint they may be, must be eradicated, is a symptom of an almost inescapable danger of artistic control. What threatens to develop in Europe as well as in the rest of the world may be called the end of the artistic subject. The artist is no longer called upon in order to express independently his experiences, visions and ideas, but has come to understand himself as a sort of a functionary who has to fulfill a social and productive duty. It is possible that this very fact destroys the true function of the arts. Certainly, the idea of the artist blindly following his intuition without thinking in technical terms and without conscientious work on his material is a romantic notion. Every true work of art has what one might call malevolently a manipulative element about itself. But it makes all the difference whether this manipulative element remains a means of realizing the essence of the work, or whether it is put into the service of molding public opinion. As an aftermath of Fascism the latter seems to become more and more emphasized, not only because of external pressure put upon the artist but because the artists themselves nourish the illusion that, by surrendering to the calls made upon them and becoming functionaries or employees, they could escape their isolation and regain contact with broad social tendencies. But art does not fulfill its function in society by acting as a social functionary. Everything will depend on whether there will be loopholes enough left to the artists in order to dodge this ever more threatening danger. It should be added, cautiously, that the consciousness of this danger today seems to increase.

2.   The aspect of being a functionary and expressing himself according to the wants and necessities of powerful social groups and tendencies is an aspect mainly affecting the artist. There is a no less dangerous tendency with regard to the attitude of the public. The foremost cultural organization of the Nazis bore the title *"Kraft durch Freude"* ("Strength through Joy"). This barbarian name, which defines the arts, as Dr. Horkheimer says in one of his studies, in terms of massage, is significant of something which probably will be alive long after the Philistines of *Kraft durch Freude* will no longer command any official organization.[8] Music, art and literature tend to become recreational activities, the means to help the tired masses to gain new strength and to get away from the drudgery of their practical existence. Fascism has taken up consciously this trend which automatically came to the fore all over the world long ago. The misery of the European post-war world as well as the vacuum left after the collapse of Nazi ideology is likely to strengthen rather than to weaken this tendency. What I

envisage here is that the arts in Europe, as far as they have contact with the broad masses, above all moving pictures, radio and popular literature, will indulge in a kind of streamlining in order to please the customer, a sort of pseudo-Americanization with poorer means and less efficiency, which even before Hitler could be noticed in European capitals such as Berlin and, to a certain extent, also Paris. The idea of being up-to-date by giving the people what they are supposed to want, or rather what amounts to the line of least resistance against big business, is likely to triumph everywhere.

3.   The trend toward collectivism for its own sake so heavily emphasized by the Nazis is likewise apt to survive within their foes. The more sacrifices the resistance forces and underground movements had to make, the more likely there are to arise demands for popular appealing art, intrinsically incompatible with the developmental phase reached by autonomous art itself. We must protect ourselves against the repressive implications of such a call for subordination and obedience of the individual to the demands of the majority and the so-called plain people, if we should not experience a revival of Nazi tendencies under an entirely different political label.

4.   There is a last danger apparently contradicting the ones I so far pointed out, but nevertheless threatening enough. I may call it the danger of the transformation of European culture into a kind of National Park, a realm tolerated and even admired, but mainly in terms of its quaintness, its being different from the general standards of technological civilization, but by this very act of tolerance being subject to its norms. Whereas we have to fear on the one side the danger of standardization and manipulation of European culture, we have to be equally on our guard against the danger of its artificial preservation, its being put on exhibition, its being enjoyed for the sake of its uniqueness rather than for any inherent qualities. What happened to certain artists of the Boulevard Montparnasse, whose colorful appearance made them lovely to look at, but at the same time put upon them the stigma of being fools, may happen to European culture as a whole. It may share the fate of old European style furniture or of European titles.

All these dangers can be met only by a strength of resistance surpassing anything non-conformist artists ever had to muster before. They must guard themselves against the leveling trend of the machinery as well as against adaptation to the market by outdated, and hence fashionable provincialism, and even by spectacular non-adaptation. Who really wants to be an artist today should neither be a commercial designer, in the broadest sense, nor a stubborn, blind specialist. His relationship to technological civilization is utterly complicated. While resisting its standardizing impact, he cannot dodge the deep and shocking experiences brought about by this civilization upon every living being. He must be in complete command of the most advanced means of artistic construction. He thus has to be both an exponent and a sworn enemy of the prevailing historical tendency. There is no recipe how to achieve this. The only thing to stick to are those inherent qualities of the work itself mentioned before. To the artist, they appear mainly in terms of inner consistency, the uncompromising realization of basic intentions. Faithful pursuit of such "realization" is not mere formalism. It works as the only means of maintaining, or regaining, that relationship between essential philosophical truth and art, or science, the abolition of which is at the hub of the Fascist spirit—provided the basic intention itself is true in terms of the underlying essential. An artist who still deserves the name should proclaim nothing, not even humanism. He should not yield to any pressure of the ever more overwhelming social organizations of our time but should express, in full command of meaning and potentialities of today's processes of rationalization, that human existence led under its command is not a human one. The humane survives today only where it is ready to challenge, by its very appearance and its determined irreconcilability, the dictate of the present man-made but merciless world.

(1945; GS, vol. 20.2, pp. 413–29)

NOTES BY RICHARD LEPPERT

Adorno wrote this text in English. He sometimes unnecessarily italicized words ("*Third Reich*" and "*Hitler Youth*"); I've rendered them in roman type. In a few instances, I have added commas for clarity and to conform to standard English usage. Finally, I have preferred to retain a few very specific mistakes ("disinterested," where "uninterested" is correct) and word choices that differ from what Adorno later came to prefer ("cultural industry" rather than "culture industry").

1. Ernst Moritz Arndt (1769–1860), poet, pamphleteer, and author of *Geist der Zeit* (4 vols., 1806–1818), one of several lengthy tracts against Napoleon and French domination of Germany. See Alfred George Pundt, *Arndt and the Nationalist Awakening in Germany* (New York: Columbia University Press, 1935); and Karl Heinz Schäfer, *Ernst Moritz Arndt als politischer Publizist: Studien zur Publizistik* (Bonn: L. Röhrscheid, 1974). Paul Anton de Lagarde (1827–1891), from 1869 professor of oriental languages at Göttingen, was both a nationalist and an anti-Semite; like Arndt, he was an advocate of Pan-Germanism. (The ideas of the pan-German movement, following its formal organization in the late nineteenth cen-

tury, had a considerable impact on Hitler.) See the lengthy entry in *Neue Deutsche Biographie*, ed. Hans Körner et al. (Berlin: Duncker and Humblot, 1982), vol. 30, pp. 409–12.

2. British-born Houston Stewart Chamberlain (1855–1927), is best known for his *Die Grundlagen des 19. Jahrhunderts* (2 vols.; 1911), a distinctly pro-Aryan and anti-Semitic tract that promoted racial purity; the book gained the attention and admiration of Adolf Hitler. The book is available in English: *Foundations of the Nineteenth Century,* trans. John Lees, 2 vols. (New York: H. Fertig, 1977). Chamberian published a worshipful biography of Richard Wagner in 1895, among other works on the composer; in 1907 he settled in Bayreuth and married Wagner's only daughter, Eva. See Geoffrey G. Field, *Evangelist of Race: The Germanic Vision of Houston Stewart Chamberlain* (New York: Columbia University Press, 1981); and Joachim Köhler, *Wagner's Hitler: The Prophet and His Disciple,* trans. Ronald Taylor (Cambridge: Polity, 2000), especially pp. 115–34, 168–75, for the connections between Cosima Wagner and Chamberlain's particular promotion of the composer, and Hitler. Köhler provides a detailed account of a meeting at Bayreuth in 1923 between Hitler and the old and ill Chamberlain, together with Eva Wagner who acted as her husband's interpreter by reading the movement of his lips.

Adorno commented on Chamberlain in "On the Question: 'What is German?'" *CM,* p. 207: His "name and development are linked to the most disastrous aspects of modern German history, the *völkisch* and anti-Semitic. It would be rewarding to understand how the sinister political function of this Germanized Englishman came about. His correspondence with his mother-in-law, Cosima Wagner, offers the richest material for such an inquiry. Chamberlain originally was a sophisticated, delicate man, extremely sensitive to the insidiousness of commercialized culture. He was attracted to Germany in general and to Bayreuth in particular by the proclaimed rejection of commercialism there. That he became a racial demagogue is neither the fault of a natural maliciousness or even of a weakness before the paranoid, power-hungry Cosima but rather of naiveté. What Chamberlain loved in German culture in comparison with the fully developed capitalism of his homeland, he took to be absolute. In it he saw an immutable, natural constitution, not the result of nonsynchronous developments in society. This led him smoothly to those *völkisch* notions, which then had incomparably more barbaric consequences than the unartistic existence he wanted to escape." The letters between Cosima Wagner and Chamberlain are available in an edition by Paul Pretzsch, *Briefwechsel 1888–1908* (Leipzig: P. Reclam, 1934).

Alfred Rosenberg (1893–1946), prominent anti-Semite idealogue, and Nazi Party member from its earliest beginnings, was much influenced by Chamberlain's writing. He is author of *Der Mythos der 20. Jahrhunderts* (1934), translated as *The Myth of the Twentieth Century: An Evaluation of the Spiritual-Intellectual Confrontations of Our Age* (Newport Beach, CA: Noontide Press, 1993), which delineates the history of the supposed racial purity of Germans, on which basis he justifies German domination of Europe. He edited the rabidly anti-Semitic Munich newspaper *Völkischer Beobachter* bought by the Nazi Party in 1923—the paper later opened editorial offices in Berlin and Vienna. During the war years Rosenberg was put in charge of bringing artwork war booty to Germany from captured territories. He was sentenced as a war criminal at the Nürnberg trials and hanged. See James Whisker, *The Philosophy of Alfred Rosenberg: Origins of the National Socialist Myth* (Costa Mesa, CA: Noontide Press, 1990); and Cecil Robert, *The Myth of the Master Race: Alfred Rosenberg and Nazi Ideology* (New York: Dodd, Mead, 1972).

3. See p. 126 n. 4.

4. The title of Horkheimer's talk was "Totalitarianism and the Crisis of European Culture." The reference to there being no common focus between science and art or between science and philosophy or religion is worked out in detail in Horkheimer's *Eclipse of Reason* (1947; reprint, New York: Continuum, 1974), based on a series of lectures delivered at Columbia University in the spring of 1944, a year in advance of the conference lecture to which Adorno refers. In his preface, Horkheimer credits Adorno: "It would be difficult to say which of the ideas originated in his mind and which in my own; our philosophy is one" (p. vii).

5. The Motion Picture Producers and Distributers of America (MPPDA), popularly known as the Hays Office, was established in 1922. Will H. Hays (1879–1954), a lawyer and activist Republican, served as its first director from 1922 to 1945. The Hays Office rated films for audience suitability, an attempt by the Hollywood studios at self-policing intended to head off government interference. In 1930 he was a co-author of the famous Production Code, in effect for more than three decades, which established industry standards for what could, and could not, be shown on the screen. See Raymond Moley, *The Hays Office* (Indianapolis: Bobbs-Merrill, 1945).

6. Adorno delivered this lecture at the same time he was drafting *Minima Moralia*, whose second part (dated 1945) uses the same quotation from Bradley as the epigraph, though quoted differently (in English): "When everything is bad it must be good to know the worst." MM, p. 83. The aphorism is from F. H. Bradley, *Appearance and Reality: A Metaphysical Essay*, 9th impression (corrected) of 2nd ed. from 1897 (Oxford: Clarendon Press, 1930), p. xii, the preface to the book's first edition (1893). Here Bradley quotes several aphorisms from what he describes as his notebook. He offers two on pessimism: "Where everything is bad it must be good to know the worst" [in slight variance with Adorno's citation in MM]; and "Where all is rotten it is a man's work to cry stinking fish." Francis Herbert Bradley (1846–1924), English philosopher, was a fellow of Merton College, Oxford. Influenced by Hegel, he was a principal spokesman for philosophical idealism, and a severe critic of British empiricism, especially that of John Stuart Mill. See Richard Wollheim, *F. H. Bradley* (Harmondsworth, OK: Penguin, 1960); and Anthony Manser, ed., *The Philosophy of F. H. Bradley* (Oxford: Clarendon Press, 1984).

7. Rudolf Wagner-Régeny (1903–1969), an exact contemporary of Adorno, Romanian born, was a German composer, as well as a pianist and clavichord player. His opera *Der Günstling*, which premiered at Dresden in 1935 under the baton of Karl Böhm, was admired and promoted by members of the Nazi Party; their support helped launch the composer's career. Later operas, however, were judged not consonant with Nazi cultural politics, and Wagner-Régeny was severely criticized—and drafted into military service in 1943. Adorno writing in 1945 is notably harder on Wagner-Régeny than more recent scholars. See David Drew, "Wagner-Régeny," in *The New Grove Dictionary of Music and Musicians*, ed. Stanley Sadie (London: Macmillan, 1980), vol. 20, pp. 150–52; and a notably sympathetic essay following the composer's death, by Dieter Härtwig, "Kongruenz von Ethos und Ästhetik: Der Komponist Rudolf Wagner-Régeny," *Das Orchester* 42 nos. 7/8 (1994), pp. 2–6.

8. *Kraft durch Freude* [KdF] was established in 1933 through the German Labor Front *[Deutsche Arbeitsfront]*, which supplanted all trade unions, as an organization for mass recreation; it was a popular and successful effort to attract the working class to National Socialism; as such it was a significant propaganda tool. KdF sponsored a variety of after-work activities, including sport, theater and cabaret, and concerts, as well as tourism, both in Germany and elsewhere in Europe. Funds to support these activities came in part from the confiscation of trade union

assets, though KdF eventually grew to become a large business enterprise. KdF commissioned two cruise liners as part of its tourism, and also subsidized the development of the Volkswagon (People's Car)—though because of the war the "beetle" did not go into civilian production until after the war, during which it was solely produced as a jeep for the military. The goals of KdF were defined by Deutsche Arbeitsfront Secretary Gerhard Starcke in 1940: "We did not send our workers on vacations aboard their own ships and build them huge seaside resorts just for the fun of it. . . . We did it only so that we might bring [them] back to [their] workplaces with new strength and purpose." *The Encyclopedia of the Third Reich*, ed. Christian Zentner and Friedemann Bedürftig, trans. Amy Hackett (New York: Macmillan, 1991), vol. 2, pp. 922–24, 1005–06 (quotation, p. 924); and James Taylor and Warren Shaw, *The Third Reich Almanac* (New York: World Almanac, 1987), p. 323.

On the Social Situation of Music

1. OUTLINE, PRODUCTION

No matter where music is heard today, it sketches in the clearest possible lines the contradictions and flaws which cut through present-day society; at the same time, music is separated from this same society by the deepest of all flaws produced by this society itself. And yet, society is unable to absorb more of this music than its ruins and external remains. The role of music in the social process is exclusively that of a commodity; its value is that determined by the market. Music no longer serves direct needs nor benefits from direct application, but rather adjusts to the pressures of the exchange of abstract units. Its value—wherever such value still exists at all—is determined by use: it subordinates itself to the process of exchange. The islands of pre-capitalistic "music making"[1]—such as the nineteenth century could still tolerate—have been washed away: the techniques of radio and sound film, in the hands of powerful monopolies and in unlimited control over the total capitalistic propaganda machine, have taken possession of even the innermost cell of musical practices of domestic music making. Even in the nineteenth century the possibility of the domestic cultivation of music—like the entirety of bourgeois private life—represented only the reverse side of a social corpus, whose surface was totally determined by production through private capital. The dialectic of capitalistic development has further eliminated even this last immediacy offered by music—in itself already an illusion, for in it the balance between individual production and understanding by society was threatened. Since Wagner's *Tristan*, this balance has been totally destroyed. Through the total absorption of both musical production and consumption by the capitalistic process, the alienation of music from man has become complete.

This process involved, of course, the objectification and rationalization of music, its separation from the simple immediacy of use which had once defined it as art and granted it permanence in contrast to its definition in terms of mere ephemeral sound. At the same time, it was this process which invested music with the power of far-reaching sublimation of drives and the cogent and binding expression of humanity. Now, however, rationalized music has fallen victim to the same dangers as rationalized society, within which class interests bring rationalization to a halt as soon as it threatens to turn against class conditions themselves. This situation has now left man in a state of rationalization which—as soon as the possibility of his further dialectic development is blocked—crushes him between unresolved contradictions. The same force of reification which constituted music as art has today taken music from man and left him with only an illusion *[Schein]* thereof. This force of reification could not simply be reconverted to immediacy without returning art to the state in which it found itself before the division of labor. Music, however, insofar as it did not submit to the command of the production of commodities, was in this process robbed of its social responsibility and exiled into an hermetic space within which its contents are removed. This is the situation from which every observation upon the social position of music which hopes to avoid the deceptions which today dominate discussions of the subject must proceed. These deceptions exist for the sake of concealing the actual situation and, further, as an apology for music which has allowed itself to be intimidated economically. They are also the result of the fact that music itself, under the superior power of the music industry developed by monopoly capitalism, became conscious of its own reification and of its alienation from man. Meanwhile, music, lacking proper knowledge of the social process—a condition likewise socially produced and sustained—blamed itself and not society for this situation, thus remaining in the illusion that the isolation of music was itself an isolated matter, namely, that things could be corrected from the side of music alone with no change in society. It is now necessary to face the hard fact that the social alienation of music— that assembly of phenomena for which an overhasty and unenlightened musical reformism employs derogatory terms such as individualism, charlatanism, and technical esotericism—is itself a matter of social fact and socially produced. For this reason, the situation cannot be corrected within music, but only within society: through the change of society. The question regarding the possible dialectic contribution which music can make toward such change remains open: however, its contribution will be slight, if it— from within its own resources—endeavors only to establish an immediacy which is not only socially restraining today, but by no means reconstruct-able or even desirable, thus contributing to the disguise of the situation. The question is further to what degree music—insofar as it might inter-vene in the social process—will be in a position to intervene as *art*. Re-gardless of the answers which might be given, here and now music is able to do nothing but portray within its own structure the social antinomies which are also responsible for its own isolation. Music will be better, the more deeply it is able to express—in the antinomies of its own formal language—the exigency of the social condition and to call for change through the coded language of suffering. It is not for music to stare in helpless horror at society: it fulfills its social function more precisely when it presents social problems through its own material and according to its own formal laws—problems which music contains within itself in the in-nermost cells of its technique. The task of music as art thus enters into a parallel relationship to the task of social theory. If the immanent devel-opment of music were established as an absolute—as the mere reflection of the social process—the only result would be a sanction of the fetish character of music which is the major difficulty and most basic problem to be represented by music today. On the other hand, it is clear that music is not to be measured in terms of the existing society of which it is the product and which, at the same time, keeps music in a state of isolation. It is the prerequisite of every historical-materialistic method which hopes to be more than a mere exercise in "intellectual history" that under no conditions is music to be understood as a "spiritual" phenomenon, abstract and far-removed from actual social conditions, which can anticipate through its imagery any desire for social change independently from the empirical realization thereof. It thus becomes obvious that the relation of present-day music and society is highly problematic in all its aspects. This relation shares its aporias with social theory; at the same time, however, it shares the attitudes which this theory expresses—or ought to express—toward these aporias. In a certain sense, the *character of cognition* is to be demanded of any music which today wishes to preserve its right to exis-tence. Through its material, music must give clear form to the problems assigned it by this material which is itself never purely natural material, but rather a social and historical product; solutions offered by music in this process stand equal to theories. Social postulates are offered, the re-lationship of which to praxis might be, to be sure, extremely mediated and difficult or which, at any rate, cannot be realized without great difficulty. It is these postulates, however, which decide whether and how the entrance into social reality might be made. The short circuit: such music is incomprehensible, esoteric-private, thus reactionary, and must, therefore, be rejected: such music is constructed upon the foundation of a romantic concept of primitive musical immediacy which gives rise to the opinion that the empirical consciousness of present-day society—a consciousness promoted in unenlightened narrow-mindedness and, indeed, promoted even to the point of neurotic stupidity in the face of class domination for the purpose of the preservation of this consciousness—might be taken as the positive measure of a music no longer alienated, but rather the property of free men. Politics must not be permitted to draw abstractions from this state of consciousness which is necessarily of central concern to the social dialectic, nor is cognition to allow the definition of its boundaries by a consciousness produced by class domination and which further as the class consciousness of the proletariat extends the wounds of mutilation by means of the class mechanism. Music is under the same obligation as theory to reach out beyond the current consciousness of the masses. Theory, however, stands in a dialectic relation to praxis, upon which it makes demands and from which it also accepts demands; in the same manner, music which has achieved self-consciousness of its social function will enter into a dialectic relation to praxis. This is to be achieved not through the self-subordination of music to "use" which it could do here and now only through definition of itself as a commodity and which would grant it only an illusion of immediacy, but rather by developing within music itself—in agreement with the state of social theory—all those elements whose objective is the overcoming of class domination. This music must do even where this development takes place in social isolation, confined to the cells of music during the period of class domination. It might be possible for the most advanced compositional production of the present—solely under the pressure of the immanent development of its problems—to invalidate basic bourgeois categories such as the creative personality and expression of the soul of this personality, the world of private feelings and its transfigured inwardness, setting in their place highly rational and transparent principles of construction. Even this music, however, would remain dependent upon bourgeois production processes and could not, consequently, be viewed as "classless" or the actual music of the future, but rather as music which fulfills its dialectic cognitive function most exactly. Within present society, such music encounters a vehement resistance which surpasses the resistance against all use music and communal music [*Gebrauchs- und Gemeinschaftsmusik*],[2] no matter how literary or political its accents might be. Nonetheless, this resistance seems to indicate that the dialectic function of this music is already perceptible in praxis, even if only as a negative force, as "destruction."

From a social perspective, present-day musical activity, production and consumption can be divided drastically into that which unconditionally recognizes its commodity character and, refusing any dialectic intervention, orients itself according to the demands of the market and that which in principle does not accept the demands of the market. A somewhat different view: music of the first category—passive and undialectic—takes its place on the side of society; the second, on the side of music. The traditional distinction between "light" and "serious" music, sanctioned by bourgeois musical culture, ostensibly corresponds to this division. But only ostensibly. For a great share of supposedly "serious" music adjusts itself to the demands of the market in the same manner as the composers of light music, even if this is done under the cover of an economically untransparent "fashion" or through the calculation of the demands of the market into production. The disguise of the market function of such music through the concept of personality or simplicity or "life" serves only to transfigure it and to increase its market value indirectly. On the other hand, it is precisely "light" music—tolerated by present-day society, despised and exploited in the same way as prostitution with which it is not compared in vain—with its "skirt seductively raised," which develops certain elements portraying the satisfaction of the drive of present society, whose official claims, however, stand in conflict to such satisfaction. In a certain sense, such music thus transcends the society which it supposedly serves. In the distinction between light and serious music, the alienation of man and music is reflected only through distortion, in the same manner, namely, as this alienation is seen by the bourgeoisie. An effort is made to exempt "serious" music from an alienation shared to an equal degree by Stravinsky's *Symphony of Psalms* and the latest hit song of Robert Stolz.[3] Blame for this alienation is assigned under the label of "kitsch" only to that music which, as an exact reaction to the constellation of drives within this society, is the only music suitable to it; it is, however, this very suitability which disavows this society. For this reason, the distinction between light and serious music is to be replaced by a different distinction which views both halves of the musical globe equally from the perspective of alienation: as halves of a totality which to be sure could never be reconstructed through the addition of the two halves.

Musical *production* which in the narrower sense does not subordinate itself unconditionally to the law of the market—that is, "serious" music with the exception of the obviously quantitatively dominant music, which likewise serves the market in disguise—is that music that expresses alienation. A rather crude scheme can be established: the first type of music is that which, without consciousness of its social location or out of indifference toward it, presents and crystallizes its problems and the solutions thereto in a merely immanent manner. To a degree, it resembles the monad of Leibniz; it "represents," to be sure, not a pre-established harmony, but certainly an historically produced dissonance, namely, social antinomies. This first type, as "modern" music is the only music which offers a serious shock to the listener, is represented essentially by Arnold Schoenberg and his school. The second type includes music which recognizes the fact of alienation as its own isolation and as "individualism" and further raises this fact to the level of consciousness; it does so, however, only within itself, only in aesthetic and form-immanent terms. It thus attempts to annul this insight without respect for actual society. For the most part, it would achieve this through recourse to stylistic forms of the past, which it views as immune to alienation, without seeing that such forms cannot be reconstituted within a completely changed society and through completely changed musical material. This music can be called *objectivism,* insofar as it—without becoming involved in any social dialectic—would like to evoke the image of a non-existent "objective" society or, in terms of its intentions, of a "fellowship." In the highly capitalistic-industrial nations, *neo-classicism* is a major component of objectivism; in the underdeveloped, agrarian countries, it is *folklore.* The most effective author of objectivism who in a highly revealing manner manifests each of these major directions—one after the other, but never simultaneously—is Igor Stravinsky. The third type is a hybrid form. Hand in hand with objectivism, this composer proceeds from the cognition of alienation. At the same time, he is socially more alert than the objectivist and recognizes the solutions offered by his colleague as illusion. He denies himself the positive solution and contents himself with permitting social flaws to manifest themselves by means of a flawed invoice which defines itself as illusory with no attempt at camouflage through attempts at an aesthetic totality. In his effort, he employs the formal language belonging in part to the bourgeois musical culture of the nineteenth century, in part to present-day consumer music. These means are used to reveal the flaws which he detects. Through his destruction of aesthetic formal immanence, this type of composer transcends into the literary realm. Extensive objective correspondences between this third type and French surrealism justify speaking in this case of *surrealistic* music. Such music was developed out of

Stravinsky's middle period—above all, out of *L'Histoire du soldat*. It has been developed most consequently in the works which Kurt Weill produced together with Bert Brecht, particularly *The Three Penny Opera* and *Mahagonny*. The fourth type involves music which attempts to break through alienation from within itself, even at the expense of its immanent form. This is normally identified as "use music." However, it is precisely this typical use music—especially as it is produced on order for radio and theater—which gives evidence of such obvious dependence upon the market that it cannot enter into the present discussion. That which demands attention is rather the effort to produce "communal music"; this direction developed out of neo-classicism and is represented by Hindemith and the proletarian choral works of Hanns Eisler.

Arnold Schoenberg decried the resistance that each new work encounters as intellectualistic, destructive, abstract and esoteric, not unlike the resistance shown toward psychoanalysis. Actually, he does manifest extensive correspondences to Freud—not, to be sure, in terms of the concrete thematic content of his music, divorced from all psychological references, but rather in terms of social structure. Like Freud and Karl Kraus,[4] whose efforts toward the purification of language find a counterpart in Schoenberg's music, this composer, also from Vienna, is to be counted among the dialectic phenomena of bourgeois individualism—taking the word in its most general sense—which work in their supposedly "specialized" areas of problems without respect for a presupposed social totality. In these areas, however, they achieve solutions which suddenly change and turn unnoticed against the prerequisites of individualism; such solutions are in principle denied to a socially oriented bourgeois reformism which must pay for its insights, aimed as they are at totality but never reaching the basis thereof, with "mediating" and—consequently—camouflaging machinations. Freud, in order to arrive at objective symbols and finally at an objective dialectic of human consciousness in history, had to carry out the analysis of individual consciousness and subconsciousness. Kraus, in order to perfect the concept of socialism in the sphere of the "superstructure" for a second time, as it were, did nothing but confront bourgeois life with its own norm of correct individual behavior, thus revealing, in turn, to individuals their own norm: according to the same scheme, Schoenberg has annulled the expressive music of the private bourgeois individual, pursuing—as it were—its own consequences, and put in its place a different music, into whose music no social function falls—indeed, which even severs the last communication with the listener. However, this music leaves all other music of the age far behind in terms of immanently musical quality and dialectic clarification of its material. He thus offers such a perfected and rational total organization that it cannot possibly be compatible with the present social constitution, which then unconsciously through all its critical representatives takes up an offensive position and calls upon nature for assistance against the attack of consciousness encountered in Schoenberg. In him, for perhaps the first time in the history of music, consciousness has taken hold of the natural material of music and seized control of it. In Schoenberg, however, the breakthrough of consciousness is not idealistic: it is not to be understood as the production of music out of pure spirit. It is much rather a type of dialectic in the strictest sense. For the movement perfected by Schoenberg proceeds from questioning how this movement is situated within the material itself. The productive force which incites this movement involves the reality of a psychic drive—the drive, namely, toward undisguised and uninhibited expression of the psyche and of the unconscious per se. This is found most precisely in the works of Schoenberg's middle period, including *Erwartung, Die glückliche Hand* and the Little Piano Pieces, which place his work in direct relationship to psychoanalysis. However, this drive is confronted by an objective problem: how can material which has achieved the highest technical development—that is, the material which Schoenberg inherited from Wagner on the one hand and, on the other, from Brahms as well—subordinate itself to radical expression of the psychic? It can do this only by submitting itself to thorough change: this namely, it must surrender all alleged connections and obligations which stand in the way of freedom of movement of individual expression; these connections are the reflection of an "agreement" of bourgeois society with the psyche of the individual which is now renounced by the sufferings of the individual. These are the traditional musical symmetrical relations in that they are based upon the technique of repetition—no matter what form it might take—and—again in agreement with Karl Kraus and also in harmony with the architectural intentions of Adolf Loos[5]—that this technique further takes the form of criticism of every type of *ornamentation.* In view of the limitation of all musical elements this criticism does not restrict itself merely to musical *architecture,* the symmetry and ornamentation of which it negates; it extends equally to the harmonic correlation of tectonic symmetrical relations and *tonality,* simultaneously touched by dissonance as the vehicle of the radical principle of expression; with the decline of the tonal scheme, *counterpoint*—previously subject to chordal limitation—is emancipated and produces that form of polyphony known as "linearity." Finally, the total homogenous *sound,* supported by the substance of traditional orchestral string tutti, is attacked. Schoenberg's really central achievement—which, by the way, has never been properly appreciated from the traditional perspective of observation, is that he, from his earliest works on, for example, in the Lieder op. 6—never behaved "expressionistically," superimposing subjective intentions upon heterogenous material in an authoritarian and inconsiderate manner. Instead, every gesture with which he intervenes in the material configuration is at the same time an answer to questions directed to him by the material in the form of its own immanent problems. Every subjective-expressive achievement of Schoenberg is simultaneously the resolution of objective-material contradictions which continued to exist in the Wagnerian technique of chromatic sequence and in the diatonic technique of variation employed by Brahms as well. Schoenberg is by no means an esoteric to be reserved for a specialized and socially irrelevant history of music, but rather a figure to be projected upon the social dialectic from the perspective of his dialectic of musical material. This is justified by the fact that he—in the form of material problems which he inherited, accepted, and continued—found present in the problems of society that produced this material and in which the contradictions of this society are defined as technical problems. That Schoenberg's solutions to technical problems are socially relevant in spite of their isolation is proven by his replacement within all his works, in spite and because of his own expressive origins, of any private fortuitousness which might have been viewed quite correctly as a type of anarchic musical production with an objective principle of order which is never imposed upon the material from the exterior, but rather extracted from the material itself and brought into relationship with it by means of an historical process of rational transparence. This is the meaning of the revolution which technologically took the form of "twelve-tone composition." In the very moment in which the total musical material is subjected to the power of expression, expression itself is extinguished—as though it were animated only by the resistance of the material, itself "alienated" and alien to the subject. Subjective criticism of instances of ornamentation and repetition leads to an objective, non-expressive structure which, in place of symmetry and repetition, determines the exclusion of repetition within the cell, i.e., the use of all twelve tones of the scale before the repetition of a tone from within the scale. This same structure further prevents the "free," arbitrary, constructively unrelated insertion of any one tone into the composition. In corresponding manner, the expressively obligatory leading tone harmonic is replaced by a complementary one. Radical freedom from all objective norms imposed upon music from the exterior is coordinated with the most extreme rigidity of immanent structure, so that music by its own forces eliminates at least within itself alienation as a matter of subjective formation and objective material. Music thus moves toward that for which Alois Hába coined the beautiful expression "musical style of freedom."[6] To be sure, music overcomes inward alienation only through the perfected expression thereof on its exterior. And if one were to assume that the immanent overcoming of the aporias of music were consistently possible, this would be nothing more than a romantic transfiguration of craftsmanship, including that of Schoenberg, and of the finest of contemporary music, tantamount to the failure to recognize these very aporias. For with the choice of text for his most recent opera *Von heute auf morgen,* a glorification of bourgeois marriage in contrast to libertinage, unreflectingly contrasting "love" and "fashion," Schoenberg nevertheless subordinates his own music to a bourgeois private sphere attacked by his music in terms of its objective character. Certain classicistic inclinations within the overall formal architecture which can be detected in Schoenberg's most recent works might well point in the same direction. Above all: the question is whether the ideal of the hermetic work of art, resting within itself, which Schoenberg inherited from classicism and to which he remains true can be reconciled with the means which he has defined and, further, whether such a concept of a work of art, as totality and cosmos, can still be upheld at all. It might well be that at their deepest level Schoenberg's works stand in opposition to this ideal; the impulse resulting from the total absence of illusion in them offers proof thereof—this impulse was expressed in his struggle against ornamentation and still more strongly in the sobriety of his present musical diction—and in the diction of the texts as well—it might well be that the secret which dwells within his work is hostility toward art: according to its implicit claims, the intention of this work is to force the autonomous work of art, as Beethoven knew it, sufficient unto itself and all-powerful in its symbolism, back into existence again by means both thoroughly and historically rationalized. However, the possibility of such reconstruction is—as in the case of Kraus's attempted reconstruction of a pure language— a doubtful undertaking. Here, and to be sure only here and not in the unpopularity of his work, Schoenberg's social insight reaches the boundary of this work; not only are the limits of his talent defined, but rather the limits of the function of talent per se. This boundary is not to be crossed through music alone. Schoenberg's student Alban Berg established residence at this boundary. In terms of compositional technique, his work represents to a certain degree the reverse line of association between Schoenberg's advanced work and that of the previous generation: Wagner,

Mahler and, in many respects, Debussy as well. However, this line is drawn from the perspective of Schoenberg's niveau, which embraces his technical achievements: extreme variation and through-construction and also the twelve-tone method are applied to older chromatic material, including the leading tone, as happens in Schoenberg's works, without "repealing" it: the expressive function is thus preserved. Even if Berg, more so than Schoenberg, remains thereby bound to bourgeois-individualistic music— in the conventional categories of style criticism: the New German school— he nonetheless breaks free of it in other areas as completely as does Schoenberg. Berg's dialectic is carried out within the realm of musical expression, which cannot be repudiated unconditionally as "individualistic," as the advocates of an empty and collectivistic New-Matter-of-Factness incessantly proclaim.[7] The question of expression can be answered rather only in concrete terms, only according to the substratus of expression, of that which is expressed, and in terms of the validity of the expression itself. If this question is seriously asked within the realm of bourgeois-individualistic music of expression, it becomes apparent that this music of expression is questionable not only as music, but as expression as well: similar to practices in many of the "psychological" novels of the nineteenth century, it is not at all the psychic reality of the subject in question which is expressed, but rather a fictive, stylized and, in many respects, counterfeited reality which is encountered in both cases. In music the interlacing of the psychological concept of expression with that of the style of romanticism is an indication of this state of affairs. If music is successful in breaking through the fictive psychological substratus thus through the Wagnerian heroic-erotic image of man, penetrating into the actual substratus, then the function of music regarding the bourgeois individual changes. It is then no longer the intention of music to transfigure the individual, establishing him as a norm, but rather to disclose his misery and his suffering, which are concealed by psychological as well as musical convention; by expressing the misery—or the vileness—of the individual without abandoning him to his isolation, but rather by objectifying this misery, music turns in the final analysis against the order of things within which it has its origins as such, just as does the expressed individual have his roots as an individual, but which in music attains to consciousness of itself and of its despair. As soon as such music—for its part sufficiently related in its content to psychoanalysis and not in vain at home in the regions of dream and insanity—eradicates the conventional psychology of expression. It decomposes the contours of the surface thereof and constructs out of the particles of musical expression a new language by means of musical immanence; this converges with Schoenberg's constructive language in spite of the totally different course by which this goal is approached. This dialectic evolves within Berg's works and it is this alone which permits an understanding of his composition of Büchner's tragedy *Wozzeck* in its full significance. A parallel to fine arts is perhaps permissible; Berg's relation to the expressive music of the late nineteenth and beginning twentieth century parallels that of Kokoschka's portraits to those of the impressionists.[8] The authentic portrayal of the individual psyche, both of the bourgeois psyche and of the proletarian psyche which is produced by the bourgeoisie, is suddenly transformed in *Wozzeck* into an intention of social criticism, without of course destroying the frame of aesthetic immanence. It is the deep paradox of Berg's work, in which social antinomy is work-immanently defined, that this critical development is possible in reference to material from the past which is now made transparent by his criticism. This can be observed in one of the most significant scenes in *Wozzeck*, the great scene in the tavern, and here Berg's method intersects with that of the surrealists. At the same time, it is this reference—at least in terms of the drama—which has protected Berg's work from total isolation and elicited a certain resonance from the bourgeois audience. Even if this resonance is rooted in the misunderstanding of *Wozzeck* as the last "music drama" of Wagnerian coinage, it permits a certain amount of that quality in *Wozzeck* which manifests a dark and dangerous current originating in the caves of the unconscious to trickle into prevailing consciousness through the channels of misunderstanding. Finally, within this context, brief reference must be made to the third representative of the Schoenberg School: Anton Webern. Unquestionable as the extraordinary musical quality of Webern's work is, the social interpretation of this work presents great difficulty and it cannot be more than touched upon here. [In Webern,] loneliness and alienation from society—conditioned in Schoenberg by the formal structure of his work—become thematic and are transformed into content: the declaration of the inexpressible and of total alienation is asserted by every sound of his music. If one were to apply the basic concept of immanent dialectics, which constitutes the foundation of the Schoenberg School, to Webern, one would have to employ a sub-title from Kierkegaard—who is sufficiently close to Webern—and speak of "dialectic lyricism."[9] For here the most extremely individual differentiation, a dissolution of the material used which musically goes far beyond Schoenberg and expressively beyond Berg, is employed for no other purpose than this: for the liberation of a type of natural language of music, of pure sound, which Webern denied without fail in the regression to a natural *material,* to tonality and to the "natural" overtone relations. To produce the image of nature within historical dialectics: that is the intention of Webern's music and the riddle which it offers. As a riddle, it offers an answer totally contrary to all nature-romanticism. This riddle will be solved only much later.

The virtuosity of Stravinsky and his followers forms an exact antithesis to the mastery of Schoenberg and his school; here the game is opposed to the absence of illusion; the seductively arbitrary change of masks, whose wearers are consequently identical but empty, is set against responsible dialectics, the substratum of which transforms itself in sudden changes. The music of objectivism is socially all the more transparent than that of the Schoenberg School, the less compactly and densely it turns upon itself in its technology. For that reason the social interpretation of objectivism must proceed from the objectivists' technical method. In every objectivist music the attempt is made to correct the alienation of music from within, that is to say, without any clear view of social reality; however, this is not attempted through further pursuit of its immanent dialectic, which is reproached as alien to nature, individualistic and overly differentiated. Absurdly enough, Stravinsky once compared Schoenberg with Oscar Wilde. The musically immanent correction of alienation is rather sought through regression to older, totally pre-bourgeois musical forms, within which an effort is made to affirm an original natural state of music—indeed, it might be said, a musical anthropology appropriate to the being of man and his bodily constitution is the objectivist goal. This explains the inclination of all objectivism to dance forms and to rhythms originating in the dance; they are thought to be elevated above historical change and accessible to every age. Objectivism distinguishes itself from the concept of stylistic history so important to romanticism, defined in an extreme formula as the "sound of legend" in Schumann; this process involves not only the contrasting of a past musical condition with the negative present-day situation as something positive which it longingly hopes to reinstitute, but even to a greater degree the construction in the past of the image of something absolutely valid which might be realized here and now just as at any other time. This is why objectivism in its theoretical pronouncements has attacked romanticism so vehemently. From a practical-musical perspective, however, all this means is that the regression of objectivism to its historical models—regardless of whether genuine or false rustic folk music, medieval polyphony or the "pre-classic" concertante style is involved—does not aim merely at the reinstitution of these models; only in exceptional cases has objectivism, in the form of stylistic copy, undertaken such reinstitution.

In the breadth of its production, however, objectivism does endeavor under the banner of "New Objectivity," dutifully emphasizing its contemporaneity and the fact that it has arrived, to apply old and presumably eternal models to its actual material: to the same harmonically free material, predisposed to polyphony and emancipated from the pressures of expression, which proceeds from the dialectic of the Schoenberg School and is taken over undialectically by objectivism. The formation of a highly differentiated material, manifesting all the signs of the division of labor, but doing so in a static naturalistic manner pre-dating the division of labor: that is, the ideal of musical objectivism.

In this process inescapable contemporary social analogies become apparent. The estate-corporative organization of a highly industrial economic context is manifested, which in objectivist music appears as a conforming image: it appears that the sovereign composer stands in free control of the supposed musical organism, in much the same way that in fascism a "leadership elite" [*Führerelite*] appears to be in control, while in truth power over the social "organism" lies in the hands of monopoly capitalism. When a dissonance is to be introduced or when a suspended note is to be resolved is decided neither by a pre-established scheme, annulled after all by the actual material, nor by structural immanence, the rational order of which is negated precisely in the name of nature, but only by the inclination, namely, the "taste" of the composer. Tempting as the analogy is and no matter how much of the true state of affairs it might reveal, it is not to be made responsible for cognition without the expression of resistance. In the Russian emigrant Stravinsky or even in a neo-classicist such as Casella, who is so very ambitious in cultural politics, the relation to fascism is beyond question.[10] The social interpretation of music, however, is not concerned with the individual consciousness of authors, but rather with the function of their work. And this is where the difficulties begin. First of all, if the association of objectivism with fascism is to be understood as something actual, categories of mediation must be found and the mediation itself must be explained. The mechanism of mediation is, however, still unknown. It could be revealed most readily by an analysis of the state of affairs in fashion, which—as demonstrated, for example, in Stravinsky's case by his generally familiar dependencies—does not permit the essential formal elements of neo-classicism to define themselves through the asking of immanent-technical questions. These elements were rather first deposited from outside the work and were then later transposed into the technical immanence of the work of art. Fashion itself, however, points back judiciously to social and economic facts. This indicates that a solution of the problem of mediation in music has by no means been found; it is rather only that the location of the problem has been designated with greater precision. And furthermore, in the interpretation of objectivism in regard to fascism, problems of content must be confronted. These difficulties are caused by the same state of alienation, the immanent-aesthetic eradication or concealment of which objectivism sets as its task. Even if it were assumed that in terms of intention and objective structure this were indeed the music of the most progressive class within monopoly capitalism, this class would still remain unable either to understand or to consume this music. In the effort of objectivism to overcome alienation only in terms of artistic imagery, alienation is permitted to continue unchanged in reality. The technical specialization of music has progressed so far that an audience is no longer in a position to comprehend this music, even when it is an objective expression of the ideology of the audience itself. In addition, ideological forces of other types, such as the concept of "education" [Bildung] as an accumulation of spiritual goods out of the past, have a far greater musical effect upon the audience than the immediate configuration of its social ideals in music; this audience is already too far removed from music to place central importance upon such configurations. It might well be that Stravinsky's music reflects upper-bourgeois ideology far more precisely than, for example, the music of Richard Strauss, the upper-bourgeois composer of the last generation; even so, the upper bourgeoisie will nonetheless suspect Stravinsky as a "destroyer" and prefer to hear Strauss in his stead—but prefer even more to hear Beethoven's Seventh Symphony. In this way, alienation complicates the social equation. It is manifested, however, in immanent-aesthetic terms as well—and this might well be the true source of the distrust of the upper bourgeoisie against "its" music. The incorrectness of the structure within itself, within which the contradiction between the affirmed formal intentions and the actual state of the material remains unresolved, corresponds to the arbitrariness—the negative arbitrariness—with which the composer disposes over his material. This he does with no preformation of the material in any objectively obligatory manner and without any unequivocal judgment upon musical justice and injustice pronounced by the inner construction of the musical constellation itself.

The greatest justice is done to the material by compositional practices such as those encountered in the significant Hungarian composer and folksong scholar Béla Bartók; he refutes the fiction of formal objectivity and goes back instead to a pre-objective, truly archaic material, which, however, is very closely related to current material precisely in its particular dissolution. Radical folklorism in the rational through-construction of his particular material is, consequently, amazingly similar to the practices of the Schoenberg School. In the realm of objectivism, however, Bartók is a totally singular phenomenon; his earlier collaborator Kodály,[11] on the other hand, falsified authentic folklore as a romantic dream image of unified-folkish life which denounces itself through the contrast of primitivizing melody and sensuously soft, late-impressionistic harmony. Stravinsky's games of masks[12] are protected from demasking of this type by his highly precise and cautious artistic understanding. It is his great and dangerous accomplishment, dangerous to himself as well, that his music uses the knowledge of its coercive antinomy in presenting itself as a game. It does this, however, never simply as a game and never as applied art: rather, it maintains a position of continual hovering between game and seriousness and between styles as well, which makes it almost impossible to call it by name and within which irony hinders any comprehension of the objectivist ideology. This, however, is the background of a despair which is permitted every expression, since no single expression suits it correctly; at the same time it brings the game of masks into relief against its dismal background. Within this oscillation a game might become seriousness at any moment and change suddenly into satanic laughter, mocking society with the possibility of a non-alienated music; it is this which makes the reception of Stravinsky as a fashionable composer whose pretention simultaneously elevates his music impossible. It is precisely the artistic security with which he recognizes the impossibility of a positive-aesthetic solution of the antinomies conditioned by society, recognizing, at the same time, the social antinomy itself which makes him suspicious in the eyes of the upper bourgeoisie. In his best and most exposed works—such as *L'Histoire du soldat*—he provokes contradiction. In contrast to all other objectivist authors, Stravinsky's superiority within his métier endangers the consistent ideological positivity of his style, as this is demanded of him by society: consequently, in his case as well, artistic logical consistence becomes socially dialectical. It is only with the *Symphony of Psalms* that he seems to have warded off the suspicion of prevailing powers against big-city "studio" art, decadence and disintegration.

The essential social function of Hindemith is the decontamination of Stravinsky's objectivism by means of the naïveté with which he assimilates it. His objectivism offers a picture of consistent seriousness; artificial security becomes artisan respectability, whereby the idea of the artisan as a "music maker" again corresponds to the ideas of a state of production not based upon the production and reproduction in music. Hindemith's satanic irony regarding "healthy humor," the health of which indicates the un-reflected state of nature in objectivism, disturbed by the grin of Stravin-sky's masks and his humor regarding aggressive irony, no matter whether it is avant-garde irony or snobbish irony, both reveal his principal recon-ciliation with social conditions. Stravinsky's despair—this totally historical despair driven to the boundary of schizophrenia in *L'Histoire du soldat*—is the expression of a subjectivity achieved only through fragments and ghosts of past objective musical language. In Hindemith, this despair is moderated to a naturalistic, unresolved, but still undialectic, melancholy, which looks upon death as an eternal state of affairs similar to numerous intentions of contemporary philosophy, evading concrete social contradic-tions under the banner of "existentialism" and thus subordinating itself willingly to the anthropological super-historical ideals of objectivism. Stra-vinsky absorbed social contradictions into artistic antinomy and gave them form; Hindemith conceals them and for that reason his blind configura-tions turn out to be filled with contradictions. The more perceptive tech-nical eye, which is able to penetrate the surface of consistently interlocking movement and infallible security of instrumentation within the acoustic inventory, locates the flaw of Hindemith's technique everywhere: it dis-covers the differences between arbitrary material employed as motifs and would-be rigidity of form; between the principal unrepeatability of the components and the forms of repetition which grant surface continuity; between terraced architecture on a large scale and the lack of discrimina-tion, along with the necessity of ordering, in the ordering of the individual terraces. All of this happens simply because "objective" architecture does not embrace the individual productive impulses as a prescribed organiza-tional principle, but rather is imposed upon them by compositional arbi-trariness, resulting in a false façade under the sign of the New Objectivity. The thematic content of objectivism here remains arbitrary, just as it is in Stravinsky and, to be sure, in the legions of his followers; it is arbitrary in the sense that it is interchangeable and replaceable according to changing ideological needs, and it is not unequivocally predetermined by a social constitution and nowhere is it that order for which music might bear wit-ness; it is rather a class order, to be concealed by music under the sign of its humanity. Now mere formal objectivity, totally lacking in content, is offered in its emptiness as thematic content, objectivity for the sake of objectivity, as is often the case in Stravinsky; this obscure vacuity is thus praised as an irrational natural force, now, as in Hindemith, it is introduced as proof of a community, as such is often formed as a petit bourgeois protest against capitalistic forms of mechanization or in the manner in which the Youth Movement would like to influence production, while simply avoiding the capitalistic production process. Now music is supposed to be an aural game, providing man with relaxation or creating community; now it should offer him cultic or existential seriousness, as in the instance when the critics demanded of Hindemith—who was then still much more aggressive—"great depth," to which he responded with the composition of Rilke's *Marienleben*.[13] The thematic contents of musical objectivism are as divergent as the interests of the prevailing forces of society and a difference such as that between upper and petit bourgeoisie—to use the concepts as vaguely as the state of social cognition still prescribes for the present—is reflected clearly enough in the objectivist product; the question of "mediation" would also have to be asked here. All objectivist music has one thing in common: the intention of *diverting attention* from social conditions. It attempts to make the individual believe that he is not lonely, but rather close to all others in a relationship portrayed for him by music without defining its own social function; it attempts to show the totality as a meaningful organization which fulfills individual destiny positively merely through its transformation into the aural medium. However, the foundation and the meaning of this state of relationship are interchangeable. Insofar as the intention of diversion is actually present and not merely the reflection of wishes within an isolated aesthetic realm, it can be looked upon as unsuccessful. The petit bourgeoisie, intensively courted by objectivism with choral societies and instrumental ensembles, "guilds of music makers" and work collectives, has accomplished nothing for the market. The distress of the capitalist crisis has referred the groups addressed by objectivism and its popularizers to other, more tractable ideologies and to those complicatedly manipulated ideologies of objectivism which are of undefined content. They will hardly feel an inclination to distinguish between the "esoteric" Schoenberg and the "music maker" Hindemith; under the label of cultural bolshevism they will reject both of them and, for their part, cling to resurrected military marches.

This anticipates the essential problematic social dilemma of those types of composers who no longer come to terms with the fact of alienation in the aesthetic image, but rather wish to overcome it in reality by including the state of actual social consciousness in the compositional process itself; they would do this through transformation of the musical *terminus a quo* into a social *terminus ad quem*. On its lower levels objectivism shows a marked tendency toward such a method; the demand for aesthetically immanent music conducive to community is transformed with continuity into a call for aesthetically elevated "use" music. When Kurt Weill as the

major representative of musical surrealism shows himself vastly superior
to such methods and to the inferior ideal of such elevation, it is because
he, better informed about the social condition, not only accepts the positive
change of society through music as a possibility, but rather because he
views the disclosure of these conditions through music as possible. He does
not present man with a primitivized art intended for use; he shows them
rather their own "use" music in the distorting mirror of his artistic
method, thus revealing it as a commodity. It is not without meaning that
the style of Weill's *Three Penny Opera* and *Mahagonny* stand in greater
proximity to *L'Histoire du soldat* than does Hindemith; it is a style based
upon montage, which abrogates the "organic" surface structure of neo-
classicism and moves together rubble and fragment or constructs actual
compositions out of falsehood and illusion, as which the harmony of the
nineteenth century has today been revealed, through the addition of intentionally false notes. The shock with which Weill's compositional practices overexposes common compositional means, unmasking them as
ghosts, expresses alarm about the society within which they have their
origin and, at the same time, it is the living negation of the possibility of
a positive communal music, which collapses in the laughter of devilish
vulgar music as which true use music is exposed. With the means of past
illusion, present compositional practices confess their own illusory nature
and in their crude radiance the coded script of social conditions becomes
legible; this prohibits not only every appeasement through an aesthetic
image—for the contradiction of this condition appears again in the image
itself—but rather approaches man so directly that he will no longer even
consider the possibility of the autonomous work of art. The qualitative
wealth of results developed out of this constellation by Weill and Brecht
is admirable; they sketch innovations of the *opera theater* in the sudden
illumination of moments which simultaneously turn dialectically against
the possibility of the opera theater per se. It is beyond question that Weill's
music is today the only music of genuine social-polemic impact, which it
will remain as long as it resides at the height of its negativity; furthermore,
this music has recognized itself as such and has taken its position accordingly. Its problem is the impossibility of remaining at this height; as a
musician, Weill must try to escape the responsibilities of a work method
which, from the perspective of music, necessarily seems "literary," similar,
in its way, to the pictures of the surrealists. The misunderstanding of the
audience which peacefully consumes the *songs** of the *Three Penny Opera*
as hit tunes, hostile as these songs are both to themselves and to this
audience, might be legitimized as a vehicle of dialectic communication. The

further course of events reveals another danger in ambiguity: illusion blends into false positivity, destruction into communal art within the realm of the status quo, and behind this mocking primitivity, conjured forth by its bitterness, comes into view the naïve-credulous primitivism of a reaching back, not to old polyphony but rather to Handelian homophony. But, as an experimenter, Weill is fundamentally so far removed from any faith in the unconsciously organic that it is hardly to be expected that he will fall victim to the dangers of the undangerous.

Communal and use music in the broadest sphere have become subject to this danger. Their activity asserts itself at the wrong place—in music rather than in society, and therefore they fail in both instances. For in capitalist society the human state of togetherness from which they proceed is a fiction and, where it might be something real, it is impotent when confronted by the capitalist process of production. The fiction of "community" in music conceals this process without changing it. At the same time, in inner-musical terms, communal music is reactionary: in the same direction as objectivism, only far more coarsely, it rejects the further dialectic movement of musical material as "individualistic" or "intellectual" and seeks instead a static concept of nature in the restitution of immediacy: the "music maker." Rather than engaging in a—certainly justified—criticism of individualism and in the correction of its immanent contradictions, while recognizing it as a necessary step in the liberation of music for mankind, recourse is taken here on all sides to a primitive, pre-individualistic stage, without any further posing of the neo-classic question regarding the reforming of material. The basic error lies in the conception of the function of music in relation to the public. The consciousness of the public is absolutized: in petit bourgeois communal music this consciousness is viewed as "nature," while class-conscious proletarian music—represented by Hanns Eisler—sees it as proletarian class-consciousness which is to be understood positively here and now. In the process it is overlooked that precisely the demands according to which production should orient itself in these cases—singability, simplicity, collective effectiveness per se—are necessarily dependent upon a state of consciousness suppressed and enchained through class domination—no one has formulated this more exactly and extremely than Marx himself—which results in fetters placed upon musically productive forces. The immanent-aesthetic results of bourgeois history, including that of the last fifty years, cannot simply be brushed aside by the proletarian theory and praxis of art, unless the desire is to eternalize a condition in art produced by class domination. The elimination of this condition within society is, after all, the fixed goal of the proletarian class struggle. In this process, the submissiveness of communal music in its relation to the present state of consciousness is revealed as deceit by this consciousness itself, for a hit song from a film about a nice little officer of the guard is given preference over popularly conceived communal music which glorifies the proletariat. The agitatory value and therewith the political correctness of proletarian communal music, for example, the choruses of Hanns Eisler, is beyond question, and only utopian-idealistic thinking could demand in its place a music internally suited to the function of the proletariat, but incomprehensible to the proletariat. However, as soon as music retreats from the front of direct action, where it grows reflective and establishes itself as an artistic form, it is obvious that the structures produced cannot hold their own against progressive bourgeois production, but rather take the form of a questionable mixture of refuse from antiquated inner-bourgeois stylistic forms, including even those of petit bourgeois choral literature and from the remains of progressive "new" music. Through this mixture, the acuteness of the attack and the coherence of every technical formulation is lost. In place of such intermediate solutions, it is conceivable that melodies of vulgar bourgeois music currently in circulation could be provided with new texts which would in this way bring about a dialectic "re-functioning." It is, nevertheless, worthy of notice that in the figure of the proletarian composer most consequent for the present, Eisler, the Schoenberg School, from which he came forth, comes into contact with efforts seemingly contrary to the School itself. If this contact is to be fruitful, it must find dialectic employment: this music must intervene actively in consciousness through its own forms and not take instructions from the passive, one-sided position of the consciousness of the user—including the proletariat.

II. REPRODUCTION, CONSUMPTION

The alienation of music from society is reflected in the antinomies of musical production: it is tangible as an actual social fact in the relation of production to *consumption*. Musical *reproduction* mediates between these two realms. It serves production, which can become immediately present only through reproduction, otherwise it would exist only as a dead text or score; [reproduction] is further the form of all musical consumption, for society can participate only in reproduced works and never only in the texts. The demand of production—understood as the demand for authenticity—and that of consumption—the demand for comprehensibility—address reproduction to the same degree and intertwine in it: the postulate of "intelligible" reproduction of the work can apply equally well to the portrayal of the text in terms of its true meaning and to the comprehensibility thereof for the listener. When production and consumption meet in this way within the innermost cells of reproduction, reproduction then becomes the most narrowly defined scene for the conflicts into which they enter with each other. If reproduction involves only alienated music, it cannot hope to reach society; as reproduction for society, it misses the essence of the works involved. For concrete reproduction is concerned— as everyday criticism would always like people to forget—neither with an eternal work per se nor with a listener dependent upon constant natural conditions, but rather with historical conditions. Not only is the consciousness of the audience dependent upon the change in social conditions and not only is the consciousness of those involved in reproduction dependent upon the state of the total musical constitution of society at a given time: the works themselves and their history change within such constitution. Their text is merely a coded script which does not guarantee unequivocal meaning and within which changing thematic contents appear along with the development of the musical dialectic, which in turn encompasses social impulses. The change within works themselves is portrayed in reproduction; this happens under the sign of radical alienation as the reduction of reproductive *freedom*. Pre-capitalist reproduction was dominated by tradition: the tradition of musical guilds, at times even the tradition of individual families. The impulse of tradition guaranteed a continuing stable relation between music and its listening public within the stability of reproduction; the work did not stand in a state of isolation from society; rather through reproduction it exerted an influence upon production, and down to the end of the eighteenth century—i.e., until the elimination of the practice of general bass through Viennese classicism—production, reproduction and improvisation intermingled without definite boundaries; even such a strictly composed formal type as the Bach fugue which, as the heir of medieval polyphony, did not subordinate itself to the general bass practice permits the interpreter full freedom in tempo and dynamics, factors only occasionally defined in the text. The regulation thereof is assigned to a tradition which remains irrational for several centuries following the introduction of tempered tuning. All this changes with the victory of the bourgeois class. The work itself establishes its independence and, in a rational system of signs, defines itself as commodity in relation to society; the tradition of interpreters and their guilds breaks off with the establishment of free competition; "schools of interpretation" are turned into collectives for learning and ideology with no responsibility toward the transmission of traditional teaching; the remnants of traditional musical practices, as, for example, they were encountered by Mahler in Vienna, are, in his words, transparent "slovenliness" *[Schlamperei].* The intervention of the interpreter in the work, still tolerated in the era before the definitive reification of the work, becomes an arbitrary and evil concern from which the rationally designed work must keep its distance. The history of musical reproduction in the last century has destroyed reproductive freedom. The interpreter has only the choice between two demands of rational character; either he must limit himself strictly to the realization, at most to the decoding, of the exact language of musical signs, or he must adjust to the demands which society as market makes upon him and within which the configuration of the work perishes. In the nineteenth century the "interpretive personality" mediated between these two demands as the last musical refuge of irrational reproduction within the capitalist process. This personality stands in a clear relation to the forms of competition and contains an equal amount of irrationality. It serves the work by producing its contents again out of the work itself within the framework of the prescriptive text and its signs; this is possible through the homogeneity of the structure of author and interpreter who are both in the same way bourgeois "individuals," and both perfect the "expression" of bourgeois individuality in the same way. Models of such interpretation are Liszt and Rubinstein, both expressive composers and, as interpreters, "re-creators." The society to which they offer music is just as individualistically constituted as they are; it recognizes itself in them, and through them it takes possession of the work offered; in the triumphs which it prepares for the virtuoso, far greater than those with which the composer is celebrated, it celebrates itself. In contrast to the nineteenth century, the decisive change experienced by contemporary musical reproduction is the destruction of the balance of individualistic society and individualistic production; the freedom of reproduction has therewith grown highly problematic, and nowhere is this seen more clearly than in the transition from competitive to monopoly capitalism. To be sure, the "interpretive personality" continues within musical life and might well be socially more effective than ever before: its function, however, has changed totally, and the sovereignty with which it asserts authority over both works and audience conceals in dictatorial fashion the abyss between free interpreter and work. However, musical production, insofar as it asserts any independence from the market, demands total subordination of the interpreter to the text, and this subordination is not restricted to present production, but rather becomes the necessary postulate of past production as well—insofar as the reproduction of older works has not become totally impossible in the light of progressive production, causing these works to lie in transparent muteness before the eyes of the strict interpreter. As a composer, Schoenberg eliminated the tonal cadence and all formal means originating in it; at the same time, however, the emancipation of representation which unquestionably belonged to these means and which consequently were not expressly defined were lost; that such means were taken for granted guaranteed the earlier interpreter his freedom. Now the text is annotated down to the last note and to the most subtle nuance of tempo, and the interpreter becomes the executor of the unequivocal will of the author. In Schoenberg this strictness has its dialectic origin in the strictness of the compositional method, according to which music is thoroughly "composed out" with no aid from a pre-existing and socially guaranteed material. In Stravinsky, on the other hand, whose note-text is no less exactly defined, the freedom of the interpreter is eliminated through the style and "taste" of objectivism. This is achieved undialectically, but with similar results. This objectivism, which of course is not purely borne out in construction, demands nonetheless total subordination of the interpreter to its objective attitude. This subordination, even if it is not totally defined in the composition and in the composer's annotation, is intended at least to result in an unemotional manner of performance, similar to that offered by mechanical instruments. The improvements and innovations in the realm of mechanical musical instruments, which make possible a more precise reproduction than that given by mediocre and uncontrolled "free" interpreters, might well have influenced the ideal of reproduction; at any rate, it has affirmed the claims of social interpretation of the conditions of musical production insofar as their immanent complex of problems has brought about the same limitation of reproductive freedom and the same tendencies toward technification and rationalization experienced outside of music in social and economic developments. The perfection of the machine and the replacement of human forces of labor through mechanical forces has become a matter of reality in music as well. These tendencies are not restricted to the reproduction of contemporary music: the historical mutation of works within the framework of ambiguous texts is not an arbitrary process, but rather obeys strictly the insights gained within the realm of musical production. Subjected to more careful observation, older and, above all, "classical" German music, if it is to be realized as its construction presents itself to the eye of today, demands the same strict reproduction as does new music, resisting every improvisational freedom of the interpreter. The demand for a neutrally adequate reproduction of the work has emancipated itself from the will of the author—which is also a difficult perspective to define—and it is precisely in such emancipation that the historical character of reproduction is responsibly revealed. If an early Beethoven piano sonata were to be played today as "freely," with such arbitrarily improvisational changes, for example, changes of the basic tempi of individual movements as it was, according to contemporary reports, by Beethoven himself at the piano, the apparently authentic manner of interpretation would strike the listener as contradictory to the meaning of the work in the face of the constructive unity of such movements. This unity has become clear only today and largely through the efforts of later production in music.

In the immanent confrontation with the work, the most progressive interpretation, oriented to the actual state of production, attains to the idea of self-suspension of the work; an open conflict with society necessarily develops, which further develops into a conflict with the audience, which feels itself represented by the interpreter in the work and, through the sacrifice of the work, this audience now feels itself expelled from the work. This process is to be observed most markedly in the best representatives of interpretation, who concentrate upon a pure reproduction of the work. The ambivalence of society regarding realization is revealed still more sharply in regard to reproduction than to production. With the perfection of technical means for the purpose of reducing the labor force and with the progressive development of the independence of music in terms of a unity of commodities subject to exchange as abstract units which then finally divorces itself totally from society, bourgeois society has not only furthered the process of musical rationalization—it is rather that only through this society did such rationalization become possible in the first place. The consequences of rationalization, however, attack the stability of bourgeois order in its basic categories; this order retreats before these consequences into a conceptual world which long ago took leave not only of immanent-musical reality, but of immanent-bourgeois reality as well. Despite this distance, this order has proven itself highly useful in the ideological concealment of the monopoly capitalist development of society. The rationalization of musical production and reproduction, the result of social rationalization, is cloaked in horror as "de-spiritualization," as if it were feared that the irrationality of the social condition which asserts itself despite all "rationalization" had become all too obvious in the light of radical artistic rationality; in so doing, "spirit" is silently equated with the bourgeois-independent private person, whose rights one would like to define ideologically with greater clarity the more they are questioned in economic and social terms. The most pedestrian antitheses are acceptable to the consumer consciousness which wishes to protect itself from the force of true reproduction in terms of its cognitive character, seeking to secure a type of music making, the major function of which is to conceal reality through dream, intoxication and inward contemplation. At the same time, such reproduction offers the bourgeoisie in aesthetic images precisely that satisfaction of drives which it prohibits them in reality; the price paid for this by the work of art, however, is its integral configuration. The organic is played off against the mechanical, inwardness against vacuity, and personality against anonymity. Objectivism, in its more conciliatory German form, attempted to counter such objections as were expressed against rational reproduction from the side of production by assimilating the lost reproductive freedom, or at least the appearance thereof in the form of "music making" [*Musikantentum*]—into the text, further developing the text out of instrumental performance methods, as though it were only the free possibility of reproduction which made production itself possible in the first place. The illusory character of this attempted mediation is disclosed by the fact that the function which would necessarily fall to reproduction is assigned to production; this makes the "text" and the concrete composition the final instance for the "music making," and the musicianship of the performer becomes a mere ornamental addition to the composition. As far as the audience is concerned, music for mere music making has always been ineffective. The will of the public was once realized in the same "interpretive personality" who served the breakthrough of individual expression in music in the nineteenth century and whose function has now undergone drastic change. This personality must now fulfill a double function. First of all, it has to establish the lost communication between work and public through the sovereignty of its "concept" by exorcizing the configuration of the work in a type of enlargement or bigger-than-life image. This image might, of course, be unsuited to the work; nonetheless, it guarantees the effect upon the public. It must further evoke the work as the expression of individual human dynamics and private animation which it, of course, no longer is. Above all other qualities, it is the ability to present works in a configuration long absent from them, indeed, which they perhaps never possessed at all, which distinguishes the "prominent" conductor. The dream image of vital fullness and uninhibited verve, of animated organic quality and direct, non-reified inwardness are provided by him corporally for those to whom capitalist economy denies in reality the fulfillment of all such wishes; and it further strengthens them in their faith in their own substance, brought to the fore by those very immortal, better to say immutable, works he [the conductor] evoked. By virtue of their education, these listeners are firmly in control of these works which, at the same time, they honor as fetishes. Such a conductor stands in an alien or negating relation to contemporary production—in strict contrast to his predecessors in the nineteenth century; from time to time he offers a modern work as a horrifying example or permits new music at most the position of a transition to the restoration of the old art of the soul. Otherwise he clings to the heroic-bourgeois past—Beethoven—or to an author such as Anton Bruckner, who unites the pomp of social event with the same claim to animation and inwardness expressed by the prominent interpreter. The same type of conductor who undertakes an insatiably engrossed celebration of the adagio of Bruckner's Eighth lives a life closely akin to that of the head of a capitalist combine, uniting in his hand as many organizations, institutes and orchestras as possible; this is the exact social corollary to the individual structure of a figure whose task it is to reduce within capitalism musical trust and inwardness to the same common denominator. Several phenomena drawn from the history of types represented by today's prominent interpreters indicate the manner in which the conductor plays the role of a total individual who dominates irresponsibly and without contradiction over the orchestral mechanism, suppressing the free competition of instrumental and vocal virtuosos. He is an *individual*, but also a "personality" who at one and the same time assumes command over music and public and in the name of the public, but without its conscious will; with gestures of command he quotes the past. Finally, his success is upheld through the gesture of command with which he counters his audience, all of this revealing, finally, the individual who ostensibly overcomes mechanization, just like the monopoly lord who conceals the rational-mechanical apparatus of individual insight in order to control everything in his own interests. His ideological domination is supported by a fame in which society reproduces his restorative-reproductive achievement again and again. Class consciousness is so precisely attuned to a fitting ideal of the interpreter that it removes interpreters who do not correspond to it, no matter how indisputable their professional qualifications and even their suggestive force might be; this was done in Vienna before the war in the same way as in present-day Milan and Berlin.

Present-day society demands of music that it serve this society as ideology in the fulfillment of its wishes, as these wishes are manifested dialectically in the problematic realm of reproduction in the figure of the "interpretive personality"—it is this demand that dominates the official musical *consumption* of bourgeois society in toto; this demand is further sanctioned by the institutions of education. In its "musical life," as it lays claim at present to its traditional locations in opera houses and concert halls, bourgeois society has concluded a type of armistice with alienated music, associating with it in carefully regulated forms of behavior. To be sure, this armistice could be terminated at any time: "musical life" reacts promptly and exactly to every change of social conditions in the bourgeoisie. For example, the expropriation of the upper middle class through inflation and other crises has expelled this stratum of society from opera and concerts, exiling its members before the radio, the distraction of which adequately expresses the atomization of the bourgeoisie and the exclusion of the bourgeois private person from public affairs: sitting in front of the loudspeaker, the bourgeoisie is subordinated to the monopoly economically and musically, even in terms of a "mixed economic operation." Because musical life registers inner-bourgeois structural changes so directly, analysis must necessarily consider the immanent differences and contradictions of the bourgeoisie. In a sphere in which the autonomous claim of isolated works of art is already broken and replaced by the needs of the market, statistics could assemble essential material for social interpretation. Such material is, however, not available. Nonetheless, observation can offer a number of findings. First of all, as far as *opera* is concerned, it has lost its actuality as a vehicle of consumption. Its primary function in the nineteenth century, that of representation, has at any rate been taken away from it for the present: the impoverished members of the middle class do not have the economic power to support such representation, nor do they any longer form a cultural unity, capable of such sublimated representation as was once to be found in the opera theater; the most they can do is to commemorate their happier years at performances of *Die Meistersinger*. The upper bourgeoisie, however, which is able and willing to engage in representation, avoids all too open presentation of itself as the dominant and economically competent stratum of society; for the moment, it restricts its representation to more exclusive circles, above all, to those in the loges, accessible to every opera glass. Furthermore, they are totally uninterested in the opera repertory and prefer to establish their musical domain in the large concert organizations which they dominate economically as well as through the politics of programming without exposing themselves to an undue degree. It is nonetheless conceivable that with progressive political development of the forms of domination in monopoly capitalism, opera could regain something of its previous social lustre. On the one hand, opera is attended in part by subscription holders from the older generation of the "educated" middle class, who experience there their own past, enjoying the triumphal bourgeois intoxication which is the particular specialty of Wagner. At the same time, by clinging to a form of art little influenced by social conditions in the breadth of its production, they are able to protest against artistic innovation and related social intentions per se. Another part of the audience which fills opera houses consists of members of other bourgeois circles, such as small merchants, and even of representatives of the artisan professions who still command a certain economic standard, but are excluded from the fruits thereof by "education" in terms of their origin and training. This is the type of opera-goer who is naturally delighted to hear the march from *Aïda* and the aria of Butterfly again—familiar to him from movies and coffee houses and on a level with his musical education; at the same time, he feels that he owes it to his actual economic position and to the possibility of social ascent to receive these bits of commodity in the place consecrated by the old bourgeois ideal of education and which grants the opera-goer, at least in his own eyes, through his presence in the opera house, something of the dignity of that education. It can be assumed that there is a considerable percentage of this type of listener present in the opera audience; this audience is, of course, subject to great modifications. Characteristic today is the total absence of the younger generation of the upper bourgeoisie and of all intellectuals and white-collar workers. The structure envisioned is primarily that encountered in the audience of a provincial opera house. In the metropolitan centers, Berlin, and Vienna as well, the bourgeoisie is still further distracted from the opera through the highly developed mechanism of diversion, so that the middle class comes less in question for the opera in those cities than in the provinces. On the other hand, opera is granted a representative dignity in the name of truly existent or fictive "foreigners" and this draws the upper bourgeoisie to it, making opera performances as "social events" possible.

The function of *concerts* within the bourgeois household is still more significant. In the concert the rather crude subject matter of the opera is absent. It manifests a baroque heritage which has remained largely unaffected by the shift of weight in inner-musical developments from the vocal to the instrumental in recent centuries. The role of opera within bourgeois humanism and idealism is only indirect and beyond question only in the greatest works of the genre, in Mozart, in *Fidelio* and in *Der Freischütz*. It is precisely the subject matter which draws the lower middle class to the opera, in which they seek something similar to a regression into pre-bourgeois culture. However, the same subject matter frightens away the upper stratum of society which finds it "primitive" and "raw." Possibly they sense the danger in the energy of the pre-bourgeois or, in any case, non-bourgeois world of the opera theater, a danger which always seeks to activate itself politically; perhaps they are interested in concealing the character of reality as a world of mere objects, as it is manifested by the opera with uncontrolled joy of discovery—they would like to conceal this precisely because it remains the character of bourgeois reality still today: the upper class retreats from this reality into "inwardness"; the more pleasant its experience, the more it distances itself from social conditions and insight into the contradictions involved therein; this insight can even be presented through music and cloaked in the illusion of immediate collectivity. The upper bourgeoisie loves concerts; in the concert hall it cultivates the humanistic-idealistic educational ideology—without compromising itself; this ideology attracts the educated class in large numbers, including its impoverished and petit bourgeois representatives. The ambiguity of "education and property" which achieves ideological reconciliation in the concert hall is expressed conspicuously in the doubling of orchestras in numerous cities: while the "philharmonic" plays for the upper bourgeoisie in expensive concerts, the exclusivity of which is guaranteed by the family subscription system, performing with highly famous guest stars and a very limited number of sanctioned, likewise ceremonial works, the "symphony orchestras" serve the middle educational stratum with cautious doses of novelties within the traditionalist program through the inclusion of resident "local" talent and for low-priced admission, as long as the economy makes such participation possible. Soloist concerts, the number of which shrinks because of increased risk to the concert agent, no longer encounter the former interest; through the reduction in number, they recede more and more from the public consciousness and restrict themselves obviously to the circle of monopolized stars. Concerts such as the offerings of the International Society for Contemporary Music,[14] which ostentatiously represent contemporary independent production, demonstrate their isolation through drastic economic measures; they are attended almost exclusively by musicians regardless of the direction of modernity that they propagate, and tickets are furnished to the audience gratis; therefore, these concerts remain within the sphere of musical production and are furthermore economically totally unproductive: they are undertakings dependent upon subvention and deficit financing. The few amateurs who support them, members of the bourgeoisie, for the most part, share in the process of economic production only indirectly or not at all, having been eliminated from it by the economic crisis. There simply is no such thing as the "consumption" of new music. Insofar as it ever experiences reproduction, this is made possible through organizations of artists among themselves who are hardly capable of bearing the economic burden or through international meetings of political flavor that prove fictive in terms both of the position taken by the individual nations toward current musical production and of their interest in "spiritual exchange," and whose contribution can no longer be predicted. Such meetings, by clinging liberalistically to the function of consumption and "exchange" for economic reasons, have sacrificed any mutually binding effect or responsibility through the compromises involved in the politics of their program, even from the perspective of musical immanence.

The consumers' *consciousness* of official musical life cannot be reduced to any simple formula. Any comment upon the ideological character of bourgeois musical consumption demands explanation. It is incorrect to believe that no actual need lies at the basis of the consumption of music; as though all musical life were nothing but some type of resounding cultural backdrop, erected by bourgeois society for the concealment of its own true purposes, while its authentic, economic-political life takes place off-stage. Regardless of the degree to which musical life assimilates such functions and no matter how great its share in the representation of the specifically "social," namely, in matters divorced from actual musical needs, these factors alone do not offer the complete picture. It is rather that the ideological power of musical consumption is all the greater, the less it is transparent as mere illusion and as a thin surface gloss and the more precisely it communicates in terms of true needs, doing so, however, in such a way that a "false consciousness" is the result and that the actual social situation is hidden from the consumer. The need for music is present in bourgeois society and this need increases with the problematic social conditions that cause the individual to seek satisfaction beyond immediate social reality, which denies him this satisfaction. This satisfaction is "ideologically" provided by musical life through its acceptance of the bourgeois tendency—dialectically produced—to flee from social reality and to reinterpret this reality for them by providing them with contents which social reality never possessed or at best lost long ago. The clinging to these contents involves the objective intention of thwarting change within society, which would necessarily unmask the true identity of these contents. The ideological essence of "musical life" is its ability to satisfy the needs of the bourgeoisie adequately—but to do so by means of a form of satisfaction which accepts and stabilizes the existing consciousness, rather than revealing through its own form social contradictions, translating them into form and cognition regarding the structure of society. When Nietzsche condemned the "intoxication" which music produces as an unproductive intoxication, incapable of activation, impure and dangerous, he correctly recognized the relation between the satisfaction of needs and ideological obscurement—the basic law of bourgeois musical practices—and further identified the unconscious as the setting of that relation. He achieved this despite the doubtfulness of his categories and the unconditional orientation of his musical concepts in terms of the work of Wagner. The association of the bourgeoisie with music takes place under the protection of the unconscious: the "legal" association within "musical life" and, to a greater degree, the "illegal" within "light music." The unconsciousness of the relation simultaneously guarantees the fetish character of music-objects; reverence, projected rather distortedly from the theological realm into the aesthetic, forbids any conscious "analyzing" concern with music, the comprehension of which is reserved for "feeling": the uncontrollability of the private-bourgeois manner of reaction to music corresponds to the fetish-like isolation of the musical structure itself. Every technological reflection which might illuminate something of the social function of music along with an explanation of its formal aspects is refused in the name of feeling; at the same time, knowledge of general and meaningless concepts of style is promoted in the name of education. Reverence and feeling cling to the celebrities of the past, before whom all criticism grows silent and in whom the bourgeoisie loves to affirm its own origins and the source of all heroism. Today, since apology is the primary obligation of official musical culture in rationalized society, equal use is made of bourgeois-revolutionary objectivity—"classicism"—and resigned bourgeois subjectivity—"romanticism"; the glorification of the victory of bourgeois ratio as well as the suffering of the individual under the sole domination of this ratio is the object of bourgeois musical life, expressed in its canonical works; the ambivalence of a feeling which finds equal satisfaction in classicism and romanticism is the ambivalence of the bourgeoisie toward its own ratio. Beyond the tension between rationally constituted objectivity and irrationally emphasized, private inwardness, the bourgeoisie registers the phases of its ascent to the heights of capitalism in "musical life." In *Die Meistersinger*, one of the most informative and, not without reason, socially popular of all works, the theme is the ascent of the bourgeois entrepreneur and his "national-liberal" reconciliation with feudalism in a type of dream displacement. The dream wish of the entrepreneur who has arrived economically makes it possible that not he is received by the feudal lord, but rather the feudal lord by the rich bourgeois; the dreamer is not the bourgeois, but the Junker, whose dream song simultaneously reestablishes lost, pre-capitalistic immediacy in contrast to the rational system of rules developed by the bourgeois "master." The suffering of the bourgeois individual under his own, and at the same time, isolated reality, the *Tristan* side of *Die Meistersinger*, is united in hatred of the petit bourgeois Beckmesser with the consciousness of the entrepreneur whose interest is worldwide economic expansion. The entrepreneur has experienced existing conditions of production as fetters upon the forces of production and perhaps already longs for monopoly in place of free competition, in the romantic image of the feudal lord. On the Festival Meadow in Act III of the opera, competition is actually no longer present; only a parody thereof is offered in the confrontation between the Junker Walther and Beckmesser. In the aesthetic triumph of Hans Sachs and the Junker, balance is achieved between the ideals of the privateer and the exporter in their struggle with each other. In Richard Strauss, the last significant bourgeois composer whose music is consumed by the bourgeoisie, international economics—as Ernst Bloch was the first to recognize—have attained the upper hand.[15] Inwardness and pessimism have been liquidated. "Ardor"—as the spirit of the entrepreneur—emancipates itself. Chromaticism and dissonance, previously means of liberation for bourgeois music from an established, irrational system and vehicle for a dialectic which attacks and transforms the material of music, lose their revolutionary-dialectical force and become, like exoticism and perversity in the subject matter, the mere emblem of worldwide economic maneuverability; technically, they are arbitrarily related as though they were ink blots which at any moment can be liquidated by the healthy optimism of the six-four chord. The material which finally emerges in Strauss's music is to a degree the primal material of all bourgeois music, diatonic-tonal, to which the bourgeoisie, in spite of all changes in structure, clings in truth as faithfully as it does to the principles of profit and interest. In Strauss this makes its appearance with some cynicism by subordinating to itself such foreign markets as literature, the Orient, antiquity and the eighteenth century.[16] There is a sharp divergence between Strauss's often and verbosely praised "technical sophistication," namely, a sophistication imposed from without and not immanent to the material, intended for the arbitrary and actually irrational "domination" of the apparatus—and an historically innocent, harmless and jovial musical substance; this divergence is not only quite suitable to the empirical state of consciousness of the upper bourgeois industrial entrepreneur around 1900, it further denotes with clarity the self-estrangement of the bourgeoisie from its own ratio, which it must intensify and curb simultaneously. Nonetheless, within the post-Wagnerian musical situation, through the social development and the immanent dialectic of Wagner's work, the alienation of musical material from society has advanced to such a degree that a productive force such as that of Strauss could not simply and unconditionally ignore the material demands and adapt itself to society. To be sure, in his best works—*Salome* and *Elektra*—the divergence is already indicated; in the music of John the Baptist and in the entire final section of *Elektra* banality is dominant, but at the beginning of *Salome*, in Elektra's monologue and in her scene with Klytemnestra, his compositional material declares as it were its independence and advances, against its will, to the very boundary of the tonal realm. This boundary is also the boundary of consumption: in the face of both works, the audience was shocked by both music and content and consequently denied them, if not the stages of all opera houses, at least a secure place in the repertory. This audience drew the line of its tolerance with Strauss and this line, in turn, affected his later work. But, in another sense, Strauss drew the line himself. Of all the composers of the bourgeoisie, he was perhaps the most class conscious; *Der Rosenkavalier* was his greatest success and in it the dialectic of material is invalidated from without. The diatonic is cleansed of all dangerous fermatas, and Octavian, the young man of good family, a trouser role, to top it off, is married to the daughter of newly ennobled wealth, while the Marschallin, simultaneously the heir of Hans Sachs and Isolde, has all the difficulty and finds consolation only in the abstract consciousness of transitoriness. With this intellectual sacrifice to consumer consciousness, Strauss's productive power is extinguished: everything that follows *Rosenkavalier* is either applied or commercial art—the break between production and consumption to which Strauss fell victim as a producer first took on extreme form only in Germany. In France, where the process of industrialization was less far advanced, thus expressing within itself the antinomies of bourgeois order less radically, both remain in harmony for a longer time. The bourgeoisie which was interested in music had extensive free time at its disposal and, trained by the painting of impressionism, it was able to follow the movement further; music, not yet isolated and not dialectical within itself by virtue of its polemic position toward society, could sublimate the means of this society within itself without making a substantial attack upon society. Even Debussy, an autonomous artist like the impressionist painters, whose technology he transposes into music, can take with him into his highly fastidious artistic method elements of bourgeois culinary music and even of salon music in terms of sound and melody. Of course, just as in Strauss, the diatonic emerges in Debussy, too— barren and archaic. This happens in his theory as well—in the dogma of natural overtones and the resulting Rousseauean diction, the consequence of the total sublimation of the primal musical material of the bourgeoisie. Ravel, with his knowing eye, can find no other means of adjustment to this situation than through psychological-literary appeasement: he resorts to gentle irony. Even in France, however, this marks the end of reconciliation. The composers of the post-Ravel generation manifest the most suspicious lack from which French artists could possibly suffer: the lack of métier. Tradition, which lasted for such a long time, has been broken; a replacement through isolated musical training in Schoenberg's sense has not yet come into being—between serious production and bourgeois consumption a vacuum is openly revealed everywhere. Production within which immanence achieved crystallization remains inaccessible; that production, however, which adjusted to consumption is rejected in its subaltern faint-heartedness by the upper bourgeoisie itself as "epigonal." The bourgeoisie thus sees itself thrown back ever more definitely upon the limited circle of "classic" production which is no longer capable of extension. The recourse to pre-liberalist classicism, the refusal even of the "moderately modern" corresponds precisely to the economic-political recourse to pre-liberalist forms, as this recourse is dialectically conditioned by liberalism itself, wherever it has no desire to move progressively beyond itself.

Below the realm of "musical life," below education and representation, stretches the vast realm of *"light"* music. Along with commercial art and song, literature for male chorus and sophisticated jazz, it extends musical life without interruption, assimilating as much from above as is accessible to it; it reaches downward into the bottomless underworld far beyond the bourgeois "hit song" *[Schlager]* and from which at only occasional junctures eruptions such as the horrifying song "Drink, Drink, Dear Brother, Drink"[17] ascend into consciousness. Light music satisfies immediate needs, not only those of the bourgeoisie, but of all of society. At the same time, however, as pure commodity, it is the most alien of all music to society; it no longer expresses anything of social misery and contradiction, but forms rather in itself one single contradiction to this society. This it does by falsifying the cognition of reality through the satisfaction of desires which it grants to man. He is forced away from reality and divorced from both music and social history. Society tolerates light music as "kitsch," which, of course, lays no claim to aesthetic rights; as a means of diversion, however, it is not subject to any criticism. Thus in its way, society adjusts to the paradox of light music which of all music at one and the same time is the closest to and the most distant from man. The same products which as daydreams fulfill the conscious and unconscious desires of men are forced upon the same people by capitalism with all its technique with no influence from those affected whatsoever; they are not asked, indeed, they have not the slightest chance of defending themselves. Light music is protected in many ways from the grasp of cognition. First of all, it is looked upon as harmless, as a minor happiness of which man must not be robbed: further, it is viewed as lacking in seriousness and unworthy of educated consideration; finally, however, the mechanism of wish fulfillment through light music is rooted so deeply in the unconscious and is assigned so cautiously to the darkness of the unconscious that this mechanism, precisely in the most important cases, is hardly accessible without the aid of theory. Reference to such an "absurd" hit song as "Who Rolled the Cheese to the Depot?"[18] makes this sufficiently clear. Such study demands highly exact interpretation—the bourgeoisie would speak of "artistic" interpretation; indeed, even very precise psychological training is called for. Observations upon technique, such as are applied to art music, reveal very little, for they are able only to characterize vulgar music in terms of its inability to develop an autonomous technique, through which it might easily have met the demands of consumption as a commodity. The place of technical analysis should be taken by an indication of the few, regressively preserved and obviously archaic-symbolic *types* and figures with which vulgar music operates; furthermore, a scheme of *depravation* should be worked out, in which only light music registers history, integrating it into the archaic mechanism of drives; finally, *changes* within light music demand description and documentation of their economic constitution; in spite of the "ahistoricism" of their types, they are extensive and important. Organized scholarship has paid no attention to any of this; the material involved has not even been philologically prepared. Such study has not gotten beyond the obvious relation between contemporary and older vulgar music, accordingly traditional dance forms, the communal song, opera buffa, and the *Singspiel*—and the confirmation of "primal motives" along with the folkloristic satisfaction that they offer. Here, however, where the invariables are completely obvious, the concern should be less with their definition than with their functional interpretation; it should be shown that the same components and the identical drive structures to which light music adjusts take on totally different meanings depending upon the given state of social progress; the same vulgar song type, for example, with the profanity of which the youthful bourgeoisie of the seventeenth and eighteenth centuries unmasked feudal hierarchy and made fun of it today serves the transfiguration and apology of the rational bourgeois profane world, whose typewriters—despite all rationalization—are transformed into music and sung—they are capable of transforming them into "immediacy." Furthermore, the formal changes encountered in all types of light music should be studied in connection with change in function. If the apocryphal character of light music complicates its social study, it could be simplified through the disappearance within it of any autonomous dialectic of production. The exposure of vulgar music need not be mediated through the technological indication of its immanent contradictions, because, in obedience to social dictates, it offers far less opposition to social categories than do independent production and educated musical life. However, the obscure realm of light music remains unexamined; there is, therefore, nothing to be gained from prejudging its topography, for the limited number of basic types, along with the drastic ideological function of many phenomena within this music, are misleading, resulting in premature anticipation of the entire sphere without definition of its "idea" with the necessary pragmatic discipline—social interpretation is thus deprived not only of its reliability, but probably of its productivity as well. Even the conceitedly summary treatment of light music remains obedient; by borrowing from it that ambiguous irony with which light music—like many contemporary films—inclines to smile at itself in order to pass by without being challenged, such observation accepts as an object of the game that which should be seen by the inexorable eye, untouched by laughter, as the fateful power of deception concentrated in light music. Until such observation becomes possible, fragmentary indications must suffice.

As old as the tension between art music and vulgar music is, it became radical only in high capitalism. In earlier epochs, art music was able to regenerate its material from time to time and enlarge its sphere by recourse to vulgar music. This is seen in medieval polyphony, which drew upon folk songs for its *cantus firmi*, and also in Mozart, when he combined peep-show cosmology with opera seria and *Singspiel*. Even the masters of the nineteenth-century operetta, Offenbach and Johann Strauss, remained sufficiently in command of the divergence between these two spheres of musical production. Today the possibility of balance has vanished and attempts at amalgamation, such as those undertaken by diligent art composers at the time when jazz was the rage, remain unproductive. There is no longer any "folk" whose songs and games could be taken up and sublimated by art; the opening up of markets and the bourgeois process of rationalization have subordinated all society to bourgeois categories. This subordination extends to ideology as well. The categories of contemporary vulgar music are in their entirety those of bourgeois rational society, which—only in order that they remain subject to consumption—are kept within the limits of consciousness imposed by bourgeois society not only upon the suppressed classes, but upon itself as well. The material of vulgar music is the obsolete or depraved material of art music. The music of Johann Strauss is set off from the art music of the time through its "genre," but this separation is not total; his waltzes leave room for harmonic differentiation and, furthermore, they are formed thematically out of small, contrasting units never subject merely to empty repetition. It is the surprising connection of these fragments which gives the Strauss waltz its charm, its "pungency," relating it at the same time to the tradition of Viennese classicism, from which it is derived via Strauss senior, Lanner[19] and Schubert. It is the decisive factor in the history of recent vulgar music that the definitive break, the sacrifice of its relation to independent production, the growing vacuity and banalization of light music corresponds exactly to the *industrialization* of production. The authors of light music were forced into mass production by inconceivably intense competition; those among them who succeeded, back before the war already, banded together in compositional trusts; they settled down in the Austrian Salzkammergut and, in carefully planned cooperation with librettists and theater directors, kept outsiders and novices at a distance. Through restriction of production to their own limited number, they established norms for the manufacture of the operetta, defining, above all, the quantity and type of the individual "numbers." At the same time, they calculated the sale of their creations in advance, avoiding for that reason all difficulties that might hinder remembrance and singing of their melodies—a practice of which the Viennese or Parisian bourgeoisie of 1880 was still capable. The sign of the industrialization of musical production was the total elimination of all contrast within melodies and the sole domination of the sequence, which of course had been employed previously as a means by which music impressed itself on the listener. Exemplary for the establishment of the new style is the waltz from *The Merry Widow;* the jubilation with which the bourgeoisie received Lehár's operetta is comparable to the success of the first department stores. Oscar Straus,[20] for example, who was still rooted in the Viennese tradition, had learned his handicraft and had exerted great effort toward a richer and more complex operetta music. However, he had to earn his living either through commercial music, from which the social effectiveness of Johann Strauss was lacking, or adjust to industrialization. Leo Fall[21] is the last composer who withdrew from this affair with some dignity. All these composers, however, were still on intimate terms with bourgeois art music, expressed within the *operetta* form itself as a unity or a "totality"—even if in a parodistic manner—which demanded of them musical architecture, strong personal contours in the characters of their works and, finally, originality and inspiration as well. The industrial development of light music annuled the last aesthetic responsibility and transformed light music into a market article. The material subject matter of the revue liquidated the subjective, formal element of the operetta and, in its appeal to the listener, the operetta was undercut by it. This it did not only by offering the audience girls*, but further by liberating it from the last demands of intellectual activity, of thinking participation in the events presented to it and in their unity. The stage thus surrenders to irresponsible play with wishes and desires, through which the revue-operetta, strangely enough, approached certain intentions of independent production. This aspect of the revue made the Viennese operetta and its Hungarian by-product institutions of serious competition. The sound film then eliminated all original musical inspiration. While a hit such as "Valencia,"[22] so as to dominate the market, was still called upon to make a distinction between the banality of its secondary maneuvers via asymmetrical, "cute" meter and other banalities, the totally rationalized factories of sound film hits with their capitalistic division of labor are excused from such efforts. No matter how their products look and sound, they are "successes"; listeners are forced to sing them to themselves, not only because the most finely tooled machinery hammers them into them, but above all, because the monopoly of the sound film prevents all other musical commodities, from which they might choose something else, from reaching them. Here monopoly capitalism has asserted itself purely and extremely; in clumsy efforts such as Bomben auf Monte Carlo,[23] it has further defined the political dimension of the omnipotence. Even if vulgar music in terms of its form and structure is thus removed from the educational categories of bourgeois society, categories about whose continuation this music is deeply concerned, it clings nonetheless to the materials of education as fetishes. The industrialization of light music and the abrasion of the bourgeois educational heritage which it accomplishes go hand in hand. It is no coincidence that at the same time in which the last chances of authentic production of light music have been eliminated, the operetta undertakes the glorification of the "creative" artist by stealing his melodies: Das Dreimäderlhaus,[24] with its abuse of Schubert's music, is a necessary component of the economic substructure of hit song fabrication, both as an advertisement and ideology, and every further development of the industrial apparatus has strengthened the fetish character of the educational heritage within which light music still lives more extremely. Frie-

derike and *Das Land des Lächelns*,[25] with all its exoticism, are sister-works; the ready-made jazz industry lives from the arrangements of "classical" music, for this heritage provides jazz with raw materials. This heritage, in turn, is strengthened, as a fetish, through the happiness of renewed encounter. The ideological function of *jazz* when it first asserted itself as the upper bourgeois form of contemporary vulgar music was to conceal the commodity character and alienated manner of production of this music; it was to be offered under the trademark of "quality goods." Jazz was to evoke the appearance of improvisational freedom and immediacy in the sphere of light music; this is why it could be so adapted so conveniently by efforts of similar intention in art music. The maneuver of jazz has been psychologically successful for years: thanks to the structure of a society whose mechanism of rationalization inevitably produces the necessity of disguising itself in the interest of turnover in the marketplace. The commodity character of jazz music is objectively evident. In jazz there can be no talk of "immediate" production; the division of labor into "inventor," proof reader, harmonizer, and specialist for instrumentation is, if possible, still further advanced in this case than in the manufacture of operetta. The apparent improvisations of *hot** music are totally the expression of set norms which can be traced back to a very few basic types: in the same manner, in jazz, freedom and rhythmic wealth are illusory from the perspective of musical immanence: metrically the eight-bar structure dominates, making use of syncopation and the interpolation of false beats[26] only as ornaments. In its harmonic-formal relations, however, this structure asserts itself without challenge, and rhythmic emancipation is restricted to the sustained quarter notes of the bass drum. Beneath the opulent surface of jazz lies the—barren, unchanged, clearly detachable—most primitive harmonic–tonal scheme with its breakdown into half- and full-cadences and equally primitive meter and form. It is socially and musically equally revealing that jazz bands and jazz composition were able to obey the fashion of military marches with ease when political reversal took place within the crisis which proclaimed the upper bourgeoisie drive of the entrepreneur in place of world-market expansion and the exotic-folkloristic corollary thereof in the vulgar music of national autarchy, which it further demanded of commercial art. The bass drum, whose previous purpose was the representation of the dance-like primal feelings of colonial peoples, now regulates the march step of local formations. The elements of musical impressionism used by jazz—the whole-tone scale, the ninth chord, chordal parallel movements—change nothing in this situation. It is not merely that they do not appear until after the dialectic of art music has left them far behind, following the exhaustion of their value as stimuli—in the same manner, vulgar music of the second half of the nineteenth century took over chromaticism from preceding romanticism. More essential, however, is that these means totally lost every formative power in jazz. All the old salon pieces, waltzes, character pieces and reveries inserted into jazz employed chromaticism only in the form of intermediate notes alien to harmony without chromaticization of the harmonic foundation itself. In like manner, in jazz, impressionistic flourishes appear only as interpolations without disturbing the harmonic-metric scheme. Light music clings rigidly to the diatonic as its "base in nature," and it is the more certain of this base the sooner it can permit itself, as jazz does, an excess under this sign.

If the scheme of depravation of light music is anticipated by its immanence in the static basic material of bourgeois art music: in tonality; and if in these terms the relation of light music to art music offers no terribly great difficulties, even in terms of social interpretation, the difficulties involved in a *theory of all types* are all the greater. Even the very basic state of affairs in light music, the division into couplet and refrain, is not easily accessible. If the historical origin thereof in the exchange between solo and choral song is considered, and if it is compared with the trick of many contemporary hits which narrate the story of their refrain in the couplet, as it were, the following interpretation seems probable: in its stereotyped figures, light music attempts to master the fact of its alienation by absorbing the reporting, observing, and detached individual, as soon as he begins the refrain, into a fictive collective. This individual, in turn, finds his significance enforced through his participation in the objectivity of the refrain; indeed, he experiences the content of the refrain text as his own content in the couplet. He then recognizes this content in the refrain with astonishment and elevation as a collective content. The psychological mechanism of hit song production, consequently, is narcissistic; the demand for arbitrary singability of hit tunes corresponds to this: in his ability to re-sing the melody with which he is manipulated, every listener identifies with the original vehicles of the melody, with leading personalities or with a collective of warriors which intones the song. He thus forgets his own isolation and accepts the illusion either that he is embraced by the collective or that he himself is a leading personality. Be that as it may, this mechanism does not prevail without exception: even if the major portion of hit song production clings to the division between couplet and refrain, several of the most successful hits of the postwar period—such as *"The Dancing Tambourine*"* and *"The Wedding of the*

Painted Doll*"27—side-stepped this division. The first of these songs is a
dance movement with trio; the second, a type of "character piece" in the
sense of the nineteenth century. In such pieces, the success of which is not
to be ascribed to their texts, the psychological mechanism cannot be defined
so easily; in "Tambourine," it might be a certain melodic contour, particularly in the trio; in the "Doll" song, the impulse of infantilism has an
influence, but such definitions are far less meaningful than psychoanalytical characteristics provoked by every hit song. This it does in order that
a second and more dangerous significance can be concealed behind the
psychoanalytic individual meaning: the social significance of the song. If,
however, in these two instrumental songs, the role of the music is so
considerable in the effect produced, one is hardly justified in ignoring this
effect in those songs with text. No method for the analysis of the psychological *effect* of music has been developed, and even Ernst Kurth's psychology of music[28] offers no sufficient instructions on this problem, which
is perhaps in reality the most important one in the social interpretation of
music. There is the further question, whether psychology in this case is
sufficient: whether the decisive categories are not rather to be provided by
social theory. The "psychology" of hit songs in the traditional sense leads
to constants in the realm of drives. Thus, in the explanation of the "absurd" type of hit, it is illuminating to make reference to anal regression
along with its sadistic components which are seldom lacking in the song
texts at hand; absurdity is portrayed as blanks created by censorship which
can, however, easily be filled in. With the definition of the anal-sadistic
structure of those hits, nothing is said about their present social function;
their effect is rather traced back to a natural disposition of drives and the
conflict thereof with society in general, an aspect which at any given time
is equally specific, while the origin and function of the hit song within
capitalism is not questioned at all. However, as long as the social dialectic
and the analysis of the structure of drives stand discretely or merely "com-
plementarily" beside each other, the concrete effect of light music has not
been seen through; it remains rather assigned to various individual disciplines, which, in the sense of bourgeois systematic scholarship, proceed in
isolation, underscoring in their separation one of the most questionable
disjunctions of bourgeois thought itself: the disjunction between nature
and history. The social interpretation of light and, in the final analysis, of
all music is faced by the one central question: what method is it to employ
to avoid still further presumption in methodology of the ambiguity of the
static state of nature—in the components of drives—and of dynamic historical quality—in its social function. If music, as it has done up to the

present, is to escape the schematism of individual psychology, if the most elementary of its effects presupposes a concrete social condition of which it offers a tendentious indication, and if nature itself does not appear in music other than in historic images, then the material character of music might offer an indication that dialectical materialism might not answer the "question" about the relation of nature and history, but that it might rather contribute to the elimination of this question both in theory and praxis.

(1932; GS, vol. 18, pp. 729–77)
Translated by Wes Blomster; revised by Richard Leppert)

NOTES BY RICHARD LEPPERT

Wes Blomster's 1978 translation of this important essay was among the first of Adorno's German musical writings to appear in English. While there is much to be admired in this translation, several problems required attention. Most important, throughout the essay a few words, phrases, and entire sentences were omitted; I have restored them. Elsewhere, Blomster inserted words, as clarification, but without brackets or any other signal to the reader; in these instances, I have either omitted the additions in those instances where clarification seemed unnecessary or retained the addition but placed it within brackets. Blomster sometimes substantially reordered Adorno's sentence structure, presumably the better to conform to conventional English usage. Where possible, I have followed Adorno's syntax in an effort to restore the text's original rhetorical impact. Blomster often repunctuated the essay, breaking up long sentences into a series of shorter ones. While this is often necessary, at other times it dilutes the power of Adorno's dialectical prose, as in instances where, in the German, a lengthy sentence is followed by one or more short ones, the latter serving rhetorically to drive home a point more dramatically. Similarly, where Adorno employs a comma, Blomster often uses a dash, which in my view tends to render Adorno's sentences too explicitly demonstrative, and which as well renders invisible Adorno's very precise occasional use of the dash. As much as possible, I have restored the original punctuation.

1. Words which occupy an important position in Adorno's vocabulary are *Musikant* and *Musikantentum*. In the total absence of corresponding English terms, they are translated here as "music maker" and "music making," using quotations marks, as Adorno himself has done with the German terms in most cases. The concepts, while not necessarily pejorative, usually convey a certain negative bite in Adorno's usage. They can refer to an extremely healthy, gifted musicianship, which is usually characterized by the lack of an intellectual dimension. The German words often evoke images of Bohemian and even gypsy musicians. [Wes Blomster]

2. Concerning *Gebrauchsmusik*, see p. 133 n. 2.

3. Robert Stolz (1880–1975), a prolific Austrian composer and conductor, wrote twenty-seven operettas and nearly 2,000 popular songs in the Viennese romantic tradition, as well as scores for numerous films; late in his life he composed music for ice reviews.

4. Regarding Karl Kraus, see p. 494 n. 12.

5. Adolf Loos (1870–1933), Austrian architect noted especially for his design of private houses. Loos was a pronounced enemy of decoration and ornamentation.

The *Sachlichkeit* [or *die Neue Sachlichkeit*] movements in early-twentieth-century German art are conventionally differentially rendered in English. In architecture the term is usually "functionalism"; in literature "realism"; and in visual art and music "New Objectivity" or "New-Matter-of-Factness." The movements are by no means identical in purpose or outlook. Adorno's references to *Neue Sachlichkeit* in music, for example, are critical of what he regarded as its aesthetic conservatism (a prime example of what he sometimes named "moderate modernism"), whereas by contrast Adorno considers Loos's architecture as notably progressive. See further n. 7, below.

6. Alois Hába (1893–1973), Czech theorist, teacher, and composer, especially noted for his microtonal (quarter-tone and sixth-tone) compositions. Regarding *"Musikstil der Freiheit,"* see his *Von der Psychologie der musikalischen Gestaltung: Gesetzmässigkeit der Tonbewegung und Grundlagen eines neuen Musikstils*, trans. Josef Löwenbach (Vienna: Universal Edition, 1925), p. 3.

7. Here begins a lengthy critical discussion of the musical *Neue Sachlichkeit* movement of the 1920s of which Hindemith was the principal composer. Adorno is repelled by the movement for the same reason he rejects the neo-classicism of Stravinsky from the same period, concerning which, see pp. 554–56. David Neumeyer, *The Music of Paul Hindemith* (New Haven: Yale University Press, 1986), p. 13: "The New Objectivity was frankly antiromantic [not the reason Adorno stood in opposition], a rejection of pre–World War expressionism and an affirmation of a new urban culture—society as a city-machine. The New Objectivity composers substituted linear, kinetic energy and deliberate formal constructivism for the nineteenth century's psychological development (motivic working and endless melody), functional harmony, and sensuous orchestral timbres." Adorno objected to what he heard as the anti-humane triumph of technocracy in the musical *Neue Sachlichkeit*.

8. The portraits by the Austrian expressionist Oskar Kokoschka (1886–1980) are noted for their intensity of psychological insight, especially through the bold use of color—and thus strikingly different from the conventionally reserved palette employed for portraits of the bourgeoisie and aristocracy alike. Adorno's contrasting Kokoschka with the more conventionally pretty impressionist images further highlights the distinctions he is wont to draw.

Kokoschka also wrote plays; the text of his *Orpheus und Eurydike* (1918) was adapted by Adorno's friend Ernst Krenek and set as an opera in 1926. He carried on a tempestuous love affair with Alma Mahler for three years, beginning in 1911, a year following the composer's death.

9. Søren Kierkegaard, *Fear and Trembling: A Dialectical Lyric, by Johannes de Silentio*, trans. Alastair Hannay (Harmondsworth, UK: Penguin, 1985).

10. Alfredo Casella (1883–1947), Italian composer, pianist, and conductor. Whereas the compositions from 1913 to 1919 reflected Casella's enthusiasm for music of the European avant-garde—including Stravinsky, Bartók, and Schoenberg—from about 1920 his music is resolutely neo-classical and conservative. Casella's opera *Il deserto tentato* (1937) openly supported Mussolini's Ethiopian campaign, hence Adorno's sarcastic comment about the composer's ambitions in the realm of cultural politics.

11. Zoltán Kodály (1882–1967), Hungarian composer, teacher, and ethnomusicologist; he published his first collection of Hungarian folk songs in 1905, a project he continued to the end of his life. He composed choral music especially, much of which consists of folksong arrangements, though his original choral compositions are for all intents and purposes indistinguishable from the arrangements.

12. Adorno often used the metaphor of masking as a sign of cultural and social

deception in modernity; in PNM, he expands upon the charge, leveled in this essay, against "Stravinsky's games of masks"; see, for example, pp. 147, 179, 184, 206.

13. The song cycle by Paul Hindemith (1895–1963), *Das Marienleben*, op. 27, for soprano solo and orchestra, sets the 1913 poems of the same name by Rainer Maria Rilke (1875–1926). Adorno highlights this work in light of the fact that it represents Hindemith's compositional turn to *Neue Sachlichkeit*. Hindemith's first version of the cycle was composed in 1922–23; he substantially rewrote it between 1936 and 1948. At the time of this essay, Adorno of course refers to the first version. For a full discussion and analysis of the different versions, see Neumeyer, *Music of Paul Hindemith*, pp. 137–67.

14. Founded in 1922, the International Society for Contemporary Music (ISCM), known in Germany as the Internationale Gesellschaft für Neue Musik (IGNM), staged its first international festival of new music in 1923, while also mounting a number of national festivals. By the time Adorno wrote this essay, ISCM was well established, though with the advent of Nazism its activities were banned in Germany.

15. Ernst Bloch, *Essays on the Philosophy of Music*, trans. Peter Palmer (Cambridge: Cambridge University Press, 1985), pp. 37–39, is essentially homologous with Adorno's discussion of Strauss, the flavor of which is evident in the following (p. 37): "It is very difficult fully to come to terms with Strauss. He is banal and presents the picture of an industrious man who can enjoy life and take it as it comes. But to compensate for and notwithstanding this, Strauss is good company to the highest degree. Even when he is merely crafty and composes fashionable successes, even amid the most frightful kitsch, he is eminently upper-class with his free and easy, sovereign, worldly manners, from which all trace of the old German petty bourgeoisie has disappeared." See also Adorno, "Richard Strauss: Born June 11, 1864," trans. Samuel Weber and Shierry Weber, *Perspectives of New Music* 3 (Fall/Winter 1965), pp. 14–32, and 4 (Spring/Summer 1966), 113–29.

16. Adorno's references to Strauss operas include *Salome* (the Orient); *Ariadne auf Naxos* (antiquity); *Der Rosenkavalier* (the eighteenth century); and *Ariadne auf Naxos* and *Elektra* (literature).

17. "Trink, trink, Brüderlein trink" (1927), music by Paul Raasch, lyrics by Wilhelm Lindemann; popular beer-hall tune which has long since achieved canonic status.

18. "Wer hat denn den Käse zum Bahnhof gerollt"; I have not located any details concerning this German novelty song.

19. Both Johann Strauss senior (1804–1849) and Joseph Lanner (1801–1843) were violinists, dance-orchestra leaders, and composers of Austrian dance music, waltzes especially. Strauss played for a time in Lanner's ensembles and orchestras—one of which Strauss led—until the two had a falling out. Thereafter, Strauss led his own Viennese orchestra which also traveled widely in Europe, unlike Lanner's which remained in Vienna, performing in coffeehouses and taverns, and for balls.

20. Oscar Straus (1870–1954), prolific Austrian operetta composer—not related to the other musical Strausses.

21. Leo Fall (1873–1925), prolific and successful Austrian operetta composer, whose works are typically melodious, as well as rhythmically inventive.

22. "Valencia," music by José Padilla, English lyrics by Clifford Grey; the original lyrics were in French. The song was introduced in the United States in the 1926 revue *The Great Temptations*. Adorno refers to this tune a number of times in various essays.

23. The German film comedy by director Hanns Schwarz and screenwriter

Franz Schulz, *The Bombardment of Monte Carlo* (1931) tells a ridiculously improbable story of a ship's captain from a fictional land who docks in Monte Carlo. Neither captain nor crew has been paid in months. Monte Carlo's Queen, moving about incognito, overhears his complaints and sells her pearls to pay his salary. The two gamble with the proceeds, win a great deal at the tables, but lose all of it on a bad bet, after which the captain threatens to shell the casino unless his money is returned. The queen, no longer hiding her identity, relieves him of his command—and the two promptly fall in love. The film's score was an early effort by Werner Heymann. Heymann left Germany after Hitler came to power; during the 1930s and 1940s he wrote scores for nearly fifty Hollywood films; he returned to Europe in 1950.

24. The highly successful pastische *Das Dreimäderlhaus* (1916) is a *Singspiel* by A. M. Willner and Heinz Reichert, with music by Franz Schubert, arranged by Heinrich Berté. The narrative, based on the novel *Schwammerl* by Rudolf Bartsch, created a fictional, if ultimately unsuccessful, hetero-normative love-life for the composer. The show was somewhat revamped for its London premiere, where it was called *Lilac Time* (1922), and again for its New York premiere, as *Blossom Time* (1921), with musical arrangements by Sigmund Romberg. Several film versions were also produced, including *Blossom Time* (1934), with Richard Tauber.

25. Adorno refers to two highly popular operettas by Franz Lehár (1870–1948): *Friederike* (1928), a tale of the ill-fated relationship between Johann Wolfgang Goethe and Friederike Brion, details of which are recounted in the poet's *Dichtung und Wahrheit*, books 10–11; and the orientalist *Das Land des Lächelns* (1929). Both were first produced in Berlin, with Richard Tauber—Lehár's favorite tenor—in the leading male roles. *Das Land des Lächelns* was a revised version of Lehár's *Die gelbe Jacke* (1923), which one critic dubbed *Monsieur Butterfly*.

26. Regarding "false beats," see p. 492 n. 1.

27. Adorno knew instrumental versions of these songs, both of which also had lyrics: "The Dancing Tambourine" (1927), music by W. C. Polla, lyrics by Phil Ponce; and "The Wedding of the Painted Doll" (1929), music by Nacio Herb Brown, lyrics by Arthur Freed.

28. Regarding Kurth, see p. 160 n. 13.

On Popular Music

[With the assistance of George Simpson]

1. THE MUSICAL MATERIAL

The two spheres of music

Popular music, which produces the stimuli we are here investigating, is usually characterized by its difference from serious music. This difference is generally taken for granted and is looked upon as a difference of levels considered so well defined that most people regard the values within them as totally independent of one another. We deem it necessary, however, first of all to translate these so-called levels into more precise terms, musical as well as social, which not only delimit them unequivocally but throw light upon the whole setting of the two musical spheres as well.

One possible method of achieving this clarification would be an historical analysis of the division as it occurred in music production and of the roots of the two main spheres. Since, however, the present study is concerned with the actual function of popular music in its present status, it is more advisable to follow the line of characterization of the phenomenon itself as it is given today than to trace it back to its origins. This is the more justified as the division into the two spheres of music took place in Europe long before American popular music arose. American music from its inception accepted the division as something pre-given, and therefore the historical background of the division applies to it only indirectly. Hence we seek, first of all, an insight into the fundamental characteristics of popular music in the broadest sense.

A clear judgment concerning the relation of serious music to popular music can be arrived at only by strict attention to the fundamental characteristic of popular music: standardization.[A] The whole structure of popular music is standardized, even where the attempt is made to circumvent standardization. Standardization extends from the most general features to the most specific ones. Best known is the rule that the chorus consists of thirty-two bars and that the range is limited to one octave and one note. The general types of hits are also standardized: not only the dance types, the rigidity of whose pattern is understood, but also the "characters" such as mother songs, home songs, nonsense or "novelty" songs, pseudo-nursery rhymes, laments for a lost girl. Most important of all, the harmonic cornerstones of each hit—the beginning and the end of each part—must beat out the standard scheme. This scheme emphasizes the most primitive harmonic facts no matter what has harmonically intervened. Complications have no consequences. This inexorable device guarantees that regardless of what aberrations occur, the hit will lead back to the same familiar experience, and nothing fundamentally novel will be introduced.

The details themselves are standardized no less than the form, and a whole terminology exists for them such as break, blue chords, dirty notes. Their standardization, however, is somewhat different from that of the framework. It is not overt like the latter but hidden behind a veneer of individual "effects" whose prescriptions are handled as the experts' secret,

A. The basic importance of standardization has not altogether escaped the attention of current literature on popular music. "The chief difference between a popular song and a standard, or serious, song like 'Mandalay,' 'Sylvia' or 'Trees,' is that the melody and the lyric of a popular number are constructed within a definite pattern or structural form, whereas the poem, or lyric, of a standard number has no structural confinements, and the music is free to interpret the meaning and feeling of the words without following a set pattern or form. Putting it another way, the popular song is 'custom built,' while the standard song allows the composer freer play of imagination and interpretation." (Abner Silver and Robert Bruce, *How to Write and Sell a Song Hit* [New York: Prentice Hall, 1939], p. 2.) The authors fail, however, to realize the externally super-imposed, commercial character of those patterns which aims at canalized reactions or, in the language of the regular announcement of one particular radio program, at "easy listening." They confuse the mechanical patterns with highly organized, strict art forms: "Certainly there are few more stringent verse forms in poetry than the sonnet, and yet the greatest poets of all time have woven undying beauty within its small and limited frame. A composer has just as much opportunity for exhibiting his talent and genius in popular songs as in more serious music" (pp. 2–3). Thus the standard pattern of popular music appears to them virtually on the same level as the law of a fugue. It is this contamination which makes the insight into the basic standardization of popular music sterile. It ought to be added that what Silver and Bruce call a "standard song" is just the opposite of what we mean by a standardized popular song.

however open this secret may be to musicians generally. This contrasting character of the standardization of the whole and part provides a rough, preliminary setting for the effect upon the listener.

The primary effect of this relation between the framework and the detail is that the listener becomes prone to evince stronger reactions to the part than to the whole. His grasp of the whole does not lie in the living experience of this one concrete piece of music he has followed. The whole is pre-given and pre-accepted, even before the actual experience of the music starts; therefore, it is not likely to influence, to any great extent, the reaction to the details, except to give them varying degrees of emphasis. Details which occupy musically strategic positions in the framework—the beginning of the chorus or its reentrance after the bridge—have a better chance for recognition and favorable reception than details not so situated, for instance, middle bars of the bridge. But this situational nexus never interferes with the scheme itself. To this limited situational extent the detail depends upon the whole. But no stress is ever placed upon the whole as a musical event, nor does the structure of the whole ever depend upon the details.

Serious music, for comparative purposes, may be thus characterized:

Every detail derives its musical sense from the concrete totality of the piece which, in turn, consists of the life relationship of the details and never of a mere enforcement of a musical scheme. For example, in the introduction of the first movement of Beethoven's Seventh Symphony the second theme (in C major) gets its true meaning only from the context. Only through the whole does it acquire its particular lyrical and expressive quality—that is, a whole built up of its very contrast with the *cantus firmus*–like character of the first theme. Taken in isolation the second theme would be disrobed to insignificance. Another example may be found in the beginning of the recapitulation over the pedal point of the first movement of Beethoven's *Appassionata*. By following the preceding outburst it achieves the utmost dramatic momentum. By omitting the exposition and development and starting with this repetition, all is lost.

Nothing corresponding to this can happen in popular music. It would not affect the musical sense if any detail were taken out of the context; the listener can supply the "framework" automatically, since it is a mere musical automatism itself. The beginning of the chorus is replaceable by the beginning of innumerable other choruses. The interrelationship among the elements or the relationship of the elements to the whole would be unaffected. In Beethoven, position is important only in a living relation between a concrete totality and its concrete parts. In popular music, position is absolute. Every detail is substitutable; it serves its function only as a cog in a machine.

The mere establishment of this difference is not yet sufficient. It is possible to object that the far-reaching standard schemes and types of popular music are bound up with dance, and therefore are also applicable to dance-derivatives in serious music: for example, the minuetto and scherzo of the classical Viennese School. It may be maintained either that this part of serious music is also to be comprehended in terms of detail rather than of whole, or that if the whole still is perceivable in the dance types in serious music despite recurrence of the types, there is no reason why it should not be perceivable in modern popular music.

The following consideration provides an answer to both objections by showing the radical differences even where serious music employs dance-types. According to current formalistic views the scherzo of Beethoven's Fifth Symphony can be regarded as a highly stylized minuetto. What Beethoven takes from the traditional minuetto scheme in this scherzo is the idea of outspoken contrast between a minor minuetto, a major trio, and repetition of the minor minuetto; and also certain other characteristics such as the emphatic three-four rhythm often accentuated on the first fourth and, by and large, dance-like symmetry in the sequence of bars and periods. But the specific form-idea of this movement as a concrete totality transvaluates the devices borrowed from the minuetto scheme. The whole movement is conceived as an introduction to the finale in order to create tremendous tension, not only by its threatening, foreboding expression but even more by the very way in which its formal development is handled.

The classical minuetto scheme required first the appearance of the main theme, then the introduction of a second part which may lead to more distant tonal regions—formalistically similar, to be sure, to the "bridge" of today's popular music—and finally the recurrence of the original part. All this occurs in Beethoven. He takes up the idea of thematic dualism within the scherzo part. But he forces what was, in the conventional minuetto, a mute and meaningless game-rule to speak with meaning. He achieves complete consistency between the formal structure and its specific content, that is to say, the elaboration of its themes. The whole scherzo part of this scherzo (that is to say, what occurs before the entrance of the deep strings in C major that marks the beginning of the trio), consists of the dualism of two themes, the creeping figure in the strings and the "objective," stone-like answer of the wind instruments. This dualism is not developed in a schematic way so that first the phrase of the strings is elaborated, then the answer of the winds, and then the string theme is mechanically repeated. After the first occurrence of the second theme in the horns, the two essential elements are alternately interconnected in the manner of a dialogue, and the end of the scherzo part is actually marked, not by the first, but by the second theme which has overwhelmed the first musical phrase.

Furthermore, the repetition of the scherzo after the trio is scored so differently that it sounds like a mere shadow of the scherzo and assumes that haunting character which vanishes only with the affirmative entry of the finale theme. The whole device has been made dynamic. Not only the themes, but the musical form itself have been subjected to tension: the same tension which is already manifest within the two-fold structure of the first theme that consists, as it were, of question and reply, and then even more manifest within the context between the two main themes. The whole scheme has become subject to the inherent demands of this particular movement.

To sum up the difference: in Beethoven and in good serious music in general—we are not concerned here with bad serious music which may be as rigid and mechanical as popular music—the detail virtually contains the whole and leads to the exposition of the whole, while, at the same time, it is produced out of the conception of the whole. In popular music the relationship is fortuitous. The detail has no bearing on a whole, which appears as an extraneous framework. Thus, the whole is never altered by the individual event and therefore remains, as it were, aloof, imperturbable, and unnoticed throughout the piece. At the same time, the detail is mutilated by a device which it can never influence and alter, so that the detail remains inconsequential. A musical detail which is not permitted to develop becomes a caricature of its own potentialities.

Standardization

The previous discussion shows that the difference between popular and serious music can be grasped in more precise terms than those referring to musical levels such as "lowbrow and highbrow," "simple and complex," "naïve and sophisticated." For example, the difference between the spheres cannot be adequately expressed in terms of complexity and simplicity. All works of the earlier Viennese classicism are, without exception, rhythmically simpler than stock arrangements of jazz. Melodically, the wide intervals of a good many hits such as "Deep Purple" or "Sunrise Serenade"[1] are more difficult to follow *per se* than most melodies of, for example, Haydn, which consist mainly of circumscriptions of tonic triads, and second steps. Harmonically, the supply of chords of the so-called classics is invariably more limited than that of any current Tin Pan Alley composer who draws from Debussy, Ravel, and even later sources. Standardization and non-standardization are the key contrasting terms for the difference.

Structural standardization aims at standard reactions. Listening to popular music is manipulated not only by its promoters, but as it were, by the inherent nature of this music itself, into a system of response-mechanisms wholly antagonistic to the ideal of individuality in a free, liberal society. This has nothing to do with simplicity and complexity. In serious music, each musical element, even the simplest one, is "itself," and the more highly organized the work is, the less possibility there is of substitution among the details. In hit music, however, the structure underlying the piece is abstract, existing independent of the specific course of the music. This is basic to the illusion that certain complex harmonies are more easily understandable in popular music than the same harmonies in serious music. For the complicated in popular music never functions as "itself" but only as a disguise or embellishment behind which the scheme can always be perceived. In jazz the amateur listener is capable of replacing complicated rhythmical or harmonic formulas by the schematic ones which they represent and which they still suggest, however adventurous they appear. The ear deals with the difficulties of hit music by achieving slight substitutions derived from the knowledge of the patterns. The listener, when faced with the complicated, actually hears only the simple which it represents and perceives the complicated only as a parodistic distortion of the simple.

No such mechanical substitution by stereotyped patterns is possible in serious music. Here even the simplest event necessitates an effort to grasp it immediately instead of summarizing it vaguely according to institutionalized prescriptions capable of producing only institutionalized effects. Otherwise the music is not "understood." Popular music, however, is composed in such a way that the process of translation of the unique into the norm is already planned and, to a certain extent, achieved within the composition itself.

The composition hears for the listener. This is how popular music divests the listener of his spontaneity and promotes conditioned reflexes. Not only does it not require his effort to follow its concrete stream; it actually gives him models under which anything concrete still remaining may be subsumed. The schematic build-up dictates the way in which he must listen while, at the same time, it makes any effort in listening unnecessary. Popular music is "predigested" in a way strongly resembling the fad of "digests" of printed material. It is this structure of contemporary popular music, which in the last analysis, accounts for those changes of listening habits which we shall later discuss.

So far standardization of popular music has been considered in structural terms—that is, as an inherent quality without explicit reference to the process of production or to the underlying causes for standardization. Though all industrial mass production necessarily eventuates in standardization, the production of popular music can be called "industrial" only in its promotion and distribution, whereas the act of producing a song hit still remains in a handicraft stage. The production of popular music is highly centralized in its economic organization, but still "individualistic" in its social mode of production. The division of labor among the composer, harmonizer, and arranger is not industrial but rather pretends industrialization, in order to look more up-to-date, whereas it has actually adapted industrial methods for the technique of its promotion. It would not increase the costs of production if the various composers of hit tunes did not follow certain standard patterns. Therefore, we must look for other reasons for structural standardization—very different reasons from those which account for the standardization of motor cars and breakfast foods.

Imitation offers a lead for coming to grips with the basic reasons for it. The musical standards of popular music were originally developed by a competitive process. As one particular song scored a great success, hundreds of others sprang up imitating the successful one. The most successful hits, types, and "ratios" between elements were imitated, and the process culminated in the crystallization of standards. Under centralized conditions such as exist today these standards have become "frozen."[B] That is, they have been taken over by cartelized agencies, the final results of a competitive process, and rigidly enforced upon material to be promoted. Noncompliance with the rules of the game became the basis for exclusion. The original patterns that are now standardized evolved in a more or less competitive way. Large-scale economic concentration institutionalized the standardization, and made it imperative. As a result, innovations by rugged individualists have been outlawed. The standard patterns have become invested with the immunity of bigness—"the King can do no wrong." This also accounts for revivals in popular music. They do not have the outworn

B. See Max Horkheimer, "Die Juden und Europa," *Zeitschrift für Sozialforschung* 8 nos. 1–2 (1939), p. 115.

character of standardized products manufactured after a given pattern. The breath of free competition is still alive within them. On the other hand, the famous old hits which are revived set the patterns which have become standardized. They are the golden age of the game-rules.

This "freezing" of standards is socially enforced upon the agencies themselves. Popular music must simultaneously meet two demands. One is for stimuli that provoke the listener's attention. The other is for the material to fall within the category of what the musically untrained listener would call "natural" music: that is, the sum total of all the conventions and material formulas in music to which he is accustomed and which he regards as the inherent, simple language of music itself, no matter how late the development might be which produced this natural language. This natural language for the American listener stems from his earliest musical experiences, the nursery rhymes, the hymns he sings in Sunday school, the little tunes he whistles on his way home from school. All these are vastly more important in the formation of musical language than his ability to distinguish the beginning of Brahms' Third Symphony from that of his Second. Official musical culture is, to a large extent, a mere superstructure of this underlying musical language, namely the major and minor tonality and all the tonal relationships it implies. But these tonal relationships of the primitive musical language set barriers to whatever does not conform to them. Extravagances are tolerated only insofar as they can be recast into this so-called natural language.

In terms of consumer-demand, the standardization of popular music is only the expression of this dual desideratum imposed upon it by the musical frame of mind of the public—that it be "stimulatory" by deviating in some way from the established "natural," and that it maintain the supremacy of the natural against such deviations. The attitude of the audience toward the natural language is reinforced by standardized production, which institutionalizes desiderata which originally might have come from the public.

Pseudo-individualization

The paradox in the desiderata—stimulatory and natural—accounts for the dual character of standardization itself. Stylization of the ever identical framework is only one aspect of standardization. Concentration and control in our culture hide themselves in their very manifestation. Unhidden they would provoke resistance. Therefore the illusion and, to a certain extent, even the reality of individual achievement must be maintained. The maintenance of it is grounded in material reality itself, for while administrative control over life processes is concentrated, ownership is still diffuse.

In the sphere of luxury production, to which popular music belongs and in which no necessities of life are immediately involved, while, at the same time, the residues of individualism are most alive there in the form of ideological categories such as taste and free choice, it is imperative to hide standardization. The "backwardness" of musical mass production, the fact that it is still on a handicraft level and not literally an industrial one, conforms perfectly to that necessity which is essential from the viewpoint of cultural big business. If the individual handicraft elements of popular music were abolished altogether, a synthetic means of hiding standardization would have to be evolved. Its elements are even now in existence.

The necessary correlate of musical standardization is *pseudo-individualization*. By pseudo-individualization we mean endowing cultural mass production with the halo of free choice or open market on the basis of standardization itself. Standardization of song hits keeps the customers in line by doing their listening for them, as it were. Pseudo-individualization, for its part, keeps them in line by making them forget that what they listen to is already listened to for them, or "pre-digested."

The most drastic example of standardization of presumably individualized features is to be found in so-called improvisations. Even though jazz musicians still improvise in practice, their improvisations have become so "normalized" as to enable a whole terminology to be developed to express the standard devices of individualization: a terminology which in turn is ballyhooed by jazz publicity agents to foster the myth of pioneer artisanship and at the same time flatter the fans by apparently allowing them to peep behind the curtain and get the inside story. This pseudo-individualization is prescribed by the standardization of the framework. The latter is so rigid that the freedom it allows for any sort of improvisation is severely delimited. Improvisations—passages where spontaneous action of individuals is permitted ("Swing it boys")—are confined within the walls of the harmonic and metric scheme. In a great many cases, such as the "break" of pre-swing jazz, the musical function of the improvised detail is determined completely by the scheme: the break can be nothing other than a disguised cadence. Hence, very few possibilities for actual improvisation remain, due to the necessity of merely melodically circumscribing the same underlying harmonic functions. Since these possibilities were very quickly exhausted, stereotyping of improvisatory details speedily occurred. Thus, standardization of the norm enhances in a purely technical way standardization of its own deviation—pseudo-individualization.

This subservience of improvisation to standardization explains two main socio-psychological qualities of popular music. One is the fact that the detail remains openly connected with the underlying scheme so that the listener always feels on safe ground. The choice in individual alterations is so small that the perpetual recurrence of the same variations is a reassuring signpost of the identical behind them. The other is the function of "substitution"—the improvisatory features forbid their being grasped as musical events in themselves. They can be received only as embellishments. It is a well-known fact that in daring jazz arrangements worried notes, dirty tones, in other words, false notes, play a conspicuous role. They are apperceived as exciting stimuli only because they are corrected by the ear to the right note. This, however, is only an extreme instance of what happens less conspicuously in all individualization in popular music. Any harmonic boldness, any chord which does not fall strictly within the simplest harmonic scheme demands being apperceived as "false," that is, as a stimulus which carries with it the unambiguous prescription to substitute for it the right detail, or rather the naked scheme. Understanding popular music means obeying such commands for listening. Popular music commands its own listening habits.

There is another type of individualization claimed in terms of kinds of popular music and differences in name bands. The types of popular music are carefully differentiated in production. The listener is presumed to be able to choose between them. The most widely recognized differentiations are those between swing and sweet and such name bands as Benny Goodman and Guy Lombardo. The listener is quickly able to distinguish the types of music and even the performing band, this in spite of the fundamental identity of the material and the great similarity of the presentations apart from their emphasized distinguishing trademarks. This labeling technique, as regards type of music and band, is pseudo-individualization, but of a sociological kind outside the realm of strict musical technology. It provides trademarks of identification for differentiating between the actually undifferentiated.

Popular music becomes a multiple-choice questionnaire. There are two main types and their derivatives from which to choose. The listener is encouraged by the inexorable presence of these types psychologically to cross out what he dislikes and check what he likes. The limitation inherent in this choice and the clear-cut alternative it entails provoke like-dislike patterns of behavior. This mechanical dichotomy breaks down indifference; it is imperative to favor sweet or swing if one wishes to continue to listen to popular music.

II. PRESENTATION OF THE MUSICAL MATERIAL

Minimum requirements

The structure of the musical material requires a technique of its own by which it is enforced. This process may be roughly defined as "plugging." The term "plugging" originally had the narrow meaning of ceaseless repetition of one particular hit in order to make it "successful." We here use it in the broad sense, to signify a continuation of the inherent processes of composition and arrangement of the musical material. Plugging aims to break down the resistance to the musically ever-equal or identical by, as it were, closing the avenues of escape from the ever-equal. It leads the listener to become enraptured with the inescapable. And thus it leads to the institutionalization and standardization of listening habits themselves. Listeners become so accustomed to the recurrence of the same things that they react automatically. The standardization of the material requires a plugging mechanism from outside, since everything equals everything else to such an extent that the emphasis on presentation which is provided by plugging must substitute for the lack of genuine individuality in the material. The listener of normal musical intelligence who hears the Kundry motif of *Parsifal* for the first time is likely to recognize it when it is played again because it is unmistakable and not exchangeable for anything else. If the same listener were confronted with an average song-hit, he would not be able to distinguish it from any other unless it were repeated so often that he would be forced to remember it. Repetition gives a psychological importance which it could otherwise never have. Thus plugging is the inevitable complement of standardization.[c]

Provided the material fulfills certain minimum requirements, any given song can be plugged and made a success, if there is adequate tie-up [sic] between publishing houses, name bands, radio and moving pictures. Most important is the following requirement: to be plugged, a song hit must have at least one feature by which it can be distinguished from any other, and yet possess the complete conventionality and triviality of all others. The actual criterion by which a song is judged worthy of plugging is par-

C. As the actual working of the plugging mechanism on the American scene of popular music is described in full detail in a study of Duncan MacDougald ["The Popular Music Industry," in *Radio Research 1941*, ed. Paul F. Lazarsfeld and Frank N. Stanton (New York: Duell, Sloan and Pearce, 1941), pp. 65–109], the present study confines itself to a theoretical discussion of some of the more general aspects of the enforcement of the material.

adoxical. The publisher wants a piece of music that is fundamentally the same as all the other current hits and simultaneously fundamentally different from them. Only if it is the same does it have a chance of being sold automatically, without requiring any effort on the part of the customer, and of presenting itself as a musical institution. And only if it is different can it be distinguished from other songs—a requirement for being remembered and hence for being successful.

Of course, this double desideratum cannot be fulfilled. In the case of actual published and plugged songs, one will generally find some sort of compromise, something which is by and large the same and bears just one isolated trademark which makes it appear to be original. The distinguishing feature must not necessarily be melodic,[D] but may consist of metrical irregularities, particular chords or particular sound colors.

Glamor

A further requirement of plugging is a certain richness and roundness of sound. This requirement involves that feature in the whole plugging mechanism which is most overtly bound up with advertising as a business as well as with the commercialization of entertainment. It is also particularly representative of the interrelationship of standardization and pseudo-individualization.

It is musical glamor: those innumerable passages in song arrangements which appear to communicate the "now we present" attitude. The musical flourishes which accompany MGM's roaring lion whenever he opens his majestic mouth are analogous to the non-leonine sounds of musical glamor heard over the air.

Glamor-mindedness may optimistically be regarded as a mental con-

---

D. Technical analysis must add certain reservations to any acceptance of listener reactions at their face value in the case of the concept of melody. Listeners to popular music speak mainly about melody and rhythm, sometimes about instrumentation, rarely or never about harmony and form. Within the standard scheme of popular music, however, melody itself is by no means autonomous in the sense of an independent line developing in the horizontal dimension of music. Melody is, rather, a function of harmony. The so-called melodies in popular music are generally arabesques, dependent upon the sequence of harmonies. What appears to the listener to be primarily melodic is actually fundamentally harmonic, its melodic structure a mere derivative.

It would be valuable to study exactly what laymen call a melody. It would probably turn out to be a succession of tones related to one another by simple and easily understandable harmonic functions, within the framework of the eight bar period. There is a large gap between the layman's idea of a melody and its strictly musical connotation.

struct of the success story in which the hardworking American settler triumphs over impassive nature, which is finally forced to yield up its riches. However, in a world that is no longer a frontier world, the problem of glamor cannot be regarded as so easily soluble. Glamor is made into the eternal conqueror's song of the common man; he who is never permitted to conquer in life conquers in glamor. The triumph is actually the self-styled triumph of the businessman who announces that he will offer the same product at a lower price.

The conditions for this function of glamor are entirely different from those of frontier life. They apply to the mechanization of labor and to the workaday life of the masses. Boredom has become so great that only the brightest colors have any chance of being lifted out of the general drabness. Yet, it is just those violent colors which bear witness to the omnipotence of mechanical, industrial production itself. Nothing could be more stereotyped than the pinkish red neon lights which abound in front of shops, moving picture theaters and restaurants. By glamorizing, they attract attention. But the means by which they are used to overcome humdrum reality are more humdrum than the reality itself. That which aims to achieve glamor becomes a more uniform activity than what it seeks to glamorize. If it were really attractive in itself, it would have no more means of support than a really original popular composition. It would violate the law of the sameness of the putatively unsame. The term glamorous is applied to those faces, colors, sounds which, by the light they irradiate, differ from the rest. But all glamor girls look alike and the glamor effects of popular music are equivalent to each other.

As far as the pioneer character of glamor is concerned, there is an overlapping and a change of function rather than an innocent survival of the past. To be sure, the world of glamor is a show, akin to shooting galleries, the glaring lights of the circus and deafening brass bands. As such, the function of glamor may have originally been associated with a sort of advertising which strove artificially to produce demands in a social setting not yet entirely permeated by the market. The post-competitive capitalism of the present day uses for its own purposes devices of a still immature economy. Thus, glamor has a haunting quality of historic revival in radio, comparable to the revival of the midway circus barker in today's radio barker who implores his unseen audience not to fail to sample wares and does so in tones which arouse hopes beyond the capacity of the commodity to fulfill. All glamor is bound up with some sort of trickery. Listeners are nowhere more tricked by popular music than in its glamorous passages. Flourishes and jubilations express triumphant thanksgiving for the music itself—a self-eulogy of its own achievement in exhorting the listener to exultation and of its identification with the aim of the agency in promoting a great event. However, as this event does not take place apart from its own celebration, the triumphant thanksgiving offered up by the music is a self-betrayal. It is likely to make itself felt as such unconsciously in the listeners, just as the child resents the adult's praising the gifts he made to the child in the same words which the child feels it is his own privilege to use.

Baby talk

It is not accidental that glamor leads to child-behavior. Glamor, which plays on the listener's desire for strength, is concomitant with a musical language which betokens dependence. The children's jokes, the purposely wrong orthography, the use of children's expressions in advertising, take the form of a musical children's language in popular music. There are many examples of lyrics characterized by an ambiguous irony in that, while affecting a children's language, they at the same time display contempt of the adult for the child or even give a derogatory or sadistic meaning to children's expressions ("Goody, Goody," "A-Tisket-a-Tasket," "London Bridge Is Falling Down," "Cry, Baby, Cry").² Genuine and pseudo-nursery rhymes are combined with purposeful alterations of the lyrics of original nursery rhymes in order to make them commercial hits.

The music, as well as the lyrics, tends to affect such a children's language. Some of its principal characteristics are: unabating repetition of some particular musical formula comparable to the attitude of a child incessantly uttering the same demand ("I Want to Be Happy");ᴱ the limitation of many melodies to very few tones, comparable to the way in which a small child speaks before he has the full alphabet at his disposal; purposely wrong harmonization resembling the way in which small children express themselves in incorrect grammar; also certain over-sweet sound colors, functioning like musical cookies and candies. Treating adults as children is involved in that representation of fun which is aimed at relieving the strain of their adult responsibilities. Moreover, the children's lan-

---

E. The most famous literary example of this attitude is "Want to shee the wheels go wound" (John Habberton, *Helen's Babies* [New York: Grosset and Dunlap, 1908] p. 9 ff). One could easily imagine a "novelty" song being based upon that phrase. [*Helen's Babies* is a novel intended for children and rife with baby talk. Adorno slightly misquotes; the sentence reads "Want to shee wheels go wound." It is repeated several times on pp. 11–12 of the U.K. edition (London: Ward, Lock, n.d.) I consulted. (rl)]

guage serves to make the musical product "popular" with the subjects by attempting to bridge, in the subjects' consciousness, the distance between themselves and the plugging agencies, by approaching them with the trusting attitude of the child asking an adult for the correct time even though he knows neither the strange man nor the meaning of time.

Plugging the whole field

The plugging of songs is only a part of a mechanism and obtains its proper meaning within the system as a whole. Basic to the system is the plugging of styles and personalities. The plugging of certain styles is exemplified in the word "swing." This term has neither a definite and unambiguous meaning nor does it mark a sharp difference from the period of pre-swing hot jazz up to the middle thirties. The lack of justification in the material for the use of the term arouses the suspicion that its usage is entirely due to plugging—in order to rejuvenate an old commodity by giving it a new title. Similarly plugged is the whole swing terminology indulged in by jazz journalism and used by jitterbugs, a terminology which, according to Hobson, makes jazz musicians wince.[F] The less inherent in the material are the characteristics plugged by a pseudo-expert terminology, the more are such auxiliary forces as announcers and commentaries needed.

There is good reason to believe that this journalism partly belongs immediately to the plugging mechanism, insofar as it depends upon publishers, agencies, and name bands. At this point, however, a sociological qualification is pertinent. Under contemporary economic conditions, it is often futile to look for "corruption," because people are compelled to behave voluntarily in ways one expected them to behave in only when they were paid for it. The journalists who take part in the promotion of a Hollywood "oomph-girl" need not be bribed at all by the motion picture industry.[3] The publicity given to the girl by the industry itself is in complete accord with the ideology pervading the journalism which takes it up. And this ideology has become the audience's. The match appears to have been made in heaven. The journalists speak with unbought voices. Once a certain level of economic backing for plugging has been reached, the plugging process transcends its own causes and becomes an autonomous social force.

Above all other elements of the plugging mechanism stands the plugging of personalities, particularly of band leaders. Most of the features actually attributable to jazz arrangers are officially credited to the conduc-

F. Wilder Hobson, *American Jazz Music* (New York: Norton, 1939), p. 153.

tor; arrangers, who are probably the most competent musicians in the United States, often remain in obscurity, like scenario writers in the movies. The conductor is the man who immediately faces the audience; he is close kin to the actor who impresses the public either by his joviality and genial manner or by dictatorial gestures. It is the face-to-face relation with the conductor which makes it possible to transfer to him any achievement.

Further, the leader and his band are still largely regarded by the audience as bearers of improvisatory spontaneity. The more actual improvisation disappears in the process of standardization and the more it is superseded by elaborate schemes, the more must the idea of improvisation be maintained before the audience. The arranger remains obscure partly because of the necessity for avoiding the slightest hint that popular music may not be improvised, but must, in most cases, be fixed and systematized.

III. THEORY ABOUT THE LISTENER

Recognition and acceptance

Mass listening habits today gravitate about recognition. Popular music and its plugging are focused on this habituation. The basic principle behind it is that one need only repeat something until it is recognized in order to make it accepted. This applies to the standardization of the material as well as to its plugging. What is necessary in order to understand the reasons for the popularity of the current type of hit music is a theoretical analysis of the processes involved in the transformation of repetition into recognition and of recognition into acceptance.

The concept of recognition, however, may appear to be too unspecific to explain modern mass listening. It can be argued that wherever musical understanding is concerned, the factor of recognition, being one of the basic functions of human knowing, must play an important role. Certainly one understands a Beethoven sonata only by recognizing some of its features as being abstractly identical with others which one knows from former experience, and by linking them up with the present experience. The idea that a Beethoven sonata could be understood in a void without relating it to elements of musical language which one knows and recognizes— would be absurd. What matters, however, is what is recognized. What does a real listener recognize in a Beethoven sonata? He certainly recognizes the "system" upon which it is based: the major-minor tonality, the interrelationship of keys which determines modulation, the different chords and their relative expressive value, certain melodic formulas, and certain structural patterns. (It would be absurd to deny that such patterns exist in serious music. But their function is of a different order. Granted all this recognition, it is still not sufficient for a comprehension of the musical sense.) All the recognizable elements are organized in good serious music by a concrete and unique musical totality from which they derive their particular meaning, in the same sense as a word in a poem derives its meaning from the totality of the poem and not from the everyday use of the word, although the recognition of this everydayness of the word may be the necessary presupposition of any understanding of the poem.

The musical sense of any piece of music may indeed be defined as that dimension of the piece which cannot be grasped by recognition alone, by its identification with something one knows. It can be built up only by spontaneously linking the known elements—a reaction as spontaneous by the listener as it was spontaneous by the composer—in order to experience the inherent novelty of the composition. The musical sense is the New—something which cannot be traced back to and subsumed under the configuration of the known, but which springs out of it, if the listener comes to its aid.

It is precisely this relationship between the recognized and the new which is destroyed in popular music. Recognition becomes an end instead of a means. The recognition of the mechanically familiar in a hit tune leaves nothing which can be grasped as new by a linking of the various elements. As a matter of fact, the link between the elements is pre-given in popular music as much as, or even to a greater extent than, the elements are themselves. Hence, recognition and understanding must here coincide, whereas in serious music understanding is the act by which universal recognition leads to the emergence of something fundamentally new.

An appropriate beginning for investigating recognition in respect of any particular song hit may be made by drafting a scheme which divides the experience of recognition into its different components. Psychologically, all the factors we enumerate are interwoven to such a degree that it would be impossible to separate them from one another in reality, and any temporal order given them would be highly problematical. Our scheme is directed more toward the different objective elements involved in the experience of recognition, than toward the way in which the actual experience feels to a particular individual or individuals.

The components we consider to be involved are the following:

a. Vague remembrance
b. Actual identification

   c.   Subsumption by label

   d.   Self-reflection on the act of recognition

   e.   Psychological transfer of recognition-authority to the object

a) The more or less vague experience of being reminded of something ("I must have heard this somewhere"). The standardization of the material sets the stage for vague remembrance in practically every song, since each tune is reminiscent of the general pattern and of every other. An aboriginal prerequisite for this feeling is the existence of a vast supply of tunes, an incessant stream of popular music which makes it impossible to remember each and every particular song.

b) The moment of actual identification—the actual "that's it" experience. This is attained when vague remembrance is searchlighted by sudden awareness. It is comparable to the experience one has sitting in a room that has been darkened when suddenly the electric light flares up again. By the suddenness of its being lit, the familiar furniture obtains, for a split second, the appearance of being novel. The spontaneous realization that this very piece is "the same as" what one heard at some other time, tends to sublate, for a moment, the ever-impending peril that something is as it always was.

It is characteristic of this factor of the recognition experience that it is marked by a sudden break. There is no gradation between the vague recollection and full awareness but, rather, a sort of psychological "jump." This component may be regarded as appearing somewhat later in time than vague remembrance. This is supported by consideration of the material. It is probably very difficult to recognize most song hits by the first two or three notes of their choruses; at least the first motif must have been played, and the actual act of recognition should be correlated in time with the apperception—or realization—of the first complete motifical "Gestalt" of the chorus.

c) The element of subsumption: the interpretation of the "that's it" experience by an experience such as "that's the hit 'Night and Day.' "[4] It is this element in recognition (probably bound up with the remembrance of the title trademark of the song or the first words of its lyrics[G] which relates recognition most intimately to the factor of social backing.

G. The interplay of lyrics and music in popular music is similar to the interplay of picture and word in advertising. The picture provides the sensual stimulus, the words add slogans or jokes that tend to fix the commodity in the minds of the public and to "subsume" it under definite, settled categories. The replacement of the purely instrumental ragtime by jazz, which had strong vocal tendencies from

The most immediate implication of this component may be the following: the moment the listener recognizes the hit as *the* so and so—that is, as something established and known not merely to him alone—he feels safety in numbers and follows the crowd of all those who have heard the song before and who are supposed to have made its reputation. This is concomitant with or follows hard upon the heels of element b). The connecting reaction consists partly in the revelation to the listener that his apparently isolated, individual experience of a particular song is a collective experience. The moment of identification of some socially established highlight often has a dual meaning: one not only identifies *it* innocently as being this or that, subsuming it under this or that category, but by the very act of identifying it, one also tends unwittingly to identify *oneself* with the objective social agencies or with the power of those individuals who made this particular event fit into this pre-existing category and thus "established" it. The very fact that an individual is capable of identifying an object as this or that allows him to take vicarious part in the institution which made the event what it is and to identify himself with this very institution.

d) The element of self-reflection on the act of identification. ("Oh, I know it; this belongs to me.") This trend can be properly understood by considering the disproportion between the huge number of lesser-known songs and the few established ones. The individual who feels drowned by the stream of music feels a sort of triumph in the split second during which he is capable of identifying something. Masses of people are proud of their ability to recognize any music, as illustrated by the widespread habit of humming or whistling the tune of a familiar piece of music which has just been mentioned, in order to indicate one's knowledge of it, and the evident complacency which accompanies such an exhibition.

By the identification and subsumption of the present listening experi-

---

the beginning, and the general decline of purely instrumental hits, are closely related to the increased importance of the advertising structure of popular music. The example of "Deep Purple" may prove helpful. This was originally a little-known piano piece. Its sudden success was at least partly due to the addition of trade-marking lyrics.

A model for this functional change exists in the field of raised entertainment in the nineteenth century. The first prelude of Bach's "Well Tempered Clavichord" [sic] became a "sacral" hit when Gounod conceived the fiendish idea of extracting a melody from the sequel of harmonies and combining it with the words of the "Ave Maria." This procedure, meretricious from its very inception, has since been generally accepted in the field of musical commercialism. [See Adorno's discussion of Gounod's *Ave Maria* in "Commodity Music Analysed," QF, pp. 37–38. (rl)]

ence under the category "this is the hit so and so," this hit becomes an object to the listener, something fixed and permanent. This transformation of experience into object—the fact that by recognizing a piece of music one has command over it and can reproduce it from one's own memory— makes it more proprietable than ever. It has two conspicuous characteristics of property: permanence and being subject to the owner's arbitrary will. The permanence consists in the fact that if one remembers a song and can recall it all the time, it cannot be expropriated. The other element, that of control over music, consists in the ability to evoke it presumably at will at any given moment, to cut it short, and to treat it whimsically. The musical properties are, as it were, at the mercy of their owner. In order to clarify this element, it may be appropriate to point to one of its extreme though by no means rare manifestations. Many people, when they whistle or hum tunes they know, add tiny up-beat notes which sound as though they whipped or teased the melody. Their pleasure in possessing the melody takes the form of being free to misuse it. Their behavior toward the melody is like that of children who pull a dog's tail. They even enjoy, to a certain extent, making the melody wince or moan.

e) The element of "psychological transfer": "Damn it, 'Night and Day' *is* a good one!" This is the tendency to transfer the gratification of ownership to the object itself and to attribute to it, in terms of like, preference, or objective quality, the enjoyment of ownership which one has attained. The process of transfer is enhanced by plugging. While actually evoking the psychic processes of recognition, identification, and ownership, plugging simultaneously promotes the object itself and invests it, in the listener's consciousness, with all those qualities which in reality are due largely to the mechanism of identification. The listeners are executing the order to transfer to the music itself their self-congratulation on their ownership.

It may be added that the recognized social value inherent in the song hit is involved in the transfer of the gratification of ownership to the object which thus becomes "liked." The labeling process here comes to collectivize the ownership process. The listener feels flattered because he, too, owns what everyone owns. By owning an appreciated and marketed hit, one gets the illusion of value. This illusion of value in the listener is the basis for the evaluation of the musical material. At the moment of recognition of an established hit, a pseudo-public utility comes under the hegemony of the private listener. The musical owner who feels "I like this particular hit (because I know it)" achieves a delusion of grandeur comparable to a child's daydream about owning the railroad. Like the riddles in an advertising contest, song hits pose only questions of recognition which anyone can answer. Yet listeners enjoy giving the answers because they thus become identified with the powers that be.

It is obvious that these components do not appear in consciousness as they do in analysis. As the divergence between the illusion of private ownership and the reality of public ownership is a very wide one, and as everyone knows that what is written "Especially for You" is subject to the clause "any copying of the words or music of this song or any portion thereof makes the infringer liable to prosecution under the United States copyright law," one may not regard these processes as being too *unconscious* either. It is probably correct to assume that most listeners, in order to comply with what they regard as social desiderata and to prove their "citizenship," half-humorously "join" the conspiracy[H] as caricatures of their own potentialities and suppress bringing to awareness the operative mechanisms by insisting to themselves and to others that the whole thing is only good clean fun anyhow.

The final component in the recognition process—psychological transfer—leads analysis back to plugging. Recognition is socially effective only when backed by the authority of a powerful agency. That is, the recognition-constructs do not apply to any tune but only to "successful" tunes—success being judged by the backing of central agencies. In short, recognition, as a social determinant of listening habits, works only on plugged material. A listener will not abide the playing of a song repeatedly on the piano. Played over the air it is tolerated with joy all through its heyday.

The psychological mechanism here involved may be thought of as functioning in this way: If some song hit is played again and again on the air, the listener begins to think that it is already a success. This is furthered by the way in which plugged songs are announced in broadcasts, often in the characteristic form of "You will now hear the latest smash hit." Repetition itself is accepted as a sign of its popularity.[I]

Popular music and "leisure time"

So far the analysis has dealt with reasons for the acceptance of any particular song hit. In order to understand why this whole *type* of music

H. Cf. Hadley Cantril and Gordon W. Allport, *The Psychology of Radio* (New York: Harper and Brothers, 1935), p. 69.

I. The same propaganda trick can be found more explicitly in the field of radio advertising of commodities. Beautyskin Soap is called "famous" since the listener has heard the name of the soap over the air innumerable times before and therefore would agree to its "fame." Its fame is only the sum-total of these very announcements which refer to it.

maintains its hold on the masses, some considerations of a more general kind may be appropriate.

The frame of mind to which popular music originally appealed, on which it feeds, and which it perpetually reinforces, is simultaneously one of distraction and inattention. Listeners are distracted from the demands of reality by entertainment which does not demand attention either.

The notion of distraction can be properly understood only within its social setting and not in self-subsistent terms of individual psychology. Distraction is bound to the present mode of production, to the rationalized and mechanized process of labor to which, directly or indirectly, masses are subject. This mode of production, which engenders fears and anxiety about unemployment, loss of income, war, has its "non-productive" correlate in entertainment; that is, relaxation which does not involve the effort of concentration at all. People want to have fun. A fully concentrated and conscious experience of art is possible only to those whose lives do not put such a strain on them that in their spare time they want relief from both boredom and effort simultaneously. The whole sphere of cheap commercial entertainment reflects this dual desire. It induces relaxation because it is patterned and pre-digested. Its being patterned and pre-digested serves within the psychological household of the masses to spare them the effort of that participation (even in listening or observation) without which there can be no receptivity to art. On the other hand, the stimuli they provide permit an escape from the boredom of mechanized labor.

The promoters of commercialized entertainment exonerate themselves by referring to the fact that they are giving the masses what they want. This is an ideology appropriate to commercial purposes: the less the mass discriminates, the greater the possibility of selling cultural commodities indiscriminately. Yet this ideology of vested interest cannot be dismissed so easily. It is not possible completely to deny that mass-consciousness can be molded by the operative agencies only because the masses "want this stuff."

But why do they want this stuff? In our present society the masses themselves are kneaded by the same mode of production as the articraft material foisted upon them. The customers of musical entertainment are themselves objects or, indeed, products of the same mechanisms which determine the production of popular music. Their spare time serves only to reproduce their working capacity. It is a means instead of an end. The power of the process of production extends over the time intervals which on the surface appear to be "free." They want standardized goods and pseudo-individualization, because their leisure is an escape from work and at the same time is molded after those psychological attitudes to which their workaday world exclusively habituates them. Popular music is for the masses a perpetual busman's holiday. Thus, there is justification for speaking of a pre-established harmony today between production and consumption of popular music. The people clamor for what they are going to get anyhow.

To escape boredom and avoid effort are incompatible—hence the reproduction of the very attitude from which escape is sought. To be sure, the way in which they must work on the assembly line, in the factory, or at office machines denies people any novelty. They seek novelty, but the strain and boredom associated with actual work leads to avoidance of effort in that leisure-time which offers the only chance for really new experience. As a substitute, they crave a stimulant. Popular music comes to offer it. Its stimulations are met with the inability to vest effort in the ever-identical. This means boredom again. It is a circle which makes escape impossible. The impossibility of escape causes the widespread attitude of inattention toward popular music. The moment of recognition is that of effortless sensation. The sudden attention attached to this moment burns itself out *instanter* and relegates the listener to a realm of inattention and distraction. On the one hand, the domain of production and plugging presupposes distraction and, on the other, produces it.

In this situation the industry faces an insoluble problem. It must arouse attention by means of ever-new products, but this attention spells their doom. If no attention is given to the song, it cannot be sold; if attention is paid to it, there is always the possibility that people will no longer accept it, because they know it too well. This partly accounts for the constantly renewed effort to sweep the market with new products, to hound them to their graves; then to repeat the infanticidal maneuver again and again.

On the other hand, distraction is not only a presupposition but also a product of popular music. The tunes themselves lull the listener to inattention. They tell him not to worry for he will not miss anything.[J]

The social cement

It is safe to assume that music listened to with a general inattention which is only interrupted by sudden flashes of recognition is not followed as a

---

J. The attitude of distraction is not a completely universal one. Particularly youngsters who invest popular music with their own feelings are not yet completely blunted to all its effects. The whole problem of age levels with regard to popular music, however, is beyond the scope of the present study. Demographic problems, too, must remain out of consideration.

sequence of experiences that have a clear-cut meaning of their own, grasped in each instant and related to all the precedent and subsequent moments. One may go so far as to suggest that most listeners of popular music do not understand music as a language in itself. If they did it would be vastly difficult to explain how they could tolerate the incessant supply of largely undifferentiated material. What, then, does music mean to them? The answer is that the language that is music is transformed by objective processes into a language which they think is their own, into a language which serves as a receptacle for their institutionalized wants. The less music is a language *sui generis* to them, the more does it become established as such a receptacle. The autonomy of music is replaced by a mere socio-psychological function. Music today is largely a social cement. And the meaning listeners attribute to a material, the inherent logic of which is inaccessible to them, is above all a means by which they achieve some psychical adjustment to the mechanisms of present-day life. This "adjustment" materializes in two different ways, corresponding to two major socio-psychological types of mass behavior toward music in general and popular music in particular, the "rhythmically obedient" type and the "emotional" type.

Individuals of the rhythmically obedient type are mainly found among the youth—the so-called radio generation. They are most susceptible to a process of masochistic adjustment to authoritarian collectivism. The type is not restricted to any one political attitude. The adjustment to anthropophagous collectivism is found as often among left-wing political groups as among right-wing groups. Indeed, both overlap: repression and crowd-mindedness overtake the followers of both trends. The psychologies tend to meet despite the surface distinctions in political attitudes.

This comes to the fore in popular music which appears to be aloof from political partisanship. It may be noted that a moderate leftist theater production such as *Pins and Needles* uses ordinary jazz as its musical medium, and that a communist youth organization adapted the melody of "Alexander's Ragtime Band" to its own lyrics.[5] Those who ask for a song of social significance ask for it through a medium which deprives it of social significance. The use of inexorable popular musical media is repressive *per se*. Such inconsistencies indicate that political conviction and socio-psychological structure by no means coincide.

This obedient type is the rhythmical type, the word rhythmical being used in its everyday sense. Any musical experience of this type is based upon the underlying, unabating time unit of the music—its "beat." To play rhythmically means, to these people, to play in such a way that even if pseudo-individualizations—counter-accents and other "differentiations"—occur, the relation to the ground meter is preserved. To be musical means to them to be capable of following given rhythmical patterns without being disturbed by "individualizing" aberrations, and to fit even the syncopations into the basic time units. This is the way in which their response to music immediately expresses their desire to obey. However, as the standardized meter of dance music and of marching suggests the coordinated battalions of a mechanical collectivity, obedience to this rhythm by overcoming the responding individuals leads them to conceive of themselves as agglutinized with the untold millions of the meek who must be similarly overcome. Thus do the obedient inherit the earth.

Yet, if one looks at the serious compositions which correspond to this category of mass listening, one finds one very characteristic feature: that of disillusion. All these composers, among them Stravinsky and Hindemith, have expressed an "anti-romantic" feeling. They aimed at musical adaptation to reality—a reality understood by them in terms of the "machine age." The renunciation of dreaming by these composers is an index that listeners are ready to replace dreaming by adjustment to raw reality, that they reap new pleasure from their acceptance of the unpleasant. They are disillusioned about any possibility of realizing their own dreams in the world in which they live, and consequently adapt themselves to this world. They take what is called a realistic attitude and attempt to harvest consolation by identifying themselves with the external social forces which they think constitute the "machine-age." Yet the very disillusion upon which their coordination is based is there to mar their pleasure. The cult of the machine which is represented by unabating jazz beats involves a self-renunciation that cannot but take root in the form of a fluctuating uneasiness somewhere in the personality of the obedient. For the machine is an end in itself only under given social conditions—where men are appendages of the machines on which they work. The adaptation to machine music necessarily implies a renunciation of one's own human feelings and at the same time a fetishism of the machine such that its instrumental character becomes obscured thereby.

As to the other, the "emotional" type, there is some justification for linking it with a type of movie spectator. The kinship is with the poor shop girl who derives gratification by identification with Ginger Rogers, who, with her beautiful legs and unsullied character, marries the boss.[6] Wish-fulfillment is considered the guiding principle in the social psychology of moving pictures and similarly in the pleasure obtained from emotional, erotic music. This explanation, however, is only superficially appropriate.

Hollywood and Tin Pan Alley may be dream factories. But they do not merely supply categorical wish-fulfillment for the girl behind the counter. She does not immediately identify herself with Ginger Rogers marrying. What does occur may be expressed as follows: when the audience at a sentimental film or [hearing] sentimental music become aware of the overwhelming possibility of happiness, they dare to confess to themselves what the whole order of contemporary life ordinarily forbids them to admit, namely, that they actually have no part in happiness. What is supposed to be wish-fulfillment is only the scant liberation that occurs with the realization that at last one need not deny oneself the happiness of knowing that one is unhappy and that one could be happy. The experience of the shop girl is related to that of the old woman who weeps at the wedding services of others, blissfully becoming aware of the wretchedness of her own life. Not even the most gullible individuals believe that eventually everyone will win the sweepstakes. The actual function of sentimental music lies rather in the temporary release given to the awareness that one has missed fulfillment.

The emotional listener listens to everything in terms of late romanticism and of the musical commodities derived from it which are already fashioned to fit the needs of emotional listening. They consume music in order to be allowed to weep. They are taken in by the musical expression of frustration rather than by that of happiness. The influence of the standard Slavic melancholy typified by Tchaikovsky and Dvořák is by far greater than that of the most "fulfilled" moments of Mozart or of the young Beethoven. The so-called releasing element of music is simply the opportunity to feel something. But the actual content of this emotion can only be frustration. Emotional music has become the image of the mother who says, "Come and weep, my child." It is catharsis for the masses, but catharsis which keeps them all the more firmly in line. One who weeps does not resist any more than one who marches. Music that permits its listeners the confession of their unhappiness reconciles them, by means of this "release," to their social dependence.

Ambivalence, spite, fury

The fact that the psychological "adjustment" effected by today's mass listening is illusionary and that the "escape" provided by popular music actually subjects the individuals to the very same social powers from which they want to escape makes itself felt in the very attitude of those masses. What appears to be ready acceptance and unproblematic gratification is actually of a very complex nature, covered by a veil of flimsy rationalizations. Mass listening habits today are *ambivalent*. This ambivalence, which reflects upon the whole question of popularity of popular music, has to be scrutinized in order to throw some light upon the potentialities of the situation. It may be made clear through an analogy from the visual field. Every moviegoer and every reader of magazine fiction is familiar with the effect of what may be called the obsolete modern: photographs of famous dancers who were considered alluring twenty years ago, revivals of Valentino films which, though the most glamorous of their day, appear hopelessly old-fashioned. This effect, originally discovered by French surrealists, has since become hackneyed. There are numerous magazines today that mock fashions as outmoded, although their popularity dates back only a few years and although the very women who appear ridiculous in the past styles are at the same time regarded as the peak of smartness in present-day fashions. The rapidity with which the modern becomes obsolete has a very significant implication. It leads to the question whether the change of effect can possibly be due entirely to the objects in themselves, or whether the change must be at least partly accounted for by the disposition of the masses. Many of these who today laugh at the Babs Hutton of 1929 not only admire the Babs Hutton of 1940 but were thrilled by her in 1929 also.[7] They could not now scoff at the Barbara Hutton of 1929 unless their admiration for her (or her peers) at that time contained in itself elements ready to tilt over into its opposite when historically provoked. The "craze" or frenzy for a particular fashion contains within itself the latent possibility of fury.

The same thing occurs in popular music. In jazz journalism it is known as "corniness." Any rhythmical formula which is outdated, no matter how "hot" it is in itself, is regarded as ridiculous and therefore either flatly rejected or enjoyed with the smug feeling that the fashions now familiar to the listener are superior.

One could not possibly offer any musical criterion for certain musical formulas today considered taboo because they are corny—such as a sixteenth on the down beat with a subsequent dotted eighth. They need not be less sophisticated than any of the so-called swing formulas. It is even likely that in the pioneer days of jazz the rhythmical improvisations were less schematic and more complex than they are today. Nevertheless, the effect of corniness exists and makes itself felt very definitely.

An adequate explanation that can be offered even without going into questions that require psychoanalytical interpretation is the following: likes that have been enforced upon listeners provoke revenge the moment the pressure is relaxed. They compensate for their "guilt" in having condoned the worthless by making fun of it. But the pressure is relaxed only as often as attempts are made to foist something "new" upon the public. Thus, the psychology of the corny effect is reproduced again and again and is likely to continue indefinitely.

The ambivalence illustrated by the effect of corniness is due to the tremendous increase of the disproportion between the individual and the social power. An individual person is faced with an individual song which he is apparently free either to accept or reject. By the plugging and support given the song by powerful agencies, he is deprived of the freedom of rejection which he might still be capable of maintaining toward the individual song. To dislike the song is no longer an expression of subjective taste but rather a rebellion against the wisdom of a public utility and a disagreement with the millions of people who are assumed to support what the agencies are giving them. Resistance is regarded as the mark of bad citizenship, as inability to have fun, as highbrow insincerity, for what normal person can set himself against such normal music?

Such a quantitative increase of influence beyond certain limits, however, fundamentally alters the composition of individuality itself. A strong-willed political prisoner may resist all sorts of pressure until methods such as not allowing him to sleep for several weeks are introduced. At that point he will readily confess even to crimes he has not committed. Something similar takes place with the listener's resistance as a result of the tremendous quantity of force operating upon him. Thus, the disproportion between the strength of any individual and the concentrated social structure brought to bear upon him destroys his resistance and at the same time adds a bad conscience for his will to resist at all. When popular music is repeated to such a degree that it does not any longer appear to be a device but rather an inherent element of the natural world, resistance assumes a different aspect because the unity of individuality begins to crack. This of course does not imply absolute elimination of resistance. But it is driven into deeper and deeper strata of the psychological structure. Psychological energy must be directly invested in order to overcome resistance. For this resistance does not wholly disappear in yielding to external forces, but remains alive within the individual and still survives even at the very moment of acceptance. Here spite becomes drastically active.

It is the most conspicuous feature of the listeners' ambivalence toward popular music. They shield their preferences from any imputation that they are manipulated. Nothing is more unpleasant than the confession of dependence. The shame aroused by adjustment to injustice forbids confession by the ashamed. Hence, they turn their hatred rather on those who point to their dependence than on those who tie their bonds.

The transfer of resistance skyrockets in those spheres which seem to offer an escape from the material forces of repression in our society and which are regarded as the refuge of individuality. In the field of entertainment the freedom of taste is hailed as supreme. To confess that individuality is ineffective here as well as in practical life would lead to the suspicion that individuality may have disappeared altogether; that is, that it has been reduced by standardized behavior patterns to a totally abstract idea which no longer has any definite content. The mass of listeners have been put in complete readiness to join the vaguely realized conspiracy directed without inevitable malice against them, to identify themselves with the inescapable, and to retain ideologically that freedom which has ceased to exist as a reality. The hatred of the deception is transferred to the threat of realizing the deception and they passionately defend their own attitude since it allows them to be voluntarily cheated.

The material, to be accepted, necessitates this spite, too. Its commodity-character, its domineering standardization, is not so hidden as to be imperceptible altogether. It calls for psychological action on the part of the listener. Passivity alone is not enough. The listener must force himself to accept.

Spite is most apparent in the case of extreme adherents of popular music—jitterbugs.

Superficially, the thesis about the acceptance of the inescapable seems to indicate nothing more than the relinquishing of spontaneity: the subjects are deprived of any residues of free will with relation to popular music and tend to produce passive reactions to what is given them and to become mere centers of socially conditioned reflexes. The entomological term jitterbug underscores this. It refers to an insect who has the jitters, who is attracted passively by some given stimulus, such as light. The comparison of men with insects betokens the recognition that they have been deprived of autonomous will.

But this idea requires qualifications. They are already present in the official jitterbug terminology. Terms like the latest craze, swing frenzy, alligator, rug-cutter indicate a trend that goes beyond socially conditioned reflexes: fury. No one who has ever attended a jitterbug jamboree or discussed with jitterbugs current issues of popular music can overlook the affinity of their enthusiasm to fury, which may first be directed against the critics of their idols but which may tilt over against the idols themselves. This fury cannot be accounted for simply by the passive acceptance of the given. It is essential to ambivalence that the subject not simply react passively. Complete passivity demands unambiguous acceptance. However, neither the material itself nor observation of the listeners supports the assumption of such unilateral acceptance. Simply relinquishing resistance is not sufficient for acceptance of the inescapable.

Enthusiasm for popular music requires willful resolution by listeners, who must transform the external order to which they are subservient into an internal order. The endowment of musical commodities with libido energy is manipulated by the ego. This manipulation is not entirely unconscious therefore. It may be assumed that among those jitterbugs who are not experts and yet are enthusiastic about Artie Shaw or Benny Goodman, the attitude of "switched on" enthusiasm prevails. They "join the ranks," but this joining does not only imply their conformity to given standards; it also implies a decision to conform. The appeal of the music publishers to the public to "join the ranks" manifests that the decision is an act of will, close to the surface of consciousness.[K]

The whole realm of jitterbug fanaticism and mass hysteria about popular music is under the spell of spiteful will decision. Frenzied enthusiasm implies not only ambivalence insofar as it is ready to tilt over into real fury or scornful humor toward its idols but also the effectuation of such spiteful will decision. The ego, in forcing enthusiasm, must over-force it, since "natural" enthusiasm would not suffice to do the job and overcome resistance. It is this element of deliberate overdoing which characterizes frenzy and self-conscious[L] hysteria. The popular music fan must be thought of as going his way firmly shutting his eyes and gritting his teeth in order to avoid deviation from what he has decided to acknowledge. A clear and calm view would jeopardize the attitude that has been inflicted upon him and that he in turn tries to inflict upon himself. The original will decision upon which his enthusiasm is based is so superficial that the

K. On the back of the sheet version of a certain hit, there appears the appeal: "Follow Your Leader, Artie Shaw."

L. One hit goes: "I'm Just a Jitterbug." ["I'm Just a Jitterbug" was recorded by Ella Fitzgerald and Chick Webb's band on 2 May 1938, in the same session at which she also recorded "A-Tisket, A-Tasket." According to Nat Shapiro, ed., *Popular Music: An Annotated Index of American Popular Songs* (New York: Adrian, 1968), vol. 4, p. 128, the first appearance of the word "jitterbug" was in the song "Jitter Bug," introduced by Cab Calloway and his orchestra in 1934, with words and music by Irving Mills, Cab Calloway, and Ed Swayze. (rl)]

slightest critical consideration would destroy it unless it is strengthened by the craze which here serves a quasi-rational purpose.

Finally, a trend ought to be mentioned which manifests itself in the gestures of the jitterbug: the tendency toward self-caricature which appears to be aimed at by the gaucheries of the jitterbugs so often advertised by magazines and illustrated newspapers. The jitterbug looks as if he would grimace at himself, at his own enthusiasm and at his own enjoyment which he denounces even while pretending to enjoy himself. He mocks himself as if he were secretly hoping for the day of judgment. By his mockery he seeks to gain exoneration for the fraud he has committed against himself. His sense of humor makes everything so shifty that he cannot be put— or, rather, put himself—on the spot for any of his reactions. His bad taste, his fury, his hidden resistance, his insincerity, his latent contempt for himself, everything is cloaked by "humor" and therewith neutralized. This interpretation is the more justified as it is quite unlikely that the ceaseless repetition of the same effects would allow for genuine merriment. No one enjoys a joke he has heard a hundred times.[M]

There is an element of fictitiousness in all enthusiasm about popular music. Scarcely any jitterbug is thoroughly hysterical about swing or thoroughly fascinated by a performance. In addition to some genuine response to rhythmical stimuli, mass hysteria, fanaticism and fascination themselves are partly advertising slogans after which the victims pattern their behavior. This self-delusion is based upon imitation and even histrionics. The jitterbug is the actor of his own enthusiasm or the actor of the enthusiastic front page model presented to him. He shares with the actor the arbitrariness of his own interpretation. He can switch off his enthusiasm as easily and suddenly as he turns it on. He is only under a spell of his own making.

But the closer the will decision, the histrionics, and the imminence of self-denunciation in the jitterbug are to the surface of consciousness, the greater is the possibility that these tendencies will break through in the

M. It would be worth while to approach this problem experimentally by taking motion pictures of jitterbugs in action and later examining them in terms of gestural psychology. Such an experiment could also yield valuable results with regard to the question of how musical standards and "deviations" in popular music are apperceived. If one would take sound tracks simultaneously with the motion pictures one could find out, i.e., how far the jitterbugs react gesturally to the syncopations they pretend to be crazy about and how far they respond simply to the ground beats. If the latter is the case it would furnish another index for the fictitiousness of this whole type of frenzy.

mass, and, once and for all, dispense with controlled pleasure. They cannot be altogether the spineless lot of fascinated insects they are called and like to style themselves. They need their will, if only in order to down the all too conscious premonition that something is "phony" with their pleasure. This transformation of their will indicates that will is still alive and that under certain circumstances it may be strong enough to get rid of the superimposed influences which dog its every step.

In the present situation it may be appropriate for these reasons—which are only examples of much broader issues of mass psychology—to ask to what extent the whole psychoanalytical distinction between the conscious and the unconscious is still justified. Present-day mass reactions are very thinly veiled from consciousness. It is the paradox of the situation that it is almost insuperably difficult to break through this thin veil. Yet truth is subjectively no longer so unconscious as it is expected to be. This is borne out by the fact that in the political praxis of authoritarian regimes the frank lie in which no one actually believes is more and more replacing the "ideologies" of yesterday which had the power to convince those who believed in them. Hence, we cannot content ourselves with merely stating that spontaneity has been replaced by blind acceptance of the enforced material. Even the belief that people today react like insects and are degenerating into mere centers of socially conditioned reflexes, still belongs to the façade. Too well does it serve the purpose of those who prate about the New Mythos and the irrational powers of community. Rather, spontaneity is consumed by the tremendous effort which each individual has to make in order to accept what is enforced upon him—an effort which has developed for the very reason that the veneer veiling the controlling mechanisms has become so thin. In order to become a jitterbug or simply to "like" popular music, it does not by any means suffice to give oneself up and to fall in line passively. To become transformed into an insect, man needs that energy which might possibly achieve his transformation into a man.

(1941)

NOTES BY RICHARD LEPPERT

Adorno wrote this essay in English. His punctuation is occasionally incorrect, in particular as regards misplaced commas that confuse the reader or distort meaning; I have corrected these mistakes. Here and there I've also inserted commas, following conventional rules, especially in those instances where misreading might otherwise result. As with other essays Adorno wrote in English, he liked to employ a comma and dash together. I have retained whichever mark best seemed to fit the context. In this essay in particular, Adorno quite often hyphenated words unnecessarily ("cross-out," "name-brands," "song-hit," "trade-mark," etc.); I have elim-inated such occurrences. Finally, I have changed his occasional use of British or non-standard orthography to American.

1. (1) "Deep Purple" (1934), music by Peter De Rose, lyrics by Mitchell Parish; first made popular as an instrumental played on the radio by Paul Whiteman. The lyrics date from 1939. (2) "Sunrise Serenade" (1938), music by Frankie Carle, lyrics by Jack Lawrence, was a major hit for Glenn Miller and his orchestra, though introduced by Glen Gray and The Casa Loma Orchestra.

2. (1) "Goody, Goody" (1936), words and music by Johnny Mercer and Matt Malneck, was a hit for Benny Goodman and his orchestra. (2) "A-Tisket A-Tasket" (1938), words and music by Ella Fitzgerald and Al Feldman, was adapted from the nursery song first published in 1879; Fitzgerald, who changed some of the lyrics from the original, recorded the tune in 1938 with the Chick Webb band; it became her first hit. For numerous documentary references to this song published throughout Fitzgerald's long career, see *The Ella Fitzgerald Companion: Seven Decades of Commentary*, ed. Leslie Gourse (New York: Schirmer, 1998); see also Stuart Nicholson, *Ella Fitzgerald: A Biography of the First Lady of Jazz* (New York: Da Capo, 1995), pp. 53–55. (3) "Cry, Baby, Cry" (1938), words and music by Jimmy Eaton, Terry Shand, Remus Harris, and Irving Melsher.

3. The "Hollywood 'oomph-girl'" was Ann Sheridan who first acquired the designator—later used more generically for other young starlets with a certain sex appeal—courtesy of the publicity machine of Warner Brothers Studios for whom she worked after 1936, following an earlier stint at Paramount.

4. "Night and Day" (1932), music and lyrics by Cole Porter, was introduced in the Fred Astaire–Claire Luce musical *Gay Divorcee*, and in the film version (1934) with Astaire and Ginger Rogers.

5. (1) *Pins and Needles* (1937) was a musical review produced by the Inter-national Ladies Garment Workers Union and using union members in the amateur cast. Words and music by Harold Rome. Highly successful, the show ran for 1,108 performances. (2) "Alexander's Ragtime Band" (1911), words and music by Irving Berlin.

6. Adorno likely has in mind two Ginger Rogers movies: *Bachelor Mother* (1939) and *Kitty Foyle* (1940), since most of his pop-culture examples in the essay were roughly contemporaneous with the essay itself. A less likely candidate is the very early Ginger Rogers movie *Office Blues* (1930), where she plays a secretary in love with her boss, who only eventually figures out that he loves her as well. Thanks to Paul Becker for his assistance on this note.

7. Dean Jennings, *Barbara Hutton: A Candid Biography* (New York: Frederick Fell, 1968), p. 17, described the famous multi-millionaire and exceedingly extrav-agant "Poor Little Rich Girl" Hutton (1912–1965), an heir to the Woolworth for-tune, as "the most conspicuous social failure of our times, and it is not entirely her fault." At age twelve she inherited $25 million, soon thereafter to be a great deal more. By the time she was in her late teens Hutton was the subject of society gossip columns; by twenty-one she had married the first of a line of European princes. Indeed, her marriage to Prince Alexis Mdivani was even discussed in Dale Carnegie's *How to Win Friends and Influence People* (see p. 59), complimenting the prince's skill at using flattery to attain his ends. Not the least cause of her notoriety lies in the fact that in 1933, during the darkest days of the Depression, her personal fortune of $45 million was made public, and at a time when Wool-worth store employees in New York were on strike over their dismal wages. By the time Adorno wrote "On Popular Music," Hutton was already romantically associated with Cary Grant, whom she married in 1942.

On Jazz

The question of what is meant by "jazz" seems to mock the clear-cut definitive answer. Just as the historical origins of the form are disappearing into the fog of the recent past, so its range is disappearing within its ambivalent use at the present moment. For the purpose of providing a crude orientation, one could concede that it is that type of dance music—whether it be used in an unmediated or slightly stylized form—that has existed since the war and is distinguished from what preceded it by its decidedly modern character, a quality which itself, however, is sorely in need of analysis. This modernity is perhaps characterized most strikingly by those resistances—differing considerably according to region—which are encountered in jazz and polarized along the lines of either its quality of mechanical soullessness or a licentious decadence. Musically, this "modernity" refers primarily to sound and rhythm, without fundamentally breaking the harmonic-melodic convention of traditional dance music. Syncopation is its rhythmic principle. It occurs in a variety of modifications, in addition to its elemental form (as the "cakewalk*," jazz's precursor, uses it), modifications which remain constantly permeated by this elemental form. The most commonly used modifications are the displacement of basic rhythm through deletions (the charleston) or slurring (ragtime); "false" rhythm, more or less a treatment of a common time as a result of three & three & two eighth-notes, with the accent always on the first note of the group which stands out as a "false" beat [Scheintakt][1] from the principal rhythm; finally, the "break*," a cadence which is similar to an improvisation, mostly at the end of the middle part two measures before the repetition of the principal part of the refrain. In all of these syncopations, which occasionally in virtuoso pieces yield an extraordinary complexity, the fundamental beat is rigorously maintained; it is marked over and over again by the bass drum. The rhythmic phenomena pertain to the accentuation and the phrasing, but not the timing of the piece, and even the accentuation consistently remains, related precisely through the bass drum and the continuo instruments which are subordinate to it, a fundamentally symmetrical one. Thus the principle of symmetry is fully respected, especially in the basic rhythmic structure *[Grossrhythmik]*. The eight-bar period, and even the four-bar half period, are maintained, their authority unchallenged. Simple harmonic and melodic symmetrical relationships correspond to this as well, broken down in accordance with half and whole closures. The sound exhibits the same simultaneity of excess and rigidity. It combines objectively maintained expressive and continuo-like elements: the violin and the bass drum are its extremes. But its vital component is the vibrato which causes a tone which is rigid and objective to tremble as if on its own; it ascribes to it subjective emotions without this being allowed to interrupt the fixedness of the basic sound-pattern, just as the syncopation is not allowed to interrupt the basic meter. In Europe the saxophone is considered representative of this sound, the instrument against which the resistance has concentrated its forces. In truth, the instrument to which so much modernistic infamy is attributed and which is supposed to perversely subject the over-stimulated Western nerves to the vitality of blacks *[Negervitalität]*, is old enough to command respect. It was already discussed in Berlioz's treatise on instrumentation;[2] it was invented during the nineteenth century when the emancipation of the art of orchestration stimulated the demand for more refined transitions between woodwinds and the brass instruments, and has been used—clearly not obligatorily—in pieces such as Bizet's *L'Arlésienne Suite*, which has long since been considered a classic. In many countries it has been used for generations in military music, and therefore is no longer shocking to anyone. Its actual significance for the practice of jazz may be secondary to that of the trumpets to which a significantly greater diversity of playing methods is available than to the saxophone and which can therefore be inserted in a manner which is functionally more comfortable and much more dependent on the basic sound-pattern. The jazz-sound itself, however, is determined not through one specific conspicuous instrument, but functionally: it is determined by the possibility of letting the rigid vibrate, or more generally by the opportunity to produce interferences between the rigid and the excessive. The vibrato itself is an interference in the precise physical sense, and the physical model is well suited for representing the historical and social phenomenon of jazz.

The technological constituent facts of the function may be understood as a symbol of a social fact; the form is dominated by the function and not by an autonomous formal law. It seems to have acknowledged itself as dance music. But at the same time it seems to be ardently attempting to proclaim its function, one that is exclusively abstract, even within the formulae of dance music, so as to be able to practice it concretely, in secret, all the more unhindered. The unequivocal function of jazz therefore presents itself to the dialectician as a puzzle. The clear elements of the material which contribute to the solving of this puzzle are as few as the forms which jazz has cultivated. Much of what is accepted as jazz—at least by the public, if not by the practitioners of jazz itself—does not come up to the standards for the crudest characteristic of rhythmic and tonal interference. This is true above all for the tangos which, rhythmically very primitive, only draw on the elementary form of syncopation without ever making it a basic principle. This is also true for that hybrid form combining jazz and march music which, since "Valencia"[3] appeared in 1925 as a *"six-eight"** piece and spread with uncommon rapidity, cultivated the march-like elements with increasing openness, and which inserted an unbroken, continuous rhythm in place of syncopation, and a homogeneous and "euphonious" tutti-sound in place of the interference. It has never been sharply differentiated from jazz practice and is played by orchestras that alternate between it and thoroughly syncopated *"hot music.*"* On the other hand, a great deal of music is perceived as being jazz or related to jazz only on the basis of its sound, without its being at all interested in the rhythmic principles of jazz. The wide public success of the *songs** of Kurt Weill was a success for jazz, although the rhythmic profiling of its melodies in accordance with the scansion of the composed verse lines is diametrically opposed to jazz practice—only the pervasive basic rhythm and the sound of the saxophone have anything to do with jazz in this case. Jazz is not what it "is": its aesthetic articulation is sparing and can be understood at a glance. Rather, it is what it is used for, and this fact clearly brings up questions whose answers will require in-depth examination. Not questions like those pertaining to the autonomous work of art, but rather like those brought to mind by the detective novel, with which jazz has in common the fact that it maintains an inexorably rigid stereotypology and at the same time does everything it can to let that stereotypology be forgotten by means of individualizing elements, which are again themselves ultimately determined by the stereotypology. Just as in the detective novel the question of the identity of the criminal is intersected with that which is implied by the whole, so in jazz the question of the alien subject, who both quivers and marches through it, is intersected by the question of what its purpose is, why it is there at all, while it asserts its existence [*Dasein*] as something self-evident which only conceals how difficult its own vindication of it must be.

If one attempts, as has been the case often enough, to consider the use value of jazz, its suitability as a mass commodity, as a corrective to the bourgeois isolation of autonomous art, as something which is dialectically advanced, and to accept its use value as a motive for the sublation [*Aufhebung*] of the object character of music, one succumbs to the latest form of romanticism which, because of its anxiety in the face of the fatal characteristics of capitalism, seeks a despairing way out, in order to affirm the feared thing itself as a sort of ghastly allegory of the coming liberation and to sanctify negativity—a curative in which, by the way, jazz itself would like to believe. No matter what the situation might be for art within the context of an approaching order of things; whether its autonomy and object quality will be retained or not—and economic considerations provide substantial grounds for the assertion that even the ideal [*richtig*] society will not be aiming to create pure immediacy—this much is in any case certain: the use value of jazz does not sublate [*aufheben*] alienation, but intensifies it. Jazz is a commodity in the strict sense: its suitability for use permeates its production in terms none other than its marketability, in the most extreme contradiction to the immediacy of its use not merely in addition to but also within the work process itself. It is subordinate to the laws and also to the arbitrary nature of the market, as well as the distribution of its competition or even its followers. The elements in jazz in which immediacy seems to be present, the seemingly improvisational moments—of which syncopation is designated as its elemental form—are added in their naked externality to the standardized commodity character in order to mask it—without, however, gaining power over it for a second. Through its intentions, whether that of appealing to an elevated "style," individual taste, or even individual spontaneity, jazz wants to improve its marketability and veil its own commodity character which, in keeping with one of the fundamental contradictions of the system, would jeopardize its own success if it were to appear on the market undisguised. However much jazz may act like a product of "New Objectivity" [*Neue Sachlichkeit*],[4] like something new, it is what any "objectivity" purports to attack most ferociously—an artistic product—and its "objectivity" is no more than a pasted-on ornament meant to deceive us about the extent to which it is merely an object.

Such deception is carried out above all in the interests of the bourgeoisie. If [the bourgeoisie] has really reserved for itself the privilege of taking pleasure in its own alienation,[5] then, in a situation which is antagonistically very advanced, this pleasure is no longer aided by the pathos of distance, a phenomenon which Nietzsche was still able to discuss in friendly terms. The more they [the bourgeoisie] decrease the distance for consciousness through community ideologies of the most varied forms, the more it grows inexorably within being.[6] Similarly, that which is alienated is endurable to them only as long as it presents itself as unconscious and "vital": that which is most alienated is what is most familiar. The function of jazz is thus to be understood as above all one which is relative to the upper class, and its more consequential forms may still be reserved—at least insofar as it is a question of a more intimate reception than merely being delivered up to loudspeakers and the bands in clubs for the masses—for the well-trained upper class, which knows the right dance steps. To it, jazz represents, somewhat like the evening clothes of the gentleman, the inexorability of the social authority which it itself is, but which is transfigured in jazz into something original and primitive, into "nature." With its individual or characteristic stylistic moments, jazz appeals to the "taste" of those whose sovereign freedom of choice is legitimated by their status. But the fact that jazz, because of its rigidity as well as its appeal to individualizing taste, is supposedly "not kitsch" allows those who consider themselves disciplined to come away from it with a good conscience. Yet the impact of jazz remains as little connected to the upper class as the latter's consciousness distinguishes itself in precise terms from that of the dominated; the mechanism of psychic mutilation upon which present conditions depend for their survival also holds sway over the mutilators themselves, and if these are similar enough to their victims in terms of drive structure, the victims thus can take some solace in the fact that they can also partake of the commodities of the dominant class to the extent that these are intended to appeal to a mutilated instinctual structure. As a surface effect and diversion, even if not as a serious ritual for amusement, jazz permeates all levels of society, even the proletariat—in Europe, only some specifically agrarian groups can be excepted from its influence. Often, the dependent lower classes identify themselves with the upper class through their reception of jazz. To them, jazz is "urbane," and, thanks to it, the white-collar employee can feel superior when he sits with his girlfriend in a beer hall. And yet in this only the "primitive" elements of jazz, the good danceable beat of the basic rhythm, are understood: the highly syncopated *hot music** is tolerated, without its penetrating more specifically into our consciousness—all the more so because the cheap dance clubs are unable to pay virtuoso orchestras, and the mediated reproduction of the music through the medium of radio is even less impressive in its effect than a live orchestra. It is, however, characteristic for jazz as a form of interference that its differentiated elements can be dispensed with without its being sublated [*aufgehoben*] or ceasing to be recognizable as jazz. Jazz is pseudo-democratic in the sense that it characterizes the consciousness of the epoch: its attitude of immediacy, which can be defined in terms of a rigid system of tricks, is deceptive when it comes down to class differences. As is the case in the current political sphere, so in the sphere of ideology, reaction is the bedfellow of such a democracy. The more deeply jazz penetrates society, the more reactionary elements it takes on, the more completely it is beholden to banality, and the less it will be able to tolerate freedom and the eruption of phantasy, until it finally glorifies repression itself as the incidental music to accompany the current collective. The more democratic jazz is, the worse it becomes.

The fact that its democratic attitude is merely an illusion can be brought to light by an analysis of its reception. There is nothing more incorrect than to think of this as a plebiscite phenomenon. The capital power of the publishers, its dissemination through radio and above all, the sound film have cultivated a tendency toward centralization which limits freedom of choice and barely allows for any real competition. Its overpowering propaganda apparatus hammers the hits into the masses for as long a period as it sees fit, although most of these are the worst examples [of jazz], until their weary memory [*Gedächtnis*] is defenselessly delivered up to them. And the weariness of their memory has in turn a retroactive effect on production. The pieces that play a decisive role in the broad social appeal of jazz are precisely not those which most purely express the idea of jazz as interference, but are, rather, technically backward, boorish dances which only contain mere fragments of these elements. These are regarded as *commercial**: after sufficient sales of the banal hits have been secured, the publishers consent to deliver a "modern"—i.e., a relatively up-to-date—*hot** piece free of charge. After all, mass consumption of *hot music** cannot be completely dispensed with—this is an expression of a certain excess of musical productive force which goes beyond the demands of the market. The orchestras clamor for *hot music**, in part to highlight their virtuosity but also in part because the perpetual repetition of the simplest things bores them to a degree which they find unbearable. At the same time, however, artisanally produced *hot music**, the relatively progressive jazz, is also necessary for the promotion of mass consumption. Just as the acceptance of *hot music** allows the upper class to maintain a clear conscience about its taste, the lack of understanding among the majority who are

shocked by this music lends to those who do listen to it the vague satisfaction of being themselves *up to date** and perhaps even confirms a sense
of having been erotically emancipated through that which is dangerously
modern or perverse. This is all mere decorum; the only melodies that find
their way into the public memory are the melodies which are the most
easily understood and the most rhythmically trivial. For their broad reception, the *hot** pieces perform at best the role of pseudo-modern painters
like van Dongen, Foujita, Marie Laurencin,[7] or, even better, of cubist advertisements.

There is one argument currently being used against this assertion. This
argument would assert that this could not be a matter of centralism or of
an illusory democracy because the propagandistic mechanism does not
function sufficiently for this. Hits cannot be "made," and therefore the
theoretical prerequisites necessary for their success could not be adequately
specified. Thus "Capri,"[8] one of the biggest hits of the recent past, was put
out by a small producer after the more important ones had rejected it, and
it supposedly made its way on its own. If one asks jazz specialists for the
reasons behind the great success of a hit, they will respond—and the
greater their business smarts, the more enthusiastic they will be in their
response—with depraved magical formulations taken from the vocabulary
of art: inspiration, the concept of genius, creativity, originality, mysterious
forces, and other irrational justifications. However transparent the motives
for this irrationalism may be, the moment of irrationality in the hit's
success cannot be overlooked. Which popular tunes are successful and
which are not can be predicted with as little certainty as can the fate of
stocks and bonds. But this irrationality represents not so much a suspension of social determination as something which is itself socially determined. For the present, theory can come up with numerous necessary,
albeit also insufficient, conditions for "success," i.e., for a piece's social
effect. Further analysis may then stumble on the "irrational" moments,
onto the question of why, in the case of two pieces which are formally
exactly alike and otherwise equivalent, one takes off and the other does
not. But analysis may not assume a creative miracle where nothing has
really been created. Provided that irrationality does not reduce itself to
unequal chances for propaganda and distribution, its arbitrary nature is
itself an expression of a total social system, whose constituent elements
include the tendency to tolerate and demand anarchistic coincidence in all
concrete individual manifestations in the midst of the most precise tendentious determinacy. In the sphere of ideology as well, monopolization
is in no way equivalent to a sublation *[Aufhebung]* of anarchy. Just as the

reality within which the hit song is heard is not ordered systematically; just as space and time are capable of exerting more control over the fate of the product form than does its own merit, so the consciousness of those who receive it is unsystematic, and its irrationality is *a priori* that of the listener. But this is not a creative irrationality; rather, it is destructive. It is not a generative force, but a recourse to false origins under the control of destruction. In an ideal society, a correlation between quality and success could perhaps be put forth, but in the false one, the absence of a correlative relationship is not so much proof of an occult quality as proof of the falseness of society.

If it is true that jazz is attempting a recourse to false origins, then the argument which revolves around the supposed irrationality of its effect loses its meaning, along with the talk about intrinsic, "archaic forces bursting forth within it," or whatever the phrases with which obliging intellectuals justify its production. The belief in jazz as an elementary force with which an ostensibly decadent European music could be regenerated is pure ideology. The extent to which jazz has anything at all to do with genuine black music is highly questionable; the fact that it is frequently performed by blacks and that the public clamors for "black jazz" as a sort of brand-name doesn't say much about it, even if folkloric research should confirm the African origin of many of its practices. Today, in any case, all of the formal elements of jazz have been completely abstractly pre-formed by the capitalist requirement that they be exchangeable as commodities. Even the much-invoked improvisations, the *hot** passages and *breaks**, are merely ornamental in their significance, and never part of the overall construction or determinant of the form. Not only is their placement, right down to the number of beats, assigned stereotypically; not only is their duration and harmonic structure as a dominant effect completely predetermined; even its melodic form and its potential for simultaneous combinations rely on a minimum of basic forms: they can be traced back to the paraphrasing of the cadence, the harmonically figurative counterpoint. The relationship between jazz and black people is similar to that between salon music and the wandering fiddle players whom it so firmly believes it has transcended—the gypsies. According to Bartók, the gypsies are supplied with this music by the cities; like commodity consumption itself, the manufacture *[Herstellung]* of jazz is also an urban phenomenon, and the skin of the black man functions as much as a coloristic effect as does the silver of the saxophone. In no way does a triumphant vitality make its entrance in these bright musical commodities; the European-American entertainment business has subsequently hired the [supposed] triumphant victors to appear as their flunkies and as figures in advertisements, and their triumph is merely a confusing parody of colonial imperialism. To the extent that we can speak of black elements in the beginnings of jazz, in ragtime perhaps, it is still less archaic-primitive self-expression than the music of slaves; even in the indigenous music of the African interior, syncopation within the example of a maintained measured time seems only to belong to the lower [social] level. Psychologically, the primal structure of jazz [*Ur-Jazz*] may most closely suggest the spontaneous singing of servant girls. Society has drawn its vital music—provided that it has not been made to order from the very beginning—not from the wild, but from the domesticated body in bondage. The sado-masochistic elements in jazz could be clearly connected to this. The archaic stance of jazz is as modern as the "primitives" who fabricate it. The improvisational immediacy which constitutes its partial success counts strictly among those attempts to break out of the fetishized commodity world which want to escape that world without ever changing it, thus moving ever deeper into its snare. He who wants to flee from a music which has become incomprehensible or form an alienating everyday situation into jazz happens upon a musical commodity system which for him is superior to the others only in that it is not so immediately transparent, but which, with its decisive, non-improvisational elements, suppresses precisely those human claims which he laid to it. With jazz, a disenfranchised subjectivity plunges from the commodity world into the commodity world; the system does not allow for a way out. Whatever primordial instinct is recovered in this is not a longed-for freedom, but rather a regression through suppression; there is nothing archaic in jazz but that which is engendered out of modernity through the mechanism of suppression. It is not old and repressed instincts which are freed in the form of standardized rhythms and standardized explosive outbursts; it is new, repressed, and mutilated instincts which have stiffened into the masks of those in the distant past.

The modern archaic stance of jazz is nothing other than its commodity character. The evidence of originality in it is that which makes it a commodity: the fixed, almost timeless stasis within movement; the mask-like stereotypology; the combination of wild agitation as the illusion of a dynamic and the inexorability of the authority which dominates such agitation. Predominant, however, is the law which is that of the market as much as it is that of myths: the illusion must constantly remain the same while at the same time constantly simulating the "new." This becomes apparent in the paradoxical demand on the composer that his work always be "just like" and yet "original," a demand which cripples all productive power. He who could accomplish both simultaneously would realize the ideal of the *commercial*.* In the irreconcilability of the two demands, however, as they are made on all commodities, one of the most deep-seated contradictions of capitalism is revealed—it is a system which must simultaneously develop and enchain productive power. Within the practice of jazz, the habitual takes pains to see that it is reinforced. The cards of jazz seem to have played themselves out: since the tango and the foxtrot, nothing new has been added to its fundamental characteristics. There has only been a modification of that which already exists. Even the "invention," the concept of which is equally problematic socially and in terms of aesthetics, remains dependent on previously successful models; it is as thoroughly and conventionally pre-formed as the basic types themselves. The "new" penetrates only occasionally, appearing as individual nuance and seen from the point of view of the individual as chance whenever it specifically expresses (always almost unconsciously) objective social tendencies, i.e., when it is precisely not individual nuance. Sometimes, although this does not happen in the majority of cases, the element of the "new" brings the greatest success, as in the case of the first *six-eight** pieces, "Valencia," or the first rumba. Such pieces are usually published against the will of the producers, since they always constitute a risk. The musical correlative of the demand for being both "just like" and "original" is, however, the fact that a successful jazz hit must unite an individual, characteristic element with utter banality on every other level. Here it is in no way a matter of the melodic shape alone; it is without exception astonishingly minor. One detail of any kind—in "Valencia" it is the slight irregularity in the meter of which the consumer is not aware—is enough. The publishers, just like any propagandists, are most concerned with the title, the beginning of the text, the first eight bars of the refrain, and the close of the refrain, which is usually anticipated as a motto in the introduction. They are indifferent to everything else, i.e., to the development of the music. The old principle of the rondo, which perhaps actually refers back to cult forms, is chosen by jazz for its ability to be memorized and thus for its marketability; throughout, the couplets or *verses** are deliberately kept two-dimensional in contrast to the refrain or the chorus.

The simultaneity of the characteristic and the banal which is marked out in jazz affects not only the jazz pieces in and of themselves. To a much greater extent, this simultaneity is realized in the relationship between production and reproduction to which jazz owes precisely its reputation for spontaneous immediacy. The piece as such—and here we may exaggerate—is banal; its reproduction is characteristic, exquisite, virtuoso, often disguising the piece to the point of unrecognizability. The composer must, oddly enough, answer for the conventional element in jazz. The one who modifies it is the arranger, who is affiliated sometimes with the publishers and sometimes with the orchestra, but who is most closely in touch with those who reproduce the music. If one were to compare the performance of a good orchestra with the actual score of the piano version, for example, one would be likely to conclude that the qualified musicians are to be found among the arrangers and not the composers. It seems almost as if material which is completely indifferent is best suited to a jazz treatment. One of the best-known virtuoso pieces for jazz, the "Tiger Rag"[9] that orchestras love to use to show off their talents, is extremely simple in terms of its composition. Thus, jazz seems to be progressive in two directions—both different with respect to the developmental tendency specific to music. One aspect is the reintroduction into the composition of those who are reproducing it. In "artistic" music, both [the composition and those who are reproducing it] are hopelessly alienated from one another; the instructions for playing the "New Music" allow no room for freedom in the process of reproducing it—indeed, the interpretation disappears completely behind the mechanical reproduction. In jazz, it seems as if the reproducer has reclaimed his rights vis-à-vis the work of art—man has reclaimed his rights over the object. This is, in any case, how jazz is understood by the more conscientious among its apologists: the sentiment of Krenek's *Jonny spielt auf* is proof of this. This sentiment is romantic, however—and Krenek was only being consistent when he followed *Jonny* with the romantic one-act piece as an epilogue.[10] The interjection of the interpreter or arranger in jazz does not permit, as the improvisations of the great stage actors still do, a real altering of the material in order to give rise to a subjective proclamation. The stimulation and the artistic piece, the new color and the new rhythm are merely inserted along with the banal—just as the jazz vibrato is inserted into the rigid sound, and syncopation in the basic meter. This element of interference in jazz is accomplished by the arrangement of the composition. But its contours remain the old ones. The schema can still be heard, even through the most digressive breaks in the arrangement. He who is reproducing the music is permitted to tug at the chains of his boredom, and even to clatter them, but he cannot break them. Freedom in reproduction is no more present here than in art music. Even if the composition were to allow it, the tradition of jazz, which is prepared to give the slightest subjective nuance its prescribed name, would not tolerate such freedom. If man is incapable of breaking through within the composition itself, then he certainly cannot do so within a reproduction which respectfully dresses up its bare walls in order to disguise its inhumanity, but which helps to prolong this inhumanity surreptitiously in doing so.

In addition, however, it seems as if one could consider the arrangement of the working process as progressive, which in jazz oscillates between production and reproduction. It presents itself as an obvious distribution of labor, which forms a "material" within a context of technical freedom and rationality without being dependent on its coincidental nature, the coincidental nature of the conditions of production or those of the performers. Somebody comes up with the "invention" or whatever is taken for one; another harmonizes it and elaborates on it; then a text develops and the rest of the music is written and seasoned with rhythm and harmony, perhaps already by the arranger at this point; finally, the whole is orchestrated by a specialist. Now, the intentionally exhibited division of labor does not take place in a systematic way in the sense of rationalization—this is just as little the case here as it is, for example, in film production. The necessity of the producer is its reason; it is subsequently turned into the "virtue" of a collective which in reality does not exist. He who presumes a late-capitalist rationality of the process of production in jazz falls victim to an illusion similar to that which is produced by the glittering machinery which the jazz orchestra, with its metal instruments and its propped-open grand piano, endeavors to imitate, and would like to romanticize the commodity "jazz" in the sense of a vague "avant-garde" quality, in the sense of the "tempo of the times." The rationalization which is so eager to declare itself through the plural of authors' names on the title pages of the piano scores functions in a highly defective manner; there can be no talk of systematic collective labor here, and the contradiction between the material and its techniques remains obvious throughout—wherein the technique itself is conspicuous as having miscarried. The division of labor originates in the fact that the "inventions" frequently stem from amateurs, from a great many outsiders to formal jazz practice, who cannot themselves orchestrate them for jazz and who often cannot even set them down or score them, while, on the other end of the process, there are the orchestras which are allied with the publishers and their particular interests. The arbitrary nature of the original material is thus in no sense the result of its technical mastery, but, instead, through it, anarchy intervenes in the process of production. It does not master the original material so much as remain independent of it and its arbitrary nature; this sets a limit for the rationality of the technique as well as for that of the result.

Jazz specialists respond to the public and to its representative in the production process; the latter, however, opposes all technical consonance on principle. If this representative were an expert, the success [of jazz] would be endangered in its origins. The division of labor in jazz merely outlines the parody of a future collective process of composition.

The amateur represents the extreme case of the public representative in the production of jazz, which as such is alienated from individuals. He is the test case for social authority in its real effect on musical practices today. He is of exemplary importance even if one wants to keep the estimate of the number of "tuned in" jazz amateurs low. The significance of this is clearly not meant to be understood in the way that jazz ideology itself represents it. The amateur is not the uncompromised and unsullied person whose originality asserts itself against the routine of the business; this idea is part of the mythic mystification of the black man. Neither does social reality, freed of image and illusion, intervene through him in the work of art. And neither is it true that through this intervention the work of art would itself become reality. As the representative of society in jazz, he is perhaps more the representative of its extremely illusory nature. Within the process of production he functions as a guarantor for the apperception of the product. His inventions are embodied within accumulated conventions. Somewhat like the businessman who, thinking he has been transformed into a poet on the occasion of a birthday celebration, will feature himself suddenly and compulsively (but not because of his literary innocence—instead he will offer an imitation of Heine or Scheffel or Wilhelm Busch),[11] the amateur in like manner imitates the clichés of current jazz music and guarantees the commercial opportunity to underbid it wherever possible. What legitimates precisely him and not just anybody in bringing this imitation into the public sphere to which he owes it is not so much the individual qualification of his ideas as it is the fact that he has mustered the necessary hysterical lack of restraint to express that which he does not suffer. He invests in the production precisely that source of unconscious musical and extra-musical associations, expectations, categories, and slippages which is eradicated in professional musicians by their training or is elevated to a conscious level and, once lost, can never again be reconstructed, but which constitutes a substantial and perhaps the decisive prerequisite for exerting an effect on the public—an invaluable component in its commercial success. The helplessness of the person who is excluded from the specialized trade, who experiences the same fear in the face of music, evinces something akin to fear as if it were a social power and, because of his fear, aspires to adapt himself to it, without, however, succeeding at it—this helplessness is just as important an ingredient [in its success] as the educated mundane consciousness of the habitué. After all, the two belong together as the constitutive elements of jazz: helplessness (the whimpering vibrato) and the average consciousness (banality). The person of the amateur is the subjective correlative of an objective formal structure. His slippages belong as much to the *a priori* of jazz as, following Karl Kraus's thoroughly verified view, typographical errors belong to the *a priori* of the newspaper.[12] Errors in musical orthography, grammar and syntax can be found in the piano scores—i.e., in the originals—of many of the most successful hits. They are continued in the finer breaks which are characteristic of high-jazz pieces for compelling reasons since, in principle, all jazz is inconsistent. If the surface has begun to close in the more recent, and especially the American, writing; if there are fewer crass errors and the dilettantes are being shut out, this should not be understood as representing "progress" in jazz. While it is beginning to split off into its two extremes, *sweet music** and the march, the core of jazz, *hot music**, is being stabilized into a middle-of-the-road line of artisanal scrupulousness and taste which restrains the improvisational elements of disruption which were sporadically present in the original conception of jazz into symphonic simplicity and grandeur. Stabilized jazz is that which presents itself as "symphonic," as autonomous art, but which thus conclusively abandons all the intentions which previously had contributed to its appearance of collective immediacy. It submits itself to the standards of art music; compared with it, however, jazz exposes itself as lagging far behind.

The "tastefulness" of jazz, the ferment of its modernity, antipole and corrective of the amateur, are artistically simple deception as much as its reverse, its immediacy. Educated taste, which tests and refines the conventional, has long since become conventional itself; modernity is based exclusively on the conventions of the music of the recent modern period. These are, roughly speaking, those of musical impressionism. The black artist Duke Ellington, who is a trained musician and the principal representative of today's "classical" stabilized jazz, has named Debussy and Delius as his favorite composers.[13] With the exception of *hot** rhythm, all the more subtle characteristics of jazz refer back to this style, and it would hardly be exaggerated to observe that this style is making its way for the first time into the broader strata of society through jazz. In Parisian nightclubs, one can hear Debussy and Ravel in between the rumbas and Charlestons. The influence of impressionism is most striking in the harmonies. Ninth-chords, *sixte ajoutée*, and other mixtures, such as the stereotypical *blue chord**, and whatever jazz has to offer in the way of vertical stimulation has been taken from Debussy. And even the treatment of melody, especially in the more serious pieces, is based on the impressionist model. The resolution into the smallest motif-formulae, which are not developed dynamically but rather statically repeated, and which are only rhythmically reinterpreted and appear to circle around an immovable center, is specifically impressionistic. But jazz deprives it of its formal sense; the impressionism which it appropriates is at the same time depraved. If, in Debussy, the melodic points form their coloration and temporal surfaces from out of themselves following the constructive command of subjectivity, in jazz they are harnessed, like in the false beat of *hot music**, into the metric-harmonic schema of the "standard" cadence of the eight-bar period. The subjective-functional distribution of the melody remains impotent by being recalled, as it were, by the eight-bar condensation into a leading-voice form which merely toys with its particulars rather than composing a new form from them; this is true in the case of the complex harmonies when they are caught again by the same cadence from which their floating resonances want to escape. Even yesterday's music must first be rendered harmless by jazz, must be released from its historical element, before it is ready for the market. Once on the market, these impressionistic trimmings function as a stimulant. Their effect, previously isolated in the concert hall and the studio, is modern: a fine nuance within a crass schema. For the broad public they are considered risqué and exciting in a way that is barely comprehensible any more; they abstractly feign progressiveness. But the individual element which is inserted into jazz through impressionism does not generate or have control over itself. It has become rigid, formulaic, spent—the individual elements are now in just the same position as social convention was previously. It is easy to rob it of its formal sense because that has already escaped of its own accord in post-Debussy epigone music; as a conventional element it can be fitted seamlessly into a convention. The individually modern element in jazz is as illusory as the collective archaic element.

The illusory character of the individual elements relates jazz to salon music, toward which impressionism itself tended in its lesser representatives. In its origins, jazz reaches deep down into the salon style. Its *expressivo* stems from this style; to put it drastically, everything in it wants to announce something soulful. The jazz vibrato was most likely taken over from the wandering fiddle player, who is then resurrected in the tango. Impressionist harmonics spill over everywhere into the sentimental harmonies of the salon. The characteristic style of the whispering jazz singers which is the most difficult to integrate into a norm is almost indistinguishable from that of the café concert. The subjective pole of jazz—subjectivity itself understood strictly in the sense of a social product and as something which has been reified into a commodity—is salon music; the subjective pole trembles from the impulses of salon music. If one wanted to describe the phenomenon of interference in jazz in terms of broad and solid concepts of style, one could claim it as the combination of salon music and march music. The former represents an individuality which in truth is none at all, but merely the socially produced illusion of it; the latter is an equally fictive community which is formed from nothing other than the alignment of atoms under the force that is exerted upon them. The effectiveness of the principle of march music in jazz is evident. The basic rhythm of the continuo and the bass drum is completely in sync with march rhythm, and, since the introduction of *six-eight** time, jazz could be transformed effortlessly into a march. The connection here is historically grounded; one of the horns used in jazz is called the Sousaphone, after the march composer. Not only the saxophone has been borrowed from the military orchestra; the entire arrangement of the jazz orchestra, in terms of the melody, bass, *obbligati*, and mere filler instruments, is identical to that of a military band. Thus jazz can be easily adapted for use by fascism. In Italy it is especially well liked, as is cubism and artisanry. The ban against it in Germany has to do with the surface tendency to reach back to pre-capitalist, feudal forms of immediacy and to call these socialism. But, characteristically enough, this ban is a powerless one. The struggle against the saxophone has been appeased by the musical organizations and the instrument industry; jazz itself continues vigorously, under other names, on the radio as well. Only the more advanced, newly objective[14] *hot music** for the upper middle classes which the layman cannot understand has fallen victim to the ban. Not only is march-like jazz music tolerated, but the new marches, as they are sometimes introduced through sound films, have themselves sprung directly from jazz.

The relationship between the salon music and march music which are mixed together in jazz has its base in the demythologizing tendency of dance itself, in the transformation of the dance into the bourgeois gait carried out whenever possible by individuals from the salons. The formal precursors of jazz before the war were referred to as *steps**: the movement of accentuating a step in the process of walking gave it its name. The history of the social function of jazz, the tendency to disenchant the dance, has yet to be written, and to be transposed subsequently into its opposite, a new magic. The gait of the bourgeois individual which is no longer connected with magic can be transformed, by the command of rhythm, into a march. Insofar as dancing is synchronous movement, the tendency to march has been present in dance from the very beginning; thus jazz is connected in its origins with the march and its history lays bare this relationship. At first, the casual gait which accompanies jazz presents itself as the opposite of the march. It seems to release the dancer from the imprisonment of exact gestures into the arbitrary nature of his everyday life, from which he no longer even escapes through dance, but which is playfully transfigured by dance as a latent order. With jazz, so it seems, the contingency of individual existence asserts itself against its social standard, with the claim that it is fraught with meaning. Jazz syncopation clearly wants to obliterate the ritualized measure; at times it sounds as if the music were sacrificing its distance and its aesthetic figurativeness and had stepped over into the physical empirical realm of regulated-arbitrary life. In film, jazz is best suited to accompany contingent actions which are prosaic in a double sense: people promenading and chatting along a beach, a woman busying herself with her shoe. In such moments, jazz is so appropriate to the situation that we are hardly conscious of it anymore. From this fact, too, stems the significance of the hits of contingency, where a chance word, as a scrap of the everyday, becomes a jacket for the music from which it spins forth: "bananas" and "cheese at the train station" and "Aunt Paula who eats tomatoes"[15] have often enough knocked their erotic and geographic competition out of the field.

This contingency can only be trusted to a very minor degree. All too willingly, the hits give their contingency a sexual meaning which is by no means an unconscious one; they all tend toward the obscene gesture. The cheese then reminds us of anal regression; the bananas provide surrogate satisfaction for the woman, and the more absurd the nonsense, the more immediate its *sex appeal**. The pace of the gait itself—language bears witness to this—has an immediate reference to coitus; the rhythm of the gait is similar to the rhythm of sexual intercourse; and if the new dances have demystified the erotic magic of the old ones, they have also—and therein at least they are more advanced than one might expect—replaced it with the drastic innuendo of sexual consummation. This is expressed in the extreme in some so-called *dance academies**, where *taxi girls** are available with whom one can perform dance steps which occasionally lead to male orgasm. Thus, the dance is a means for achieving sexual satisfaction and at the same time respects the ideal of virginity. The sexual moment in jazz is what has provoked the hatred of petit bourgeois ascetic groups.

This sexual moment is, however, deliberately emphasized in all jazz. In contrast to the practice of psychoanalysis but using its terminology, one would like to designate the symbolic representation of sexual union as the manifest dream content of jazz, which is intensified rather than censored by the innuendo of the text and the music. One cannot free oneself of the suspicion that the crude and easily transparent sexual secretiveness of jazz conceals a secondary, deeper, and more dangerous secret. The first instance would not differentiate itself at all from what provided the material for older operettas like the *Walzertraum;*[16] the character of modernity which is inherent in jazz would not be affected by it. The second secret, however, may be assumed to be a social one. In order to expose the latent dream structure, one may insist on the interrelatedness of jazz and contingency. Its social significance does not merge into the sexual meaning; the social must be forced from the sexual. Even socially, jazz has at first a simple solution in store. This is its rondo component, that of the couplet and refrain which it shares with traditional simple vocal music. The *couplet* and *refrain* are called in English the *verse** and the *chorus**, and the name and subject matter betray the old relationship between the single lead singer or principal dancer and the collective. In the verse, the individual speaks as if in isolation, precisely out of the contingency of his individuality; he is modest, reporting unobtrusively, not in the tone of the communal hymn, in order then to be confirmed and socially objectified in the chorus, which responds to the question expressed musically by the partial closure. This ritual is addressed to individuals as its public. The intended, unconscious process which the public performs is thus one of establishing identification. The individual in the audience experiences himself primarily as a couplet-ego, and then feels himself transformed *[aufgehoben]* in the refrain; he identifies himself with the collective of the refrain, merges with it in the dance, and thus finds sexual fulfillment. So much for the well-known dream content of jazz; it resembles that of film, which has been treated as with fantasy again and again with all due trivial esprit. Like the films which correspond to it, it illustrates the primacy of society vis-à-vis the individual, who nonetheless experiences himself as the measure in the process. The production process is significant; it realizes the primacy of the refrain over the couplet in that it is always written first and as the principal component; the couplet is found later, only subsequently; the individual, the "hero" of the verse, is an indifferent element in its production. The

verse often tells a simpleminded history of the development of the refrain just to provide a point of connection for the refrain. In orchestral
arrangements, the verse retreats altogether; the piece begins with the refrain and the couplet is used only once in the rondo—only the chorus is
permitted to take part in the repetition and variations. Only it is sung.
Contrary to this, the piano scores which are aimed more at the private
sphere contain the complete text and musically give the couplet as well
as the refrain.

If theory wants to go beyond such findings to penetrate the center of the
social function of jazz, or, to put it in psychological terms, its latent dream
content—that is, to point out the concrete historically determined constellation of social identification and sexual energy for which it is an
arena—it must formulate the problem of contingency with regard to *hot
music**, even though this music, at least in Europe, has reached only a
fraction of the general public. *Hot music** can be contrasted to the minimum of march and salon music as the achievable maximum; the "idea" of
jazz can be construed from it if it is to be construed at all. The scope of
the *hot** elements extends from the artfully executed improvisation via
the *break** and false beats to the elemental component, the syncopation
which seems to stumble out of the basic rhythm. The maintained beat is
contrasted to it as the normative standard. These can lay a greater claim
to being the subject of jazz than does its archaic rudiment, the couplet;
individual contingency is embodied in their excess departures from the
norm. This jazz subject is inept and yet is inclined toward improvisation;
it is contrasted as Self against the abstract superimposed authority and yet
can be exchanged arbitrarily. It lends this authority expression without
softening it by this expression—in this way it is paradoxical. The fact that
it is itself preformed conventionally and only appears to be self-sufficient
forces one to conclude, as does the musical expression of *hot** passages,
that this subject is not a "free," lyrical subject which is then elevated into
the collective, but rather one which is not originally free—a victim of the
collective. Here the sense of jazz's original refrain/couplet relationship
reappears in its own time, for the lead singer or principal dancer is nothing
other than a—perhaps superseded—human sacrifice. In this context, it
may be decisively illuminating that the only important composer who is
at all close to jazz is Stravinsky, whose principal work, *Le Sacre du printemps*, famous for its artful syncopation, makes the subject of the work a
human sacrifice, that of the principal dancer—a sacrifice which the music

not so much interprets as ritualistically accompanies. The sacrificial meaning of the jazz subject is now clearly mitigated under the pressure of dream censorship. It falls out of the collective just as syncopation does from the regular beat; it does not want to be engulfed in the prescribed majority, which existed before the subject and is independent of it, whether out of protest or ineptitude or both at once—until it finally is received into, or, better, subordinated to the collective as it was predestined to be; until the music indicates, in a subsequently ironic manner as the measures grow rounder, that it was a part of it from the very beginning; that, itself a part of this society, it can never really break away from it; indeed, that its seeming ineptitude is really a virtuosity of adaptation; that its "not-being-able-to" (and this is clearly tied in with the sexual meaning here) really indicates an "ability to," an "also-being-able-to," indeed, an "ability to do it better."

The most precise precursor of this jazz subject took shape on the prewar variety stage—therefore the historical question of the extent to which the first tap-dances stem from the variety theater is factually of the utmost importance for a comprehensive theory of jazz. The eccentric may be taken as a model for the jazz subject—one of the oddest and most famous pieces of art music, a Debussy prelude that appeared before World War I, which is similar to jazz bears the title *General Lavine, eccentric*, with the subtitle, *dans le mouvement et le style d'un Cake-walk* ("following the movement and style of a *cakewalk**").[17] The eccentric can first of all be understood as the strict antithesis of the clown. If the clown is the one whose anarchistic and archaic immediacy cannot be adapted to the reified bourgeois life, and becomes ridiculous before it—fragmentary, but at the same time allowing it to appear ridiculous—the eccentric certainly is just as much excluded from instrumental regulation, from the "rhythm" of bourgeois life. He is the crank and recluse, as much as the clown, and may well verge on the ridiculous. But his exclusion manifests itself immediately—not as powerlessness, but rather as superiority, or the appearance of it; laughter greets the eccentric only to die away in shock, and, with his ridiculousness, that of society also elegantly drops out of sight. The rhythm of his arbitrariness is subordinated without a rupture to a greater, more lawful rhythm; and his failure is located not below, but above the standard: to obey the law and yet be different. This type of behavior is taken over, bound up with the gradual abandonment of the traces of playful superiority and liberal difference, by the *hot** subject. Even externally, the jazz practice of the best orchestras always maintains eccentric elements. The juggling acts of the drummers, the lightning-fast switch from one instrument to another, improvisations which sound ridiculously off-beat at first and sound right only once the last beat has sounded, a systematic stumbling over and turning around one another which is both ingenious and futile—the more virtuoso jazz practice has all this in common with the practice of the eccentric. The rhythmic categories of *hot music** are themselves eccentric categories. The syncopation is not, like its counterpart, that of Beethoven, the expression of an accumulated subjective force which directed itself against authority until it had produced a new law out of itself. It is purposeless; it leads nowhere and is arbitrarily withdrawn by an undialectical, mathematical incorporation into the beat. It is plainly a "coming-too-early," just as anxiety leads to premature orgasm, just as impotence expresses itself through premature and incomplete orgasm. The syncopation is completely relativized by the basic rhythm, which is maintained steadfastly from the very beginning, rigidly in accordance with the beat, and modified only in terms of emphasis—or, more precisely, the basic meter and, once again as in the case of impotence, jeered at: it expresses the derision and the suffering from it likewise in a murky ambiguity. As a clown, the *hot** ego begins to follow too weakly the standard of the collective which has been unproblematically set, reeling with uncertainty like many of the figures of the American film grotesque genre, such as Harold Lloyd and occasionally Chaplin himself. The decisive intervention of jazz lies in the fact that this subject of weakness takes pleasure precisely in its own weakness, almost as if it should be rewarded for this, for adapting itself into the collective that made it so weak, whose standard its weakness cannot satisfy. In psychological terms, jazz succeeds in squaring the circle. The contingent ego as a member of the bourgeois class is blindly abandoned on principle to social law. By learning to fear social authority and experiencing it as a threat of castration—and immediately as fear of impotence—it identifies itself with precisely this authority of which it is afraid. In exchange, however, it now suddenly belongs to it and can "dance along." The *sex appeal** of jazz is a command: obey, and then you will be allowed to take part. And the dreamthought, as contradictory as reality, in which it is dreamt: I will only be potent once I have allowed myself to be castrated. The relationship between the jazz subject represented by *hot** jazz elements and social authority, the prescribed metric law, is ambivalent from a material-musical perspective as well as from a social-psychological one. Anxiety causes the subject to drop out and go into opposition, but opposition by an isolated individual, who represents himself in his isolation as purely socially determined, is an illusion. Out of anxiety, individuality, like syncopation, is once again relinquished, which is itself pure anxiety; it sacrifices an individuality which it does not really possess, feels itself, as a mutilated subject, at one with the mutilating authority, and transfers this authority onto itself in such a way that it now believes itself to be "able." The opposing ego remains a part of the total society, it is only concealed from itself at first, and the performance of jazz is not so much its dialectical modification and "transformation," properly speaking, as it is the rigid ritual of the exposure of its social character. The elements of its weakness are inscribed in the "parodic" or comic elements which are peculiar to the *hot** sections—without, however, anyone knowing what exactly is being parodied. They represent at the same time, and still in the sense of eccentricity, the playful superiority of the individual over society, which precisely because of its exact knowledge of the rules of its game can dare not to strictly maintain them. Only this ironic excess is suspect in jazz, and this is indicated by its hatred for squeaks and dissonance—but not the adaptation of syncopation; only it is eliminated within fascism, but not the model of its rhythmic development. For the specification of the individual in jazz never was and never will be that of a thriving productive power, but always that of a neurotic weakness, just as the basic models of the "excessive" *hot** subject remain musically completely banal and conventional. For this reason, perhaps, oppressed peoples could be said to be especially well-prepared for jazz. To some extent, they demonstrate for the not yet adequately mutilated liberals the mechanism of identification with their own oppression.

Jazz, the amalgam of the march and salon music, is a false amalgam: the amalgam of a destroyed subjectivity and of the social power which produces it, eliminates it, and objectifies it through this elimination. This is also true in coloristic terms of the unity of the pseudo-liberated and pseudo-immediate and of the march-like collective basic meter; the subjective-expressive sound; a subjective tone which dissolves itself by revealing its mechanical aspect. Of all the instruments, this coloration is most genuinely recognizable in the unbearable Wurlitzer organ. In it, the character of the jazz vibrato comes definitively to the fore. The other sound characteristics of jazz—the muted distortions of the horns, the chirping and vibrating tonal repetitions of the plucked instruments, the banjo and the ukulele, and even the harmonica—are functionally equivalent to it in so far as they all modify an "objective" sound, but still only to the extent that this sound remains inevitably manifest; it is perhaps ironicized, but mostly it ironicizes the whimpering which is helplessly testing itself within it. The objective sound is embellished by a subjective expression, which is unable to dominate it and therefore exerts a fundamentally ridiculous and heart-rending effect. The elements of the comical, the grotesque, and the anal which are inherent in jazz can therefore never be separated from the sentimental elements. They characterize a subjectivity which revolts against a collective power which it itself *is;* for this reason its revolt seems ridiculous and is beaten down by the drum just as syncopation is by the beat. Only those positions which are characterized by irony, when it is directed against just anyone, and which suspects the expression of subjectivity when it doesn't matter whose it is, are unable to tolerate this sound. Then there appears in its place the militaristically noble, demonically harmonious elements of the symphonic jazz marches, whose sheer compactness will no longer concede even the semblance of humanity its gap. At this point, jazz will have split off along the two poles of its origins, while, in the middle, *hot music,** too soon condemned to classical status, will continue its meager specialized existence. Once this happens, jazz will be beyond redemption.

(1936; GS, vol. 17, pp. 74–100)
Translated by Jamie Owen Daniel; modified by Richard Leppert

NOTES BY RICHARD LEPPERT;
ADDITIONAL NOTES BY JAMIE OWEN DANIEL [JOD]

1. Adorno regards *Scheintakt* as a kind of syncopation. He chooses the word, which he uses repeatedly, as part of a larger rhetorical ploy to emphasize what he regards as the thorough "falseness" of the German dance-band music—fundamentally what he means here by "jazz"—that is the subject of his essay. J. Bradford Robinson, "The Jazz Essays of Theordor Adorno: Some Thoughts on Jazz Reception in Weimar Germany," *Popular Music* 13 no. 1 (January 1994), p. 12, points out that the term was coined by Weimar Germany's jazz theorists to account for what is now known as a secondary rag: "*Scheintakte,* or 'pseudo-bars,' are created when crotchets or quavers are grouped in threes within a 4/4 metre and allowed to produce three-beat patterns extending over the normal bar lines." Robinson points out that Adorno misunderstood the nature of the *Scheintakt* when he described it as a combination of 3 + 3 + 2 eighth-notes within a single 4/4 measure (which is the Charleston rhythm); in fact, the *Scheintakt* must extend across a bar line, otherwise it cannot be heard as such. Robinson acknowledges Adorno's larger point, that the *Scheintakt* ultimately resolves into the basic 4/4 of the piece.

2. Hector Berlioz, *Treatise on Instrumentation,* ed. Richard Strauss, trans. Theodore Front (1843; 2nd ed. 1855; 1948 reprint New York: Dover, 1991), pp. 399–400, under the category "New Instruments."

3. See p. 435 n. 22.

4. Adorno here makes a dismissive reference to the artistic and literary movement known as "New Objectivity," fashionable during the Weimar period, of which he was critical. As John Willet has pointed out in his excellent study of the period: "[A] '*Sache*' is a fact, a matter, a 'thing' in the more abstract sense. Its quality of '*Sachlichkeit*' then implies objectivity in the sense of a neutral, sober, matter-of-fact approach, thus coming to embrace functionalism, utility, absence of

decorative frills." John Willet, *Art and Politics in the Weimar Period: The New Sobriety, 1917–1933* (New York: Pantheon, 1978,), p. 112. See further p. 437 n. 7. [jod]

5. The reference here is to a much-cited passage from Walter Benjamin's essay "The Work of Art in the Age of Mechanical Reproduction," in *Illuminations*, trans. Harry Zohn (New York: Schocken, 1969), p. 242, written during the same period: "Its [mankind's] self-alienation has reached such a degree that it can experience its own destruction as an aesthetic pleasure of the first order." For the importance of Benjamin's essay to Adorno's jazz essay—Adorno had hoped to see both essays published together as a pair—see Jamie Owen Daniel, "Introduction to Adorno's 'On Jazz,'" *Discourse: Theoretical Studies in Media and Culture* 12 no. 1 (Fall/Winter 1989–90), pp. 39–44. [jod]

6. This "being" is meant in the sense of everyday reality, and not in the sense of a transcendent Heideggerian "Being." [jod]

7. Kees van Dongen (1877–1968) was a fauvist painter well known for his portraits of women. In 1908 he joined "Die Brücke," the expressionist painters' group founded in 1905. Tsuguji Fujita (1886–1968) was a Japanese expatriate painter who spent nearly all of his career in Paris. Marie Laurencin (1883–1956), likewise active in Paris, was a painter, watercolorist, and printmaker; as subjects, she favored women, to whom she gave melancholic expression. Adorno's assessment of these artists is founded on the same critique he waged against "moderate modern" *[gemässigte Moderne]* composers like Hindemith. See, for example, ISM, pp. 191–92.

8. "Isle of Capri," with lyrics by Jimmy Kennedy, music by Will Grosz, was published in 1934. Guy Lombardo introduced the song in the United States. It achieved hit status in 1935 via a recording by singer-trumpeter Joe "Wingy" Manone. In England, the song was introduced by Lew Stone's orchestra, with Nat Gonella as vocalist. Thanks to Steve Gilmartin for identifying the song title.

9. "Tiger Rag," published in 1917, has been recorded many times. Jelly Roll Morton (1890–1941) claimed authorship, though this has been disputed by some of his contemporaries. See Edward A. Berlin, *Ragtime: A Musical and Cultural History* (Berkeley and Los Angeles: University of California Press, 1980), p. 183 n. 16.

10. Ernst Krenek's (1900–1991) jazz-influenced *Jonny spielt auf*, an opera in two acts on a text by Krenek, was premiered in Leipzig on 10 February 1927. (It was hugely successful in the short run, receiving more than four hundred performances in German theaters in the 1927–28 season, though it faded quickly thereafter.) *Jonny* was quickly followed by two one-act operas, and a one-act operetta, all three on texts by the composer: *Der Diktator* in 1926 (Krenek later acknowledged that Mussolini served as his model), *Das geheime Königreich* in 1927, and *Schwergewicht, oder Die Ehre der Nation* (1927). All three were premiered together in Wiesbaden on 6 May 1928. Adorno's reference to the "romantic one-act piece as an epilogue," strictly speaking could apply to any one of them but on balance likely refers to *Der Dictator* as regards both its libretto and music. See further John L. Stewart, *Ernst Krenek: The Man and His Music* (Berkeley and Los Angeles: University of California Press, 1991), pp. 80–92. (Adorno's correspondence with Krenek began in 1929.)

11. Adorno names three German artists whose works are known for their humor. Heinrich Heine (1797–1856), whose poetry is often trenchantly ironic and satirical, and commonly directed at German culture, which rendered him a controversial figure. Heine also wrote a number of prose works, including political essays. Joseph Victor von Scheffel (1826–1886), likewise a poet as well as novelist,

is best known for his *Der Trompeter von Säckingen* (1854), a comic epic poem, and for the popular sentimental historical novel *Ekkehard* (1855). Wilhelm Busch (1832–1908) was both a poet and a painter; he wrote satiric verse which he illustrated by drawings. He is regarded as the first fully professional comic-strip artist. He is best known for his *Max und Moritz*, forerunner of "The Katzenjammer Kids." Busch's work emphasizes farce, but with the dark potential for violence.

12. Karl Kraus (1874–1936), Austrian critic-journalist, dramatist, and poet; he was a skilled satirist and wrote in a highly idiomatic style, making him difficult to translate. Adorno cites him often. In particular, see "Morals and Criminality: On the Eleventh Volume of the Works of Karl Kraus," NL, vol. 2, pp. 40–57, concerning the continued relevance of Kraus's *Sittlichkeit und Kriminalität* (1908). In Adorno's words, Kraus "is a critic of ideology in the strict sense: he confronts consciousness, and the form of its expression, with the reality it distorts. . . . He was guided by the profound, if unconscious, insight that when they are no longer rationalized, evil and destructiveness stop being wholly bad and may attain something like a second innocence through self-knowledge" (p. 43); and Kraus "is not rendered obsolete by the worse things that came after him because he had already recognized the worst in the moderately bad and had revealed it by reflecting it. Since then the average has revealed itself to be the worst, the ordinary citizen to be Eichmann" (p. 52).

Regarding Adorno's comment about typographical errors, Adorno may have had in mind the following anecdote Kraus published in his satirical journal *Die Fackel* (1912), titled "I Believe in the Printer's Gremlin" ["Ich glaube an den Druckfehlerteufe"]:

> A hitherto unknown tragedy by Shakespeare was recently announced in the advertising columns of a Skt. Gallen newspaper. It said that the municipal theatre of Skt. Gallen was going to perform "King Lehar," a tragedy in five acts by W. Shakespeare.
> This is no laughing matter. It's horrible. The printer was not trying to make a joke. The word that he was not supposed to set, the association that got into his work, is the measure of our time. By their misprints shall ye know them. What may be read here *is* a Shakespearean tragedy.

(Kraus regarded Lehár's operettas as inane; the irony of the misprint is apparent in the fact that the editor doesn't know the difference between the work of a second-rate composer and one of literature's greatest tragedies.) The translation of this excerpt from *Die Fackel* appears in *In These Great Times: A Karl Kraus Reader*, ed. Harry Zohn, trans. Joseph Fabry et al. (Montreal: Engendra Press, 1976), p. 69. See further Edward Timms, *Karl Kraus: Apocalyptic Satirist: Culture and Catastrophe in Habsburg Vienna* (New Haven: Yale University Press, 1986).

13. Duke Ellington's music was connected to music by Debussy and Delius as early as 1932, in a critical essay on Ellington by R. D. Darrell, "Black Beauty," published in *disques*, pp. 152–61. This essay is reprinted in *The Duke Ellington Reader*, ed. Mark Tucker (Oxford: Oxford University Press, 1993), pp. 57–65. Tucker, p. 57, points out that "Black Beauty" was the first critical assessment of Ellington's music. Its impact was significant, and the views expressed were thereafter repeated. The following year Wilder Hobson in an essay in *Fortune* (August 1933), "Introducing Duke Ellington," suggests that Ellington was reported to have commented, "I'll have to find out about this Delius," after hearing composer Percy Grainger repeat the connection (the essay is reprinted in *Duke Ellington Reader*, pp. 93–98; the quotation appears on p. 95). Enzo Archetti, "In Defense of Ellington and His 'Reminiscing in Tempo,'" *American Music Lover* (1936),

claimed that "Ellington is known to be a great admirer of Delius' works" (*Duke Ellington Reader*, p. 124; see also p. 125 n. 3, concerning Ellington and Delius). Simply stated, it seems clear that Ellington was first introduced to Delius through remarks by Darrell and Grainger. In Mark Tucker's words, "Although there is no compelling evidence showing that Ellington was influenced by Delius, since the thirties many critics have linked the two composers" (p. 125 n. 3, q.v.). For that matter, Ellington was also linked to Ravel and Stravinsky, though Adorno's concern is to associate him with what he regarded as warmed-over impressionism. The purported link between Ellington and Debussy did not receive the stress in the music press that was accorded to Ellington and Delius.

14. Another reference to "New Objectivity," then very much in vogue. See n. 4, above. [jod]

15. The reference is to lines from popular commercial hits of the period. [jod]

16. *Ein Walzertraum* (1907) is by Oscar Straus (1870–1954), the Austrian operetta composer and conductor. His operetta *Der tapfere Soldat* (1908), based on George Bernard Shaw's *Arms and the Man*, was popular in the United States as *The Chocolate Soldier*.

17. Claude Debussy, Préludes, Book II (1913), number six in a collection of twelve pieces.

Farewell to Jazz

The regulation that forbids the radio from broadcasting "Negro jazz" may have created a new legal situation; but artistically it has only confirmed by its drastic verdict what was long ago decided in fact: the end of jazz music itself. For no matter what one wishes to understand by white or by Negro jazz, here there is nothing to salvage. Jazz itself has long been in the process of dissolution, in retreat into military marches and all sorts of folklore. Moreover, it has become stabilized as a pedagogical means of "rhythmic education," and with this has visibly renounced the aesthetic claims that it admittedly never ever made on the consciousness of the producers and consumers of dance, but did make in the ideology of the clever art composers who at one time thought they could be fertilized by it. They have to look around for something else and are certainly already doing so; but in the surviving clubs the last interjected false bar [Schein-takt],[1] the last muted trumpet, if not unheard, will soon die away without a shock.

It is not big-city degeneration, deracinated exoticism, and certainly not, as naïve people think, the bizarre quality of stimulating or clashing asphalt harmonies that appears in jazz and is vanishing along with it. Jazz no more has anything to do with authentic Negro music, which has long since been falsified and industrially smoothed out here, than it is possessed of any destructive or threatening qualities. Even the disrespectful use of themes from Beethoven or Wagner, which is intended to irritate and seemed to hint at a revolutionary undertone, is in truth nothing but the expression of the impoverishment of a music fabrication that became so standardized and attuned to consumption that it lost its last little bit of freedom, the musical inspiration, which it then stole wherever it could find it—one might think of a sort of "patent-evasion"—rather cleverly incorporating the pleasure of the cultivated person who is permitted to stumble across his cultural heritage in a club. Rather, what hollowed jazz out is its own stupidity.[2] What is stamped out, along with it, is not the musical influence of the Negro race on the northern one; nor is it cultural Bolshevism. It is a piece of bad arts and crafts.

Jazz was the *Gebrauchsmusik*[3] of the *haute bourgeoisie* of the post-war period. Two things, in tandem, guaranteed its success. For one thing, it was available for immediate consumption; it registered the development of art music only in stunted reflexes, generally of impressionist harmonies. It remained danceable, on and on, even for the unmusical person, thanks to the basic rhythm, always marked by the bass drum, even where the audacious cadences of *hot music**, syncopation as principle, and the burgeoning joy brought on by triple rhythms inserted into a four-beat meter seem to loosen all the bonds of upbringing and custom *[Zucht und Sitte]*. Nothing was difficult to understand, and if the factory-made product seemed alien to the consumer, it was equally easy to use. Its excesses, however, recalled the erotic ones of the cinema, those undressing scenes, dubious trips to the beach, and ambiguous situations, all of which, under the dictates of a censorship that is deeply ingrained in them, stop short of final consequences. But at the same time, jazz presented itself as progressive, modern, and up-to-date. There was a world-economic resonance in the cheap foreign locales that could be imported at will from Montevideo, Waikiki, and Shanghai. The petit-bourgeois narrowness of dance lessons, polka, and galop[4] seemed left far behind; the sexless saxophone, squawking, declared its quasi-agreement with risqué things, and the harmonies, now mellow, now biting, not only had a stimulating effect but evoked distant memories, at once scary and comforting, of new music's realm of dissonance, which was otherwise avoided so assiduously and with which, it seemed, one could safely associate only here. As if that were not enough, as arts and crafts, jazz was characterized by the fact that, despite its transparently industrial origins, it was distinguished superficially from "vulgar" music; that consumption could be disguised as art appreciation. The concertizing "jazz symphony orchestras" are the obvious expression of this. Or, even more to the point: the technique of improvisation, which developed together with syncopation and the false bar *[Scheintakt]*. The virtuoso saxophonist or clarinetist, or even percussionist, who made his audacious leaps in between the marked beats of the measure, who distorted the accents and dragged out the sounds in bold glissandi—he, at least, should have been exempted from industrialization. His realm was considered to be the realm of freedom; here the solid wall between production and reproduction was evidently demolished, the longed-for immediacy restored, the alienation of man and music mastered out of vital force.

It was not, and the fact that it was not constituted the betrayal and the downfall of jazz. The reconciliation of art music and music for common use [Gebrauchsmusik], of consumability and "class," of closeness to the source and up-to-date success, of discipline and freedom, of production and reproduction is untrue in all its aspects. Indeed, all the elements of "art," of individual freedom of expression, of immediacy are revealed as mere cover-ups for the character of consumer goods. In jazz, the charm of the ninth chords, of the endings on seventh chords, and of the whole-tone daubings are shabby and worn out; it conserves a decaying modernity of the day before yesterday. No different, on second glance, are those achievements of jazz in which people thought they perceived elements of a fresh beginning and spontaneous regeneration—its rhythms. First, syncopation is new for popular music, but by no means for art music. In a master like Brahms, for example, it is accomplished with incomparably greater richness and penetrating depth of construction than in the jazz writers, in whose work—as the "textbooks" of *hot music** unwittingly but all the more drastically reveal—the apparent variety of rhythmic constructs can be reduced to a minimum of stereotypical and standardized formulae. But then—and this explains the stereotypical quality—the rhythmic achievements of jazz are mere ornaments above a metrically conventional, banal architecture, with no consequences for the structure, and removable at will. The bass drum, for which the capers of the other instruments are of no consequence, is already one expression of this. But above all, the way the compositions themselves are constructed. For the schema of the eight-measure period, with its bisection into half- and full stop, the old, cheap schema of dance music—much more meager, for example, than the formally rich waltzes of the great Johann Strauss—is thoroughly in force in jazz. The "false bars," which essentially constituted the supposed rhythmic charm of jazz, have their essence precisely in the fact that rhythmically free, improvisational constructions complement each other in such a way that, taken together, they fit back into the unshaken schema after all. Hence, for example, to cite only the simplest and most frequent case in point, two measures in three-eight and a measure in two-eight are combined sequentially to make a four-four measure, as marked out by the drum. And what is true of the individual measure is true, as well, of the musical period, as can easily be observed in its harmonic and melodic articulation. If someone had wanted to take the syncopation and rhythmically improvisational impulses to their logical conclusion, then the old symmetry would have broken apart; but along with it the tonal harmonic structure, as is actually the case in the jazz experiments of Stravinsky. But then jazz would have lost its consumability and easy comprehensibility, and would have turned into art music. In vain, for those same conclusions, drawn from the dissolution of the old tonal periodicity, had been arrived at long before, more thoroughly, by art music, before anyone even thought of jazz. Jazz didn't take this kind of risks; it contented itself with the boredom of its false effects. Very characteristic, how easily it was able to part with its ferment, syncopation, i.e., the movement of emphasis away from the "good part of the measure" *[vom guten Taktteil]* of metrical time. Kurt Weill, whom people used to like to link with jazz on account of the sound of the saxophone, sacrificed syncopation and false bars in the conscious search for accessibility and made the primitively symmetrical speech accents of song verses his metric rule. But for the last two years, with an eagerness that will not redound to their credit, and that people have already seen through, the jazz manufacturers have already been switching to the kind of patriotic kitsch that now—and perhaps not by accident—has been overtaken by a government verdict at the same time as jazz, precisely because it is closely related to it. The military march has long been lying in wait underneath the colorful arabesques of jazz. But the social stratum that has consumed jazz until now, even if it has not been convinced of its aesthetic inferiority, will be all the more inclined to give it up politically, because in the context of what is possible to do between two four-beat measures, jazz is simply unable to offer any variety.

What it was possible to learn from jazz is the emancipation of the rhythmic emphasis from metrical time; a decent, if very limited and specialized thing, with which composers had long been familiar, but which, through jazz, may have achieved a certain breadth in reproductive practice. Otherwise not much will be left of it, other, perhaps, than the memory of the few pieces that had the élan of first beginnings, like *"Kitten on the Keys*"[5] or the singing of The Revelers,[6] and of an era that was petrified into history with a single blow. Jazz has left behind a vacuum. There is no new *Gebrauchsmusik* to take its place, and it will not be easy to launch one. But this vacuum is not the worst thing. In it is expressed, wordlessly, like the alienation of art and society, a kind of overall state of reality that words are lacking to express. This vacuum may be wordless, but it is no false consciousness. Perhaps in the silence it will grow loud.

(1933; GS, vol. 18, pp. 795–99)
Translated by Susan H. Gillespie

NOTES BY RICHARD LEPPERT

1. See p. 492 n. 1.

2. Adorno uses an English neologism, *Stupidität*. [translator's note]

3. Adorno's use of *Gebrauchsmusik* in this instance serves the purpose of driving a wedge between the *haute bourgeois* sense of (socially autonomous) art music, and jazz as a music that has the "social function" which art music supposedly lacks—an issue that is complicated for Adorno to the extent, paradoxically, that he sees autonomy as part and parcel of art music's critical social function, while at the same time acknowledging that autonomy is turned against itself once it is adopted as a component of the cultural capital of artworks by the very *haute bourgeois* (in this instance) from whom it distances itself. On *Gebrauchsmusik*, see p. 133 n. 2.

4. The polka and galop were popular social dances in nineteenth-century Germany. The galop was a very fast 2/4 dance.

5. "Kitten on the Keys" (1921), music by Zez Confrey (1895–1971), was a popular novelty piece often performed by both Confrey and pianist-bandleader Vincent Lopez. Confrey performed it at Paul Whiteman's famous Aeolian Hall concert in New York in 1924, where Gershwin also premiered *Rhapsody in Blue*. Confrey's recording of the fast-paced showpiece is available on various reissues.

6. Concerning The Revelers, see p. 275 n. 5; and "Revelers" and "Shannon Four," in *Encyclopedia of Recorded Sound in the United States*, ed. Guy A. Marco and Frank Andrews (New York: Garland, 1993), pp. 586, 621.

Kitsch

As little as it may otherwise hit the mark, in the case of ideas that are immersed in history, to refer back to a word's lexical meaning, the term "kitsch" has grown so remote from its lexical meaning that the latter may once again enlighten by being pointed to as a forgotten secret. If the interpretation is correct that derives the word from the English *sketch*,[1] then this would mean, first of all, the quality of being unrealized, merely hinted at. This may lead deeper than all notions of the non-genuine, illusory, by themselves, ever could. In music, at any rate, all real kitsch has the character of a *model*. It offers the outline and draft of objectively compelling, pre-established forms that have lost their content in history, and for which the unfettered artist, cast adrift, is not able to fashion the content on his own. Hence the illusory character of kitsch cannot be unambiguously traced to the individual inadequacy of the artist, but, instead, has its own objective origin in the downfall of forms and material into history. Kitsch is the precipitate of devalued forms and empty ornaments from a formal world that has become remote from its immediate context. Things that were part of the art of a former time and are undertaken today must be reckoned as kitsch. On the other hand, the objectivity of kitsch is the source of its justification. For kitsch precisely sustains the memory, distorted and as mere illusion, of a formal objectivity that has passed away. Kitsch is a kind of receptacle of mythic basic materials of music, as they appear only in it, transformed, as the most advanced results of music's dialectic, but are otherwise lost. Hence kitsch is to be preferred to all music of the *juste milieu* [happy medium].

Of course, one must make distinctions. The recuperation of kitsch holds good, in truth, only in the musical underworld of operettas, hit songs, and vaudeville songs; and the anonymous domain underneath that under-world, the marches and drinking songs, sentimental tunes and ditties for servant girls. Ultimately it applies to aspects of moderate, formerly serious music that have meanwhile become transparent and, today, recognizable as kitsch, relinquish their secret—the way, for example, the riddle of mu-sical *Jugendstil*, from whose idea the entire Richard Strauss might be con-structed, could be solved using Lassen's "Stell auf den Tisch die duftenden Reseden" [Put the Sweet-Smelling Mignonettes on the Table].[2] For "mod-erate Kitsch"—the expression is Karl Kraus's[3]—no rescue is possible. For the rights of kitsch can be invoked only over the head of the composer, only when he himself didn't mean anything by it. But as soon as the composition itself makes claims and wants to be subjectively formed, but succumbs to kitsch, the power of kitsch-objectivity within it is over and done with. Someone once spoke of good bad books and bad good books. The difference is precisely applicable here. Good bad music: that is *"Tea for Two*,"*[4] the trio from *"Sunflower*"*[5] from the time of the inflation; later *"The Dancing Tambourine*,"*[6] perhaps even *The Three Musketeers*.[7] Bad good music does not need to be enumerated here. It is kitsch too—unrealized, illusory, living on false emotions. But the power of the dead forms has absconded from it. It had best be eliminated.

Impossible to grasp the concept "kitsch" in a free-floating aesthetic way. The social moment is essentially constitutive of it. For by serving up past formal entities as contemporary, it has a social function—to deceive people about their true situation, to transfigure their existence, to allow intentions that suit some powers or other to appear to them in a fairy-tale glow. All kitsch is essentially ideology. Thus, in the nineteenth century, musical kitsch transfigured the existence of bourgeois and proletarians, who are absorbed in class struggle, by means of a *romanticism* that, once it had died out as great art, was good enough to transform the living room into a saloon with *Eliland* and *The Trumpeter of Säckingen*.[8] In the more spa-cious and secure *Lebensraum* of that time, all kitsch resonated with a metaphysics of death, as it was summarized in Tristan's renunciation and "May God protect you, it would have been so beautiful."[9] Today, when the moderate security of the bourgeoisie is a thing of the past, the function of kitsch has changed. It no longer leaves any room for death. Now it has merely to conceal and transfigure, and it must satisfy with an altogether different alacrity the concrete wishes of tormented individuals. Concealment notwithstanding, the real class relations stand out ever more starkly—for example, when for about a year now hit songs of the type "Blonde-haired Inge"[10] have been flourishing, which try, with sound movies and revues, to fool the girl at the typewriter into thinking she is a queen. Hard to believe how quickly kitsch responds to need. I once demonstrated the connection between "Ich küsse Ihre Hand, Madame" [I kiss your hand, Madame][11] and stabilization. With the onset of the economic crisis, the song came out about the one white chrysanthemum that often says as much as a whole bouquet[12]—evidently for reasons of thrift. The "Gigolo"[13] serves the ideological linkage of economic need with political reaction. Are the military hit songs an accident, or the beats of a new nativism that we are being served up today?

Music is very much a part of all this. It is assigned the task, above all, of eliciting the impression of collective commitment by means of the preservation of old and superannuated formal types; of employing individual means of expression—such as romantic harmonies and today, already, impressionist harmonies—at a moment when they have come loose from their original formal contexts and can circulate like a kind of musical small change; of utilizing melodic arcs that still bear traces of their former emotional significance conventionally, as mere phrases. In the process, the linking of the characteristic and the banal remains the task and paradox of all genuine kitsch music. If, on the one hand, it needs the characteristic in order to be noticed and remembered, at the same time it is only banality that allows it to be comprehended at all, without conscious concentration, usually "subconsciously" in the psychoanalytic sense. It clings faithfully to ancient, actually probably ritual schemas like that of stanza and refrain. It has a preference for harmonies that were once especially exposed and striking, such as the diminished-seventh chord or, nowadays, the whole-tone scale. It also differentiates itself from every individual formal creation by virtue of the fact that it is constructed in types. As soon as a new type turns up—"Valencia":[14] six-eighth step; "Heidelberg": fast march;[15] "Wenn der weisse Flieder . . ." [When the White Lilac . . .]:[16] pseudo folk song—a large group of similar compositions is created that sometimes drive out the originals; or a type emerges in innumerable examples simultaneously. What is absolutely excluded is the penetration of any stirrings of compositional independence into the kitsch region. On the other hand, good prospects exist for ideas that hew strictly to the bounds of convention, like the triple meter in "Valencia."

The worst kitsch is kitsch with "class," which is not recognizable in advance, but has compositional ambition. The only means of tearing off its mask is *technical* critique—elements of kitsch in music that is intended as "serious" always give themselves away by technical anomalies. True, the latter only provide the point of departure: technical anomaly does not necessarily need to be kitsch.

There is no general criterion for kitsch, for the concept is itself a frame that is always only filled historically and has its actual justification only in polemics. Today the term has long since been adopted by the *juste milieu* and has, itself, become an ideological means of defending a moderate "culture" of the musical that no longer possesses any power. Thus the talk about kitsch itself begins to be kitschy, as it succumbs to the very historical dialectic from which its object emerged. Since contempt for low music as the true realm of the subconscious in music no longer helps, and the critique of anomaly in serious and aspiring music is always more compelling than the allegation of kitsch, which presupposes a closed, compelling musical language, people will gradually learn to avoid such talk—after it has been made clear what it means.

(c. 1932; GS, vol. 18, pp. 791–94)
Translated by Susan H. Gillespie

NOTES BY RICHARD LEPPERT

1. For this history, see Jochen Schulte-Sasse, "Kitsch" in *Historisches Wörterbuch der Philosophie*, ed. Joachim Ritter and Karl Gründer (Basel: Schwabe, 1976), vol. 4, cols. 843–46.

2. Eduard Lassen (1830–1904) was a Belgian composer born in Copenhagen and active in Germany. He wrote several operas but is especially known for his many songs, which were popular at the end of the nineteenth century. "Stell auf den Tisch die duftenden Reseden" *(Allerseelen)* is from his Lieder op. 85, on a text by Hermann von Gilm (1812–1864), which was also set by Richard Strauss, op. 10 no. 8.

3. See p. 494 n. 12.

4. "Tea for Two," music by Vincent Youmans, words by Irving Caesar; from the 1923 musical *No, No Nanette;* the New York premiere occurred in 1925.

5. I have not located this tune, which presumably dates to around 1923, the height of *Inflationszeit*.

6. "Dancing Tambourine" (1927), music by W. C. Polla, words by Phil Ponce.

7. A successful American musical, *The Three Musketeers*, based on Alexandre Dumas's *Les trois Mousquetaires* (1844), premiered in New York in 1928; music by Rudolf Friml, words by P. G. Wodehouse and Clifford Grey. However, Adorno is almost certainly referring to *Drei Musketiere*, produced in Berlin in 1929, music by Ralph Benatzky, text by Ernst Welisch and Rudolf Schanzer. Benatzky's own tunes were apparently interspersed with borrowed American songs. (Whereas Adorno cites the American pop tunes in their original English, he gives this musical in German, suggesting that it is the Berlin show rather than the New York production to which he refers.)

8. *Eliland* is a song cycle by the German composer Alexander von Fielitz (1860–1930); it is his best-known work. *Der Trompeter von Säckingen* (1884), an opera by the Alsatian composer Viktor E. Nessler (1841–1890), was immensely popular in Germany and is noted for its sentimental tunes.

9. The lines, "B'hüt dich Gott, es wär so schön gewesen, Behüt dich Gott, es hat nicht sollen sein!" form the chorus of a three-stanza poem by Josepf Viktor von Scheffel (1826–1886), whose syrupy and sentimental epic *Der Trompeter von Säckingen* served as the basis for the opera by Nessler. The text appears in the opera and also in a separate song-setting by the German composer Franz Wilhelm Abt (1819–1885), op. 213 no. 2.

10. "Wenn Ich die Blonde Inge: Cha-Cha-Cha" (c. 1929), music and lyrics by Friedrich Schwarz. Recorded by "Red" Roberts in 1930.

11. The song, long on sentiment, music by Ralph Erwin, words by Fritz Rotter, takes its name from a late silent film (1929)—but with music—of the same name, with Marlene Dietrich playing a woman who must choose between two men. Performed by Harry Liedke, the tune became a hit. A recording, arranged for orchestra and humming backup chorus, is available on the CD *Orchestre Grand Café* HRCD 8093.

12. The German word for bouquet is *Strauss*. Adorno is almost certainly employing a pun at the expense of Richard Strauss, whose work is critiqued earlier in the essay.

13. Probably the medium tempo tune "Schöner Gigolo" (1929), music by Leonello Casucci, words by Julius Brammer; the English version, words by Irving Caesar, is "Just a Gigolo" (1929); a recording of an instrumental arrangement is available on the CD identified in n. 11, above.

14. See p. 435 n. 22.

15. There are a number of old pop tunes of this name. Adorno may be referring to the well-accented 6/8 allegro "Heidelberg Stein Song" from the musical *The Prince of Pilsen*, which premiered in New York in 1903; music by Gustave Luders, words by Frank Pixley. The musical was successful in London and was also taken to France in 1907.

16. "Wenn der weisse Flieder wieder blüht: Lied u. Slow-Fox [Trot]," music by Franz Doelle, words by Fritz Rotter. Published in Cologne, 1928; available in an instrumental version on the CD identified in n. 11, above.

Music in the Background

In our immediate life there is no longer a place for music. Anyone who, by himself, wanted to sing out loud in the street would run the risk of being arrested as a disturber of the peace. If you hum under your breath, abstracted from external things, you may run into a car at any moment. And don't the three boy scouts [*Wandervögel*][1] look sad and stiff as they take their place in the market square and sing along with their out-of-tune guitar chords, as if they were wandering minstrels—these secondary school students. Only political action can possibly unleash the physical reality of song for a few brief hours. We are far from Naples, not only in space, but in time. If, there, all speech still soars toward song; if the fruit seller, bearing his wares on a heathen altar-cart, offers up hymns before it; here at home the street vendors have long since become ambulant posters. If you are looking for music, you have to step outside the space of immediate life, because it no longer is one, and find the lost immediacy where it costs the price of admission, at the opera, at a concert.

All the same, it is has not been entirely eliminated. Certainly, the organ-grinder and the backyard musician are archaic vestiges. They have their own law and their own history, at cross-purposes with society, and their obscure existence counts for nothing in its eyes. The islands of house music are located rather close to the shimmering frozen lake of self-conscious artistic practice. But exiled Music herself, pushed to the edge of existence, holds out loyally there: music as background.

It is, after the death of the silent film and its consoler, the movie-house orchestra, the music of the cafés or, in the ritualistically preferred language of today, the establishments with live entertainment. It has survived the radios, even without outside assistance; cafés and pubs with their own band always draw a bigger crowd than those with nothing but a loudspeaker. It

506

costs the listener nothing; it is included in the price of the coffee, the hot chocolate, the vermouth; he barely notices it. If he does notice it, he feels himself buoyed up as a visitor to an expensive establishment. Music belongs; it may have been shooed off the street, but not to the distant reaches of formalized art. Rather, it keeps the customers company—the tired ones with their stimulating drink, the busy ones at their negotiations, even the newspaper readers; even the flirts, if there still are any.

The first characteristic of background music is that you don't have to listen to it. No stillness surrounds it with an insulating layer. It seeps into the murmur of the conversations. If an unfortunate tenor bellows out his Italian canzonettas, we experience him as intrusive. The silence lasts only the couple of seconds until the next order is taken. Art connoisseurs who go "Shhh!"—here they are implacably exposed as comical.

In *piano* passages the music wants to disappear altogether. Then you can hear the clatter of spoons and cups, mingled with the glockenspiel, maybe the high notes of the piano; the phrases of the cello fall away, lost. In *forte* passages, the music climbs like a rocket. Its arcs glisten over the listeners until they sit there, abandoned once more, in the gray of their cigarette puffs. They are not an audience. Scarcely ever will one of them comment on the quality of the music that is offered. Nor are they in a musical mood. The music scarcely touches their inner stirrings. Rather: it is an objective event among, above them. The coldness from table to table; the strangeness between the young gentleman and the unknown girl across from him, who waits for the looks that will give her permission to be offended. All this is not, for the life of you, eliminated by the music, but instead caught up and bound together. The gentleman will certainly not dare to accost the girl here, in the expensive establishment with live entertainment. But coldness, desire, the strangeness of the closeness between the two—the music transports it with an abrupt gesture into the stars, like the name of Ariadne abandoned.[2] The accosted girls themselves do not need to pay attention to it. As soon as it gets too loud, they remove their bodies from the astral event with the cry: Waiter! The bill! And strike the glass with their spoon. This, however, is simultaneously the sound of café music.

Has anyone ever listened carefully to this sound? Connoisseurs know how to differentiate between a Parisian-style band, a salon band, and certain others. The differences are of a rather subtle kind. The sound is common to all—Hindemith created his worthy monument to it in the first Donaueschingen chamber works.[3] One cannot speak of an orchestra; the endlessness of the string choir, the colors of the wind instruments, the resonance of the brass are lacking. Ergo, chamber music, one thinks, and at once becomes aware of the impossibility. Here is no intertwining play of instruments entering by turns. There is only a melody of the uppermost voice—the soloist presents himself as a "wandering fiddler *[Stehgeiger]*." The piano is not employed like a piano in chamber music; it is the "conductor," with foundation and harmony, perhaps the last heir in European music to the figured bass. This gaudy sound has something splendidly shabby about it. It is as bright as tinsel; but it tears in your hand. It wants to represent orchestras and yet is dominated by the piano; there is scarcely any place where the demand that things should be "appropriate to the material" is so heedlessly rendered ridiculous as here. Like the *Stephanie Gavotte*,[4] it pretends to chamber-musical refinements—but in the end it only means "wandering fiddler," for the pizzicati get lost. Nowhere has music become so wholly appearance as in the café. But in appearance, it is preserved. It must, or so it seems, be thus emancipated from all human seriousness and all genuineness of artistic form if it is still to be tolerated by human beings amidst their daily affairs without frightening them. But it is its appearance that lights up for them. No—that lights them up. They do not change in it, but their image changes. It is brighter, sharper, more clearly defined. When café music falls silent, it sounds as if a miserly waiter is turning off a couple of electric bulbs. Background music is an acoustic light source.

For what is non-genuine, appearance-like about it, the designated technical term is "arrangement." No original compositions are played, no piece as it is conceived. Everything is in arrangements for the salon orchestra, which falsifies and alters it. It softens grandly conceived passages into intimacy, blows up tender ones with tremolo and vibrato. The works dissolve in all this, and dissolved works, by those once-famous, then forgotten masters, are the right ones for background music. The question is only whether they stop at dissolution. In dissolution the works fall silent. Here they become audible once again. Not, it is true, they themselves, in their structured form. But the ruins of their sound have been joined together in a second, strangely transparent form. The piano does not simply replace the missing horns; the previous fullness has itself become shabby and is therefore passed on to the piano. The first fiddler does not make the noble melody ordinary with his soloistic intrusiveness; it has already lost its noble character and therefore abandons itself to the fiddler. The truly noble melody will shine like a star against the background: one hears it as music.

For the rest, however, the café arranges bouquets of dead flowers. The joints between the brittle sounds into which they are layered are not firmly bonded. Through them shimmers the mysterious allegorical appearance that arises whenever fragments of the past come together in an uncertain surface. What is true for the vertical sound is no less true horizontally, for the passage of time. The cafés are the site of potpourris. The latter are constructed out of the fragments of the work, its best-loved melodies. But they awaken the ruins to new, ghostly life. If our art music lingers in the comforting realm of Orpheus—here its echo sounds from Euridice's mournful region. Its glow is netherworldly. It can remain unnoticed because it is unreal. But it is not a black shadow, rather a bright one, like milk glass. One can, as it were, hear vaguely through this music, through to the next room. This is why it shines.

One would think that music in the background, unnoticed music, should not present itself other than as accompaniment—as good ballet music, in contrast to pantomimes, creates a complement of rhythms, colors, sounds and saves the music for the dance up on the stage. Far from true. Since in the café, after all, the melodies wander around as ghosts, one need not fear any disturbance from them, no matter how present they are. For they are quoted from the unconscious memory of the listeners, not introduced to them. The greater the ecstasies, the more perfect the emotional calm of the hearers over whose heads they drift. There are masters—truly masters—whose greatness first becomes entirely evident in this odd transformation of passionate appearance into the cold comfort of reality. Puccini is the most prominent among them. One could think that *Bohème, Butterfly, Tosca* were created with the thought of imaginary potpourris that do not emerge until the last tear from the operatic catastrophes has dried up. But Grieg, too, is not to be sneezed at, with pieces like "To Spring." Tchaikovsky is suitable; naturally Mignon and Margarete. Carmen defies all ghostly doings. Faced with Schubert, café music becomes blasphemous. Strange that the new dances don't want to fit in, either. Their function is too fresh for them to allow themselves to be used as background yet. The best are the melodies with the great unbroken arcs, like the arias of Butterfly and Rodolfo.[5] Anyone who, moved, is startled out of his conversation or thoughts after all, and who looks in that direction, is transformed into Georg Heym's suburban dwarf: "he looks up to the great green bell of heaven, where silent meteors cross far away."[6]

(c. 1934; GS, vol. 18, pp. 819–23)
Translated by Susan H. Gillespie

NOTES BY RICHARD LEPPERT

1. *Wandervogel* was a scout-like organization founded around 1895; its name was changed in 1901 to "Wandervogel Committee for Schoolboy Excursions." After 1933 the organization was merged with the Hitler Jugend. Though the Wandervögel Leagues were officially dissolved by the Nazi regime, individual groups in some instances remained in contact with their members and served as nuclei for opposition to the Third Reich. "Wandervogel," in *The Encyclopedia of the Third Reich*, ed. Christian Zentner and Friedemann Bedürftig, trans. Amy Hackett (New York: Macmillan, 2001), vol. 2, pp. 1017–18.

2. Ariadne was abandoned by Theseus, whom she loved, on the island of Naxos, after she had helped him escape the labyrinth following his successful slaying of the feared Minotaur. Ariadne was eventually rescued by Bacchus. From Ovid, *Metamorphoses*, trans. Rolfe Humphries (Bloomington: Indiana University Press, 1955), 8:169–82.

3. The Donaueschingen Festival was one of the most important all-new-music festivals of the twentieth century, and perhaps the longest-lived, though it has gone through a number of transformations. Hindemith, who served as a principal administrator of the festival between 1923 and 1926, very successfully premiered a number of his chamber works there, including works as stylistically different as the Second String Quartet (1921) and the Kammermusik No. 1 (1922). Adorno's wry reference is almost certainly to this latter work, whose finale includes quotations from a foxtrot written by the cabaret composer Wilm-Wilm, and ends with a siren; the work's twelve instruments include accordion, trumpet, and percussion. Adorno may also have in mind the jazzy solo piece *1922 — Suite for Piano*, op. 26, with movements marked: march, shimmy, nocturne, Boston, and ragtime. See also p. 133 n. 2.

4. See p. 316 n. 7.

5. Adorno names the principal female roles, and one principal male role, from several standard repertory romantic operas, all of which were supplied by their composers with arias lending themselves to transformation into café music; these include Mignon from Ambroise Thomas's opera of the same name, Margarete from Gounod's *Faust*, and Rodolfo from Puccini's *La Bohème*. The sort of music that Adorno has in mind was often recorded, sans vocal parts—the melodic lines being relocated, where necessary, to the first violins—and mass marketed as "opera without words" in the 1950s and '60s. Indeed, the orchestral arrangements of this sort tended to be overstocked with strings: the recording orchestras led by André Kostelanetz and Mantovani were among the more prominent, together with 101 Strings.

6. Georg Heym (1887–1912), German expressionist poet. The lines Adorno cites are the last two from his eleven-stanza poem "Die Vorstadt" [The Suburb]. Georg Heym, *Gesammelte Gedichte*, ed. Carl Seelig (Zürich: Verlag der Arche, 1947), pp. 8–9.

4

COMPOSITION, COMPOSERS, AND WORKS

Commentary

Richard Leppert

In art we can read off clearly the ambivalence of all progress.

I believe in the strict knowability of music—because music is itself
knowledge, and in its way very strict knowledge.

> Adorno, *Beethoven: The Philosophy of Music*

Adorno's work is tightly focused on the history of Western modernity
from its ascendancy in the late eighteenth century to its late phase in the
aftermath of World War II. His social and sociological concerns were principally defined by the history and impact of the bourgeoisie, from the
class's dramatic emergence in the early decades of the nineteenth century,
and its foundation in economic and cultural capitalism, to its saturation
and colonization of the subject and subjectivity. Adorno saw modernity as
a period of more or less permanent crisis as regards the deeply ironic
relation between, on the one hand, the general possibility for human happiness and emancipation as a result of the highest ideals of the Enlightenment and the technological advancements of the Industrial Revolution,
and, on the other, the actual general failure to realize either. Adorno saw
modernity as a long history of lost opportunity in the face of myriad
catastrophes. Arguably, the French Revolution[1] constituted in capsule form
the history of the following century and a half: making claim for eman-

---

1. ISM, p. 62: "If we listen to Beethoven and do not hear anything of the
revolutionary bourgeoisie—not the echo of its slogans, the need to realize them,
the cry for that totality in which reason and freedom are to have their warrant—we
understand Beethoven no better than does one who cannot follow the purely musical content of his pieces, the inner history that happens to their themes." And
on p. 210: "The din of the bourgeois revolution rumbles in Beethoven." A similar
statement occurs in AT, p. 349. Tia DeNora, *Beethoven and the Construction of
Genius: Musical Politics in Vienna, 1792–1803* (Berkeley and Los Angeles: University of California Press, 1995), makes clear that the relationship between Beethoven and Enlightenment humanism cannot be staged on the basis of the social
class which supported these views, in Vienna the established aristocracy, rather
than the middle class. Adorno's concern, however, is not patronage, but the discursive implications of Beethoven's music.

cipation and general rights, it turned on its own ideals and degenerated into a bloodbath, to be followed by dictatorship, general war, and "restoration," ironically culminating in the 1848 revolutions with the hegemonic bourgeoisie asserting its "rights," highly particular, against the emerging working classes in an increasingly urbanized Europe.[2] Adorno's own childhood occurred in the shadow of World War I, and his early maturity witnessed the impact of Nazism, anti-Semitism, exile, the Holocaust, and the Stalinist show trials and the resulting mass executions. His experience in the American "paradise" suggested what was to come after the defeat of fascism, a world dominated by technologically accomplished forms of mass culture whose purpose was to sell. As he saw things, happiness and emancipation devolved to little more than advertising slogans and Cold War propaganda. He left America at the height of the McCarthy Hearings: late modernity as witch hunt. His years back in Germany provided no special comfort; there he witnessed the German Economic Miracle (scathingly characterized by writers like Heinrich Böll and Günther Grass), structured on versions of mass culture and late capitalism. For Adorno, modernity and catastrophe were one, the bitter irony of which resided in the fact that modernity at its beginning had posited something fundamentally different, which might have been realized but was not.

Adorno spent his life pursuing the impact of two conflicting concerns: insisting that the happiness claimed as a vast marketing scheme was a mask worn by domination, and at the same time suggesting that happiness was still discernable, hence possible, if—sad to say—barely. Happiness for Adorno was social. Personal happiness in the face of general social unhappiness (injustice) was false by definition; it resided in the realm of selfish privilege, a socio-psychic gated community. Adorno regarded art as the repository for the faint image of a happiness otherwise unavailable, while insisting that art could not provide what society denied.

Art with any claim to truth estranged itself from the here and now, because merely to aestheticize present reality perpetuated modernity's lie. But estrangement created aporia: the more autonomous the art, the greater its remove from people, themselves increasingly conditioned to receive aestheticized representations of market will. If autonomous art turned

2. See Rose Rosengard Subotnik's excellent account, "Adorno's Diagnosis of Beethoven's Late Style: Early Symptom of a Fatal Condition," in *Developing Variations: Style and Ideology in Western Music* (Minneapolis: University of Minnesota Press, 1991), p. 18, regarding the French Revolution, Napoleon, and the aftermath of both as regards Adorno's account of Beethoven.

away in order to reference something better, it risked losing touch with the human subjects on whose behalf it acted. Adorno struggled with this dilemma throughout his career, finding only near the very end of his life—discernible in hints and not much more—a possible path other than the one he had long walked, that is, other than one marked by the increasingly absolute divisions of autonomous from non-autonomous art, and high culture from mass culture. Nonetheless, Adorno's last writings, which acknowledge potentially utopian comportment in film and television, and in what he termed *"une musique informelle,"* are anticipated in much earlier work, and notably in his work on music (that on Mahler is perhaps the clearest in this regard).

Adorno's account of musical modernity and its social stakes is framed by two composers, more or less at the beginning and end of the historical period, Beethoven and Schoenberg, with four other composers occupying his attention as well, Wagner, Mahler, Berg, and Stravinsky, though to be sure he wrote about many others, but far less attentively. Stated altogether too simplistically, of the six composers named, two—Wagner and Stravinsky—are "present" as negative foils to the others. But despite Adorno's sustained, at times scathing, critique of Wagner and Stravinsky, it must be noted that he offered a dialectical account of all six composers, however "shaded" to one or the other side of the equation his account of any one of them. Moreover, Adorno did not waste words on composers whom he didn't take seriously. This is to suggest, simply, that Wagner's genius and Stravinsky's multifaceted talent (Adorno would not accuse him of genius) were not lost on him. And in particular, Adorno was quite clear when he discerned progressive elements in their work, though what he principally recognized was regressive. Similarly, he acknowledged regressive elements in Beethoven, Mahler, Berg, and Schoenberg—though among these composers Berg especially was accorded Adorno's almost untarnished admiration.

In all instances, Adorno's musical criticism concerns the relation of the composer's works to the overriding question of its truth content, in relation to modernity and the state of the subject. This is a tall order for the works and for Adorno, and defines the very nature and substance of his aesthetic theory, marking his singular contribution to social and musical discourse. His concerns are social, aesthetic, and philosophical; any response to these concerns comes from the musical works directly: immanently—not the least reason that Adorno is far more concerned with music's production than its reception. That is, Adorno's musical criticism is defined by what is specifically musical; his concern is musical sound as such and its social-philosophical import. This section sketches how Adorno goes about his task, and what he hears in the works of the composers he focuses on.

Beethoven   Adorno's aesthetic privileges extremes. Extremes exhibit clarity, the quality of standing out, determined by a relation to the conventional whose principles are, by whatever means, exceeded or violated, engaged and denaturalized. Accordingly, only by understanding the conventional will we hear the extreme as such. Two essays in this volume amply clarify Adorno's approach: the almost fragmentary "Late Style in Beethoven," barely five pages in length, which addresses in essence the entirety of Beethoven's so-named Third Period, hence a great number of works (only a couple of which he mentions even barely); and the fully fleshed out essay "Alienated Masterpiece: The *Missa Solemnis*," which is focused in considerable detail on a single work.

"LATE STYLE IN BEETHOVEN" (1937; pp. 564–68) addresses catastrophe; Adorno likens late work to bitter, spiny fruit—whose affect, in a word, is anti-culinary. Adorno is keen to undercut accounts of late work that link it to particular forms of subjectivity associated with old age; he insists that the principle of late work is not to be found in psychology. Indeed, the dimension that interests him is not personal history but history as such: the late works of significant artists bear the ravages of history. Adorno suggests, in this regard, that Beethoven's late works are not saturated with expression (as we might expect); instead they keep their distance from us, remaining mysterious, and thereby providing an indication of the inadequacy of psychological explanation (to which, for example, Richard Strauss's "Four Last Songs" all too well, by contrast, offer themselves, in my view).

To address the riddle of late works, Adorno considers not the composer's mental-emotional state, but the works themselves. His chief interest at first glance seems off the mark, namely, the role played by conventions, in which history is congealed but also rendered invisible to the extent that conventions function as second nature.[3] In Beethoven's late-works' use of convention, Adorno finds exactly the opposite of what we might expect,

---

3. Ibid., p. 29: "Convention signifies for Adorno the impervious, unyielding, or to use Nietzsche's term, the *immergleich* aspect of external reality, that aspect which the subject cannot alter, obscure, or efface, even through the creation of an artistic surface.... Even the arbitrariness with which the subject wrenches convention out of its obscurity reflects the subject's deference to the objective, since arbitrariness is not characteristic of a rational subject but is rather a facet of force, the quality that, along with collectivity, Adorno's subject associates with objective reality."

not a rejection or refusal of conventions (for this would in fact be what is actually conventional in Beethoven) but a notable adherence to them. That is, it is the conventional in Beethoven's late work that (ironically, startlingly) estranges them, renders them enigmatical—and which at the same time renders inadequate psychoanalytical-subjectivist readings. "The works are full of decorative trill sequences, cadences, and *fiorituras.* Often convention appears in a form that is bald, undisguised, untransformed" (p. 565).

Adorno amplifies the point in his unfinished Beethoven monograph: "In Beethoven's late style there is altogether something like a tendency towards dissociation, decay, dissolution, but not in the sense of a process of composition which no longer holds things together: the dissociation and disintegration themselves become artistic means."[4] He further suggests that there occurs a splitting into extremes between polyphony and monody, what he terms "a dissociation of the middle," resulting in "the withering of harmony." The harmony that survives seems mask- or husk-like, "a convention keeping things upright, but largely drained of substance." Adorno remarked harmony's relative powerlessness to determine these works' forward trajectory: "Harmony suffers the same fate in late Beethoven as religion in bourgeois society: it continues to exist, but is forgotten."[5]

Adorno finds expression in the late works in their expressionlessness, and subjectivity in its apparent lack—apparently lacking to the extent that by denying a direct outpouring of subjectivity, which is what's expected, subjectivity is referenced the more profoundly. By this means, the separation of subject from (musical) object is acknowledged—the very separation that determined the flawed nature of the subject and modernity alike, the gap which the artwork serves to bridge. In other words, the late work "cast[s] off the appearance of art" (p. 566) and by that means becomes greater art still, its negativity divulging the awful truth while, as art, nonetheless positing the hope for reconciliation.

No composer ever succeeded in dominating his musical materials more than Beethoven. Indeed, for Adorno, it is this quality that marks the composer himself as the (invariably flawed) modern subject, conditioned by

4. B, p. 189.
5. Ibid., pp. 156, 158. Subotnik, "Adorno's Diagnosis of Beethoven's Late Style," p. 32, points out that estrangement in music "requires interfering with the perception of coherence in structural and syntactical elements, something Beethoven's late style found many ways of doing."

rational powers through which he forced musical materials to do his bidding. But the late work is different. Reflective, it is produced at life's end, when "touched by death, the hand of the master sets free the masses of material that he used to form; its tears and fissures, witnesses to the finite powerlessness of the I confronted with Being, are its final work" (p. 566). The egotistical "I" recognizes in the end that the nature from which it separated itself in order to become a subject is now about to reclaim the "I" as its own in spite of everything. Death and reconciliation, to be sure, but something else, besides. The composer continues to compose, to rework the material, which is to say that he continues to assert his subjecthood but one that recognizes and valorizes a different and non-antagonistic subject-object relation. "Thus in the very late Beethoven the conventions find expression as the naked representation of themselves" (p. 566).[6]

Adorno understands musical material, in one sense "natural," to be always already historical. The composer, as it were, inherits the material: the "possibilities" immanent to the material are in place when the composer approaches it, as determined by prior use. Hence musical "nature" is fundamentally not natural; it is humanly constructed yet both part of and different from the subject. Moreover, the musical material is resistant to the composer's actions and in two ways. First, it is literally foreign to the composer, a "substance" different from the human, which the subject will shape. Second, it carries with it a certain historical contingency and inevitability; it "demands" to be shaped in some ways at the expense of others. The artwork worthy of the name, however, does not acquiesce to standardized comportment; to do so would render the effort to make art (to discern truth content) moot by definition, since standardization is a hallmark of modern domination which the standardized artwork serves merely to aestheticize, thereby perpetuating modernity's lie. But to subvert standardization requires an effort literally against the "expectations" of the material: as it were, against the force of history itself. The truth of the work is not to overcome the subject-object polarity, except, so to speak, negatively, by revealing the polarity for what it is by "working" the materials to suggest in acoustic-sensuous form how the separation of subject from object can at once be acknowledged and overcome, in acoustic-sensuous form, without losing sight of the fact that the bridging occurs in an artwork and not in society, and therefore fails, except as a hope for something better, as the representation of what might be.

6. See also B, pp. 123–61, aphorisms and notes addressing late style, and pp. 186–93, focused on the late quartets.

This is the fundamental argument that determines Adorno's account of Middle Period Beethoven, for Adorno the last historical moment in modernity when an aesthetic bridge between subject and object could legitimately be structured within works, not as a reflection of reality but as a reminder of a *socially* (and not merely aesthetically) realizable aspiration.[7] With the failure of the Enlightenment, the demand for aesthetic truth, as a repository for social truth, became all the more urgent. (After Beethoven, social crisis was mirrored in an aesthetic one.[8] Schoenberg broke the aesthetic impasse, if only temporarily, while the social crisis advanced with increasing ferocity; he recognized the impossibility, and irresponsibility, of positing even aesthetic reconciliation without at the same time preserving in art the image of what had been lost in actuality.) One of the outcomes— tricks, perhaps—of great artworks is that they take on the appearance of something organic, of a totality, their organicism the result of the domination of the materials by the artist. In this respect, even the most progressive composers' aesthetic authority contains an authoritarian element, in effect bespeaking the assertive claim, "That's how it is." Still, Adorno notes the necessity of this fatal flaw: "This is the tribute Beethoven was forced to pay to the ideological character whose spell extends even to the most sublime music ever to mean freedom by continued unfreedom."[9] Late work, like the new music Adorno admired, never relinquishes its claim to being *in*organic, and by that means the very violence necessary to wield the materials into a work is made visible, part and parcel of its truth con-

7. Eugene Lunn, *Marxism and Modernism: An Historical Study of Lukács, Brecht, Benjamin, and Adorno* (Berkeley and Los Angeles: University of California Press, 1982), p. 258: "Adorno interpreted the emancipation of individual musical 'subjects' within compositions of Beethoven's second period ('subjects' whose motivic development over time generates the musical logic of the whole work), as expressions of the revolutionary universalist aspirations of the European bourgeoisie at the point at which they seemed most capable of concrete realization"; see also Martin Jay, *Adorno* (Cambridge: Harvard University Press, 1984), pp. 141–44.

8. Rose Rosengard Subotnik, "The Historical Structure: Adorno's 'French' Model for the Criticism of Nineteenth-Century Music," in *Developing Variations: Style and Ideology in Western Music* (Minneapolis: University of Minnesota Press, 1991), p. 207, points out that Adorno regards the division between the Second and Third Periods of Beethoven's work to signal an epistemic change of Foucauldian proportion. Adorno treats nineteenth-century music "less as a gradual decline from Beethovenian achievement than as a single unit or system, the essentials of which are established early in the century and remain more or less constant thereafter."

9. ISM, p. 210. Cf. AT, p. 245, regarding the first movement: "The entrance of the reprise in the Ninth Symphony, which is the result of the symphonic process, celebrates its original introduction. It resonates like an overwhelming 'Thus it is.'"

tent.[10] Thus the sense of Adorno's comment in *Aesthetic Theory*, "Beethoven's late works mark the revolt of one of the most powerful classicistic artists against the deception implicit in the principle of his own work."[11]

Adorno saw in Beethoven the reenactment of Hegelian philosophy. In his fragmentary Beethoven monograph, he returns to this connection repeatedly, of which the following is characteristic: "Beethoven's music is Hegelian philosophy: but at the same time it is truer than that philosophy. That is to say, it is informed by the conviction that the self-reproduction of society as a self-identical entity is not enough, indeed that it is false. Logical identity as immanent to form—as an entity at the same time fabricated and aesthetic—is both constituted and criticized by Beethoven. Its seal of truth in Beethoven's music lies in its suspension: through transcending it, form takes on its true meaning. This formal transcendence in Beethoven's music is a representation—not an expression—of hope."[12]

Beethoven's "connection" to Hegel is manifested in the relation of his music to Absolute Spirit, a utopian construct of oneness in which the subject, as a particular, progresses forward and is ultimately reconciled to the all and preserved in it—a striving progression evident, for example, in sonata form development sections.[13] Adorno, to be sure, notices both the idealism and ideology in Hegel; and he suggests that Beethoven does as well. Beethoven's music provides an *image* of the reconciliation between

10. See further Shierry Weber Nicholsen, *Exact Imagination, Late Work: On Adorno's Aesthetics* (Cambridge: MIT Press, 1997), pp. 40–43; and Robert W. Witkin, *Adorno on Music* (New York: Routledge, 1998), pp. 65–69.

11. AT, p. 298. Subotnik, "Adorno's Diagnosis of Beethoven's Late Style," p. 22, however, points out that Adorno recognized the harbingers of late style in some of Beethoven's Middle Period works.

12. B, p. 14. In a note to himself in the Beethoven monograph, B, p. 8, Adorno comments: "The task of the book will be to resolve the riddle of humanity as a dialectical image."

13. Colin Sample, "Adorno on the Musical Language of Beethoven," *Musical Quarterly* 78 no. 2 (Summer 1994), p. 383: "Development in Beethoven is for Adorno precisely equivalent to the Hegelian notion of the self-reflection of absolute spirit." This essay is an extended review of the German edition of Adorno's Beethoven monograph. See also the lengthy review by Stephen Hinton, "Adorno's Unfinished *Beethoven*," *Beethoven Forum* 5 (Lincoln: University of Nebraska Press, 1996), pp. 139–53. Both are excellent. Hinton, p. 140, points out that Adorno began the book, never to be completed, in 1933, the year the Nazis came to power. Hinton does not regard this as coincidence, pointing out that up to this time nearly all of Adorno's work had been on living composers. He suggests that Adorno's Beethoven project is likely a response to the fact that in 1933 the National Socialists claimed Beethoven as one of their own. The connection Adorno draws between Beethoven's music and emancipation directly counters the composer's colonization by the fascists.

the subject and Absolute Spirit, the particular and the universal, without simply positing that it is so.

But not quite. Adorno subjects Beethoven to dialectical critique, if less relentlessly than he does Hegel. For starters, there is the problem of the symphonic recapitulation which returns the subject whole and intact—but profoundly self-assertive. Subjecthood is projected, but aggressively, even violently.[14] The subject's foundation in domination is underscored, so that the Hegelian reconciliation between subject and Absolute Spirit, as it were, negates itself in a falsehood papered over by the inevitability of the music's forward march—what Adorno calls Beethoven's ostentation, a "prefiguration of mass culture, which celebrates its own triumphs." Beethoven sometimes sounds contrived, as if the effects have been calculated, which Adorno likens to a "moment of ham-acting." He suggests that at times Beethoven's genius employs compositional technique to "manufacture transcendence." And in a note to himself he confides: "the manipulation of transcendence, the *coercion*, the violence. This is probably the deepest insight I have yet achieved into Beethoven. It is profoundly connected to the nature of art as appearance."[15]

Adorno's conception of late work is shaped by his sense of the performance medium of the works he has in mind—chamber music, and especially the string quartet, in contrast to orchestral music, whether symphony or concerto. He addressed the relationship of late style and genre in a chapter of *Introduction to the Sociology of Music*.[16] He suggests that chamber music's "inner character" is determined by its distribution among several musicians, and that the act of its performance seems as much dedicated to the musicians themselves as to the audience. Chamber musicians, such as quartet players with one player to a part, in effect are exposed; with no place to "hide," they can't shrink back. Each stands out, solely responsible for the "voice" assigned to his or her instrument. This fact projects the demand for and claim to expertise. It marks individual accomplishment. Yet individuality as such, the defining characteristic of the great

14. Subotnik, "Adorno's Diagnosis of Beethoven's Late Style," p. 21: "In fact, the recapitulation seems to confirm the rational irresistibility of the subject's determination to return to itself, since it nearly always seems to emerge as the logical outcome and resolution of what has preceded."

15. B, pp. 77–78 (original emphasis). Cf. p. 17: "Out of the recapitulation Beethoven produced the identity of the non-identical. Implicit in this, however, is the fact that while the recapitulation is in itself positive, the tangibly conventional, it is *also* the moment of untruth, of ideology."

16. ISM, pp. 85–103.

solo-concerto literature of the nineteenth century, is detrimental to chamber music discourse. The individual's role must be subordinated to that of the whole: each voice must be heard and must, in effect, hear its others. Adorno argued that chamber music is the sonoric embodiment of a sociality otherwise disappearing from modern society. Chamber music—and he had the string quartet in the forefront of his mind—represented for him a kind of utopian social balance between the promulgation of individuality, on the one hand, and the relation of individuality to the enactment of community, on the other.

Throughout his writing, Adorno labored to understand the sociocultural import of Western individuality in both its philosophical and practical functions—dating as far back as the Homeric Odysseus and culminating in what he would surely recognize today in human types as diverse as media stars, Wall-Street MBAs, sports tycoons (both owners and players), and celeb-status musicians of all types. Adorno saw individuality as the foundation of history, as the defining principle of the Western subject. He viewed it dialectically, as something both paradoxical and contradictory, at once liberating and enslaving. Individuality constituted the basis of social organization, yet individuality in its competitive, appetitive, ultimately solipsistic drive was ironically anti-social, anti-communal, and fundamentally self-privatizing. For Adorno chamber music, both as sound and as a social phenomenon, was a site of momentary refuge, a place of promise, imagination, and perhaps memory, where another kind of individuality might be thought, seen, and indeed heard. In chamber music he located a space for a lost sociability, where each musical voice was heard by mutual consent, and where being heard was not defined by the competitive survival of the fittest, the loudest, the most clever. In chamber music, as a principle of musical organization, Adorno heard and saw musical conversation, musical give and take, musical sharing, musical support of intertwining voices: in short, an enactment of mutual respect and friendship. In chamber music Adorno could imagine the possibility of what otherwise seemed unavailable: a society that was actually social (or sociable).

The issue wasn't defined simply by what went on among the four players; the effects he projected involved chamber music's audience as well, to the extent that listening to chamber music tends to offer less opportunity for culinary reception than, say, orchestral music with its dramatic climaxes and stunning array of sonoric effects. Adorno clearly understood that the audience for chamber music was largely privileged. It was small, typically economically and educationally elite; its audience was "comfortable." Paradoxically, the audience for chamber music constituted the embodied reminder of the profoundly unequal society that Adorno saw chamber music itself sonorically re-imagining in more democratic form. Yet he was neither romantic nor cynic, either about music or political sociology. As he put it, "Chamber music is specific to an epoch in which the private sphere, as one of leisure, has vigorously parted from the public-professional sphere."[17]

Chamber music does not eschew the competition inherent in, say, the concerto: the four string parts of the quartet do after all interrupt one another, one part struggling against the momentary hegemony of another, for example. Further, the audience sees this in the physical gestures necessary to make one instrument heard with or against or above another— the biting attack of bow against string, maybe of pizzicato, or *col legno* use of the bow, introducing a new sonority like an exclamation or an insistence against the prevailing discourse. We can *see* all this: the players do things with their bodies that have visual and aural consequences. String quartets, in other words, are not the musical equivalents of love feasts.

But neither are quartets analogous to TV's *Battle of the Network Stars* or *Survivor*—acoustic contests of the musically fittest. Quartets engender competition, and in part depend upon it, but they limit competition's seeming demand to win by the other's defeat by remaining within preordained formal boundaries of a composition that in the end fails as music unless the parts work to produce a whole. Adorno commented, "The first step in playing chamber music well is to learn not to thrust oneself forward but to step back. What makes a whole is not boastful self-assertion on the several parts—that would produce a barbarian chaos—but self-limiting reflection." Chamber music in essence "practices courtesy."[18]

By contrast, the nineteenth-century concerto commonly depends for its impact on the thrall within which the audience is held on account of the soloist's ability to claim our attention as the one and only. That is, the concerto's success is defined by the soloist in opposition to the orchestra. It is not the orchestra that thrills us, no matter how well it plays, but the soloist. Indeed, if the soloist is sufficiently commanding, the orchestra increasingly serves to underscore the soloist. The conductor's scopophilic magnetism is transferred to the soloist. The conductor, metaphor for the orchestral body itself, is undercut. If the soloist disappoints the audience

17. Ibid., p. 86.
18. Ibid., p. 87.

by performing unconvincingly or poorly, however, it's not the conductor or orchestra who "wins" the competition, because the music is of course scored so that only one "victor"—or none at all—is possible.

In chamber music, by contrast, competitiveness is circumscribed both sonorically and visually: there is no single hero upon whom to focus our eyes and ears. And this in turn demands a different response to the music, and a different reason for coming to hear the music: chamber music is radically social. We attend it not only for what it is but also for what it is not. Adorno explains this, paradoxically, as chamber music's "purposelessness." We aren't here to see and hear enacted the titanic force of individual will, but to experience a productive labor of (more or less) equals make sound without a winning voice, literally and metaphorically to make a harmony and a socio-musical polyphony. We're here to witness a dialogue, a conversation, the sonoric analogue to a shared meal, one of life's most profound of simple pleasures: a mutual nourishment. Adorno argued that chamber music doesn't surrender to the teleology of the ending, the drive for closure, the move toward the final thrill of the last climax. Instead, it sonorically and visually marks process—what he calls "pure doing." We don't invite a friend to eat with us in order to get to the dessert; it's the entire act of eating *and* the pleasure of the encounter as such that activates the happiness of sharing food. So also with chamber music.

Adorno pointed out that "Beethoven's symphonies are simpler than [his] chamber music despite their substantially more lavish apparatus."[19] Musically speaking, Adorno regarded the Ninth Symphony as backward-looking when compared to the late quartets.[20] "Musical conversation" in the Ninth Symphony—let's stick with the last movement—is really, after all, literally (a) speech, which, though beginning with some hesitancy, a bit of review, and some apparent searching, "finds" its true theme and rhetorical pace in the "Ode to Joy" which is nothing if not overwhelming, authoritative, and dangerously authoritarian for all its musical and textual claims in the name of liberal emancipation. The late quartets by contrast will have none of this; they provide no guarantees, no sonoric formulas about process leading inevitably to resolution, and final closure. And they never make speeches. Neither are they therefore philosophically abstract.

19. Ibid., p. 94.
20. B, p. 97: "The Ninth Symphony is not a late work [i.e., despite its date of composition], but a reconstruction of the *classical* Beethoven (with the exception of some parts of the last movement and, above all, of the trio of the third [*sic*, i.e., second] movement)" (original emphasis).

They are dialogic attempts to transcend the very claims of liberal individuality triumphantly shouted out in military rhythmic punctuations during the choral finale of the Ninth Symphony. Adorno called chamber music the "music of inwardness" at the same time that he saw the danger in that quality, to the extent that it provided refuge for the self-satisfaction of the pharisee, or as a locus where privileged people could falsely imagine they had escaped from an uglier external world that the music itself in fact acknowledged by its very difference from the world. As he put it: "The quality of works of art is the revenge of the false social condition, no matter what position they take in regard to it."[21]

"ALIENATED MASTERPIECE: THE MISSA SOLEMNIS" (1959; pp. 569–83) attempts a rescue of a work that Adorno acknowledged has been neutralized as canonic, as cultural goods, but which nonetheless remains "enigmatically incomprehensible" and which "offers no justification for the admiration accorded it" (p. 569).[22] Adorno seeks, as with his famous Bach essay,[23] to "break through the aura of irrelevant worship which protectively surrounds [the Missa Solemnis] and thereby perhaps to contribute something to an authentic aesthetic experience of it beyond the paralyzing respect of the academic sphere" (p. 570).

21. ISM, p. 95. Cf. James Brown, "The Amateur String Quartet," Musical Times 68 (1927), a serialized "how-to" essay intended to guide the training of teen-aged string players, most of which involves practical suggestions not relevant here. But here and there Brown anticipates Adorno, and in a treatise on performance rather than a book of academic sociology of music. At the end he identifies what characterizes the uniqueness of the string quartet as an ensemble. He botches it just a bit, for the word he chooses is "aristocratic." But Brown redeems himself, and at considerable verbal length, by getting at exactly what Adorno later better stated: "string quartet playing is perhaps the most perfect expression, in terms of music, of that precious human quality which we call courtesy"; and he goes on to link quartet playing to sociality itself. "Perhaps instead of 'music,'" he says, "I should say 'social music'; that is to say, music performed by several people together," the point of which he specifies brilliantly: "It is impossible to extricate the 'social' joy from the 'musical' joy [of string quartet playing], because they are actually the same thing" (p. 908). The social courtesy of the string quartet—the music, the making of the music—is musical doing with others. It is a simulacrum of happiness. See also Barbara Hanning, "Conversation and Musical Style in the Late Eighteenth-Century Parisian Salon," Eighteenth-Century Studies 22 no. 3 (Summer 1989), pp. 512–28, which considers the development of style dialogue in instrumental chamber music as a mirror of salon etiquette. Works by Haydn, as well as by lesser composers, are discussed.

22. By his own account, Adorno never succeeded in penetrating the enigma of the Missa Solemnis, which he points out in the foreword to his essay collection Moments musicaux, GS, vol. 17, p. 12.

23. Adorno, "Bach Defended against His Devotees" (1951), PR, pp. 133–46.

A work's enigmatic character, as Peter Uwe Hohendahl points out, is incompatible with discursive knowledge; yet discursive language necessarily re-enters in the form of philosophical reflection about the work's enigmaticalness, itself part and parcel of the non-conceptual logic that organizes a work's truth content.[24] Like the late quartets, the *Missa Solemnis* (composed 1819–23) keeps its distance, while largely staying within established musical conventions. Adorno emphasizes less the work's traditionalism than the archaism of Beethoven's occasional use of modal harmony, in essence referencing now-estranged old conventions. Yet the work is fundamentally different from the late quartets to the extent that it eschews their intellectualism in favor of "an inclination to splendidness and tonal monumentality" (p. 573). The work's difficulty, Adorno suggests, resides in the music's meaning, as well as the effect on the listener of the fact that the music doesn't always even sound like Beethoven. Beethoven abandons developing variations in favor of "kaleidoscopic mixing and supplementary combinations." Motifs appear and reappear "in changing light" while remaining nonetheless identical (p. 574). Internal development is supplanted by sectional divisions that are imitative but separate from what surrounds them, which Adorno likens to renaissance polyphonic works. The whole seems stylized (the "Benedictus" excepted), and the apparent absence of spontaneity further gives the work an archaic, remote quality.[25]

Adorno's principal concern is to relate the *Missa Solemnis* to history, specifically, to the question of belief which, in modernity, is under severe strain, such that the will to believe is insufficient to overcome history's force. But at the same time, the humanistic Enlightenment subject, not least in the face of the increasingly apparent failure of its foundational ideals, finds itself an inadequate substitute. Thus in one sense the archaism

24. Peter Uwe Hohendahl, *Prismatic Thought: Theodor W. Adorno* (Lincoln: University of Nebraska Press, 1995), pp. 237–39. See also Peter Osborne, "Adorno and the Metaphysics of Modernism: The Problem of a 'Postmodern' Art," in *The Problems of Modernity: Adorno and Benjamin*, ed. Andrew Benjamin (New York: Routledge, 1989), pp. 32–35; and Max Paddison, *Adorno's Aesthetics of Music* (Cambridge: Cambridge University Press, 1993), p. 15.

25. Carl Dahlhaus, *Ludwig van Beethoven: Approaches to His Music*, trans. Mary Whittall (Oxford: Clarendon Press, 1991), pp. 194–201, provides a structural-processural reading of the *Missa Solemnis* strikingly similar to Adorno's, though Dahlhaus only briefly touches on the work's meaning, his discussion being principally formalist criticism. Dahlhaus is fundamentally critical, even dismissive, of Adorno's social semiotics of music, in regard to which see *Schoenberg and the New Music: Essays by Carl Dahlhaus*, trans. Derrick Puffett and Alfred Clayton (Cambridge: Cambridge University Press, 1987), pp. 243–44.

of the *Missa Solemnis* plaintively hails a past that is not recoverable—
Adorno cites the remark by his teacher Eduard Steuermann that Beethoven
had the fugue subject "repeat the word Credo as if the isolated man had
to assure himself and others of his actual belief by this frequent repetition"
(p. 577). In other words, the *Missa Solemnis* is constituted not by the
affirmation of belief but by the dilemma of its potential impossibility—
and in the face of the acute desire for what may not be. The musical
archaism references loss in the form of a lament; in the absence of belief
(that which can no longer be believed), the subject stands radically alone,
caught in aporia, reasserting "Credo" unconvincingly. Here Adorno forcefully rejects any universalizing interpretation of Beethoven the Modern
to the effect that "his is a mass for Unitarians" (p. 577). The limitations
of the "I" are asserted throughout the work by means of the insistent
stylization principle which, in undercutting spontaneity, diminishes the
expressiveness associated with subjectivity. Adorno notes the Mass's feeling of indirectness, goallessness, or lack of forward movement, which contributes to its enigmatic quality, all the more evident in the moment of its
historical locus in an outwardly confident modernity.

Adorno calls the *Missa Solemnis* a work of "exclusion" and "permanent
renunciation," qualities that stamp it "in a principal sense with the mark
of impotence. It is the impotence not merely of the mightiest composer
but of an historical position of the intellect which, of whatever it dares
write here, can speak no longer or not yet" (pp. 579–80). It is precisely
impotence that enshrines the work's vitality; the truth Beethoven reveals
in this aporia is the limitation of the bourgeois spirit which, through acknowledgment, is transcended: "Something in his own genius, the deepest
part of it, refused to reconcile in a single image what is not reconciled" (p.
580).[26] In other words, the ideological foundation of triumphant affirmation of the Middle Period symphonies is rejected in the *Missa Solemnis*
in favor of a "measure of success" in the truth of failure.[27] As Rose

26. See also Adorno, B, pp. 138–41, a series of notes and aphorisms concerning
this work; Paddison, *Adorno's Aesthetics of Music*, pp. 234–40; and Alastair Williams, *New Music and the Claims of Modernity* (Aldershot, UK: Ashgate, 1997),
pp. 22–26.
27. Cf. B, pp. 99–100: "Art-works of the highest rank are distinguished from
the others not through their success—for in what have they succeeded?—but
through the manner of their failure. For the problems within them, both the immanent, aesthetic problems and the social ones (and, in the dimension of depth,
the two kinds coincide), are so posed that the attempt to solve them must fail,
whereas the failure of lesser works is accidental, a matter of mere subjective in-

Rosengard Subotnik points out, "Implicit in Beethoven's late style, as Adorno analyzes it, is the eventual dissolution of all the values that made bourgeois humanism the hope of a human civilization."[28]

Wagner   On 4 May 1938 Adorno, writing to Benjamin from New York, where he had arrived the previous February, told his friend that "the Wagner is finished," in reference to what would eventually be shaped into a small monograph, *In Search of Wagner,* published only in 1952, at the end of his American sojourn. Adorno sent Benjamin the draft manuscript (not the final version), parts of which he had got to him already in February.[29] In June 1938, having read it, Benjamin gave Adorno his assessment: "As far as I can see, you have never written anything with quite the same pregnant physiognomy as this piece. Your portrait of Wagner is totally convincing from head to toe. The way in which you have captured the interplay of gesture and attitude in the man is masterly," an impression that Benjamin amplifies at length—but not without qualification, though he also refers to the text's "enormous richness and [its] most astonishing perspicacity." The monograph's famously agonistic tone was not lost on Benjamin, who wonders in his letter whether Adorno had always thus reacted to Wagner, a question around which he creates a compelling image. Benjamin comments that he would like to imagine a grassy plot which someone knew well from playing there since childhood, where, as an adult, he stands again and "suddenly and unexpectedly finds that it has now become the allotted place for a pistol duel to which he has been challenged by a personal enemy. The kind of tensions such a situation would surely produce also seem to persist

---

capacity. A work of art is great when it registers a failed attempt to reconcile objective antinomies. That is its truth and its 'success': to have come up against its own limit."

28. Subotnik, "Adorno's Diagnosis of Beethoven's Late Style," p. 17. On the historical necessity of late style, see p. 24. For a general overview of Adorno's work on Beethoven, see Witkin, *Adorno on Music,* pp. 50–69.

29. CC, p. 248. It's not clear whether Adorno had in fact sent Benjamin the full draft, since Benjamin in his reply to Adorno, p. 257, remarks that "an excerpt is no pleasure to a lover of manuscripts." (The letter date is incorrectly printed as March instead of May.) Adorno began writing ISW in the fall of 1937, completing it in about six months, during which time he moved from England to the United States. Four chapters (1, 6, 9, 10, with brief accounts of the others) were published in the Institute's journal, *Zeitschrift für Sozialforschung* 8 Heft 1–2 (1939–40), pp. 1–48, under the title "Fragmente über Wagner." ISW, though published only long after it was written, was Adorno's first book-length musical study. See CC, p. 237, for the letter from Benjamin, 11 February 1938, acknowledging receipt of the manuscript.

throughout your Wagner book." A little later Benjamin is still more direct: "the fundamental conception behind your Wagner, which God knows is quite a powerful one, is essentially polemical."[30]

Essentially, Benjamin accused Adorno's *Wagner* with what Adorno five months later would accuse Benjamin: lack of mediation.[31] The polemics in effect overwhelm the dialectics. The progressive aspects of Wagner, though acknowledged by Adorno, are insufficiently set in tension with the regressive tendencies that principally define the study. Benjamin takes issue with the binary progressive-regressive, suggesting that the concept of progressiveness is disturbingly linear—and hinting perhaps at its affinity with historicism. Instead, Benjamin invokes a process of "salvation," essentially on the grounds that salvation's form is cyclical rather than linear or "progressive." His precise meaning is difficult to grasp at first reading, not least because he makes reference to private conversations between the two men a few months earlier in what would turn out to be their last face-to-face meeting. At the very least, it is clear that Benjamin is searching for a more nuanced account of Wagner, for he points to the inadequacy of Adorno's separation of the progressive from the regressive "like the sheep from the goats."[32] The point is that such separation renders invisible the tension between the two that by necessity ultimately informs the whole. That is, the issue is not to create two columns, the good and the bad, but to un-

---

30. Ibid., pp. 257–58. It is fair to suggest, however, that what strikes readers, including Benjamin, as polemical is itself a reflection of the saturation of Wagner-worship into "general consciousness"—which to be sure has hardly died away even today. On this point, see Rose Rosengard Subotnik, "The Role of Ideology in the Study of Western Music," in *Developing Variations: Style and Ideology in Western Music* (Minneapolis: University of Minnesota Press, 1991), p. 8: "Suppose Wagner were a young composer coming up for tenure at a major American university today, and that he had, for example, voiced the same sort of ideas about American blacks as the actual Wagner did about Jews. Wouldn't there at least be some of us who were disposed to feel that no amount of craft could be sufficient to overcome the negative force of such an ideology, and even that the music produced by a mind espousing such an ideology must in some sense be a flawed human vision?" Subotnik goes on to suggest the need to develop rigorous critical methods that permitted the investigation of the relation between ideology and craft, and she credits Adorno with having the temerity of attempting just that. On a related point, see Subotnik's important and ground-breaking essay, "Kant, Adorno, and the Self-Critique of Reason: Toward a Model for Music Criticism," ibid., p. 58.

31. CC, p. 283, letter to Benjamin, 10 November 1938. Adorno is critiquing Benjamin's Baudelaire essay, part of the *Arcades* project. He draws direct comparison, as regards the lack of mediation, to the phantasmagoria section of ISW, chapter 6, pp. 85–96. Walter Benjamin, *The Arcades Project,* trans. Howard Eiland and Kevin McLaughlin (Cambridge: Belknap Press of Harvard University Press, 1999).

32. Benjamin is here quoting Adorno against himself; see ISW, p. 47.

derstand how the two function together as part of the work's totality. Benjamin wryly drives the point home by making a direct reference to Adorno's *Indianer Joe:* "you must allow me to surprise you in body and soul with your own favorite image from Indian Joe about unearthing the hatchet and provoking a fight." Simply stated, Benjamin argues for a "salvation, undertaken from the perspective of the philosophy of history," a task incompatible with a perspective focused, "unconditionally," upon progress and regress.[33]

Neither Benjamin nor Adorno is prepared to hand over Wagner to the fascists as their poster boy; both acutely perceive nonetheless that Wagner is being so claimed. The "salvation"—better, rescue—of Wagner, in Benjamin's characteristically messianic terminology, in other words, has the ring of saving Wagner from himself, given the tendencies within his work that Adorno finds so compatible with fascist regression.[34] Benjamin sug-

33. CC, pp. 258–59. See further Gyorgy Markus, "Adorno's Wagner," *Thesis Eleven* 56 (February 1999), p. 27, on Adorno's own conception of rescuing Wagner's music. The fundamental point of Markus's thoughtful and important essay is to argue that Adorno fails in this attempt, notably on the basis of what drives the enterprise in the first place: Adorno's critique of Wagner's music as commodity. Essentially, Markus suggests that Adorno not only misreads Marx on the commodity form, but also uses the term with an extreme degree of abstractness and lack of specificity as applied to Wagner's music, p. 42: "The programme of a commodity analysis of art does not succeed, because Adorno is unable to interconnect the aesthetic characteristics of the works analysed with anything historically-socially more specific than the most broadly conceived (and, as I shall argue, misconceived) general structure of the commodity form." Indeed, Markus suggests that Adorno's use of the commodity-form concept in ISW could be appropriately applied to both progressive and regressive music—a judgment with which Adorno would disagree only in degree, to the extent that he insisted that all music bears the scars of modernity's social regression.

34. Adorno, "Wagner, Nietzsche, and Hitler," *Kenyon Review* 9 no. 1 (Winter 1947), p. 157, a review of the fourth volume of Ernest Newman's *Life of Richard Wagner*, is insistent on the question of Wagner's relation to recent German history: "Wagner, as a human being, crystallized to an amazing extent the Fascist character long before Fascism was ever dreamed of. . . . In private life the artist resembled, more specifically, the Fascist agitator." See also the thoughtful, and notably sympathetic, though hardly uncritical, review of ISW by John Deathridge in *19th Century Music* 7 no. 1 (Summer 1983), pp. 81–85: "No one seriously interested in Wagner or the history of Wagnerism can afford to ignore this astonishing book. . . . It probably did more than any other single publication to clear the Wagnerian air in Germany after the Second World War. In a sense Adorno is trying literally to face the music. His book is an examination of moral conscience that projects history into the deepest crevices of Wagner's work" (p. 84). Markus, "Adorno's Wagner," p. 26, while acknowledging the book's anti-fascism, alludes to its "often censorious rather than critical tone" and its reach "beyond the limits of legitimate criticism." He cites, for example, Adorno's suggested connection of *Gesamtkunst-*

gests that Adorno's Wagner study hands over the composer to those who would only too happily claim him—and despite the fact that, after reading Adorno's manuscript, Benjamin readily admits finding salvation for Wagner "utterly problematic." Both Benjamin (no musician) and Adorno fully appreciate Wagner's genius, which in Benjamin's view must add up to more than Adorno ultimately allows, in regard to which he asks Adorno whether, in his critique, he hasn't compromised fundamental parts of his own philosophy of music, in particular the idea of music as protest and opera as consolation. Benjamin, in short, calls for "a redemption of Wagner."[35]

Adorno took his time crafting a reply to Benjamin, doing so only in early August, and briefly. Thanking Benjamin graciously, and commenting on his own further "constant alternations and improvements," he acknowledged: "I am forced to respond rather laconically, if only because I cannot help agreeing with you"—but for reasons different from Benjamin's opening presumption that Adorno had known Wagner's work since childhood (in fact, he only studied Wagner under Berg's direction). But in the end, Adorno fundamentally rejects Benjamin's critique, insisting that his Wagner study already possessed "more of a cyclical form in your own sense than you are ready to credit."[36] The fact that fourteen years later Adorno published the text in a form close to what Benjamin had read, and again in paperback in 1964 fixing only some printing errors, indicates the degree to which Adorno held to his original ground.

Wagner presents a topic of staggering proportion, given the number, length, and complexity of his operas and music dramas, as well as his voluminous writings, not to mention the secondary literature. Yet Adorno "dispenses" with Wagner in 134 pages (in the German edition). The notable brevity, together with the polemical tone, is part and parcel of Adorno's strategic rhetorical purpose, mobilized to respond to Wagner—and Wagnerism—in contemporary German history. *In Search of Wagner*

---

werk to political totalitarianism as "unjustifiable exaggerations." "Nevertheless," he adds, "the initial German reaction to the publication of this booklet, treating it mainly as a crude attack upon Wagner fuelled by resentment, was completely illegitimate."

35. CC, pp. 258–59. Thomas Mann, *The Story of a Novel: The Genesis of Doctor Faustus*, trans. Richard Winston and Clara Winston (New York: Alfred A. Knopf, 1961), pp. 94–95, tells of reading the Wagner manuscript, which Mann clearly admired, while noting "its somewhat stiff attitude toward the subject, which [however] never entirely passes over to the negative side."

36. CC, all quotations p. 265, letter dated 2 August 1938. See also p. 268 n. 1.

is a political tract no less than a sociological and aesthetic critique. Adorno is responding to historical necessity of the most urgent variety, as is abundantly evident in the opening chapter, "Social Character," whose subject is the anti-Semitism attached to Wagner's personal behavior, writings, and compositions, and, in this regard, Wagner's relation to the history of the emergent catastrophe. Closely related, and linked in his mind to the fascists' aestheticization of politics, Adorno pursues a theme he will continue to explore throughout the book: the link between pleasure and death in Wagner.[37]

In "Gesture," his second chapter, Adorno focuses on one gesture in particular: striking a blow. The blow he describes is musical; its impact is on listeners, namely, the invitation to identify with the aggressor. Adorno opens with an attention-getting metaphor: "It would be rewarding to examine the heaps of rubbish, detritus and filth upon which the works of major artists appear to be erected, and to which they still owe something of their character, even though they have just managed to escape by the skin of their teeth."[38]

The musical principle behind the effect of a beating, or striking a blow, is the leitmotif which "thunders at [the listener] in endless repetitions to hammer its message home" and in the process of repetition evades "the necessity to create musical time."[39] Two mutually supportive, mutually regressive tendencies here come together: repetition and the lack of development. Simply stated, the leitmotif stands in radical opposition to sonata form. Development in time, and time in development, hallmarks of the social progressiveness that Adorno associates with Beethoven as expressions of the Enlightenment subject, are brought to stasis.[40] Time is

---

37. ISW, p. 14.

38. Ibid., p. 28. Adorno's metaphor of striking a blow first appears on p. 30.

39. Ibid., pp. 32, 37. Cf. Adorno, "On the Score of 'Parsifal'" (1956), trans., with commentary, by Anthony Barone, *Music and Letters* 76 no. 3 (August 1995), p. 384: "Long-windedness was always characteristic of Wagner; it is associated with both his evocative use of gesture and an inclination to talk the listener to death." This aphoristic "essay," only three pages long, was first published as a program note; Anthony Barone provides an excellent commentary, pp. 387–97. Barone's discussion of Adorno's treatment of *Parsifal* as late style, at once similar to and different from his treatment of Beethoven in this regard, is particularly informative.

40. Adorno, not surprisingly, has been criticized for valorizing thematic development over the thematic transformation that occurs in Wagner. Adorno suggests that such transformation is limited to harmonic sequencing techniques; see ISW, pp. 46–47. Carl Dahlhaus, *Between Romanticism and Modernism: Four Studies in the Music of the Later Nineteenth Century*, trans. Mary Whittall (Berkeley

stood still; history ends—or, better, is denied. History's denial returns us to myth, a prehistory that claims permanence, but which in fact promotes the permanent regression of the subject under terms ironically defined by the commodity form in modernity.[41] Adorno, in other words, explains Wagner's music as an aestheticization of market production: the ever-same promoting itself as the ever-new, as advertising for the corruption of the subject, but of a particularly sinister kind: in Wagner musical logic is replaced by a compositional technique described as "a sort of gesticulation [as opposed to an expressive gesture], rather in the way that agitators substitute linguistic gestures for the discursive exposition of their thoughts."[42] Under these conditions, art doesn't reveal; it obfuscates and regresses to the status of fetish—or to what Adorno calls "Phantasmagoria," borrowing from Marx, the subject of an entire chapter of the monograph.[43]

---

and Los Angeles: University of California Press, 1980), p. 46, describes the "real sequence" as "an expository procedure, a means of elaborating a musical idea which in itself . . . needs no continuation and would not tolerate conventional 'rounding off' in a closed period."

Of Wagner's melodic writing, Adorno comments, ISW, p. 57: "Wagner's melody is in fact unable to make good its promise of infinity since, instead of unfolding in a genuinely free and unconstrained manner, it has recourse to small-scale models and by stringing those together provides a substitute for true development." Williams, *New Music and the Claims of Modernity*, pp. 26–27, offers a summary of typical critiques of Adorno; Harold Blumenfeld, *"Ad vocem Adorno," Musical Quarterly* 70 no. 2 (Spring 1984), pp. 526–28, takes Adorno to task in particularly strident terms on this matter, but fails to acknowledge the nuance immanent to Adorno's critique. For a notably spirited defense of ISW, see Fredric Jameson, *Late Marxism: Adorno, or the Persistence of the Dialectic* (London: Verso, 1990), pp. 221–22. For general accounts of Adorno's Wagner criticism, see Paddison, *Adorno's Aesthetics of Music*, pp. 243–53; and Witkin, *Adorno on Music*, pp. 70–93.

41. ISW, p. 46, suggests that Wagner's scores anticipate film music. See the expansion of this remark by Gary Tomlinson, *Metaphysical Song: An Essay on Opera* (Princeton: Princeton University Press, 1999), p. 146. See also Tomlinson's consideration of *Parsifal* as phantasmagoria, pp. 131–33. On Wagner and the commodity form, per Adorno, see the excellent essay by John Deathridge, "Postmortem on Isolde," *New German Critique* 69 (Fall 1996), especially pp. 123–26. Finally, on Adorno's account of Wagner in relation to the Culture Industry, see Andreas Huyssen, "Adorno in Reverse: From Hollywood to Richard Wagner," *New German Critique* 29 (Spring/Summer 1983), pp. 29–38; and Karin Bauer, *Adorno's Nietzschean Narratives: Critiques of Ideology, Readings of Wagner* (Albany: State University of New York Press, 1999), pp. 117–71, passim.

42. ISW, p. 34; and p. 42: "Whereas Wagner's music incessantly arouses the appearance, the expectation and the demand for novelty, strictly speaking nothing new takes place in it."

43. Ibid., chapter 6, pp. 85–96.

Adorno devotes the entire next chapter to the leitmotif,[44] which he refers to as "miniature pictures" whose "supposed psychological varia-tions involve only a change of lighting"—and here he suggests that they bear the true stamp of the *idée fixe*, in essence outdoing Berlioz by some distance—pictures so fundamentally static, according to Adorno, that they negate the very psychological dynamism whose purpose they might otherwise usefully serve in the narrative.[45] In short, the leitmotif is rendered positivistic, as a sign or slogan of and for What Is. The result is the regression of the listener, with apparent social consequences: "technological hostility to consciousness is the very foundation of the music drama. It combines the arts in order to produce an intoxicating brew."[46] Adorno likens Wagnerian leitmotifs to component parts of factory-assembled products: musical Fordism.[47] *Gesamtkunstwerk*, pos-ited as a totality, is a mask that pretends a unity of subject and object rather than faces squarely the social rupture it so avidly works to deny— yet a pretense true in the negative sense that *Gesamt*-totality is achieved only in death rendered alternately heroic and tragic, but also transfigur-ative and posited as pleasurable. A utopia arrived at through death serves the interests of society as it is, rather than what society might be-come.

In the chapter devoted to "Sonority," Adorno for the first time acknowl-edges Wagner-the-progressive, pointing to the "sovereign subjectivity" of dissonance over resolution in Wagner; "in the progressive harmonic sec-tions, accents fall consistently on the dissonances, not the resolutions," upending convention.[48] Similarly, in the chapter on "Color," Adorno force-fully presents as progressive Wagner's integral use of instrumental timbre, which he credits as "the domain" of Wagner's subjectivity.[49] As Max Pad-dison has pointed out, Adorno regards as progressive, and even revolu-tionary, Wagner's increasing control of the musical material.[50] But Adorno also points out that Wagner uses orchestration for what he terms "a flight from the banal," or in essence as padding, distraction, "by means of which the composer hopes to escape the market requirements of the commodity

44. Ibid., chapter 3, pp. 43–61, the longest in the book.
45. Ibid., p. 45.
46. Ibid., p. 100.
47. Ibid., p. 49.
48. Ibid., pp. 65, 67.
49. Ibid., p. 72.
50. Paddison, *Adorno's Aesthetics of Music*, p. 251.

known as opera." This practice, an effort to replace essence with appearance, in the end fails.[51]

"WAGNER'S RELEVANCE FOR TODAY" (1963; pp. 584–602) reaffirms the stance toward the composer that Adorno adopted in his early monograph, while in a sense going beyond it in light of a change in (essentially German) consciousness about Wagner. Specifically, Adorno points to a loss of the authoritative hold that Wagner enjoyed even a generation earlier. Alluding to the connection between Wagner and National Socialism—which Adorno argued was immanent to both Wagner the person and his music—Adorno insists that the revival of this linkage in the future remains a possibility. Nevertheless, what has changed about Wagner is "his work itself, in itself," a striking claim indeed. Adorno here invokes a relation, invariably historical, between a work and its audience. Hearing itself is historical; history determines a way of hearing. As a result, any of the myriad qualities immanent to a work either emerge or recede in relation to historical change. The historically present demands a different hearing of Wagner than was the case, say, a generation earlier: "As spiritual entities, works of art are not complete in themselves. They create a magnetic field of all possible intentions and forces, of inner tendencies and countervailing ones, of successful and necessarily unsuccessful elements. Objectively, new layers are constantly detaching themselves, emerging from within; others grow irrelevant and die off. One relates to a work of art . . . by deciphering within it things to which one has a historically different reaction" (pp. 586–87). Adorno observes his own attraction-repulsion reaction, in fact not different in kind but in degree to what he had voiced years earlier, and in relation to the progressive and regressive traits of the works themselves. He acknowledges that the attraction relation must be tempered by the historical knowledge of the previous decades; the works' reception history in the Third Reich, in other words, cannot be swept aside as though it were wholly an external misfortune to which the works succumbed, and precisely because the works in Adorno's view hailed this reception from within themselves.

Wagner the progressive stands *musically* against his own time, that is, against the anti-modernist, nostalgia-ridden German version of arts and crafts, anchored in "folk" idioms, and early-music revivals—movements, from Adorno's perspective, all too adaptable to fascist nationalist *Volk* ideology situated alike in ahistorical mythologizing of the musical past and musical regression. Adorno also credits Wagner's music with a

51. ISW, pp. 82, 98.

degree of erotic freedom utterly unlike anything heard previously in German music, just as Adorno attacks the "petit bourgeois" reaction that favors musical and "self-righteous purity" (p. 587). Adorno regards *Siegfried* as Wagner's most modern opera, and on that account the least popular among the *Ring* music dramas. He argues for Wagner's modernity on the basis of what he terms the composer's "uncompromising musical nominalism," that is, Wagner's elevation of the primacy of the specific work and its internal workings-out above any demands or "requirements" of any externally imposed form. Wagner "was the first to draw the consequences from the contradiction between traditional forms, indeed the traditional formal language of music as a whole, and the concrete artistic tasks at hand" (p. 588). Here Adorno comes very close to crediting Wagnerian opera with the quality otherwise ascribed only to instrumental music of the nineteenth century: autonomy, a music that, before anything else, responds to the demands of its material. (Wagner's departure from conventional operatic forms—forms within the form—of recitative, aria, and ensemble, raises the stakes of the matter and also further highlights his modernity.) It is precisely this factor in Wagner that establishes for Adorno the crucial link to Schoenberg. The *Ring* music dramas especially, "thoroughly modern works," exceed the ahistorical mythology of their libretti ("cheap and phony . . . a romanticism of false beards and bull's-eye windows"): in their mythic world modern violence breaks through and shatters the complacency of the bourgeois façade. Such marks Wagner's relevance for today.[52] When violence thus "expresses itself in pure form, unobscured, in all its terror and entrapment" (p. 589), Wagner's mythologies are indicted as myth in spite of themselves. Precisely this paradox, if not contradiction, guarantees Wagner's relevance to the extent that his work aesthetically expresses what remains, as it were, unfinished, a history yet to be adequately confronted. Wagner's mythology, in other words, invokes history, and this invocation is all the more important to the extent that the invocation occurs under the duress of the musical score, even in spite of it.

Adorno cites Wagner's dissonance in this regard, which in essence puts consonance to a test that consonance cannot pass, as Schoenberg would for the first time insist a generation later. Adorno then credits Wagner with something he refused to grant him in the earlier Wagner monograph. He

52. Precisely this reading defined the famous Pierre Boulez–Patrice Chéreau *Ring* cycle, performed at Bayreuth, 1976.

brings up Wagner's use of sequencing techniques, the repetition of leit-motifs "on a higher level, generally with dynamic, intensifying effect." That is, what Adorno had previously critiqued as the ever-same, he reconsiders here as a compositional procedure that produced variation with "great subtlety," a component part of the various works' internal organization (p. 591). In place of established formal principles, aria notably, Wagner establishes the orchestra itself (orchestration, instrumental color, and texture) as a form-giving element of the music drama, a point Adorno made in *In Search of Wagner* but here elaborated (pp. 593–95).

Adorno closes his essay with a cogent and insistent reminder of Wagner and regression, in effect, reasserting the points stressed earlier: Wagner's contradictions are forgotten at considerable peril to the future. And so to end, he returns to the ending: the final act of *Götterdämmerung*, where he recognizes a kind of regressive triumph. The music of the end of the world is not up to the task; in essence it remains conventionally aesthetic, as it were, too beautiful; as such the music fatalistically affirms as inevitable the myth's narrative, as though it could not be otherwise. As a result, Adorno suggests, myth itself triumphs in the end, a triumph of death. And yet everything about the *Ring* is historical. The "challenge" today revolves around the need—which must fail in the end—to negotiate successfully the work's contradictions which constitute nevertheless its real truth. "If it is true about Wagner that no matter what one does, it is wrong, the thing that is still most likely to help is to force what is false, flawed, antinomical out into the open, rather than glossing over it and generating a kind of harmony to which the most profound element in Wagner is antithetical" (p. 600).[53]

53. Wagner's relevance for today is a principal subject of a special issue of *New German Critique* 69 (Fall 1996). David J. Levin, "Wagner and the Consequences—An Introduction," pp. 4–5: "Wagner is problematic not simply as author, architect, composer, impresario, and yes, anti-Semite, but also—to use an ungainly phrase from contemporary cultural theory—as an erratically polyvalent cultural signifier, one that threatens to veer all too readily from one univalence to another." In this regard, and in the same journal issue, see Marc A. Weiner, "Reading the Ideal," pp. 53–83, which considers Wagnerian anti-Semitism, and invokes the much-reported exchange on this topic at a Columbia University conference in 1995 between Edward Said and conductor Daniel Barenboim. (Barenboim had unsuccessfully attempted to perform Wagnerian excerpts with the Israel Philharmonic, despite a ban in Israel on performing Wagner in effect since the orchestra was founded immediately after the Second World War.) Weiner considers the paradox and challenge that Adorno articulates in "Wagner's Relevance for Today," though his conclusion, p. 83, does not exceed Adorno's: "Perhaps in recognizing the fact

Mahler   Adorno's *Mahler: A Musical Physiognomy*, like the Wagner book, is a small monograph (158 pp. in the German edition); as with the earlier study, there are no musical examples, though nearly two hundred passages are both cited and discussed. Here Adorno relies on myriad footnotes, keyed to scores, that direct the reader to the musical material. Adorno never leads the reader through the musical processes, start to finish, of any composition or even an entire movement; instead his focus is on telling details which are in turn related to the whole, linked to parallel usage in other compositions by Mahler or other composers, from Beethoven through Brahms, and on to Schoenberg and Berg, among others. The result is stunning. This is not a book easily grasped without an acute knowledge of Mahler, whose works Adorno knew extremely well and precisely. Principal attention is paid to the symphonies, *Des Knaben Wunderhorn, Kindertotenlieder*, and *Das Lied von der Erde*.

Fundamentally, Adorno's Mahler is a progressive, but at odds with the progressive core in Wagner. Whereas Wagner's musical progressiveness lay in his looking forward, as it were anticipating a new modernity, Mahler's looked backward and wrung from the "old" (the increasingly worn-out musical language of the nineteenth century) the contradiction of its confrontation with history—in a later essay on the composer, Adorno noted that Mahler "has absolutely nothing in common with the idea of originality."[54] As in the case of Beethoven and Wagner, Adorno regards Mahler's efforts, paradoxically, as successful failures. That is, in the end there is no breakthrough in the music because there is no breakthrough in society.[55] The truth of Mahler, the character of his greatness, is his

---

that the music dramas are imbued with the very material they themselves seek to deny, we can today effect a redemption from Wagner's desire for totality, and thus find ourselves in a position other than one on either of the polar extremes of his social tracts and aesthetic accomplishments—in an ideological and aesthetic space that is not that of a Mime or a Siegfried, but perhaps, of both—a social and aesthetic position of codependence that may well have constituted Wagner's most fundamental fear, but that, ironically, the agonizing polarizations of his social theory and wonderfully enigmatic music dramas repeatedly and dialectically imply."

54. Adorno, "Mahler," QF, p. 84.

55. Precisely this point determines Adorno's account of musical style, which he addresses briefly in DE, pp. 130–31: "Style represents a promise in every work of art. . . . [The] promise held out by the work of art that it will create truth by lending new shape to the conventional social forms is as necessary as it is hypocritical. It unconditionally posits the real forms of life as it is by suggesting that fulfillment lies in their aesthetic derivatives. To this extent the claim of art is always ideology too. However, only in this confrontation with the tradition of which style

ability to imagine something different, paradoxically by using the detritus of an exhausted musical vocabulary, as it were, against itself. In Mahler Adorno hears the acoustic trace of hope's realization: "It is music's nature to overreach itself. Utopia finds refuge in its no-man's-land."[56] Mahler's musical forms develop from the form of society itself, as do those of all music. Here and elsewhere Adorno likens Mahlerian form to that of the nineteenth-century large-scale novel, even using the term "novel-symphony" [Romansymphonik] and "epic" to describe them: dramatic works with characters.[57] The society immanent to the music assures that the music will ultimately remain tied to that against which it protests—an entanglement that art would breach, if it could. Thus Mahler's works "are rooted in what music seeks to transcend."[58] Formally, as Rose Rosengard Subotnik has pointed out, Mahler invokes Beethovenian totality but negatively—as an "as-if," a totality invoked but recognizably, irretrievably lost—by "constructing enormous symphonic patterns out of elements too discontinuous to effect any large-scale unity."[59] Adorno hears Mahler's

---

is the record can art express suffering. That factor in a work of art which enables it to transcend reality certainly cannot be detached from style; but it does not consist of the harmony actually realized. . . . It is to be found in those features in which discrepancy appears: in the necessary failure of the passionate striving for identity."

56. M, p. 6.

57. M, p. 72, and Adorno, "Mahler," p. 87. Concerning Adorno's sense of the epic nature of Mahler's work, see Nicholson, *Exact Imagination*, pp. 208–09; and Williams, *New Music and the Claims of Modernity*, pp. 29–30. See also John Williamson, "Mahler, Hermeneutics and Analysis," *Music Analysis* 10 no. 3 (October 1991), pp. 357–73, an overview of recent studies of Mahler, which come in the wake of Adorno's monograph.

58. M, p. 6.

59. Subotnik, "Historical Structure," p. 208. The phrase "as-if" is Adorno's own; see ISM, p. 108. Artworks for Adorno provide an illusion of truth. Their illusory character emerges from the demand for structural unity or wholeness, which in turn defines the artwork's autonomy from society, that is, art's determinate negation of society. In art, however, unity is usually feigned rather than fully achieved, and in any event unity runs the risk of disguising social antagonism. The semblance or illusory nature of artworks carries with it an element of (necessary) deceit as a precondition of its protest. Part of art's truth, of course, is its own guilt.

Morton Schoolman, "Toward a Politics of Darkness: Individuality and Its Politics in Adorno's Aesthetics," *Political Theory* 25 no. 1 (February 1997), pp. 61–62: "Art is ambiguous. As the image of reconciliation, art creates an illusion. As the subtle articulation of the nonidentity of being, art exposes the illusion and reveals an insurmountable barrier to reconciliation and the violence to nature and difference meted out by the quest for reconciliation. . . . Paradoxically, Adorno is

protest in his works' perpetual motion, what he terms their "aimlessly circling, irresistible movements [which] . . . are always images of the world's course."[60] Simply put, Mahler renders problematic the apparent forward motion of frenetic modernity, trapped in activity, the "vain commotion" of a general unfreedom. Mahler's musical motion accuses socially defined and vain commotion. "Hope in Mahler always resides in change," a struggle against "blind functioning. . . . Mahler's symphonies plead anew against the world's course. They imitate it in order to accuse,"[61] and in the end decline to offer a counterfeit reconciliation between subject and object.

Mahler's utopia is "the forward motion of the past and the not-yet-past in becoming." It looks back in order to discern a better future, which can only come about if the past is faced squarely. Mahler brushes history against the grain, and by so doing he finds an Otherness, whose conventionally hidden presence he brings forward into view—that "which is not immanence yet arises from immanence."[62] Otherness develops from estranging the familiar, by what Adorno termed a "positive negation." For example, as Mahler himself noted, if he wanted a soft, subdued sound, he gave it to an instrument that can only produce it with difficulty, "often only by forcing itself and exceeding its natural range. I often make the basses and bassoon squeak on the highest notes, while my flute huffs and puffs down below."[63] Adorno hears Mahler's extremes as an invocation of the present-past used against itself. Nowhere does Mahler's pursuit of otherness come more significantly into play than in his incorporation of the musically banal and vulgar ("His symphonies shamelessly flaunt what rang in all ears, scraps of melody from great music, shallow popular songs, street ballads, hits").[64]

Adorno long lamented the social causes and effects of musical division, the increasingly absolute separation of light or popular music from its

---

saying, art 'achieves reconciliation,' provides an idea of what our relation to nature ought to be, only by showing through the history of artworks that every image of reconciliation is a lie." See also Lambert Zuidervaart, *Adorno's Aesthetic Theory: The Redemption of Illusion* (Cambridge: MIT Press, 1991), pp. 168–69, 178-80.

60. M, p. 6.
61. Ibid., pp. 6–7.
62. Ibid., p. 14.
63. Ibid., p. 16. The Mahler citation Adorno quotes is from Natalie Bauer-Lechner, *Recollections of Gustav Mahler*, ed. Peter Franklin, trans. Dika Newlin (New York: Cambridge University Press, 1980), p. 160.
64. M, p. 35.

"serious" twin, noting already in his early essay "On the Social Situation of Music" (1932) that present-day society officially despised and exploited popular music "in the same way as prostitution with which it is not compared in vain." Yet in a certain sense, light music "transcends the society which it supposedly serves" to the extent that its debasement exposes modernity's social truth, as it were, in spite of itself (p. 395). Adorno insists that the distinction between light and serious music be replaced by one that acknowledges "both halves of the musical globe equally from the perspective of alienation: as halves of a totality which to be sure could never be reconstructed through the addition of the two halves" (p. 395). (Music cannot pretend to put the world back together again without rendering itself ideological, and merely affirming what is, as opposed to what might be.)

Mahler sets these musics against each other, in extreme tension, producing for the effort "the scandal of all bourgeois musical aesthetics."[65] It is the tension between the musics that matters, not simply the incorporation of the banal and vulgar (Adorno's words) with the supposedly elevated. As a result, both musics are changed: "nothing sounds as it was wont to; all things are diverted as if by a magnet. What is worn out yields pliantly to the improvising hand; the used parts win a second life as variants."[66] And here Adorno employs a striking metaphor, that of a used car (this from a man who never drove), kept going by the skill of the driver who tends it. Adorno invokes the motion of the ultimate machine of modernity, but directs it toward a destination, a goal. Activity for a purpose: "Just as the chauffeur's knowledge of his [own] old second-hand car can enable him to drive it punctually and unrecognized to its intended destination, so can the expression of an exhausted melody, straining under the pressure of E-flat clarinets and oboes in the upper register, arrive at places which the approved musical language could never safely reach. Such music really crystallizes the whole, into which it has incorporated the vulgarized fragments, into something new, yet it takes its material from regressive listening" (all quotations pp. 314–15, "Fetish-Character" essay).

Adorno's allusion to punctuality, like his allusion to the rattle-trap car's

---

65. Cf. AT, p. 41: "Mahler's music is progressive just by its clumsy and at the same time objective refusal of the neo-romantic intoxication with sound, but this refusal was in its own time scandalous, modern perhaps in the same way as were the simplifications of van Gogh and the fauves vis-à-vis impressionism."

66. Cf. M, p. 36: "In his musical vagrancy [Mahler] picks up the broken glass by the roadside and holds it up to the sun so that all the colors are refracted. . . . In the debased and vilified materials of music he scratches for illicit joys."

being driven "unrecognized," are critical to his larger point. The musically worn-out is transformed by Mahler into the otherness of its "better half." The scandal of Mahler's use of the banal and vulgar, in other words, develops from his insistence on treating them as though they were not different, lesser, from their other, and despite the fact that their otherness remains other, however fully incorporated into the "punctual" movement of the work as a whole. What goes unrecognized is not the otherness of banality and vulgarity but the fact of their worn-out character—precisely what Mahler needs and "keeps going" in order to reach his destination, defined by a utopia of truth that emerges from lies exposed.[67] Otherness arises from victims and victimization, the losers in "progress," with whom Mahler identifies.[68] This otherness of the Other is manifested by Mahler always against the triumphant that has subsumed it by means of a musical language that has ejected what didn't coincide with aesthetic rationalization and conventionalized control over the materials: "The shabby residue left by triumph accuses the triumphant. Mahler sketches a puzzle composed of the progress that has not yet begun, and the regression that no longer mistakes itself for origin."[69]

The musical "atmosphere" of Mahler's music is, in a word, familiar, not the least of the reasons why the otherness he insistently projects is at the same time so defamiliarizing. What is new, Adorno argues, is the tone of Mahler's music, his charging tonality with an expressiveness for which it was no longer constituted. Tone is stretched to the limits; Adorno cites score markings, such as *kreischend* (screeching) for a woodwind passage in the scherzo of the Seventh Symphony. Harmonic teleology, the forward inevitability of tonality, with its cultural-musical association with progress, is achieved in Mahler only by force—sonic violence, rendered honest. Harmony is made expressive against its own expression by being unbalanced. The same effect occurs with his sudden shifts between major and minor, thereby undermining the hegemony of one or the other, rendering messy the neat binary, each containing its other in paradox if not contradiction. In other words, Mahler thrusts forward the non-identical that lurks in the shadow of musical identity, the mannerism of the idiosyncratic procedure

67. M, p. 17: "If the Other is not to be sold off, it must be sought incognito, among lost things."
68. Adorno, "Mahler," p. 96: "The expression of suffering, his own and of those who have to bear the burdens, no longer knuckles under at the behest of the sovereign subject which insists that things must be so and not otherwise. This is the source of the offence he gives."
69. M, p. 17.

being "the scar left behind by expression in a language no longer capable of expression."[70] Accordingly, tonality, immanently critiqued by the otherness of the imposed juxtapositions of major to minor, is at the same time made expressive, and made also to prefigure the modern: "Mahler's minor chords, disavowing the major triads, are masks of coming dissonances." Major-minor dualism, made a principal issue, constitutes a general that cannot absorb (and hide) the particular; as a result the general itself, major tonality, is rendered different, strange. "What is general in Mahler's compositions in the end are the deviations themselves."[71] Mahler's music stresses its own inauthenticity, which becomes the hallmark of authenticity itself to the extent that it gives lie to what claims to be authentic; as such, Mahler's music is "the enemy of all illusion."[72] Desperately, his music holds onto what culture has cast off as unworthy, mutilated. The artwork, "chained to culture, seeks to burst the chain and show compassion for the derelict residue; in Mahler each measure is an opening of arms."[73]

"MAHLER TODAY" (1930; pp. 603–11) provides a glimpse of Adorno's later Mahler monograph as regards both substance and style. The essay, though brief, ranges widely over Mahler's instrumental and vocal music, picking up one or two details from one work, then moving on to another, weaving in and out, while weaving a considerably insightful tapestry of why Mahler matters. Adorno's essay reacts to the then-conventional wisdom that Mahler was passé as a (supposedly) late romantic who had been left in the dust by modernism. Adorno suggests that Mahler had been "adroitly overcome" (p. 603)—but not dealt with. The substance of his

70. Ibid., pp. 20–22; the quotation appears on p. 22. Adorno, p. 26, suggests that for Mahler "minor is the particular, major the general; the Other, the deviant, is, with truth, equated with suffering. In the major-minor relationship, therefore, the expressive content is precipitated in sensuous, musical form."

71. Ibid., p. 26. Adorno, "Mahler," pp. 85–86, refers to Mahler's tonal chords as "cryptograms of modernism, guardians of the absolute dissonance which after him became the very language of music."

72. M, p. 30.

73. Ibid., p. 38. Cf., p. 39: "Not despite the kitsch to which it is drawn is Mahler's music great, but because its construction unties the tongue of kitsch, unfetters the longing that is merely exploited by the commerce that kitsch serves"; see further pp. 61–62. Adorno's admiration for Mahler is tempered by his consideration of the composer's weaknesses; see especially his critique of the Eighth Symphony, pp. 138–39, which he wryly names "the official magnum opus," and notes its "ostentatious cardboard, the giant symbolic shell," the "aborted, objectively impossible resuscitation of the cultic. . . . The dogmatic content from which it borrows its authority is neutralized in it to a cultural commodity. In reality it worships itself."

argument is to identify what remains in Mahler for moderns to confront: their own social, cultural, and musical past and present, set in extreme dialectical tension, the details of which Adorno precisely identifies. "The genuine significance of Mahler that can be discovered for today lies in the very violence with which he broke out of the same musical space that today wants to forget him" (p. 604).

"MARGINALIA ON MAHLER" (1936; pp. 612–18) addresses death. The essay was written in commemoration of the twenty-fifth anniversary of the composer's passing, but also in connection with Adorno's own personal loss the year before of his beloved aunt, Agathe Calvelli-Adorno (on 26 June 1935), who lived with Adorno's parents and was an integral member of the household throughout his childhood. "Marginalia on Mahler," cites the *Kindertotenlieder* in order to invoke remembrance as history, and history as a rescue attempt of "what is possible, but has not yet been." In Mahler Adorno hears the reconfiguration of the past into hopes and innocent dreams of all who have lived, and especially the unselfconscious vitality, energy, and spontaneity of the very young. He perceives this not as a gesture of blind nostalgia and melancholy, but precisely as a dream of something better but unfulfilled: remembrance as a responsibility toward the dead on behalf of the living and those who have not yet been born.

In a sudden shift, Adorno takes up the "formal law," the "extensive totality," that defines Mahler's music, which he identifies as the variant, but of a different sort than occurs in music by, say, Beethoven, Brahms, or Schoenberg. In place of more or less strict formal development following from a posited theme which, as subject, has the agency to define whatever follows in its wake, Mahler produces "music as immediacy, prior to any canon of objectification, [which] seeks to produce itself spontaneously." Mahler's principle of variant "as small divergence and prosaic irregularity lets [themes] . . . emerge flexibly from each other, disappear into each other." In this regard, and invoking childhood against the properly formal bourgeois adult world, Adorno suggests that Mahler "draws on a musical never-never land—a time when there were not yet any themes as firm possessions" (p. 613). Mahler's "never-never land" looks forward, not back; he is a modern, a realized subject whose music advances as a result of his own heightened state of consciousness. The explicitly historical consciousness that defines his subjecthood is evident in the degree to which his musical modernity is informed by a musical past—what Adorno names "fragments," in the sense of "ruins" or "wreckage" [*Trümmer*]—that is a constant point of reference: reworked and transformed. "Now the old formal walls stand as an allegory not so much of what has been as of what is to come" (p. 614). Mahler's purpose is humane; he employs an increasingly inhumane musical language—one of affirmation and aestheticization of the here and now—against itself, in an effort to remember (and re-member) what might have been, and what might be.

Mahler is a dealer in detritus, one who picks from the scrap heap of the present, and having a particular taste for the trashy; something of a naif and visionary, he finds new uses for this junk, ways of assembling the scraps so that they both retain the look of what they were when he found them and also gain a new essence, often profound and invariably meaningful, as he sets them in tension with the aesthetic principles of the artwork, but not without affecting the "mold" into which they are put, a mold unmade not least by their presence. Adorno suggests that we may laugh at the joke of their inclusion—their parodic import—but as a reader of Freud he knows full well the seriousness that lies at the heart of comedy. Not least, the vulgar and banal in Mahler produces the tendency to re-materialize (objectify) the reality which nineteenth-century musical aesthetics otherwise all too often worked hard to etherialize and, hence, ironically to reify. Mahler returns music to the here and now precisely to insist on the profound inadequacy of what is. Not least, the banal and vulgar, intruding into the aesthetic glories of the late-romantic language of bourgeois self-affirmation, forcefully announce to the bourgeois audience just who has been left out of this equation, very much as if the servants insisted on helping themselves to the cornucopia laid out on the sideboard buffet, inserting themselves into line, plates in hand, alongside their social betters. The Mediterranean, swarthy urbanite: mandolin. The Austrian peasant: cowbells. Rather like an accordion band on the White House lawn playing "Hail to the Chief." Mahler knew the social semiotics of sound. And he knew the effects of sound intrusions. "Mahler's brittleness, however, defines his truth as a historical-philosophical line of demarcation" (p. 616). Yet it is leading in the wrong direction simply to suggest that Mahler's music intends to scandalize the Viennese bourgeoisie and attack their self-satisfied complacency. At the essay's end Adorno returns to his opening theme of remembrance and reformulates it: remember the living. He posits a "community of lovers." Mahler's setting in tension of high art and low functions as more than a sonoric comeuppance of privilege because the everyday itself is transformed, raised up, just as a high and mighty is taken to task (and maybe taken down a peg) by the presence of its otherwise suppressed Other. But the real point is that Mahler acknowledged and valorized difference without valorizing the current state of either the high or the low. Instead, his sprawling symphonies posit a utopia that develops both by articulating the inadequacy of the here and now and positing an alternative—without, however, pretending that current reality has been rendered moot.[74] The lack of an organic totality that defines Mahler's musical structures acts to prevent such wishful thinking. Mahler, Adorno insists, works to reverse the direction of history's forward march: "He promises victory to the losers. All his symphonic music is a reveille. Its hero is the deserter" (p. 617)—words Adorno wrote in protest and provocation while witnessing German rearmament in preparation for general war.[75]

Berg   Alban Berg, Adorno's composition teacher, profoundly affected Adorno and his understanding of music, music's social responsibility, and music's capacity, and that of art more generally, to tell the truth—indirectly.[76] Throughout his writing on music Adorno stressed details, a "habit" acquired from Berg—what in 1931 Adorno termed "Berg's principle of the infinitesimal; the principle of the smallest transition."[77] If Schoenberg's music proceeds from the principle of transition, Berg's does so from the "imperceptible transition," via extreme—and highly expressive—nuance. Adorno notes the tiny units from which his music is structured and whose infinitesimal size permits their interchange "at will re-

74. What Adorno once said of Berg holds true for Mahler. Adorno, "Alban Berg" (1956), SF, p. 79: "The greatest works of art do not exclude the lower depths, but kindle the flame of utopia on the smoking ruins of the past."

75. Cf., M, pp. 166–67, the final lines of this monograph; Adorno returns to the *"Rewelge"* [reveille]: "Mahler's music has sympathized with the social outcasts who vainly stretch out their hands to the collective. . . . Only those cast from the ranks, trampled underfoot, the lost outpost, the one buried 'where the shining trumpets blow,' the poor 'drummer boy,' those wholly unfree for Mahler embody freedom. Bereft of promises, his symphonies are ballads of the defeated, for 'Nacht ist jetzt schon bald'—soon the night will fall." Regarding *Rewelge*, see p. 618 n. 9.

76. Adorno, AB, p. 13, described his first meeting in 1924 with Berg in Frankfurt after the performance of three excerpts from *Wozzeck:* "If I try to recall the impulse that drew me spontaneously to him I am sure it was exceedingly naive, but it was related to something very essential about Berg: the *Wozzeck* pieces, above all the introduction to the March and then the March itself, struck me as a combination of Schoenberg and Mahler, and at the time that was my ideal of genuine new music." On Berg's teaching composition to Adorno, see pp. 32–33.

77. Adorno, "Berg and Webern—Schönberg's Heirs," *Modern Music* 8 no. 2 (January/February 1931), p. 32. The subtitle Adorno gave to his Berg monograph named the composer: *Master of the Smallest Link [Berg, der Meister des kleinsten Übergangs].* Adorno, "Schöne Stellen," GS, vol. 18, p. 699, describes the interpretation and experience of music from the details to the whole—and vice versa—in terms of "exact imagination." On this point, see Nicholsen, *Exact Imagination*, p. 5.

gardless of their differences." Adorno connects Berg to romanticism at the level of structure, to the extent that each work unfolds "like a plant": organically.[78] But unlike that of romantic music, Berg's expressiveness is defined by the austerity of his works' construction. Berg's music is highly calculated, formally precise, exact.[79]

"THE OPERA WOZZECK" (1929; pp. 619–26) addresses expression in music generally, in order to mark the exact manner in which it emerges in Berg's opera, namely, as an objective image of the subjective. Adorno points out that virtually all music is expressive; but to say just that much provides little insight. He points to the commonplace that nineteenth-century music is the canonic locus of musical subjectivism, but then suggests that romanticism's subjectivism disguises subjectivity itself, to the extent that it treats expression as "the image of a single experience, an isolated impulse" (p. 621). It is Berg's purpose, Adorno writes, to rediscover what lies beneath the mask: "real humanity." That is, Berg drives "the musical-psychological process to a deep level where the unity of the surface relations of consciousness no longer prevails, but where the objective characters, in their solitariness, clamber out of the abyss of subjectivity. Here they are seized by the formal work, by virtues of its construction" (p. 621).

Wozzeck, psychologically charged in the extreme, its truth seemingly bursting forth spontaneously through its anti-hero, is rationalized to the nth degree. Moreover, Wozzeck's narrative and music together function as a unit intent on engaging the subject's fate, and in ways distinctly different from canonic late romantic opera, verismo notably (small irony),

---

78. Adorno, "Berg and Webern—Schoenberg's Heirs," p. 32.

79. See the discussions, passim, in Dave Headlam, The Music of Alban Berg (New Haven: Yale University Press, 1996); and Douglas Jarman, The Music of Alban Berg (London: Faber and Faber, 1979); and, for Adorno's account of Berg, see the somewhat general essay by Raymond Geuss, "Berg and Adorno," in The Cambridge Companion to Berg, ed. Anthony Pople (Cambridge: Cambridge University Press, 1997), pp. 38–50.

There are numerous commentaries on the formal design of Wozzeck; see George Perle, The Operas of Alban Berg, vol. 1, Wozzeck (Berkeley and Los Angeles: University of California Press, 1980), especially pp. 38–92, on the formal design, and pp. 93–129, on representation and symbol in the music; Douglas Jarman, Alban Berg: Wozzeck (Cambridge: Cambridge University Press, 1989), pp. 41–68; Anthony Pople, "The Musical Language of Wozzeck," in The Cambridge Companion to Berg, ed. Anthony Pople (Cambridge: Cambridge University Press, 1997), pp. 145–64; and Theo Hirsbrunner, "Musical Form and Dramatic Expression in 'Wozzeck,'" in Alban Berg: Wozzeck, ed. Nicholas John (London: John Calder, 1990), pp. 25–36.

where the grimness of social reality is made not only palatable but distinctly pleasurable by a music adequate to the meager task of reaffirming injustice as a fact of fate—was ever poverty made more pretty and pleasurable, more apparently "right" (and less accounted for), than in the opening act of *La Bohème?* Berg speaks against this order without surrendering the sensuousness conventional to opera, and via what Adorno elsewhere referred to as Berg's "sonoral economy. . . . there is not one note, not a single instrumental line that is not absolutely requisite for the realization of the musical meaning—and coherence."[80] "It is precisely because opera, as a bourgeois vacation spot *[bürgerliche Erholungsstätte]*, allowed itself so little involvement in the social conflicts of the nineteenth century that it was able to mirror so crassly the developing tendencies of bourgeois society itself."[81] Adorno credits Berg with "greatheartedness" *[Grossherzigkeit]*, not compassion: Berg isn't interested in handing out alms; he is committed to "total identification."[82]

80. AB, p. 85.

81. Adorno, "Bourgeois Opera" (1955), SF, p. 23. Adorno, "Alban Berg," p. 70, tells of walking the streets of Berlin with Berg late into the night following the opera's highly successful premiere—consoling the composer who assumed that if the (bourgeois) audience liked the work he must have done something wrong. Adorno repeats this story, with variation, in AB, p. 10. According to a note in CC, p. 120, Adorno also attended the second performance, a week later, together with Walter Benjamin who, like Adorno, was much affected by the opera. Adorno soon thereafter published a lengthy and glowing review, "Alban Berg: Zur Uraufführung des 'Wozzeck,'" *Musikblätter des Anbruchs* 7 Heft 10 (December 1925); reprinted in GS, vol. 18, pp. 456–64.

In ISM, p. 74, Adorno suggests that *Wozzeck*, by some incredible fluke, managed to impress its structural authenticity upon a public unable to understand it structurally: "It is conceivable that in the case of *Wozzeck* . . . [as in Schoenberg's *Moses und Aron*] neither the details nor their structural connection were fully understood, but that the phenomenon fashioned by the compositorial force conveyed that force to an audience whose ears would have been unable to account for it in the particular." Concerning this passage, Rose Rosengard Subotnik commented to me, in a private communication, that "this has always struck me as one of the most potentially inconsistent and astonishing admissions in Adorno's writings. He provides an explanation here that would account for the public's favor on terms that Berg could accept. But this explanation comes at the cost of an enormous discrepancy with the rest of Adorno's writings: that somehow, in this one exceptional case, the audience could gauge the authenticity of a work without any basis for actually understanding the music. I'm not saying Adorno was wrong about *Wozzeck:* but the exception he makes for it does open up questions in relation to other parts of his work. Why, for instance, is such an instantaneous perception of authenticity to be trusted—and what happens if applied to other jagged works that may not be so well constructed (including popular music)?"

82. Adorno, "Alban Berg," p. 72.

Adorno repeatedly points to Berg's compositional nuance, the subtlety of the opera's effects, the lack of a "fuss." He suggests that the score has the precision and clarity of an architectural drawing, while insisting that the work's full richness can only be discerned in performance. Berg's compositional skill occurs in the absence of what Adorno considered by then the major crutch of music, tonality—a crutch in two senses: as the musical sign of the broken, and as a second-nature, de-historicized device for pretending its own inevitability. In the absence of the powerful organizing principles tonality affords, Berg composed a musically coherent stage work of considerable length by other means, namely, by employing "the traditional thematic-motivic techniques of Viennese classicism applied to their full extent and as never before to the stage."[83] Adorno references Berg's adaptive use of forms borrowed from absolute music—sonata, passacaglia, scherzo, fugue, rondo, etc.—which organize the opera's fifteen scenes, evenly divided among the three acts. (Each closed form nonetheless functions as a fragment; as historical-formal aesthetic detritus, none is capable of functioning as an organic totality to the extent that each is linked to the narrative—what came before and what will follow.) While recognizing the critical role these forms and procedures play in the long haul, Adorno is really after something else, and not only because (as Berg himself maintained) these forms and procedures are neither (or at least not consistently) heard nor intended to be, however evident they may be in retrospect, and particularly with the advantage of the score.[84] Indeed, the fact of their relative inaudibility serves Berg's larger purpose; their "original" semiotics are exposed for their actual emptiness. But as with Mahler, Berg reappropriates them against their own history.[85] Adorno valorizes what he terms the music's inner construction, its fabric. The *autonomy* of Berg's opera music develops on account of the text, not in spite of it,

83. AB, p. 86.
84. For Berg's own comments on the musical forms employed in *Wozzeck* and their impact, or lack thereof, on the audience, see his brief "A Word about 'Wozzeck,'" from 1927, reprinted in Jarman, *Alban Berg: "Wozzeck,"* pp. 152–53. See also Berg's quite lengthy 1929 lecture on *Wozzeck*, reprinted on pp. 154–70, an analysis which relates the musical structure to the dramatic narrative.
85. Thus the passacaglia with its twenty-one variations that anchors scene 4 of act 1, between the sadistic, controlling, and mad Doctor and Wozzeck, his "patient," victim of the Doctor's ambitions, and whom the Doctor, in an acute gesture of transference, accuses of having *"eine schöne fixe Idee."* Conventionally, a passacaglia's ground bass drives the teleological force of harmonic movement. Berg's use of atonality, by contrast, robs the structure of this affirmative teleology, and exposes a darker image: obsession with variations.

and to the extent that Berg's expressionism, entirely musical, attends so carefully to the text's import yet without serving it as a kind of programmatic description. In other words, Berg's striking modernity depends on the tension between a music that adheres to the social necessity of its own autonomy—not the least function of a formal structure anchored in absolute instrumental music—while addressing the most urgent of social necessities, the degraded state of the subject. The truth of Berg's music is its insistence on musical truth in the face of social untruth, its claim on behalf of the subject expressed with the intensity of aesthetic expressionism: not a cry of pain but a *musical* cry of pain, which gives meaning to the impulse by invoking modernity's attack not only on the body but also on the soul. If conventional opera aestheticizes surfaces, puts on a pretty, and even thrilling, face for suffering, all too often that face remains a mask. Berg's opera delineates the soul whose suffering knows no measurable depth. Berg's music does not gain market share for pain; he offers no Bellini or Donizetti mad scene in which suffering is the blessed cause of beauty itself, beauty's sine qua non. Instead, Berg provides a full-face gaze onto cruelty and pain, yet with his degraded subject's personal dignity still precariously intact. His music refuses to satisfy conventional expectations of opera aesthetics, yet distinctly privileges and valorizes musical beauty—but under history's duress. Berg's operas resonate in this respect with the Grand Tradition which they otherwise do so much to belie.

Berg's characters speak musically, yet not quite. In a marked gesture against operatic tradition, he demands of his singers that they perform, as it were, "unmusically," but with the utmost musical precision: *Sprechstimme* or *Sprechgesang*. Between speech and song, a liminal space between drama and opera. Opera's "voice" reverses itself, becoming songless and speechful. (Or at least it would were this nearly impossible performance requirement fully realizable.) In the process, aesthetics is not pushed off stage, but its role is radically redefined. Specifically, the second nature of operatic absurdity is denaturalized; the suspension of disbelief that is presumably necessary when taking one's seat before the curtain is called into question. Berg insists on drawing attention to the artifice of the artwork, to aesthetics, as unnatural, and by that means to direct his listeners to the very nature of musical expression in opera. The centrality of this effort is organized around what the listener commonly attended opera to forget: the stark reality and actual suffering that is, not coincidentally, opera's favorite subject. "The creation is so complete that nothing is required of the listener beyond a taut readiness to receive what is given with such prodigality. No one should shrink from a love that unreservedly searches out humanity where it is neediest."[86] *Sprechstimme* is the musical voice reduced to a desperate metaphoric whisper, where an acoustic aesthetic lives on but cannot struggle into the open and still remain true to itself.

Schoenberg and Stravinsky   Adorno's *Philosophy of New Music*[87] establishes a link between these two central figures of musical modernism such that it makes sense to discuss them together. *Philosophy of Modern Music* constitutes an account of the state of music, and society, in the then-present which defines both the book's necessity and the specific form it takes. Schoenberg and Stravinsky together form a force-field of difference, a constellation explained in terms of an extreme dialectical relation by means of which to discern both the truth of music today (the truth that is the lie of Stravinsky) and a music that is actually true to the modernity it critically confronts (Schoenberg). Adorno, quoting Hegel in his opening paragraph, cites the function of "meaningful juxtaposition" and "opposing extremes": "For only in such extremes can the essence of this music be defined; . . . [these extremes] alone permit the perception of its truth content." Schoenberg and Stravinsky represent themselves but also the outer and opposite limits of music's engagement with the present.[88]

In the introduction to *Philosophy of Modern Music* Adorno takes up the common charge that new music is all head and no heart, that its alleged intellectualism (its difficulty) comes at the explicit sacrifice of emotion. He regards this less as an accurate account of music (whose intellectualism he neither denies nor apologizes for) and more the reflection of subjects constituted by the Culture Industry. Artworks strive to produce historical consciousness that society would prefer to do without. As he puts it, art

86. AB, p. 88.

87. The book's title, *Philosophie der neuen Musik*, is given as *Philosophy of Modern Music* in the English edition. The various inadequacies of this translation have been described by several scholars. See Blumenfeld, "*Ad vocem* Adorno," pp. 522–23; Robert Hullot-Kentor, "Popular Music and Adorno's 'The Aging of the New Music,'" *Telos* 77 (Fall 1988), p. 80; and Gillian Rose, *The Melancholy Science: An Introduction to the Thought of Theodor W. Adorno* (New York: Columbia University Press, 1978), p. 195. The English translation breaks the text into numerous subtitled sections which in the original appear solely in the table of contents. Robert Hullot-Kentor is preparing a new translation of *Philosophy of New Music* for the University of Minnesota Press.

PNM was written in two phases: the Schoenberg study, pp. 29–133, in 1941, and the Stravinsky section, pp. 135–217, together with the introduction, pp. 3–28, in 1948; the book was published in 1949. Adorno himself regarded PNM as an "extended appendix" to DE, as he remarked in the preface, p. xiii.

88. PNM, p. 3, translation modified. In fact, each of the book's three sections opens with an epigraph from Hegel.

vehemently opposes false clarity. "Art is able to aid enlightenment only by relating the clarity of the world consciously to its own darkness."[89] It sees through the supposed humanitarianism of art delivered as comfort food, a disguise, a mask for inhumanity. But as he often noted, art paid a price for its heightened autonomy, for wanting to "tell" a story few wanted to hear, namely, the cost of its increasing irrelevance in popular consciousness. Accordingly, art's truth "withers," surviving only as a "cultural obligation," and as such is neutralized. This aporia notwithstanding, Adorno insists on music's task in the face of such dismal odds: "The inhumanity of art must triumph over the inhumanity of the world for the sake of the humane. . . . All of its beauty is in denying itself the illusion of beauty."[90]

89. Ibid., p. 15. On the matter of Schoenberg and intellectualism, see also Adorno, "Arnold Schoenberg, 1874–1951" (1953), PR, pp. 150, 152.

90. PNM, pp. 132–33. For other comments of this sort, see pp. 20–22, 46, 112–17. The most sustained critique of Adorno's concept of the autonomy of the artwork, central to his aesthetic theory, is by Peter Bürger, especially in his monograph *Theory of the Avant-Garde*, trans. Michael Shaw (Minneapolis: University of Minnesota Press, 1984); and "Adorno's Anti-Avant-Gardism," *Telos* 86 (Winter 1990–91), 49–60. Adorno considers autonomy a salient feature for a work's truth content; at the same time he acknowledges that autonomous art both affirms and critiques society. Art's affirmative impulse comes through its commodity character; that is, in a very direct sense, even the autonomy of art has been commodified. Adorno, "Culture and Administration" (1960), trans. Wes Blomster, in *The Culture Industry: Selected Essays on Mass Culture*, ed. J. M. Bernstein (London: Routledge, 1991), p. 102, points to art's neutralization as a result of its autonomy. "Today manifestations of extreme artistry can be fostered, produced and presented by official institutions; indeed art is dependent upon such support if it is to be produced at all and find its way to an audience. Yet, at the same time, art denounces everything institutional and official. . . . That which is so provokingly useless in culture is transformed into tolerated negativity or even into something negatively useful—into a lubricant for the system." See also Adorno's comments on this issue in ISM, p. 41.

Lambert Zuidervaart, "The Social Significance of Autonomous Art: Adorno and Bürger," *Journal of Aesthetics and Art Criticism* 48 no. 1 (Winter 1990), p. 61, points out, in an excellent assessment of both Adorno and Bürger, that "the autonomy of art is viewed as an 'evil' necessary for some greater good" by both men. Whereas Adorno regards autonomy as a sine qua non of avant-garde art, Bürger, *Theory of the Avant-Garde*, p. 22, argues that the avant-garde represents an attack on the bourgeois institution of art, that is, on "the productive and distributive apparatus and also . . . the ideas about art that prevail at a given time and that determine the reception of works. The avant-garde turns against both—the distributive apparatus on which the work depends, and the status of art in bourgeois society as defined by the concept of autonomy." Bürger treats the concept of art's autonomy as part and parcel of bourgeois ideology; as such it is the goal of avant-garde art—a goal that in the end failed—to excise autonomy and return art to life praxis. Adorno argues that an artwork's truth content is immanent to the work; Bürger on the other hand insists on examining the issue with regard to the work's

Art cannot promote happiness except by insisting that what is advertised as pleasure isn't.

Adorno opens the Schoenberg essay, just as he opens his introduction and the later Stravinsky section, with an invocation of history. Specifically, he insists on the historicity of musical material, in opposition to long-conventional accounts—in modernity dating back at least to Rameau, and ultimately leading back to Pythagoras—that regarded musical materials as natural, in terms of their physical properties. As regards music, a cultural practice, natural properties treated as such do not reveal music's connection to society. Further to the point, music's materials, myriad in the extreme, are not universally and synchronically available for use. At a given time and place, and for a particular function or purpose, only certain materials can be used. "The actual compositional material . . . is as different from [the sum of all sounds at the disposal of the composer] . . . as is language from its total supply of sounds."[91] The sounds of the past are, after all, commonly heard as antiquated, and not only by experts. But for Adorno the matter is not properly understood as one of untimeliness or antiquation but as one of falseness. Modern music's technical procedures reveal conventional techniques and sounds as "impotent clichés."[92] They no longer structure truth.

Stravinsky's music "avoids the dialectical confrontation with the musical progress of time," what Adorno regards as the basis of all great music of the common practice period, that is, epistemic modernity.[93] The rhyth-

---

function within the social institutions through which art is realized and received—in other words, for Bürger the work's social significance is determined by its use/usefulness. Zuidervaart, p. 69, is critical of the positions established by both men, but in the end he argues on behalf of a mediated notion of autonomy, suggesting that it be understood in two different but complementary ways: purpose and function: "'Purpose' pertains to the fulfillment of human needs and desires within a society. 'Function' pertains to the institutionalized operations whereby human purposes are met or denied. . . . Adorno's concept of autonomy loses sight of this distinction."

See also the excellent discussion of the autonomy principle by Lydia Goehr, *The Quest for Voice: On Music, Politics, and the Limits of Philosophy* (Berkeley and Los Angeles: University of California Press, 1998), chaps. 3 and 4. Zuidervaart, *Adorno's Aesthetic Theory*, pp. 88–89, 217–47, provides further valuable background, and critique, of Adorno's autonomy principle, factoring in as well Bürger's work.

91. PNM, p. 32.
92. Ibid., p. 34.
93. Ibid., p. 187. See further pp. 194–97. Cf. Adorno, "Criteria of New Music" (1957), SF, p. 191: "There is no doubt that for Stravinsky, too, time was the problem of music, strictly speaking; that was his greatness. But objectively, his music de-

mic violence of *Le Sacre* engages musical time by wresting it into the form of an acute propulsiveness which, though leaving the dancer's body constantly at odds with itself, nonetheless progresses forward to its own sacrifice, foretold in the music's domination of its movements and the irrelevance of subjectivity accompanying this "progress." The lack of synchronicity between music and the body's "natural movements" (i.e., part nature, part second nature) constitutes a truth of the modern subject but renders the insight moot by two means: by valorizing the gestures in an unproblematic, if nonetheless mythic, timelessness, and by garbing all of it in the musical costume of a radical modernity. In time, out of time. The pulsating march toward sacrifice.

A great deal of the Schoenberg section actually constitutes a critique of Schoenberg or, more precisely, of twelve-tone technique, a basic account of which I delineated in my commentary to part 1. What strikes Adorno as the regressive tendency in twelve-tone technique's progressive engagement with the history of modernity is, as with Enlightenment generally, the degree to which its extreme rationalization unwittingly delivers itself back to myth—the mythic power of numbers, what Adorno calls a "number game" whose agency over composers borders on superstition. The means becomes the goal;[94] spontaneity is sacrificed on the altar of mathematical control. Thus dissonances, for Adorno a sine qua non for the expression of suffering and hence of modern artwork's truth content, in twelve-tone compositions are reduced to so much increasingly conventionalized raw material, the historicity of dissonance thereby returned to nature, or regressed to second nature as the anticipated and expected sound of "modern" music.[95]

Adorno focuses on Stravinsky as a musical reactionary whose modernity is confined to the mask of style.[96] Borrowing from Schoen-

---

spairs of being able to annul time through articulation, through the process of what Hegel called statement *[Setzung]* and negation. . . . Instead of confronting the passage of time and its terrors so as to give it its due, and instead of standing his ground, he manipulates time. . . . His music, which is praised for its rhythms, is the opposite of rhythmic. It does not intervene in time; it makes no attempt to shape time by being shaped by it, but instead ignores it. The illusion of timelessness is installed at the expense of the nonillusory aspect of music, its temporal dialectic."

94. PNM, p. 66. Cf. "Arnold Schoenberg, 1874–1951," p. 166.

95. PNM, p. 86.

96. Donald B. Kuspit, "Critical Notes on Adorno's Sociology of Music and Art," *Journal of Aesthetics and Art Criticism* 33 no. 3 (Spring 1975), p. 323: "For Adorno, Stravinsky typifies a regressive reactionary, a 'neo-naive,' as Adorno terms it, restoring the artistic forms of the past in a simple format much as one might restore a monarch, for the sake of appearances, to a throne with no power."

berg's essay "New Music, Outmoded Music, Style and Idea" (1946),[97] Adorno calls style an accessory, "worn" for an occasion. He understands style as an historical category (Bach's style, for example); Stravinsky, he argues, likewise recognizes the historicity of style but ignores the consequences of this history; hence he employs style not as an integral demarcator of music *in* history but as decorative resonance, as it were, "history" as in Disneyland. Stravinsky borrows style like a tourist who passes pleasurably from Frontierland to Tomorrowland, from one ersatz façade to another. To the extent that history and the past revert to mere quotation (not the least regressive feature of postmodernism, though that's a different matter), history is in fact forgotten, and the presentness of the present is all the more inscribed and naturalized.

In one sense Stravinsky's mining of the musical past might be regarded as a form of insistence on music's autonomy. But for Adorno this is inauthentic to the extent that music's autonomy is not founded on reification. While mining for musical ore necessarily admits to music's historicity, it refuses to face that history's consequences in the present—in diametrical opposition to Berg's invocation of past musical procedures (if hardly styles).[98] Stravinsky, as it were, checks time on the clock of music's prehistory (modernized archaism or stylized primitivism) or history (neo-classicism), while averting his eyes to the demand of the hour at hand. Borrowing a line from his friend Rudolf Kolisch, Adorno refers to Stravinsky's neo-classical works as simply "music about music."[99] The hour at hand demands more, specifically attention to modernity's victims. Stravinsky acknowledges the subject, but perversely, as grist for ritual sacrifice on behalf of the collective *(Le Sacre)* or the butt of life's cruel joke (Adorno's opinion of *Petrouchka*); Stravinsky's music, in short, identifies with the aggressor.[100]

The polemical tone of Adorno's Stravinsky critique is by no means evident throughout the essay. In fact, it comes into the forefront only near

97. Arnold Schoenberg, "New Music, Outmoded Music, Style and Idea," in *Style and Idea: Selected Writings of Arnold Schoenberg,* ed. Leonard Stein; trans. Leo Black (New York: St. Martin's, 1975), especially pp. 121–24. Adorno further commented on this issue, citing Schoenberg, in AT, p. 206; and in "Arnold Schoenberg, 1874–1951," p. 154: "Although Schoenberg's music is not intellectual, it does demand musical intelligence. . . . Schoenberg's music honours the listener by not making any concessions to him."

98. See PNM, pp. 212, 216–17.

99. Ibid., pp. 182, 206.

100. Ibid., pp. 143–48. Note the sharp distinctions Adorno draws on the issue of victims and victimization is his accounts of Schoenberg's *Erwartung* and *Die glückliche Hand,* pp. 42–51, and the two Stravinsky ballets, pp. 140–60. Adorno's

the book's end, beginning with a subsection called "Der letzte Trick,"[101] in a discussion of Stravinsky's neo-classicism, which Adorno regards with near total contempt, as a total capitulation to the here and now and to the Culture Industry. Adorno calls the *Pulcinella Suite* a "somewhat graceful insult to Pergolesi," addressed to listeners who prefer their music to be always already familiar—and also modern: "This indicates the willingness inherent in this music to be used as fashionable commercial music," which Adorno names a "penchant for conciliation" and a "universal necrophilia [as] . . . the last perversity of style." What results are "quotable musical goods," totally and completely conformist.[102]

Whereas Adorno provides a sustained dialectical account of Schoenberg's music, the dialectics in the Stravinsky section are notably muted. Only occasionally does Adorno elucidate progressive elements, and then grudgingly, such as in a lengthy footnote (!) that describes the jazz elements (i.e., dance music as described in part 3) in *Histoire du soldat* and other like compositions whose (almost unwitting) trashiness exposes the truth about its model—he concedes Stravinsky's transformation of the standardized elements into "stylized ciphers of decay."[103] Faint praise.[104]

---

critique of *Le Sacre* is largely centered on the insistent rhythms which take control of the work, and which Adorno hears as immutably rigid and as "convulsive blows and shocks" (p. 155) that mirror the subject caught in the nightmare of a Fritz Lang–like *Metropolis* of machines and machine-efficient technocratic domination. See pp. 154–57, 178. Cf. Adorno, "Stravinsky: A Dialectical Portrait" (1962–63), QF, p. 166: "His percussion effects are no less than assassination attempts, echoes of archaic war drums, blows of the sort that sacrificial victims and slaves have to endure." Much of Adorno's critique of Stravinsky and his music's impact on listeners, centered on schizophrenia, narcissism, and infantilism, is anchored in Freudian social psychology, which, to be sure, is often somewhat essentialist. See, especially, PNM, pp. 160–68, 174–79, 183–84, and 197.

101. PNM, pp. 203–09.

102. Ibid., pp. 203–05.

103. Ibid., p. 171. Cf. his comments about progressive elements in the Symphony in Three Movements, p. 211. Adorno, "Stravinsky: A Dialectical Portrait," p. 147, addresses Stravinsky's move away from neo-classicism and toward serial composition, and without retracting "anything I wrote in 1947." Adorno responds to criticisms leveled against the Stravinsky section of PNM. Only in the last few pages does he give Stravinsky any "due" by noting the dialectical elements in Stravinsky's music—for example, citing the important role he gives to percussion (p. 167: "he invested the percussion with emotion"); his inventive use of wind instruments; in general, his acute awareness of the sound appropriate to a situation; and the insightfulness regarding the subject's alienation in *Histoire du soldat*. But again, for the most part Adorno didn't change his mind on Stravinsky.

104. Subotnik, "Role of Ideology in the Study of Western Music," pp. 7–8:

In "TOWARD AN UNDERSTANDING OF SCHOENBERG" (1995, rev. 1967; pp. 627–43) Adorno argues for the composer's continued relevance, while accounting for the impediments standing in the way of a public regard for his music. Whereas Adorno's attempted "rescue" of Wagner

---

"Adorno's grounds of rejection [of Stravinsky] *are* based on an ideological predisposition, but at least the ideology involved is not hidden. It is explicit in virtually every sentence that Adorno writes and thus readily available for our own evaluation. . . . And second, however much Adorno doubts the absolute existence of autonomous musical structure or dislikes Stravinsky's musical structures in particular, he does not ignore the latter but directs considerable attention to their internal workings."

For additional discussion of PNM, see Paddison, *Adorno's Aesthetics of Music*, pp. 44–47, 265–71; Williams, *New Music and the Claims of Modernity*, pp. 31–42, especially strong and detailed on the Stravinsky section of PNM, provides a good overview of the responses to Adorno's Stravinsky critique—in regard to which, it's worth pointing out that the Schoenberg section of PNM has produced remarkably little controversy. James L. Marsh, "Adorno's Critique of Stravinsky," *New German Critique* 28 (Winter 1983), pp. 147–64 presents Stravinsky as a progressive—for example, arguing for the musical "playfulness" of *Petrouchka*, as opposed to what Adorno reads as the depravity of the comic and grotesque principal subject. Marsh's salvage operation is compromised by his inadequate engagement of Adorno's critique of Stravinsky's neo-classical works. Nancy Weiss Hanrahan, "Negative Composition," *Philosophy and Social Criticism* 15 no. 3 (1989), pp. 273–90, focuses solely on the Schoenberg material. Robert Craft, "A Bell for Adorno," in *Prejudices in Disguise: Articles, Essays, Reviews* (New York: Alfred A. Knopf, 1974), pp. 91–102, is a fairly scathing review (no surprise given the author's long, personal association with Stravinsky) of the English edition of PNM; thus, p. 93: "a mind of exceptional subtlety is in hiding somewhere in this loftily wrongheaded philosophy." Two recent monographs provide overviews of PNM: Christopher J. Dennis, *Adorno's "Philosophy of Modern Music"* (Lewiston, ME: Edwin Mellen Press, 1998), fundamentally a detailed précis of PNM; and a more critically engaged study by Bhesham R. Sharma, *Music and Culture in the Age of Mechanical Reproduction* (New York: Peter Lang, 2000).

David Roberts, *Art and Enlightenment: Aesthetic Theory after Adorno* (Lincoln: University of Nebraska Press, 1991), sees Adorno's dialectical comparison of Schoenberg and Stravinsky in PNM as prefiguring the modernism-postmodernism debates. In a related vein, Michael Chanan, *Musica Practica: The Social Practice of Western Music from Gregorian Chant to Postmodernism* (London: Verso, 1994), pp. 247–48, posits that Stravinsky's borrowing ("kleptomania") from the broad terrain of music history is postmodern before the fact, which Chanan reads as a progressive gesture against the tyranny of historical teleology.

Finally, see Albrecht Rietmüller, "Theodor W. Adorno und der Fortschritt in der Musik," in *Das Projekt Moderne und die Postmoderne* (Regensburg: Bosse, 1989), pp. 15–34, principally a consideration of Adorno's articulation of progress and regression; and Giselher Schubert, "Adornos Auseinandersetzung mit der Zwölftontechnik Schönbergs," *Archiv für Musikwissenschaft* 46 no. 3 (1989), pp. 235–54, which explores the development of Adorno's critique of twelve-tone technique.

came in a certain sense in spite of the composer, his attempted rescue of Schoenberg is, by contrast, on behalf of a man and his music that Adorno unambiguously admired. But there's something more. Adorno senses that "people who care about music at all should care about [Schoenberg]" (p. 629). In other words, by fulfilling his felt responsibility toward Schoenberg, Adorno offers something in return: the richness of Schoenberg's music, whose import for Adorno is second to none, and which he considers essentially the equal of Beethoven's, specifically in light of the historical urgency that Schoenberg directly confronts.

The listener must bring to Schoenberg two things: a willing regard for music "as a living and internally meaningful sequence of events," and a "relatively good command" (p. 629) of Western pre-Schoenberg classical music—in other words, a familiarity with tonal music, its conventions and repertory (it's not lost on Adorno that this is no small order). He points out that Schoenberg's music "wants to be apprehended spontaneously as an organic structural complex of sounds" (p. 629). In this respect, Schoenberg's perceived relation to his audience was entirely traditional, as was his disappointment in his apparent failure to obtain an audience.

In a sense, Adorno's essay constitutes an explanation of the question, "Why is Schoenberg's music so difficult to understand?" which he took up any number of times during his career, either directly or indirectly. In other words, Adorno's intent is pedagogical. By way of explaining impediments to understanding, he hopes to open doors to Schoenberg. His explanations are linked invariably to history and subject-formation in modernity—against which Schoenberg's music protests. Adorno's argument on behalf of Schoenberg is that his music proffers insight, but that the difficulty appended to the insight emerges from our not wishing to hear the truth the music speaks.

The difficulty with Schoenberg's music is at once musical and historical, the one informing the other. His music engages tradition (tonality) but without offering the comforts that adhere to the traditional tonal conventions established for upwards of 350 years, and which exercise powerful agency on listener's expectations. Indeed, Adorno paraphrases a comment made years earlier in his essay "On Popular Music" to the effect that such music "hears for the listener" (p. 442)—a remark often cited in critiques of Adorno's stance on popular music. Here he applies the judgment to tonal music *tout court*: "traditional music listened for the listener" (p. 630). Tonality projects powerful forward movement through its harmonic rhythm; but an important contributing factor to tonality's teleology is the degree to which our ears are trained to anticipate the movement. Indeed, we do so as second nature. Schoenberg's music disrupts tonality's teleology. In its place each musical structure demands to be considered and understood on the basis solely of its own inner workings, without tonality's road map as a guide. No "universal" script exists to outline where the listener will be taken, yet each work is scripted with exacting attention. Each work makes musical sense as a rationally produced aesthetic object.

A critical component of his music's import is its requirement to be met by the listener halfway: Schoenberg "no longer allows us to abandon ourselves to pure harmony, or to doze in a mood." Nevertheless, Schoenberg's music presumes intersubjective engagement, which requires that music "finally outgrow its baby shoes" (p. 630). His is not music designed for "easy listening" (Adorno used the phrase in English)—in a word, not background. Schoenberg's music makes demands on listeners which, if met, offer much in return. Adorno regards the structural complexity and precision of Schoenberg's music utopian to the extent that it (perhaps naïvely) is necessarily addressed to fully realized subjects; accordingly, it provides no extraneous enticements as self-advertisement for itself. The extraordinary care in composing honors the subject via an intersubjectivity constructed on the principle that only the most cogent and attentive working out is worthy of either Schoenberg himself or his listener. Further, the care with which Schoenberg approaches the musical materials respects that which his rational powers otherwise seek to dominate. His music, in other words, enacts a reconciliation with the object world which his music attempts to express and make sense of. The aesthetic domination he necessarily enacts (necessary in that without his willful command the work would not exist) is mediated by the respect shown the materials in the compositional process, which precisely and patiently reveals what is immanent—but otherwise only latent—in these materials: "Schoenberg leaves nothing unformed; every tone is developed from within the law of motion of the thing itself" (p. 630). With Schoenberg, "everything that makes a sound has its logic" (p. 632).

But logic—the manifestation of a non-instrumental aesthetic—is not what our ears are culturally trained for. Music as entertainment is the dominant paradigm—whether on the radio in the car or at the office, or coming from the home entertainment center (Mahler playing softly at upscale cocktail parties). At most, to the extent that listening under such circumstances occurs at the level of consciousness, it comes "as a sequence of isolated sensual stimuli" (p. 632). This observation leads Adorno back to tonality which evolved, he suggests, "as a result of the subject's need for expression" (p. 633). But as tonality's conventions were established, the composer's expressive agency was circumscribed as much as it was enabled; enabled by a sonic script whose conventions provided a common sonoric vocabulary; disabled by the "compulsory" constraints on expression, whose very expressiveness, after all, depended not on cliché and repetition, but on the affective power of the non-standardized. (Adorno here describes the tension between schema and originality, which he accounts for in terms of structural duality—surface and depth.)

Convention is a surface manifestation. Only at the level of the "subcutaneous, a structure under the skin" (p. 634), is truth realized by the composer, and experienced by the listener—precisely the level of music for which listeners are increasingly ill equipped, even as regards traditional tonal music. With Schoenberg the problem is exacerbated; his music is, as it were, turned inside out: the musically subcutaneous breaks through to the surface; the musical inside defines everything. There is no "surface" of familiarity and anticipation easing access or providing entertainment value. Schoenberg's music is emancipated from layers of historical convention, but its freedom threatens listeners anchored in the sonoric assurance of traditional music, and despite the fact that traditional music deceives us about the reality it aesthetically reenacts. "This music denies the very thing we have been accustomed . . . to expect from music as the magical art: consolation." What it offers instead, simply, is truth—"without the crutches of the familiar, but also without the deception of praise and false positivity." But herein lies an alternate and non-passive form of consolation: "the strength to do this, not illusion, is what is consoling about it" (all quotations p. 638).

What Schoenberg releases are "the forces of unrestrained, emancipated, authentic expression" (p. 639); paradoxically he does so via a compositional process of extreme control. Schoenberg's expressiveness is marked by spontaneity not in spite of the control he exercises on the material, but because of it. This is what renders his music art. The depth of his music's expressiveness is determined by the degree to which it is planned as an intentional act involving procedural decisions, which arise at the same time from his extreme heightened sensitivity toward and valorization of expression itself as definitive of the subject in whose name his music speaks. Expression in art depends on the articulation of a sense of the spontaneous—"planned" expression affects manipulation. Nevertheless, composition results from intention, realized through control of materials which themselves are *made* expressive. Schoenberg's genius, Adorno suggests, results from his commitment and ability to accomplish this monumental task while remaining true to the musical materials (not least by steadfastly refusing the fallback to the tried and true, which would merely manipulate the materials in order to perpetuate sounds in league with the history that envelops them). Schoenberg's genius—and Adorno uses that word—is that his music's spontaneity is artifactual but also objectively true. That is, for all his works' structural precision, Schoenberg himself interacts with these materials with a spontaneity characteristic of a subject worthy of the name. He doesn't so much manipulate the materials as engage them. Engagement, as opposed to manipulation, is a mark of respect.

Adorno senses respectful engagement in Schoenberg's use of formal variation, the defining characteristic of his compositional procedure. In his use of twelve-tone writing, the musical material is "completely emancipated"; thematic material freed of tonal chains is formed and reformed with a spontaneity that is real, and not merely represented, which results in a level of expressiveness rarely matched. "This alone, and not any supposedly mathematical operations, is what matters" (p. 640). The expressiveness of Schoenberg's music reflects the composer's acute control over compositional process, yet his thematic variations seem to emerge spontaneously. The result mirrors the accord between the composer and his materials. "The purpose of the whole, its entire raison d'être, is that, using material that is in every case preformed in the strictest fashion, one can now compose quite freely and unrestrainedly, without there being any danger of dissociation" (p. 640).

"DIFFICULTIES" (1964, 1966; pp. 644–79), the final, late essay in this collection (based on a lecture) returns to the challenges facing composers in late modernity, the central issue that frames Adorno's philosophy of music and his musical aesthetics. Composers confront the aporia of an exhausted musical language: "Every triad that a composer still utilizes today already sounds like a negation of the dissonances that have meanwhile been set free" (p. 647), yet not only the traditionalists adhere to tonality. Even members of the avant-garde feel tonality's magnetic pull— tonality's ahistorical false promise that things aren't what we know them to be. Krenek goes back to tonality, only soon to recognize the futility of his wishful thinking, something Adorno names Krenek's "great aesthetic-moral accomplishment" (p. 647). Even Schoenberg dabbles with tonality's self-assurance. Others launch themselves into musical modernity only to pull back—out of fear or horror at what such aesthetic modernism reveals?—and as though the choice to retreat to tonality's (unsafe) safe haven were without consequence: Strauss, about whom Adorno comments,

"The person who commits himself to what is older only out of despair at the difficulties of the new is not comforted, but becomes the victim of his helpless nostalgia for a better era that, finally, never actually existed" (p. 648).

But the reactionary's retreat reveals an objective truth, namely, that the musical techniques of the avant-garde (what Adorno calls the "technical productive forces of music") have outrun composers' ability to respond to them; their own subjective musicality lags behind, and not least due to the pull—and deep, comforting attraction—of the musical past, again: tonality, and everything that sticks to this most powerful of sonoric-semantic magnets. A profoundly unequal relation marks "the development of the technical forces of production and the human responses, the capacity to use, control, and make sensible use of these techniques" (p. 648). One of the principal reasons for the imbalance is social; technology advances, but subjects regress. As Adorno put it, we are conquering space while becoming increasingly infantile. Adorno does not pretend an answer, except to the extent that the first principle of the cure is diagnosis of the condition. Looking back at musical composition since 1920, he points to efforts to develop, from musical material, idiom, and technique, those compositional processes which will "relieve" the composing subject of the crushing burdens imposed by modernity's prevailing conditions. He alludes to the aporia reached by composers like Schoenberg in his move from tonality to atonality, and to the frustrations that led him to slow his output to a crawl during much of the teens; and Berg, whose output was so small that he stopped using opus numbers so as not to embarrass himself because they were so low.

"Relief" from compositional aporia arrived first in the form of twelve-tone technique, and, thereafter, in more radicalized form, in integral serialism that reached the peak of its canonic status by the time Adorno delivered his lecture. The point of his intense critique of integral serialism—not to mention serialism generally, once its underlying principles had become instrumentally rationalized—is that the "relief" purportedly offered to the composer by these compositional procedures is a false "cure." The alleged promise of a set method or technique for composing modern music in the end grants only deception. And worse, the very subjecthood of the composer is surrendered in the bargain in exchange for an assumed perfection in the form of antiseptic musical objectivity. In short, the "help" offered by the system threatens to overwhelm the composer. "He is subjected to a set of laws that are alien to him and that he can scarcely catch up with" (p. 657).

John Cage (once a student of Schoenberg) entered the fray. But Adorno sees in Cageian indeterminacy the mirror image of the absolutely determined: another temporary and ultimately false relief: "Pure chance, it is true, breaks stolid, inescapable necessity, but is as external to living hearing as the latter" (p. 658); and he suggests that the very ease of movement by many serialist composers to radical indeterminacy suggests as much. So in the end we are caught on the horns of a dilemma, the juncture at which Adorno ends the first part of his long essay by loosely quoting the playwright Grabbe: "For nothing but despair alone can save us." Adorno regards the musical (and social) situation to be precarious: "perhaps only that music is still possible which measures itself against this greatest extreme, its own falling silent" (p. 660).[105]

Yet to the end Adorno remained faithful alike to the subject, however bent low and compromised, and to a music in whose sounds might be posited the acoustic trace of a reconciliation of the particular with the universal, of the subject with its others. Adorno chose to imagine utopia, and in that imagining he delineated not the pipe dream of a fool, but the conscious remembrance of harmony, however fleeting, whether in his memories of childhood or in, say, Mahler's sonic evocations of young life recalled. Modernity, like the new music, was growing old; Adorno's faithful adherence to the possibility of something better was not.

105. In the lecture-essay's second part, Adorno turns back once more to the state of listening and the listening subject in late modernity—that is, to the aporia confronting not the composer but the one who hears what the composer writes. Thus, near the end of his career, he revisits issues he had defined decades earlier at his career's beginning: "Why Is the New Art So Hard to Understand?" Adorno's diagnostics and his diagnosis have not changed, but the condition he identifies has, and for the worse, insofar as he understands it. At the heart of the social condition of new-music listening in late modernity lies what Adorno names tonality's "power of resistance" (p. 663), the details about which organize the remainder of his discussion: "The listening ear, calibrated to that harmony [i.e., tonality], feels overwhelmed when it is supposed to follow on its own the specific processes of the individual compositions, in which the relationship between the universal and the particular is articulated each time" (p. 669).

Late Style in Beethoven

The maturity of the late works of significant artists does not resemble the kind one finds in fruit. They are, for the most part, not round, but furrowed, even ravaged. Devoid of sweetness, bitter and spiny, they do not surrender themselves to mere delectation. They lack all the harmony that the classicist aesthetic is in the habit of demanding from works of art, and they show more traces of history than of growth. The usual view explains this with the argument that they are products of an uninhibited subjectivity, or, better yet, "personality," which breaks through the envelope of form to better express itself, transforming harmony into the dissonance of its suffering, and disdaining sensual charms with the sovereign self-assurance of the spirit liberated. In this way, late works are relegated to the outer reaches of art, in the vicinity of document. In fact, studies of the very late Beethoven seldom fail to make reference to biography and fate. It is as if, confronted with the dignity of human death, the theory of art were to divest itself of its rights and abdicate in favor of reality.

Only thus can one comprehend the fact that hardly a serious objection has ever been raised to the inadequacy of this view. The latter becomes evident as soon as one fixes one's attention not on the psychological origins, but on the work itself. For it is the formal law of the work that must be discovered, at least if one disdains to cross the line that separates art from document—in which case every notebook of Beethoven's would possess greater significance than the Quartet in C-sharp Minor. The formal law of late works, however, is, at the least, incapable of being subsumed under the concept of expression. From the very late Beethoven we have extremely "expressionless," distanced works; hence, in their conclusions, people have elected to point as much to new, polyphonically objective construction as to that unrestrainedly personal element. The work's ravaged character does not always bespeak deathly resolve and demonic humor, but is often ultimately mysterious in a way that can be sensed in pieces that have a serene, almost idyllic tone. The incorporeal spirit does not shy away from dynamic markings like *cantabile e compiacevole* or *andante amabile*. In no case can the cliché "subjective" be applied flatly to his stance. For, in general, in Beethoven's music, subjectivity—in the full sense given to it by Kant—acts not so much by breaking through form, as rather, more fundamentally, by creating it. The *Appassionata* may stand here as one example for many: admittedly more compact, formally tighter, more "harmonious" than the last quartets, it is, in equal measure, also more subjective, more autonomous, more spontaneous. Yet by comparison the last works maintain the superiority of their mystery. Wherein does it lie?

The only way to arrive at a revision of the [dominant] view of late style would be by means of the technical analysis of the works under consideration. This would have to be oriented, first of all, toward a particularity that is studiously ignored by the popularly held view: the role of conventions. This is well known in the elderly Goethe, the elderly Stifter;[1] but it can be seen just as clearly in Beethoven, as the purported representative of a radically personal stance. This makes the question more acute. For the first commandment of every "subjectivist" methodology is to brook no conventions, and to recast those that are unavoidable in terms dictated by the expressive impulse. Thus it is precisely the middle Beethoven who, through the creation of latent middle voices, through his use of rhythm, tension, and other means, always drew the traditional accompanying figures into his subjective dynamics and transformed them according to his intention—if he did not indeed develop them himself, for example in the first movement of the Fifth Symphony, out of the thematic material, and thus free them from convention on the strength of their own uniqueness. Not so the late Beethoven. Everywhere in his formal language, even where it avails itself of such a singular syntax as in the last five piano sonatas, one finds formulas and phrases of convention scattered about. The works are full of decorative trill sequences, cadences, and *fiorituras*. Often convention appears in a form that is bald, undisguised, untransformed: the first theme of the Sonata op. 110 has an unabashedly primitive accompaniment in sixteenths that would scarcely have been tolerated in the middle style; the last of the Bagatelles contains introductory and concluding measures that resemble the distracted prelude to an operatic aria—and all of this mixed in among some of the flintiest strata of the polyphonic landscape, the most restrained stirrings of solitary lyricism. No critique of Beethoven, and perhaps of late styles altogether, could be adequate that

interpreted the fragments of convention as merely psychologically motivated, the result of indifference to appearances. For ultimately, the content
of art always consists in mere appearance. The relationship of the conventions to the subjectivity itself must be seen as constituting the formal law
from which the content of the late works emerges—at least to the extent
that the latter are ultimately taken to signify more than touching relics.

This formal law is revealed precisely in the thought of death. If, in the
face of death's reality, art's rights lose their force, then the former will
certainly not be able to be absorbed directly into the work in the guise of
its "subject." Death is imposed only on created beings, not on works of
art, and thus it has appeared in art only in a refracted mode, as allegory.
The psychological interpretation misses this. By declaring mortal subjectivity to be the substance of the late work, it hopes to be able to perceive
death in unbroken form in the work of art. This is the deceptive crown of
its metaphysics. True, it recognizes the explosive force of subjectivity in
the late work. But it looks for it in the opposite direction from that in
which the work itself is striving; in the expression of subjectivity itself.
But this subjectivity, as mortal, and in the name of death, disappears from
the work of art into truth. The power of subjectivity in the late works of
art is the irascible gesture with which it takes leave of the works themselves. It breaks their bonds, not in order to express itself, but in order,
expressionless, to cast off the appearance of art. Of the works themselves
it leaves only fragments behind, and communicates itself, like a cipher,
only through the blank spaces from which it has disengaged itself. Touched
by death, the hand of the master sets free the masses of material that he
used to form; its tears and fissures, witnesses to the finite powerlessness
of the I confronted with Being, are its final work. Hence the overabundance
of material in *Faust II* and in the *Wanderjahre*,[2] hence the conventions
that are no longer penetrated and mastered by subjectivity, but simply left
to stand. With the breaking free of subjectivity, they splinter off. And as
splinters, fallen away and abandoned, they themselves finally revert to
expression; no longer, at this point, an expression of the solitary I, but of
the mythical nature of the created being and its fall, whose steps the late
works strike symbolically as if in the momentary pauses of their descent.

Thus in the very late Beethoven the conventions find expression as the
naked representation of themselves. This is the function of the often-
remarked-upon abbreviation of his style. It seeks not so much to free the
musical language from mere phrases, as, rather, to free the mere phrase
from the appearance of its subjective mastery. The mere phrase, unleashed

and set free from the dynamics of the piece, speaks for itself. But only for a moment, for subjectivity, escaping, passes through it and catches it in the harsh light of its intention; hence the *crescendi* and *diminuendi,* seemingly independent of the musical construction, that are often jarring in the very late Beethoven.

No longer does he gather the landscape, deserted now, and alienated, into an image. He lights it with rays from the fire that is ignited by subjectivity, which breaks out and throws itself against the walls of the work, true to the idea of its dynamism. His late work still remains process, but not as development; rather as a catching fire between the extremes, which no longer allow for any secure middle ground or harmony of spontaneity. Between extremes in the most precise technical sense: on the one hand the monophony, the *unisono* of the significant mere phrase; on the other the polyphony, which rises above it without mediation. It is subjectivity that forcibly brings the extremes together in the moment, fills the dense polyphony with its tensions, breaks it apart with the *unisono,* and disengages itself, leaving the naked tone behind; that sets the mere phrase as a monument to what has been, marking a subjectivity turned to stone. The caesuras, the sudden discontinuities that more than anything else characterize the very late Beethoven, are those moments of breaking away; the work is silent at the instant when it is left behind, and turns its emptiness outward. Not until then does the next fragment attach itself, transfixed by the spell of subjectivity breaking loose and conjoined for better or worse with whatever preceded it; for the mystery is between them, and it cannot be invoked otherwise than in the figure they create together. This sheds light on the nonsensical fact that the very late Beethoven is called both subjective and objective. Objective is the fractured landscape, subjective the light in which—alone—it glows into life. He does not bring about their harmonious synthesis. As the power of dissociation, he tears them apart in time, in order, perhaps, to preserve them for the eternal. In the history of art late works are the catastrophes.

(1937; GS, vol. 17, pp. 13–17)
Translated by Susan H. Gillespie

NOTES BY RICHARD LEPPERT

1. Adalbert Stifter (1805–1868), prolific Austrian short-story writer and novelist best known for his bildungsroman *Der Nachsommer* [1857; "Indian Summer"] and the epic historical novel, set in the twelfth century, *Witiko* (1865–67).

His writing is classically reserved and displays sensitivity to nature and life led simply. See Eric A. Blackall, *Adalbert Stifter: A Critical Study* (Cambridge: Cambridge University Press, 1948).

2. Both *Faust II* and *Wilhelm Meisters Wanderjahre* are late works. *Faust II* was published posthumously in 1832, the year of Goethe's death; Goethe began *Wanderjahre* in 1821 and completed it in 1829.

Alienated Masterpiece

The *Missa Solemnis*

Neutralization of culture—the words have the ring of a philosophical concept. They posit as a more or less general reflection that intellectual constructs have forfeited their intrinsic meanings because they have lost any possible relation to social praxis and have become that which aesthetics retrospectively claims they are—objects of pure observation, of mere contemplation. As such they ultimately lose even their own aesthetic import; their aesthetic truth content disappears along with their tension vis-à-vis reality. They become cultural goods, exhibited in a secular pantheon in which contradictions, works which would tend to destroy each other, find a deceptively peaceful realm of co-existence, e.g., Kant and Nietzsche, Bismarck and Marx, Clemens Brentano and Büchner.[1] This wax museum of great men finally admits its own disconsolateness in the innumerable ignored pictures of each museum and in the editions of the classics in miserly locked-up bookcases. But no matter how widespread the consciousness of all this has meantime become, it is still as difficult as ever to grasp this phenomenon in its entirety, at least if one ignores the fashion of biographical writing which reserves a niche for this queen and that microbe hunter. For there is no superfluous work of Rubens in which at least the cognoscenti would not admire the incarnate value and no house poet of the Cotta Firm[2] in whose work there are no non-contemporarily successful verses awaiting resurrection. Every now and then, however, it is possible to name a work in which the neutralization of culture has expressed itself most strikingly; a work, in fact, which in addition is also famous, which occupies an uncontested place in the repertoire even while it remains enigmatically incomprehensible; and one which, whatever else it may conceal, offers no justification for the admiration accorded it. No less a work than Beethoven's *Missa Solemnis* belongs in this category. To speak seriously of this work can mean nothing less than, in Brecht's terms, to alienate it; to break through the aura of irrelevant worship which protectively surrounds it and thereby perhaps to contribute something to an authentic aesthetic experience of it beyond the paralyzing respect of the academic sphere. This attempt necessarily requires criticism as its medium. Qualities which have been assigned without any thought by traditional consciousness to the *Missa Solemnis* must be tested in order to prepare for a recognition of its content, a recognition which to this day is still missing. This effort is not one of *debunking**, of tearing down recognized greatness for the sake of tearing something down. The disillusioning gesture which pulls down from the heights the very thing it attacks is by that very act subservient to the substance of that which it pulls down. Instead, criticism with regard to a work of such demand and with regard to the total *oeuvre* of Beethoven, can only be a means of penetrating the work. It is the fulfillment of a duty vis-à-vis the work and not a means of gaining malicious satisfaction from knowing that once again there is one less great work in the world. It is necessary to point this out, because neutralized culture makes certain that the names of the authors are taboo while the constructs themselves are no longer perceived in their original contents. Rather they are merely consumed as socially acceptable works. Rage is immediately provoked whenever reflection about the work threatens to touch the authority of the author.

This situation must be anticipated whenever one prepares to say something heretical about a composer of the highest authority, one whose power is comparable only to the philosophy of Hegel and is still undiminished at a time when the historical preconditions of his work are irrevocably lost. But Beethoven's power of humanity and of demythologization demands by its very existence the destruction of mythical taboos. There is, of course, among musicians an underground tradition of critical reserve about the *Missa*. They have also long known that Handel is no Bach and that the actual compositional qualities of Gluck are questionable. Only fear of established public opinion made them keep their own opinions to themselves. So too they have known that there is something peculiar about the *Missa Solemnis*. Little truly penetrating has been written about it. Most of what has been written makes general pronouncements of awe about an immortal *chef d'oeuvre*, and it is easy to note the embarrassment of these writers which prevents them from stating wherein this supposed greatness actually lies. The neutralization of the *Missa* to cultural produce is reflected in such writings, but it is not overcome. Hermann Kretzschmar, who comes from a generation of music historians which had not yet cast off the experiences of the nineteenth century, expressed the most significant admiration for this work. According to his writing, the earliest performances of the work, before its official acceptance into Valhalla, made no lasting impression. He sees the chief difficulty in the "Gloria" and "Credo" and supports his view with reference to the large number of short musical images which require the listener to organize them into a unity. Kretzschmar has at least named one of the alienating symptoms which the *Missa* exhibits. On the other hand, he has overlooked the manner in which this symptom is connected to the essence of the composition and has, therefore, expressed the erroneous opinion that the resultant musical difficulties could be overcome by the use of an enclosure of these short sections by powerful major themes in both the long movements. But this is as little the case as asserting, for example, that the listener comprehends the *Missa* as soon as he has present in mind the preceding parts in concentrated form in accordance with the principle of comprehending the great symphonic movements of Beethoven. The listener then supposedly follows in this manner the creation of unity from diversity. This unity itself is of a completely different type from the productive power of fantasy in the *Eroica* and in the Ninth Symphony. It is not a crime to doubt that his unity is so obviously comprehensible.

Indeed, the historical fate of this work is an alienating factor. It could only be performed twice during Beethoven's lifetime; once, but in incomplete form, in Vienna in 1824, together with the Ninth Symphony, and a second time that same year in Petersburg in complete form. Up to the beginning of the 1860s, it was performed only occasionally. It was more than thirty years after the composer's death that it achieved its current standing. The difficulties of interpretation—above all in the treatment of the vocal parts, and not, in most sections any particular musical complexities—are not sufficient reason for this late discovery. Contrary to legend, the last quartets, which are in many ways far more exposed and far more demanding, found from the outset a respectable reception. But Beethoven had lent his own authority directly on behalf of the *Missa* in a manner decidedly different from his usual custom. He designated it *"l'oeuvre le plus accompli,"* his most successful work, when he offered it for subscription, and he wrote over the "Kyrie" the words "from the heart—may it go to hearts," a confession the like of which one may search for in vain in all the other printed editions of Beethoven's works. It is not possible to treat his own attitude to his work either lightly or to accept it blindly. The tone of that remark is conjuring, as if Beethoven had sensed something of the incomprehensible, reserved, and enigmatic quality of the *Missa* and had tried through the force of his will (as that force of will had ever stamped the content of his music) to force the work externally upon those whom it did not of its own power compel. This would hardly be conceivable if the work did not itself contain a secret quality which Beethoven believed justified him in influencing the history of this work. But when it had eventually established itself it was much aided by what had become in the meantime the unassailable prestige of the composer. His major sacred work was vouchsafed as a sister work the same admiration accorded to the Ninth Symphony without anyone daring to ask questions which might merely reveal the lack of depth of the questioner, as in the fairy tale of the emperor's new clothes.

The *Missa* would never have attained to an unquestioned place in the repetoire if it had caused a drastic shock, like *Tristan*, by its difficulty. But that is not the case. If one ignores the occasionally unusual demands made on the singing voice, a demand the work shares with the Ninth Symphony, the work may be seen to contain little that exceeds the circumference of traditional musical language. Very large parts are homophonous and even the fugues and fugati fit without difficulty into the thorough-bass pattern. The progressions of the harmonic intervals and with them the surface context, are seldom if ever problematic. The *Missa Solemnis* was composed far less against prevailing compositional traditions than are the late quartets and the *Diabelli* Variations; above all, it does not fall under Beethoven's final conception of style as derived from the quartets and variations, the five late sonatas and the bagatelle cycles. The *Missa* is distinguished more by certain archaicizing moments of harmony—church modes—rather than by the advanced compositional daring of the great Grosse Fuge. Not only did Beethoven always keep a stricter separation among the compositional genres than one suspects, but he also incorporated in them temporally different stages of his *oeuvre*. If the symphonies are in many respects simpler than the major works of the chamber music because of or despite the richer resources of the orchestra, the Ninth Symphony is clearly different and returns retrospectively to the classical symphonies of Beethoven without the sharp edges of the last quartets. In his late period the composer did not, as one might think, blindly follow the dictates of his inner ear, nor did he forcibly estrange himself from the sensual aspect of his work. Instead, he disposed sovereignly over all the possibilities which had grown up in the history of his composing. Desensualization was but one of these possibilities. The *Missa* shares with the last quartets an occasional abruptness, i.e., the lack of transitions. Otherwise there are few similarities. Altogether it reveals a sensuous aspect quite opposed to the intellectualized late style, an inclination to splendidness and tonal monumentality which usually is lacking in that late style. This aspect is incorporated technically in the process which in the Ninth Symphony is restricted to brief moments of ecstasy, doubling the parts through brasses, above all the trombones but also the French horns, which carry the melody. The frequently powerful octaves are related to this aspect as well, coupled with harmonic bass effects of the type contained in the well known "Die Himmel rühmen des Ewigen Ehre" and decisively in the passage "Ihr stürzt nieder" in the Ninth Symphony, later important in Bruckner. Clearly it is to no small extent these sensuous high points, an inclination to the tonally overwhelming, which gave the *Missa* its authority and helped its audiences over their own lack of understanding.

The real difficulty is greater than any of these. It is one of content, of the meaning of the music. It can perhaps be best formulated by asking whether someone ignorant of the work would recognize the *Missa*, apart from certain sections, as a work of Beethoven. If one played it to those who had never heard any part of it and had them guess who the composer was, one could expect some surprises. As little as the so-called imprint (*Handschrift*) of a composer forms a central criterion, its absence nevertheless reveals all the more that something isn't quite right. If one searches among Beethoven's other works of church music, one encounters this absence of the Beethoven imprint again. It is significant how difficult it is even to dredge up his *Christ on the Mount of Olives* or the by no means early C Major Mass, op. 86. The latter could, by contrast to the *Missa*, scarcely be attributed to Beethoven even in separate sections or phrases. Its indescribably tame "Kyrie" would seem at most to indicate a weak Mendelssohn. But throughout this work there are sections which reappear in the much more demandingly formed and more splendidly planned *Missa*. These include the dissolution into often short, hardly symphonically integrated parts, a lack of decisive thematic inspirations which otherwise characterize each work of Beethoven, and a lack of discharging dynamic developments. The C Major Mass reads as if Beethoven had decided only with difficulty to feel his way into what was for him a strange genre. It is as if his humanism rebelled against the heteronomy of the traditional liturgical text and as if his composition of this text surrendered to a routine which cost it all its genius. In order to get to the enigma of the *Missa* at all it will be necessary to call to mind this moment of his early church music. In the *Missa*, of course, it becomes a problem against which he struggles, wearing out his strength, but it helps in identifying something of the conjuring nature of the work. The problem cannot be separated from the paradox of Beethoven composing a mass at all. If one could understand fully why he did it, one would certainly be able to understand the *Missa.*

It is customary to assert that the *Missa* far exceeds the traditional form of the mass and to accord it the entire wealth of the secular compositions. Even in the music volume of the *Fischer-Lexicon* recently edited by Rudolf Stephan, which otherwise does away with many conventional platitudes, the piece is credited with being an "extraordinarily artistic thematic work."[3] In so far as one can talk about such work in the *Missa* at all, it utilizes a method of kaleidoscopic mixing and supplementary combinations exceptional in Beethoven. The motifs do not change with the dynamic pull of the composition—it has no such pull—but rather constantly reappear in changing light though they are always identical. The idea of exploded form may apply to the external dimensions at best, and Beethoven doubtless considered this idea when he contemplated concert performance. But the *Missa* does not at all break out of the pre-planned objectivity of the model through any subjective dynamic, nor does it create the totality in symphonic spirit out of itself. On the contrary, the consequent denial of all this removes the *Missa* from any direct connection with Beethoven's other works, with the exception of his previously mentioned earlier church music. The internal construction of this music, its fever, is radically different from everything which distinguishes Beethoven's style. It is itself archaic. The form is not achieved through developing variations from basic motifs, but arises largely from sections imitative in themselves, similar to the method of the Netherlandish composers around the middle of the fifteenth century, and it is uncertain how well Beethoven knew their work. The formal organization of the whole work is not that of a process developing through its own impetus—it is not dialectical—but seeks accomplishment by a balance of the individual sections, of the movements, ultimately through contrapuntal enclosure. All the estranging characteristics can be seen in this light. The fact that Beethoven did not use his own type of themes in the *Missa*—who after all can sing a passage from it the way one can sing a passage from any one of the symphonies or from *Fidelio*—can be explained by the exclusion of the organizational principle of development. It is only wherever a presented theme is developed and has, therefore, to be recognizable in its subsequent development, that it needs plastic form. Such an idea was foreign to the *Missa* as well as to medieval music. One need only compare the Bach "Kyrie" with that of Beethoven. In Bach's fugue there is an incomparably memorable melody which suggests the image of humanity as a procession dragging itself along while bowed down under the heaviest of burdens. In Beethoven's work there are complexes almost without melodic profile which delineate the harmony and avoid expression with a gesture of monumentality. This comparison leads to a real paradox. According to the current if questionable view, Bach, in recapitulating the objective-closed musical world of the Middle Ages, had brought the fugue to its pure and authentic form even if he was not the creator of this musical form. The fugue was as much his product as he was the product of its spirit. He stood in a direct relationship to the fugue. For that reason many of his fugue themes, with the possible exception of his speculative late works, have a kind of freshness and spontaneity about them comparable only to the cantabile-like inspirations of the subjective composers. At the historic moment of Beethoven's creativity, however, that form of musical organization, the reflection of which Bach still regarded as an *a priori* of his compositions, was no longer valid. With it disappeared a harmony of the musical subject and the musical forms which had permitted something akin to naïveté in Schiller's sense of the word. The objectivity of the musical forms with which Beethoven worked in the *Missa* is mediated and problematic—an object of reflection. The first part of the "Kyrie" includes Beethoven's own standpoint of subjective-harmonious being. But since this standpoint is also immediately pushed into the horizon of sacred objectivity, it takes on a mediated character as well, separated from the composed spontaneity—it is stylized. For that reason the smooth harmonious opening section of the *Missa* is more remote and less eloquent than the contrapuntal learnedness of Bach. That is particularly true of the actual fugues and fugati themes of the *Missa*. They have a peculiar character of quotation as if they had been built according to models. One could speak of compositional topics analogous to the widespread literary custom in antiquity, or of the treatment of music according to latent patterns through which the objective demand is strengthened. That is very likely responsible for the peculiar incomprehensibility, for the withdrawnness from any primary completion, which is characteristic of these fugue themes and is then also encountered in their further development in the work. The first fugal section of the *Missa*, the "Christe eleison" in B minor, is an example of this and at the same time demonstrates the work's archaicizing tone.

In point of fact, the work stands removed both from all subjective dynamics as well as from expression. The "Credo" hurries over the "Crucifixus"—in Bach this is one of the expressive high points—marking it, however, with a very striking rhythm. Only at the "Et sepultus est," at the end of the Passion itself, does the section reach an expressive concentration in thoughts about the frailty of the human being, however, and

not about the Passion of Christ. But that pathos cannot be attributed to
the contrast of the following "Et resurrexit" which, at an analogous point
in Bach, reaches toward the extreme of that emotion. Only one section,
one which has also become the most famous of the work, is an exception
to this, and that is the "Benedictus," the chief melody of which suspends
stylization. The prelude to this section is a piece of intensely deep harmonious proportions having an equivalent only in the twentieth of the
Diabelli Variations. But the "Benedictus" melody itself, rightly praised as
inspired, resembles the variation theme of the E-flat Major Quartet, op.
127. The entire "Benedictus" reminds one of that custom attributed to
certain artists in the late Middle Ages—those who are said to have included
their own portraits somewhere on their tabernacles for the host so that
they would not be forgotten. But even the "Benedictus" remains true to
the color of the entire work. It is divided into sections by intonations, like
the other sections, and the polyphony always paraphrases the chords figuratively. That in turn is the result of the planned thematic looseness of
the compositional process. It permits the themes to be treated imitatively
yet to be conceived harmoniously in keeping with the basic homophonous
consciousness of Beethoven and his era. The process of archaicizing was
to respect the limits of Beethoven's musical experience. The great exception
is the "Et vitam venturi" of the "Credo" in which Paul Bekker correctly
saw the nucleus of the entire work.[4] It is a polyphonically fully developed
fugue; in certain details, particularly in harmonic twists, it is related to the
finale of the *Hammerklavier* Sonata, leading into a grand development.
Therefore, it is also quite explicit melodically and heightened to an extreme
by its intensity and power. This piece—perhaps the only one which is
entitled to the epithet "explosive"—is the most difficult one in terms of
complexity and performance, but together with the "Benedictus" is the
simplest by virtue of the directness of the effect.

It is no accident that the transcendental moment of the *Missa Solemnis*
does not refer to the mystical content of transubstantiation but to the hope
of eternal life for humanity. The enigma of the *Missa Solemnis* is the tie
between an archaism which mercilessly sacrifices all Beethoven's conquests
and a human tone which appears to mock precisely this archaism. That
enigma—the combination of the idea of the human with a somber aversion
to expression—can perhaps be deciphered by assuming that there is in the
Missa a tangible taboo which determines its reception—a taboo about the
negativity of existence, derived from Beethoven's despairing will to survive. The *Missa* is expressive wherever it addresses or literally conjures up
salvation. It usually cuts off that expression wherever evil and death dom-

inate in the text of the mass, and precisely through this suppression the *Missa* demonstrates the gradually dawning superior power of the negative; despair and yet anxiety of having that despair become manifest. The "Dona nobis pacem" assumes in a certain sense the burden of the "Crucifixus." The expressive potential is accordingly held back. The dissonant parts are only rarely the bearers of this expression (e.g., in the "Sanctus" before the allegro opening of the "Pleni sunt coeli"). The expression clings much more often to the archaic portions, to the scale sequences of the old church modes, to the awe about the past, as if the suffering were to be thrown back into the transitory realm. Not the modern but the ancient is expressive in the *Missa*. The human idea asserts itself in this work, as it did in the works of the later Goethe, only by virtue of convulsive, mythic denial of the mythical abyss. It calls upon positive religion for help whenever the lonely subject no longer trusted that it could of itself, as pure human essence, dispel the forward-surging chaos of conquered and protesting nature. The recourse to mention of Beethoven's subjective piety as an explanation of the fact that the composer, emancipated to the extreme and self-reliant, tended toward traditional form, is as unsatisfying as the opposite extreme found in the academic sphere. There the explanation for this which is offered claims that his religiosity in this work, which subjects itself with zealous discipline to the liturgical purpose, extends beyond dogma to a kind of universal religiosity. The claim, therefore, is made that his is a mass for Unitarians. But confessions or announcements of subjective piety in relation to Christology have been repressed by the work. In the section where the liturgy dictates unavoidably the "I believe," Beethoven, according to Steuermann's[5] astonishing observation, betrayed the opposite of such certainty by having the fugue theme repeat the word Credo as if the isolated man had to assure himself and others of his actual belief by this frequent repetition. The religiosity of the *Missa*, if one can speak unconditionally of such a thing, is neither that of one secure in belief nor that of a world religion of such an idealistic nature that it would require no effort of its adherent to believe in it. Expressed in more modern terms, it is a matter for Beethoven of whether ontology, the objective intellectual organization of existence, is still possible. It is a question of whether the musical salvation of such ontology in the realm of subjectivism and the return to the liturgy is intended to effect this salvation in a manner paralleled only in Kant's evocation of the ideas of God, Freedom, and Immortality. In its aesthetic form the work asks what and how one may sing of the absolute without deceit, and because of this, there occurs that compression which alienates it and causes it to approach incomprehensibility.

This is so perhaps because the question which it asks itself refuses even musically the valid answer. The subject then remains exiled in its finiteness. The objective cosmos can no longer be imagined as an obligatory construct. Thus the *Missa* balances on point of indifference which approaches nothingness.

Its humanistic aspect is defined by the plenitude of chords in the "Kyrie" and extends to the construction of the concluding section, the "Agnus Dei," which prefigures the "Dona nobis pacem," the plea for inner and outer peace. Beethoven superscribed the section with the equivalent German words, and the piece once more breaks out expressively after the threat of war allegorically presented by tympani and trumpets. Already at the "Et homo factus est," the music begins to warm as if breathed upon. But these are the exceptions. Most of the time, despite stylization, the work proceeds in tone and style back toward something unexpressed, undefined. This aspect, resulting from the mutually contradictory forces in the work, is perhaps the one which interferes most with its comprehension. Having been conceived in a flat and undynamic manner, the *Missa* is not arranged according to pre-classical "terraces." In fact, it often erases even the slightest contours. Short inserts frequently do not converge into the whole nor do they stand on their own; rather they rely upon their proportions to other parts. The style is contrary to the spirit of the sonata and yet not as much traditionally ecclesiastical as secular in a rudimentary ecclesiastical language dredged up from memory. The relationship to this language is as deflected as it is to Beethoven's own style. It is distantly analogous to the position of the Eighth Symphony with regard to Haydn and Mozart. Except in the "Et vitam venturi" fugue, even the fugue sections are not genuinely polyphonic but are also in no measure homophonously melodious in the manner of the nineteenth century. While the category of totality, which in Beethoven's works is always the major one, results in other works from the internal development of the individual parts, it is retained in the *Missa* only at the price of a kind of leveling. The omnipresent stylization principle no longer tolerates anything which is truly unique and whittles the character of the work down to the level of the scholastic. These motifs and themes resist being named. The lack of dialectical contrasts, which are replaced by the mere opposition of closed phrases, weakens at times the totality. That is particularly obvious in conclusions of movements. Because no direction is traversed, because no individual resistance has been overcome, the trace of the accidental is carried over to the entire work itself, and the phrases, which no longer terminate in a specific goal prescribed by the thrust of the particular, frequently end exhausted; they cease without achieving the security of a conclusion. Despite an external manifestation of powerfulness, all this nevertheless causes a feeling of mediation to prevail, a feeling which is at an equal distance both from a liturgical connection and from compositional fantasy. It rather brings about that enigmatic quality which at times, as in the brief allegro and presto sections of the "Agnus," borders on the absurd.

After all that has been written above, it might appear that the *Missa*, characterized in all its uniqueness, could now be understood. But the dark quality of the work, perceived as such, does not brighten without further analysis. To understand that one does not understand is the first step toward understanding but is not understanding itself. The above-mentioned characteristics of the work can be confirmed by listening to it, and the attention which is concentrated on those characteristics may prevent a disoriented listening, but by themselves they do not allow the ear spontaneously to perceive a musical purpose or meaning in the *Missa*. If it exists at all, such a meaning lies precisely in the resistance to such spontaneity. This much at least is certain: the alienating aspects of the work do not disappear in the presence of the comfortable formula which asserts that the autonomous fantasy of the composer chose a heteronomous form removed from his will and fantasy, and that the specific development of his music had thereby been hindered. For it would seem apparent that Beethoven did not try in the *Missa* to legitimize himself in a genre not familiar to him as well as in his "actual" works. This kind of legitimation has been attempted before in the history of music. But in Beethoven's case, there was an attempt not to overburden that unfamiliar genre. Instead, each measure of the work as well as the length of the process of composition—unusual for Beethoven—shows the most insistent effort on the composer's part. But the effort is not, as in his other works, directed at the accomplishment of the subjective intention, but rather at its exclusion. The *Missa Solemnis* is a work of such exclusion, of permanent renunciation. It is already to be counted among those efforts of the later bourgeois spirit which no longer hope to conceive and form in any concrete manner the universally human, but which strive instead to accomplish this end through abstraction, through the process of exclusion of the accidental by means of maintaining a firm grasp on a universal which had gone astray in the reconciliation with the particular. The metaphysical truth in this work becomes a residue, as in Kantian philosophy the contentless simplicity of the pure "I think." This residual nature of truth, the rejection of the permeation of the particular, condemns the *Missa Solemnis* not merely to being enigmatic, but stamps it in a principal sense with the mark of impotence. It is the impotence not merely of the mightiest composer but of an historical position of the intellect which, of whatever it dares write here, can speak no longer or not yet.

But what compelled Beethoven, that immeasurably deep human being in whom the power of subjective creation rose to the hubris of the human being as the creator to the opposite of all this, to self-limitation? It was certainly not the psychology of this man who could traverse at one and the same time the composition of the *Missa* and the composition of works entirely its opposite. It was rather a pressure in the thing itself, which Beethoven, resisting to be sure to the last, obeyed and obeyed with all his energy. Here we find something common to both the *Missa* and to the last quartets in their intellectual structuring. They share a common avoidance. The musical experience of the late Beethoven must have become mistrustful of the unity of subjectivity and objectivity, the roundness of symphonic successes, the totality emerging from the movement of all the parts; in short, of everything that gave authenticity up to now to the works of his middle period. He exposed the classical as classicizing. He rejected the affirmative, that which uncritically endorsed Being in the idea of the classically symphonic. He rejected that trait which Georgiades in his article on the finale of the *Jupiter* Symphony called ceremonial.[6] He must have felt the untruth in the highest demand of classical music, that untruth which asserts that the essence of the contradictory motion of all the parts which disappears in that essence is itself the positive, the affirmative. At this moment he transcended the bourgeois spirit whose highest musical manifestation was his own work. Something in his own genius, the deepest part of it, refused to reconcile in a single image what is not reconciled. Musically this may have become concretized in a greater resistance to filigreed structure and the principle of development. It is related to the hostility which developed poetic sensibility had early seized upon in Germany toward dramatic complexity and intrigue. It is a sublimely plebeian hostility, inimical to all that is aristocratic and it was Beethoven who for the first time imbued German music with this feeling. Intrigue in the theater had always had something foolish about it. Its activity seemed to emanate from above, from the author and his idea, and was never motivated from below, from out of the characters themselves. The activity of the thematic work may have sounded to Beethoven's inner ear like the machinations of the courtiers in Schiller's plays, of costumed wives and broken jewel cases, and stolen letters. There is something realistic, in a true meaning of that word, in Beethoven which is not satisfied with conflicts so obviously contrived, with manipulated antitheses which all classicism creates and which are supposed to transcend all details but which instead are thrust upon those details as if by decree. Marks of this arbitrariness can be found in the decisive phrases of the developments in even the Ninth Symphony. The late Beethoven's demand for truth rejects the illusory appearance of the unity of subjective and objective, a concept practically at one with the classicist idea. A polarization results. Unity transcends into the fragmentary. In the last quartets this takes place by means of the rough, unmediated juxtaposition of callow aphoristic motifs and polyphonic complexes. The gap between both becomes obvious and makes the impossibility of aesthetic harmony into the aesthetic content of the work; makes failure in a highest sense a measure of success. In its way even the *Missa* sacrifices the idea of synthesis. But in so far as it refuses the subject, the listener, entry or access to the music and the subject or listener is no longer secure in the objectivity of the form and cannot produce this form unbroken out of himself, it is prepared now to pay for its human universality by having the individual soul be silent, perhaps already submissive. That, and not the concession to ecclesiastical tradition or the will to please Archduke Rudolf, his pupil, may lead to an explanation of the *Missa Solemnis*. The autonomous subject, that subject which otherwise cannot know itself capable of objectivity, secedes from freedom to heteronomy. Pseudo morphosis to an alienated form, at one with the expression of alienation itself, is supposed to accomplish what otherwise would be incapable of accomplishment. The composer experiments with strict style because formal bourgeois freedom is not sufficient as a stylization principle. The composition unremittingly controls whatever is to be filled out by the subject under such externally dictated stylization principles. Not only is each motion which opposes this principle subjected to rigorous criticism, but each more concrete version of the objectivity itself, which degrades it to romantic fiction, is also so criticized, and either as a skeleton, real, tangible, or concrete it nonetheless disappears into that fiction. This dual criticism, a kind of permanent selection process, imposes upon the *Missa* its remote silhouette-like character. It brings the work despite its full resonance into such a rigorous contradiction to sensuous appearance as in the ascetic last quartets. The aesthetically fragile in the *Missa Solemnis*, the denial of conspicuous organization in favor of an almost cuttingly strict question as to what is at all still possible, corresponds in its deceptively closed surface to the open fractures which the last quartets demonstrate. The tendency to an archaicization which here is still tempered, is shared by the *Missa* with the late style of almost all great composers from Bach to Schoenberg. They have all, as exponents of the bourgeois spirit, reached the limits of that spirit without, however, in the bourgeois world ever being able to climb beyond it on their own. All of them had to dredge up the past in the anguish of the present as sacrifices to the future. Whether this sacrifice was fruitful in Beethoven's case, whether the essence of that which was left out is really the cipher of a realized cosmos, or whether as in the later attempts to reconstruct objectivity, the *Missa* already failed, all this can be judged only if historical-philosophical reflection on the structure of the work were to penetrate even into the innermost compositional cells. The fact that today, after the developmental principle has been driven to its historical conclusion and has lost its meaningfulness, composing sees itself obliged to segmentation of parts, to articulations restricted by fields without any thought given to the methodology of the *Missa*'s composition, encourages us to take Beethoven's plea in the greatest of his works for more than merely a plea.

(1959; GS, vol. 17, pp. 145–61)

Translated by Duncan Smith; modified by Richard Leppert

NOTES BY RICHARD LEPPERT

1. Clemens Brentano (1778–1842), German poet, novelist, and dramatist, helped initiate the Heidelberg Romantic school which promoted folklore and history. His sister, and friend of Goethe, was Bettina von Arnim. With Achim von Arnim he edited *Des Knaben Wunderhorn* (1805–08), a collection of German folk poetry, which later served as the textual source for numerous lieder set by composers from Schubert to Anton Webern, those by Mahler being the most famous. Georg Büchner (1813–1837), proto-expressionist dramatist, wrote only three plays, including *Woyzeck* (unfinished; first published only in 1879), the source for Berg's opera. His other two plays were *Dantons Tod* (1835) and *Leonce und Lena* (1836).

2. The Cotta Firm was a prominent German publishing house first established in the second half of the seventeenth century. The firm reached its apogee under Johann Friedrich Cotta (1764–1832), who published Fichte, Goethe, Hegel, Herder, Kleist, Jean Paul, A. W. Schlegel, Tieck, and Wieland. In 1798 Cotta established the *Allgemeine Zeitung*, the leading German newspaper of the nineteenth century. (In the course of the century the paper's offices moved from Tübingen to Stuttgart, Ulm, Augsburg, and, finally, Munich.)

3. Rudolf Stephan, *Music*, vol. 5 of *Das Fischer Lexikon: Enzyklopädie des Wissens* (Frankfurt am Main: Fischer Verlag, 1957); available in English in an expanded version: *Music A to Z*, ed. Jack Sacher, trans. Mieczyslaw Kolinski et al. (New York: Grosset and Dunlap, 1963); see p. 156: "The form of the Mass has

been greatly expanded, chiefly in the contrapuntal passages; the instrumental writing is considerably intensified, and the technical difficulties for both singers and instrumentalists are very much more severe. . . . [The *Missa* is] outstanding for [its] extremely ingenious thematic elaboration."

4. See Paul Bekker, *Beethoven,* trans. M. M. Bozman (London: J. M. Dent and Sons, 1932), p. 274: "The finale of this 'Divine Heroic Symphony' reaches its climax in the *Et vitam venturi.* . . . It is perhaps the climax of the whole tremendous *Missa solemnis.*"

5. Concerning Steuermann, see p. 159 n.3.

6. I have not located any essay concerning the finale of the *Jupiter* Symphony by Thrasybulos Georgiades.

Wagner's Relevance for Today

Of the countless aspects with which Wagner's work presents us, I select one at random, as is unavoidable for the lecture form: the question of Wagner's relevance for today, of the perspective of present-day consciousness toward his work—assuming that one can speak generally of such a perspective.[1] What is meant is advanced consciousness: consciousness that is equal to the Wagnerian oeuvre and that itself occupies an advanced standpoint in its development. Almost thirty years ago I wrote a book, *In Search of Wagner*, of which four chapters appeared in the *Zeitschrift für Sozialforschung* in 1939. The entire book did not appear until much later, in 1952, shortly after my return to Germany. Today I would formulate many things in the book differently. Its central problem, that of the relation between societal aspects on the one hand and compositional and aesthetic aspects on the other, might have to be argued more profoundly within the subject matter than it was then. But I am not distancing myself from the book, nor am I abandoning the conception. With regard to Wagner the situation has changed generally. Therefore, I would like to present—not as a revision of what I once thought, but as a way of taking into account what has newly come to our attention about Wagner—some divergences from the old text.

We have gained distance over the past thirty years. Wagner no longer represents, as he did in my youth, the world of one's parents, but that of one's grandparents instead. A rather commonplace symptom: I can still remember quite well from my childhood how my mother lamented the demise of Italian vocal art that was caused by the Wagnerian style of singing. Today that style is itself beginning to die out; it is exceedingly difficult to locate any singers who are up to it. The well-known and hypocritically criticized system of guest singers, by which a handful of the most famous Wagner singers are lent around, so to speak, from one new production to the next, is not just an aberration. The opera is beginning to regress to precisely that phase that had shown itself, in light of Wagner, to be outdated. Wagner no longer possesses the boundless authority of the earlier time. But what rose up against that authority was not so much a critically interventionary consciousness, in disagreement with the triumphal lord, as a reactive one: the ambivalence one feels toward a formerly beloved object that must now be consigned to the past, whatever the cost. At any rate, we have gained much freedom toward Wagner as an object of consideration: the affective tie to him has loosened.

If, thanks to this freedom, I may now make some comments about the historical changes in the attitude toward Wagner's art, I cannot ignore the political aspect. Too much catastrophe has been visited on living beings for a consideration that purports to be purely aesthetic to close its eyes to it. Yet the position of consciousness toward Wagner may also change politically. The form of nationalism that he embodied, especially in his work, exploded into National Socialism, which could draw on him, via Chamberlain and Rosenberg,[2] for its rationalization. With the integration of nations into blocs this is no longer so immediately threatening; therefore it also begins to recede in the work. However, one must not overestimate this. As the National Socialist potential continues to smolder within the German reality, now as then, so it is still present in Wagner. This begins to touch on the most serious difficulty he affords for present-day consciousness. The stormy applause that one may still encounter following a performance of, say, *Die Meistersinger,* the self-affirmation of the public, which it hears from within Wagner's music, still has something about it of the old virulent evil; the question of whether and how Wagner should be performed can be separated only wrenchingly from the acknowledgment of such demagogy. At an earlier time I attempted to localize this demagogy precisely in the purely musical-aesthetic form. But, if I am allowed to express myself so personally, perhaps my criticism has now earned me the right to emphasize what has outlasted it. My own experience with Wagner does not exhaust itself in the political content, as unredeemable as the latter is, and I often have the impression that in laying it bare I have cleared away one level only to see another emerge from underneath, one, admittedly, that I was by no means uncovering for the first time. At any rate, the private objections to Wagner's person and way of life that are still all the rage have something unspeakably subaltern about them; anyone who drags them out gets sweaty hands. If I, too, previously included his person among the subjects under discussion, it was because I was thinking of his social character—the private individual as the exponent and locus of social tendencies—not of the individual in his psychological arbitrariness, upon whom so many people imagine they are qualified to pass judgment. If the connection is not made between the power of artistic production that was concentrated in him and the society, whatever accusations are made against him are pure philistinism, not far removed from the contemptible genre of fictionalized biographies. It is well to remind ourselves, as a corrective, of the great biography by Newman[3]—anything but semi-official—which justifiably emphasized how dishonest was the indignation over Wagner's extravagance, for example, in view of the fact that during all the years he spent in emigration the theaters earned a fortune at his expense, while he had to do without.

The merely aesthetic anti-Wagnerianism rode the tide of the so-called neo-classical movement—politically not at all progressive—which is linked primarily to the name of Igor Stravinsky. This movement is not only chronologically passé; it also suffers from internal exhaustion. As the perceptible sign of its capitulation, the late Stravinsky himself made use of the very technique against which his movement had originally honed its polemical edge: that of the Schoenberg School. This has to do not only with the mood of the times, but also with the deficiency that is intrinsic to neo-classicism; its historical impossibility becomes a compositional defect. The tendency that is now emerging in opposition to neo-classicism, and exposing by contrast the decorative weakness that is implicit in the latter, is producing many things that have more to do with Wagner than with those individuals who for the last thirty or forty years have enjoyed playing the role of his opponents. The Second Vienna School, that of Arnold Schoenberg, which exercises a decisive influence on the most recent contemporary music, took Wagner as its immediate point of departure. This was precisely one of the things people used to like to criticize in the very early Schoenberg as a cheap way of discrediting the mature musician.

But what has changed about Wagner, in the interim, is not merely his impact on others, but his work itself, in itself. This is what forms the basis of his relevance; not some posthumous second triumph or the well-justified defeat of the neo-baroque. As spiritual entities, works of art are not complete in themselves. They create a magnetic field of all possible intentions and forces, of inner tendencies and countervailing ones, of successful and necessarily unsuccessful elements. Objectively, new layers are constantly detaching themselves, emerging from within; others grow irrelevant and die off. One relates to a work of art not merely, as is often said, by adapting it to fit a new situation, but rather by deciphering within it things to which one has a historically different reaction. The position of consciousness toward Wagner that I experience as my own whenever I encounter him, and which is not only mine, is even more deserving of the appellation "ambivalent" than the earlier position—an oscillation between attraction and repulsion. This only points back to the Janus-like character of the work itself. Undoubtedly, every art of significance exhibits something like this, Wagner's especially. As progressive and regressive traits are intertwined in his work, so also in his reception. After what has occurred, it is self-evident that one assumes a defensive posture toward him politically. This was true even beforehand and has remained so in view of the possibility of a reawakening of the powers that, like their patron goddess Erda, should better have gone on sleeping. In this regard, reality takes precedence over art. Still open is the question of how the appropriate defensiveness relates to the possibility of performing Wagner. One cannot, by the way—and here I touch on something central—simply imagine that it is possible to separate out the ideological element in Wagner and hold on to pure art as a kind of purified substrate. For the demagogic, the proselytizing, the collective-narcissistic gesture reaches right into the inner complexion of his music; here the suspect element is amalgamated with its opposite. But on the other hand—and this is a part of the ambivalence of the position of consciousness—among those resisting Wagner we find all those individuals, even today, who have simply not kept up musically. Among them is his greatest critic, Nietzsche. The anti-Wagnerian movement, the first large-scale incidence of *ressentiment* against modern art in Germany, has formed a fatal alliance with folk music (so-called) and young people's music, devotees of recorders and the like; their preferred tactic has been to compare him unfavorably with newly unearthed composers like Heinrich Schütz and to mobilize against him forces that would counter his highly differentiated and complex art with stupefaction. There is something like a right-wing, petit bourgeois opposition to Wagner. It may be that he was resisted by a good bourgeois element, namely, insistence on the responsibility and autonomy of the individual, but also by a bad one, a stuffy and dense narrow-mindedness to which Wagner is unalterably opposed. His music is free erotically to a degree shared by very few other things that were ever admitted into the German pantheon. Orthodox opinion, very early on, responded to this aspect of Wagner by committing the sin of self-righteous purity.

Ambivalence is a relation toward something one has not mastered; one behaves ambivalently toward a thing with which one has not come to terms. In response to this, the first task at hand would be, quite simply, to experience the Wagnerian work fully—something that to this day, despite all the external successes, has not been accomplished. *Tristan, Parsifal,* the most significant elements of the *Ring* are always more praised than truly appreciated. It is grotesque that in the *Ring,* then as now, *Die Walküre* still plays the most prominent role, on account of such selections as "Winterstürme wichen dem Wonnemond," or Wotan's farewell and the magic fire—in other words, on account of what in Vienna are called *Stückerl,* or little numbers. As such, they fly in the face of the Wagnerian idea. The incomparably greater architecture of *Siegfried,* in contrast, has never quite found its way into the public consciousness. At best, the opera-going public suffers through it as a cultural monument. The works of Wagner that have failed to win the appreciation of the public are precisely the most modern ones, those the most boldly progressive in technique and therefore the farthest removed from convention. Their modernity should not be misconceived as superficial, as a matter of the means they employ, simply because they make greater use of dissonances, enharmonic and chromatic elements, than the others. Wagnerian modernity is of a different order; it towers decisively over everything it leaves in its wake. Wagner is the first case of uncompromising musical nominalism, if I may use the philosophical term: his work is the first in which the primacy of the individual work of art and, within the work, the primacy of the figure in its concrete, elaborated reality, are established fundamentally over any kind of scheme or externally imposed form. He was the first to draw the consequences from the contradiction between traditional forms, indeed the traditional formal language of music as a whole, and the concrete artistic tasks at hand. The contradiction had already made itself felt, rumblingly, in Beethoven, and in essential ways generated his late style. Wagner, then, realized without reservation that the binding, truly general character of musical works of art is to be found, if at all, only through the medium of their particularity and concretion, and not by recourse to any kind of general types. Therefore, contrary to the opinion of the mass-distributed book on Wagner by Hans Gál,[4] Wagner's criticism of the opera carries very great weight, both theoretically and artistically. It must not be trivialized by the simplistic assertion that Wagner was just another opera composer, basically no different from others, who had come up with some secondary theories to use for his private propagandistic purposes. His verdict that opera was childish, his desire that music should finally come of age, cannot be appealed. Opera, as a form, is something historically emergent and transitory. Merely to locate Wagner's place within the genre is to deny the dynamic that is inherent in the history of this form. It is no accident that number operas, when they occur today, as in the *Rake* of Stravinsky, are possible only in a refracted mode, as stylization. Even anti-Wagnerians who return, in this manner, to the number operas recognize or acknowledge, in the irony with which they resurrect the numbers and set pieces, that the verdict Wagner imposed on such categories remains in force. He clearly faced the contradiction between the general and the particular in music, which until then had been crystallizing in mere unconsciousness, and his *ingenium* made its incorruptible decision that nothing general should exist except in the extreme of particularity.

This, however, touches not only the form but also the content of Wagner's art. In him, the artistic consciousness of an antagonistic, internally contradictory world was radicalized. The traditional forms are as poorly adapted to this artistic consciousness as fossilized relations are to critical insight. In this sense, what he did was productive. More than that. In the introduction to Hegel's philosophy of history, which has become popular under the title *Reason in History*,[5] I found this sentence: "Mere desire, the wildness and brutality of the will, has no place in the theater and the sphere of world history." This theorem of Hegel's, who was not only aesthetically but also philosophically a classicist, is one to which Wagner did not adhere. In this, Wagner, who in his youth, before he converted to the ideas of Schopenhauer, is known to have been decisively influenced by Feuerbach, was quite the revolutionary Young Hegelian. His music shudders with the unrelieved violence that lives on today in the world order. One can raise all imaginable sorts of objections to the Wagnerian mythology, exposing it as cheap and phony, as a romanticism of false beards and bull's-eye windows. Nevertheless, in comparison to all more moderate, detachedly realistic or classicist art, his work—especially the *Ring*—retains its decisive truth in this mythological moment: that in it violence breaks through as the same law that it was in the prehistoric world. In these thoroughly modern works, prehistory persists as modernity itself. This splinters the façade of the bourgeois surface, and through the cracks there shines enough of what has only now become fully evolved and recognizable to suffice as proof of Wagner's relevance for today. Admittedly, his gesture, the thing his music is arguing for—and Wagner's music, not merely his texts, is always arguing for something—is a gesture in favor of mythology. He becomes, one might say, an advocate of violence, just as his principal work glorifies Siegfried, the man of violence. But when, in his work, violence expresses itself in pure form, unobscured, in all its terror and entrapment, then the work, despite its mythologizing tendency, is an indictment of myth, willingly or not. This is shown by Siegmund's indescribable emigré-music in the opening passages of the second act of *Die Walküre*. Richard Strauss is the source of the divinatory statement that Wagner strove to deliver us from myth by means of the leitmotif. One might conclude from this that the leitmotif—quasi-rational, identifying, unity-creating—brings to a halt the blind, diffuse, and deadly ambiguity of myth, which Wagner's surging sound reproduces. Through self-consciousness, myth becomes something qualitatively different; the imaginative recollection of destruction marks its boundary.

That Wagner makes the case for myth, but accuses it through his creation, may provide the key to his dual character. His immediate relevance for today is not of the species of merely artistic renaissances. It approaches us from the vicinity of something unfinished, like many things from the nineteenth century, a prime example being Ibsen. This can be illustrated by a series of examples, several of which I shall adduce. First, Wagnerian harmony. Gál's book denies its relationship to modern harmony, to atonality, in stark contradiction to the fact that modern harmony was developed by Schoenberg, after *Verklärte Nacht*, as a continuation of Wagner's. It is self-evident that Wagner was not atonal, and it would never have occurred to me to assert anything of the kind. All the tones and their combinations, even at their most daring, for example in *Tristan* and *Parsifal*, can be explained in accordance with the traditional teachings of harmony. At issue is a tendency, a potential—not what one finds literally in the notes, but what they tend toward—and this, indeed, has decisively to do with atonality. The preponderance of each particular harmonic event over harmonic reference points, over triads and seventh chords, presages what will later come into its own as a consistent atonality that completely does away with the reference points. In Wagner dissonance preponderates qualitatively, if not yet quantitatively. It has more power, more substantiality than consonance, and this points compellingly in the direction of the new music. On various occasions, Heinrich Schenker, in his books, accused Wagner, whom he could scarcely abide, of having destroyed the *Urlinie*, the basic line, despite his use of correct harmonic procedures. Schenker, in his odd terminology, means only that the skeletal structure of the entire musical progression along orderly steps within the usual functional harmony of thorough-bass and corresponding melody is lacking. The observation is correct, but Schenker's emphasis is wrong. As a retrograde proponent of the power of skeletons, of abstract generalities in music, he failed to hear precisely in the supposed destruction, the emancipation of music from its merely skeletal, abstract organization toward an organization located in its specific forms, the irresistibly new element that was the precondition of everything that was to come. The feeling of leaving solid ground behind, of drifting into uncertainty, is precisely what is exciting and also compelling about the experience of Wagnerian music. Its innermost composition, the thing one might, by analogy to painting, call its *peinture*, can in fact be apprehended only by an ear that is willing to cast itself, as the music does, into uncertainty. Here we may state that what is relevant for today is precisely what went unrecognized then and was therefore neither understood nor appreciated.

I would like to elaborate on this principle by means of a technical detail; for it is impossible to speak—rather than gossip—about artistic phenomena if one does not at least provide a perspective on their concrete technical complexion. It has become customary to emphasize the principle of the sequence in the mature works of Wagner; I myself did so at one time. By sequence is meant the repetition of abbreviated motifs—in Wagner the leitmotifs—on a higher level, generally with dynamic, intensifying effect. The spinning out of the music, its essential fiber or texture, thus works more or less with the repetition of given elements, in contrast to the essential technique of Viennese classicism, which, borrowing Arnold Schoenberg's term, can be called the technique of developing variation. But however many sequences there are in Wagner, they by no means represent the sole principle; and above all, they are already varied, frequently and with great subtlety, in themselves. A perfect example would be the famous beginning of *Tristan*, two sequencings of one model. By the third extension of the sequence, it is already varied—minimally, but in a harmonic-modulatory sense decisively—in comparison with the original model, and only thus is it led back to the *forte*-entry in the reformulated dominant of the tonic A minor. The sequence principle in Wagner is by no means a crutch. It follows from the chromaticism, the prevalence of the minor second that pervades the entire musical material, at least in the works of the type to which I am referring. On the one hand, the sequence principle is intended to create the context that has vanished as a result of chromaticism, i.e., the abandonment of articulation by harmonic steps that carry a different weight. But on the other hand—and this shows the close and modern way in which Wagner conforms to his own material—chromaticism itself embodies something not altogether dissimilar to the sequential principle; the repetition of the smallest intervals corresponds to the repetition of individual musical events as they follow each other within the sequence. The identity of the elements in the sequence, which follow one another, is very closely related to the identity of the chromatic steps. Thus even the principle of the sequence is not a mechanical thing, as we musicians

592   /   Composition, Composers, and Works

may conclude all too hastily; it is much more profoundly connected to the problems and tasks of the internal organization of Wagner's music than I was capable of comprehending thirty years ago.

In other of Wagner's works, it is true, things work quite differently; in these—the less chromatic works—the sequential principle plays no central role at all. The understanding of Wagner that is due and would be relevant for today would have to inquire into their structure. In *Die Meistersinger*, extensive musical differentiation is combined with a general absence of chromaticism, and frequently with a deemphasizing of sequences in favor of a colorful variety of individual forms. The continuity is created, over long stretches, by an unconstrained redrawing of the dramatic curve from moment to moment. The intact diatonic tonal structure makes it possible to dispense with surface links. In this way, the music achieves a concreteness of the irregular that traditional music never dreamed of. This would remain prototypical for Schoenberg, for Berg, and for the most recent tendency: the trend toward structures that are free, yet dense. The idea of a unity of constantly changing situations, which in Wagner still oriented itself to the requirements of the dramatic action, has, to this day, not been fully realized. It would provide the ideal model for a truly informal process of composition utilizing characteristic models that would be both differentiated from each other and necessarily complementary. In Wagner, naturally, nothing of the kind is yet present in pure, developed form, nor is it intended. The dramatic action was more important to him than the constructive structure, but the objective tendency toward the latter is unmistakable.

These complicated structural matters, which I have barely touched upon, bring me to the problem of so-called form in Wagner. It would be good to start with a bit of terminological order, without, however, overemphasizing it in a pedantic way. Many musical concepts, including the concept of rhythm, but particularly that of form, are used ambiguously and are often twisted to such a degree that they come to mean everything and nothing. If Wagner did away with given, familiar forms in opera such as the aria, recitative, or ensemble, it does not therefore follow that his music has no form, that it is, as the nineteenth century stridently complained, formless. This objection remains petty and reactionary, even if validated by the authority of Nietzsche. What is true about it is that peculiar sensation of floating—that the music has, so to speak, no solid ground under its feet. In Wagner, form grows aerial roots; he reacted allergically to that element within it that the restorationist language of the twentieth century would call ontological. But music that appears to swing back and forth in the air, as if held in the hand of an invisible puppeteer, has something static about it, just as Wagner's supposedly so dynamic sequential principle terminates in a feeling of eternal sameness. In the most recent music, which draws so near to painting and the graphic arts, the trend toward the static becomes quite marked—here, too, something is fully realized that Wagner had envisioned earlier.

The accusation of formlessness misses the point by confusing everything that is not oriented toward traditional forms with lack of organization. In fact, without following any abstract scheme, Wagner's music is organized, articulated, architectonically thought through in the highest degree. It was the great accomplishment of Alfred Lorenz,[6] who is undeservedly forgotten, to have been the first to see this. To deny that there is a formal problem in Wagner, as Gál does, is simply an expedient way of eliminating, or resolving, the problem by ignoring it. No sooner had the orientation toward given formal norms disappeared than the task of organizing music compellingly in and of itself became inescapable. True, the formal types that Lorenz proposed, the bow or arch form and the concept of the bar[7]—to which he surely gave too much emphasis, even if it is not completely unimportant in Wagner—are themselves much too abstract: mathematical, graphlike outlines that fall short of Wagner's developmental principle and thus of a material theory of musical forms. As a particular case in point, the art of transitions, which Wagner equated with the art of composition, cannot be adequately explained by diagrams. The task of the Wagner interpretation that is needed would be to describe, down to the details, how his forms, without borrowing, express, develop, and create themselves with compelling necessity from within. This occurs perhaps most splendidly in *Siegfried*—an unbroken ascending curve, further articulated so that each of the three acts contains an additional ascent, the strongest of these in the third act: altogether, probably the high point of Wagner's oeuvre. I would like to make the heretical suggestion that someone should attempt a separate production of the third act of *Siegfried* by itself, so that viewers could devote themselves to it with complete concentration; not until then will we be able fully to comprehend the riches it contains.

In connection with form I would like to say a few things about color and orchestration. Wagner's mastery as an orchestrator is unquestioned even by his opponents. The idea of extended instrumentation[8] has long been recognized in Wagner: translating the most delicate network of the composition into a correspondingly delicate network of instrumental colors and clarifying it in the process. The orchestration, the tone colors become a means of making the course of the musical events visible down to its most subtle details. To this extent it already creates form. But this must be further elaborated. Wagner's art of orchestration does not exhaust itself in small-scale effects; it also answers the large-scale formal problem I have described above. Perhaps one can say that whatever Wagner did away with, in terms of general schemes, he replaced with the wholly new, thoroughly individualized dimension he gave to orchestration. Color itself became architectonic. For this, too, *Siegfried* offers perhaps the best example. Even the pitch levels, high and low, are articulated in the course of the music in such a way that in the individual acts, as in the work as a whole, an uplift in the music corresponds to a rise in the pitch level. What Wagner achieves in the differentiation of color through its dissolution into the tiniest elements, he complements by combining the smallest values constructively to create something like integral color. His tendency is to take the tone, once it has been broken down into minimal units, and create great tonal surfaces, like unbroken fields; to take the fragments into which the sword has been shattered, as Siegfried says in the enigmatic sword songs, and forge them back together into great homogeneous units. Only infinitesimally small elements can be combined flawlessly into such wholes. Anyone who is familiar with the formal problems of painting will have no trouble recognizing the relationship this musical duality of differential and integral techniques bears to impressionism. The unbroken tonal surface based on the breaking down of tones is one of the most important characteristics of Wagner's method: the creation of totality by means of its reduction to minute models of the particular, which then, because they approach liminal values, can be combined continuously into one another; indeed, properly speaking, they actually generate the great dense tonal surfaces. This is what lends Wagnerian sound its rounded, enveloping quality, the phenomenon that I have referred to, using a philosophical term, as totality, and that one might, from a technical point of view, better call the tonal surface. No other composer knows it in as unbroken and richly nuanced a way as Wagner. The integral tonal surface, the melding of differentiated tones into fields, is another thing that has attained its first full realization today in the idea of the incorporation of tone into the total musical construction.

Wagner's orchestration also makes evident how many of the prevalent objections against him either always missed the mark or have been rendered obsolete by history. Our parents accused him of being noisy; the complaint, oddly enough, has continued to accompany the history of the development of modern music. As it happens, word has gotten around that the covered orchestra in Bayreuth was hardly meant to encourage noise. But here, too, it would be better to begin at the extreme, with the noise itself, to emphasize the creative brilliance of Wagner's sound in those instances where it stands in opposition to the mean of moderate enjoyment, and simply cannot be listened to with delectation. At times, Wagner mobilizes extremes of loudness. Not often; anyone who knows the scores knows how sparing he is with the *fortissimo*. But when it does turn *fortissimo*, then in fact something happens resembling a protest against the moderate cultural consensus Wagner denounced in the knights of *Tannhäuser* and ridiculed in the guilds of *Die Meistersinger*. Barbarism can no more be equated with loudness, in his music, than the representation of myth can be equated with the direct expression of barbarism. Barbarism ceases to be barbaric through its reflection in great art; it becomes distanced, is even, if you will, criticized. Where Wagner goes to the extreme, it has a precise function: the objectification of the chaotic, undomesticated element that his works confront unreservedly. The violence of Wagnerian sound, where it occurs, is the violence of its content.

Wagner's peculiar transcendence vis-à-vis culture—he always stands simultaneously above and below it—is one of his eminently German characteristics. But anything that has such an integral aesthetic function as the sound described above finds in this its inner justification, becomes intrinsically beautiful. On recent occasions (for example, at a compellingly melodious performance of *Götterdämmerung* by Karajan in Vienna), I have noticed something remarkable: in the final act of the *Ring*, the only passages that seem noisy are those that are not resolved compositionally, in which the musical events do not fully correspond to the volume of sound—such as, for example, the overextended and compositionally uneventful climax of Siegfried's funeral march. The latter would seem altogether problematic; it is not coincidental that it recalls Liszt. The conquest, following Wagner, of extreme positions of musical expression and construction has, as it were, justified his loudness after the fact; it is no accident that works on the threshold of the new music, such as Schoenberg's *Gurrelieder* and Strauss's *Elektra*, with their tendency to triple *fortissimos*, show an affinity to Wagner. At the same time, however, his own art of orchestration is never heavily applied. Everywhere the phrase is transparent, everything can be heard, in contrast to a number of works from Strauss's middle period. If it is true that in Wagner the art of orchestration and tonal color is subordinated to the creation of the compositional fiber, then this implies that its goal is not murkiness or overblown sound but the clear representation of the musical events, which, because they are no longer self-explanatory within an overall scheme, require additional means for their clarification. Only by hearing Wagner from this perspective does one hear him correctly. He is already guided by the instrumentational ideal of clarity, which later led via Mahler to Schoenberg and the new music. It follows from the principle of the tonal realization of the musical structure. The *Siegfried Idyll,* which introduces the themes of the third act in *Siegfried* in a soloistic, chamber music setting, provides the proof by example.

Light is even shed on certain eccentricities of Wagner's composition that arouse displeasure nowadays: for example, the overly long narratives, the tendency toward musical loquaciousness. In view of the difficulty inherent in reducing the rich content of the *Edda*[9] Siegfried narrative to theatrical form, the repetition of things that occurred beforehand and are already known (in narratives like Wotan's lengthy excursus in the second act of *Die Walküre,* or the repetition of long-familiar items in the riddle scene between Wotan and Mime in the first act of *Siegfried*) seem superfluous. Nor can we ignore the bothersome and discomfiting quality of certain long speeches, including Gurnemanz's tale of Amfortas and Klingsor, which are perhaps necessary from a dramatic point of view. There should be no prejudging the question whether contemporary Wagner interpretation should not finally decide to edit passages such as these when the harmonic structure allows it, despite the collective howls of the cultural keepers of the Grail. But if, in the process, such extraordinary things as that speech of Wotan's to Brünnhilde were to be sacrificed to the red pencil, it would only confirm the difficulty of the position of present-day consciousness toward Wagner; namely, that as I have said, what is magnificent in his work cannot be cleanly divided from what is questionable. One can scarcely be had without the other; his truth content and those elements that legitimate criticism has found questionable are mutually interdependent. The uncertainty with which a self-conscious performance practice approaches him is caused, not least of all, by the fact that there is no way around this interweaving of the true and the false in his work. In any case, it was Wagner's profound sense of form that created those narratives. The fundamental conception of the *Ring* is not actually dramatic, but correlative, narrative, like the original from which it was taken. If one wanted to draw out the paradox, one might speak, in regard to the entire *Ring* and other works of the mature Wagner, of epic theater—although the rabid anti-Wagnerian Brecht would not have wanted to hear this and would be at my throat. Wagner's instinct sensed clearly that epics—in which subjectivity, the free individual human being, does not yet exist but arises only as the antithesis to fate—do not permit dramatization in the true sense. In this Wagner was cleverer than Hebbel,[10] who thought himself so much cleverer and was so much better educated. But the epic tendency does not merely follow from the content. One could, after all, object that Attic tragedy also concerned itself with epic materials and that it succeeded in translating them wholly into the dramatic form. The entirety of the *Ring*, which was conceived after all as a *chef d'oeuvre* and which one must begin by accepting as such, has something predecided, predetermined about it—a consequence of the Schopenhauerism in which its entire musical fiber is steeped. Step by step, what was to be expected and cannot happen otherwise is fulfilled. If in Hegel history meant progress in the consciousness of freedom, then in Wagner, who sided with Hegel's antipode, Schopenhauer, the *Ring* was a phenomenology of the spirit as fate. Consequently his work lacks the element of freedom, of openness, that constitutes drama. From Senta's ballad to the great narrative of Gurnemanz, the work is therefore interlarded with reports and ballads, sometimes in the manner of the great lieder art of the earlier nineteenth century. (I note only in passing that so far as I know the extremely productive inquiry into a relationship between Wagner and certain songs of Schubert has not been undertaken.) The narratives signify that what is occurring is reported truthfully, that it already existed as something predetermined. This points once more to the insight that Wagner's music, which—in contrast to traditional music that works with solid, extant forms—defines itself as dynamic, as continually in a state of becoming, ultimately turns static, in the final analysis because its absolute dynamism lacks the other, antithetical element against which it could become genuinely dynamic. One would have some difficulty identifying, in Wagner's music, contrasting themes in the sense of Beethoven. A related element is the music's organization into fields. We know from studying logic that without solidity there can be no dynamics, that where everything flows nothing happens; the peculiar convergence between the philosophy of Heraclitus and that of his antipodes, the Eleatics, speaks to this fact.

In Wagner unceasing change—both an asset and a liability—ends in constant sameness. This is already embodied in his most striking musical material. For chromaticism—the principle par excellence of dynamics, of unceasing transition, of going further—is in itself nonqualitative, undifferentiated. One chromatic step resembles another. To this extent, chromatic music always has an affinity to identity. If a bit of speculation in the mode of the philosophy of history is allowed—and I would be the last to gainsay it—one might go so far as to surmise that Wagner's compositional process prophesied the dawning horror of the transition from a society that had reached the apogee of its dynamism to one that had again turned rigid, become utterly reified: a new feudalism, to use Veblen's term.

Also in this context, I would like to treat another dubious element in Wagner that again substantiates the close relationship between what is inadequate and what is grandiose in his work. I am again thinking of *Götterdämmerung*. It can hardly by denied that its final act is weak, falls short of its subject. Wagner conceives no music of world destruction adequate to the one he prophesies. It falls off, fails to fulfill the expectation of the maximal catastrophe that it has aroused, despite the gruesomeness of passages like Gutrune's scene before the corpse is brought back. Thus, for example, to take only the most obvious example, Brünnhilde's final song is infinitely weaker, somehow fractured, when compared to the fairly analogous one of Isolde. I used to explain this evident weakness as a result of the leitmotif-machine, the necessity of working with the preexisting, decades-old motific material, which the fully developed compositional style of the late Wagner has left far behind. But that is too superficial. The circular, inescapable nature of the conception of the tetralogy—already indicated by the word *ring* in the title—excludes from the start everything qualitatively different, even where it would have been required aesthetically at the critical juncture. Something similar was already going on in the *Meistersinger* quintet, where Wagner's sense of form tells him he needs to break out of the circle, so he launches into an indescribably melodic thought that does not derive from the machinery; however, he does not spin out the new idea in a logical manner, doesn't pursue it along the lines of its dynamic force, but instead busies himself once more with the already rather shopworn themes from the complex surrounding the Prize Song. The same things that I have just described for you a bit sketchily in the third act of *Götterdämmerung* are quite literally valid for great philosophy, specifically Hegel's *Phenomenology of Spirit*, to which I have referred elsewhere. The last chapter of this work is called "Absolute Knowledge." The unwitting reader, who has chewed his way through the *Phenomenology*, hopes that in the end absolute knowledge will actually be revealed in the identity of subject and object, and there he will finally have it. But when one reads the chapter, one is sorely disappointed and, what's more, can imagine the scorn Hegel felt for such extravagant hopes even when kindled by his own philosophy. Absolute knowledge proves to be little more than a kind of recapitulation of the foregoing book; the quintessence of that motion of the spirit in which it purportedly came to itself without the absolute itself ever having been expressed, since, if one follows Hegel, the latter was, in fact, never capable of being expressed as a result. In short, musically speaking, it is a reprise, with the element of disappointment that characterizes all reprises. So, too, in *Götterdämmerung*. The absolute, redemption from myth, even when it takes the form of catastrophe, is possible only as a reprise. Myth is catastrophe in permanence. What does away with it brings it to fulfillment, and death, which is the end of the bad infinite, is at the same time absolute regression.

If I have succeeded in giving at least some sense of the fact that the aesthetic weakness here is bound up with the core conception, which is of something circling within itself, fatefully self-contained, foreclosing the realization of the thing it nonetheless promises, then it is possible to understand why Wagner's so-called aesthetic errors are not correctable at will. It is not an individual weakness of Wagner's that is responsible for them. They can be criticized only by stepping outside the bounds of aesthetics. To talk about errors may sound pedantic, but as soon as one speaks of truth, in regard to artworks of the highest order, one must also speak of error: otherwise one takes them to be nonbinding. Wagner's aesthetic weaknesses spring from the metaphysics of repetition, from the idea that "This is the way things are, and always will be; you don't escape, there is no way to escape." This leads to the problem of performing Wagner today, about which I would like to say a few words at least. The problem is antinomical. What is true of the narrative passages and of the third act of *Götterdämmerung* is true of everything that is hard to bear in Wagner. The problem is deeply embedded in the heart of the thing itself. If one removes the bothersome element, one violates the work, is forced to go beyond it, and with every step one takes this leads to discrepancies, friction, unsatisfying effects. But if one does not remove it, one is not only succumbing to antiquarianism, but is compelled to show all sorts of things— and by things I mean not only lilac bushes,[11] but music, from sequences to entire formal elements—that are no longer possible as they stand. Finally, attempts to flee from such antinomies into the timeless—the idea of which, it is true, is suggested by Wagner's mythology—are hopeless. Everything in Wagner has its temporal core. Like a spider, his mind sits amidst the powerful web of nineteenth-century exchange relationships. Even the subtly seductive Spitzwegian[12] quality of the second act of *Die Meistersinger* has its function within the whole; it belongs to the almost irresistible but contaminated attempt to invent a mythological recent past for the German people, on which they could then become intoxicated. For this reason the surrealistic attempts at a resolution are perhaps adequate after all, despite the outdated character of the surrealism of the '20s and

'30s. They attempt not to mythologize Wagner in the sense of timelessness, but to explode his temporal core, to show Wagner himself as in the
grip of history or, as we nowadays say all too readily, to alienate him. I
like Max Ernst's idea: to have King Ludwig II amusing himself in the cave
of the Venusberg.[13] The latest parodistic and aggressive interpretation of
the second act of *Die Meistersinger* in Bayreuth—I have not seen the
production myself—seems to be in a similar vein. If it is true about Wagner
that no matter what one does, it is wrong, the thing that is still most likely
to help is to force what is false, flawed, antinomical out into the open,
rather than glossing over it and generating a kind of harmony to which
the most profound element in Wagner is antithetical. For that reason, only
experimental solutions are justified today; only what injures the Wagner
orthodoxy is true. The defenders of the Grail shouldn't get so worked up
about it; Wagner's precise instructions exist and will continue to be handed
down for historians. But the rage that is unleashed by such interventions
proves that they strike a nerve, precisely that layer where the question of
Wagner's relevance for today is decided. One should also intervene without
question in conspicuously nationalistic passages like the final speech of
Hans Sachs. In the same way, one should liberate the musical dramas from
the stigma of the disgraceful Jewish caricatures Mime and Beckmesser—
at least through the accents set by the production. If Wagner's work is
truly ambivalent and fractured, then it can be done justice only by a performance practice that takes this into account and realizes the fractures
instead of closing them cosmetically.

It should be asked whether Wagner's relevance for today, as I have
attempted to illuminate it from widely divergent angles, isn't, in the familiar phrase, merely artistic, something that is ultimately confined to
technical matters. The concept that is implied here of a technique separable
from truth content is shallow. But I would like to address the truth content
directly. If there is a formula to be found for it, it would be a music that
is dark despite all its color and that points to the calamitous fate of the
world by representing it. Even the barbaric aspects of Wagner's work are
an expression of this: the culture that is shattered there the way Siegfried
breaks the anvil of Mime's smithy is not yet a culture at all. Truly the
world spirit behaved like the Wagnerian unfolding of total negativity. Even
today there is nothing of more serious concern than this; this is why
Wagner remains a serious matter. This is affirmed, for the last time perhaps, by the profound affinity between the poetic texts—whether or not
one considers them successful—and their compositional realization. Such
affinity has not been achieved by any art in the grand style since then.

Music became specialized, and it is music's curse, from the point of view of the philosophy of history, that the process of specialization cannot be reversed at will, and yet impairs the relevance and authenticity of the resulting works. The fractures in the Wagnerian work are themselves already the consequence of a claim to totality that is not contented with the specialized artwork, in which Wagner, too, participated through technology. His artistry, his craft, those traits that already enchanted Nietzsche, should be held up in contrast to dull handiwork in order that we might again learn everything from them. In Wagner they serve a vision of the whole that criticizes not only the opera of former times, with its division into different jurisdictions, but also society, with its division of labor, its guilds and orders, as it exists down to the present day. When the whole of history is shown as circling within itself, as something within which history has not yet begun, it protests wordlessly against this very fact. His friend Bakunin[14] heard this within him when he listened to the *Holländer* and said: "That was only water, what must this music become when one day it deals with fire!" That Wagner could not succeed equally in the representation of fire is itself a piece of metaphysics; driven by its own metaphysics, his music took itself back into itself. But because it does not, in the end, realize what it has promised, it is therefore fallible, given into our hands incomplete, as something to be advanced, unfinished in itself. It awaits the influence that will advance it to self-realization. This would seem to be its true relevance for our time.

(1963; GS, vol. 16, pp. 543–64)
Translated by Susan H. Gillespie

NOTES BY SUSAN H. GILLESPIE
AND RICHARD LEPPERT [RL]

1. This essay is drawn from a lecture given in September 1963 during the Berliner Festspielwochen.

2. See p. 388 n. 2.

3. Ernest Newman, *The Life of Richard Wagner*, 4 vols. (New York: Alfred A. Knopf, 1933–1947).

4. Hans Gál, *Richard Wagner: Versuch einer Würdigung* (Frankfurt am Main: Fischer, 1963); in English as *Richard Wagner*, trans. Hans-Hubert Shönzeler (New York: Stein and Day, 1976). Gál (1890–1987) was an Austrian composer and teacher.

5. Volume I of Georg Wilhelm Friedrich Hegel's *Vorlesungen über die Philo-sophie der Geschichte* [Lectures on the Philosophy of History] was titled *Die Ver-nunft in der Geschichte: Einleitung in die Philosophie der Weltgeschichte* [Reason in History: Introduction to the Philosophy of World History]. It is not identical

to the compilation published in English as *Reason in History* (New York: Liberal Arts Press, 1953).

6. Alfred Lorenz (1868–1939) is the author of *Das Geheimnis der Form bei Richard Wagner* [The Secret of Form in Richard Wagner], 4 vols. (Berlin: Hesse, 1924–34).

7. Lorenz's term *Bogenform* (bow or arch form) denotes a musical form that is roughly symmetrical, i.e., ABA or ABCBA. The "bar" stanza is the formal strophic design, AAB, based on German medieval *Minnesang*. Lorenz's analysis of the extended use of this form in *Die Meistersinger* was influential in reestablishing its importance for later composers as well.

8. *Ausinstrumentieren*, also translated as "integrated instrumentation."

9. The *Edda* are Old Norse poems assembled in two thirteenth-century collections known as the *Prose* (or *Younger*) *Edda* and the *Poetic* (or *Elder*) *Edda*. The *Poetic Edda*, one of Wagner's narrative sources for the *Ring*, includes the oldest versions of what later became the *Nibelungenlied*. See *The Poetic Edda*, trans. Carolyne Larrington (Oxford: Oxford University Press, 1996). See also W. J. Henderson, *Richard Wagner: His Life and His Dramas*, 2nd ed. rev. (New York: G. P. Putnam's Sons, 1901), pp. 372–77, 384–87. [rl]

10. Christian Friedrich Hebbel (1813–1863), poet and playwright, known for his psychological dramas; Adorno's reference is to Hebbel's *Die Niebelungen Trilogie* (1862): *Der Gehörnte Siegfried, Siegfrieds Tod*, and *Kriemhilds Rache*. See Sten G. Flygt, *Friedrich Hebbel* (New York: Twayne, 1968); and Edna Purdie, *Friedrich Hebbel: A Study of His Life and Work* (London: Oxford University Press, 1932). [rl]

11. A reference to the lilac monologue in the second act of *Die Meistersinger*.

12. Carl Spitzweg (1808–1885) was a German Biedermeier painter specializing in sentimental, as well as humorous, low- and village-life genre subjects. [rl]

13. I have not located any reference to Ludwig II amusing himself in the cave of the Venusberg in Ernst's writing, or in his extremely prolific graphic art, painting, or sculpture. It's possible that Adorno's reference is to a remark made by Ernst in an interview. [rl]

14. Mikhail Aleksandrovich Bakunin (1814–1876), Russian political agitator and anarchist. He spent time in Germany in the 1840s, including in Berlin where he associated with the politically radical Young Hegelians. He was living in Paris at the time of the February 1848 revolution, in which he was directly, if briefly, engaged. He remained a revolutionary throughout his life; he joined the First International, held in Geneva in 1868, though he was expelled in 1872 after a dispute with Marx, with whom he had earlier been on close terms. His friendship with Wagner dates from 1848. See Ernest Newman, *The Life of Richard Wagner, 1848–1860*, vol. 2 (New York: Alfred A. Knopf, 1937), pp. 49–51. [rl]

Mahler Today

The currently dominant consciousness is at odds with Mahler. Twenty
years ago, his symphonic music may have looked like the colossal painting
of a music of the future, larger than the eye of a single bourgeois individual
could behold; like the gamble of a man with an obsessively progressive
program whose aims and accomplishments, in the trendy phrase, did not
coincide. But today we pass hurriedly by his oeuvre, maintaining that we
have long since left it behind us, while in actuality we are only making
haste not to look at it too closely. The musician who was once ridiculed
for using car horns and sirens, like an impudent dadaist, is no longer
objective [sachlich] enough for the most gray-bearded conservatory types,
and every better music history seminar considers itself to be more modern
than he as it recites its concepts of play of movement [Bewegungsspiel]
and process music [Ablaufmusik], of pre-classical and neo-classical polyphony.[1] No romanticism, not even Pfitzner's,[2] has been as adroitly overcome as Mahler's, about which it is not even possible to state with certainty
whether it actually is romantic. The fact that a work has become un-
modern before it was properly modern would, in itself, not be sufficient
proof that people are behaving falsely toward it. But in the profoundly
analogous case of Schoenberg, who was consigned to the future as a lonely
prophet until it was concluded that he had been surpassed as a lonely
artiste, the reactionary trick is very transparent, and suggests that we
should look for related motives in the contemporary mood of opposition
to Mahler. Similarly, whole groups of formulae are common to the fight
against Schoenberg and against Mahler—the Jewish intellectual whose
deracinated intellect ruins oh-so-beneficent Nature; the despoiler of ven-
erably traditional musical goods, which are either turned into banalities or
corroded, pure and simple; the abstract fanatic with the will, discovered by

Riemann, "to accomplish something unheard-of,"[3] who is burning down the lovely greensward all around us, on which everyone else feels so good—Mahler, like Schoenberg, is the butt of all these accusations, as if the radical dialectical rupture of the newer music did not fall between them. But regardless of the state of the unbroken line of defense against the thoroughly different heads of the two Viennese Schools, the wild impact of every Mahler symphony, which immediately compels an audience that is perceptibly distancing itself from *Heldenleben* and *Domestica*;[4] the shock that always emanates anew from Mahler, whereas his contemporaries, without exception, are fatally transparent; the unsolved secret that distances his music compositionally from every other late romantic, *Neudeutsch*,[5] or impressionist work make the fashionable aversion to Mahler objectively incommensurate and reveal its logic, which is contradicted by the real effect, to be purposely ideological. Mahler has not been overcome, he has been *repressed*. The bourgeois music culture of the prewar world has reconstituted itself and strictly rejects everything that is not in keeping with its moderate peacefulness. Everything that does not fit in is regarded as crazy and esoteric, or banal and kitsch. But precisely a situation that would like to bury the explosive productive power of music is ripe to be measured by its extremes. What is decisive today is what occurs above the immanence of musical life, in Schoenberg's sphere, or beneath that immanence in deepest depravity. The genuine significance of Mahler that can be discovered for today lies in the very violence with which he broke out of the same musical space that today wants to forget him. Admittedly, Mahler's breakout from bourgeois musical space is not unambiguous and can be truly understood only from within the dialectical opposition to the thing from which it launched itself; not as flight. Mahler was no Gauguin and did not go looking for Tahiti, although the exoticism of the *Lied von der Erde*, which is so disparate from all earlier Mahler, has a much more real foundation than any inclination toward impressionist values, which have no place in Mahler's compositional development and do not occur even in the *Lied von der Erde*, whose pentatonic structure he handles in the sense of basic constructive forms and renders imperceptible as a stimulant. As the fir trees and stream of the *Lied von der Erde* belong to the landscape of Southern Tyrol, the only song since Schubert to grasp the earth; as even the porcelain glazes *[Lasuren]* it describes could have been mined from the contrast of the red mountains and the dense blue of the sky, whose late-afternoon encounter the brittle china would preserve—so every gaze of Mahler's observing, recognizing music holds fast to the world that he painfully transcends. This says, above all, that Mahler wanted to salvage the integrity *[Geschlossenheit]* of the very music to which he was bidding farewell. Over and over again, people have remarked upon the disproportion that exists in his work between lonely subjectivity and its objective language; have stumbled over the willed simplicity, taken harsh irony and ambivalent sentiment as the stigmata of mannerism. But an art is no more condemned, as a whole, by the concept of mannerism than Mahler is condemned by the psychological evidence of typical formulae, which he developed as vocables of his emotional language. If, perhaps, mannerism always appears in art where the objective images so overwhelm man that his right to form them subjectively declines and he attempts, instead, to hold fast to them through repetition and name-giving, then the conventionally criticized "problematic" of Mahler and all the mannerist elements of his form are based in an objective constellation. His constellation is so constituted that he attempts the salvation of the formal cosmos of Western music by thinking together the ruined fragments of its lowest level and its highest truth contents. For Mahler, the depraved essence underneath the form is the only place where the true images are stored, to which form speaks in vain. He picks them up as one picks up potsherds along the road, their fractured mass reflecting the sun in a way the well-preserved, full soup tureen hardly could. It is not stifled pantheistic love of created beings and Nature, not a romantic return to lost simplicity that is occurring in Mahler's work when it inclines toward lower things. Rather, he is searching for the higher contents in their downward plunge through history in the place where they appear to him here and now. The ruins of moderate, formed musical practice are transparent for him right through to the starry heavens that once shone down upon it. His predilection for Dostoyevsky[6] is grounded, not in a vague, pitying psychological mood, but in the cognition and form of the work. His work is centered on the point of interference *[Indifferenzpunkt]*[7] between the higher and the lower, between theological images and a lost, wholly illusory profanation. He sees their coincidence *[Indifferenz]* in the totality of a closed and embracing work, and in it, precisely, he believes he is preserving the formal immanence of the nineteenth century. He does not set out the extremes in order to construct their common meaning out of the resulting figure; he bends them together violently, so that they penetrate each other. This is what is meant by Mahler's *dynamism*, by the pathos that so roughly injects song and dance and folklore, by the sobbing, unrestrained excess of emotion, by the continually fresh improvisation. The underworld of music is mobilized against the disappearing world of the starry heavens, in order for the latter to be moved and to be a corporeal presence among humankind.

Magnificent paradox of Mahler—the same dynamic that wants to bind the extremes into a formal totality bursts the sphere of art itself, in an unmediated way, and becomes an iconoclasm that wants to inject the vanquished images forcibly into the current reality of humankind. Here the Eighth Symphony is revealed. That you can't build a cathedral without a congregation and with materials that have been completely disqualified—this is something every jackass knows, just as, in Brahms's words, any jackass can hear the similarity between the concluding theme of his First Symphony and that of Beethoven's Ninth—both of which, indeed, were dared for the sake of the same iconoclasm, to which, later, Mahler's breathless symphonic practice is dedicated, down to its last feverish note. But when someone erects a great tent camp of revolt on the place that has been designated for a cathedral, with the same dimensions; when sermon and choir and organ rally the populace to attack, then no architectural police should dare to approach and mount their objections on the grounds of good taste, by order of the building bureau. Mahler's *ecclesia militans* is a salvation army, better than the real thing, not moderated in a petit-bourgeois way, not retrospectively proselytizing, but ready and willing to summon the oppressed into proper battle for the things of which they have been robbed and which they, alone, are still capable of achieving. The language with which the organization and discipline of that army are described is not bad because it is outmoded and overthrown. But because it is outmoded and bad and overthrown, it is given the power of organization and discipline. It is a language not of signs, but of passwords and commands; it is no accident that horn signals are its favorite words. This is how things stand with Mahler's romanticism. With romanticism, in the case of Mahler, we have identified nothing more than when we accuse socialism of romanticism—namely, at best its historical-dialectical origin. But utopia ceases to be romantic as soon as it actually takes the productive forces of the lower [elements] into its power.

It is the task of future formal analyses and most particularly of future performances of Mahler's music to demonstrate all this in the concrete. For Mahler is radically distinguished from romanticism precisely by the fact that his work does not, in place of contents, have free-floating ideologies for which it strives. Instead, what it objectively means is fully realized in the material. It was concealed by the circumstances of the time in which it originally appeared. Schoenberg gave the Mahlerian *expressivo* a magnificent historical–philosophical interpretation, in the broadest sense, right down to the programmatic framework of the symphonies: as a means of making *graspable* the alien things we encounter. So it is indeed. Neither the interpretations of the movements, which are so divergent that in printed program descriptions one can often find those of the Second and Third Symphony reversed, and never quite know when exactly Nature is awakening from its wintry rigidity and what the animals have to say to each other,[8] nor the characterizing phrases indicating the [manner of] musical performance are qualitatively different from the incomparably more important musical markings that are intended to ensure the plasticity and comprehensibility of that performance.[9] Schoenberg's system of indicating the principal and secondary voices, today an index of the strictest construction, is prefigured in Mahler's *hervortretend* [literally, "becoming more prominent"] and *zurücktretend* ["becoming less prominent"]. And comprehensibility is virtually the principle of Mahler's instrumentation, through which it is so sharply differentiated from the more homogeneous and diffuse group sound of late romanticism—especially Strauss. However, it would be a mistake to sever Mahler summarily from romanticism, the way he has been summarily categorized, until now, as belonging to it. He remains dialectically linked to it, after all. His work wants to be understood in layers. The external layer, with which it protected itself and which probably grew to be a part of it from the time of its inception, communicates with romanticism. Those relationships have been explored to excess. Mahler's form results from the contest between his substance and that romantic layer, which for him, at any rate, may perhaps still have meant a guarantee of objectivity, until it finally disintegrated in the face of the terrible seriousness of the last works. As surface, the romantic layer has fallen away for us over time—much as time, after Mahler's death, did for him what he himself intended in the conscious course of his development. Hence for us the relationship between individual theme and symphonic form, the "problem" of Mahler in the ordinary way of thinking about him, already appears much changed. It makes good sense that Mahler's themes are not symphonic themes of the kind whose concept we are accustomed to deriving from Beethoven; that they are not organized in symmetrical relations among motifs. If the objectivity of the symphonic theme in Beethoven was overthrown by the subjectivity of the lied, as we encounter it in Wagner, who tries in vain to objectify the subjectively unique cells of song, without being able to attack their uniqueness, so that he is forced to repeat them as sequences, Mahler takes up this lied-thematic at the point when it can no longer be sustained even in sequences, when it falls out of any formal immanence into the looseness of improvisation. What he finds is an archaic banality; it is located prior to the constitution of the harmonically symmetrical relationships and corrodes them. Mahler's dynamism comes magnificently to the fore in these themes, which remain "open." In other words, neither is the form created out of them through repetitive work with repeated motifs, nor are they statically arrayed alongside each other, as in folk-like efforts. The boundaries that separate them have been removed; one follows the other in continuously fresh production. This by no means signifies that work with motifs has disappeared; on the contrary, Mahler's incommensurable thematic production almost always has its foundation in relations among motifs, which occasionally, in the Sixth Symphony and in the *Lied von der Erde*, become graspable. But the relations among motifs are usually *latent*—are not principles of the architecture but cells from which the totality grows without ever being constructed according to its abstract measure. The principle of basic form as a latent thematic unity that is scarcely ever revealed in the surface context of the whole and only shimmers through occasionally— this constructive principle, which is the first to have truly breached the law of the preexisting formal surface, is already essentially developed in Mahler. It is here, not in harmony, melody, or instrumentation, or even in a legendary ease of understanding that in Mahler finally only exists as a misunderstanding, that his genuine significance for today is to be found. Here, too, is his true point of contact with Schoenberg. Using completely different material, the two composers have developed the same intentions toward formal creation—Mahler with the archaically corroded material of romanticism; Schoenberg with material that is driven forward dialectically; both in protest against the bourgeois symmetry of form, to which they oppose the free contours of the freshly trodden landscape of the imagination. In addition, both share, as a dialectical means of advancing from the preexisting into the untrodden, the *technique of variation*. While in Schoenberg it is an aspect of execution, which gradually subdues the whole form, in Mahler it grows out of song, as a means of strophic monody, but rather quickly erases the boundaries of the stanza and conjoins the thematic complexes, which, like villages, grow together into a big city according to an unknown plan. Mahler's variation is the rule of dynamic improvisation, which cannot be permanently fixed. It draws all formal schemata into itself. In the first movement of the Third Symphony, introduction and exposition are ambiguous in their relationship to each other, and remain so in the double development and recapitulation. In the Fourth Symphony, the recapitulation masks itself in variations behind the development. The Fifth Symphony, by dint of the principle of variation, has two first movements, as it were, and dissolves the symphonic beginning into the side-by-side of two dynamic complexes, which relate to each other like two counterpoints bisected in time. The finale of the Sixth Symphony, perhaps the most powerful formal being in Mahler's realm, finally melts the crust of form, which the first movement had hardened dialectically, as if whole geographic regions were glowing volcanically and their settlements were pitching into each other in a river of fire. The march rhythm becomes the signal of the catastrophe, and the tragic expression of the movement—who will ever forget the sound of the half-note tenth chords that continue the principal theme?—is justified from within the form itself. This is no tale of eternal love and resurrection of an overblown All-Nature, but a tale of the end of the symphonic sonata, or, to call the intentional object by its proper name, the end of the order that bore the sonata. Never, with the possible exception of van Gogh's paintings, has the crisis of the bourgeois world been cast in aesthetic images in a way that does greater justice to the material or is less literary; and never with a greater revolutionary impulse than in this movement. It is the caesura in Mahler's development, and everything that comes after it breaks out of the preestablished musical space. The first movement of the Seventh Symphony answers the finale of the Sixth as if from the other shore of the river that is their common border; over it, swaying, stretch the pontoons for Mahler's dream battalions. From the shore of the Seventh, the archaic world that provided the impulse for the revolt already appears ghostly and insubstantial; hence this symphony, the first unromantic one from Mahler's hand, simultaneously became the first to be officially romantic, with the *ronde* and rondo of the first *Nachtmusik* and the shadows of a scherzo, from which the damned lament of the oboe sounds more terrible than all of romanticism's noble sorrow; its images are lost. Or perhaps not entirely lost. Unfathomable profundity of Mahler, that in the serenade of the second *Nachtmusik* he shyly salvages what has just seemed to sink into bottomless maelstroms; what remains of the dream of romanticism is the fleeting trace that flutters, like a brightly colored pennant, over the uncertain gray of the present.[10] This is the source of the strange organization of hope in the Eighth Symphony, which has its powerful right not as a neo-religious cantata, but rather as an improvisational storming of the trembling transcendental images. This right has been strengthened by the last works, which lay the foundation for the outbreak of hope, the daring "It is accomplished," out of all the heaviness that weighs on the abandoned human individual, who dies unconsoled, without a form to embrace him. The perfected hopelessness of the *Lied von der Erde*, for which nothing remains but the memory of a girl's laughter, is the reality that alone legitimizes the dream, which ascends from uncertainty upward into uncertainty.

It is also our reality. That it rouses itself from the disintegrating dream, not remaining content with intentionless modesty; that it is at once starkly moved and driven to exceed itself—this is what constitutes Mahler's significance for today. It is present in the formal language of our music; truly all of it, for just as it has been begotten by the extremes, so it has its effect in the extremes. If Schoenberg's contents are very closely related to Mahler's, only interpellated in a different language, then Mahler's language, for its part, is located as a medium between the poles of contemporary opera. The ländler scene in *Wozzeck*[11] and "Can't help a dead man" from *Mahagonny*[12] meet in Mahler's murky, dimly lit tone. More important than the recognizable relationships to Mahler's style are the more hidden ones of his compositional method. All contemporary compositional technique lies ready in Mahler's work under the thin cover of the late romantic language of expression. It needs only authentic interpretation to bring it out. Mahler's work is not historical. His musical figure is present among us and his contents should be, too, if people were not anxiously endeavoring to paste over the cracks that cut through the objective world despite all objectivity; their sense becomes legible in Mahler's works.

(1930; GS, vol. 18, pp. 226–34)
Translated by Susan H. Gillespie

NOTES BY RICHARD LEPPERT

1. In M, Adorno explains Mahler's sense of counterpoint in explicit distinction to textbook conservatory models: "By polyphony [Mahler] obviously means the tendency toward chaotic, unorganized sound, the unregulated, fortuitous simultaneity of the 'world,' the echo of which his music, through its artistic organization, seeks to become. What he loved in polyphony was that which gave offense to . . . 'pedantry'" (p. 112; see further to p. 115). It is in this regard that *Bewegungsspiel* is invoked, as opposed to the pejorative invocation of *Ablaufmusik*, that is, a polyphony that is fundamentally technical and unimaginative. The neologism *Ablaufmusik* is difficult to render in English; *Ablauf* means, in addition to process, discharge, drain, and flow.

2. Hans Pfitzner (1869–1949), late-romantic German composer and conductor, chiefly remembered for his opera *Palestrina* (1912–15), which he designated a "musical legend" rather than an opera.

3. Hugo Riemann (1849–1919), German musicologist. Adorno elsewhere cited this phrase (which I have not located in Riemann's writing).

4. Richard Strauss's tone poem *Ein Heldenleben*, op. 43 (1897–98), and his *Symphonia domestica*, op. 53 (1902–03).

5. The so-named late-nineteenth-century New German school included Richard Strauss and Max Reger; Adorno is particularly emphasizing the distinction between Mahler and Strauss. On the same point, see Adorno, "Mahler," QF, pp. 98–99.

6. See p. 617 n. 5.

7. Adorno seems to be alluding here to physics, specifically wave theory. The term *interference* means "the mutual action of two waves or streams of vibration, as of sound, light, etc., in reinforcing or neutralizing each other according to their relative phases on meeting" (*Webster's New World Dictionary of the American Language*, 1964). [translator's note]

8. Adorno is referring to the original and various programs for the Second and Third Symphonies, all of which Mahler eventually discarded. The specific images Adorno invokes, with notable irony, are drawn from the composer's program outlines for the six movements of the Third (e.g., "What the meadow-flowers tell me," and "What the creatures of the forest tell me," for the second and third movements, respectively). However, in his much later Mahler monograph, Adorno takes a different tack with respect to the Third Symphony and its sometime programmatic references to animals and nature. Specifically, Adorno advances an argument, fleshed out in detail in AT, pp. 61–78, concerning the subject's separation from nature and natural beauty, and the desire for reconciliation with the otherness of nature, as with what Adorno names the "animal symbolism" of the Third Symphony's scherzo (M, pp. 8–9): "The music comports itself like animals: as if its empathy with their closed world were meant to mitigate something of the curse of closedness. It confers utterance on the speechless by imitating their ways in sound. . . . Through animals humanity becomes aware of itself as impeded nature and of its activity as deluded natural history." For Mahler, "the animal realm is the human world as it would appear from the standpoint of redemption." This last point was first advanced in DE.

9. By *charakterisierenden Vortragsbezeichnungen* Adorno means those general words or phrases that Mahler used to characterize a movement or section, such as *Kräftig*, or *Lustig im Tempo und keck im Ausdruck*—to cite examples from the Third Symphony; by *musikalischen Bezeichnungen* he means the more specific performance markings for dynamics, accents, etc.

10. The Seventh Symphony is in five movements, the second and fourth of which are marked *Nachtmusik*. Adorno's wry reference to the Seventh being designated "officially romantic" likely stems from the subtitle sometimes attached to the work—and not by Mahler—"Song of the Night," as well as from a suggestion made to Mahler, following the Prague premiere, that the first *Nachtmusik* movement was suggestive of a *Nachtwanderung*, or night walk, a popular topos in romantic poetry. See Constantin Floros, *Gustav Mahler: The Symphonies*, trans. Vernon Wicker (Portland: Amadeus, 1993), p. 198.

11. *Wozzeck*, act 2, scene 4, structured as a scherzo/ländler, the orchestral introduction of which is distinctly Mahler-like. Mahler-like procedures are evident throughout the scene in both the orchestral and vocal writing, and the whole is tinged with irony, notably the stand-out ländler quotations. Adorno comments (M, p. 46): "Berg is the legitimate heir of this spirit; in the *Ländler* in *Wozzeck*, which urges the poor folk into an ungainly, subservient dance, is mingled a clarinet rhythm from the Scherzo of the Fourth Symphony. The prevalent ideology of the true, beautiful, and good, with which Mahler's music first made common cause, is inverted into valid protest. Mahler's humanity is a mass of the disinherited."

12. The line Adorno quotes from Kurt Weill's *Aufstieg und Fall der Stadt Mahagonny* (1930), "Können einem toten Mann nicht helfen," is repeatedly sung during the finale while the city burns amidst social degradation and cynicism, and following the gratuitous execution of Jim Mahoney.

Marginalia on Mahler

On the occasion of the twenty-fifth anniversary of his death,
May 18, 1936

Tombstone inscription
Heart that cannot hold itself
Tear that holds the light
Downfall—thou exaltation—
Burst the stone and the world.

Why Mahler, following those poems by Rückert, wrote the *Kindertoten-lieder*, I understood the first time in my life when someone I loved died.[1] The feeling in them, bent to the breaking point in a powerful bow, out of tenderness for what we hold closest and loss into the greatest distance, does not find its measure in individual misfortune of the sort that consigns children to the dead. Yet the dead may well be our children. The aura of what has not become that encircles those who died young like a halo of apparent happiness does not fade for adults either. But it is not able to enclose their distracted and abandoned life otherwise than by making it smaller. This happens to the dead through memory. It strokes the hair of the helpless, gives sustenance to the destroyed mouth, watches over the sleep of those who will never again awake. As they are defenseless, at the mercy of our memory, so our memory is the only help that is left to them. They pass away into it, and if every deceased person is like someone who was murdered by the living, so he is also like someone whose life they must save, without knowing whether the effort will succeed. The rescue of what is possible, but has not yet been—this is the aim of remembrance. It is the law that is given to the *Lied von der Erde*. When the music of the fourth movement looks back on beauty with a few bars of the clarinets, it is as if through remembrance all the happiness that never was has been preserved in miniature in these measures. The dead are transfigured into children, for whom the possible would still be possible, because they have not been. In the *Kindertotenlieder*, this transfiguration is notated in full. "Often I think they have only gone out."[2] Not because they were children, but because uncomprehending love can only comprehend death as if the last farewell were that of children who will come home again. We can hope for the dead only as if for children.

If we were to risk the attempt to state in a single word the formal law of Mahler's music—that extensive totality which eludes the spell of formula more thoroughly than any other—one would like to call this law the variant. It is as fundamentally different from the variation in the sense of Beethoven, Brahms, or even Schoenberg as Mahler's conjuring gestures are different from every kind of formal immanence. For his variant, unlike the variation, knows no established and formally binding model against which it could test itself by dialectical incursions. Rather, his attempt to break out of the bourgeois musical space is realized technically when he refuses to recognize the theme as objectification, as a musical thing, as it were. It is shattered into fragments, into those banalities that are so aggravating to moderate taste; but the fragments of the object world are hurled into the lava flow of intention, so that they lose whatever form has congealed within. Mahler draws on a musical never-never land—a time when there were not yet any themes as firm possessions. Hence he himself knows no fixed themes; the variant as small divergence and prosaic irregularity lets them all emerge flexibly from each other, disappear into each other. Music as immediacy, prior to any canon of objectification, seeks to produce itself spontaneously. For this reason, it is irresponsible to assign him, stylistically and self-righteously, to the nineteenth century, just because he wrote horn movements and gave some of his earlier pieces explanations with which the works themselves have no more in common than Bach has with Brockes.[3] Admittedly, this historical tendency has its good, i.e., its bad side. For the despised romantic was sufficiently unromantic to undertake the return to immediacy not in the name of the restitution of some long-lost states of being, but with the force of his own state of consciousness. His critique of musical reification is not one that forgets the reality of this reification and sallies forth against it like a Don Quixote in musical costume. His dealings with reified music are strictly spoken, with such strictness that the music bursts asunder. Its fragments and the fragments of the emotions that accompany it are his material, over which symphonic reason rules in a planned and powerful way. To transpose the exploded world of objects, by means of its own productive tendencies, into one that is humanly immediate—that is his will, and the improvisational variant comes closer to an action that is informed by reality, yet ready for change, than the neo-classically total stylistic purpose, which finds it easy enough to negate the whole of existence in order to maintain it more conveniently in its present state. Mahler leaves it where it is, but burns it out from within. Now the old formal walls stand as an allegory not so much of what has been as of what is to come. The Mahler-haters have understood correctly that the falling hammer of the Sixth Symphony is meant for them.

"And sing until the moon shines bright in the black firmament."[4] This is the landscape of the late Mahler. For this firmament has the blackness of lacquered Japanese boxes, with their painted golden moon; a precious, but at the same time an imitated, already all-too-familiar, outworn thing. But the intoxicated singer takes it seriously. He brings it close to his eye—now the sky has the blackness of the end of the world, and the moon shines down like the torch of judgment, close enough to touch, as close as ordinary things used to be. The stumbling singer stretches the goblet of his music toward it. Is this the satanic gesture of a person who has lost hope, is no longer moved by any Spring, and with a final gulp sacrifices all the joy of existence to his own destruction? Or is it the draught of reconciliation, offered by dying Earth herself, who no longer has need of any Spring because her true, winterless time is finally at hand? No one could know the answer. But in Mahler's music both things may be implicit: that as a brittle allegory that overreaches itself, the gesture of final, satanic defiance may signify reconciliation; that for the person who has lost hope, the nearby blaze of destruction may shine like the faraway light of redemption. The fine flakes at the end of the *Lied von der Erde* are equally ambiguous. A lonely soul can freeze to death in them, in a panic, dissolved into pure being; and they can equally well be the blessed whiteness of rapture—snow [as] the ultimate good that remains of existence, linking the redeemed to Being, while striking the window as a starry hope for the living. The elective affinity with Dostoyevsky goes to the heart of it. In Mahler Ivan Karamasov[5] found his music. But it alone is his true language.

An early poem by Werfel contains the word *entlächelnd* [smiling away from].[6] It could have been a fugitive from Mahler's music. For just as here, for once, subjectivity implicitly expects of language something the latter is incapable of giving; as the body of the word is stretched too far and torn, but its tears stand as signs of an intention toward the real that is hostile to language—this is how Mahler's music behaves at every instant. Its banal aspect, from the point of view of content, appears as fragments of the world of musical things. Yet at the same time it is produced by the ego, whose drive to express itself immediately, indeed to reproduce Being, whose documentary will is oblivious to choice and, weary of moderate musical articulation, dares to expect of it so much humane expression that it dissolves and, in the process, becomes something banal. But Mahler is "smiling away" from something in a more precise sense of the word, as well—that of a bafflingly false transcendence. That a worldly gesture like smiling can be intensified to such a degree of infinitude that it seems more than worldly; that with a blasphemous shout it steals the appearance of the supernatural, but that this appearance nevertheless elicits the response "It is accomplished," in which the Eighth Symphony exults with such childlike force—this happens in Mahler's profane sacred music. But when a smile nevertheless flits across a face like a cloud, only to disappear in the distance, leaving clarity behind; then Mahler's music greets the world in passing, airily, as a cloud. "Smiling away" is the gesture of farewell. Every work of Mahler's, from the *Gesellenlieder* [Songs of a Wayfarer] to the Ninth Symphony, is saying farewell. Thus, in the theme of its adagio, the violin climbs into its cloud-heaven with a secondary motif in four steps, each one bigger than a man, in his weakness, could ascend—the greeting of someone who is disappearing. Of someone who is destroyed? Alive? In lieu of an answer, the gesture remains behind, as speechless as a legend. One would need to have the most disbelieving and the most believing ears to interpret it.

Mahler the ambiguous—above the banal themes he sometimes wrote "with parody" and sometimes "without any parody." Where the indication is lacking, exalted reason struggles with the embarrassing question, Did he mean it seriously or not? It is embarrassing because reason thinks it has to worry about remaining serious in the wrong place, while, at the same time, its humor is out of place even where there is actually something to be laughed at. But Mahler's music refuses to answer his question. This means that its banality is parody and seriousness at one and the same time. In banality, the world of things that behaves as if it is eternal, natural, and confirmed succumbs to laughter, and the visible rupture makes it recognizable as artificial, damaged, and shabby. But the rupture, for its part, is quite serious and literal—legible as the trace of man, who, in his vain strivings, has made all this and for whom it has now disintegrated. It is legible as the trace of the damage that can be repaired if only you have pieced the fragments together the right way; of everything that is impoverished and discarded, that has everything to gain and hence, perhaps, will one day inherit everything. Exalted reason is accustomed to call this "literary." But with this we have said as much about Mahler as if we were to call "literary" the grenades that once invaded the secure structure of the cathedral of Reims. Except that Mahler's music serves a different purpose than they did.

Isn't it striking that the people who have so much to say about new "links" of music to the collective, to customary practice, refuse to give their blessing to Mahler's music and in its presence turn into implacable advocates of the very *l'art pour l'art* that they are otherwise so eager to ignore, as they hasten to advance their daily agenda?—While Mahler, to this very day, has remained the only exemplary composer who realistically stands outside the space of aesthetic autonomy, and—what is more—whose music could be used truthfully and by living human beings, not ideological *Wandervögel*?[7] Don't those link-lovers care more about the link *per se* than about the contents on whose behalf the collective is mobilized? Indeed, in their eyes, do not *any* contents appear fundamentally suspect that are more than a fetishization of the link itself? The future fate of Mahler's music will tell us a thing or two about this.

His music is the first to substantiate the recognition that the fate of the world is no longer dependent on the individual; and at the same time it substantiates this as individual recognition and in the emotional categories of the individual human being. This is why it is so easy to insult it by calling it brittle. But its brittleness is "correct false consciousness"; no aesthetic form that is concerned with true humanity and not the fiction of the individual would be able to deny the individual as a stage in history, and any aesthetic form that does so becomes a lie in the process. Mahler's brittleness, however, defines his truth as a historical-philosophical line of demarcation. In the words of the profoundly similar Frank Wedekind,[8] he was not an "art-artist." Rather, the movement of society presented itself to his music in its true sacrifice and concrete measure—the individual drive and its conflicts. The valid evidence for this is the conception of the Mahlerian march, as it already appears, compellingly, in the first movement of the Third Symphony, for example. The march is meant for the collective and for moving in solidarity—but heard from the perspective of the individual. It does not give orders so much as it carries you along; and if it carries along even the meanest things and those that are the most mutilated, it does not itself mutilate. The individual who is carried along is not eliminated. The community of lovers is made available to him. The human being survives in the march on the strength of the variant, the determining asymmetry—this is what makes it so completely impossible to misuse Mahler's music. The men who otherwise were simply forced to die when they fell out of line, the line above Strasbourg's trenches; the nighttime sentry, the [soldier] who is laid to rest in the beauty of the cornets, and the poor little drummer boy—Mahler forms them out of freedom. He promises victory to the losers. All his symphonic music is a reveille *[Rewelge]*.[9] Its hero is the deserter.

Translated by Susan H. Gillespie

(1936; GS, vol. 18, pp. 235–40)

NOTES BY RICHARD LEPPERT

1. Adorno refers to the death the previous year (on 26 June 1935) of his aunt, Agathe Calvelli-Adorno, who had lived with Adorno's parents since Adorno's childhood. He was very close to her.

Friedrich Rückert (1788–1866) is best known as a lyric poet, though he also wrote epic poetry, historical plays, and Aristophanic comedies. He wrote the *Kindertotenlieder* in 1834, following the death of his two children; the poems were published posthumously in 1872. Rückert was also a scholar of several Eastern languages.

2. The opening line from the fourth of the five *Kindertotenlieder* (1901–04).

3. Barthold Hinrich Brockes (1680–1747), German poet; author of the libretto for the Passion oratorio *Der für die Sünden der Welt gemarterte und sterbende Jesus* (1712), set by a number of composers, including Handel in the early eighteenth century. Bach used parts of the Brockes text for his *St. John Passion*. Brockes wrote a great deal of nature poetry.

4. From the penultimate stanza of "Der Trunkene im Frühling" [The Drunkard in Spring], the fifth song from *Das Lied von der Erde* (1909), after Li-Tai-Po. Adorno's text following his quotation of this line at once describes and interprets the poem.

5. Fyodor Dostoyevsky, *The Brothers Karamazov* (1880), the last of his major works. Adorno's reference is to the two most famous chapters in this long novel, "The Grand Inquisitor" and "The Devil. Ivan's Nightmare." In the first, Ivan confronts Christ, in the second the Devil, and in both he wrestles with fundamental dilemmas of moral philosophy, beginning with the question of God's existence. Both chapters constitute arguments for denial. Through the novel's other principal characters the opposite claim is articulated, but, in the end, final judgment remains ambiguous. It is the ambiguity of answers to such ultimate existential questions that Adorno sees as the link between Mahler's music and Dostoyevsky's character. See also "Novel," in M, pp. 61–80.

6. Franz Werfel (1890–1945) was an expressionist poet, playwright, and nov-

618 / *Composition, Composers, and Works*

elist. He married Alma Mahler, the composer's widow, in 1929. They emigrated to the United States in 1940, having earlier left Germany for France.

The neologism *entlächelnd* appears in the poem "Alte Dienstboten" [Old Servants], in the collection *Einander* (1913–14): "Die alten Mägde haben gütige Hüte auf, / Mild von Vergangenheit und kaum entlächelnd mehr." The richly image-laden German is difficult to capture in English, but roughly: "The old servant women now wear kindly hats, / Softened by time and hardly any more capable of refusing a smile." Franz Werfel, *Das lyrische Werk*, ed. Adolf D. Klarmann (Frankfurt am Main: S. Fischer, 1967), p. 183. Adorno repeats this remark in M, p. 132: "The word *entlächelnd* in an early poem by Werfel gives the same impression of a departing smile. Such a feeling inhabits the motive type of the first violins in the consequent phrase marked *mit Empfindung* (with feeling) of the Adagietto of the Fifth."

German is rather free in allowing the formation of new words that combine a prefix and a verb or noun—in this case *ent-* (meaning: forth, from, out, away, dis-) and *lächeln* (to smile). Some compounds formed in this way fall easily into place in German—but not *entlächeln*, which retains the strangeness and awkwardness of a neologism. Adorno's comment that "the body of the word is stretched too far and torn" refers precisely to this awkwardness and strangeness. There is no evident way to translate the term *entlächeln* into a unique term in English, since English does not have the same grammatical capacity, and hence analogous constructions, for example "dis-smiling," are nonsensical. [translator's note]

7. See p. 510 n. 1.

8. Frank Wedekind (1864–1918), German expressionist playwright. His dramas *Erdgeist* and *Die Büchse der Pandora* served Alban Berg as the textual sources for *Lulu*.

9. Adorno's reference is to the title of a song from Mahler's *Des Knaben Wunderhorn* (1892–1901), "Rewelge: The Dead Drummer," the penultimate song from among the *Wunderhorn* texts that he set; it was composed in 1899. The reference, however oblique, is critical to his essay's import; see the discussion, p. 546.

The Opera *Wozzeck*

The composition of an opera based on the tragic drama *Wozzeck*, which proves itself by the power of both the word and the [theatrical] setting, cannot be justified merely by insight into the play and belief in the possibility of a music that is assumed to be implicit in the passion of the action and the darkness of its backdrop. Neither pathos nor mood opens the fragment to music. Rather, the times made it ripen into composition—its age. The hundred years that lie between *Wozzeck* and today have hollowed out cavities within the drama, have made its fragmentary character more acute by taking away the immediacy of the attack that it previously mounted and that carried it along from one fragment to the next. In today's society, it is no more appropriate to pay primary attention to the paralysis of the petit bourgeois individual in the face of his domination by the bourgeoisie—since the suffering of that individual has long since entered into the class struggle and turned against the permanence of that bourgeoisie— than a drama's surface form is truthfully sustainable if its form is constructed solely around that individual. However, the suffering of the oppressed human being has no more been assuaged by the class struggle, up to now, than art that takes this suffering as its subject is lost. From such a contradiction springs the music of *Wozzeck*. That the tragic drama collapsed as a totality makes it accessible to music, which enters through the cracks and catches fire more easily on the old material of the sentence structure than it would be able to with self-assertive living material. The fact that its cells contain truth justifies the effort the music devotes to *Wozzeck*, its will to generate from within itself new forms to replace the drama's old collapsed ones. Music and the word meet in the power of suffering, and the music salvages a suffering that may have been intended in *Wozzeck*'s words but that the verbal drama no longer supports. In the

619

same way, Mahler, to whom Berg is closer in a purely musical sense than anyone else is, undertook to preserve the vanishing contents of the *Wunderhorn* songs. Walter Benjamin correctly remarked on the analogy between Berg's method and Karl Kraus's treatment of the lyrics of Matthias Claudius.[1] All this is intended to indicate that the alternative that Berg's opera production is said to represent nowadays does not characterize *Wozzeck*. The person who is interested in salvaging the objective contents of past works is unlikely to pursue the subjective psychological impulses that may be found in the material. But if he becomes aware of the human motivation for that salvaging in himself, he will not simply ban human essence from the compass of his music. Berg's *Wozzeck* is not a musical drama; neither is it an opera-musical in the sense of that *Neue Sachlichkeit*[2] that makes the singing individuals into mere contrapuntal figures in a fugal system that hovers above their heads without ever touching them directly. It is quite necessary to distinguish the opera from both of these things. On the one hand, *Wozzeck*, with its musical visions of anxiety, its murky landscape and gurgling pond, has been seen psychologically and even impressionistically, and has reminded some people of Wagner or Debussy. Others have allowed themselves to be misled by the suite, the passacaglia, and the triple fugue, and have discovered in *Wozzeck*, as everywhere else, the revival of old forms with which people nowadays attempt to disguise and distract from the rupture of musical consciousness.[3] Against all this, Berg's *Wozzeck* adopts the stance of a *real humanity*, one that falls completely outside the abstract schema of an alternative. In order to describe this stance, it is necessary to critique the concept of *"Ausdrucksmusik,"* or music of expression, which nowadays is applied much too vaguely, although with a certain polemical justification. Whether a particular music is psychological is not decided by whether it expresses something. The concept of the expressionless has its authentic application in the most powerful moments of the musical—where music attains imageless presence. All expressionless music that fails to attain imageless presence is nothing but the empty shell of something expressed that has remained absent. Admittedly, it can gain power through this very silencing; but it is never the power of the expressionless. There is, consequently, scarcely any music that could be said to be expressionless, and precisely Bach, the unattainable goal of all objective will in modernism, delved deeply into the realm of expression.[4] The objective character of music is essentially determined by what is expressed in it. In the nineteenth century, which is the terrain of music of expression in the specific sense, music reproduces, within continuously shifting boundaries, the course of human experience—even if it is the image of a single experience, an isolated impulse. The expression of pre-Beethovenian music, however, is aimed at objective characters of being itself, in which the variety of human experience may participate, but with which it is by no means identical. The eighteenth-century *Affektenlehre* [Theory of the Affects] is quite clear about this. However, if whatever truth there is in objective characters continues to exist in altered form even under the mantle of musical subjectivism, then a procedure is legitimized that cuts through that mantle and grasps anew the contents beneath it. This occurs in Berg's *Wozzeck*. Others, aware of the crisis of musical subjectivism, have denied the situation of the latter and made a fresh start, as if the eighteenth century were commencing with them. Berg holds out in the situation in which he finds himself, drives it to destruction and grasps, among its decayed ruins, the objective characters. More than in any correspondence of musical style, his relationship to Schoenberg is revealed in the dialectical movement that Berg performs in the realm of musical subjectivism, in order to destroy it. He destroys the music drama by realizing it to the fullest. He arrives at construction by driving the musical-psychological process to a deep level where the unity of the surface relations of consciousness no longer prevails, but where the objective characters, in their solitariness, clamber out of the abyss of subjectivity. Here they are seized by the formal work *[Gebilde]*, by virtue of its construction. Between *Wozzeck* and psychoanalysis there exists not mere similarity, but a family relationship. Like analysis, Berg's music begins with sleep and the dream—not the illusory dream of romantic remoteness, but the dream as a ghostly simulacrum that arises from the lost depths of the human being and grasps the construction interpretively. Berg's music is not lacking in images. But its images are derived from an archaic realm, childhood, the dense dream rather than bright, contemporary life, and the music seizes the images not reproductively, but with the attack of recollection. The radical disintegration of the coherent musical surface corresponds, in Berg, to the dissolution of the surface structure of consciousness under analysis, the destruction of the coherent course of consciousness that analysis brings about as a consequence of taking seriously the idea of coherence and of understanding every experience from within the totality of psychic life, until it perceives totality itself as a transparent illusion. It is a style that pulverizes substance into the tiniest particles, in order to create its form from the construction of their transition. Just as, finally, the psychoanalytic process uncovers *residues of existence* that can no longer be derived from the process itself and that make the all-powerful nature of the process illusory, so Berg's music—

a process, like analysis, and entirely functional—uncovers essential remnants of existence. It adheres to them, and they are the measure of the opera's objectivity. Despite all its subjective dynamics, *Wozzeck*, in reality, is an objective act performed in the space of subjectivity. One can recognize the Austrian and even a relationship to Schubert in the acceptance of fate's inevitability in music that does not seek to influence fate, of its own volition, but offers consolation as it faithfully accepts it. Only in this way does the choice of the text become fully understandable. For it is only his passivity that makes the soldier Wozzeck into the bearer of the fateful action that the music means and transcends. For this reason, the petit bourgeois individual is needed here once again: his suffering discloses objective characters that are not yet evident today in the action of the collective. Wozzeck's private pathology is the entry portal for the objective characters, as little suited to traditional psychology as Berg's music is to the psychology of romanticism. His dominant emotion, fear, is at the same time the foundational emotion of the opera. The astonishment with which he imagines himself "on the track of many things" and hears the Freemasons marching underground resembles the astonishment of a music that, shuddering, finds archaic dream material under the earth.

The *construction* of *Wozzeck*, however, is only the means of grasping this dream material before it dissolves into the atmosphere and drifts away in moods. Not that the music of *Wozzeck* generates contents from within itself. Here craftsmanship is at work, internally consistent and ready to recover the contents it encounters. The readiness for reception as the measure of technique can be defined no better than Alban Berg himself did in a letter. "I know," he wrote, "when I look at the score, *how* objectively that was composed—admittedly always with an effort to make sure that the other person doesn't notice anything and feels as romantically comfortable as in a good armchair with nails that don't protrude and glue that doesn't stink while it holds it together." Craft-like autonomy, in other words, is merely the strict joining of a means to absorb the intentions, lest they slip away from it. At the same time, however, Berg's comments are a critique of the practice of the *Neue Sachlichkeit*, as dictated by his humane stance. Here, too, a peculiar dialectic is at work, one that Berg discovered, and quite productively. For ordinary objectivity is characterized by the fact that it is visible as objectivity; that, to remain within the metaphor, the nails do stick out, the glue does stink; that the technical apparatus runs on idle like a blinking machine. But objectivity that establishes itself as its own raison d'être is objectively inaccurate; for the true balance of any construction lies in the fact that no part of the whole is supposed to emancipate itself. Where the parts are balanced against each other, the construction as such no longer announces itself. This does not mean that the internal consistency of the material is negated, nor that music is once again expected to be decorative. But if everything perfect points beyond its kind, then surely this is true of compositional technique, whose perfection is not unquestioned until it becomes comprehensible as a figure for what is meant. As Berg, by means of the perfection of the psychological music drama, breaks through to the objective truth contents, the construction, whose perfection no longer leaves a room for a single free note, is transformed into its opposite and makes room for those very contents. This explains the fact that no unprejudiced listener notices, or is supposed to notice, very much in the way of variations and fugues. They are saturated with expression; their purpose is to carry the expression coherently. The armchair with which Berg compares the opera is no practical lounge chair for the comfortable audience, but the seat of demons. It resembles van Gogh's chair.[5] It fits together, it has its proportions and perspectives, but it is seen from too close up or from below, so askew, so strangely does it stand in space. Not in the room; in the storm. It stands up to a terrible procession of phenomena that emerge from their darkness to corporeal horror. The path to them passes through childhood. It can be followed in *Wozzeck*'s numerous songs—the hunting song, in which the nomad's ancient right to booty falls into bourgeois order like a meteor; in Marie's lullaby and her ballad of the gypsy that comes for the child who won't go to sleep, a spirit that kills anyone who lays eyes on it; in the lyre songs about the daughter who has attached herself to the coachmen and the wagoners, the maid who doesn't wear long dresses, because they aren't suitable for her but also because she rebels against being brought up.[6] Grown-ups don't sing the way these songs do; it is how children sing in the dark, in order to banish fear. In the songs themselves are quivering fear and at the same time the hope of banishing it. This subterranean folklore also reverberates in the distorted tonality of the songs, which does not conserve the recently departed romanticism, but quotes from a preexisting, long-vanished one—as children do in their songs. Above the mythical realm into which *Wozzeck*'s music sinks a hundred shafts, the emotion of sorrow rises powerfully. In it, the endless emotional world of weakness is held up to judgment. The way this sorrow rises above the foundering demons, with mad military music, with drums and clarinets— the nineteenth century never heard anything like it. *Wozzeck*'s expression has nothing whatsoever to do with *Tristan*'s. The depth of the sleep from which all the music here wrests itself loose, groaning; this startle reflex

624 / *Composition, Composers, and Works*

and jumpiness, the thumping, the "Too near" in the scene of Wozzeck and Andres in the field, when Marie is murdered—all this could no more be contained in psychological expression than the tone of Berg's orchestra sounded at that time, in which all the colors return as if bewitched with blackness, drained and dreamlike. Only Schoenberg's *Erwartung* explored this realm. In *Wozzeck*, its entire geography is mapped out. For the music is as wholly constructed as any by Stravinsky or Hindemith from this period—only richer by all the layers of the depth dimension. Its construction originates in motif cells, as the contents of the work are cell-like. The way these cells develop out of each other binds them to the psychological process that they ultimately destroy. The means of their transition is that of the infinitely small. The motifs transform seamlessly into each other; each new one retains elements of the old, as its residue. The simple individual tone often becomes the glue that holds the motif parts together. The instrumentation proceeds in the same manner. For all the continuous change and even reversal, tonal substance is carried over from each tone to the next, and is only gradually dissolved in it. The functional essence of a harmony that despite all the freedom of its chord construction does not, in the end, completely renounce the tension between dominant and tonic can be explained in the same way. No nails protrude—the power of *Wozzeck* resides entirely in the power of transition. The dialectic of this musical style, which everywhere translates the constancy of what has been into the alien perspective of what is becoming, can be distinguished in relation to Schoenberg. Berg starts from the most advanced Schoenberg, who was his teacher, and from that starting point he sinks wide-ranging roots, as it were, into the past, in order to retrieve the mythical images that he finds in himself as his authentic possession. Despite all the energy of this forward thrust, *Wozzeck* also, at the same time, draws the line backward to *Mahler*. Not only do the shapes of the themes often resemble him; not only does Berg follow Mahler when he carries along the lower, cast-off music, or rather reawakens it as subterranean folklore. What recalls Mahler, above all, is the architectonically incommensurable, wholly organic type of symphonic expansion. But where in Mahler, often enough, the brittle program had to fill the gaps, here in Berg it is accomplished compellingly by the dramatic structure. When the musical construction founders under the power of the expressive moment, then the dramatic construction embraces the moment perceptibly, in its stead. The latter becomes extremely dense in the first scene in the tavern, probably the core element in the [opera's] conception. Here suffering individual and demonic folklore run smack up against each other, only to penetrate each other in the counterpoint of the scherzo, which Mahler might have struggled his whole life long to achieve. After the second act is the opera's caesura, which can be felt in the splendid moments of silence during the curtain's fall, and then at the beginning of the third act during its rise. If music, always and forever, has utilized the pause as an element of its form—Berg was the first to make silence into a musical actor, the empty beating of time. In seconds, the expressionless; just as in the murder scene, once again, he composed out the filled silence with the rising voices of the muted trombones, with terror. The entire third act skirts the abyss; the music contracts and counts the minutes until death. Then it throws itself into the orchestral epilogue and is reflected as distantly, in the children's scene of the conclusion, as the blue of the sky appears at the bottom of a well. This reflex alone indicates hope in *Wozzeck*—weak, undetermined, made murky by the light of the tragic irony that makes the child on the hobbyhorse ride to the corpse of its mother, but evident after all. It illuminates the character of the opera softly, and late. Its character is *Passion.*[7] The music does not suffer within the human being, does not, itself, participate in his actions and emotions. It suffers over him; only for this reason is it able, like the music of the old passion plays, to represent every emotion without ever having to assume the mask of one of the characters of the tragic drama. The music lays the suffering that is dictated by the stars above bodily onto the shoulders of the human being, the individual, Wozzeck. In wrapping him in suffering so that it touches him wholly, it may hope that he will be absolved of that which threatens ineluctably in the rigid eternity of the stars.

(1929; GS, vol. 18, pp. 472–79)
Translated by Susan H. Gillespie

NOTES BY RICHARD LEPPERT

1. Adorno, "Reminiscence," in AB, pp. 25–26: "Benjamin, who was rather indifferent to music and who in his youth had nursed a certain animosity towards musicians, said to me with real insight after a performance of *Wozzeck* that as a composer Berg had treated Büchner's drama in a manner similar to Kraus's treatment of Claudius and Göcking. Berg's literary sensibility told him that one could not just compose these works the way Verdi did his librettos." Matthias Claudius (1740–1815), German writer and poet and friend of Lessing, Herder, and Goethe, is also regarded as the father of German popular journalism. His poetry addresses the small details of ordinary life, precisely the matters that, along with his gift for satire, caught Kraus's eye. Kraus himself wrote poetry of a similar sort on topics

like "The Day," and "Rapid Transit"; his lyrics are marked with a distinctly dark edge, where the mundane shows its hideous underside. Leopold Friedrich von Göcking (or Goeckingk) (1748–1828) was a German rococo poet and epigrammatist.

2. Adorno amplifies this point in his 1932 essay, "On the Social Situation of Music"; see p. 401. Adorno has in mind music of the 1920s, by Hindemith in particular, but likely as well works by Kurt Weill.

3. Adorno is alluding to the neo-classic revivalism among what he termed the "moderate moderns" in general, and Stravinsky in particular. See PNM, pp. 203–09.

4. See Adorno, "Bach Defended against His Devotees," PR, especially pp. 142–46.

5. Vincent van Gogh (1853–1890), "The Chair and the Pipe" (1889–90), London, National Gallery, inv. no. 3862. See the discussion in Richard Leppert, *Art and the Committed Eye: The Cultural Functions of Imagery* (Boulder: Westview/ HarperCollins, 1996), pp. 69–70.

6. Adorno's references are the various scenes in Büchner's unfinished play which exists in four fragmentary drafts. Regarding the specific "songs" to which Adorno refers, see Georg Büchner, *Complete Works and Letters*, ed. Walter Hinderer and Henry J. Schmidt, trans. Henry J. Schmidt (New York: Continuum, 1986): the hunting song, p. 233 (from draft 2, scene 1); Marie's lullaby, p. 202 (draft 4, scene 2); ballad of the gypsy, p. 205 (draft 4, scene 4); lyre songs, p. 230 (draft 1, scene 10); the maid who doesn't wear long dresses, p. 220 (draft 1, scene 17).

7. Adorno uses the Latinate term "Passion," which refers specifically to the passion of Christ. [translator's note]

Toward an Understanding
of Schoenberg

Arnold Schoenberg firmly counted on living to be eighty, and on that day he planned to announce publicly his long-accomplished reconciliation with Thomas Mann.[1] A serious illness, together with a crisis during which he believed his heart had already stopped beating and he had, as it were, already died, did not dent his confidence. He lived as if there were still an endless wealth of time available to him. Again and again, he postponed the conclusion of his two monumentally conceived works, the oratorio *Die Jakobsleiter* and the biblical opera *Moses und Aron*, which accompanied him for decades. At most, he occasionally joked about having made himself a Five- or Ten-Year Plan for their completion, only to devote himself to other pressing conceptions. One may reflect on why the two great choral works remained fragments—patchwork like everything else, he said—and on whether the task itself, of once more musically shaping a comprehensive totality of meaning, poses difficulties that mocked even the inexhaustible strength of the Master. This inexhaustibility is manifested in his big-hearted time-wasting, his readiness to yield to every productive impulse, no matter how distant from his musical center. At the end of the bourgeois era, the capacity to bring forth the entire world aesthetically from within oneself, from the subject, was embodied, once again, in a few individuals; as it had been vouchsafed to the greatest artists of the beginning of the epoch, to Michelangelo, or Shakespeare perhaps. Like Schoenberg, Picasso also produces with unquenchable youthfulness, as if the genius of History were making up in the sphere of aesthetics, in the substance of the individual, for what it withholds from society in its reality. That Schoenberg nevertheless had to depart from us, only a few days after one of his twelve-tone works, the "Dance around the Golden Calf," gave the lie, at its premiere in Darmstadt, to the received wisdom that this music

627

is asocial and does not speak to human beings—this seems symbolic of the fact that it was not to be after all; that the out-of-joint world would not permit it to the one person who, in his subjective capacity, would have been capable of it; that, in a word, the artist's accomplishment is not, as genius theory teaches, within his power, but instead depends largely on the objective conditions of the form and content of the work.

The duty is all the greater to compensate, to some extent, not for what the artist failed to accomplish, but for what the structure of existence denied to him. There is scarcely anyone to whom this responsibility is owed as much as to Schoenberg. For more than fifty years, the relationship of the public to his *oeuvre* was uncertain, skewed, and full of hostility. That his music demands of the listener such great powers of concentration, so much combinatorial capacity, as much intelligence as went into it, is reflected in the resistance of all those who are incapable of this, and who blame their incapacity on the work, which is considered to be abstract, intellectual, constructed, or outlandish. Ever more rationalizations were found for withdrawing from him. First there was the era of the scandal, during which all worthy citizens were united in the observation that "that is not music"—a remark that still betrays a closer connection than "I don't understand that," which is now *de rigueur.* Then, beginning approximately in the 1920s, came a time when Schoenberg was considered washed up and old-fashioned and was thrust back into the past before anyone had learned to perform him properly, much less hear him. In this period, every proper Philistine believed he had overcome Schoenberg, no longer because he was complicated, but because he was linked with others. This followed the formula, which has meanwhile proved so tried and true politically, that encourages the idiocy for which differentiation, intellection, and truth no longer exist and that feels comfortable asserting its power in the world, not only in order to annihilate whatever it hates, but also to feel superior doing it and to imagine that regressing to an earlier state is better than trying to attain a higher one. After the defeat of National Socialism, Schoenberg's twelve-tone technique was discovered and adopted, with many omissions and without doing justice to the function for the sake of which it was conceived. He was degraded to the inventor of a system that was more or less convenient to operate, a stimulating companion for likethinking hobbyists. Again, people exempted themselves from the only thing that was important, his living music. Finally, all the defensive motifs have come together and are proliferating ineradicably. Therefore, one should simply try to state the case concerning the composer Schoenberg himself, and why people who care about music at all should care about him.

Perhaps the moment is favorable, not to talk about Schoenberg's historical achievements, nor to interpret his music from the vantage point of the philosophy of history, but rather to point directly to its quality. For the musical situation we are in forces us to reflect on what has been repressed—something whose meaning, compared to the rest of musical production, even its antagonists are aware of, in principle. One must only be able and willing to regard music as a living and internally meaningful sequence of events and have a relatively good command of the categories of traditional, pre-Schoenbergian music. However different his melodies, with their large intervals, may be from the ones to which we are accustomed; however different the many-toned chords sound; however refracted the colors and irregular the forms are—Schoenberg's music resembles every other great music of the past in this respect, that it wants to be apprehended spontaneously as an organic structural complex of sounds. It would never have occurred to Schoenberg himself to think of it as anything else. When the not exactly avant-garde public of Naples proved to be less than enthusiastic about *Pierrot lunaire*, or when a comic opera with a highly complex structure failed to become the darling of the public in Frankfurt, Schoenberg could hardly understand it.[2] He thought of his music as music like that of the Masters, nothing else. His listener must also have something of this naïveté, which is characteristic not only of Schoenberg's private behavior but also of Schoenberg as an artistic type, all the while people are trying to persuade the listener of the opposite.

Schoenberg's music will reveal itself more easily, the more one forgets the formulae that have been attached to his work. Above all, it is necessary to clear away the false expectations with which listeners go after the phenomenon, instead of abandoning themselves to it in a kind of tensile passivity. The difference between Schoenberg and traditional music might be demonstrated with the help of a *bon mot* of Schumann's that one can tell whether a person is musical by his ability to continue performing a piece more or less correctly when someone forgets to turn the page. This, precisely, is not possible in the case of Schoenberg. By no means because his music is "not music," is chaotic and governed by chance. Rather, traditional music was stamped through and through by the schema of tonality; it moved within harmonic, melodic, and formal paths that were pre-drawn by this schema. It was as if every musical particular was subordinated to an established generality. By listening appropriately, starting from there, one would be able to deduce the development of its particulars in detail and to find one's way with relative ease. Traditional music listened for the listener. This, precisely, is over and done with in Schoenberg. The musical context wants to be understood purely from within itself, without lightening the listener's burden by means of an already available system of coordinates within which the particular is nothing but minimal variation. In this music, the only thing that still matters is the particular, the now and here of the musical events, their own inner logic. Perhaps, in truth, it requires greater concentration for us to measure this music against a generality that does not determine it than we would need to pursue it on its own. But we stand under the spell of that generality.

In addition, it is true that there is a richness of imagination compared to which most of the technical aspect of traditional music, even the most lauded, seems childlike and simplistic. Schoenberg fulfilled the Wagnerian wish that music should finally outgrow its baby shoes. He no longer allows us to abandon ourselves to pure harmony, or to doze in a mood. The ear must identify his music in order to feel it. In particular, his music presupposes an ability that it is hardly possible to acquire in traditional music elsewhere than through Bach—the ability to follow the various melodic lines simultaneously and in their relationship to each other. Even the individual chords are internally polyphonically organized down to the last note. The listener must not just receive them as mere tonal stimuli, but must listen into them, as it were, must feel out all the tensions and shadings that each one of these chords contains. Compared with this kind of intellectual effort, which, properly understood, is immediate, and not a task of reflective thinking, the outwardly alienating features of Schoenberg's music carry hardly any weight. The melodies with the unaccustomed intervals; the so-called dissonances, which in truth are only many-toned chords; the supposed disintegration, which is nothing but the lack of the crutches of an accustomed symmetry—all these are merely byproducts of Schoenberg's music. Once the hearer has understood them starting from their inner principle, he will quite naturally accept their sensual and tonal deviations from the conventional. The decisive thing is the density of composition, which no one ever conceived of before—its concreteness, not its abstraction. Schoenberg leaves nothing unformed; every tone is developed from within the law of motion of the thing itself. This was already true of the young Schoenberg, at least of the works between op. 6 and op. 10, in which tonality is still outwardly respected and whose sounds no longer have anything disturbing about them today. Nevertheless, the First Chamber Symphony, op. 9, in E major, is probably still just as difficult as it was sixty years ago. If someone wants to get close to Schoenberg, not just inform himself about him in a music-historical sense, he should immerse himself, above all, in these earlier works, where beneath the shell of the traditional musical idiom all the forces are evolving that would later burst that shell and lay the foundation for a new musical material. He should let the twelve-tone rows be straight or crooked and focus first on the shapes whose immediacy and spontaneity will not allow any thought of a system to arise. Once he has truly made these his own— and nothing stands in his way, as long as he approaches the task with love and a good ear—then the dreaded later works will not pose more riddles than every work of art does, if in fact it is one.

Schoenberg, whose intellectualism is legend, was, as a type, a naïve artist. If the term musical vagrant[3] *[Musikant]* had not been so shamefully abused to glorify an unenlightened and uncritical performance, it could be applied to his origins. He bubbled over with music just like any other denizen of the Viennese-Slavic-Hungarian cultural milieu. Only the irresistible force of his talent, with which, in his words, his courage could not keep pace, and by no means a speculative turn of mind drove him step by step beyond the circle within which he was at home. He often said, and Anton von Webern has confirmed, that he introduced the great innovations only hesitantly, almost against his will. The best impression of Schoenberg's fund of musical idioms is the one given by works that precede the evolution of what is generally known as his style—for example the *Gurrelieder*. They do not borrow more from Wagner than any youthful work of a great composer does from his predecessors—Beethoven from Haydn. In fact, only a rather dull and externally oriented musicality will fail to perceive the difference between this musical language and Wagner's. It is thoroughly lacking the element of the self-reflexive, the self-admiring, as it were. Everything is turned much more toward the thing than toward the ego, with an apparently altruistic warmth that is completely without the addictive tone of Wagner. The choral work of the twenty-six-year-old already differentiates itself from contemporary composers like Richard Strauss by the modest, honest style in which it is through-composed, and above all harmonically developed—a style that derives its effect purely from the musical form and disdains effects in favor of compositional integrity.

In the melodic warmth of the young Schoenberg, an extraordinarily expansive force is gathering. Soon it no longer tolerates the melodic arcs within the circumscribed boundaries of even-numbered periods and conventional intervals. At a time when Schoenberg was still writing tonally, for example in the First String Quartet, op. 7, in D minor, the pure intensity of expression is already pushing beyond them. Like the Lieder op. 6, composed at the same time, the quartet already shows Schoenberg's authentic sound explicitly. Using the example of this same First Quartet, in an extraordinarily instructive essay entitled "Why Is Schoenberg's Music So Hard to Understand?" Alban Berg, Schoenberg's student who became a master himself, already developed the reasons for the difficulty of understanding Schoenberg—and its justification. The most important of these reasons is the contrapuntal imagination. "Every thematic idea," writes Berg, citing music historian Egon Wellesz, "is immediately invented with all its contrapuntal voices." The challenge to the public consists only in the fact that all of this "also wants to be heard."[4]

What is exceptional about this method of composition, already in the First Quartet, is its complete formal thoroughness. Nothing is left to chance, nothing is splashing along in the musical current; rather, every voice, indeed every accompanying figure is profiled in the extreme. Everything that makes a sound has its logic. Themes, when they are no longer in the foreground, become models for accompaniments; accompaniments that at first appear very modest are germ cells of later themes. At the same time, the sculptural quality of the music is always maintained; that is, the principal events are distinguished as sharply as possible from the incidental. But the incidental does not run alongside the real course of the composition, without getting involved. Rather, it is determined right down to the details by the composition's structure. Hence Schoenberg's music demands the opposite of what the title of a well-known American radio program called *"easy listening*."* The ear that does not want to be helplessly left behind must voluntarily perform the entire work of composition once again, independently. But the habit of listening that is dominant, and that is perhaps growing even stronger thanks to the culture industry, the business of music that is wholly or completely entertainment, is calibrated to perceive music in a more or less de-concentrated way, as a sequence of isolated sensual stimuli. There is reason to believe that even so-called classical music is in great measure consumed in this fashion. Both the universally familiar quality of the works that are repeated over and over again, and the well-established and familiar language that they use are contributing factors. Schoenberg broke with all of this. He disdains the usual fare. His music is not satisfied with the language it finds at hand, but instead creates its own, out of itself.

This is often followed by the rhetorical question, Is that really necessary, and not just unrestrained and arbitrary individualism? If you have the task of introducing a group of listeners to the New Music, and if, for some reason, you play a few bars of Beethoven's Sonata op. 111 in between, a pleasant ripple runs through the rows. It seems to say, How beautiful, why can't we leave it at that? Must we really be confronted with the other? This is in fact the central question. Historicism, the reference to the development that brought things to this point, does not suffice. For nowhere is it written that its progression should automatically contain a measure of greater wisdom. One must try to respond starting from the thing itself. The music in which we are still immediately living—and it does begin with Bach, after all—labors from its inception under an internal difficulty, a contradiction. On the one hand it is tied into a system, the system of triads, keys, and their relationships. On the other hand, the subject is trying to express itself in it; instead of every norm that is merely imposed externally, it wants to generate the regularities from within. Certainly, one must not imagine the relationship between tonality and composition, between the system that held sway, more or less, for 350 years and subjectivity solely as a contradiction. Tonality evolved ever more over the course of the centuries as a result of the subject's need for expression. It changed so much that in terms of the individual harmonic events, for example, the step from the boldest parts of Strauss's *Elektra* to Schoenberg appears quite small. At the same time, tonality has also determined the impulses of composers. The most powerful formal types that music has crystallized out of itself, and in which it has found fulfillment, the fugue and the sonata, are generated by tonality down to the most intimate details. Despite this, the great composers, in particular, have always felt dissatisfaction with the external, compulsory moment in music, which imposed constraints on what they themselves actually wanted. The greatest fully polyphonic works of Bach, such as the *Well-Tempered Clavier*, the *Art of Fugue*, and individual pieces from *The Musical Offering*, bear witness to this dissatisfaction. For this reason, Bach drew on the polyphonic arts of the medieval Low Countries, which were already archaic in his era, in order to overcome the gravity of the schema by dint of the complete integration of all the voices, as it appears in his work even in the dance movements; so that the music, as it were, owes nothing to anything except what it itself is, here and now.

This tradition, which disappeared again immediately after Bach's death, and which corresponded, over the course of the centuries, to a tendency toward dissonance, was taken up again by the late Beethoven, and then again by Schoenberg. The latter, however, with a decisive difference. In traditional music, and precisely in the great constructive composers like

Bach, Mozart, Beethoven, Brahms, there was always still the attempt to achieve something like a balance between the schema and the uniqueness of each work of through-composed music. This resulted in a peculiar duality in the structure. One part is on the surface. This is the part that is reached by the usual analyses based on the *basso continuo* schema and the theories of modulation and musical forms, and that is fully expressed in the general relations of tonality. But underneath this there is the second part, which Schoenberg called subcutaneous, a structure under the skin, which derives the whole from very specific germ cells and which first generates the more profound, true unity. Only this inner structure makes a difference in the work's actual quality, but it, precisely, is barely perceived in traditional music by most listeners. It is essentially defined by what is called thematic work, which originally developed out of the economy-of-motif technique in the fugue and then unfolded above all in the sonata developments. Masters like Brahms already scarcely wrote a note that was not thematic, that did not refer to a latent basic material. Heinrich Schenker, otherwise a sworn enemy of modern music, was the first to reveal this subcutaneous structure, above all in Beethoven.

Now, the event in the case of Schoenberg is nothing else than the break-through of the subcutaneous, that what is inside is turned out. This explains why the effort of Schoenberg, and the effort of his listeners, are needed. Artistic invention cannot, in the long run, stand to orient itself according to two concurrent sets of laws that are always growing farther apart, the external, traditional one, and its own. It strives to forge what has been imposed externally, which was by no means meaningless and accidental, but which gradually paled, into something entirely internal. Already in Bach, certainly in Beethoven, the balance was precarious, and the abysses of the latest Beethoven are those of the irreconcilability of the two principles. It convinced Beethoven ultimately to forego the appearance of reconciliation and instead to oppose the bedrock of tonality with the enlivening subjective elements starkly and in an unmediated way. In Schoenberg, however, who bore within himself the entire heritage of romanticism, subjective differentiation and above all the urge to let pass only those things that he was able to fill entirely from within himself have become extreme. He is not only, as a constructive musician, the executor of the Beethoven-Brahms tradition, but equally the executor of Wagner, who, by the usual stylistic standards, was his point of departure. The overwhelming compulsion to express himself refused to allow him, as it refused to allow his contemporaries, the expressionists, any compromise with the traditional schema. That Schoenberg's music was turned inside out means above all that everything decorative, ornamental, not purely of the thing itself, was unbearable for him, as, for example, in the architecture of his friend Adolf Loos, who coined the first slogans for what is today known as Functionalism [*Sachlichkeit*].[5] Schoenberg literally experiences the external musical structure as a false façade, and it has to fall, in order for what is functionally necessary to become audible.

In addition, the expressive element as such, which originally dominates him, has been linked since the inception of the newer music with so-called dissonance. The more the consonances declined, becoming mere building blocks in the tonal schema, the more completely the power of subjective expression passed to dissonance. Anyone who wants to understand what compels Schoenberg to dismantle the musical façade must listen once to one of those early lieder, in which, instead of adding ornaments, expression reveals itself with a previously unknown directness, and dissonance is joined with dense construction—for example in "Lockung" [Temptation] from op. 6. This song is not even polyphonic; it resembles the Brahmsian type, with a motivically through-composed piano accompaniment. But although there is no diversity of complex voices to be followed simultaneously, it is not easy to follow the song unless the intensity of expression carries you away beyond it. The reason for this is the fact that in Schoenberg not only the simultaneous, but the sequential is worked through much more densely and variously than in traditional music. His allergy to everything mechanical applied, first of all, to external symmetry and repetition. The principle of thematic work, to which everything in his music is subordinated, demands unceasing variation. Rarely does he form simple, continuous, unbroken themes, and in their construction he disdains the comfortable expedient of easily comprehensible sequences. Usually the themes, in themselves, are already forged out of contrasting elements bound together by means of relations among motifs. Thus the song's introduction consists of three short phrases, all of which, it is true, are very closely related to the others, but which at the same time form a very sharp contrast: first the rising principal motif; then a kind of urgent following, pressing after; finally a sort of cadencing little concluding phrase that turns into a half-conclusion and leads to the beginning of the song. The themes of the mature, radical Schoenberg are not constructed any differently; they are just as irregular, except that the vestiges of tonal pillars are now lacking. Actually the step that was needed in order to reach atonality was a small one; what is essential is already contained in the tonal pieces. The music of Schoenberg that was indebted to the lieder tradition of Brahms and Mahler only needed to give itself a shake in order to reveal itself as what it is today considered to be.

Schoenberg displayed particular sensitivity in his relation to tonality. He always avoided producing the tonal center of gravity by means of the usual and by now really worn-out expedient of the cadence, i.e., the sequence of the fourth or some comparable interval, the dominant, and the tonic. This sensitivity was something he shared, to a greater or lesser degree, with many composers of his generation. Only he drew the full consequences from it. He was not, like Richard Strauss, for example, satisfied with startling effects in the sequence of chords; nor with concluding flourishes[6] instead of cadences. Instead, he rewrote tonality; he achieved the effect of keys by constructive harmonic means, with ever-fresh, powerful intervals similar to those that had already played a role in the diatonic Brahms. The tonal relations are stretched to the extreme; it is they that recreate the principle of tonality, afresh, purely from within the compositional events. But with this the events are rendered so powerful that soon they actually no longer need the points of tonal contact at all. Combining Wagnerian and Brahmsian tendencies, Schoenberg allowed the so-called secondary intervals to emerge more and more, until ultimately he endowed even the chromatic accidentals of the key with the character of powerful fundamental steps. In the end, every sound became autonomous, all tones enjoyed equal rights, and the reign of the tonic triad was overthrown. The music's internal tensions rend the mantle of tonality, and with it much that was interwoven with it. Without the resistance of this mantle, they would scarcely have attained the force and concentration with which they now manifest themselves.

But once music is divested of this mantle, something like the musical realm of freedom really opens up. It is one of the riddles of human musical consciousness that only a very few dared to rejoice in this freedom. Hardly had it been accomplished than a fateful call for new bondage went out— as if the unobstructed horizon of the possible that Schoenberg opened up had not given music the joy of an unsuspected richness of imagination; as if, in this new, liberated language of music, music had not, for the first time, actually arrived at the youth that Busoni eulogized,[7] and that is then denied, ironically, precisely in the name of the young. If the term "New Music" is more than a chronological label, if something of utopia really resonates in it, then it deserves to be applied to the period of emancipated composition that Schoenberg inaugurated around 1907. As soon as the conflict between the subjective impulse and the language of music has been removed, music assumes a second immediacy, which sometimes recalls the radical primitivism of the Fauves[8] and other avant-garde painting from the first decade of the twentieth century. The scale of expression expands. Schoenberg finds sounds and shadings for experiences of the strange, the untrodden, which were totally unavailable to the congealed emotional stereotypes of previous music, including the expressive daubings of Richard Strauss. The last movement of the Second String Quartet, the first predominantly atonal piece, in which Schoenberg symbolically omitted the key signature altogether, remained the unrivaled prototype of this kind of freedom. The poem that he selected for the movement, the "Rapture" ["Entrückung"] from George's *Seventh Ring,* is the representation of an ecstasy that transports the poet across the barrier of individuation. The last lines are, "I stride across monstrous abysses, / I feel how above a last cloud / I swim in a sea of crystal brilliance— / I am but a spark of holy fire / I am but a roaring of the holy voice." This is the sort of spiritual landscape in which this music transpires, and it carries it within itself.

Now, at first, the techniques of thematic work that form the subcutaneous structure recede completely. Schoenberg abandons himself purely to the moment. He strings together, in the most colorful variety, forms that he has learned in the strict school of variation work. The contrasts, which are compressed into the most limited space, become bigger than we have ever known them to be, as if ordinary musical logic were making room for a process of free association similar to the one that Schoenberg's fellow countryman Freud was simultaneously discovering as the road to the psychologically subcutaneous, the subconscious. This is the most arresting thing, for example, about the beginning of the famous first piano piece from op. 11. It falls into the same period as the quartet movement "Rapture" and the George lieder op. 15. But Schoenberg also resisted repetition in the sense that he never duplicates the type and spiritual form of a work. This, perhaps more than anything else, defines his inexhaustibility—an inexhaustibility not of applications but of primary images, of a kind that music before him probably experienced only in Beethoven. In his desire to present the thing itself, naked and undistorted, Schoenberg, in the Piano Pieces, sacrificed the poetic element of composition, the magic, what Benjamin called the aura,[9] which had blazed up in the Second Quartet as if saying good-bye. The search for the subcutaneous leads him to a kind of protocol of expression, which confronts the listener almost soberly, without perspective, without anything transfiguring, and shocks him. It is probably this transition, the transformation of the expressionist into an objective ideal of composition, that along with the technical aspects makes it hardest for people with traditional leanings to do justice to Schoenberg's mature works. This music denies the very thing we have been accustomed, since Shakespeare's days, to expect from music as the magical art: consolation. In the era of music's emancipation it claims to be nothing more than the voice of truth, without the crutches of the familiar, but also without the deception of praise and false positivity. The strength to do this, not illusion, is what is consoling about it. One could say that Schoenberg translated the Old Testament ban on images into music. This alienates us, where his tone is concerned.

But the ban also has its technical aspect. The consoling aspect of music, the feeling of security derived from its embracing structure, an all-enveloping, integral architecture created by formal construction and thematic work, by the mutual responsiveness of all its parts, the relationship among the totality of elements. In the Piano Pieces op. 11 and in a series of other works, among which the most consequential is probably the monodrama *Erwartung*, Schoenberg, who had previously brought the art of thematic work to its highest level, abandoned it entirely. In general, his development proceeds by contradictions. He never relied on what he had already achieved. No longer is his music held together as if with iron clamps. It breathes out. Its form composes itself from the involuntary combination of its temporal moments. This, in turn, creates difficulties of the most unfamiliar kind. Not only does the affirmative, confirming aspect vanish, spiritually, but the sensual ear must also learn to combine completely contrasting elements that are apparently aphoristically unrelated, must learn to leap with the music, as it were. The individual musical forms are much farther removed from each other than ever before. The unity becomes a unity of extremes. The listener must sharpen his feeling for the forms, for the way a compact voice-leading, for example, is suddenly followed by a figure that is completely broken up *[völlig aufgelösten Figur]*; for what necessity reigns in such a case; for the way a musical phrase is formed out of sharp contrasts. With this manner of proceeding, Schoenberg, surprisingly enough, reaches back to Mozart, who, unlike Beethoven, often combines similarly contrasting motifs into individual themes. In Mozart the contrasts are held together by tonality; in Schoenberg there are no bridges. Nothing helps except to carry out, without reservation, the inner synthesis of the mutually contradictory. This challenge is inseparably linked with the idea of expressionism, which inspires the works of this period. Schoenberg liberates the expression of the psychological as something that exceeds moderate normalcy. Twenty years before the term "borderline situation" was invented, his music pushes in that direction, into a realm that the business of hardened culture has not yet appropriated. Schoenberg's music is no state of normalcy. It takes place in a realm that is otherwise ringed around with taboos and that the conventional language of art does not reach. Abruptly, unrestrained outbursts alternate with tenderness from that legend that compares the soul, as it floats away, with a butterfly fluttering off. In Schoenberg's own formulation, such music says something that can only be said through music. The final piano piece from op. 19, for example, which Schoenberg notated in 1911 on the day of Gustav Mahler's funeral, partakes of this spirit. It is simultaneously the model for all the music of his student Anton von Webern.

At every level in Schoenberg, forces of a polar nature are at work—the forces of unrestrained, emancipated, authentic expression; and the force of a through-construction that attracts to itself even the least detail, the fleeting tremor. These two trunks of his music have a secret common root, like intuition [*Anschauung*] and thought in Kant. This root is musical spontaneity, which prefers to avoid everything given, would rather owe everything to itself, the totality as well as the individual element, the single inspiration as well as the large form. But just as these divergent elements spring, most profoundly, from the same impulse, so Schoenberg's music has also labored at their reunification. One could virtually describe the history of his work as the effort to achieve this reunification by way of the most acute sharpening of the contradictions. This effort was necessary. For as with every step forward, there is a price to pay for musical progress. Music has as one of its indispensable tasks the overcoming of the temporal dimension through articulation. This task recedes for as long as music entrusts itself, without looking forward or backward, to the pure present, without any architecture of repetition. Hence the disconcerting brevity of the Piano Pieces. In the period of free atonality into which they fall, which led to what was probably the greatest intensity of Schoenberg's productive powers, he often, for this reason, drew on the sung and spoken word to articulate longer temporal stretches. This was the case in the lieder op. 15, 20, and 22; in the two works for the stage *Erwartung* and *Die glückliche Hand,* and finally in the monodramas *Pierrot lunaire* and the unfinished oratorio *Die Jakobsleiter.* The only exceptions are the [Five] Orchestral Pieces op. 16, where, for the first time, he transferred the subtle arts of thematic work, which he had so greatly intensified in the first two quartets and the First Chamber Symphony, to the now fully emancipated musical material.

From this vantage point it is possible to understand what the twelve-tone technique, in which Schoenberg composed during the last thirty years of his life, means. It is nothing else but the synthesis of a completely emancipated material, which has been cleansed of tonal rudiments, and the equally thoroughly applied principle of thematic work, or, if one prefers, the primacy of variation. In a word, it is the very attempt to synthesize Schoenberg's two fundamental intentions, the explosively anti-conventional one and the cohesively constructive one, into one and the same method of proceeding. This alone, and not any supposedly mathematical operations, is what matters. Now, truly, every note becomes, as it were, thematic. But where everything is thematic, the concept of the thematic loses its meaning in comparison to mere transition or non-cohesive episodes. Nothing is thematic any longer—namely, more thematic than anything else. The twelve-tone technique does justice to this state of affairs. It does not recognize a single free note, not one that would not have its place in the context of the row that is composed, in each case, of twelve different notes, and that individually carries each twelve-tone piece. But this all-powerful thematic work is no longer, as in the earlier works and in the tradition of Viennese classicism, the content of the composition itself, but merely its precondition. It is an organizational principle to which the music is subjected before it even begins. Hence the twelve-tone technique does not replace tonality, as is falsely claimed again and again. It is nothing that is to be noticed or should be noticed; on the contrary, if the row itself, as such, were to stand out, it would permit a non-artistic peek into the workshop, at the site where the form is only intended to stand in for itself. The preliminary form takes shape in such a way that the series is not simply reeled off again and again—even that would be something merely external and mechanical—but rather is subjected to all the inflections that are made possible by a highly developed variation technique. Some of these inflections go back to methodological means of the old Netherlandish polyphony, such as the crab canon. But the purpose of the whole, its entire raison d'être, is that, using material that is in every case pre-formed in the strictest fashion, one can now compose quite freely and unrestrainedly, without there being any danger of dissociation. It is now possible to compose in wide-spanned, large formal arcs, which are stable, without any borrowings from traditional types of forms. Schoenberg, the builder, organizes the material; Schoenberg the composer places it wholly in the service of the individual compositional intention. If this aim, namely the establishment of a medium for completely free expression, is neglected, as it is in the efforts of some young composers, who read the twelve-tone technique as nothing but a rationalization schema, then the whole thing misses its mark and degenerates into fetishism. But in spite of his unexampled control of the material, Schoenberg's genius never succumbed to the temptation to elevate technique into an end in itself. This is not the place to speak of later tendencies that extended and then once again rescinded this technique.

The difficulties that Schoenberg had to endure can scarcely be exaggerated. Once again, as happened repeatedly in his life, he had to forget what he knew how to do in order to be able to do it truthfully. The first piece in pure twelve-tone technique that he published is a waltz that today sounds almost angular in its awkwardness and therefore doubly touching. But he did not leave it at that for long. Thereafter Schoenberg, in one of his most reticent works, the Wind Quintet, intensified his polyphonic capacity, thanks to the twelve-tone technique, to the point where it became a kind of renewed pure style [*reiner Satz*], and he acquired the freest command of that technique, as well. The most important documents of this effort are the Chamber Suite op. 29, the Third String Quartet, and the Variations for Orchestra op. 31. Just this once, as he began to plow over the entire musical material, he sought shelter in older, traditional forms and made distant contact with the neo-classicism of the 1920s. There are gigues, rondos—in the Third Quartet an almost paradigmatically overstated one—movements with variations. This results in certain contradictions, since, after all, the traditional forms referred implicitly to the very tonality whose trace is extinguished by the twelve-tone organization of the material. Moreover, it seems not entirely consonant with aesthetic economy when issues that have been moved up into the organization of the material and resolved there are duplicated in the foreground of an openly thematic composition. Schoenberg's inexhaustible strength took on even this challenge. The powerful first movement of the Third Quartet already has hardly anything to do with traditional forms, despite its sonata outline. Rather, it is held together—a rare exception in Schoenberg—by a continuously varied ostinato figure. On yet other occasions, Schoenberg has harnessed the threat of domination by his own technique in vocal compositions; in the comic opera *Von heute auf morgen,* with its metallic brilliance, and then in *Moses und Aron,* the biblical work of which he completed two acts at the beginning of the 1930s. Afterward, he returned to the thing that today has probably become most closely identified with him, instrumental music as nourished by the string quartet type. The twelve-tone technique, treated with sovereign command and hence once again already unobtrusive, combines powerful forms that, while they may share with more familiar forms the ferment of the musical context that creates meaning, no longer have anything schematic about them.

The most exemplary is probably the Fourth Quartet, each of whose four movements expresses the spirit of traditional quartet movements in pure form. The first movement is uncorked sonata spirits; the second corresponds to an intermezzo; the third, adagio, brings a double sequence of open recitative and closed song; the last evokes the rondo playfully and non-pedantically. The passionate tone of the adagio is that of resistance against the grayness that dominated Europe at the time this music was being written in America.

In the very last pieces, then, Schoenberg's twelve-tone music reestablished an immediate connection with his boldest, expressionist phase. Of the String Trio he said, half in jest, that he had composed his whole illness into it, including the nurses. *Die Überlebende von Warschau* is probably the only work of art of that epoch that, along with Picasso's *Guernica*, was capable of looking unflinchingly at its most extreme horror and yet was aesthetically compelling. That Schoenberg, at a time in which the possibility of art itself, in its very essence, became questionable, still composed music that does not seem impotent and vain in light of the reality, confirms, in the end, what he once began.

(1955/1967; GS, vol. 18, pp. 428–45)
Translated by Susan H. Gillespie

NOTES BY RICHARD LEPPERT

1. See the introduction, p. 9 n. 25, regarding Schoenberg's break with Mann.
2. Adorno is referring to Schoenberg's *Von heute auf morgen*, which premiered in Frankfurt on 1 February 1930.
3. *Musikant* stands in relation to *Musiker* roughly as does fiddler to violinist. The point of Adorno's word choice is clarified in the following sentence, which firmly connects Schoenberg to Central European musical tradition, and thereby opposes the common judgment that Schoenberg's music was unfathomable and freakish. At the same time, the sense of vagrancy attached to *Musikant* acknowledges the fact that Schoenberg was an outsider to the culture within which he was firmly rooted, much like downtrodden street musicians, hurdy-gurdy players, for example.
4. Berg's essay, "Warum ist Schönbergs Musik so schwer verständlich?" was first published in *Musikblätter des Anbruchs* in 1924. Egon Wellesz (1885–1974) was an Austrian composer and musicologist; he studied with Schoenberg and also published a brief biography of his teacher in 1921, translated into English in 1924. He was a close friend of Webern.
5. Concerning Loos, see p. 433 n. 5.
6. Adorno's word is *Pointen*, in apparent reference to rhetoric, where the word means a concluding flourish.
7. Ferruccio Busoni (1866–1924), composer and pianist, in 1907 published a short tract, in German, *Entwurf einer neuen Ästhetik der Tonkunst*, available in translation as *Sketch of a New Esthetic of Music*, in *Three Classics in the Aesthetics*

of Music, trans. Theodore Baker (1911; reprint, New York: Dover, 1962), pp. 73–102. Busoni waxes eloquent on what he regards as the youth of Western music, "hardly four hundred years old," remarking that "young as it is, this child, we already recognize that it possesses one radiant attribute which signalizes [sic] it beyond all its elder sisters." Music's singularity is its freedom; music *"floats on air!* . . . It is well-nigh incorporeal. Its material is transparent. It is sonorous air. It is almost Nature herself. It is—free" (p. 77, original emphasis). Much of the tract rails against prevailing nineteenth-century compositional convention, the rule of what he calls the "lawgivers" who hinder music's development. Music's "natural" freedom, in other words, is unacknowledged and weighted down.

8. Fauvism was a movement in French painting at the beginning of the twentieth century noted for its use of bright, unmediated color and aggressively expressive style. The first fauvist exhibition occurred in Paris in 1905. The principal painters associated with fauvism included Henri Matisse, André Derain, and Maurice de Vlaminck.

9. Walter Benjamin, "The Work of Art in the Age of Mechanical Reproduction," in *Illuminations,* ed. Hannah Arendt, trans. Harry Zohn (New York: Schocken, 1969), pp. 217–51. Essentially "aura" refers to the magical or cultic value that appends to unique art objects (p. 223: "The uniqueness of a work of art is inseparable from its being imbedded in the fabric of tradition"). Benjamin's examples include oil painting, sculpture, etc.—as opposed to mass-produced art forms for which, in effect, no "original" exists, such as film, and which do not demand worshipful, contemplative attention from consumers. See my comments, pp. 241–44.

Difficulties

I. IN COMPOSING

In 1934, Brecht wrote a text with the title "Five Difficulties in Writing the Truth."[1] I am going against my habit of not attaching myself to other people's titles, although I would not be able to count the difficulties that today stand in the way of composing. But probably the difficulties that Brecht described in his essay, which has become famous, are those not only of the writer but of the musician as well—the degeneration of so-called cultural production into ideology. He described accurately an experience that is not restricted to a single medium, namely that today there is something about all art that causes consternation. You feel the earth quake beneath your feet, and it is no longer possible to hold forth in your medium as naïvely as an admittedly dubious legend would have had artists do in happier days. However, the ideological moments that are reflected in the various arts are by no means only of a material kind; rather, they extend to the aesthetic construction of the thing itself. This should justify, to some extent, the application of Brecht's theme to music, independent of him. Obviously, the questions are posed here in an essentially different way than in literature. Music is not an object and not conceptual; hence some concrete ideological references are lacking. The intellectual [das Geistige] is certainly not exhausted in such references, nor in the representation of some social interests or other, independent of its own truth or legitimacy. Otherwise, the theory with which Brecht, too, identified himself would not be possible. The intellectual—art and thought alike—has an immanent lawfulness that has its own specifically determined relation to truth content. Moreover, the situation has changed fundamentally compared to that which prevailed thirty years ago, when Brecht wrote this text. The political opportunities that he regarded as immediately present or soon-to-be-realized, and against which he measured everything, no longer exist in that way. The political realm that seemed to him to be the guarantor of truth, that of the East, has itself meanwhile become thoroughly overgrown with ideological matter. There, as is well known, people take the concept of ideology, which was originally meant critically, as a positive claim, as if everything intellectual *[alles Geistige]*, including theory, were ultimately only a means of imposing authority. I retain only this much of Brecht's conception: that, like writing, composition is also linked to objective difficulties the likes of which were scarcely known before; that these difficulties have to do essentially with the position of art in society; and that one cannot escape them by ignoring them.

There is one statement in the Brecht text, at any rate, that I would like to take as an immediate point of departure. It refers to naïve artists and intellectuals. Of them he says, "Undeterred by the powerful, but also not deterred by the screams of the violated, they daub away at their images. The senselessness of their behavior generates a 'profound' pessimism within them, which fetches a good price and to which other people might more justifiably lay claim, given these Masters and these sales. Meanwhile, it is not easy to discern that their truths are of the sort that apply to chairs or the rain; ordinarily they sound quite different, like truths about important things. For the creation of artistic form, after all, consists precisely in lending importance to a thing. It is only on close examination that one realizes they are merely saying, 'A chair is a chair,' and, 'No one can do anything about the fact that rain falls downward.' " Something of these statements, which are meant sardonically, and with which Brecht tries to denounce artists and intellectuals who are not directly politically engaged, also applies to music.[2] If we musicians, undeterred, behave intransigently, or, as Brecht says maliciously, "daub away at" our compositions as if nothing had transpired, then music threatens to become indifferent. The sorrow and senselessness that it still expresses is in danger of becoming inconsequential, of itself turning into a kind of ornament, as Brecht prophesies in these statements. However, the implied optimism that lurks behind his critique of this aspect is utterly groundless. The artist has as little cause to be optimistic toward the world as the state of the world justifies such optimism. If one turns Brecht's malice against himself, there is a piece of conformism in the very fact that he pokes fun at pessimism. Along with the negative, the critical aspects are already as muffled as in the official ideology of the Soviet empire. If there is something that is ideology, then [it is] the official optimism, the cult of the positive. Only art that stands up to what is dark and threatening has any chance at all of telling the truth. But if it, particularly music, were to try to intervene, as Brecht expected it to do in these theses concerning the writer, it finds itself blocked. Music as such cannot intervene immediately. Even if you put it to work for purposes of haranguing,[3] the effect remains uncertain. It is no accident that it then attaches itself to some political texts or other. Nor, in my opinion, is it an accident that certain compositions written more than thirty years ago by the late, highly gifted Hanns Eisler, which served aggressive political propaganda in ways that were extremely intensive and considered, including their tone and their character—that these compositions, so far as I know, are no longer performed even in the East. Probably, they would fall victim over there to the verdict of corrosive cultural Bolshevism.

On the other hand, the statement that most of the images only say that a chair is a chair and rain falls downward also applies to most music. To the extent that music is made in an unreflected way, to the extent that it does not, itself, recognize its difficulties as preconditions and incorporate them, it degenerates into the mere repetition of things that have already been said a hundred times, a kind of tautology of the world. Moreover, it surrounds things with an aura and in the best case affirms sorrowfulness as something that is unalterable and possibly obliged to be such [So-sein Sollendes].[4] In this sense, one can say of music, too, that it is infected by the increasing character of ideology. The possibility of escaping the difficulties by relying on the tried and true and simply continuing on as before is excluded.

I could imagine some of you interjecting, "If this business of composing is such a frightfully precarious and difficult thing that you have to make a special trip here to lecture us about it, and throw up your hands and exclaim, 'God, is this difficult, is this difficult!' then why do all of you even bother? Why don't you stay home and earn an honest living and make music more or less according to the accepted models that, after all, still make many of us happy?" This trivial argument must be taken seriously, at least to the extent that it cannot be dismissed with a vague gesture that says "anyone who thinks like that is out of step with the times." For this reason, I would like at least to suggest why attempts to go on speaking the traditional language of music are stricken with impotence. I refer you to Jean Sibelius. He wanted something of this kind. Nowhere did he go beyond the limits of the existing, traditional tonal means. In spite of which—this much must be conceded—he found something like an individual style. But individual style, by itself, is not yet a blessing or an achievement; one must look to see what is realized in it. As an aside, it is absolutely never permissible to judge works of art starting from their so-called style, but always and exclusively according to what they crystallize out within themselves, *"on their own merit*,"* as they would say in England. But in a demonstrable technical sense—one, at any rate, that can be demonstrated among musicians—all of Sibelius's works turned out so brittle, so inadequate, that his attempt should be regarded as precisely what people are otherwise all too eager to criticize in modern music—as an experiment with a negative outcome. One should jettison the opinion that new music is a matter of what its opponents call fashion, or what the wild men among them refer to as a straitjacket—that the composers have accommodated themselves to whatever happens to be *"up to date*"* at the moment, or, to use the favorite phrase, that they are mere fellow travelers. The impossibility of continuing to move musically within the tradition is objectively set. It is not based on a lack of talents that are capable of making proper use of the traditional methods; although it is striking that, for the most part, composers who today still compose traditionalistically are no longer even capable of doing so correctly according to the traditional standard, but fail in this regard at every turn. The traditional means, and above all the forms of coherence that they create, are affected, altered by the subsequently discovered means and forms of musical form-creation. Every triad that a composer still utilizes today already sounds like a negation of the dissonances that have meanwhile been set free. It no longer has the immediacy that it once had and that is asserted by its contemporary usage; rather, it is historically mediated. It contains its own antithesis. When this antithesis, this negation, remains silent, every such triad, every traditionalistic turn toward the positive lie, with its forced and frantic affirmation, becomes the equivalent to the talk of a *heile Welt,* an undamaged world, that is quite common in other cultural spheres. There is no primal meaning to be recreated in music. About thirty years ago, Ernst Krenek, after wild, atonal outbursts, tried to write tonally again. His theory was that this primal meaning was immanent in tonality, and that it should be reestablished. Krenek recognized—a great aesthetic-moral accomplishment—the impossibility of this attempt and gave it up after several years of passionate effort; and once again took as his starting point the radical intentions that he pursued in his first compositional period. The explanation for such phenomena is probably that even the tonal means, which he at times regarded as natural, primal givens and wanted to reestablish, were not such original givens at all, but themselves something historically emergent, evolved, developed, and hence also transitory.

The methods that are linked to the traditional language of music have become retrospectively problematic as a result of those that were discovered later—namely, they have become schematic. One hears, through what is newer, weaknesses of the old that were once hidden. There are very many things that sound stereotyped that were not stereotyped at the time. Richard Wagner, who was very *alert** in these matters, already registered this. Disrespectfully, but forthrightly, he said that in some of Mozart's pieces he could hear the dishes clatter on the table—*Tafelmusik,* even where it was by no means intended as such. It was possible to follow this schema as long as it was not evident as such, as long as it was still of a piece with the self-evident preconditions of composing. But once composing, and the relationship of the composer to the schemas, has lost its virginity, then the schemas not only emerge baldly and annoyingly, but lead in many places to anomalies, contradict the moments that have meanwhile been emancipated. Even Richard Strauss, in his purportedly unique, so-called personal style, failed, approximately from the time of the *Alpine* Symphony and the *Frau ohne Schatten,* as a result of the fact that he no longer took any notice of the objective tendencies of the music of his era. The person who commits himself to what is older only out of despair at the difficulties of the new is not comforted, but becomes the victim of his helpless nostalgia for a better era that, finally, never actually existed.

On the other hand, one should not dispense with reactionary objections in the manner of an apologist, but should learn the measure of correct insights that they offer, which so frequently give them the advantage over moderate, progressive cultural liberalism. The objective development of the musical material and of musical methods—one could say the level of development of the technical productive forces of music—has unquestionably outrun the subjective forces of production, i.e., the form of the response of the composers themselves. The invention of many technical principles and systems of the last forty years could be understood, from a certain distance, as an attempt to balance the disproportion between the objective development of music and what I, speaking casually, would like to call subjective musicality. In the process, something occurs that very much resembles society as a whole, where, indeed, glaringly unequal relations have emerged between the development of the technical forces of production and the human responses, the capacity to use, control, and make sensible use of these techniques. That human beings, on the one hand, are conquering space, while on the other they are regressing psychologically to an absurd extent, becoming infantile, is the most blatant expression of this state of affairs. But it also extends to artistic practice, down to its most subtle details. As early as the generation of Schoenberg, Stravinsky, and Bartók, inaccurately dubbed modern classicists, there were composers who in their own manner of responding were not able to cope with their innovations and hence somehow put a brake on themselves. I will name one of the greatest talents, with the greatest integrity—Béla Bartók. Any thought of him having accommodated himself to the market or watered his wine for the sake of the public is out of the question. Bartók once told me in a radio conversation that we had for the municipal station in New York that he was unable to get away from tonality; that this was self-evident in an artist who, like himself, had his roots in folk music. You may take my word for it that Bartók, who, out of protest against Fascism, had gone into emigration and poverty, did not allow himself to be infected by any *Blut-und-Boden* ideology.[5] But under the compulsion of origin and tradition, which ultimately proved more powerful than his own productively musical achievement, he had evidently lost contact with what he had dared in his boldest works, for example the two sonatas for violin and piano. The issue is a more general one. Even Richard Strauss, who boasted that in *Elektra* he had gone to the outer limit of tonality, later nevertheless said that tonality was a natural law that one must, in principle, not infringe upon. There is even a statement already attributed to Richard Wagner to the effect that at one time, in *Tristan*, he had committed unique extravagances that should be neither repeated nor imitated by others. In other words, this breach between the direction in which the subconscious drives the composers and the language in which they emerged dates back at least one hundred years. Most recently, it has been bleakly documented in the self-revocation of Hindemith, who either no longer acknowledged his best works or rewrote them in a very moderate sense, as if under censorship. Even in the boldest and most consequential composer of the period, in Schoenberg, there are at least symptoms of this breach to be observed. Again and again, he played with the material of tonality, and it was by no means only secondary works that he wrote tonally, but, even among his late works, such significant ones as the Second Chamber Symphony or the *Kol nidre.* In an essay that bears the title *"On revient toujours"*—namely *à ses premiers amours*—he attempted to justify this theoretically, more or less admitted that he actually felt drawn back to the thing from which he had launched himself.[6]

Today, the discrepancy between the subjective state of composition and the technical development that is identified by catchwords like integral composition and electronics has grown infinite. Compositional subject and compositional objectivity face each other across an abyss. This often leads to an opposite result compared to the previous generation. Composers frequently capitulate to the means, which they must utilize without really composing with them. Hence the first difficulty would be to achieve an appropriate relationship to the state of technique, either by the composers utilizing and forming the latter in accordance with the state of their own consciousness, or by their pushing their self-criticism so far that they catch up with the state of technique. How this should be done is something for which there are no general rules. I only mention the difficulty in order to focus attention on it, instead of repressing it. Naturally this is much easier said than done. Technique has its own specific gravity; every attempt to meld it with subjective experience threatens to water it down. All composers who are worth anything—really all—have, then, also been overtaken by profound insecurity in the face of the difficulty. Perhaps the answer to this would be that security is absolutely no ideal. Possibly such insecurity provides better preconditions for legitimate art than a feeling of security that is guaranteed by nothing in external or internal reality.

Among other things, as one of the difficulties of writing the truth, Brecht mentioned the art of making the truth practicable, of bringing it to the people as a weapon, so to speak. If one wanted to express this in a more or less illusionary way, the sentence applies musically to the phenomenon that there is no longer any such thing as a securely established space for composing, in which music would have its place. What Paul Valéry wrote many years ago about sculpture, that as a result of the loss of its relation to architecture it had become homeless, problematic, is true both literally and figuratively of music as well.[7] This is not, by any means, to warm up the humbug about the incomprehensibility of modernism. I mean something deeper, the position of music *per se* in contemporary society, the position of its spirit in relation to the objective one of the epoch. The chaotic situation of the contemporary concert within official musical life, for example, where a piece of music is performed without anyone—neither the composer, nor the conductor, nor the presenter—having a proper idea where it belongs, why it is being played in this particular place together with these other pieces, what it is actually supposed to do for the listener— this chaotic, museum-like situation of the concert business is the most striking expression of this. The anonymity of the concert, its anarchic element, is not the guarantor of freedom, as one might suppose, but instead introduces the work of art into emptiness and arbitrariness. The lack of functionality communicates itself to the work of art as the consciousness of something chaotic and as disorientation. This has nothing to do with music's serving some heteronymous practical purpose, with making an audience wax enthusiastic or disciplining it—luckily for it, music has divested itself of teleological relations. What is shattered, instead, is the adequacy between music and its place in society. What has become uncertain is what it means for the experience of the people to whom it is displayed. At the same time, music is no longer capable of absorbing that human experience in any way. If I said that composing feels the earth quake beneath its feet, then this is probably the explanation. Voltaire's statement "Où il n'y a pas le vrai besoin il n'y a pas le vrai plaisir" [Where there is no real need there is no real pleasure] is certainly also true of art. Where a thing no longer has within itself an objective social need—by which I mean not that it satisfies an external need, but rather that it reflects one within itself—the thing itself becomes hollow. What the opponents of the new music like to term its experimental character is generally the effort to come to terms with this situation of being hollowed out, as a result of owning up to the situation of the quaking earth and, if possible, trying to objectify it precisely by means of the work of art.

Permit me to say a few words about this concept of the experimental, which will be discomfiting to some of you with regard to so many things about new and newest music. It would be superficial to think that the experimental is the uncertain, is what is built on air and can be destroyed tomorrow; and to take the non-experimental for what is certain. It is precisely that which does *not* experiment, which keeps right on going as if it were still possible to do so, which continues to compose as if the old preconditions were still secure, that is consigned, with apodictic certainty, to downfall and oblivion. The experimenter still has more chances to last and to survive than the man who steers clear of experiment and behaves like a saver in an inflationary period who puts his wealth into gilt-edged stocks and bonds that are then inevitably devalued. However, this is not true in reverse. The experimental is not automatically within the truth, but can equally well end in failure; otherwise the concept of the experiment would have no sensible meaning at all. It is undeniable that many so-called experiments already discount, in themselves, the possibility of their failure, present themselves from the outset as if they didn't quite believe in themselves and were giving the game up for lost before the first move is made. Experimental, in the legitimate sense, means nothing other than art's self-conscious power of resistance against what is conventionally forced upon it from the outside, by consensus.[A] The conclusion from all this would not

A. In light of the most recent developments this may be qualified. Lately, compositional methods are frequently specifically termed experimental whose own

652 / *Composition, Composers, and Works*

be that one should, for example, set up nature preserves for the experimental in musical life and leave everything else, as always, to traditional music. Rather, both should be granted the same organizational preconditions, so that modern, radical music does not in fact become relegated to the specialty that its enemies then denounce.

Speaking immanently, in a musical sense, the lack of a pre-existing and embracing musical space now appears as the loss of objectively pre-existing musical *language.* The paradoxical difficulty of all music today is that every music that is written is subject to the compulsion to create its own language for itself, while language, as something that by virtue of its very concept exists beyond and outside of composition, as something that carries it, cannot be created purely by the will of the individual. The paradox defines concretely the difficulty with which one has to deal. I attempted to grasp the phenomenon many years ago, in *Philosophy of New Music,* by citing one of Kafka's parables in which he tells of a theater director who, himself, not only has to lead his ensemble and paint his scenery, but also actually has to beget his actors so that some day they will act and behave the way he has in mind. This Kafkaesque parable has meanwhile been revealed as the objective precondition of all composing.[8]

There has been no lack of attempts to come to terms with this difficulty by trying to restore music to its place in society. All of them have failed; it is time to admit this failure without reservation, without illusions. That all composers worth considering no longer make use of any but the most radical musical possibilities; that there is probably no longer any seriously gifted composer who would commit himself to the ominous moderate modernism is related to this. As proof of this failure I cite the entire realm of the sing-and-play movement, of young people's music; but also what is taking place following the official line of the Eastern Bloc. It is not the affair of art to make a social place for itself. It finds itself within the structure of social reality, but is unable on its own to influence the latter in any essential way. Up until the threshold of the present, art presupposed what in Hegel is called the Substantial, objective like-mindedness *[Gleichsinnigkeit].* Even now, the structure of a society must still be able to be connected with the composers' consciousness and subconscious, even if under extreme tension. Beethoven did not accommodate himself to the ideology of the often-cited rising bourgeoisie of the era of 1789 or 1800; he partook of its spirit. Hence his unsurpassed achievement, even though already dur-

---

results, the composed work itself, cannot be predicted either in the process of composing or in the imagination of the composer.

ing his lifetime this achievement, the inner coincidence with society, was by no means simply identical with external reception. But where the inner coincidence is lacking and is imposed by force or fiat, the result is merely conformity on the part of the composer, in other words something heteronomous. This is regularly at the expense of musical quality, of the music's stature. The music becomes foolish. By giving in to a state of humanity that does not keep pace with its own development, music at once commits itself to the regressive tendencies of society, to the steadily increasing liquidation of the individual in a world that, due to the concentration of ever greater power complexes, is moving toward total administration. Everything that in music attributes to itself the ethos of community inclines toward totalitarian forms of society. The difficulties of composing can be mastered, not by casting sidelong glances at a social space, as even Brecht still did, but, if at all, then only by proceeding from the thing itself—by giving the compositions themselves such a compelling quality that as a result they acquire an objectivity that would also, ultimately, partake of social meaning after all. Without this trust, as problematic as it may be, it is no longer possible to write a single note.

But this does not put an end to the difficulties. The general insight is a frame; it orients the composers to some extent, but by no means gives them comfort. It is just as difficult, purely from the point of view of the individual who is composing without preconceptions, to achieve objectivity in fact, as it would be bad and untruthful for the composer to accept an external source of responsibility. One is in a desperate situation: better to analyze it than to avoid it by stubborn naïveté. The only thing that today can provide any starting point for artists is their subjective capacity for response. For to be musical, in a higher sense, is not a merely subjective characteristic, but is precisely the capacity to innervate something of music's objective compulsions, in which, ultimately, the social compulsions are also contained. That is the reasonable foundation of the trust about which I spoke. If we say of a person that he is musical, we are not thinking just of a talent that is more or less natural and cannot be pursued beyond that point, but rather of his capacity to perceive the objectivity of music, its structural context. Even in the intellectualized notion of musicality, this is retained. But this very capacity for response by the subject became problematic. The individual is not something that exists purely in itself, but is always also mediated, always also a piece of social illusion and no last thing *[kein Letztes]*. The tendency of the times, indeed, has so weakened the ego that in many instances it is no longer quite master of its own responses. Today, what the breaches between subjective musical responses and objective technological conditions often conceal is merely the weakness of the subject. The composer who intones, "I am no snob, I don't go along with these fashions; I rely on my own instinct and do what I wish and can and nothing else"—this composer will, in general, probably be no snob, to the extent that it is an achievement not to be one. Instead, he will simply reproduce the residues of the conventions of the past and will think he hears his own voice in what is only a triply refracted echo.

If one examines the musical development since, say, 1920, as a whole from the perspective that I have identified here, the developments that are to be taken seriously are almost exclusively efforts to develop, out of the form of musical objectivity, i.e., from the material, idiom, and technique, methods of proceeding that *relieve [entlasten]* the subject, which no longer has confidence in itself alone, because it is bent over and crushed by all those difficulties. The musical history of the past forty years seems to me to be in large part a history of attempts at musical relief. Allow me to clarify this briefly for you.

The concept of relief *[Entlastung]*, as some spokesmen for the musical youth movement, for instance Wilhelm Ehmann, have adopted it, together with some twelve-tone musicians in America, quite innocently, and as Arnold Gehlen uses it, in a principled way and with great positive emphasis, in his anthropological sociology,[9] is not consistent with the idea of the through-composed work of art toward which, on the other hand, all of these techniques ultimately strive. The decrease in effort, the relief, always means a preponderance of dead matter, of elements that have not passed through the subject, that are externally thing-like and ultimately alien to art. Still, the attempts at relief have their sound reason—precisely that the difficulties of composing out of pure freedom, out of a kind of all-sided actuality of hearing, are now scarcely surmountable. That was possible, evidently, only during the short period of the explosion, during the heroic period of the new music, as it comprises the middle works of Schoenberg, from the Piano Pieces op. 11 to the Lieder op. 22, and the contemporaneous creations of the young Webern and the young Alban Berg. These three composers are classic composers of modernism only because at the time they were not classicists—because they got by without externally imposed rules, purely with the compositional form of response, with the way their immediate imagination worked. This could be demonstrated even in the origin of some of the works of this phase. Schoenberg composed his boldest and most advanced work, the monodrama *Erwartung*, in two weeks, evidently in a kind of trance, not so very differently from the way the automatic writing of the surrealists would later be intended; really by means of an explosion of the subconscious.[10] The extraordinarily rapid emergence of such works corresponds to the brevity of the phase during which people composed in this way. Afterwards, Schoenberg experienced a very long, seven-year hiatus in his creative output. In Berg's case, something similar is indicated by the fact that the quantum of his production remained so small. There has scarcely ever been a musician of comparable stature who left behind as few works as he did. Already beginning with *Wozzeck*, he no longer added any more opus numbers, because, as he told me once, he was embarrassed that the opus numbers of the more than forty-year-old composer were so low. In Webern's case, the miniature formats testify to something analogous. Evidently he could bear the boundless inner tension without relief only by renouncing the possibility of musical articulation over long stretches of time, although the longing for long, composed-out time never relinquished its lifelong hold on him. Even Schoenberg could not hold out with purely spontaneous, unrelieved, purely self-reliant composition. Here, it may also be a factor that the unexampled spontaneity of such works cannot be preserved over time, and also that his critical consciousness became aware of a series of illogical and anomalous elements in the freely created works that he did not feel he could correct critically except by a certain process of rationalization. Under this last aspect, one should have a look at the Four Piano Pieces of my friend René Leibowitz,[11] which apply this kind of rationalization to the model of the pieces in Schoenberg's op. 23 [Five Piano Pieces], which with the exception of the last are not yet twelve-tone. They transpose, as it were, the ideas of these pieces into twelve-tone technique; a noteworthy attempt. Examining it, one can confirm both the progress through the system of relief, the greater consistency, continuity, and also the price that had to be paid for it, the loss of the immediacy of those middle works by Schoenberg. In fact, the first great phenomenon of relief was the twelve-tone technique. My recently deceased teacher Eduard Steuermann[12] once expressed this very simply with the statement that the row procedure should help to accomplish what the ear could not achieve at every moment. The transition to this point took place early in the heroic period of free atonality. Webern reported that in the Bagatelles op. 9, one of his most significant and successful works, he wrote down the notes that had already come up in these very brief works, in order to avoid them and in their place to use others that were still unutilized: in other words, to avoid repeated notes. This occurred in approximately 1909, but already implies the idea, if not yet the systematic development, of the twelve-tone technique, derived simply from the naïve practice of the composer. Almost impossible to say where the immanent achievement of the ear ends and the external relief begins. Who would dare to begrudge the composer Webern that innocent list of already-used notes? But one must assume something like a threshold phenomenon, a transformation of quantity into quality—that the necessity of such rationalization suddenly becomes alienated from itself, that it confronts the composer and his hearing as something external. Then the music is forcibly subjected to order; the order no longer follows purely from the musical events. By rationalizing the latter, from among which, after all, it is simultaneously emerging, the order is also imposed on them. It is no accident that in the early period of the twelve-tone technique so many older forms were pressed into service, despite their obvious lack of congruence with the atonal material; and that right down to the micro structure so many things resurfaced at that time that were still forbidden, with good reason, for example in the use of sequences, retained rhythmic patterns, and the like.

One can interpret the serial development that set in with such vehemence after Schoenberg's death as a critique of those illogical elements. The serial principle, from the perspective of twelve-tone music, means that everything that projected heterogeneously into what was composed and pre-formed by twelve-tone-ness—everything independent of the twelve-tone technique, all the material and structural traces of the old tonal idiom, are removed. Stockhausen formulated this accurately and strikingly when he said that in terms of his musical language Schoenberg, despite all the innovations, was actually still tonal. The serial school wanted to radicalize the twelve-tone principle, which they regarded, in a sense, as a merely partial reordering of the materials. They wanted to extend it to all the musical dimensions, to elevate it to totality. Absolutely everything is to be determined, even the dimensions of rhythm, meter, tonal color, and overall form, which in Schoenberg had still been free. In doing so, the serial composers took as their starting point the thesis that because all musical phenomena, including pitch and tonal color, are, in their acoustical regularity, ultimately temporal relations, they must all be able to be reduced compositionally to a single common denominator—time. From a series's given, original material, which should be as brief as possible, everything—every note, every rest, duration, pitch, color should strictly follow. It may remain open whether the equation actually works; whether one can simply identify objective physical time, according to the rate of vibration and overtone relations, with musical time, the feeling of musical duration, which is essentially subjectively mediated. The serial composers encountered this problem a long time ago. The most advanced among them, Boulez and Stockhausen, are laboring at it with great intensity. What is of greater concern to me is the idea of total determination as such. It is already implicit in the twelve-tone technique, to the extent that it is not clear why this and that dimension should be strictly determined in it, and others not. Accordingly, one may perhaps say that the serialists did not arbitrarily concoct mathematicizations of music, but confirmed a development that Max Weber, in the sociology of music,[13] identified as the overall tendency of more recent musical history—the progressive rationalization of music. It is said to have reached its fulfillment in integral construction. If from a given basic material absolutely everything else, in fact, were to follow, then this would be the greatest relief of the composer that can possibly be imagined. He would then only have to obey what is contained in his series, and would be delivered from all cares.

But this does not leave one with a good feeling. The reification that is already perceptible in the twelve-tone technique, the disempowerment of the living, listening act as the authentic constituent of music, is so intensified that it threatens to destroy all meaningful context. I recall a young composer who brought me a composition in Darmstadt, perhaps as much as fourteen years ago, that appeared to me as the craziest gibberish.[14] You couldn't make out any up and down, front and back, logic and setting—no articulation of the phenomenon at all that you could grasp. When I asked him how everything related to everything else, what the musical meaning of a phrase was, where it ended and began, and other such elementary questions about structure, the young man demonstrated to me that some number of pages later there was a pause that corresponded to a single note in a particular place, and so on in that vein. He had truly, as Philistine enemies envision it, reduced the whole thing to a mathematical example, which may even have been correct—it was too boring for me to figure it out—but which absolutely no longer translated into any recognizable and compelling musical context. The subject, on which music is thrown back in the absence of a social space, and which was supposed to be relieved by all these machinations, is not only relieved but virtually eliminated. But along with it also the control that it exercises and that helps to constitute musical objectivity. If it were seriously just a matter of composing out what a series like this contains within it, then—the joke is as cheap as the thing itself—one could compose better with an electronic computer than by troubling a composer. The help he is offered threatens to overwhelm him. He is subjected to a set of laws that are alien to him and that he can scarcely catch up with. The resulting music, however, becomes something deaf and vacant. What I forecast years ago as the aging of new music is literally occurring. At the time, some of my Kranichstein[15] colleagues were angry with me; today I can say that the best of them, at any rate, are largely of one mind with me in this diagnosis.

Into this situation of serialism barged John Cage; it explains the extraordinary effect that he had. His principle of chance, which is familiar to you under the name of aleatory music, wants to break out of the total determinism, the integral, obligatory musical ideal of the serial school. He, the American, was not pressured in the same way, not compelled by the same historical necessity as the musicians of the European tradition, who exist within the context of the obligatory style, the general onward march of the rationalization of music. But even the principle of indeterminacy that Cage introduced remained as alien to the ego as its apparent opposite, serialism. It, too, belongs in the category of relief for the weakened ego. Pure chance, it is true, breaks stolid, inescapable necessity, but is as external to living hearing as the latter. Cage once formulated it very logically, saying than when one hears Webern, one always only hears Webern, but in truth what one wants to hear is not him, but the sound. With this, he, similarly, argues for an almost physical, thing-like objectivity, such as serial music was. This, by the way, also explains the fact that so many serial composers went over without a hitch to the principle of indeterminacy. The Hungarian composer György Ligeti, who is as perceptive as he is truly original and significant, observed correctly that in their effect the extremes of absolute determination and absolute chance coincide. Statistical generality becomes the law of composition, a law that is alien to the ego. Certainly the absolute indeterminacy of Cage and his school is not exhausted in it. It has a polemical meaning; it comes close to the dadaist and surrealist actions of the past. But their "happenings*," in keeping with the political situation, no longer have any politically demolishing content and hence tend to take on a sectarian, séance-like quality—while everyone believes they have participated in something uncanny, nothing at all happens, no ghost appears. It is Cage's contribution, which cannot be exaggerated, to have sown doubts regarding the extremes of musical logic, the blind ideal of complete domination over nature in music; hardly uninfluenced by "action painting*." What he himself offers in his most radical works is nevertheless not as different as one might suppose from studying the program, even if his best pieces, like the piano Concerto, still emit an extraordinary shock that stubbornly resists all neutralization. Hardly any other composer of our time has achieved that. But the most serious difficulty is that despite everything there is no going back. If, in contrast to the twelve-tone technique, the serial principle, and aleatory music, one simply sought to get a fresh grasp on substantive freedom, i.e., free atonality in the sense of Schoenberg's expectation, one would almost necessarily capitulate to reaction.

Against the techniques of relief, one should hold fast to the ideal of something that Heinz-Klaus Metzger called a-serialism, and for which I suggested the term informal music. Mindful of the impossibility of painting a picture of the so-called positive anywhere, I will forego describing it in detail, particularly since if you are interested you can learn about my ideas on the subject from the essay "Vers une musique informelle," which may be found at the end of *Quasi una fantasia*.[16] However, I shall at least identify models of the difficulties that also confront the ideal of the informal. In the most advanced and acoustically sensitive compositions today there is a yawning discrepancy between the blocks that have been joined together, layered, so to speak, and are often astonishingly through-composed in themselves, and the overall structure. It is as if there were no mediation connecting the unprecedented articulation of the details with the equally magnificently through-composed totality; as if the two things were joined together according to principles of construction, but as if these principles of construction were not capable of realization in living phenomena. Mediation is lacking in the banal, as well as in the strict sense. In the banal sense, links are lacking between the individual sounds, in which everything is concentrated. In the strict sense, the events in themselves do not want to transcend themselves; the structure remains largely abstract in relation to them. Until now, integration frequently has become impoverishment. One can observe, along with an extreme increase in compositional means, a kind of regression to homophony. As I described this, borrowing an expression of Boulez's, blocks are being added together, rather than lines being drawn. Hardly any harmonic tensions are created; hardly any complementary harmonies; hardly any monodic, much less polyphonic lines. This shrinkage is out of all proportion to the compositional expenditure of means and construction. It may have something to do with what one can call the preponderance of extras, of the extra-musical in the most recent music, which Schnebel identified as one of the most characteristic phenomena of its development. It is as if music, by using noise, bruitistic effects, and then optical, especially mimetic ones, wanted to make up part of what it is temporarily blocked from achieving in the way of immanent unfolding.[17] Those actions, however, frequently have something aimless about them. Dada turns into *l'art pour l'art*, and this is hard to reconcile with the idea of dada. Frequently a music is assembled that actually doesn't want to go anywhere. Against this it is argued, above all by electronic composers, that it is a matter of providing materials. If I once said that electronic compositions sounded like Webern on a Wurlitzer,[18] that is unquestionably out of date. But on the other side there is always some primitiveness of results that remains unmistakable in relation to the technical effort. In general, it is probably difficult to develop means independent of the purpose, the quality of what is composed with them. I would like to mention at least one symptom that struck me recently and that perhaps also has something to do with the complex of difficulties— the phenomenon of the restraining of impulses; that music is constantly moving, wanting to develop, but breaks off again as if under a spell. Whether this spell expresses the one that we live under, whether it, too, is a symptom of ego-weakness or compositional inadequacy, is something on which I would not like to pass judgment.

I only wanted to make you aware of all this; not to prophesy or postulate anything. Music today sees itself faced with an alternative, that between the fetishism of the material and the process, on the one hand, and unfettered chance, on the other. A statement by Christian Dietrich Grabbe occurred to me that once greatly impressed me: "For nothing but despair alone can save us."[19] Everything lies with spontaneity, i.e., the involuntary reaction of the compositional ear, *quand même*. But if one composes in deadly earnest, one must ultimately ask whether it is not all becoming ideological nowadays. Therefore, one must confront the possibility of its falling silent non-metaphorically and without the consolation that it cannot go on that way. What Beckett expresses in his dramas, and above all in his novels, which sometimes babble like music, has its truth for music itself. Perhaps only that music is still possible which measures itself against this greatest extreme, its own falling silent.

(1964; GS, vol. 17, pp. 253–73)

II. IN UNDERSTANDING NEW MUSIC

For H. H. Stuckenschmidt on the occasion of his 65th birthday

In the chapter "Instructions for Listening to New Music," in the book *Der getreue Korrepetitor*,[20] I had essentially confined myself, in the interest of practical musical aims, to purely technical matters that create difficulties in understanding new music. By comparison, I had de-emphasized the sociological aspect. Without question, it cannot be separated from the immanently musical aspect, as I should like to emphasize in opposition to some currently virulent tendencies in the sociology of music. Specifically musical problems cannot be avoided, unless the sociology of music wants to narrow itself to the identification of subjective responses, without regard to the object. At the same time, the social aspect also has an element of independence. On the one hand, society provides the frame for all music and musical practice. The person who speaks of reception without also considering the overall structure into which the music falls, along with the possibility or impossibility of its reception, would be thinking abstractly in the bad sense. On the other hand, social conditions extend deep into the apparently purely musical difficulties of hearing. I recall, merely as a general factor that works against the reception of new music, something that I once, in a different context, called "half-cultivation" [*Halbbildung*],[B] which corresponds to the administration of spirit and its transformation into a cultural product. From the beginning, it is against the possibility of understanding an art that does not want to submit to those mechanisms, or even resists them. Were one to focus only on the technical issues of listening, one would tacitly assume at least the potential for a relationship between the listeners and the new music, and the will to such a relationship. But this assumption, which is self-evident in technical analysis, is entirely problematic when it comes to the social relationship between the public and energetically progressive music. Kierkegaard spoke of aesthetic seriousness. Perhaps the expression itself was already reactive. Perhaps as long as something of the kind existed it was not necessary to talk about it at all, and instead the more seriously art was taken, the more it was seen as mere play. Meanwhile, the proponents of entertainment music ply us, as apologists, with *Weltanschauung* and even with Riesman's theory of the other-directed individual.[21] In any case, aesthetic seriousness and the disposition to distraction, whose present-day predominance is not at all new, point in opposite directions. The latter forms an *a priori* of unapproachability, before it even comes to a concrete conflict between listening and the living phenomenon of new music.

Meanwhile, the explanations for the disproportion between it and understanding remain unsatisfying. I refer in this regard to a number of earlier works on the same subject, such as the one I published before 1933 in the Essen theater journal *Der Scheinwerfer* [The Spotlight], under the title "Why Is the New Art So Hard to Understand?" Generally, the catchword "alienation" is applied. This is associated with the notion that from approximately the middle of the nineteenth century the progressive autonomy of art caused the latter to become more and more distant from human beings—the leap that falls between Heine and Baudelaire in lyric

B. Cf. Adorno, "Theorie der Halbbildung," GS, vol. 8, pp. 93–121.

poetry. It also thoroughly dominates music; *Tristan* is generally considered to be its moment. This thesis, which has already become a cliché, takes the fact of the matter as its explanation. If one divests the argument of its trappings and cultural ballast, what is left is that people are alienated from the new music because they are alienated from it. I would like to try to go at least a little way beyond this sterile method of dealing with the question, or at least suggest one. Unquestionably, there has, at times, existed an adequacy between listeners and music, in rough terms, and among rather exclusive strata. Admittedly, in the most significant instances since Bach, it was probably by no means as self-evident as a romantically retrospective imagination paints it. People who believe they are thinking socially when they condemn modern music on account of its asocial character should be forced to desist by the fact that even on the greatest heights of musical history it was not a blessed equivalency that held sway. At least one may say, without too much temerity, that the adequacy between the hearers and what was heard is confined to the era of tonality, specifically in its largely diatonic form. Given the highly artificial character of the church modes and the no less artificial late medieval polyphony, the equivalence is highly uncertain in music before the era of figured bass—to the extent that we can even imagine it by means of living, participatory listening. The ideal that music should or must be generally understood, which is frequently assumed as unproblematic, has its own socio-historical index. It is democratic; it was scarcely in force under feudalism. At that time, what one might call the disciplinary function of music, in the sense of Plato and Augustine, was foregrounded, as opposed to universal understanding or purported enjoyment. At that time, consequently, music was also characteristically regarded as a kind of secret science. No scores, but only voices have come down to us, presumably in order to keep the *misera plebs* far away from the alchemist's kitchen of counterpoint. After *Tristan*, more recently, the temporary and precarious agreement began to falter once again.

No doubt some things were, and are still being made up for. With imperceptible slowness, works from the period after the revocation of the understanding are being responded to. But this reception should not be overrated. There is a considerable difference whether people simply put up with works because they have now become fifty, sixty, or seventy years old, or whether they really understand them. A performance of Schoenberg's First Chamber Symphony will no longer cause a scandal nowadays. In the meanwhile, the public has become accustomed to altogether different things, and the piece in question, after all, contains numerous parts and elements that moderate the shocks. One should nevertheless assume that the work, which has an extraordinarily difficult texture, is just as little understood, in the strict sense, or "listened through" as in the years when it was written, prior to 1910. A really detailed study of the reception of the mature works of Wagner would already be timely and productive. It would probably show that, on the one hand, certain epiphenomena in Wagner, sometimes of a kind that contradicted his ideal, and, on the other hand, the ideological gesture of the whole, were understood. However, the elements of composition, themselves, were probably much less well understood in their context. Let me recall a state of affairs that Richard Strauss mentioned in his revision of Berlioz's treatise on instrumentation, with respect to Wagner, and that applies even more to Strauss himself. The latter speaks of the *al fresco* treatment of the orchestra in the magic fire of *Walküre*. Tonal complexes like this are already conceived in such a way as not to be perceived with the same precision in each of their sounds as pre-Wagnerian music, but rather, as it were, from a certain distance. A certain vagueness of perception is presumed, indeed composed into it; the phenomenon that is written down and the one that is really perceived are by no means identical. This suggests a sociological speculation that Benjamin applied analogously to Baudelaire: that since that leap after the middle of the nineteenth century, music, to the extent that it belongs to modernism, already addresses itself to listeners who do not pay such close attention and—one may extrapolate—consequently do not understand so very precisely either. Historical changes in the act of understanding, accordingly, would have been endorsed by compositional technique.

With the era of tonality I was referring to that of major-minor tonality, as it gained acceptance after the beginning of the seventeenth century. That within its zone the traditional understanding, or at least what seems to itself to be understanding, holds sway, raises questions in retrospect. Musicology, in the meanwhile, knows or suspects that major-minor tonality, which corresponds to the dominance of the Ionian and Aeolian church modes, is much older in folk music than its official approbation by modern figured-bass music since the end of the sixteenth century. Accordingly, the major-minor feeling would have been alive much longer than the progress of the musical material would have us believe. Actual listening may never have followed the church modes as much as it did major and minor. In musical pre-consciousness and in the collective subconscious, tonality, although, for its part, it is also a historical product, seems to have become something like second nature. This would probably explain its eminent power of resistance in the consciousness of listeners when it comes to the comprehension of forms that, for their part, followed with complete logical consistency and necessity from the immanent development of tonality as the language of music.

In order to picture the difficulties in the comprehension of new music, one must ask oneself the question *e contrario:* where does the capacity for resistance of tonality as a musical language come from? First, one will probably have to recall the fact that to a great extent tonality was the result of an involuntary, unguided process of development. One will not easily be able to fend off the thought of the principles of the bourgeois money economy, which also originated, as Max Weber demonstrated in *Wirtschaft und Gesellschaft,* from the immanent lawfulness of pre-bourgeois, feudal society, the accounting of the patrimonial system.[22] In the apologetics of the new music it is easy to forget that tonality is no merely established system of sounds, but rather corresponded quite precisely to the concept of the objective spirit. It mediated between a musical language that was more or less immediately and spontaneously spoken—if the expression is permitted—by human beings, and norms that had crystallized out within this language. That balance between language and norms has now been revoked by the new music, approximately since the first works of fully implemented atonality. It no longer permits a language-like regularity, nor does it resemble the way most people listen, pre-artistically, in a rather childlike fashion. The spoken and the literarily objectified languages of words have also separated; only, in music, the break is much more radical. The difference between tonality and the emancipated material of today—that of the twelve equally entitled and tempered half-tones (we may leave aside the quarter- and semi-tones here) is not the superficial difference between the one system, the one organization scheme and another, but is the difference between a sedimented language on the one hand, and on the other a procedure that has passed through the conscious will of emancipated consciousness.

New music's revocation of the collective agreement is itself an essential aspect of the new material, even though the latter, for its part, developed out of the law of movement of the old music. In order not to succumb to the gravitational pull of music's linguistic aspects, its gesture would like to divest itself of linguistic elements altogether, to construe the context purely from within itself, in accordance only with the demands of the concrete work. There were social reasons why this occurred—the traditional, given, idiomatic language of music clashed with individual differentiation in music, in which the process of differentiation of bourgeois society is manifested. The aspect of commonality in the tonal language increasingly emerged as one of the comparability of everything with everything, of leveling and convention. The simplest sign of this is the way the principal chords of the tonal system can be inserted at innumerable points, as a kind of form of equivalence, in which something that is always identical stands in for something that is always different, without, themselves, having to be modified. This comparability of the aspect of musical language increasingly put itself at the disposal of the consumer character, as its vehicle. Or, as I suspect, it is possible that the same principle that was at work in bourgeois-era consumer thinking may also have been involved, from the beginning, in the comparability and exchangeability of tonal markers. Gradually, in any case, the consumer character spread itself over the entire language of music. This became unendurable; what had once been language, in music, turned into clatter. Romanticism had an unwavering sense of that. The usual subjective invectives against romantic individualism and subjectivism are generally nothing but an exalted-sounding ideology for that stiff and mechanical essence that human beings revolted against as long as the idea of freedom meant anything substantive to them. What seemed individualistic about the protest against the dominance of tonality, in the name of freedom of expression, is actually itself social protest, directed at the selling out of musical language to profit, against its debasement into ideology.

Cocteau was not the first to point out that the development of the new painting, since impressionism, can only be understood in relation to photography. Painting, as it relates to optical form-creation, becomes what refuses to be incorporated into photographic technique, and, at the same time, resistance against the transformation of the world into its own cheap imitation, which is being perfected nowadays. The relation of art music to light music is analogous—like Pierre Boulez, I definitively reckon jazz, which is completely misplaced when it is thrown together with avant-garde tendencies, as people like to do in Germany, to the latter. Light music expands to excess, and the culture industry sucks more and more of the products of so-called high culture into itself, with or without arranging and jazzing them up. By itself, the never-ending repetition of standards that have been stamped "classical" and given brand names like "*The Emperor**" already transforms them into hits. In much late romantic, ostensibly serious music, there is already a gradual transition to light music; I have attempted to demonstrate this in the case of Tchaikovsky. Fifty years ago, Franz Schreker was still modern; at the time, Paul Bekker described him as the authentic exponent of modernism in opera.[23] Many of his achievements in sound, which fascinated musicians at that time, have meanwhile sunk to the level of pop music.

But the more the realm of entertainment expands, the more music and musical elements are affected, the more emphatic, objectively, is the need of composers for something un-disfigured. One must become conscious of a paradox: the very things that are disparaged as intellectual refer to things that have not yet been subjected to treatment by the rationalized enterprise, that do not yet bear the fingerprints of universal communication. It is not so much that the meanwhile over-taxed alienation is the cause of the difficulty of understanding modern music, as that modern music itself, in order not to play along with the general bleating, turns its barbs against the listener, disavows the usual notions of immediacy and the natural. Disgust at banality, in the name of taste, has always been artistically productive—never merely aestheticism, also a guardian of morality in art. But in the meanwhile, such disgust is no longer limited to individual objectionable phrases and tonal combinations, but has spilled over onto the entire worn-out material.

In my opinion, however, the core of an explanation for the difficulty of understanding new music lies in tonality's power of resistance. One would have to understand *by what means* it became second nature. Its similarity to language is not, alone, sufficient to explain this. One must refer back to the function that tonality exercised for so long, that of a certain resolution between the universal and the particular in music. August Halm, whose works are almost entirely forgotten today, was probably the first to pose the question of the universal and the particular in music explicitly.[24] While tonality, like spoken language, could draw on general formulae, ranging from the individual sound to the sequence of intervals to the overall architecture, it was flexible enough to offer, in the combination of these elements, space for the particular; in other words, for specific, characteristic individual coinage and individual expression. True, tonality had pre-organized all phenomena in the sense of an objective language, similar to the languages of words. But at the same time it contained innumerable possibilities for combinations, and above all the possibility of being saturated with expression, so that the particular could enter into every universal, indeed frequently was engendered by the universal. For Nietzsche, this capacity was something he already no longer experienced as self-evident. He was of the opinion, which by the way is hardly defensible, that music's capacity to express the particular was merely a matter of convention. He did not take the objective spirit in tonality seriously enough; he underestimated its substantive nature—astonishing in a person who thought about music as tonally as he did. The other side of this kind of objectivity in tonal music is an aspect that may have provided the decisive impulse that ultimately led new music to revoke the *contrat social*. My friend Rudolf Kolisch, in an American work[25] that is much too little known in Germany, described the basic characters to which the types of Beethoven's tempi correspond. In this way, he arrived at a discrete number of such basic characters and tempi. At first, the result is shocking; it seems a bit mechanistic and overly mathematical in relation to Beethoven's gigantic oeuvre. But if you turn the tables, if you understand Kolisch's view as potentially critical, you will find that great tonal music actually bears some resemblance to a puzzle. The movements of the greatest composers are based on a discrete number of *topoi*, of more or less rigid elements, out of which they are constructed. The aspect of the organic, the developing, which is central to Viennese classicism, proves, in light of these *topoi*, to be largely an art of appearances. Music represents itself as if one thing were developing out of the other, but without any such development literally occurring. The mechanical aspect is covered up by the art of composition, but is incomparably more powerful than believers in culture can feel good about. It is as profoundly related to the spirit of the natural sciences as to that of the bourgeoisie. Similarly, with a certain amount of naïveté, the great philosophical systems beginning with Plato have had recourse again and again to such mechanical means, against which the pathos of the spirit, which dominates in them, should have rebelled. The discomfort with this aspect of music, kaleidoscopic and mechanistically constructed from individual parts, drove in the direction of a music that wanted to be free of it. Bourgeois consciousness, on the other hand, always thinks about constructing as much as possible from a minimum of parts, after the pattern of the labor processes that began with the era of factory production. There is a stubborn if unacknowledged pleasure in this kind of procedure—that of regressive repetition. Tonality, outliving itself, provides for this within bourgeois art. The latter no more rebelled against it than the bourgeoisie was truly revolutionary. To this extent, the new music really brings traditional music before a court of justice.

Nevertheless, the advantage of the tonal idiom—which admittedly did not have to compete with any other—was that at its height, from Bach to early romanticism, it not only, as a schema, embraced the particular, but, as one could demonstrate in the case of Beethoven, encouraged it, indeed engendered the form of the particular from within itself. For hundreds of years, the specific emotions and individual impulses, the so-called inspirations, which were independently pre-formed by tonality, more or less demanded the organizing principles of the latter. Without making light of it, we must remind ourselves what a leap the new music entailed, not merely on account of its qualitative difference, but above all by dint of what it lost in tonality. Only by not covering this up is it possible to understand the sense in which modern music is radical, and why it is that people resist it so fiercely. The function that tonality fulfilled for many hundreds of years can no longer be so easily fulfilled; it must, if such a thing is even possible, be recreated in each individual instance. This is the main reason for the shock. To differentiate, in this zone, between things that are integral to music and things that are social would be superficial and external. The problems of musical structure, of the relationship between the universal and the particular in music, are unselfconscious manifestations of profound social processes. The universal and the particular cannot be brought back together arbitrarily; nor can tonality, as people once imagined, be recuperated. With its downfall it pays back its own debt, the repressive element that does violence to the individual impulse. One can probably picture what is at stake most easily by remembering that precisely the great tonal composers, Bach, Mozart, Beethoven, had a desire for dissonance that shows through again and again, but is kept within bounds by the figured bass.

Accordingly, the main difficulty in the reception of new music would be that this equilibrium—Schoenberg spoke of homeostasis; in accepting it as an ideal he was a thoroughly traditional composer—is no longer automatically provided by the order of the material. Modern music knows no prestabilized harmony between the universal and the particular, and cannot know it, for the sake of its own truth. The universal is open, deschematized, but problematic, always yet to be discovered, from the formulation of the individual impulse all the way up to the construction of the whole. It has turned out that in the course of development the particular, which was possessed of enormous power in the spontaneous beginnings of the new music, has also been affected by this constellation. I remind you of the simple observation that the real, concrete through-construction of details in fully integrated music is inferior to the through-construction of details in free atonality or even in late tonality. This is related to the crisis of inspiration that Eduard Steuermann, as well as Ernst Krenek, identified. As in the Hellenistic period, after the decay of the Greek *polis*, the emancipated individual did not grow stronger but shriveled up, found less and less room for its realization, and finally was reduced to the ideal of living in secret; this is evidently what is occurring in music. Its chaotic aspect, which is what most people find frightening about it, is conditioned by the fact that the prestabilized harmony of the universal and the particular has disintegrated. The listening ear, calibrated to that harmony, feels overwhelmed when it is supposed to follow on its own the specific processes of the individual compositions, in which the relationship between the universal and the particular is articulated each time.

Here, now, the social aspect plays a flagrant role that extends to the internal structure of the music. It is no accident that tonality was the musical language of the bourgeois era. The harmony of the universal and the particular corresponded to the classical liberal model of society. As in the latter, totality, as the *invisible hand**, took over by means of the individual, spontaneous events, and over their heads. The universal resolution of tension that it effected was intended to make the sum, the balance of credits and debits, come out even. Homeostasis, balance, and the equivalency of credits and debits are immediately the same. This model was never adequate to reality, but was to a large extent ideology. It evolved in such a way that it was increasingly unable to satisfy itself on its own, and demanded interventions. Similarly, one could interpret the history of the new music as one of interventions by a critical, planning will into the apparently autarchic mechanism of tonality. Since the latter has ceased to exist, there is aesthetic interventionism in music, with all the difficulties and disproportionalities that necessarily accompany such permanent intervention. The more intervention and planning, the more the old model is hollowed out, or becomes a pure pretext. The universal character of tonality, which no longer has any transparent relation to the particular, is divested of all substantiality and becomes a limiting convention. This is how composers, for more than a century, have perceived the classical cadence formula of the subdominant to dominant to tonic.

The idea of the resolution of tension, of harmony in the artistic sense, is becoming ever more ideological, in proportion as reality, through the universal, accords to the particular less and less of what the latter has been promised and promises itself. In an overall circumstance in which it has become entirely doubtful whether it has any meaning at all, an artistic process that—however indirectly—presents and transfigures the whole as something meaningful is no longer tolerable. Instead, people who are confronted by demystification respond, like a mirror reflex, by hating *it*, instead. Aesthetic ties are a lie because the real ties have become a lie. Here is probably where we must seek the deepest motivation for the revocation of the collective consensus. Let me remind you of an experience that plays a role here and that Schoenberg already stumbled across—that of musical stupidity, as he emphasized it, for example, in Verdi's sequences, full of disdain for the way a musical idea that was previously expressed is repeated two, three, or however many more times. This element of stupidity is nothing other than reified consciousness that draws a veil of deception, with musical babbling, over the real social contradictions. Schoenberg's statement that art should not be decorative, but true, in agreement with Adolf Loos, was not a naturalistic program: properly understood, he is making an indictment of reified consciousness. The refusal to comprehend new music is the unconscious and hence all the more stubborn defense of that reified consciousness. Its social solidification is misunderstood as the eternity of the natural. It is these real contradictions, which contemporary society cannot see beyond, that stem society's consciousness and back it up toward the supposedly blessed era of tonality. This false consciousness is rehearsed by the culture industry, which brings the already arrested bourgeois imagery to a halt, freezes it. That which would be the voice of society in art is for this very reason anathema to society; not the least reason for the difficulty of listening to new music.

In this context I would like to draw attention to something that has not been seen correctly in either its social or its aesthetic relevance, but that recently emerged in crass form on the occasion of a discussion in Frankfurt. The resistance to the new music is especially focused on opera. Opera is popular, on the whole, with people who would like to participate in cultivation, but who evade the claims of active intellectual participation that cultivation would impose on them and prefer to relax in the passive reception of an everlasting sameness. The opera is the hearth and home of culture consumers and hence the bulwark of resistance against new music. The concept of "modern opera" contains irresolvable contradictions. The idea of opera of the type that is savored by the public cannot be reconciled with the means of the new music.[26] The revolutionary Schoenberg, consequently, dismissed that operatic ideal with the two one-act operas *Erwartung* and *Die glückliche Hand*. So, although in a totally different, less abrupt way, did Stravinsky, with *Renard* and the *Histoire du soldat*. In the realm of the theater, the new music is especially pressed to enter into a very close alliance with so-called experimental productions.

The difficulties in the comprehension of new music are, on the one hand, those of lack of understanding in the strict sense, conditioned by the lack of easy-to-understand communication formulae, but also by the lack of a musical logic—however illusionary it may be—that would be analogous to discursive logic. True, this kind of logic may never have prevailed in traditional music in as strict a sense as the idiom would have it appear;

but new music dismisses even its appearance. In exchange, in its authentic products, the new music is much more logically organized—literally and no longer metaphorically—than traditional music. But this very kind of uncompromisingly logical organization hurts the purportedly relaxed and, in truth, distracted consciousness of the listeners. The new formal works, even though they rarely cause scandals nowadays, still provoke, beyond mere incomprehension, aggressive emotions in response to the aggression that they themselves commit. Radical right-wing political groups all disparage modern music. The latter is opposed in all its technical characteristics—dissonance, remote intervals, open form—to the ordinary, spiritual-ideological concept of harmony. It recalls the very things about which what Herbert Marcuse called the affirmative character of culture deceives us.[27] The rage at it is incorporated into something more comprehensive, the socio-psychological syndrome of the authoritarian personality. The latter hates everything deviant *per se*, especially specific content; everything is supposed to conform. New music, however, is absolute deviance. As such, it poses the problem that it can scarcely be comprehended truthfully without some relation to the thing from which it deviates. But be this as it may, the rage to which I refer is concerned not so much with a rebellion against specific contents or structures as with a form of reaction that precedes all of that: the defense against whatever is alien. The less it is possible to grasp the content, the less it conforms to ordinary experience, the stronger this kind of reaction against it. The sworn enemies of new music are generally those who understand nothing about it. It is not like certain avant-garde literature, which violates specific taboos; it violates the *a priori* agreement with the world. Hence the resistance against it is worldwide.

A few words may be said about the specifically social aspects of reception. There is a lot of talk about the disappearance of a stratum of genuine connoisseurs. Whatever truth there may be in this is not to be understood quantitatively. In absolute terms, if you were to want to count them and did so, there are probably more connoisseurs today than there were before, merely as a result of the increased population. However, the number of connoisseurs has probably decreased, not only in relation to size of the population as a whole, but in relation to the number of people who are drawn into music's sphere of activity, who are reached by music. This, in combination with changes in the overall structure of the population, leads to a shift in behavior toward music, first as regards the newer music, and then the older music, as well. I refer to the peculiar role played by the concept of the classical, as it is reflected in the ever-present division into classical and popular music. In the opinion of innumerable people, modern music has not replaced traditional music; pop music has replaced serious music. Evidently, the authority of the stratum that knows music has diminished. This stratum, to borrow an expression from Habermas, has become the bearer of the ideology of an elite that either is or imagines itself to be in decline; or at any rate styles itself as such.[28] Culture that supposes it is resisting barbarism frequently assists the latter by its reactionary worldview. Thirty years ago, when I introduced the concept of regressive listening, I did not mean, as Herr Wiora[29] accused me of meaning, in the face of my explicit assertions to the contrary, a general step backward in listening, but the listening of regressed, obsessively socially adjusted individuals, whose ego formation has failed, and who do not understand works of art autonomously, but rather in collective identification. The regression of listening does not mean that it has regressed in comparison with a previously higher standard. Rather, the overall relationship between adequate listeners and inadequate listeners shifted in favor of the latter. The individuals who today collectively dominate musical consciousness are regressive in the socio-psychological sense. In Germany, the musical youth movement[30] bears a large share of the blame for this. By making everything pedagogical, while maintaining the illusion of an engagement with serious music, it lowered ambitions, established the primacy of playing along over listening—basically the primacy of the audience over the thing itself—and ultimately cheated the public out of what would have done it honor. Above all, the understanding of great chamber music from Haydn to Webern has decayed. The capacity to listen to chamber music, however, is one of the most important preconditions for understanding new music. By listening to chamber music, one can learn the concentrated quickness of response, the leaps even to remote places, that new music demands. Mono-thematic music with terraced dynamics and a strong motor component prevents this. There is a loss of the capacity to make qualitative distinctions. The problem of making everything pedagogical is a general one, familiar to pedagogy as well. To this way of thinking it is more important how a thing is presented to people, and who takes care of its communication and popularization, than what is going to be presented to them. Again and again, one can encounter the excessive and compulsive concern about this.

I mentioned the decrease in the capacity for concentration. This touches a nerve. Because the new, highly qualified music is more specific and more articulated in all of its events, one cannot swim along in it. It demands *more* concentration, at least on the face of it, than traditional music, which people, admittedly, also did not understand, but they didn't notice, while with modern music they believe they do notice it. On the other hand, the capacity for concentration is unquestionably declining, for many reasons—the often-cited flood of stimuli is only one of them. Music itself and the anthropological structure of its audience develop out of each other. New music, as a whole, postulates—as consciousness of tension—experience, the dimension of happiness and suffering, the capacity for the extreme, for what has not already been pre-formed, in order, as it were, to salvage what is being destroyed by the apparatus of the administered world. But the listeners, as socially pre-formed individuals, are scarcely capable of this any longer. The new music speaks both for them and past them. But the notion of seriousness that characterizes it is suspect to the all-powerful mechanism of repression. Seriousness is taken as an attack, a shock, and is therefore registered as its opposite, as a joke. In this regard there is probably no longer any difference today in the perception of significant older and newer music. Except that older music in Europe is shielded by prestige, and by virtue of its idiomatic traits allows people to prattle along inwardly, while in newer music the seriousness, the lack of playing along dares to come out nakedly into the open. This makes it, in the strict sense, the heir of what was once termed classical.

In the demand for concentration, new music commits an offense against one of the main ideological props of the dominant musical culture, the irrationality of music, which is said to appeal purely to the emotions. The distinction between emotion and intellect, which has long since been cast on the scrap heap by psychology, survives stubbornly in vulgar usage. The common notions of intellectually and emotionally colored music are a fa-çade that must be torn down. What is called intellectual is usually just something that demands the work and effort of listening, the force of attention and memory, actually love: in other words, emotion; and what is called emotion is usually just the reflex of a passive mode of behavior that savors music as a stimulus without having any specific or, if you will, naïve relation to it, to what is heard concretely. In traditional music it was apparently possible to get along without this effort; in the new music one is completely disoriented without it. In its significant products, it struggles against the backwardness of the ideology of emotion, which in any case was always the complement of bourgeois rationalism. It mobilizes the anti-intellectualism that society is hatching and that nowadays is popping up all over. Related to this are certain encouragements to return to the folk song; their nationalistic influence is unmistakable. Young people, including and especially the long-haired ones, resist this, with good reason. Only in the process they tend to be drawn into the illusionary context, because the thing that mobilizes them musically against the *establishment** is nothing but the dross from the consumer culture that they would like to escape.

The effort that is required to grasp new music is not one of abstract knowledge, nor is it one of acquaintance with some systems or other, with theorems, much less with mathematical procedures. It is essentially imagination, what Kierkegaard called the speculative ear.[31] The prototype of genuine experience of new music is the capacity to combine divergent things, to create unity, in tandem with the music, in true variety. It is no accident that modernism originated in the emancipation of the multiplicity of independent voices, of polyphony unbound. But precisely imagination is among the anthropological traits that are atrophying, in comparison with socially acknowledged traits such as integration, skillful compromise, and functioning. One may suppose that the new music makes people feel ashamed, feel that they are being regarded as something they are not, yet feel they should be. While many composers, in keeping with the general spiritual disorientation, are flirting with positivism—for example, with communication and information theory—new music is incompatible with the dominant positivism of the general life feeling, which wants people to cast off the burden of the ego. The resistance against this defines new music, at least in one decisive dimension, although there are also others, in which one must suspect something like latent conformity. These latter tendencies seem to prepare the contact with the listeners by loosening, softening the strictness of the musical diction—that the composers themselves, but now with musical intent, make music as regressive as the people who hear it already are. But one must not overemphasize this tendency, as if a new harmony were being created between music and the audience. There are strict limits to this kind of harmony. Music is not able, on its own, to close the historical breach. It has its proper social place only where it puts its own stamp, as resolutely as possible, on the breach. Otherwise it does not do justice to the truth. No path leads out of the paradox that music cannot even desire the closing of the breach; its own content today is the critical one, antithetical to society. Hence all efforts to encourage understanding of new music, even my own words, are somehow at odds with it, as if we were committing an offense against its own intention, as if with our explanations we were removing fangs that are essential to it. Nevertheless, it must want to reach people. For even in its most inaccessible form, it is a social entity and is threatened with irrelevance as soon as that thread to the listener is broken off. The intention of being understood and the hesitancy in this respect are equally integral to it. One cannot escape this contradiction by thinking about it. The only thing one can do is to elevate it to the level of consciousness, to speak it; at best there remains the hope of a music whose power compels the understanding of those who now feel indifference or animosity.

(1966; GS, vol. 17, pp. 272–91)
Translated by Susan H. Gillespie

NOTES BY RICHARD LEPPERT

1. Bertolt Brecht, "Fünf Schwierigkeiten beim Schreiben der Wahrheit," in Bertolt Brecht, *Mutter Courage und ihre Kinder: Eine Chronik aus dem Dreissig-jährigen Krieg, Brecht Versuche* 9 no. 21 (Berlin: Suhrkamp, 1949), pp. 85–96. Brecht wrote the essay in 1934; it appeared in the anti-fascist paper *Unsere Zeit*. Brecht addresses the difficulties attending the writing of truth under fascism, while at the same time insisting that the difficulties are present as well "in den Ländern der bürgerlichen Freiheit" (p. 85). The difficulties, briefly, are: (1) the courage to write the truth; (2) the intelligence to recognize the truth; (3) the art of making truth more available as a weapon; (4) the judgment to choose people who can effectively use the truth; and (5) the cunning necessary to spread the truth widely.

2. The passage Adorno quotes is from the second of the five difficulties, "the intelligence to recognize the truth," pp. 86–87. However obliquely, Adorno is addressing more than Brecht in the discussion that follows; specifically, he is responding as well to the (in)famous and notably gratuitous remark by Lukács in the 1962 preface to the reissue of his *Theory of the Novel* about the purported impotent pessimism of intellectuals, who all the while live the good life in the "Grand Hotel Abyss"—and naming Adorno—concerning which, see pp. 67–68.

3. Adorno uses an ironic German neologism, *haranguieren*, based on the English. [translator's note]

4. Adorno may be referring to the concept of *Sein-sollendes* in Hegel (especially as it is worked out in *Philosophy of Right* [1821]), meaning something which "has to be." Alternately, if rather less likely, he may be referring to the work of Austrian philosopher Alexius Meinong (1853–1920), in particular his object theory, in which *sein sollen* constitutes the being of what is an obligation. Either way, Adorno's deeply ironic "So-sein-Sollendes" would refer to an alleged duty or obligation of music to affirm sorrowfulness as if it were ontological.

5. *Blut und Boden* [Blood and Soil], also referred to, derisively, as *Blubo*, was coined by Oswald Spengler in *The Decline of the West* (1918–1922) and became a convenient propaganda catch-phrase for National Socialism, one of its numerous references to blood as a mythic symbol of Aryan purity and German nationalism. The phrase was adopted by Richard Walther Darré (1895–1953), who promoted the German peasantry as the backbone of the Reich and as a bulwark against capitalism, urbanism, and—ironically—industrialism. Darré was *Reichsbauern-führer* and appointed Minister for Food and Agriculture in 1933, a post he lost in 1942 due to incompetence. Darré was a pig breeder—he extolled pigs in his writings—and a pronounced anti-Semite. His books include *Das Bauerntum als Le-bensquell der nordischen Rasse* (1928), *Um Blut und Boden* (1929), and *Neuadel aus Blut und Boden* (1930). His *Aufbruch des Bauerntums: Reichsbauerntagsreden*

1933 bis 1938 (1942) includes the essays "Wo der Jude herrscht, muss der Bauer sterben," and "Die Verfälschung des Sozialismus durch den jüdischen Marxismus."

6. Arnold Schoenberg, *"On Revient Toujours"* (1948), in *Style and Idea: Selected Writings of Arnold Schoenberg,* ed. Leonard Stein, trans. Leo Black (New York: St. Martin's, 1975), pp. 108–10: "But a longing to return to the older style was always vigorous in me; and from time to time I had to yield to that urge. This is how and why I sometimes write tonal music. To me stylistic differences of this nature are not of special importance. I do not know which of my compositions are better; I like them all, because I liked them when I wrote them" (pp. 109–10).

7. Paul Valéry, "The Problem of Museums," in *Degas, Manet, Morisot,* trans. David Paul (New York: Pantheon, 1960), p. 206: "Painting and Sculpture, says my Demon of Analysis, are both foundlings. Their mother, Architecture, is dead. So long as she lived, she gave them their place, their function and discipline. They had no freedom to stray. They had their exact allotted space and given light, their subjects and their relationship."

8. Adorno's Kafka citation in PNM appears on p. 104 n. 46; see Franz Kafka, *The Diaries of Franz Kafka,* vol. 2: *1914–1923,* ed. Max Brod, trans. Martin Greenberg (New York: Schocken, 1949), p. 222.

9. The concept of *Entlastung,* "relief," "giving relief," or "relief from" appears in the magnum opus of the German anthropologist-sociologist and philosopher Arnold Gehlen, *Man: His Nature and Place in the World,* trans. Clare McMillan and Karl Pillemer (New York: Columbia University Press, 1988). In *Man,* first published in 1940, Gehlen, in attempting to account for the fundamental features that distinguish the human species, articulated the basic requirements for human existence, which he viewed as precarious. Gehlen posed the question: "How can such a vulnerable, needy, exposed being possibly manage to survive?" The answer: through the higher functions of consciousness, imagination and language, which in turn feed into Gehlen's central "concept of *action*" which articulates the complicated mutually reinforcing relationship between mind and body in the struggle for existence. "The category of relief . . . means that the functions of thought and imagination have achieved their level of versatility through primary visual and tactile experiences interwoven with language, that they develop the experiences gained through sight and touch in an easier, or freer, form" (p. 12). He later amplifies: Man "is flooded with stimulation, with an abundance of impressions, which he must somehow learn to cope with. He cannot rely upon instincts for understanding his environment. He is confronted with a 'world' that is surprising and unpredictable in its structure and that must be worked through with care and foresight, must be experienced. By relying on his own means and efforts, man must find *relief* from the burden of overwhelming stimulation; he must transform his deficiencies into opportunities for survival" (p. 28, original emphasis). Gehlen sees human creativity, which incorporates what he calls "world-openness," as a means by which to achieve this relief necessary for survival, a means of compensating for the "deficiencies in his organic structure" (p. 32). Relief develops by a "working through" of the world that comes about through the interaction of physical body (he cites hands, eyes, and the sense of touch) and the imagination—the homology with John Locke is obvious. Finally, language permits the personal experience to be broadened beyond the self. Language—and imagination—produce the consciousness ultimately critical to survival, concerning which, see the chapter "The Law of Relief: The Role of Consciousness," pp. 54–64.

Wilhelm Ehmann (1904–1989), German choral and brass-choir director and musicologist; his research focused principally on choral church music. The second volume of his *Die Chorführung,* 2 vols. (Kassel: Bärenreiter, 1949) was published in translation, based on the 3rd German ed. (1956) as *Choral Directing,* trans. George D. Wiebe (Minneapolis: Augsburg, 1968). What Adorno is getting at Ehmann makes clear in his opening: "Through music making the body is awakened and supported in its original proportions, its parts are harmoniously related to each other and consequently begins [sic] to sound. According to this, sickness is a musical dissonance in the human body which can be cured again through consonant music. In the singing activities and choral work of our own time we should experience a freeing of the whole person through a harmonious body-soul relationship within ourselves. Man, in his total complexity, must become vibrant within himself and must find his 'own tone.' All mental and physical inhibitions, suppressions, and 'cramped-in' feelings are to be dissolved in this harmony. The singer uses his body both *to sustain life* and *to cultivate his art.* He can never escape from himself, for with his physical life he either furthers or hinders his artistic life" (p. 2, original emphasis).

10. Automatic writing was expounded by, among others, surrealist writers André Breton (1896–1966) and Philippe Soupault (1897–1990), who promoted the unconscious as a seat of creative energy. They attempted to write in a state of trance, committing to paper whatever passed through this state of altered consciousness. The first published example, co-authored by Breton and Soupault, was *"Les Champs magnétiques"* (1920).

11. See p. 201 n. 10. Adorno refers to Leibowitz's Four Pieces for Piano op. 8 (1943).

12. Steuermann died 11 November 1964; see Adorno's tribute, "Nach Steuermanns Tod," GS, vol. 17, pp. 311–17, written in the same year.

13. Max Weber, *The Rational and Social Foundations of Music,* ed. and trans. Don Martindale, Johannes Riedel, and Gertrude Neuwirth (Carbondale: Southern Illinois University Press, 1958).

14. Cf. pp. 172–73.

15. Kranichsteiner Musikinstitut was the name used by the Darmstadt Internationales Musikinstitut between 1949 and 1962.

16. See pp. 110–11.

17. German avant-garde composer Dieter Schnebel's own music pushed beyond the conventional boundaries of the musical to include speech and gesture. Schnebel became increasingly concerned with visual effects and, eventually, solely with the sight of music, in which its aurality as such disappears—"visible music," so to speak: music that could be seen but did not sound. The impact of Cage is obvious. See Dieter Schnebel, "Visible Music," in *Classic Essays on Twentieth-Century Music: A Continuing Symposium,* ed. Richard Kostelanetz and Joseph Darby (New York: Schirmer, 1996), pp. 283–95. In this essay Schnebel comments, "Visible music is music that requires an audience because its spatial, tonal, and 'gestic' nature expands into the optical sphere" (p. 283); the principal arenas of visible music which, in essence, act as a *supplément* to music's aurality include music in space, music in action, music as theater, music with images (film), and notation (musical graphics).

18. This remark appears in "The Aging of the New Music," p. 195.

19. Christian Dietrich Grabbe (1801–1836), German dramatist. Adorno slightly mis-recalls the passage in question. It appears in the 1831 drama *Napolean oder die hundert Tage,* at the beginning of the play's penultimate scene—act 5, scene 6—and is spoken to Napoleon by the commander of his infantry, Count von Lobau, now facing defeat: "Verwünschte Übermacht—kann denn weder Geist noch Verzweiflung gegen sie retten?" [Accursed superiority—can neither spirit nor despair

save us in the face of them?] which Adorno recalls as "Denn nichts als nur Verzweiflung kann uns retten."

20. *Der getreue Korrepetitor: Lehrschriften zur musikalischen Praxis* (1963)
[The Faithful Music Coach; GS, vol. 15, pp. 157–402] has not yet appeared in
English. The collection contains eight essays, six of which are what Adorno calls
"Interpretationsanalysen neuer Musik" involving compositions by Schoenberg
(Fantasy for Violin with Piano Accompaniment, op. 47), Berg (a lengthy discussion
of the Violin Concerto), and, especially, Webern (lieder and chamber music).

21. David Riesman et al., *The Lonely Crowd: A Study in the Changing American Character* (New Haven: Yale University Press, 1950); and its sequel, *Faces in
the Crowd: Individual Studies in Character and Politics* (New Haven: Yale University Press, 1952). From *The Lonely Crowd*, pp. v–vi: "My major thesis . . . is
that the conformity of earlier generations of Americans of the type I term 'inner-
directed' was mainly assured by their internalization of adult authority. The
middle-class urban American of today, the 'other-directed,' is, by contrast, in a
characterological sense more the product of his peers—that is, in sociological terms,
his 'peer-groups.'" Throughout these studies Riesman prominently cites the role
of the mass media in shaping the individual, and he also acknowledges the pioneering work carried out by scholars like Adorno and Lazarsfeld and a few others
like them involved in audience studies (p. 99)—though to lump Adorno with Lazarsfeld is obviously problematic. Adorno in essence points to an irony: apologists
for mass entertainment cite Riesman despite the fact that he is ultimately critical
of the role it plays in character formation, specifically its role in advancing social
conformism. In essence, Riesman's position is congruent with Herbert Marcuse's
later *One-Dimensional Man: Studies in the Ideology of Advanced Industrial Society* (Boston: Beacon Press, 1964).

On the subject of music, for example, Riesman, *The Lonely Crowd*, pp. 220–
21, discusses the research of "a graduate student at the University of Chicago"—
no less than Howard C. Becker, his M.A. thesis, "The Professional Dance Musician
in Chicago" (1949)—concerning consumer attitudes toward popular singers. "'I
like Dinah Shore because she's so sincere,' or 'that's a very sincere record,' or 'You
can just feel that he [Frank Sinatra] is sincere.'" Concerning which Riesman comments: "While it is clear that people want to personalize their relationships to their
heroes of consumption and that their yearning for sincerity is a grim reminder of
how little they can trust themselves or others in daily life, it is less clear just what
it is that they find 'sincere' in a singer or other performer. . . . The popular emphasis on sincerity . . . means that the source of criteria for judgment has shifted
from the content of the performance and its goodness or badness, aesthetically
speaking, to the personality of the performer. He is judged for his attitude toward
the audience, an attitude which is either sincere or insincere."

22. Max Weber, *Economy and Society: An Outline of Interpretative Sociology*,
ed. Guenther Roth and Claus Wittlich, trans. Ephraim Fischoff et al., 3 vols. (New
York: Bedminster, 1968), based on the 4th German edition. The discussion to which
Adorno refers is treated in detail in volume 3.

23. Franz Schreker (1878–1934), Austrian composer noted especially for his
stage works. At various times throughout his career he experimented with modernist compositional techniques while never really abandoning the nineteenth century. By the time of his death his reputation as a modernist was already in notable
decline.

24. August Halm (1869–1929), German composer, critic, and musicologist,
whose extensive writings focus especially on Bach, Beethoven, and Bruckner.
Adorno greatly admired Halm's work and cited him a number of times. For a list

of Halm's published scholarship, see the biographical entry in *Die Musik in Geschichte und Gegenwart* (Kassel and Basel: Bärenreiter, 1956), vol. 5, cols. 1378–79.

25. Rudolf Kolisch, "Tempo and Character in Beethoven's Music," trans. Arthur Mendel, *Musical Quarterly* 39 nos. 2–3 (April/July 1943), pp. 169–87, and 291–312. See also the commentary on this essay by Regina Busch, ". . . den Genuss klassischer Musik wieder verschaffen," in *Beethoven und die Zweite Wiener Schule*, ed. Otto Kolleritsch (Vienna: Universal, 1992), pp. 103–21.

26. Adorno amplifies these points in "Opera," ISM, pp. 71–84, and "Bourgeois Opera," SF, pp. 15–28.

27. Herbert Marcuse, "The Affirmative Character of Culture" (1937), in *Negations: Essays in Critical Theory*, trans. Jeremy J. Shapiro (Boston: Beacon, 1968), pp. 88–133, 277–80.

28. Adorno seems to be referring to Jürgen Habermas, *The Structural Transformation of the Public Sphere: An Inquiry into a Category of Bourgeois Society* (1962), trans. Thomas Burger, with the assistance of Frederick Lawrence (Cambridge: MIT Press, 1989).

29. Walter Wiora (1906–1997), German musicologist, best known in North America for his *The Four Ages of Music*, trans. M. D. Herter Norton (New York: Norton, 1965), the current "age" being one of "technology and global industrial culture." I have not located the precise reference in Wiora, but the listener and listening are discussed at some length in his *Komponist und Mitwelt* (Kassel: Bärenreiter, 1964).

30. For example, Wilhelm Ehmann. See n. 9, above.

31. Søren Kierkegaard's sole reference to the "speculative ear" *[speculative Øre]* comes in a footnote in the lengthy chapter "The Immediate Stages of the Erotic or the Musical Erotic," in *Either/Or: A Fragment of Life* [1843], trans. David F. Swenson and Lillian Marvin Swenson (Princeton: Princeton University Press, 1944), vol. 1, p. 99n; and, in the Danish edition, *Enten-Eller*, in *Samlede Værker*, 3rd ed., ed. A. B. Drachmann et al. (Copenhagen: Gyldendal, 1962), vol. 2, p. 115 n. 1. The essay principally concerns a detailed discussion of Mozart's *Don Giovanni* as a metaphor to the eroticism immanent to human nature. Kierkegaard is discussing Elvira's aria of passionate outrage against Don Giovanni, her seducer, in the act 1 aria "Ah! Chi mi dice mai." He suggests that the music's power lies in the fact that Giovanni, who has taken control of her despite her outrage, constitutes a deeply ironic—indeed, mocking—internalized presence at the core of her being: "As love transforms its object, so also does indignation. She is possessed by Don Juan." Kierkegaard clarifies his observation in a lengthy footnote which opens: "In my opinion, Elvira's aria and the situation should be interpreted thus: Don Juan's incomparable irony ought not to be something external, but should be concealed in Elvira's essential passion. They must be heard simultaneously. As the speculative eye sees things together, so the [listener's] speculative ear should hear things together."

Bibliography

Note: The bibliography is selective, consisting of the works cited in the introduction and commentary sections of this book. Sources cited solely in the notes to Adorno's essays are not included.
The bibliography is arranged as follows:
    I. Adorno Bibliographies
    II. Adorno: Primary Sources Consulted
       a) Books (including collections of essays and of letters)
       b) Individual Essays, Reviews, etc.
    III. Secondary Sources on Adorno Consulted
    IV. Tertiary Sources Consulted

I. ADORNO BIBLIOGRAPHIES

Several excellent, comprehensive bibliographies of both primary and secondary Adorno sources are available, as follows:

Görtzen, René. "Theodor W. Adorno: Vorläufige Bibliographie seiner Schriften und der Sekundärliteratur." In *Adorno-Konferenz 1983*. Edited by Ludwig von Friedeburg and Jürgen Habermas, pp. 402–71. Frankfurt am Main: Suhrkamp, 1983. Includes a chronological listing of Adorno's published monographs, as well as published reviews, and location in GS. Posthumously published work is also included.

Jarvis, Simon. *Adorno: A Critical Introduction*, pp. 261–75. New York: Routledge, 1998.

Lang, Peter Christian. "Kommentierte Auswahlbibliographie 1969–1979." In *Materialien zur ästhetischen Theorie Th. W. Adornos: Konstruktion der Moderne*. Edited by Burkhardt Lindner and W. Martin Lüdke, pp. 509–56. Frankfurt am Main: Suhrkamp, 1979.

Nordquist, Joan. *Theodor Adorno: A Bibliography*. Social Theory: A Bibliographic Series, no. 10. Santa Cruz, CA: Reference and Research Services, 1988. Superseded by the 1994 revision (below), except for secondary work published prior to 1988, none of which is included in the later edition.

———. *Theodor Adorno (II): A Bibliography.* Social Theory: A Bibliographic Series, no. 35. Santa Cruz, CA: Reference and Research Services, 1994. A bibliography of primary and secondary materials available in English. English-language reviews of translations of Adorno monographs are included, as well as a list of dissertations and theses on Adorno. Keyword indexed.

Paddison, Max. *Adorno's Aesthetics of Music,* pp. 330–64. Cambridge: Cambridge University Press, 1993. Paddison is the best source concerning Adorno's writing on music (excluding most of Adorno's reviews of books, music scores, and concerts, many of which are listed in GS, vol. 19, pp. 648–52) and related secondary literature. Includes a chronological list of Adorno's principal music essays and monographs (1921–69), citing both the original place of publication and the item's location in the GS, as well as English translation, where available.

Pettazzi, Carlo. "Bibliographie zu Th. W. Adorno," In *Theodor W. Adorno.* Edited by Heinz Ludwig Arnold, pp. 176–93. 2d ed. enlarged. Munich: Edition Text + Kritik, 1983. Emphasis on Italian sources. Includes a list of published reviews of Adorno's monographs.

Schultz, Klaus. "Vorläufige Bibliographie der Schriften Theodor W. Adornos." In *Theodor W. Adorno zum Gedächtnis: Eine Sammlung.* Edited by Hermann Schweppenhäuser, pp. 178–239. Frankfurt am Main: Suhrkamp, 1971.

Wiggershaus, Rolf. *The Frankfurt School: Its History, Theories, and Political Significance.* Translated by Michael Robertson, pp. 715–71. Cambridge: MIT Press, 1995. A general bibliography of the Frankfurt School and the individuals associated with it.

Zuidervaart, Lambert. *Adorno's Aesthetic Theory: The Redemption of Illusion,* pp. 351–80. Cambridge: MIT Press, 1991.

II.   ADORNO: PRIMARY SOURCES CONSULTED

The original date of publication (or, in some instances, authorship) is indicated in brackets at the end of each listing. If applicable, the location in the GS is also provided. Adorno sometimes published subsequent editions of monographs, but the revisions are seldom substantial. Later editions are not indicated, although English translations are usually based on the most recent edition.

a) Books (including collections of essays and of letters)

Aesthetic Theory. Edited by Gretel Adorno and Rolf Tiedemann. Translated by Robert Hullot-Kentor. Minneapolis: University of Minnesota Press,

1997. Also: Translated by C. Lenhardt. London: Routledge and Kegan Paul, 1984. [1970; GS, vol. 7.]

Alban Berg: Master of the Smallest Link. Translated by Juliane Brand and Christopher Hailey. Cambridge: Cambridge University Press, 1991. [1968; GS, vol. 13, pp. 321–494.]

The Authoritarian Personality. [With Else Frenkel-Brunswik, Daniel J. Levinson, and R. Nevitt Sanford.] New York: Harper and Brothers, 1950. [1950; GS 9.1, pp. 143–509.]

Beethoven: The Philosophy of Music. Edited by Rolf Tiedemann. Translated by Edmund Jephcott. Stanford: Stanford University Press, 1998. [1993]

Briefwechsel. [With Ernst Krenek.] Edited by Wolfgang Rogge. Frankfurt am Main: Suhrkamp, 1974.

The Complete Correspondence, 1928–1940 [of Theodor W. Adorno and Walter Benjamin]. Edited by Henri Lonitz. Translated by Nicholas Walker. Cambridge: Harvard University Press, 1999. [1994]

Composing for the Films. [With Hanns Eisler.] Introduction by Graham McCann. London: Athlone Press, 1994. [1947; GS, vol. 15, pp. 7–155.]

Critical Models: Interventions and Catchwords. Translated by Henry W. Pickford. New York: Columbia University Press, 1998. [1963, 1969; GS, vol. 10.2, pp. 455–799.]

Dialectic of Enlightenment. [With Max Horkheimer.] Translated by John Cumming. New York: Continuum, 1972. [1944; GS, vol. 3.]

Gesammelte Schriften. Edited by Rolf Tiedemann et al. 20 vols. in 23. Frankfurt am Main: Suhrkamp, 1970–1986.

In Search of Wagner. Translated by Rodney Livingstone. London: Verso, 1984. [1952; GS, vol. 13, pp. 7–148.]

Introduction to the Sociology of Music. Translated by E. B. Ashton. New York: Continuum, 1988. [1962; GS, vol. 14, pp. 168–433.]

Kompositionen. Edited by Heinz-Klaus Metzger and Rainer Riehn. 2 vols. Munich: Edition Text + Kritik, 1980.

Mahler: A Musical Physiognomy. Translated by Edmund Jephcott. Chicago: University of Chicago Press, 1992. [1960; GS, vol. 13, pp. 149–319.]

Minima Moralia: Reflections from Damaged Life. Translated by E. F. N. Jephcott. London: Verso, 1978. [1951; GS, vol. 4.]

Moments musicaux. GS, vol. 17, pp. 7–161. [1964]

Negative Dialectics. Translated by E. B. Ashton. New York: Continuum, 1983. [1966; GS, vol. 6, pp. 7–412.]

Notes to Literature. Edited by Rolf Tiedemann. Translated by Shierry Weber Nicholsen. 2 vols. New York: Columbia University Press, 1991–92. [1958, 1961, 1965, 1974; GS, vol. 11.]

Philosophy of Modern Music. Translated by Anne G. Mitchell and Wesley V. Blomster. New York: Continuum, 1985. [1949; GS, vol. 12.]

Prisms. Translated by Samuel Weber and Shierry Weber. Cambridge: MIT Press, 1981. [1955; GS, vol. 10.1, pp. 9–287.]

Quasi una fantasia: Essays on Modern Music. Translated by Rodney Living-
stone. London: Verso, 1992. [1963; GS, vol. 16, pp. 249–540.]
Der Schatz des Indianer-Joe. Singspiel nach Mark Twain. Edited by Rolf
Tiedemann. Frankfurt am Main: Suhrkamp, 1979.
Sound Figures. Translated by Rodney Livingstone. Stanford: Stanford Uni-
versity Press, 1999. [1959; GS, vol. 16, pp. 7–248.]

b) Individual Essays, Reviews, etc.

"The Aging of the New Music." Translated by Robert Hullot-Kentor and Fred-
eric Will. *Telos* 77 (Fall 1988), pp. 95–116. And this volume, pp. 181–202.
[1955; GS, vol. 14, pp. 143–67.]
"Alban Berg." SF, pp. 69–79. [1956; GS, vol. 16, pp. 85–96.]
"Alban Berg: Zur Uraufführung des 'Wozzeck.'" [1925; GS, vol. 18, pp. 456–
64.]
"Alienated Masterpiece: The *Missa Solemnis.*" Translated by Duncan Smith.
Telos 28 (Summer 1976), pp. 113–24. And this volume, pp. 569–83. [1959;
GS, vol. 17, pp. 145–61.]
"Analytical Study of the NBC *Music Appreciation Hour.*" *Musical Quarterly*
78 no. 2 (Summer 1994), pp. 325–77. [1938–40]
"Anton von Webern." SF, pp. 91–105. [1959; GS, vol. 16, pp. 110–25.]
"Arbeitsprobleme des Komponisten: Gespräch über Musik und soziale Situa-
tion." [With Ernst Krenek.] [1930; GS, vol. 19, pp. 433–39.]
"Arnold Schoenberg, 1874–1951." PR, pp. 147–72. Also in: *The Adorno
Reader.* Edited by Brian O'Connor, pp. 280–303. Oxford: Blackwell, 2000.
[1953; GS, vol. 10.1, pp. 152–80.]
"Bach Defended against His Devotees." PR, pp. 133–46. [1951; GS, vol. 10.1,
pp. 138–51.]
"Berg and Webern—Schoenberg's Heirs." *Modern Music* 8 no. 2 (January/
February 1931), pp. 29–38. [1930; GS, vol. 18, pp. 446–55.]
"Berg's Discoveries in Compositional Technique." QF, pp. 179–200. [1961; GS,
vol. 16, pp. 413–32.]
"Bourgeois Opera." SF, pp. 15–28. Also in: *Opera through Other Eyes.* Trans-
lated by David J. Levin. Edited by David J. Levin, pp. 25–43. Stanford:
Stanford University Press, 1994. [1955; GS, vol. 16, pp. 24–39.]
"Chaplin Times Two." Translated by John Mac Kay. *Yale Journal of Criticism*
9 no. 1 (Spring 1996), pp. 57–61. [1930/1964; GS, vol. 10.1, pp. 362–66.]
"Classicism, Romanticism, New Music." SF, pp. 106–22. [1959; GS, vol. 16,
pp. 126–44.]
"Commitment." NL, vol. 2, pp. 76–94. Also in: *The Essential Frankfurt School
Reader.* Translated by Francis McDonagh. Edited by Andrew Arato and Eike
Gebhardt, pp. 300–18. New York: Continuun, 1982. [1962; GS, vol. 11, pp.
409–30.]
"Commodity Music Analysed." QF, pp. 37–52. [1955; written 1934–40; GS,
vol. 16, pp. 284–97.]

"Criteria of New Music." SF, pp. 145–96. [1957; GS, vol. 16, pp. 170–228.]

"Cultural Criticism and Society." PR, pp. 17–34. Also in: *Critical Sociology: Selected Readings*. Edited by Paul Connerton, pp. 258–76. Harmondsworth: Penguin, 1976; and *The Adorno Reader*. Edited by Brian O'Connor, pp. 195–210. Oxford: Blackwell, 2000. [1951; GS, vol. 10.1, pp. 11–30.]

"Culture and Administration." Translated by Wes Blomster. *Telos* 37 (Fall 1978), pp. 93–111. Also in: *The Culture Industry: Selected Essays on Mass Culture*. Edited by J. M. Bernstein, pp. 93–113. London: Routledge, 1991. [1960; GS, vol. 8, pp. 122–46.]

"Culture Industry Reconsidered." Translated by Anson G. Rabinbach. In *The Culture Industry: Selected Essays on Mass Culture*. Edited by J. M. Bernstein, pp. 85–92. London: Routledge, 1991. Also in: *The Adorno Reader*. Edited by Brian O'Connor, pp. 230–38. Oxford: Blackwell, 2000; and *Critical Theory and Society: A Reader*. Edited by Stephen Eric Bronner and Douglas MacKay Kellner, pp. 128–35. New York: Routledge, 1989. [1963; GS, vol. 10.1, pp. 337–45.]

"The Curious Realist: On Siegfried Kracauer." NL, vol. 2, pp. 58–75. [1964; GS, vol. 11, pp. 388–408.]

"The Curves of the Needle." Translated by Thomas Y. Levin. *October* 55 (Winter 1990), pp. 49–55. And this volume, pp. 271–76. [1927/1965; GS, vol. 19, pp. 525–29.]

"The Dialectical Composer." Translated by Susan H. Gillespie. This volume, pp. 203–09. [1934; GS, vol. 17, pp. 198–203.]

"Difficulties." Translated by Susan H. Gillespie. This volume, pp. 644–79. [1964, 1966; GS, vol. 17, pp. 253–91.]

"Education after Auschwitz," CM, pp. 191–204. [1967; vol. 10.2, pp. 674–90.]

"The Essay as Form." NL, vol. 1, pp. 3–23. Also in: *The Adorno Reader*. Translated by Robert Hullot-Kentor and Frederic Will. Edited by Brian O'Connor, pp. 91–111. Oxford: Blackwell, 2000. [1958; GS, vol. 11, pp. 9–33.]

"Extorted Reconciliation: On Georg Lukács' *Realism in Our Time*." NL, vol. 1, pp. 216–40. [1958; GS, vol. 11, pp. 251–80.]

"Farewell to Jazz." Translated by Susan H. Gillespie. This volume, pp. 496–500. [1933; GS, vol. 18, pp. 795–99.]

"The Form of the Phonograph Record." Translated by Thomas Y. Levin. *October* 55 (Winter 1990), pp. 56–61. And this volume, pp. 277–82. [1934; GS, vol. 19, pp. 530–34.]

"Free Time." CM, pp. 167–75. Also in: *The Culture Industry: Selected Essays on Mass Culture*. Edited by J. M. Bernstein, pp. 162–70. London: Routledge, 1991. [1969; GS, vol. 10.2, pp. 645–55.]

"Funktion der Farbe in der Musik." In *Darmstadt-Dokumenta I*. Edited by Heinz-Klaus Metzger and Rainer Riehn, pp. 263–312. Musik-Konzepte Sonderband: Die Reihe über Komponisten. Munich: Edition Text + Kritik, 1999. [1966 lecture.]

"Gebrauchsmusik." [1924; GS, vol. 19, pp. 445–47.]

"The George-Hofmannsthal Correspondence, 1891–1906." PR, pp. 187–226. [1942; GS, vol. 10.1, pp. 195–237.]

"How to Look at Television." *Quarterly of Film, Radio and Television* 8 (Spring 1954), pp. 213–35. Also in: *The Culture Industry: Selected Essays on Mass Culture.* Edited by J. M. Bernstein, pp. 136–53. London: Routledge, 1991. See also by its alternate title, "Television and the Patterns of Mass Culture."

Interview. "Of Barricades and Ivory Towers." *Encounter* 23 no. 3 (September 1969), pp. 63–69. [1969]

"Is Art Lighthearted?" NL, vol. 2, pp. 247–53. [1967; GS, vol. 11, pp. 599–606.]

"Is Marx Obsolete?" Translated by Nicolas Slater. *Diogenes* 64 (Winter 1968), pp. 1–16. [c. 1968]

"Jazz." In *Encyclopedia of the Arts.* Edited by Dagobert R. Runes and Harry G. Schrickel, pp. 511–13. New York: Philosophical Library, 1946.

"Kitsch." Translated by Susan H. Gillespie. This volume, pp. 501–05. [c. 1932; GS, vol. 18, pp. 791–94.]

"Late Style in Beethoven." Translated by Susan H. Gillespie. *Raritan: A Quarterly Review* 13 no. 1 (Summer 1993), pp. 102–07. And this volume, pp. 564–68. [1937; GS, vol. 17, pp. 13–17.]

"Little Heresy." Translated by Susan H. Gillespie. This volume, pp. 318–24. [1965; GS, vol. 17, pp. 297–302.]

"Mahler." QF, pp. 81–110. [1961; GS, vol. 16, pp. 323–38.]

"Mahler Today." Translated by Susan H. Gillespie. This volume, pp. 603–11. [1930; GS, vol. 18, pp. 226–34.]

"Marginala on Mahler." Translated by Susan H. Gillespie. This volume, pp. 612–18. [1936; GS, vol. 18, pp. 235–40.]

"Marginalia to Theory and Praxis." CM, pp. 259–78. [1969; GS, vol. 10.2, pp. 759–82.]

"The Mastery of the Maestro." SF, pp. 40–53. [1958; GS, vol. 16, pp. 52–67.]

"The Meaning of Working through the Past." CM, pp. 89–103. [1959; GS, vol. 10.2, pp. 555–72.]

"Memorandum: Music in Radio." Unpublished. Paul F. Lazarsfeld papers, Columbia University. [June 1938]

"Motifs." QF, pp. 9–36. [1927–37, 1951; GS, vol. 16, pp. 259–83.]

"Music and Language: A Fragment." QF, pp. 1–6. [1956–57; GS, vol. 16, pp. 251–56.]

"Music and New Music." QF, pp. 249–68. Also translated by Wes Blomster, in *Telos* 43 (Spring 1980), pp. 124–38. [1960; GS, vol. 16, pp. 476–92.]

"Music and Technique." SF, pp. 197–214. Also translated by Wes Blomster, in *Telos* 32 (Summer 1977), pp. 79–94. [1958; GS, vol. 16, pp. 229–48.]

"Music in the Background." Translated by Susan H. Gillespie. This volume, pp. 506–10. [c. 1934; GS, vol. 18, pp. 819–23.]

"Music, Language, and Composition." Translated by Susan H. Gillespie. *Musical Quarterly* 77 no. 3 (Fall 1993), pp. 401–14. And this volume, pp. 113–26. [1956; GS, vol. 16, pp. 649–64.]

"The Musical Climate for Fascism in Germany." [c. 1945; GS, vol. 20.2, pp. 430–40.]

"New Music, Interpretation, Audience." SF, pp. 29–39. [1957; GS, vol. 16, pp. 40–51.]

"Odysseus or Myth and Enlightenment." [With Max Horkheimer.] Chapter from *Dialectic of Enlightenment.* Translated by Robert Hullot-Kentor. *New German Critique* 56 (Spring/Summer 1992), pp. 109–41. [1944; GS, vol. 3, pp. 61–99.]

"On Jazz." Translated by Jamie Owen Daniel. *Discourse* 12 no. 1 (Fall/Winter 1989–90), pp. 45–69. And this volume, pp. 470–95. [1936; GS, vol. 17, pp. 74–100.]

"On Popular Music." [With the assistance of George Simpson.] *Studies in Philosophy and Social Science* 9 (1941), pp. 17–48. And this volume, pp. 437–69. [1941]

"On Some Relationships between Music and Painting." Translated by Susan Gillespie. *Musical Quarterly* 79 no. 1 (Spring 1995), pp. 66–79. [c. 1964; GS, vol. 16, pp. 628–42.]

"On Subject and Object." CM, pp. 245–58. Also in: *The Essential Frankfurt School Reader.* Edited by Andrew Arato and Eike Gebhardt, pp. 497–511. New York: Continuun, 1982; and *The Adorno Reader.* Edited by Brian O'Connor, pp. 137–51. Oxford: Blackwell, 2000. [1969; GS, vol. 10.2, pp. 741–58.]

"On the Contemporary Relationship of Philosophy and Music." Translated by Susan H. Gillespie. This volume, pp. 135–61. [1953; GS, vol. 18, pp. 149–76.]

"On the Fetish-Character in Music and the Regression of Listening." In *The Frankfurt School Reader.* Edited by Andrew Arato and Eike Gebhardt, pp. 270–99. New York: Continuum, 1982. And this volume, pp. 288–317. [1938; GS, vol. 14, pp. 14–50.]

"On the Problem of Musical Analysis." Translated by Max Paddison. *Music Analysis* 1 no. 2 (July 1982), pp. 169–87. And this volume, pp. 162–80. [1969]

"On the Question: 'What Is German?'" CM, pp. 205–14. [1965; GS, vol. 10.2, pp. 691–701.]

"On the Score of 'Parsifal.'" Translated, with commentary, by Anthony Barone. *Music and Letters* 76 no. 3 (August 1995), pp. 384–97. [1956/57; GS, vol. 17, pp. 47–51.]

"On the Social Situation of Music." Translated by Wes Blomster. *Telos* 35 (Spring 1978), pp. 128–64. And this volume, pp. 391–436. [1932; GS, vol. 18, pp. 729–77.]

"On the Use of Foreign Words." NL, vol. 2, pp. 286–91. [GS, vol. 11, 640–46.]

"On Tradition." *Telos* 94 (Winter 1993–94), pp. 75–82. [1966; GS, vol. 10.1, pp. 310–20.]

"Opera and the Long-Playing Record." Translated by Thomas Y. Levin. *October* 55 (Winter 1990), pp. 62–66. And this volume, pp. 283–87. [1969; GS, vol. 19, pp. 555–58.]

"The Opera *Wozzeck*." Translated by Susan H. Gillespie. This volume, pp. 619–26. [1929; GS, vol. 18, pp. 472–79.]

"Opinion Delusion Society." CM, pp. 105–22. [1961; GS, vol. 10.2, pp. 573–94.]

"Parataxis: On Hölderin's Late Poetry." NL, vol. 2, pp. 109–49. [1964; GS, vol. 11, pp. 447–91.]

"Perennial Fashion—Jazz." PR, pp. 119–32. Also in: *The Adorno Reader*. Edited by Brian O'Connor, pp. 267–79. Oxford: Blackwell, 2000; and *Critical Theory and Society: A Reader*. Edited by Stephen Eric Bronner and Douglas MacKay Kellner, pp. 199–209. New York: Routledge, 1989. [1953; GS, vol. 10.1, pp. 123–37.]

"Philosophy and Teachers." CM, pp. 19–35. [1962; GS, vol. 10.2, pp. 474–94.]

"Prologue to Television." CM, pp. 49–57. [1952/53, 1962; GS, vol. 10.2, pp. 507–17.]

"The Psychological Technique of Martin Luther Thomas' Radio Addresses." Also: Stanford University Press, 2000. [1943; GS, vol. 9.1, pp. 7–141.]

"The Radio Symphony." In *Radio Research 1941*. Edited by Paul F. Lazarsfeld and Frank N. Stanton, pp. 110–39. New York: Duell, Sloan and Pearce, 1941. And this volume, pp. 251–70. [1941]

"Resignation." CM, pp. 289–93. Also translated by Wes Blomster, in *Telos* 35 (Spring 1978), pp. 165–68; and *The Culture Industry: Selected Essays on Mass Culture*. Edited by J. M. Bernstein, pp. 171–75. London: Routledge, 1991. [1969; GS, vol. 10.2, pp. 794–99.]

Review of *American Jazz Music*, by Wilder Hobson, and *Jazz Hot and Hybrid*, by Winthrop Sargeant. With the assistance of Eunice Cooper. *Studies in Philosophy and Social Science* 9 (1941), pp. 167–78. [1941; GS, vol. 19, pp. 382–99.]

"The Schema of Mass Culture." In *The Culture Industry: Selected Essays on Mass Culture*. Edited by J. M. Bernstein, pp. 53–83. London: Routledge, 1991. [1942; GS, vol. 3, pp. 299–335.]

"Schöne Stellen." [1965; GS, vol. 18, pp. 695–718.]

"Scientific Experiences of a European Scholar in America." Translated by Donald Fleming. In *The Intellectual Migration: Europe and America, 1930–1960*. Edited by Donald Fleming and Bernard Bailyn, pp. 338–70. Cambridge: Belknap Press of Harvard University Press, 1969. Also in: CM, pp. 215–42. [1969; GS, vol. 10.2, pp. 702–38.]

"A Social Critique of Radio Music." *Kenyon Review* 7 no. 2 (Spring 1945), pp. 208–17.

"Sociology and Empirical Research." Translated by Graham Bartram. In

Critical Sociology: Selected Readings. Edited by Paul Connerton, pp. 237–57. Harmondsworth: Penguin Books, 1976. [1957; GS, vol. 8, pp. 196–216.]

"Some Ideas on the Sociology of Music." SF, pp. 1–14. [1958; GS, vol. 16, pp. 9–23.]

"The Stars Down to Earth." In *Adorno: The Stars Down to Earth and Other Essays on the Irrational in Culture.* Edited, with introduction, by Stephen Crook, pp. 34–127. New York: Routledge, 1994. Also in: *Telos* 19 (Spring 1974), pp. 13–90. [1957; GS, vol. 9.2, pp. 7–120.]

"Stravinsky: A Dialectical Portrait." QF, pp. 145–75. [1962; GS, vol. 16, pp. 382–409.]

"Taboos on the Teaching Vocation." CM, pp. 177–90. [1965; GS, vol. 10.2, pp. 656–73.]

"Television and the Patterns of Mass Culture." In *Mass Culture: The Popular Arts in America.* Edited by Bernard Rosenberg and David Manning White, pp. 474–88. Glencoe, IL: Free Press, 1957. See also by its alternate title, "How to Look at Television."

"Television as Ideology." CM, pp. 59–70. [1953; GS, vol. 10.2, pp. 518–32.]

"Theory of Pseudo-Culture." Translated by Deborah Cook. *Telos* 95 (Spring 1993), pp. 15–38. [1959; GS, vol. 8, pp. 93–121.]

"Thesis upon Art and Religion Today." 1945; reprint. *Kenyon Review* 18 nos. 3–4 (Summer/Fall 1996), pp. 236–40. [1945; GS, vol. 11, pp. 647–53.]

"To Describe, Understand and Explain." [Discussion with Lucien Goldmann.] In *Cultural Creation in Modern Society,* by Lucien Goldmann. Translated by Bart Grahl, pp. 130–47. St. Louis: Telos Press, 1976. [1968]

"Toward an Understanding of Schoenberg." Translated by Susan H. Gillespie. This volume, pp. 627–43. [1955/1967; GS, vol. 18, pp. 428–45.]

"Transparencies on Film." Translated by David J. Levin. In *The Culture Industry: Selected Essays on Mass Culture.* Edited by J. M. Bernstein, pp. 154–61. London: Routledge, 1991. Also in: *New German Critique* 24–25 (Fall/Winter 1981–82), pp. 199–205. [1966; GS, vol. 10.1, pp. 353–61.]

"A Typology of Music Listening." Unpublished. Paul F. Lazarsfeld papers, Columbia University. 17 pp. MS. [c. 1938]

"Über die musikalische Verwendung des Radios." [1963; GS, vol. 15, pp. 369–401.]

"Vers une musique informelle." QF, pp. 269–322. [1961/1963; GS, vol. 16, pp. 493–540.]

"Wagner, Nietzsche, and Hitler." Review of *Life of Richard Wagner,* vol. 4, by Ernest Newman. *Kenyon Review* 9 no. 1 (Winter 1947), pp. 155–62. [1947; GS, vol. 19, pp. 404–12.]

"Wagner's Relevance for Today." Translated by Susan H. Gillespie. *Grand Street* 11 no. 4 (1993), pp. 33–59. And this volume, pp. 584–602. [1963; GS, vol. 16, pp. 543–64.]

"What National Socialism Has Done to the Arts." This volume, pp. 373–90. [1945; GS, vol. 20.2, pp. 413–29.]

"Why Is the New Art So Hard to Understand?" Translated by Susan H. Gillespie. This volume, pp. 127–34. [1931; GS, vol. 18, pp. 824–31.]

"Why Still Philosophy." CM, pp. 5–17. [1962; GS, vol. 10.2, pp. 459–73.]

"Words from Abroad." NL, vol. 1, pp. 185–99. [1959; GS, vol. 11, pp. 216–32.]

III. SECONDARY SOURCES ON ADORNO CONSULTED

Agger, Ben. *A Critical Theory of Public Life: Knowledge, Discourse and Politics in an Age of Decline.* London: Falmer Press, 1991.

———. "On Happiness and the Damaged Life." In *On Critical Theory.* Edited by John O'Neill, pp. 12–23. New York: Seabury, 1976.

Arato, Andrew, and Eike Gebhardt. "Esthetic Theory and Cultural Criticism." In *The Essential Frankfurt School Reader.* Edited by Andrew Arato and Eike Gebhardt, pp. 185–224. New York: Continuum, 1982.

Arnold, Heinz Ludwig, ed. *Theodor W. Adorno.* 2nd ed. enlarged. Munich: Edition Text + Kritik, 1983.

Barron, Stephanie, with Sabine Eckmann, eds. *Exiles + Emigrés: The Flight of European Artists from Hitler* [exhibition catalogue, Los Angeles County Museum of Art]. New York: Harry N. Abrams, 1997.

Bauer, Karin. *Adorno's Nietzschean Narratives: Critiques of Ideology, Readings of Wagner.* Albany: State University of New York Press, 1999.

Baugh, Bruce. "Left-Wing Elitism: Adorno on Popular Culture." *Philosophy and Literature* 14 no. 1 (April 1990), pp. 65–78.

Benhabib, Seyla. "Critical Theory and Postmodernism: On the Interplay of Ethics, Aesthetics, and Utopia in Critical Theory." In *The Handbook of Critical Theory.* Edited by David M. Rasmussen, pp. 327–39. Oxford: Blackwell, 1996.

Benjamin, Andrew, ed. *The Problems of Modernity: Adorno and Benjamin.* London: Routledge, 1989.

Berman, Russell A. "Adorno, Marxism and Art." *Telos* 34 (Winter 1977–78), pp. 157–66.

———. *Modern Culture and Critical Theory: Art, Politics, and the Legacy of the Frankfurt School.* Madison: University of Wisconsin Press, 1989.

Blomster, Wes. "Sociology of Music: Adorno and Beyond." *Telos* 28 (Summer 1976), pp. 81–112.

Blumenfeld, Harold. "*Ad Vocem* Adorno." *Musical Quarterly* 70 no. 2 (Spring 1984), pp. 515–37.

Borio, Gianmario. "Die Positionen Adornos zur musikalischen Avantgarde zwischen 1954 und 1966." In *Adorno in seinen musikalischen Schriften,* pp. 163–79. Rogensburg: G. Bosse, 1987.

Born, Georgina. "Against Negation, for a Politics of Cultural Production: Adorno, Aesthetics, the Social." *Screen* 34 no. 3 (Fall 1993), pp. 223–42.

Boulez, Pierre. "T. W. Adorno." In *Orientations: Collected Writings by Pierre*

Boulez. Edited by Jean-Jacques Nattiez. Translated by Martin Cooper, pp. 517–18. Cambridge: Harvard University Press, 1986.

Brinkmann, Reinhold, and Christoph Wolff, eds. *Driven into Paradise: The Musical Migration from Nazi Germany to the United States.* Berkeley and Los Angeles: University of California Press, 1999.

Brown, Lee B. "Adorno's Critique of Popular Culture: The Case of Jazz Music." *Journal of Aesthetic Education* 26 no. 1 (Spring 1992), pp. 17–31.

Brunkhorst, Hauke. "Theodor W. Adorno: Aesthetic Constructivism and a Negative Ethic of the Non-Forfeited Life." Translated by James Swindal. In *The Handbook of Critical Theory.* Edited by David M. Rasmussen, pp. 305–22. Oxford: Blackwell, 1996.

Buck-Morss, Susan. *The Origin of Negative Dialectics: Theodor W. Adorno, Walter Benjamin, and the Frankfurt Institute.* New York: Free Press, 1977.

Bürger, Peter. "Adorno's Anti-Avant-Gardism." *Telos* 86 (Winter 1990–91), pp. 49–60.

———. *Theory of the Avant-Garde.* Translated by Michael Shaw. Minneapolis: University of Minnesota Press, 1984.

Chadwick, Nick. "Mátyás Seiber's Collaboration in Adorno's Jazz Project, 1936." *British Library Journal* 21 no. 2 (Fall 1995), pp. 259–88.

Collins, Jim. *Uncommon Cultures: Popular Culture and Post-Modernism.* New York: Routledge, 1989.

Cook, Deborah. *The Culture Industry Revisited: Theodor W. Adorno on Mass Culture.* Lanham, MD: Rowman and Littlefield, 1996.

Cooper, Harry. "On *Über Jazz:* Replaying Adorno with the Grain." *October* 75 (1996), pp. 99–133.

Craft, Robert. "A Bell for Adorno." Review of *Philosophy of Modern Music,* by Theodor W. Adorno. In *Prejudices in Disguise: Articles, Essays, Reviews,* pp. 91–102. New York: Alfred A. Knopf, 1974.

Crook, Stephen. "Introduction: Adorno and Authoritarian Irrationalism." In *Adorno: The Stars Down to Earth and Other Essays on the Irrational in Culture.* Edited by Stephen Crook, pp. 1–33. New York: Routledge, 1994.

Deathridge, John. Review of *In Search of Wagner* by Theodor W. Adorno. *19th Century Music* 7 no. 1 (Summer 1983), pp. 81–85.

Dennis, Christopher J. *Adorno's "Philosophy of Modern Music."* Lewiston, ME: Edwin Mellen Press, 1998.

Eagleton, Terry. "Art after Auschwitz: Theodor Adorno." In *The Ideology of the Aesthetic,* pp. 341–65. Oxford: Blackwell, 1990.

Engh, Barbara. "After 'His Master's Voice,'" *New Formations* 38 (Summer 1999), pp. 54–63.

Etzkorn, K. Peter. "Sociologists and Music." In *Music and Society: The Later Writings of Paul Honigsheim.* Edited by K. Peter Etzkorn, pp. 3–40. New York: John Wiley and Sons, 1973.

Feher, Ferenc. "Negative Philosophy of Music—Positive Results." Translated by Zoltan Feher. *New German Critique* 4 (Winter 1975), pp. 99–111.

―――. "Rationalized Music and Its Vicissitudes (Adorno's Philosophy of Music)." *Philosophy and Social Criticism* 9 no. 1 (Spring 1982), pp. 43–65.

Forst, Rainer. "Justice, Reason, and Critique: Basic Concepts of Critical Theory." In *Handbook of Critical Theory.* Edited by David M. Rasmussen, pp. 138–62. Oxford: Blackwell, 1996.

Gendron, Bernard. "Theodor Adorno Meets the Cadillacs." In *Studies in Entertainment: Critical Approaches to Mass Culture.* Edited by Tania Modleski, pp. 18–36. Bloomington: Indiana University Press, 1986.

Geulen, Eva. "Theodor Adorno on Tradition." In *The Actuality of Adorno: Critical Essays on Adorno and the Postmodern.* Edited by Max Pensky, pp. 183–93. Albany: State University of New York Press, 1997.

Geuss, Raymond. "Berg and Adorno." In *The Cambridge Companion to Berg.* Edited by Anthony Pople, pp. 38–50. Cambridge: Cambridge University Press, 1997.

Giddens, Anthony. *The Nation-State and Violence.* Vol. 2 of *A Contemporary Critique of Historical Materialism.* Berkeley and Los Angeles: University of California Press, 1985.

Gillespie, Susan H. "Translating Adorno: Language, Music, and Performance." *Musical Quarterly* 79 no. 1 (Spring 1995), pp. 55–65.

Gracyk, Theodore A. "Adorno, Jazz, and the Aesthetics of Popular Music." *Musical Quarterly* 76 no. 4 (Winter 1992), pp. 526–42.

Grassl, Markus, and Reinhard Kapp, eds. *Darmstadt-Gespräche: Die Internationalen Fereinkurse für Neue Musik in Wien.* Vienna: Böhlau, 1996.

Gross, Harvey. "Adorno in Los Angeles: The Intellectual in Emigration." *Humanities in Society* 2 no. 4 (Fall 1979), pp. 339–51.

Haack, Helmut. "Adornos Sprechen über Musik." In *Adorno und die Musik.* Edited by Otto Kolleritsch, pp. 37–51. Graz: Universal Edition, 1979.

Habermas, Jürgen. "The Entwinement of Myth and Enlightenment: Re-Reading *Dialectic of Enlightenment.*" Translated by Thomas Y. Levin. *New German Critique* 26 (Spring/Summer 1982), pp. 13–30.

―――. "A Generation Apart from Adorno." Interview by J. Früchtl. Translated by James Swindal. *Philosophy and Social Criticism* 18 no. 2 (1992), pp. 119–24.

Haggin, B. H. *Music in the Nation.* New York: William Sloane Associates, 1949.

Hailey, Christopher. "Defining Home: Berg's Life on the Periphery." In *The Cambridge Companion to Berg,* edited by Anthony Pople, pp. 5–23, 259–65. Cambridge: Cambridge University Press, 1997.

Hamilton, Carol V. "All That Jazz Again: Adorno's Sociology of Music." *Popular Music and Society* 15 no. 3 (Fall 1991), pp. 31–40.

Hanrahan, Nancy Weiss. "Negative Composition." *Philosophy and Social Criticism* 15 no. 3 (1989), pp. 273–90.

Hansen, Miriam. "Introduction to Adorno, 'Transparencies on Film' (1966)." *New German Critique* 24–25 (Fall/Winter 1981–82), pp. 186–98.

―――. "Mass Culture as Hieroglyphic Writing: Adorno, Derrida, Kracauer."

New German Critique 56 (Spring/Summer, 1992), pp. 43–73. Also in: *The Actuality of Adorno: Essays on Adorno and the Postmodern*. Edited by Max Pensky, pp. 83–110. Albany: State University of New York, 1997.

———. "Of Mice and Ducks: Benjamin and Adorno on Disney." *South Atlantic Quarterly* 92 no. 1 (Winter 1993), pp. 27–61.

Harding, James Martin. *Adorno and "A Writing of the Ruins": Essays on Modern Aesthetics and Anglo-American Literature and Culture*. Albany: State University of New York Press, 1997.

Heilbut, Anthony. *Exiled in Paradise: German Refugee Artists and Intellectuals in America from the 1930s to the Present*. Berkeley and Los Angeles: University of California Press, 1983, 1997 (new postscript).

Held, David. *Introduction to Critical Theory: Horkheimer to Habermas*. Berkeley and Los Angeles: University of California Press, 1980.

Hewitt, Andrew. "A Feminine Dialectic of Enlightenment? Horkheimer and Adorno Revisited." *New German Critique* 56 (Spring/Summer, 1992), pp. 143–70.

Hinton, Stephen. "Adorno's Unfinished *Beethoven*." Review of *Beethoven: Philosophie der Musik*, by Theodor W. Adorno. *Beethoven Forum* 5, pp. 139–53. Lincoln: University of Nebraska Press, 1996.

Hohendahl, Peter Uwe. "*Dialectic of Enlightenment* Revisited: Habermas's Critique of the Frankfurt School." In *Reappraisals: Shifting Alignments in Postwar Critical Theory*, pp. 99–130. Ithaca: Cornell University Press, 1991.

———. *Prismatic Thought: Theodor W. Adorno*. Lincoln: University of Nebraska Press, 1995.

———. *Reappraisals: Shifting Alignments in Postwar Critical Theory*. Ithaca: Cornell University Press, 1991.

Huhn, Tom, and Lambert Zuidervaart, eds. *The Semblance of Subjectivity: Essays in Adorno's Aesthetic Theory*. Cambridge: MIT Press, 1997.

Hullot-Kentor, Robert. "Back to Adorno." *Telos* 81 (Fall 1989), pp. 5–29.

———. "The Impossibility of Music: Adorno, Popular and Other Music." *Telos* 87 (Spring 1991), pp. 97–117.

———. "Notes on *Dialectic of Enlightenment*: Translating the Odysseus Essay." *New German Critique* 56 (Spring/Summer 1992), pp. 101–08.

———. "The Philosophy of Dissonance: Adorno and Schoenberg." In *The Semblance of Subjectivity: Essays in Adorno's Aesthetic Theory*. Edited by Tom Huhn and Lambert Zuidervaart, pp. 309–19. Cambridge: MIT Press, 1997.

———. "Popular Music and Adorno's 'The Aging of the New Music.'" *Telos* 77 (Fall 1988), pp. 79–94.

———. "Translator's Introduction," AT, pp. xi–xxi.

Huyssen, Andreas. "Adorno in Reverse: From Hollywood to Richard Wagner." *New German Critique* 29 (Spring/Summer 1983), pp. 8–38.

———. *After the Great Divide: Modernism, Mass Culture, Postmodernism*. Bloomington: Indiana University Press, 1986.

Israel, Nico. "Damage Control: Adorno, Los Angeles, and the Dislocation of Culture." *Yale Journal of Criticism* 10 no. 1 (Spring 1997), pp. 85–113.

Jachec, Nancy. "Adorno, Greenberg and Modernist Politics." *Telos* 110 (Winter 1998), pp. 105–18.

Jameson, Fredric. "Introduction to T. W. Adorno." In *The Legacy of the German Refugee Intellectuals*. Edited by Robert Boyers, pp. 140–43. New York: Schocken, 1972.

———. *Late Marxism: Adorno, or, the Persistence of the Dialectic*. London: Verso, 1990.

———. "Reification and Utopia in Mass Culture." *Social Text* 1 (1979), pp. 130–48.

Jarvis, Simon. *Adorno: A Critical Introduction*. New York: Routledge, 1998.

Jay, Martin. *Adorno*. Cambridge: Harvard University Press, 1984.

———. "Adorno and Kracauer: Notes on a Troubled Friendship." In *Permanent Exiles: Essays on the Intellectual Migration from Germany to America*, pp. 217–36. New York: Columbia University Press, 1985.

———. "Adorno in America." *New German Critique* 31 (Winter 1984), pp. 157–82. Also in *Permanent Exiles: Essays on the Intellectual Migration from Germany to America*, pp. 120–37. New York: Columbia University Press, 1985.

———. *The Dialectical Imagination: A History of the Frankfurt School and the Institute of Social Research, 1923–1950*. Boston: Little, Brown, 1973.

———. "The Extraterritorial Life of Siegfried Kracauer." In *Permanent Exiles: Essays on the Intellectual Migration from Germany to America*, pp. 152–97. New York: Columbia University Press, 1985.

———. "The Frankfurt School in Exile." In *Permanent Exiles: Essays on the Intellectual Migration from Germany to America*, pp. 28–61. New York: Columbia University Press, 1985.

———. "Mass Culture and Aesthetic Redemption: The Debate between Max Horkheimer and Siegfried Kracauer." In *On Max Horkheimer: New Perspectives*. Edited by Seyla Benhabib, Wolfgang Bonss, and John McCole, pp. 365–86. Cambridge: MIT Press, 1993.

———. "Mimesis and Mimetology: Adorno and Lacoue-Labarthe." In *The Semblance of Subjectivity: Essays in Adorno's Aesthetic Theory*. Edited by Tom Huhn and Lambert Zuidervaart, pp. 29–53. Cambridge: MIT Press, 1997.

———. "The Permanent Exile of Theodor W. Adorno." *Midstream* 15 (December 1969), pp. 62–69.

———. *Permanent Exiles: Essays on the Intellectual Migration from Germany to America*. New York: Columbia University Press, 1985.

Jhally, Sut. "Advertising as Religion: The Dialectic of Technology and Magic." In *Cultural Politics in Contemporary America*. Edited by Ian Angus and Sut Jhally, pp. 217–29. New York: Routledge, 1989.

Kadelbach, Gerd. "Persönliche Begegnungen mit Theodor W. Adorno im Frankfurter Funkhaus." In *Politische Pädagogik: Beiträge zur Humanisie-*

rung der Gesellschaft. Edited by Friedhelm Zubke, pp. 49–56. Weinheim: Deutscher Studien, 1990.

Kellner, Douglas. "Critical Theory Today: Revisiting the Classics." *Theory, Culture and Society* 10 no. 2 (May 1993), pp. 43–60.

Klemm, Eberhardt. "Zur vorliegenden Ausgabe." In *Komposition für den Film.* Vol. 4, of Hanns Eisler, *Gesammelte Werke,* ser. 3, pp. 5–24. Leipzig: VEB Deutscher Verlag für Musik, 1977.

Knapp, Gerhard. *Theodor W. Adorno.* Berlin: Colloquium, 1980.

Kogawa, Tetsuo. "Adorno's 'Strategy of Hibernation.'" *Telos* 46 (Winter 1980–81), pp. 147–53.

Kolleritsch, Otto, ed. *Adorno und die Musik.* Graz: Universal Edition, 1979.

Krahl, Hans-Jürgen. "The Political Contradictions in Adorno's Critical Theory." *Telos* 21 (Fall 1974), pp. 164–67.

Kraushaar, Wolfgang, ed. *Frankfurter Schule und Studentenbewegung: Von der Flaschenpost zum Molotowcocktail, 1946–1995.* 3 vols. Hamburg: Rogner and Bernhard, 1998.

Kuspit, Donald B. "Critical Notes on Adorno's Sociology of Music and Art." *Journal of Aesthetics and Art Criticism* 33 no. 3 (Spring 1975), pp. 321–27.

Lazarsfeld, Paul F. "An Episode in the History of Social Research: A Memoir." In *The Intellectual Migration: Europe and America, 1930–1960.* Edited by Donald Fleming and Bernard Bailyn, pp. 270–337. Cambridge: Belknap Press of Harvard University Press, 1969.

Leibowitz, René. "Der Komponist Theodor W. Adorno." In *Zeugnisse: Theodor W. Adorno zum sechzigsten Geburtstag,* pp. 355–59. Edited by Max Horkheimer. Frankfurt am Main: Europäische Verlagsanstalt, 1963.

Levin, Thomas Y. "The Acoustic Dimension: Notes on Cinema Sound." *Screen* 25 no. 3 (May/June 1984), pp. 55–68.

———. "For the Record: Adorno on Music in the Age of Its Technological Reproducibility." *October* 55 (Winter 1990), pp. 23–47.

———. "Nationalities of Language: Adorno's *Fremdwörter,* An Introduction to 'On the Question: What Is German?'" *New German Critique* 36 (Fall 1985), pp. 111–19.

Levin, Thomas Y., with Michael von der Linn. "Elements of a Radio Theory: Adorno and the Princeton Radio Research Project." *Musical Quarterly* 78 no. 2 (Summer 1994), pp. 316–24.

Lindstrom, Fred B., and Naomi Lindstrom. "Adorno Encounters Cu-Bop: Experimental Music as a Task for Critics and Their Audiences." *Sociological Perspectives* 29 no. 2 (April 1986), pp. 284–304.

Lowenthal, Leo. "The Left in Germany Has Failed." Interview by Peter Glotz. Translated by Benjamin Gregg. In *An Unmastered Past: The Autobiographical Reflections of Leo Lowenthal.* Edited by Martin Jay, pp. 247–60. Berkeley and Los Angeles: University of California Press, 1987.

———. "Recollections of Theodor W. Adorno." Translated by Sabine Wilke. In *An Unmastered Past: The Autobiographical Reflections of Leo Lowen-*

thal. Edited by Martin Jay, pp. 201–15. Berkeley and Los Angeles: University of California Press, 1987. Also in: Leo Lowenthal, *Critical Theory and Frankfurt Theorists: Lectures—Correspondence—Conversations,* pp. 62–72. New Brunswick: Transaction, 1989.

———. "Theodor W. Adorno: An Intellectual Memoir." In *An Unmastered Past: The Autobiographical Reflections of Leo Lowenthal.* Edited by Martin Jay, pp. 183–200. Berkeley and Los Angeles: University of California Press, 1987.

———. "The Utopian Motif in Suspension: A Conversation with Leo Lowenthal." Interview by W. Martin Lüdke. Translated by Ted R. Weeks. In *An Unmastered Past: The Autobiographical Reflections of Leo Lowenthal.* Edited by Martin Jay, pp. 237–46. Berkeley and Los Angeles: University of California Press, 1987.

Löwy, Michael, and Eleni Varikas. "'The World Spirit on the Fins of a Rocket': Adorno's Critique of Progress." Translated by Martin Ryle. *Radical Philosophy* 70 (March/April 1995), pp. 9–15.

Lunn, Eugene. *Marxism and Modernism: An Historical Study of Lukács, Brecht, Benjamin, and Adorno.* Berkeley and Los Angeles: University of California Press, 1982.

MacRae, D. G. "Frankfurters." Review of *Negative Dialectics,* by Theodor W. Adorno. *New Society* 27 no. 599 (28 March 1974), p. 786.

Markus, Gyorgy. "Adorno's Wagner." *Thesis Eleven* 56 (February 1999), pp. 25–55.

Marsh, James L. "Adorno's Critique of Stravinsky." *New German Critique* 28 (Winter 1983), pp. 147–69.

Martin, David. "Dr. Adorno's Bag of Tricks." Review of *Minima Moralia: Reflections from Damaged Life,* by Theodor W. Adorno. *Encounter* 47 no. 4 (October 1976), pp. 67–76.

Mayer, Günter. "Adorno und Eisler." In *Adorno und die Musik.* Edited by Otto Kolleritsch, pp. 133–55. Graz: Universal Edition, 1979.

McCann, Graham. "New Introduction." In *Composing for the Films,* by Theodor W. Adorno and Hanns Eisler, pp. vii–xlvii. London: Athlone Press, 1994.

Menke, Christoph. "Critical Theory and Tragic Knowledge." Translated by James Swindal. In *The Handbook of Critical Theory.* Edited by David M. Rasmussen, pp. 57–73. Oxford: Blackwell, 1996.

Metzger, Heinz-Klaus. "Just Who Is Growing Old?" *Die Reihe 4: Young Composers,* pp. 63–80. Bryn Mawr, PA: Theodore Presser, 1960.

Metzger, Heinz-Klaus, and Rainer Riehn, eds. *Darmstadt-Dokumente I.* Musik-Konzepte Sonderband: Die Reihe über Komponisten. Munich: Edition Text + Kritik, 1999.

———. *Theodor W. Adorno: Der Komponist.* Musik-Konzepte 63–64. Munich: Edition Text + Kritik, 1989.

Miller, James. "Is Bad Writing Necessary? George Orwell, Theodor Adorno, and the Politics of Language." *Lingua Franca* 9 no. 9 (December/January 2000), pp. 33–44.

Motte, Diether de la. "Adornos musikalische Analysen." In *Adorno und die Musik*. Edited by Otto Kolleritsch, pp. 52–63. Graz: Universal Edition, 1979.

Morrison, David E. "The Beginning of Modern Mass Communication Research." *Archives Européennes de Sociologie* 19 no. 2 (1978), pp. 347–59.

———. "Kultur and Culture: The Case of Theodor W. Adorno and Paul F. Lazarsfeld." *Social Research* 45 no. 2 (Summer 1978), pp. 331–55.

Nägele, Rainer. "The Scene of the Other: Theodor W. Adorno's Negative Dialectic in the Context of Poststructuralism." In *Postmodernism and Politics*. Edited by Jonathan Arac, pp. 91–111. Minneapolis: University of Minnesota Press, 1986).

Nesbitt, Nick. "Sounding Autonomy: Adorno, Coltrane and Jazz." *Telos* 116 (Summer 1999), pp. 81–98.

Nicholsen, Shierry Weber. *Exact Imagination, Late Work: On Adorno's Aesthetics*. Cambridge: MIT Press, 1997.

Nye, William P. "Theodor Adorno on Jazz: A Critique of Critical Theory." *Popular Music and Society* 12 no. 4 (Winter 1988), pp. 69–73.

O'Neill, Maggie, ed. *Adorno, Culture and Feminism*. London: Sage, 1999.

Osborne, Peter. "Adorno and the Metaphysics of Modernism: The Problem of a 'Postmodern' Art." In *The Problems of Modernity: Adorno and Benjamin*. Edited by Andrew Benjamin, pp. 23–48. New York: Routledge, 1989.

Paddison, Max. *Adorno's Aesthetics of Music*. Cambridge: Cambridge University Press, 1993.

———. *Adorno, Modernism and Mass Culture: Essays on Critical Theory and Music*. London: Kahn and Averill, 1996.

———. "The Critique Criticised: Adorno and Popular Music." In *Popular Music: 2: Theory and Method*. Edited by Richard Middleton and David Horn, pp. 201–18. Cambridge: Cambridge University Press, 1982.

———. "The Language-Character of Music: Some Motifs in Adorno." *Journal of the Royal Musical Association* 116 no. 2 (1991), pp. 267–79.

Paetzold, Heinz. "Adorno's Notion of Natural Beauty: A Reconsideration." In *The Semblance of Subjectivity: Essays in Adorno's Aesthetic Theory*. Edited by Tom Huhn and Lambert Zuidervaart, pp. 213–35. Cambridge: MIT Press, 1997.

Pattison, Robert. *The Triumph of Vulgarity: Rock Music in the Mirror of Romanticism*. New York: Oxford University Press, 1987.

Pensky, Max, ed. *The Actuality of Adorno: Critical Essays on Adorno and the Postmodern*. Albany: State University of New York Press, 1997.

Pepper, Ian. "From the 'Aesthetics of Indifference' to 'Negative Aesthetics': John Cage and Germany, 1958–1972." *October* 82 (Fall 1997), pp. 31–47.

Pepper, Thomas. *Singularities: Extremes of Theory in the Twentieth Century*. Cambridge: Cambridge University Press, 1997.

Pickford, Henry W. Preface to *Critical Models: Interventions and Catchwords*, by Theodor W. Adorno, translated by Henry W. Pickford, pp. vii–xii. New York: Columbia University Press, 1998.

Quinn, Richard. "Playing with Adorno: Improvisation and the Jazz Ensemble." *Yearbook of Comparative and General Literature* 44 (1996), pp. 57–67.

Rasmussen, David M. "Critical Theory and Philosophy." In *Handbook of Critical Theory*. Edited by David M. Rasmussen, pp. 11–38. Oxford: Blackwell, 1996.

Rietmüller, Albrecht. "Theodor W. Adorno und der Fortschritt in der Musik." In *Das Projekt Moderne und die Postmoderne*, pp. 15–34. Edited by Wilfred Gruhn. Regensburg: Bosse, 1989.

Rifkin, Adrian. "Down on the Upbeat: Adorno, Benjamin and the Jazz Question." *Block* 15 (1989), pp. 43–47.

Roberts, David. *Art and Enlightenment: Aesthetic Theory after Adorno*. Lincoln: University of Nebraska Press, 1991.

Robinson, J. Bradford. "The Jazz Essays of Theodor Adorno: Some Thoughts on Jazz Reception in Weimar Germany." *Popular Music* 13 no. 1 (January 1994), pp. 1–25.

———. "Jazz Reception in Weimar Germany: In Search of a Shimmy Figure." In *Music and Performance during the Weimar Republic*. Edited by Bryan Gilliam, pp. 107–34. Cambridge: Cambridge University Press, 1994.

Rocco, Christopher. "Between Modernity and Postmodernity: Reading *Dialectic of Enlightenment* against the Grain." *Political Theory* 22 no. 1 (February 1994), pp. 71–97.

Rose, Gillian. *The Melancholy Science: An Introduction to the Thought of Theodor W. Adorno*. New York: Columbia University Press, 1978.

Rosen, Philip. "Adorno and Film Music: Theoretical Notes on *Composing for the Films*." *Yale French Studies* 60 (1980), pp. 157–82.

Sample, Colin. "Adorno on the Musical Language of Beethoven." Review of *Beethoven: Philosophie der Musik*, by Theodor W. Adorno. *Musical Quarterly* 78 no. 2 (Summer 1994), pp. 378–93.

Sandner, Wolfgang. "Popularmusik als somatisches Stimulans: Adornos Kritik der 'leichten Musik.'" In *Adorno und die Musik*. Edited by Otto Kolleritsch, pp. 125–32. Graz: Universal Edition, 1979.

Scheible, Hartmut. *Theodor W. Adorno: Mit Selbstzeugnissen und Bilddokumenten*. Reinbek bei Hamburg: Rowohlt, 1989.

Schibli, Sigfried. *Der Komponist Theodor W. Adorno*. Frankfurt am Main: Frankfurter Bund für Volksbildung, 1988.

Schmidt, James. "Language, Mythology, and Enlightenment: Historical Notes on Horkheimer and Adorno's *Dialectic of Enlightenment*." *Social Research* 65 no. 4 (1998), pp. 807–38.

Schnebel, Dieter. "Einführung in Adornos Musik." In *Adorno und die Musik*. Edited by Otto Kolleritsch, pp. 15–19. Graz: Universal Edition, 1979.

Schönherr, Ulrich. "Adorno and Jazz: Reflections on a Failed Encounter." *Telos* 87 (Spring 1991), pp. 85–96.

Schoolman, Morton. "Toward a Politics of Darkness: Individuality and Its Politics in Adorno's Aesthetics." *Political Theory* 25 no. 1 (February 1997), pp. 57–92.

Schubert, Giselher. "Adornos Auseinandersetzung mit der Zwölftontechnik Schönbergs. *Archiv für Musikwissenschaft* 46 no. 3 (1989), pp. 235–54.

Sharma, Bhesham R. *Music and Culture in the Age of Mechanical Reproduction.* New York: Peter Lang, 2000.

Slater, Phil. *Origin and Significance of the Frankfurt School: A Marxist Perspective.* London: Routledge and Kegan Paul, 1977.

Smith, David Norman. "The Beloved Dictator: Adorno, Horkheimer, and the Critique of Domination." *Current Perspectives in Social Theory* 12 (1992), pp. 195–230.

Subotnik, Rose Rosengard. "Adorno's Diagnosis of Beethoven's Late Style: Early Symptom of a Fatal Condition." In *Developing Variations: Style and Ideology in Western Music*, pp. 15–41. Minneapolis: University of Minnesota Press, 1991.

———. "The Challenge of Contemporary Music." In *Developing Variations: Style and Ideology in Western Music*, pp. 265–93. Minneapolis: University of Minnesota Press, 1991.

———. "The Historical Structure: Adorno's 'French' Model for the Criticism of Nineteenth-Century Music." In *Developing Variations: Style and Ideology in Western Music*, pp. 206–38. Minneapolis: University of Minnesota Press, 1991.

———. "Kant, Adorno, and the Self-Critique of Reason: Toward a Model for Music Criticism." In *Developing Variations: Style and Ideology in Western Music*, pp. 57–83. Minneapolis: University of Minnesota Press, 1991.

———. "The Role of Ideology in the Study of Western Music." In *Developing Variations: Style and Ideology in Western Music*, pp. 3–14. Minneapolis: University of Minnesota Press, 1991.

———. "Toward a Deconstruction of Structural Listening: A Critique of Schoenberg, Adorno, and Stravinsky." In *Deconstructive Variations: Music and Reason in Western Society*, pp. 148–76. Minneapolis: University of Minnesota Press, 1996.

———. "Why Is Adorno's Music Criticism the Way It Is? Some Reflections on Twentieth-Century Criticism of Nineteenth-Century Music." In *Developing Variations: Style and Ideology in Western Music*, pp. 42–56. Minneapolis: University of Minnesota Press, 1991.

Sullivan, Michael, and John T. Lysaker. "Between Impotence and Illusion: Adorno's Art of Theory and Practice." *New German Critique* 57 (Fall 1992), pp. 87–122.

Tar, Zoltán. *The Frankfurt School: The Critical Theories of Max Horkheimer and Theodor W. Adorno.* New York: John Wiley and Sons, 1977.

Theodor W. Adorno. Special Issue: *New German Critique* 56 (Spring/Summer 1992).

Thomas, Calvin. "A Knowledge That Would Not Be Power: Adorno, Nostalgia, and the Historicity of the Musical Subject." *New German Critique* 48 (Fall 1989), pp. 155–75.

Tiedemann, Rolf. "Historical Materialism or Political Messianism? An Interpretation of the Theses 'On the Concept of History.'" In *The Frankfurt School: Critical Assessments*. Edited by Jay Bernstein, vol. 2, pp. 111–39. London and New York: Routledge, 1994.

Townsend, Peter. "Adorno on Jazz: Vienna versus the Vernacular." *Prose Studies* 11 no. 1 (May 1988), pp. 69–88.

Volpacchio, Florindo. "The Unhappy Marriage of Music and Emancipation: Reply to Kentor." *Telos* 87 (Spring 1991), pp. 118–23.

Weber, Samuel. "Translating the Untranslatable." In *Prisms,* by Theodor W. Adorno, translated by Samuel Weber and Shierry Weber, pp. 9–15. Cambridge: MIT Press, 1981.

Wellmer, Albrecht. *The Persistence of Modernity: Essays on Aesthetics, Ethics, and Postmodernism.* Translated by David Midgley. Cambridge: MIT Press, 1991.

Whitebook, Joel. "Fantasy and Critique: Some Thoughts on Freud and the Frankfurt School." In *The Handbook of Critical Theory.* Edited by David M. Rasmussen, pp. 287–304. Oxford: Blackwell, 1996.

———. "From Schoenberg to Odysseus: Aesthetic, Psychic, and Social Synthesis in Adorno and Wellmer." *New German Critique* 58 (Winter 1993), 45–64.

Wiggershaus, Rolf. *The Frankfurt School: Its History, Theories, and Political Significance.* Translated by Michael Robertson. Cambridge: MIT Press, 1995.

———. *Theodor W. Adorno.* Munich: C. H. Beck, 1987.

Wilcock, Evelyn. "Adorno, Jazz and Racism: 'Über Jazz' and the 1934–7 British Jazz Debate." *Telos* 107 (Spring 1996), pp. 63–80.

———. "Adorno's Uncle: Dr. Bernard Wingfield and the English Exile of Theodor W. Adorno, 1934–38." *German Life and Letters* 49 no. 3 (July 1996), pp. 324–38.

———. "Alban Berg's Appeal to Edward Dent on Behalf of Theodor Adorno, 18 November 1933." *German Life and Letters* 50 no. 3 (July 1997), pp. 365–68.

Wilke, Sabine, and Heidi Schlipphacke. "Construction of a Gendered Subject: A Feminist Reading of Adorno's *Aesthetic Theory.*" In *The Semblance of Subjectivity: Essays in Adorno's Aesthetic Theory.* Edited by Tom Huhn and Lambert Zuidervaart, pp. 287–308. Cambridge: MIT Press, 1997.

Williams, Alastair. *New Music and the Claims of Modernity.* Aldershot, UK: Ashgate, 1997.

Witkin, Robert W. *Adorno on Music.* New York: Routledge, 1998.

Wohlfarth, Irving. "Hibernation: On the Tenth Anniversary of Adorno's Death." *Modern Language Notes* 94 no. 5 (December 1979), pp. 956–87.

Wolin, Richard. "Benjamin, Adorno, Surrealism." In *The Semblance of Subjectivity: Essays in Adorno's Aesthetic Theory.* Edited by Tom Huhn and Lambert Zuidervaart, pp. 93–122. Cambridge: MIT Press, 1997.

———. "The De-Aestheticization of Art: On Adorno's *Aesthetische Theorie.*" *Telos* 41 (Fall 1979), pp. 105–27.

―――. *The Terms of Cultural Criticism: The Frankfurt School, Existentialism, Poststructuralism.* New York: Columbia University Press, 1992.

―――. "Utopia, Mimesis, and Reconciliation: A Redemptive Critique of Adorno's *Aesthetic Theory.*" *Representations* 32 (Fall 1990), pp. 33–49.

Wood, Michael. "Adorno's Ascetic Formula. *Kenyon Review* 18 nos. 3–4 (Summer/Fall 1996), pp. 222–28.

Zipes, Jack. "Adorno May Still Be Right." *Telos* 101 (Fall 1994), pp. 157–67.

Zuidervaart, Lambert. *Adorno's Aesthetic Theory: The Redemption of Illusion.* Cambridge: MIT Press, 1991.

―――. "The Social Significance of Autonomous Art: Adorno and [Peter] Bürger." *Journal of Aesthetics and Art Criticism* 48 no. 1 (Winter 1990), pp. 61–77.

IV. TERTIARY SOURCES CONSULTED

Note: Some of the sources cited below discuss Adorno, but only as a secondary focus.

Attali, Jacques. *Noise: The Political Economy of Music.* Translated by Brian Massumi. Minneapolis: University of Minnesota Press, 1985.

Ayars, Christine Merrick. *Contributions to the Art of Music in America by the Music Industries of Boston, 1640 to 1936.* New York: H. W. Wilson, 1937.

Bakhtin, Mikhail. *Rabelais and His World.* Translated by Hélène Iswolsky. Bloomington: Indiana University Press, 1984.

Bate, Philip. "Saxophone." In *The New Grove Dictionary of Music and Musicians.* London: Macmillan, 1980. Vol. 16, pp. 534–39.

Baudrillard, Jean. "The Art Auction: Sign Exchange and Sumptuary Value." In *For a Critique of the Political Economy of the Sign.* Translated by Charles Levin, pp. 112–22. St. Louis: Telos Press, 1981.

Bauer-Lechner, Natalie. *Recollections of Gustav Mahler.* Edited by Peter Franklin. Translated by Dika Newlin. New York: Cambridge University Press, 1980.

Benjamin, Walter. *The Arcades Project.* Translated by Howard Eiland and Kevin McLaughlin. Cambridge: Belknap Press of Harvard University Press, 1999.

―――. "Theses on the Philosophy of History." In *Illuminations.* Edited by Hannah Arendt. Translated by Harry Zohn, pp. 253–64. New York: Schocken, 1969.

―――. "The Work of Art in the Age of Mechanical Reproduction." In *Illuminations.* Edited by Hannah Arendt. Translated by Harry Zohn, pp. 217–51. New York: Schocken, 1969.

Berg, Alban. "A Lecture on 'Wozzeck.'" In *Alban Berg: "Wozzeck,"* by Douglas Jarman, pp. 154–70. Cambridge: Cambridge University Press, 1989.

―――. "A Word about 'Wozzeck.'" In *Alban Berg: "Wozzeck,"* by Douglas Jarman, pp. 152–53. Cambridge: Cambridge University Press, 1989.

Berg, Alban, and Arnold Schoenberg. *The Berg-Schoenberg Correspondence: Selected Letters.* Edited by Juliane Brand, Christopher Hailey, and Donald Harris. Translated by Juliane Brand and Christopher Hailey. New York: Norton, 1987.

Bergmeier, Horst J. P., and Rainer E. Lotz. *Hitler's Airwaves: The Inside Story of Nazi Radio Broadcasting and Propaganda Swing.* New Haven: Yale University Press, 1997.

Berliner, Paul F. *Thinking in Jazz: The Infinite Art of Improvisation.* Chicago: University of Chicago Press, 1994.

Betz, Albrecht. *Hanns Eisler Political Musician.* Translated by Bill Hopkins. Cambridge: Cambridge University Press, 1982.

Bloom, Allan. *The Closing of the American Mind: How Higher Education Has Failed Democracy and Improverished the Souls of Today's Students.* New York: Simon and Schuster, 1987.

Bloomfield, Terry. "Resisting Songs: Negative Dialectics in Pop." *Popular Music* 12 no. 1 (January 1993), pp. 13–31.

Blum, Cinzia Sartini. *The Other Modernism: F. T. Marinetti's Futurist Fiction of Power.* Berkeley and Los Angeles: University of California Press, 1996.

Borio, Gianmario. "New Technology, New Techniques: The Aesthetics of Electronic Music in the 1950s." *Interface: Journal of New Music Research* 22 no. 1 (1993), pp. 77–87.

Bottum, J. "The Soundtracking of America." *Atlantic Monthly* (March 2000), pp. 56–70.

Boulez, Pierre. "Alea." Translated by David Noakes and Paul Jacobs. *Perspectives of New Music* 3 no. 1 (Fall/Winter 1964), pp. 42–53.

———. "L'informulé." *Revue d'esthétique* 8 (1985), pp. 25–29.

Brewster, Ben. "From Shklovsky to Brecht: A Reply." *Screen* 15 no. 2 (Summer 1974), pp. 82–102.

Brown, James. "The Amateur String Quartet." *Musical Times* 68 (1927), pp. 508–09, 600–02, 714–16, 798–800, 907–09, 1078–81.

Bruce, Robert. *How to Write a Hit Song and Sell It.* New York: Lexington Press, 1945.

Brush, Pete. "Telephone Psychics See Money in Their Futures." *Los Angeles Times,* 28 March 1997, p. D-7.

Buhler, James, and David Neumeyer. Review of *Strains of Utopia: Gender, Nostalgia, and Hollywood Film Music,* by Caryl Flinn, and *Settling the Score: Music and the Classical Hollywood Film,* by Kathryn Kalinak. *Journal of the American Musicological Society* 47 no. 2 (Summer 1994), pp. 364–85.

Carnegie, Dale. *How to Win Friends and Influence People.* New York: Simon and Schuster, 1937.

Chanan, Michael. *Musica Practica: The Social Practice of Western Music from Gregorian Chant to Postmodernism.* London: Verso, 1994.

Dahlhaus, Carl. *Between Romanticism and Modernism: Four Studies in the*

Music of the Later Nineteenth Century. Translated by Mary Whittall. Berkeley and Los Angeles: University of California Press, 1980.

————. *Ludwig van Beethoven: Approaches to His Music.* Translated by Mary Whittall. Oxford: Clarendon Press, 1991.

————. *Schoenberg and the New Music: Essays by Carl Dahlhaus.* Translated by Derrick Puffett and Alfred Clayton. Cambridge: Cambridge University Press, 1987.

Deathridge, John. "Post-mortem on Isolde." *New German Critique* 69 (Fall 1996), pp. 99–126.

DeLong, Thomas A. *Pops: Paul Whiteman, King of Jazz.* Piscataway, NJ: New Century, 1983.

De Nora, Tia. *Beethoven and the Construction of Genius: Musical Politics in Vienna, 1792–1803.* Berkeley and Los Angeles: University of California Press, 1995.

DeVeaux, Scott. *The Birth of Bebop: A Social and Musical History.* Berkeley and Los Angeles: University of California Press, 1997.

Downie, Andrew. "Papal Visit: Vatican's Endorsement Deal Leaves Many Mexicans Uneasy." *The Houston Chronicle,* 22 January 1999, p. 18.

Edström, Olle. "Fr-a-g-me-n-ts: A Discussion on the Position of Critical Ethnomusicology in Contemporary Musicology." *Svenskt Tidskrift för Musikforskning* 79 (1997), no. 1, pp. 9–68.

————. "'Vi skall gå på restaurang och höra musik': Om reception av restaurangmusik och annan 'mellanmusik'" ["We Shall Go to a Restaurant and Listen to Musik": About Reception of Music Played in Restaurants and Other Middle Music]. *Svensk Tidskrift för Musikforskning* (1989), pp. 77–112.

Ehrlich, Cyril. *Social Emulation and Industrial Progress—The Victorian Piano.* New Lecture Series, no. 82. Belfast: Queen's University, 1975.

Eisler, Hanns. *Hanns Eisler, A Rebel in Music: Selected Writings.* Edited by Manfred Grabs. New York: International, 1978.

Ewbank, Henry L., and Sherman P. Lawton. *Broadcasting: Radio and Television.* New York: Harper and Brothers, 1952.

Ewen, Stuart. *All Consuming Images: The Politics of Style in Contemporary Culture.* New York: Basic Books, 1988.

Ewen, Stuart, and Elizabeth Ewen. *Channels of Desire: Mass Images and the Shaping of American Consciousness.* New York: McGraw-Hill, 1982.

Fink, Robert. "Elvis Everywhere: Musicology and Popular Music Studies at the Twilight of the Canon." *American Music* 16 no. 2 (Summer 1998), pp. 135–79.

Fiske, John. *Reading the Popular.* Boston: Unwin Hyman, 1989.

————. *Understanding Popular Culture.* Boston: Unwin Hyman, 1989.

Fiske, John, and John Hartley, *Reading Television.* London: Metheun, 1978.

Foucault, Michel. *The Order of Things: An Archaeology of the Human Sciences.* New York: Vintage Books, 1970.

Frith, Simon. *Performing Rites: On the Value of Popular Music.* Cambridge: Harvard University Press, 1996.

Goehr, Lydia. "Music and Musicians in Exile: The Romantic Legacy of a Double Life." In *Driven into Paradise: The Musical Migration from Nazi Germany to the United States.* Edited by Reinhold Brinkmann and Christoph Wolff, pp. 66–91. Berkeley and Los Angeles: University of California Press, 1999.

———. *The Quest for Voice: Music, Politics, and the Limits of Philosophy.* Berkeley and Los Angeles: University of California Press, 1998.

Gorbman, Claudia. "Hanns Eisler in Hollywood." *Screen* 32 no. 3 (Fall 1991), pp. 272–85.

———. *Unheard Melodies: Narrative Film Music.* Bloomington: Indiana University Press, 1987.

Gracyk, Theodore A. *Rhythm and Noise: An Aesthetics of Rock.* Durham, NC: Duke University Press, 1996.

Greenberg, Clement. "Avant-Garde and Kitsch." In *Mass Culture: The Popular Arts in America.* Edited by Bernard Rosenberg and David Manning White, pp. 98–107. Glencoe, IL: Free Press, 1957.

Grunwald, Edgar A., ed. *Variety Radio Directory 1939–1940.* New York: Variety, 1939.

Hall, Stuart, and Tony Jefferson, eds. *Resistance through Rituals: Youth Subcultures in Post-War Britain.* London: Hutchinson, 1976.

Hanning, Barbara. "Conversation and Musical Style in the Late Eighteenth-Century Parisian Salon." *Eighteenth-Century Studies* 22 no. 3 (Summer 1989), pp. 512–28.

Headlam, Dave. *The Music of Alban Berg.* New Haven: Yale University Press, 1996.

Hebdige, Dick. *Subculture: The Meaning of Style.* London: Methuen, 1979.

Hegel, G. W. F. *Phenomenology of Spirit.* Translated by A. V. Miller. Oxford: Oxford University Press, 1977.

Hinton, Stephen. "Hindemith and Weill: Cases of 'Inner' and 'Other' Direction." In *Driven into Paradise: The Musical Migration from Nazi Germany to the United States.* Edited by Reinhold Brinkmann and Christoph Wolff, pp. 261–78. Berkeley and Los Angeles: University of California Press, 1999.

Hirsbrunner, Theo. "Musical Form and Dramatic Expression in 'Wozzeck.'" In *Alban Berg: Wozzeck.* Edited by Nicholas John, pp. 25–36. London: John Calder, 1990.

Hirsch, E. D., Jr. *Cultural Literacy: What Every American Needs to Know.* Boston: Houghton Mifflin, 1987.

Hirsch, E. D., Jr., Joseph F. Kett, and James Trefil. *The Dictionary of Cultural Literacy.* 2d ed. rev. Boston: Houghton Mifflin, 1993.

Horkheimer, Max. "Art and Mass Culture." *Studies in Philosophy and Social Science* 9 (1941), pp. 290–304.

———. "The Social Function of Philosophy." In *Critical Theory: Selected Es-*

says. Translated by Matthew J. O'Connell, et al. pp. 253–72. New York: Continuum, 1982.

———. "Traditional and Critical Theory." In *Critical Theory: Selected Essays.* Translated by Matthew J. O'Connell, pp. 188–243. New York: Continuum, 1982.

Horowitz, Joseph. *Understanding Toscanini: How He Became an American Culture-God and Created a New Audience for Old Music.* New York: Alfred Λ. Knopf, 1987.

Jarman, Douglas. *Alban Berg: "Wozzeck."* Cambridge: Cambridge University Press, 1989.

———. *The Music of Alban Berg.* London: Faber and Faber, 1979.

Kater, Michael H. *Different Drummers: Jazz in the Culture of Nazi Germany.* New York: Oxford University Press, 1992.

Kerman, Joseph. "How We Got into Analysis, and How to Get Out." In *Write All These Down: Essays on Music*, pp. 12–32. Berkeley and Los Angeles: University of California Press, 1994.

Kornhauser, Arthur W., and Paul F. Lazarsfeld. *The Techniques of Market Research from the Standpoint of a Psychologist.* Institute of Management Series, no. 16. New York: American Management Association, 1935.

Lazarus, Neil. "Hating Tradition Properly." *New Formations* 38 (Summer 1999), pp. 9–30.

Levin, David J. "Wagner and the Consequences—An Introduction." *New German Critique* 69 (Fall 1996), pp. 3–5.

Liebman, Stuart. "On New German Cinema, Art, Enlightenment, and the Public Sphere: An Interview with Alexander Kluge." *October* 46 (Fall 1988), pp. 23–59.

Lippman, Edward. *A History of Western Musical Aesthetics.* Lincoln: University of Nebraska Press, 1992.

Longhurst, Brian. *Popular Music and Society.* Cambridge: Polity Press, 1995.

Lott, Eric. "Love and Theft: The Racial Unconscious of Blackface Minstrelsy." *Representations* 39 (Summer 1992), pp. 23–50.

Lowe, Donald M. *The History of Bourgeois Perception.* Chicago: University of Chicago Press, 1982.

Lukács, Georg. *History and Class Consciousness: Studies in Marxist Dialectics.* Translated by Rodney Livingstone. Cambridge: MIT Press, 1971.

———. *The Theory of the Novel: A Historico-Philosophical Essay on the Forms of Great Epic Literature.* Translated by Anna Bostock. Cambridge: MIT Press, 1971.

MacDonald, J. Frederick. "'Hot Jazz,' the Jitterbug, and Misunderstanding: The Generation Gap in Swing 1935–1945." In *American Popular Music: Readings from the Popular Press.* Vol. 1: *The Nineteenth Century and Tin Pan Alley.* Edited by Timothy E. Scheurer, pp. 151–60. Bowling Green, OH: Bowling Green State University Popular Press, 1989.

MacDougald, Duncan, Jr. "The Popular Music Industry." In *Radio Research*

1941, edited by Paul F. Lazarsfeld and Frank N. Stanton, pp. 65–109. New York: Duell, Sloan and Pearce, 1941.

Mann, Thomas. *Doctor Faustus: The Life of the German Composer Adrian Leverkühn as Told by a Friend*. Translated by H. T. Lowe-Porter. New York: Alfred A. Knopf, 1948.

———. *The Story of a Novel: The Genesis of Doctor Faustus*. Translated by Richard Winston and Clara Winston. New York: Alfred A. Knopf, 1961.

Marcuse, Herbert. "Marcuse and the Frankfurt School: Dialogue with Herbert Marcuse." Interview by Bryan Magee. In *Men of Ideas*, by Bryan Magee, pp. 60–73. New York: Viking Press, 1978.

———. "A Note on Dialectic." In *The Essential Frankfurt School Reader*. Edited by Andrew Arato and Eike Gebhardt, pp. 444–51. New York: Continuum, 1982.

———. "Remarks on a Redefinition of Culture." In *Science and Culture: A Study of Cohesive and Disjunctive Forces*. Edited by Gerald Holton, pp. 218–35. Boston: Houghton Mifflin, 1965.

Martin, Peter. *Sounds and Society: Themes in the Sociology of Music*. Manchester: Manchester University Press, 1995.

Marx, Karl, and Frederick Engels. *The German Ideology. Part One*. Edited by C. J. Arthur. New York: International, 1970.

McCaughan, Michael. "Pope's Visit Gives Some a Chance for Financial Gain." *The Irish Times*, 21 January 1999, p. 13.

McClary, Susan. "Terminal Prestige: The Case of Avant-Garde Music Composition." *Cultural Critique* 12 (Spring 1989), pp. 57–81.

McGuigan, Jim. *Cultural Populism*. London: Routledge, 1992.

Middleton, Richard. *Studying Popular Music*. Milton Keynes, UK: Open University Press, 1990.

Negus, Keith. *Popular Music in Theory: An Introduction*. Hanover, NH: Wesleyan University Press, 1997.

Nietzsche, Friedrich, *Werke*. Edited by Karl Schlechta. 4 vols. Munich: C. Hanser, 1954–65.

Perle, George. *The Operas of Alban Berg*. Vol. 1: *Wozzeck*. Berkeley and Los Angeles: University of California Press, 1980.

Piccone, Paul. "The Crisis of One-Dimensionality." *Telos* 35 (Spring 1978), 43–54.

Pople, Anthony. "The Musical Language of *Wozzeck*." In *The Cambridge Companion to Berg*. Edited by Anthony Pople, pp. 145–64. Cambridge: Cambridge University Press, 1997.

Postman, Neil. *Amusing Ourselves to Death: Public Discourse in the Age of Show Business*. New York: Viking, 1985.

Robinson, William S. "Radio Comes to the Farmer." In *Radio Research 1941*. Edited by Paul F. Lazarsfeld and Frank N. Stanton, pp. 224–94. New York: Duell, Sloan and Pearce, 1941.

Roell, Craig H. *The Piano in America, 1890–1940*. Chapel Hill: University of North Carolina Press, 1989.

Russolo, Luigi. *The Art of Noises*. Monographs in Musicology, no. 6. Translated by Barclay Brown. New York: Pendragon, 1986.

Said, Edward W. *Musical Elaborations*. New York: Columbia University Press, 1991.

Schoenberg, Arnold. "Modern Music on the Radio." In *Style and Idea: Selected Writings of Arnold Schoenberg*. Edited by Leonard Stein. Translations by Leo Black, pp. 151–52. New York: St. Martin's, 1975.

———. "New Music, Outmoded Music, Style and Idea." In *Style and Idea: Selected Writings of Arnold Schoenberg*. Edited by Leonard Stein. Translations by Leo Black, pp. 113–24. New York: St. Martin's, 1975.

Shusterman, Richard. "Form and Funk: The Aesthetic Challenge of Popular Culture." *British Journal of Aesthetics* 31 no. 3 (July 1991), pp. 203–13.

Silver, Abner, and Robert Bruce. *How to Write and Sell a Song Hit*. New York: Prentice Hall, 1939.

Small, Christopher. *Musicking: The Meanings of Performing and Listening*. Hanover, NH: University Press of New England, 1998.

Spaeth, Sigmund. *Great Symphonies: How to Recognize and Remember Them*. Garden City, NY: Garden City Publishing, 1936.

Suchman, Edward A. "Invitation to Music: A Study of the Creation of New Music Listeners by the Radio." In *Radio Research 1941*. Edited by Paul F. Lazarsfeld and Frank N. Stanton, pp. 140–88. New York: Duell, Sloan and Pearce, 1941.

Thomson, Virgil. "Jazz." *American Mercury* 2 no. 8 (August 1924), pp. 465–67.

———. *The Musical Scene*. New York: Alfred A. Knopf, 1945.

Tomlinson, Alan. "Introduction: Consumer Culture and the Aura of the Commodity." In *Consumption, Identity, and Style: Marketing, Meanings, and the Packaging of Pleasure*. Edited by Alan Tomlinson, pp. 1–38. London: Routledge, 1990.

Tomlinson, Gary. *Metaphysical Song: An Essay on Opera*. Princeton: Princeton University Press, 1999.

Volpacchio, Florindo, and Frank Zappa. "The Mother of All Interviews: Zappa on Music and Society." *Telos* 87 (Spring 1991), pp. 124–36.

Wagner, Richard. "What Is German?" In *Richard Wagner's Prose Works*. Volume 4. Translated by William Ashton Ellis, pp. 149–69. 1895. Reprint, New York: Broude Brothers, 1966.

Wainwright, David. *Broadwood, by Appointment: A History*. London: Quiller, 1982.

Walser, Robert. *Running with the Devil: Power, Gender, and Madness in Heavy Metal Music*. Hanover, NH: Wesleyan University Press, 1993.

Wayne, Mike. "Television, Audiences, Politics." In *Behind the Screens: The Structure of British Broadcasting in the 1990s*. Edited by Stuart Hood, pp. 43–64. London: Lawrence and Wishart, 1994.

Weiner, Marc A. "Reading the Ideal." *New German Critique* 69 (Fall 1996), pp. 53–83.

Whiteman, Paul, and Mary Margaret McBride. *Jazz*. New York: J. H. Sears, 1926.

Willet, John. *The New Sobriety, 1917–1933: Art and Politics in the Weimar Period*. London: Thames and Hudson, 1978.

Williamson, John. "Mahler, Hermeneutics and Analysis." *Music Analysis* 10 no. 3 (October 1991), pp. 357–73.

Wolin, Richard. *Walter Benjamin: An Aesthetic of Redemption*. New York: Columbia University Press, 1982.

Wolzogen, Hans von. *Guide to the Music of Richard Wagner's Tetralogy: The Ring of the Niebelung: A Thematic Key*. Translated by Nathan Haskell Dole. New York: G. Schirmer, 1905.

Source and Copyright Acknowledgments

All essays by Adorno in this volume appear by permission of the Theodor W. Adorno Archiv.

Theodor W. Adorno, *Gesammelte Schriften*, vol. 14, *Dissonanzen. Musik in der verwalteten Welt.* ©Vandenhoeck & Ruprecht, Göttingen 1956. Alle Rechte bei und vorbehalten durch Suhrkamp Verlag, Frankfurt am Main. "On the Fetish-Character in Music and the Regression of Listening" ("Über den Fetishcharakter in der Musik und die Regression des Hörens"), pp. 14–50. "The Aging of the New Music" ("Das Altern der Neuen Musik"), pp. 143–67.

Theodor W. Adorno, *Gesammelte Schriften*, vol. 16, *Musikalische Schriften I-III.* © Suhrkamp Verlag, Frankfurt am Main 1978. "Wagner's Relevance for Today" ("Wagners Aktualität"), pp. 543–64. "Music, Language, and Composition" ("Musik, Sprache und ihr Verhältnis im gegenwärtigen Komponieren"), pp. 649–64.

Theodor W. Adorno, *Gesammelte Schriften*, vol. 17, *Musikalische Schriften IV: Moments musicaux. Neu gedruckte Aufsätze 1928–1962.* © Suhrkamp Verlag, Frankfurt am Main 1982. "Late Style in Beethoven" ("Spätstil Beethovens"), pp. 13–17. "On Jazz" ("Über Jazz"), pp. 74–108. "Alienated Masterpiece: The *Missa Solemnis*" ("Verfremdetes Hauptwerk. Zur Missa Solemnis"), pp. 145–61.

Theodor W. Adorno, *Gesammelte Schriften*, vol. 17, *Musikalische Schriften IV: Impromptus. Zweite Folge neu gedruckter musikalischer Aufsätze.* © Suhrkamp Verlag, Frankfurt am Main 1982. "The Dialectical Composer" ("Der dialektische Komponist"), pp. 198–203. "Difficulties" ("Schwierigkeiten. I. Beim Komponieren. II. In der Auffassung neuer Musik"), pp. 253–91. "Little Heresy" ("Kleine Häresie"), pp. 297–302.

Theodor W. Adorno, *Gesammelte Schriften*, vol. 18, *Musikalische Schriften V: Theorie der neuen Musik.* © Suhrkamp Verlag, Frankfurt am Main 1984.

"On the Contemporary Relationship of Philosophy and Music" ("Über das gegenwärtige Verhältnis von Philosophie und Musik"), pp. 149–76.

Theodor W. Adorno, *Gesammelte Schriften*, vol. 18, *Musikalische Schriften V: Komponisten und Kompositionen.* © Suhrkamp Verlag, Frankfurt am Main 1984. "Mahler Today" ("Mahler heute"), pp. 226–34. "Marginalia on Mahler" ("Marginalien zu Mahler"), pp. 235–40. "Toward an Understanding of Schoenberg" ("Zum Verständnis Schönbergs"), pp. 428–45. "The Opera *Wozzeck*" ("Die Oper Wozzeck"), pp. 472–79. "On the Social Situation of Music" ("Zu gesellschaftlichen Lage der Musik"), pp. 729–77. "Kitsch" ("Kitsch"), pp. 791–94. "Farewell to Jazz" ("Abschied vom Jazz"), pp. 795–99. "Music in the Background" ("Musik im Hintergrund"), pp. 819–23. "Why Is the New Art So Hard to Understand?" ("Warum is die neue Kunst so schwer verständlich?"), pp. 824–31.

Theodor W. Adorno, *Gesammelte Schriften*, vol. 19, *Musikalische Schriften VI.* © Suhrkamp Verlag, Frankfurt am Main 1984. "The Curves of the Needle" ("Nadelkurven"), pp. 525–29. "The Form of the Phonograph Record" ("Die Form der Schallplatte"), pp. 530–34. "Opera and the Long-Playing Record" ("Oper und Langspielplatte"), pp. 555–58.

Theodor W. Adorno, *Gesammelte Schriften*, vol. 20.2, *Vermischte Schriften II.* © Suhrkamp Verlag, Frankfurt am Main 1986. "What National Socialism Has Done to the Arts," pp. 413–29.

"The Aging of the New Music" ("Das Altern der Neuen Musik"). Translated by Robert Hullot-Kentor and Frederic Will. *Telos* 77 (Fall 1988), pp. 95–116. By permission of Telos Press.

"Alienated Masterpiece: The *Missa Solemnis*" ("Verfremdetes Hauptwerk. Zur Missa Solemnis"). Translated by Duncan Smith. *Telos* 28 (Summer 1976), pp. 113–24. By permission of Telos Press.

"The Curves of the Needle" ("Nadelkurven"). Translated by Thomas Y. Levin. *October* 55 (Winter 1990), pp. 49–55. Used by permission.

"The Form of the Phonograph Record" ("Die Form der Schallplatte"). Translated by Thomas Y. Levin. *October* 55 (Winter 1990), pp. 56–61. Used by permission.

"Late Style in Beethoven" ("Spätstil Beethovens"). Translated by Susan H. Gillespie. *Raritan: A Quarterly Review* 13 no.1 (Summer 1993), pp. 102–07. Used by permission.

"Music, Language, and Composition" ("Musik, Sprache und ihr Verhältnis im gegenwärtigen Komponieren"). Translated by Susan H. Gillespie. *Musical Quarterly* 77 no. 3 (Fall 1993), pp. 401–14. By permission of Oxford University Press.

"On Jazz" ("Über Jazz"). Translated by Jamie Owen Daniel. *Discourse* 12 no. 1 (Fall/Winter 1989–90), pp. 45–69. Used by permission.

"On the Fetish-Character in Music and the Regression of Listening" ("Über den Fetishcharakter in der Musik und die Regression des Hörens"). In *The Frankfurt School Reader.* Edited by Andrew Arato and Eike Gebhardt, pp. 270–99. New York: Continuum, 1982. By permission of The Continuum Publishing Company.

"On the Problem of Musical Analysis" ("Zum Probleme der musikalischen Analyse"). Translated by Max Paddison. *Music Analysis* 1 no. 2 (July 1982), pp. 169–82. By permission of Blackwell Publishers.

"On the Social Situation of Music" ("Zu gesellschaftlichen Lage der Musik"). Translated by Wes Blomster. *Telos* 35 (Spring 1978), pp. 128–64. Used by permission of Telos Press.

"Opera and the Long-Playing Record" ("Oper und Langspielplatte"). Translated by Thomas Y. Levin. *October* 55 (Winter 1990), pp. 62–66. Used by permission.

"Wagner's Relevance for Today" ("Wagners Aktualität"). Translated by Susan H. Gillespie. *Grand Street* 11 no. 4 (1993), pp. 33–59. By permission of Grand Street Press.

The publisher apologizes for any errors or omissions in this list and requests notification of any additions or corrections that should be incorporated in the next edition or reprint of this volume.

Index

Adorno's quicksilver dialectic and aphoristic proclivities present challenges to the indexer. This index is necessarily selective but does attempt to reflect the range of topics touched upon—sometimes only glancingly—in the essays.

Page numbers printed in roman type refer to essays by Adorno; numbers in italics refer to the introduction and commentaries by Richard Leppert and the notes by Leppert and the translators. Substantive discussions occurring in the notes are indexed; unannotated references to secondary literature are not. "Serious" artworks are entered under their authors; "popular" works, under their titles.

(the) absolute, *86*, 116; *Missa Solemnis* and, 577; music's attempt to possess, 144; as sound, 140
absolute music, 192
action painting, *658*
administration, 43–44, *45n141*; of spirit, 661; and the subject, 57; total, *653*
Adorno, Theodor Wiesengrund: and the academy, *10, 73–75, 77*; Adorno-Benjamin Debate, *240–50*; aesthetics, *31, 72–73, 104, 330n6, 338, 357n64, 561*; American reception of, *12n34, 76*; and Berg, *4, 4n9, 14, 14n39*, 176–77, *515, 546*; in California, *8, 8n22, 70n224*; champions aesthetic modernism, *92*; changes name, *2*; charged with elitism, 47, *47n149*, 220–21; childhood, *2, 11, 514*; as composer, *14, 14–15n40*; critique of American research methods, *58n179*, 216–217,

216n12; difficulty, *vii, xiv*; early maturity, *514*; emigrates to U.S., *7*, in England, *7, 349*; and essay form, *65, 65n206*; Eurocentrism, *14n37*; exaggeration in, 64–65, *64n202*, 247, 248; on exile, *13n35*; and gender issues, *25–26n72*; Habermas on, *1*, "half-Jew," *7*; and Hegel, *179n6*; influence, *vii*; intellectual training, *2–4*; "Jewish impulse" in, *23*; language, *ix, xiv, 12, 13n35*, 65–67; life, *1–18*; Lukács's critique of, *68, 68n219, 675n2*; marries, *7*; and music, *vii, xiii*; musical analyses, 104–7; musical journalism, *5*; on musical modernity, *515*; musical referents in, *39n122, 63n198*; musical training, *4*; musical understanding, 105; musical writings, *76–77*; naïveté, *7*; and new music, 15–16; *oeuvre, 13–14*; parameters of thought, *23*;

Adorno, Theodor Wiesengrund
(*continued*)
parataxis in, *63, 63n198;* parents,
2, 7n21; pessimism, *68, 68n220;*
politics, *73;* and popular culture,
76, 77, 347; posthumous career,
73, 75–82; presentism, *viii;*
publications and recordings of music by, *15n40;* public critique of, *69;*
as public intellectual, *17, 17n44,*
62n193; quietism, *72;* relations
with Schoenberg, *5;* reluctance to
leave Germany, *7;* return to Germany, *10–11, 12;* rhetoric, *358n65,*
360; self-confidence, *3;* and '60s
student movement, *18, 18n46;* sociology of music, *73–74;* as structural listener, *105;* and Thomas
Mann, *9, 9n25, 9–10n27, 531n35;*
translation of, *xiii–xv, 24n70,*
62n194, 76; U.S. citizenship, *11;*
university studies, *4;* and Wagner,
585, 587; writing, *vii, xiii–xivn2,*
61–67, 65n208, 76; youthful appearance, *3. See also* Adorno,
Theodor Wiesengrund, works of
Adorno, Theodor Wiesengrund,
works of: *Aesthetic Theory, 17, 62,*
71, 75–76, 97, 103, 520; Against
Epistemology: A Metacritique, 17;
"The Aging of the New Music,"
101, 107, 111; "Alban Berg,"
546n74, 548n81; Alban Berg: Mas-
ter of the Smallest Link, 105, 106,
168, 176–77, 548n81; "Alban Berg:
Zur Uraufführung des 'Wozzeck',"
548n81; "Analytical Study of the
NBC *Music Appreciation Hour,*"
214n3; "Antwort des Fachidioten,"
287n8, "Anton von Webern," *91–*
92n15; "Arnold Schoenberg, 1874–*
1951," 552n89; The Authoritarian
Personality (senior author), *8,*
13n34; "Bach Defended against his
Devotees," *525, 525n23; Beethoven:*
The Philosophy of Music, 14, 520,
520nn12, 13; "Berg and Webern—
Schoenberg's Heirs," *546n77;*
"Berg's Discoveries in Compositional Technique," *100n25;* "Bourgeois Opera," *237n53, 286n5,*
548n81, 679n26; "Classicism, Romanticism, New Music," *361n75;*
"Commitment," *70–71;* "Commodity Music Analyzed," *361n76, 363,*
455nG; Composing for the Films
(with Eisler), *8, 286n2, 331, 365–*
71; "The Concept of the Unconscious in the Transcendental Theory of Mind," *5–6;* "Criteria of
New Music," *102–3n29, 361n75,*
553–54n93; "Culture and Administration," *43n135, 57, 552n90;*
"Culture Industry Reconsidered,"
44, 57; Current of Music: Ele-
ments of a Radio Theory, 214n3;
"The Curves of the Needle," *233–*
34; "The Dialectical Composer,"
112; Dialectic of Enlightenment
(with Horkheimer), *8, 21–34,*
24n70, 58, 76, 157, 226, 327; "Education after Auschwitz," *223n30;*
"The Essay as Form," *65n206;* essay collections, *14;* "Farewell to
Jazz," *330–31, 359–60;* "The Form
of the Phonograph Record," *331;*
"Four- Hands, Once Again," *xiii;*
"Free Time," *61;* "The Function of
Color in Music," *110n44; Der ge-*
treue Korrepetitor, 660, 678n20;
"How to Look at Television," *11;*
In Search of Wagner, 9, 528–35,
528n29, 529nn30, 31, 584; Intro-
duction to the Sociology of Music,
14, 93–94, 95n21, 101, 228, 333,
333n16, 356, 521; "Is Art Lighthearted?" *364n82;* "Is Marx Obsolete?" *52n164; The Jargon of Au-*
thenticity, 17; "Jazz," *356n62;*
"Kierkegaard: Construction of the
Aesthetic," *6;* "Late Style in Beethoven," *516–25;* literary essays, *17;*
"Little Heresy," *250;* "Mahler,"
610n5; "Mahler Today," *543–44;*

"Marginalia on Mahler," *544–46;* "Marginalia to Theory and Praxis," *72n232;* "The Mastery of the Maestro," *246n77;* "The Meaning of Working through the Past," *17n44, 18;* "Memorandum: Music in Radio," *218–19, 219n20; Minima Moralia: Reflections from Damaged Life, 8, 24, 25, 35, 37, 38, 39–40, 46, 62, 64, 66, 81, 364, 389n6;* "Motifs," *362;* "The Musical Climate for Fascism in Germany," *327n1, 328, 328n3;* "Music and Language: A Fragment," *85;* "Music and New Music," *93n18, 101n27;* "Music and Technique," *110n42, 286n2;* "Music in the Background," *331, 371–72;* "Music, Language, and Composition," *85–92;* "Musik im Fernsehen ist Brimborium," *287n8;* "Nach Steuermanns Tod," *677n12; Negative Dialectics, 17, 30, 32, 33, 62, 71, 75–76;* "New Music, Interpretation, Audience," *95–96n22, 239–40;* "Notes on Philosophical Thinking," *28n79;* "Of Barricades and Ivory Towers," *72n232;* "On the Contemporary Relationship of Philosophy and Music," *96–101;* "On the Fetish-Character in Music and the Regression of Listening," *219, 240–50, 331;* "On Jazz," *331, 349–58, 355–56n62, 356n63;* "On the Musical Employment of Radio," *281n1;* "On Popular Music," *214n3, 331, 336–48, 558;* "On Some Relationships between Music and Painting," *88n4;* "On the Problem of Musical Analysis," *101–7;* "On the Question: What is German?" *11, 11n32, 13n35, 286n4, 388n2;* "On the Score of 'Parsifal'," *532n39;* "On the Social Situation of Music," *5, 42, 331, 333n12, 332–36;* "On the Use of Foreign Words," *65, 65n209;* "On

Tradition," *77–81;* "Opera," *679n26;* "Opera on the Long-Playing Record," *236–39;* "The Opera Wozzeck," *547–51;* "Parataxis: On Hölderlin's Late Poetry," *63n198;* "Perennial Fashion—Jazz," *330, 350–51n50, 352n52, 352–53n53;* "Philosophy and Teachers," *223n30; Philosophy of Modern Music, 8, 13, 15–16, 100, 121, 148–49, 151, 152, 551, 551n87, 652;* "Prologue to Television," *47n148;* "Psychoanalysis Revised," *13;* "The Psychological Technique of Martin Luther Thomas' Radio Address," *342n31;* "The Radio Symphony," *214, 218–30, 340;* "Reminiscence," *625n1;* "Resignation," *72;* "Richard Strauss: Born June 11, 1864," *287n11;* "Der Schatz des Indianer-Joe: Singspiel nach Mark Twain," *15n40, 355n60, 530;* "Schema of Mass Culture," *49n157, 53n166, 329–30n6, 340;* "Schöne Stellen," *227, 227–28n37, 546n77;* "Scientific Experiences of a European Scholar in America," *215–16, 215–16n10;* "A Social Critique of Radio Music," *214n3;* "Sociology and Empirical Research," *216n12, 217–18n17;* "Die stabilisierte Musik," *200n3;* "The Stars Down to Earth," *11, 57–60;* "Stravinsky: A Dialectical Portrait," *276n2, 556n100;* String Quartet no. 1, *14, 14n39;* "Taboos on the Teaching Vocation," *223–24n30;* "Television as Ideology," *57n178;* "Theorie der Halbbildung," *661nB;* "Theory of Pseudo-Culture," *226n34;* "To Describe, Understand, and Explain" (with L. Goldmann), *89n8;* "Toward an Understanding of Schoenberg," *557–61;* "Transparencies on Film," *239n55;* "A Typology of Music Listening," *228n40;* "Über

Adorno, Theodor Wiesengrund,
works of *(continued)*
die musikalische Verwendung des
Radios," *226n33;* "Valéry Proust
Museum," *287n12;* "Vers une musique informelle," *110–11, 110n44;*
"Wagner, Nietzsche, and Hitler,"
530n34; "Wagner's Relevance for
Today," *535–37;* "What National
Socialism Has Done to the Arts,"
327–29; "Why Is the New Art So
Hard to Understand?" *93–95, 661;*
"Why Still Philosophy," *22n60,
38, 38n121, 41n126, 42;* "Words
from Abroad," *65, 65–66n209,
66n214; Zu einer Theorie der musikalischen Reproduktion: Aufzeichnungen, ein Entwurf und zwei
Schemata, 214n3;* "Zu einer Umfrage, Neue Oper und Publikum,"
286n5
advertising, *50, 50n160, 61, 72, 133;*
as art, *51n162;* and Culture Industry, *304;* and music, *295;* triumph
of, *53. See also* "plugging"
aesthetic residue, *103, 169*
aesthetics, *5, 68, 73, 73n235, 74–75,
77, 80, 240, 268, 290;* and analysis,
168; necessity of, *98n24;* of popular music, *346n39;* sphere of, *142,
627. See also* art
aesthetic seriousness, *661, 673*
aesthetic wholeness, *250*
affections, doctrine of, *621*
Affektenlehre, 621
affirmative music, *93–94, 115, 580*
age: in reception of popular music,
459
agency, *55n170, 57*
Agger, Ben, *62–63*
aleatoric music, *16, 172, 658*
"Alexander's Ragtime Band," *460,
469n2*
alienation, *129, 291;* as catchword,
661; and *Missa Solemnis, 579;* of
music from man, *199, 391;* vented
in laughter, *314*

aloofness, *381–82*
ambivalence, *587;* of listeners to popular music, *464–65, 466*
America: Adorno on, *12;* German arrogance toward, *12;* inequalities in,
79
"American Bandstand," *248*
amusement: as prolongation of work,
48
analysis, musical, *102–7, 162–80;*
abuses, *105–6;* antagonism toward,
162; autonomy of, *169;* crisis in,
178; decay of, *298;* elemental, *170–
71, 172, 179n13;* essential element
of art, *169;* a form in its own
right, *102, 167;* goes beyond facts,
169; home ground of tradition, *163;*
immanence, *166;* legitimacy of,
172; particulars in, *106;* potential
effect on composition, *178;* quantification in, *106;* reified, *170;* reveals work's "problem," *104;* and
reverence, *422;* singularity and
generality of, *177;* and structural
listening, *164;* task of, *173;* and
work's truth content, *107, 167*
Anderson, Laurie, *330n6*
anti-intellectualism, *382, 673*
antinomies, social, *396;* in Berg, *402*
anti-reason, *21*
anti-Semitism, *23, 351n51, 374,
388n2*
anti-Wagnerism, *123, 376, 587;* and
neo-classicism, *586*
aphorism: Adorno's fondness for, *62*
apology: and official musical culture,
422
aporia(s), *400, 514*
architecture, musical, *398*
Arendt, Hannah, *2n3*
Ariadne, *507, 510n2*
Armstrong, Louis, *356, 356–57n64*
arrangements, *298–300*
arrangers, *451–52*
art: adaptation to social consciousness, *132;* anticipates emancipation,
41; bad conscience of, *200;* be-

tween seriousness and light-heartedness, *364n82;* and the Catholic Church, 377; and cognition, 96; concealing function of, 130; as consumer goods, *328, 328n2,* 377–78; de-aestheticization of, *318, 330n6;* demythification, *243, 248;* diagnostic role of, 95; disconnected from prevailing consciousness, 130; distinguished from mass culture, *47–48;* and domination of nature, 192; encapsulated, 132; enigmaticalness, *97–98;* for sale, *80;* and history, 97; hostility toward, in Schoenberg, 400; and ideology, 132; lost immediacy of, 129; and natural beauty, *31;* and political commitment, *70–71;* possibility of, 642; and praxis, *70–71;* presuppositions of, 652; as processual, *104;* production and consumption, *94;* and propaganda, *134n2,* 384; pseudo-Americanization of, 386; *raison d'être, 138, 183;* recreational use of, *385–86;* and science, *192–93;* and society, 198, 296; task of, 131; and the unconscious, 192; understandability demanded, 129; useful, 131. *See also* aesthetics
art for art's sake. See *l'art pour l'art*
artist: modern, psychic makeup of, 128; after Nazism, *386–87;* as social functionary, 385
art music. *See* "serious music"
art nouveau, 190
l'art pour l'art, 128, 134n2, 616, 659
arts and crafts, *80,* 189; and jazz, 497
artwork: artifice of, in Berg, *550;* auratic, *243;* as commodity, *47–48, 412;* dialectical, *243;* double character of, *89;* embodies contradictions, *36;* expressiveness of, *90–91, 91n14;* as force-field organized around problem, 173; as form of cognition, *179n6;* hermetic, 400; historical relation with audience,

535; and horror, 200; and instrumentalized reason, *90;* life cycle of, 586; naturalness of, *89;* organicism of, *519;* social culpability of, *41n127;* stripped of meaning, 377–78; technologization of, *193;* truth content of, *88–89, 103,* 280; usefulness of, *553n90;* vulgarization of, 298
asceticism, *109–10,* 291
a-serialism, 659
"as-if": in Mahler, *539, 539n59*
astrology, *57–60;* pseudo-rational, *58;* rhetoric of, *60;* spontaneity lacking in, *59*
atonality, *93, 127,* 173; up-ends convention, *94;* and Schoenberg, 635
Attali, Jacques, *234n51*
audience: agency, *369;* antagonism to, 300; and new music, 380; primacy of, 672
aura, 301, 646; of artwork, *242, 243, 244, 261, 265, 312;* of the commodity, 266; and Schoenberg, 637
Auschwitz, *223–24n30*
Ausdrucksmusik, 620
Austria: economic backwardness, as boon to Berg and Webern, 199
authenticity, *115, 346–47;* of musical work, *87, 119;* replaced by reproducibility, *241*
authoritarian personality, 671
automatic writing, *654, 677n10*
autonomy: of art, *128, 347, 514–15, 552, 552–53n90, 661–62;* in Berg, 549; confused with heteronomy, 122; and Mahler, 616; of music, *87, 221n23;* and reification, *555;* of sounds, in Schoenberg, 636; of the subject, *20, 55–56;* surrender of, 157; turned against itself, *500n3;* of Wagnerian opera, *536*
avant-garde, *101;* and art's autonomy, *552–53n90;* direction of, *111n48;* in Germany, 380; isolation of, *95n21;* resignation of, 158

avant-garde art: Adorno's faith in, *249;* defies consumer expectation, *94–95*
awe, 140

Bach, Johann Sebastian, 147, 320, 570; *The Art of the Fugue,* 633; complete integration of voices in, 633; and expression, 620, *626n4;* forgetting of, 182; fugue in, 412, 575; impression of mechanicalness given by, 171; late instrumental works, 152, 633; Mass in B minor, 574–75; *The Well-Tempered Clavier,* 294, 455nG, 633
background music, 506–9; characteristics of, 507; arrangements ubiquitous in, 508
"bad good music," 502
Bakhtin, Mikhail, *354*
Bakunin, Mikhail, 601, *602n14*
banality: in jazz, 483; power of, 292
band leaders, 451–52
"barbarism of perfection," 246, 301
Barenboim, Daniel, *537n53*
Barone, Anthony, *532n39*
barrel organ, 279
Bartók, Béla, 477; archaic material in, 405; and Brahms, 184; and objectivism, 406; no accommodation to market, 649; *Out of Doors,* 184; separation from past, 184; sonatas for violin and piano, 649; tonality indispensable to, 184; Violin Concerto no. 2, 184; Violin Sonata no. 1, 184
Battisti, Cesare, 183, *201n5*
Baudelaire, Charles, 661, 663
Bayreuth (Festspielhaus): covered orchestra in, 595
"beat," 460
"beautiful passages," 227–28, *228n38,* 292
beauty, 381; demand for, as fascist ideology, *329. See also* natural beauty

Becker, Howard C., *678n21*
Beckett, Samuel, 660
Beckmann, Max, 273, *276n4*
becoming: in Beethoven, 172; in music, 115, 171; as negation, in Berg, 177
Beethoven, Ludwig van, 99, 147, 298, 496, *516–28;* articulate unity in, 261; atomistic forms in, 125; and bourgeois ideology, 652; and bourgeois revolution, *513n1;* Brahms's analyses of, 163; concretion, 167; convention, 565–66; demand for truth, 581; dynamics in, 164; form, 188; germinal cells in, 171; greatness, 294; and Hegel, 144, 167, 176, 520, 570; "homophonous consciousness," 576; indifference of material in, 171; interpretive practices of, 415; and Kant, 167; late style, *516,* 564–67, 572–73, 634; listened to in terms of Tchaikovsky, 266; "manufactured transcendence" in, *521;* middle period, *519,* 527, 565; as model for philosophy of music, 144; musical processes, *102;* mystery, in late works, *516,* 565; and the Nazis, 374, *520n13;* "ostentation" in, *521;* performance rules, 164; principle of variation in, 255, 255nH; priority of becoming in, 172; projection of subjecthood, *521, 521n14;* on the radio, 220–21, 225, 252–68; reconstruction of tonality in, 167; score markings, *102,* 164; simplicity and richness in, 258; "standard classic," 253; and the subject, 123, *517, 519,* 565, 575, 578, 581, 657; syncopation in, 490; tempi, 667; tension and resolution in, 321; themes in, 176, 607; titanism, 167. *See also* Beethoven, Ludwig van, works of
Beethoven, Ludwig van, works of: Bagatelles, op. 33, 113; Bagatelles,

op. 126, 565; bagatelle cycles, 572; *Christ on the Mount of Olives,* 573; church music, 573, 574; *Fidelio,* 419; *Grosse Fuge,* op. 133, 572; late piano sonatas, 572; late quartets, 524–25, 571, 572; *Leonore* overture, 299; Mass in C major, op. 86, 573; *Missa Solemnis,* 525–28, 569–82; Piano Sonata no. 14 ("Moonlight"), 368; Piano Sonata no. 21 ("Waldstein"), 255nH; Piano Sonata no. 23 ("Appassionata"), 172, 255nH, 439, 565; Piano Sonata no. 26 ("Les Adieux"), 141; Piano Sonata no. 29 ("Hammerklavier"), 576; Piano Sonata no. 32 (op. 111), 10n27, 565, 633; symphonies, 524, 527, 572; String Quartet, op. 127, 576; String Quartet, op. 131, 564; Symphony no. 3 ("Eroica"), 175–76, 256, 571; Symphony no. 4, 294; Symphony no. 5, 220, 226, 256, 262–63, 267–68, 299, 440–41, 565; Symphony no. 7, 256, 294, 405, 439; Symphony no. 8, 578; Symphony no. 9, 115, 172, 519, 524–25, 524n20, 571, 572, 573, 581; Variations on a Waltz by Diabelli, op. 120, 168, 572, 576; Violin Sonata, op. 47 ("Kreutzer"), 328, 378

"be happy," 60

Bekker, Paul, 257, 665–66; on *Missa Solemnis,* 576, 583n4; on opera, 285, 287n10

belief, question of: and *Missa Solemnis,* 526–27, 577–78

Benjamin, Walter, 2, 4, 40–41, 63, 240–50, 305, 348–49, 620, 637, 643n9, 663; critique of Adorno's Wagner monograph, 528–31; dialectic, 244; on imagination, 169; *One-Way Street,* 322; *The Origin of German Tragic Drama,* 282n8; "The Paris of the Second Empire in Baudelaire," 243–44, 529n31; on

quotations, 332, 323n5; theory of mass art, 241; "The Work of Art in the Age of Mechanical Reproduction," 240–50, 493n5

Berg, Alban, 4, 4n9, 322, 323n6, 400–402, 546–51, 654; abandonment of opus numbers, 562, 655; Adorno's admiration for, 515; Adorno's early analyses of, 176–77; *Altenberg-Lieder,* op. 4, 181; attention to text, in *Wozzeck,* 549–50; autonomous logic and Wagnerian language in, 123–24; compared to Kokoschka, 402; craftsmanship, 622; dialectic, 401–2, 624; dream material in, 621, 622; and expressionism, 550; expressiveness, 547; forms borrowed from absolute music, in *Wozzeck,* 549, 549n84, 620; "greatheartedness," 548; images from childhood, 621; influence on Adorno, 546; and Mahler, 620, 624–25; and musical beauty, 550; musical-linguistic forms in 125; and opera, 237n53; orchestration, 151, 624; "permanent dissolution" in, 177, 180n21; praises Adorno's String Quartet no. 1, 14, 14n39; precarious existence of, 199; and previous generation, 401–2; and romanticism, 547; and Schoenberg, 621, 624, 632; on Schoenberg's difficulty, 133n1; on Schoenberg's String Quartet no. 1, 133n1; seriousness, 124; silence, 625; sonoral economy, 548; and tradition, 92; "unhygienic" aspect, 100n25; "Warum ist Schönbergs Musik so schwer verständlich?" 131n1, 632; *Wozzeck,* 4, 92, 402, 546n76, 547–57, 548n81, 610, 611n11, 619–25

Berlioz, Hector: *idée fixe,* 534; *Treatise on Instrumentation,* 260, 471, 663

Bernstein, Leonard, 330n6

best-sellers (musical), 294
Bildung, 405
Bizet, Georges, 283, 286n1;
    L'Arlésienne, 471; "March of the
    Toreadors" (Carmen), 318
blackface minstrelsy: parallels with
    jazz, 353n53
black music: falsification of, 496; and
    jazz, 477
blacks, 351, 351n51, 352, 353, 354,
    354n57, 355, 356n62, 358
Der Blaue Reiter, 188, 201n11
Bloch, Ernst, 4, 423; on R. Strauss,
    435n15
Blomster, Wes, ix, 433
"Blonde-haired Inge," 503
blow, striking a (Wagnerian gesture),
    532
Blut und Boden, 649, 675n5
body, 30, 30n87, 61; and the female
    voice, 274; modernity's attack on,
    550; musician's, as topic of "musi-
    cal" discourse, 248; natural move-
    ments, 554
Bomben auf Monte Carlo, 429, 435–
    36n23
boredom, 48, 449, 458; inescapability
    of, 459; as "objective desperation,"
    61
Boulez, Pierre, 16, 536n52, 657, 659,
    665; Adorno on, 101; on Adorno,
    16n43; composition in segments,
    124–25; integral rationalization
    replaces composition, 187; Struc-
    ture 1A, 101; systematicity in,
    156; traditional idioms discarded,
    187
Bourgeois, Jeanne Florentine, 276n6
bourgeois categories, 394
bourgeois consciousness, 667
bourgeoisie: decultivation of, in Ger-
    many, 376–82; and jazz, 473–74;
    musical life, 408, 417–33; privilege,
    328
bourgeoisie, upper: musical prefer-
    ences, 405
bourgeois money economy, 664

bourgeois music, 93
"bourgeois sadism," 244
bourgeois society, 664–65; need for
    music in, 421; rhythm of, 144
bourgeois spirit: Beethoven's tran-
    scendence of, 580
Bradley, F.H., 381, 389n6
Brahms, Johannes, 606, 634; late
    works influenced by musical anal-
    ysis, 163; motivic economy in, 163;
    Symphony no. 1, 268, 298; synco-
    pation in, 498
Brecht, Bertolt, 4, 134n2, 242, 243,
    249, 355, 366, 650, 653; anti-
    Wagnerian, 596; collaboration with
    Weill, 397; on disengaged artists,
    644–46; "Five Difficulties in Writ-
    ing the Truth," 644–46, 675n1
Brentano, Clemens, 569, 582n1
Brinkmann, Donald: demarcation be-
    tween aesthetic and natural, 142
Brockes, Barthold Hinrich, 613,
    617n3
Brown, James: on "social joy" of
    string quartet playing, 525n21
Brown, Lee B., 354n57
Bruce, Robert, 337–38, 339
Bruckner, Anton, 99, 150, 417, 573;
    Symphony no. 8, 417
Brunkhorst, Hauke, 2
Büchner, Georg, 402, 569, 582n1,
    625n1, 626n6
Buck-Morss, Susan, 19n48, 27,
    34n106, 35, 35n110, 64n201
bureaucratic thinking, 33
Bürger, Peter, 552n90
Busoni, Ferruccio, 636, 642–43n7

café music, 507–8. See also back-
    ground music
cafés: as settings for music, 372, 506
Cage, John, 563, 658; European reac-
    tions to, 111–12n48
Calvelli-Adorno, Agathe, 2, 617n1
Calvelli-Adorno della Piana, Maria, 2
canon, 80
capitalism, late, 44

Carnegie, Dale: *How to Win Friends and Influence People*, 59, 59n185
Casella, Alfredo, 404, 434n10
Cassirer, Ernst, 7
catastrophe, European, 199–200
Central Europe, musical tradition of: and Schoenberg, 631, 642n3
Chadwick, Nick, 349n46
Chamberlain, Houston Stewart, 374, 388n2, 585
chamber music, 259–60, 521–25, 525n21; audience for, 522–23; capacity to listen to, 672; and late style, 521–22; "practices courtesy," 523; purposelessness, 524; and radio, 252, 252nC; as utopian, 522
chamber symphony, 257, 257nK
Chanan, Michael, 557n104
change, 17, 21, 332
Chaplin, Charlie, 244; *Modern Times*, 51
charity: substitute for justice, 26
Chéreau, Patrice, 536n52
Chladni, Ernst Florens Friedrich, 280, 281–82n7
chromaticism, 423; appropriated in popular music, 431; and identity, 597; in Wagner, 119, 591
church modes. *See* modes
cinema. *See* film
class domination, 394
"classical" music, 135, 430, 671
classicism, 422; Viennese, 144, 155, 320, 640, 667; principle of economy in, 170
classics, 79, 79n246
class struggle, 619
Claudius, Matthias, 620
Cocteau, Jean, 258, 269–70n1, 665
coherence, musical, 121, 192
collectivism, musical: in Germany, 382
color (musical): discovery of, 299; in modern dance music, 313; in popular music, 306; in Wagner, 593–94. *See also* tone-color composition; *Tonfarbenmusik*

commercialization of life, 44
commercials: common currency of youth, 51n162
commodity: exchange value of, 296–97; and subject, 51–52
commodity fetishism, 50n160, 61; Marx's definition, 296. *See also* fetishism
commodity listening, 293. *See also* listening
common practice period, 86, 89, 98. *See also* tonality
communal music, 397, 410–11
communication: art as instrument of, 242; and language, 66
community: and art, 132; for community's sake, 197; as musical fashion, 410
community, spirit of: in Germany, 382
competition: domination's twin, 26n74
composers, 158, 649; challenges of late modernity, 561; choices facing, 136; consciousness of, 162; insecurity, 384, 650; and musical material, 111, 205; Nazi, 383; need for self-reflexivity, 101; and technique, 650; training of, 196–97
composition: with a computer, 657; difficulties, 644–60; motivic-thematic, 166, 170; reduced to control, 196; space for, 651–52, 653. *See also* compositional process
compositional process, 121; articulated by "intonations," 124; convergence with analytical process, 168; mechanization of, 335; unconscious production of relationships in, 162. *See also* composition
computer, composition with, 657
concentration, 139; demanded by new music, 672–73. *See also* listening: deconcentrated
concepts, musical: invariance of, 114
concerto, 521–22, 523–24

concerts: in bourgeois musical life, 419–21; chaotic situation of, 650

conductor, 416–17, 523–24; fetish character of, 302; as monopolist, 417; as "personality," 417; relationship with orchestra, 222n26, 301–2. *See also* Toscanini, Arturo

connoisseurs, musical, 671

consciousness: bourgeois, 667; of consumer, 53n167, 131, 133, 665; emancipated, 129; reified, 56n171, 670; temporal, 143; transformation of, by art, 71

consolation: denied by Schoenberg, 560, 638

constellation: organizational principle in Adorno's writing, 63–64, 64n201

constructivism, 125, 127

constructivists, pointillist, 191; oblivious to temporal interrelations, 188

consumer: betrayal of, 307; consciousness of, 53n167, 131, 133, 665; incomprehension of new art, 95; self-worshipping, 296; value of 47

consumer "choice," 46–47

consumer goods: abstractly exchangeable, 128

consumerism, American: domination by other means, 327

consumption, 131; as deindividuating, 50; heroes of, 678n21; musical, 411, 417–33

contemplation, aesthetic, 242

contradiction, 36n114, 37; in art, 35–36

convention, 145–46, 516n3; in late Beethoven, 516–17, 518, 560, 565–66; and subjectivity, 566

Cornelius, Hans, 6

Cotta Firm, 569, 582n2

counterpoint, 151, 152, 201n4; emancipation of, 398

Craft, Robert, 557n104

craft-ideology relation, 529n30

Critical Theory, *vii*, 18–32, 76; characteristic discourse of, 22; and happiness, 72; Horkheimer on, 19–22; Lukács on, 68; "messages in bottles," 70; not a system, 19; public critique of, 69; and social change, 68–70; theory-praxis relation, 69–70, 69n223

criticism, musical, 77; and analysis, 168; fulfillment of duty to the work, 570; shortcomings, 197

Crook, Stephen, 58n179

crying, 363, 462

cubism, 127

"cultural bustle," 21

cultural goods: exchange value, 296

Cultural Studies, British, 54

culture, 42; affirmative character of, 671; as business, 45; as commodity, 50–51n162; condition of, since European catastrophe, 199–200; dumbing down of, 328; and fascism, 374; neutralization of, 377, 569–70; promoted by radio, 220

Culture Industry, 42–61, 42n133, 134n2, 361, 365, 377, 551, 665; Adorno's position criticized, 47; and advertising, 304; choice of term, 43, 43n135; and false consciousness, 670; leisure time governed by, 95; lies promulgated by, 54; pleasure proffered by, 48; public functions, 55; as repetition, 47; and spontaneity, 384; and subjectivity, 57; threatened acquisition of new music, 181

cunning, 28, 28n79

cynicism: and fascism, 379; and transformation of the Germans, 378

dada, 658, 659

Dahlhaus, Carl: on Adorno, 526n25; on *Missa Solemnis*, 526n25; on sequence, 532–33n40

Dallapiccola, Luigi, 158, 161n20

dance: and the bourgeois gait, 485–86; derivatives, in serious music, 440–

41; disenchantment of, and jazz, 485–86

dance craze, 344

"The Dancing Tambourine," 431–32, 436n27, 502

Daniel, Jamie Owen, *ix*, 493n5

Darmstadt International Vacation Courses on New Music, 15, 16n43, 73, 76, 172, 657. *See also* Kranichstein

Darré, Richard Walther, 675n5

Darrell, R. D., 494n13

death, 544, 566, 612–13; absolute regression, 599

Deathridge, John, 530n34

Debussy, Claude, 206, 267, 353, 424–25, 483, 484; attacked by H. Schenker, 166; Bartók and, 184; Boulez and, 125; "General Lavine, eccentric" (*Préludes*, Book II), 489, 495n17

"decomposition," musical, 305–6

deconcentration, 305. *See also* listening: deconcentrated

"Deep Purple," 455nG, 469n1

Delius, Frederick, 353, 483, 494–95n13

DeLong, Thomas A., 349–50n47

Dennis, Christopher J., 557n104

DeNora, Tia, 513n1

Dent, Edward, 7

desire, 29; Hegel on, 589; in hit songs, 338

details, musical, 319–22, 323n3, 324n8; deified and reified, on radio, 266; impatience with, 322, 323n4; in popular music, 438–41

developing variations, 173; abandoned in *Missa Solemnis*, 526; as superfluous, 124

development: as art of appearances, 667; dynamic, 170–71; meaningfulness lost, 582; and structural listening, 221n23; as superfluous, 124; in time, 532

deviation-schema relationship: and musical analysis, 165

dialectical materialism, 433

dialectic of the Enlightenment, 142, 145–46. *See also* Adorno, works of: *Dialectic of Enlightenment*; Enlightenment

dialectics, *vii*, 20n52, 32–40; agony conceptualized, 34; and articulation of otherness, 33; historical, 145; in Plato's *Symposium*, 120; of modernity, 80

difference, 79; as marketing technique, 46

differentiation, 129; escape from, 130

Disney: references in Adorno and Benjamin, 249–50

dissociation: in late Beethoven, 517

dissonance, 423; emancipation of, 118; in jazz, 306; in twelve-tone music, 554; in Wagner, 590

distraction, aesthetic, 242, 343; bound to mode of production, 458; disposition to, 661; not universal, 459nJ

(the) divine, music as manifestation of, 140–41. *See also* music: theological aspect

division of labor, 392; and compositional technique, 153; intellectual, 20, 135

"dominance-tonality," 206, 209n7

domination, 25–26, 28, 30–31

Donaldson, Walter, 293, 316n5

Donaueschingen Festival, 507, 510n3

Dongen, Kees van, 476, 493n7

Don Quixote, 613

Dostoyevsky, Fyodor, 605; *The Brothers Karamazov*, 614, 617n5

Das Dreimäderlhaus, 429, 436n24

Dvořák, Antonin, 462; "Humoresque," 360n74

dynamics: absolute, 256; in Beethoven's Symphony no. 5, 258–59; restricted by radio, 257, 257nJ

Eagleton, Terry, 39n123, 64

"easy listening," 559; Schoenberg as antithesis of, 632

écriture, 88n4

ecstasy: stylized, 309
Edda, 596, 602n9
Edström, Olle, 221n23
Ehmann, Wilhelm, 654, 676–77n9
Ehrlich, Cyril, 232n48
Einstein, Albert, 155
Eisenstein, Sergei, 370
Eisler, Hanns, 70n224, 286n2, 365–
    371, 366n88, 410–11, 646; prole-
    tarian choral works, 397; and the
    Second Viennese School, 411
élan vital, cult of, 379
Eleatic philosophers, 597
electronic music, 660; contradictory
    tendencies in, 101; "Webern on a
    Wurlitzer," 194–95
elemental analysis. See analysis: ele-
    mental
Eliland, 502, 505n8
Ellington, Duke, 353, 483, 494–95n13
emancipation: in Adorno's aesthetics,
    73, 73n235; of musical material,
    188–89; obstructed by Culture In-
    dustry, 57; and Schoenberg, 155–
    56; as slogan, 514
emigration, internal, 384
Engh, Barbara, 233n50
enjoyment: diversionary function of,
    291; illusory, 292
Enlightenment, 26, 144; failure of,
    519; and myth, 29–30; totalizing,
    30. See also dialectic of the En-
    lightenment
entertainment, 661; and mode of
    production, 458; ubiquity of, 300–
    301
Ernst, Max, 600, 602n13
Ervin, Sam, 44n137
essay form, 65, 65n206
estrangement, 12n34, 517n5; in
    Missa Solemnis, 574
"exact imagination," 322
exchange economy, 22
exchange value, 296–97
experience, musical: obscurity of, 218;
    transformed into object, 456

(the) experimental, 651; no "nature
    preserves" for, 652
expression, 145–46, 342; aesthetics
    of, 116–17; and density of experi-
    ence, 191; intensification of, 146;
    as miming of suffering, 91n14;
    music of, 620; refusal of, in new
    music, 109, 191; taboo against, 381
expressionism, 127, 634–35, 638
expressionlessness, 117, 119, 620,
    625; in late Beethoven, 517, 564;
    in Wozzeck, 620
expressiveness: of music, 102; of mu-
    sical atoms, on radio, 265
extremes: in Adorno's aesthetics, 516;
    in late Beethoven, 567

fact-value relationship, 20, 36
failure: as distinguishing great art-
    works, 527, 527–28n27; as mea-
    sure of success, 581; and Missa
    Solemnis, 582
Fall, Leo, 428, 435n21
false beats: in jazz, 430, 470, 484,
    492n1, 496, 497, 498, 499
false consciousness, 154; "correct," in
    Mahler, 616
fame: and advertising, 457
family: in Adorno's social psychol-
    ogy, 24; and the phonograph, 272
fantasy, power of: in Beethoven, 571
fascism: and aestheticization of poli-
    tics, 532; and America, 373; effect
    on German intellectual climate,
    154; and hatred of thinking, 381;
    and mass media, 56n170, 342; sur-
    vival of, 327. See also Nazism
fashion: and fury, 463
Les Fauves, 637, 643n8
fear, 29; organization of, 29n84
Federal Republic of Germany. See
    Germany
Feher, Ferenc, 103n31
fetish character, 298, 393; of music
    objects, 422. See also fetishism
fetishism, 194; and music, 252, 294–

303; revolts against, 308. *See also* commodity fetishism

Feuerbach, Ludwig, 589

film, 45, 49, 239n55, 303–4, 370; disconnected from life, 48; jazz in, 486; Nazi, 244. *See also* film industry; film music; sound film

film industry, 241 45, 367–68

film music, 125, 286n2, 332, 335, 365–71; melody in, 367–68; new aesthetic for, 367; and sensuousness, 370; in silent pictures, 368–69, 368n95

Fink, Robert, 345n38

(the) folk, disappearance of, 427. *See also Volk*

folk art: in industrialized settings, 129. *See also* folklore

folklore: and Bartók, 406; demonic, in Berg, 625; and objectivism, 396

force-field: organizational principle in Adorno's writing, 63, 64

Ford, John: *The Grapes of Wrath*, 49, 49n156

foreign words, 65–67

form: Adorno's concepts of, 88; architectonic-schematic theory of, 177–78; in Beethoven, 125; defined historically, 178; as destiny of musical content, 117; enigmatic, in new art, 127; exploded, 574; law of, 101; material theory of, 177, 178; musical, 87, 115; symphonic, in classical period, 254

form-content relationship, 320

forms, large: stratification of, 124

Foujita, Tsuguji, 476, 493n7

fragmentation: defining characteristic of postmodernity, 52

France: industrialization in 424; tradition broken in, 425

Frankfurt School, vii, 5. *See also* Critical Theory

freedom, 314; and Beethoven, 207; contradiction of, 198; and Critical Theory, 22; illusion of, 53–54n168;

of the individual, 57; lacking in Wagner, 597; musical, 636; in musical reproduction, 412, 413, 414, 480–81

Freire, Paulo, 223

French Revolution: as encapsulation of later history, 513–14

Freud, Sigmund, 545, 637; Adorno's reading of, 23–24; *Moses and Monotheism*, 155, 160n17. *See also* psychoanalysis

Frith, Simon, 346n39

frontier, musical: disappearance of, 191

fugue, 575; generated by tonality, 633

fury: and jitterbugs, 465–66, 467

futurism, 127, 131

Gál, Hans, 588, 590, 593, 601n4

"gallant" style, 182

game shows, epistemology of, 52

Ganzheitspsychologie, 180n16

garage bands: and social critique, 345n36

Gauguin, Paul, 604

"gaze" of music, 139

Gebrauchskunst, 132. See also *Gebrauchsmusik*

Gebrauchsmusik, 133–34n2, 497, 499, 500n3. *See also* use music

Gehlen, Arnold, 654, 676n9

Gendron, Bernard, 348

genius, theory of, 628

genre: and analysis, 169

George, Stefan, 126n5, 205, 208n5; "Entrückung," 637

Georgiades, Thrasybulos, 580, 583n6

German Economic Miracle, 514

Germany: Adorno's posthumous reputation in, 73–74; break between production and consumption, 424; enduring Nazi potential in, 585; hostility toward dramatic intrigue, 580; imperialism, 375, 379; jazz in, 357–60, 665; mass-culture debates

Germany (continued)
in, 43n134; mass psychosis in, 342; middle classes, 376–82; musical culture in, 378–79; musical life before Hitler, 374; postwar climate, 10; ressentiment against modern art in, 587

Gershwin, George, 319; Rhapsody in Blue, 268, 350n47

Gesamtkunstwerk: as mask, 534

Gestalt, aesthetic, 117

gesture(s): and gesticulation, in Wagner, 533; in music, 139; sedimented history, 98

Geulen, Eva, 77n241

Giddens, Anthony, 78n243

"Gigolo," 503, 505n13

Gillespie, Susan H., 63, 63n198, 324n8

"giving the masses what they want," 458

glamor, musical, 448–50; and the childlike, 450–51; and the song of the common man, 449

Gluck, Christoph Willibald, 570

Göcking, Leopold Friedrich von, 625–26n1

God, name of, 114. See also name, naming

Goehr, Lydia, x, 12n34, 238n54, 553n90

Goethe, Johann Wolfgang von, 381, 565, 577; Elective Affinities, 2; Faust II, 566, 568n2; paid lip service by Nazis, 374; Wilhelm Meisters Wanderjahre, 566, 568n2

Goldmann, Lucien, 89n8

"good bad music," 345, 502

Goodman, Benny, 344, 446, 466

Gorbman, Claudia, 371n106

Gould, Glenn, 238n54

Gounod, Charles: "Ave Maria," 360, 361, 362, 455nG; Faust, 509, 510n5

Grabbe, Christian Dietrich, 660, 677–78n17

Gracyk, Theodore A., 346n39, 347n41

Grainger, Percy, 494–95n13

grammar, musical, 98

gramophone. See phonograph

great music, idea of, 261; bound up with bourgeois era, 137; as force for synthesis, 290; and Wagner, 123

Greenberg, Clement: "Avant-Garde and Kitsch," 363, 363–64n82

Grieg, Edvard: as café music, 509; "To Spring," 509

Grofé, Ferde, 350n47

Gross, Harvey, 13n34

gypsies, 477

Hába, Alois, 400, 434n6

Habberton, John: Helen's Babies, 450nE

Habermas, Jürgen, 1, 68, 73, 672, 679n28

Hacker, Friedrich, 11, 57

Haecker, Theodor, 199, 202n16

Haggin, B. H., 230, 230n45

"half-cultivation," 661, 661nB

Halm, August, 666, 678–79n24

Handel, George Frideric, 570; graspable without analysis, 168; provocatively healthy, 292

Hangmen Also Die, 367

Hanning, Barbara, 525n21

Hanrahan, Nancy Weiss, 557n104

Hansen, Miriam, 239n55, 355n61; on Disney references in Adorno and Benjamin, 249–50

Hanslick, Eduard, 139; The Beautiful in Music, 126n4, 159nn4, 6, 376

happenings, 658

happiness, 291, 462, 553; at heart of Critical Theory, 23, 72; instinct for, 29n83; mediated, 20; and music, 86, 343, 343n32; as slogan, 514; as social, 514; thought as, 72

Harburger, Walter, 145

Harding, James, 351n51, 359n71

Hardt, Petra Christina, xi

harmony, modern: origins, 119, 590

harmony, tonal, 87; in late Beet-

hoven, *517;* in popular music, *442.*
See also tonality

Haydn, Joseph: and Mozart, 165–66; preference for the "gallant," 290

Hays Office, 381, *389n5*

hearing: dominated by sight, *368;* as historical, *535;* infantile, 308; masochism in, 311. *See also* listening

"hear-stripe," *218–19, 218n19,* 251. *See also* noise

Hebbel, Friedrich, 597, *602n10*

Hegel, Georg Wilhelm Friedrich, 22, 381, 652; absolute knowledge in, 598; and Beethoven, 144; dialectics of, *34–35; Phenomenology of Spirit,* 141, 598; *Philosophy of Right, 675n4; Reason in History,* 589, *601n5*

Heilbut, Anthony, 215

"Heidelberg," 503, *505n15*

Heine, Heinrich, 661

Hellenistic period, 668

Heraclitus, 597

Heym, Georg, 509, *510n6*

high fidelity: and Adorno's critique of radio music, *218n19*

Hindemith, Paul, 406–8, *434n7,* 624; adaptation to reality in, 461; contradictions in, 407; Donaueschingen chamber works, 507, *510n3;* and *Gebrauchsmusik, 134n2,* 397; *Das Marienleben,* 408, *435n13;* melancholy in, 407; objectivism decontaminated, 406; renunciation of new music, 183, 649

Hinton, Stephen, *520n13*

Hirsch, E. D., Jr., *52–53n165*

"His Master's Voice," 274, *276n7,* 277, 278

historicism, *40;* parody's reversion to, 120

history, *40–42;* absence of, in radical serialists, *108–9;* belongs to victors, *40;* denial of, in Wagner, *533;* and kitsch, *364;* as music's truth, *99;* objectification of, *56;* and philosophy, *40*

Hitler, Adolf, 374, 375; and musical culture, 379. *See also* Nazism

hit songs, 305–6; anal-sadistic structure of, 432; distinguishing feature obligatory in, 447–48; harmonic vocabulary, *339;* life cycle of, 459; as listener's property, 456; "mistakes" in, 307; novelty in, *338–39;* origin and function of, within capitalism, 432; psychological mechanism of production, 431–32; repetition of, 447; response appropriate to, 318–19; rules for writing, *338;* sameness of, *337, 343. See also* "plugging"; popular music; standardization

hobbies, 17, *61,* 193

Hobson, Wilder, 451, *451nF, 494n13*

Hohendahl, Peter Uwe, 526

Hölderlin, Friedrich, 147

Holocaust, 149–50

homeostasis, 668, 669

homophony: regression to, 659

hook: in hit songs, *338–39, 343;* and pseudo-individuation, *339*

Horkheimer, Max, *4, 6, 42,* 213, 349, 377; collaboration with Adorno, 24–25, *24n70;* on Critical Theory, 19–22; *Eclipse of Reason, 389n4;* on radio, *56n170*

"hot" music, 475–76, 488, 490, 492, 497, 498

house music, 391, 506

House Un-American Activities Committee, *365n86*

housing projects, 45

How to Write and Sell a Song Hit (Silver and Bruce), *337, 338,* 438nA

How to Write a Hit Song and Sell It (Bruce), *337–38, 339*

Hullot-Kentor, Robert, *ix, 27n76, 29n84, 63n197, 68n220, 328n2, 332n11,* 345–46

(the) humane, 328, 378; Mahler and, *545;* survival of, 387

humanism: in Beethoven, *329*, *378*; and German music, *378*; and opera, *419*

Hutton, Barbara, *463*, *469n7*

Huxley, Aldous, *289*, *315–16n1*

Huyssen, Andreas, *54–55n169*, *363–64n82*

"Ich küsse Ihre Hand, Madame," *503*, *505n11*

idealism, German, *347*

identity: homogenization of, *46*; spurious foundation of, *50*

identity and non-identity: in music, *188*

ideology: concept of, *645*; and music, *646*; ubiquity of, *660*

imagination, exact, *322*

"immanent criticism," *37*, *74*

immediacy: of effect, in new and older art, *128–29*; lost, *506*; and Mahler, *544*, *613*; musical, *394*

impressionism, *503*, *604*; in painting, *131*, *193*, *402*, *424*

improvisation, *356n64*

inclusion, feeling of: denied to listener by Schoenberg, *99*, *150*

indeterminacy, *658*; mirror image of the absolutely determined, *563*

individual: bourgeois, *401*; and detail in artwork, *250*; liquidation of, *245*, *293*, *297*, *298*, *653*; in Mahler, *616*; other-directed, *661*; shrivelling of, *668*; and society, *24*; subordination of, *386*; suffering of, *422*, *423*, *619*, *622*, *624*, *625*. *See also* individuality

individuality: collapse of, *198–99*; as foundation of history, *522*; illusion of, *485*; liquidation of, *315*; reduced to abstraction, *465*; sacrifice of, *297*; and solo-concerto literature, *522*. *See also* individual

infantilization, *329–30n6*; *450–51*, *562*

Institute of Social Research (Frankfurt), *5*, *10*, *11*; Adorno's directorship, *16–17*; Marxist orientation, *6*

instrumental reason, *28*; Adorno's struggle against, *33*; Critical Theory's critique of, *70*

instrumentation, *151*

instruments: infantile, *307*; mechanical, *414*

intellect and emotion, false distinction between, *673*

intellectual(s): Nazis' murder of, *373*; role of, *vii*, *21*

International Society for Contemporary Music (ISCM), *435n13*; concerts of, *420*

interpretation, *412–17*; and history, *98*; and musical analysis, *102*; progressive, *415*; required by music and language, *115*; and the riddle of music, *139*; schools of, *412–13*

interpreter. *See* performer

"interpretive personality." *See* performer

intersubjectivity: loss of, in radio performance, *224*; musically constructed, *328*

inwardness: liquidation of, *423*

irrationality, *476–77*

"Isle of Capri," *476*, *493n8*

Israel Philharmonic, *537n53*

Jameson, Frederic, *20n52*, *23n64*, 44

Jay, Martin, 2, *2–3n4*, 18, *63–64*, *90n13*; on characteristics of Adorno's thought, *23*; on Culture Industry, 55

jazz, *137*, *251*, *283*, *309*, *331–32*, *335*, *349–58*, *470–92*, *496–99*, *665*; Adorno's definition, *349*; Adorno's writings on, *331*; alien subject in, *472*; as amalgam of march and salon music, *491*; and art composers, *496*; and blacks, *477*, *496*; "break" in, *445*, *470*, *488*; business of, *295*; castration symbolism, *352*; characteristic sound, *471*, *491*; "classical" music as raw material for, *430*; commercial, *305*; commodity character, *430*, *473*; constitutive ele-

ments, 483; and contingency, 487; and corniness, 463–64; couplet and refrain in, 487–88; as cultural hybrid, 354n57; and dance, 472, 485–86, 497; disrespectful use of themes in, 496; division of labor in, 481; "eccentric" elements in, 489 90, 491; end of, 496; equivocal function of, 472; and fascism, 485; *Gebrauchsmusik* of the haute bourgeoisie, 497; in Germany, 357–60, 485, 496; harmonies in, 497, 498; helplessness in, 483; "hot," 355, 474–76, 483; and human sacrifice, 488; ideological function, 430; impressionist elements in, 430, 431, 483–84; improvisation in, 354, 356–57n64, 430, 445; industrial product, 360; irony in, 492; in Italy, 485; and Jews, 355–56n62; latent dream content, 487–88; and march music, 430, 485–86, 499; (un)marketability, 356, 473; melody in, 484; modernity of, 470; and nationality, 353; and otherness, 351; and the performer, 355, 356–57n64; primal structure of, 478; production and reproduction in, 479–80, 481, 497–98; "progressive" elements in, 349, 355, 484; pseudo-democratic, 475; and psychic mutilation, 474; reception, 475–76; sameness and newness in, 478; saxophone in, 471; seeming immediacy of, 473; sexual moment in, 486–87, 490; and social authority, 474; stabilized, 483, 496; subjective pole of, 485; sweet, 483; symmetry in, 471; syncopation in, 470, 486; and upper class, 474; vacuum left by, 499; vibrato in, 471, 483, 484, 491. *See also* jazz amateur(s); jazz subject; popular music
jazz amateur(s), 310, 481–83
jazz subject, 488–89, 490–91, 492; eccentric as model for, 488–89, 491
Jephcott, Edmund, 39n122

Jhally, Sut, 50n160
jitterbug(s), 249n78, 308–9, 451, 465–66, 467–68, 466nL, 467nM; and Nazi rallies, 344, 344n33; and self-caricature, 467
Jöde, Fritz, 204, 208n3
Johann Wolfgang Goethe University (Frankfurt): Adorno's studies at, 4
John Paul II (pope), 44n137
Jugendstil, musical, 502

Kafka, Franz, 159–60n12; 184, 652, 676n8; place of music in, 115, 136
Kagel, Mauricio, 284, 286–87n6
Kandinsky, Wassily: "On the Spiritual in Art," 188; friendship with Schoenberg, 201n11
Kant, Immanuel, 565, 569, 577; Adorno's study of, 2–3; intuition and thought in, 639
Karajan, Herbert von, 595
Karamazov, Ivan: and Mahler, 614, 617n5
Karplus, Gretel, 7
Kater, Michael H., 359
"keep smiling," 49, 309
Kierkegaard, Søren, 67n218, 183, 402, 661, 674, 679n31; *Stages on Life's Way*, 157, 160–61n19
King, Carole, 345n37
The King of Jazz, 354
kitsch, viii, 285, 332, 360–64, 361–62n77, 364n82, 364–65n85, 395, 425, 501–4; with "class," 504; and forgetting, 361; lexical meaning, 501; linkage of characteristic and banal, 503; and metaphysics of death, 502; moderate, 502; negative eternity of, 131; patriotic, in Germany, 359, 499; precipitate of devalued forms, 501; public's alleged desire for, 133; and remembering, 363; social function, 502; talk about, 504
"Kitten on the Keys," 499, 500n5
Klangfarbenmelodien, 151, 160n14. *See also* tone-color composition

Kluge, Alexander, 239n55
knowledge: musical, 376; as posses-
sion, 53; reduced to raw data, 52
Kodály, Zoltán, 406, 434n11
Kogawa, Tetsuo, 23n64
Kokoschka, Oskar, 402, 434n8
Kolisch, Rudolf, 5, 179n3, 555, 667,
679n25
Kolisch Quartet, 178–79n3; playing
from memory, 165
Kolleritsch, Otto, x, 316n7
Kracauer, Siegfried, 2–4, 67n218
Kraft durch Freude, 385, 389–90n8
Krahl, Hans-Jürgen, 68–69, 69n221
Kramer, Larry, x, 316n8
Kranichstein, 658, 677n14. *See also*
Darmstadt International Vacation
Courses on New Music
Kraus, Karl, 483, 494n12, 502, 620,
625n1; *Die Fackel*, 322, 323n6,
494n12; *The Last Days of Man-
kind*, 183, 201n5; purification of
language in, 397, 400; and Schoen-
berg, 397, 398
Krenek, Ernst, 121, 434n8; on crisis
of inspiration, 668; debates with
Adorno, 5; *Jonny spielt auf*, 480,
493n10; return to tonality, 561;
Symphony no. 2, 121
Kretzschmar, Hermann: on *Missa
Solemnis*, 570–71
"Kreutzer" Sonata (Beethoven): and
the humane, 378
Kulturbolschewismus, 380, 381, 383,
646
Kurth, Ernst: concept of musical
space in, 150, 160n13; psychology
of music, 432
Kuspit, Donald B., 554–55n96

Lang, Fritz, 556n100
language, 33; and idea of objectivity,
125–26; instrumentalization of, 63;
intention-less, 114; music's emancipation from, 146; and otherness,
66; reshaped by Culture Industry,
67; signifying, 114, 115, 116

language-like elements in music, 145;
allergy to, 122; negation of, 123;
ostracized as alien, 121; in Schoenberg, 121, 155, 156
Lassen, Eduard: "Stell auf den Tisch
die duftenden Resenden," 502,
504n2
late style, late work, 582; of Bach,
147; of Beethoven, 147, 516–25,
564–67; and catastrophe, 567; conventions in, 565; and genre, 521;
of R. Strauss, 516; and Wagner's
Parsifal, 532
laughter: in cinema, 244–45, 245n75
Laurencin, Marie, 476, 493n7
Lazarsfeld, Paul, 213, 213n1, 215,
217, 333, 678n21
Lazarus, Neil, 81–82
Léhar, Franz, 436n25; *Friederike*, 429–
30; *Das Land des Lächelns*, 430;
The Merry Widow, 428
Leibowitz, René, 187, 201n10; Four
Pieces for Piano, op. 8, 655,
677n11
leisure time: and work, 133, 458–59
leitmotif, 170, 171, 537, 590; rendered positivistic, 534. *See also*
Wagner, Richard
Leppert, Richard, 626n5
Levin, David J., 537n53
Levin, Thomas Y., 233n49, 361–
62n77, 368n95, 369n96
liberal democracy, 70
Ligeti, György, 658
light music. *See* popular music
linearity, 398
listeners: betrayal of, 248; consciousness of, 302; diminished spontaneity of, 339; "emotional," 343–44;
pseudoactivity of, 300; as purchas-
ers, 291; resistance to popular music, 464; theory of, 452–68; typology of, 228–29, 228n40
listening: atomistic, 226, 261–2, 303,
305, 318, 319; deconcentrated, 247,
305, 632; disempowerment of, 657;
and freedom, 314; institutionaliza-

tion of, 447; in late modernity, 563n105; manipulated, 442; mass, 463; modern habits of, 95; new possibilities in, 312; participatory, 662; and rage, 311; regressive, 97, 246, 252, 303–15, 672; responsible, 250; socially conditioned, 240, 661. *See also* structural listening

Liszt, Franz, 595; as interpreter, 413; *Mazeppa*, 184, 201n6

Lloyd, Harold, 490

logic, musical, 670; as caricature of logic, 196; in Schoenberg, 559

Lombardo, Guy, 349, 361n74, 446

loneliness, 238–39

Loos, Adolf, 398, 433–34n5, 635, 670

Lorenz, Alfred, 593, 602nn7, 8

Los Angeles Times, 57

Lott, Eric, 353n53

lottery, 49–50

Lowenthal, Leo, 3, 18, 45, 67n218, 71, 224n30; on Culture Industry, 50

Ludwig II (king of Bavaria), 600

Lukács, Georg, 56, 56n172, 67–68, 262nN, 675n2; Adorno on, 68n219; Lowenthal on, 71

lyric poetry, 661–62

MacDougald, Duncan, Jr., 340–41, 447nC

MacRae, D.G., 75–76

macrocosm and microcosm, 45

Mahler, Gustav, 174–75, 538–46, 563, 603–10, 612–17, 639; "animal symbolism" in, 611n8; (in)authenticity in, 543; banal aspect, 614–15; and Berg, 610, 611n11; compositional method, 610; and Dostoyevsky, 605, 614, 617n5; form, 605, 607, 608; fragments as material for, 614, 615; incorporation of the vulgar, 540; lost totality evoked in, 539; and musical progress, 315; notation, 607; "novelistic" form in, 539; and otherness, 540, 542, 545; outbreak

of hope in, 609; parody in, 615; polyphony, 610n1; and regressive listening, 315; and remembrance, 544, 545; and reveille, 546, 546n75, 617, 618n9; "romanticism" of, 603, 606, 607, 609; and Schoenberg, 603–4, 606, 608; significance of, 544, 608, 610; themes, 314–15, 607–8, 613; tonality in, 542–43, 543nn70, 71; on tradition, 413; unoriginality, 538; principle of variant in, 544, 613, 617; variation technique, 608

Mahler, Gustav, works of: *Kindertotenlieder*, 544, 612–13; *Des Knaben Wunderhorn*, 618n9; *Lieder eines fahrenden Gesellen*, 615; *Das Lied von der Erde*, 604, 608, 609, 612, 614; Symphony no. 2, 607; Symphony no. 3, 607, 608, 611n8, 616; Symphony no. 4, 175, 180nn18, 19, 608, 611n11; Symphony no. 5, 608, 618n6; Symphony no. 6, 608, 609, 614; Symphony no. 7, 317n14, 542, 609, 611n10; Symphony no. 8, 543n73, 606, 615; Symphony no. 9, 615

Mann, Thomas, 9, 9n25, 9–10n27, 627; on Adorno's Wagner monograph, 531n35

march music: echoed in symphonic music, 142; in jazz, 430, 485–86, 499; in Mahler's Symphony no. 3, 616

Marcuse, Herbert, 4, 36–37, 46–47, 79n246, 671, 678n21, 679n27; on Adorno's writing, 67

Markus, Gyorgy, 530n33, 530–31n34

Marinetti, F. T., 231–32, 231n47, 243n69

marketing. *See* "plugging"

"marketplace of ideas," 32

Marsh, James L., 557n104

Martin, David, 65nn205, 208

Marx, Karl, 569; Lowenthal on, 71

Marx Brothers, 136; *A Night at the Opera*, 159n2, 314

Marxism, 23, 24; linked with psycho-analysis, in Critical Theory, 23–24n65

masochism, 311

mass culture, viii, 297; avant-garde of, 345; critique of, 345; globalization of, 96; grip of, 57; late modifications of Adorno's position on, 43; and music, 330–72; potential progressiveness of, 249

masses, 20–21, 244; Adorno as champion of, 47n149; consciousness of, 394; listening habits, 304, 342, 343; musical condition of, 289, 292; as objects, 458; reaction to art, 242; subjecthood, 243

material, musical, 129, 146, 428, 437–446, 518; Beethoven's domination of, 517–18; expansion of, 190; historically produced, 129, 553; and musical language, 195–96; purification of, 182; ransacked for sensory stimulation, 190; rooted in tonality, 186; Schoenberg's approach to, 559; as second nature to musical subject, 145; set free, in late work, 566

mathematics, 130, 121, 194

McCarthy hearings, 514

means: enthroned as end, 31

mediation, 116, 140, 141, 404–5; feeling of, in Missa Solemnis, 579; and new music, 659; of subject and object, 125

Meinong, Alexius, 675n4

Meissner, David, x

melancholy, Slavic, 462

melody: "abuse" of, 456; as ghost, in café music, 509; in jazz, 484; layman's idea of, 448; in popular music, 441–42; as property, 294; solo, 319; in Wagner, 533n40. See also theme(s)

Melting Pot, 79, 79n245

memory, 612

Mendelssohn, Felix, 573

Menke, Christoph, 20

Merton College, Oxford, 7

Messiaen, Olivier, 156, 187

Metropolis, 556n100

Metzger, Heinz-Klaus, 107n38, 169, 200n1, 659

Michelangelo, 627

Middleton, Richard, 347n42

mimesis, 89, 90n13

Mistinguett, 274, 276n6

"moderate modernism," 197–98, 493n7, 626n3, 652

modernity, 514; Adorno's focus, 513; aging of, 563; and the commodity fetish, 95; constituted by othering, 29; incomprehensibility of, 95; music in, viii, 85, 96, 515, 674; as permanent crisis, 513

Modern Times, 51

modes, 663; in Missa Solemnis, 572; Plato on, 289–90

moments: defined, 179n4; as departure point for analysis, 175

monopoly capitalism: and aesthetic perception, 249n78; concealment of, 415

montage, 121, 242, 370; in Weill, 409

monumentality: in Missa Solemnis, 526, 573

"more": premise of modern ideology, 50

Mozart, Wolfgang Amadeus, 648; The Magic Flute, 290, 335; The Marriage of Figaro, 284; operas, 284, 419, 427; Symphony no. 39 (E-flat major), 299; Symphony no. 40 (G minor), 263; Symphony no. 41 ("Jupiter"), 580

MTV, 248

music: and cognition, 393, 513; background, 289, 506–9; as commodity, 245, 248, 332, 391; crisis of, 135, 147; dignity of, 97, 136, 138, 147; as drug, 257–58; enigmatic character of, 137, 138, 140, 141;

and history, *86, 91, 98,* 144, 147;
humanization of, 145; and impulse,
288, 314, 660; informal, 110–11,
515, 659; intentions, *87, 88,* 114–
15, 116, 117; interpretation of,
115, 139; and language, *85, 91, 92,*
98, 113–14, 117, 120, 122, 126,
146–47, 192, 279–80, 444, 652; as
a language *sui generis,* 142, 145,
636; mass behavior towards, 460–
62; meaning and, *viii,* 21, 74, *85–*
86, 87, 103, 139, 140, 192, 193,
460, 651; under Nazism, 374–84;
and painting, *88,* 476, *493n7;* pedagogy, 221, 222, *222n26,* 223,
223n28, 319; petrifaction of, 235–
36, 279; and philosophy, *vii,* 96–
101, 135–61, 329; phonograph-
specific, 277, *281n3;* potpourris,
509; and praxis, 77, 394; primitive
concepts in, *86,* 113–14; primitivism and, *91,* 292, 303, 637; proletarian, 397, 410–11; radio-specific,
277, *281n1; raison d'être,* 136,
138, 150, 152, 158; rationalization
of, 190, 191, 415, 657; reception,
219, 221, 247, 293, 661; and signification, 114; and society, *96,* 146–
47, *332–36,* 391–433; social position, 650–51, 661, 674; and sport,
312; structure, *110,* 164, 668, 669;
and technology, *219,* 283; theological aspect, *85,* 114, 136, 14041; and
thought, *85–86,* 144; time in, *99,*
143–44; truth of, *104,* 142, 145,
147, 329; typologies, 176, 247,
395, 437; ubiquity of, 135–36,
220n22, 372n108; and writing,
236, 279–80. *See also* musical life;
new music; popular music
musicality, *91,* 653
musical life, 77, 135, 371–72, 383,
650; and the bourgeoisie, 417–33;
and fetishism, 293–95
musical sound: as focus of Adorno's
criticism, 515–16

musica perennis, 183
"Music Appreciation Hour" (NBC
radio program), 221–23
music drama: Berg and, 621
"music-festival music," 153, 182–83
musicology, 73–74, 77
musique concrète, 194, *201n14,*
286n6
musique informelle. See music: informal

name, naming, *99, 324n8;* and music:
116, 140, 141, 146, 322
Naples, 506
National Socialism. *See* fascism, Nazism
natural beauty, *31–32,* 90. *See also*
beauty
nature: and art, *88n6;* domination
of, 25; freedom from, *364;* and
history, in bourgeois thought,
432–33; longing for, *31;* rupture
from, *34;* and second nature,
87n3
Nazism: and the arts, 373–90; cultural consequences, 327–29; mentality of, 375; rationalization, 585;
surviving traces, 373. *See also* fascism
NBC (radio network). *See* "Music
Appreciation Hour"
negative dialectic, *3. See also*
Adorno, works of: *Negative Dia-*
lectics
negative thinking: Marcuse on, *36*
negativity, 313; confronted by
Schoenberg, 150
Negus, Keith, *346n40*
neo-classicism, 80, 143, 320; and anti-
Wagnerism, 586; feebleness of, 184;
and objectivism, 396; reversion to
historicism, *91;* Schoenberg and,
148, 641
"Nero complex," *126n3*
Nesbitt, Nick, *357n64*
Netherlandish composers, 574

Neue Sachlichkeit. See New Objectivity

new art: difficulty of, 127, 130, 131, 133; lacks immediacy, 128; and the past, *81, 81n251;* rejection of beauty in, 181; understanding proscribed, 132. *See also* new music

New German School, 169, 401, 604, *610n5*

Newman, Ernest, *530n34,* 586, *601n3*

new music, 87, 100, 107, 114, 420, 636, 647, 654, 659, 660–75; Adorno and, *viii, 110n44;* aging of, 181–200, 636, 657–58; and aggression, 671; and alienation, 152, *281n1;* chords in, 129; estrangement from, *92–93,* 184, *239–40,* 667; hope for, 675; and human suffering, 199; intellectualism, *551, 552n89;* lacks immediacy of effect, *93,* 98; and language, 118, 124, 194, 664–65; and the past, *91, 96,* 186, 196; performance of, *95–96n22;* and radio, *239–40;* rage against, 671; reception, 289, 662; and regression, 191; renunciation of masterpieces, 182; and the theater, 284, *286n5*

New Objectivity, 401, 407, *434n7, 492–93n4,* 620, 635; Berg's critique of, 622; and jazz, 473; and objectivism, 404

Nice (France), 273

Nietzsche, Friedrich, 138, 258, *329n4,* 474, 569; *Also sprach Zarathustra,* 379; *The Birth of Tragedy from the Spirit of Music, 269n1;* on music's intoxication, 421–22; "prison-house of language," 67, *67n216;* and Wagner, 314, *317n13,* 587, 592, 601

"Night and Day," 454, *469n4*

noise, 231–32; background, in radio, *218–19*

notation, 139, 279, 307; and interpretation, 163, 414

novels, psychological, 401

number operas, 588–89. *See also* opera

Nye, William P., *351n51*

objectification, 56; in new music, 107

objectivism, 109, 121, 396, 403–8; and fascism, 404; and reproductive freedom, 416

objectivity, 92, 125, 191; bourgeois-revolutionary, 422; musical, 144

Odysseus, *28–29*

Offenbach, Jacques, 427

Ohnesorg, Benno, 69

Old Testament: ban on images, 638

ontology: possibility of, for Beethoven, 577; musical, 142, 144

opera, 314, 418–19, 531, 670; absurdity of, *550;* as anachronism, 236, *237n53;* in bourgeois humanism, 419; broadcast, 284, *287n8;* as consolation, *531;* as cult object, 284; and the long-playing record, 283–87; modern, 670; as museum, 285; potential resurrection of, 286; romantic, *510n5,* 547; social position of, 418–19, 420; updated, 236–37, 284; "voice" of, *550;* Wagner and, 585, 588. *See also* number operas

opera theater, 409

operetta, 335, 427, 428–30

orchestras: "philharmonic" and "symphony" distinguished, 420

ornamentation: criticism of, 398, 399, 400

"O sole mio," 285, *287n9*

othering: aesthetic transcendence of, 89

"Our Miss Brooks," *57n178*

Paddison, Max, *ix, 5n10, 62n195,* 88, *88nn 4, 6, 101,* 178, *221n3, 332n11, 359n71,* 534; on Adorno's musical analyses, *104–5;* on "irritation value" in Adorno's writing, 64; on nature and second nature, *87n3*

painting, 121, 139, 189, 476, 665
pan-German movement, 375, 387–88n1
Passion: in *Wozzeck*, 625, 626n7
pathos: collective, 151; of distance, 301, 474
Patti, Adelina, 2
Peale, Norman Vincent, 36
"Penny Serenade," 361n74
Pepper, Thomas Adam, x, 348n43
perception, acoustical, 368
performance, musical, 246, 287n6, 298, 301
performer, musical, 90, 97n23, 102, 412–17; experience of, 162; analytical consciousness in, 168
Pergolesi, Giovanni Battista, 556
Pfitzner, Hans, 603, 610n2
phantasmagoria, 533, 533n41
philosophical aesthetics. *See* aesthetic theory
philosophy: claim to totality, 38; and music, 96–101, 135–61; necessity of, 22n60, 33; practice of, 38–39n121; role of, 32
phonograph, 233–34, 233n50, 271–75, 276 nn3, 4, 277–80, 283–86; prehistory of, 279, 281n4
photography, 245, 271, 277; and painting, 665
piano, 232, 273
piano, electric. *See* pianola
pianola, 278, 281n3, 282n9
Picasso, Pablo, 200, 627; *Guernica*, 149, 642
Pickford, Henry W., 17
Pins and Needles, 460, 469n5
Plato: *Republic*, 289–90; *Symposium*, 120, 126n6
pleasure, 48, 49, 50, 60, 292
"plugging," 456; of popular songs, 336, 339–40, 341, 447–48; of styles and personalities, 451–52. *See also* advertising
polyphony: medieval, 427; obstacle to musical understanding, 252nC; and twelve-tone technique, 151

Popper, Karl, 74
popular music, *viii*, 248, 289, 290, 330–72, 425–33, 437–68; Adorno's essays on, 331; and advertising, 454nG; complexity in, 441–42; and false collectivity, 335–36; "hears for the listener," 339, 442–43; hybrid nature of, 348; listening habits prescribed by, 442, 446; mass hysteria about, 466, 467; "ownership" of, 457; predigested, 443; progressive function, 333–34; reception, 304–5; relation to older forms, 426–27; romantic individualism mummified, 311; and "selling out," 347, 347n41; and sincerity, 678n21; as social cement, 460; and spite, 464–65; study of, 334–35, 426; types of, 347, 426, 427, 431, 438; wish fulfillment and, 426. *See also* hit songs; jazz; standardization
popular-resistance theory, 54–55
positivism, 674; Adorno's critique of, 74, 74n237
postmodernism, 555
praxis, *vii*, 67–74, 69n223, 72n232, 200; musical, 365–67
Princeton Radio Research Project, 7, 213–14, 213n1, 214n2, 331; Adorno on, 215–16, 217
production, 129, 130–31, 133, 415, 458, 644; artistic, 379, 384; forces of, 51–52, 648; musical, 391–411
progress, 27, 290; musical, 196, 315, 639
proletariat. *See* masses
promesse de bonheur, 34, 291, 328
Proust, Marcel, 285, 287nn9, 12
pseudo-individualization, 445–46
pseudomorphosis, 120, 139, 581
psychoanalysis, 401; Adorno's interest in, 24; "in reverse," 50; Schoenberg and, 398; and *Wozzeck*, 621. *See also* Freud, Sigmund

Puccini, Giacomo: as background music, 509, *510n5*; *La Bohème*, 509, *510n5*; *Madama Butterfly*, 419, 509; *Tosca*, 509
"Püppchen," 304, *316n10*

quiz shows. *See* game shows
quotation, 265, 308, *324n8*, *555*; Benjamin on, 322, *323n5*; and radio music, 263–65

race, *351–52*
Rachmaninoff, Sergei, *8n22*; piano concertos, 319; Prélude in C-sharp minor, 115, *126n3*, *360n74*
racism, *351–52*, *351n51*, 355, *355n60*
radicalism: musical, 190; "official," 107, *107n39*, 108
radio, 135, *218–228*, 314; and collectivity, *257nK*; Horkheimer on, *56n170*; Nazi ban on "Negerjazz," 359; and new music, *239*; and the symphony, 251–70; in U.S., *214–15*
radio ham, 309
Radio Research Project. *See* Princeton Radio Research Project
radio symphony, 251–70. *See also* radio; symphonic music; symphony
Rasmussen, David M., *21n55*
rationality, teleological, 138
Ratz, Erwin, 174–75, *180n17*
Ravel, Maurice, 425, 483
reality, 130; art and, 131–32, 381
reason: as its own other, *30*; and suffering, *41*. *See also* instrumental reason
recapitulation: in Beethoven, 299, 521, *521nn14*, *15*; in Mahler, 608; in sonata form, 155
reception: social aspects, 671
recognition: in a Beethoven sonata, 452–53; components of, 453–57; and mass listening, 342, 452–57; moment of, 459
record(s), phonograph: albums, 278–

79, 290; and availability of music, *239n55*; collecting, *234n51*, 238; as commodities, *238n54*; form of, 277–82, 285; industrial production of, 271, *341*; long-playing, *237–38*, 283–87; "messages in bottles," *236*; as models for performance, 301; and photographs, 271, 278; physicality, 234–36, 271, 277–80; repeatability, 279, 285; second life of, 285; and time, 235, 279
redemption, 39
Reger, Max, 206
regression, psychological, 648
reification, 121, 128, 130, 145, 299; Mahler's critique of, 613; and music, 392; positive, *56n172*
relativism: and fascism, 379
relief, concept of, 654, *676n9*
renunciation, 29
repetition, 57, 398, 452, 599, 639; in *Modern Times*, *51*; regressive tendency, 532, 667
representation, 364
reproduction, musical, 411–15; technological, 271–75, 277–80, 283–86
resistance, 71, 200, *343*; to music, 394; to popular music, 464
Revelers (singing act), 273, *276n5*, 499
revolution, 70
rhythm: and jazz, 360, 498; in new music, 129, 153; in popular music, 441
riddle: of humanity, *520n12*; posed by music, 122
Riemann, Hugo, 170, 604, *610n3*; on Schoenberg, 204, *208n4*
Riesman, David, 661, *678n21*
Rietmüller, Albrecht, *557n104*
Rilke, Rainer Maria, 115, 408, *435n13*
Ritter, Johann Wilhelm, 280, *282n9*
Roberts, David, *557n104*
Robinson, J. Bradford, *357–58*, *357n65*, *358–59n69*, *359–60n72*, *492n1*

Rockefeller Foundation, 213
Rogers, Ginger, 461, 462, 469n6
romanticism, 109, 143, 194, 255, 322,
    363, 401, 422, 431, 473, 502, 503,
    536, 545, 603–9, 613, 634, 667; at-
    tacked by objectivism, 403; late,
    91, 100, 100n25, 203, 253, 319,
    665; and reification, 298
romanticization: promoted by radio,
    265–66
rondo: in jazz, 479, 487–88
Rose, Gillian, 56n171
Rosen, Philip, 371, 371n105
Rosenberg, Alfred, 374, 383, 388n2,
    585
Rottweiler, Hektor (pseudonym for
    Adorno), 331, 351n51
Rubens, Peter Paul, 569
Rubinstein, Anton, 413
Rückert, Friedrich, 612, 617n1
ruins, 508–9; musical, 371–72, 391;
    in Mahler, 544
Russia: rejection of non-utilitarian
    art in, 132
Russolo, Luigi, 231

Sade, Marquis de, 30, 30n86
sado-masochistic character, 297
Said, Edward W., 246n77, 537n53
salon music, 300; and jazz, 477, 484–
    85, 491
Sample, Colin, 520n13
Sargeant, Winthrop, 331n10
Satie, Erik, 269–70n1
saxophone, 351–52, 355, 499; Bizet's
    use of, 283, 286n1; history of, 471
scar, 81, 81n250; stupidity as, 28n79
Schaeffer, Pierre, 201n14
Scheible, Hartmut, xiii
Schenker, Heinrich, 104, 116, 165–
    66, 167, 178n2; and Beethoven,
    166, 634; and Wagner, 590
Schiller, Friedrich, 580
Schmidt, James, 56n170
Schnebel, Dieter, 659, 677n17
Schoenberg, Arnold, 118, 124, 125,
    148–60, 171, 200, 203–9, 315, 380,

414, 519, 551–63, 627–42, 654,
655, 668; "air of catastrophe" in,
112, 204; and Beethoven, 558;
"blackboard musician," 270n1; and
bourgeois individualism, 397–98;
and Brahms, 398, 399, 636; career
of, 112, 641; classicistic inclinations in, 400; conservatism, 187;
counterpoint, 151–52; demands
musical intelligence, 555n97; difficulty, 558, 638; early works, 150,
204, 630; and Einstein, 155; expressionist phase, 150, 638; extremes in, 203; and Freud, 397,
637; greatness, 148, 189, 561, 641;
hostility toward art, 400; interpretation, 149; and Karl Kraus, 397,
398; late works, 100–101, 147, 149,
153, 155; and Mahler, 608, 636,
639; melodies, 629; and Mozart,
638; musical-linguistic forms in,
125; on musical stupidity, 669–70;
naïveté, 149, 629, 631; paintings
by, 201n11; principle of variation
in, 561, 608, 635, 640; refuses to
be enjoyed, 292; resistance to, 203;
on radio music, 225–26n32; and
romanticism, 634; reception, 148,
628; remoteness of, 4, 96, 99–101;
sculptural quality, 632; sense of
space in, 100; stage works, 206,
670; and Thomas Mann, 627; and
tonality, 562, 636; and tradition,
155, 558–59, 641; and twelve-tone
technique, 107–8, 184, 628; and
Wagner, 123, 204, 398, 399, 536,
630, 631
Schoenberg, Arnold, works of: *Das
Buch der hängenden Gärten* (op.
15), 208n5, 637, 639; Chamber
Symphony no. 1 (op. 9), 118, 119,
186, 257nK, 630–31, 639, 662–63;
Chamber Symphony no. 2 (op.
38a), 649; "Dance Around the
Golden Calf" (*Moses und Aron*),
149, 150, 155, 627–28; *Erwartung*
(op. 17), 92, 190, 203, 398,

Schoenberg, Arnold, works of *(cont.)*
555n100, 624, 638 639, 654, 670;
Fünf Orchesterstücke, op. 16, 92,
204, 639; *Die glückliche Hand* (op.
18), 201n12, 203, 398, 555–
56n100, 639, 670; *Gurrelieder*, 595,
631; *Herzgewächse* (op. 20), 639;
Die Jakobsleiter, 627; Klavierstücke, op. 11, 150, 637, 638, 639;
Klavierstücke, op. 23, 655; Kleine
Klavierstücke, op. 19, 398, 639;
Kol Nidre (op. 39), 649; Lieder, op.
6, 148, 204, 399, 632, 635; Lieder,
op. 22, 639; "Lockung" (Lieder, op.
6, no. 7), 204, 635; *Moses und
Aron*, 149, 186, 627, 641; "On revient toujours," 649, 676n6; "Peripetie" (Orchesterstücke, op. 16, no.
4), 204, 208n1; Phantasy for violin
and piano (op. 47), 174, 180n15;
Pierrot lunaire (op. 21), 5, 92, 206,
629, 639; String Quartet no. 1 (op.
7), 133n1, 632, 639; String Quartet
no. 2 (op. 10), 119, 126n5, 148,
637, 639; String Quartet no. 3 (op.
30), 641; String Quartet no. 4 (op.
37), 186, 642; String Trio (op. 45),
642; Suite, op. 29, 641; *Die Überlebende von Warschau* (op. 46),
149–50, 642; Variations for
Orchestra (op. 31), 641; *Verklärte
Nacht* (op. 4), 118, 190, 590; *Von
heute auf morgen* (op. 32), 400,
641; Wind Quintet (op. 26), 151,
641
Schoenberg circle. *See* Second Viennese School
Schönberg, Arnold. *See* Schoenberg,
Arnold
Schönherr, Ulrich, 357n64
Schoolman, Morton, 539–40n59
Schopenhauer, Arthur, 68, 123; and
Wagner, 144, 589
Schrecker, Franz, 665–66, 678n23
Schubert, Franz, 255nI, 292, 319,
428, 429, 604; arranged, 299,
316n8; and café music, 509; "Sere-

nade," 300; Symphony no. 8
("Unfinished"), 264, 293; and
Wozzeck, 622
Schubert, Giselher, 557n104
Schulte-Sasse, Jochen, x, 67n216
Schütz, Heinrich, 587
Schumann, Robert, 143, 403, 629
score, musical, 102; as picture, 163
Second Viennese School, *viii*, 108,
329, 396, 586; Adorno and, 110
Sedlmayr, Hans, 153, 160n16
Seiber, Mátyás, 349n46, 358
Sekles, Bernhard, 4
sequence, 428, 533n40; in Wagner,
591–92, 593
serialism, 91, 107, 109, 125, 151,
172, 188,562, 656; canonization of,
16, 100, 108
"serious music," 135, 137, 292; characterized, 439; and popular music,
427, 665
Sex Pistols, 335–36n15
sexuality: and jazz rhythms, 352
Shakespeare, William, 627
Sharma, Bhesham R., 557n104
Shaw, Artie, 344, 466, 466nK
sheet music, 341, 358
Sibelius, Jean, 646, 647
Sievier, Bruce, 351n51
silence, 289, 563, 660; in Webern, 97,
137
Silver, Abner, 337
Simpson, George, 331, 331n9
sing-and-play movement, 652. *See
also* young people's music
singing: Italian, 584; Wagnerian, 584–
85
singing voice: demands on, in *Missa
Solemnis*, 572; and fetishism, 294–
95; and the phonograph, 274
Les Six, 269n1
skepticism: Hegel on, 35
sociability: musically constructed,
328
social theory: and music, 393
society: liberal model of, 669; regressive tendencies in, 653

Society for Private Musical Performances (Vienna), 165, *178n3*
sociology, American: Adorno's critique of, 216–17, *216n12*
sociology of music, *222n27*, 335, 660–61; of Max Weber, 145, 657
soloist: as predetermined "winner" in concerto, *523–24*
song hits. *See* hit songs
soul, suffering of: in *Wozzeck*, 550
sound: electronic production of, 121–22; homogenous, 398–99
sound film, 429
sound intensity, 256–61
sound recording: and listening, 233–38; technical liabilities, 235. *See also* phonograph; record(s); reproduction
Sousa, John Philip: and the saxophone, 352
space, musical: and color, 150–51; and film, *369n96*; and musical language, 652; and Schoenberg, 99–100
space, symphonic, 224, 257
space-time, musical, 142, 143
Spaeth, Sigmund, *226n34*
spatiality. *See* space, musical
speaking voice: and musical gesture, 113
Spengler, Oswald, *675n5*
Sphinx, 205, 206
spirit, 200, 415, 661
Spitzweg, Carl, 599, *602n12*
spontaneity, 452, 468, 526, 639, 660; loss of, 46, 266, 301; sacrificed, in twelve-tone music, 554
Sprechgesang. See Sprechstimme
Sprechstimme, 550–51
"speculative ear," 674, *679n31*
standardization: in popular music, 337, 338, 339, 340, 341, 438, 441–44; subversion of, 518. *See also* hit songs; popular music
star principle, 293–94
stars: in "classical" music, 340
star worship, 340

"Stell auf den Tisch die duftenden Reseden," 502, *504n2*
Stephan, Rudolf, 166, 572, *582–83n3*
"Stephanie Gavotte," 299, *316n7*, 508
Steuermann, Eduard, 4, 137, *159n3*, 301, 655, *677n12*; on the Credo of the *Missa Solemnis*, 527, 577; on the crisis of inspiration, 668
Stifter, Adalbert, 565, *567–68n1*
Stockhausen, Karlheinz, 16, 657; *Gesang der Jünglinge*, *101n27*, *361n75*; on Schoenberg, 656
Stolz, Robert, 395, *433n3*
Strasbourg, 617
Straus, Oscar, 428, *435n20*, *495n16*
Strauss, Johann, 427, 428, 498
Strauss, Richard, 169, 260, 267, 405, 423–24, 502, 561–62, 631, 636, 637; Adorno's antipathy towards, 333; attacked by H. Schenker, 166; and bourgeois comfort, 329, *329n4*; class consciousness of, 424; compromises with Nazism, 380; failure of, 424, 648; and opera, 285; purveyor of cultural goods, 379; and tonality, 649; and Wagner, 123, 590, 663. *See also* Strauss, Richard, works of
Strauss, Richard, works of: *An Alpine Symphony*, 648; *Elektra*, 118, 379, 424, 595, 633, 649; *Four Last Songs*, 516; *Die Frau ohne Schatten*, *329n4*, 379, 648; *Ein Heldenleben*, 604; *Der Rosenkavalier*, 284, 329, *329n4*, 379, 424; *Salome*, 379, 424; *Symphonia domestica*, 604
Stravinsky, Igor, 91, 156, *269–70n1*, 396, 403–6, 461, 551–63, 624; Adorno's rejection of, *556–57n104*; despair in, 406, 407; dialectical elements in, *556n103*; as "destroyer," 405; elimination of subjectivity in, 272, *276n2*; evasion of time in, 553–54, *553–54n93*; instrumenta-

Stravinsky, Igor *(continued)*
   tion, *556n103;* and jazz, 488–89,
   553–54, 556; masks in, *403, 406;*
   and mechanical instruments, *278,
   318n3;* music about music, *555;*
   and neo-classicism, 586; regression
   to pre-bourgeois forms, *120, 403;*
   renunciation of new music, *183;* as
   tourist among styles, *555;* and
   twelve-tone technique, *556n103,*
   586
Stravinsky, Igor, works of: *L'Histoire
   du soldat, 397, 406, 407, 556,
   670; Petrouchka, 555, 556n100;
   Pulcinella* Suite, *556; The Rake's
   Progress,* 589; *Renard, 670;
   Le Sacre du printemps, 181,
   488, 554, 555, 556n100; Symphony in Three Movements,
   556n103; Symphony of Psalms,*
   395, 406
string quartet, *521, 522, 523*
Strindberg, August, 183
structural listening, 164, 178, 220–
   21, *221n23,* 228, 250, 318, 336
Stuckenschmidt, H. H., *276n1,* 660
Stückerl, 588
student movement (1960s), *18,
   18n46, 69*
stupidity, *28n79;* musical, 148, 669–
   70
Stuttgart Week of New Music, *107*
style, musical, *538–39n55*
subcutaneous structure: in Beethoven, 634; in Schoenberg, 634,
   637
(the) subject, *20, 30, 37, 45, 46, 56,
   109, 111, 121,* 146, *198, 320, 550,
   563;* Adorno's fidelity to, *563;* artistic, 385; and the commodity, *51–
   52;* and compositional objectivity,
   649; and dehumanization, *328;*
   elimination of, 657; formation,
   222, 336; future of, *347;* as limit
   of reification, *57;* in *Missa Solemnis,* 578, 581; and musical material, 125, 189; and modernity, *vii,*

96; and object, *34, 207, 250;* relation to nature, *25, 26, 28, 31, 90,
   236, 364;* "speaking" of, *146, 250;*
   state's domination of, *342;* weakness of, 653
subjecthood: expressed through song,
   338
subjectivism, 114, 621
subjectivity, *31, 32, 57,* 478, *566–67;*
   bourgeois, 422. *See also* intersubjectivity
subjectivization: of music, 145
subject-object relation: in late Beethoven, *518*
Subotnik, Rose Rosengard, *ix–x,
   51n162, 106n36, 111n46, 514n2,
   516n3, 517n5, 519n8, 520n11,
   521n14, 527–28, 528n28, 529n30,
   539, 539n59;* on Adorno's praxis,
   72n232; on Adorno's rejection of
   Stravinsky, *556–57n104;* on perceived authenticity of *Wozzeck,
   548n81;* on Schoenberg's ugliness,
   330n6; on structural listening,
   221n23
success story, American, 448–49
Suchman, Edward A., *228–29n40*
suffering, *vii,* 4, 40, 191, 332, 393,
   401; and art, *41;* in *Wozzeck,* 619
"Sunflower," 502
surrealism, 127, 658; and Wagner,
   599–600
surrealistic music, 396–97
surrealists, 402, 654, *677n10*
Swift, Christopher, *67n218*
Swinburne, Algernon Charles, 115
"swing," 451. *See also* jazz
symphonic music, *252nC,* 265, 267–
   69
symphony: characteristics, 253–56;
   and radio, 251–70; romantic, 253,
   255–56
syncopation, 313, 350, 430, 470, 486,
   497, 498, 499; as premature orgasm, in jazz, 490
synthesis: sacrificed in *Missa Solemnis,* 581

talent, function of, 400

talking machines, 271, 272. *See also* phonograph

tango, 472

taste, musical, 288, 289, 297–98

Tchaikovsky, Piotr Ilyich, 462, 665; as café music, 509; radio listeners' preference for, 266; *Romeo and Juliet*, 319; Symphony no. 5 (op. 64), 294, 361n74

"Tea for Two," 502

technical development, 313, 378

Technik: two senses distinguished, 283, 286n2

technique, *110, 562, 650*; instrumental, *350*

technology, *viii, 49*, 195, 277; and art, 193; fetishizing of, *28*; and modern consciousness, 231; and musical consumption, 232–33; reproductive, *241*; and Schoenberg, 207. *See also* phonograph, radio

telephone psychics, *60–61n189*

tension, resolution of, 669

theme(s), 186, 254nG, 262nM, 264–65, 496, 532n40, 574, 640; as cultural property, 226, 226n34; symphonic, 262, 263–64. *See also* Beethoven, Ludwig van; Mahler, Gustav

theory, *72*, 252; in the marketplace, *32*; traditional, *19–20*

theory-praxis relation, 71–72, 72n232. *See also* praxis, theory

Third Program, 135, *159n1*

Thomas, Ambroise: *Mignon*, 509, *510n5*

Thomas, Calvin, 347–48, 348n43

Thomson, Virgil: on jazz, *353n54*; on music's inescapability, 220n22; on radio music, 219n20, 224, 225; on recording, 235n52

thought, *20, 38, 39–40, 72, 90n13*; possibility of, *21, 39*

The Three Musketeers, 502, 505n7

"Tiger Rag," 480, 493n9

Tillich, Paul, 6

time, *108;* musical, *99*, 143–44, *236, 532;* in recordings, 279

time consciousness: suspension of, in Beethoven, 256

timelessness, illusion of: in Stravinsky, *554n93*

Tin Pan Alley, *337, 340, 341–42n30;* as "song factory," *341*, 462

Titanic, 362

Tomlinson, Alan, *53–54n168*

Tomlinson, Gary, 237n53, 238n54

tonality, 113, 145, 306, 321, 398, 558–59, 562, 647, 649; and bourgeois era, 669; dominance of, 665; exhaustion of, *561*; expressive possibilities, 666–68; general and particular in, 629–30, 667–69; immanent dynamism of, *109*; language-like, *86*; and new music, *87*; and objective spirit, 664; regression of, *93*; reification of, *86*; as second nature, *87*, 663, 666; spatial consciousness in, 150; and the subject, *560*, 633

tone-color composition, 122. *See also* color (musical); *Tonfarbenmusik*

tone-mass, 275, 276n8

Tonfarbenmusik, 189, *201n12*. See also *Klangfarbenmelodien*, tone-color composition

Toscanini, Arturo, 293; as fetish, *246, 246n77*; and radio, 222n26, 227

totality, 621; and Beethoven, 578, 580; philosophical, *52*; social, *20, 24, 35, 73n235*, 229, 250, *513n1;* in Wagner, 594, 601

Townsend, Peter, *358n65*

tradition, *73–82*, 412–13; as forgetting, 155; and modernity, *78, 78n243;* in post-traditional world, 647; resistance to, 196

transition, concept of, 186

Tristan chord, 190

The Trumpeter of Säckingen, 502, 505n8

truth, *33, 142*, 378, 579

742 / *Index*

truth content, *108, 111, 167, 169,
347, 515;* of artworks, *88–89,
89n8, 90, 95, 179n6,* 280, *332*
Tucker, Mark, *494–95n13*
twelve-tone technique, *107, 108, 157,
158, 184–86, 206,554, 562,* 640;
extinction of expression in, 399;
meaning of, *639–40;* Stravinsky's
use of, *556n103,* 586; Webern and,
655–56

ugliness, 329, *329nn5, 6*
unconscious, 163; and bourgeois musical life, 422
understanding, 128, 193; history of,
663; musical, 268, 453; and perception of wholes, 318; retrospective,
104
"unintentional truth," *34n106*
unity: of subjective and objective,
581
universal and particular, 320, 321,
563, 563n105, 589
use music, 397; failure of, 410; in
Weill, 409. See also *Gebrauchsmusik*
use value, 296–97
utopia, *60, 563, 79n245;* and music,
85–86

"Valencia," *429, 435n22, 472, 479,
503–4*
Valéry, Paul, 188, 193, 650, *676n7*
van Gogh, Vincent, 609, 623, *626n5*
Varèse, Edgard: and technology, 194
variety theater: and jazz, 489
Verdi, Giuseppe: *Aïda,* 419; sequences in, 670
*Verein für musikalische Privatauf-
führungen (Wien),* 165, *178n3*
verismo, 547
Vernunft and *Verstand:* distinguished,
33. See also instrumental reason;
reason; understanding
vibrato, *350, 350n49;* in café music,
508; in jazz, 471
Vienna: Adorno's dislike of, 4

violins, 260, 295
virtuoso, 301–2
visual arts, 139. *See also* painting
Volk, 388n2. See also folk
Volkswagen, *390n8*
Voltaire, 651

Wagner, Eva, *388n2*
Wagner, Richard, 92, 116, 123, 131,
267, 496, *528–37, 584–601;* anti-
Semitism, *529n30,* 532, 600; atonal
tendency in, 590; and boredom,
269n1; and bourgeois intoxication,
419; chromaticism in, 119, 591,
597; erotic freedom in, *535–36,*
587; and fascism, 327–28, 374–77,
585; and film music, *533n41;* form,
592–94; grandiosity, 598; image of
man in, 401; leitmotif in, *103, 169–
70, 171, 534, 537,* 590; magnitude
of sound in, 258, 590; modernity
of, 588; "musical nominalism" in,
536, 588; and myth, *536,* 589–90,
599; and novelty, *533n42;* orchestration, *534–35, 537,* 593–96; performance of, 587, 599–600;
pleasure and death in, *532;* progressive elements in, *534, 535–36;*
reception of, 284, 327–28, 663;
"rescued" from his regressive tendencies, *529, 530, 530n33,* 531;
and Schopenhauer, 123, 144, 589,
597; true and false in, 596; truth
content, 600; turn towards language in, 122–23; violence in, 589
Wagner, Richard, works of: *Der flie-
gende Holländer,* 597, 601; *Götterdämmerung, 537, 595,* 598–99; *Die
Meistersinger von Nürnberg,* 300,
418, 422–23, *585, 592, 595,* 598,
600; *Parsifal,* 314, 447, *532n39,*
588, 590, 596, 597; *Der Ring des
Nibelungen, 170, 171, 375, 536,
537, 588, 596, 597; Siegfried, 536,
588, 593, 594, 596; Siegfried-Idyll,*
596; *Tannhäuser, 595,* 600; *Tristan
und Isolde,* 118, 119, 222–23, *391,*

423, 572, 588, 589, 590, 591, 623,
649, 662; *Die Walküre*, 588, 589–
90, 596

Wagner-Régeny, Rudolf, 383, *389n7*

Ein Walzertraum, 487, *495n16*

Wandervögel, 506, *510n1*, 616

Weber, Carl Maria von: *Der Freischütz*, 419

Weber, Max, 273, *276n3*; sociology
of music, 145, 657; *Wirtschaft und
Gesellschaft*, 664, *678n22*

Webern, Anton (von), 156, 173, 185,
187, 199, 315, 402–3, 631, 639,
654, 655; Adorno's admiration for,
91–92n15; Boulez and, 125; Cage
on, 658; "dialectic lyricism," 402;
Five Movements for String Quartet, op. 5, 157, 185; silences in, 97,
137; Six Bagatelles for String
Quartet, op. 9, 168, 173, *179n8*,
655; and twelve-tone technique,
655–56

"The Wedding of the Painted Doll,"
431–32, *436n27*

Wedekind, Frank, 616, *618n8*

Weill, Kurt, 4, 333, 383, 408–10,
472, 499; *Aufstieg und Fall der
Stadt Mahagonny*, 397, 409, 610,
611n12; *The Three-Penny Opera*,
397, 409

Weimar Republic. *See* Germany

Weiner, Marc A., *537–38n53*

Wellesz, Egon, 632, *642n4*

Weltanschauung, 661

"Wenn der weisse Flieder wieder
blüht," 503

Werfel, Franz, 614, *617–18n6*

Whiteman, Paul, 268, 349, *349–
50n47*, 353–54, *358*

whole, musical, 194, 290, 291, 319;
perception of, 318; in popular music, 439

whole-part relationships, 306, *250*,
441; in Beethoven's symphonic
movements, 255–56; in jazz,
356–57n64; in musical analysis,
174, 175; in radio symphony, 262–
63

"Who Rolled the Cheese to the Depot?" *334*, 426, *435n18*

Wiesengrund, Oskar, 2, *7n21*

Wilcock, Evelyn, *351n51*, *355–56n62*,
358n67

Wilde, Oscar, *329n4*, 403

Willet, John, *492–93n4*

Williams, Alastair, 107, *557n104*

Wiora, Walter, 672, *679n29*

Witkin, Robert, *528n28*

Wohlfarth, Irving, 70

Wolf, Hugo, 204, *208n2*

Wolin, Richard, *70n224*, *73n235*, *97–
98n24*, 242, *330n6*

Wolzogen, Hans von, *103*, *103n32*,
169

work of art. *See* artwork

Wurlitzer organ, 195, *350n49*, 491,
660

young people's music, 652, 654. *See
also* youth movement (musical)

youth: and new music, 191

youth movement (musical): in Germany, 320, 382, 408, 672. *See also*
young people's music

Zappa, Frank, *335–36n15*

Zuidervaart, Lambert, *64n201*, *91n14*,
552–53n90

Compositor: Binghamtom Valley Composition
Text: 10/13 Aldus
Display: Aldus
Printer: Sheridan Books, Inc.
Binder: Sheridan Books, Inc.